Eighth Edition

The American
DEMOCRACY

Texas Edition

Thomas E. Patterson

Bradlee Professor of Government and the Press
John F. Kennedy School of Government
Harvard University

Gary M. Halter

Professor of Political Science
Texas A&M University

Boston   Burr Ridge, IL   Dubuque, IA   Madison, WI   New York   San Fra
Bangkok   Bogotá   Caracas   Kuala Lumpur   Lisbon   Lo
Milan   Montreal   New Delhi   Santiago   Seoul

Higher Education

THE AMERICAN DEMOCRACY: TEXAS EDITION
Published by McGraw-Hill, a business unit of The McGraw-Hill Companies, Inc., 1221 Avenue of the Americas, New York, NY, 10020. Copyright © 2008 by The McGraw-Hill Companies, Inc. All rights reserved. No part of this publication may be reproduced or distributed in any form or by any means, or stored in a database or retrieval system, without the prior written consent of The McGraw-Hill Companies, Inc., including, but not limited to, in any network or other electronic storage or transmission, or broadcast for distance learning.
Some ancillaries, including electronic and print components, may not be available to customers outside the United States.

This book is printed on acid-free paper.

1 2 3 4 5 6 7 8 9 0 DOW/DOW 0 9 8 7 6

ISBN: 978-0-07-321936-3
MHID: 0-07-321936-3

Vice President and Editor-in-Chief: *Emily Barrosse*
Publisher: *Lyn Uhl*
Sponsoring Editor: *Monica Eckman*
Developmental Editor: *Angela W. Kao*
Editorial Assistant: *Jessica Badiner*
Marketing Manager: *Pamela S. Cooper*
Managing Editor: *Jean Dal Porto*
Senior Project Manager: *Catherine R. Iammartino*
Art Director: *Jeanne Schreiber*
Art Editor: *Emma C. Ghiselli*
Lead Designer: *Gino Cieslik*
Senior Photo Research Coordinator: *Alexandra Ambrose*
Senior Supplement Producer: *Louis Swaim*
Senior Media Project Manager: *Michele Borrelli*
Media Producer: *Sean Crowley*
Senior Production Supervisor: *Carol Bielski*
Composition: *10/12 Sabon, by Techbooks*
Printing: *45# New Era Matte, R. R. Donnelley & Sons*

Credits: The credits section for this book begins on page C1 and is considered an extension of the copyright page.

Library of Congress Cataloging-in-Publication Data
Patterson, Thomas E.
    The American democracy/Thomas E. Patterson, Gary M. Halter.–8th ed., Texas ed.
      p. cm.
    ISBN-13: 978-0-07-321936-3 (pbk. alk. paper)
    ISBN-10: 0-07-321936-3 (pbk.: alk. paper)
      1. United States–Politics and government–Textbooks. I. Halter, Gary M. II. Title.
    JK276.P37 2006
    320.473–dc22   2006047178

www.mhhe.com

ABOUT
THE AUTHOR

Thomas E. Patterson is Bradlee Professor of Government and the Press in the John F. Kennedy School of Government at Harvard University. He was previously Distinguished Professor of Political Science in the Maxwell School of Citizenship at Syracuse University. Raised in a small Minnesota town near the Iowa and South Dakota borders, he attended South Dakota State University as an undergraduate and served in the military in Vietnam before enrolling at the University of Minnesota, where he received his Ph.D. in 1971.

He is the author of numerous book and articles, which focus mainly on elections and the media. His book *The Vanishing Voter* (2002) describes and explains the long term decline in Americans' electoral participation. An earlier book, *Out of Order* (1994), received national attention when President Clinton said every politician and journalist should be required to read it. In 2002, *Out of Order* received the American Political Science Association's Graber Award for the best book of the past decade in political communication. Another of Patterson's books, *The Mass Media Election* (1980), received a *Choice* award as Outstanding Academic Book, 1980-1981. Patterson's first book, *The Unseeing Eye* (1976), was selected by the American Association for Public Opinion Research as one of the fifty most influential books of the past half-century in the field of public opinion.

His research has been funded by major grants from the National Science Foundation, the Markle Foundation, the Smith-Richardson Foundation, the Ford Foundation, the Knight Foundation, The Carnegie Corporation, and the Pew Charitable Trusts.

Gary Halter is a native of Amarillo and Wichita Falls, Texas. He earned his BA degree from Midwestern University and his PhD from the University of Maryland. He is a Professor of Political Science at Texas A&M University in College Station, Texas. He served as a member of the city council for five years and as mayor for six years. He has worked as a consultant to many city councils in Texas and other states on goal setting and policy making. Dr. Halter is the author of *Government & Politics of Texas: A Comparative Approach,* published by McGraw-Hill, and with Harvey Tucker he is co-author of the *Texas Legislative Almanac* published by Texas A&M Press in 1997 and 2001.

CONTENTS IN BRIEF

List of Boxes XXII
Preface for the Instructor XXIV
Preface for the Student: A Guided Tour XXI
Acknowledgments XXV

PART ONE Foundations 3

1   American Political Culture: Seeking a More Perfect Union 4
2   Constitutional Democracy: Promoting Liberty and Self-Government 34
3   Federalism: Forging a Nation 66
4   Civil Liberties: Protecting Individual Rights 96
5   Equal Rights: Struggling Toward Fairness 130

PART TWO Mass Politics 163

6   Public Opinion and Political Socialization: Shaping the People's Voice 164
7   Political Participation and Voting: Expressing the Popular Will 188
8   Political Parties, Candidates, and Campaigns: Defining the Voters' Choice 212
9   Interest Groups: Organizing for Influence 244
10 The News Media: Communicating Political Images 272

PART THREE Governing Institutions 299

11 Congress: Balancing National Goals and Local Interests 300
12 The Presidency: Leading the Nation 336
13 The Federal Bureaucracy: Administering the Government 372
14 The Federal Judicial System: Applying the Law 402

PART FOUR Public Policy 434

15 Economic and Environmental Policy: Contributing to Prosperity 436
16 Welfare and Education Policy: Providing for Personal Security and Need 472
17 Foreign and Defense Policy: Protecting the American Way 498

PART FIVE Texas Government and Politics 526

18 Introduction to Texas Government 528
19 The State Constitution 546
20 Participation Politics and Interest Groups in Texas Politics 564
21 Political Parties and Elections in Texas 586
22 The Texas Legislature 618
23 The Office of Governor and State Agencies in Texas 660
24 The Court System in Texas 696
25 Local Governments in Texas 724

Appendixes A
Glossary G1
Notes N1
Credits C1

CONTENTS

List of Boxes XXII
Preface for the Instructor XXIV
Preface for the Student: A Guided Tour XXI
Acknowledgements XXV

PART ONE   Foundations   3

1   American Political Culture: Seeking a More Perfect Union   4

Political Culture: The Core Principles of American Government   7

America's Core Values: Liberty, Equality, and Self-Government   9
  The Power of Ideals   11
  The Limits of Ideals   13

Politics: The Resolution of Conflict   17
  The Social Contract   18
  The Rules of American Politics   21

Political Power: The Control of Policy   24
  Authority   25
  Theories of Power   26

The Concept of a Political System and This Book's Organization   29
Summary   31
Study Corner   32

2   Constitutional Democracy: Promoting Liberty and Self-Government   34

Before the Constitution: The Colonial and Revolutionary Experiences   37
  "The Rights of Englishmen"   37
  The Declaration of Independence   38
  The Articles of Confederation   39
  Shays's Rebellion: A Nation Dissolving   40

Negotiating Toward a Constitution   42
  The Great Compromise: A Two-Chamber Congress   42
  The North-South Compromise: The Issue of Slavery   42
  A Strategy for Ratification   44
  The Ratification Debate   45
  The Framers' Goals   46

Protecting Liberty: Limited Government   47
  Grants and Denials of Power   48
  Using Power to Offset Power   48
  Separated Institutions Sharing Power: Checks and Balances   49
  The Bill of Rights   51
  Judicial Review   56

Providing for Self-Government   55
  Democracy Versus Republic   55
  Limited Popular Rule   56

Altering the Constitution: More Power to the People   58
Constitutional Democracy Today   62
Summary   63
Study Corner   64

3   Federalism: Forging a Nation   66

Federalism: National and State Sovereignty   68
  The Argument for Federalism   70
  The Powers of the Nation   73
  The Powers of the States   74

Federalism in Historical Perspective   75
  An Indestructible Union (1789–1865)   75
  Dual Federalism and Laissez-Faire Capitalism (1865–1937)   78
  Toward National Citizenship   83

Federalism Today   84
  Interdependency and Intergovernmental Relations   85
  Government Revenues and Intergovernmental Relations   86
  A New Federalism: Devolution   88

The Public's Influence: Setting the Boundaries of Federal-State Power   92
Summary   93
Study Corner   94

4   Civil Liberties: Protecting Individual Rights   96

Freedom of Expression   99
  The Early Period: The Uncertain Status of the Right of Free Expression   100
  The Modern Period: Protecting Free Expression   101
  Free Expression and State Governments   103
  Libel and Slander   106
  Obscenity   108

Freedom of Religion   109
  The Establishment Clause   109
  The Free-Exercise Clause   111

The Right of Privacy   112
  Abortion   112
  Sexual Relations Among Consenting Adults   114
  The Continuing Issue of Privacy Rights   114

Rights of Persons Accused of Crimes   115
  Selective Incorporation of Procedural Rights   116
  Limits on Defendants' Rights   117
  Crime, Punishment, and Police Practices   120

Rights and the War on Terrorism   123
  Detention of Enemy Combatants   123
  Surveillance of Suspected Terrorists   125

The Courts and a Free Society   126
Summary   127
Study Corner   128

5 Equal Rights: Struggling Toward Fairness 130

The Struggle for Equality 132
African Americans 132
Women 135
Native Americans 137
Hispanic Americans 138
Asian Americans 143
Other Groups and Their Rights 144

Equality Under the Law 147
Equal Protection: The Fourteenth Amendment 147
Equal Access: The Civil Rights Acts of 1964 and 1968 149
Equal Ballots: The Voting Rights Act of 1965, as Amended 150

Equality of Result 152
Affirmative Action: Workplace Integration 152
Affirmative Action in the Law 154
School Integration: Busing 156

Persistent Discrimination: Superficial Differences, Deep Divisions 157

Summary 159
Study Corner 160

PART TWO   Mass Politics 163

6 Public Opinion and Political Socialization: Shaping the People's Voice 164

The Nature of Public Opinion 166
How Informed Is Public Opinion? 167
The Measurement of Public Opinion 168

Political Socialization: How Americans Learn Their Politics 173
The Process of Political Socialization 173
The Agents of Political Socialization 173

Frames of Reference: How Americans Think Politically 176
Cultural Thinking: Common Ideas 176
Ideological Thinking: The Outlook of Some 177
Group Thinking: The Outlook of Many 179
Partisan Thinking: The Line That Divides 182

The Influence of Public Opinion on Policy 184

Summary 185
Study Corner 186

7 Political Participation and Voting: Expressing the Popular Will 188

Voter Participation 190
Factors in Voter Turnout: The United States in Comparative Perspective 191

Why Some Americans Vote and Others Do Not 197

Conventional Forms of Participation Other Than Voting 200
Campaign Activities 201
Lobbying Group Contributions 201
Community Activities 202
Attending to the News 202
Virtual Participation 204

Unconventional Activism: Social Movements and Protest Politics 205

Participation and the Potential for Influence 207

Summary 209
Study Corner 210

8 Political Parties, Candidates, and Campaigns: Defining the Voters' Choice 212

Party Competition and Majority Rule: The History of U.S. Parties 214
The First Parties 214
Andrew Jackson and Grassroots Parties 215
Republicans Versus Democrats: Realignments and the Enduring Party System 216
Today's Party Alignment and Its Origins 217
Parties and the Vote 220

Electoral and Party Systems 220
The Single-Member-District System of Election 221
Politics and Coalitions in the Two-Party System 222
Minor Parties 224

Party Organizations 227
The Weakening of Party Organizations 227
The Structure and Role of Party Organizations 228

The Candidate-Centered Campaign 233
Campaign Funds: The Money Chase 233
Organization and Strategy: Hired Guns 233
Voter Contacts: Pitched Battle 236

Parties, Candidates, and the Public's Influence 238

Summary 241
Study Corner 242

9 Interest Groups: Organizing for Influence 244

The Interest-Group System 247
Economic Groups 247
Citizens' Groups 251
A Special Category of Interest Group: Governments 254

Inside Lobbying: Seeking Influence Through Official Contacts 255
Acquiring Access to Officials 256
Webs of Influence: Groups in the Policy Process 258

Outside Lobbying: Seeking Influence Through Public Pressure 260

Constituency Advocacy: Grassroots Lobbying 261
Electoral Action: Votes and PAC Money 261

The Group System: Indispensable but Biased 265

The Contribution of Groups to Self-Government: Pluralism 265
Flaws in Pluralism: Interest-Group Liberalism and Economic Bias 266
A Madisonian Dilemma 267

Summary 269
Study Corner 270

10 The News Media: Communicating Political Images 272

Historical Development: From Partisanship to Objective Journalism 275

The Politics of America's News Media 276

Newspapers 276
Broadcast News 277
Cable Television 282
The Internet 283

The News Media as Link: Roles the Press Can and Cannot Perform Well 286

The Signaling Role 286
The Common-Carrier Role 288
The Watchdog Role 288
The Public-Representative Role 291

Organizing the Public in the Media Age 294
Summary 295
Study Corner 296

**PART THREE
Governing Institutions** 299

11 Congress: Balancing National Goals and Local Interests 300

Congress as a Career: Election to Congress 303

Using Incumbency to Stay in Congress 304
Pitfalls of Incumbency 307
Safe Incumbency and Representation 309
Who Are the Winners in Congressional Elections? 310

Congressional Leadership 311

Party Leadership in Congress 312
Committee Chairs: The Seniority Principle 316
Oligarchy or Democracy: Which Principle Should Govern? 317

The Committee System 317

Committee Membership 318
Committee Jurisdiction 319

How a Bill Becomes Law 320

Committee Hearings and Decisions 320
From Committee to the Floor 322
Leadership and Floor Action 322
Conference Committees and the President 323

Congress's Policymaking Role 324

The Lawmaking Function of Congress 324
The Representation Function of Congress 327
The Oversight Function of Congress 329

Congress: Too Much Pluralism? 332
Summary 333
Study Corner 334

12 The Presidency: Leading the Nation 336

Foundations of the Modern Presidency 339

Asserting a Claim to National Leadership 340
The Need for Presidential Leadership of an Activist Government 342

Choosing the President 344

The Primary Elections 349
The National Party Conventions 349
The Campaign for Election 349

Staffing the Presidency 353

Presidential Appointees 354
The Problem of Control 358

Factors in Presidential Leadership 358

The Force of Circumstance 359
The Stage of the President's Term 360
The Nature of the Issue: Foreign or Domestic 360
Relations with Congress 362
Public Support 365

Summary 368
Study Corner 370

13 The Federal Bureaucracy: Administering the Government 372

Federal Administration: Form, Personnel, and Activities 374

The Federal Bureaucracy in Americans' Daily Lives 376
Types of Administrative Organizations 376
Federal Employment 378
The Federal Bureaucracy's Policy Responsibilities 380

Development of the Federal Bureaucracy: Politics and Administration 381

Small Government and the Patronage System 381
Growth in Government and the Merit System 382
Big Government and the Executive Leadership System 383

The Bureaucracy's Power Imperative 385

The Agency Point of View 386
Sources of Bureaucratic Power 386

Bureaucratic Accountability 388

Accountability Through the Presidency 390
Accountability Through Congress 393
Accountability Through the Courts 394
Accountability Within the Bureaucracy Itself 395

Reinventing Government? 396
Summary 398
Study Corner 400

14 The Federal Judicial System: Applying the Law 402

The Federal Judicial System 404
   The Supreme Court of the United States 408
   Other Federal Courts 409
   The State Courts 411

Federal Court Appointees 413
   The Selection of Supreme Court Justices
      and Federal Judges 413
   Justices and Judges as Political Officials 415

The Nature of Judicial Decision Making 417
   The Constraints of the Facts 417
   The Constraints of the Law 418

Political Influences on Judicial Decisions 420
   Outside Influences on Court Decisions 420
   Inside Influences: The Justices' Own Political Beliefs 423

Judicial Power and Democratic
   Government 423
   The Debate over the Proper Role of the Judiciary 424
   The Judiciary's Proper Role: A Question of Competing
      Values 430

Summary 431
Study Corner 432

PART FOUR
Public Policy 434

15 Economic and Environmental Policy: Contributing to Prosperity 436

The Public Policy Process 438
   Emergence of Policy Issues 438
   Resolution of Policy Issues 440

Government as Regulator of the
   Economy 442
   Efficiency Through Government Intervention 443
   Equity Through Government Intervention 447
   The Politics of Regulatory Policy 448

Government as Protector of the
   Environment 450
   Conservationism: The Older Wave 450
   Environmentalism: The Newer Wave 452

Government as Promoter of Economic
   Interests 456
   Promoting Business 456
   Promoting Labor 456
   Promoting Agriculture 457

Fiscal Policy: Government as Manager of
   Economy, I 457
   Taxing and Spending Policy 457
   The Process and Politics of Fiscal
      Policy 461

Monetary Policy: Government as Manager of
   Economy, II 465
   The Fed 466
   The Politics of the Fed 467
Summary 468
Study Corner 470

16 Welfare and Education Policy: Providing for Personal Security and Need 472

Poverty in America: The Nature of the
   Problem 475
   The Poor: Who and How Many? 475
   Living in Poverty: By Choice or Chance? 476

The Politics and Policies of Social
   Welfare 477
   Social Insurance Programs 480
   Public Assistance Programs 481
   Culture, Welfare, and Income 485

Education and Equality of Opportunity:
   The American Way 489
   Public Education: Leveling Through the Schools 489
   Public School Issues 490
   The Federal Role in Education: Political Differences 492

The American Way of Promoting the General
   Welfare 494

Summary 494
Study Corner 496

17 Foreign and Defense Policy: Protecting the American Way 498

The Roots of U.S. Foreign and Defense
   Policy 501
   The United States as Global Superpower 501
   The Cold War and Vietnam 502
   Disintegration of the "Evil Empire" 502
   A New World Order 503
   The War on Terrorism 504
   The Iraq War 506

The Military Dimension of National Security
   Policy 509
   Military Power, Uses, and Capabilities 509
   The Politics of National Defense 513

The Economic Dimension of National
   Security Policy 514
   A Changing World Economy 514
   America's Global Economic Goals 515

A New World 521
Summary 522
Study Corner 524

PART FIVE   Texas Government and Politics   526

18 Introduction to Texas Government 528

Texas: A Land of Contrasts 530

Settlement Patters in Texas History 530
- *The Tejanos or Mexican Settlers* 530
- *Anglo Settlers* 531
- *German Immigrants* 532

Urban and Rural Contrasts 532

Population Growth and the Changing Climate of Texas Politics 533

Minority Groups 533
- *Hispanic Americans* 534
- *African Americans* 535
- *Asian Americans* 535

The Political Culture of Texas 536

The Economy of Texas 541

Summary 543

Study Corner 544

19 The State Constitution 546

Texas Constitutions 547
- *Constitutions Under the Republic of Mexico* 548
- *The Republic of Texas Constitution of 1836* 548
- *The Statehood Constitution of 1845* 548
- *The Civil War and Reconstruction Constitutions of 1861, 1866, and 1869* 549
- *The Constitution of 1876* 549
- *State Constitutions as Reflections of Texas Culture* 550

Political Culture and Institutions 550

Principles of Constitutional Government 550

Characteristics Common to State Constitutions 551
- *Separation of Powers* 551
- *Bill of Rights* 552
- *Supreme Law of the State* 552

Comparing the Structure of State Constitutions 552

Amending and Revising State Constitutions 555
- *Patterns of Constitutional Change* 558
- *Amending the Texas Constitution* 558

Summary 561

Study Corner 562

20 Participation Politics and Interest Groups in Texas Politics 564

Voter Turnout in Texas 567
- *Poll Tax and Annual Registrations* 570
- *White Primary* 571
- *Gender Discrimination* 571
- *Social and Economic Factors* 572

- *Party Competition* 573
- *Regional Variations* 573
- *Other Factors Affecting Voter Turnout* 573

Interest Groups in State Politics 574

State Regulation of Interest Groups 576

Techniques Used by Interest Groups 577
- *Lobbying* 577
- *Electioneering* 578

Factors Determining the Strengths of Interest Groups 579
- *Leadership and Organization* 580
- *Geographic Distribution* 580
- *Money* 580

The Varying Strength of Interest Groups 580
- *Economic Diversity* 581
- *Political Party Competition* 581
- *Professionalism of the State Legislature and Government Fragmentation* 581

Summary 583

Study Corner 584

21 Political Parties and Elections in Texas 586

Fifty State Party Systems 587

Party Ideology 591

Democratic and Republican Party Strength in Texas 592

The One-Party Era in Texas 592

Party Realignment in Texas 593
- *The Beginning of Change* 593
- *The Election of John Tower* 594
- *The Election of Bill Clements* 594
- *The "Conversion" and Election of Phil Gramm* 595
- *The Move Toward Republican Parity with the Democrats, 1988 94* 595
- *Governor Bush and the Republican Dominance, 1995–2001* 595
- *Republican Dominance in 2002–04* 596

The Strength of the Republican Party 597

The Death of the Yellow Dog Democrat? 598

Party Dealignment 599

Elections and Election Cycles 600
- *Election Cycles* 601
- *Ballot Form* 601
- *Ballot Access to the November General Election* 601
- *Political Differences between Open and Closed Primary Systems* 606
- *Runoff Primary Elections* 607
- *The Administration and Finance of Primary Elections* 608
- *Absentee and Early Voting* 608

Campaigns 609
- *Political Consultants* 612
- *Money in Campaigns* 612

Summary 615

Study Corner 616

22 The Texas Legislature 618
The Size of the Texas Legislature 620
Methods of Election 620
Reapportionment and Redistricting Issues 625
    Equity of Representation 625
    Minority Representation 627
    Political and Racial Gerrymandering 627
Impact of Redistricting 628
Re-redistricting in 2003 628
Qualifications for Legislators 631
Getting Elected 634
Turnover in State Legislatures 638
Characteristics of State Legislatures 640
    Term Limits 640
    Sessions 640
    Salaries 641
Formal Procedures of the Legislature 644
    Leadership Positions in the Texas
       Legislature 644
    Committees in the House and Senate 647
    Formal Rules: How a Bill Becomes a
       Law 649
    Major and Minor Calendars and Bills 649
    Legislative Workload and Logjams 652
Informal Rules 652
Role Playing 653
    Representational Roles 654
    Partisan Roles 654
Rating the Texas Legislature 655
Summary 656
Study Corner 657

23 The Office of Governor and State Agencies in Texas 660
Roles of the Governor 662
Qualifications for Governor 662
Salary 666
PostGubernatorial Offices 666
Succession to Office and Acting Governor 666
Removal from Office 667
Formal Powers of the Governor 668
    Tenure 668
    Appointive and Executive Powers 670
    Budgetary Powers 675
    Legislative Powers 677
    Judicial Powers 678
    Military Powers 679
Powers of the Texas Governor Compared 679
Informal Powers 680
    Party Leadership 681
    The Governor's Staff 681

Administrative Agencies of State Government 682
    Agencies with Elected Officials 682
    Single-Head Agencies 686
    Boards and Commissions 688
    Legislative Agencies 689
    Other State Agencies and Boards 690
Sunset Review 691
    State Employees 691
Summary 693
Study Corner 694

24 The Court System in Texas 696
Court Decision Making 697
Judicial Federalism 698
Trial and Appellate Courts 699
The Structure of State Courts 700
    Magistrate or Minor Courts 700
    County Courts 700
    District Courts 702
    Appellate Courts 702
    Supreme Courts 702
Judicial Selection 703
Issues in Judicial Selection in Texas 703
    Familiar Names 704
    Straight–Ticket Voting 704
    Campaign Contributions 705
    Minority Representation 706
    Conclusions on Elected Judges 706
The "Appointive-Elective" System in Texas 707
Is There a Best System? 708
Removal and Discipline of Judges 710
The Legal System 710
    Grand Jury 711
    Petit Jury 712
Crime and Punishment in Texas 712
    The Crime Rate 713
    Factors Contributing to Crime 713
    The Effect of Punishment on Crime
       Rates 714
    The Death Penalty 716
    The Harris County Factor 718
Summary 721
Study Corner 722

25 Local Governments in Texas 724
"Creatures of the State" 726
General Law Cities and Home Rule 728
Incorporation: The Process of Creating a City 729

Forms of City Government 730

Mayor-Council Government 730
Council-Manager Government 731

Role of the Mayor 732

Role of the City Manager 733

The Commission Form of Government 734

Methods of Electing City Councils and
   Mayors 735

Election of City Councils 735
Election of Mayors 738
Nonpartisan Elections 738

Voter Turnout in City Elections 739

County Governments 740

Urban and Rural Counties 741
The Structure of County Government 742

Weaknesses of County Government in Texas 744
Possible Reform of County Government 746

Special District Governments 747

School Districts 748
Issues in School Politics 749

Summary 754
Study Corner 755

Appendixes A

Glossary G1

Notes N1

Credits C1

Index I1

List of boxes

Leaders

Chapter 1   Thomas Jefferson
             Sandra Day O'Connor
Chapter 2   James Madison
             John Marshall
Chapter 3   Alexander Hamilton
             Frederick Douglass
Chapter 4   Oliver Wendell
             Holmes Jr.
Chapter 5   Martin Luther King Jr.
             Cesar Estrada Chavez
Chapter 6   George Gallup
Chapter 7   Susan B. Anthony
             Samuel Adams
Chapter 8   Andrew Jackson
             Abraham Lincoln
Chapter 9   Pat Robertson
Chapter 10   Jody Williams
Chapter 11   John McCain
             Nancy Pelosi
Chapter 12   George Washington
Chapter 13   Herbert Hoover
Chapter 14   John Marshall
Chapter 15   Adam Smith
             Rachel Carson
             Alan Greenspan
Chapter 16   Franklin D. Roosevelt
             Marian Wright Edelman
Chapter 17   Mary Edwards Walker
             Dwight D. Eisenhower
Chapter 18   Sam Houston
Chapter 19   Bill Ratliff

How the U.S. Compares

Chapter 1   Personal Freedom and
             Self Reliance
Chapter 2   Checks and Balances
Chapter 3   Federal vs. Unitary
             Government
Chapter 4   Law and Order
Chapter 5   Inequality and Women
Chapter 6   National Pride
Chapter 7   Voter Turnout
Chapter 8   Party Systems

Chapter 9   Groups: A Nation of
             Joiners
Chapter 10   Partisan Neutrality as a
             News Value
Chapter 11   Legislative Leadership
             and Authority
Chapter 12   Systems of Executive
             Policy Leadership
Chapter 13   Educational
             Backgrounds of
             Bureaucrats
Chapter 14   Judicial Power
Chapter 15   Global Economic
             Competitiveness
Chapter 16   Children Living in
             Poverty
Chapter 17   The Burden of Military
             Spending

How Texas Compares

Chapter 18   Comparison of Growth
             Rates of the Fifteen Most
             Populous States
             Political Subcultures
             Per Capita Income in
             2002 for the Fifteen Most
             Populous States
Chapter 19   Constitutional
             Amendments Among the
             States
Chapter 20   Voter Turnout Among
             the Fifteen Populous
             States
             Party Competition in the
             States
             Primary Systems Among
             the States
Chapter 21   Limitations on Campaign
             Contributions in
             Statewide Races
Chapter 23   Term Limits for Governor

States in the Nation

Chapter 1   A College Education
Chapter 2   Direct Democracy: The
             Initiative and
             Referendum
Chapter 3   Federal Grants-in-Aid to
             the States
Chapter 4   The Death Penalty

Chapter 5   Black and Latino
             Representation in State
             Legislatures
Chapter 6   Conservatives and
             Liberals
Chapter 7   Voter Turnout in
             Presidential Elections
Chapter 8   Public Funding of State
             Elections
Chapter 9   Limits on PAC
             Contributions
Chapter 10   In the News, or Out?
Chapter 11   Women in the State
             Legislatures
Chapter 12   Electoral Votes in the
             2004 Election
             Divided Power in the
             Executive
Chapter 13   The Size of State
             Bureaucracies
Chapter 14   Principal Methods of
             Selecting State Judges
Chapter 15   Federal Taxing and
             Spending: Winners and
             Losers
Chapter 16   The Declining Number of
             Families on Welfare
Chapter 17   The All-Volunteer
             Military's Recruits

Debating the Issues

Chapter 1   Should the United States
             have a Temporary
             Workers Program for
             Mexican Citizens?
Chapter 2   Is Warrantless
             Domestic Surveillance
             Constitutional When
             Authorized Only by the
             President?
Chapter 3   Should the Federal
             Government Have the
             Authority to Prevent
             States from Legalizing
             Marijuana Use for
             Medical Purposes?
Chapter 4   Should "Under God" be
             Removed from the
             Pledge of Allegiance?
Chapter 5   Should Same-Sex
             Marriage be Legalized?
Chapter 6   Should Representatives
             Lead on the Basis of
             Opinion Polls?

Chapter 7   Should Voting through the Internet be Allowed?

Chapter 8   Should There be Limits on Campaign Contributions?

Chapter 9   Have Interest Groups Hijacked the Initiative Process?

Chapter 10   Should Reporters be Protected from Having to Reveal Sources of National Secrets?

Chapter 11   Should Partisan Gerrymandering be Abolished?

Chapter 12   Should the Electoral College be Abolished?

Chapter 13   The Case of Iraq's Weapons of Mass Destruction: Did the CIA Play Politics?

Chapter 14   Should all the Florida Ballots have been Counted?

Chapter 15   Should the United States have Supported the Kyoto Agreement?

Chapter 16   Are Tax Cuts for High Income Taxpayers Good for America?

Chapter 17   Should U.S. Forces Stay in Iraq?

Chapter 19   Should Gay Marriage Be Banned?

Chapter 21   Do Campaign Contributions Buy Influence with the Governor?

Chapter 22   Should the Legislature Meet in Annual Sessions?

Chapter 24   Should Members of Legislature Be Paid a Living Wage?

Chapter 25   Should an Alternative to Evolution Be Taught in Public Schools?

Political Culture

Chapter 1   Religion and American Ideals

Chapter 2   Liberty and the Bill of Rights

Chapter 3   Large Versus Small Republics

Chapter 4   Procedural Due Process and Personal Liberty

Chapter 5   Private Discrimination: Liberty or Equality?

Chapter 6   Americans' Ideologies

Chapter 7   Voting and Self Government

Chapter 8   Parties, Political Equality, and Self-Government

Chapter 9   Interest Groups, Liberty, and Equality

Chapter 10   Liberty, Self-Government, and a Free Press

Chapter 11   Congress and Self-Government

Chapter 12   Executive Power and Liberty

Chapter 13   Bureaucracy, Liberty, and Self-Government

Chapter 14   Judicial Review and Liberty

Chapter 15   Liberty and Equality through the Economy

Chapter 16   Education and Equality

Chapter 17   Foreign Policy and America's Ideals

Chapter 18   Texas as a Majority-Minority State

Chapter 19   Constitutional Change in Texas

Chapter 20   Voting Rights

             Election Cycles

             Lobbying Texas Style

             Money Spent By Lobby Groups

             Grassroots or Astroturf?

Chapter 21   Judge Upholds "Sore Loser" Law

Chapter 22   You Better Be Good—the Lobby Is Watching

Chapter 23   The Weak Governor In Texas

Chapter 24   The Application of Court Rulings

Chapter 25   Advantages of Decentralized Governments

             The Creation of Impact Texas

Media & Politics

Chapter 1   Comedy News: The Daily Show

Chapter 2   Are Bloggers Today's Pamphleteers

Chapter 3   Local Self-Governance and Media Consolidation

Chapter 4   Christian News Broadcasting

Chapter 5   Religious Insult or Cultural Expression

Chapter 7   The Decline of Broadcast News and the Television News Audience

Chapter 8   Fox: News with a Partisan Twist

Chapter 10   The Twilight of Investigative Reporting

Chapter 11   C-SPAN

Chapter 13   National Public Radio and the Corporation for Public Broadcasting

Chapter 17   Global Television and Foreign Policy

Chapter 21   Texas Blogs: The New Vocal Minority?

Chapter 22   Texas Legislature Blogs

Get Involved!

Chapter 1   American Ideals and Civic Participation

Chapter 2   Speak Up

Chapter 3   Step Up

Chapter 4   Stand Up

Chapter 5   Stand Up

Chapter 6   Inform Yourself

Chapter 7   Register and Vote

Chapter 8   Commit Yourself

Chapter 9   Join Up

Chapter 10   Communicate

Chapter 11   Working on the Inside

Chapter 12   Every Four Years

Chapter 13   Serve

Chapter 14   Sit, When Called

Chapter 15   Do Your Part

Chapter 16   Lend a Helping Hand

Chapter 17   Serve Your Country

Chapter 18   Who Governs?

Chapter 19   Concepts from the Bill of Rights in the Texas Constitution

Chapter 20   New Efforts to Limit Voting Rights—Voter ID Cards

             The Texas Public Utility Commission

Chapter 22   Know Your State Representative and Senator

             Competition in State Legislative Races

             From Lawmaker to Lobbyist in one Short Step: Harvest Time

Chapter 23   Campaign Money Used to Pay Members of Governor's Staff

             Democratic Control and Bureau Cratic Responsiveness

Chapter 24   Justice For Sale?

             Does the Death Penalty Reduce Crime?

Chapter 25   More Books Than Anyone Can Read, Just Do It Right, and Sick Horses

Preface for the Instructor

Recent years have brought changes barely imaginable not so long ago—the war on terrorism, economic globalization, and soaring budget deficits to name a few. In this text, I have sought to capture these and other dynamic features of American politics.

REACHING OUT TO THE STUDENT

This text is dedicated to helping students learn, including nurturing their capacity for critical thinking and civic participation. I have tried to write a text that expands students' horizons as well as one that informs their thinking, a text that they will want to read as opposed to one they are simply required to read. Four features of the text support this effort:

Narrative Style

This is a narrative-based text. Unlike a text that piles fact upon fact and thereby squeezes the life out of its subject, the narrative style aims to bring the subject to life. Politics doesn't have to be dull. Politics has all the elements of drama with the added feature of affecting the lives of real people.

The narrative style is an expository form that allows for the presentation of a lot of material but always as part of a larger point. The details buttress the narrative, highlighting the main ideas. Pedagogical studies have shown that the narrative style is a superior method for teaching a complex science such as political science. It promotes student learning by bringing the key points squarely into view.

Studies also show that students read attentively for a longer period of time when a text is narrative in form. In contrast with a text that compartmentalizes its material, a narrative text draws students into the material, piquing their interest. The strength of a narrative text, however, is not simply that it is more interesting to read. Its deep strength is that it disciplines the writer. Nothing is more discouraging to students than to encounter material of uncertain significance. The narrative form forces the writer to organize the material so that every piece has a purpose. The fact that partisanship affects Supreme Court appointments is important in itself, but it gains signifance when explained in the context of the openness of the American legal system, whereby political controversies often become also judicial ones.

Critical Thinking

A pedagogical goal of this text is to help students think critically. Critical thinking is the most important skill that a student can acquire from exposure to the social sciences. Students cannot learn to think critically by engaging in list making or rote memorization. Critical thinking is a cultivated skill that students develop by reflecting on what they have read, by resolving challenges to their assumptions, and by confronting vexing issues. To this end, I have structured the discussion in ways that encourage students to reflect as they read. In the first chapter, for example, I discuss the inexact meanings, conflicting implications, and unfinished promise of Americans' most cherished ideals, including liberty and equality. The discussion includes the "Chinese Exclusion," a grotesque and not widely known chapter in our history that can lead students to think about what it means to be an American.

Two of the book's boxed features have critical thinking as their purpose. Each chapter has a "How the United States Compares" box and a "States in the Nation" box. The United States is the world's oldest democracy but also one of its most distinctive. America's political processes and policies are different in many respects from those found elsewhere. The American states, too, differ from each other, despite being part of the same union. Students invariably gain a better understanding of their nation or state when they become aware of how it differs from others. When students discover, for example, that the United States has a higher child poverty rate than other Western democracies, they naturally want to know why this is the case.

Citizen Involvement

Of the academic disciplines, political science is most closely connected to a role that Americans share—that of citizen. Citizenship is a right and entails a duty. Young Americans recognize the responsibility of citizenship but do not always know how to act on it. Many of them also do not see what theorists like Aristotle and John Stuart Mill saw: that acts of citizenship enlarge the individual as well as the community.

Each chapter of this text includes two participation suggestions. The first is a "Participate!" entry at the end of each chapter. The second is a more substantial "Get Involved!" box within each chapter. Citizenship is partly a state of mind, and the initial "Get Involved!" boxes seek to foster this outlook. In Chapter 2, for example, the student is urged to participate in the classroom—to "speak up"—as a means of developing communication skills that can enhance civic participation. Subsequent "Get Involved!" boxes suggest a civic or political activity in which the student can engage.

Politics as Discipline and Practice

I have attempted in this book to present American government through the analytical lens of political science but in a way that captures the vivid world of politics. I regularly reminded myself while writing the book that only a tiny percentage of introductory students are interested in an academic political science career. Most students take the course because they are required to do so or because they like politics. I have sought to write a book that will deepen political interest in the second type of student and kindle it in the first type. I had a model for this kind of book in mind: V.O. Key's absorbing *Politics, Parties, and Pressure Groups,* which I had read years earlier as an undergraduate. Professor Key was a consummate scholar with a deep love of politics who gently chided scholars whose interest in political science was confined to the "science" part.

My hope is that the readers of this text will learn, as I did as an undergraduate, to value what political science provides, and to relish what politics offers. The body of this book is shaped by the systematic knowledge that political science has developed. The spirit of this book is defined by the challenging nature of politics—the ongoing struggle of Americans to find agreeable ways to govern themselves. This struggle fills many pages of the text, most pointedly in the "Debating the Issues" box that appears in each chapter. These boxes present opposing opinions on current issues, including immigration, global warming, warrantless wiretaps, same-sex marriage, tax cuts, and the Iraq conflict.

POLITICAL CULTURE AND OTHER REGULARITIES IN AMERICAN POLITICS

Political science is a complex science in the sense that the objects of study are too intricate and fluid to be reduced to a couple of mathematical formulas. Indeed, politics includes such a wide range of human activity that political scientists have studied it through a variety of analytical tools: legal analysis, historical analysis, cultural analysis, political psychology, political sociology, rational choice, institutional analysis, organizational analysis, and so on.

Nonetheless, the systematic study of American politics has yielded an impressive body of knowledge. Political scientists have identified several tendencies that are a basis for a systematic understanding of the U.S. political system. These tendencies are introduced in the first chapter and developed in subsequent ones. If students can be expected to forget many of the points made in this book, they may at least come away with an understanding of the regularities of American politics:

- Enduring ideals that are the basis of Americans' political identity and culture and that are a source of many of their beliefs, aspirations, and conflicts.

- Extreme fragmentation of governing authority that is based on an elaborate system of checks and balances that serves to protect against abuses of political power but also makes it difficult for political majorities to assert power when confronting an entrenched or intense political minority.

- Many competing groups, which are a result of the nation's great size, population diversity, and economic complexity and which exercise considerable influence—sometimes to society's benefit and sometimes to its detriment—on public policy.

- Strong emphasis on individual rights, which results in substantial benefits to the individual and places substantial restrictions on majorities.

- Preference for the marketplace as a means of allocating resources, which has the effect of placing many economic issues beyond the reach of political majorities.

All these regularities figure prominently in this book, but the first one I listed has a special niche. As Tocqueville, Bryce, Hartz, Rossiter, and other observers have stressed, Americans' deep-rooted political beliefs are the basis of their unity. Americans are a diverse people with origins in many lands. Their nation was founded on a set of principles—including liberty, self-government, equality, and individualism—that became the people's unifying bond. When an American confronts an everyday situation and responds by saying "It's my right," he or she is responding in a way that is distinctly if not uniquely American. And when all such patterned behaviors are taken into account, they constitute a unique political perspective—an *American* political perspective.

Although this text's primary focus is U.S. political institutions and processes, they operate within the context of the nation's political culture. How might one explain, for example, the fact that the United States is the only affluent democracy without government-provided medical care for all? Or why Americans, though deeply divided over the conflict in Iraq, universally believe the Iraqi people would be better off if they lived in a democracy? Or why issues such as stem-cell research and biological evolution are larger controversies in the United States than in other Western democracies? Or, as a final example, why lobbying groups have more political clout in the United States than anywhere else?

No analysis of American institutions or processes can fully answer these questions. Americans' deep-rooted beliefs about politics must also be taken into account. Government-provided health care for all, as an example, is at odds with American individualism, which emphasizes self-reliance—a reason why Presidents Roosevelt and Johnson backed away from proposing such a program and why Presidents Truman and Clinton failed miserably when they did so. Americans govern themselves differently than do other people because they have different beliefs about the purposes of government. Indeed, each of the other regularities on the list above is a prominent feature of U.S. politics *because* they stem from cultural beliefs. The prominence in U.S. politics of the marketplace, of interest groups, of individual rights, and of checks and balances owes in significant part to Americans' deep-seated ideas about the proper way to govern.

This fact is one of the major lessons students can derive from a course on U.S. government because it is the link between today's politics and those of the past and the future. What is it—if not a desire for a fuller measure of liberty, equality, self-government, and self-realization—that connects today's citizens with other generations of Americans? This recognition can also lead students to seek a more active part in civic life. America's principles—and the political, economic, and social relationships they idealize—must be constantly renewed and enlarged through principled leadership and citizen action.

The significance of political culture in this text is apparent in the "Political Culture" box of each chapter. These boxes challenge students to think about the encompassing nature of America's political culture. The box in the opening chapter, for example, examines the connection between Americans' political ideals and their religious practices.

NEW TO THIS EDITION

The chapters have been thoroughly updated to include recent scholarship and the latest developments at home and abroad. The largest changes were occasioned by the 2006 midterm election and the Iraq conflict, which have altered American politics far more than anyone would have predicted two years ago, when the previous edition was published. The role of the Internet in American politics continues to feature ever more prominently in the text's instructional content. Each chapter includes one or more World Wide Web icons (identified by a computer mouse alongside which "WWW" appears). Each icon indicates the presence on the text's website of material (self-tests, simulations, and graphics) that is relevant to the topic being discussed.

The chapters also include Historical Background icons that signal content on key historical moments. "Learning from history" contributes to students' understanding of contemporary politics and to their development as citizens. The Cold War was ending as today's undergraduates were being born but its impact on American politics did not expire with the death of the Soviet Union. Students also learn when asked to think more deeply about things they believe they already know. Every student is familiar with the war on terrorism, but not all of them have thought about its impact on civil liberties, foreign relations, or the constitutional balance between Congress and the presidency.

This edition includes several new box features. The "Get Involved!" and "Political Culture" boxes mentioned earlier are new. So, too, are the "Media and Politics" boxes. The extraordinary changes in how we get our news are addressed in these boxes. Jon Stewart's "The Daily Show" is examined in one of these boxes; Christian broadcasting is discussed in another. A box feature entitled "Leaders" is also new. Each chapter has one or more of these boxes, which highlight the contributions of exemplary Americans. The text's other box features—"How the United States Compares" and "States in the Nation"—are holdovers from the previous edition.

Another holdover is the "Study Corner" that appears at the end of each chapter. We introduced this feature in the last edition, and the response has been uniformly favorable. Each Study Corner is a two-page study guide that includes the chapter's key terms, a self-test, a critical-thinking exercise, and book and web references, as well as a political participation suggestion.

Finally, in response to suggestions from instructors that have found many of today's students to be less than voracious readers, I have shortened this edition of the text, not by cutting content but by tightening the discussion. I did a line-by-line edit of the entire book, looking to take out words, phrases, examples, or sentences that could be excised without loss of meaning. I also rewrote and tightened whole sections of several chapters. In doing this, I came to understand the truth in Thomas Jefferson's apology to John Adams for writing him a lengthy letter. Wrote Jefferson: "I didn't have time to write a short letter, so I wrote a long one instead." Streamlining takes more time, but the result is a clearer, more vigorous rendition. This edition of the text has roughly fifty fewer pages than the previous one.

SUPPLEMENTS PACKAGE

This text is accompanied by supplementary materials. Please contact your local McGraw-Hill representative or McGraw-Hill Customer Service (800-338-3987) for details concerning policies, prices, and availability, as some restrictions may apply.

For Students and Instructors

OnLine Learning Center with PowerWeb
Visit our website at www.mhhe.com/pattersontad8.

This website contains separate instructor and student areas. The instructor area contains the instructor's manual, test bank, and PowerPoints, while the student area hosts a wealth of study materials such as additional Internet resources, concept lists, practice tests, essay questions, and thinking exercises. All chapter-by-chapter material has been updated for the new edition.

PoliCentral Introducing PoliCentral! McGraw-Hill is excited to bring you PoliCentral, a new dynamic, interactive site filled with simulations, debate tools, participation activities, and video, audio, and speech activities.

Debate! Citizenship and Debate! Voting & Elections CD-ROMS
Political Science comes alive through **Debate!** McGraw-Hill's **Debate!** CD-ROM provides instant access to some of the most important and interesting documents, images, artifacts, audio recordings, and videos available on topics in political science. You can browse the collection across critical thinking questions, media types, subjects, or your own custom search criteria. Each source opens into our Source window, packed with tools that provide rich scholarly contexts, interactive explorations, and access to a printable copy for each source.

While examining any of these sources, you can use our notebook feature to take notes, bookmark favorite sources, and save or print copies of all the sources for use outside of the archive (for example, inserting them into PowerPoint). After researching a particular theme or time period, you can use our **Debate!** outlining tool to walk you through the steps of composing a debate or presentation.

Through its browsing and inspection tool, **Debate!** helps you practice the art of political debate using a rich collection of multimedia evidence. This process of political science investigation follows three simple but engaging steps: **ask,** where you use our browsing panels to search and filter the sources; **research,** where you use the Source Browser and Source Window's tools to examine the sources in detail; and **debate,** where you can practice outlining arguments using selected sources from the collection.

For Instructors

Instructor's Manual/Test Bank
Available online, the instructor's manual includes the following for each chapter: learning objectives, focus points and main points, a chapter summary, a list of major concepts, a lecture outline, alternative lecture objectives, class discussion topics, and a list of Internet resources. The test bank consists of approximately fifty multiple-choice questions, and five suggested essay topics per chapter, with answers given alongside the questions. This tool also offers multimedia components, such as PowerPoint presentations, photographs, maps, and charts.

McGraw-Hill American Government Lecture Launchers
Lecture Launchers provide approximately two to three minutes of chapters-specific video to help instructors "launch" their lecture. Round-table discussions, famous speeches, and everyday stories are followed by two "Pause and Think" questions per clip aimed at the heart of new debate. These invite students to consider who sets policy and how they can get involved. In addition to reinforcing the basics, these short video clips focus on civic involvement and consider the Framers of the Constitution. Available in VHS and DVD, with selected clips also available on PoliCentral.com.

PageOut
At www.mhhe.com/pageout, instructors can create their own websites. PageOut requires no prior knowledge of HTML; simply plug the course information into template and click on one of sixteen designs. The process leaves instructors with a professionally designed website.

PRIMIS Online
Instructors can use this text as a whole, or they can select specific chapters and customize the text to suit their specific classroom needs. The customized text can be created as a hardcopy or as an e-book. Also available in this format are custom chapters on **"California Government"** and **"Texas Government."**

For Students

Study Guide
Each chapter includes the following: learning objectives, focus and main points (to help direct students' attention to key material), chapter summary, major concepts (listed and defined), annotated Internet resources, analytical-thinking exercises, and test review questions—approximately ten true-false, fifteen multiple-choice, and five essay topics. The answers are provided at the end of each chapter.

2006 Midterm Election Update
    by Richard Semiatin of American University
This supplement details the 2006 election. Richard Semiatin analyzes the context of the election and the role of the Bush administration. This supplement also contains information on major election issues, on the media campaign, on money and fund-raising, on voter participation, and finally on the results and implications of the election.

YOUR SUGGESTIONS ARE INVITED

The American Democracy has been in use in college classrooms for more than a dozen years. During that time, the text (including its concise edition, *We the People*) has been adopted at more than eight hundred colleges and universities. I am extremely grateful to all who have used it. I am particularly indebted to the many instructors and students over the years who have sent me recommendations or corrections. Professors William Plants and Michael Treleavan, for example, caught errors in the previous edition that are corrected in this one. Alexandre Cournol, a Florida International University undergraduate, was among the students who sent thoughtful notes. You can contact me at the John F. Kennedy School, Harvard University, Cambridge, MA 02138, or by e-mail: thomas_patterson@harvard.edu.

Thomas E. Patterson

Preface for the Student: A Guided Tour

This book describes the American political system, one of the most interesting and intricate systems in the world. The discussion is comprehensive; a lot of information is packed into the text. No student could possibly remember every tiny fact or observation that each chapter contains, but the main points of discussion are easily grasped if you make the effort.

The text has several features that will help you identify and understand the major points of discussion. For example, each chapter has an opening story that illustrates a central theme of the chapter, followed by a brief summary of the chapter's main ideas.

The guided tour presented here describes the organization and special features of your text.

Thomas E. Petterson

Opening Illustration

A narration of a compelling event introduces the chapter's main ideas.

CHAPTER 1

One hears people say that it is inherent in the habits and nature of democracies to change feelings and thoughts at every moment. . . . But I have never seen anything like that happening in the great democracy on the other side of the ocean. What struck me most in the United States was the difficulty experienced in getting an idea, once conceived, out of the head of the majority.

Alexis de Tocqueville[1]

At 8:47 A.M. on September 11, 2001, a hijacked American Airlines passenger jet slammed into one of the twin towers of New York City's World Trade Center. Twenty minutes later, a second hijack jet hit the other tower. A third hijacked jet then plowed into the Pentagon in Washington, D.C. Within two hours, the World Trade Center collapsed, killing all still inside, including police and firefighters who bravely into the buildings to help in the evacuation. Three thousand were murdered that September morning, the highest death toll attack on American soil by a foreign adversary. The toll would have higher if not for the bravery of passengers aboard United Airlines who fought with its hijackers, causing the plane—which was a Washington, D.C.—to crash in a barren Pennsylvania field.

That evening, a somber George W. Bush addressed the nation Americans to stay calm and resolute, President Bush said: "America geted for an attack because we're the brightest beacon for freedom tunity in the world." Sprinkled throughout his speech were time-honored American ideals: liberty, the will of the people, justice of law. "No one will keep that light from shining," said Bush.

The ideals that guided Bush's speech would have been familiar eration of Americans. These ideals have been invoked when America gone to war, declared peace, celebrated national holidays, launched icy initiatives, and asserted new rights.[2] The ideals contained in were the same ones that had punctuated the speeches of George Washington, Abraham Lincoln, Susan B. Anthony and Franklin D. Roosevelt, Luther King Jr., and Ronald Reagan.

The ideals were also there at the nation's beginning, when into words in the Declaration of Independence and the Constitution the practical meaning of these words has changed greatly during two centuries the United States has been a sovereign nation. When of the Constitution began the document with the words "We the did not have all Americans equally in mind. Black slaves, women, out property did not have the same rights as propertied white me

A supporter of Oregon's Death with Dignity law holds a sign outside the federal courthouse in Portland, Oregon, where a hearing on the U.S. Justice Department's challenge to the law is being held. This type of struggle between the power of the federal government and the power of a state government has been repeated countless times in American history, a reflection of the U.S. federal system that vests sovereignty in both the national and state governments. In this particular case, the state, Oregon, prevailed. The U.S. Supreme Court in 2006 ruled that Attorney General John Ashcroft had exceeded his authority in trying to invalidate the Oregon law.

88   PART ONE   Foundations

in which constitutional authority is divided between a national government and state governments: each government is assumed to derive its powers directly from the people and therefore to have sovereignty (final authority) over the policy responsibilities assigned to it. The federal system consists of nation *and* states, indivisible yet separate.[3]

This chapter on American constitutionalism focuses on federalism. The nature of the relationship between the nation and the states was the most pressing issue when the Constitution was written in 1787. This chapter describes how that issue helped shape the Constitution. The chapter's closing sections discuss how federalism has changed throughout the nation's history and conclude with a brief overview of contemporary federalism. The main points presented in the chapter are these:

- *The power of government must be equal to its responsibilities.* The Constitution was needed because the nation's preceding system (under the Articles of Confederation) was too weak to accomplish its expected goals, particularly those of a strong defense and an integrated economy.

- *Federalism—the Constitution's division of governing authority between two levels, nation and states—was the result of political bargaining.* Federalism was not a theoretical principle, but a compromise made necessary in 1787 by the prior existence of the states.

- *Federalism is not a fixed principle for allocating power between the national and state governments, but a principle that has changed over time in response to new political needs.* Federalism has passed through several distinct stages in the course of the nation's history.

- *Contemporary federalism tilts toward national authority,* reflecting the increased interdependence of American society. However, there is a current trend toward reducing the scope of federal authority.

FEDERALISM: NATIONAL AND STATE SOVEREIGNTY

At the time of the writing of the Constitution, some of America's top leaders were dead set against the creation of a strong national government. When rumors circulated that the delegates to the constitutional convention were planning to propose such a government, Patrick Henry, an ardent believer in state-centered government, said that he "smelt a rat." After the convention had adjourned, he realized that his fears were justified. "Who authorized

Main Points

The chapter's three or four main ideas are summarized in the opening pages.

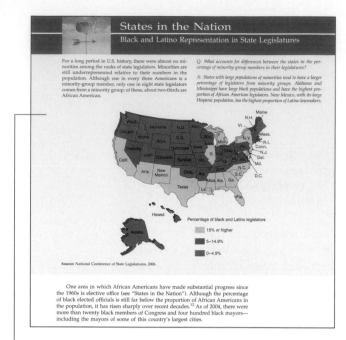

"States in the Nation" Boxes

Each chapter has a box that compares the fifty states on some aspect of politics.

"Debating the Issues" Boxes

Each chapter has a box that introduces a current controversy and includes opposing opinions on the issue.

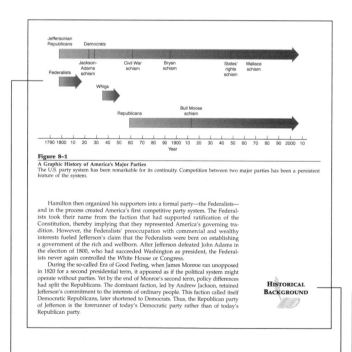

Figures and Tables

Each chapter has figures and tables that relate to points made in the discussion.

Reference Icons

These icons reference material that is of historical importance or available on the text's website.

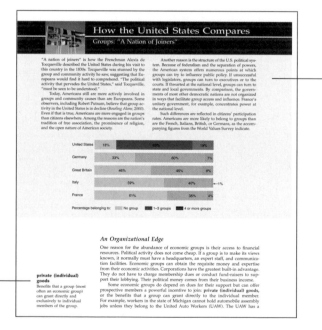

"How the United States Compares" Boxes

Each chapter has a box that compares the United States with other countries in regard to a major political feature.

Key Terms

Each key term is defined in the margin near its reference in the text.

Get Involved!

Register and Vote

Some observers take comfort in low-turnout elections. They claim that the country is better off if less interested and less knowledgeable citizens stay home on election day. In a 1997 cover story in *Atlantic Monthly*, Robert Kaplan wrote: "The last thing America needs is more voters—particularly badly educated and alienated ones—with a passion for politics." The gist of this age-old argument is that low turnout protects society from erratic or even dangerous shifts in power. However, America's voters have not acted whimsically. Except for an interlude in the 1780s, when the Articles of Confederation governed the United States, erratic voting has not been a persistent source of political instability.

On the other hand, a low participation rate can be a problem. In general, the smaller the electorate, the less representative it is of the public as a whole. Polls indicate that the outcomes of elections would in some instances have changed if turnout had been substantially higher. And even if greater voter turnout would not have altered the outcomes, campaign platforms have always been tailored to those who vote. As the political scientists Steve Rosenstone and Mark Hanson note in *Mobilization, Participation, and Democracy in America* (1993): "The idle go unheard: They do not speak up, define the agenda, frame the issues, or affect the choices leaders make."

Voting can strengthen democracy in other ways. When people vote, they are more attentive to politics and are better informed about issues affecting them. As the philosopher John Stuart Mill theorized a century ago, voting also deepens community involvement. Studies indicate that voters participate more frequently in community affairs and are more likely to work with others on community projects. Of course, these associations say more about the type of person who votes than about the effect of voting. But recent evidence, as Harvard University's Robert Putnam notes in *Bowling Alone* (2000), "suggests that voting itself encourages volunteering and other forms of good citizenship."

Voting among young adults in particular has declined. When eighteen- to twenty-one-year-old citizens gained eligibility to vote in the 1972 election, nearly 50 percent of them voted. In 2000, less than 35 percent did so. The hotly contested 2004 election, waged against the backdrop of a soft economy and turmoil in Iraq, produced increased turnout among young adults, although the level was substantially below that of 1972. Unless increased turnout among young voters can be sustained, the overall voting rate will continue to stagnate, because the oldest generation, those who grew up during the Depression and World War II, participate at very high rates.

Changes in registration laws have made it easier for students to vote if they choose to do so. Voting is not a time-consuming task, and the benefits to the individual and society are considerable. Have you registered yet?

Why Some Americans Vote and Others Do Not

Even though turnout is lower in the United States than in other major Western democracies, some Americans vote regularly while others seldom or never vote. Among the explanations for these individual differences are civic attitudes, age, and education and income.

Civic Attitudes

Americans differ greatly in their feelings about politics. Some have almost no interest in politics. **Apathy** is the term used to describe a general lack of concern with politics. Just as some people would not attend the Super Bowl if it were free and being played across the street, some Americans would not bother to vote even if a ballot were delivered to their door. Other Americans, however, have a strong sense of **civic duty**—the belief that they are obliged to participate in public affairs.

apathy
A feeling of personal disinterest in or unconcern with politics.

civic duty
The belief of an individual that civic and political participation is a responsibility of citizenship.

"Get Involved!" Boxes

Each chapter has a box that provides suggestions for getting involved in civic and political activity.

LEADERS

SANDRA DAY O'CONNOR

In 1981, Sandra Day O'Connor became the first woman to be appointed to the U.S. Supreme Court, where she served for a quarter century before retiring in 2006. Toward the end of her tenure, she was widely regarded as the Court's most influential member. A pragmatic jurist, she was the swing vote on an ideologically divided Court. She cast the deciding vote in many 5-4 decisions, usually but not consistently siding with its more conservative members. A graduate of Stanford Law School, O'Connor faced discrimination because of her gender. One firm offered her a job as a legal secretary but not as an attorney. She eventually started her own practice and later served as assistant attorney general in Arizona. She ran successfully for a seat in the Arizona legislature and subsequently was appointed to the Arizona Court of Appeals before being nominated by President Ronald Reagan for a seat on the U.S. Supreme Court. As a member of the Court, O'Connor cast the deciding vote in leading cases involving key issues such as affirmative action, federalism, and abortion. O'Connor's policy influence reflects Tocqueville's observation that sooner or later most political issues in America become also judicial issues. O'Connor's career is testament to the importance in America of constitutionalism—the idea that the power of government over individuals is subject to judicial oversight.

"Leaders" Boxes

Each chapter has one or more boxes highlighting the contributions of exemplary Americans.

Political Culture

Religion and American Ideals

The United States is a nation established in 1776 on a set of principles—liberty, equality, and self-government. These ideals derived in part from broad lessons of history, the direct experiences of the colonists, and treatises such as those of Locke and Rousseau. Religious beliefs also played a major part.

Many of the early colonists came to America in order to practice their religions freely. Church and state in Europe were joined. Government there sided with a particular religion—Roman Catholicism in France and Spain, Anglicanism in England. Rhode Island's founder, the Reverend Roger Williams, was a Calvinist who left his native England for reasons of religious freedom. Williams was the first to assert that church and state in America ought to be separate. Williams argued that salvation required an acceptance of God, which is meaningful only if it is an act of free will—and this is impossible if religion is imposed on the individual by the state. To Williams and others, religious liberty and political liberty were inseparable. The prevalence of this view is apparent in the First Amendment to the Constitution, which at once provides for freedom of political expression *and* for religious freedom.

Liberty is not the only American ideal with a religious basis. Equality was considered God's work: "all men are created equal." Every individual was a child of God and thus equal in His eyes. (This belief posed a dilemma for slaveholders, who finessed it by claiming that slaves either were soulless or were secondary beings in God's "natural order.") Self-government, too, had a religious foundation, though a Protestant one. Unlike the Catholic Church, which was hierarchical in its organization, with the Pope and bishops at its head, many Protestant sects had self-governing congregations. Their democratic operation affected their members' views on the proper form of government.

America, said the British writer G. K. Chesterton, is "a nation with the soul of a church" and "the only country founded on a creed." He could have added that America is also a nation that emulated a religious model in its governing document. The first colonists formed religious communities governed by written covenant, a model for the written Constitution drafted and ratified by Americans more than a century later.

Forty years later, the English philosopher John Locke used Hobbes's idea of a social contract to argue *against* absolutism. In his *Second Treatise on Civil Government* (1690), Locke claimed that all individuals have certain natural (or inalienable) rights, including those of life, liberty, and property. Such rights, Locke wrote, belonged to people in their natural state before government was created. When people come together in order to have the protection that only organized government can provide, they retain these rights. People enter into the social contract—they agree to be governed—in order to safeguard their rights. Accordingly, government is obliged to provide this protection. If it fails to do so, Locke argued, the people can rightfully rebel against it and create a new government.

Three-quarters of a century later, the French philosopher Jean Jacques Rousseau extended the idea of a social contract to include popular rule. Like Locke, Rousseau despised absolute government. "Man was born free, but everywhere he is in chains" are the opening words of Rousseau's *Social Contract* (1762). Rousseau claimed that people in their natural state are innocent and happy. Accordingly, the only legitimate government is one that governs in their interest and with their consent. The people, in Rousseau's view, were sovereign. Government was not the sovereign authority; government was merely the instrument for carrying out the people's laws. Rousseau worried, however, that the people would act selfishly and proposed a limit on popular sovereignty. It would be legitimate only if people acted in the common interest—what Rousseau called "the general will."

"Political Culture" Boxes

Each chapter has a box that examines the connection between the American political culture and a chapter topic.

Media & Politics

Comedy News: *The Daily Show*

Long before baseball or football enjoyed its reputation as America's national pastime, political humor occupied that spot. The United States was founded on a rejection of political authority—that of the British monarch—and poking fun at the nation's leaders is nearly an American birthright. Every generation could relate to these words of humorist Will Rogers: "I don't make jokes. I just watch the government and report the facts." Writer Mark Twain echoed this sentiment: "Reader, suppose you were an idiot, and suppose you were a member of Congress. But I repeat myself."

The acknowledged king of political comedy today is Jon Stewart. His program, *The Daily Show*, attracts roughly 1.5 million viewers, ranking it near the top of the ratings for a cable news program. Like Rush Limbaugh's radio talk show (see Chapter 10), which soared in the ratings during the 1990s when the conservative Limbaugh feasted off the actions of Democrat President Bill Clinton, the liberal Stewart's television show has risen in popularity based on his swipes at Republican President George W. Bush. In one telling moment, Stewart looked blankly at the television screen for seemingly endless seconds before blurting out "Please say, please say, you're kidding me." This followed a videotape of National Security Advisor Condoleeza Rice admitting to Congress that she had read a classified briefing titled "Bin Laden Determined to Attack Inside the United States" a month before the September 11, 2001, terrorist attacks on the World Trade Center and the Pentagon. Rice had earlier claimed that no one in the Bush administration could possibly have foreseen the attacks.

Unlike most hosts of shows with a partisan twist, Stewart takes occasional potshots at his preferred party. Following a report about prisoner abuse by U.S. military personnel, Stewart commented: "The prisoner scandal is yet another election year problem for President Bush. And, with the economy still struggling, combat operations in Iraq dragging on, and the 9-11 hearings revealing damning information, even an opponent of limited political skill should be able to capitalize on those problems. The Democrats, however, chose to nominate John Kerry."

The Daily Show's formula is a mixture of comedy and the day's news events. More than half of the program's audience is under 40 years, which is the opposite of the age distribution of the audience for broadcast network newscasts. But if *The Daily Show* is helpful in getting today's young adults to pay attention to news, it might not be helpful in getting them involved in politics. A recent study by Jody Baumgartner and Jonathan Morris, political scientists at East Carolina University, found that youthful viewers of *The Daily Show*, as compared with youthful viewers of broadcast network news, had more negative views of candidates and of the electoral process.

Political humor dates to the Greeks, but few societies have embraced it as fully as have Americans. Part of the reason is rooted in the American political culture. Liberty, equality, and self-government are assertions of individualism as pitted against traditional deference to the high, the mighty, the rich, and the well-born. As Mark Twain noted of arrogant leaders, "Against the assault of laughter nothing can stand."

Theories of Power

Who has power in America? Who, in the end, decides the policies that the U.S. government pursues? Do the people themselves hold this power, or does it reside in the hands of a relatively small group of influential people, either within or outside of government?

This issue is compelling because the ultimate question of any political system is the question of who governs. Is power widely shared and used for the benefit of the many, or is it narrowly held and used to the advantage of the few? The issue is compelling for a second reason: power is easy to define but hard to locate. Consider, for example, the votes that a member of Congress casts. Are these votes an expression of the member's power, or are they an expression of the power of groups on whom the member depends for reelection?

The pattern of political power in America has been shown to differ substantially across individuals, institutions, and policy areas. As a result, there is no single theory of how power in America is held and exercised. Instead, four broad theories predominate (see Table 1-3). None of these theories describes every aspect of American politics, but each applies in some situations.

"Media and Politics" Boxes

Some chapters have a box that examines politics as presented through the media, particularly the newer media.

"Self-Test" Icons

These identify the website where self-test and other support items can be found.

Summary

A short discussion, organized around the chapter's main points, summarizes each chapter's content.

Summary

Self-Test www.mhhe.com/pattersontad8

A political interest group is composed of a set of individuals organized to promote a shared political concern. Most interest groups owe their existence to factors other than politics. These groups form for economic reasons, such as the pursuit of profit, and maintain themselves by making profits (in the case of corporations) or by providing their members with private goods, such as jobs and wages. Economic groups include corporations, trade associations, labor unions, farm organizations, and professional associations. Collectively, economic groups are by far the largest set of organized interests. The group system tends to favor interests that are already economically and socially advantaged.

Citizens' groups do not have the same organizational advantages as economic groups. They depend on voluntary contributions from potential members, who may lack interest and resources or who recognize that they will get the collective good from a group's activity even if they do not participate (the free-rider problem). Citizens' groups include public-interest, single-issue, and ideological groups. Their numbers have increased dramatically since the 1960s despite their organizational problems.

Organized interests seek influence largely by lobbying public officials and contributing to election campaigns. Using an inside strategy, lobbyists develop direct contacts with legislators, government bureaucrats, and members of the judiciary in order to persuade them to accept the group's perspective on policy. Groups also use an outside strategy, seeking to mobilize public support for their goals. This strategy relies in part on grassroots lobbying—encouraging group members and the public to communicate their policy views to officials. Outside lobbying also includes efforts to elect officeholders who will support group aims. Through political action committees (PACs), organized groups now provide nearly a third of all contributions received by congressional candidates.

The policies that emerge from the group system bring benefits to many of society's interests, and in some instances these benefits also serve the collective interest. But when groups can essentially dictate policies, the common good is not served. The majority's interest is subordinated to group (minority) interests. In most instances, the minority consists of individuals who already enjoy a substantial share of society's benefits.

STUDY CORNER

Key Terms

air wars (p. 236)
candidate-centered politics (p. 213)
grassroots party (p. 215)
hard money (p. 231)
hired guns (p. 233)
money chase (p. 233)
multiparty system (p. 221)
nomination (p. 227)
packaging (of a candidate) (p. 235)

party-centered politics (p. 213)
party coalition (p. 223)
party competition (p. 214)
party organizations (p. 227)
party realignment (p. 217)
political party (p. 213)
primary election
  (direct primary) (p. 227)
proportional representation (p. 221)

prospective voting (p. 220)
retrospective voting (p. 220)
service relationship (p. 231)
single-member districts (p. 221)
soft money (p. 231)
split ticket (p. 219)
two-party system (p. 220)

Self-Test

1. The formation of political parties:
   a. acts as a support for an elitist government.
   b. makes it difficult for the public to participate in politics.
   c. can mobilize citizens to collective action to compete for power with those who have wealth and prestige.
   d. can function as an alternative to free and open media.

2. A major change in party activity in the South since the 1960s is:
   a. the emergence of a viable third party.
   b. a sharp decline in voter turnout.
   c. a decline in the level of two-party competition in state and local elections.
   d. a switch to support of Republican candidates in presidential elections.

3. The chief electoral factor supporting a two-party system in the United States is:
   a. proportional representation.
   b. multimember election districts.
   c. single-member districts with proportional voting.
   d. single-member districts with plurality voting.

4. The high cost of campaigns in the United States is largely related to:
   a. televised ads.
   b. developing a colorful website.
   c. organizing door-to-door canvassing efforts.
   d. the legal and accounting expenses related to filing information about campaign donors and expenditures with the Federal Elections Commission.

5. In recent decades state political party organizations in the United States have:
   a. become weaker and less effective.
   b. taken over control and direction of the national parties.
   c. been hurt by services provided by the national party organizations.
   d. become more professional in staffing and support of statewide races.

6. European and American political parties differ in which of the following ways?
   a. the degree to which they are party-centered as opposed to candidate-centered.
   b. the nature of their party organizations: the extent to which they are organized at the local and national levels and the amount of power that exists at each of these levels.
   c. the type of electoral system in which they elect their candidates to office.
   d. all of the above.

7. The coalitions of voters that make up the Republican and Democratic parties are virtually identical. (T/F)

8. Primary elections helped strengthen party organizations in the United States. (T/F)

9. U.S. political parties are organized from the bottom up, not the top down. (T/F)

10. Modern-day parties in the United States are described in the text as having more of a service than a power relationship with candidates. (T/F)

Critical Thinking

Why are elections conducted so differently in the United States than in European democracies? Why are the campaigns so much longer, more expensive, and more candidate-centered?

Study Corner

A two-page section at the end of each chapter includes (as shown on the example page) key terms, a self-test, and a critical-thinking exercise; the second page (not shown) has suggested readings, annotated references to relevant websites, and a guide to civic and political participation.

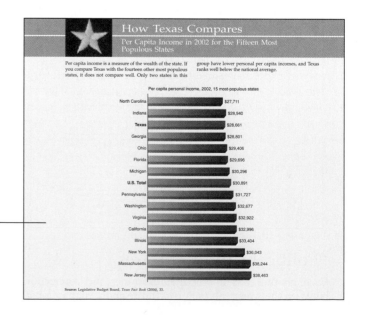

How Texas Compares

Per Capita Income in 2002 for the Fifteen Most Populous States

Per capita income is a measure of the wealth of the state. If you compare Texas with the fourteen other most populous states, it does not compare well. Only two states in this group have lower personal per capita incomes, and Texas ranks well below the national average.

Per capita personal income, 2002, 15 most-populous states

State	Income
North Carolina	$27,711
Indiana	$28,940
Texas	$28,661
Georgia	$28,801
Ohio	$29,406
Florida	$29,696
Michigan	$30,296
U.S. Total	$30,891
Pennsylvania	$31,727
Washington	$32,677
Virginia	$32,922
California	$32,996
Illinois	$33,404
New York	$36,043
Massachusetts	$38,244
New Jersey	$38,463

Source: Legislative Budget Board, Texas Fact Book (2004), 33.

"How Texas Compares" boxes

Each Texas government chapter contains some of these boxes, which compare Texas with other states.

Acknowledgments

Nearly two decades ago, when planning the first edition of *The American Democracy*, my editor and I concluded that it would be enormously helpful if a way could be found to bring into each chapter the judgment of those political scientists who teach the introductory course year in and year out. Thus, in addition to soliciting general reviews from a select number of expert scholars, we sent each chapter to a dozen or so faculty members at U.S. colleges and universities of all types—public and private, large and small, two-year and four-year. These political scientists, 213 in all, had well over a thousand years of combined experience in teaching the introductory course, and they provided countless good ideas.

Since then, scores of other political scientists have reviewed subsequent editions. These many reviewers will go unnamed here, but my debt to all of them remains undiminished by time.

For this new, eighth edition, I again received an enormous amount of sound advice. Reviewers are the lifeblood of a text, and I was fortunate to have the assistance of a skilled group of scholars. I am deeply grateful to each and all of them for their help:

Fabian Biancardi, Riverside Community College

John P. Burke, University of Vermont

John Carhart, Texa A & M University at Galvestan

Cecilia Castillo, Texas State University—San Mono

June Cheatham, Richland College

Denise DeGarmo, Southern Illinois University

Doris Jones, Tarrant County College

Andrew Karch, University of Texas at Austin

Lisa Langenbach, Middle Tennessee State University

Joel Lieske, Cleveland State University

Mark C. Miller, Clark University

David Putz, Kingwood College

Regina Swopes, Northeastern Illinois University

Albert Waite, Central Texas College

Kevin Walsh, Broward Community College

David G. Wigg, St. Louis Community College/Florissant Valley

I also want to thank those at McGraw-Hill who contributed to the eighth edition. Monica Eckman, my editor, always at the top of her game, topped even that this time. If this edition is the best yet, Monica deserves the credit. Her professional skill and inspired ideas over the past few editions have exceeded what any author could reasonably expect. Angela Kao and Jessica Badiner shared the role of editorial coordinator, offering keen suggestions and ably handling the supplements. Katherine Bates and Jennifer Reed, marketing managers for the book, worked hard to ensure that the text meets instructors' needs.

I would also like to thank the book's lead project manager, Cathy Iammartino. She carefully oversaw the book's production and skillfully prodded me about deadlines. Mary Roybal was, once again, a copyeditor with a deft and seamless touch. Toni Michaels did the photo research, providing a marvelous set of choices. I would also like to thank Carol Bielski, production supervisor; Gino Cieslik, designer; and Kate Boylan, media project manager.

At Harvard, I had the diligent and cheerful support of my extraordinary faculty assistant, Kate Tighe, who helped update the text and copied endless drafts of it. Tezeta Tulloch served as my in-house proofreader, meticulously correcting errors of all kinds. Alex Patterson was my photo advisor; his keen eye is behind the final photo selections in this edition. I owe each of them a deep thanks.

Thomas Patterson

To, Alex and Leigh

PART 1

FOUNDATIONS

The British statesman William Gladstone in 1878 declared that the U.S. Constitution was "the most wonderful work ever struck off at a given time by the brain and purpose of man." The U.S. Constitution is, indeed, a remarkable document. Its lasting power alone is testament to the skill and foresight of those who wrote it. Since 1787, the United States has been governed throughout by the same constitution, which is now the world's oldest constitution still in force. France has had fourteen constitutions during the same period in which the United States has had just one.

Part One of this book examines the constitutional foundations of American government. The discussion begins in Chapter 1 with an exploration of the cultural ideals that underlie the U.S. constitutional system.

Chapters 2 and 3 describe how the writers of the Constitution devised institutional structures designed to enhance and preserve these ideals, which include liberty, equality, and self-government. A central theme of these chapters is that basic constitutional issues are never fully settled. Rather, they are recurring sources of debate, and each generation is forced to find new answers.

Constitutional government is also a matter of individual rights, of a system in which people have basic freedoms that are constitutionally protected from infringement by government. Although these rights are rooted in principle, they are achieved through politics. Chapter 4 discusses how civil liberties—for example, free speech—are protected both from and through political action. Chapter 5 examines the degree to which Americans' rights are affected by differences in areas such as gender and race.

PART ONE OUTLINE

1   American Political Culture:
    Seeking a More Perfect Union 4

2   Constitutional Democracy:
    Promoting Liberty and
    Self-Government 34

3   Federalism: Forging a Nation 66

4   Civil Liberties: Protecting
    Individual Rights 96

5   Equal Rights: Struggling Toward
    Fairness 130

American Political Culture:
Seeking a More Perfect Union

Chapter Outline

Political Culture: The Core
Principles of American
Government

America's Core Values: Liberty,
Equality, and Self-Government
The Power of Ideals
The Limits of Ideals

Politics: The Resolution of Conflict
The Social Contract
The Rules of American Politics

Political Power: The Control
of Policy
Authority
Theories of Power

The Concept of a Political System
and This Book's Organization

CHAPTER 1

One hears people say that it is inherent in the habits and nature of democracies to change feelings and thoughts at every moment. . . . But I have never seen anything like that happening in the great democracy on the other side of the ocean. What struck me most in the United States was the difficulty experienced in getting an idea, once conceived, out of the head of the majority.

Alexis de Tocqueville[1]

At 8:47 A.M. on September 11, 2001, a hijacked American Airlines passenger jet slammed into one of the twin towers of New York City's World Trade Center. Twenty minutes later, a second hijacked passenger jet hit the other tower. A third hijacked jet then plowed into the Pentagon building in Washington, D.C. Within two hours, the World Trade Center towers collapsed, killing all still inside, including police and firefighters who had rushed bravely into the buildings to help in the evacuation. Three thousand Americans were murdered that September morning, the highest death toll ever from an attack on American soil by a foreign adversary. The toll would have been even higher if not for the bravery of passengers aboard United Airlines flight 93, who fought with its hijackers, causing the plane—which was aimed toward Washington, D.C.—to crash in a barren Pennsylvania field.

That evening, a somber George W. Bush addressed the nation. Urging Americans to stay calm and resolute, President Bush said: "America was targeted for an attack because we're the brightest beacon for freedom and opportunity in the world." Sprinkled throughout his speech were allusions to time-honored American ideals: liberty, the will of the people, justice, and the rule of law. "No one will keep that light from shining," said Bush.

The ideals that guided Bush's speech would have been familiar to any generation of Americans. These ideals have been invoked when Americans have gone to war, declared peace, celebrated national holidays, launched major policy initiatives, and asserted new rights.[2] The ideals contained in Bush's speech were the same ones that had punctuated the speeches of George Washington and Abraham Lincoln, Susan B. Anthony and Franklin D. Roosevelt, Dr. Martin Luther King Jr., and Ronald Reagan.

The ideals were also there at the nation's beginning, when they were put into words in the Declaration of Independence and the Constitution. Of course, the practical meaning of these words has changed greatly during the more than two centuries the United States has been a sovereign nation. When the writers of the Constitution began the document with the words "We the People," they did not have all Americans equally in mind. Black slaves, women, and men without property did not have the same rights as propertied white men.

5

When terrorists attacked the World Trade Center towers on September 11, 2001, President George W. Bush, as America's political leaders have done throughout the nation's history, evoked the country's enduring ideals. Here, people look out at the former site of the World Trade Center. The rebuilt site will include a memorial to the nearly three thousand Americans who died in the attacks.

Nevertheless, America's ideals have been remarkably enduring. Throughout their history, Americans have embraced the same set of core values. They have quarreled over the meaning and practice of these ideals, but they have never seriously questioned the principles themselves. As historian Clinton Rossiter concluded, "There has been in a doctrinal sense, only one America."[3]

This book is about contemporary American politics, not U.S. history or culture. Yet American politics today cannot be understood apart from the nation's heritage. Government does not begin anew with each generation; it builds on the past. In the case of the United States, the most significant link between past and present lies in the nation's founding ideals. The Frenchman Alexis de Tocqueville was among the first to see that the main tendencies of American politics cannot be explained without taking into account the country's core beliefs. "Habits of the heart" was Tocqueville's description of Americans' ideals.[4]

This chapter briefly examines the principles that have helped shape American politics since the country's earliest years. The chapter also explains basic concepts—such as power, pluralism, and constitutionalism—that are important in the study of American politics. The main points made in this chapter are these:

- *The American political culture centers on a set of core ideals—liberty, equality, self-government, individualism, diversity, and unity—that serve as the people's common bond.* These mythic principles have a substantial influence on what Americans will regard as reasonable and acceptable and on what they will try to achieve.

- *Politics is the process that determines whose values will prevail in society.* The play of politics in the United States takes place in the context of democratic procedures, constitutionalism, and capitalism and involves elements of majority, pluralist, bureaucratic, and elitist rule.

- *Politics in the United States is characterized by a number of major patterns, including a highly fragmented governing system, a high degree of pluralism, an extraordinary emphasis on individual rights, and a pronounced separation of the political and economic spheres.*

POLITICAL CULTURE: THE CORE PRINCIPLES OF AMERICAN GOVERNMENT

The people of every nation have a few great ideals that characterize their political life, but, as James Bryce observed, Americans are a special case.[5] Their ideals are the basis of their national identity. Other people take their identity from the common ancestry that led them gradually to gather under one flag. Thus, long before there was a France or a Japan, there were French and Japanese people, each a kinship group united through blood. Even today, it is kinship that links them. There is no way to become fully Japanese except to be born of Japanese parents. Not so for Americans. They are a multitude of people from different lands—England, Germany, Ireland, Africa, Italy, Poland, Mexico, and China, to name just a few (see Figure 1–1). Americans are linked not by blood but by allegiance to a set of commonly held ideals such as liberty and equality.

These ideals are habits of mind, a customary way of thinking about the world. They help Americans live and work together harmoniously. They are part of what social scientists call **political culture,** a term that refers to the characteristic and deep-seated beliefs of a particular people about government and politics.[6]

political culture
The characteristic and deep-seated beliefs of a particular people.

America's core ideals are rooted in the European heritage of the first white settlers. They arrived during the Enlightenment period, when people were awakening to the idea of human progress. These settlers were not, as is sometimes claimed, seeking to create in America an entirely new way of life. Their ideas about society were shaped by the European culture they had experienced. But the settlers also did not seek to reproduce in America exactly what they had known in Europe. They wanted to build upon that which they admired about the Old World and to leave behind that which they disliked.[7] Many of them, for example, were trying to escape religious persecution. They came to America for the chance to worship freely.

Europeans

Their vision of society changed as they discovered the possibilities that America offered. The opportunities provided by the New World's vast open lands and its great distance from European rulers gave ordinary people a level of personal freedom unthinkable in the Old World. There was in America no titled

The United States was founded on a set of ideals that have served to unify its people, whose immigrant origins trace to every corner of the world. America's diversity is evident here, as Los Angeles's Mayor-elect Antonio Villaraigosa leads his supporters to city hall for his inauguration in 2005.

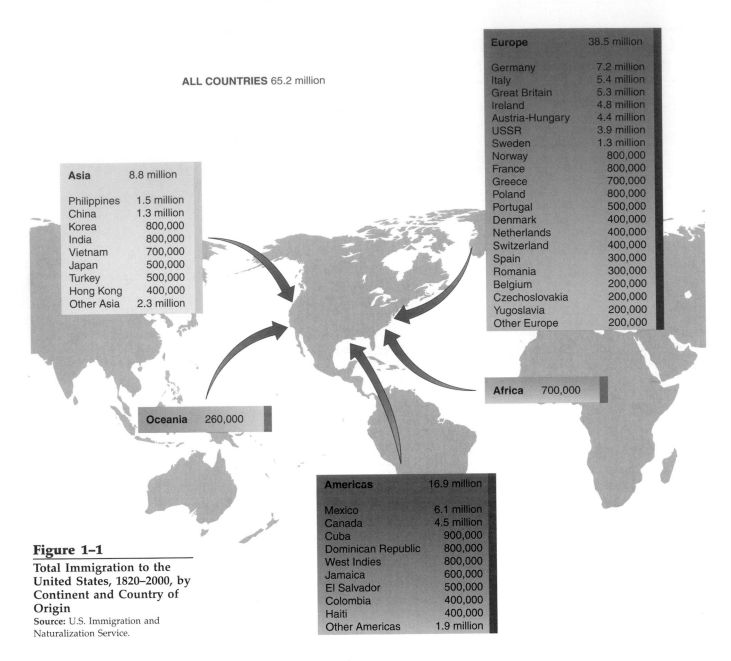

ALL COUNTRIES 65.2 million

Europe	38.5 million
Germany	7.2 million
Italy	5.4 million
Great Britain	5.3 million
Ireland	4.8 million
Austria-Hungary	4.4 million
USSR	3.9 million
Sweden	1.3 million
Norway	800,000
France	800,000
Greece	700,000
Poland	800,000
Portugal	500,000
Denmark	400,000
Netherlands	400,000
Switzerland	400,000
Spain	300,000
Romania	300,000
Belgium	200,000
Czechoslovakia	200,000
Yugoslavia	200,000
Other Europe	200,000

Asia	8.8 million
Philippines	1.5 million
China	1.3 million
Korea	800,000
India	800,000
Vietnam	700,000
Japan	500,000
Turkey	500,000
Hong Kong	400,000
Other Asia	2.3 million

Africa	700,000

Oceania	260,000

Americas	16.9 million
Mexico	6.1 million
Canada	4.5 million
Cuba	900,000
Dominican Republic	800,000
West Indies	800,000
Jamaica	600,000
El Salvador	500,000
Colombia	400,000
Haiti	400,000
Other Americas	1.9 million

Figure 1–1

Total Immigration to the United States, 1820–2000, by Continent and Country of Origin

Source: U.S. Immigration and Naturalization Service.

nobility that held nearly all the power and nearly all the wealth. Ordinary Americans acquired land and acted independently. In the end, the colonists revolted against their European masters—engaging in the first successful large-scale rebellion in human history driven largely by a vision of a wholly different society. The United States was a nation founded abruptly in 1776 on a set of principles that were proclaimed in The Declaration of Independence:[8]

> We hold these truths to be self-evident, that all men are created equal; that they are endowed by their Creator with certain unalienable rights; that among these, are life, liberty, and the pursuit of happiness. That, to secure these rights, governments are instituted among men, deriving their just powers from the consent of the governed; that, whenever any form of government becomes destructive of these ends, it is the right of the people to alter or to abolish it, and to institute a new government, laying its foundation on such principles, and organizing its powers in such form, as to them shall seem most likely to effect their safety and happiness.

Subsequent generations of Americans have embraced these principles while discovering that they require constant renewal and rethinking. The principles themselves are timeless. Their meaning in practice is not. The Great Depression of the 1930s, for example, forced Americans to reconsider the everyday realities of personal liberty. One-fourth of the labor force lost their jobs, and another one-fourth could not find full-time employment. Homes were lost to creditors, and food was scarce. It became harder for Americans to think of personal freedom as simply a matter of freedom *from* government, and they turned *to* government for help in dealing with economic hardship. In his 1941 State of the Union Address, President Franklin D. Roosevelt spoke to people's hopes when he declared that "freedom from want" was among Americans' fundamental liberties.

The September 11, 2001 terrorist attacks on U.S. soil have challenged Americans once again to rethink the practice of liberty. How much leeway should they give their government in its war on terrorism? How much personal freedom should they surrender so that the nation is not once again attacked on a massive scale? Should Americans allow their government to comb citizens' telephone records in the hope of identifying those individuals that might seek to harm the country? Should Americans allow their government to comb citizens' bank accounts and travel records in the hope of finding indicators of suspicious behavior? Such questions have shaped the American governing experience since the nation's beginning. *A defining characteristic of the U.S. political system is Americans' pursuit of the political ideals upon which the nation was founded and that continue to serve as Americans' common bond.*

AMERICA'S CORE VALUES: LIBERTY, EQUALITY, AND SELF-GOVERNMENT

An understanding of America's ideals begins with the recognition that the individual rather than the government is the cornerstone of society. Government exists to serve the people. No clearer statement of this principle exists than the reference in the Declaration of Independence to "unalienable rights"—freedoms that belong to each and every person and that cannot lawfully be denied by government.

Liberty, equality, and self-government are widely regarded as America's core political ideals (see Table 1–1). **Liberty** is the principle that individuals should be free to act and think as they choose, provided they do not infringe unreasonably on the freedom and well-being of others. The United States, as historian Louis Hartz said, was "born free."[9] The Declaration of Independence rings with the proclamation that people are entitled to "Life, Liberty and the Pursuit of Happiness." The preamble to the Constitution declares that the U.S. government was founded to secure "the Blessings of Liberty to ourselves and our Posterity." The Statue of Liberty stands in New York harbor as the symbol of the American people, and the "Star-Spangled Banner" rings out with the words "land of the free."

For early Americans, liberty was nearly a birthright. Ordinary people did not have to accept the European system of absolute government and aristocratic privilege when greater personal liberty was as close as the next area of unsettled land. Not surprisingly, they were determined, when forming their own government, to protect personal liberty. The First Amendment of the Constitution prohibits laws that would infringe on individual freedom: "Congress shall make no law respecting the establishment of religion, or prohibiting the free exercise thereof; or abridging the freedom of speech, or of the press; or the right of the people to peaceably assemble, and to petition the Government for a redress of grievances."

#2, #3

liberty
The principle that individuals should be free to act and think as they choose, provided they do not infringe unreasonably on the rights and freedoms of others.

TABLE 1–1	America's Core Political Ideals The United States was founded on a set of political ideals that have served as its people's common bond. Foremost among these ideals are liberty, equality, and self-government	
IDEAL	**DESCRIPTION**	**ORIGIN (IN PART)**
Liberty	The principle that individuals should be free to act and think as they choose, provided they do not infringe unreasonably on the rights and freedoms of others.	Colonial America's vast open lands offered a degree of liberty unattainable in Europe; the American Revolution was fought over liberty.
Equality	The notion that all individuals are equal in their moral worth, in their treatment under the law, and in their political voice.	Colonial America's openness made Europe's aristocratic system unenforceable; greater personal opportunity in America fostered a sense of social equality.
Self-government	The principle that the people are the ultimate source and proper beneficiary of governing authority and must have a voice in how they are governed.	Colonial America had a degree of self-government; Americans' sense of personal freedom and equality led them to want self-determination in public affairs as well.

Americans' demand for liberty has persisted throughout the country's history. Observers from Tocqueville onward have seen fit to note that liberty in America, as in no other country, is ingrained in people's thinking. Americans' chief concern, wrote Tocqueville, "is to remain their own masters."

A second American political ideal is **equality**—the notion that all individuals are equal in their moral worth and so are entitled to equal treatment under the law. America provided its white settlers a new level of equality. Europe's rigid aristocratic system based on land ownership was unenforceable in frontier America. Almost any free citizen who wanted to own land could obtain it. It was this natural sense of equality that Thomas Jefferson expressed so forcefully in the Declaration of Independence: "We hold these truths to be self-evident, that all men are created equal."

Equality, however, has always been a less clearly defined concept than liberty. Even Jefferson professed not to know its exact meaning. A slave owner, Jefferson distinguished between free citizens, who were entitled to equal rights, and slaves, who were not. After slavery was abolished, Americans continued to argue over the meaning of equality, and the debate continues today. Does equality require that wealth and opportunity be widely shared? Or does it merely require that artificial barriers to advancement be removed? Despite differing opinions about such questions, an insistence on equality is a distinctive feature of the American experience. Americans, said Bryce, reject "the very notion" that some people might be "better" than others merely because of birth or position.[10] And perhaps no ideal has so inspired Americans to political action as has their desire for fuller equality. The abolition and suffrage movements were rooted in this ideal. The more recent civil rights movements of black Americans, women, Hispanics, gays, and other groups also are testaments to the power of the ideal of equality.

Self-government, America's third great political ideal, is the principle that people are the ultimate source of governing authority and must have a voice in how they are governed. "Governments," the Declaration of Independence proclaims, "deriv[e] their just powers from the consent of the governed." In his Gettysburg address, Lincoln extolled a government "of the people, by the people, for the people."

equality
The notion that all individuals are equal in their moral worth, in their treatment under the law, and in their political voice.

self-government
The principle that the people are the ultimate source and proper beneficiary of governing authority; in practice, a government based on majority rule.

Americans' belief in self-government originated in colonial America. The Old World was an ocean away, and European governments had no option but to allow the American colonies a degree of self-determination. Out of this experience came the dream of a self-governing nation. It was an ideal that captured the imagination even of those in the lower ranks of society. Ordinary people willingly risked their lives in the cause of self-government during the American Revolution. The ensuing federal and state constitutions were based on the idea that government is properly founded on the will of the people. "We the People" is the opening phrase of the Constitution of the United States.

At no time in the nation's history has national leadership been conferred except through the vote. At various times and places elsewhere in the world, governing power has been seized by brute force. The United States has an unbroken history of free elections as the legitimate means of acquiring governmental power. Etched in a corridor of the nation's Capitol building are the words Alexander Hamilton spoke when asked about the foundation of the nation's government: "Here, sir, the people govern."

LEADERS

THOMAS JEFFERSON

Thomas Jefferson was the principal author of the Declaration of Independence. It was Jefferson who at age thirty-three coined the renowned words "Life, Liberty and the Pursuit of Happiness." A man of contradictions, Jefferson owned slaves while arguing for human equality and liberty. Elected to the presidency in 1800, Jefferson was a proponent of states' rights and of a strict interpretation of the national government's constitutional powers. Yet he overlooked the Constitution, which had no authorization for such an act, in purchasing the Louisiana Territory from the French Emperor Napoleon in 1803, doubling the area of the United States. A reserved man who was a better writer than public speaker, Jefferson dedicated much of his life to the betterment of his home state of Virginia. He drafted the state's Bill of Rights, which included a provision for religious freedom—a right not guaranteed in all states at the time. After retiring to his Monticello estate following his two terms as president, Jefferson designed and founded the University of Virginia, calling it one of his greatest achievements. To Jefferson, the success of the American experiment in self-government rested ultimately on an educated citizenry.

Although liberty, equality, and self-government are the core American political ideals, the American Creed—the set of core values that define the nation's political culture—also includes other principles. **Individualism** is a commitment to personal initiative, self-sufficiency, and material accumulation. It is related to the idea of liberty, which makes the individual the foundation of society, and is buttressed by the idea of equality, which holds that everyone should be given a fair chance to succeed. Individualism stems from the belief that people who are free to pursue their own path and are not unfairly burdened can attain their fullest potential. Individualism has roots in the country's origins as a wilderness society. The early Americans developed a pride in their "rugged individualism," and from this experience grew the idea that people ought to try to make it on their own.

Unity and diversity are also part of the American creed. **Unity** is the principle that Americans are one people and form an indivisible union. **Diversity** holds that individual and group differences should be respected and that these differences are themselves a source of strength. These two principles, which acknowledge at once both the differences and the oneness that are part of the American experience, are expressed in the phrase *E pluribus unum* ("One out of many").

individualism
The idea that people should take the initiative, be self-sufficient, and accumulate the material advantages necessary for their well-being.

unity
The principle that Americans are one people and form an indivisible union.

diversity
The principle that individual and group differences should be respected and are a source of national strength.

The Power of Ideals

Ideals serve to define the boundaries of action. They do not determine exactly what people will do, but they affect what people will regard as reasonable and desirable. Why, for example, does the United States spend relatively less money on government programs for the poor than do other fully industrialized democracies,

How the United States Compares
Personal Freedom and Self-Reliance

The United States was labeled "the country of individualism *par excellence*" by William Watts and Lloyd Free in their book *State of the Nation*. They were referring to the emphasis that Americans place on self-reliance and personal freedom.

In European democracies, such views also prevail but are moderated by a greater acceptance of welfare programs. The difference between the American and European cultures reflects their differing political traditions. America was an open country ruled by a foreign power, and its revolution was fought largely over the issue of personal liberty. In European revolutions, equality was also at issue, because wealth was held by hereditary aristocracies. Europeans' concern with equality was gradually translated into a willingness to use government as a means of redistributing wealth. An example is government-paid medical care for all citizens.

Even today, Americans are more likely than Europeans (and Canadians as well) to rank personal freedom ahead of economic security, as indicated by a multination survey released in 2004 by the Pew Research Center for the People

and the Press. Respondents were asked, "What's more important in society today—that everyone be free to pursue their life's goals without interference from government, or that government play an active role in society so as to guarantee that nobody is in need?" Following are the percentages of respondents in each country who said "free to pursue their life's goals" was the higher priority:

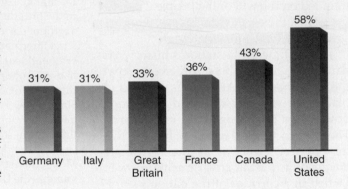

Germany 31%   Italy 31%   Great Britain 33%   France 36%   Canada 43%   United States 58%

including Germany, France, Switzerland, the Netherlands, Spain, Britain, Sweden, Italy, and Japan? Are Americans so much better off than these other people that they have less need for welfare programs? The answer is no. Of all these countries, the United States has the most poverty, in both relative and absolute terms. The United States spends less on social welfare chiefly because of its cultural emphasis on liberty and individualism. Americans have resisted giving government a larger social welfare role because of their deep-seated belief in self-reliance and limited government (see "How the United States Compares").

Of course, social welfare policy is not simply an issue of cultural differences. The welfare issue, like other issues, is part of the rough-and-tumble of everyday politics. There are always powerful interests aligned on both sides of important issues. In the United States, the Republican party, business groups, antitax groups, and others have resisted the expansion of the government's social welfare role, while the Democratic party, unions, minority groups, and others have from time to time argued for greater intervention. Nevertheless, Americans' belief in individualism, which has no exact equivalent in European society, has played a defining role in shaping U.S. welfare policy.

The distinctiveness of this cultural belief is clear from a recent survey that asked respondents in different countries whether it is more important "that everyone be free to pursue their life's goals without interference from government" or "that government play an active role in society so as to guarantee that nobody is in need." Americans were much less likely than Europeans to say that it is more important to ensure that "nobody is in need."[11] Americans do not necessarily have less sympathy for the poor; rather, they place more emphasis on personal responsibility than do Europeans.[12]

The structure of U.S. society helps promote the American dream of success—for example, by encouraging young people to attend college. Shown here are New York University students celebrating their commencement.

The importance of individualism to American society also is evident in the emphasis on equal opportunity. If individuals are to be entrusted with their own welfare, they must be given a fair chance to succeed on their own. Nowhere is this philosophy more evident than in the country's elaborate system of higher education, which includes nearly three thousand two-year and four-year institutions and is designed to accommodate nearly every individual who wants to pursue a college education. About a fourth of the nation's adult citizens have a college degree, the world's highest rate. Even the American state (see "States in the Nation") that has the lowest proportion—West Virginia, where one in every six adults has a degree—has a higher percentage of college graduates than does the average European country.

Of course, the idea that success is within equal reach of all Americans who strive for it is far from accurate. Young people who grow up in abject poverty and without adequate guidance know all too well the limits on opportunity. In some inner-city areas, teenage boys are more likely to spend time in jail than to spend time in college.

The Limits of Ideals

Cultural beliefs originate in a country's political and social practices, but they are not perfect representatives of these practices. They are mythic ideas—symbolic positions taken by a people to justify and give meaning to their way of life.[13] Myths contain elements of truth, but they are not the full truth.

High ideals do not come with a guarantee that a people will live up to them. The clearest proof of this failing in the American case is the human tragedy that began nearly four centuries ago and continues today. In 1619 the first black slaves were brought in chains to America. Slavery lasted 250 years. Slaves in the field worked from dawn to dark (from "can see, 'til can't"), in both the heat of summer and the cold of winter. The Civil War brought an end to slavery but not to racial oppression. Slavery was followed by the Jim Crow era of legal segregation: black people in the South were forbidden by law to use the same schools,

HISTORICAL BACKGROUND

States in the Nation

A College Education

Reflecting their cultural beliefs of individualism and equality, Americans have developed the world's most extensive college system. Every state has at least eight colleges within its boundaries. No European democracy has as many colleges as either California (322) or New York (320). The extensive U.S. college system has enabled large numbers of Americans to earn a college degree. About one in four American adults is a college graduate. Even the states that rank low on this indicator have a higher percentage of college graduates than do most European countries.

Q: Why do the northeastern and western coastal states have a higher percentage of adults with college degrees?

A: The northeastern and western coastal states are more affluent and urbanized than most states. Thus, young people in these states can better afford the costs of college and are more likely to need a college degree for the work they intend to pursue.

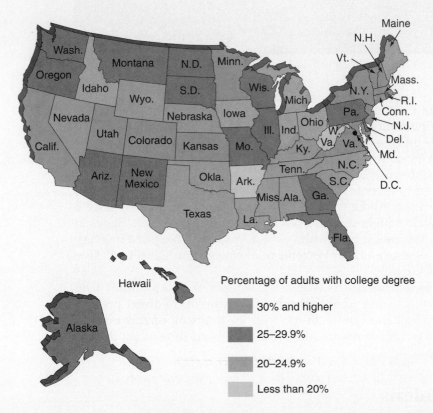

Percentage of adults with college degree

- 30% and higher
- 25–29.9%
- 20–24.9%
- Less than 20%

Source: U.S. Bureau of the Census, 2006. Based on percentage of adults twenty-five years of age or older with a college degree.

hospitals, restaurants, and restrooms as white people. Those who spoke out against this system were subjected to beatings, firebombings, castrations, rapes, and worse—hundreds of African Americans were lynched by white vigilantes in the early 1900s. Today African Americans have equal rights under the law, but in fact they are far from equal. Compared with whites, blacks are twice as likely to live in poverty, twice as likely to be unable to find a job, and twice as likely to die in infancy.[14] There have always been at least two Americas, one for whites and one for blacks.

During the era of racial segregation in the South, this sign at the entrance to the Memphis public zoo meant that it was Tuesday—the only day black people were allowed to go to the zoo. On the other six days of the week, the sign excluded black people from entering.

Despite the lofty claim that "all men are created equal," equality has never been an American birthright. In 1882, Congress suspended Chinese immigration on the assumption that the Chinese were an inferior people. Calvin Coolidge in 1923 asked Congress for a permanent ban on Chinese immigration, saying that people "who do not want to be partakers of the American spirit ought not to settle in America."[15] Not until 1965 was discrimination against the Chinese and other Asians (and Hispanics as well) effectively eliminated from U.S. immigration laws (Figure 1–2).

The claim that the United States is a gigantic melting pot is a blend of fact and fiction. No other nation has so fully opened its doors to groups from around the world. Even today, Americans are more likely than Europeans to support immigration. They also have a better opinion of recent immigrants (see Figure 1–3). For example, compared with French people's view of North African immigrants, Americans are nearly twice as likely to say that Hispanic immigrants are having

WWW.MHHE.COM/PATTERSONTAD8

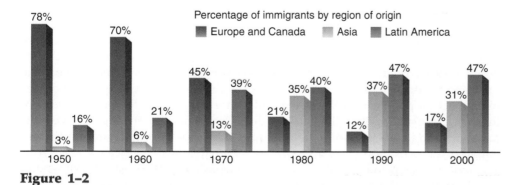

Figure 1–2

The Changing Face of Immigration
Until 1965, immigration laws were biased in favor of European immigrants. The laws enacted in 1965 increased the proportion of immigrants from Asia and Latin America.
Source: U.S. Immigration and Naturalization Service, 2006. Percentages are totals for each decade, e.g., the 2000 figures are for the 1991–2000 period.

Figure 1–3

Opinion of the Influence on Society of Recent Immigrants

Americans are more likely than most Europeans to believe that recent immigrants have had a positive influence on their society.
Source: The Pew Research Center for the People and the Press, Global Attitudes Survey, 2005. Respondents were asked about immigration from a particular region (Middle East and North America, in the case of the European countries; Mexico and Latin America, in the case of the United States).

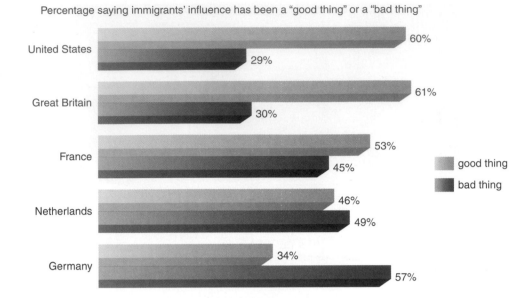

Percentage saying immigrants' influence has been a "good thing" or a "bad thing"

United States — good thing 60%, bad thing 29%
Great Britain — good thing 61%, bad thing 30%
France — good thing 53%, bad thing 45%
Netherlands — good thing 46%, bad thing 49%
Germany — good thing 34%, bad thing 57%

a positive influence on society. Nevertheless, established groups in America have never fully embraced new arrivals. When Irish, Italian, and Eastern European immigrants reached this country's shores in large numbers in the nineteenth and early twentieth centuries, they encountered nativist elements that assailed their customs and religions. Many Americans, including some members of Congress, wanted Catholics and Jews completely barred from entry. During the last third of the twentieth century, Asian and Hispanic immigrants encountered stiff opposition in some parts of the country. After the September 11, 2001, terrorist attacks on the World Trade Center and the Pentagon, polls indicated that most Americans wanted Middle East immigration sharply reduced or stopped entirely.

Resistance to immigrant groups is not among the stories that Americans like to tell about themselves.[16] Such lapses of historical memory can be found among all peoples, but the tendency to rewrite history is perhaps exaggerated in the American case because Americans' beliefs are so idealistic (see Table 1–2). How could a nation that upholds the ideal of human equality have barred the Chinese, enslaved the blacks, betrayed the Indians, and subordinated women?

One reason America's ideals do not match reality is that they are general principles, not fixed rules of conduct. They derive from somewhat different experiences and philosophical traditions, and there are points at which they conflict. Equality, for instance, emphasizes fairness and the opportunity for all to partake of society's benefits, whereas liberty emphasizes personal freedom and threats posed to it by political power. Conflict between these ideals is inevitable. Take the issue of affirmative action. Proponents say that only through aggressive affirmative action programs will women and minorities receive the equal treatment in the job market to which they are entitled. Opponents say that aggressive affirmative action infringes unreasonably on the liberty of the employer and the initiative of the work force. Each group can say that it has America's ideals on its side, and no resort to logic can persuade either side that the opposing viewpoint should prevail.

Americans' ideals, despite their inexact meanings, conflicting implications, and unfulfilled promise, have had a strong impact on Americans' politics. If racial, gender, ethnic, and other forms of intolerance constitute the sorriest chapter in the nation's history, the centuries-old struggle of Americans to create a

IN TEACHING THE AMERICAN STORY TO CHILDREN, HOW IMPORTANT IS THE FOLLOWING THEME?	ESSENTIAL/VERY IMPORTANT	SOMEWHAT IMPORTANT	SOMEWHAT UNIMPORTANT/ VERY UNIMPORTANT/ LEAVE IT OUT OF THE STORY
With hard work and perseverance, anyone can succeed in America.	83%	14%	4%
Our founders limited the power of government so government would not intrude too much into the lives of its citizens.	74	19	8
America is the world's greatest melting pot in which people from different countries are united into one nation.	73	21	5
America's contribution is one of expanding freedom for more and more people.	71	22	6
Our nation betrayed its founding principles by cruel mistreatment of blacks and American Indians.	59	24	17
Our founders were part of a male-dominated culture that gave important roles to men while keeping women in the background.	38	28	35

TABLE 1–2 **Telling the American Story to Children** Americans' values and myths are reflected in their preferences in teaching children about the nation's history.

Used by permission of the Survey of American Political Culture, James Davison Hunter and Carol Bowman, directors, Institute for Advanced Studies in Culture, University of Virginia.

more equal society is among the finest chapters. Few nations have battled so relentlessly against the insidious discrimination that stems from superficial human differences such as the color of one's skin. High ideals are more than mere abstractions. They are a source of human aspiration and, ultimately, of political and social change.

POLITICS: THE RESOLUTION OF CONFLICT

Cultural ideals help shape what people expect from politics and inspire people to work together for a collective purpose. Politics, however, is more than shared ideals and common efforts. Politics is also a struggle for power and advantage. Commenting on the competitive nature of politics, political scientist Harold Lasswell described it as the struggle over "who gets what, when, and how."[17] **Politics** is the process through which a society settles its conflicts.

Political conflict has two primary sources. One is *scarcity*. Even the richest societies do not have enough wealth to satisfy everyone's desires. Conflict over the distribution of resources is the predictable result. Consider, for example, the issue of school quality. Affluent suburban districts have better schools than do poor inner-city districts. Lacking a strong local tax base, inner-city residents have pressured state governments to provide equal funding to all schools. Residents of suburban communities have fought this arrangement, fearing that it would increase their taxes and weaken their local schools.

Differences in values are the other main source of political conflict. People see issues differently as a result of differences in their beliefs, experiences, and interests. Abortion is an issue of freedom of choice for some and an issue of murder for others. People bring to politics a wide range of conflicting standards—about

politics
The process through which a society makes its governing decisions.

Social contract theory holds that people agree to be governed in order to protect their rights and interests. Neither the government nor the people always hold up their side of the bargain. Shown here are some of the thousands of New Orleans residents that were abandoned by government as Hurricane Katrina roared in from the Gulf Coast. A much smaller number of New Orleans residents took advantage of the chaos to loot city homes and businesses.

social contract

A voluntary agreement by individuals to form government, which is then obliged to act within the confines of the agreement.

abortion, the environment, crime and punishment, the poor, the economy, and countless other issues.

The Social Contract

Politics operates by a set of "rules" that determine whose voice will prevail when conflict arises over resources and values. Without such rules, people would be constantly at each other's throats, and society would dissolve into chaos and lawlessness.

For a long period of world history, the rules of politics were stacked against ordinary people. They had no say in their governing and were at the mercy of those in authority. Government was controlled by absolute monarchs, whose word was law. Some of these rulers were tyrants, and many taxed their subjects heavily to raise large armies and erect great palaces.

Roughly four centuries ago, ideas about the proper form of government began to change. Ironically, one of the theorists who contributed to this development was an advocate of absolute rule. In *Leviathan* (published in 1651), the English philosopher Thomas Hobbes argued that government rests on a **social contract** in which ordinary people surrender the freedom they would have in a state of nature in return for the protection that a sovereign ruler can provide. People give up their freedom, Hobbes said, because life in its natural state is "nasty, brutish, and short"—the weak are constantly preyed upon by the strong. Thus, people seek the protection of a strong ruler whom they must obey, even if a particular ruler turns out to be cruel or capricious. The alternative—an endless "war of all against all"—is worse.

Thomas Hobbes-
Social Contract
"nasty, brutish, short"

Debating the Issues

Should the United States Have a Temporary Worker Program for Mexican Citizens?

Although the United States is a nation of immigrants, it has not always been welcoming of new immigrant groups. At the turn of the twentieth century, American industry had a huge shortage of workers, and immigration was encouraged—but only for the able-bodied. Strict inspection standards denied entry to the weak and the infirm. Some Americans, the so-called Nativists, even wanted to deny admission to all Catholics and Jews arriving from southern and eastern Europe, declaring their beliefs and customs "un-American." Immigration is still a contentious issue, particularly in regard to the illegal entry of Mexican citizens. While they are a source of inexpensive labor and are sought by employers, these immigrants place a burden on local schools and other public institutions and services. Early in his second term, President George W. Bush proposed

legislation that would tighten security on the Mexican border while creating a temporary worker program that would enable more than 10 million otherwise illegal immigrants to work in the United States for a period not to exceed six years. The guest worker program would relieve pressures on the Mexican government stemming from high unemployment in Mexico. In turn, the Mexican government would assist in preventing Mexicans from illegally gaining entry into the United States.

President Bush's proposal sparked an immediate and heated debate. Much of the opposition to his plan came from members of his own political party. Below are portions of Bush's announcement and part of a reaction to it by a Republican member of Congress. Which position do you find more persuasive? Why?

 Yes

As we enforce our immigration laws, comprehensive immigration reform also requires us to improve those laws by creating a new temporary worker program. This program would create a legal way to match willing foreign workers with willing American employers to fill jobs that Americans will not do. Workers would be able to register for legal status for a fixed period of time, and then be required to go home. This program would help meet the demands of a growing economy, and it would allow honest workers to provide for their families while respecting the law. This plan would also help us relieve pressure on the border. By creating a legal channel for those who enter America to do an honest day's labor, we would reduce the number of workers trying to sneak across the border....

The program that I propose would not create an automatic path to citizenship, it wouldn't provide for amnesty—I oppose amnesty. Rewarding those who have broken the law would encourage others to break the law and keep pressure on our border.... I support increasing the number of annual green cards that can lead to citizenship [but do not support] amnesty.... In this new century, we must continue to welcome immigrants, and to set high standards for those who follow the laws to become a part of our country. Every new citizen of the United States has an obligation to learn our customs and values, including liberty and civic responsibility, equality under God and tolerance for others, and the English language.

—*George W. Bush, President of the United States*

No

Let's take the President's first claim: "we will not be able to effectively enforce our immigration laws until we create a temporary worker program." Really? That is, cannot the United States government stop illegal aliens from getting to our soil? The challenge is not catching *every single person,* but stopping enough to make the trip into the U.S. costly and to reverse many of the side effects of massive illegal immigration (cultural bifurcation, social service hemorrhaging, downward wage pressure, etc.). The President's next line: "The program that I propose would not create an automatic path to citizenship, it wouldn't provide for amnesty—I oppose amnesty." ... What the White House is trying to do is to confuse amnesty with a "path to citizenship," so that

when the public hears "no path to citizenship," it thinks "no amnesty." ... The President's new plan is still amnesty in two respects. First, it protects persons who have broken the law from the punishment prescribed by the law (deportation) while offering them a privilege that few get (living and working in the U.S.). Second, does anyone really think that at the end of six years they'll go home or that Congress will have the political will to make them? Six years from now, after we've secured the border and gotten tough on interior enforcement, there will be tremendous political pressure to go soft on the "guest workers" who have been here for years.

—*Tom Tancredo, U.S. Representative (R-Colo.)*

Political Culture

Religion and American Ideals

The United States is a nation established in 1776 on a set of principles—liberty, equality, and self-government. These ideals derived in part from broad lessons of history, the direct experiences of the colonists, and treatises such as those of Locke and Rousseau. Religious beliefs also played a major part.

Many of the early colonists came to America in order to practice their religions freely. Church and state in Europe were joined. Government there sided with a particular religion—Roman Catholicism in France and Spain, Anglicanism in England. Rhode Island's founder, the Reverend Roger Williams, was a Calvinist who left his native England for reasons of religious freedom. Williams was the first to assert that church and state in America ought to be separate. Williams argued that salvation required an acceptance of God, which is meaningful only if it is an act of free will—and this is impossible if religion is imposed on the individual by the state. To Williams and others, religious liberty and political liberty were inseparable. The prevalence of this view is apparent in the First Amendment to the Constitution, which at once provides for freedom of political expression *and* for religious freedom.

Liberty is not the only American ideal with a religious basis. Equality was considered God's work: "all men are created equal." Every individual was a child of God and thus equal in His eyes. (This belief posed a dilemma for slaveholders, who finessed it by claiming that slaves either were soulless or were secondary beings in God's "natural order.") Self-government, too, had a religious foundation, though a Protestant one. Unlike the Catholic Church, which was hierarchical in its organization, with the Pope and bishops at its head, many Protestant sects had self-governing congregations. Their democratic operation affected their members' views on the proper form of government.

America, said the British writer G. K. Chesterton, is "a nation with the soul of a church" and "the only country founded on a creed." He could have added that America is also a nation that emulated a religious model in its governing document. The first colonists formed religious communities governed by written covenant, a model for the written Constitution drafted and ratified by Americans more than a century later.

Forty years later, the English philosopher John Locke used Hobbes's idea of a social contract to argue *against* absolutism. In his *Second Treatise on Civil Government* (1690), Locke claimed that all individuals have certain natural (or inalienable) rights, including those of life, liberty, and property. Such rights, Locke wrote, belonged to people in their natural state before government was created. When people come together in order to have the protection that only organized government can provide, they retain these rights. People enter into the social contract—they agree to be governed—in order to safeguard their rights. Accordingly, government is obliged to provide this protection. If it fails to do so, Locke argued, the people can rightfully rebel against it and create a new government.

Three-quarters of a century later, the French philosopher Jean Jacques Rousseau extended the idea of a social contract to include popular rule. Like Locke, Rousseau despised absolute government. "Man was born free, but everywhere he is in chains" are the opening words of Rousseau's *Social Contract* (1762). Rousseau claimed that people in their natural state are innocent and happy. Accordingly, the only legitimate government is one that governs in their interest and with their consent. The people, in Rousseau's view, were sovereign. Government was not the sovereign authority; government was merely the instrument for carrying out the people's laws. Rousseau worried, however, that the people would act selfishly and proposed a limit on popular sovereignty. It would be legitimate only if people acted in the common interest—what Rousseau called "the general will."

John Locke

Rousseau
– Social
Contract

These ideas—that people have individual rights and should have a say in their government—sparked the American Revolution of 1776. The basic principle of contract theory—that the power of leaders is limited by a set of rules—was embodied in the Constitution of the United States, written in 1787.

The Rules of American Politics

The major rules of American politics—democracy, constitutionalism, and capitalism—establish a political process that is intended to promote self-government, defend individual rights, and protect property.

Democracy Rousseauist idea

democracy
A form of government in which the people govern, either directly or through elected representatives.

Democracy is a set of rules intended to give ordinary people a significant voice in government. The word *democracy* comes from the Greek words *demos*, meaning "the people," and *kratis*, meaning "to rule." In simple terms, **democracy** is a form of government in which the people govern, either directly or through elected representatives (see Chapter 2). A democracy thus is different from an **oligarchy** (in which control rests with a small group, such as top-ranking military officers or a few wealthy families) and from an **autocracy** (in which control rests with a single individual, such as a king or dictator).

oligarchy
A form of government in which control rests with a few persons.

autocracy
A form of government in which absolute control rests with a single person.

Democratic government rests on the Rousseauist idea that legitimate authority stems from the consent of the governed, which in practice has come to mean majority rule through voting in elections. More direct forms of democracy exist, such as the town meeting in which citizens vote directly on issues affecting them, but the impracticality of such an arrangement at the national level has made majority rule through elections the operating principle of modern democracies.

Majority rule through the vote does not take the same form in all democracies. The U.S. electoral system was established in a period when the power of government—whether it rested with a king or the majority—was greatly feared. To protect against abuses of power, the writers of the U.S. Constitution devised an elaborate system of checks and balances. Authority was divided among the executive, legislative, and judicial branches so that each branch could serve as a check on the power of the others and could balance their power with its own power (see Chapter 2). Indeed, *extreme fragmentation of governing authority is a defining characteristic of the American political system*. One result of this constitutional arrangement is that majority rule is less direct in the United States than in many democratic countries, including those of Europe. In the European democracies, a majority has the power in a single election to place executive and legislative power in the hands of a single group of representatives (see Chapter 2). In the United States, however, elections for the president, the Senate, and the House of Representatives are separate, and the terms of office for these officials are staggered. Thus, for a majority to exercise control in the United States, it must have enough strength and lasting power to dominate a series of elections.

Democracy—the idea of a government of, for, and by the people—is an organizing principle of the American political system. In practice, democracy—along with its accompanying feature, majoritarianism—is most clearly evident in elections when Americans through their votes choose their representatives.

LEADERS

SANDRA DAY O'CONNOR

In 1981, Sandra Day O'Connor became the first woman to be appointed to the U.S. Supreme Court, where she served for a quarter century before retiring in 2006. Toward the end of her tenure, she was widely regarded as the Court's most influential member. A pragmatic jurist, she was the swing vote on an ideologically divided Court. She cast the deciding vote in many 5-4 decisions, usually but not consistently siding with its more conservative members. A graduate of Stanford Law School, O'Connor faced discrimination because of her gender. One firm offered her a job as a legal secretary but not as an attorney. She eventually started her own practice and later served as assistant attorney general in Arizona. She ran successfully for a seat in the Arizona legislature and subsequently was appointed to the Arizona Court of Appeals before being nominated by President Ronald Reagan for a seat on the U.S. Supreme Court. As a member of the Court, O'Connor cast the deciding vote in leading cases involving key issues such as affirmative action, federalism, and abortion. O'Connor's policy influence reflects Tocqueville's observation that sooner or later most political issues in America become also judicial issues. O'Connor's career is testament to the importance in America of constitutionalism—the idea that the power of government over individuals is subject to judicial oversight.

constitutionalism
The idea that there are definable limits on the rightful power of a government over its citizens.

socialism
An economic system in which government owns and controls many of the major industries.

Constitutionalism

The concept of democracy implies that the will of the majority should prevail over the wishes of the minority. If taken to the extreme, however, this principle would allow a majority to ride roughshod over the minority. Such action could deprive the minority even of its liberty, a clearly unacceptable outcome. Individuals have rights and freedoms that cannot lawfully be denied by the majority.

Constitutionalism is a set of rules that restricts the lawful uses of power. In its original sense, constitutionalism in Western society referred to a government based on laws and constitutional powers.[18] **Constitutionalism** has since come to refer specifically to the Lockean idea that there are limits to the rightful power of government over citizens. In a constitutional system, officials govern according to law, and citizens have basic rights that government cannot take away or deny.[19] Free speech is an example. Government is prohibited by the First Amendment from interfering with the lawful exercise of free speech. No right is absolute, which means that some restrictions are allowed. No student, for example, has a First Amendment right to shout loudly and disrupt a classroom. Nevertheless, free speech is broadly protected by the courts. During the buildup to war with Iraq in 2003, tens of thousands of antiwar demonstrators took to the streets. Despite instances in which protesters were intimidated by police or arrested for disorderly conduct, those who opposed the government's pursuit of the war had the opportunity to express their views freely without the threat of being sent to prison.

The constitutional tradition in the United States is at least as strong as the democratic tradition. In fact, *a defining characteristic of the American political system is its extraordinary emphasis on individual rights.* Issues that in other democracies would be resolved through elections and in legislative bodies are, in the United States, decided in courts of law as well. As Tocqueville noted, there is hardly a political issue in the United States that does not sooner or later become also a judicial issue.[20] Abortion rights, nuclear power, busing, toxic waste disposal, and welfare services are among the scores of issues that in recent years have played out in part as questions of rights to be settled through the courts.

Capitalism

Just as democracy and constitutionalism are systems of rules for allocating costs and benefits in American society, so too is capitalism. Societies have adopted alternative ways of organizing their economies. One way is **socialism,** which

Free speech is a familiar aspect of constitutionalism. This anti-gun control rally took place in Austin, Texas.

assigns government a large role in the ownership of the means of production, in regulating economic decisions, and in providing for the economic security of the individual. Under the form of socialism practiced in democratic countries, such as Sweden, the government does not attempt to manage the overall economy. Under **communism,** the government owns most or all major industries and also takes responsibility for overall management of the economy, including production quotas, supply points, and pricing.

Capitalism, an alternative method for distributing economic costs and benefits, holds that the government should interfere with the economy as little as possible. Firms are allowed to operate in a free and open marketplace, and individuals are expected to rely on their own initiative to establish their economic security. Firms decide what they will produce and the price they will charge for their goods, while consumers decide what they will buy at what price. Meanwhile, following a Lockean principle, private property rights are vigorously protected through government action.

Like the rules of democracy and constitutionalism, the rules of capitalism are not neutral. Whereas democracy responds to numbers and constitutionalism responds to individual rights, capitalism responds to wealth. "Money talks" in a capitalist system, which means, among other things, that wealthier people will have by far the greater say not only in economic matters but in political ones as well. Most Americans see nothing wrong with this arrangement and, compared with Europeans, are more likely to accept limits on government action in the area of the economy.

For all practical purposes, this outlook places many kinds of choices that in other countries are decided collectively beyond the reach of political majorities in the United States. Although Americans complain that their taxes are too high, they are taxed at substantially lower rates than are Europeans (see Figure 1–4). This situation testifies to the extent to which Americans believe wealth to be more properly allocated through the economic marketplace than through government policy. *A major characteristic of the American*

communism
An economic system in which government owns most or all major industries and also takes responsibility for overall management of the economy.

capitalism
An economic system based on the idea that government should interfere with economic transactions as little as possible. Free enterprise and self-reliance are the collective and individual principles that underpin capitalism.

Figure 1–4

Level of Taxation
Americans pay less in taxes
than do Europeans.
Source: OECD. 2006. Percentages
based on all taxes (national and
subnational) relative to a country's
Gross Domestic Product (GDP).

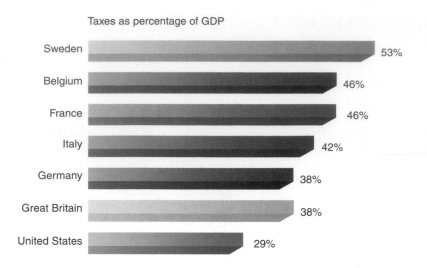

Taxes as percentage of GDP

Sweden — 53%
Belgium — 46%
France — 46%
Italy — 42%
Germany — 38%
Great Britain — 38%
United States — 29%

system is a relatively sharp distinction between what is political, and therefore to be decided in the public arena, and what is economic, and therefore to be settled in the private realm.

POLITICAL POWER: THE CONTROL OF POLICY

power
The ability of persons or institutions to control policy.

public policy
A decision of government to pursue a course of action designed to produce an intended outcome.

totalitarian government
A form of government in which the leaders claim complete dominance of all individuals and institutions.

authoritarian government
A form of government in which leaders, though they admit to no limits on their powers, are effectively limited by other centers of power in the society.

Rules are necessary in politics because the stakes are high. Individuals who decide how society will be governed have **power,** a term that refers to the ability of persons or institutions to control public policy.[21] **Public policy** is a decision by government to follow a course of action designed to produce a particular outcome. Persons or institutions with sufficient power can determine which side will prevail in policy disputes.

Some governments exercise absolute power. **Totalitarian governments** assert complete dominance over individuals and the institutions of society. They determine the culture, control the media, direct the economy, dictate what can and cannot be taught in schools, define family relations, and decide which religions—if any—can be practiced openly. In fact, virtually no area of life is beyond their sphere of control, which leads them to one-party rule and the use of fear, intimidation, and force to subdue the population. Germany under Adolf Hitler and the Soviet Union under Josef Stalin were totalitarian regimes. Millions of people in both countries were deemed enemies of the state and were imprisoned, tortured, or murdered.

Harsh rule is also characteristic of **authoritarian governments.** Although authoritarian governments include totalitarian ones, it is useful to distinguish regimes such as Nazi Germany from regimes that, though they admit to no limits on their power, are effectively limited by other strong institutions in the society, such as churches, corporations, or wealthy families. The governments that have resulted periodically from military coups in Africa and South America usually are authoritarian in form. Although authoritarian regimes repress political opponents and restrict free expression, they refrain from asserting full authority, recognizing that any such claim could antagonize powerful institutions that might drive them out of office.

Unlike authoritarian governments, democratic governments are characterized by ongoing competition for power among a range of interests. This tendency is particularly pronounced in the case of the United States. The country's settlement by people of different lands and religions, its great size and geographical variation, and its economic complexity have made the United States a diverse nation. Perhaps no country has more competing interests than the United States. *Competition for power among a great many interests of all kinds is a major characteristic of American politics.* Indeed, America's great diversity helps explain why its political life is not a life-and-death struggle. In *Federalist* No. 10, James Madison argued that government is most dangerous when a single group is powerful enough to gain full political control. In such cases, the group will use government to further its interests at the expense of all others in society. Because the United States is so diverse, however, no single group can hope to achieve full control. This forces groups to work together to exercise power, a process that requires each group to accommodate the interests of the others.

Nevertheless, as in every society, power in America is the means of controlling public policy. Americans who have enough power can levy or cut taxes, permit or prohibit abortions, protect or take away private property, provide or refuse health benefits, impose or relax trade barriers, make war or declare peace. With so much at stake, it is not surprising that Americans, like people elsewhere, seek power as a means of achieving their policy goals.

Adolf Hitler's Nazi Germany was a brutal totalitarian regime responsible for the deaths of millions of people.

Authority

Political power can reside with private individuals and organizations as well as in the hands of those who occupy government positions. A case in point is the power exercised by the National Rifle Association (NRA) over gun control policy. NRA members are strongly opposed to restrictions on gun ownership and back up their position through the power of their votes and their money. Although Congress has the authority to enact stricter controls on guns, many of its members are reluctant to antagonize the NRA.

Nevertheless, U.S. officials do have a special kind of power as a result of the positions they hold. When government officials exercise power, it is called **authority**, defined as the recognized right of an individual, organization, or institution to make binding decisions. By this definition, government is not the only source of authority: parents have authority over their children; professors have authority over their students; firms have authority over their employees. However, government is a special case. Government's authority extends to all people within its geographical boundaries and can be used to redefine the authority of the parent, the professor, or the firm. Government's authority is also the most coercive. It includes the power to arrest and imprison, and even to legally punish by death those who violate its rules.

Government needs coercive power to ensure that its laws will be obeyed. Without this power, lawlessness would prevail—as it does in Colombia, where drug lords control large areas of the country. Yet this power can itself be abused, as when government uses force to intimidate opponents. The challenge, as Madison noted, is to grant government the authority necessary to prevent lawlessness while confining its authority to lawful purposes.

authority
The recognized right of an individual or institution to exercise power.

Media & Politics
Comedy News: *The Daily Show*

Long before baseball or football enjoyed its reputation as America's national pastime, political humor occupied that spot. The United States was founded on a rejection of political authority—that of the British monarch—and poking fun at the nation's leaders is nearly an American birthright. Every generation could relate to these words of humorist Will Rogers: "I don't make jokes. I just watch the government and report the facts." Writer Mark Twain echoed this sentiment: "Reader, suppose you were an idiot, and suppose you were a member of Congress. But I repeat myself."

The acknowledged king of political comedy today is Jon Stewart. His program, *The Daily Show,* attracts roughly 1.5 million viewers, ranking it near the top of the ratings for a cable news program. Like Rush Limbaugh's radio talk show (see Chapter 10), which soared in the ratings during the 1990s when the conservative Limbaugh feasted off the actions of Democrat President Bill Clinton, the liberal Stewart's television show has risen in popularity based on his swipes at Republican President George W. Bush. In one telling moment, Stewart looked blankly at the television screen for seemingly endless seconds before blurting out "Please say, please say, you're kidding me." This followed a videotape of National Security Advisor Condoleeza Rice admitting to Congress that she had read a classified briefing titled "Bin Laden Determined to Attack Inside the United States" a month before the September 11, 2001, terrorist attacks on the World Trade Center and the Pentagon. Rice had earlier claimed that no one in the Bush administration could possibly have foreseen the attacks.

Unlike most hosts of shows with a partisan twist, Stewart takes occasional potshots at his preferred party. Following a report about prisoner abuse by U.S. military personnel, Stewart commented: "The prisoner scandal is yet another election year problem for President Bush. And, with the economy still struggling, combat operations in Iraq dragging on, and the 9-11 hearings revealing damning information, even an opponent of limited political skill should be able to capitalize on those problems. The Democrats, however, chose to nominate John Kerry."

The Daily Show's formula is a mixture of comedy and the day's news events. More than half of the program's audience is under 40 years, which is the opposite of the age distribution of the audience for broadcast network newscasts. But if *The Daily Show* is helpful in getting today's young adults to pay attention to news, it might not be helpful in getting them involved in politics. A recent study by Jody Baumgartner and Jonathan Morris, political scientists at East Carolina University, found that youthful viewers of *The Daily Show,* as compared with youthful viewers of broadcast network news, had more negative views of candidates and of the electoral process.

Political humor dates to the Greeks, but few societies have embraced it as fully as have Americans. Part of the reason is rooted in the American political culture. Liberty, equality, and self-government are assertions of individualism as pitted against traditional deference to the high, the mighty, the rich, and the well-born. As Mark Twain noted of arrogant leaders, "Against the assault of laughter nothing can stand."

Theories of Power

Who has power in America? Who, in the end, decides the policies that the U.S. government pursues? Do the people themselves hold this power, or does it reside in the hands of a relatively small group of influential people, either within or outside of government?

This issue is compelling because the ultimate question of any political system is the question of who governs. Is power widely shared and used for the benefit of the many, or is it narrowly held and used to the advantage of the few? The issue is compelling for a second reason: power is easy to define but hard to locate. Consider, for example, the votes that a member of Congress casts. Are these votes an expression of the member's power, or are they an expression of the power of groups on whom the member depends for reelection?

The pattern of political power in America has been shown to differ substantially across individuals, institutions, and policy areas. As a result, there is no single theory of how power in America is held and exercised. Instead, four broad theories predominate (see Table 1–3). None of these theories describes every aspect of American politics, but each applies in some situations.

TABLE 1–3	**Theories of Power: Who Governs America?** There are four theories of power in America, each of which must be taken into account in any full explanation of the nation's policies.

THEORY	DESCRIPTION
Majoritarianism	Holds that numerical majorities determine issues of policy
Pluralism	Holds that policies are effectively decided through power wielded by special interests that dominate particular policy areas
Elitism	Holds that policy is controlled by a small number of well-positioned, highly influential individuals
Bureaucratic rule	Holds that policy is controlled by well-placed administrators within the government bureaucracy

Majoritarianism: Government by the People

A basic principle of democracy is the idea of majority rule. **Majoritarianism** is the notion that the majority prevails not only in the counting of votes but also in the determination of public policy.

Majorities do sometimes rule in America. Their power is perhaps most evident in those states that offer voters the opportunity to decide directly on policy initiatives, which then become law if they receive a majority vote. The majority's influence is also felt indirectly through the decisions of elected representatives. When Congress in 1996 passed a welfare reform bill that included provisions requiring able-bodied welfare recipients to accept a job or job training after a two-year period or face the loss of their welfare benefits, it was acting in accord with the thinking of the majority of Americans who believe that employable individuals should be self-reliant. A more systematic assessment of the power of majorities is provided by Benjamin Page and Robert Shapiro's study of the relationship between majority opinions and more than three hundred policy issues. On major issues particularly, the researchers found that when majority opinion changed, policy tended to change in the same direction.[22]

Majorities do not always rule in America, however. In many policy areas, majority opinion either is nonexistent or is ignored by policymakers. There are only a few issues at any moment that have the general public's attention and an even smaller number that the public really cares about. Thus, majoritarianism cannot account for most government policies. Other explanations are required in these instances.

Pluralism: Government by Groups

One such explanation is provided by the theory of **pluralism,** which focuses on group activity and holds that many policies are effectively decided through power wielded by diverse (plural) interests.

Many policies are in fact more responsive to the interests of particular groups than to majority opinion. Farm subsidies, for example, are determined more by pressures from agricultural groups than by the opinions of the general public. For pluralists, the issue of whether interest-group politics serves the public good centers on whether a diverse range of interests is served. Pluralists contend that it is misleading to view society only in terms of majorities. They see society as primarily a collection of separate interests. Farmers, broadcasters, college students, and multinational corporations have different needs and, according to the pluralist view, should have a disproportionate say in policies that directly affect

majoritarianism
The idea that the majority prevails not only in elections but also in policy determination.

pluralism
A theory of American politics that holds that society's interests are substantially represented through the activities of groups.

Get Involved!

America's Ideals and Civic Participation

Author Theodore H. White described America as a nation "in search of itself." He was speaking of Americans' efforts to live up to the high promise of the principles on which the nation was founded. Liberty, equality, and self-government are demanding ideals that can be diminished if citizens are inactive and uncaring.

Signs of the need for vigilance are all around you. They can be found in Americans' questioning of the responsiveness of their government: what is the meaning of self-government if officials are more receptive to the demands of powerful interest groups than to the concerns of ordinary people? The signs can be seen in concerns raised by the war on terrorism: what is the meaning of liberty when America's security is threatened by terrorist groups or when citizens' civil liberties are weakened in the name of fighting terrorism? The signs also can be seen on college campuses throughout the country: what is the meaning of equality when a college education is less readily available to young adults whose families lack money? The list could go on, but the point would be the same: Americans are a people in search of a fuller realization of their nation's founding ideals.

With so much at stake for the individual and for the nation, why do so many citizens sit on the sidelines, forgoing opportunities to contribute? It is not for lack of opportunity. With its tradition of free expression and free association, the United States is a country where the barriers to citizen participation are relatively low. Moreover, any number of civic and political arenas—from the college to the church to the political party—desire and welcome volunteers. The "Get Involved" boxes in subsequent chapters suggest some ways you can make a difference through your participation.

them. Thus, as long as many groups have influence in their own area of interest, government is responding to the interests of most Americans. Pluralists such as Robert Dahl have argued that this is in fact the way the American political system operates most of the time.[23]

Critics argue that pluralists wrongly assume that the public interest is somehow represented in a system that allows special interests, each in its own sphere, to set public policy (see Chapter 9). Any such outcome, they say, represents the triumph of minority rule over majority rule. Critics also say that society's underprivileged groups are unable to compete effectively because of their lack of organization and money. They see a group system biased in favor of wealthy interests.

Elitism: Government by a Few

elitism

The view that the United States essentially is run by a tiny elite (composed of wealthy or well-connected individuals) who control public policy through both direct and indirect means.

Elite theory offers in varying degrees a pessimistic view of the U.S. political system. **Elitism** holds that power in America is held by a small number of well-positioned, highly influential individuals. A leading proponent of elite theory was sociologist C. Wright Mills, who argued that key policies are decided by an overlapping coalition of select leaders, including corporate executives, top military officers, and centrally placed public officials.[24] Other proponents of elite theory have defined the core group somewhat differently, but their contention is the same: America is governed not by majorities or by a plurality of groups but by a small number of well-placed and privileged individuals.

Proponents of elite theory differ, however, in the extent to which they believe elites control policy for their own purposes. Some theorists, including G. William Domhoff, hold the view that elites operate behind the scenes in order to manipulate government for selfish ends.[25] Other theorists claim that elites, in part to protect their privileged positions and in part out of a sense of obligation, pursue policies that serve others' interests as well as their own. One such view holds that competing elites appeal to voters for support and, in the process, adopt policy positions favored by large blocs of voters.[26]

Unquestionably, certain policies are effectively controlled by a tiny circle of influential people. The nation's monetary policy, for example, is set by the decisions of the Federal Reserve Board ("the Fed"), which meets in secrecy and decides the interest rates that banks pay for the loans they receive from the Federal Reserve. These rates in turn affect the interest rates that banks charge for their loans to customers. The Fed is very responsive to the concerns of bankers. What is less clear is the Fed's responsiveness to the concerns of consumers.

The Federal Reserve Board of Governors is a government body that through its interest-rate policies exerts a substantial influence on the American economy. The board meets in secrecy and is an example of the influence of political elites.

Bureaucratic Rule: Government by Administrators

A fourth theory holds that power resides in the hands of career government bureaucrats. The leading proponent of the theory of **bureaucratic rule** was the German sociologist Max Weber, who argued that all large organizations tend toward the bureaucratic form, with the result that decision-making power devolves to career administrators whose experience and knowledge of policy issues exceed those of elected officials.[27] Another sociologist, Roberto Michels, propounded the "iron law of oligarchy," concluding that power inevitably gravitates toward experienced administrators at the top of large-scale organizations, even in the case of organizations that aim to be governed democratically.[28]

Bureaucratic politics raises the possibility of a large, permanent government run by unaccountable administrators. Elections come and go, but the bureaucrats who staff executive agencies stay on. As public policy issues have become increasingly complex, these bureaucrats often are the most knowledgeable on these issues and also are well-positioned to influence their resolution. Modern government could not function without career bureaucrats, but in most cases they are not instruments of the majority. They tend instead to act in ways that will promote their own agency and its programs (see Chapter 13).

bureaucratic rule
The tendency of large-scale organizations to develop into the bureaucratic form, with the effect that administrators make key policy decisions.

Who Does Govern?

The perspective of this book is that each of these theories—majoritarianism, pluralism, elitism, and bureaucratic rule—must be taken into account in any full explanation of politics and power in America. As subsequent chapters will demonstrate, some policies are decided by majority influence, whereas others reflect the influence of special interests, bureaucrats, or elites.

THE CONCEPT OF A POLITICAL SYSTEM AND THIS BOOK'S ORGANIZATION

As the foregoing discussion suggests, American government is based on a great many related parts. It is useful to regard these components as constituting a **political system.** The parts are separate, but they connect with one another,

political system
The various components of American government. The parts are separate, but they connect with one another, affecting how each performs.

Figure 1–5

The American Political System
This book's chapters are organized within a political-system framework.

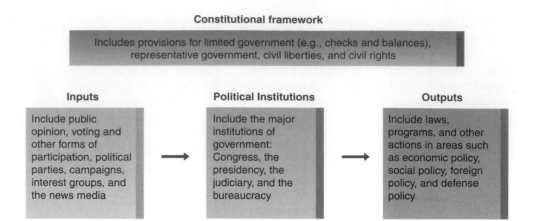

Constitutional framework

Includes provisions for limited government (e.g., checks and balances), representative government, civil liberties, and civil rights

Inputs	Political Institutions	Outputs
Include public opinion, voting and other forms of participation, political parties, campaigns, interest groups, and the news media	Include the major institutions of government: Congress, the presidency, the judiciary, and the bureaucracy	Include laws, programs, and other actions in areas such as economic policy, social policy, foreign policy, and defense policy

affecting how each performs. Political scientist David Easton, who was a pioneer in this conception of politics, said that it makes little sense to study political relations piecemeal when they are, in reality, "interrelated."[29]

The complexity of government has kept political scientists from developing a fully explanatory model of the political system, but the concept of politics as a system is useful for instructional purposes. To view politics as a system is to emphasize the connections between the parts and the ways change in one area affects the others. It is a dynamic conception in that the political system is constantly changing in response to new conditions and to the interplay of its various parts.

The political-system approach characterizes this book, beginning with the organization of its chapters (see Figure 1–5). The political system operates against the backdrop of a constitutional framework that defines how power is to be obtained and exercised. This structure is the focus of the opening chapters, which examine how the Constitution defines, in theory and practice, the institutions of government and the rights of individuals. Another part of the political system is *inputs:* the demands people and organizations place on government and the support they provide for institutions, leaders, and policies. These inputs are explored in chapters on public opinion, political participation, political parties, interest groups, and the news media. The functioning of governing officials is addressed in chapters on the nation's *political institutions*—Congress, the presidency, the federal bureaucracy, and the federal courts. Some of the discussion in these chapters is devoted simply to describing these institutions, but most of the discussion explores their interrelationships and how their actions are affected by inputs and by the constitutional system in which they operate. Throughout the book, but particularly in the closing chapters, attention is given to the political system's *outputs*—policy decisions that are binding on society. These decisions, which are made by political institutions in response to inputs, affect American life in many areas, including the economy, the environment, social welfare, education, foreign affairs, and national defense.

The chapters are collectively designed to convey a reliable body of knowledge that will enable the reader to think systematically about the nature of the American political system. This body of knowledge derives from the full range of methodological approaches that political scientists have applied to the study of politics. Political science, unlike some academic disciplines, has been defined more by its subjects of inquiry than by a particular methodology. Normative theory, historical reasoning, legal analysis, and cultural analysis are among the strains, along with political psychology, political sociology, and political economy. Rational choice theory, organizational theory, and institutional analysis are other strains. Each approach can illuminate certain aspects of politics. For example, rational choice theory is based on the assumption that actors pursue their interests rationally and has proved to be a powerful model to describe, for instance, the behavior of elected officials as they seek to position themselves for reelection. As another example, cultural analysis is a powerful lens through which to view the values that motivate political action.

Political scientists have uncovered numerous tendencies in American political behavior, institutions, and processes. Five of these tendencies have been iden- #10
tified in this opening chapter as deserving special attention:

- Enduring cultural ideals that are Americans' common bond and a source of their political goals

- Extreme fragmentation of governing authority that is based on an elaborate system of checks and balances

- Many competing interests that are the result of the nation's great size, population diversity, and economic complexity

- A strong emphasis on individual rights, which is a consequence of the nation's political traditions

- A relatively sharp separation of the political and economic spheres that has the effect of placing many economic issues outside the reach of political majorities

Underlying this book's concern with the broad patterns of the American political system is a question that must be asked of any democracy: what is the relationship of the people to their government? The answer to this question is the foundation not only of a reasonable assessment of the state of American democracy but also of good citizenship. Responsible citizenship depends finally on an informed perspective, on a recognition of how difficult it is to govern effectively and yet how important it is to try. It cannot be said too often that the issue of governing is the most difficult issue facing any society. Nor can it be said too often that governing is a quest and a search, not a resolved issue. The Constitution's opening phrase, "We the People," is a call to Americans to join in that quest. E. E. Schattschneider said it clearly: "In the course of centuries, there has come a great deal of agreement about what democracy is, but nobody has a monopoly on it and the last word has not been spoken."[30]

Summary

Self-Test www.mhhe.com/pattersontad8

The United States is a nation that was formed on a set of ideals. Liberty, equality, and self-government are foremost among these ideals, which also include the principles of individualism, diversity, and unity. These ideals became Americans' common bond and today are the basis of their political culture. Although they are mythic, inexact, and conflicting, these ideals have had a powerful effect on what generation after generation of Americans has tried to achieve politically for themselves and others.

Politics in the United States plays out through rules of the game that include democracy, constitutionalism, and capitalism. Democracy is rule by the people, which in practice refers to a representative system of government in which the people rule through their elected officials. Constitutionalism refers to rules that limit the rightful power of government over citizens. Capitalism is an economic system based on a free-market principle that allows the government only a limited role in determining how economic costs and benefits will be allocated.

Politics is the process by which it is determined whose values will prevail in society. The basis of politics is conflict over scarce resources and competing values. Those who have power win out in this conflict and are able to control governing authority and policy choices. In the United States, no one faction controls all power and policy. Majorities govern on some issues, while groups, elites, and bureaucrats each govern on other issues.

#10

STUDY CORNER

Key Terms

authoritarian government (*p. 24*)
authority (*p. 25*)
autocracy (*p. 21*)
bureaucratic rule (*p. 29*)
capitalism (*p. 23*)
communism (*p. 23*)
constitutionalism (*p. 22*)
democracy (*p. 21*)
diversity (*p. 11*)

elitism (*p. 28*)
equality (*p. 10*)
individualism (*p. 11*)
liberty (*p. 9*)
majoritarianism (*p. 27*)
oligarchy (*p. 21*)
pluralism (*p. 27*)
political culture (*p. 7*)
political system (*p. 29*)

politics (*p. 17*)
power (*p. 24*)
public policy (*p. 24*)
self-government (*p. 10*)
social contract (*p. 18*)
socialism (*p. 22*)
totalitarian government (*p. 24*)
unity (*p. 11*)

Self-Test

1. American political culture centers on a set of core ideals that includes all **except** which of the following?
   a. socialism
   b. liberty
   c. equality
   d. self-government

2. Compared with citizens in European democracies, Americans:
   a. emphasize individualism.
   b. feel that success in life is determined by forces outside their control.
   c. are willing to use government to redistribute economic resources.
   d. a and b.
   e. all of the above.

3. When people are able to control policy decisions and prevail in political conflicts, they are said to have:
   a. political culture.
   b. political power.
   c. pluralism.
   d. diversity.

4. America's commitment to the principle of constitutionalism means:
   a. the majority can decide all policy issues.
   b. there are limits on the rightful power of government over citizens.
   c. direct democracy will be favored over representative democracy.
   d. a "mixed economy" must be upheld at all costs.

5. Which one of the following is **not** among the four theories of power concerning who governs America mentioned in the text?
   a. majoritarianism
   b. pluralism
   c. aristocratic rule
   d. bureaucratic rule

6. Which of the following statements are true about American ideals?
   a. They do not fully match what happens in reality.
   b. There is inevitable conflict between these ideals.
   c. Americans have no interest in putting the ideals into practice.
   d. only a and b
   e. only b and c

7. Cultural beliefs are mythical in the sense that they are based on wishful thinking and serve no useful purpose for society. (T/F)

8. Historically, America has been relatively free from racial and ethnic discrimination. (T/F)

9. Authority can be defined as the recognized right of an individual, organization, or institution to make binding decisions. (T/F)

10. Americans have the world's most extensive system of college education. (T/F)

Critical Thinking

How are Americans' beliefs about liberty, equality, and self-government related to their preference for constitutionalism? For capitalism? For democracy?

Suggested Readings

Dahl, Robert. *On Democracy*. New Haven, Conn.: Yale University Press, 1998. A handbook on democracy by a leading advocate of pluralism.

Domhoff, G. William. *Who Rules America? Power and Politics*, 4th ed. New York: McGraw-Hill, 2002. A critical assessment of American government by a leading proponent of elite theory.

Ferguson, Robert A. *Reading the Early Republic*. Cambridge, Mass.: Harvard University Press, 2004. Argues that America has always been a country trying to reach its ideals.

Katz, Michael B., and Mark J. Stern. *One Nation Divisible: What America Was and What It's Becoming*. New York: Russell Sage Foundation, 2006. A penetrating look at the transformation of American society during the twentieth century.

Lipset, Seymour Martin. *American Exceptionalism: A Double-Edged Sword*. New York: Norton, 1996. Argues that Americans' tendency to view society in idealized terms is a source of both alienation and progress.

Schuck, Peter H. *Diversity in America: Keeping Government at a Safe Distance*. Cambridge, Mass.: Belknap Press of Harvard, 2003. A far-reaching analysis of when diversity does and does not serve America's interests.

Stout, Jeffrey. *Democracy and Tradition*. Princeton, N.J.: Princeton University Press, 2004. An analysis of the moral claims associated with democracy.

White, John Kenneth. *The Values Divide*. Washington, D.C.: CQ Press, 2002. A look at Americans' values in a time of change.

List of Websites

http://www.conginst.org/
A site that provides up-to-date survey data on the American political culture.

http://www.loc.gov/
The Library of Congress website; it provides access to over seventy million historical and contemporary U.S. documents.

http://www.stateline.org/
A University of Richmond/Pew Charitable Trusts site dedicated to providing citizens with information on major policy issues.

http://www.tocqueville.org/
Includes biographical and other references to Alexis de Tocqueville and his writings.

Participate!

The American political culture includes a belief in liberty, equality, and self-government. As a prelude to getting involved in public affairs, reflect on what these ideals mean to you. What types of political activity are associated with each of these ideals? Thinking of your own experiences, what have you done to promote these ideals? What might you consider doing in the future to promote them?

Extra Credit

For up-to-the-minute *New York Times* articles, interactive simulations, graphics, study tools, and more links and quizzes, visit the text's Online Learning Center at www.mhhe.com/pattersontad8.

Constitutional Democracy:
Promoting Liberty and Self-Government

Chapter Outline

Before the Constitution: The Colonial and Revolutionary Experiences
"The Rights of Englishmen"
The Declaration of Independence
The Articles of Confederation
Shays's Rebellion: A Nation Dissolving

Negotiating Toward a Constitution
The Great Compromise: A Two-Chamber Congress
The North-South Compromise: The Issue of Slavery
A Strategy for Ratification
The Ratification Debate
The Framers' Goals

Protecting Liberty: Limited Government
Grants and Denials of Power
Using Power to Offset Power
Separated Institutions Sharing Power: Checks and Balances
The Bill of Rights
Judicial Review

Providing for Self-Government
Democracy Versus Republic
Limited Popular Rule
Altering the Constitution: More Power to the People

Constitutional Democracy Today

CHAPTER 2

The people must be governed by a majority, with whom all power resides.
But how is the sense of this majority to be obtained?

Fisher Ames (1788)[1]

On the night of June 17, 1972, a security guard at the Watergate apartment-office complex in Washington, D.C., noticed that the latch on the door to the Democratic party's national headquarters had been taped open. He called the police, who captured the five burglars inside. As it turned out, the men had links to Republican President Richard Nixon's Committee to Re-elect the President. Nixon called the incident "bizarre" and denied that anyone on his staff had had anything to do with the break-in.

The reality was that the Watergate break-in was part of an orchestrated campaign of "dirty tricks" designed to ensure Nixon's reelection. The dirty-tricks campaign included wiretaps, tax audits, and burglaries of Nixon's political opponents (the "enemies list"), who included journalists and antiwar activists in addition to Democrats. Although the Nixon White House managed for a time to hide the truth, the facts of the dirty-tricks campaign gradually became known. During Senate investigative hearings, a White House assistant revealed that Nixon had tape-recorded all his telephone calls and personal conversations in the Oval Office. Nixon at first refused to release the tapes but then made public what he claimed were "all the relevant" ones. Congress demanded additional tapes, as did the special prosecutor who had been appointed to investigate criminal aspects of the Watergate affair. In late July the U.S. Supreme Court, which included four justices appointed by Nixon, unanimously ordered the president to supply sixty-four additional tapes. The tapes were incriminating, and two weeks later, on August 9, 1974, Richard Nixon resigned from office, the first president in U.S. history to do so.

Nixon's downfall was owed in no small measure to the handiwork two centuries earlier of the writers of the Constitution. They were well aware that power could never be entrusted to the goodwill of leaders. "If angels were to govern men," James Madison wrote in *Federalist* No. 51, "neither external nor internal controls on government would be necessary." Madison's point, of course, was that leaders are not angels and, as mere mortals, are subject to temptation and vice, including a lust for power—hence the Framers' insistence on constitutional checks on power, as when they gave Congress the authority to impeach and remove the president from office.

The writers of the Constitution were determined through their system of checks and balances to protect liberty from the threat of a too-powerful government.

The Senate Judiciary Committee holds hearings on allegations of illegal acts by President Richard Nixon. The congressional investigation led to Nixon's resignation.

limited government

A government that is subject to strict limits on its lawful uses of power, and hence on its ability to deprive people of their liberty.

self-government

The principle that the people are the ultimate source and proper beneficiary of governing authority; in practice, a government based on majority rule.

The Framers sought a **limited government:** one that is subject to strict limits on its lawful uses of power. They also had a second and somewhat competing objective. They wanted **self-government:** a government based on the people and subject to their control. Self-government requires that the majority through its representatives have the power to rule. However, limited government requires that majority rule stop at the point where it infringes on the legitimate rights and interests of the minority. This consideration led the Framers to forge a Constitution that provides for majority rule but has built-in restrictions on the majority's power.

This chapter describes how the principles of self-government and limited government are embodied in the Constitution and explains the tension between them. The chapter also indicates how these principles have been modified in practice in the course of American history. The main points of this chapter are these:

- *America during the colonial period developed traditions of limited government and self-government.* These traditions were rooted in governing practices, philosophy, and cultural values.

- *The Constitution provides for limited government mainly by defining lawful powers and by dividing those powers among competing institutions.* The Constitution, with its Bill of Rights, also prohibits government from infringing on individual rights. Judicial review is an additional safeguard of limited government.

- *The Constitution in its original form provided for self-government mainly through indirect systems of popular election of representatives.* The Framers' theory of self-government was based on the notion that political power must be separated from immediate popular influences if sound policies are to result.

- *The idea of popular government—in which the majority's desires have a more direct and immediate impact on governing officials—has gained strength since the nation's beginning.* Originally, the House of Representatives was the only institution subject to direct vote of the people. This mechanism has been extended to other institutions and, through primary elections, even to the nomination of candidates for public office.

BEFORE THE CONSTITUTION: THE COLONIAL AND REVOLUTIONARY EXPERIENCES

Early Americans' admiration for limited government was based partly on their British heritage. Unlike other European governments of the time, Britain did not have an absolute monarchy. The Parliament was an independent body with lawmaking powers, and British subjects had certain rights, including that of jury trial. This tradition carried over to the American colonies. In each colony there was a right to trial by jury. There was also freedom of expression, although of a limited kind. Not all colonies, for example, granted freedom to all religions. The colonies also had a degree of self-government. Each had an elected representative assembly, which was subject to British oversight but nonetheless had substantial legislative powers.

The colonists also had the example of Native American governments, particularly that of the Iroquois Confederacy. The Confederacy was a union of the Mohawk, Oneida, Onondaga, Cayuga, and Seneca tribes, governed by a fifty-member council made up of representatives of the five tribes. To protect each tribe's interest, the confederacy's constitution included a system of checks and balances—a feature that would become a hallmark of the U.S. Constitution. Historians disagree over the influence of the Iroquois Confederacy on colonial thought, but Benjamin Franklin and Thomas Jefferson were among the colonial leaders who wrote approvingly of its governing system.

"The Rights of Englishmen"

The Revolutionary War was partly a rebellion against Britain's failure to respect its own tradition of limited government in the colonies. Many of the colonial charters had conferred upon Americans "the rights of Englishmen," but Britain showed progressively less respect for these rights as time went on. Until the period after the French and Indian War (1755–1763), the colonists had viewed

HISTORICAL BACKGROUND

This 1790s colored engraving by William Birch depicts a Philadelphia street scene. Philadelphia's role in the birth of the American nation is rivaled only by Boston's contribution.

Drafting the Declaration of Independence, a painting by J. L. Ferris. Benjamin Franklin, John Adams, and Thomas Jefferson (standing) drafted the historic document. Jefferson was the principal author; he inserted the inspirational words about liberty, equality, and self-government. Jealous of the attention that Jefferson later received, Adams declared that there wasn't anything in Jefferson's words that others hadn't already said.

themselves as loyal subjects of the British King. In fact, the colonists had fought alongside British soldiers to drive the French out of the Western territories. At the end of the war, however, Britain for the first time imposed heavy taxes on the colonies. The war with France, which was also waged in Europe, had created a budget crisis in Britain. Taxing the colonies was a way to reduce the debt. The first such tax was a stamp tax on colonial newspapers and business documents. The colonists were not represented in the British Parliament that imposed the tax, and they responded angrily. "No taxation without representation" became their rallying cry.

Although Parliament backed down and repealed the Stamp Act, it then passed the Townshend Act, which imposed taxes on all glass, paper, tea, and lead. The colonists again responded angrily and Parliament again backed down, except for a tax on tea, which was kept to show the colonies that Britain was still in charge of their affairs. The tea tax sparked an act of defiance that became known as the "Boston Tea Party." In December 1773, under the cover of darkness, a small band of patriots disguised as Native Americans boarded an English ship in Boston Harbor and dumped its cargo of tea overboard.

In 1774, the colonists met in Philadelphia at the First Continental Congress to decide what they would demand from Britain. They called for free assembly, an end to the British military occupation, their own councils for the imposition of taxes, and trial by local juries. (British authorities had resorted to shipping "troublemakers" to London for trial.) King George III rejected their demands, and in 1775 British troops and colonial minutemen clashed at Lexington and Concord. Eight colonists died on the Lexington green in what became known as "the shot heard 'round the world." The American Revolution had begun.

The Declaration of Independence

Although grievances against Britain were the immediate cause of the American Revolution, ideas about the proper form of government were also on the colonists' minds.[2] The century-old theory of John Locke was particularly influential. Locke held that people have **inalienable rights** (or **natural rights**)—including those of life, liberty, and property—and can rebel against a ruler who tramples on these rights (see Chapter 1).

Thomas Jefferson declared that Locke "was one of the three greatest men that ever lived, without exception," and Jefferson paraphrased Locke's ideas in key passages of the Declaration of Independence:

> We hold these truths to be self-evident, that all men are created equal, that they are endowed by their Creator with certain unalienable rights, that among these are life, liberty and the pursuit of happiness.
>
> That to secure these rights, governments are instituted among men, deriving their just powers from the consent of the governed.
>
> That whenever any form of government becomes destructive of these ends, it is the right of the people to alter or to abolish it, and to institute a new government.

inalienable (natural) rights

Those rights that persons theoretically possessed in the state of nature, prior to the formation of governments. These rights, including those of life, liberty, and property, are considered inherent and, as such, are inalienable. Since government is established by people, government has the responsibility to preserve these rights.

Media & Politics

Are Bloggers Today's Pamphleteers?

At the time of the writing of the Constitution, the news as we know it today did not exist. A major newspaper printed at most a few hundred copies of each issue, and there were no full-time reporters. Often, the newspaper owner did everything, from covering local events to hand-printing the copies. Most of what newspapers printed was not even news by today's standards, consisting mainly of ship manifests and government notices. Not until the 1830s, when the invention of the hand-cranked rotary press made it possible to print newspapers at low cost, was the first full-time reporter hired—and he was brought over from England by a New York newspaper to write sensational stories about street crime.

At the time of the nation's founding, the most influential writers were pamphleteers, not journalists. Thousands of pamphlets urging a break with Britain appeared in the decade before the American Revolution. Their authors usually published anonymously to hide their identity from British authorities. Thomas Paine, the most influential pamphleteer of the age, was no exception. When his pamphlet *Common Sense*, which sold over a hundred thousand copies, first appeared, it had no name on it. "We have the power to begin the world over again," wrote Paine, who also penned the famous line: "These are the times that try men's souls." Paine would later go to France to foment revolution there, at one point landing in jail for his writings.

Are bloggers today's equivalent of revolutionary America's pamphleteers? Like the pamphleteers, bloggers are not regular journalists and engage in advocacy rather than straightforward reporting. They are a product of the Internet and of the opportunity created by the traditional media's reluctance (with a few exceptions, such as Fox News) to take stands on controversial issues. The bloggers themselves are a diverse lot. Some write from a conservative perspective, others from a liberal perspective. Some are careful in their use of facts, others are careless or deceptive. A few have a substantial audience, but most have only a small one. What they, like the colonial-era pamphleteers, have in common is a commitment to promoting a point of view.

As with pamphleteering, the price of entry to the blogging world is small. All it takes is the creation of a website and a willingness to spend long hours writing commentary and posting messages and stories. This fact, combined with the tendency of some bloggers to stretch the truth, has led conventional journalists to claim that bloggers are not "real journalists." Yet they are part of the news process—and not just because they post news stories on their websites. It was bloggers who first recognized that a racially laden comment by Senate Republican leader Trent Lott was big news—big enough that it would eventually force Lott to resign his leadership post. And it was bloggers who first identified as forgeries the government documents CBS's Dan Rather held up as proof that President George W. Bush had shirked his National Guard duties during the 1970s. Within months, Rather was forced into premature retirement from his job as anchor of the CBS Evening News.

The Declaration was a call to revolution rather than a framework for a new form of government, but the ideas it contained—liberty, equality, individual rights, self-government, lawful powers—became the basis, eleven years later, for the Constitution of the United States. (The Declaration of Independence and the Constitution are reprinted in their entirety in the appendixes of this book.)

The Articles of Confederation

The first government of the United States was based not on the Constitution but on the Articles of Confederation. The Articles, which were adopted during the Revolutionary War, created a very weak national government that was subordinate to the states. The colonies had always been governed separately, and their people considered themselves Virginians, New Yorkers, or Pennsylvanians as much as they thought of themselves as Americans. Moreover, they were leery of a powerful central government. The American Revolution was sparked by grievances against the arbitrary policies of King George III, and Americans were in no mood to replace him with a strong national authority of their own making.

Under the Articles of Confederation, each state retained its "sovereignty, freedom and independence." There was a national Congress, but its members were appointed and paid by their respective state governments. Each of the thirteen

HISTORICAL BACKGROUND

This is a portion of Thomas Jefferson's handwritten draft of the Declaration of Independence, a formal expression of America's governing ideals.

states had one vote in Congress, and the agreement of nine states was required to pass legislation. Moreover, any state could block constitutional change: the Articles of Confederation could be amended only by unanimous approval of the states.

The American union held together during the Revolutionary War out of necessity. The states had either to cooperate or to surrender to the British. But once the war ended, the states felt free to go their separate ways. Several states sent representatives abroad to negotiate their own trade agreements with foreign nations. New Hampshire, with its eighteen-mile coastline, even established its own navy. In a melancholy letter to Thomas Jefferson, George Washington wondered whether the United States deserved to be called a nation.

Congress was expected to provide for the nation's defense and establish the basis for a general economy, but the Articles of Confederation did not give it the powers necessary to achieve these goals. The Articles prohibited Congress from interfering in the states' commerce policies, and the states were soon engaged in ruinous trade wars. The Articles also denied to Congress the power to tax, and as a result it had no money with which to build a navy or hire an army.

Shays's Rebellion: A Nation Dissolving

By 1784, the nation was unraveling. Congress was so weak that its members often did not bother to attend its sessions.[3] Finally, in late 1786, a revolt in western

County courthouses in Massachusetts in 1786 were the scenes of brawls between angry farmers and citizens who supported the state's attempts to foreclose on farmers' property because of unpaid debts. The violence of Shays's Rebellion convinced many political leaders that anarchy was spreading and that a more powerful national government was required to stop it.

Massachusetts prompted leading Americans to conclude that the country's government had to be changed. A ragtag army of two thousand farmers armed with pitchforks marched on county courthouses to prevent foreclosures on their land. Many of the farmers were veterans of the Revolutionary War; their leader, Daniel Shays, had been a captain in the Revolutionary army. They had been given assurances during the Revolution that their land, which lay fallow because they were away at war, would not be confiscated for unpaid debts and taxes. They were also promised the back pay owed to them for their military service. (Congress had run out of money during the Revolution.) Instead, they received no back pay, and heavy new taxes were levied on their farms. Many farmers faced the loss of their property and even jail because they could not pay their creditors.

Shays's Rebellion frightened wealthy interests, who called on the governor of Massachusetts to put down the revolt. He in turn asked Congress for help, but it had no army to send. The governor finally raised enough money to hire a militia that put down the revolt, but Shays's Rebellion made it clear that Congress and the army were weak and that civil unrest was spreading. Fear that anarchy would overtake the country was widespread. An emergency meeting of five states in Annapolis led to a plea to Congress to authorize a constitutional convention of all the states to be held the following spring in Philadelphia. Congress authorized the convention but placed a restriction on it: the delegates were to meet for "the sole and express purpose of revising the Articles of Confederation."

NEGOTIATING TOWARD A CONSTITUTION

The delegates to the Philadelphia constitutional convention ignored the instructions of Congress. They drafted a plan for an entirely new form of government. Prominent delegates (among them George Washington, Benjamin Franklin, and James Madison) were determined from the outset to establish an American nation built on a strong central government.

The Great Compromise: A Two-Chamber Congress

Virginia (large-state) Plan

A constitutional proposal for a strong Congress with two chambers, both of which would be based on numerical representation, thus granting more power to the larger states.

New Jersey (small-state) Plan

A constitutional proposal for a strengthened Congress but one in which each state would have a single vote, thus granting a small state the same legislative power as a large state.

Great Compromise

The agreement at the constitutional convention to create a two-chamber Congress with the House apportioned by population and the Senate apportioned equally by state.

North-South Compromise

The agreement over economic and slavery issues that enabled northern and southern states to settle differences that threatened to defeat the effort to draft a new constitution.

Debate at the constitutional convention of 1787 began over a plan put forward by the Virginia delegation, which was dominated by strong nationalists. The **Virginia Plan** (also called the **large-state plan**) called for a two-chamber Congress that would have supreme authority in all areas "in which the separate states are incompetent," particularly defense and interstate trade. The Virginia Plan also provided that representation in both chambers would be based on size. Small states such as Delaware and Rhode Island would be allowed only one representative in the lower chamber, while large states such as Massachusetts and Virginia would have more than a dozen.

The Virginia Plan was sharply attacked by delegates from the smaller states. They rallied around a counterproposal made by New Jersey's William Paterson. The **New Jersey Plan** (also called the **small-state plan**) called for a stronger national government with the power to tax and to regulate commerce among the states; in most other respects, however, the Articles would remain in effect. Congress would have a single chamber in which each state, large or small, would have a single vote.

The debate over the New Jersey and Virginia Plans dragged on for weeks before the delegates reached what is now known as the **Great Compromise.** It provided for a bicameral (two-chamber) Congress: the House of Representatives would be apportioned among the states on the basis of population, and the Senate would be apportioned on the basis of an equal number of votes (two) for each state. This compromise was critically important. The small states would not have agreed to join a union in which their vote was always weaker than that of large states, a fact reflected in Article V of the Constitution: "No state, without its consent, shall be deprived of its equal suffrage in the Senate."

The North-South Compromise: The Issue of Slavery

The separate interests of the states were also the basis for a second major agreement: the **North-South Compromise** on economic issues. The southern states feared that the states of the North, which were more numerous and had a larger population, would use their numerical majority in Congress to tax them unfairly. If Congress imposed high tariffs on manufactured goods imported from Europe in order to protect domestic manufacturers, the South would be disadvantaged since U.S. manufacturing was largely based in the North. Then, if Congress also imposed high tariffs on agricultural exports, the South would again be disadvantaged because it was the prime source of agricultural exports, which, if taxed, would be more expensive and therefore of less interest to European buyers. The South's delegates were also concerned that northern representatives in Congress would tax or even bar the importation of slaves.

After extended debate, a compromise was reached. Congress was to be prohibited by the Constitution from taxing exports but could tax imports. In addition,

Southern delegates at the constitutional convention sought assurances that Congress would not bar the importation and sale of slaves and that their slave-based agricultural economy would be protected. The photo shows a Civil War–era building in Atlanta that was a site of slave auctions.

Congress would be prohibited until 1808 from passing laws to end the slave trade. However, the most controversial trade-off was the so-called "Three-Fifths Compromise." For purposes of apportionment of taxes and seats in the U.S. House of Representatives, each slave was to count as less than a full person. Northern delegates had argued against the counting of slaves because they did not have legal rights. Southern delegates wanted to count them as full persons for purposes of apportioning House seats (which would have the effect of increasing the number of southern representatives) and to count them as non-persons for purposes of apportioning taxes (which would have the effect of decreasing the amount of federal taxes levied on the southern states). The delegates finally settled on a compromise that included both taxation and apportionment but counted each slave as three-fifths of a person. Although the southern states did not get all that they wanted, they got the better end of the bargain. If slaves had not been counted at all, the southern states would have had only slightly more than 35 percent of House seats. With the compromise, they held nearly 45 percent of the seats, giving them considerable power over national policy.

These compromises have led critics to claim that the Framers of the Constitution had no objections to slavery. In fact, most of the delegates were deeply troubled by it, recognizing the stark inconsistency between the practice of slavery and the Lockean ideals that all persons are entitled to liberty and equality. "It is inconsistent with the principles of the Revolution," Maryland's Luther Martin stated. George Mason, a Virginian and a slaveholder, said: "[Slaveholders] bring the judgment of heaven on a country."[4] Benjamin Franklin and Alexander Hamilton were among the delegates who were involved in antislavery organizations.

Figure 2–1

African Americans as a Percentage of State Population, 1790
At the writing of the Constitution, African Americans (most of whom were slaves) were concentrated in the southern states.
Source: U.S. Bureau of the Census.

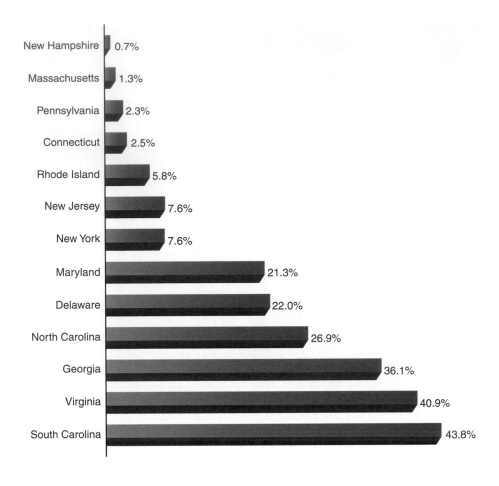

State	Percentage
New Hampshire	0.7%
Massachusetts	1.3%
Pennsylvania	2.3%
Connecticut	2.5%
Rhode Island	5.8%
New Jersey	7.6%
New York	7.6%
Maryland	21.3%
Delaware	22.0%
North Carolina	26.9%
Georgia	36.1%
Virginia	40.9%
South Carolina	43.8%

Yet the southern states' dependence on slavery was a reality that the delegates had to confront if there was to be a union of the states. The northern states had few slaves, whereas the southern economies were based on slavery (see Figure 2–1). John Rutledge of South Carolina asked during the convention debate whether the North regarded southerners as "fools." Southern delegates declared that they would form their own union rather than join one that banned slavery.

A Strategy for Ratification

The compromises over slavery and the structure of the Congress took up most of the four months that the convention was in session. Some of the other issues, such as the structure and powers of the federal judiciary, were the subject of surprisingly little debate.

There remained a final issue, however: would those Americans not attending the convention support the proposed Constitution? The delegates realized that ratification was not a sure thing. Congress had not authorized a wholesale restructuring of the federal government and had in fact created a barrier to any such plan. In authorizing the Philadelphia convention, Congress had stated that any proposed change in the Articles would have to be "agreed to in Congress" and then "confirmed by [all of] the states." The delegates recognized that if unanimous consent was required, the Constitution had no chance of ratification. Rhode Island had refused even to send a delegation to the convention. In a bold move, the delegates established their own ratification process. They instructed Congress to submit the document directly to the states, where it would become law after having been approved by at least nine states in special ratifying conventions of popularly elected delegates. It was a masterful strategy. There was little hope that all thirteen state legislatures would approve the Constitution, but nine states through conventions might be persuaded to ratify it. Indeed, North Carolina and Rhode Island were steadfastly opposed to the new union and did not ratify the Constitution until the eleven other states had ratified it and begun the process of establishing the new government.

The Ratification Debate

The debate over ratification was contentious. The **Anti-Federalists** (as opponents of the Constitution were labeled) raised arguments that still echo in American politics. They claimed that the national government would be too powerful and would threaten self-government in the separate states and the liberty of the people. Many Americans had an innate distrust of centralized power and worried that the people's liberty could be eclipsed as easily by a distant American government as it had been by the British king. The fact that the Constitution contained no bill of rights heightened this concern. Did its absence indicate that the central government would be free to define for itself what the people's rights would be?

The presidency was another source of contention. No such office had existed under the Articles, and some worried that it would lead to the creation of an American monarchy. The fact that the president would be chosen by electors appointed by the states lessened but did not eliminate this concern.

Even the motives of the men who wrote the Constitution came under attack. They were men of wealth and education and had acted in response to debtors' riots. Would the Constitution become a tool by which the wealthy ruled over those with little or no money? And who would bear the burden of additional taxation? For Americans struggling with local and state tax payments, the thought of paying national taxes as well was not appealing.

Most Anti-Federalists acknowledged a need to strengthen national commerce and defense. What they opposed was the creation of a powerful national government as the mechanism. They favored a revision of the Articles of Confederation, which in their opinion could accomplish these goals without the risk of establishing a government that could threaten their liberties, their livelihoods, and their local interests. (The Anti-Federalist argument is discussed further in Chapter 3.)

The **Federalists** (as the Constitution's supporters called themselves) responded with a persuasive case of their own. Their strongest arguments were set forth by James Madison and Alexander Hamilton, who along with John Jay wrote a series of essays that were published in a New York City newspaper under the pen

Anti-Federalists
A term used to describe opponents of the Constitution during the debate over ratification.

Federalists
A term used to describe proponents of the Constitution during the debate over ratification.

LEADERS

JAMES MADISON

(1751–1836)

James Madison is called the "father of the Constitution." Madison himself rejected that label, saying that the Constitution was the work of "many heads and many hands." Nevertheless, Madison had the clearest ideas about how to structure the U.S. government, and he guided debate at the constitutional convention of 1787. His *Federalist Papers* contributed to the Constitution's ratification. Later, Madison assisted Thomas Jefferson in forming a political party that aimed to promote ordinary citizens as opposed to the rich and powerful—the forerunner of today's Democratic party. He served as secretary of state during Jefferson's presidency and, in 1808, succeeded Jefferson as president. Europe was in the midst of the Napoleonic Wars, and Madison was unsuccessful in asserting America's neutrality. In 1812, the British invaded Washington, D.C., burning the Capitol and forcing Madison to flee to Maryland. The British withdrew and later were defeated by General Andrew Jackson at New Orleans, leading Americans to claim victory in the War of 1812. Madison completed his second presidential term in 1817. After leaving office, he spoke out often against the growing states'-rights sentiment in the South that eventually would plunge the nation into the Civil War over the issue of slavery. Preservation of the Union was his dying wish.

name Publius. (The essays, collectively referred to as *The Federalist Papers*, are widely acknowledged as a brilliant political treatise.) Madison and Hamilton argued that the government of the Constitution would correct the defects of the Articles; it would have the power necessary to forge a secure and prosperous union. At the same time, because of restrictions on its powers, the new government would endanger neither the states nor personal liberty. In *Federalist* Nos. 47, 48, 49, 50, and 51, for example, Madison explained how the separation of national institutions was designed to both empower and restrict the federal government. (The Federalist argument is discussed further in Chapter 3.)

Whether the ratification debate changed many minds is unclear. Historical evidence suggests, however, that a majority of ordinary Americans opposed the Constitution's ratification. But their voice in the state ratifying conventions was smaller than that of wealthier interests, which in the main supported the change. The pro-ratification forces were also bolstered by the widespread assumption that George Washington, the most trusted and popular American leader, would become the first president. In the view of historians, the fact that Washington had presided over the Philadelphia convention and the assumption that he would become the chief executive tipped the balance in favor of ratification.

Delaware was the first state to ratify the Constitution, and Connecticut, Georgia, and New Jersey followed, an indication that the Great Compromise had satisfied several of the small states. In the early summer of 1788, New Hampshire became the ninth state to ratify. The Constitution was law. But neither Virginia nor New York had ratified it, and a stable union without these major states was almost unthinkable. As large in area as many European countries, they conceivably could survive as independent nations. They nearly did choose a separate course. In both states, the Constitution barely passed, and then only after the Federalists promised to support a bill of rights designed to protect individual liberty from the power of the central government.

WWW.MHHE.COM/PATTERSONTAD8

The Framers' Goals

The Englishman James Bryce ranked America's written constitution as its greatest contribution to the practice of government. The Constitution offered the world a new model of government in which a written document defining the state's lawful powers would be a higher authority than the actions of any political leader or institution.

constitution

The fundamental law that defines how a government will legitimately operate.

A **constitution** is the fundamental law that defines how a government will legitimately operate—the method for choosing its leaders, the institutions through which these leaders will work, the procedures they must follow in making policy, and the powers they can lawfully exercise. The U.S. Constitution is exactly such a law. It is the highest law of the land. Its provisions define how power is to be acquired and how it can be used.

The Constitution embodied the Framers' vision of a proper government for the American people (see Table 2–1). One of the Framers' goals was the creation of a national government strong enough to meet the nation's needs, particularly in the areas of defense and commerce. Another goal was to preserve the states as governing entities. Accordingly, the Framers established a system of government (federalism) in which power is divided between the national government and the states. Federalism is discussed at length in Chapter 3, which also explains how the Constitution laid the foundation for a strong national government.

The Framers' other goals were to establish a national government that was restricted in its lawful uses of power (limited government) and that gave the people a voice in their governance (self-government). These two goals and the story of how they were written into the Constitution are the focus of the rest of this chapter.

TABLE 2–1	Major Goals of the Framers of the Constitution

1. To establish a government strong enough to meet the nation's needs—an objective sought through substantial grants of power to the federal government in areas such as defense and commerce (see Chapter 3)

2. To establish a government that would not threaten the existence of the separate states—an objective sought through federalism (see Chapter 3) and through a Congress connected to the states through elections

3. To establish a government that would not threaten liberty—an objective sought through an elaborate system of checks and balances

4. To establish a government based on popular consent—an objective sought through provisions for the direct and indirect election of public officials

PROTECTING LIBERTY: LIMITED GOVERNMENT

A challenge facing the Framers of the Constitution was how to control the coercive force of government. Government's unique characteristic is that it alone can legally arrest, imprison, and even kill people who break its rules. Force is not the only basis of effective government, but government must be able to use force to prevent lawless elements from taking over society. The dilemma is that government itself can use its force to brutalize and intimidate its opponents. "It is a melancholy reflection," James Madison wrote to Thomas Jefferson shortly after the Constitution's ratification, "that liberty should be equally exposed to danger whether the government has too much or too little power."[5]

The men who wrote the Constitution sought to establish a government strong enough to enforce national interests, including defense and commerce among the states (see Chapter 3), but not so strong as to destroy liberty. Limited government is built into the Constitution through both grants of political power and restrictions on that power (see Table 2–2).

TABLE 2–2	Constitutional Provisions for Limited Government The U.S. Constitution creates an elaborate governing structure designed to protect against the abusive exercise of power—in short, to create a limited government.
MECHANISM	**PURPOSE**
Grants of power	Powers granted to the national government; accordingly, powers not granted it are denied it unless they are necessary and proper to the carrying out of the granted powers.
Separated institutions sharing power	The division of the national government's power among three branches, each of which is to act as a check on the powers of the other two.
Federalism	The division of political authority between the national government and the states, enabling the people to appeal to one authority if their rights and interests are not respected by the other authority.
Denials of power	Powers expressly denied to the national and state governments by the Constitution.
Bill of Rights	The first ten amendments to the Constitution, which specify rights of citizens that the national government must respect.
Judicial review	The power of the courts to declare governmental action null and void when it is found to violate the Constitution.
Elections	The power of the voters to remove officials from office.

Grants and Denials of Power

grants of power
The method of limiting the U.S. government by confining its scope of authority to those powers expressly granted in the Constitution.

The Framers chose to limit the national government in part by confining its scope to constitutional **grants of power.** Congress's lawmaking powers are specifically listed in Article I, Section 8 of the Constitution. Seventeen in number, these listed powers include, for example, the powers to tax, to establish an army and navy, to declare war, to regulate commerce among the states, to create a national currency, and to borrow money. Powers *not* granted to the government by the Constitution are in theory denied to it. In a period when other governments had unrestricted powers, this limitation was remarkable.

denials of power
A constitutional means of limiting government by listing those powers that government is expressly prohibited from using.

The Framers also used **denials of power** as a means to limit government, prohibiting certain practices that European rulers had routinely used to intimidate political opponents. The French king, for example, could imprison a subject indefinitely without charge. The U.S. Constitution prohibits such action: citizens have the right to be brought before a court under a writ of habeas corpus for a judgment as to the legality of their confinement. The Constitution also forbids Congress and the states from passing ex post facto laws, under which citizens can be prosecuted for acts that were legal at the time they were committed.

As a further denial of power, the Framers made the Constitution difficult to amend, thereby making it hard for those in power to increase their lawful authority by changing the Constitution. An amendment could be proposed only by a two-thirds majority in both chambers of Congress or by a national constitutional convention called by two-thirds of the state legislatures. Such a proposal would then become law only if ratified by three-fourths of state legislatures or state conventions. In all but one case (the Twenty-first Amendment), state legislatures have done the ratifying. The national constitutional convention as a means of proposing amendments has never been used.

Using Power to Offset Power

Although the Framers believed that grants and denials of power could act as controls on government, they had no illusion that written words alone would suffice. As a consequence, they sought to control government by dividing its powers among separate institutions.[6]

separation of powers
The division of the powers of government among separate institutions or branches.

The idea of a **separation of powers** had been proposed decades earlier by the French theorist Montesquieu. His reasoning was widely accepted in America, and when the states drafted new constitutions after the start of the Revolutionary War, they built their governments around this concept. Pennsylvania was an exception, and its experience only seemed to prove the necessity of separated powers. Unrestrained by an independent judiciary or executive, Pennsylvania's all-powerful legislature ignored basic rights and freedoms: Quakers were disenfranchised for their religious beliefs, conscientious objectors to the Revolutionary War were prosecuted, and the right of trial by jury was eliminated.

In *Federalist* No. 10, Madison asked why governments often act according to the interests of overbearing majorities rather than according to principles of justice. He attributed the problem to "the mischiefs of faction." People, he argued, are divided into opposing religious, geographical, ethnic, economic, and other factions. These divisions are natural and desirable in that free people have a right to their personal opinions and interests. Yet factions can themselves be a source of oppressive government. If a faction gains full power, it will use government to advance itself at the expense of all others. (*Federalist* No. 10 is widely regarded as the finest political essay ever written by an American. It is reprinted in the appendixes at the back of this book.)

The Constitution was written in Philadelphia during the summer of 1787 in the East Room of the Old Pennsylvania State House, where the Declaration of Independence had been signed a decade earlier. George Washington presided over the constitutional convention, but in this role he was expected to remain neutral during the debate and thus he played a less active part in shaping the Constitution than did some other delegates.

Out of this concern came the Framers' special contribution to the doctrine of the separation of powers. They did not believe that it would be enough, as Montesquieu had suggested, to divide the government's authority strictly along institutional lines, granting all legislative power to the legislature, all judicial power to the courts, and all executive power to the presidency. This total separation would make it too easy for a single faction to exploit a particular area of political power. A faction that controlled the legislature, for example, could enact laws ruinous to other interests. A better system of divided government would be one in which political power could be applied forcibly only when institutions agreed on its use. This system would require separate but overlapping powers. Because no one faction could easily gain control over all institutions, factions would have to work together, a process that would require each of them to respect the interests of the others.[7]

Separated Institutions Sharing Power: Checks and Balances

The Framers' concept of divided powers has been described by political scientist Richard Neustadt as the principle of **separated institutions sharing power**.[8] The separate branches are interlocked in such a way that an elaborate system of **checks and balances** is created (see Figure 2–2). No institution can act decisively without the support or acquiescence of the other institutions. Legislative, executive, and judicial powers in the American system are divided in such a way that they overlap: each of the three branches of government checks the others' powers and balances those powers with powers of its own. As natural as this system now might seem to Americans, most democracies are of the parliamentary type, with executive and legislative power combined in a single institution rather than vested in separate ones. In a parliamentary system, the majority in the legislature selects the prime minister, who then serves as both the legislative leader and the chief executive (see "How the United States Compares").

Shared Legislative Powers

Under the Constitution, Congress has legislative authority, but that power is partly shared with the other branches and thus checked by them. The president

separated institutions sharing power

The principle that, as a way to limit government, its powers should be divided among separate branches, each of which also shares in the power of the others as a means of checking and balancing them. The result is that no one branch can exercise power decisively without the support or acquiescence of the others.

checks and balances

The elaborate system of divided spheres of authority provided by the U.S. Constitution as a means of controlling the power of government. The separation of powers among the branches of the national government, federalism, and the different methods of selecting national officers are all part of this system.

#12

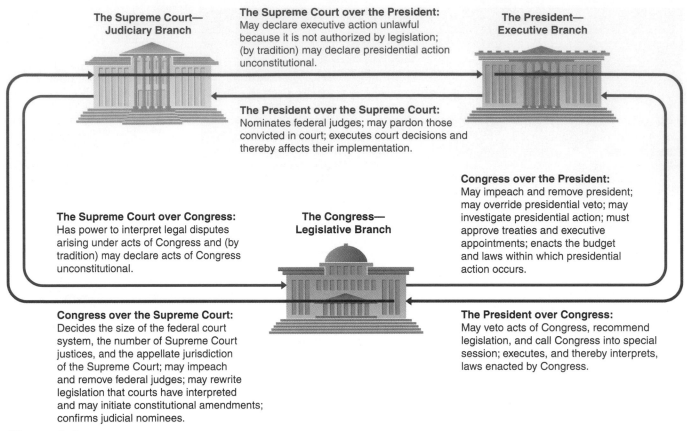

The Supreme Court—
Judiciary Branch

The Supreme Court over the President:
May declare executive action unlawful
because it is not authorized by legislation;
(by tradition) may declare presidential action
unconstitutional.

The President—
Executive Branch

The President over the Supreme Court:
Nominates federal judges; may pardon those
convicted in court; executes court decisions and
thereby affects their implementation.

Congress over the President:
May impeach and remove president;
may override presidential veto; may
investigate presidential action; must
approve treaties and executive
appointments; enacts the budget
and laws within which presidential
action occurs.

The Supreme Court over Congress:
Has power to interpret legal disputes
arising under acts of Congress and (by
tradition) may declare acts of Congress
unconstitutional.

The Congress—
Legislative Branch

Congress over the Supreme Court:
Decides the size of the federal court
system, the number of Supreme Court
justices, and the appellate jurisdiction
of the Supreme Court; may impeach
and remove federal judges; may rewrite
legislation that courts have interpreted
and may initiate constitutional amendments;
confirms judicial nominees.

The President over Congress:
May veto acts of Congress, recommend
legislation, and call Congress into special
session; executes, and thereby interprets,
laws enacted by Congress.

Figure 2–2

The System of Checks and Balances
This elaborate system of divided spheres of authority was provided by the U.S. Constitution as a means of controlling the power of government. The separation of powers among the branches of the national government, federalism, and the different methods of selecting national officers are all part of this system.

can veto acts of Congress, recommend legislation, and call special sessions of Congress. The president also has the power to execute—and thereby interpret—the laws Congress makes.

The Supreme Court has the power to interpret acts of Congress that are disputed in legal cases. The Court also has the power of judicial review: it can declare laws of Congress void when it finds that they are not in accord with the Constitution.

Within Congress, there is a further check on legislative power: for legislation to be passed, a majority in each house of Congress is required. Thus, the Senate and the House of Representatives can block each other from acting.

Shared Executive Powers

Executive power is vested in the president but is constrained by legislative and judicial checks. The president's power to make treaties and appoint high-ranking officials, for example, is subject to Senate approval. Congress also has the power to impeach and remove the president from office. In practical terms, Congress's greatest checks on executive action are its lawmaking and appropriations powers. The executive branch cannot act without laws that authorize its activities or without the money that pays for these activities.

How the United States Compares

Checks and Balances

All democracies place constitutional limits on the power of government. The concept of rule by law, for example, is characteristic of democratic governments but not of authoritarian regimes. Democracies differ, however, in the extent to which political power is restrained through constitutional mechanisms. The United States is an extreme case in that its government rests on an elaborate system of constitutional checks and balances. The system employs a separation of powers among the executive, legislative, and judicial branches. It also includes judicial review, the power of the courts to invalidate actions of the legislative or executive branch. These constitutional restrictions on power are not part of the governing structure of all democracies.

Most democracies have parliamentary systems, which invest both executive and legislative leadership in the office of prime minister. Britain is an example of this type of system. Parliament under the leadership of the prime minister is the supreme authority in Britain. Its laws are not subject to override by Britain's high court, which has no power to review the constitutionality of parliamentary acts.

In parliamentary systems, moreover, either there is only one legislative chamber or, if there are two, power resides primarily in one chamber. The British House of Lords, for example, has only a limited ability to check the actions of the British House of Commons, which the prime minister heads. In the United States, the two legislative chambers—the House and the Senate—are coequal bodies. Because legislation can be enacted only with the approval of both houses, each serves as a check on the other.

COUNTRY	SEPARATION OF EXECUTIVE & LEGISLATIVE POWERS?	JUDICIAL REVIEW?
Belgium	No	Yes
Canada	No	Yes
France	Yes	No
Germany	No	Yes
Great Britain	No	No
Italy	No	Yes
Japan	No	Yes
Mexico	Yes	Yes
United States	Yes	Yes

The judiciary's major check on the presidency is its power to declare an action unlawful because it is not authorized by the legislation that the executive claims to be implementing.

Shared Judicial Powers

Judicial power rests with the Supreme Court and with lower federal courts, which are subject to checks by the other branches of the federal government. Congress is empowered to establish the size of the federal court system, to restrict the Supreme Court's appellate jurisdiction in some circumstances, and to impeach and remove federal judges from office. More important, Congress can rewrite legislation that the courts have misinterpreted and can initiate amendments when it disagrees with the courts' rulings on constitutional issues.

The president has the power to appoint federal judges with the consent of the Senate and to pardon persons convicted in the courts. The president also is responsible for executing court decisions, a function that provides opportunities to influence the way rulings are carried out.

The Bill of Rights

Although the delegates to the Philadelphia convention discussed the possibility of placing a list of individual rights (such as freedom of speech and the right to a fair trial) in the Constitution, they ultimately decided that such a list

Political Culture

Liberty and the Bill of Rights

Of America's founding ideals, none was more prominent in the thinking of the Constitution's Framers than liberty. The American Revolution had been won in the name of freedom—of both the country and its people. The Constitution was designed to solidify that victory.

The writers of the Constitution were products of the Enlightenment, a movement that emphasized reason and humanism—the ideas that society could be organized sensibly and should be organized around the individual as opposed to a ruler or the state. Emphasis on the individual meant that government had to be controlled because historically it had been an instrument of oppression. The Framers recognized that government must have coercive power in order to carry out those actions necessary for a civil society, but they also saw that government could be used by unscrupulous leaders to strip others of their liberty. Accordingly, the Framers created an intricate form of government built around checks and balances that would make it difficult for any individual or faction to exploit the power of government to advance its own ends at the expense of others.

The Bill of Rights was added to the Constitution despite the Framers' belief that it was unnecessary. In their view, the Constitution denied to the federal government any power not granted to it. From this perspective, there was no need, for example, for a guarantee of religious freedom because government was not authorized to deny people the right to worship as they pleased. The Framers feared, moreover, that any listing of rights would become a means of denying people rights that were not listed.

Most constitutional scholars believe that, on balance, the Bill of Rights has enhanced personal liberty. It had the effect of transforming abstract rights (for example, "the right to life, liberty and the pursuit of happiness") into concrete legal rights, thus giving people a basis for judicial action should their legal rights be abridged or denied. If you speak your mind publicly or are charged with a criminal offense, for example, you have a specific constitutional provision under which to claim your right. The Sixth Amendment, for example, gives you a right to counsel if you are accused of a crime. Of course, authorities sometimes ignore restrictions in the Bill of Rights and often get away with it. Nevertheless, the fact that the Bill of Rights contains specific guarantees increases the likelihood that authorities will respect them. By refusing to allow a suspect to talk with an attorney, for example, authorities run the risk of having a judge dismiss their case because of a constitutional violation.

was unnecessary because of the doctrine of expressed powers: government could not lawfully engage in actions, such as the suppression of speech, that were not authorized by the Constitution. Moreover, the delegates argued that a bill of rights was undesirable because government might feel free to disregard any right that was inadvertently left off the list or that emerged at some future time.

These arguments did not persuade leading Americans who believed that no possible safeguard of liberty should be omitted. "A bill of rights," Jefferson argued, "is what the people are entitled to against every government on earth, general or particular, and what no just government should refuse or rest on inference." Jefferson had included a bill of rights in the constitution he wrote for Virginia at the outbreak of the Revolutionary War, and all but four states had followed Virginia's example.

Opposition to the exclusion of a bill of rights led to its addition to the Constitution. Madison himself introduced a series of amendments during the First Congress, ten of which were soon ratified by the states. These amendments, traditionally called the **Bill of Rights,** include rights such as freedom of speech and religion and due process protections (such as jury trial and legal counsel) for persons accused of crimes. (These rights, termed *civil liberties*, are discussed at length in Chapter 4.)

Bill of Rights
The first ten amendments to the Constitution. They include rights such as freedom of speech.

The Bill of Rights is a precise expression of the concept of limited govern-ment. In consenting to be governed, the people agree to accept the authority of government in certain areas but not in others; the people's constitutional rights cannot lawfully be denied by governing officials.

Judicial Review

The writers of the Constitution both empowered and limited government. But who was to decide whether officials were operating within the limits of their constitutionally authorized powers? The Framers did not specifically entrust this power to a particular branch of government, although they did grant the Supreme Court the authority to decide on "all cases arising under this Consti-tution." Moreover, at the ratifying conventions of at least eight of the thirteen states, it was claimed that the judiciary would have the power to nullify actions that violated the Constitution.[9]

Nevertheless, because the Constitution did not explicitly grant the judici-ary this authority, the principle had to be established in practice. The oppor-tunity arose with an incident that occurred after the election of 1800, in which John Adams lost his bid for a second presidential term after a bitter campaign against Jefferson. Between November 1800, when Jefferson was elected, and March 1801, when he was inaugurated, the Federalist-controlled Congress cre-ated fifty-nine additional lower-court judgeships, enabling Adams to appoint loyal Federalists to those positions before he left office. However, Adams's term expired before his secretary of state could deliver the judicial commissions to all the appointees. Without this authorization, an appointee could not take office. Knowing this, Jefferson told his secretary of state, James Madison, not to deliver the commissions. William Marbury was one of those who did not receive his commission, and he asked the Supreme Court to issue a writ of mandamus (a court order directing an official to perform a specific act) that would force Madison to deliver it.

Marbury v. Madison (1803) became the foundation for judicial review by the federal courts. Chief Justice John Marshall wrote the *Marbury* opinion, which declared that Marbury had a legal right to his commission. The opinion also said, however, that the Supreme Court could not issue him a writ of mandamus because it lacked the constitutional authority to do so. Congress had passed ordinary legislation in 1789 that gave the Court this power, but Marshall noted that the Constitution prohibits Congress from expanding the Supreme Court's authority except through a constitutional amendment. That being the case, Marshall argued, the legislation that provided the authorization was constitu-tionally invalid.[10] In striking down this act of Congress on constitutional grounds, the Court asserted its power of judicial review—that is, the power of the judiciary to decide whether a government official or institution has acted within the limits of the Constitution and, if not, to declare its action null and void.

Marshall's decision was ingenious because it asserted the power of judicial review without creating the possibility of its rejection by either the executive or the legislative branch. In declaring that Marbury had a right to his commission, the Court in effect said that President Jefferson had failed in his constitutional duty to execute the laws faithfully. But because it did not order Jefferson to deliver the commission, he had no opportunity to refuse to comply with the Court's judgment. At the same time, the Court reprimanded Congress for pass-ing legislation that exceeded its constitutional authority. Congress also had no way to retaliate. It could not force the Court to accept the power to issue writs of mandamus if the Court itself refused to do so.

HISTORICAL BACKGROUND

judicial review
The power of courts to decide whether a govern-mental institution has acted within its constitutional powers and, if not, to declare its action null and void.

Debating the Issues

Is Warrantless Domestic Surveillance Constitutional When Authorized Only by the President?

Based on the principle of checks and balances, the U.S. Constitution is designed to limit the ability of officials to act on their own in ways that infringe on personal liberty. This principle was at issue in the 2006 congressional hearings into whether President George W. Bush had exceeded his constitutional and statutory powers by authorizing warrantless phone-taps. After the terrorist attacks of September 11, 2001, Bush authorized the National Security Agency (NSA), without first obtaining a court order, to intercept international phone calls and e-mails placed from or received in the United States. The Foreign Intelligence Surveillance Act (FISA) of 1978 had prohibited such surveillance. Moreover, the Fourth Amendment protects individuals from unjustified searches. Ordinarily, officials are not allowed to spy on U.S. citizens without obtaining a warrant from a judge who has reviewed and approved the proposed surveillance. The Bush administration tried to keep NSA's surveillance program secret. When it became known, the Administration argued that the president was acting within his lawful powers. Members of Congress questioned that claim, and congressional hearings were held.

On the hearings' opening day, Attorney General Alberto Gonzalez defended the surveillance program, while Senator Patrick Leahy, the ranking minority member on the Senate Judiciary Committee, was among the senators who questioned its legality. Which argument do you find more convincing? Where would you draw the line on the limits of presidential power in time of war?

Yes

The Constitution charges the President with the primary responsibility for protecting the safety of all Americans, and the Constitution gives the President the authority necessary to fulfill this solemn duty.... The President authorized the terrorist surveillance program in response to the deadliest foreign attack on American soil, and it is designed solely to prevent the next al Qaeda attack. After all, the goal of our enemy is to blend in with our civilian population in order to plan and carry out future attacks within America. We cannot forget that the September 11th hijackers were in our country, living in our communities.... The President's authority to take military action—including the use of communications intelligence targeted at the enemy—does not come merely from his constitutional powers. It comes directly from Congress as well. Just a few days after the attacks of September 11th, Congress enacted a joint resolution to support and authorize the military response to the attacks on American soil.... Some contend that even if the President has constitutional authority to engage in the surveillance of our enemy during an armed conflict, that authority has been constrained by Congress with the passage in 1978 of the Foreign Intelligence Surveillance Act (FISA). It is a serious question whether, consistent with the Constitution, FISA may encroach upon the President's Article II powers during the current armed conflict with al Qaeda by prohibiting the terrorist surveillance program....

Many people ask why the President elected not to use FISA's procedures for securing court orders for the terrorist surveillance program. We have to remember that what is at issue is a wartime intelligence program designed to protect our Nation from another attack in the middle of an armed conflict. It is an "early warning system" with only one purpose: to detect and prevent the next attack on the United States from foreign agents hiding in our midst. It is imperative for national security that we can detect reliably, immediately, and without delay whenever communications associated with al Qaeda enter or leave the United States. That may be the only way to alert us to the presence of an al Qaeda agent in our country and to the existence of an unfolding plot.... The key question under the Fourth Amendment is not whether there was a warrant, but whether the search was reasonable. Determining the reasonableness of a search for Fourth Amendment purposes requires balancing privacy interests with the Government's interests and ensuring that we maintain appropriate safeguards. Although the terrorist surveillance program may implicate substantial privacy interests, the Government's interest in protecting our Nation is compelling. Because the need for the program is reevaluated every 45 days and because of the safeguards and oversight, the al Qaeda intercepts are reasonable.

—*Alberto Gonzalez, Attorney General of the United States*

No We all agree that we should be wiretapping al Qaeda terrorists—of course we should. Congress has given the President authority to monitor these messages legally, with checks to guard against abuses when Americans' conversations and email are being monitored. But instead, the President has chosen to do it illegally, without those safeguards. . . . The President and the Justice Department have a constitutional duty to faithfully execute the laws. They do not write them. They do not pass them. They do not have unchecked power to decide what laws to follow and what laws to ignore. They cannot violate the law or the rights of ordinary Americans. In America no one, not even the President, is above the law. . . . [FISA] expressly states that it provides the "exclusive" source of authority for wiretapping for intelligence purposes. Wiretapping that is not authorized under that statute is a federal crime. That is what the law says, and that is what the law means. This law was enacted to define how domestic surveillance for intelligence purposes may be conducted while protecting the fundamental liberties of Americans. Two or more generations of Americans are too young to know this from their experience, but there's a reason we have the FISA law. It was enacted after decades of abuses by the Executive, including the wiretapping of Dr. Martin Luther King Jr. and other political opponents of earlier government officials, and the White House "horrors" of the Nixon years, during which another President asserted that whatever he did was legal because he was the President. . . . I have many questions for the Attorney General. But first, I have a message to give him and the President. It is a message that should be unanimous, from every Member of Congress regardless of party and ideology. Under our Constitution, Congress is the co-equal branch of Government that makes the laws. If you believe we need new laws, you can come to us and tell us. If Congress agrees, we will amend the law. If you do not even attempt to persuade Congress to amend the law, you must abide by the law as written. That is as true for this President as it is for any other American. That is the rule of law, on which our Nation was founded, and on which it endures and prospers.

—*Patrick Leahy, U.S. Senator (D-Vt.)*

PROVIDING FOR SELF-GOVERNMENT

"We the People" is the opening phrase of the Constitution. It expresses the idea that in the United States the people will have the power to govern themselves. In a sense, there is no contradiction between this idea and the Constitution's provisions for limited government, because individual *liberty* is an essential element of *self-government*. If people cannot express themselves freely, they cannot be self-governing. In another sense, however, the contradiction is clear: restrictions on the power of the majority are a denial of its right to govern society as it sees fit.

The Framers believed that the people deserved and required a voice in their government, but they worried that the people would become inflamed by a passionate issue or fiery demagogue and act rashly. To the Framers, the great risk of popular government was **tyranny of the majority**: the people acting as an irrational mob that tramples on the rights of the minority. Their fear was not without foundation. The history of democracies was filled with examples of majority tyranny, and there were even examples from the nation's brief history. In 1786, for instance, debtors had gained control of Rhode Island's legislature and made paper money a legal means of paying debts, even though existing contracts called for payment in gold. Creditors were then hunted down and held captive in public places so that debtors could come and pay them in full with worthless paper money. A Boston newspaper wrote that Rhode Island should be renamed Rogue Island.

tyranny of the majority
The potential of a majority to monopolize power for its own gain to the detriment of minority rights and interests.

Democracy Versus Republic

No form of self-government could eliminate completely the threat to liberty of majority tyranny, but the Framers believed that the danger would be greatly diminished by creating a republican government as opposed to a democratic

LEADERS

JOHN MARSHALL

(1755–1835)

John Marshall forcefully expressed his nationalist views in important Supreme Court decisions during his thirty-four years as chief justice, the longest tenure in that position in U.S. history. Marshall served for a time as John Adams's secretary of state and in the House of Representatives before his appointment by Adams to the position of chief justice. At the time of Marshall's appointment, the Supreme Court was perceived as a feeble branch of the federal government. Marshall changed that belief. An ardent nationalist, Marshall steered the Court through a series of decisions that established it as a powerful institution and helped lay the foundation for a strong Union. Despite philosophical differences with the presidents who succeeded Adams, Marshall dominated the Court throughout his long tenure, persuading newly appointed justices to back him on key constitutional issues. Marshall saw himself as a Framer of the Constitution, the ongoing architect of the work begun in Philadelphia during the summer of 1787. Although a distant cousin of Thomas Jefferson, the two were bitter opponents. Marshall's first landmark decision, *Marbury v. Madison* (1803), which established the principle of judicial review, was a rebuke of President Jefferson's executive authority. Their ongoing dispute peaked in 1807 during the trial of Aaron Burr, who had been justly accused of treason by the Jefferson administration. Marshall presided over the trial and acquitted Burr, ruling that a single eyewitness was insufficient grounds for conviction.

government.[11] Today, the terms **democracy**, **republic**, and **representative government** are often used interchangeably to refer to a system of government in which political power rests with the people through their ability to choose representatives in free and fair elections. To the writers of the Constitution, however, a *democracy* and a *republic* were different forms of government.

By the term *democracy*, the Framers meant a government in which the power of the majority is unlimited, whether exercised directly (as in the case of town meetings open to all citizens) or through a representative body. The majority's rule is absolute. Should it decide to act tyrannically—to run roughshod over the minority—there is nothing in the laws to stop it. By the term *republic*, the Framers meant a government that is based on majority rule but protects the minority through a guarantee of individual rights and other checks on majority power. The purpose of republican government is to limit the power of the majority, not as a means of preventing the people from governing themselves but as a means of safeguarding minority rights and interests. The majority rules, but it does so within prescribed limits.[12]

The Framers believed that a republican government is superior to a democratic one. They also believed that a

democracy

A form of government in which the people rule, either directly or through elected representatives.

republic

Historically, the form of government in which representative officials met to decide on policy issues. These representatives were expected to serve the public interest but were not subject to the people's immediate control. Today, the term *republic* is used interchangeably with *democracy*.

republic, to work well in practice, requires virtuous representatives—lawmakers who have an enlightened sense of the public interest. In this respect, their outlook was similar to that of the English theorist Edmund Burke (1729–97). In his *Letter to the Sheriffs of Bristol*, Burke argued that representatives should act as public **trustees;** they are obliged to serve the interest of those who elect them, but the nature of this interest is for the representatives, not the voters, to decide. Burke was concerned with the ease with which a majority can think like a mob, and he claimed that representatives should not surrender their judgment to frenzied majorities.

Limited Popular Rule

The Constitution provided that all power would be exercised through representative institutions. There was no provision for any form of direct popular participation in the making of policy decisions. In view of the fact that the United States was much too large to be governed directly by the people in popular assemblies, a representative system was necessary. The Framers went beyond what was necessary, however, and placed officials at a considerable distance from the people they represented (see Table 2–3).

The House of Representatives was the only institution that would be based on direct popular election—its members would be elected to serve for two years by a vote of the people. Frequent and direct election of House members was intended to make government sensitive to the concerns of popular majorities.

U.S. senators would be appointed by the legislatures of the states they represented. Because state legislators were popularly elected, the people would be choosing their senators indirectly. Every two years, a third of the senators would be appointed to six-year terms. The Senate was expected to check and balance the House, which, by virtue of the more frequent and direct election of its members, presumably would be more responsive to popular opinion.

Presidential selection was an issue of considerable debate at the Philadelphia convention. Direct election of the president was twice proposed and twice rejected because it linked executive power directly to popular majorities. The Framers finally chose to have the president selected by the votes of electors (the so-called **Electoral College**). Each state would have as many **electoral votes** as it had members in Congress and could select its electors by any method it chose. The president would serve four years and be eligible for reelection.

The Framers decided that federal judges and justices would be appointed rather than elected. They would be nominated by the president and confirmed through approval by the Senate. Once confirmed, they would "hold their offices during good behavior." In effect, they would be allowed to hold office for life unless they committed a crime. The judiciary was a "guardian" institution that would uphold the rule of law and serve as a check on the elected branches of government.[13]

These differing methods of selecting national officeholders would not prevent a determined majority from achieving unchecked power, but control could not be attained quickly. Unlike the House of Representatives, institutions such as the Senate, presidency, and judiciary would not yield to an impassioned majority in a single election. The delay would reduce the likelihood that government would degenerate into mob rule driven by momentary passions.

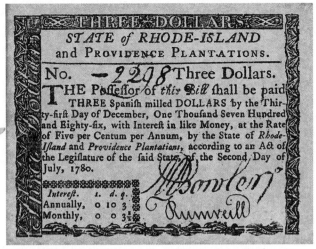

Rhode Island was nicknamed "Rogue Island" for its disregard of property rights. Shown here is the Rhode Island three-dollar bank note, which came to be worth no more than the paper on which it was written and yet was used to pay off gold debts.

representative democracy
A system in which the people participate in the decision-making process of government not directly but indirectly, through the election of officials to represent their interests.

trustees
Elected representatives whose obligation is to act in accordance with their own consciences as to what policies are in the best interests of the public.

Electoral College
An unofficial term that refers to the electors who cast the states' electoral votes.

TABLE 2–3	**Methods of Choosing National Leaders** Fearing the concentration of political power, the Framers devised alternative methods of selection and terms of service for national officials.	

OFFICE	METHOD OF SELECTION	TERM OF SERVICE
President	Electoral College	4 years
U.S. senator	State legislature	6 years (one-third of senators' terms expire every 2 years)
U.S. representative	Popular election	2 years
Federal judge	Nominated by president, approved by Senate	Indefinite (subject to "good behavior")

electoral votes
The method of voting that is used to choose the U.S. president. Each state has the same number of electoral votes as it has members in Congress (House and Senate combined). By tradition, electoral voting is tied to a state's popular voting. The candidate with the most popular votes in a state (or, in a few states, the most votes in a congressional district) receives its electoral votes.

HISTORICAL BACKGROUND

Altering the Constitution: More Power to the People

The Framers' conception of self-government was at odds with what the average American in 1787 had come to expect. Every state but South Carolina held annual legislative elections, and several states also chose their governors through direct annual election. Not long after ratification of the Constitution, Americans began to challenge the Constitution's restrictions on majority rule (see Table 2–4).

Jeffersonian Democracy: A Revolution of the Spirit

Thomas Jefferson, who otherwise admired the Constitution, was among the prominent Americans who questioned its provisions for self-government—and it was Jefferson who may have spared the nation a bloody conflict over the issue of popular sovereignty. Under John Adams, the second president, the national government increasingly favored the nation's wealthy interests. Adams publicly indicated that the Constitution was designed for a governing elite, while Alexander Hamilton suggested that Adams might have to use force to suppress radical dissent.[14] Jefferson asked whether Adams, with the aid of a strong army, planned soon to deprive ordinary Americans of their liberty. Jefferson challenged Adams in the next presidential election and, upon defeating him, hailed his victory as the "Revolution of 1800."

Although Jefferson was a champion of the common people, he had no clear vision of how a popular government might work in practice. Jefferson saw Congress, not the presidency, as the institution better suited to representing majority opinion.[15] Jefferson also had no illusions about a largely uneducated population's readiness for playing a large governing role and feared the consequences of inciting the masses to confront the moneyed class. But Jefferson did found the nation's first political party (the forerunner of today's Democratic party), which served to link like-minded leaders and thus act as a bridge across divided institutions of power. By and large, however, Jeffersonian democracy was a revolution of the spirit. Jefferson taught Americans to look on national government institutions as belonging to all, not just to the privileged few.[16]

TABLE 2–4	**Measures Taken to Make Government More Responsive to Popular Majorities** The U.S. Constitution created barriers designed to limit direct popular influence on government. Subsequent changes were designed to lower these barriers and increase the power of voting majorities.
EARLIER SITUATION	**SUBSEQUENT DEVELOPMENT**
Separation of powers, as a means of dividing authority and blunting passionate majorities	Political parties, as a means of uniting authorities and linking them with popular majorities
Indirect election of all national officials except House members, as a means of buffering officials from popular influence	Direct election of U.S. senators and popular voting for president (linked to electoral votes), as a means of increasing popular control of officials
Nomination of candidates for public office through political party organizations	Primary elections, as a direct means of selecting party nominees

Pictured here is the Old Senate Chamber, where the U.S. Senate met until 1859, when a new and larger chamber was constructed. The Old Senate Chamber was the scene of heated debates over slavery. Daniel Webster, Henry Clay, and John C. Calhoun gained national reputations here. After the Senate vacated the chamber, it was occupied by the U.S. Supreme Court until 1935, when the Court's own building across the street from the Capitol was completed. Not until 1914 were U.S. senators chosen by direct vote of the people.

Jacksonian Democracy: Linking the People and the Presidency

Not until the election of Andrew Jackson in 1828 did the country have a powerful president who was willing and able to involve the public more fully in government. Jackson carried out the constitutional revolution that Jeffersonian democracy had foreshadowed.

Jackson recognized that the president was the only official who could legitimately claim to represent the people as a whole. Unlike the president, members of Congress were elected from separate states and districts rather than from the entire country. Yet the president's claim to popular leadership was weakened by the fact that the president was chosen by electors rather than by the voters. Jackson's ingenious solution was to have each state give its electoral votes to whichever candidate got the most popular votes in the state. This arrangement, still in effect, places the selection of the president in the voters' hands in most elections. The candidate who gets the most popular votes nationally is also likely to finish first in enough states to win a majority of the electoral votes. Since Jackson's time, only three candidates—Rutherford B. Hayes in 1876, Benjamin Harrison in 1888, and George W. Bush in 2000—have won the presidency after losing the popular vote. (The Electoral College is discussed further in Chapter 12.)

The Progressives: Senate and Primary Elections

The Progressive era of the early 1900s brought another wave of democratic reforms. The Progressives rejected the Burkean idea of representatives as trustees, instead embracing the idea of representatives as **delegates**—officeholders who are obligated to respond directly to the expressed opinions of the people they represent.

delegates
Elected representatives whose obligation is to act in accordance with the expressed wishes of the people they represent.

States in the Nation

Direct Democracy: The Initiative and Referendum

In some states, citizens through their votes can directly enact or defeat legislation. This legislation is placed on the ballot through either the referendum (where the state legislature places a legislative proposal on the ballot) or the initiative (where citizens by gathering enough signatures on petitions place a legislative proposal on the ballot). The map identifies states that have the least restrictive forms of the initiative or referendum—that is, states that place no substantial limit (except for judicial review) on what citizens can directly decide through their votes.

Q: Why are southern and northeastern states less likely to have the initiative and referendum than states in other areas?

A: The initiative and referendum were introduced in the early 1900s by the Progressives, who sought to weaken the power of political bosses and give voters a larger voice in their governance. In the Northeast, party machines had enough strength in state legislatures to block their enactment. In the South, these devices were blocked by the white establishment, which feared that blacks and poor whites would make use of them.

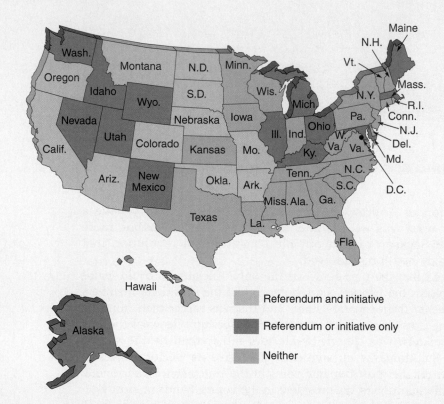

Source: Compiled by author from multiple sources.

The Progressives sought to place power more directly in the hands of the people.[17] They succeeded in changing the way some state and local governments operate. Progressive reforms at state and local levels included the initiative and the referendum, which enable citizens to vote directly on legislative issues (see "States in the Nation"). Another Progressive reform was the recall election, which enables citizens through petition to force an officeholder to

Get Involved!

Speak Up

The classroom provides an everyday opportunity to develop a skill that is basic to effective citizenship—the ability to speak clearly and persuasively. To the Greek philosopher Aristotle, rhetoric was the defining skill of citizenship. Aristotle did not define rhetoric as it is often used today, as a derisive term for speech that is long on wind and short on reason. Rather, he saw rhetoric as a tool in the search for truth, a form of persuasion that flourished when people were free to speak out in face-to-face settings. Rhetoric was a means of clarifying discussion and of bringing people to agreement. Aristotle saw it as a forensic device for determining which claims are true and which are false. He believed it was the foundation of self-government. If citizens lack the ability to talk and reason things through effectively, they will not act wisely.

Formal education in Ancient Greece emphasized rhetorical training that, in certain city-states, followed Aristotle's model. Many of the Framers of the U.S. Constitution were familiar with Aristotle's model, as indeed were many American schoolchildren until a century or so ago, when the importance of rhetoric was downgraded to make room for teaching other subjects. Nevertheless, the ability to speak and write effectively is as much a hallmark of the effective citizen today as it was a century ago in the United States or in Ancient Greece.

The college classroom is a place to develop rhetorical skills. Speak up in the classroom when you have a point to make and can support it. Rhetorical skills are honed only through practice, and few settings offer more opportunities for practice than the classroom. Like playing soccer or computer games, speaking is a skill that needs to be developed. The payoff extends beyond your experiences as a citizen. Most of the people you will meet in life—whether in the classroom, the workplace, a church or civic group, or a political cause—will know you largely by the words they hear you speak. The conclusions they draw will affect their inclination to look to you for leadership.

submit to reelection before the regular expiration of his or her term. (In 2003 a recall election in California resulted in the election of actor Arnold Schwarzenegger as the state's new governor.)

The Progressives also instigated two changes in federal elections. One was the direct election of U.S. senators, who before the Seventeenth Amendment was ratified in 1913 had been chosen by state legislatures and were widely perceived as agents of big business (the Senate was nicknamed the "Millionaires' Club"). Senators who stood to lose their seats in a direct popular vote had blocked earlier attempts to change the Constitution. However, the Senate was persuaded to support an amendment following pressure from the Progressives and revelations that corporate bribes had influenced the selection of several senators. The second change was the **primary election,** which gives rank-and-file voters the power to select party nominees. In the early 1900s, nearly all states adopted the primary election as a means of choosing nominees for at least some federal and state offices. Before this change, nominees were selected by party leaders.

The Progressive era spawned attacks on the Framers. A prominent criticism was laid out in historian Charles S. Beard's *An Economic Interpretation of the Constitution.*[18] Arguing that the Constitution grew out of wealthy Americans' fears of the debtor rebellions and noting that many of the Framers were themselves wealthy men, Beard claimed that the Constitution's elaborate systems of power and representation were devices for keeping power in the hands of the rich. Beard's thesis was challenged by other historians, and he later acknowledged that he had not taken the Framers' full array of motives into account. Their conception of separation of powers, for example, was a

primary election

A form of election in which voters choose a party's nominees for public office. In most states, eligibility to vote in a party's primary election is limited to voters who are registered members of the party.

governing principle that had earlier been incorporated into state constitutions. Although the Framers did not have great trust in popular rule, to conclude that they were foes of democracy would be a mistake. They were intent on balancing the demand for self-government with the requirement for limited government, believing that unchecked majority rule could lead to oppressive government.

Since the Progressive era, no major structural changes have taken place in the process by which Americans elect their leaders. Nevertheless, the question of how best to achieve self-government in practice continues to engage Americans. During the 1960s, for example, public demands led to fairer voter-registration laws, including the elimination of literacy tests and poll taxes, which were devices designed to keep minorities and poor people from voting. More recent efforts include the term-limit movement, which seeks to limit the length of time the same individual can hold a particular public office. Through the relationships they build with powerful groups, incumbent officeholders today enjoy a huge advantage over their electoral challengers (see Chapters 8 and 11). Congressional incumbents are able to raise far more money for their campaigns than their challengers can raise. One result has been increasingly lopsided election outcomes. Upwards of 95 percent of congressional incumbents win reelection—most by margins of two-to-one or greater. Term limits would reduce the advantage of incumbency, thus shifting power in campaigns from moneyed interests to the voters.

CONSTITUTIONAL DEMOCRACY TODAY

constitutional democracy

A government that is democratic in its provisions for majority influence through elections, and constitutional in its provisions for minority rights and rule by law.

The type of government created in the United States in 1787 is today called a **constitutional democracy.** It is *democratic* in its provisions for majority influence through elections and *constitutional* in its requirement that power gained through elections be exercised in accordance with law and with due respect for individual rights.

By some standards, the American system of today is a model of *self-government.*[19] The United States schedules the election of its larger legislative chamber (the House of Representatives) and its chief executive more frequently than does any other democracy. In addition, it is the only major democracy to rely extensively on primary elections rather than party organizations for the selection of party nominees. The principle of popular election to office, which the writers of the Constitution regarded as a prerequisite of popular sovereignty but a method to be used sparingly, has been extended further in the United States than anywhere else.

By other standards, however, the U.S. system is less democratic than many others. Popular majorities must work against the barriers to influence devised by the Framers—the elaborate system of divided powers, staggered terms of office, and separate constituencies. In fact, the link between an electoral majority and a governing majority is less direct in the American system than in nearly all other democratic systems. In the European parliamentary democracies, for example, legislative and executive power are not separated, are not subject to close check by the judiciary, and are acquired through the winning of a legislative majority in national elections. The Framers' vision was a different one, dominated by a concern with *liberty* and therefore with controls on political power. It was a response to the experiences they brought with them to Philadelphia in the summer of 1787.

Summary

The Constitution of the United States is a reflection of the colonial and revolutionary experiences of the early Americans. Freedom from abusive government was a reason for the colonies' revolt against British rule, but the English tradition also provided ideas about government, power, and freedom that were expressed in the Constitution and, earlier, in the Declaration of Independence.

The Constitution was designed in part to provide for a limited government in which political power would be confined to proper uses. The Framers wanted to ensure that the government they were creating would not itself be a threat to freedom. To this end, they confined the national government to expressly granted powers and also denied it certain specific powers. Other prohibitions on government were later added to the Constitution in the form of stated guarantees of individual liberties in the Bill of Rights. The most significant constitutional provision for limited government, however, was a separation of powers among the three branches. The powers given to each branch enable it to act as a check on the exercise of power by the other two, an arrangement that during the nation's history has in fact served as a barrier to abuses of power.

The Constitution, however, made no mention of how the powers and limits of government were to be judged in practice. In its historic ruling in *Marbury v. Madison*, the Supreme Court assumed the authority to review the constitutionality of legislative and executive actions and to declare them unconstitutional and thus invalid.

The Framers of the Constitution, respecting the idea of self-government but distrusting popular majorities, devised a system of government that they felt would temper popular opinion and slow its momentum so that the public's "true interest" (which includes a regard for the rights and interests of the minority) would guide public policy. Different methods were advanced for selecting the president, the members of the House and Senate, and federal judges as a means of insulating political power against momentary majorities.

Since the adoption of the Constitution, the public gradually has assumed more direct control of its representatives, particularly through measures that affect the way officeholders are chosen. Presidential popular voting (linked to the Electoral College), direct election of senators, and primary elections are among the devices aimed at strengthening the majority's influence. These developments are rooted in the idea, deeply held by ordinary Americans, that the people must have substantial direct influence over their representatives if government is to serve their interests.

STUDY CORNER

Key Terms

Anti-Federalists (*p. 45*)
Bill of Rights (*p. 52*)
checks and balances (*p. 49*)
constitution (*p. 46*)
constitutional democracy (*p. 62*)
delegates (*p. 59*)
democracy (*p. 56*)
denials of power (*p. 48*)
Electoral College (*p. 57*)
electoral votes (*p. 58*)

Federalists (*p. 45*)
grants of power (*p. 48*)
Great Compromise (*p. 42*)
inalienable (natural) rights (*p. 38*)
judicial review (*p. 53*)
limited government (*p. 36*)
New Jersey (small-state) Plan (*p. 42*)
North-South Compromise (*p. 42*)
primary election (*p. 61*)
representative democracy (*p. 57*)

republic (*p. 56*)
self-government (*p. 36*)
separated institutions sharing
  power (*p. 49*)
separation of powers (*p. 48*)
trustees (*p. 57*)
tyranny of the majority (*p. 55*)
Virginia (large-state) Plan (*p. 42*)

Self-Test

1. The principle of checks and balances in the U.S. system of government:
   a. requires the federal budget to be a balanced budget.
   b. provides that checks cashed at U.S. banks will be honored as legal tender.
   c. was a principle invented by the Progressives.
   d. allows the majority's will to work through representative institutions but places checks on the power of those institutions.

2. The U.S. Constitution provides for limited government mainly:
   a. through direct election of representatives.
   b. through indirect systems of popular election of representatives.
   c. by defining lawful powers and by dividing those powers among competing institutions.
   d. by making state law superior to national law when the two conflict.

3. The U.S. Constitution provides for self-government mainly:
   a. through direct and indirect systems of popular election of representatives.
   b. by defining the lawful powers of government.
   c. by dividing governing powers among competing institutions.
   d. by giving the majority absolute power to govern as it pleases.

4. Shays's Rebellion called attention to:
   a. the lack of ability of Congress under the Articles of Confederation to put down popular rebellion.
   b. Americans' anger with Britain over "taxation without representation."

   c. inability of the states under the Articles to bring the American Revolution to a successful conclusion.
   d. the conditions that were leading to mutiny on U.S. naval vessels.

5. The addition of the Bill of Rights to the U.S. Constitution meant that:
   a. a list of individual rights would be protected by law.
   b. the Anti-Federalists no longer had any reason to oppose the adoption of the Constitution.
   c. the national government could infringe on the rights of the states.
   d. the state governments could infringe on the rights of the national government.

6. Of the issues taken up during the constitutional convention, which one consumed the most time and attention?
   a. structure of the presidency
   b. structure of Congress
   c. structure and powers of the federal judiciary
   d. ratification of the new Constitution

7. The Framers of the Constitution feared political apathy more than tyranny of the majority. (T/F)

8. The idea of popular government—in which the majority's desires have a more direct and immediate impact on public policy—has gained strength since the nation's beginning. (T/F)

9. The Supreme Court decision in *Marbury v. Madison* gave courts the power to declare governmental action null and void when it is found to violate the Constitution. (T/F)

10. The Virginia Plan (also known as the large-state plan) called for a Congress with equal representation of each state but with greatly strengthened powers. (T/F)

Critical Thinking

How does the division of power in the U.S. political system contribute to limited government? How do the provisions for representative government (the various methods of choosing national officials) contribute to limited government?

Suggested Readings

Beard, Charles S. *An Economic Interpretation of the Constitution*. New York: Macmillan, 1941. Argues that the Framers had selfish economic interests uppermost in their minds when they wrote the Constitution.

Edling, Max M. *A Revolution in Favor of Government*. New York: Oxford University Press, 2003. Argues that the Framers intended the Constitution to create a strong government.

Ellis, Joseph J. *Founding Brothers: The Revolutionary Generation*. New York: Vintage, 2002. A riveting account of the lives of America's leading Founders.

Federalist Papers. Many editions, including a one-volume paperback version edited by Isaac Kramnick (New York: Penguin, 1987). A series of essays written by Alexander Hamilton, James Madison, and John Jay under the pseudonym Publius. The essays, published in a New York newspaper in 1787–88, explain the Constitution and support its ratification.

Hardin, Russell. *Liberalism, Constitutionalism, and Democracy*. New York: Oxford University Press, 1999. Analysis of the great ideas that underlie the Constitution.

Holcombe, Randall G. *From Liberty to Democracy*. Ann Arbor: University of Michigan Press, 2002. An interpretive history of the transformation of American government.

McGerr, Michael. *A Fierce Discontent: The Rise and Fall of the Progressive Movement in America, 1870–1920*. New York: Free Press, 2005. Assessment of the Progressive movement's contribution to American democracy.

Tocqueville, Alexis de. *Democracy in America*, vols. 1 and 2, ed. J. P. Mayer. New York: Doubleday/Anchor, 1969. A classic analysis (originally published 1835–40) of American democracy by an insightful French observer.

Wilentz, Sean. *The Rise of American Democracy: Jefferson to Lincoln*. New York: W.W. Norton, 2005. An account of how democratic ideas triumphed over aristocratic ones.

List of Websites

http://www.nara.gov/
The National Archives site; includes an in-depth look at the history of the Declaration of Independence.

http://odur.let.rug.nl/~usa/P/aj7/about/bio/jackxx.htm
A site that focuses on Andrew Jackson and his role in shaping U.S. politics.

http://www.yale.edu/lawweb/avalon/constpap.htm
Includes documents on the Constitution, the American Revolution, and the Constitutional Convention.

http://www.yale.edu/lawweb/avalon/presiden/jeffpap.htm
A site that includes the papers of Thomas Jefferson. His autobiography is among the available materials.

Participate!

In recent years, as a means of checking the power of elected officials, a number of states and localities have imposed a limit on the number of terms that representatives can serve. Although the term-limit movement has slowed, there are still opportunities to get involved on either side of the issue. If you favor term limits and want to get involved, you might start by examining the website of U.S. Term Limits (www.termlimits.org). If you oppose term limits, you could begin by looking at the Common Cause site (www.commoncause.org).

Extra Credit

For up-to-the-minute *New York Times* articles, interactive simulations, graphics, study tools, and more links and quizzes, visit the text's Online Learning Center at www.mhhe.com/pattersontad8.

(Self-Test Answers: 1. d 2. c 3. a 4. a 5. a 6. b 7. F 8. T 9. T 10. F)

Federalism:
Forging a Nation

Chapter Outline

Federalism: National and State Sovereignty
The Argument for Federalism
The Powers of the Nation
The Powers of the States

Federalism in Historical Perspective
An Indestructible Union (1789–1865)
Dual Federalism and Laissez-Faire Capitalism (1865–1937)
Toward National Citizenship

Federalism Today
Interdependency and Intergovernmental Relations
Government Revenues and Intergovernmental Relations
A New Federalism: Devolution

The Public's Influence: Setting the Boundaries of Federal-State Power

CHAPTER 3

The question of the relation of the states to the federal government is the cardinal question of our Constitutional system. It cannot be settled by the opinion of one generation, because it is a question of growth, and each successive stage of our political and economic development gives it a new aspect, makes it a new question.

—Woodrow Wilson[1]

In late 2001, Attorney General John Ashcroft directed federal agents to take action that would stop Oregon physicians from prescribing federally controlled drugs to assist terminally ill patients in committing suicide. Ashcroft sought to void the Oregon law that permits physician assistance in cases where a patient, in the judgment of at least two doctors, has less than six months to live, is suffering painfully, and is mentally competent to decide whether to end his or her life. Ashcroft's action was not the first federal attempt to nullify the Oregon law. Congress had twice initiated action—in one instance, a bill passed in the House but failed to come up for a vote in the Senate.

Oregon's voters had approved the assisted-suicide law in a statewide referendum, becoming the first state (and, as of 2007, the only state) to do so. A majority of Oregon's voters had been persuaded by the argument that no public benefit derives from requiring the dying to accept prolonged suffering. Opponents had countered that society's interest in preserving life outweighs a patient's desire to die, that doctors and relatives in some instances might persuade terminally ill patients to accept death against their will, and that depressed patients who asked to die should be treated for their depression (after which they might choose to live). In filing suit against the Oregon law, the U.S. Department of Justice argued that "there are important medical, ethical and legal distinctions between intentionally causing a patient's death and providing sufficient dosages of pain medications to eliminate or alleviate pain."

In 2006, the U.S. Supreme Court decided the issue in Oregon's favor, ruling that its physicians could not be punished for prescribing the drugs in question. The Court held in *Gonzales v. Oregon* that federal law did not grant Ashcroft "the extraordinary authority" he had claimed in trying to regulate medical practice. The Court did not repudiate Congress's power to regulate drugs, but it did reject Ashcroft's claim to that authority in the area of physician-assisted suicide.[2]

The controversy surrounding Oregon's Death with Dignity Act is one of thousands of disagreements over the course of American history that have hinged on whether national or state authority should prevail. Americans possess what amounts to dual citizenship: they are citizens both of the United States and of the state where they reside. The American political system is a *federal system,*

A supporter of Oregon's Death with Dignity law holds a sign outside the federal courthouse in Portland, Oregon, where a hearing on the U.S. Justice Department's challenge to the law is being held. This type of struggle between the power of the federal government and the power of a state government has been repeated countless times in American history, a reflection of the U.S. federal system that vests sovereignty in both the national and state governments. In this particular case, the state, Oregon, prevailed. The U.S. Supreme Court in 2006 ruled that Attorney General John Ashcroft had exceeded his authority in trying to invalidate the Oregon law.

in which constitutional authority is divided between a national government and state governments: each government is assumed to derive its powers directly from the people and therefore to have sovereignty (final authority) over the policy responsibilities assigned to it. The federal system consists of nation *and* states, indivisible yet separate.[3]

This chapter on American constitutionalism focuses on federalism. The nature of the relationship between the nation and the states was the most pressing issue when the Constitution was written in 1787. This chapter describes how that issue helped shape the Constitution. The chapter's closing sections discuss how federalism has changed throughout the nation's history and conclude with a brief overview of contemporary federalism. The main points presented in the chapter are these:

- *The power of government must be equal to its responsibilities.* The Constitution was needed because the nation's preceding system (under the Articles of Confederation) was too weak to accomplish its expected goals, particularly those of a strong defense and an integrated economy.

- *Federalism—the Constitution's division of governing authority between two levels, nation and states—was the result of political bargaining.* Federalism was not a theoretical principle, but a compromise made necessary in 1787 by the prior existence of the states.

- *Federalism is not a fixed principle for allocating power between the national and state governments, but a principle that has changed over time in response to new political needs.* Federalism has passed through several distinct stages in the course of the nation's history.

- *Contemporary federalism tilts toward national authority, reflecting the increased interdependence of American society.* However, there is a current trend toward reducing the scope of federal authority.

FEDERALISM: NATIONAL AND STATE SOVEREIGNTY

At the time of the writing of the Constitution, some of America's top leaders were dead set against the creation of a strong national government. When rumors circulated that the delegates to the constitutional convention were planning to propose such a government, Patrick Henry, an ardent believer in state-centered government, said that he "smelt a rat." After the convention had adjourned, he realized that his fears were justified. "Who authorized

them," he asked, "to speak the language of 'We, the People,' instead of 'We, the States'?"

The question of "people versus states" was precipitated by the failure of the Articles of Confederation. The government under the Articles (see Chapter 2) was a union of states rather than also a union of people. As a result, for example, the government had no power to tax citizens. The states alone had this power. Congress had the power to pass laws affecting the states but, although they were obliged in principle to obey, they were independent enough to ignore national laws that they deemed disagreeable or inconvenient. Georgia and North Carolina, for example, contributed no money at all to the national treasury between 1781 and 1786. The national government could do little more than beg them to pay their allotted share of the costs of defense, diplomacy, and other national programs.

The only realistic solution to this problem—if the United States was to be a nation in more than name only—was a government that had direct power over the people. If individuals were ordered to pay taxes, for example, they would ordinarily do so. The alternatives to not paying—imprisonment or loss of property—were less appealing.

Although the creation of a national government based directly on the people was therefore a goal of the writers of the Constitution, they also wanted to preserve the states as governing bodies. The states were already in existence, had their own constitutions, and enjoyed popular support. When Virginia's George Mason said he would never agree to a union that abolished the states, he was speaking for virtually all the delegates. The Philadelphia convention therefore devised a system of government that came to be known as **federalism.** Federalism is the division of **sovereignty,** or ultimate governing authority, between a national government and regional (that is, state) governments. Each directly governs the people and derives its powers from them.

American federalism is basically a system of divided authority (see Figure 3–1). The system gives states the power to address local issues in ways of their own

federalism

A governmental system in which authority is divided between two sovereign levels of government: national and regional.

sovereignty

The ultimate authority to govern within a certain geographical area.

#1

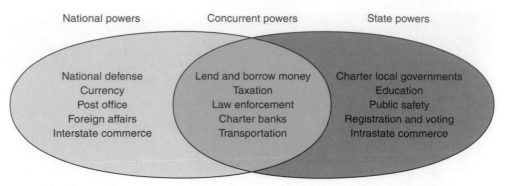

National powers | Concurrent powers | State powers

National defense
Currency
Post office
Foreign affairs
Interstate commerce

Lend and borrow money
Taxation
Law enforcement
Charter banks
Transportation

Charter local governments
Education
Public safety
Registration and voting
Intrastate commerce

Figure 3–1

Federalism as a Governing System: Examples of National, State, and Concurrent Powers
The American federal system divides sovereignty between a national government and the state governments. Each is constitutionally protected in its existence and authority, although their powers overlap somewhat even in areas granted to one level (for example, the federal government has a role in education policy).

choosing. At the same time, federalism gives the national government the power to decide matters of national scope. Although there is some overlap between state and national action, there is also a division of responsibilities. The national government has primary responsibility for national defense and the currency, among other things, while the states have primary responsibility for policy areas such as public education and police protection. The national and state governments also have some concurrent powers (that is, powers exercised over the same policy areas); for example, each has the power to raise taxes and borrow money.

A federal system is different from a **confederacy,** the type of government established by the Articles. A confederacy is a union in which the states alone are sovereign—the authority of the central government is derived from the states, which can, at will, redefine its authority. Federalism is also different from a **unitary system,** in which sovereignty is vested solely in the national government. Under a unitary system, the people are citizens or subjects only of the national government. The other governments in such a system have only as much authority as the national government allows them to have. The national government even has the power to abolish them as governing bodies. In contrast, a federal system invests sovereignty—final authority—in both the national and state governments. Each level of government has a permanent existence and authority that is independent of that of the other level.

Federalism was invented in America in 1787. It was different not only from a confederate or a unitary system but also from any form of government the world had known. The ancient Greek city-states and the medieval Hanseatic League were confederacies. The governments of Europe were unitary in form. The United States of America would be the first nation to be governed through a true federal system.

The Argument for Federalism

Unlike many other decisions made at the Philadelphia convention, the choice of federalism had no clear basis in political theory. Federalism was a practical necessity: there was a need for a stronger national government, and yet the states existed and were intent on retaining their sovereignty. Nevertheless, the Framers

confederacy
A governmental system in which sovereignty is vested entirely in subnational (state) governments.

unitary system
A governmental system in which the national government alone has sovereign (ultimate) authority.

How the United States Compares

Federal Versus Unitary Governments

Federalism involves the division of sovereignty between a national government and subnational (such as state) governments. It was invented in 1787 in order to maintain the preexisting American states while establishing an effective central government. Since then a number of other countries have established a *federal* government, but most countries have a *unitary* government, in which all sovereignty is vested in the national government.

However, even within these alternative political systems there are important differences. In Germany's federal system, for example, the states have limited lawmaking powers but do have broad authority in determining how national laws are implemented. By comparison, the U.S. federal system grants substantial lawmaking powers to the states except in specified areas such as national defense and currency.

Unitary systems also differ. In Britain, the national government has delegated substantial authority to regions; Scotland, for example, has its own parliament, which exercises lawmaking powers. In France, on the other hand, political authority is highly centralized.

In nearly all federal systems, the national legislature has two chambers—one apportioned by population (as in the case of the U.S. House of Representatives) and one

apportioned by geographical area (as in the case of the U.S. Senate). The U.S. Senate is a pure federal institution in the sense that each state has the same number of senators. In some federal systems, such as Germany's, the states are not equally represented even in the geographically apportioned chamber.

Unitary systems typically have but a single national legislative chamber, which is apportioned by population—there is no constitutional justification for a second chamber based on geography.

COUNTRY	FORM OF GOVERNMENT
Canada	Federal
France	Unitary
Germany	Federal
Great Britain	Modified unitary
Italy	Modified unitary
Japan	Unitary
Mexico	Modified federal
Sweden	Unitary
United States	Federal

developed arguments for the superiority of this type of political system. Federalism, they said, would protect liberty, moderate the power of government, and provide the foundation for an effective national government.

Protecting Liberty

Theorists such as Locke and Montesquieu had not proposed a division of power between national and local authorities as a means of protecting liberty. Nevertheless, the Framers came to look upon federalism as part of the Constitution's system of checks and balances (see Chapter 2). Alexander Hamilton argued in *Federalist* No. 28 that the American people could shift their loyalties back and forth between the national and state governments in order to keep each under control. "If [the people's] rights are invaded by either," Hamilton wrote, "they can make use of the other as the instrument of redress."

Moderating the Power of Government

To the Anti-Federalists (opponents of the Constitution), the sacrifice of the states' power to the nation was as unwise as it was unnecessary. They claimed that a distant national government could never serve the people's interests as well as the states could. Liberty *and* self-government, they argued, were enhanced by

LEADERS

ALEXANDER HAMILTON

(1757–1804)

Born an illegitimate child, Alexander Hamilton left his native West Indies in his teens for New York. A brilliant student and essayist, Hamilton joined the Revolutionary Army, distinguishing himself in early fighting around New York, and became aide to General George Washington—the beginning of a relationship that would serve both men well. After the war, Hamilton pursued a career in law and politics and went to the 1787 Philadelphia convention as a New York delegate. A firm believer in a strong national government, Hamilton contributed to the Constitution's ratification through his *Federalist Papers* essays. Appointed the nation's first secretary of the treasury by President Washington, he fought with Secretary of State Thomas Jefferson over the direction of national policy. In a brilliant political move, Hamilton agreed to locate the nation's capital at the tip of Virginia in exchange for Jefferson's support of the consolidation of state debts at the federal level. This financial system, along with the creation of the First Bank of the United States, enabled Hamilton to establish a national fiscal policy. Creditors at home and abroad henceforth would place their trust in the federal government. His dispute with Jefferson led to the creation of America's first political parties—the Republicans, founded by Jefferson, and the Federalists, founded by Hamilton. When John Adams replaced Washington as president, Hamilton stayed on as secretary of the treasury, a situation that became uncomfortable when several members of Adams's cabinet showed more loyalty to Hamilton than to Adams. In 1804, Hamilton was fatally wounded in a pistol duel with Aaron Burr, a political and personal foe.

state-centered government. In support of their contention, the Anti-Federalists turned to Montesquieu, who had concluded that a small republic is more likely than a large one to respect and respond to the people it governs. When government encompasses a small area, he argued, its leaders are in closer touch with the people and have a greater concern for their welfare.

James Madison took issue with this claim. In *Federalist* No. 10, Madison argued that whether a government serves the common good is a function not of its size but of the range of interests that share political power. The problem with a smaller republic, Madison claimed, is that it is likely to have a dominant faction—whether it be large landholders, financiers, an impoverished majority, or some other group—that is strong enough to take full control of government and to use this power to advance its selfish interests. A large republic is less likely to have such an all-powerful faction. If financiers are strong in one area of a large republic, they are likely to be weaker elsewhere. The same will be true of farmers, merchants, laborers, and other interests. A large republic, Madison concluded, would impede the efforts of any single group to gain control and would force groups to compromise and work together. "Extend the sphere," said Madison, "and you take in a greater variety of parties and interests; you make it less probable that a majority of the whole will have a common motive to invade the rights of other citizens."

Strengthening the Union

The most telling argument in 1787 for a federal system, however, was that it would overcome the deficiencies of the Articles. The Articles had numerous flaws (including a very weak executive and a judiciary subservient to the state courts), and two of them were fatal: the government had neither the power to tax nor the power to regulate commerce.

Under the Articles, Congress was given responsibility for national defense but was not granted the power to tax, so it had to rely on the states for the money to maintain an army and a navy. During the first six years under the Articles, Congress asked the states for $12 million but received only $3 million—not even enough to pay the interest on Revolutionary War debts. By 1786 the national government was so desperate for funds that it sold the navy's ships and had fewer than a thousand soldiers in uniform—this at a time when England had an army in Canada and when Spain occupied Florida.

HISTORICAL BACKGROUND

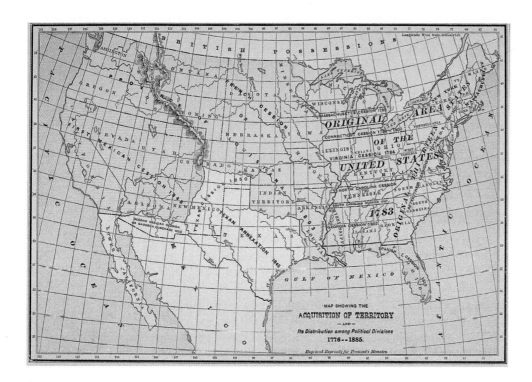

MAP SHOWING THE
ACQUISITION OF TERRITORY
— AND —
Its Distribution among Political Divisions
1776--1885.

It could take weeks to travel overland or by ship from the most distant points in the American states. The great size of America compared with European countries was used as an argument by both those who favored a strong union and those who opposed it.

Congress also was expected to shape a national economy, yet it was powerless to do so because the Articles prohibited it from interfering with the states' commerce policies. States were free to do whatever they wanted, and they took advantage of the situation by imposing trade barriers on each other. Connecticut, for example, placed a higher tariff on manufactured goods from its trading rival Massachusetts than it placed on the same goods shipped from England.

The Articles of Confederation showed the fallacy of the adage "That government is best which governs least." The consequences of an overly weak authority were abundantly clear: public disorder, economic chaos, and inadequate defense.

The Powers of the Nation

The Philadelphia convention met to decide the powers of the national government. The delegates had not been sent to determine how state government should be structured. Accordingly, the U.S. Constitution focuses on the lawful authority of the national government, which is provided through *enumerated and implied powers.* Authority that is not granted to the national government is left— or "reserved"—to the states. Thus, the states have *reserved powers.*

Enumerated Powers

Article I of the Constitution grants to Congress seventeen **enumerated (expressed) powers.** These powers were intended by the Framers to be the basis for a government strong enough to forge a union that was secure in its defense and stable in its commerce. Congress's powers to regulate commerce among the states, to create a national currency, and to borrow money, for example, would provide a foundation for a sound national economy. Its power to tax, combined with its authority to declare war and establish an army and a navy, would enable it to provide for the common defense. In addition, the

enumerated (expressed) powers

The seventeen powers granted to the national government under Article I, Section 8 of the Constitution. These powers include taxation and the regulation of commerce as well as the authority to provide for the national defense.

#3

Constitution prohibits the states from actions that would interfere with the national government's exercise of its lawful powers. Article I, Section 10 forbids the states to make treaties with other nations, raise armies, wage war, print money, or make commercial agreements with other states without the approval of Congress.

The writers of the Constitution recognized that the lawful exercise of national authority would at times conflict with the actions of the states. In such instances, national law was intended to prevail. Article VI of the Constitution grants this dominance in the so-called **supremacy clause,** which provides that "the laws of the United States . . . shall be the supreme law of the land."

Implied Powers

The Framers of the Constitution also recognized that a narrow definition of national authority would result in a government incapable of adapting to change. Under the Articles of Confederation, Congress was strictly confined to those powers expressly granted to it, which limited its ability to respond effectively to the country's changing needs after the Revolutionary War. Concerned that the enumerated powers by themselves might be too restrictive of national authority, the Framers added the **"necessary and proper"** clause or, as it later came to be known, the **elastic clause.** Article I, Section 8 gives Congress the power "to make all laws which shall be necessary and proper for carrying into execution the foregoing [enumerated] powers." This grant gave the national government **implied powers:** the authority to take action that is not expressly authorized by the Constitution but that supports actions that are so authorized.

The Powers of the States

The Framers' preference for a sovereign national government was not shared in 1787 by all Americans. Although Anti-Federalists recognized a need to strengthen defense and interstate commerce, they feared the consequences of a strong central government. The interests of the people of New Hampshire were not identical to those of Georgians or Pennsylvanians, and the Anti-Federalists argued that only state-centered government would protect and preserve the differences. Self-government, they claimed, would be weakened if power resided with a distant national government.

The Federalists responded by saying that the national government would have no interest in depriving the states of their liberty or of their right to self-government in local matters.[4] The national government would take responsibility for establishing a strong defense and for promoting a sound economy, while the states would retain nearly all other governing functions, including oversight of public morals, education, and safety.

This argument did not persuade the Anti-Federalists that their fear of an overly powerful national government was baseless. The supremacy and "necessary and proper" clauses were particularly worrisome, because they provided a constitutional basis for future expansions of national authority. Such concerns led to demands for a constitutional amendment that would protect the states against encroachment by the national government. Ratified in 1791 as the Tenth Amendment to the Constitution, it reads: "The powers not delegated to the United States by the Constitution, nor prohibited by it to the States, are reserved to the States." The states' powers under the U.S. Constitution are thus called **reserved powers.**

---

supremacy clause
Article VI of the Constitution, which makes national law supreme over state law when the national government is acting within its constitutional limits.

"necessary and proper" (elastic) clause
The authority granted Congress in Article I, Section 8 of the Constitution "to make all laws which shall be necessary and proper" for the implementation of its enumerated powers.

implied powers
The federal government's constitutional authority (through the "necessary and proper" clause) to take action that is not expressly authorized by the Constitution but that supports actions that are so authorized.

reserved powers
The powers granted to the states under the Tenth Amendment to the Constitution.

Get Involved!

Step Up

The U.S. federal system of government offers an array of channels for political participation. Vital governing decisions are made at the national, state, and local levels, all of which provide opportunities for citizens to make a difference.

Another participatory arena is close at hand: the college campus. Most colleges and universities support a variety of activities in which students can engage. Student government is one such opportunity; another is the student newspaper. Most colleges and universities offer a wide range of groups and sponsored programs, from debate clubs to fraternal organizations. Many students do not avail themselves of these opportunities, and among those who do, many see the opportunities as offering only a temporary advantage.

The theorist John Stuart Mill (1806–73) thought differently, arguing that public activity has several benefits. One benefit is that people are better able to promote and protect their interests when they are actively involved. Participation also enables people to contribute to their community. Mill suggested yet a third benefit—the one for which he is noted. Mill contended that the active individual is the more virtuous citizen in that he or she will be more socially skilled, more personally assured, and more ethically aware. Community participation helps individuals develop their abilities and understand the interests of others. In a word, the active citizen is more enlightened than the passive one. Mill's belief in the role of participation in personal development led him to support women's rights. In an era when women had few rights, Mill was a passionate advocate of sexual equality.

If you are not now active in campus groups, consider joining one. If you join—or if you already belong to such a group—take full advantage of the participatory opportunities it provides. The benefits will extend beyond your college years.

FEDERALISM IN HISTORICAL PERSPECTIVE

Since ratification of the Constitution over two centuries ago, no aspect of it has provoked more frequent or bitter conflict than federalism. By establishing two levels of sovereign authority, the Constitution created competing centers of power and ambition, each of which was sure to claim disputed areas as belonging within its realm of authority.

Conflict between national and state authority was also ensured by the brevity of the Constitution. The Framers deliberately avoided detailed provisions, recognizing that brief phrases would lend flexibility to the government they were creating. The document does not define, for example, the difference between *inter*state commerce (which the national government is empowered to regulate) and *intra*state commerce (which is reserved for regulation by the states).

Not surprisingly, federalism has been a contentious and dynamic system, its development determined less by constitutional language than by the strength of contending interests and by the country's changing needs. Federalism can be viewed as having progressed through three historical eras, each of which has involved a different relationship between the nation and the states.

An Indestructible Union (1789–1865)

The issue during the first era, which lasted from the Constitution's beginnings in 1789 through the end of the Civil War in 1865, was the Union's survival. Given the state-centered history of America before the Constitution, it was inevitable that the states would dispute national policies that threatened their particular interests.

A first dispute over federalism was whether the Constitution allowed the creation of a Bank of the United States (shown here in an early-nineteenth-century painting). The Constitution had a clause authorizing the printing of currency but not the establishment of a bank itself.

**HISTORICAL
BACKGROUND**

The Nationalist View: McCulloch v. Maryland

A first dispute over federalism arose when President George Washington's secretary of the treasury, Alexander Hamilton, proposed that Congress establish a national bank. Thomas Jefferson, Washington's secretary of state, opposed the bank on the grounds that its activities would benefit the interests of the rich at the expense of the interests of ordinary people. Jefferson claimed that the bank was unlawful because the Constitution did not expressly authorize the creation of a national bank. Hamilton and his supporters claimed that because the federal government had constitutional authority to regulate currency, it had the "implied power" to establish a national bank.

Hamilton's view prevailed when Congress in 1791 established the First Bank of the United States, granting it a twenty-year charter. Although Congress did not renew the charter when it expired in 1811, Congress decided in 1816 to establish the Second Bank of the United States. State and local banks did not want competition from a national bank and sought help from their state legislatures. Several states, including Maryland, levied taxes on the U.S. Bank's operations within their borders, hoping to drive it out of existence by making it unprofitable. Edwin McCulloch, who was in charge of the Maryland branch of the U.S. Bank, refused to pay the Maryland tax and the resulting dispute was heard by the Supreme Court.

The chief justice of the Supreme Court, John Marshall, was a strong nationalist, and in *McCulloch v. Maryland* (1819) the Court ruled decisively in favor of national authority. It was reasonable, Marshall concluded, to infer that a government with powers to tax, borrow money, and regulate commerce could establish a bank in order to exercise those powers properly. Marshall's argument was a clear statement of *implied powers*—the idea that through the "necessary and proper" clause the national government's powers extend beyond a narrow reading of its enumerated powers.

Marshall also addressed the meaning of the Constitution's supremacy clause. The state of Maryland argued that, even if the national bank was a legal entity, it had the sovereign authority to tax it. The Supreme Court rejected Maryland's position, concluding that valid national law prevailed over conflicting state law. Because

#4

the national government had the power to create the bank, it also could protect the bank against actions by the states, such as taxation, that might destroy it.[5]

The *McCulloch* decision served as precedent for later rulings in support of national power. In *Gibbons v. Ogden* (1824), for example, the Marshall-led Court rejected a New York law granting a monopoly on a ferry that operated between New York and New Jersey, concluding that New York had encroached on Congress's power to regulate commerce among the states. The Court also ruled that Congress's commerce power extended *into* a state when commerce between two or more states was at issue.[6]

Marshall's opinions asserted that legitimate uses of national power took precedence over state authority and that the "necessary and proper" clause and the commerce clause were broad grants of national power. As a nationalist, Marshall was providing the U.S. government the legal justification for expanding its power in ways that fostered the development of the United States as a nation rather than as a collection of states. This constitutional vision was of utmost significance. As Justice Oliver Wendell Holmes Jr. noted a century later, the Union could not have survived if each state had been allowed to determine for itself the extent to which it would accept national authority.[7]

The States'-Rights View: The **Dred Scott** *Decision*

Although John Marshall's rulings helped strengthen national authority, the issue of slavery posed a growing threat to the Union's survival. Fearing that northern members of Congress might move to abolish slavery, southern leaders did what others have done throughout American history: they devised a constitutional argument to fit their political desires. John C. Calhoun of South Carolina argued that the Constitution had created "a government of states . . . not a government of individuals."[8] This line of reasoning led Calhoun to his famed "doctrine of nullification," which declared that each state had the constitutional right to nullify a national law.

WWW.MHHE.COM/PATTERSONTAD8

In 1832 South Carolina invoked this doctrine, declaring "null and void" a tariff law that favored northern interests. President Andrew Jackson retorted that South Carolina's action was "incompatible with the existence of the Union," a position that was strengthened when Congress authorized Jackson to use military force if necessary against South Carolina. The state backed down when Congress amended the tariff act to reduce its impact on the South.

The clash foreshadowed a confrontation of far greater scope and consequence: the Civil War. It would not break out for another thirty years, but in the interim, conflicts over states' rights intensified. Westward expansion and immigration into the northern states were tilting power in Congress toward the free states, which increasingly signaled their determination to outlaw slavery in the United States at some future time. Attempts to find a compromise acceptable to both the North and the South were fruitless.

The Supreme Court's infamous *Dred Scott* decision (1857), written by Chief Justice Roger Taney, an ardent states'-rights advocate, intensified the conflict. Dred Scott, a slave who had lived in the North for four years, applied for his freedom when his master died, citing a federal law—the Missouri Compromise of 1820—that made slavery illegal in a free state or territory. The Supreme Court ruled against Scott, claiming that slaves were "property" and that persons of African descent were barred from citizenship and thereby could not sue for their freedom in federal courts. The Court also invalidated the Missouri Compromise. The Court ruled that, because slaves were property and because property could be taken into any state or territory, Congress could not outlaw slavery in any part of the United States.[9]

LEADERS

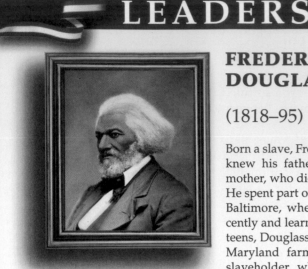

FREDERICK DOUGLASS

(1818–95)

Born a slave, Frederick Douglass never knew his father and rarely saw his mother, who died when he was seven. He spent part of his early childhood in Baltimore, where he was treated decently and learned to read. In his early teens, Douglass was sent to work on a Maryland farm owned by a brutal slaveholder, who whipped Douglass mercilessly. It took Douglass more than two years to find an opportunity to escape north to Massachusetts, where he joined the antislavery movement and discovered that he had unusual oratorical skill. As his speaking fame grew, Douglass toured the North and Europe, creating support for abolition. He argued that the Constitution should be read as a mandate for freedom for all. As much as he despised the slave states, Douglass was a fervent advocate of saving the Union, arguing that to abandon the Union would mean abandoning those enslaved in the South. After the Civil War ended, Douglass pushed for constitutional amendments that would give equal rights to former slaves.

The Taney Court's decision drew an angry response in the North and contributed to a sectional split in the nation's majority party, the Democrats. In 1860, the Democratic party's northern and southern wings nominated separate candidates for the presidency, which split the Democratic vote, enabling the Republican candidate, Abraham Lincoln, to win the presidency with only 40 percent of the popular vote. Lincoln had campaigned on a platform that called, not for an immediate end to slavery, but for its gradual abolition through payments to slaveholders. Nevertheless, southern states saw Lincoln's election as a grave threat to their sovereignty. By the time Lincoln assumed office, seven southern states, led by South Carolina, had left the Union. Four more states were to follow. In justifying his decision to wage war on the secessionists, Lincoln said, "The Union is older than the states." In 1865, the superior strength of the Union army settled by force the question of whether states are required to accept national authority.

Dual Federalism and Laissez-Faire Capitalism (1865–1937)

Although the Civil War preserved the Union, new challenges to federalism were surfacing. Constitutional doctrine held that certain policy areas, such as interstate commerce and defense, belonged exclusively to the national government, whereas other policy areas, such as public health and intrastate commerce, belonged exclusively to the states. This doctrine, known as **dual federalism,** was based on the idea that a precise separation of national and state authority was both possible and desirable. "The power which one possesses," said the Supreme Court, "the other does not."[10]

American society, however, was in the midst of changes that raised questions about the suitability of dual federalism as a governing concept. The Industrial Revolution had given rise to large business firms, which were using their economic power to dominate markets and exploit workers. Government was the logical counterforce to this economic power. Which level of government—state or national—would regulate business?

There was also the issue of the former slaves. The white South had lost the war but was hardly of a mind to share power with newly freed slaves. Would the federal government be allowed to intervene in state affairs to ensure the fair treatment of African Americans?

Dual federalism became a barrier to an effective response to these issues. From the 1860s through the 1930s, the Supreme Court held firm to the idea that there was a sharp line between national and state authority and, in both areas, a high wall of separation between government and the economy. This era of

dual federalism

A doctrine based on the idea that a precise separation of national power and state power is both possible and desirable.

The American Civil War was the bloodiest conflict the world had yet known. Ten percent of fighting-age males died in the four-year war, and uncounted others were wounded. The death toll—618,000 (360,000 from the North, 258,000 from the South)—exceeded that of the American war dead in World War I, World War II, the Korean War, and the Vietnam War combined. This death toll was in a nation with a population only one-ninth the size it is today.

federalism was characterized by state supremacy in racial policy and business supremacy in commerce policy.

The Fourteenth Amendment and State Discretion

Ratified after the Civil War, the Fourteenth Amendment was intended to protect the newly freed slaves from discriminatory actions by state governments. A state was prohibited from depriving "any person of life, liberty, or property without due process of law," from denying "any person within its jurisdiction the equal protection of the laws," and from abridging "the privileges or immunities of citizens of the United States."

Supreme Court rulings during subsequent decades, however, helped to undermine the Fourteenth Amendment's promise of liberty and equality for all. The Court held, for example, that the Fourteenth Amendment did not substantially limit the power of the states to determine the rights to which their residents were entitled.[11] Then, in *Plessy v. Ferguson* (1896), the Court issued its infamous "separate but equal" ruling. A black man, Homer Adolph Plessy, had been convicted of violating a Louisiana law that required white and black citizens to ride in separate railroad cars. The Supreme Court upheld his conviction, concluding that state governments could require blacks to use separate railroad cars and other accommodations as long as those facilities were "equal" in quality to those reserved for use by whites. "If one race be inferior to the other socially," the Court concluded, "the Constitution of the United States cannot put them on the same plane." The lone dissenting justice in the case, John Marshall Harlan, had harsh words for his colleagues: "Our Constitution is color-blind and neither knows nor tolerates classes among citizens. . . . The thin disguise of 'equal' accommodations . . . will not mislead anyone nor atone for the wrong this day done."[12]

HISTORICAL BACKGROUND

Political Culture

Large Versus Small Republics

During the debate over ratification of the Constitution, Americans argued over whether liberty, equality, and self-government would be better protected by the states or by the nation. The Anti-Federalists argued that a small republic was closer to the people and therefore would do more to protect individuals' rights. Arguing for the Federalists, James Madison countered by saying that a large republic was preferable because its wide diversity of interests would require compromise and tolerance among various groups.

Which view—that of the Anti-Federalists or that of the Federalists—is better supported by history? Have America's founding ideals been better nurtured through state governments or through the national government? For a long period in U.S. history, the answer was one-sided. As political scientist William Riker noted, state-centered government before and after the Civil War was the tool by which white

Americans dominated black Americans, first through slavery and later through institutionalized racism (for example, the separation by law of black and white children attending public schools). As Madison prophesied, a smaller republic makes it easier for a particular faction to run roughshod over another.

Legal racial discrimination is now a thing of the past, and state governments are much less likely to side with one faction against others. How would you judge today's situation? In your view, which level of government—federal or state—is more likely to protect and enhance the ideals of liberty, equality, and self-government? Which level of government is more likely to promote the interests of a particular group at the expense of other groups? In what areas of public policy—taxation, education, public safety, and so on—do you think your opinion is most supported?

With its *Plessy* decision, the Court undercut the Fourteenth Amendment and allowed southern states to segregate the races. Black children were forced into separate schools that seldom had libraries and usually had few teachers. Hospitals for blacks had few doctors and nurses and almost no medical supplies and equipment. Legal challenges to these discriminatory practices were generally unsuccessful. The *Plessy* ruling had become a justification for the separate and *unequal* treatment of black Americans.

Judicial Protection of Business

Through its rulings after the Civil War, the Supreme Court also provided a constitutional basis for uncontrolled economic power. A majority of the Court's justices believed in laissez-faire capitalism (which holds that business should be "allowed to act" without interference), and they interpreted the Constitution in ways that frustrated government's attempts to regulate business activity. In 1886, for example, the Court decided that corporations were "persons" within the meaning of the Fourteenth Amendment and thus their property rights were protected from substantial regulation by the states.[13] The irony was inescapable. A constitutional amendment that had been enacted to protect the liberty of newly freed slaves was ignored for this purpose but used instead to protect fictitious persons—business corporations.

The Court also weakened the national government's regulatory power by narrowly interpreting its commerce power. The Constitution's **commerce clause** says that Congress shall have the power "to regulate commerce" among the states but does not spell out the economic activities included in the grant of power. When the federal government invoked the Sherman Antitrust Act (1890) in an attempt to break up a monopoly on the manufacture of sugar, the Supreme Court blocked the action, claiming that interstate commerce covered only the "transportation" of goods, not their "manufacture."[14] Manufacturing was deemed

commerce clause

The clause of the Constitution (Article I, Section 8) that empowers the federal government to regulate commerce among the states and with other nations.

After the Civil War Reconstruction, the white majority in the South used the power of government to enforce creation of a two-race society in which the public schools and other public facilities for blacks were inferior to those for whites.

part of intrastate commerce and thus, according to the dual federalism doctrine, subject to state regulation only. However, because the Court had previously decided that the states' regulatory powers were restricted by the Fourteenth Amendment, the states for the most part were also denied the authority to regulate manufacturing activity.

Although the national government subsequently made some headway in business regulation, the Supreme Court remained an obstacle. An example is the case of *Hammer v. Dagenhart* (1918), which arose from a 1916 federal act that prohibited the interstate shipment of goods produced by child labor. The act was popular because factory owners were exploiting children, working them for long hours at low pay. Citing the Tenth Amendment, the Court invalidated the law, ruling that factory practices could be regulated only by the states.[15] However, in an earlier case, *Lochner v. New York* (1905), the Court had prevented a state from regulating labor practices, concluding that such action was a violation of firms' property rights.[16]

In effect, the Court had negated the principle of self-government. The people, through their representatives, were denied the power to act decisively in the economic realm—neither Congress nor the state legislature was allowed to regulate the marketplace. America's corporations, with the Supreme Court as their shield, were the controlling authority.[17]

National Authority Prevails

Judicial supremacy in the economic sphere ended abruptly in 1937. For nearly a decade, the United States had been mired in the Great Depression, which President Franklin D. Roosevelt's New Deal was designed to alleviate. The Supreme Court, however, had ruled much of the New Deal's economic recovery legislation unconstitutional. A constitutional crisis of historic proportions seemed inevitable until the Court suddenly reversed its position. In the process, American federalism was fundamentally and forever changed.

HISTORICAL BACKGROUND

Between 1865 and 1937, the Supreme Court's rulings severely restricted national power. Narrowly interpreting Congress's constitutional power to regulate commerce, the Court forbade Congress to regulate child labor and other aspects of manufacturing.

The Great Depression revealed clearly that Americans had become a national community with national economic needs. By the 1930s, more than half the population lived in cities (compared to a fifth in 1860), and more than ten million workers were employed by industry (compared to one million in 1860). Urban workers typically were dependent on landlords for their housing, on farmers and grocers for their food, and on corporations for their jobs. Farmers were more independent, but they too were increasingly a part of a larger economic network. Farmers' income depended on market prices and shipping and equipment costs.[18]

This economic interdependence meant that no area of the economy was immune from damage if things went wrong. When the depression hit in 1929, its effects could not be contained. At the depths of the Great Depression, one-fourth of the nation's work force was unemployed and another fourth could find only part-time work.

The states by tradition had responsibility for helping the unemployed, but they were nearly penniless because of declining tax revenues and the growing need for welfare assistance. Roosevelt's New Deal programs were intended to alleviate Americans' suffering. The National Industry Recovery Act (NIRA), for example, called for coordinated action by major industries and for a federal jobs program. Economic conservatives strenuously opposed such programs. They accused Roosevelt of trying to lead the country into communism and found an ally in the Supreme Court. In *Schecter v. United States*, just as it had done in previous New Deal cases, the Supreme Court in a 5-4 ruling held that the NIRA was unconstitutional.[19]

Frustrated by the Court's opposition, Roosevelt in 1937 proposed that Congress expand the Supreme Court by passing legislation that would permit an additional justice to be appointed whenever a seated member passed the age of seventy. Roosevelt would then be able to appoint enough new justices to swing the Court to his side. Congress rejected Roosevelt's plan, but the controversy ended with "the switch in time that saved nine." For reasons that have never been made fully clear, Justice Owen Roberts switched sides on New Deal cases, giving the president a 5-4 majority on the Court.

Within months, the Court upheld the 1935 National Labor Relations Act, which gave employees the right to organize and bargain collectively.[20] In passing

During the Great Depression, shantytowns were erected in most cities by people who had lost their jobs and homes. State and local governments could not cope with the enormous problems created by the Great Depression, so the federal government stepped in with its New Deal programs, greatly changing the nature of federal-state relations.

the act, Congress had claimed that labor-management disputes disrupted the nation's economy and therefore could be regulated through the commerce clause. In upholding the act, the Supreme Court in effect granted Congress the authority to apply its commerce powers broadly.[21] During this same period, the Court also loosened its restrictions on Congress's use of its taxing and spending powers.[22] These decisions removed the constitutional barrier to increased federal authority, a change the Court later acknowledged when it said that Congress's commerce power is "as broad as the needs of the nation."[23]

In effect, the Supreme Court had finally recognized the obvious: that an industrial economy is not confined by state boundaries and must be subject to national regulation. It was a principle that business itself also increasingly accepted. The nation's banking industry, for example, was saved in the 1930s from almost complete collapse by the creation of a federal regulatory agency, the Federal Deposit Insurance Corporation (FDIC). By insuring depositors' savings against loss, the FDIC stopped the panic withdrawals that had forced many banks to close.

Toward National Citizenship

The fundamental change in the constitutional doctrine of federalism as applied to economic issues that took place in the 1930s was paralleled by similar changes in other areas, including civil rights and civil liberties. In *Brown v. Board of Education* (1954), for example, the Supreme Court held that states could not require black children to attend public schools separate from those for white children (see Chapter 5).[24] Another example is the Supreme Court's 1967 *Miranda* ruling, which requires police officers in all states to inform crime suspects of their rights at the time of arrest (see Chapter 4).[25]

Of course, important differences remain in the rights and privileges of the residents of the separate states, as could be expected in a federal system. The death penalty, for example, is legal in some states but not others, and states differ greatly in terms of their services, such as the quality of their public schools. Nevertheless, national citizenship—the notion that Americans should be equal in their rights and opportunities regardless of the state in which they live—is a more encompassing idea today than it was in the past.

Media & Politics

Local Self-Governance and Media Consolidation

America's federal system of government is prized for promoting self-government at the national, state, and local levels. But what happens if the information about public affairs at any of these levels begins to dry up? How can people govern themselves if they have difficulty finding out what government is doing? This concern is being voiced in some communities as a result of media consolidation and cost-cutting. Confronted with Internet and cable competition for advertising dollars and audiences, many local newspapers and television stations have sharply reduced their local news reporting. At one time, nearly every local news outlet had a reporter assigned solely to the coverage of local government. Few local news organizations today have such a reporter, and in some places city hall is only rarely in the news.

The problem is most acute in the medium of radio. In recent decades, truly local stations—those that are locally owned and operated and that aim to serve local needs—have declined sharply in number. Major corporations now own most radio outlets. A giant in the field is Clear Channel Communications, which owns more than 1,200 stations nationwide. Only a tiny fraction of the content on Clear Channel stations originates locally. Instead, their content is produced centrally, a much more profitable enterprise because the same item can be used in many outlets. Clear Channel stations also rely on technology that allows announcers to act as if they are broadcasting locally when they actually are in a studio halfway across the country.

A tragic incident in 2002 demonstrated how this media structure can adversely affect a community. In the early hours of a January morning, a Canadian Pacific Railway train carrying highly toxic ammonia derailed in Minot, North Dakota. Ammonia liquid spilled from tank cars, and a cloud of toxic gas spread slowly through the city. Local officials had improperly programmed the emergency alert system that would have automatically interrupted programming on the city's broadcast radio stations. When they called the local stations directly to get them to inform residents of the danger, no one was at the stations to pick up the phone. All six local stations were owned by Clear Channel, which was operating them remotely. One Minot resident died from exposure to ammonia gas, and more than one hundred people had to be taken to the hospital.

Of course, a single event does not fully define the implications of media consolidation. It can be argued that Americans prefer the slicker radio programming that a large corporation like Clear Channel can provide. It also can be said that a city like Minot, which has a population of roughly thirty-five thousand people, could not otherwise support six separate stations. Nevertheless, to the degree that self-government in a federal system requires citizens' awareness of local affairs, recent media trends are troublesome. Americans have a media system that is more equipped to tell them what is happening halfway around the world than to inform them of what is happening halfway across town.

FEDERALISM TODAY

Since the 1930s, the relation of the nation to the states has changed so fundamentally that dual federalism is no longer even a roughly accurate description of the American situation.

An understanding of the nature of federalism today requires a recognition of two countervailing trends. The first trend is a long-term *expansion* of national authority that began in the 1930s and continued for the next half century. The national government now operates in many policy areas that were once almost exclusively within the control of states and localities. The national government does not dominate in these policy areas, but it does play a significant role. Much of this national influence stems from social welfare policies enacted in the 1960s as part of President Lyndon Johnson's Great Society program, which included initiatives in health care, public housing, nutrition, welfare, urban development, and other areas previously reserved to states and localities.

The second, more recent trend involves a partial *contraction* of national authority. Known as *devolution*, this trend involves the "passing down" of authority from the national government to the state and local levels. Devolution has reversed the decades-long increase in federal authority, but only in some areas and then only to a moderate degree.

In short, the national government's policy authority has expanded greatly since the 1930s, even though that authority has been reduced somewhat in recent years. We will explain each of these two trends in more detail.

Interdependency and Intergovernmental Relations

Interdependency is a reason that national authority increased dramatically in the twentieth century. Modern systems of transportation, commerce, and communication transcend local and state boundaries. These systems are national—and even international—in scope, which means that problems affecting Americans living in one part of the country are likely to affect Americans living elsewhere. This situation has required Washington to assume a larger policy role. National problems ordinarily require national solutions.

Interdependency has also encouraged national, state, and local policymakers to work together to solve policy problems. This collaborative effort has been described as **cooperative federalism**.[26] The difference between this system of federalism and the older dual federalism has been likened to the difference between a marble cake, whose levels flow together, and a layer cake, whose levels are separate.[27]

Cooperative federalism is based on shared policy responsibilities rather than sharply divided ones. An example is the Medicaid program, which was created in 1965 as part of President Johnson's Great Society initiative and provides health care for the poor. The Medicaid program is jointly funded by the national and state governments, operates within eligibility standards set by the national government, and gives states some latitude in determining the benefits that recipients receive. The Medicaid program is not an isolated example. Literally hundreds of policy programs today are run jointly by the national and state governments. In many cases, local governments are also involved. The following characteristics describe these programs:

- Jointly funded by the national and state governments (and sometimes by local governments)

- Jointly administered, with the states and localities providing most of the direct service to recipients and a national agency providing general administration

- Jointly determined, with both the state and national governments (and sometimes the local governments) having a say in eligibility and benefit levels and with federal regulations, such as those prohibiting discrimination, providing an element of uniformity to the various state and local efforts

Cooperative federalism should not be interpreted to mean that the states are powerless and dependent. States have retained most of their traditional authority. Nearly 95 percent of the funding for public schools, for example,

cooperative federalism
The situation in which the national, state, and local levels work together to solve problems.

The devastation caused by Hurricane Katrina in 2005 predictably brought federal, state, and local governments together in the reconstruction effort. Cooperative federalism is a term used to describe such joint efforts. Like any governing arrangement, however, cooperative federalism does not ensure success. In the case of Katrina, the scope of the natural disaster overwhelmed the capacity of the nation's governments, leading to widespread criticism of officials at all levels. Shown here is New Orleans' famed Canal Street, covered by floodwaters.

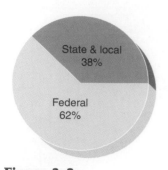

Figure 3–2

Federal, State, and Local Shares of Government Tax Revenue
The federal government raises more tax revenues than all state and local governments combined.
Source: U.S. Department of Commerce, 2006.

is provided by states and localities, which also set most of the education standards, from teachers' qualifications to course requirements to the length of the school day. Moreover, the policy areas dominated by the states—such as education, law enforcement, and transportation—tend to be those that have the most direct impact on people's daily lives. Finally, contrary to what many Americans might think, state and local governments have nearly six times as many employees as the federal government.

Nevertheless, the federal government's involvement in policy areas traditionally reserved for the states has increased its influence on policy and diminished state-to-state policy differences. Before the enactment of the federal Medicaid program in 1965, for example, poor people in many states were not entitled to government-paid health care. Now most poor people are eligible for health benefits regardless of where in the United States they live.

Government Revenues and Intergovernmental Relations

The interdependency of American society—the fact that developments in one area affect what happens elsewhere—is one of two major reasons why the federal government's policy role has expanded greatly since the early twentieth century. The other reason is the federal government's superior taxing capacity. States and localities are in an inherently competitive situation with regard to taxation. A state that raises taxes too high will lose residents and firms to states where taxes are lower. People and businesses are much less likely to move to another country in search of a lower tax rate. The result is that the federal government raises more tax revenues than do all fifty states and the thousands of local governments combined (see Figure 3–2).

Fiscal Federalism

fiscal federalism
A term that refers to the expenditure of federal funds on programs run in part through states and localities.

grants-in-aid
Federal cash payments to states and localities for programs they administer.

The federal government's revenue-raising advantage has helped make money the basis for many of the relations between the national government and the states and localities. **Fiscal federalism** refers to the expenditure of federal funds on programs run in part through state and local governments.[28] The federal government provides some or all of the money for a program through **grants-in-aid** (cash payments) to states and localities, which then administer the program.

The pattern of federal assistance to states and localities during the last half-century is shown in Figure 3–3. Federal grants-in-aid increased dramatically during this period. A sharp rise occurred in the late 1960s and early 1970s as a result of President Johnson's Great Society programs. Roughly one in every five dollars spent by local and state governments in recent decades has been raised not by them, but by the government in Washington (see "States in the Nation").

Cash grants to states and localities have extended Washington's influence on policy decisions. State and local governments can reject a grant-in-aid, but if they accept it they must spend it in the way specified by Congress. Also, because most grants require states to contribute matching funds, the federal programs in effect determine how states will allocate some of their own tax dollars. Federal grants have also pressured state and local officials to accept broad national goals, such as the elimination of racial and other forms of discrimination. A building constructed with the help of federal funds, for example, must be accessible to persons with disabilities.

Nevertheless, federal grants-in-aid also serve the policy interests of state and local officials. While these officials have often complained that federal grants

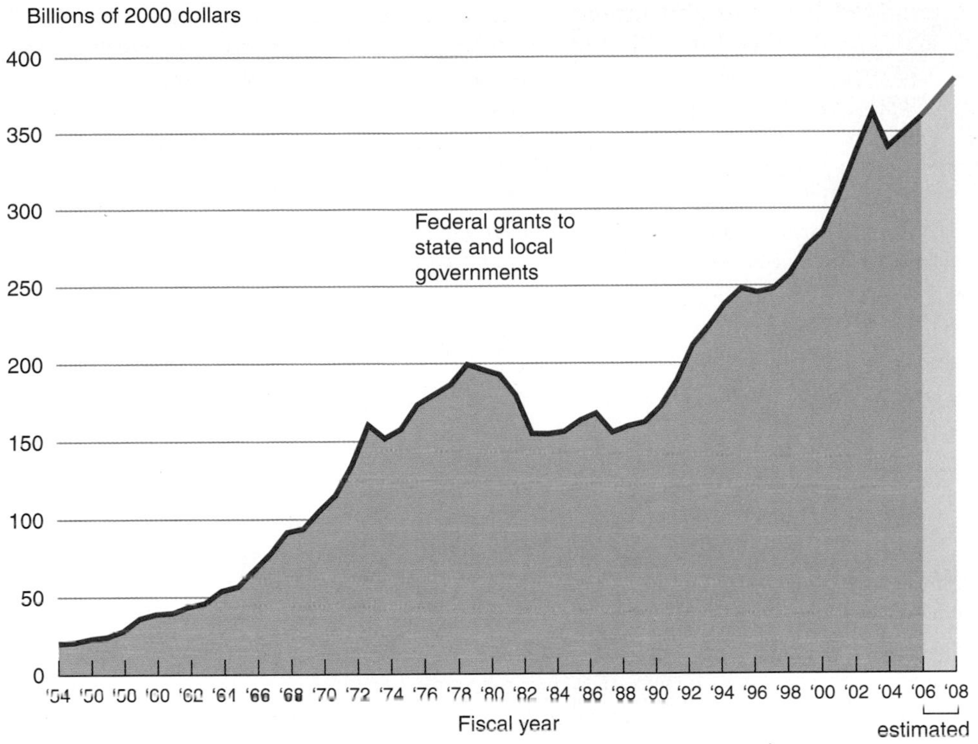

Billions of 2000 dollars

Federal grants to
state and local
governments

Fiscal year

estimated

Figure 3–3

**Federal Grants to State
and Local Governments**
Federal aid to states and
localities has increased
dramatically since the 1950s.
Source: Office of Management and
Budget, 2006. Figure is based on
constant (2000) dollars in order to
control for the effect of inflation.

contain too many restrictions and infringe too much on their authority, they have
been eager to obtain the money because it permits them to offer services they
could not otherwise afford. An example is a 1994 federal grant program that
enabled local governments to put seventy-five thousand additional police
officers on the streets.

Categorical and Block Grants

State and local governments receive two major types of assistance, categorical
grants and block grants. These differ in the extent to which Washington defines
the conditions of their use.

Categorical grants are more restrictive. They can be used only for a designated activity. An example is funds directed for use in school lunch programs.
These funds can be used only in support of school lunches; they cannot be
diverted for other school purposes, such as the purchase of textbooks or the hiring of teachers. **Block grants** are less restrictive. The federal government specifies the general area in which the funds must be used, but state and local officials
select the specific projects. A block grant targeted for the health area, for example, might give state and local officials leeway in deciding whether to use the
money for hospital construction, medical equipment, or some other health care
activity.

State and local officials have naturally preferred federal money that comes
with fewer strings attached and thus have favored block grants. On the other
hand, members of Congress have at times preferred categorical grants, because
this form of assistance gives them more control over how state and local officials
spend federal funds. Recently, however, officials at all levels have looked to block
grants as the key to a more workable form of federalism. This tendency is part
of a larger trend—devolution.

categorical grants
Federal grants-in-aid to
states and localities that can
be used only for designated
projects.

block grants
Federal grants-in-aid that
permit state and local
officials to decide how the
money will be spent within
a general area, such as
education or health.

States in the Nation

Federal Grants-in-Aid to the States

Federal assistance accounts for a significant share of state revenue, but the variation is considerable. New Mexico (with a third of its total revenue coming from federal grants-in-aid) is at one extreme. Nevada (a seventh of its revenue) is at the other.

Q: Why do states in the South, where anti-Washington sentiment is relatively high, get more of their revenue from the federal government than most other states?

A: Many federal grant programs are designed to assist low-income people, and poverty is more widespread in the South. Moreover, southern states traditionally have provided fewer government services, and federal grants therefore constitute a larger proportion of their budgets.

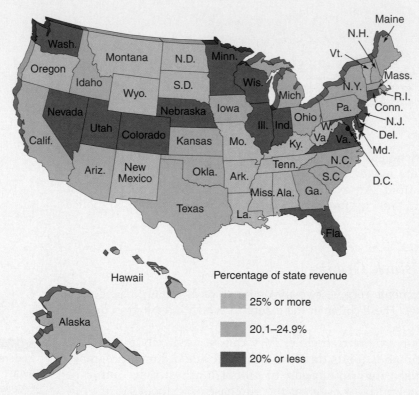

Percentage of state revenue

25% or more

20.1–24.9%

20% or less

Source: U.S. Bureau of the Census, 2006.

A New Federalism: Devolution

devolution

The passing down of authority from the national government to the state and local governments.

Devolution embodies the idea that American federalism will be strengthened by a partial shift in authority from the federal government to the state and local governments. Devolution is attributable to both practical and political developments.[29]

Budgetary Pressures and Public Opinion

As a practical matter, the growth in federal assistance had slowed by the early 1980s. The federal government was facing huge budget deficits, and awarding

CHAPTER 3   Federalism   89

large new grants-in-aid to states and localities was not feasible. As budgetary pressures intensified, relations among national, state, and local officials became increasingly strained. A slowdown in the annual increase in federal assistance had forced states and localities to pay an increasingly larger share of the costs of joint programs. As state and local governments raised taxes or cut other services to meet the costs of joint programs, taxpayer anger intensified. Some grant programs that had not been very popular before the budget crunch, such as food stamps and public housing, now came under even heavier criticism.

By the early 1990s, American federalism was positioned for a change. Two decades earlier, three-fourths of Americans had expressed confidence in Washington's ability to govern effectively. Less than half the public now held this view. A 1993 CBS News/New York Times survey indicated that 69 percent of Americans believed that "the federal government creates more problems than it solves."

The Republican Revolution

When the Republican party scored a decisive victory in the 1994 congressional elections, Newt Gingrich declared that "1960s-style federalism is dead." Republican lawmakers proposed to cut some programs, but, even more, they sought to increase state and local control.

That Republicans would lead the move to a more decentralized form of federalism was no surprise. Although members of both parties had supported expansions of federal authority, Republicans had more often questioned the overall result. Republican presidents Richard Nixon and Ronald Reagan, for example, proposed versions of a "new federalism" in which some areas of public policy for which the federal government had assumed responsibility would be returned to states and localities.

Upon taking control of Congress in 1995, Republican lawmakers acted to reduce *unfunded mandates,* federal programs that require action by states or localities but provide no or insufficient funds to pay for it. For example, states and localities are required by federal law to make their buildings accessible

When the 1994 elections were over, Newt Gingrich declared that "1960s-style federalism is dead." As Speaker of the House of Representatives, Gingrich helped enact major changes in federal-state relations. Gingrich (on the left) is shown with Senate majority leader Robert Dole.

to the physically handicapped, but Washington pays only part of the cost of these accommodations. In the Unfunded Mandates Reform Act of 1995, Congress eliminated some of these mandates, although under threat of a presidential veto it exempted those that deal with civil rights. The GOP-controlled Congress also took action to lump additional categorical grants into block grants, thereby giving states more control over how federal money would be spent.

The most significant legislative change came in 1996, when the Republican Congress enacted the sweeping Welfare Reform Act. Its key element, the Temporary Assistance for Needy Families block grant (TANF), ended the decades-old program that granted cash assistance to every poor family with children. TANF restricts a family's eligibility for federal assistance to five years, and after two years a family head normally has to go to work for the benefits to continue. Moreover, TANF gives states wide latitude in setting benefit levels, eligibility criteria, and other regulations affecting aid to poor families. TANF also places states in charge of developing training and education programs that will move people off of welfare and into jobs. (TANF and other aspects of the 1996 welfare reform legislation are discussed further in later chapters.)

After passage of the 1996 Welfare Reform Act, congressional efforts to reduce federal authority declined sharply. Welfare had been the main target of Republican lawmakers, and other large initiatives were politically more difficult to accomplish. Nevertheless, devolution had enabled states and localities to recapture some of the authority they had lost since the 1930s. Yet, devolution had not succeeded in rolling back the great majority of the federal domestic programs instituted since the 1930s. The fact is, there are substantial limits on the amount of power that can reasonably be returned to the states. Because of the increased interdependency of American society, the states will never again have the level of autonomy that they enjoyed until the early twentieth century.

Devolution, Judicial Style

In the five decades after the 1930s, the Supreme Court granted Congress broad discretion in the enactment of policies affecting state and local governments. In *Garcia v. San Antonio Authority* (1985), for example, the Court held that federal minimum wage standards apply as well to employees of state and local governments.[30] States and localities are prohibited from paying their own workers less than the federally mandated minimum wage.

In recent years, however, the Supreme Court has moved to restrict somewhat Congress's power to enact laws binding on the states. Turnover in the Court's membership has placed control in the hands of Republican-appointed conservative justices who believe Congress has overstepped its constitutional authority in some areas.[31] In *United States v. Lopez* (1995), for example, the Court cited the Tenth Amendment in striking down a federal law that prohibited the possession of guns within 1,000 feet of a school. Congress had justified the law as an exercise of its commerce power, but the Court stated that the ban had "nothing to do with commerce, or any sort of economic activity."[32] Two years later, in *Printz v. United States* (1997), the Court struck down that part of the federal Handgun Violence Prevention Act (the so-called Brady bill) that required local law-enforcement officers to conduct background checks on prospective handgun buyers. The Court concluded that the provision violated the Tenth Amendment in that it ordered state officials, in this case police officers, to "enforce a federal regulatory program."[33] Congress can require federal officials to take such action, but it cannot order state officials to do so.

Debating the Issues

Should the Federal Government Have the Authority to Prevent States from Legalizing Marijuana Use for Medical Purposes?

Federalism has led to countless disputes between states and the national government. One current dispute is whether the states should have the authority to create medical exceptions to the federal ban on marijuana. In a 1996 ballot initiative, California voters passed a law permitting doctors to prescribe marijuana to relieve pain and other ailments. Nearly a dozen other states enacted similar laws. However, a federal law—the Controlled Substances Act (CSA)—bans marijuana use entirely. In *Gonzales v. Raich* (2005), the Supreme Court upheld the federal ban by a 6-3 vote. Even though the marijuana in question had been raised and consumed locally, the Court concluded that Congress had the power to ban it through its authority to regulate commerce among the states. When the ruling was announced, some state and local officials said they would not enforce the ban. Patients then would be at risk of arrest only if their marijuana use came to the attention of federal law enforcement officials.

Justice John Paul Stevens wrote the majority opinion in *Gonzales v. Raich*. Justice Sandra Day O'Connor wrote a dissenting opinion. Portions of their arguments are provided below. Do you think the commerce clause justifies the outlawing of state laws that permit the local use of medical marijuana? Where do you stand more generally on the issue of medical marijuana? Do you think state and local officials who refuse to enforce the federal ban are acting improperly?

Yes

Congress' power to regulate purely local activities that are part of an economic "class of activities" that have a substantial effect on interstate commerce is firmly established. If Congress decides that the "total incidence" of a practice poses a threat to a national market, it may regulate the entire class. Of particular relevance here is *Wickard v. Filburn* where, in rejecting the appellee farmer's contention that Congress' admitted power to regulate the production of wheat for commerce did not authorize federal regulation of wheat production intended wholly for the appellee's own consumption, the Court established that Congress can regulate purely intrastate activity that is not itself "commercial," *i.e.*, not produced for sale, if it concludes that failure to regulate that class of activity would undercut the regulation of the interstate market in that commodity. The similarities between this case and *Wickard* are striking. In both cases, the regulation is squarely within Congress' commerce power because production of the commodity meant for home consumption, be it wheat or marijuana, has a substantial effect on supply and demand in the national market for that commodity. In assessing the scope of Congress' Commerce Clause authority, the Court need not determine whether respondents' activities, taken in the aggregate, substantially affect interstate commerce in fact, but only whether a "rational basis" exists for so concluding. Given the enforcement difficulties that attend distinguishing between marijuana cultivated locally and marijuana grown elsewhere, and concerns about diversion into illicit channels, the Court has no difficulty concluding that Congress had a rational basis for believing that failure to regulate the intrastate manufacture and possession of marijuana would leave a gaping hole in the CSA.

—*John Paul Stevens, Associate Justice of the U.S. Supreme Court*

No

There is simply no evidence that homegrown medicinal marijuana users constitute, in the aggregate, a sizable enough class to have a discernable, let alone substantial, impact on the national illicit drug market or otherwise to threaten the CSA regime. Explicit evidence is helpful when substantial effect is not visible to the naked eye. And here, in part because common sense suggests that medical marijuana users may be limited in number and that California's Compassionate Use Act and similar state legislation may well isolate activities relating to medicinal marijuana from the illicit market, the effect of those activities on interstate drug traffic is not self-evidently substantial. . . . The Court's [declarations] amount to nothing more than a legislative insistence that the regulation of controlled substances must be absolute. They are asserted without any supporting evidence—descriptive, statistical, or otherwise. . . . [S]imply because Congress may conclude a particular activity substantially affects interstate commerce does not necessarily make it so. Indeed, if declarations like these suffice to justify federal regulation, and if the Court today is right about what passes rationality review before us, then our decision in *Morrison* should have come out the other way. In that case, Congress had supplied numerous findings regarding the impact gender-motivated violence had on the national economy. . . . If, as the Court claims, today's decision does not break with precedent, how can it be that voluminous findings, documenting extensive hearings about the specific topic of violence against women, did not pass constitutional muster in *Morrison*, while the CSA's abstract, unsubstantiated, generalized findings about controlled substances do?

—*Sandra Day O'Connor, Associate Justice of the U.S. Supreme Court*

The Supreme Court has also used the Eleventh Amendment to trim Congress's authority over state governments. The Eleventh Amendment protects a state against being sued without its consent in federal court by a private citizen. In *Kimel v. Florida Board of Regents* (2000)[34] and *Board of Trustees of the University of Alabama v. Garrett* (2002),[35] the Supreme Court held that states cannot be sued by their own employees for violations of federal age and disability discrimination laws. The Court ruled that, although states must comply with these laws and can be sued by the federal government for violating them, they cannot be sued by their own employees because age and disability discrimination are not among the forms of discrimination protected from state action by the Fourteenth Amendment. On the other hand, gender is a protected category, which is why the Supreme Court in *Nevada Department of Human Resources v. Hibbs* (2003) held that state governments can be sued for violations of the federal Family and Medical Leave Act (FMLA), which provides unpaid leave and job retention to employees caring for a new baby or a seriously ill family member. The Court said that FMLA was enacted primarily to protect women employees from discrimination and accordingly was "appropriate legislation" under the Fourteenth Amendment.[36]

Although recent Court rulings have limited Congress's discretion to some extent, they have not fundamentally rolled back the increase in federal authority that began during the 1930s. The Supreme Court has not retreated from the principle established then that Congress's commerce and spending powers are broad and substantial.[37] This principle has enabled the federal government, through its grants-in-aid and its regulatory policies, to exercise its authority in policy areas once reserved for the states. American federalism, even with devolution, is a far different governing system today than it was prior to the 1930s.[38] The states remain powerful governing bodies, but they operate within a system in which federal authority is pervasive. In 2005, for example, the Supreme Court upheld the power of Congress to prohibit marijuana use even for medical purposes. Nearly a dozen states, including California, had passed laws enabling patients, with a physician's prescription, to grow and use marijuana. Although the marijuana was not shipped across state lines, the Supreme Court in *Gonzales v. Raich* (2005) held that the commerce clause allows Congress to ban marijuana even in states that have authorized it for medical use only.[39]

THE PUBLIC'S INFLUENCE: SETTING THE BOUNDARIES OF FEDERAL-STATE POWER

Public opinion had a decisive influence on the ebb and flow of federal power during the twentieth century. As changes occured in Americans' attitudes toward the federal government and the states, the balance of power between these two levels of government also shifted.

During the Great Depression, when it was clear that the states would be unable to help, Americans turned to Washington for relief. For people without jobs, the fine points of the Constitution were of little consequence. President Roosevelt's programs, though a radical departure from the past, quickly gained public favor. A 1936 Gallup poll indicated, for example, that 61 percent of Americans supported Roosevelt's social security program, whereas only 27 percent opposed it. This support reflected a new public attitude: the federal government, not the states, was expected to take the lead in protecting Americans from economic hardship.[40]

The second great wave of federal social programs—Lyndon Johnson's Great Society—was also driven by public demands. Income and education levels had risen dramatically after the Second World War, and Americans wanted more and better services from government.[41] When the states were slow to respond, Americans pressured federal officials to act. The Medicare and Medicaid programs, which were created in 1965 and provide health care for the elderly and the poor, respectively, are examples of Washington's response. So, too, is increased federal aid in areas such as education, housing, and transportation.

Public opinion was also behind the rollback of federal authority in the 1990s. Americans' dissatisfaction with federal deficits and policies provided the springboard for the Republican takeover of Congress in the 1994 midterm election, which led to policies aimed at devolving power to the states.[42] The capstone program of this devolution was the widely popular 1996 Welfare Reform Act.

The public's role in defining the boundaries between federal and state power would come as no surprise to the Framers of the Constitution. For them, federalism was a pragmatic issue, one to be decided by the nation's needs rather than by inflexible rules. James Madison predicted as much when he said Americans would look to whichever level of government was more responsive to their interests. Indeed, each succeeding generation of Americans has seen fit to devise a balance of federal and state power that would serve its needs. Historian Daniel Boorstin said that the true genius of the American people is their pragmatism, their willingness to try new approaches to self-government when the old ones stop working.[43] In few areas of governing has Americans' pragmatism been more apparent than in their approach to federalism.

Summary

Self-Test www.mhhe.com/pattersontad8

A foremost characteristic of the American political system is its division of authority between a national government and state governments. The first U.S. government, established by the Articles of Confederation, was essentially a union of the states.

In establishing the basis for a stronger national government, the U.S. Constitution also made provision for safeguarding state interests. The result was the creation of a federal system in which sovereignty was vested in both national and state governments. The Constitution enumerates the general powers of the national government and grants it implied powers through the "necessary and proper" clause. Other powers are reserved to the states by the Tenth Amendment.

From 1789 to 1865, the nation's survival was at issue. The states found it convenient at times to argue that their sovereignty took precedence over national authority. In the end, it took the Civil War to cement the idea that the United States was a union of people, not of states. From 1865 to 1937, federalism reflected the doctrine that certain policy areas were the exclusive responsibility of the national government whereas responsibility in other policy areas belonged exclusively to the states. This constitutional position validated the laissez-faire doctrine that big business was largely beyond governmental control. It also allowed the states to discriminate against African Americans in their public policies. Federalism in a form recognizable today began to emerge in the 1930s.

In the areas of commerce, taxation, spending, civil rights, and civil liberties, among others, the federal government now plays an important role, one that is the inevitable consequence of the increasing complexity of American society and the interdependence of its people. National, state, and local officials now work closely together to solve the country's problems, a situation described as cooperative federalism. Grants-in-aid from Washington to the states and localities have been the chief instrument of national influence. States and localities have received billions in federal assistance; in accepting federal money, they also have accepted both federal restrictions on its use and the national policy priorities that underlie the granting of the money.

The issue of the relationship between the nation and the states has changed somewhat as a result of devolution—a shift of power downward to the states. This change, like changes throughout U.S. history, sprang from the demands of the American people.

STUDY CORNER

Key Terms

block grants (*p. 87*)
categorical grants (*p. 87*)
commerce clause (*p. 80*)
confederacy (*p. 70*)
cooperative federalism (*p. 85*)
devolution (*p. 88*)

dual federalism (*p. 78*)
enumerated (expressed) powers (*p. 73*)
federalism (*p. 69*)
fiscal federalism (*p. 86*)
grants-in-aid (*p. 86*)
implied powers (*p. 74*)

"necessary and proper" (elastic)
  clause (*p. 74*)
reserved powers (*p. 74*)
sovereignty (*p. 69*)
supremacy clause (*p. 74*)
unitary system (*p. 70*)

Self-Test

1. Describing the United States as having a federal system of government means that:
   a. the states are not included in the power arrangement.
   b. constitutional authority for governing is divided between a national government on the one hand and the state governments on the other.
   c. the states are not bound by the rules and regulations of the national government.
   d. constitutional authority for governing is placed entirely in the hands of the states rather than the national government. *Confederacy*
   e. America set up the exact same type of governing structure as Britain except for the establishment of a monarchy.

2. The significance of the Preamble of the Constitution reading "We the People" rather than "We the States" is that:
   a. there was to be no change in the power relationship between the states and the nation in the new Constitution.
   b. the new Constitution symbolically recognized the people for winning the Revolutionary War.
   c. the states would not have to pay their war debts.
   d. the national government under the Constitution would have direct power over the people, which it did not have under the Articles of Confederation.

3. Which type of power was given to the states under the Constitution?
   a. the power to declare war
   b. supremacy over the national government
   c. reserved power
   d. necessary and proper power

4. The Supreme Court's opinion in *McCulloch v. Maryland:*
   a. ruled in favor of state-centered federalism.
   b. affirmed that national law is supreme over conflicting state law.
   c. established the principle of judicial review.
   d. declared the "necessary and proper" clause unconstitutional.

5. All **except** which one of the following describe trends in government revenues and intergovernmental relations in the United States?
   a. The federal government raises more revenues than all state and local governments combined.
   b. Unlike states and localities, the federal government controls the American dollar and has a nearly unlimited ability to borrow money to cover its deficits.
   c. The states possess the organizational resources to make fiscal federalism a workable arrangement.
   d. Financial assistance from the federal government to the states is gradually being eliminated.

6. The concept of devolution is used to explain:
   a. the current trend to shift authority from the federal government to state and local governments.
   b. the necessity for keeping federal and state spheres of responsibility absolutely separate from each other.
   c. a failed political revolution.
   d. increased recognition that the industrial economy is not confined by state boundaries and must be subject to national regulation.

7. Categorical grants allow the states more flexibility and discretion in the expenditure of funds than block grants do. (T/F)

8. The primary goal of the writers of the Constitution was to establish a national government strong enough to forge a union secure in its defense and open in its commerce. (T/F)

9. Dual federalism is the idea that the national and state governments should not interfere in each other's activities. (T/F)

10. Fiscal federalism involves the states raising money for programs and the federal government administering the programs. (T/F)

Critical Thinking

How have interdependency and the federal government's superior taxing power contributed to a larger policy role for the national government? Do you think these factors will increase or decrease in importance in the future? What will this trend mean for the future of American federalism? (You might find it helpful to think about these questions in the context of a specific policy area, such as the terrorist threat facing the country.)

Suggested Readings

Beer, Samuel H. *To Make a Nation: The Rediscovery of American Federalism.* Cambridge, Mass.: The Belknap Press of Harvard University, 1993. An innovative interpretive framework for understanding the impact of federalism and nationalism on the nation's development.

Chopra, Pran. *Supreme Court Versus the Constitution: A Challenge to Federalism.* Thousand Oaks, Calif.: Sage Publications, 2006. A look at the Supreme Court's view of federalism.

Cornell, Saul. *The Other Founders: Anti-Federalism and the Dissenting Tradition in America.* Chapel Hill: University of North Carolina Press, 1999. An analysis of Anti-Federalist thought, its origins, and its legacy.

Elkins, Stanley, and Eric McKitrick. *The Age of Federalism: The Early American Republic, 1788–1800.* New York: Oxford University Press, 1993. An award-winning book on the earliest period of American federalism.

Ross, William G. *A Muted Fury: Populists, Progressives, and Labor Unions Confront the Courts, 1890–1937.* Princeton, N. J.: Princeton University Press, 1993. A valuable study of the political conflict surrounding the judiciary's laissez-faire doctrine in the period 1890–1937.

Teaford, John. *The Rise of the States: Evolution of American State Government.* Baltimore, Md.: Johns Hopkins University Press, 2002. A historical assessment of state government that spans the past century.

Walker, David B. *The Rebirth of Federalism*, 2d ed. Chatham, N. J.: Chatham House Publishers, 2000. An optimistic assessment of the state of today's federalism.

List of Websites

http://lcweb2.loc.gov/ammem/amlaw/lawhome.html
A site containing congressional documents and debates from 1774 to 1873.

http://www.csg.org/
The site of the Council of State Governments; includes current news from each of the states and basic information about their governments.

http://www.temple.edu/federalism/
The site of the Center for the Study of Federalism, located at Temple University; offers information and publications on the federal system of government.

http://www.yale.edu/lawweb/avalon/federal/fed.htm
A documentary record of the *Federalist Papers,* the Annapolis convention, the Articles of Confederation, the Madison debates, and the U.S. Constitution.

Participate!

Federalism can be a contentious system in that a policy outcome may depend on whether the issue is settled at the national or the state level. Oregon's physician-assisted suicide law (see the chapter's opening example) is a case in point. Consider writing a letter to your member of Congress expressing your view of what ought to be done in this case. In its 2005 decision, the Supreme Court indicated that Congress could enact legislation explicitly banning the use of controlled substances for the purpose of physician-assisted suicide. Congress could also choose not to take action, in which case the Supreme Court's ruling would continue to govern what states can do in this area. In writing your letter, you should resolve two issues: your own position on physician-assisted suicide, and whether you believe an issue of this type is properly decided at the state or the federal level. Note that your opinion on the issue may be at odds with your opinion on whether state or federal authority should prevail—for example, you may conclude that the issue should be decided by each state for itself even though you personally oppose physician-assisted suicide.

Extra Credit

For up-to-the-minute *New York Times* articles, interactive simulations, graphics, study tools, and more links and quizzes, visit the text's Online Learning Center at www.mhhe.com/pattersonad8.

(Self-Test Answers: 1. b   2. d   3. c   4. b   5. d   6. a   7. F   8. T   9. T   10. F)

Civil Liberties:
Protecting Individual Rights

Chapter Outline

Freedom of Expression
The Early Period: The Uncertain Status of the Right of Free Expression
The Modern Period: Protecting Free Expression
Free Expression and State Governments
Libel and Slander
Obscenity

Freedom of Religion
The Establishment Clause
The Free-Exercise Clause

The Right of Privacy
Abortion
Sexual Relations Among Consenting Adults
The Continuing Issue of Privacy Rights

Rights of Persons Accused of Crimes
Selective Incorporation of Procedural Rights
Limits on Defendants' Rights
Crime, Punishment, and Police Practices

Rights and the War on Terrorism
Detention of Enemy Combatants
Surveillance of Suspected Terrorists

The Courts and a Free Society

CHAPTER 4

A bill of rights is what the people are entitled to against every government on earth, general or particular, and what no just government should refuse, or rest on inference.

—*Thomas Jefferson*[1]

Robert and Sarisse Creighton and their three children were asleep when FBI agents and local police broke into their home in the middle of the night. Brandishing guns, the officers searched the house for a relative of the Creightons who was suspected of bank robbery. When asked to show a search warrant, the officers said, "You watch too much TV." The suspect was not there, and the officers left as abruptly as they had entered. The Creightons sued the FBI agent in charge, Russell Anderson, for violating their Fourth Amendment right against unlawful search.

The Creightons won a temporary victory when the U.S. Circuit Court of Appeals for the Eighth Circuit—noting that individuals are constitutionally protected against warrantless searches unless officers have good reason ("probable cause") for a search and unless they have good reason ("exigent circumstances") for conducting that search without a warrant—concluded that Anderson had been derelict in his duty. In the judgment of the appellate court, Anderson should have sought a warrant from a judge, who would have decided whether a search of the Creightons' home was justified.

The Supreme Court of the United States overturned the lower court's ruling. The Court's majority opinion stated: "We have recognized that it is inevitable that law enforcement officials will in some cases reasonably but mistakenly conclude that probable cause is present, and we have indicated that in such cases those officials . . . should not be held personally liable." Justice John Paul Stevens and two other justices sharply dissented. Stevens accused the Court's majority of showing "remarkably little fidelity" to the Fourth Amendment.[2] Civil liberties groups claimed that the Court's decision gave police an open invitation to invade people's homes on the slightest pretext. On the other hand, law enforcement officials praised the decision, saying that a ruling in the Creightons' favor would have made them hesitant to pursue suspects for fear of a lawsuit whenever the search failed to produce the culprit.

As this case illustrates, issues of individual rights are complex and political. No right is absolute. For example, the Fourth Amendment protects Americans not from *all* searches but from *unreasonable* searches. The public would be unsafe if law officials could never pursue a suspect into a home. Yet the public would also be unsafe if police could invade homes anytime they wanted. The challenge for a civil society is to establish a level of police authority that balances the demands of public safety with those of personal freedom. The balance point, however, is always subject to dispute. Did FBI agent Anderson have sufficient cause for a warrantless search of the Creightons' home? Or was his evidence so weak that his forcible entry constituted an unreasonable search? Not even the justices of the Supreme Court could agree on these questions. Six justices sided with Anderson, and three backed the Creightons' position.

This chapter examines issues of **civil liberties,** specific individual rights, such as freedom of speech and protection against self-incrimination, that are constitutionally protected against infringement by government. As seen in Chapter 2, the Constitution's failure to enumerate individual freedoms led to demands for the **Bill of Rights** (see Table 4–1). Enacted in 1791, these first ten amendments to the Constitution specify certain rights of life, liberty, and property that the national government is obliged to respect. A later amendment, the Fourteenth, became the basis for protecting these rights from actions by state and local governments.

Rights have full meaning only as they are protected in law. A constitutional guarantee of free speech, for example, is worth no more than the paper on which it is written if authorities can stop people from speaking freely. Judicial action is important in defining what people's rights mean in practice and in setting limits on official action. In some areas, the judiciary devises a specific test to determine whether government action is lawful. A test applied in the area of free

civil liberties
The fundamental individual rights of a free society, such as freedom of speech and the right to a jury trial, which in the United States are protected by the Bill of Rights.

Bill of Rights
The first ten amendments to the Constitution, which set forth basic protections for individual rights to free expression, fair trial, and property.

TABLE 4–1	The Bill of Rights: A Selected List of Constitutional Protections
	The Bill of Rights refers to the first ten amendments to the Constitution, which include protections of individual rights.

FIRST AMENDMENT

Speech: You are free to say almost anything except that which is obscene, slanders another person, or has a high probability of inciting others to take imminent lawless action.

Assembly: You are free to assemble, although government may regulate the time and place for reasons of public convenience and safety, provided such regulations are applied evenhandedly to all groups.

Religion: You are protected from having the religious beliefs of others imposed on you, and you are free to believe what you like.

FOURTH AMENDMENT

Search and seizure: You are protected from unreasonable searches and seizures, although you forfeit that right if you knowingly waive it.

Arrest: You are protected from arrest unless authorities have probable cause to believe you have committed a crime.

FIFTH AMENDMENT

Self-incrimination: You are protected against self-incrimination, which means that you have the right to remain silent and to be protected against coercion by law enforcement officials.

Double jeopardy: You cannot be tried twice for the same crime if the first trial results in a verdict of innocence.

Due process: You cannot be deprived of life, liberty, or property without proper legal proceedings.

SIXTH AMENDMENT

Counsel: You have a right to be represented by an attorney and can demand to speak first with an attorney before responding to questions from law enforcement officials.

Prompt and reasonable proceedings: You have a right to be arraigned promptly, to be informed of the charges, to confront witnesses, and to have a speedy and open trial by an impartial jury.

EIGHTH AMENDMENT

Bail: You are protected against excessive bail or fines.

Cruel and unusual punishment: You are protected from cruel and unusual punishment, although this provision does not protect you from the death penalty or from a long prison term for a minor offense.

speech, for example, is whether general rules (such as restrictions on the time and place of a public gathering) are applied fairly. Government officials do not meet this test if they apply one set of rules for groups that they like and a harsher set of rules for those they dislike.

Issues of individual rights have become increasingly complex. The writers of the Constitution could not possibly have foreseen the United States of the early twenty-first century, with its huge national government, enormous corporations, pervasive mass media, urban crowding, and vulnerability to terrorist acts. These developments are potential threats to personal liberty, and the judiciary in recent decades has seen fit to expand the rights to which individuals are entitled. However, these rights are constantly being balanced against competing rights and society's collective interests. The Bill of Rights operates in an untidy world where people's highest aspirations collide with their worst passions, and it is at this juncture that issues of civil liberties arise. Should an admitted murderer be entitled to recant a confession? Should the press be allowed to print military secrets whose publication might jeopardize national security? Should extremist groups be allowed to publicize their messages of prejudice and hate? Such questions are among the subjects of this chapter, which focuses on these points:

Protesters line the route as President George W. Bush passes by in his limousine during the Inaugural Parade marking the start of his second term. Freedom of expression is widely regarded as the most basic of rights because other aspects of a free society, such as open and fair elections, are dependent on it.

- *Freedom of expression is the most basic of democratic rights, but, like all rights, it is not unlimited.* Free expression recently has been strongly supported by the Supreme Court.

- *"Due process of law" refers to legal protections (primarily procedural safeguards) designed to ensure that individual rights are respected by government.*

- *During the last half-century particularly, the civil liberties of individual Americans have been substantially broadened in law and given greater judicial protection from action by all levels of government.* Of special significance has been the Supreme Court's use of the Fourteenth Amendment to protect these individual rights from action by state and local governments.

- *Individual rights are constantly being weighed against the demands of majorities and the collective needs of society.* All political institutions are involved in this process, as is public opinion, but the judiciary plays the central role in it and is the institution that is most partial to the protection of civil liberties.

FREEDOM OF EXPRESSION

Freedom of political expression is the most basic of democratic rights. Unless citizens can openly express their political opinions, they cannot properly influence their government or act to protect their other rights. As the Supreme Court concluded in 1984, "The freedom to speak one's mind is not only an aspect of individual liberty—and thus a good unto itself—but also is essential to the common quest for truth and the vitality of society as a whole."[3]

freedom of expression
Americans' freedom to communicate their views, the foundation of which is the First Amendment rights of freedom of conscience, speech, press, assembly, and petition.

The First Amendment provides the foundation for **freedom of expression**—the right of individual Americans to hold and communicate views of their choosing. For many reasons, such as a desire to conform to social pressure or a fear of harassment, Americans do not always choose to express themselves freely. Moreover, freedom of expression, like other rights, is not absolute. It does not entitle individuals to say or do whatever they want, to whomever they want, whenever they want. Free expression can be denied, for example, if it endangers national security, wrongly damages the reputations of others, or deprives others of their basic freedoms. Nevertheless, the First Amendment provides for freedom of expression by prohibiting laws that would abridge the freedoms of conscience, speech, press, assembly, and petition.

Free expression is vigorously protected by the courts. Today, under most circumstances, Americans can freely express their political views without fear of governmental interference. In earlier times, however, Americans were less free to express their opinions.

The Early Period: The Uncertain Status of the Right of Free Expression

HISTORICAL BACKGROUND

The first attempt by the U.S. government to restrict free expression was the Sedition Act of 1798, which made it a crime to print harshly critical newspaper stories about the president or other national officials. Thomas Jefferson called the Sedition Act an "alarming infraction" of the Constitution and, upon replacing John Adams as president in 1801, pardoned those who had been convicted under it. Because the Supreme Court did not review the sedition cases, however, the judiciary's position on free expression was an open question. The Court also did not rule on free speech during the Civil War era, when the government severely restricted individual rights.

In 1919 the Court finally ruled on a free-expression case. The defendant had been convicted under the 1917 Espionage Act, which prohibited forms of dissent, including the distribution of antiwar leaflets, that could harm the nation's effort in World War I. In *Schenck v. United States* (1919), the Court unanimously upheld the constitutionality of the Espionage Act. In the opinion written by Justice Oliver Wendell Holmes, the Court said that Congress could restrict speech that was "of such a nature as to create a clear and present danger" to the nation's security. In a famous passage, Holmes argued that not even the First Amendment would permit a person to falsely yell "Fire!" in a crowded theater and create a panic that could kill or injure innocent people.[4]

Although the *Schenck* decision upheld a law that limited free expression, it also

LEADERS

OLIVER WENDELL HOLMES JR.

(1841–1935)

Oliver Wendell Holmes Jr. was nominated for the Supreme Court in 1901 by President Theodore Roosevelt and served for more than three decades. The son of a famous writer and physician, Holmes was a leading intellectual force on the Court. An advocate of judicial restraint, he nonetheless argued that the law had to keep pace with society. He helped lay the foundation for an interpretation of the First Amendment that limited government's ability to restrict free expression. Holmes famously wrote that the First Amendment would not protect a person "falsely shouting fire in a theater and causing a panic" but that government also did not have blanket authority to limit free speech. Upon his death, Holmes left his estate to the U.S. government. In one of his Court opinions, he had written: "Taxes are the price we pay for civilization."

Get Involved!
Stand Up

"Get up, stand up: stand up for your rights!" These are the words of one of reggae icon Bob Marley's best-known songs.

American citizens enjoy an impressive array of personal liberties, including the right to speak freely. Yet studies find that many Americans do not exercise that right when they think it will bring them into conflict with authorities or associates. Social pressure—and in some cases fear of retribution—leads them to stay silent when they hear opinions or slurs they think are wrong. Alexis de Tocqueville noted this tendency when he toured America in the 1830s. Tocqueville said that he knew of no country in the world where people were freer to think and speak for themselves. But then he added, "I know of no country in which there is so little independence of mind and real freedom of discussion as in America." Tocqueville attributed the tendency to Americans' embrace of majority opinion. Within that opinion, he said, there is room for disagreement. Outside it, there is social isolation.

Consider, for example, opinions on the Iraq war, which vary sharply across society and yet tend to be similar among people who talk with each other regularly. It is rare for someone who opposes the war, but whose acquaintances or work associates support it to express his or her view openly and often. The same is true of someone who supports the war but is surrounded by people who oppose it.

One effect of this tendency is to lead those who hold the majority opinion to believe that others think as they do and that their opinion is therefore the only proper one. The failure of citizens to openly express their opinions also means forgoing the personal liberty that the Constitution provides and that other Americans have sacrificed to preserve at critical moments in the nation's history. Tocqueville identified yet another effect of citizen silence. By failing to speak their minds, citizens empower government to think for them. Tocqueville wrote:

> It does not break wills, but it softens them, bends them, and directs them; it rarely forces one to act, but it constantly opposes itself to one's acting; it does not destroy, it prevents things from being born; it does not tyrannize, it hinders, compromises, enervates, extinguishes, dazes, and finally reduces [citizens] to being nothing more than a herd of timid and industrious animals of which the government is the shepherd.

Tocqueville may have overstated his case, but the point is a valid one. As a citizen, you have more to lose than to gain by failing to exercise your right of free expression. Stand up for what you believe. Stand up for your rights.

established a standard—the **clear-and-present-danger test**—for determining when government had exceeded its constitutional authority to restrict speech. Political speech that was a clear and present danger could be banned by government. Speech that did not pose such a danger could *not* be banned. (The clear-and-present-danger test was later replaced by the imminent lawless action test, which is discussed later in the chapter.)

The Modern Period: Protecting Free Expression

Until the twentieth century, the tension between national security interests and free expression was not a pressing issue in the United States. The country's great size and ocean barriers provided protection from potential enemies, minimizing concerns about internal subversion. World War I, however, intruded on America's isolation, and World War II brought it to an abrupt end. Since then, Americans' rights of free expression have been defined largely in the context of national security concerns.

Free Speech

During the cold war that developed after World War II, many Americans believed that the Soviet Union was bent on destroying the United States, and the Supreme Court allowed government to limit certain types of expression.

clear-and-present-danger test
A test devised by the Supreme Court in 1919 in order to define the limits of free speech in the context of national security. According to the test, government cannot abridge political expression unless it presents a clear and present danger to the nation's security.

HISTORICAL BACKGROUND

In 1951, for example, the Court upheld the convictions of eleven members of the U.S. Communist party who had been prosecuted under a law that made it illegal to express support for the forceful overthrow of the U.S. government.[5] By the late 1950s, however, fear of internal communist subversion was subsiding, and the Supreme Court expanded the scope of free speech.[6] The Court implicitly embraced a legal doctrine first outlined by Justice Harlan Fiske Stone in 1938. Stone argued that First Amendment rights of free expression are the basis of Americans' liberty and ought to have a "preferred position" in the law. If government can control what people know and say, it can manipulate their opinions and thereby deprive them of the right to govern themselves. Therefore, government should be broadly prohibited from restricting free expression.[7]

This philosophy has led the Supreme Court to rule that government officials must show that national security is directly and substantially imperiled before they can lawfully prohibit citizens from speaking out. For example, during the Vietnam era, despite the largest sustained protest movement in America's history, not a single individual was convicted solely for criticizing the government's war policy. (Some dissenters were found guilty on other grounds, such as inciting riots and assaulting the police.)

symbolic speech
Action (for example, the waving or burning of a flag) for the purpose of expressing a political opinion.

The Supreme Court's protection of **symbolic speech** has been less substantial than its protection of verbal speech. For example, the Court in 1968 upheld the conviction of a Vietnam protester who had burned his draft registration card. The Court concluded that the federal law prohibiting the destruction of draft cards was intended primarily to protect the military's need for soldiers, not to prevent people from criticizing government policy.[8]

The Supreme Court, however, has not granted the government broad power to restrict symbolic speech. In 1989, for example, the Court ruled that the symbolic burning of the American flag is a lawful form of expression. The ruling came in the case of Gregory Lee Johnson, who had set fire to a U.S. flag outside the hall in Dallas where the 1984 Republican National Convention was being held. The Supreme Court rejected the state of Texas's argument that flag burning is, in every instance, an imminent danger to public safety. "If there is a bedrock principle underlying the First Amendment," the Court ruled in the *Johnson* case, "it is that the Government may not prohibit the expression of an idea simply because society finds the idea itself offensive or disagreeable."[9] (A year later the Court struck down a new federal statute that would have made it a federal crime to burn or deface the flag.[10])

Press Freedom and Prior Restraint

Freedom of the press has also received strong judicial protection in recent decades. In *New York Times Co. v. United States* (1971), the Court ruled that the *Times*'s publication of the "Pentagon papers" (secret government documents revealing that officials had deceived the public about aspects of the Vietnam War) could not be blocked by the government, which claimed that publication would hurt the war effort. The documents had been illegally obtained by antiwar activists, who then gave them to the *Times*. The Court ruled that "any system of prior restraints" on the press is unconstitutional unless the government can clearly justify the restriction.[11]

prior restraint
Government prohibition of speech or publication before the fact, which is presumed by the courts to be unconstitutional unless the justification for it is overwhelming.

The unacceptability of **prior restraint**—government prohibition of speech or publication before the fact—is basic to the current doctrine of free expression. The Supreme Court has said that any attempt by government to prevent expression carries "a 'heavy presumption' against its constitutionality."[12] News organizations are legally responsible after the fact for what they report or say (for

The Supreme Court has ruled that flag burning is a constitutionally protected form of free expression. Shown here is a scene outside California's San Quentin Prison in 2005. The crowd is burning the American flag to protest the execution of convicted murderer Stanley Williams, whose case attracted national attention.

example, they can be sued by an individual whose reputation is wrongly damaged by their words), but generally government cannot stop the media in advance from reporting their views. One exception is the reporting on U.S. military operations during wartime. The courts have allowed the government to censor reports filed by journalists who are granted access to the battlefront. The courts have also upheld the government's authority to ban uncensored publications by certain past and present government employees, such as CIA agents, who have knowledge of classified information and programs.

Free Expression and State Governments

In 1790 Congress rejected a proposed constitutional amendment that would have applied the Bill of Rights to the states. Thus, the freedoms provided in the Bill of Rights initially were protected only from action by the national government.[13] The effect was that the Bill of Rights had limited meaning to the lives of ordinary Americans because state and local governments carry out most of the activities, such as law enforcement, in which people's rights are at issue.

Not until the twentieth century did the Supreme Court begin to protect individual rights from infringement by state and local governments. The instrument for this change was the **due process clause of the Fourteenth Amendment** to the Constitution.

due process clause (of the Fourteenth Amendment)
The clause of the Constitution that has been used by the judiciary to apply the Bill of Rights to the actions of state governments.

The Fourteenth Amendment and Selective Incorporation

The Fourteenth Amendment, ratified in 1868, includes a clause that forbids a state from depriving any person of life, liberty, or property without due process of law (due process refers to the legal procedures, such as the right to a lawyer, that have been established as a means of protecting individuals' rights). Six decades later, the Supreme Court in *Gitlow v. New York* (1925) decided that the Fourteenth Amendment applied to state action in the area of free expression. Although the Court upheld Benjamin Gitlow's conviction for violating a New York law making

	Selective Incorporation of Rights of Free Expression In the 1920s and 1930s, the Supreme Court selectively incorporated the free-expression provisions of the First Amendment into the Fourteenth Amendment so that these rights would be protected from infringement by the states.		
TABLE 4–2			
SUPREME COURT CASE		**YEAR**	**CONSTITUTIONAL RIGHT AT ISSUE**
Gitlow v. New York		1925	Fourteenth Amendment protection of free expression
Fiske v. Kansas		1927	Free speech
Near v. Minnesota		1931	Free press
Hamilton v. Regents, U. of California		1934	Religious freedom
DeJonge v. Oregon		1937	Freedom of assembly and of petition

it illegal to advocate the violent overthrow of the U.S. government, the Court said that the states were not completely free to limit expression:

> For present purposes we may and do assume that freedom of speech and of the press—which are protected by the First Amendment from abridgement by Congress—are among the fundamental personal rights and "liberties" protected by the due process clause of the Fourteenth Amendment from impairment by the states.[14]

selective incorporation
The absorption of certain provisions of the Bill of Rights (for example, freedom of speech) into the Fourteenth Amendment so that these rights are protected by the federal courts from infringement by the states.

There is no indication that Congress, when it passed the Fourteenth Amendment after the Civil War, meant it to protect First Amendment rights from state action. The Supreme Court justified its new interpretation in the *Gitlow* case by referring to **selective incorporation**—the incorporation into the Fourteenth Amendment of certain provisions of the Bill of Rights so that these rights can be protected by the federal courts from infringement by the states. The Court reasoned that the Fourteenth Amendment's due process clause would be largely meaningless if states had the power to stop their residents from speaking openly.

This interpretation of the Fourteenth Amendment provided the Court with a legal basis for striking down state laws that infringed unreasonably on other forms of free expression. But the Supreme Court can act only in the context of specific cases; it does not have the constitutional authority to issue blanket rulings. Accordingly, the incorporation of additional rights by the Court did not occur until appropriate cases arose and reached the Court on appeal from lower courts. Within a dozen years (see Table 4–2), the Court had received four cases that enabled it to invalidate state laws restricting expression in the areas of speech (*Fiske v. Kansas*), press (*Near v. Minnesota*), religion (*Hamilton v. Regents, University of California*), and assembly and petition (*DeJonge v. Oregon*).[15] The *Near* decision is the best known of these rulings. Jay Near was the publisher of a Minneapolis weekly newspaper that regularly made defamatory attacks on blacks, Jews, Catholics, and labor union leaders. His paper was closed down on authority of a state law banning "malicious, scandalous, or defamatory" publications. Near appealed the shutdown, and the Supreme Court ruled in his favor, saying that the Minnesota law was "the essence of censorship."[16]

Limiting the Authority of the States to Restrict Expression

Since the 1930s, the Supreme Court has broadly protected freedom of expression from action by the states and by local governments, which derive their authority from the states. The Court has held that the states cannot restrict free

Exercising their right of free speech and assembly, antiabortion protesters gather outside a government building. Individuals do not have a constitutional right to demonstrate in any place at any time, but government is required to accommodate requests for marches and other displays of free expression.

expression except when it is almost certain to provoke immediate lawless action such as a rampage or riot. A leading free speech case was *Brandenburg v. Ohio* (1969). The appellant was a Ku Klux Klan member who, in a speech delivered at a Klan rally, said that "revenge" might have to be taken if the national government "continues to suppress the white Caucasian race." He was convicted under an Ohio law, but the Supreme Court reversed the conviction, saying that the First Amendment prohibits a state from suppressing speech that advocates the unlawful use of force "except where such advocacy is directed to inciting or producing imminent lawless action, and is likely to produce such action."[17]

This test—the likelihood of **imminent lawless action**—is a severe limit on the government's power to restrict expression. It is rare for words alone to incite others to engage in immediate unlawful action. In effect, Americans are free to say almost anything they want on political issues. This protection includes hate speech. In a unanimous 1992 opinion, the Court struck down a St. Paul, Minnesota, ordinance making it a crime to engage in speech likely to arouse "anger or alarm" on the basis of "race, color, creed, religion or gender." The Court said that the First Amendment prohibits government from "silencing speech on the basis of its content."[18] This protection of hate *speech* does not, however, extend to hate *crimes,* such as assault, motivated by racial or other prejudice. A Wisconsin law that provided for increased sentences for hate crimes was challenged as a violation of the First Amendment. In a unanimous 1993 opinion, the Court said that the law was aimed at "conduct unprotected by the First Amendment" rather than the defendant's speech.[19]

In a key case involving freedom of assembly, the U.S. Supreme Court in 1977 upheld a lower-court ruling against local ordinances of Skokie, Illinois, that had been invoked to prevent a parade there by the American Nazi party.[20] Skokie had a large Jewish population, including many survivors of Nazi Germany's

imminent lawless action test

A legal test that says government cannot lawfully suppress advocacy that promotes lawless action unless such advocacy is aimed at producing, and is likely to produce, imminent lawless action.

concentration camps. The Supreme Court held that the right of free expression takes precedence over the mere *possibility* that the exercise of that right might have undesirable consequences. Before government can lawfully prevent a speech or rally, it must demonstrate that the event will cause harm and also must demonstrate the lack of alternative ways (such as assigning police officers to control the crowd) to prevent the harm from happening.

The Supreme Court has recognized that freedom of speech and assembly may conflict with the routines of daily life. Accordingly, individuals do not have the right to hold a public rally at a busy intersection during rush hour, nor do they have the right to immediate access to a public auditorium or the right to turn up the volume on loudspeakers to the point where they can be heard miles away. The Court has held that public officials can regulate the time, place, and conditions of public assembly, provided that these regulations are reasonable and are applied evenhandedly to all groups, including those that hold unpopular views.[21]

In general, the Supreme Court's position is that the First Amendment makes any government effort to regulate the *content* of a message highly suspect. In the flag-burning case, Texas was regulating the content of the message— contempt for the flag and the principles it represents. Texas could not have been regulating the act itself, for the Texas government's own method of disposing of worn-out flags is to burn them. But a content-neutral regulation (no public rally can be held at a busy intersection during rush hour) is acceptable as long as it is reasonable and does not discriminate against certain groups or ideas.

Libel and Slander

libel

Publication of material that falsely damages a person's reputation.

slander

Spoken words that falsely damage a person's reputation.

The constitutional right of free expression is not a legal license to avoid responsibility for the consequences of what is said or written. If false information that greatly harms a person's reputation is published (**libel**) or spoken (**slander**), the injured party can sue for damages. If it were easy for public officials to claim defamation and win large amounts of money, individuals and organizations would be reluctant to criticize those in power. As it happens, U.S. slander and libel law is based on the assumption that society has an interest in encouraging citizens and news organizations to speak out. Accordingly, public officials can be attacked nearly at will without fear that the writer or speaker will have to pay them damages for slander or libel. (The courts are less protective of the writer or speaker when allegations are made about a private citizen. What is said about private individuals is considered to be less basic to the democratic process than what is said about public officials.)

The Supreme Court has held that true statements disseminated by the media have "full constitutional protection."[22] In other words, factually accurate statements, no matter how damaging they might be to a public official's career or reputation, are a protected form of expression. Even false or conjectural statements enjoy considerable legal protection. In *New York Times Co. v. Sullivan* (1964), the Supreme Court overruled an Alabama state court that had found the *New York Times* guilty of libel for printing an advertisement that criticized Alabama officials for mistreating student civil rights activists. Even though some of what was alleged was false, the Supreme Court ruled in favor of the *Times*, saying that libel of a public official requires proof of actual malice, which was defined as a knowing or reckless disregard for the truth.[23] It is very difficult to prove that a publication has acted with reckless or deliberate disregard for the truth. In fact, no federal official has won a libel judgment against a news organization in the four decades since the *Sullivan* ruling.

Debating the Issues

Should Flag Burning Be Declared Unconstitutional?

Few Americans believe that the burning of the American flag is an acceptable form of protest. Even fewer would choose to burn the flag as a symbol of their disagreement with U.S. policy. Yet, flag burning has been a leading political issue since the Supreme Court in 1989 held that burning the flag is a constitutionally protected form of expression. Since then, Congress has tried several times to initiate a constitutional amendment that would ban flag burning. If such an amendment were ratified, courts would be obliged to uphold it. In 2006, Congress came within one vote in the Senate of obtaining the two-thirds majority in each chamber that is necessary to send a flag-burning amendment to the states for ratification. The congressional debate was heated as proponents of reverence for the flag faced off against proponents of free expression. Below are the statements of two of the senators who took opposite sides on the issue.

Where do you stand on the issue? Is flag burning so disrespectful of a revered national symbol that it should be made a federal crime? Or does the First Amendment's guarantee of free expression take precedence?

Yes

I was preparing for this debate and thinking about the Lincoln Memorial. What if somebody today, yesterday, or some other time had taken spray paint and sprayed on the Lincoln Memorial: "We want freedom" or "Death to tyrants" or "Down with the flag"? Let's say they wrote that in big spray paint on the Lincoln Memorial and defaced the memorial and then was caught and was brought to trial and claimed: Wait a minute, I have a first amendment right to say what I want to say, and I believe it is important that I say it anywhere, and I want to say it on the Lincoln Memorial. . . . We would all recognize that as being something wrong, violating the law, and something there should be a law against. We don't have a problem with a person standing on the Lincoln Memorial and shouting at the top of his lungs for as long as he wants whatever he wants to say—if it is about the war in Iraq, if it is about the President, if it is about somebody in the Senate, if it is about myself, if it is about the Chair, if it is about anything he wants. We don't have any problem with that. But if he defaces the memorial, we do. It is interesting, that was the dissent Justice Stevens used in the *Texas v. Johnson* case. He made that same point. We have no problem with a person speaking on the Lincoln Memorial. We have a problem with him defacing the Lincoln Memorial. We have no problem with people speaking against the flag. We have a problem with them defacing the flag.

—*Sam Brownback, U.S. senator (R-Kansas)*

No

Let me make one thing clear at the outset. Not a single Senator who opposes the proposed constitutional amendment, as I do, supports burning or otherwise showing disrespect to the flag. Not a single one. None of us think it is "OK" to burn the flag. None of us view the flag as "just a piece of cloth." On those rare occasions when some malcontent defiles or burns our flag, I join everyone in this Chamber in condemning that action. But we must also defend the right of all Americans to express their views about their Government, however hateful or spiteful or disrespectful those views may be, without fear of their Government putting them in jail for those views. America is not simply a Nation of symbols, it is a Nation of principles. And the most important principle of all, the principle that has made this country a beacon of hope and inspiration for oppressed peoples throughout the world, is the right of free expression. This amendment threatens that right, so I must oppose it. We have heard at various times over the years that this amendment has been debated that permitting protestors to burn the American flag sends the wrong message to our children about patriotism and respect for our country. I couldn't disagree more with that argument. We can send no better, no stronger, no more meaningful message to our children about the principles and the values of this country than if we oppose efforts to undermine freedom of expression, even expression that is undeniably offensive. When we uphold First Amendment freedoms despite the efforts of misguided and despicable people who want to provoke our wrath, we explain what America is really about. Our country and our people are far too strong to be threatened by those who burn the flag. That is a lesson we should proudly teach our children.

—*Russell Feingold, U.S. senator (D-Wisc.)*

Justin Timberlake and Janet Jackson during their performance at Super Bowl XXXVIII in Houston, February 2004, just before he pulled off the fabric covering her chest. The incident prompted the Federal Communications Commission to fine the CBS network for violating broadcast decency standards.

Obscenity

Obscenity is a form of expression that is not protected by the First Amendment and thus can be prohibited by law. However, the Supreme Court has found it difficult to define with precision the criteria by which material is to be judged obscene. The Court set forth the first explicit test for obscenity in *Roth v. United States* (1957) by saying that material is obscene if "taken as a whole" it appeals to "prurient interest" and has no "redeeming social value." This assessment was to be made from the standpoint of "the average person, applying contemporary community standards."[24] However, the test proved unworkable in practice. Even the justices of the Supreme Court, when they personally examined allegedly obscene material, argued over whether it appealed to prurient interest and was without redeeming social value. In the end, they usually concluded that the material at issue had at least some social significance.

In *Miller v. California* (1973), the Court narrowed "contemporary community standards" to the local level. The Court said that what might offend residents of "Mississippi might be found tolerable in Las Vegas."[25] But even this test proved too restrictive. The Court subsequently ruled that material cannot be judged obscene simply because the "average" local resident might object to it. "Community standards" were to be judged in the context of a "reasonable person"— someone whose outlook is broad enough to evaluate the material on its overall merit rather than its most objectionable feature. The Court later also modified its content standard, saying that the material must be of a "particularly offensive type."[26] These efforts illustrate the difficulty of defining obscenity and, even more, of establishing a clear legal standard that the courts can apply consistently when obscenity cases arise.

The Supreme Court has distinguished between obscene materials in public places and those in the home. A unanimous ruling in 1969 held that what adults read and watch in the privacy of their homes cannot be made a crime.[27] The Court created an exception to this rule in 1990 by upholding an Ohio law making it a crime to possess pornographic photographs of children.[28] The Court reasoned that the purchase of such material encourages producers to use children in the making of pornographic materials, which is a crime. Consistent with this reasoning, the Court in *Ashcroft v. Free Speech Coalition* (2002) held that pictures of adults digitally altered to look like children cannot be banned because children are not used in the production of this type of material.[29]

Children have also been a consideration in court cases involving material transmitted on cable television or over the Internet. On several occasions, Congress has passed legislation (for example, the 1998 Child Online Protection Act) that would restrict the transmission of sexually explicit material that children can access. The Supreme Court has held that the restrictions, though well intentioned, have been so broad that they would ban material adults have a constitutional right to view if they so choose.[30] The Court has directed officials to find less restrictive ways to keep such material from being seen by children. An example is the federal requirement that cable operators must scramble the signal of channels that convey sexually explicit material if a subscriber requests it.

FREEDOM OF RELIGION

Free religious expression is the precursor of free political expression, at least within the English tradition of limited government. England's Glorious, or Bloodless, Revolution of 1689 centered on the issue of religion and resulted in the Act of Toleration, which gave members of all Protestant sects the right to worship freely and publicly. The English philosopher John Locke (1632–1704) extended this principle, arguing that legitimate government could not inhibit free expression, religious or otherwise. The First Amendment reflects this tradition, providing for freedom of religion along with freedom of speech, press, assembly, and petition.

In regard to religion, the First Amendment reads: "Congress shall make no law respecting an establishment of religion, or prohibiting the free exercise thereof." The prohibition on laws aimed at "establishment of religion" (the establishment clause) and its "free exercise" (the free-exercise clause) applies to states and localities through the Fourteenth Amendment.

HISTORICAL BACKGROUND

The Establishment Clause

The **establishment clause** has been interpreted by the courts to mean that government may not favor one religion over another or support religion over no religion. (This position contrasts with that of a country such as England, where Anglicanism is the official, or "established," state religion, though no religion is prohibited.) The Supreme Court's interpretation of the establishment clause has been described as maintaining a "wall of separation" between church and state. The Court held in *Engel v. Vitale* (1962) that the establishment clause prohibits the reciting of prayers in public schools.[31] A year later the Court struck down Bible readings in public schools.[32]

Religion is a powerful force in American life, and the Supreme Court's ban on religious teaching in public school classrooms has evoked strong opposition. An Alabama law attempted to circumvent the prayer ruling by permitting public schools to set aside one minute each day for silent prayer or meditation. In 1985 the Court declared the law unconstitutional, ruling that "government must pursue a course of complete neutrality toward religion."[33] The Court in 2000 reaffirmed the ban by extending it to include organized student-led prayer at public school football games.[34]

establishment clause
The First Amendment provision stating that government may not favor one religion over another or favor religion over no religion, and prohibiting Congress from passing laws respecting the establishment of religion.

Media & Politics
Christian News Broadcasting

Until the 1930s, when the Great Depression altered the nation's course, religion was a powerful force in American politics. The Protestant-Catholic divide was embedded in the conflict between the major parties, and religious impulses inspired many of the great political movements, including the abolitionist and suffragist movements. The severe economic downturn that occurred during the 1930s shifted politics squarely toward economic issues, and the resulting party realignment blurred many long-standing religious splits.

Stirrings of a new politics of religion began in the 1960s, when the Supreme Court held that the First Amendment's ban on the establishment of religion precluded prayer and Bible readings in public schools. When the Supreme Court in 1973 declared that the right to privacy permitted a woman to choose abortion in the first trimester of pregnancy, religion once again took a place at the center of American politics.

This trend can be seen in the spread of Christian-format news broadcasting—news with a religious point of view, typically that of Christian fundamentalism. Christian broadcasting is one of the most rapidly growing forms of media and dominates some media markets in the South. There are now more than two thousand self-described Christian radio stations, double the level of a decade ago. Audience ratings for Christian radio have increased markedly. Although Christian programming is less evident on television, it can be found

there as well—most notably in the Pat Robertson–founded Christian Broadcasting Network. The network's main news program is Robertson's *700 Club*, a mix of news, interviews, and religious messages. Robertson's program attracts roughly one million viewers, which is a large audience by the standards of cable television.

Whether aired on radio or television, Christian news broadcasting differs from traditional news. Top stories are covered but are given a religious slant. In an interview on PBS's *The News Hour with Jim Lehrer*, Ed Sossen of KIXL, a Christian radio station in Austin, Texas, said: "We do the same kinds of things—traffic, news, weather, sports—that another radio station would give, we just do it from a Christian perspective and hopefully people find that comforting." Sossen commented about judicial appointment hearings: "[We don't advocate] fair, impartial Supreme Court justices. We want somebody who agrees with us." On the abortion issue, Christian news broadcasts side openly with the pro-life position. Marvin Olasky, a Christian news journalist who was interviewed on the same *News Hour* program as Sossen, said: "We won't try to balance a story between the abortionists and a pro-life person."

What's your awareness and opinion of Christian broadcasting? Have you listened often enough to have an opinion about whether its news programming, in addition to serving religious purposes, also meets people's information needs? Why do you think it does, or does not?

The Supreme Court also has banned religious displays on public property when the purpose of such a display is overtly religious and lacks a historical context. Because of the prominence of religion in American life, many public buildings sport religious symbolism. For instance, a statue of Moses holding the Ten Commandments stands in the rotunda of the Library of Congress building, which opened in 1897. Legal challenges to such displays are unlikely to succeed. In *Van Orden v. Perry* (2005), for example, the Supreme Court rejected a suit asking for the dismantling of a display of the Ten Commandments on a monument on the grounds of the Texas State Capitol. The Court noted that the display had been installed nearly a half-century earlier, had been paid for by a nonreligious group, and had not previously been the subject of dispute.[35] On the other hand, in *McCreary County v. American Civil Liberties Union* (2005), the Supreme Court struck down displays of the Ten Commandments on the walls of two Kentucky courthouses. The displays were recent and had initially hung by themselves on the courtroom walls. Only after county officials were sued did they mount a few historical displays alongside the religious ones. The Supreme Court concluded that the officials had religious purposes in mind when they erected the displays and thus had to remove them.[36]

The Supreme Court generally has taken a pragmatic approach to religious controversies, permitting some establishment activities while disallowing others. For instance, the Court has allowed states to pay for secular textbooks used in church-affiliated schools[37] but has not allowed them to pay part of the salaries of the teachers in such schools.[38] Such distinctions are based on judgments of whether government action involves "*excessive* entanglement with religion."[39] In allowing public funds to be used by religious schools for secular textbooks but not for teachers' salaries, the courts have indicated that, whereas it is relatively easy to determine whether the content of a particular textbook promotes religion, it would be much harder to determine whether a particular teacher was promoting religion in the classroom.[40]

In a key 2002 decision, however, the Supreme Court upheld an Ohio law that allows students in Cleveland's failing public schools to receive a tax-supported voucher to attend private or parochial school. The Court's majority argued in *Zelman v. Simmons-Harris* that the program did not violate the establishment clause because students had a choice between secular and religious education. Four members of the Court dissented sharply with the majority's reasoning. Justice Stevens said the ruling had removed a "brick from the wall that was once designed to separate religion from government."[41] A piece of the brick was restored in 2004 when the Court in *Locke v. Davey* held that publicly funded scholarships can be denied to students pursuing religious careers. At issue was a state of Washington scholarship program that excluded otherwise eligible students who were studying for the ministry. The state justified the exclusion on grounds that the use of public funds to educate ministers would involve it in the establishment of religion.[42]

The Free-Exercise Clause

The First and Fourteenth Amendments also prohibit government interference with the free exercise of religion. The idea underlying the **free-exercise clause** is clear: Americans are free to believe what they want. However, they are not always free to act on their beliefs. The courts have allowed government interference in the exercise of religious beliefs when such interference is the secondary result of an overriding social goal. An example is the legal protection of children with life-threatening illnesses whose parents refuse to permit medical treatment on religious grounds. A court may order that such children be given medical assistance because the social good of saving their lives overrides their parents' free-exercise rights.

free-exercise clause
A First Amendment provision that prohibits the government from interfering with the practice of religion or prohibiting the free exercise of religion.

The First Amendment's protection of free expression includes religious freedom, which has led the courts to hold that government cannot in most instances promote or interfere with religious practices.

In a few circumstances, the free-exercise clause has been the basis for allowing certain individuals to disobey otherwise valid laws. The Supreme Court ruled in 1972 that Amish families did not have to abide by a state law requiring children to attend school until they were sixteen years of age because the law conflicted with the centuries-old Amish religious practice of having children leave school and begin work at an early age.[43] In upholding free exercise in such cases, the Court may be said to have violated the establishment clause by granting preferred treatment to people who hold a particular religious belief. The Court has recognized the potential conflict between the free-exercise and establishment clauses and, as in other such situations, has tried to strike a reasonable balance between the competing claims.

When the free-exercise and establishment clauses cannot be balanced, the Supreme Court has been forced to choose. In 1987 the Court overturned a Louisiana law requiring that creationism (the Bible's account of how the world was created) be taught along with the theory of evolution in public school science courses. Creationism, the Court concluded, is a religious doctrine, not a scientific theory; thus, its inclusion in public school curricula violates the establishment clause by promoting a religious belief.[44] In 2005, a federal judge barred a Pennsylvania public school district from requiring that intelligent design (the belief that God has guided evolution) be taught in science classes along with evolution. The judge concluded that the theory of intelligent design is a disguised version of creationism, has no basis in science, and violates the First Amendment's establishment clause. Some religious groups argue that such decisions trample on the free exercise of religion because children are required to study the theory of evolution even though it conflicts with their beliefs about creation.

THE RIGHT OF PRIVACY

Until the 1960s, Americans' constitutional rights were confined largely to those listed in the Bill of Rights. This situation prevailed despite the Ninth Amendment, which reads "The enumeration in the Constitution, of certain rights, shall not be construed to deny or disparage others retained by the people." In 1965, however, the Supreme Court added to the list of individual rights, declaring that Americans have "a right of privacy." This judgment arose from the case of *Griswold v. Connecticut*, which challenged a state law prohibiting the use of birth control devices, even by married couples. The Supreme Court struck down the statute, concluding that a state had no business interfering with a married couple's decision regarding contraception. The Court did not invoke the Ninth Amendment but reasoned instead that the freedoms in the Bill of Rights imply an underlying right of privacy. The Court held that individuals have a "zone of [personal] privacy" that government cannot lawfully infringe upon.[45]

Abortion

The right of privacy was the basis for the Supreme Court's ruling in *Roe v. Wade* (1973), which gave women full freedom to choose abortion during the first three months of pregnancy.[46] In overturning a Texas law banning abortion except to save the life of the mother, the Court said that the right to privacy is "broad enough to encompass a woman's decision whether or not to terminate her pregnancy."

After *Roe*, antiabortion activists sought to reverse the Court's ruling. Attempts at a constitutional amendment that would ban abortions were unsuccessful, which prompted abortion foes to seek other ways to restrict the

Abortion rights activists demonstrate outside the Supreme Court while the justices inside hear arguments on Pennsylvania's controversial abortion law. By a 5-4 vote, the Court narrowly reaffirmed the principle that a woman has the right to choose abortion during the early months of pregnancy.

practice. They campaigned successfully to prohibit the use of government funds to pay for abortions for poor women. Then, in *Webster v. Reproductive Health Services* (1989), the Supreme Court upheld a Missouri law that prohibits abortions from being performed in Missouri's public hospitals and by its public employees.[47]

The *Webster* decision was followed in 1992 by the Pennsylvania abortion case *Planned Parenthood v. Casey*, which antiabortion advocates had hoped would reverse the *Roe* precedent. Instead, by a 5-4 margin, the Supreme Court upheld the principle that a woman has a right to abortion in the earliest months of pregnancy. The Court said that "the essential holding of *Roe v. Wade* should be retained and once again reaffirmed."[48]

However, the Court also said that a state can impose regulations that do not place an "undue burden" on women seeking an abortion. In this vein, the Court upheld a provision of the Pennsylvania law that requires a minor to have parental or judicial consent before obtaining an abortion. But the Court applied its "undue burden" standard in 2006 to strike down by unanimous vote a New Hampshire law that had no medical emergency exception to its parental-consent requirement.[49] However, the question of what constitutes a medical emergency is not one on which the Supreme Court's justices agree. In *Stenberg v. Carhart* (2000), the Court invalidated a Nebraska law that prohibited so-called partial-birth abortion (in which the fetus's life is terminated during delivery) even if the mother's life or health was in danger.[50] The Court's majority said that the procedure is sometimes the most appropriate way to protect the mother's health. However, the case was decided by a narrow 5-4 margin, which prompted congressional Republicans in 2003 to pass a federal law banning partial-birth abortion and holding doctors criminally liable if they perform the procedure even when the woman's health is at risk. In 2006, the Supreme Court accepted for review two cases where the federal law on partial-birth abortions was at issue. The fact that Justice Sandra Day O'Connor, the swing vote in the Nebraska case, had since been replaced on the Supreme Court by the more conservative Samuel Alito led some observers to speculate that the Court was likely to reverse its position on partial-birth abortion.

Sexual Relations Among Consenting Adults

Although it was widely said at the time that the Supreme Court's 1965 *Griswold* ruling on contraceptive use took "government out of people's bedrooms," a clear exception remained. All states prohibited sexual relations between consenting adults of the same sex. A number of states eliminated this prohibition over the next two decades, and others stopped enforcing it. Nevertheless, in a 1986 Georgia case, *Bowers v. Hardwick*, the Supreme Court held that the right of privacy did not extend to homosexual acts among consenting adults.[51]

In 2003, however, the Court reversed itself and in the process struck down the sodomy laws of the thirteen states that still had them. The ruling came in response to a Texas law prohibiting consensual sex between adults of the same sex. In *Lawrence v. Texas*, the Court in a 6-3 vote concluded that the Texas sodomy law violated privacy rights protected by the due process clause of the Fourteenth Amendment. The Court said: "The petitioners are entitled to respect for their private lives. The State cannot demean their existence or control their destiny by making their private sexual conduct a crime."[52] The decision was hailed by gay and lesbian rights groups but condemned by some religious leaders, who said that it would open the door to same-sex marriage (see Chapter 5).

The Continuing Issue of Privacy Rights

The right of privacy is a broad issue that extends into many areas, including but not limited to personal medical and financial records. In most of these areas, the "zone of privacy" that is constitutionally protected has yet to be defined and likely will be subject to adjustment as technology and lifestyles change. The Supreme Court undoubtedly will extend privacy protection into new areas and deny it in others, as it did with the issue of "the right to die." In a 1997 case involving a Washington state law that prohibited physician-assisted suicide, the Court held that "liberty" in the Fourteenth Amendment does not include the constitutional right to doctor-assisted suicide.[53] At the same time, the Court hinted

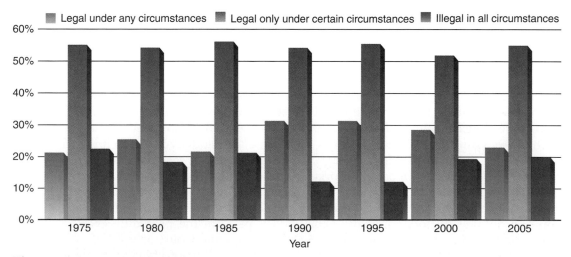

Figure 4–1

Americans' Opinions on Abortion
Since abortion was judged a constitutional right in 1973, public opinion on the issue has not changed greatly.
Source: Gallup polls, various dates.

that states have the authority to permit physician-assisted suicide if they should decide to do so. Oregon has such a law, which the Court upheld in a 2005 ruling (see Chapter 3).

Privacy questions are among the most contentious in American politics because of the moral issues they raise. The abortion issue, for example, has provoked intense debate for more than three decades. The American public is divided on the issue (see Figure 4–1), and there are many activists on both sides. As with other rights, the abortion issue is not only, or even primarily, fought out in the courts. Abortion opponents have waged demonstrations outside clinics in an effort to stop the practice. Some of these protests have erupted in violent acts against women trying to enter the clinics. In 1994, Congress passed a law making it illegal to block the entrance to abortion clinics or otherwise prevent people from entering. (The Supreme Court upheld the law, concluding that it regulated abortion protesters' actions as opposed to their words and thus did not violate their right to free speech.)[54]

RIGHTS OF PERSONS ACCUSED OF CRIMES

Due process refers to legal protections that have been established to preserve the rights of individuals. The most significant form of these protections is **procedural due process;** the term refers primarily to procedures that authorities must follow before a person can legitimately be punished for an offense.

The U.S. Constitution provides for several procedures designed to protect a person from wrongful arrest, conviction, and punishment. According to Article I, Section 9, any person taken into police custody is entitled to seek a writ of habeas corpus, which requires law enforcement officials to bring the suspect into court and to specify the legal reason for the detention. The Fifth and Fourteenth Amendments provide generally that no person can be deprived of life, liberty, or property without due process of law. Specific procedural protections for the accused are spelled out in the Fourth, Fifth, Sixth, and Eighth Amendments:

- *The Fourth Amendment* forbids the police to conduct searches and seizures unless they have probable cause to believe that a crime has been committed.
- *The Fifth Amendment* protects against double jeopardy (being prosecuted twice for the same offense); self-incrimination (being compelled to testify against oneself); indictment for a crime except through grand jury proceedings; and loss of life, liberty, and property without due process of law.
- *The Sixth Amendment* provides the right to have legal counsel, to confront witnesses, to receive a speedy trial, and to have a trial by jury in criminal proceedings.
- *The Eighth Amendment* protects against excessive bail or fines and prohibits the infliction of cruel and unusual punishment on those convicted of crimes.

These protections have been subject to interpretation. The Sixth Amendment, for example, provides the right to have legal counsel. But what if a person cannot afford a lawyer? For most of the nation's history, poor people had virtually no choice but to act as their own attorney. They had a right to a lawyer but had no money with which to hire one. Today, if a person is accused of a serious crime and cannot afford a lawyer, the government must provide one. This change came about not through a constitutional amendment but through Supreme Court rulings that expanded the protections provided by the Sixth Amendment.

procedural due process
The constitutional requirement that government must follow proper legal procedures before a person can be legitimately punished for an alleged offense.

Political Culture
Procedural Due Process and Personal Liberty

"The history of liberty has largely been the history of the observance of procedural guarantees," said Justice Felix Frankfurter in *McNabb v. United States* (1943). No system of justice is foolproof. Even in the most careful systems, innocent people have been wrongly accused, convicted, and punished with imprisonment or death. But the scrupulous application of procedural safeguards, such as a defendant's right to legal counsel, greatly increases the likelihood that justice will prevail.

However, as past police scandals in Dallas, Los Angeles, New York, and several other cities would indicate, constitutional guarantees are no assurance that people will be treated justly. In Dallas, dozens of people, many of them Hispanics,

were accused of peddling drugs after having been set up by police officers, who planted fake evidence while arresting them. Some were held in jail for months before being cleared of wrongdoing. Wrongful arrests and cooked-up evidence are not by any means the norm in U.S. law enforcement, but they occur with enough frequency to be a cause of concern to anyone committed to the principle of legal justice.

What do you think can be done to safeguard individuals' due process rights? Do you share the view of social theorists who say that when procedural due process is violated, the fault lies more with a public that is willing to tolerate abuses than with the few errant law enforcement officials who commit these abuses?

Selective Incorporation of Procedural Rights

For most of the nation's history, the procedural protections in the Bill of Rights applied only to the actions of the national government. States in their criminal proceedings were not bound by them. There were limited exceptions, such as a 1932 Supreme Court ruling that a defendant charged in a state court with a crime carrying the death penalty had to be provided with an attorney.[55] Nevertheless, even as the Court was moving to protect free-expression rights from state action in the 1930s, it held back on doing the same for the rights of the accused. The Court claimed that free-expression rights were more deserving of federal protection because they are "the indispensable condition of nearly every other form of freedom."[56]

This view changed abruptly in the 1960s when the Supreme Court broadly required states also to safeguard procedural rights. Changes in public education and communication had made Americans more aware of their rights, and the civil rights movement dramatized the fact that rights were administered unequally: the poor and minority group members had many fewer rights in practice than did other Americans. In response, the Supreme Court in the 1960s "incorporated" Bill of Rights protections for the accused by ruling that these rights are protected against state action by the Fourteenth Amendment's guarantee of due process of law (see Table 4–3).

The selective incorporation process began with *Mapp v. Ohio* (1961). Dollree Mapp's home had been entered by Cleveland police, who, though they failed to find what they were seeking, happened to discover some pornographic material. Mapp's conviction for its possession was overturned by the Supreme Court on the grounds that she had been subjected to unreasonable search and seizure.[57] The Court ruled that illegally obtained evidence could not be used in state courts. Two years later, the Court's decision in *Gideon v. Wainwright* (1963) required the states to furnish attorneys for poor defendants in all felony cases. Clarence Gideon, an indigent drifter, had been convicted and sentenced to prison in Florida for breaking into a poolroom. He successfully appealed on the grounds that he had been denied due process because he could not afford to pay an attorney.[58] During the 1960s, the Court also ruled that defendants in state criminal proceedings cannot be compelled to testify against themselves,[59] have the right to

| TABLE 4–3 | **Selective Incorporation of Rights of the Accused** In the 1960s, the Supreme Court selectively incorporated the fair-trial provisions of the Fourth through Eighth Amendments into the Fourteenth Amendment so that these rights would be protected from infringement by the states. |

SUPREME COURT CASE	YEAR	CONSTITUTIONAL RIGHT (AMENDMENT) AT ISSUE
Mapp v. Ohio	1961	Unreasonable search and seizure (Fourth)
Robinson v. California	1962	Cruel and unusual punishment (Eighth)
Gideon v. Wainwright	1963	Right to counsel (Sixth)
Malloy v. Hogan	1964	Self-incrimination (Fifth)
Pointer v. Texas	1965	Right to confront witnesses (Sixth)
Miranda v. Arizona	1966	Self-incrimination and right to counsel (Fifth and Sixth)
Klopfer v. North Carolina	1967	Speedy trial (Sixth)
Duncan v. Louisiana	1968	Jury trial in criminal cases (Sixth)
Benton v. Maryland	1969	Double jeopardy (Fifth)

remain silent and to have legal counsel when arrested,[60] have the right to confront witnesses who testify against them,[61] must be granted a speedy trial,[62] have the right to a jury trial,[63] and cannot be subjected to double jeopardy.[64] The best known of these cases is *Miranda v. Arizona* (1966), which arose when Ernesto Miranda confessed during police interrogation to kidnap and rape. The Supreme Court overturned his conviction on the grounds that he had not been informed of his rights to remain silent and to have legal assistance. This ruling led to the development of the "Miranda warning" that police are now required to read to suspects: "You have the right to remain silent. . . . Anything you say can and will be used against you in a court of law. . . . You have the right to an attorney." (Miranda was subsequently retried and convicted on the basis of evidence other than his confession.)

In a 2000 case, *Dickerson v. United States,* the Supreme Court reaffirmed the *Miranda* decision, saying that it was an established "constitutional rule" that could not be eliminated by ordinary legislation.[65] The Court further strengthened the Miranda precedent in *Missouri v. Siebert* (2004). This ruling came in response to a police strategy of questioning suspects first and then reading them their Miranda rights, followed by a second round of questioning. In such instances, suspects who admitted wrongdoing in the first round of questioning tended also to do so in the second round. The Court concluded that the strategy was intended "to undermine the Miranda warnings" and was not permissible.[66]

Limits on Defendants' Rights

In the courtroom, the rights to counsel, to confront witnesses, and to remain silent are of paramount importance. Before the courtroom phase in a criminal proceeding, the main protection is the Fourth Amendment's restriction on illegal search and seizure. This restriction holds that police must have suspicion of wrongdoing (and, sometimes, a judge's permission) before they can search your person, your car, or your residence, although involvement in an offense (such as driving faster than the speed limit) can lead to a permissible search that uncovers wrongdoing of another kind (such as drug possession). Without search and seizure protection, individuals could be subject to unrestricted police harassment and intimidation, characteristics of a totalitarian state, not a free society.

The Fourth Amendment, however, does not provide blanket protection against searches. In 1990, for example, the Supreme Court held that police roadblocks to check drivers for signs of intoxication are legal as long as the action is systematic and not arbitrary (for example, stopping only young drivers would be unconstitutional). The Court justified its decision by saying that roadblocks serve a public safety purpose.[67] However, the Court does not allow the same types of roadblocks to check for drugs. In *Indianapolis v. Edmund* (2001), the Court held that narcotics roadblocks, because they serve a general law enforcement purpose rather than one specific to highway safety, violate the Fourth Amendment's requirement that police have suspicion of wrongdoing before they can search an individual's auto.[68] The Court has also held that police may not use a thermal-imaging device to detect the presence in a home of heat sources that might be related to the production of illegal drugs. Police cannot enter a home without a warrant based on suspicion of wrongdoing, and the Court said that searches based on modern technology must meet the same standard.[69]

The Fourth Amendment protects individuals in their persons as well as in their homes and vehicles. In *Ferguson v. Charleston* (2001), for example, the Court held that patients in public hospitals cannot be forced to take a test for illegal drugs if the purpose is to turn over to the police those patients who test positive. Such action, said the Court, constitutes an illegal search of the person.[70] The rule is somewhat different when it comes to students in public schools. Authorities have more latitude in this situation. For example, the Court in *Board of Education of Independent School District No. 92 of Pottawatomie County v. Earls* (2002) held that random drug testing of high school students involved in extracurricular activities does not violate the ban on unreasonable searches.[71]

The Exclusionary Rule

exclusionary rule

The legal principle that government is prohibited from using in trials evidence that was obtained by unconstitutional means (for example, illegal search and seizure).

In general, the Supreme Court in recent decades has reduced but not eliminated the protections afforded to the accused by *Mapp* and other 1960s rulings. The 1960s Court was dominated by liberal justices who saw fit to expand individual rights. Turnover in the Court's membership moved it in a conservative direction and toward positions that give law enforcement officials more leeway in their handling of criminal suspects. The change can be seen in the application of the **exclusionary rule,** which bars the use in trials of evidence obtained in violation of a person's constitutional rights. The rule was formulated in a 1914 Supreme Court decision,[72] and its application was expanded in federal cases. The *Mapp* decision extended the exclusionary rule to state trial proceedings. Subsequent decisions of the Supreme Court broadened its application to the point where almost any type of illegally obtained evidence was considered inadmissible in a criminal trial. In the 1980s, the Supreme Court reversed the trend by placing restrictions on the rule's application, concluding that illegally obtained evidence can sometimes be admitted in trials if the procedural errors are inadvertent or if the prosecution can show that it would have discovered the evidence anyway.[73]

Recent decisions have also lowered the standard that must be met for a lawful search and seizure to occur. In the 1960s, the Court developed the principle that police had to have a solid basis ("probable cause") for believing that an individual was involved in a specific crime before they could stop a person and engage in search-and-seizure activity. This principle has been modified, as illustrated by *Whren v. United States* (1996), which upheld the conviction of an individual who had been found with drugs in the front seat of his car. The police had no evidence (no "probable cause") indicating that drugs were in the car, but they suspected that the driver was involved in drug dealing and used a minor traffic infraction as a pretext to stop and check him. The Supreme Court accepted defense arguments that the police had no clear evidence to back their suspicion, that the traffic infraction was not the real reason the individual was stopped, and that police usually do not stop a person for the infraction in question (turning a corner without signaling). However, the Court concluded that the officers' motive was irrelevant, as long as an officer in some situations might reasonably stop a car for the infraction that occurred. Thus, the stop-and-search action was deemed to meet the Fourth Amendment's reasonableness standard.[74]

In general, the Court's goal has been to weaken the exclusionary rule without giving police unduly broad discretion. However, this objective could be changing. The Court appears to be in the process of narrowing the exclusionary rule to the point where it would apply only to the most outrageous instances of police misconduct. In *Hudson v. Michigan* (2006), the Court overthrew "the knock-and-announce" rule, which began in thirteenth century England. Under this rule, police with a search warrant are supposed to knock on the door and announce their presence before entering a suspect's house. Detroit police did not do so when they entered the home of Booker Hudson, and he sought to have his conviction for drug possession tossed out on grounds that the evidence was obtained illegally. In rejecting his position in a 5-4 ruling, the Court's majority argued that the knock-and-announce rule is no longer necessary because the police today are more professional and because individuals whose homes or persons are illegally searched can bring civil suit against the police. In a dissenting opinion, Justice Stephen Breyer ridiculed this idea, saying that the Court's majority could not "cite a single reported case" in which someone whose home had been barged into by police had been awarded damages worth noting.[75]

Habeas Corpus Appeals

Legal protection for the accused has also been reduced by a restriction on habeas corpus appeals to federal courts by individuals who have been convicted of crimes in state courts. (Habeas corpus gives defendants access to federal courts in order to argue that their rights under the Constitution of the United States were violated when they were convicted in a state court.) A 1960s Supreme Court precedent gave prisoners the right to have their appeal heard in federal court unless they had "deliberately bypassed" the opportunity to first make their appeal in state courts.[76]

This precedent was overturned in 1992 when the Court held that inmates can lose the right to a federal hearing even if a lawyer's mistake is the reason they failed to first present their appeal properly in state courts.[77] Another significant habeas corpus setback for inmates occurred in 1993 when the Supreme Court held that federal courts cannot overturn a state conviction on the basis of constitutional error unless the prisoner can demonstrate that the error contributed to the conviction.[78] Previously, the burden of proof had been on the state: it had to prove that the error did not affect the case's outcome. In *Felker v. Turpin* (1996), the Court upheld a recently enacted federal law that prohibited in most cases federal habeas corpus appeals by state prison inmates who have already filed one such appeal.[79]

Through these decisions, the Supreme Court has sought to prevent frivolous and multiple federal court appeals. State prisoners had used habeas corpus appeals to contest even small issues, and some inmates—particularly those on death row—had filed appeal after appeal. An effect is the clogging of the federal courts and a delay in hearing other cases. A majority of Supreme Court justices concluded that a more restrictive policy toward these appeals is required. They held that it is fair to ask inmates to first pursue their options in state courts and then, except in unusual cases,[80] to confine themselves to a single federal appeal. At the same time, the Court has taken steps to ensure that meritorious appeals are heard. In two 2003 cases, for example, the Court expressed concern that lower federal courts in some instances were not being sufficiently careful in identifying legitimate appeals.[81]

Despite modifications of the appeal process and the exclusionary rule, there has not been a return to the lower procedural standards that prevailed before the 1960s. Many of the vital precedents established in that decade remain in effect, including the most important one of all: the principle that procedural protections guaranteed to the accused by the Bill of Rights must be observed by the states as well as by the federal government.

WWW.MHHE.COM/PATTERSONTAD8

Crime, Punishment, and Police Practices

The theory and practice of procedural guarantees are often two quite different things, as Adrienne Cureton discovered on January 2, 1995. She is a plainclothes police officer who, with a uniformed partner, was called to the scene of a domestic dispute. A struggle ensued, and her partner radioed for help. When the officers arrived, Cureton and her partner had already handcuffed the homeowner. The officers barged in and mistook Cureton, an African American, for the other person involved in the dispute. They grabbed her by the collar, dragged her by the hair onto the porch, and clubbed her repeatedly with flashlights, despite her screams that she was a police officer.[82]

There is no reliable estimate of how often Americans' rights are violated in practice, but infringements of one sort or another are commonplace. Minorities and the poor are the more likely victims. *Racial profiling* (the assumption that certain groups are more likely to commit particular crimes) is a common police practice and results in the unequal treatment of minorities. An American Civil Liberties Union study found that 80 percent of the motorists stopped and searched by Maryland State Police on Interstate 95 were minorities and only 20 percent were white, despite the fact that white motorists constituted 75 percent of all drivers and were just as likely as minority motorists to violate the traffic laws. A 1999 report by the New Jersey Attorney General's Office revealed a similar pattern in that state. African Americans refer mockingly to a traffic infraction they call DWB—"driving while black."

Another issue of justice in America is whether adherence to proper legal procedures produces reasonable outcomes. The Eighth Amendment prohibits "cruel and unusual punishment" of those convicted of crime, but judgments in this area are subjective. Although the Supreme Court has ordered officials to relieve inmate overcrowding and to improve prison facilities in a few instances, it has concluded that inmates cannot sue over prison conditions unless prison officials show "deliberate indifference" to the conditions.[83] The severity of a sentence can also be an Eighth Amendment issue. The Supreme Court in 1991 upheld a conviction under a Michigan law that mandated life imprisonment without parole for a nonviolent first offense involving 1.5 pounds of cocaine.[84] More recently, the Court upheld a conviction under California's "three strikes and you're out" law that sent a twice previously convicted felon to prison for life without parole for shoplifting videotapes worth $100.[85] Although many people would regard such penalties as too severe, the Supreme Court has seldom invoked the Eighth Amendment's prohibition on cruel and unusual punishment. The Court has allowed Congress and the state legislatures to decide

States in the Nation

The Death Penalty

Most crimes and punishments in the United States are defined by state law. Nowhere is this more obvious than in the application of the death penalty. Some states prohibit it, and others apply it liberally. Texas, Florida, and Virginia are far and away the leaders in its application. Roughly a third of all executions in the past quarter-century have taken place in Texas alone.

Q: What do many of the states that prohibit capital punishment have in common?

A: States without the death penalty are concentrated in the North. Most of these states are relatively affluent, rank high on indicators of educational attainment, and have a small minority-group population.

Number of executions, 1976–2006

- More than 10
- 10 or fewer
- Have statute, no executions
- No death penalty statute

Source: Death Penalty Information Center, 2006.

the appropriate penalties for crime, believing that it lacks the capacity to devise consistent rules that would differentiate between acceptable and unacceptable levels of punishment.

However, the Supreme Court in two recent decisions did invoke the Eighth Amendment to narrow the use of the death penalty. In *Atkins v. Virginia* (2002), the Court outlawed the death penalty for the mentally retarded, saying that it constitutes "cruel and unusual punishment." The Court noted that nearly all countries in the world prohibit such executions.[86] In 2005, the Court also cited global practices in declaring it unconstitutional to put juveniles to death. The Court's majority wrote in *Roper v. Simmons* that "the United States is the only country in the world that [gave] official sanction to the juvenile death penalty."[87]

How the United States Compares
Law and Order

Individual rights are a cornerstone of the American governing system and receive strong protection from the courts. The government's ability to restrict free expression is severely limited, and the individual's right to a fair trial is protected through elaborate due process guarantees.

According to Amnesty International, a watchdog group that monitors human rights achievements and violations around the world, the United States has a good record in terms of its constitutional protection of civil liberties. A number of countries in Asia, Africa, Eastern Europe, the Middle East, and Latin America are accused by Amnesty International of "appalling human rights catastrophes" that include the execution, torture, and rape of persons accused of crime or regarded as opponents of the government. Amnesty International does not rank the United States as high as the countries of northern Europe in terms of respect for human rights. Among other problems, Amnesty International faults police in the United States for "excessive force" in their treatment of prisoners and faults U.S. immigration officials for the forcible return of asylum seekers to their country of origin without granting them a hearing.

Although human rights groups admire America's elaborate procedural protections for those accused of crime, they are critical of its sentencing and incarceration policies. The United States is the world leader in the number of people it places behind bars and in the length of sentences for various categories of crime. Defenders of U.S. policy say that although overall crime rates are about the same here as elsewhere, there is more violent crime in America. Critics reply that although the murder rate is high in the United States, it is also true that more than half of the people in prison were convicted of nonviolent offenses, such as drug use or a crime against property. Whatever the reasons, the United States is rivaled only by Russia in the proportion of its people who are in prison.

Incarceration rates (per 100,000 inhabitants)

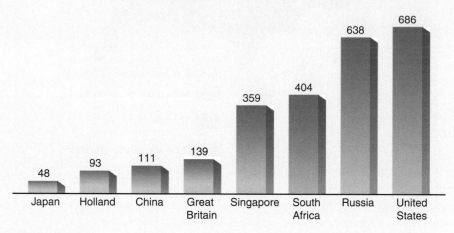

Source: The Sentencing Project, 2004.

Recently, the Supreme Court left open an Eighth Amendment challenge to how states carry out executions.[88] At issue is the mix of chemicals used in lethal injection. Studies indicate that the current mix can cause excruciating pain before death occurs. Visible signs of the prisoner's pain are masked by a paralyzing drug that is part of the mix. If this challenge is upheld, states could still use lethal injection to execute prisoners but would have to devise an acceptable chemical mix before being permitted to do so.

Sentencing issues have also arisen in the context of the Sixth Amendment's guarantee of trial by jury. Until recently, the courts applied this right only to the question of a defendant's guilt or innocence and not also to sentencing. However, in *Ring v. Arizona* (2002), the Supreme Court held that the right of jury trial prohibits a judge from deciding whether the death penalty will be imposed in a capital case. The Court ruled that only a jury could make this determination.[89] This principle was expanded in *Blakley v. Washington* (2004) to include sentences that are longer than the law prescribes. The Supreme Court held that the Sixth Amendment requires that a jury decide whether aggravating factors, such as the cruelty of a crime, justify a harsh sentence.[90] The *Blakley* ruling was widely criticized on grounds that it would overburden the legal system by requiring a second jury trial whenever the prosecution seeks to imprison someone for an unusually long period.

However, the issue of punishment is primarily a political one as opposed to a judicial one. The pressure for harsher sentences has come mainly from elected officials rather than from judges. Being "tough on crime" is a popular political stance, and Congress and most state legislatures during the past two decades have enacted stiffer penalties for crimes while also limiting the ability of judges to reduce the penalties, as in cases where the defendant has no prior criminal record. As a result, the number of federal and state prisoners has more than doubled since 1990. In fact, the United States has the largest per capita prison population in the world (see "How the United States Compares") Russia is the only country that is even close to the United States in terms of the number of its people who are imprisoned. On a per capita basis, the United States has five times as many of people in jail as Great Britain does.

As the prison population has increased and sentencing has become more severe, debate over America's criminal justice system has intensified. The severest criticisms have been directed at the death penalty and the incarceration of nonviolent drug users. In these areas, U.S. policies are at odds with those of other industrialized countries, nearly all of which prohibit the death penalty and rely more heavily on treatment programs than on prisons in dealing with drug offenders. Critics also cite studies showing that minorities and the poor receive harsher sentences than middle-class white persons convicted of comparable crimes.

RIGHTS AND THE WAR ON TERRORISM

In time of war, the courts have allowed government to exercise authority that would not be permitted in peacetime. After the Japanese attack on Pearl Harbor in 1941, for example, President Franklin D. Roosevelt ordered the forced relocation of tens of thousands of Japanese Americans living on the West Coast to detention camps in Arizona, Utah, and other inland locations. Congress endorsed the policy, and the Supreme Court upheld it.[91] Another Supreme Court ruling during World War II denied a U.S. citizen arrested as a Nazi collaborator a court trial after the government decided to try him before a military tribunal.[92]

After the terrorist attacks of September 11, 2001, precedents such as these were invoked by the Bush administration, which declared that customary legal protections must be altered if the war on terrorism was to be waged successfully. "[There is] the necessity for certain types of action . . . when we are in danger," said Solicitor General Theodore Olson.

Detention of Enemy Combatants

The Bush administration soon announced its policy for handling "enemy combatants"—individuals judged to be engaged in terrorism directed at the United States. They were to be detained without access to lawyers or family

In the aftermath of the September 11, 2001, terrorist attacks, Arab Americans were subjected to ethnic profiling at airports and other locations. Shown here is an Arab American protesting the practice of profiling.

members until the president chose to release them. The Administration also claimed the authority to round up and hold in secret any individuals living in the United States who were suspected of having terrorist ties. Hundreds of individuals, nearly all of Middle Eastern descent, were taken into custody. Although nearly all of them were eventually cleared of wrongdoing by the FBI, some were held for months and others were deported for immigration violations. A lawsuit forcing the government to explain why these individuals were detained was dismissed by the Supreme Court; the Bush administration claimed that release of the information would divulge the methods by which U.S. agencies identify suspected terrorists.[93]

As the war on terrorism shifted into military operations in Afghanistan and then Iraq, the United States had a need to detain and interrogate the enemy soldiers it captured. Some prisoners were sent to a detention facility created at the U.S. Naval Base at Guantanamo Bay on the tip of Cuba. Others were imprisoned in Afghanistan, Iraq, and elsewhere. Requests by lawyers and international agencies like the Red Cross to see the detainees were denied or strictly limited. President Bush claimed that the detainees were enemy combatants rather than prisoners of war and accordingly did not have the legal protections provided either by U.S. law or by the Geneva Convention. President Bush did not publicly announce that the prisoners would be subject to harsh interrogation, but such treatment was practiced at Abu Ghraib prison in Iraq and at Guantanamo Bay and was alleged to have taken place at secret CIA prisons in undisclosed locations.

In 2004, the Supreme Court issued its first ruling on these various practices, holding that the Guantanamo Bay detainees had the right to challenge their detention in court. The Court reasoned that the naval base, though in Cuba, is on land leased to the United States, and therefore under the jurisdiction of U.S. courts.[94] In a second 2004 case (*Hamdi v. Rumsfeld*), the Court ruled that one of the Guantanamo Bay detainees, who was a U.S. citizen by virtue of being born in the United States though he was raised in Saudi Arabia, had the right to be heard in U.S. courts. The Court said that, though the government could hold the prisoner as an enemy combatant, he had the constitutional right to use the U.S. courts to challenge his detention. The Court said that a citizen was entitled to a "fair opportunity to rebut the government's factual assertions before a neutral [judge]" and that "essential constitutional promises may not be eroded" because of the security situation. The Court went on to say: "As critical as the government's interest may be in detaining those who actually pose an immediate threat to the national security of the United States during ongoing international conflict, history and common sense teach us that an unchecked system of detention carries the potential to become a means of oppression and abuse of others who do not present that sort of threat."[95]

Two years later, the Court issued its sharpest rebuke yet of the Bush administration's detention policies. In a ruling almost unprecedented in its challenge to a president's war-time authority, the Court held that the detainees were protected both by the U.S. Uniform Code of Military Justice and by the Geneva

The war on terrorism has raised important civil liberties issues, including the president's authority to conduct wiretaps without a judicial warrant and to deny enemy combatants the protection of U.S. law and the Geneva Convention. Although the courts have deferred in some cases to President Bush's war-time authority as commander-in-chief, the courts have also struck down some of his policies on constitutional grounds. Shown here are college students in Washington, D.C., turning their backs on Attorney General Alberto Gonzales as he speaks in defense of the Bush administration's wiretapping policies. The words on their sign were uttered by Benjamin Franklin during the American Revolution.

Convention. At issue was the Bush administration's use of secret military tribunals to try detainees. In these trials, detainees were to have no right to see the evidence against them and would not necessarily be allowed to gather evidence or call witnesses that might exonerate them. The Court held in *Hamdan v. Rumsfeld* (2006) that the tribunals were unlawful. In its opinion, the Court wrote that "the Executive is bound to comply with the Rule of Law. . . ."[96] In essence, the Court said that a war-time president does not have blanket authority to ignore U.S. and international law. In response to the ruling, President Bush negotiated legislation, which Congress enacted in 2006, that grants legal protections to detainees held by the U.S. military. However, at Bush's insistence, the legislation excluded CIA interrogations conducted overseas, an exception that the Supreme Court could conceivably rule upon in the future.

Surveillance of Suspected Terrorists

After the September 11 terrorist attacks and in response to the Bush administration's request for expanded surveillance powers, Congress passed the USA Patriot Act, which lowered the standard for judicial approval of wiretapping when terrorist activity was at issue. The law also allowed information from intelligence surveillance to be shared with criminal investigators when evidence was found of criminal activity unrelated to terrorism. Previously, such information could be shared only if it was obtained by the stricter standards that officials must follow in criminal investigations. The new law also gave government increased authority to examine medical, financial, and student records and allowed the government, in specified situations, to secretly search homes and offices.

Critics claimed that the USA Patriot Act was at odds with America's constitutional tradition. "No one is questioning the government's authority to prosecute spies and terrorists," said Ann Beeson of the American Civil Liberties Union, "but we do not need to waive the Constitution to do so."[97] For their part, officials said that the September 11 attacks had forced a change in the rules. "The danger that darkened the United States and the civilized world on September 11 did not pass with the atrocities committed that day," said Attorney General John Ashcroft.

The Bush administration promised to act with restraint in its exercise of the new powers, and congressional oversight committees were generally satisfied with its actions until the *New York Times* revealed in late 2005 that President Bush without judicial approval had secretly authorized the National Security Agency (NSA) to wiretap international phone calls and email messages originating in the United States. Such wiretaps are expressly prohibited by the Foreign Intelligence Surveillance Act (FISA) of 1978. Bush rejected allegations that he had broken the law, saying that he had acted legally under his war-time powers as commander-in-chief and under authority implicitly granted him by the Patriot Act.

The question of governing authority—whether the Bush administration's NSA surveillance activities are within or outside the law—is only now being heard in lower courts. The first such ruling occurred in August of 2006; the district judge in that case held that President Bush had exceeded his statutory and constitutional authority in ordering wiretaps without a judicial warrant. Most analysts believe, however, that a definitive judgment on this issue will not come until the Supreme Court itself decides the issue or unless the White House persuades Congress to change the laws governing intelligence-gathering wiretaps.

Other surveillance issues are certain to be reviewed by the judiciary in the coming years. Lower court decisions on various aspects of the USA Patriot Act so far have been mixed. One ruling held, for example, that crime-related information obtained in domestic intelligence operations could be shared with law-enforcement officials. However, another ruling held that government without judicial consent cannot require Internet or telephone companies to turn over customer records and then block them from revealing publicly that they have done so.[98]

THE COURTS AND A FREE SOCIETY

The United States was founded on the idea that individuals have an innate right to liberty—to speak their minds, to worship freely, to be secure in their homes and persons, to be assured of a fair trial. Americans embrace these freedoms in the abstract. In particular situations, however, many Americans would prefer policies that diminish the freedom of those who hold minority views or look and act differently than most Americans. After the September 11 terrorist attacks, for example, polls indicated that a third of Americans felt Arab Americans should be placed under special surveillance and that half felt Arab Americans should be required to carry special identification cards. Two fifths said they would ban college lectures by speakers who argue that aspects of U.S. foreign policy have contributed to terrorist activity.

The judiciary is not isolated from the public mood. Judges inevitably are required to balance society's need for security and public order against the rights of the individual. Nevertheless, judges can ordinarily be expected to be more protective of individual rights than either elected officials or the general public. How far the courts will go in protecting a person's rights depends on the facts of the case, the existing status of the law, prevailing social needs, and the personal views of the judges. Nevertheless, most judges and justices regard the protection of individual rights as a constitutional imperative, which is the way the Framers saw it. The Bill of Rights was created in order to transform the abstract idea that individuals have inalienable rights to life, liberty, and happiness into a set of specified constitutional rights, thereby bringing them under the protection of courts of law.[99]

Summary

In their search for personal liberty, Americans added the Bill of Rights to the Constitution shortly after its ratification. These amendments guarantee certain political, procedural, and property rights against infringement by the national government. Freedom of expression is the most basic of democratic rights. People are not free unless they can freely express their views. Nevertheless, free expression may conflict with the nation's security needs during times of war and insurrection. The courts at times have allowed government to limit expression substantially for purposes of national security. In recent decades, however, the courts have protected a wide range of free expression in the areas of speech, press, and religion.

The guarantees embodied in the Bill of Rights originally applied only to the national government. Under the principle of selective incorporation of these guarantees into the Fourteenth Amendment, the courts extended them to state governments, though the process was slow and uneven. In the 1920s and 1930s, First Amendment guarantees of freedom of expression were given protection from infringement by the states. The states continued to have wide discretion in criminal proceedings until the early 1960s, when most of the fair-trial rights in the Bill of Rights were given federal protection.

Due process of law refers to legal protections that have been established to preserve individual rights. The most significant form of these protections consists of procedures or methods (for example, the right of an accused person to have an attorney present during police interrogation) designed to ensure that an individual's rights are upheld. A major controversy in this area is the breadth of the exclusionary rule, which bars the use in trials of illegally obtained evidence. The right of privacy, particularly as it applies to the abortion issue, is also a source of controversy, as is the issue of constitutional rights in the pursuit of the war on terrorism.

Civil liberties are not absolute but must be balanced against other considerations (such as national security or public safety) and against one another when different rights conflict. The judicial branch of government, particularly the Supreme Court, has taken on much of the responsibility for protecting and interpreting individual rights. The Court's positions have changed with time and conditions, but the Court has generally been more protective of and sensitive to civil liberties than have elected officials or popular majorities.

STUDY CORNER

Key Terms

Bill of Rights (*p. 98*)
civil liberties (*p. 98*)
clear-and-present-danger test (*p. 101*)
due process clause (of the Fourteenth Amendment) (*p. 103*)
establishment clause (*p. 108*)

exclusionary rule (*p. 118*)
freedom of expression (*p. 100*)
free-exercise clause (*p. 111*)
imminent lawless action test (*p. 105*)
libel (*p. 106*)
prior restraint (*p. 102*)

procedural due process (*p. 115*)
selective incorporation (*p. 104*)
slander (*p. 106*)
symbolic speech (*p. 102*)

Self-Test

1. The _____ Amendment, as interpreted by the Supreme Court after 1925, provides protection of individual rights from the actions of a repressive state government.
   a. Fourteenth
   b. Tenth
   c. Fifth
   d. Fourth
   e. First

2. The exclusionary rule holds that:
   a. people who are biased against the defendant may be excluded from serving on a jury.
   b. a court can order or constrain an action by an individual.
   c. evidence obtained from an illegal search and seizure cannot be used in a trial.
   d. "fighting words" can be excluded from constitutional protection.

3. The U.S. Bill of Rights as originally approved and interpreted protected individual liberties from violation by:
   a. state government only.
   b. the national government only.
   c. both national and state governments.
   d. all levels of government in the United States.

4. The establishment clause prohibits government from:
   a. establishing exceptions to the Bill of Rights.
   b. interfering in any matters where the church and the state conflict.

c. favoring one religion over another or supporting religion over no religion.
   d. interfering with a person's practice of religion.

5. The right to privacy was the basis for the Supreme Court ruling in:
   a. *Roe v. Wade.*
   b. *Mapp v. Ohio.*
   c. *Miranda v. Arizona.*
   d. *Schenck v. United States.*

6. The term that refers primarily to procedures that authorities must follow before a person can legitimately be punished for an offense is:
   a. the three-point test.
   b. the right to privacy.
   c. procedural due process.
   d. substantive due process.
   e. suspension of the writ of habeas corpus.

7. Sexual material that is offensive to any one individual in society is automatically deemed obscene and is not protected under the First Amendment. (T/F)

8. Modern Americans' rights of free expression have been defined largely in the context of national security concerns. (T/F)

9. In order to win a libel suit, public officials must prove that a news organization or journalist acted with knowing or reckless disregard for the truth. (T/F)

10. The Supreme Court supported the effort of the state of Texas to outlaw the burning of the U.S. flag. (T/F)

Critical Thinking

What is the process of selective incorporation, and why is it important to the rights you possess today?

Suggested Readings

Abraham, Henry J. *Freedom and the Court*. New York: Oxford University Press, 2003. A comprehensive analysis of the Supreme Court's work on civil rights and civil liberties.

Cohen, David B., and John W. Wells, eds. *American National Security and Civil Liberties in an Era of Terrorism*. New York: Palgrave Macmillan, 2004. A balanced set of essays on the current tensions between national security and civil liberties.

Epstein, Lee, and Thomas G. Walker. *Constitutional Law for a Changing America*, 5th ed. Washington, D.C.: Congressional Quarterly Press, 2004. An accessible introduction to U.S. constitutional law.

Hull, N. E. H., and Peter Charles Hoffer. *Roe v. Wade: The Abortion Rights Controversy in American History*. Lawrence: University Press of Kansas, 2001. A thorough

assessment of both sides of the abortion conflict, beginning with the *Roe v. Wade* decision.

Perry, Michael J. *Religion in Politics: Constitutional and Moral Perspectives*. New York: Oxford University Press, 1997. A legal and philosophical analysis of the role of religion in politics.

Schwarz, John E. *Freedom Reclaimed: Rediscovering the American Vision*. Baltimore, Md.: Johns Hopkins University Press, 2005. An impassioned argument for an expansive view of liberty, both from and through government action.

Vestal, Theodore H. *The Eisenhower Court and Civil Liberties*. Westport, Conn.: Praeger, 1993. A look at the Supreme Court that greatly expanded the rights of the criminally accused.

List of Websites

http://www.fepproject.org/
Includes information and opinions on a wide range of free-expression policy issues.

http://www.aclu.org/
The American Civil Liberties Union site; it provides information on current civil liberties and civil rights issues, including information on recent and pending Supreme Court cases.

http://www.findlaw.com/casecode/supreme.html
An excellent source of information on Supreme Court and lower-court rulings.

http://www.ncjrs.org/
The site of the National Criminal Justice Reference Service, a federally funded organization that compiles information on a wide range of criminal-justice issues.

Participate!

Although their right of free expression is protected by law, Americans often choose not to exercise this right for fear of social pressure or official reprisal. Yet constitutional rights tend to wither when people fail to exercise them. Think of an issue that you favor but that is unpopular on your campus or in your community. Consider writing a letter expressing your opinion to the editor of your college or local newspaper. (Practical advice: Keep the letter short and to the point; write a lead sentence that will get readers' attention; provide a con-

vincing argument for your position; be sure to sign the letter and provide a return address so the editor can contact you if there are questions.)

Extra Credit

For up-to-the-minute *New York Times* articles, interactive simulations, graphics, study tools, and more links and quizzes, visit the text's Online Learning Center at www.mhhe.com/pattersontad8.

(Self-Test Answers: 1. a   2. c   3. b   4. c   5. a   6. c   7. F   8. T   9. T   10. F)

Equal Rights:
Struggling Toward Fairness

Chapter Outline

The Struggle for Equality
  African Americans
  Women
  Native Americans
  Hispanic Americans
  Asian Americans
  Other Groups and Their Rights

Equality Under the Law
  Equal Protection: The Fourteenth
    Amendment
  Equal Access: The Civil Rights Acts of
    1964 and 1968
  Equal Ballots: The Voting Rights Act of
    1965, as Amended

Equality of Result
  Affirmative Action: Workplace Integration
  Affirmative Action in the Law
  Busing: School Integration

Persistent Discrimination:
Superficial Differences, Deep
Divisions

CHAPTER 5

I have a dream that one day this nation will rise up and live out the true meaning of its creed: "We hold these truths to be self-evident: that all men are created equal."

Martin Luther King Jr.[1]

The producers of ABC television's *Primetime Live* put hidden cameras on two young men, equally well dressed and groomed, and then sent them on different routes to do the same things—search for an apartment, shop for a car, look at albums in a record store. The cameras recorded people's reactions to the two men. One was usually greeted with smiles and quick service. The other man was more often greeted with suspicious looks and was sometimes made to wait. Why the difference? The explanation was straightforward: the young man who was routinely well received was white; the young man who was sometimes treated poorly was an African American.

The Urban Institute conducted a more substantial experiment. It included pairs of specially trained white and black male college students who were the same in all respects—education, work experience, speech patterns, physical builds—except for their race. The students responded individually to nearly five hundred classified job advertisements in Chicago and Washington, D.C. The black applicants got fewer interviews and received fewer job offers than did the white applicants. An Urban Institute spokesperson said, "The level of reverse discrimination [favoring blacks over whites] that we found was limited, was certainly far lower than many might have been led to fear, and was swamped by the extent of discrimination against black job applicants."[2]

These two experiments suggest why some Americans are still struggling to achieve equal rights. In theory Americans have equal rights, but in reality they are not now equal nor have they ever been. African Americans, women, Hispanic Americans, the disabled, Jews, Native Americans, Catholics, Asian Americans, gays and lesbians, and members of other minority groups have been victims of discrimination in fact and in law. The nation's creed—"all men are created equal"—has encouraged minorities to demand equal treatment. But inequality is built into almost every aspect of U.S. society. For example, compared with whites, African Americans with correctable health problems are significantly less likely to receive coronary-artery bypass surgery, to receive a kidney transplant, or to undergo surgery for early-stage lung cancer.[3]

civil rights, or **equal rights**
The right of every person to equal protection under the laws and equal access to society's opportunities and public facilities.

This chapter focuses on **equal rights,** or **civil rights**—terms that refer to the right of every person to equal protection under the laws and equal access to society's opportunities and public facilities. Chapter 4 explained that civil liberties refer to specific *individual* rights, such as freedom of speech, that are protected from infringement by government. Equal rights, or civil rights, have to do with whether individual members of differing *groups*—racial, sexual, and the like—are treated equally by government and, in some areas, by private parties. To oversimplify, civil liberties deal with issues of personal freedom, and civil rights deal with issues of equality.

Although the law refers to the rights of individuals first and to those of groups in a secondary and derivative way, this chapter concentrates on groups because the history of civil rights has been largely one of group claims to equality. The chapter emphasizes these points:

- *Disadvantaged groups have had to struggle for equal rights.* African Americans, women, Native Americans, Hispanic Americans, Asian Americans, and others have all had to fight for their rights in order to come closer to equality with white males.

- *Americans have attained substantial equality under the law.* They have, in legal terms, equal protection under the laws, equal access to accommodations and housing, and an equal right to vote. Discrimination by law against persons because of race, sex, religion, or ethnicity is now almost nonexistent.

- *Legal equality for all Americans has not resulted in de facto equality.* African Americans, women, Hispanic Americans, and other traditionally disadvantaged groups have a disproportionately small share of America's opportunities and benefits. Existing inequalities, discrimination, and political pressures still are major barriers to their full equality. Affirmative action is a policy designed to help the disadvantaged achieve a fuller degree of equality.

THE STRUGGLE FOR EQUALITY

Equality has always been the least fully developed of America's founding concepts. Not even Thomas Jefferson, who had a deep admiration for the "common man," believed that a precise meaning could be given to the claim of the Declaration of Independence that "all men are created equal."[4]

The history of America shows that disadvantaged groups have rarely achieved a greater measure of justice without a struggle.[5] Their gains have nearly always followed intense and sustained political action, such as the civil rights movement of the 1960s, that has forced entrenched interests to relinquish or share their privileged status (see Chapter 7).

Disadvantaged groups have a shared history of political exclusion, struggles for empowerment, and policy triumphs, but each has a distinctive history as well, as is evident in a brief review of the equal rights efforts of African Americans, women, Native Americans, Hispanic Americans, Asian Americans, and other groups.

African Americans

No Americans have faced greater hardship than have black Americans. Their ancestors came to this country as slaves after having been captured in Africa, shipped in chains across the Atlantic, and sold in open markets in Charleston, Boston, and other seaports.

Two police dogs attack a black civil rights activist (*center left*) during the 1963 Birmingham demonstrations. Such images of hatred and violence shook many white Americans out of their complacency about the plight of African Americans.

The Civil War ended slavery—but not racism. When federal troops withdrew from the South in 1877, the region's white majority took over the state governments, passing laws that kept blacks from voting. Even more punitive were laws that prohibited black citizens from using the same public facilities as whites.[6] In *Plessy v. Ferguson* (1896), the Supreme Court endorsed these laws, ruling that "separate" facilities for the two races did not violate the Constitution as long as the facilities were "equal."[7] The *Plessy* decision became a justification for the separate and *unequal* treatment of African Americans. For example, black children were forced into separate schools that rarely had libraries and had few teachers.

Black Americans challenged these discriminatory practices through legal action, but not until the late 1930s did the Supreme Court begin to respond. The Court began modestly by ruling that where no separate public facilities existed for African Americans, they must be allowed to use those reserved for whites. When Oklahoma, which had no law school for blacks, was ordered to admit Ada Sipuel as a law student in 1949, it created a separate law school for her—she sat alone in a roped-off corridor of the state capitol building. The white students, meanwhile, continued to meet at the University of Oklahoma's law school in Norman, twenty miles away. The Supreme Court then ordered the law school to admit her to regular classes. The law school did so but roped off her seat from the rest of the class and stenciled the word "colored" on it. She was also forced to eat alone in a roped-off area of the law school's cafeteria.[8]

The Brown Decision

Substantial judicial intervention on behalf of African Americans finally occurred in 1954 with *Brown v. Board of Education of Topeka*. The case began when Linda Carol Brown, a black child in Topeka, Kansas, was denied admission to an all-white elementary school that she passed every day on her way to her all-black school, which was twelve blocks farther. In its decision, the Court reversed its *Plessy* doctrine by declaring that racial segregation of public schools "generates

LEADERS

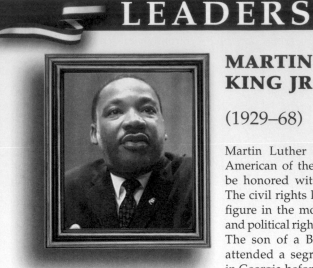

MARTIN LUTHER KING JR.

(1929–68)

Martin Luther King Jr. is the only American of the twentieth century to be honored with a national holiday. The civil rights leader was the pivotal figure in the movement to gain legal and political rights for black Americans. The son of a Baptist minister, King attended a segregated public school in Georgia before going to Morehouse College, a traditional African American institution. He later earned a doctorate from Boston University before taking a pastorate in Montgomery, Alabama.

Already active on civil rights issues, King used rhetorical skills and nonviolent protest to galvanize the black community and sweep aside a century of governmental discrimination. High points were a protest march in Salem, Alabama, that exposed white brutality and a triumphal gathering of a quarter million supporters on the Washington Mall. His leadership inspired other groups, including women and Hispanics, to assert their rights. The recipient of the Nobel Peace Prize in 1964 (the youngest person ever to receive that honor), King was assassinated in Memphis in 1968 as he was preparing to lead a protest march on behalf of the city's sanitation workers.

[among black children] a feeling of inferiority as to their status in the community that may affect their hearts and minds in a way unlikely ever to be undone. . . . Separate educational facilities are inherently unequal."[9]

A 1954 Gallup poll indicated that a substantial majority of southern whites opposed the *Brown* decision. The same poll found that a slim majority of whites outside the South agreed with the decision.

The Black Civil Rights Movement

After *Brown*, the struggle of African Americans for their rights became a political movement. Perhaps no single event turned national public opinion so dramatically against segregation as a 1963 march led by Dr. Martin Luther King Jr. in Birmingham, Alabama. As the nation watched on television in disbelief, police officers led by Birmingham's sheriff, Eugene "Bull" Connor, attacked King and his followers with dogs, cattle prods, and fire hoses.

The modern civil rights movement peaked with the triumphant March on Washington for Jobs and Freedom of August 2, 1963. It attracted 250,000 marchers, one of the largest gatherings in the history of the nation's capital. "I have a dream," the Reverend King told the gathering, "that my four little children will one day live in a nation where they will not be judged by the color of their skin but by the content of their character." A year later, after a months-long fight in Congress marked by every parliamentary obstacle that racial conservatives could muster, the Civil Rights Act of 1964 was enacted. The legislation provided African Americans and other minorities with equal access to public facilities and prohibited job discrimination. President Lyndon Johnson, who had been a decisive force in the battle to pass the Civil Rights Act, called for new legislation that would also end racial barriers to voting. Congress answered with the 1965 Voting Rights Act.

The Aftermath of the Civil Rights Movement

Although the most significant progress in history toward the legal equality of all Americans occurred during the 1960s, Dr. King's dream of a color-blind society has remained elusive.[10] Even the legal rights of African Americans do not, in practice, match the promise of the civil rights movement. Studies have found that African Americans accused of crime are more likely to be convicted and to receive stiff sentences than are white Americans on trial for comparable offenses. Federal statistics indicate, for example, that black Americans account for more than 75 percent of crack cocaine convictions but only about 35 percent of crack cocaine users.[11] It is hardly surprising that many African Americans believe that the nation has two standards of justice, with a harsher standard for blacks than for whites.

States in the Nation

Black and Latino Representation in State Legislatures

For a long period in U.S. history, there were almost no minorities among the ranks of state legislators. Minorities are still underrepresented relative to their numbers in the population. Although one in every three Americans is a minority-group member, only one in eight state legislators comes from a minority group; of these, about two-thirds are African American.

Q: What accounts for differences between the states in the percentage of minority-group members in their legislatures?

A: States with large populations of minorities tend to have a larger percentage of legislators from minority groups. Alabama and Mississippi have large black populations and have the highest proportion of African American legislators. New Mexico, with its large Hispanic population, has the highest proportion of Latino lawmakers.

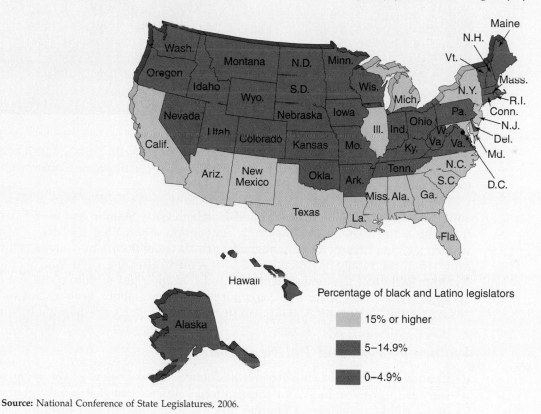

Percentage of black and Latino legislators

15% or higher

5–14.9%

0–4.9%

Source: National Conference of State Legislatures, 2006.

One area in which African Americans have made substantial progress since the 1960s is elective office (see "States in the Nation"). Although the percentage of black elected officials is still far below the proportion of African Americans in the population, it has risen sharply over recent decades.[12] As of 2006, there were five hundred black mayors and more than forty black members of Congress, including one U.S. senator, Barack Obama of Illinois.

Women

The United States carried over from English common law a political disregard for women, forbidding them to vote, hold public office, or serve on juries.[13] Upon marriage, a woman essentially lost her identity as an individual and could not

The majority of women with preschool children work outside the home, a situation that has increased demand for government support of day care centers, parental leave, and other support programs and services.

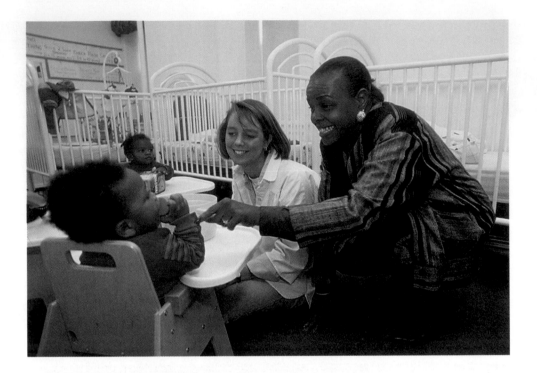

own and dispose of property without her husband's consent. Even a wife's body was not fully hers. A wife's adultery was declared by the Supreme Court in 1904 to be a violation of the husband's property rights![14]

The first women's rights convention in America was held in 1848 in Seneca Falls, New York, after Lucretia Mott and Elizabeth Cady Stanton had been barred from the main floor of an antislavery convention. Thereafter, the struggle for women's rights became closely aligned with the abolitionist movement. However, when the Fifteenth Amendment was ratified after the Civil War, women were not included; the amendment declared that the right to vote could not be abridged on account of race or color but said nothing about gender. Not until passage of the Nineteenth Amendment in 1920 did women gain the right to vote.

Women's Legal and Political Gains

Ratification of the Nineteenth Amendment encouraged leaders of the women's movement to propose in 1923 a constitutional amendment that would guarantee equal rights for women. Congress rejected that proposal and several subsequent ones. In 1973, however, Congress approved the Equal Rights Amendment (ERA) and submitted it to the states for ratification or rejection. The ERA failed by three states to receive the three-fourths majority required for ratification.[15] Nevertheless, the ERA helped bring women's rights to the forefront at a time when developments in Congress and the courts were contributing significantly to legal equality for women. Among the congressional initiatives were the Equal Pay Act of 1963, which prohibits sex discrimination in salary and wages by some categories of employers; Title IX of the Education Amendment of 1972, which prohibits sex discrimination in education; and the Equal Credit Act of 1974, which prohibits sex discrimination in the granting of financial credit.

Women are also protected by Title VII of the Civil Rights Act of 1964, which bans gender discrimination in employment. This protection extends to sexual harassment. Lewd comments and unwelcome advances are part of the workplace reality for many American women. However, the courts have held, and with increasing firmness, that companies and government agencies can be sued if they do not make an effort to prevent this type of behavior.[16] In a 2006 decision, the Supreme Court strengthened employees' protection by making it easier for them to sue an organization that retaliates against them for filing a sexual harassment complaint. The case involved a woman who, after filing a complaint against her supervisor, was removed from her job as a forklift operator and assigned a less desirable position.[17]

Women have made substantial gains in the area of appointive and elective offices.[18] In 1981, President Reagan appointed the first woman to serve on the Supreme Court, Sandra Day O'Connor. When the Democratic party in 1984 chose Geraldine Ferraro as its vice presidential nominee, she became the first woman to run on the national ticket of a major political party. The elections of California's Dianne Feinstein and Barbara Boxer in 1992 marked the first time that women occupied both U.S. Senate seats of a state. Despite such signs of progress, women are still a long way from political equality with men.[19] Women occupy roughly one in six congressional seats and one in five statewide and city council offices (see "How the United States Compares").

Although women are underrepresented in political office, their vote is increasingly powerful. Until the 1970s, the voting patterns of women and men were nearly alike. Today, there is a substantial **gender gap:** women and men

gender gap
The tendency of women and men to differ in their political attitudes and voting preferences.

How the United States Compares
Inequality and Women

The one form of inequality common to all nations is that of gender: nowhere are women equal to men in law or in fact. But there are large differences between countries. A study by the Population Crisis Committee ranked the United States third overall in women's equality, behind only Sweden and Finland. Based on five measures—jobs, education, social relations, marriage and family, and health—the study rated the status of U.S. women at 82.5 percent that of men.

The inequality of women is underscored by their underrepresentation in public office. In no country do women comprise as many as half the members of the national legislature. The Scandinavian countries rank highest in terms of the percentage of female lawmakers. Other northern European countries have lower levels, but their levels are higher than in the United States. The accompanying figure indicates the approximate percentage of seats held by women in the largest chamber of each country's national legislature.

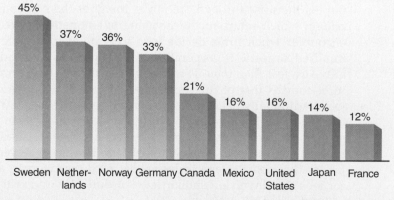

Percentage of legislative seats held by women

Sweden 45%
Netherlands 37%
Norway 36%
Germany 33%
Canada 21%
Mexico 16%
United States 16%
Japan 14%
France 12%

Source: For non–U.S. countries, Inter-Parliamentary Union; for United States, U.S. House of Representatives.

Figure 5–1

The Gender Gap in Congressional Voting
Women and men differ, on average, in their political behavior. For example, women are more likely than men to vote Democratic, as shown by the difference between the women's vote and the men's vote for Democratic candidates in U.S. House races.
Source: National Election Studies (1988–1998); multiple polls (2000–2004); 2006 figure based on preliminary data.

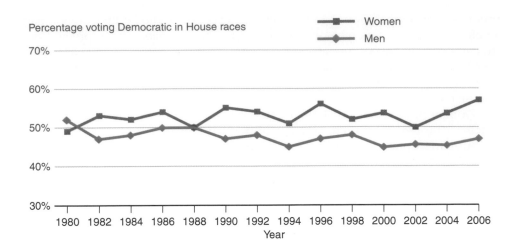

differ in their opinions and their votes. Women are more supportive than men of government programs for the poor, minorities, children, and the elderly. They also have a greater tendency to cast their votes for Democratic candidates (see Figure 5–1). The gender gap is discussed further in Chapter 6.

Job-Related Issues: Family Leave, Comparable Worth, and Sexual Harassment

In recent decades, increasing numbers of women have sought employment outside the home. Government statistics indicate that employment-age women are six times more likely to work outside the home compared with a half-century ago. Women have made gains in many traditionally male-dominated fields. For example, women now make up more than a third of the new lawyers and physicians that graduate each year. The change in women's work status is also reflected in education statistics. A few decades ago, more white, black, and Hispanic men than women were enrolled in college. Today, the reverse is true, with more women than men of each group enrolled. A U.S. Education Department report issued in 2006 showed that women are ahead of men in more than just college enrollment. Compared with men, they are more likely to complete their degree, to do it in a shorter period, and to get better grades.[20]

Although women have made gains in the workplace, they have not achieved equality when it comes to jobs. Women increasingly hold managerial positions but, as they rise through the ranks, many of them encounter the so-called *glass ceiling*, which refers to the invisible but nonetheless real barrier that women encounter when firms decide who to appoint to the top positions. Of the five hundred largest U.S. corporations, only 2 percent are headed by women. Women also earn less than men. The average pay for full-time female employees is about three-fourths that of full-time male employees. One reason is that many of the jobs traditionally held by women, such as office secretary, pay less than many of the jobs traditionally held by men, such as truck driver. Attempts by women's groups to change this tendency have been largely unsuccessful. Only a tiny percentage of firms and municipalities have instituted a policy of *comparable worth*. Under this policy, wage scales are set such that women and men get equal pay for jobs that involve a similar level of difficulty and that require a similar level of training or education.[21]

Women gained a major victory in the workplace when Congress passed the Family and Medical Leave Act in 1993. It provides for up to twelve weeks of unpaid

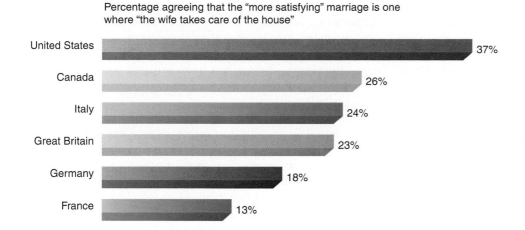

Percentage agreeing that the "more satisfying" marriage is one where "the wife takes care of the house"

Country	Percentage
United States	37%
Canada	26%
Italy	24%
Great Britain	23%
Germany	18%
France	13%

Figure 5–2

Opinions on Women's Role in Marriage
Americans are more likely than Western Europeans to believe that the "more satisfying" marriage is one where "the wife takes care of the house and children" rather than one where "the husband and wife both have jobs."
Source: Global Attitudes Survey (2002) by the Pew Research Center for the People and the Press.

leave for employees to care for a new baby or a seriously ill family member. Upon return from leave, the employee ordinarily must be given the original or an equivalent job position with equivalent pay, benefits, and other employment terms. These provisions apply to men as well as women, but women were the instigating force behind the legislation and are its primary beneficiaries because they still bear the larger share of responsibility for sick and young family members.

Traditional practices are reflected in Americans' attitudes toward the role of women in society. Roughly two in five adults say that the preferred marriage is one where the wife stays home to take care of the house. This opinion is more prevalent in the United States than in Europe (see Figure 5–2), even though women's legal and employment gains in the United States have been at least as impressive as those in Europe.

Native Americans

When white settlers began arriving in America in large numbers during the seventeenth century, an estimated ten million Native Americans were living in the territory that would become the United States. By 1900, the Native American population had plummeted to less than one million. No people in human history suffered a steeper loss. Diseases brought by white settlers took the largest toll on the various Indian tribes, but wars and massacres contributed. "The only good Indian is a dead Indian" is not simply a hackneyed expression from cowboy movies. It was part of a strategy of westward expansion, as settlers and U.S. troops alike mercilessly drove the eastern Indians from their ancestral lands to the Great Plains and later took those lands as well. Even well-intentioned policies failed. Reservation lands in some instances were divided into farming plots in the naive belief that Native Americans would readily adjust to an agricultural life based on private property rights.

Today, Native Americans number more than one million, about half of whom live on or close to reservations set aside for them by the federal government. Reservations are governed by treaties signed when they were established. State governments have no direct authority over federal reservations, and the federal government's authority is limited by the terms of a particular treaty. Although U.S. policy toward the reservations has varied over time, the current policy is to promote self-government and economic self-sufficiency.[22] Preservation of Native American cultures is also a policy goal. For example, Native American children can now be taught in their own languages; at an earlier time in schools run by the Bureau of Indian Affairs, children were required to use English.

Native Americans are less than half as likely to attend college as other Americans, their life expectancy is more than ten years lower than the national average, and their infant mortality rate is more than three times higher than that of white Americans. In recent years, some Native American tribes have erected gaming casinos on reservation land. The casinos have brought jobs and income to the reservations but have also brought controversy—traditionalists argue that the casinos are destroying tribal cultures.

The civil rights movement of the 1960s at first did not include Native Americans. Then, in the early 1970s, militant Native Americans occupied the Bureau of Indian Affairs in Washington, D.C., and later seized control of the village of Wounded Knee on a Sioux reservation in southwestern South Dakota, exchanging gunfire with U.S. marshals. These episodes highlighted the grievances of Native Americans and may have contributed to legislation that in 1974 granted Native Americans living on reservations greater control over federal programs that affect them. Native Americans had already benefited from the legislative climate created by the 1960s civil rights movement: in 1968, Congress enacted the Indian Bill of Rights, which gives Native Americans on reservations constitutional guarantees similar to those given to other Americans.

In recent years Native Americans have filed suit to reclaim lost ancestral lands and have won a few settlements. But they stand no realistic chance of getting back even those lands that had been granted to them by federal treaty but later were sold off or seized forcibly by federal authorities. Native Americans were not even official citizens of the United States until passage of an act of Congress in 1924. Their citizenship status came too late to be of much help; their traditional way of life had already largely disappeared.

Hispanic Americans

The fastest-growing minority in the United States is Hispanic Americans, that is, people of Spanish-speaking background. Hispanics recently surpassed African Americans as the nation's largest racial or ethnic minority group. More than 35 million Hispanics live in the United States, an increase of 40 percent over the 1990 census. They have emigrated to the United States primarily from Mexico and the Caribbean islands, mainly Cuba and Puerto Rico. About half of all Hispanics in the United States were born in Mexico or claim a Mexican ancestry. Hispanics are concentrated in their states of entry; thus Florida, New York, and New Jersey have large numbers of Caribbean Hispanics, while California, Texas, Arizona, and New Mexico have many immigrants from Mexico. More than half the population of Los Angeles is of Hispanic—mostly Mexican—descent.

Legal and Political Action

Hispanic Americans have benefited from laws and court rulings aimed primarily at protecting other groups. Although the Civil Rights Act of 1964 was largely a response to the condition of black people, its provisions against discrimination apply broadly to other groups.

Nevertheless, Hispanics had their own civil rights movement. Its most publicized actions were the farm workers' strikes of the late 1960s and the 1970s that aimed at achieving basic labor rights for migrant workers. Migrants were working long hours for low pay, were living in shacks without electricity or plumbing, and were unwelcome in many local schools as well as in some local hospitals. Farm owners at first refused to bargain with the workers, but a well-organized national boycott of California grapes and lettuce forced that state to pass a law giving migrant workers the right to bargain collectively. The strikes were led in

California by Cesar Chavez, who himself grew up in a Mexican American migrant family. Chavez's tactics were copied in other states, particularly Texas, but the results were less successful.

The Hispanic civil rights movement has also pursued social and political goals. Hispanics have had some success, for example, in pressuring federal, state, and local governments to increase spending on bilingual education programs. They also succeeded in getting Congress to enact legislation requiring states to provide bilingual ballots in local areas where there is a sizeable concentration of non-English speaking residents.

Hispanics are one of the country's oldest ethnic groups. Some Hispanics are the descendants of people who helped colonize the areas of California, Texas, Florida, New Mexico, and Arizona before those areas were annexed by the United States. However, most Hispanics are recent immigrants or their descendants.

LEADERS

CESAR ESTRADA CHAVEZ

(1927–93)

Cesar Chavez led the first successful farm workers' strike in U.S. history. Founder of the United Farm Workers of America, Chavez was called "one of the heroic figures of our time" by Robert F. Kennedy and is widely regarded as the most influential Latino leader in modern U.S. history. A migrant worker as a child, Chavez knew firsthand the deprivations suffered by farm laborers. Like Martin Luther King Jr., Chavez was an advocate of nonviolent protest, and he organized food boycotts that eventually caused agricultural firms to improve wages and working conditions for farm workers. In 1994, Chavez was posthumously awarded the Presidential Medal of Freedom, the highest civilian honor an American can receive.

A significant number—roughly ten million by some estimates—are in the United States illegally. In past eras, immigration authorities could more easily control new arrivals because most of them arrived by ship through a port of entry, such as Ellis Island. Most Hispanics have arrived by land, many of them crossing illegally from Mexico. U.S. authorities have had little success in stopping this influx. Most of the illegal aliens have come to America seeking jobs, and they now make up an estimated 5 percent of the U.S. workforce. They have had broad support

When Congress in 2006 seemed on the verge of enacting legislation that would crack down on illegal immigrants, most of whom are from Mexico, pro-immigrant rallies were held in nearly every American city with a sizeable Hispanic population. The rally in Los Angeles was the largest in the city's history. Even in locations more distant from Mexico the rallies were large and enthusiastic. The scene here is of the rally in Lincoln, Nebraska, where the flags of the United States and Mexico were readily visible.

in the Hispanic community, which has sought to ease immigration restrictions and to expand the rights and privileges of illegal aliens—positions that are at odds with those held by many Americans.

In response to growing political pressure over the issue of illegal aliens, President George W. Bush in 2006 urged Congress to enact a guest-worker program. Under Bush's plan, workers who are in the United States illegally could enroll in the program, which would allow them to work in the country for up to six years. Other noncitizens could enter the United States as guest workers if they had a job waiting for them. The program was intended to address the nation's labor needs while simultaneously reducing illegal immigration by increasing border surveillance and by raising penalties on employers who hire undocumented aliens. Bush's plan had business community support and was backed by many congressional Democrats, although some Democrats wanted citizenship at the end of six years for guest workers who held jobs and stayed free of crime. Bush's plan won the backing of the Senate but got derailed in the House of Representatives. House Republicans insisted, as a precondition of support for a guest-worker program, that U.S. borders first be secured against illegal entry, that current laws against hiring illegal aliens be enforced rigorously, and that illegal residents be identified and deported.

As Congress was debating the legislation, large rallies—ones reminiscent of the 1960s civil rights movement—were taking place in nearly every American city with a sizeable Hispanic population. The rally in Los Angeles drew an estimated half million marchers, reputedly the largest such gathering in the city's history. The mostly Hispanic demonstrators had taken to the streets to protest what they feared was a pending crackdown on illegal immigrants. The scale and spontaneity of the rallies caught even seasoned political observers by surprise; it was a demonstration of Hispanic political solidarity unlike anything previously seen.

Growing Political Power

More than four thousand Hispanic Americans nationwide hold public office. Hispanics have been elected to statewide office in several states, including New Mexico and Arizona. About twenty Hispanic Americans currently serve in the House of Representatives.

Hispanic Americans are a growing political force. By the middle of the century, Hispanics are projected to become the largest racial or ethnic group in California. Their political involvement, like that of other immigrant groups, will increase as they become more firmly rooted in society. At present, about half of all Hispanics are not registered to vote, and only about a third actually vote, limiting the group's political power. Nevertheless, the sheer size of the Hispanic population in states such as Texas and California makes the group a potent force, as was evident in the 2006 election when both the Republicans and the Democrats mounted massive efforts to woo Hispanic voters.

With the exception of the conservative Republican-leaning Cuban Americans of southern Florida, Hispanics lean toward the Democratic party (see Figure 5–3). However, Hispanics are not a cohesive

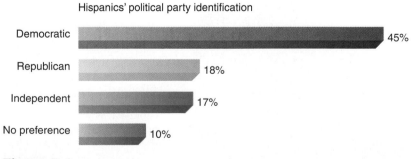

Figure 5–3

Hispanics' Party Identification
Hispanics' party loyalties lean heavily toward the Democratic party.
Source: "2005 National Latino Survey," Latino Coalition, December 2005.

voting bloc in the same way that African Americans are. Blacks of all income levels are solidly Democratic; among Hispanics, Democratic support is concentrated among those of lower income. Opinion surveys show that Hispanics tend to be relatively liberal on economic issues and relatively conservative on social issues. These tendencies suggest that Hispanics will lean Democratic in the near future but divide more evenly between the parties as their average income rises.[23]

Asian Americans

Chinese and Japanese laborers were brought into western states during the late 1800s to work in mines and to build railroads. When the need for this labor declined, Congress in 1892 ordered a temporary halt to Asian immigration. Over the next three decades, informal agreements kept all but a few Asians from entering the country. In 1930, Congress completely blocked the entry of Japanese. Japan had protested a California law that prohibited persons of Japanese descent from buying property in the state. Rather than finesse what was called "the California problem," Congress bluntly told Japan that its people were not wanted in the United States.[24]

Discrimination against Asians did not ease substantially until 1965, when Congress enacted legislation that adjusted the immigration quotas to favor those who had previously been assigned very small numbers. This change in the law was a product of the 1960s civil rights movement, which increased public awareness of all forms of discrimination. Asian Americans now number about twelve million, or roughly 4 percent of the total U.S. population. Most Asian Americans live on the West Coast, particularly in California. China, Japan, Korea, India, Vietnam, and the Philippines are the ancestral homes of most Asian Americans.

The rights of Asian Americans have been expanded primarily by court rulings and legislation, such as the Civil Rights Act of 1964, that were initiated in response to the demands of other minorities. In some instances, however, the actions of Asian Americans have strengthened the rights of other minorities. In *Lau v. Nichols* (1974), a case initiated by a Chinese American family, the Supreme Court ruled unanimously that placing public school children for whom English is a second language in regular classrooms without special assistance is a violation of the Fourteenth Amendment's equal protection clause, because it denies them an equal educational opportunity.[25] Although the Court did not mandate bilingual instruction as the form of that assistance and later held that bilingual courses are not required, the *Lau* decision did lead many schools to establish bilingual instruction. Since then, some states have restricted its use. In California, the limitation was enacted in 1998 through Proposition 227, which requires children for whom English is a second language to take their courses in English after their first year in school, though other forms of assistance and waivers are permitted in some cases.

Many Asian Americans hold responsible positions in the professional and technical fields, a reflection of educational attainment. However, Asian Americans are substantially underrepresented in managerial positions, as are other minority groups.

Asian Americans are an upwardly mobile group. The values of most Asian cultures include family-oriented self-reliance, which, in the American context, has included an emphasis on academic attainment. For example, Asians make up a disproportionate share of the students at California's leading public universities, which base admission primarily on high school grades and standardized test scores. However, Asian Americans are still underrepresented in certain areas of the workplace. According to U.S. government figures, Asian Americans account for about 5 percent of professionals and technicians, slightly more than their percentage of the total population. Yet they hold less than 2 percent of managerial jobs; past and present discrimination has kept them from obtaining their fair share of top business positions. They are also underrepresented politically.[26] Not until 1996, for example, was an Asian American elected governor of a state other than Hawaii.

Other Groups and Their Rights

The 1964 Civil Rights Act (discussed further later in the chapter) prohibits discrimination by sex, race, or national origin. This act classified women and racial and ethnic minorities as legally protected groups, enabling them to pursue their rights in court. As these minority groups gained success, other groups began to make their own claims for protection from discrimination that is rooted in prejudicial attitudes or assumptions.

Older Americans

Older Americans are one such group. The Age Discrimination Act of 1975 and the Age Discrimination in Employment Act of 1967 prohibit discrimination against older workers in hiring for jobs in which age is not clearly a crucial factor in job performance. More recently, mandatory retirement ages for most jobs have been eliminated by law.

However, forced retirement for reasons of age is permissible if it is justified by the nature of a particular job or by the performance of a particular employee. As these exceptions to federal age–discrimination laws indicate, older Americans are not as fully protected by law as women and minority-group members are. Age discrimination is not among the forms of discrimination prohibited by the U.S. Constitution.[27] As a result, although the federal government has granted substantial legal protections to older residents, it is not bound by the Constitution to do so.

Disabled Americans

Disabled Americans are also protected from discrimination. Roughly forty million Americans have a physical or mental disability that prevents them from performing a critical function, such as seeing, hearing, or walking. A goal of the disabled is equal access to society's opportunities. This was facilitated by the 1990 Americans with Disabilities Act, which grants the disabled the same employment and other protections enjoyed by other disadvantaged groups. In addition, the Education for All Handicapped Children Act of 1975 mandates that all children, however severe their disability, must receive a free, appropriate education. Before the legislation, four million children with disabilities were getting either no education or an inappropriate one (as in the case of a blind child who is not taught Braille). Although the disabled have substantial legal protections, they, like the elderly, are not a constitutionally protected group. Accordingly, government actions that have the effect of discriminating against the disabled, are in some cases legal, although the courts have required governments to take reasonable steps to provide the disabled with access to public services and facilities.[28]

Gays and Lesbians

A group that has historically been the object of hostility and discrimination is gays and lesbians. Until recently, they typically responded by trying to hide their sexual orientation. Some still do so, but many gays and lesbians now openly pursue a claim to equal protection under the law.

Gays and lesbians gained a significant legal victory when the Supreme Court in *Romer v. Evans* (1996) struck down a Colorado constitutional amendment that nullified all existing and any new legal protections for homosexuals. In a 6-3 ruling, the Court said that the Colorado law violated the Constitution's guarantee of equal protection because it subjected individuals to employment and other discrimination simply because of their sexual preference. The Court concluded that the law had no reasonable purpose but was instead motivated by hostility toward homosexuals.[29] In *Lawrence v. Texas* (2003), the Court handed gays and lesbians another victory by invalidating state laws that prohibited sexual relations between consenting adults of the same sex (see Chapter 4).[30]

These gains have been partially offset by setbacks. In 2000, for example, the Supreme Court held that the Boy Scouts, as a private organization that has a right to free association, can ban gays because the Scout creed forbids homosexuality.[31] Gays and lesbians who are open about their sexual preference are also barred from serving in the military. However, they can serve under the military's "don't ask, don't tell" (or "don't harass, don't pursue") policy. As long as they do not by words or actions reveal their sexual preference, they are allowed to enlist and stay in the service. In turn, soldiers are instructed not to inquire about others' sexual orientation, nor are they to try to entrap those they suspect of being gay or lesbian. The courts have upheld the military's ban, citing the unusually close physical proximity with minimal privacy that occurs in the military. An attempt by U.S. law schools to force a change in the policy by prohibiting the military from recruiting on their premises collapsed when the Supreme Court in 2006 upheld a law that withholds federal funds from colleges that do not give military recruiters the same access to students that they give to recruiters for other employers.[32]

Gay and lesbian couples are currently seeking the same legal status that the law extends to opposite-sex married couples. During the past decade, same-sex couples have succeeded in getting some states, cities, and firms to extend employee benefits, such as health-care insurance, to their employees' same-sex partners. These arrangements, however, do not extend to things such as inheritance and hospital visitation rights, which are reserved by state law for married couples and their families. In 2000, Vermont legalized the civil union of same-sex couples, thereby granting them the same legal rights as those held by opposite-sex married couples. In 2004, upon order of the state's high court, Massachusetts gave same-sex couples the right to marry.

The claim that gay and lesbian couples should have the same legal rights as opposite-sex married couples has been strongly contested. Even before Vermont authorized same-sex unions, Congress passed the Defense of Marriage Act, which defines marriage as "a legal union of one man and one woman as husband and wife." This 1996 law authorizes states to deny marital rights to a same-sex couple that has been granted these rights by another state. Under the U.S. Constitution's "full faith and credit clause," states are required to recognize the laws and contracts of other states, although Congress can create exceptions, as it did with the Defense of Marriage Act.

Debating the Issues

Should Same-Sex Marriage Be Legalized?

The Massachusetts Supreme Judicial Court in 2003 declared that the state's constitution requires that same-sex couples be given the same opportunity to marry as opposite-sex couples. The court ordered the state legislature to enact a law to that effect within six months. In 2004, Massachusetts became the first state to allow same-sex marriage. Four years earlier, Vermont had authorized civil unions for same-sex couples, which provided them with many of the same legal rights enjoyed by opposite-sex married couples. Widespread public debate accompanied these policy developments, particularly same-sex marriage.

Yes

The Massachusetts Supreme Judicial Court ruled that the rights, protections, and responsibilities afforded by civil marriage should not be denied to any resident of that state. It is a great victory for the seven couples represented by the Gay & Lesbian Advocates & Defenders, for every gay and lesbian couple in Massachusetts—and for all fair-minded people who believe every American deserves equal treatment under the law. The opening statement of the court's decision says it all: "The exclusive commitment of two individuals to each other nurtures love and mutual support; it brings stability to our society." This decision affirms the inherent value and social benefit that committed, loving relationships between gay and lesbian people bring to society at large—and utterly dismisses the claims made by the anti-gay industry that granting basic protections and rights to same-sex families somehow threatens the fabric of our society. My partner of 22 years and I have experienced firsthand the benefits a loving, mutually supportive relationship has had on our three children. It's gratifying to see the Massachusetts court acknowledge relationships like ours—and we look forward to a day when every state recognizes the benefit of treating relationships like ours equally under the law.

—*Joan Garry, Executive Director, Gay and Lesbian Alliance Against Defamation*

No

Across times, cultures, and very different religious beliefs, marriage is the foundation of the family. The family, in turn, is the basic unit of society. Thus, marriage is a personal relationship with public significance. Marriage is the fundamental pattern for male-female relationships. It contributes to society because it models the way in which women and men live interdependently and commit, for the whole of life, to seek the good of each other. The marital union also provides the best conditions for raising children: namely, the stable, loving relationship of a mother and father present only in marriage. The state rightly recognizes this relationship as a public institution in its laws because the relationship makes a unique and essential contribution to the common good. Laws play an education role insofar as they shape patterns of thought and behavior, particularly about what is socially permissible and acceptable. . . . When marriage is redefined so as to make other relationships equivalent to it, the institution of marriage is devalued and further weakened. The weakening of this basic institution at all levels and by various forces has already exacted too high a social cost.

—*U.S. Conference of Catholic Bishops*

Social conservatives have sponsored ballot initiatives to prohibit same-sex marriage. In 2004, voters in eleven states overwhelmingly approved bans on such marriages. Voting in the eight states that considered the ban in 2006 was less one-sided. The margin of victory was less than 60 percent in some states and Arizona voters rejected a same-sex marriage ban, becoming the first electorate to do so.

Aside from the issue of same-sex marriage, Americans have become more accepting of gay and lesbian relationships. Support for civil unions has been increasing gradually in opinion polls, which also indicate most Americans now believe that partners in same-sex relationships should get the same employee benefits as

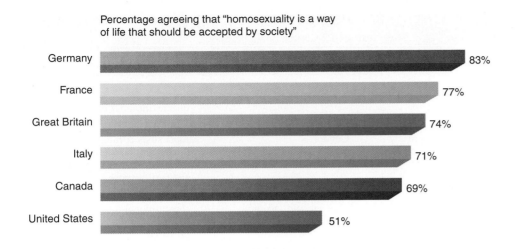

Percentage agreeing that "homosexuality is a way of life that should be accepted by society"

Germany	83%
France	77%
Great Britain	74%
Italy	71%
Canada	69%
United States	51%

Figure 5–4

Opinions on Gay and Lesbian Lifestyles
Americans are less likely than Western Europeans to believe that society should accept gay and lesbian lifestyles.
Source: Global Attitudes Survey (2002) by the Pew Research Center for the People and the Press.

spouses do.[33] For its part, Congress has not taken the issue of same-sex unions beyond the Defense of Marriage Act. An attempt by congressional conservatives in 2006 to initiate a constitutional amendment to ban same-sex marriage fell far short of getting the requisite two-thirds vote in the House and Senate. Yet Americans, perhaps because of their deeper religious beliefs (see Chapter 6), are less supportive of gay and lesbian lifestyles than are Europeans (see Figure 5–4). One thing is sure: issues of gay and lesbian rights, including same-sex marriage and civil union, will be a focus of political action and controversy for the foreseeable future.

EQUALITY UNDER THE LAW

The catchphrase of nearly every group's claim to a more equal standing in American society has been "equality under the law." Once they are secure in their legal rights, people are in a stronger position to insist that their rights be respected and find it easier to pursue equality in other arenas, such as the economic sector. Americans' claims to legal equality are embodied in a great many laws, a few of which are particularly noteworthy.

Equal Protection: The Fourteenth Amendment

The Fourteenth Amendment, which was ratified in 1868, declares in part that no state shall "deny to any person within its jurisdiction the equal protection of the laws." Through this **equal-protection clause,** the courts have protected groups such as African Americans and women from discrimination by state and local governments.

The Fourteenth Amendment's equal-protection clause does not require government to treat all groups or classes of people the same way in all circumstances. By law, for example, twenty-one-year-olds can drink alcohol but twenty-year-olds cannot. The judiciary allows such inequalities because they are held to be "reasonably" related to a legitimate government interest. In applying this **reasonable-basis test,** the courts require government only to show that a particular law is reasonable. For example, the courts have held that the goal of reducing fatalities from alcohol-related accidents involving young drivers is a valid reason for imposing a twenty-one-year minimum age requirement for the purchase of alcohol.

equal-protection clause
A clause of the Fourteenth Amendment that forbids any state to deny equal protection of the laws to any individual within its jurisdiction.

reasonable-basis test
A test applied by courts to laws that treat individuals unequally. Such a law may be deemed constitutional if its purpose is held to be "reasonably" related to a legitimate government interest.

TABLE 5–1	Levels of Court Review for Laws That Treat Americans Differently		
TEST	**APPLIES TO**		**STANDARD USED**
Strict scrutiny	Race, ethnicity		Suspect category—assumed unconstitutional in the absence of an overwhelming justification
Intermediate scrutiny	Gender		Almost suspect category—assumed unconstitutional unless the law serves a clearly compelling and justified purpose
Reasonable basis	Other categories (such as age and income)		Not suspect category—assumed constitutional unless no sound rationale for the law can be provided

strict-scrutiny test
A test applied by courts to laws that attempt a racial or ethnic classification. In effect, the strict-scrutiny test eliminates race or ethnicity as a legal classification when it places minority-group members at a disadvantage.

suspect classifications
Legal classifications, such as race and national origin, that have invidious discrimination as their purpose and therefore are unconstitutional.

intermediate-scrutiny test
A test applied by courts to laws that attempt a gender classification. In effect, the test eliminates gender as a legal classification unless it serves an important objective and is substantially related to the objective's achievement.

The reasonable-basis test does not apply, however, to racial or ethnic classifications, particularly when these categories serve to discriminate against minority-group members (see Table 5–1). Any law that treats people differently because of race or ethnicity is subject to the **strict-scrutiny test,** under which such a law is presumed unconstitutional in the absence of an overwhelmingly convincing argument that it is necessary. The strict-scrutiny test has virtually eliminated race and ethnicity as permissible classifications when the effect is to place a hardship on members of a minority group. The Supreme Court's position is that race and national origin are **suspect classifications**—in other words, that legal classifications based on race and ethnicity are assumed to have discrimination as their purpose and are presumed unconstitutional.

The strict-scrutiny test emerged after the 1954 *Brown* ruling and became a basis for invalidating laws that discriminated against black people. As other groups, especially women, began to organize and assert their rights in the late 1960s and early 1970s, the Supreme Court gave early signs that it might expand the scope of suspect classifications to include gender. In the end, however, the Court announced in *Craig v. Boren* (1976) that sex classifications were permissible if they served "important governmental objectives" and were "substantially" related to the achievement of those objectives.[34] The Court thus placed sex distinctions in an intermediate (or almost suspect) category, to be scrutinized more closely than some other classifications (for example, income or age level) but, unlike racial classifications, justifiable in some instances. In *Rostker v. Goldberg* (1980), for example, the policy of male-only registration for the military draft was upheld on grounds that the exclusion of women from *involuntary* combat duty serves a legitimate and important purpose.[35]

The inexactness of the **intermediate-scrutiny test** has led some scholars to question its usefulness as a legal principle. Nevertheless,

Although women are excluded by law from having to register for the draft, they are eligible to enlist voluntarily in the U.S. military. Shown here is a U.S. woman soldier controlling the crowd on the streets of Mosul, Iraq. Roughly 2 percent of American military casualties in the Iraq conflict have been women.

Political Culture

Private Discrimination: Liberty or Equality?

The courts have ruled that private organizations are often within their rights in discriminating against individuals because of color, gender, creed, national origin, or other characteristics. The Fifth and Fourteenth Amendments only prohibit discrimination by government bodies.

Jews, Catholics, and blacks are among the groups that historically have been denied membership in private clubs and organizations. The most celebrated recent incident was the decision of the Boy Scouts of America (BSA) to revoke the membership of Scoutmaster James Dale. Dale is gay, and the BSA excludes homosexuals from membership.

Dale's suit against the BSA went to the Supreme Court, which ruled in 2000 that the BSA, as a private organization, had the right to deny membership to gays.

Issues of liberty and equality are at the forefront of such cases. Liberty is enhanced when private organizations are free to pick their members. But equality is diminished when people are denied opportunities because of their physical characteristics or lifestyles.

What's your opinion on the Dale–BSA dispute? What general limits, if any, would you impose on the discriminatory acts of private organizations?

when evaluating claims of sex discrimination, the judiciary applies a stricter level of scrutiny than is required by the reasonable-basis test. Rather than giving government broad leeway to treat men and women differently, the Supreme Court has struck down most of the laws it has recently reviewed that contain sex classifications. A leading case is *United States v. Virginia* (1996), in which the Supreme Court determined that the male-only admissions policy of Virginia Military Institute (VMI), a 157-year-old state-supported college, was unconstitutional. The state had developed an alternative program for women at another college, but the Court concluded that it was no substitute for the unique education and other opportunities that attendance at VMI could provide. (The VMI decision also had the effect of ending the all-male admissions policy of the Citadel, a state-supported military college in South Carolina.)[36]

Equal Access: The Civil Rights Acts of 1964 and 1968

The Fourteenth Amendment applies only to action by government. It does not prohibit discrimination by private parties. As a result, for a long period in the nation's history, owners could legally bar black people from restaurants, hotels, and other accommodations, and employers could freely discriminate in their job practices. Since the 1960s, however, private firms have had much less freedom to discriminate for reasons of race, sex, ethnicity, or religion.

Accommodations and Jobs

The Civil Rights Act of 1964, which is based on Congress's power to regulate commerce, entitles all persons to equal access to restaurants, bars, theaters, hotels, gasoline stations, and similar establishments serving the general public. The legislation also bars discrimination in the hiring, promotion, and wages of employees of medium-size and large firms. A few forms of job discrimination are still lawful under the Civil Rights Act. For example, an owner-operator of a small business can discriminate in hiring his or her coworkers, and a religious school can take the religion of a prospective teacher into account.

The Civil Rights Act of 1964 has nearly eliminated the most overt forms of discrimination in the area of public accommodations. Some restaurants and hotels may provide better service to white customers, but outright refusal to serve African Americans or other minority-group members is rare. Such a refusal is a violation of the law and could easily be proved in many instances. It is harder to prove discrimination in job decisions; accordingly, the act has been less effective in rooting out employment discrimination—a subject that we will discuss in detail later in this chapter.

Housing

In 1968, Congress passed civil rights legislation designed to prohibit discrimination in housing. A building owner cannot refuse to sell or rent housing because of a person's race, religion, ethnicity, or sex. An exception is allowed for owners of small multifamily dwellings who reside on the premises.

Despite legal prohibitions on discrimination, housing in America remains highly segregated. Less than a third of all African Americans live in a neighborhood that is mostly white. One reason is that the annual income of most black families is substantially below that of most white families. Another reason is banking practices. At one time, banks contributed to housing segregation by redlining—refusing to grant mortgage loans in certain neighborhoods. This practice drove down the selling prices of homes in these neighborhoods, which led to an influx of African Americans and an exodus of whites. Redlining is prohibited by the 1968 Civil Rights Act, but many of the segregated neighborhoods that it helped create still exist. Studies indicate that minority status is still a factor in the lending practices of some banks. A report of the U.S. Conference of Mayors indicated that, among applicants with average or slightly higher incomes relative to their community, Hispanics and African Americans were twice as likely as whites to be denied a mortgage.[37]

Equal Ballots: The Voting Rights Act of 1965, as Amended

Free elections are perhaps the foremost symbol of American democracy, yet the right to vote has only recently become a reality for many Americans, particularly African Americans. Although they appeared to have gained that right in 1870 with ratification of the Fifteenth Amendment, southern whites invented a series of devices, including whites-only primaries, poll taxes, and rigged literacy tests, to keep them from registering and voting. For example, almost no votes were cast by African Americans in North Carolina between the years 1920 and 1946.[38]

Barriers to black participation in elections began to crumble in the mid-1940s, when the Supreme Court declared that whites-only primary elections were unconstitutional.[39] Two decades later, the Twenty-fourth Amendment outlawed poll taxes.

The major step toward equal voting rights for African Americans was passage of the Voting Rights Act of 1965, which forbids discrimination in voting and registration. The legislation empowers federal agents to register voters and to oversee participation in elections. The Voting Rights Act, as interpreted by the courts, also prohibits the use of literacy tests as a registration requirement. Although civil rights legislation has seldom had a large and immediate impact on people's behavior, the Voting Rights Act was an exception. In the 1960 presidential election, voter turnout among African Americans was barely 30 percent

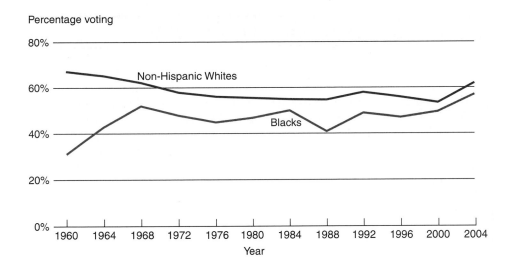

Percentage voting

Non-Hispanic Whites

Blacks

Year

Figure 5–5

Voter Turnout in Presidential Campaigns Among Black and White Americans, 1960–2004
Voter turnout among black Americans rose dramatically during the 1960s as legal obstacles to their voting were removed.
Source: U.S. Bureau of the Census. Figures based on percent of voting-age population that voted.

nationwide (see Figure 5–5). In 1968, three years after passage of the legislation, the turnout rate exceeded 40 percent.

Congress has renewed the Voting Rights Act several times, most recently in 2006. The act includes a provision that compels states and localities to clear with federal officials any electoral change that has the effect, intended or not, of reducing the voting power of a minority group. One way to reduce the power of a group's votes is to spread members of the group across election districts so that their number in any given district is too small to constitute a voting majority. When congressional district boundaries were redrawn after the 1990 census (see Chapter 11), the amendment became the basis for the creation of districts that included a majority of Hispanic or African American voters. The result was the election of an unprecedented number of minority-group members to Congress in 1992, when the number of Hispanic and African American representatives jumped from 27 to 63.

However, in three separate cases that were each decided by a 5-4 margin, the Supreme Court ruled that the redistricting of several congressional districts in Texas, North Carolina, and Georgia violated the Fourteenth Amendment because race had been the "dominant" consideration in their creation. The Court held that the redistricting violated the equal-protection rights of white voters and ordered the three states to redraw the districts.[40] Nevertheless, in *Easley v. Cromartie* (2001), the Court granted states more leeway in creating racially imbalanced districts. At issue was a North Carolina district that was drawn with the goal of creating a safe Democratic district, which, in this instance, produced a district with a large proportion of black voters. The Court, which had long allowed partisan redistricting, ruled that, if such redistricting incidentally creates a minority-dominated district, as was the case with the North Carolina district in question, the action does not violate the Fourteenth Amendment.[41] But in a 2006 case (*League of United Latin American Voters v. Perry*), the Court held that partisan redistricting that comes at the expense of minority-group members can be unlawful. The case involved Texas's 23rd congressional district, which was drawn in a way that deliberately diluted the power of Hispanic voters. In ordering Texas to redraw the district, the Court said: "The troubling blend of politics and race—and the resulting vote dilution of a group that was beginning to [overcome] prior electoral discrimination—cannot be sustained."[42]

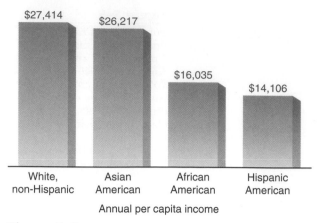

Figure 5–6

U.S. per Capita Income, by Race and Ethnicity
The average income of white Americans is substantially higher than that of most other Americans.
Source: U.S. Bureau of the Census, 2006.

de facto discrimination
Discrimination on the basis of race, sex, religion, ethnicity, and the like that results from social, economic, and cultural biases and conditions.

de jure discrimination
Discrimination on the basis of race, sex, religion, ethnicity, and the like that results from a law.

equality of result
The objective of policies intended to reduce or eliminate the effects of discrimination so that members of traditionally disadvantaged groups will have the same benefits of society as do members of advantaged groups.

affirmative action
A term that refers to programs designed to ensure that women, minorities, and other traditionally disadvantaged groups have full and equal opportunities in employment, education, and other areas of life.

EQUALITY OF RESULT

America's disadvantaged groups have made significant progress toward equal rights, particularly during the past few decades. Through acts of Congress and rulings of the Supreme Court, most forms of government-sponsored discrimination—from racially segregated public schools to gender-based pension plans—have been banned.

However, civil rights problems involve deeply rooted conditions, habits, and prejudices and affect whole categories of people. For these reasons, a new civil rights policy rarely produces a sudden and dramatic change in society. Despite their greater equality in law, America's traditionally disadvantaged groups are still substantially unequal in their daily lives. Consider the issue of income disparity (see Figure 5–6). The average Hispanic or African American's income is less than 60 percent of the average white person's income.

Such disparities reflect **de facto discrimination,** discrimination that is a consequence of social, economic, and cultural biases and conditions. This type of discrimination is different from **de jure discrimination,** which is discrimination based on law, as in the case of the state laws that forced black and white children to attend separate schools during the pre-*Brown* period. De facto discrimination is the more difficult type to root out because it is embedded in the structure of society.

Equality of result is the aim of policies intended to reduce de facto discriminatory effects. Such policies are inherently controversial because many Americans believe that government's responsibility extends no further than the removal of legal barriers to equality. This attitude reflects the culture's emphasis on personal *liberty*—the freedom to choose one's associates, employees, neighbors, and classmates. Nevertheless, a few policies—notably affirmative action and busing—have been implemented to achieve equality of result.

Affirmative Action: Workplace Integration

The difficulty of converting newly acquired legal rights into everyday realities is illustrated by the 1964 Civil Rights Act. Although the legislation prohibited discrimination in employment, women and minorities did not suddenly obtain jobs for which they were qualified. Many employers continued to favor white male employees. Other employers adhered to established employment procedures that kept women and minorities at a disadvantage; membership in many union locals, for example, was handed down from father to son. Moreover, the Civil Rights Act did not require employers to prove that their hiring practices were unbiased. Instead, the burden of proof was on the woman or minority-group member who had been denied a particular job. It was costly and often difficult for individuals to prove in court that their sex or race was the reason they had not been hired. In addition, a victory in court helped only the individual in question; these case-by-case settlements did not affect the millions of other women and minorities facing job discrimination.

A broader remedy was obviously required, and the result was the emergence during the late 1960s of affirmative action programs. **Affirmative action** is a deliberate effort to provide full and equal opportunities in employment, education,

Since its inception in the 1960s, affirmative action policy has been a source of contentious debate but also a source of progress for women and minorities.

and other areas for members of traditionally disadvantaged groups. Affirmative action requires corporations, universities, and other organizations to establish programs designed to ensure that all applicants are treated fairly. Affirmative action also places the burden of proof on the providers of opportunities, who, to some extent, must be able to demonstrate that any disproportionate granting of opportunities to white males is the result of necessity (such as the nature of the job or the locally available labor pool) and not the result of systematic discrimination against women or minorities.

Few issues in recent decades have sparked more controversy than has affirmative action, a reflection of the public's ambivalence about the policy.[43] Most Americans say that they favor granting women and minorities equal opportunities, but they also express opposition to programs that would give preferential treatment to women and minorities (see Figure 5–7).

"In order to overcome past discrimination, do you favor or oppose affirmative action programs designed to help blacks, women, and other minorities get better jobs and education?"

"We should make every possible effort to improve the position of blacks and other minorities, even if it means giving them preferential treatment."

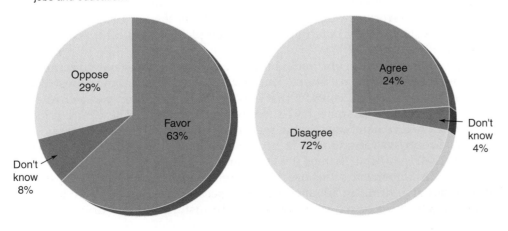

Oppose 29%
Favor 63%
Don't know 8%

Agree 24%
Disagree 72%
Don't know 4%

Figure 5–7

Opinions on Affirmative Action

Most Americans support affirmative action when it comes to programs that will give women and minorities an equal chance at opportunities but oppose it when it comes to programs that will give them preferential treatment.

Source: The Pew Research Center for the People and the Press, May 14, 2003.

TABLE 5–2	Key Decisions in the History of Affirmative Action Policy

YEAR	ACTION
1969	Nixon administration's Department of Labor initiates affirmative action policy
1978	Supreme Court in *Bakke* invalidates rigid quotas for medical school admissions but does not invalidate affirmative action
1980	Supreme Court in *Fullilove* upholds a quota system for minority-owned firms in granting of federal contracts
1980s	Supreme Court in a series of decisions narrows situations in which preferential treatment of minorities will be permitted
1995	Supreme Court in *Adarand* eliminates fixed quotas in the granting of government contracts, reversing the *Fullilove* (1980) precedent
2003	Supreme Court in *Gratz v. Bollinger* and *Grutter v. Bollinger* upholds affirmative action but invalidates formula-based (quota-like) programs.

Affirmative Action in the Law

Most issues that pit individuals against each other in a struggle over society's benefits eventually end up in the courts, and affirmative action is no exception (see Table 5–2). The policy was first tested before the Supreme Court in *University of California Regents v. Bakke* (1978). Alan Bakke, a white man, was denied admission to a medical school that on the basis of a race-based quota system had admitted several minority-group applicants with lower admission test scores. Bakke sued, and the Supreme Court ruled in his favor without invalidating the principle of affirmative action. The Court held that quotas were unconstitutional but said that race could be among the factors taken into account in schools' efforts to create a diverse student body.[44] The *Bakke* ruling was followed by a decision that affirmed the use of quotas in a different context. In *Fullilove v. Klutznick* (1980), the Court upheld a congressional spending bill that included the requirement that 10 percent of the funds for building projects be awarded to minority-owned firms.[45]

These rulings strengthened affirmative action as national policy. However, the appointment of more conservative judges to the Supreme Court during the 1980s narrowed the policy's scope. In 1986, for example, the Court held that preferential treatment for minorities could be justified only in cases where discrimination had been severe and in ways that did not endanger the employment rights of white workers (thus limiting, for example, the use of race rather than seniority as the basis for determining which employees would be terminated in the case of job layoffs).[46]

However, the most substantial blow to advocates of affirmative action was a 1995 decision, *Adarand v. Pena*. The case arose when Adarand Constructors filed suit over a federal contract that was awarded to a Hispanic-owned company even though Adarand had submitted a lower bid. The Court ruled in Adarand's favor, thereby reversing the *Fullilove* precedent. The Court said that set-aside contracts for minority firms are lawful only when the firms involved have themselves been harmed by discrimination. The Court outlawed rules (such as the 10 percent set-aside of government contracts for minority-owned firms) that give firms an advantage simply because the owners' race is that of a people who have been discriminated against historically. The Court also held that, even in situations where a particular firm has been harmed by discrimination, the remedy must be "narrowly tailored" to the situation—that is, the remedy must be in proportion to the harm done to the firm.[47]

Adarand marked the end of an era. By holding that affirmative action must address specific acts of discrimination and be designed to correct those specific acts, the Court effectively brought a halt to federal contracts that gave preference to applicants on the basis of race or gender. The Court had earlier halted such contracts at the state and local government levels.

Both advocates and opponents of affirmative action wondered whether race- and gender-based college admission programs would be the next ones struck down by the Supreme Court. In 2003, in what many observers saw as the most important affirmative action ruling since the *Bakke* decision three decades earlier, the Court made its position known. At issue were two University of Michigan affirmative action admission policies: Michigan's point system for undergraduate admission, which granted twenty points (out of a total of 150 possible points) to minority applicants, and its law school admission process, in which race (along with other factors such as work experience and extracurricular activities) was taken into account in admission decisions. The case attracted national attention, including the involvement of major U.S. corporations, which argued that programs such as those at the University of Michigan contributed to their goal of finding well-educated minorities to fill managerial positions.

Opponents of affirmative action hoped that the Court would strike down the Michigan policies, effectively ending the use of race as a factor in college admissions. Indeed, by a 6-3 vote in *Gratz v. Bollinger,* the Supreme Court did strike down Michigan's undergraduate admissions policy because its point system assigned a specific weight to race.[48] However, by a 5-4 vote in *Grutter v. Bollinger,* the Court upheld the law school's program, concluding that it was being applied in a limited and sensible manner and furthered Michigan's "compelling interest in obtaining the educational benefits that flow from a diverse student body." The Court's majority opinion said further that the law school's policy "promotes 'cross-racial understanding,' helps to break down racial stereotypes, and enables [a] better understand[ing of] persons of different races."[49]

Thus, affirmative action remains a part of national education policy. Both sides of the issue recognize, however, that the Supreme Court's narrow 5-4 majority in the 2003 case means that the issue has not yet been fully settled.

Most Americans know that, whatever the future of affirmative action, the issue of equal opportunity is not one that can be ignored. The nation and its states and communities, as well as its corporations and institutions, have a stake in giving people of all backgrounds a reasonable chance to succeed. Innovative approaches to this challenge have emerged. An example is a Texas policy on college admissions. Recognizing the disparity in the quality of its public schools and other factors that result in lower average scores on standardized tests for minorities, the state established a policy that guarantees admission at a University of Texas institution to any Texas high school student who graduates in the top 10 percent of his or her class. This approach initially faced little opposition even from critics of affirmative action, but opposition has increased as a result of growing enrollment pressure at Texas's flagship universities and the widening perception that students at weaker high schools have an unfair advantage.

The University of Michigan was the focus of national attention in 2003 as a result of its affirmative action admissions programs. Shown here are demonstrators from both sides of the issue. In its 2003 ruling, the Supreme Court upheld the use of race as a factor in admissions but rejected the use of a "point system" as the method of applying it.

The Texas policy reveals a major reason why issues of education, job, and other opportunities are so contentious. Almost every conceivable method of allocating society's benefits—whether through the public sector or the private sector, and however fair they might at first appear—inevitably leave some Americans feeling as if they were unfairly treated. And at that point, such policies invariably become political issues.[50]

Busing: School Integration

The 1954 *Brown* ruling mandated an end to forced segregation of public schools. Government would no longer be permitted to prevent minorities from enrolling in white schools. However, government was not required by the *Brown* decision to compel minority children and white children to attend school together. Fifteen years after *Brown*, because of neighborhood segregation, fewer than 5 percent of America's black children were attending schools that were predominately white. This situation set the stage for one of the few public policies to force whites into regular contact with blacks: the forced busing of children out of their neighborhoods for the purpose of achieving racial balance in the schools.

In *Swann v. Charlotte-Mecklenburg County Board of Education* (1971), the Supreme Court ruled that the busing of children was an appropriate way to integrate schools that were segregated because past discrimination had contributed to the creation of racially separate neighborhoods.[51] Unlike *Brown*, which affected mainly the South, *Swann* applied also to northern communities where blacks and whites lived separately in part because of discriminatory housing ordinances and real estate practices. *Swann* triggered protests even larger than those accompanying the *Brown* decision. Angry and sometimes violent demonstrations lasting weeks occurred in Charlotte, Detroit, Boston, and other cities.

Forced busing had mixed results. For a time, it helped reduce the level of segregation in America's schools; at the high point, nearly 40 percent of minority children were attending a school where most of the students were white. Studies found that busing improved racial attitudes among school children and improved the performance of minority children on standardized tests without diminishing the performance of white classmates.[52] However, these achievements came at a high cost. For many children, forced busing meant long hours riding buses each day to and from school. Moreover, busing contributed to white flight to private schools and to the suburbs, which were protected by a 1974 Supreme Court decision that prohibited busing across school district lines unless those lines had been drawn for the purpose of keeping the races apart.[53] As white students left city schools, it became harder to achieve racial balance through busing and harder as well to gain public support for school spending.

In the past fifteen years, courts have ended most forced busing, saying it was intended as a temporary solution to the problem of segregated schools.[54] Many communities were allowed to devise alternative approaches. Some of them have increased their spending on neighborhood schools in poorer areas. Others have instituted voluntary busing programs that give minority children a choice among district schools. The most controversial of the newer programs give all students a choice among schools but take race into account when assigning children to them.[55] Children might be denied their first choice if granting it would upset the racial balance. The Supreme Court recently agreed to review two such programs, Louisville's and Seattle's, which were challenged by parents who believe that race should have no part at all in determining their

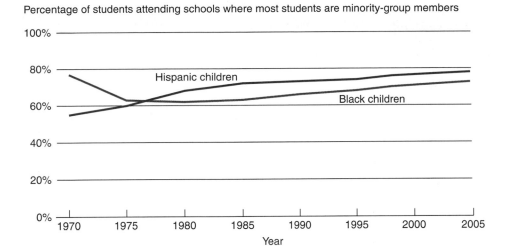

Percentage of students attending schools where most students are minority-group members

Figure 5–8

Segregation in Public Schools Has Been Increasing In the past two decades, racial and ethnic segregation in America's public schools has increased. More than two-thirds of black and Hispanic children today attend a school in which most of the students are members of a minority group. An increase in the number of white non-Hispanic students attending private schools and a decrease in racial busing are factors in the trend. **Source:** U.S. Department of Education, 2006.

children's school assignment. Regardless of how the Court rules on this dispute, the national effect will likely be small. As a result of cutbacks in forced busing, white flight to private and suburban schools, and other factors, segregation of America's schools has been rising steadily since the late 1980s (see Figure 5–8). Today, less than a third of Hispanic and black children attend a school that is predominately white.

PERSISTENT DISCRIMINATION: SUPERFICIAL DIFFERENCES, DEEP DIVISIONS

In 1944, Swedish sociologist Gunnar Myrdal gained fame for his book *An American Dilemma*, whose title referred to deep-rooted racism in a country that idealized equality.[56] Since then, legal obstacles to the mixing of the races have been nearly eliminated, and public opinion has softened significantly. In the early 1940s, a majority of white Americans believed that black children should not be allowed to go to school with white children; today less than 5 percent of white Americans express this belief. There are also visible signs of black progress. In the past two decades, increasing numbers of African Americans have attended college, earned undergraduate degrees, obtained jobs as professionals and managers, and moved into suburban neighborhoods.

Nevertheless, true equality for all Americans remains elusive. The realities of everyday American life are still very different for its white and black citizens. For example, a black child born in the United States has more than twice the chance of dying before reaching his or her first birthday than a white child does. The difference in the infant mortality rates of whites and African Americans reflects differences in their nutrition, medical care, and education—in other words, differences in their access to the most basic resources of a modern society.

The history of equality in America is one of progress and of setbacks and, always, of new challenges. The latest challenge is the treatment of Arab Americans and Muslims in the aftermath of the terrorist attacks of September 11, 2001. Shortly afterward, a radio talk-show host suggested that recent immigrants from the Middle East should be deported, a message eerily reminiscent of what some people once said about Irish Americans and, more recently, Hispanics. Other

Get Involved!

Speak Out

Martin Niemoller was decorated for valor while fighting for Germany in World War I. After the war, he became a Lutheran minister. He initially supported Adolf Hitler's rise to power in 1930s Germany but later became disillusioned with Nazi ideology and spoke against it from the pulpit, an action that led to his confinement in a concentration camp during World War II. When the war ended, he wrote a poem lamenting the German people's unwillingness to stand up for what is right:

First they came for the communists, and I did not speak out—

because I was not a communist;

Then they came for the socialists, and I did not speak out—

because I was not a socialist;

Then they came for the trade unionists, and I did not speak out—

because I was not a trade unionist;

Then they came for the Jews, and I did not speak out—

because I was not a Jew;

Then they came for me—

and there was no one left to speak out.

America is no stranger to discrimination. It began with the introduction of slavery four centuries ago and continues today. Disadvantaged groups have had to fight to achieve a fuller measure of equality. It is not surprising that they would choose to fight. No people in human history have thought second-class status acceptable. What is somewhat surprising is the failure of dominant groups in America to fully embrace the principle of a society of equals. If the economic self-interest of the slaveholder somehow made slavery understandable, though no less abominable, what could possibly underlie discrimination today except raw prejudice?

No American goes through life without witnessing discrimination. It can be as simple as a racial, ethnic, or religious slur. Citizens are obliged to speak out against such expressions, even when they are voiced by friends, neighbors, or coworkers. Robert Dole had the courage to do so. Believing that some individuals within his party were exploiting racial and ethnic prejudice, Dole in his acceptance speech at the 1996 Republican National Convention said that his party had no room for them. Pointing to the back of the convention hall, Dole said "the exits . . . are clearly marked." Dole might have lost a few votes that night, but his point was unimpeachable: discrimination has no place in a nation that claims equality as a birthright.

Americans took the law into their own hands. The Los Angeles Police Department alone recorded more than 150 hate-crime incidents directed against Americans of Middle Eastern origin. Mosques in many U.S. cities were defaced. There was even a bizarre case of malicious misidentification. A Sikh spiritual center in upstate New York was set ablaze by four hooligans because they thought the Sikhs were Arabs who supported Osama bin Laden and his terrorist network. The Sikh spiritual center was named Gobind Sadan, which they thought stood for "go bin Laden."

Although the great majority of Americans have a lot more sense than is displayed by a violent few, many do not necessarily embrace fully the notion that the United States is "one people and one nation." They accept the idea in the abstract but often find it difficult to apply in everyday life. The color of a person's skin or the accent in a person's voice can lead them to respond differently to someone they meet, whether on the street, in a store, on the job, or in the house next door.

Equality is a difficult idea in practice because it requires people to shed preconceived and often deeply embedded notions about how other people think, behave, and feel. Nearly everyone has difficulty seeing beyond superficial differences—whether those differences relate to skin color, national origin, religious preference, sex, or lifestyle—to the shared humanity that unites people of all backgrounds. Myrdal called discrimination "America's curse." He could have broadened the generalization. Discrimination is civilization's curse, as is evident in the scores of ethnic, national, and religious conflicts that have marred human history. But America is a special case because, as Lincoln said in his Gettysburg address, it is a nation founded "on the proposition that all men are created equal." No greater challenge faces America, today as throughout its history, than the challenge of living up to that proposition.

Summary  Self-Test www.mhhe.com/pattersontad8

During the past few decades, the United States has undergone a revolution in the legal status of its traditionally disadvantaged groups, including African Americans, women, Native Americans, Hispanic Americans, and Asian Americans. Such groups are now provided equal protection under the law in areas such as education, employment, and voting. Discrimination by race, sex, and ethnicity has not been eliminated from American life, but it is no longer substantially backed by the force of law.

Traditionally disadvantaged Americans have achieved fuller equality primarily as a result of their struggle for greater rights. The Supreme Court has been an important instrument of change for minority groups. Its ruling in *Brown v. Board of Education* (1954), which declared racial segregation in public schools to be an unconstitutional violation of the Fourteenth Amendment's equal-protection clause, was a major breakthrough in equal rights. Through its busing, affirmative action, and other rulings, the Court also has mandated the active promotion of integration and equal opportunity.

However, because civil rights policy involves general issues of social values and the distribution of society's resources, questions of civil rights are politically explosive. For this reason, legislatures and executives as well as the courts have been deeply involved in such issues, at times siding with established groups and other times backing the claims of underprivileged groups.

In recent decades, affirmative action programs—programs designed to achieve equality of result for African Americans, women, Hispanic Americans, and other disadvantaged groups—have been a civil rights battleground. Affirmative action has had the strong support of civil rights groups and has won the qualified endorsement of the Supreme Court, but it has been opposed by those who claim that it unfairly discriminates against white males. Busing is another issue that has provoked deep divisions within American society, although the era of large-scale forced busing of schoolchildren for the purpose of achieving racial integration is nearly over.

Despite extraordinary gains during recent decades, true equality for all Americans has remained an elusive goal. Tradition, prejudice, and the sheer difficulty of transforming society stand as obstacles to the fuller achievement of America's most challenging ideal—justice for all.

STUDY CORNER

Key Terms

affirmative action (*p. 152*)
civil rights (*p. 132*)
de facto discrimination (*p. 152*)
de jure discrimination (*p. 152*)

equality of result (*p. 152*)
equal-protection clause (*p. 147*)
equal rights (*p. 132*)
gender gap (*p. 136*)

intermediate-scrutiny test (*p. 148*)
reasonable-basis test (*p. 147*)
strict-scrutiny test (*p. 148*)
suspect classifications (*p. 148*)

Self-Test

1. The term *civil rights* refers to:
   a. treating groups equally under the law.
   b. protecting an individual's right to religious belief.
   c. protecting public safety.
   d. permitting marriage by justices of the peace.

2. The Supreme Court of the United States:
   a. has never tolerated discriminating against people on the basis of their race.
   b. outlawed discrimination based on race in the *Plessy* case.
   c. refused to hear the law case involving school segregation in Topeka, Kansas, because Kansas was not considered part of the South.
   d. in *Brown v. Board of Education* prohibited the practice of separate public schools for the purposes of racial segregation.

3. The legal test that in some cases (such as the legal consumption of alcohol) allows government to treat people differently based on their characteristics (such as age) is called:
   a. reasonable-basis test.
   b. strict-scrutiny test.
   c. suspect classification standard.
   d. none of the above.

4. Government policies that have been implemented to eliminate discrimination with the goal of achieving "equality of result" include:
   a. redlining.
   b. affirmative action.
   c. busing.
   d. a and b only.
   e. b and c only.

5. Regarding job-related issues, women:
   a. have made gains in many traditionally male-dominated fields.
   b. have achieved gains in the workplace through programs such as day care and parental leave.
   c. are less likely than men to be promoted to top-level corporate jobs.
   d. hold a disproportionate number of the lower-wage jobs in society.
   e. all of the above.

6. Regarding affirmative action, Supreme Court decisions in the 1980s and 1990s have:
   a. moved to outlaw it entirely.
   b. moved to narrow its application to specific past acts of discrimination.
   c. asked Congress to clarify the policy.
   d. asked the president to clarify the policy.

7. De facto discrimination is much harder to overcome than de jure discrimination. (T/F)

8. The history of discrimination against Hispanics is virtually the same as the history of discrimination against African Americans, which helps account for the similarity of their political and economic situations. (T/F)

9. In recent years, the struggle for equal rights has been extended to the elderly but not to the disabled or to children. (T/F)

10. Asian Americans have made such great progress in overcoming discrimination that the percentage of Asian Americans in top managerial positions and elected political offices is greater than the percentage of Asian Americans in the U.S. population. (T/F)

Critical Thinking

What role have political movements played in securing the legal rights of disadvantaged groups? How has the resulting legislation contributed to a furtherance of these groups' rights?

Suggested Readings

Anderson, Terry H. *The Pursuit of Fairness: A History of Affirmative Action.* New York: Oxford University Press, 2005. A comprehensive look at the affirmative action issue.

Armor, David. *Forced Justice: School Desegregation and the Law.* New York: Oxford University Press, 1996. An evaluation that concludes that the federal courts have overstretched their legal mandate by requiring school integration rather than simply school desegregation.

Chang, Gordon H., ed. *Asian Americans and Politics.* Stanford, Calif.: Stanford University Press, 2001. A broad look at the political engagement of Asian Americans.

Nagel, Joane. *American Indian Ethnic Renewal: Red Power and the Resurgence of Identity and Culture.* New York: Oxford University Press, 1997. Explores the meaning of activism for Native Americans' ethnic identification.

Pinello, Daniel R. *Gay Rights and American Law.* New York: Cambridge University Press, 2003. A careful study of recent appellate-court decisions dealing with gay rights issues.

Reeves, Keith. *Voting Hopes or Fears? White Voters, Black Candidates, and Racial Politics in America.* New York: Oxford University Press, 1997. A critical assessment of race and politics in American society.

Rosen, Ruth. *The World Split Open: How the Modern Women's Movement Changed America.* New York: Viking, 2000. A historian's assessment of the women's rights movement.

Stavans, Ilan. *The Hispanic Condition: Reflections on Culture and Identity in America.* New York: HarperPerennial, 1996. An analysis of the behavioral and cultural differences and similarities among the major Hispanic groups.

Willingham, Alex. *Beyond the Color Line?* New York: Brennan Center for Justice, 2002. A set of articles on race and representation.

List of Websites

http://www.airpi.org/
The website of the American Indian Policy Center, which was established by Native Americans in 1992; includes a political and legal history of Native Americans and examines current issues affecting them.

http://www.naacp.org/
The website of the National Association for the Advancement of Colored People (NAACP); includes historical and current information on the struggle of African Americans for equal rights.

http://www.nclr.org/
The website of the National Council of La Raza (NCLR), an organization dedicated to improving the lives of Hispanics; contains information on public policy, immigration, citizenship, and other subjects.

http://www.rci.rutgers.edu/~cawp/
The website of the Center for the American Woman and Politics (CAWP) at Rutgers University's Eagleton Institute of Politics.

Participate!

Think of a disadvantaged group that you would like to assist. It could be one of the federal government's designated groups (such as Hispanics), one of the other groups mentioned in the chapter (such as the disabled), or some other group (such as the homeless). Contact a college, community, national, or international organization that seeks to help this group and volunteer your assistance. (The Internet provides the names of thousands of organizations, such as Habitat for Humanity, that are involved in helping the disadvantaged.)

Extra Credit

For up-to-the-minute *New York Times* articles, interactive simulations, graphics, study tools, and more links and quizzes, visit the text's Online Learning Center at www.mhhe.com/pattersontad8.

(Self-Test Answers: 1. a   2. d   3. a   4. e   5. e   6. b   7. T   8. F   9. F   10. F)

PART 2

MASS POLITICS

W e are concerned about public affairs, but preoccupied with our private lives, Walter Lippmann wrote. Nevertheless, democracy requires citizens to have an active and influential role in their governing. Citizens are most powerful when they join together in common purpose. This joining together comes during elections and through intermediaries such as political parties, interest groups, and the media.

The chapters in Part Two explore these avenues of citizen politics. Chapter 6 examines the way Americans think politically and the effect of their opinions on government. Chapter 7 describes the nature and impact of political and civic participation. Chapter 8 looks at parties, candidates, elections, and campaigns. Interest groups are the subject of Chapter 9, and the news media are addressed in Chapter 10.

All democracies depend on these instruments of popular influence, but the United States does so in relatively unique ways. For example, America's political parties are among the weakest in the world, while its interest groups and media are among the strongest. The consequences are significant. Political action enables Americans to make their voices heard, but the precise nature of this activity determines whose voices will be heard the loudest.

PART TWO OUTLINE

6 Public Opinion and Political Socialization: Shaping the People's Voice 164

7 Political Participation: Activating the Popular Will 188

8 Political Parties, Candidates, and Campaigns: Defining the Voters Choice 212

9 Interest Groups: Organizing Influence 244

10 The News Media: Communicating Political Images 272

Public Opinion and Political Socialization:
Shaping the People's Voice

Chapter Outline

The Nature of Public Opinion
How Informed Is Public Opinion?
The Measurement of Public Opinion

Political Socialization: How Americans Learn Their Politics
The Process of Political Socialization
The Agents of Political Socialization

Frames of Reference: How Americans Think Politically
Cultural Thinking: Common Ideas
Ideological Thinking: The Outlook of Some
Group Thinking: The Outlook of Many
Partisan Thinking: The Line That Divides

The Influence of Public Opinion on Policy

CHAPTER 6

> To speak with precision of public opinion is a task not unlike coming
> to grips with the Holy Ghost.
>
> —*V.O. Key Jr.*[1]

As the U.S. troop buildup in the Persian Gulf region continued into 2003, most Americans were unsure of the best course of action. They had been hearing about Saddam Hussein for years and had concluded that he was a brutal tyrant and a terrorist threat. A majority expressed a willingness to support a war in Iraq if President George W. Bush deemed it necessary. But Americans had differing opinions on when and whether war would occur. Some wanted to give United Nations inspectors ample time to investigate Iraq's weapons program before a final decision on war was made. Others preferred to hold off on making the decision for war until the United States could line up international support. Still others supported more immediate action but preferred a bombing campaign to the launching of a ground war that might result in high casualties among U.S. forces.

Nevertheless, once the bombs started dropping on Iraq and U.S. ground troops poured into Iraq from their staging base in Kuwait, Americans strongly supported the action. Polls indicated that roughly 70 percent backed President Bush's decision to use military force against Iraq, with 20 percent opposed and 10 percent undecided.

The Iraq war is a telling example of the influence of public opinion on government: public opinion rarely forces officials to take a particular course of action. If President Bush had decided that the Iraq situation could have been resolved through UN weapons inspectors, public opinion would have supported his decision. A majority of Americans would also have supported the president if he had decided that war made sense only if it had broad international support or was limited to an air war.

Although public opinion has a central place in democratic societies because of a belief that public policy should reflect the will of the people, public opinion is seldom an exact guide to policy. Political leaders ordinarily enjoy leeway in choosing a course of action. Rather than fighting a war against Iraq, for example, President Bush could have decided to concentrate on finishing the war begun earlier in Afghanistan. Concentrations of Al Qaeda and Taliban fighters were still operating in Afghanistan, and terrorist leader Osama bin Laden was still at large. Bush also had the option of a law-enforcement response to the terrorist threat. He could have decided to pump resources into a worldwide police and intelligence effort aimed at finding and eliminating terrorist cells. The September 11, 2001, terrorist attacks on the World Trade

Center and the Pentagon had created an expectation among Americans that the Bush administration would act decisively to counter the terrorist threat. But it was largely up to the president and his advisers to decide the precise nature of the response.

This chapter discusses public opinion and its influence on the U.S. political system. A major theme is that public opinion is a powerful yet inexact force in American politics.[2] The policies of the U.S. government cannot be understood apart from public opinion; at the same time, as stated above, public opinion is not a precise determinant of public policy. The main points made in this chapter are these:

- *Public opinion consists of those views held by ordinary citizens that are openly expressed.* Public officials have many means of gauging public opinion but increasingly have relied on public opinion polls to make this determination.

- *The process by which individuals acquire their political opinions is called political socialization.* This process begins during childhood, when, through family and school, Americans acquire many of their basic political values and beliefs. Socialization continues into adulthood, during which peers, political institutions and leaders, and the news media are major influences.

- *Americans' political opinions are shaped by several frames of reference. Four of the most important are ideology, group attachments, partisanship, and political culture.* These frames of reference form the basis of political consensus and conflict among the general public.

- *Public opinion has an important influence on government but ordinarily does not directly determine what officials will do.* Public opinion works primarily to place limits on the choices made by officials.

THE NATURE OF PUBLIC OPINION

Public opinion is a relatively new concept in the history of political thought. Not until pressures began to mount in the 1700s for representative government was there a need for a term to refer to what ordinary people thought about politics. The first English-speaking philosopher to write at length about public opinion was Jeremy Bentham (1748–1832).[3] Originally an advocate of government by an enlightened elite, Bentham came to believe that the public's views had to be taken into account if leaders were to govern properly.

Public opinion is now a widely used term, but it is a term that is often used inexactly. A common mistake is the assumption that "the public"—meaning the whole citizenry—actually has an opinion on most issues of public policy. In fact, most issues do not attract the attention of even a majority of citizens. Agricultural conservation programs, for example, are of intense interest to some farmers, hunters, and environmentalists but of little interest to most people. This pattern is so pervasive that opinion analysts have described America as having *many* publics.[4]

On numerous issues, there is literally no majority opinion. On some issues, such as agricultural conservation programs, a form of *pluralist* democracy usually prevails. Government responds to the views of particular groups. In other cases, *elitist* opinion prevails. On the question of U.S. relations with Finland, for example, there is little likelihood that ordinary citizens would know or care what the U.S. government does. In such instances, the policy opinions of an elite group of business and policy leaders ordinarily prevail. *Majority* opinion also can be decisive, but its influence normally is confined to a few broad issues that elicit widespread attention and concern, such as war, social security, and employment. This situation may suggest a limited role for popular majorities, but such issues, though few in number, typically have the greatest impact on society as a whole.

Hence, any definition of the term *public opinion* cannot be based on the assumption that all citizens, or even a majority, are actively interested in and hold a preference about all aspects of political life. **Public opinion** can be defined as the politically relevant opinions held by ordinary citizens that they express openly.[5] This expression need not be verbal. It could also take the form, for example, of a protest demonstration or a vote for one candidate rather than another. The crucial point is that a person's private thoughts on an issue become public opinion when they are expressed openly.

How Informed Is Public Opinion?

A practical obstacle to government by public opinion is that people have differing opinions; in responding to one side of an issue, government is compelled to reject other preferences. Public opinion can also be contradictory. Polls indicate, for example, that most Americans would like better schools, health care, and other public services while also favoring a reduction in taxes (see Figure 6–1). Which opinion of the people should govern—their desire for more services or their desire for lower taxes?

Another limitation is that people's opinions, even on issues of great importance, are often misinformed. In the buildup to the U.S. invasion of Iraq in 2003, for example, polls revealed that more than half of the American public wrongly believed that Iraq had close ties to the terrorist network Al Qaeda and that Iraqis were among the nineteen terrorists who had flown airplanes into the World Trade Center and the Pentagon on September 11, 2001. Moreover, despite opposition to the war on the

Lee Miringoff heads the Marist College's Institute for Public Opinion. With him are students as they call New York State residents to get their opinions on public issues. Polling is now nearly synonymous with public opinion. A wide variety of public and private organizations conduct polls for clients and, in some cases, do so simply to discover how people across the nation, within a state, or in a community are responding to events of the moment.

public opinion
The politically relevant opinions held by ordinary citizens that they express openly.

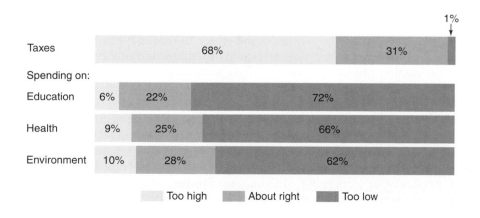

	Too high	About right	Too low
Taxes	68%	31%	1%
Spending on:			
Education	6%	22%	72%
Health	9%	25%	66%
Environment	10%	28%	62%

Figure 6–1

Opinions on Taxing and Spending
People's opinions can be contradictory. Americans say, for example, that taxes are too high and yet also say, when asked about specific policy areas, that government is spending too little.
Source: National Opinion Research Center, University of Chicago.

Public opinion includes contradictory elements. According to surveys, for example, most Americans say they want lower taxes but also say they want more public services. At a Boston rally, this demonstrator expresses anger with President Clinton's tax-increase legislation while also demanding that government provide free health care.

part of most Europeans, Asians, South Americans and Africans, one-fourth of Americans wrongly believed that world opinion favored the war. Americans who held such views were more supportive of the Iraq war than were other Americans.[6]

Most Americans are not closely attentive to politics and therefore do not possess a lot of factual information. Americans are not unique in this respect, but in some areas they are less informed than citizens of most other Western democracies. In a seven-country survey, Americans ranked next to last (ahead of only Spaniards) in their ability to respond correctly to five factual questions about prominent world leaders and developments.[7] Despite America's leading role in the world, most Americans are less informed about international affairs than are most Europeans.

Even many college-educated Americans lack basic information about public affairs. A survey of Ivy League students found that one-third could not identify the British prime minister, half could not name both U.S. senators from their state, and three-fourths could not identify Abraham Lincoln as the author of the phrase "a government of the people, by the people, and for the people."[8]

Of course, citizens do not always have to be well informed about an issue to have a reasonable opinion about it. Opinions derive largely from people's values and interests.[9] People can have sound opinions on the abortion issue, for example, without precise knowledge of what courts and lawmakers have done on the issue. Nevertheless, the public's lack of information limits the role that public opinion can play in policy formulation. The choice among policy options in some cases requires an understanding of the consequences of the different options. Citizens usually lack this type of information.

The Measurement of Public Opinion

Woodrow Wilson once said he had spent nearly all his adult life in government and yet had never seen a "government." What Wilson was saying, in effect, was that government is a system of relationships. A government is not a building or a person—it is not tangible in the way that a car or a bottle of soda is. So it is with public opinion. No one has ever seen a "public opinion," and thus it cannot be measured directly. It must be assessed indirectly.

Election returns are a traditional method of assessing public opinion. Journalists and politicians routinely draw conclusions about what citizens are thinking by how they vote. Letters to the editor in newspapers, email messages to elected officials, and the size of crowds at mass demonstrations are other means of judging public opinion. All these indicators are useful guides for policymakers. None of them, however, is a precise indicator of what the broad public is thinking. Elections offer citizens only a yes-no choice between the candidates, and different voters will have chosen the same candidate for different reasons. As for letter writers and demonstrators, they are nearly always *unrepresentative* of the population as a whole. Fewer than 1 percent of Americans participate each year in a mass demonstration, and fewer than 10 percent write to the president or a member of Congress. Studies have found that the opinions of letter writers and demonstrators are more extreme than those of most citizens.

Get Involved!

Inform Yourself

During the buildup to the U.S. invasion of Iraq, polls revealed that more than half of the American public incorrectly believed that the Iraq regime had close ties to the terrorist network Al Qaeda. More than half also wrongly believed that Iraqis were among the nineteen terrorists who had flown airplanes into the World Trade Center and the Pentagon on September 11, 2001, and one-fourth wrongly thought that America's invasion of Iraq had the backing of most of the rest of the world.

Americans are generally uninformed about global affairs. The war on terrorism has increased their understanding of some parts of the world, but Americans typically have had less interest in what is occurring elsewhere than have comparably educated people in other countries. Analysts suggest that America's "ocean isolation" is a reason why its citizens are insular. Unlike Europeans, Americans are not surrounded by a host of other countries. But ocean isolation is not a complete explanation. Americans share a border with Canadians and Mexicans, for example, but know much less about Canada and Mexico than Canadians and Mexicans know about the United States.

International terrorism and the increasing globalization of the economy suggest that Americans should pay more attention to the larger world in which they live. Many Americans, for example, were puzzled when their country was targeted for terrorist attacks on September 11, 2001. Their initial impulse was to say that the country had been attacked because it represents freedom. As Americans discovered, however, that explanation was incomplete. The terrorists had specific grievances against the United States, including its policies in the Middle East. The terrorists' decision to target innocent civilians to express their discontent was cowardly and despicable, but as Americans came to understand during the months after the attacks, it was not rooted in envy.

Citizenship entails responsibilities, one of which is to stay informed about problems and developments that affect the community, the state, and the nation. As an informed citizen, you will be better able to make judgments about policy issues, to choose wisely when voting during elections, and to recognize situations that call for greater personal involvement. Fortunately, you have access to one of the most substantial news systems in the world. News about public affairs is virtually at your fingertips—through your computer, on television, and in the newspaper. Spending only a small amount of time each day following the news will enable you to be a more effective and involved citizen.

Public Opinion Polls

In an earlier day, indicators such as elections and letters to the editor were the only means by which public officials could gauge what the public was thinking. Today, they also rely on opinion polls or surveys, which provide a more systematic method of estimating public sentiment.[10]

In a **public opinion poll**, a relatively few individuals—the **sample**—are interviewed in order to estimate the opinions of a whole **population**, such as the residents of a city or the citizens of a country. If a sufficient number of individuals are chosen at random, their views will tend to be representative—that is, roughly the same as the views held by the population as a whole.

How is it possible to measure the thinking of a large population on the basis of a relatively small sample? How can interviews with, say, one thousand Americans provide a reliable estimate of what 300 million are thinking? The answer is found in the laws of probability. Consider the hypothetical example of a huge jar filled with a million marbles, half of them red and half of them blue. If a blindfolded person reaches into the jar, the probability of selecting a marble of a given color is fifty-fifty. And if one thousand marbles are chosen in this random way, it is likely that about half of them will be red and about half will be blue. Opinion sampling works in the same way. If respondents are chosen at random from a population, their opinions will approximate those of the population as a whole.

Random selection is the key to scientific polling, which is based on *probability sampling*—a sample in which each individual in the population has a

public opinion poll
A device for measuring public opinion whereby a relatively small number of individuals (the sample) are interviewed for the purpose of estimating the opinions of a whole community (the population).

sample
In a public opinion poll, the relatively small number of individuals who are interviewed for the purpose of estimating the opinions of an entire population.

population
In a public opinion poll, the people (for example, the citizens of a nation) whose opinions are being estimated through interviews with a sample of these people.

Debating the Issues

Should Representatives Lead on the Basis of Opinion Polls?

A fundamental principle of democracy is that public opinion ought to be the foundation of government. However, the role that public opinion should play in specific policy decisions is, and always has been, a subject of dispute. James Madison distinguished between the public's momentary passions and its enduring concerns, arguing that government is obliged to represent only the latter. In contrast, the Jacksonians and Progressives had a strong faith in the judgment of ordinary citizens and a distrust of entrenched elites. With the advent of the public opinion poll, it became possible to measure citizens' policy views more directly. Should policymakers follow the polls in making their decisions? Some analysts have held that leaders should act in close accord with the polls. Other analysts have argued that polls measure fleeting opinions about topical issues and that leaders in any event are obliged only to respond to the people's deep and enduring beliefs.

Sixty-eight percent of Americans think they should have a great deal of influence on the decisions of elected and government officials in Washington, but fewer than one in ten (9%) believe they do.... Who instead do Americans think bends the ears of the politicians and officials in the Capitol? According to the public, money talks. Nearly six in ten [say] that politicians pay a great deal of attention to their campaign contributors when making decisions about important issues.... Fifty-four percent of Americans expect their officials to follow what the majority wants, even if it goes against the officials' knowledge and judgment. Fewer (42%) want officials to use their own judgment if it goes against the wishes of the majority.... If we all lived in small New England towns, then perhaps town hall meetings would be a realistic means of injecting public opinion into the national debate. However, when it takes one western senator a whole year to travel to every single county in his or her home state, it is clear that the limits imposed by geography and time necessitate a continuing place for polling in public policy.

—*Bill McInturff and Lori Weigel, pollsters*

True statesmen are not merely mouthpieces for opinion polls. British historian Lord Acton recognized that the will of the majority could be and often is just as tyrannical as the will of a monarch, and in some cases more dangerous because the error has the support of the masses. Thus he observes, "It is bad to be oppressed by a minority, but it is worse to be oppressed by a majority," and "The will of the people cannot make just that which is unjust." ... In the United States we have compelling historical and contemporary examples of the majority siding with what were, in retrospect, clear-cut cases of injustice. The legalization and promotion of slavery by governments are a prime example, and stand as a stark rebuke to elected officials who think they ought to represent the people without regard to their own conscience. Today, there are a number of hotly contested issues—such as abortion, stem cell research, and, now, marriage—whose partisans often make appeals based on poll data. Our elected officials follow the shifting temper of the electorate with rapt attention. But is this how we ask our elected officials to lead? ... [T]oo many political leaders have settled on an inadequate answer: the will of the people (and the pollsters).

—*Jordon J. Ballor, Acton Institute*

known probability of being chosen at random for inclusion. A scientific poll is different from the surveys found on many Internet sites; those who respond to such surveys are selecting themselves for the poll rather than being selected randomly by the pollster. A scientific poll is also different from the "people-in-the-street" interviews that news reporters sometimes conduct. Although a reporter may say that the opinions of those interviewed represent the views of the local population, this claim is clearly faulty. Interviews conducted on a downtown street at the noon hour, for example, will include a disproportionate number of business employees taking their lunch break. Housewives, teachers, and factory workers are among the many groups that would be underrepresented in such a sample.

The science of polling is such that the size of the sample, as opposed to the size of the population, is the key to accurate estimates. Although it might be assumed that a much larger sample would be required to poll accurately the people of the United States as opposed to the residents of Georgia, the sample requirements are nearly the same. Consider again the example of a huge jar filled with marbles, half of them red and half of them blue. If one thousand marbles were randomly selected, about half would be red and about half would be blue, regardless of whether the jar held one million, ten million, or one hundred million marbles. On the other hand, the size of the sample—the number of marbles selected—does matter. If only ten marbles were drawn, it might happen that five would be of each color but, then again, it would not be unusual for six, seven, or even eight of them to be of the same color. However, if one thousand marbles were drawn, it would be highly unusual for six hundred of the marbles, much less seven hundred or eight hundred of them, to be of the same color.

The accuracy of a poll is expressed in terms of **sampling error,** the degree to which the sample estimates might differ from what the population actually thinks. The larger the sample, the smaller the sampling error, which is usually expressed as a plus-or-minus percentage. For example, a properly drawn sample of one thousand individuals has a sampling error of roughly plus or minus 3 percent. Thus, if 55 percent of a sample of one thousand respondents say they intend to vote for the Republican presidential candidate, then the probability is high that between 52 percent and 58 percent (55 percent plus or minus 3 percent) of all voters actually plan to vote Republican.

The impressive record of the Gallup poll in predicting the outcome of presidential elections indicates that the theoretical accuracy of polls can be matched in practice. The Gallup organization has polled voters in every presidential election since 1936 (eighteen elections in all) and has erred badly only once: it stopped polling several weeks before the 1948 election and missed a late voter shift that carried Harry Truman to victory.

sampling error
A measure of the accuracy of a public opinion poll. The sampling error is mainly a function of sample size and is usually expressed in percentage terms.

President Harry Truman holds up the early edition *Chicago Tribune* with the headline "Dewey Defeats Truman." The *Tribune* was responding to analysts' predictions that Dewey would win the 1948 election. A Gallup poll a few weeks before the election had shown Dewey with a seemingly insurmountable lead. The Gallup Organization decided that it did not need to do another poll closer to the election, a mistake that it has not since repeated.

LEADERS

GEORGE GALLUP

(1901–84)

George Gallup has been called the father of the public opinion poll. Gallup began his career as a college professor at Drake University after earning a Ph.D. from the University of Iowa. Within a few years, he had taken a job at the New York advertising firm of Young & Rubicam, where he developed pioneering methods for measuring media impact. In 1935, he started a polling firm. The firm distinguished itself by touting "scientific polling"—polls based on systematic sampling. A year later, Gallup's method proved itself in dramatic fashion. The nation's best-known poll of the time, the *Literary Digest* poll, predicted a Republican landslide in the 1936 presidential election. Gallup's poll indicated a landslide for incumbent Democratic President Franklin D. Roosevelt. Roosevelt's victory made Gallup nationally known and gave instant credibility to both his organization and his polling method. Gallup lectured and wrote throughout his career, claiming repeatedly that polls could serve democracy by enabling political leaders to better understand what the public is thinking. Gallup said: "Polling is merely an instrument for gauging public opinion. When a president or any other leader pays attention to poll results, he is, in effect, paying attention to the views of the people. Any other interpretation is nonsense." The Gallup Organization remains the world's best-known survey firm.

WWW.MHHE.COM/PATTERSONTAD8

Problems with Polls

Although pollsters assume that their samples are drawn from a particular population, it is seldom the case that everyone in that population has a chance of becoming part of the sample. Only rarely does a pollster have a list of all individuals in a population from which to draw a sample. An expedient alternative is a sample based on telephone numbers. Pollsters use computers to randomly pick telephone numbers, which are then dialed by interviewers to reach households. Within each of these households, a respondent is then randomly selected. Because the computer is as likely to pick one telephone number as any other and because more than 90 percent of U.S. homes have a telephone, a sample selected in this way is assumed to be representative of the population. Nevertheless, some Americans do not have phones and many of those who are called are not home or refuse to participate. Such factors reduce the accuracy of telephone polling. In fact, although telephone polls continue to provide precise predictions of elections, pollsters are increasingly worried about the future of telephone polling. The percentage of Americans that refuse to participate in telephone surveys has increased sharply in recent decades and the use of cell phones—which are not included in computer-based telephone sampling—has risen significantly.

The accuracy of polling is also diminished when respondents are questioned about a topic they are unfamiliar with or have not thought about. In this case, respondents tend to answer the question but the only reason that they have an answer is because the pollster has asked them for one. In such cases, pollsters are measuring what scholars call "nonopinions."

Question wording can also affect poll results, particularly on sensitive issues. For example, an NBC News/Wall Street Journal poll found that two-thirds of Americans favor federal funding for research on human embryonic stem cells whereas a poll conducted for the Conference on Catholic Bishops found that only a fourth of Americans favor such funding. The wide difference in the two polls is explained by question wording. The NBC News/Wall Street Journal's poll question asked directly about government funding whereas the Conference of Catholic Bishops' poll question stressed the fact that stem cells are taken from human embryos.[11]

Despite these and other sources of error, the poll or survey is the most relied-upon method of measuring public opinion. More than one hundred organizations are in the business of conducting public opinion polls. Some, like the Gallup Organization, conduct polls that are then released to the news media by syndication. Most large news organizations also have their own in-house polls; one of the most prominent of these is the CBS News/New York Times poll. Some polling firms specialize in conducting surveys for candidates and officeholders.

POLITICAL SOCIALIZATION: HOW AMERICANS LEARN THEIR POLITICS

Analysts have long been interested in how public opinion originates. The learning process by which people acquire their political opinions, beliefs, and values is called **political socialization.** Just as a language, a religion, or an athletic skill is acquired through a learning process, so too are people's political orientations. Americans grow up to believe that free elections are the proper method of choosing leaders. People in some parts of the world are accustomed to other methods, which they find perfectly acceptable.

For most Americans, the socialization process starts in the family with exposure to the political loyalties and opinions of their parents. The schools later contribute to the process, as do the mass media, friends, work associates, and other agents. Political socialization is a lifelong process.

The Process of Political Socialization

The process of political socialization in the United States has several major characteristics. First, although socialization continues throughout life, most people's political outlook is substantially influenced by their childhood learning. That which is learned first is often lodged most firmly in a person's mind. Basic ideas about race, gender, and political affiliation, for example, are often formed uncritically in childhood, much in the way belief in a particular religion—typically the religion of one's parents—is acquired.

A second characteristic of political socialization is that its effect is cumulative. Early learning affects later learning. Individuals have psychological defenses that protect beliefs acquired earlier in life. Many people, for example, remain lifelong Republicans or Democrats even as their personal lives or political conditions change in ways that might logically lead them to identify with the other party. Of course, political change can and does occur. Historically, major shifts in political orientation have occurred around major upheavals and have been concentrated among younger adults because their beliefs are less firmly rooted than are those of older adults. The **age-cohort tendency** holds that a significant change in the pattern of political socialization is typically concentrated among younger citizens. For example, President Franklin Roosevelt's New Deal, which sought to alleviate the economic hardship of the Great Depression, prompted many younger Republicans, but not many older ones, to shift their loyalty to the Democratic party.

The Agents of Political Socialization

The socialization process takes place through a variety of agents, including family, schools, mass media, peers, and political leaders and events. It is helpful to consider briefly some of these **agents of socialization** and how they affect political learning.

Families

The family is a powerful agent of socialization because it has a near-monopoly on the attention of the young child, who places great trust in what a parent says. By the time the child is a teenager and is not likely to listen to any advice a parent might offer, many of the beliefs and values that will stay with the child throughout life are already in place. Many adults are Republicans or Democrats today largely because their parents backed that party. They can give all sorts of reasons

political socialization
The learning process by which people acquire their political opinions, beliefs, and values.

age-cohort tendency
The tendency for a significant break in the pattern of political socialization to occur among younger citizens, usually as the result of a major event or development that disrupts preexisting beliefs.

agents of socialization
Those agents, such as the family and the media, that have a significant impact on citizens' political socialization.

How the United States Compares
National Pride

Americans are justifiably proud of their nation. It is the oldest continuous democracy in the world, an economic powerhouse, and a diverse yet harmonious society.

What Americans may not recognize, because it is so much a part of everyday life in America, is the degree to which they are bombarded with messages and symbols of their nation's greatness. Political socialization in the United States is not the rigid program of indoctrination that some societies impose on their people. Nevertheless, Americans receive a thorough political education. Their country's values are impressed on them by every medium of communication: newspapers, daily conversations, television, movies, books. After the terrorist attacks of September 11, 2001, these tendencies reached new heights. The NBC television network outfitted its peacock logo with stars and stripes, and computer-generated flags festooned the other networks' broadcasts.

The words and symbols that regularly tell Americans of their country's greatness are important to its unity. In the absence of a common ancestral heritage to bind them, Americans need other methods to instill and reinforce the idea that they are one people. As discussed in Chapter 1, America's political ideals have this effect, as do everyday reminders such as the flying of the flag on homes and private buildings, a practice that is almost uniquely American. (Elsewhere, flags are rarely displayed except on public buildings.)

One indicator of Americans' political socialization is their high level of national pride. Harvard University's Pippa Norris (in Marian Sawer's edited volume *The People's Choice*) constructed an index of national pride based on

people's admiration for their country's political, economic, artistic, sporting, scientific, and other achievements. Americans ranked at the top, as shown by the following chart, which is based on Norris's index:

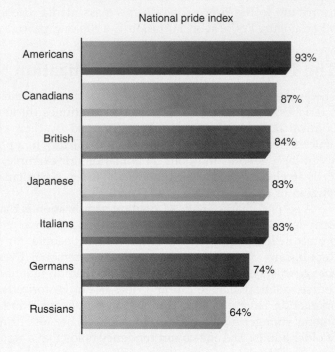

National pride index

Americans	93%
Canadians	87%
British	84%
Japanese	83%
Italians	83%
Germans	74%
Russians	64%

for preferring their party to the other, but the reasons come later in life. The loyalty comes first, during childhood. The family also contributes to basic orientations that, while not directly political, have political significance. For example, American families tend to be more egalitarian than families in other nations, and American children often have a voice in family decisions. Basic American values such as equality and individualism have roots in patterns of family interaction.[12]

Schools

The school, like the family, affects children's basic political beliefs. Teachers at the elementary level extol the exploits of national heroes such as George Washington, Abraham Lincoln, and Martin Luther King Jr. and praise the country's economic and political systems.[13] Although students in the middle and high school grades receive a more nuanced version of American history, it tends to emphasize the nation's great moments—for example, its decisive role in the two world wars. U.S. schools are probably more instrumental in building support for the nation than are the schools in other democracies. The Pledge of Allegiance, which is

Students in a North Carolina school reciting the Pledge of Allegiance. Such childhood socialization experiences can have a profound impact on an individual's basic political beliefs.

recited daily in many U.S. schools, has no equivalent in European countries. Schools also contribute to Americans' sense of social equality. Most American children, regardless of family income, attend public schools and study a fairly standard curriculum. In many countries, schoolchildren are separated at an early age, with some placed in vocational classes while others are slotted in courses that will lead them to attend college.

Mass Media

The mass media are another powerful socializing agent. The themes and images that dominate the media affect people's perceptions of their world. For example, repeated exposure to crime on television can lead people to believe that society itself is more violent than it actually is. Similarly, people's perceptions of political leaders are affected to some extent by how those leaders are represented in the media. When leaders are regularly portrayed as manipulative, for example, people tend to regard them as self-serving.[14]

Peers

Peer groups—friends, neighbors, and coworkers—tend to reinforce what a person already believes. One reason is that most people trust the opinions of their friends and associates. Many individuals also are unwilling to deviate too far from what their peers think. In *The Spiral of Silence*, Elisabeth Noelle-Neumann contends that most individuals are reluctant to express contrary opinions. One effect, she argues, is to make prevailing opinions appear to be more firmly and widely held than they actually are.[15]

Political Institutions and Leaders

Citizens look to political leaders and institutions, particularly the president and political parties, as guides to opinion.[16] In the period immediately after the terrorist attacks on the World Trade Center and the Pentagon on September 11, 2001,

Religion is a powerful socializing force in American life. Churches, synagogues, mosques, and temples are places where Americans acquire values and beliefs that can affect their opinions about politics. Shown here are Muslim men gathering to pray at a mosque in Garden Grove, California. Traditionally, men and women have prayed in different parts of the mosque. Some U.S. mosques have integrated their prayer services and a few have allowed women to lead prayer sessions—changes that have been sharply criticized by traditionalists.

many Americans were confused about who the enemy was and what the response should be. That state of mind changed dramatically ten days later after a televised speech by President Bush in which he identified the Al Qaeda and Taliban forces in Afghanistan as the immediate target of what would become a war on terrorism. In polls taken immediately after the speech, nine of every ten Americans said they shared Bush's views.

Churches

Beginning with the Puritans in the seventeenth century, churches have played a substantial role in shaping Americans' social and political opinions. Most Americans say they believe in God, most attend church at least occasionally, and most belong to a religion that includes teachings on the proper form of society. Moreover, most Americans say that religion has answers to many of the problems facing today's society. In these and other respects, churches and religion are a more powerful force in the United States than in most other Western countries.

Scholars have not studied the impact of churches on political socialization as closely as they have studied influences such as schools and the media.[17] Nevertheless, churches are a significant source of political attitudes, including those related to society's obligations to children, the poor, and the unborn. (The impact of religion is discussed further in a later section of this chapter.)

FRAMES OF REFERENCE: HOW AMERICANS THINK POLITICALLY

What are the frames of reference that guide the political thinking of Americans? The question is an important one. Shared opinions enable people to find common cause. The opinions of millions of Americans would mean little if everyone's ideas were different. But if enough people think the same way, they may decide to work together to promote their view.

Among the frames of reference through which Americans think about politics are cultural values, ideology, group attachments, and partisanship, as the following discussion will explain.

Cultural Thinking: Common Ideas

As was discussed in Chapter 1, Americans embrace a common set of ideals. Principles such as liberty, equality, and individualism have always meant somewhat different things to Americans but nonetheless are a source of agreement. For example, government programs aimed at redistributing wealth from the rich to the poor are popular among Europeans but are less appealing to Americans, who have a deeper commitment to individualism.

States in the Nation

Conservatives and Liberals

In the United States, self-identified conservatives substantially outnumber those who call themselves liberals. Only in twelve states and the District of Columbia are liberals greater or nearly equal in number to conservatives.

Q: Why is the concentration of conservatives especially high in the southern, plains, and mountain states?

A: The southern, plains, and mountain states are less urbanized. Accordingly, their residents traditionally have been less dependent on and less trusting of government.

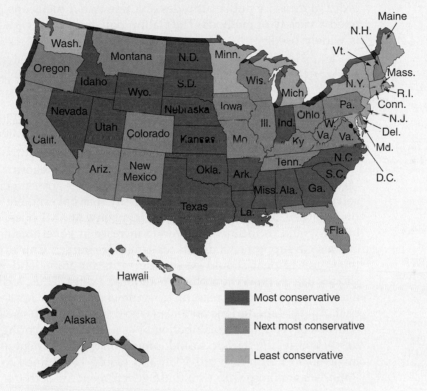

- Most conservative
- Next most conservative
- Least conservative

Source: CNN exit polls, 2000. Classification based on the difference in the proportions of self-identified conservatives and liberals in each state.

There are limits, of course, to the degree to which Americans' basic beliefs shape their policy opinions. For more than three centuries, African Americans were inferior by law to white Americans, despite the American creed that "all men are created equal." Such inconsistencies speak to the all-too-human capacity to voice one idea and live another. Nevertheless, Americans' political ideals have a powerful influence on their opinions.

Ideological Thinking: The Outlook of Some

Analysts sometimes use words such as *liberal* and *conservative* to describe how ordinary Americans think about politics (see "States in the Nation"). These are ideological terms, as are terms such as socialism and communism. An **ideology** is a consistent pattern of political attitudes that stems from a core belief. The core

ideology
A consistent pattern of opinion on particular issues that stems from a core belief or set of beliefs.

belief of socialism, for example, is that society should ensure that every person's basic economic needs are met. Accordingly, a socialist would support public policies that provide for economic security, such as a government-guaranteed minimum annual income for all families.

America's major ideologies are rooted in beliefs about equality and liberty. The importance that people attach to one or the other of these ideals and the degree to which they think government involvement promotes or impedes it affect their ideological stance. Economic liberals, for example, look to government to create a more equal society than that which results from unregulated markets or untaxed incomes. In contrast, economic conservatives believe that too much government involvement in the economy undermines personal liberty and initiative.

Today, ideological conflict in the United States centers on the scope of government involvement in the economic realm and in the area of social values. In order to measure public attitudes on these two dimensions, pollsters have developed a variety of methods. The Gallup poll employs a two-question method that is widely used:

1. Some people think the government is trying to do too many things that should be left to individuals and businesses. Others think that government should do more to solve our country's problems. Which view is closer to your own?

2. Some people think the government should promote traditional values in our society. Others think that the government should not favor any particular set of values. Which view is closer to your own?

The Gallup poll's two questions are used to categorize Americans into four ideological types. **Liberals** are those who say that government should do more to solve the country's problems and who say that government ought not to support traditional values at the expense of less conventional ones. Thus, for example, a liberal would be inclined to favor an increase in government-provided health care and also to support civil unions for same-sex couples. **Conservatives** are those who think government should be sparing in its programs and who feel government should use its power to uphold traditional values. Thus, a conservative would be likely to oppose an increase in government-provided health care and to oppose civil unions. **Libertarians** are those who are reluctant to use government either as a means of economic redistribution or as a means of favoring particular social values. Thus, a libertarian would prefer that government not get more deeply involved in health-care provision and would be inclined to permit civil unions. **Populists** are those who would use government for both the purpose of economic redistribution and the purpose of guarding traditional values. Thus, a populist would be inclined to support increased health-care spending and to oppose civil unions. (To determine your ideology by this method, see "Political Culture.")

Of these four types, conservatives are the largest group. The proportion of Americans in each category, however, has been found to change as national conditions change. After the economy turned downward in 2000, for example, the number of populists and liberals rose as Americans increasingly looked to government for answers to their economic problems.[18]

Although ideology is a component of public opinion, its scope can be overstated. Any attempt to neatly categorize Americans by ideology must confront the inconvenient fact that most people want government to solve some problems and want other problems left to the private sector. Many citizens are neither consistently pro-government nor consistently anti-government when it comes to questions of how best to solve the nation's problems.

Moreover, as illustrated by the earlier example of people who favor steep tax cuts while also wanting more spending on government services, some citizens hold incompatible opinions. Thus, by a strict definition of what constitutes a

liberals
Those who believe government should do more to solve the nation's problems but reject the notion that government should favor a particular set of social values.

conservatives
Those who believe government tries to do too many things that should be left to firms and individuals but look to government to uphold traditional values.

libertarians
Those who believe government tries to do too many things that should be left to firms and individuals and who oppose government as an instrument of traditional values.

populists
Those who believe government should do more to solve the nation's problems and who look to it to uphold traditional values.

Political Culture

Americans' Ideologies

In the United States, the key dimensions of political conflict center on the extent of government intervention in the economic marketplace and in the maintenance of traditional values. Government intervention in either sphere has implications for liberty—the amount of freedom you should have in deciding on your lifestyle and in making economic choices. Government intervention in the economic sphere can also affect equality—government has been the principal means of providing economic security for those vulnerable to market forces.

You can test your ideology—and thus in a way your conception of liberty and equality—by asking yourself the two measurement questions used in Gallup surveys:

1. Some people think the government is trying to do too many things that should be left to individuals and businesses. Others think that government should do more to solve our country's problems. Which view is closer to your own?
   a. Government is doing too much.
   b. Government should do more.
2. Some people think the government should promote traditional values in our society. Others think that the government should not favor any particular set of values. Which view is closer to your own?
   a. Government should promote traditional values.
   b. Government should not favor particular values.

If you had been a respondent in a poll that asked these questions, you would have been classified as a *conservative* if you agreed with the first statement of each question (1a and 2a); a *liberal* if you agreed with the second statement of each question (1b and 2b); a *libertarian* if you agreed with the first statement of the first question (1a) and the second statement of the second question (2b); and a *populist* if you agreed with the second statement of the first question (1b) and the first statement of the second question (2a).

political ideology—a *consistent* pattern of political attitudes—many Americans do not have one. Studies indicate that no more than a third of Americans hold consistent opinions across a broad range of issues.[19]

If only a minority of Americans can be classified as true ideologues, ideology nonetheless remains a useful way to talk about broad patterns of opinion. Ideological terms help to describe the choices that Americans make and the conflicts that divide them. Beginning with the New Deal, for example, liberal attitudes—a preference for government action—dominated. Later, Americans became less trusting of government and more worried about its financial cost. Conservative opinions gained strength. Most recently, Americans have been split between those who want government to do less and those who want it to do more. Some observers believe, in fact, that Americans are today wider apart ideologically than at any time in recent decades. (Chapters 8 and 11 will discuss this topic further in the context of splits between Republicans and Democrats.)

Group Thinking: The Outlook of Many

For most citizens, groups are a more important frame of reference than is ideology.[20] Many Americans see politics through the lens of the group or groups that define who they are. Farmers, for example, care a lot more about agricultural issues than do members of other groups. And although farmers are more likely than most Americans to oppose government benefit programs, they favor farm subsidies. Their ideological opposition to "big government" suddenly disappears when their own benefits are at issue.

Because of the country's great size, its settlement by various immigrant groups, and its economic pluralism, Americans are a very diverse people. Later chapters examine group tendencies more fully, but it is useful here to mention a few major group orientations: religion, class, region, race and ethnicity, gender, and age.

Religion

Religious beliefs have always been a source of solidarity among group members and a source of conflict with outsiders. As Catholics and Jews came to America in large numbers in the nineteenth and early twentieth centuries, they encountered intense hostility from some Protestants. Today, Catholics, Protestants, and Jews have similar opinions on most policy issues.

Nevertheless, important religious differences remain, although the opposing sides are not always the same. Fundamentalist Protestants and Roman Catholics oppose legalized abortion more strongly than do mainline Protestants and Jews. This split reflects differ-

Economic class as related to jobs and incomes affects Americans' opinions on a range of social and economic issues. Shown here is a work crew constructing formed wooden beams.

ent religious teachings about when human life begins, whether at conception or at a later stage in the development of the fetus. Religious doctrine also affects opinions on poverty programs. Catholics and Jews are more supportive of such programs than Protestants are. An obligation to help the poor is a larger theme in Catholic and Jewish teachings; self-reliance is a larger part of Protestant thought.

The most powerful religious force in contemporary American politics is the so-called religious right, which consists primarily of individuals who see themselves as born-again Christians and who view the Bible as infallible truth. Their views on issues such as gay rights, abortion, and school prayer differ significantly from those of the population as a whole. A Time/CNN survey found that born-again Christians are a third more likely than other Americans to agree that "the Supreme Court and the Congress have gone too far in keeping religious and moral values like prayer out of our laws, schools, and many areas of our lives."

Class

Economic class has less influence on political opinion in the United States than in Europe, but it is nevertheless related to opinions on certain economic issues. For example, lower-income Americans are more supportive of social welfare programs, business regulation, and progressive taxation than are Americans in higher-income categories.

 An obstacle to class-based politics in the United States is that people with similar incomes but differing occupations do not share the same opinions. Support for collective bargaining, for example, is substantially higher among factory workers than among small farmers, service workers, and workers in the skilled crafts, even though the average income of members of all these groups is similar. The interplay of class and opinion is examined more closely in Chapter 9, which discusses interest groups.

Region

For a long period, region nearly defined American politics. The North and South were divided over the issue of race, which spilled over into issues such as education and welfare policy. Racial progress has diminished the regional divide, as has the relocation of millions of Americans from the Northeast and Midwest to the South and West. The policy beliefs of these newcomers tend to be less conservative than those of people native to these regions. Nevertheless, regional differences are still evident in the areas of social welfare, civil rights, and national defense. Residents of the southern, mountain, and Great Plains states have more conservative opinions on these issues than do Americans elsewhere—a reflection of longs-tanding regional attitudes about government. The differences are large enough that when analysts talk about "red states" (Republican bastions) and "blue states" (Democratic bastions), they basically are referring to regions. The red states are concentrated in the South, Great Plains, and Rocky Mountains. The blue states are found mostly in the Northeast, the northern Midwest, and the West Coast.

Race and Ethnicity

As Chapter 5 pointed out, race and ethnicity have a significant influence on opinions. Whites and African Americans, for example, differ on issues of integration: black people more strongly support affirmative action, busing, and other measures designed to promote racial equality and integration. Racial and ethnic groups also differ on economic issues, largely as a result of differences in their economic situations. Law enforcement is another area in which different opinions exist. Opinion polls reveal that blacks are far less likely than whites to trust the police and the judicial system.

Gender

Although male-female differences of opinion are small on most issues, gender does affect opinion in some policy areas. For example, women are somewhat more supportive than men of abortion rights and affirmative action. A Gallup poll found a 63 percent to 53 percent breakdown in support for affirmative action. The difference is even larger on some social welfare issues, such as poverty and education assistance. Compared with men, women have more liberal opinions on these issues, reflecting their greater economic vulnerability and their traditional responsibility for childcare. A Washington Post/ABC News poll found, for example, that women were 20 percent more likely than men to favor increased spending for public education.

Women and men also differ in their opinions on the use of military force. In nearly every case, women are less supportive of military action than men are. The terrorist attacks on the World Trade Center and the Pentagon on September 11, 2001, produced an exception to the normal pattern. Men and women were almost equally likely (90 percent and 88 percent, respectively) to favor a military response. But they differ in expected ways when questioned about the Iraq conflict. Women are less likely than men to think that military intervention in Iraq was worthwhile (see Figure 6–2).

Differences such as these contribute to the gender gap discussed in Chapter 5. Women and men do not differ sharply in their political views, but they differ enough to respond somewhat differently to issues, events, and candidates.

Age

Age has always affected opinions, but the gap between young and old is widening. In her book *Young v. Old*, political scientist Susan MacManus notes that the elderly tend to oppose increases in public school funding while supporting increases in social security and Medicare (government-assisted

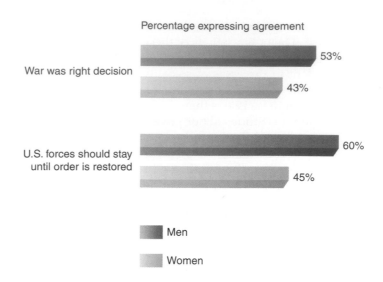

Figure 6–2

Gender and the Iraq Conflict

Compared with men, women are somewhat less inclined to support military force as a means of resolving international conflicts. This difference has been evident in polls on support for the Iraq war, as these examples illustrate.

Source: (In order of questions) Pew Research Center for the People and the Press, February 2005; ABC News/Washington Post poll, November 2005.

medical care for retirees). MacManus predicts that issues of age will increasingly dominate American politics and that the elderly will have the political clout to prevail. They vote at a much higher rate than do young people, are better organized politically (through groups such as the powerful AARP), and are increasing in number as a result of lengthened life spans (the so-called graying of America).[21]

Crosscutting Cleavages

Although group loyalty can have a powerful impact on people's opinions, this influence is diminished when identification with one group is offset by identification with other groups. In a pluralistic society such as the United States, groups tend to be "crosscutting"—that is, each group includes individuals who also belong to other groups, where they encounter different people and opinions. Crosscutting cleavages encourage individuals to appreciate and understand differences, which leads them toward moderate opinions. By comparison, in societies such as Northern Ireland, where group loyalties are reinforcing rather than crosscutting, opinions are intensified by personal interactions. Catholics and Protestants in Northern Ireland live largely apart from each other, differing not only in their religions but also in their income levels, neighborhoods of residence, ethnicities, and loyalties to the government. The result is widespread mistrust between Northern Ireland's Catholics and Protestants.

Partisan Thinking: The Line That Divides

In the everyday world of politics, no source of opinion more clearly divides Americans than that of their partisanship. Figure 6–3 provides examples, but these show only a few of the differences. On nearly every major political issue, Republicans and Democrats have views that are at least somewhat different. In many cases, such as spending programs for the poor, the differences are substantial.

Party identification refers to a person's ingrained sense of loyalty to a political party. Party identification is not formal membership in a party but rather an emotional attachment to a party—the feeling that "I am a Democrat" or "I am a

party identification
The personal sense of loyalty that an individual may feel toward a particular political party.

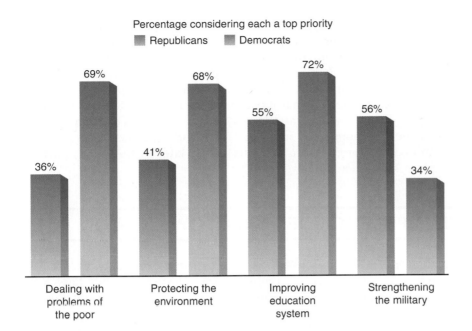

Percentage considering each a top priority

■ Republicans   ■ Democrats

36%	69%	41%	68%

Dealing with problems of the poor — Protecting the environment — Improving education system — Strengthening the military

55%   72%   56%   34%

Figure 6–3

Partisanship and Issue Opinions
Republicans and Democrats differ significantly in their policy opinions and priorities.
Source: Pew Research Center for the People and the Press, 2006.

Republican." Scholars and pollsters typically have measured party identification with a question of the following type: "Generally speaking, do you think of yourself as a Republican, a Democrat, an Independent, or what?" About two-thirds of adults call themselves Democrats or Republicans. Of the one-third who prefer the label "Independent," most say they lean toward one party or the other and tend to vote primarily for that party's candidates.

Early studies concluded that party loyalties were highly stable and seldom changed over the course of adult life.[22] Subsequent studies have shown that party loyalties are more fluid than originally believed; they can be influenced by the issues and candidates of the moment.[23] Nevertheless, most adults do not switch their party loyalties easily, and a substantial proportion never waver from their initial commitment to a party, which can often be traced to childhood influences.

Once acquired, partisanship affects how people perceive and interpret events. An example is the differing opinions of Republicans and Democrats about U.S. military intervention in Kosovo in 1999 and in Iraq in 2003. Democrats were more supportive of the first war, while Republicans were more supportive of the second. While differences in the nature and purpose of these wars might partially explain this split, partisanship clearly does. The first of these conflicts was initiated by a Democratic president, Bill Clinton, while the second was begun by a Republican president, George W. Bush.

For most people, partisanship is not simply blind faith in the party of their choice. Some Republicans and Democrats know very little about their party's policies

Senator John McCain (R-Ariz.) stumps in Oregon for the reelection of George W. Bush in 2004. A party maverick on some issues, McCain understood that his support of Bush was necessary if he was to build the Republican support he would need should he run for the presidency himself in 2008. Partisanship is one of the strongest influences on citizens' political opinions.

and unthinkingly embrace its candidates. However, party loyalties are not randomly distributed across the population but instead follow a pattern that would be predicted from the parties' histories. The Democratic party, for example, has been the driving force behind social welfare and workers' rights policies, while the Republican party has spearheaded probusiness and tax reduction policies. The fact that most union workers are Democrats and most businesspeople are Republicans is not a coincidence. Their partisanship is rooted in their economic self-interest.[24] This and other issues of partisanship are examined in more detail at various points later in this book, particularly in Chapters 7, 8, 11, and 12.

THE INFLUENCE OF PUBLIC OPINION ON POLICY

Yet unanswered in our discussion is a central question about public opinion: what impact does it have on government? The question does not have a firm or final answer. In any society of appreciable size, self-government takes place through representative institutions. The people themselves do not directly decide issues of policy but instead entrust them to elected and appointed officials. Governing decisions are complex, as are the factors that go into them, including the influence of public opinion.

Some observers claim that officials are relatively insensitive to public opinion—that they are so entrenched in their positions that, however much they claim to serve the people, they actually pay little attention to what ordinary citizens think.[25] This assessment undoubtedly applies to some officials and some issues.

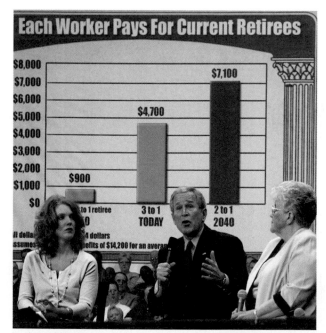

In his 2005 State of the Union address, President Bush outlined key provisions of his plan to partially privatize social security. Here, he argues for it at a town-hall style meeting at the University of Notre Dame. A year later, the proposal was dead as Republican lawmakers abandoned it out of fear that it would cost them votes in the 2006 midterm election.

However, the most comprehensive study ever conducted on the relationship between public opinion and policy concluded that public opinion does in fact sway government. The study examined fifty years of polls and policy decisions and found that when public opinion on an issue changed, policy usually changed in the direction of the change in public opinion. In the case of major issues, this pattern was particularly evident—in such cases, policy typically aligned with public opinion.[26]

However, a more recent study by Lawrence Jacobs and Robert Shapiro found a widening gap between public opinion and policy, apparently because elected officials of both parties have tilted toward the more extreme positions favored by powerful groups within their respective parties (such as the Christian right within the Republican party and lifestyle liberals within the Democratic party).[27] Jacobs and Shapiro nonetheless conclude that officials remain sensitive to public opinion on many issues, particularly those that could become campaign issues. As the midterm congressional elections approached in 2006, for example, a number of congressional Republicans backed away from President Bush's controversial proposal to change the social security program to allow workers to put some of their social security taxes into private investment accounts. Many congressional Republicans who had initially supported his plan changed their minds when polls showed declining support for the proposal and for the president.

If elections heighten officials' attention to public opinion, so do particular issues. There are certain actions that officials shy away from for fear of public retribution. Tax hikes are a prime example. Politicians ordinarily will go to great lengths—including borrowing huge amounts of money to shift the problem to future generations—to avoid a major tax increase. Angry taxpayers are officeholders' worst nightmare.

Such examples, however, do not provide an answer to the question of whether public officials are *sufficiently* responsive to public opinion. This question is complicated by the fact that it is partly a normative one—the answer rests on beliefs about the proper relationship between people's opinions and government policies. As discussed in Chapter 2, some theorists hold that representatives should base their policy decisions on what they believe will best serve the people's interests, while others claim that the people themselves are the best judge of their interests and that it is the representative's duty to pay close heed to the people's demands. The question is also complicated by the fact that politics involves attempts to influence public opinion. Citizens' opinions are not fixed. They can be activated, changed, and crystallized through political action. Political leaders invest enormous amounts of money and time in an effort to get citizens to see things their way.

In fact, one of the best indicators of the power of public opinion is the great effort made by political leaders to harness it in support of their goals. In American politics, popular demand for a policy is a powerful argument for that policy. For this reason and others, great effort is made to organize and represent public opinion through elections (Chapter 7), political parties (Chapter 8), interest groups (Chapter 9), the news media (Chapter 10), and political institutions (Chapters 11 through 14).

Summary

 Gelf Toot www.mhhe.com./pattersontad8

Public opinion can be defined as those opinions held by ordinary citizens that they openly express. Public officials have many ways of assessing public opinion, such as the outcomes of elections, but they have increasingly come to rely on public opinion polls. There are many possible sources of error in polls, and surveys sometimes present a misleading portrayal of the public's views. However, a properly conducted poll can be an accurate indication of what the public is thinking and can dissuade political leaders from thinking that the views of the most vocal citizens (such as demonstrators and letter writers) are also the views of the broader public.

The process by which individuals acquire their political opinions is called political socialization. During childhood, the family and schools are important sources of basic political attitudes, such as beliefs about the parties and the nature of the U.S. political and economic systems. Many of the basic orientations that Americans acquire during childhood remain with them in adulthood, but socialization is a continuing process. Major shifts in opinion during adulthood are usually the consequence of changing political conditions; for example, the Great Depression of the 1930s was the catalyst for wholesale changes in Americans' opinions on the government's economic role. Short-term fluctuations in opinion can result from new political issues and problems. Individuals'

opinions in these cases are affected by prior beliefs, peers, political leaders, and the news media. Events themselves are also a significant short-term influence on opinions.

The frames of reference that guide Americans' opinions include cultural beliefs, such as individualism, which affect what people will find politically acceptable and desirable. Opinions can also stem from ideology, although most citizens do not have a strong and consistent ideological attachment. In addition, individuals develop opinions as a result of group orientations, notably religion, income level, occupation, region, race, ethnicity, gender, and age. Partisanship is perhaps the major source of political opinions; Republicans and Democrats differ in their voting behavior and views on many policy issues.

Public opinion has a significant influence on government but seldom determines exactly what government will do in a particular instance. Public opinion serves to constrain the policy choices of officials. Some policy actions are beyond the range of possibility because the public will not accept change in existing policy or will not seriously consider policy that seems clearly at odds with basic American values. Evidence indicates that officials are somewhat attentive to public opinion on highly visible and controversial issues of public policy.

STUDY CORNER

Key Terms

age-cohort tendency (*p. 174*)
agents of socialization (*p. 174*)
conservatives (*p. 178*)
ideology (*p. 177*)
liberals (*p. 178*)

libertarians (*p. 178*)
party identification (*p. 182*)
political socialization (*p. 173*)
population (*p. 169*)
populists (*p. 178*)

public opinion (*p. 167*)
public opinion poll (*p. 169*)
sample (*p. 169*)
sampling error (*p. 171*)

Self-Test

1. The process by which individuals acquire political opinions is called:
   a. public opinion polling.
   b. efficacy.
   c. selective incorporation.
   d. political socialization.
   e. sampling error.

2. Most studies on the influence of ideology on public opinion agree that:
   a. most people think of themselves as liberals.
   b. most people think of themselves as libertarians.
   c. most people think of themselves as isolationists.
   d. only a minority of Americans truly understand and apply ideological frames of reference.

3. Public officials increasingly rely on what way to assess public opinion?
   a. talk show ratings
   b. election outcomes
   c. public opinion polls
   d. what editorial writers in newspapers are saying about the public
   e. mail received by elected representatives in Washington, D.C.

4. Compared to Europeans, Americans are substantially more likely to form political opinions based on their:
   a. religious beliefs.
   b. economic class.

c. party identification.
d. occupation.
e. age.

5. According to your text, a person who favors economic individualism and traditional social values can be labeled a:
   a. liberal.   *Gov. involve - Not social values*
   b. conservative.   *Not fav. Gov -trad. S Values*
   c. libertarian.
   d. populist.   *Gov involve*
   e. nationalist.

6. The political opinions of males and females differ most significantly on issues of:
   a. the environment.
   b. crime and the judicial system.
   c. the use of military force.
   d. global trade.

7. In general, the larger the size of the sample in a poll, the smaller the sampling error. (T/F)

8. Most American citizens apply a fully developed ideological frame of reference to political issues. (T/F)

9. When asked whether they are liberal, conservative, or moderate, most Americans describe themselves as liberal. (T/F)

10. Most Americans pay close attention to and are well informed about the workings of their government. (T/F)

Critical Thinking

What factors limit the influence of public opinion on the policy choices of public officials?

Suggested Readings

Alvarez, R. Michael, and John Brehm. *Hard Choices, Easy Answers: Values, Information, and American Public Opinion.* Princeton, N.J.: Princeton University Press, 2002. An analysis that argues that what citizens know about politics is assessed in the context of their values and beliefs.

Asher, Herbert. *Polling and the Public*, 6th ed. Washington, D.C.: Congressional Quarterly Press, 2004. A guide to public opinion poll methods and analysis.

Canes-Wrone, Brandice. *Who Leads Whom? Presidents, Policy, and the Public.* Chicago: University of Chicago Press,

2005. A look at recent presidents and their policies in the context of public opinion.

Green, Donald, Bradley Palmquist, and Eric Schickler. *Partisan Hearts and Minds*. New Haven, Conn.: Yale University Press, 2002. An analysis that concludes partisanship powerfully affects how citizens respond to candidates and issues.

Jacobs, Lawrence, and Robert Shapiro. *Politicians Don't Pander*. Chicago: University of Chicago Press, 2000. An analysis that concludes politicians are not driven by polls.

MacManus, Susan A. *Young v. Old: Generational Combat in the Twenty-first Century*. Boulder, Colo.: Westview Press, 1996. A study of the emerging conflict in the political self-interest of younger and older Americans.

Stimson, James. *Tides of Consent: How Public Opinion Shapes American Politics*. New York: Cambridge University Press, 2004. An analysis of trends in public opinion and their political impact.

Zaller, John R. *The Nature and Origins of Mass Opinion*. New York: Cambridge University Press, 1992. A superb analysis of the nature of public opinion.

List of Websites

http://www.policy.com/

A nonpartisan site that provides a wealth of information about current public issues.

http://www.people-press.org/

Website of the Pew Research Center for the People and the Press; it includes an abundance of recent polling results, including cross-national comparisons.

http://www.princeton.edu/~abelson/

The Princeton Survey Research Center's site; it offers results from surveys conducted by a variety of polling organizations.

http://www.publicagenda.org/

The nonpartisan Public Agenda's site; it provides opinions, analyses, and educational materials on current policy issues.

Participate!

At the website of a polling organization such as the Pew Research Center for the People and the Press (www.people-press.org), examine the poll results on a current policy issue. Study the extent to which opinions differ, if at all, between men and women and between Republicans and Democrats. Would an informal poll of the people you know result in a similar distribution of opinion? Why or why not?

Extra Credit

For up-to-the-minute *New York Times* articles, interactive simulations, graphics, study tools, and more links and quizzes, visit the text's Online Learning Center at www.mhhe.com/pattersontad8.

Political Participation:
Activating the Popular Will

Chapter Outline

Voter Participation
Factors in Voter Turnout: The United
    States in Comparative Perspective
Why Some Americans Vote and Others
    Do Not

Conventional Forms of
Participation Other Than Voting
Campaign Activities
Community Activities
Attending to the News
Virtual Participation

Unconventional Activism: Social
Movements and Protest Politics

Participation and the Potential
for Influence

CHAPTER 7

We are concerned in public affairs, but immersed in our private ones.

—*Walter Lippmann*[1]

At stake in the 2006 midterm election was control of the U.S. House and Senate. Which party would have the leading voice on legislation affecting education, health, welfare, and the environment? Which party would be entrusted with legislative oversight of America's involvement in Iraq? With so much at stake, it might be thought that citizens would have been eager to cast their ballots for the party of their choice. Voter turnout was in fact higher than in the previous midterm election. Nevertheless, tens of millions of American adults did not vote in the 2006 midterm election. Despite a concerted get-out-the-vote campaign by the political parties, news media, and civic groups, the number of people who did not vote was much greater than the number who voted for either party.

Voting is a form of **political participation**—involvement in activities intended to influence public policy and leadership. Political participation involves other activities in addition to voting, such as joining political groups, writing to elected officials, demonstrating for political causes, and giving money to political candidates.

Democratic societies are distinguished by their emphasis on citizen participation. The concept of self-government is based on the idea that ordinary people have a right and a duty to participate in the affairs of state. As it happens, the pattern of participation in the United States is somewhat different than in other democracies, as this chapter will show. The major points made in this chapter are these:

political participation
Involvement in activities intended to influence public policy and leadership, such as voting, joining political groups, writing to elected officials, demonstrating for political causes, and giving money to political candidates.

- *Voter turnout in U.S. elections is low in comparison with that of other democratic nations.* The reasons for this difference include the nature of U.S. election laws, particularly those pertaining to registration requirements and the scheduling of elections.

- *Most citizens do not participate actively in politics in ways other than voting.* Only a small proportion of Americans can be classified as political activists.

- *Most Americans make a sharp distinction between their personal lives and national life.* This attitude reduces their incentive to participate and contributes to a pattern of participation dominated by citizens of higher income and education.

VOTER PARTICIPATION

suffrage
The right to vote.

**HISTORICAL
BACKGROUND**

At the nation's founding, **suffrage**—the right to vote—was limited to property-owning males. Tom Paine ridiculed this policy in *Common Sense*. Observing that a man whose only item of property was a jackass would lose his right to vote if the jackass died, Paine asked, "Now tell me, which was the voter, the man or the jackass?" It was not until 1840 that all states extended suffrage to property-less white males, a change made possible by their continued demand for the vote and by the realization on the part of the wealthy that the nation's abundance and openness were natural protections against an assault on property rights by the voting poor.

Women did not secure the vote until 1920, with the ratification of the Nineteenth Amendment. In the 1870s, Susan B. Anthony tried to vote in her hometown of Rochester, New York, asserting that she had a right to do so as a U.S. citizen. She was arrested for "illegal voting" and told that her proper place was in the home. By 1920, men had run out of excuses for keeping the vote from women. As Senator Wendell Phillips observed: "One of two things is true: either woman is like man—and if she is, then a ballot based on brains belongs to her as well as to him. Or she is different, and then man does not know how to vote for her as she herself does."[2]

African Americans had to wait nearly fifty years longer than women to be granted full suffrage. Blacks seemed to have won the right to vote with passage of the Fifteenth Amendment after the Civil War, but as explained in Chapter 5, they were effectively disenfranchised in the South by a number of electoral tricks, including poll taxes and literacy tests. The poll tax was a fee of several dollars that had to be paid before a person could register to vote. Because most blacks in the South were too poor to pay it, the poll tax effectively barred them from voting. Not until the ratification of the Twenty-fourth Amendment in 1964 was the poll tax outlawed in federal elections. Supreme Court decisions and the

After a hard-fought, decades-long campaign, American women finally won the right to vote in 1920.

TABLE 7–1	Opinions on Obligations of Citizens	Americans rank voting as one of the essential obligations of citizenship.		
	ESSENTIAL OBLIGATION	VERY IMPORTANT OBLIGATION	SOMEWHAT IMPORTANT	PERSONAL PREFERENCE
Treating all people equally regardless of race or ethnic background	57%	33%	6%	4%
Voting in elections	53	29	9	9
Working to reduce inequality and injustice	41	42	12	6
Being civil to others with whom we may disagree	35	45	14	6
Keeping fully informed about the news and other public issues	30	42	19	10
Donating blood or organs to help with medical needs	20	37	18	26
Volunteering time to community service	16	42	26	16

Source: Used by permission of the 1996 Survey of American Political Culture, James Davison Hunter and Carol Bowman, Directors, Institute for Advanced Studies in Culture, University of Virginia.

Voting Rights Act of 1965 swept away other legal barriers to fuller participation by African Americans.

In 1971, the Twenty-sixth Amendment extended voting rights to include citizens eighteen years of age or older. Previously, nearly all states had restricted voting to those twenty-one years of age or older.

Factors in Voter Turnout: The United States in Comparative Perspective

Today nearly any American adult—rich or poor, man or woman, black or white—who is determined to vote can legally and actually do so. Most Americans embrace the symbolism of the vote, saying that they have a duty to vote in elections (see Table 7–1). However, many Americans shirk this duty. Millions choose not to vote regularly, a tendency that sets Americans apart from citizens of most other Western democracies.

Voter turnout is the proportion of adult citizens who actually vote in a given election. Since the 1960s, the voter turnout in presidential elections has averaged about 55 percent (see Figure 7–1). Turnout is even lower in the

voter turnout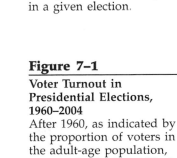
The proportion of persons of voting age who actually vote in a given election.

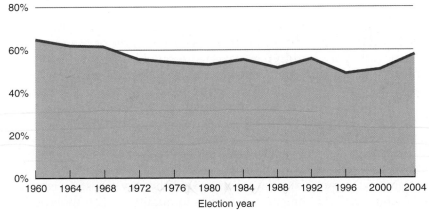

Percentage of adults who voted

Figure 7–1

Voter Turnout in Presidential Elections, 1960–2004
After 1960, as indicated by the proportion of voters in the adult-age population, turnout declined steadily. In the past two decades, turnout has fluctuated, depending on the issues at stake in the particular election.
Source: U.S. Bureau of the Census. Figures based on percent of voting-age adults who voted.

LEADERS

SUSAN B. ANTHONY

(1820–1906)

Susan B. Anthony's name is nearly synonymous with women's right to vote—and well it should be. She spent much of her adult life fighting for women's suffrage, even at the risk of arrest. When she was in her twenties, she moved to upstate New York and almost immediately became politically active. Like many of the women who would lead the movement for women's rights, her first crusade was with the temperance movement, which sought to ban the sale of alcohol because of the hardship alcoholism imposed on women and children. She next joined the abolitionist movement, which sought an end to slavery. After the Civil War, she teamed up with an old friend and fellow activist, Elizabeth Cady Stanton, to demand equal pay and voting rights for women. She twice went to the polls in her hometown of Rochester, New York, to assert her right to vote and twice was arrested. By then, Anthony was a national figure who lectured widely on women's suffrage. She died a decade before women gained the right to vote in the United States, but she, as much as any American, made women's suffrage a reality.

midterm congressional elections that take place between presidential elections. Midterm election turnout has not reached 50 percent since 1920, and has seldom topped the 40 percent mark since 1970. After one midterm election, cartoonist Rigby showed an election clerk eagerly asking a stray cat that had wandered into a polling place, "Are you registered?"[3]

Nonvoting is far more prevalent in the United States than in nearly all other democracies (see "How the United States Compares"). In recent decades, turnout in major national elections has averaged more than 90 percent in Belgium and more than 80 percent in France, Germany, and Denmark.[4] The disparity in turnout between the United States and other nations is not as great as these official voting rates suggest. Some nations calculate turnout solely on the basis of eligible adults, whereas the United States has traditionally based its figures on all adults, including noncitizens and other ineligible groups. Nevertheless, even when such statistical disparities are corrected, turnout in U.S. elections is relatively low.

Contributing to the relatively low turnout in U.S. elections are registration requirements, the frequency of elections, and the lack of clear-cut differences between the political parties.

Registration Requirements

registration
The practice of placing citizens' names on an official list of voters before they are eligible to exercise their right to vote.

Before Americans are allowed to vote, they must be registered—that is, their names must appear on an official list of eligible voters. **Registration** began around 1900 as a way of preventing voters from casting more than one ballot during an election. Fraudulent voting was a favorite tactic of political party machines in communities where the population was too large for residents to be personally known to poll watchers. However, the extra effort involved in registering placed a burden on honest citizens. Because they could now vote only if they had registered beforehand, those people who forgot or otherwise failed to do so found themselves unable to participate on election day. Turnout in U.S. elections declined steadily after registration was instituted.

Although other democracies also require registration, they place this responsibility on government. In most European nations, public officials have the duty to enroll citizens on registration lists. When someone moves to a new address, for example, the postal service will notify registration officials of the change. The United States—in keeping with its individualistic culture—is one of the few democracies in which registration is the individual's responsibility. In addition, registration laws have traditionally been established by the state governments, and some states make it difficult for citizens to qualify. Registration periods and

Although Americans have voted in relatively low numbers in recent U.S. elections, the turnout rate increased in 2004 and 2006 in response to the issues of the moment. Here, voters stand in a long line waiting to cast their ballot at a polling place in Fort Mill, South Carolina.

locations usually are not highly publicized.[5] Eligibility can also be a problem. In most states, a citizen must reside at an address for a minimum period, usually thirty days, before becoming eligible to register. It is estimated that turnout in the United States would be roughly 10 percentage points higher if it had European-style registration.[6]

States with a tradition of lenient registration laws have a higher turnout than most states. Idaho, Maine, Minnesota, New Hampshire, Wisconsin, and Wyoming, which are states that allow people to register at their polling place on election day, have high turnout rates. Those states that have erected the most barriers are in the South, where restrictive registration was originally intended to prevent black people from voting. These historical differences continue to be reflected in state voter turnout (see "States in the Nation").

In 1993, in an effort to increase registration levels nationwide, Congress enacted a voting registration law known as "motor voter." It requires states to permit people to register to vote when applying for a driver's license and when applying for benefits at certain state offices. Registration is not automatic in these situations; the citizen must take the time to fill out an application form. Moreover, the motor voter law does not help citizens who do not drive or do not otherwise have contact with an appropriate state agency. The law has raised registration levels somewhat, but voter turnout has not increased sharply since the law was enacted. Clearly, the registration requirement is only one factor contributing to America's low turnout rate.

Frequency of Elections

The United States holds more elections than any other nation. No other democracy has elections for the lower chamber of its national legislature (the equivalent of the U.S. House of Representatives) as often as every two years, and none schedules

How the United States Compares
Voter Turnout

The United States ranks near the bottom among the world's democracies in the percentage of eligible citizens who participate in national elections. One reason for the low voter turnout is that individual Americans are responsible for registering to vote, whereas in most other democracies voters are automatically registered by government officials. In addition, unlike some other democracies, the United States does not encourage voting by holding elections on the weekend or by imposing penalties, such as fines, on those who do not participate.

Another factor affecting voter turnout rate in the United States is the absence of a major labor or socialist party, which would serve to bring lower-income citizens to the polls. America's individualist culture and its electoral system (see Chapter 8) have inhibited the establishment of a major labor or socialist party. In democracies where such parties exist, the turnout difference between upper- and lower-income groups is relatively small. In the United States, however, lower-income persons are much less likely to vote than are higher-income persons.

COUNTRY	APPROXIMATE VOTER TURNOUT	AUTOMATIC REGISTRATION?	SOCIAL DEMOCRAT, SOCIALIST, OR LABOR PARTY?	ELECTION DAY A HOLIDAY OR WEEKEND DAY?
Belgium	90%	Yes	Yes	Yes
Germany	85	Yes	Yes	Yes
Denmark	85	Yes	Yes	No
Italy	80	Yes	Yes	Yes
Austria	80	Yes	Yes	Yes
France	80	No	Yes	Yes
Great Britain	60	Yes	Yes	No
Canada	60	Yes	Yes	No
Japan	60	Yes	Yes	Yes
United States	55	No	No	No

Source: Developed from multiple sources. Turnout percentages are a rough average of national elections during the past two decades.

elections for chief executive as often as every four years.[7] In addition, elections of state and local officials in the United States are often scheduled separately from national races. Four-fifths of the states elect their governors in nonpresidential election years,[8] and 60 percent of U.S. cities hold elections of municipal officials in odd-numbered years.[9] Finally, the United States uses primary elections to select the party nominees. In other democracies, party leaders pick them.

The high frequency of U.S. elections places a burden on citizens. Americans are asked to vote two to three times as often as Europeans, which increases the likelihood that they will not participate in each election.[10] Moreover, elections in the United States are traditionally held on Tuesday, which means that most adults must find time before or after work to get to the polls. Many European nations hold their elections on Sunday or declare election day a national holiday, making it easier for working people to vote.

Party Differences

A final explanation for lower voter turnout in the United States is the nation's party system. Most European democracies have three or more significant

States in the Nation

Voter Turnout in Presidential Elections

The United States has a low voter turnout relative to most other Western democracies. However, the state-to-state variation is considerable. In a few states, including Minnesota and New Hampshire, nearly seven in ten adults vote in presidential elections. In contrast, there are a few states, including Hawaii and Texas, where barely more than four in ten adults vote.

Q: Why does the South have lower turnout than other regions? Why do states in the Southwest have relatively low turnout rates?

A: Southern states have more poverty and a tradition of more restrictive registration laws (dating to the Jim Crow era of racial segregation). Both factors are associated with lower voting rates. States with large populations of recent immigrants, including the states of the Southwest, also tend to have lower voting rates.

Source: Compiled by author from various sources; based on recent midterm and presidential elections.

political parties that have formed along class and social divisions and sometimes along religious and ethnic divisions as well. Labor and social democratic parties abound in Europe, as do middle-class, environmental, and right-wing parties. European voters have a range of choices. They are likely to find a party that closely fits their interests, perhaps even one they can support enthusiastically.

The United States has only two major parties, the Republicans and the Democrats. Each has its enthusiastic supporters, yet each party, to get the majority support it needs to win, must have broad support. The major

Volunteers at a community event attempt to interest citizens in registering so that they can vote in the next election. Nearly all democracies have automatic voter registration. The United States does not, which makes voter registration efforts an important factor in election turnout.

American parties do not completely avoid aligning with certain groups, but they try to attract a sizable share of votes from nearly all groups in order to gain the 50 percent or more of the vote that they need for an election victory. As a consequence, some Americans feel that the parties' candidates are too much alike to represent a real choice, which diminishes their incentive to participate in elections.[11]

At times, Americans do see large differences between the parties (see Figure 7–2). In the 2004 presidential election, for example, which was waged against the backdrop of a weak economy and the controversial war in Iraq, Americans thought a lot was at stake in the choice between the Republicans and the Democrats. Four years earlier, however, with the economy strong and the nation not at war, Americans were less convinced that it made much difference which party won the presidency. Americans voted at a much lower rate in 2000 than they did in 2004. The 2000 election was more typical. In most U.S. elections, most adults believe that the outcome will not substantially affect their future or that of the nation. (Chapter 8 has a fuller discussion of the American two-party system and its consequences.)

Figure 7–2

The Perceived Effect of Electing a Republican or a Democratic President
Many Americans believe that the country will not be greatly affected by whether the Republican or Democratic presidential candidate is elected. However, the proportion holding this belief shrinks when, as in the 2004 campaign, Americans think important issues are at stake in the election.
Source: The Vanishing Voter Project, Shorenstein Center on the Press, Politics and Public Policy, Harvard University. Published by permission of project director.

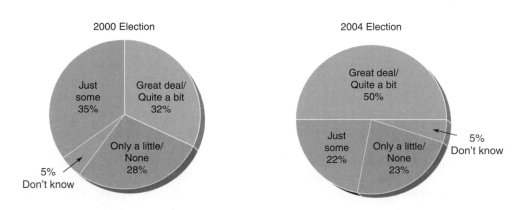

Get Involved!

Register and Vote

Some observers take comfort in low-turnout elections. They claim that the country is better off if less interested and less knowledgeable citizens stay home on election day. In a 1997 cover story in *Atlantic Monthly*, Robert Kaplan wrote: "The last thing America needs is more voters—particularly badly educated and alienated ones—with a passion for politics." The gist of this age-old argument is that low turnout protects society from erratic or even dangerous shifts in power. However, America's voters have not acted whimsically. Except for an interlude in the 1780s, when the Articles of Confederation governed the United States, erratic voting has not been a persistent source of political instability.

On the other hand, a low participation rate can be a problem. In general, the smaller the electorate, the less representative it is of the public as a whole. Polls indicate that the outcomes of elections would in some instances have changed if turnout had been substantially higher. And even if greater voter turnout would not have altered the outcomes, campaign platforms have always been tailored to those who vote. As the political scientists Steve Rosenstone and Mark Hanson note in *Mobilization, Participation, and Democracy in America* (1993): "The idle go unheard: They do not speak up, define the agenda, frame the issues, or affect the choices leaders make."

Voting can strengthen democracy in other ways. When people vote, they are more attentive to politics and are better informed about issues affecting them. As the philosopher John Stuart Mill theorized a century ago, voting also deepens community involvement. Studies indicate that voters participate more frequently in community affairs and are more likely to work with others on community projects. Of course, these associations say more about the type of person who votes than about the effect of voting. But recent evidence, as Harvard University's Robert Putnam notes in *Bowling Alone* (2000), "suggests that voting itself encourages volunteering and other forms of good citizenship."

Voting among young adults in particular has declined. When eighteen- to twenty-one-year-old citizens gained eligibility to vote in the 1972 election, nearly 50 percent of them voted. In 2000, less than 35 percent did so. The hotly contested 2004 election, waged against the backdrop of a soft economy and turmoil in Iraq, produced increased turnout among young adults, although the level was substantially below that of 1972. Unless increased turnout among young voters can be sustained, the overall voting rate will continue to stagnate, because the oldest generation, those who grew up during the Depression and World War II, participate at very high rates.

Changes in registration laws have made it easier for students to vote if they choose to do so. Voting is not a time-consuming task, and the benefits to the individual and society are considerable. Have you registered yet?

Why Some Americans Vote and Others Do Not

Even though turnout is lower in the United States than in other major Western democracies, some Americans vote regularly while others seldom or never vote. Among the explanations for these individual differences are civic attitudes, age, and education and income.

Civic Attitudes

Americans differ greatly in their feelings about politics. Some have almost no interest in politics. **Apathy** is the term used to describe a general lack of concern with politics. Just as some people would not attend the Super Bowl if it were free and being played across the street, some Americans would not bother to vote even if a ballot were delivered to their door. Other Americans, however, have a strong sense of **civic duty**—the belief that they are obliged to participate in public affairs.

apathy
A feeling of personal disinterest in or unconcern with politics.

civic duty
The belief of an individual that civic and political participation is a responsibility of citizenship.

Debating the Issues

Should Voting Through the Internet Be Allowed?

As nonvoting has increased and Internet use has spread, it was only a matter of time before voting through the Internet would be considered. In 2000, Arizona voters had the opportunity to be the first to vote online. The election was the state's Democratic presidential primary. Several states are considering online voting for all elections, and the U.S. military has established a pilot online voting option for troops overseas.

Advocates see online voting as the answer to a downward trend in voter turnout. Not everyone agrees that Internet voting is the solution, however. Opponents say that Internet voting would lead to a sharp increase in election fraud. They also note that Internet voting would disadvantage groups, primarily the poor and minorities, that have unequal access to the Internet.

Yes Few benefits of online interactivity are of such potential importance—or are so often overlooked—as the Internet's promise for improving democracy. . . . Voting is an important example of an information activity that could be improved with the help of the Internet. Where I live, we vote for judges, but I often don't know who deserves my ballot, since little information about their judicial records is readily available. I look forward to an Internet-based alternative. Instead of voting in person or mailing in an absentee ballot, I expect to be able to vote from my PC. While pondering the choices at my leisure, I'll be able to see what the candidates say about themselves, listen to speeches they've given, check their judicial records, read or watch news reports, survey their endorsements or the recommendations of nonpartisan groups, or even ask individuals I trust who they intend to vote for—all electronically. The result will be a better-informed vote, and probably greater participation. I'm an optimist about information technology because I've seen how it can improve the effectiveness of businesses and how it's beginning to positively influence education. It's no secret that many governments could be more efficient and responsive, and I'm confident that PCs and the Internet will play a welcome role in improving civic life and political dialogue around the world.

—*Bill Gates, chair, Microsoft Corporation*

No Internet voting initially presents itself as a benevolent new platform for election administration, with the potential to reach voters not currently engaged in the process. But given the inequities of access to the Internet, "remote" Internet voting—voting via the Internet in a nonpolling-place environment such as a home, office or library—results in discrimination. . . . Whites are more likely to have Internet access from home than most racial and ethnic minorities have from *any* location. . . . Even if special pains were taken to create cybervillages in publicly accessible locations, remote Internet voting would be less likely among minority voters. By making voting more convenient for voters who have ready access—predominantly white—a bias is set up that boosts the potential turnout for connected voters while diluting the power of individual minority voters' ballots. . . . By confining Internet voting to polling places, you immediately bring parity to the process, while gaining time to address the complex issues of how to bridge the digital divide. Otherwise, the premature use of remote Internet voting will result in an America where all voters are created equal, but some are more equal than others.

—*Deborah Phillips, chair and president, Voting Integrity Project*

Apathy and a sense of civic duty are attitudes that are usually acquired during childhood and adolescence as a result of parental influence. When parents vote regularly and take an active interest in politics, their children usually grow up thinking that political participation is important. When parents never vote and show almost no interest in public affairs, their children are likely to be politically apathetic.

TABLE 7–2	Opinions on Election Politics Americans are generally dissatisfied with election politics.		
	AGREE	**DISAGREE**	**DON'T KNOW**
Political candidates are more concerned with fighting each other than with solving the nation's problems.	70%	26%	4%
Most political candidates will say almost anything in order to get themselves elected.	78	18	4
Political campaigns today seem more like theater or entertainment than like something to be taken seriously.	65	30	5
Interest groups and donors who give large sums of money to political campaigns have way too much influence on what candidates do once they are elected.	80	16	4

Source: National poll by The Vanishing Voter Project, Joan Shorenstein Center on the Press, Politics, and Public Policy, John F. Kennedy School of Government, Harvard University, October 20–24, 2000. Used by permission of project director.

Yet a third attitude bears on political participation. **Alienation** is the term that describes a sense of personal powerlessness, the notion that government is unresponsive to or uncaring of citizens like oneself. Politically alienated Americans have low participation rates.[12] Many of them regard voting as a complete waste of time because they are convinced that officials pay no attention to people like them. Alienation can be traced to childhood socialization, but, more so than apathy or civic duty, it has adult roots as well. America's pursuit of the Vietnam War, for example, alienated many young adults. Voter turnout fell in 1968 and in 1972—the two presidential elections in which the Vietnam War was most intensely debated.

Fewer than 10 percent of Americans today are so thoroughly alienated from politics that they have no interest whatsoever in participating. However, most Americans are at least somewhat disenchanted with election politics. They believe, for example, that money plays too large a role in determining who gets elected and that candidates routinely make campaign promises they do not intend to keep (see Table 7–2). Such beliefs ordinarily do not stop people from voting. Nevertheless, a small percentage of Americans are so disgusted with how U.S. campaigns are conducted that they stay home on election day.

alienation
A feeling of personal powerlessness that includes the notion that government does not care about the opinions of people like oneself.

Age

When viewers tuned in MTV at various times in the 2004 presidential campaign, they might have thought at first that they had selected the wrong channel. Rather than a video of their favorite rock star, they saw the presidential candidates urging young people to vote.

The candidates had targeted the audience most in need of a reminder. Young adults are much less likely to vote than are middle-aged citizens. Even senior citizens, despite the infirmities of old age, have a far higher turnout rate than do

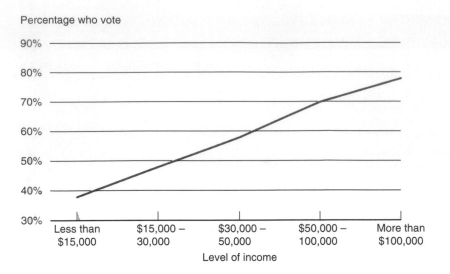

Figure 7–3

Voter Turnout and Level of Income, 2004
Americans of lower income are much less likely to vote than those of higher income. The gap in these voting rates is greater in the United States than in other western democracies.
Source: U.S. Bureau of the Census, 2006.

voters under the age of thirty. Young people are less likely to have the political concern that can accompany lifestyle characteristics such as homeownership, a permanent career, and a family.[13] In fact, citizens under the age of thirty have the lowest voter turnout rate of any major demographic group.

Education and Income

Americans at the top levels of education attainment are twice as likely to vote in a presidential election as those at the bottom levels. The same difference describes Americans at the top and bottom income levels (see Figure 7–3). It is no surprise that education and income make a difference in voter participation. Achievement in these areas contributes to an interest in public affairs and a belief that a person can make a difference politically.[14]

Education and income also affect participation rates in European democracies, but to a lesser degree. Europeans with less education and lower income are encouraged to participate by the presence of class-based organizations and traditions—strong socialist or labor parties, politically oriented trade unions, and class-based political ideologies. The United States does not have, and never has had, a major socialist or labor party. Although the Democratic party by and large represents the working class and the poor, it is more attentive to the middle class, which, because of its size and voting regularity, is the key to victory in U.S. elections. Americans in the bottom third by income are more likely than those in the top third to believe that election outcomes have no appreciable effect on their lives.[15]

CONVENTIONAL FORMS OF PARTICIPATION OTHER THAN VOTING

In one sense, voting is an unrivaled form of citizen participation. Free and open elections are the defining characteristic of democratic government, so voting is regarded as the most basic duty of citizens. Furthermore, most citizens in most democracies vote in elections. No other active form of political participation is so widespread.

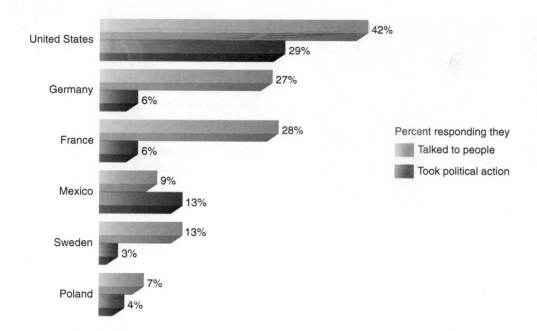

United States 42%
29%

Germany 27%
6%

France 28%
6%

Mexico 9%
13%

Sweden 13%
3%

Poland 7%
4%

Percent responding they
☐ Talked to people
■ Took political action

Figure 7–4

Campaign Activity
Although Americans are less likely to vote in elections than citizens elsewhere, they are more likely to engage in other campaign activities, such as trying to influence the vote choice of others. **Source:** Surveys by Comparative Studies of Electoral Systems, 2001–4. Reported in Russell J. Dalton, "The Myth of the Disengaged American," CSES Report, October 25, 2005, web release. Sixteen other countries were included in surveys; none had a higher participation rate than the United States.

In another sense, however, voting is a limited form of involvement. Citizens have the opportunity to vote only at a particular time, and only on the choices listed on the ballot. Other activities, such as working on a campaign or joining a civic group, provide the citizen with a fuller opportunity to participate.

Campaign Activities

Working for a candidate or attending election rallies requires a lot more time than voting does. Not surprisingly, the proportion of citizens who engage in such activities is relatively small. Fewer than one in twenty adult Americans say they worked for a party or a candidate within the past year.[16]

Nevertheless, campaign participation is higher in the United States than in Europe. A five-country comparative study found that Americans were more likely to contribute money and time to election campaigns than were citizens of Germany, Austria, the Netherlands, and Great Britain.[17] A more recent study of twenty-three countries found that the United States ranked first in terms of citizens' efforts to influence other voters (see Figure 7–4). One reason why Americans are more active in campaigns, even though they vote at a lower rate, is that they have more opportunities to become active.[18] The United States is a federal system with campaigns for national, state, and local offices. A citizen who wants to participate is almost certain to find an opportunity at one level of office or another. Most of the governments in Europe are unitary in form (see Chapter 3), which means that there are fewer elective offices and thus fewer campaigns in which citizens can participate.

Lobbying Group Contributions

As government has extended its reach into more areas of American life, political activity outside the context of elections has increased substantially. Thousands of interest groups now actively lobby government on almost every conceivable policy and program. Lobbying activities once were conducted without much involvement by ordinary citizens, but that is no longer the case. Lobbying groups encourage citizens to place pressure on policymakers and to contribute money to

The Internet has vast but as yet unrealized potential as an instrument of mass political participation. Shown here is Markos Moulitsas Zuniga, who aided in the creation of presidential candidate Howard Dean's "meetups"—supporters connected with each other through the Internet. Zuniga runs a political web log called Daily Kos.

support the groups' activities. Millions of Americans every year play their part. In fact, Americans are more likely than citizens elsewhere to contribute money, usually in the form of annual dues, to lobbying groups. These donations support professionally run organizations that contact government officials and otherwise attempt to influence policy decisions.[19] Examples of such groups are the National Organization for Women, Common Cause, the Christian Moral Government Fund, the American Association of Retired Persons, and the National Conservative Political Action Committee. Chapter 9 discusses lobbying groups in more detail.

Community Activities

Many Americans participate in public affairs not through campaigns and political parties but through local organizations such as parent-teacher associations, neighborhood groups, business clubs, church-affiliated groups, and hospital auxiliaries. The actual number of citizens who participate actively in a community group is difficult to estimate, but the number is surely in the tens of millions. The United States has a tradition of local participation that goes back to colonial days. Moreover, compared with cities and towns in Europe, localities in the United States have more authority over policy issues, which is an added incentive to participation. Because of increased mobility and other factors, Americans may be less tied to their local communities than in the past and therefore less involved in community action. Nevertheless, half of Americans claim that they volunteer time to groups and community causes, compared with 20 percent or less in most European countries. Young American adults have increasingly engaged in community volunteer work. A 2003 survey of the nation's college students by Harvard University's Institute of Politics found that more of them were interested in, and active in, community volunteering than in election volunteering.

In a widely publicized book titled *Bowling Alone*, Harvard's Robert Putnam claims that America has been undergoing a long-term decline in its **social capital** (the sum of the face-to-face civic interactions among citizens in a society).[20] Putnam attributes the decline to television and other factors that draw people inward and away from participation in civic and political groups. Not all scholars accept Putnam's interpretation of trends in civic involvement (some indicators point toward a rise in certain types of participation), but no one challenges his assumption about the importance of civic participation. It brings people together, gives them an understanding of other points of view, and builds skills that make them more effective citizens.

social capital
The sum of the face-to-face interactions among citizens in a society.

Attending to the News

Informed participation is a democratic ideal, and news is the means by which most citizens try to keep abreast of public affairs. Although news consumption is an individual activity rather than a form of collective action, it is nonetheless a vital part of democratic citizenship. And it is a form of citizenship that increasingly is practiced by fewer and fewer adults.

Media & Politics

The Decline of Broadcast News and of the Television News Audience

Broadcast news once dominated the U.S. news system. Each evening, most television households tuned in the nightly network news. In most markets at the dinner hour, news was the only choice viewers had. Network newscasts on ABC, CBS, and NBC had an 80 percent market share—tens of millions of viewers. Today, their market share is less than half that. The introduction of cable television produced a fragmented marketplace with multiple news outlets that compete for viewers' attention not only with each other but also with entertainment programming.

Fewer Americans today watch television news regularly. Cable news, available around the clock, is a boon for those interested in television news. But cable television also enables viewers to easily ignore the news by making entertainment programming available at the click of a remote.

News exposure is particularly low among young adults. Why is it the case that less than half of young adults have a television news habit? Part of the answer can be found in their home environment during their childhood. Before the age of cable television, most American children were regularly exposed to news broadcasts. They did not have an inborn interest in news, but because most of their parents watched it, they were exposed to it. By the time they reached voting age, most had acquired a television news habit. After cable television came along, children had less exposure to television news. Even in homes where parents tuned in the evening news rather than an entertainment program, the children often were in a separate room watching entertainment programming on a second television set. A study by the Shorenstein Center on the Press, Politics, and Public Policy at Harvard University found that only 39 percent of the cable generation, compared with 59 percent of the broadcast generation, said that the news was a "daily part of home life" when they were growing up. The study also found that whether adults watch television news depends in large part on whether they were exposed to it regularly as children. Like many other habits, a news habit ordinarily is acquired early in life. Many of today's young adults never developed a news habit and, if past tendencies are a guide, might never develop one. The consequence could be a citizenry that is hard to reach and poorly informed.

Americans spend a huge number of hours attending to the media. Next to sleeping and working, media use absorbs the largest share of people's time. However, only a fraction of this use involves news consumption—in fact, news audiences in the United States have been shrinking (see Figure 7–5). Because of cable television, the Internet, computer games, and other forms of newer media, the news faces stiff competition for people's time and attention. Newspapers have lost readers to television news, which in turn has lost viewers to entertainment telecasts. Before cable television became widely available in the 1980s, many television viewers had no media alternative to watching a newscast during the dinner hour. With cable, viewers always have a variety of program choices, and many viewers simply prefer entertainment content to news content. Although the Internet has become a source of news for an increasing number of Americans, most Internet users do not depend on it for news—and some of those who do rarely go beyond the headlines they come across.

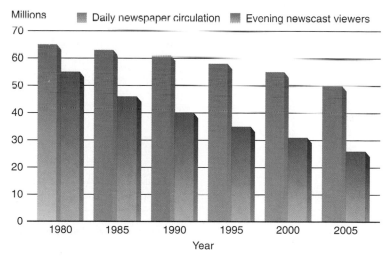

Figure 7–5

The Declining News Audience
For decades, Americans have relied mostly on the daily newspaper and the broadcast networks' evening newscasts as their major sources of national news. The audiences for both these media have declined sharply since 1980 as a consequence of competition from cable television and the Internet.
Source: Estimated by author from multiple sources.

Americans fall into three groups of nearly equal size based on their attention to news. About a third of the public follows the news on a daily basis; most of these citizens read the daily paper and also watch television newscasts. Another third follows the news intermittently, scanning a paper's news sections once in a while or catching an occasional newscast or webcast. The final third pays no appreciable attention to news in any form except when an extraordinary event occurs. This last group is the one that is growing in size, and the reason is simple: most young adults do not have much interest in news. News habits usually are formed by early adulthood, and today's young adults show less interest in the news than their predecessors. Fewer than one in five adults under thirty years of age, for example, read a daily newspaper, half the percentage of a few decades ago. Although young adults increasingly cite alternative sources of political information, such as late-night comedy shows, most of these sources contain minimal news. Studies have found that young adults who depend on alternative sources for their news are less informed about public affairs than other citizens are.[21]

Virtual Participation

The prospect of an entire generation of politically inattentive citizens is disturbing to many observers. Yet there is a glimmer of hope—the Internet. It is used more heavily by younger people and is packed with political information and participation possibilities.

It is unclear whether the Internet will actually serve as an entry into the world of politics for large numbers of citizens. Most people use it primarily for entertainment, school assignments, shopping, and personal and workplace communication. Nevertheless, thousands of websites feature news or politics. There have been remarkable examples of citizen mobilization through the Internet, none more successful than MoveOn, which claims two million "online activists," many of them young people. Internet use during the 2004 Democratic presidential nominating campaign provided a glimpse into the medium's potential (see Table 7–3). One-third of Internet users engaged in some form of election-related activity, such as sending or receiving campaign e-mails. A relatively small number—4 percent of Internet users—made use of election-related blogs or chat rooms, but the Internet was for some Americans a significant point of contact with the campaign. Howard Dean's candidacy, though ultimately unsuccessful,

TABLE 7–3 **Online Campaign Activities** During the 2004 Democratic presidential nominating campaign, nearly one-third of online users claimed to have engaged in a campaign-related activity online.

USED INTERNET TO:	PERCENTAGE OF ONLINE USERS
Get candidate issue information	18%
Send/receive campaign e-mails	18
Get information on local activities	10
Visit websites of political groups	9
Visit candidate websites	8
Engage in chats, discussions, blogs	4
Any of these six activities	30

Source: Pew Research Center for the People and the Press, January 2004.

caught the imagination of Internet users, and he raised millions of dollars for his campaign through the Internet.

The full impact of the Internet on citizen participation is not likely to become clear until its technological capacity is developed further and another generation of computer-savvy children reaches voting age.[22] Some analysts believe the Internet will usher in an era of unprecedented citizen involvement and influence. Other analysts are less optimistic, noting that the Internet has hundreds of thousands of websites, most of which have little or nothing to do with public affairs. They note further that users have almost complete control of web content. These analysts doubt that citizens will avail themselves of the Internet's political material unless they are otherwise interested in public affairs.

UNCONVENTIONAL ACTIVISM: SOCIAL MOVEMENTS AND PROTEST POLITICS

During the era of absolute monarchies, the public resorted to protest as a way of expressing dissatisfaction with its rulers. Tax and food riots occurred with some frequency. When democratic governments came into existence, the vote gave citizens a way to express their views in a regular and less disruptive way.

However, voting is double-edged. Although the vote gives citizens a degree of control over government, *the vote also gives government a degree of control over citizens.*[23] Because government officials are freely chosen by the people, they can claim that their policies reflect the will of the people and therefore must be respected and obeyed. The power of the vote is also limited by the choices listed on the ballot. In the American case, citizens who are dissatisfied with both the Republican party and the Democratic party have no realistic way to exercise power through the vote.

Social movements are an alternative form of influence. **Social movements,** or **political movements** as they are sometimes called, refer to broad efforts to achieve change by citizens who feel that government is acting improperly.[24] These efforts are sometimes channeled through conventional forms of participation, such as political lobbying, but citizens can also take to the streets in protest against government. In 2003, as the Bush administration was preparing for war with Iraq, protest demonstrations were held in many U.S. cities, including Washington and San Francisco. Two percent of adult Americans said they participated in an antiwar demonstration. Many of them were young adults. Participants in social movements are younger on average than nonparticipants, a reversal of the pattern for voting.[25]

Social movements do not always succeed, but they sometimes force government into action. For example, the timing and scope of the landmark 1964 Civil Rights Act and 1965 Voting Rights Act can be explained only as a response by Congress to the pressure created by the

social (political) movements
Active and sustained efforts to achieve social and political change by groups of people who feel that government has not been properly responsive to their concerns.

The high point of the civil rights movement was Dr. Martin Luther King Jr.'s "I Have a Dream" address on the capitol mall in Washington, D.C., on August 28, 1963. A quarter of a million people, the largest gathering on the mall to that date, turned out for the rally.

Figure 7–6

Protest Activity
Despite the significance of protest activity in U.S. history, Americans are less likely to protest than are citizens of many other democracies. Of twenty-three countries surveyed, the United States ranked eighteenth in level of protest activity. Only selected countries are included in this figure.
Source: Surveys by Comparative Studies of Electoral Systems, 2001–4. Reported in Russell J. Dalton, "The Myth of the Disengaged American," CSES Report, October 25, 2005, web release.

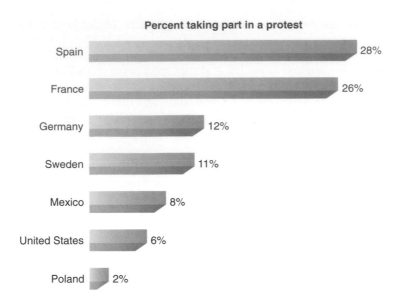

Percent taking part in a protest

- Spain — 28%
- France — 26%
- Germany — 12%
- Sweden — 11%
- Mexico — 8%
- United States — 6%
- Poland — 2%

civil rights movement. Another effective social movement in the 1960s was that of the farm workers, whose protests led to improved conditions for migrant workers.

Political protests have taken on new forms in recent years. Protest was traditionally a desperate act that began, often spontaneously, when a group had lost hope that it could succeed through more conventional methods. Today, however, protest is usually a calculated act—a means of bringing added attention and impetus to a cause.[26] These tactical protests often involve a great deal of planning, including, in some instances, the busing of thousands of people to Washington for a rally staged for television. Civil rights, environmental, agricultural, and pro- and antiabortion groups are among those that have staged tactical protests in Washington within the past few years.

Protest politics has a long history in America, dating to the Boston Tea Party and earlier. It would be no exaggeration to claim that the United States was founded on a protest movement that sparked a revolution against Britain. Despite this tradition, however, protest activity is less common in the United States than in many Western democracies (see Figure 7–6). Spain, France, Germany, Sweden, and Ireland are among the countries that have higher rates of participation in political protests.

Public support for protest activity is also relatively low in the United States. For reasons that are not fully clear, Americans often side with the authorities against protesters. The Vietnam War protests, which in limited cases were accompanied by the burning of draft cards, enjoyed only marginal public support outside the circle of protesters. When unarmed student protesters at Kent State University and Jackson State University were shot to death in May 1970 by members of the National Guard, a majority of Americans polled blamed the students, not the guardsmen, for the tragedy.

The public was more accepting of protests against the 2003 war in Iraq (see Figure 7–7). Even after the fighting had begun, according to an ABC News/Los Angeles Times poll, three in every five

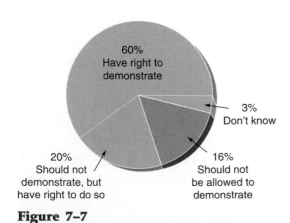

- 60% Have right to demonstrate
- 3% Don't know
- 20% Should not demonstrate, but have right to do so
- 16% Should not be allowed to demonstrate

Figure 7–7

Americans' Opinions of Iraq War Protests
A majority supported the right of antiwar protesters to demonstrate, although some Americans felt they should not be allowed to do so.
Source: ABC News/Washington Post poll, March 23, 2003.

Americans said they saw the protests as "a sign of a healthy democracy." Still, almost two in five felt that "opponents of the war should not hold antiwar demonstrations"; about half of these said that antiwar demonstrations should be banned. In another poll, about a third of respondents said that protesters were "the kind of people who tend to blame America first."[27]

Nonetheless, there is a basic acceptance of protest activity. Rarely are protesters attacked by those who disagree with their actions, and most Americans display at least some understanding of protest as part of America's tradition of free expression. In that sense, protest is seen as something to be allowed, if not universally admired.

PARTICIPATION AND THE POTENTIAL FOR INFLUENCE

Although Americans claim that political participation is important, many of them do not practice what they preach. Most citizens show little interest in participation except to vote, and a significant minority cannot even be persuaded that voting is worth their time. However, Americans are not completely apathetic: many millions of them contribute to political causes, and more than a hundred million vote in presidential elections.

Yet sustained political activism does not engage a large proportion of the public. Moreover, many of those who do participate are drawn to politics by a habitual sense of civic duty rather than by an intense concern with current issues. The emphasis that American culture places on individualism tends to diminish interest in political participation. "In the United States, the country of individualism *par excellence*," William Watts and Lloyd Free write, "there is a sharp distinction in people's minds between their own personal lives and national life."[28] Although wars and severe recessions can lead Americans to look to government for help, most people under most conditions expect to solve their own problems. This is not to say that Americans have a disdain for collective action. In their communities particularly, citizens frequently take part in collective efforts to support a local hospital, improve the neighborhood, and the like. But most Americans tend not to see their material well-being as being closely linked to partisan political activity.

This tendency contributes to a class bias in American politics. For one thing, it helps maintain a relatively sharp distinction between that which is properly public (political) and that which is properly private (economic). Americans, as political scientist Robert Lane notes, prefer to see benefits distributed primarily through the economic marketplace rather than through the policies of government.[29] For example, access to medical care

LEADERS

SAMUEL ADAMS

(1722–1803)

In time, Samuel Adams's second cousin, John Adams, would become more famous, rising to the position of president of the United States. But it was Samuel Adams who meant more to the founding of the United States. He organized and led the Boston Tea Party, a defiant and dramatic protest against British rule of the American colonies. Samuel Adams was a brilliant student, earning a bachelor's degree and a master's degree from Harvard College—this in an era when few enjoyed the privilege of a college education. His father owned a brewery, which Samuel Adams took over upon his father's death. (In the 1980s, a new beer was launched in Boston bearing Samuel Adams's name.) Adams's real passion, however, was politics. From the start, he was a radical voice, constantly questioning and challenging the legitimacy of British authority. He was among the signers of the Declaration of Independence and during his career served in Congress and as Massachusetts state legislator, lieutenant governor, and governor. Adams sided with the anti-Federalists in the debate over ratification of the Constitution, finally agreeing to support it when a Bill of Rights was promised.

Protesters demonstrate (in 2003) against the war in Iraq. Although protest movements are an American tradition, they do not routinely receive strong public support.

Political Culture

Voting and Self-Government

On election day, officials unfailingly urge Americans "to get out and vote." Some of these officials are not to be taken seriously. On the whole, U.S. elections are conducted fairly and openly with the support of tens of thousands of public-minded officials and volunteer poll watchers. Lurking in the shadows, however, are policies that serve to depress the vote. The worst abuses, such as whites-only primaries and poll taxes, are in the past. But official obstacles to voting are still part of the electoral system. For example, registration in most states closes two or more weeks in advance of election day. Many officials in these states have no interest in adopting the election-day registration policy that is currently in effect in six states. They prefer a smaller voter turnout because it is more manageable and predictable. Another obstacle is early poll closings. Half the states close the polls before 8 P.M., which disadvantages people who are at work during daylight hours.

Some states are just as cavalier in counting the vote. In 2000, George W. Bush won the presidency on the basis of a 537-vote victory in Florida, where tens of thousands of ballots went uncounted. Although Congress soon thereafter passed legislation that provided money and set standards to increase the likelihood that a vote that is cast will actually be counted, Florida and other states have been slow to acquire balloting systems with a low error rate. Well over a million ballots cast in the 2004 presidential election went uncounted, with the highest percentage of wasted ballots typically concentrated in poor or minority areas. In Chicago, for example, the error rate has been three times higher in African American neighborhoods, where older and less reliable ballot methods have been used. Even where the balloting machinery is up-to-date, there are not always enough machines to handle the number of voters. In 2004 in some Ohio locations, voters stood in line for hours waiting to cast a ballot because not enough polling booths had been set up. Some observers concluded that in some precincts the shortage was a deliberate ploy by officials to hold down the vote in those districts.

More so than in most Western democracies, voting in the United States has been subject to political manipulation. America's electoral history is replete with examples of public policies designed to deny or suppress the vote. Voting has been treated as a privilege rather than an inalienable right, as something to be earned (or, in some cases, arbitrarily withheld) rather than something so intrinsic to citizenship that government makes every reasonable effort to promote its exercise.

What, in your opinion, explains the historical tendency? Do you think Americans' claim to self-government has been diminished by the tendency?

---

in the United States, unlike in Europe where government-provided health care is available to all, is to some degree based on a person's ability to pay for it. Roughly forty-five million Americans do not have access to adequate health care because they cannot afford health insurance.

Lower-income Americans are a relatively weak force in the nation's politics. They are less likely to have the financial resources and communication skills that encourage participation in politics and make it personally rewarding. Among citizens who are most active in politics, three times as many have incomes in the top third as in the bottom third.[30] This difference is much greater than in other Western democracies, where poorer citizens are assisted through automatic voter registration and by the presence of class-based political organizations. The poor in the United States must arrange their own registration and must choose between two political parties that are attuned primarily to middle-class interests.

The low participation rate of lower-income Americans reduces their influence on public policy. Studies indicate that representatives are more responsive to the demands of participants than to those of nonparticipants.[31] Although it must be kept in mind that participants do not always promote only their own narrow interests, it would be a mistake to conclude that large numbers of people regularly support policies that would mainly benefit others. For example, a turning point in the defeat of President Bill Clinton's health care reform proposal, which would have extended health care coverage to nearly all Americans, came when middle-class taxpayers decided that it might increase the cost and reduce the quality of their own medical care. According to Time/CNN polls, support for the Clinton plan dropped from 57 percent to 37 percent between September 1993 and July 1994. Although this decline reflected a loss of support among all groups, the drop was particularly severe among middle- and higher-income people who already had health insurance, through either an individual policy or an employment-related group policy.

In sum, the pattern of individual political participation in the United States parallels the distribution of influence that prevails in the private sector. Those who have the most power in the marketplace also have the most power in the political arena. However, the issue of individual participation is only one piece of the larger puzzle of who rules America and for what purposes. Subsequent chapters will supply additional pieces.

Summary

Self-Test www.mhhe.com/pattersontad8

Political participation is involvement in activities designed to influence public policy and leadership. A main issue of democratic government is the question of who participates in politics and how fully they participate.

Voting is the most widespread form of active political participation among Americans. Yet voter turnout is significantly lower in the United States than in other democratic nations. The requirement that Americans must personally register in order to establish their eligibility to vote is one reason for lower turnout among Americans; other democracies place the burden of registration on government officials rather than on the individual citizen. The fact that the United States holds frequent elections also discourages some citizens from voting regularly. Finally, the major American political parties, unlike many of those in Europe, do not clearly represent the interests of opposing economic classes; thus, the policy stakes in American elections are lower. Some Americans do not vote because they think that policy will not change greatly regardless of which party holds power.

Only a minority of citizens engage in the more demanding forms of political activity, such as work on community affairs or on behalf of a candidate during a political campaign. The proportion of Americans who engage in these more demanding forms of activity exceeds the proportion of

Europeans who do so. Nevertheless, only about one in every four Americans will take an active part in a political organization at some point in their lives. Most political activists are individuals of higher income and education; they have the skills and material resources to participate effectively and tend to take a greater interest in politics. More than in any other Western democracy, political participation in the United States is related to economic status.

Social movements are broad efforts to achieve change by citizens who feel that government is not properly responsive to their interests. These efforts sometimes take place outside established channels; demonstrations, picket lines, and marches are common means of protest. Protesters are younger and more idealistic on average than are other citizens, but they are a very small proportion of the population. In addition, protest activities do not have a high level of public support, despite the country's tradition of free expression.

Overall, Americans are only moderately involved in politics. While they are concerned with political affairs, they are mostly immersed in their private pursuits, a reflection in part of a cultural belief in individualism. The lower level of participation among low-income citizens has particular significance in that it works to reduce their influence on public policy and leadership.

STUDY CORNER

Key Terms

alienation (*p. 199*)

apathy (*p. 197*)

civic duty (*p. 197*)

political participation (*p. 189*)

registration (*p. 194*)

social capital (*p. 202*)

social (political) movements (*p. 205*)

suffrage (*p. 190*)

voter turnout (*p. 191*)

Self-Test

1. Low voter turnout in U.S. elections compared to other democracies is explained by all except:
   a. differences in registration requirements.
   b. use of the secret ballot.
   c. frequency of elections.
   d. differences in the political party systems.

2. Unconventional political activism includes all except:
   a. participating in a social movement.
   b. taking part in a political demonstration or march.
   c. practicing civil disobedience.
   d. doing volunteer work for a political candidate or party.

3. Which group has the lowest voter turnout level?
   a. high-income Americans.
   b. college-educated Americans.
   c. young adult Americans.
   d. Americans with a strong sense of civic duty.

4. In European democracies, voting registration is:
   a. purely an individual's responsibility.
   b. the responsibility of government officials.
   c. taxed, although the tax is only a small amount in most European countries.
   d. open only to citizens 30 years of age and older in most European countries.

5. In comparison with citizens of European democracies, Americans are more likely to:
   a. vote in national elections.
   b. join labor unions.

   c. participate in community activities.
   d. regard protest as the most patriotic form of participation.

6. All of the following statements describe political participation in America except which one?
   a. Many people who participate in politics often do so from a sense of civic duty.
   b. America's culture of individualism discourages a reliance on political involvement.
   c. There are more barriers to regular participation in elections in the United States than in Europe.
   d. Americans place more emphasis on the public (political) sphere as a means of attaining their social and economic goals than they place on the private (economic) sphere.

7. More than in other Western democracies, political participation in the United States is related to income level. (T/F)

8. People who participate in social movements tend to be younger than nonparticipants. (T/F)

9. As a result of the increase in the number of college-educated adults, Americans today read more newspapers than ever before. (T/F)

10. With regard to election campaigns, Americans are more likely than Europeans to contribute money and to volunteer their time to help a candidate or party. (T/F)

Critical Thinking

Why does economic class—differences in people's incomes—make such a large difference in political participation levels? What are the policy consequences of this difference?

Suggested Readings

Bimber, Bruce, and Richard Davis. *Campaigning Online: The Internet in U.S. Elections.* New York: Oxford University Press, 2003. A careful study of citizens' use of the Internet in elections.

Burns, Nancy, Kay Lehman Schlozman, and Sidney Verba. *The Private Roots of Public Action: Gender, Equality, and Public Action.* Cambridge, Mass.: Harvard University Press, 2001. An analysis of gender differences in political participation.

Leighley, Jan. *Strength in Numbers: The Political Mobilization of Racial and Ethnic Minorities.* Princeton, N.J.: Princeton University Press, 2001. A study of the factors that motivate blacks and Hispanics to participate.

Patterson, Thomas E. *The Vanishing Voter.* New York: Knopf, 2002. A study of the decline in electoral participation and what might be done to reverse the trend.

Putnam, Robert. *Bowling Alone.* New York: Simon and Schuster, 2000. A provocative analysis of the trend in civic participation.

Schudson, Michael. *The Good Citizen: A History of American Civic Life.* New York: Free Press, 1998. A thoughtful history of civic participation in America.

Skocpol, Theda. *Diminished Democracy: From Membership to Management in American Civic Life.* Norman: University of Oklahoma Press, 2003. An analysis of the trend away from active membership in civic and political organizations.

Zukin, Cliff, Scott Keeter, Molly Andolina, Krista Jenkins, and Michael X. Delli Carpini. *A New Engagement: Political Participation, Civic Life, and the Changing American Citizen.* New York: Oxford University Press, 2006. A comprehensive study that concludes that young adults are finding ways other than election politics to exercise citizenship.

List of Websites

http://www.rockthevote.org/

Rock the Vote is an organization dedicated to helping young people realize and utilize their power to affect the civic and political life of their communities.

http://www.umich.edu/~nes/

The University of Michigan's National Election Studies (NES) site; provides survey data on voting, public opinion, and political participation.

http://www.vanishingvoter.org/

Harvard University's election study site; provides information on voter participation.

http://www.vote-smart.org/

Project Vote Smart includes information on Republican and Democratic candidates and officials; also has the latest in election news.

Participate!

If you are not currently registered to vote, consider registering. You can obtain a registration form from the election board or clerk in your community of residence. There are several websites that contain state-by-state registration information. One such site is www.vanishingvoter.org. If you are already registered, consider participating in a registration or voting drive on your campus. Although students typically register and vote at relatively low rates, they will often participate if encouraged by other students to do so.

Extra Credit

For up-to-the-minute *New York Times* articles, interactive simulations, graphics, study tools, and more links and quizzes, visit the text's Online Learning Center at www.mhhe.com/pattersontad8.

(Self-Test Answers: 1. b   2. d   3. c   4. b   5. c   6. d   7. T   8. T   9. F   10. T)

Political Parties, Candidates, and Campaigns:
Defining the Voter's Choice

Chapter Outline

Party Competition and Majority Rule: The History of U.S. Parties
The First Parties
Andrew Jackson and Grassroots Parties
Republicans Versus Democrats: Realignments and the Enduring Party System
Today's Party Alignment and Its Origins
Parties and the Vote

Electoral and Party Systems
The Single-Member-District System of Election
Politics and Coalitions in the Two-Party System
Minor Parties

Party Organizations
The Weakening of Party Organizations
The Structure and Role of Party Organizations

The Candidate-Centered Campaign
Campaign Funds: The Money Chase
Organization and Strategy: Hired Guns
Voter Contacts: Pitched Battle

Parties, Candidates, and the Public's Influence

CHAPTER 8

Political parties created democracy and . . . modern democracy is unthinkable save in terms of the parties.

E. E. Schattschneider[1]

Toe-to-toe, they slugged it out in states and districts across the breadth of America, each side saying that it had the better answer to America's problems. One side claimed that the fighting in Iraq was a key link in the war on terrorism—that America would be safe only if it took the fight to the enemy. The other side portrayed the Iraq invasion as an ill-conceived venture that had increased the terrorist threat while taking a heavy toll on America's soldiers. And Iraq was but one of the issues separating the two sides: among the others were jobs, taxes, education, immigration, health, abortion, budget deficits, and the environment.

The scene of this showdown was the 2006 midterm election. The two sides were the Republican party and the Democratic party, each with a slate of House and Senate candidates that carried its message into cities and towns across America.

A **political party** is an ongoing coalition of interests joined together in an effort to get its candidates for public office elected under a common label.[2] By offering a choice between policies and leaders, parties give voters a chance to influence the direction of government. "It is the competition of [parties] that provides the people with an opportunity to make a choice," political scientist E. E. Schattschneider wrote. "Without this opportunity popular sovereignty amounts to nothing."[3]

This chapter examines political parties and the candidates who run under their banners. U.S. campaigns are **party-centered politics** in the sense that the Republican and Democratic parties compete across the country election after election. Yet campaigns are also **candidate-centered politics** in the sense that individual candidates devise their own strategies, choose their own issues, and form their own campaign organizations. The following points are emphasized in this chapter:

- *Political competition in the United States has centered on two parties, a pattern that is explained by the nature of America's electoral system, political institutions, and political culture.* Minor parties exist in the United States but have been unable to compete successfully for governing power.

- *To win an electoral majority, candidates of the two major parties must appeal to a diverse set of interests; this necessity normally leads them to advocate moderate and somewhat overlapping policies.* Only during periods of stress are America's parties likely to present the electorate with starkly different choices.

political party

An ongoing coalition of interests joined together to try to get their candidates for public office elected under a common label.

party-centered politics

Election campaigns and other political processes in which political parties, not individual candidates, hold most of the initiative and influence.

candidate-centered politics

Election campaigns and other political processes in which candidates, not political parties, have most of the initiative and influence.

213

- *U.S. party organizations are decentralized and fragmented.* The national organization is a loose collection of state organizations, which in turn are loose associations of autonomous local organizations. This feature of U.S. parties can be traced to federalism and the nation's diversity, which have made it difficult for the parties to act as instruments of national power.

- *The ability of America's party organizations to control nominations and election to office is weak, which in turn enhances the candidates' role.*

- *Candidate-centered campaigns are based on the media and utilize the skills of professional consultants.* Money, strategy, and televised advertising are key components of today's presidential and congressional campaigns.

PARTY COMPETITION AND MAJORITY RULE: THE HISTORY OF U.S. PARTIES

Through their numbers, citizens have the potential for great influence, but that potential cannot be realized unless citizens have the capacity to act together. Parties give them that capacity. When Americans go to the polls, they have a choice between the Republican and Democratic parties. This **party competition** narrows their options to two and in the process enables people with different backgrounds and opinions to unite behind a single alternative. In casting a majority of its votes for one party, the electorate chooses that party's candidates, philosophy, and policies over those of the opposing party.

The history of democratic government is synonymous with the history of parties. When the countries of Eastern Europe gained their freedom more than a decade ago, one of their first steps toward democracy was the legalization of parties. When the United States was founded over two centuries ago, the formation of parties was also a first step toward the building of its democracy. The reason is simple: it is the competition among parties that gives popular majorities a chance to influence how they will be governed.[4] Stated differently, political parties are the instrument that allows the principle of self-government to be realized in practice. If there were no mechanism like the party to enable citizens to make their voices heard collectively, they would be powerless—each unable to be heard loud enough to get the government's attention.

The First Parties

America's early leaders mistrusted parties. George Washington in his farewell address warned the nation of the "baneful effects" of parties, and James Madison likened parties to special interests. However, Madison's misgivings about parties gradually gave way to a grudging admiration; he recognized that they enabled like-minded people to exercise collective power.

America's parties originated in the rivalry within George Washington's administration between Thomas Jefferson, a supporter of states' rights and small landholders, and Alexander Hamilton, a promoter of strong national government and commercial interests (see Figure 8–1). When Hamilton's ideas prevailed in Congress, Jefferson and his followers formed a political party, the Republicans. By adopting this label, which was associated with popular government, the Jeffersonians sought to portray themselves as the rightful heirs to the American Revolution's legacy of self-government and political equality.

Democratic nominee John Kerry is surrounded by party faithful during the 2004 presidential campaign.

party competition

A process in which conflict over society's goals is transformed by political parties into electoral competition in which the winner gains the power to govern.

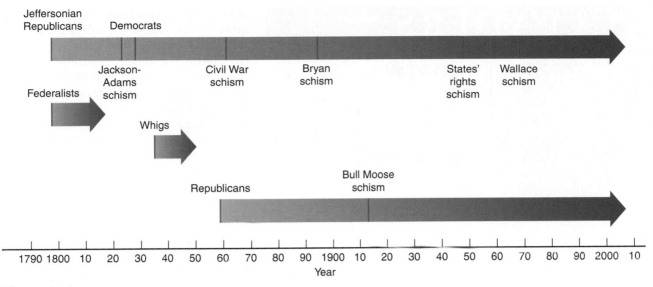

Figure 8–1

A Graphic History of America's Major Parties
The U.S. party system has been remarkable for its continuity. Competition between two major parties has been a persistent feature of the system.

Hamilton then organized his supporters into a formal party—the Federalists—and in the process created America's first competitive party system. The Federalists took their name from the faction that had supported ratification of the Constitution, thereby implying that they represented America's governing tradition. However, the Federalists' preoccupation with commercial and wealthy interests fueled Jefferson's claim that the Federalists were bent on establishing a government of the rich and wellborn. After Jefferson in the election of 1800 defeated John Adams, who had succeeded Washington as president, the Federalists never again controlled the White House or Congress.

During the so-called Era of Good Feeling, when James Monroe ran unopposed in 1820 for a second presidential term, it appeared as if the political system might operate without parties. Yet by the end of Monroe's second term, policy differences had split the Republicans. The dominant faction, led by Andrew Jackson, retained Jefferson's commitment to the interests of ordinary people. This faction called itself Democratic Republicans, later shortened to Democrats. Thus, the Republican party of Jefferson is the forerunner of today's Democratic party rather than of today's Republican party.

HISTORICAL BACKGROUND

Andrew Jackson and Grassroots Parties

For all its shortcomings, competition between parties is the only system that can regularly mobilize collective influence on behalf of the many who are individually powerless against those few who have extraordinary wealth and status.

This realization led Jackson during the 1820s to develop a **grassroots party.** Whereas Jefferson's party had been well organized only at the leadership level, Jackson sought a party that was built from the bottom up. Jackson's Democratic party consisted of organizations at the local, state, and national

grassroots party
A political party organized at the level of the voters and dependent on their support for its strength.

LEADERS

ANDREW JACKSON
(1767–1845)

Andrew Jackson rose to national fame when, as a major general, he defeated the British at the Battle of New Orleans during the War of 1812. A Tennessee native and slaveholder, he won the presidency in 1828 after having lost in 1824 despite receiving the most popular votes. Jackson disliked the political elite that had governed America until his presidency, and he was determined to give ordinary citizens more influence in government. He failed in an attempt to eliminate the Electoral College, but he succeeded in turning the Democratic party into a grassroots organization. The term "Jacksonian Democracy" became synonymous with his belief that ordinary people were capable of governing themselves. Jackson's relationship with Congress was stormy; he believed that the president, not Congress, was the proper spokesman for the people. When Congress rejected Martin Van Buren, Jackson's choice, as ambassador to Britain, Jackson got even by picking Van Buren as his running mate in 1832. When Jackson stepped down from the presidency four years later, Van Buren succeeded him.

levels, with membership open to all eligible voters. These organizations, along with more liberal suffrage laws, contributed to a nearly fourfold rise in voter turnout during the 1830s.[5] At the peak of Jacksonian democracy, Alexis de Tocqueville wrote, "The People reign in the American political world as the Deity does in the universe."[6] Although Tocqueville exaggerated the people's true power, he caught the spirit of popular government that was behind the development of grassroots parties under Andrew Jackson.

In this period, a new opposition party, the Whigs, emerged to challenge the Democrats. The Whigs were a catchall party. Its followers were united not by a coherent philosophy of their own but by their opposition for one reason or another to the policies of the Jacksonian Democrats.

Competition between the Whigs and the Democrats was relatively short-lived. During the 1850s the slavery issue began to tear both parties apart. The Whig party withered, and a northern-based new party, calling itself Republican, arose as the main challenger to the Democrats. In the 1860 presidential election, the Democratic party's northern faction nominated Stephen A. Douglas, who held that the question of whether a new territory would permit slavery was for its voters to decide, while the southern faction nominated John C. Breckinridge, who called for legalized slavery in all territories. The Democratic vote split sharply along regional lines between these two candidates—with the result that the Republican nominee, Abraham Lincoln, who had called for the gradual elimination of slavery, was able to win the presidency with only 40 percent of the popular vote. Lincoln's election prompted the southern states to secede from the Union, which led to the Civil War. For the first and only time in the nation's history, the party system had failed to peaceably resolve Americans' conflicting goals.[7] The issue of slavery proved too explosive to be settled through electoral competition.

Republicans Versus Democrats: Realignments and the Enduring Party System

After the Civil War, the nation settled into the pattern of competition between the Republican and Democratic parties that has lasted through today. The durability of these two parties is due not to their ideological consistency but to their remarkable ability to adapt during periods of crisis. By abandoning at these crucial times their old ways of doing things, the Republican and Democratic parties have repeatedly remade themselves—with new bases of support, new policies, and new public philosophies.

These periods of great political change are known as *realignments*. A **party realignment** involves four basic elements:

#3

1. The disruption of the existing political order because of the emergence of one or more unusually powerful and divisive issues
2. An election contest in which the voters shift their support strongly in favor of one party
3. A major change in policy brought about through the action of the stronger party
4. An enduring change in the party coalitions, which works to the lasting advantage of the dominant party

party realignment

An election or set of elections in which the electorate responds strongly to an extraordinarily powerful issue that has disrupted the established political order. A realignment has a lasting impact on public policy, popular support for the parties, and the composition of the party coalitions.

Realignments are rare. They do not occur simply because one party wrests control of government from the other. They involve deep and lasting changes in the party system that affect not just the most recent election but later ones as well. By this standard, there have been three clear-cut realignments since the 1850s.

The first of these, the Civil War realignment, brought about a thorough change in the party system. The Republicans replaced the Democrats as the nation's majority party. The Republicans dominated the larger and more populous North, while the Democratic party was left with a stronghold in what became known as "the Solid South." During the next three decades, the Republicans held the presidency except for Grover Cleveland's two terms of office and had a majority in Congress for all but four years.

The 1896 election resulted in a second realignment of the Republican-Democratic party system. Three years earlier, an economic panic following a bank collapse had resulted in a severe depression. The Democrat Cleveland was president when the crash happened, and people blamed him and his party. In the aftermath, the Republicans made additional gains in the Northeast and Midwest, solidifying their position as the nation's dominant party. During the four decades between the 1890s realignment and the next one in the 1930s, the Republicans held the presidency except for Woodrow Wilson's two terms and had a majority in Congress for all but six years.

#3

The Great Depression of the 1930s triggered yet another realignment of the American party system. The Republican Herbert Hoover was president during the stock market crash of 1929, and many Americans blamed Hoover, his party, and its business allies for the economic catastrophe that followed. The Democrats became the country's majority party. Their political and policy agenda called for an expanded role for the national government. Franklin D. Roosevelt's presidency was characterized by unprecedented policy initiatives in the areas of business regulation and

LEADERS

ABRAHAM LINCOLN

(1809–65)

Abraham Lincoln had been a member of Congress from Illinois before he was elected to the presidency in 1860. Homely and gangly, Lincoln is regarded by many as America's greatest president for his principled leadership during the Civil War. Lincoln's accomplishments are all the more remarkable in that, unlike earlier presidents, he came from a humble background. His father was a frontiersman, his mother died when he was ten, and he was largely self-schooled. His greatest legacy is the preservation of the American Union. The Emancipation Proclamation and the Gettysburg Address are two of his other legacies. He was assassinated at Ford's Theater in the nation's capital shortly after the start of his second term as president. Lincoln was the first Republican elected to the presidency, and his successful pursuit of victory in the Civil War led to a party realignment that solidified the GOP's status as the nation's majority party.

The new order begins: Franklin D. Roosevelt rides to his inauguration with outgoing president Herbert Hoover after the realigning election of 1932.

social welfare (see Chapter 3). His election in 1932 began a thirty-six-year period of Democratic presidencies that was interrupted only by Dwight D. Eisenhower's two terms in the 1950s. In this period the Democrats also dominated Congress, losing control only in 1947–48 and 1953–54.

The reason realignments have such a substantial effect on future elections is that they affect voters' *party identification* (see Chapter 6). Young voters in particular tend to identify with the newly ascendant party, and they retain that identity, giving the party a solid base of support for years to come. First-time voters in the 1930s came to identify with the Democratic party by a two-to-one margin, establishing it as the nation's majority party and enabling it to dominate national politics for the next three decades.[8]

Today's Party Alignment and Its Origins

A party realignment inevitably loses strength over time as the issues that gave rise to it decline in importance. By the late 1960s, with the Democratic party divided over the Vietnam War and civil rights, it was apparent that the era of New Deal politics was ending.[9]

The change was most dramatic in the South. The region had been solidly Democratic at all levels since the Civil War, but the Democratic party's leadership on civil rights angered white conservatives.[10] In the 1964 presidential election, five southern states voted Republican, and the South is now a Republican bastion in presidential politics. The Republican party also made gains, though more gradually, in elections for other offices. Today most top officials in the southern states are Republicans.

More slowly and less completely, the northeastern states have become more Democratic. The shift is partly attributable to the growing size of minority populations in the Northeast. But it is also due to the declining influence of the Republican party's moderate wing, which was concentrated in these states. As southern conservatives became Republican in ever larger numbers, the party's stands on social issues such as abortion and affirmative action tilted toward the right, reducing the party's appeal among northeastern voters.

Party conflict also extended to federal spending on education, health, and economic security programs. The Democrats, who had started nearly all of these programs, defended them, while Republicans attacked them as being too expensive. Taxing and spending became perennial campaign issues, resulting in a further alignment of liberals against conservatives.

The GOP (short for "Grand Old Party" and another name for the Republican party) gained the most from these changes in party politics. Since 1968, Republicans have held the presidency for twice as many years as the Democrats have. Also, since 1994, the GOP has controlled the House and Senate for more years than the Democrats have. Republicans, after trailing the Democrats for decades, have also narrowed the gap in terms of party identification (see Figure 8–2). In 2004, Democratic identifiers outnumbered Republican identifiers by only 2 percentage points in the Gallup poll, the smallest margin ever recorded by that organization. By 2006, however, the Democrats' lead had

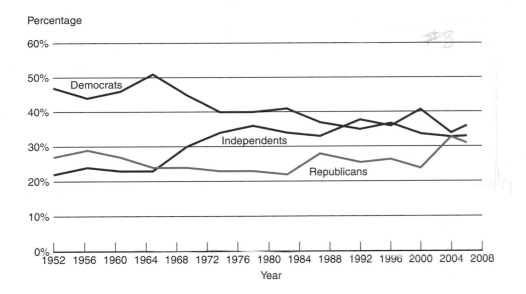

Percentage

Figure 8-2

Partisan Identification
After trailing for decades, Republican identifiers nearly reached parity with Democratic identifiers in 2004, only to fall behind again as Iraq and other issues worked to the Democrats' advantage. Of the roughly one-third of voters who describe themselves as Independents, most also say they "lean" toward one of the two major parties. The leaners divide almost evenly between the two parties.
Source: National Election Studies, 1952–2000, Gallup surveys, after 2000.

widened to 5 percentage points, apparently in response to growing discontent with the Bush administration's handling of the conflict in Iraq and other issues.[11]

The general shift toward the Republican party is not a party realignment in the traditional sense. Rather than occurring abruptly in response to a disruptive issue, as was the case in the 1860s, 1890s, and 1930s realignments, the change has taken place slowly and somewhat fitfully. For a period in the 1970s, for example, Republican support weakened. Further, the partisan intensity that marks a full-scale party realignment has at times been missing. The percentage of self-described Independent voters rose sharply during the 1960s and early 1970s, as did the number of voters casting a **split ticket,** that is, casting a ballot on which their vote for different offices is divided between Democratic and Republican candidates. Some analysts described these developments as a *dealignment*—a partial but enduring weakening of partisanship.[12]

Partisanship is not as strong today as in peak periods such as the 1930s, but it has staged a comeback since the 1970s. Conflict between Republican and Democratic officeholders in Washington has intensified since that decade (see Chapters 11 and 12), and the gap in the policy opinions of Republican and Democratic party identifiers has widened (see Chapter 6). In addition, fewer voters today cast a split ticket. When all offices—local, state, and federal—are taken into account, ticket splitting is still relatively common, with about half of all voters casting such a ballot. Ticket splitting among candidates for federal office, however, has declined by nearly half since its peak in the 1970s (see Figure 8–3). Today, fewer than 20 percent of voters back one party's candidate for president and the other party's candidate for the House of Representatives. The fact that more than four of five voters now back the same party's presidential and congressional candidates is a sure sign of robust partisanship.

Analysts are divided in their opinions on where the party system is heading. Some predict a period of Republican dominance as the GOP consolidates its recent gains and adds to them.[13] Others foresee a resurgent Democratic party fueled by the increasing voting power of minority groups, particularly blacks and Hispanics.[14] One thing is virtually certain: as they have for over 150 years, Americans will continue to look to the Republican and Democratic parties for

split ticket
The pattern of voting in which the individual voter in a given election casts a ballot for one or more candidates of each major party.

Figure 8–3

Split-Ticket Voting in Presidential and Congressional Races
The level of split-ticket voting, as measured by the percentage who backed one party's candidate for president and the other party's candidate for the House of Representatives, has declined in recent elections. The change reflects an increased level of partisanship among America's voters.
Source: National Election Studies.

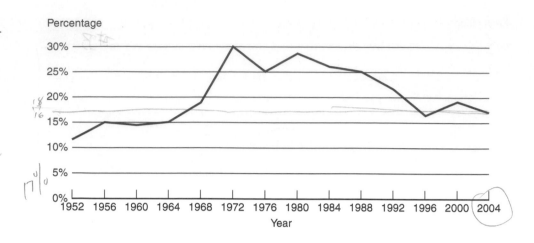

political leadership. The enduring strength and appeal of the two major parties is a hallmark of American politics.

Parties and the Vote

The power of party is at no time clearer than when, election after election, Republican and Democratic candidates reap the vote of their party's identifiers. In the 2004 presidential election, George W. Bush had the support of 93 percent of Republican party identifiers, while John Kerry garnered the votes of 89 percent of self-identified Democrats. Major party candidates do not always do that well with party loyalists, but it is relatively unusual—in congressional races as well as in the presidential race—for a party nominee to get less than 80 percent of the partisan vote.

Nevertheless, some voters in every election are swayed by the issues of the moment. Voters respond to issues both prospectively and retrospectively. **Prospective voting** occurs when the voter chooses a candidate on the basis of what the candidate promises to do if elected. In contrast, **retrospective voting** is based on a judgment about past performance—the situation in which a voter supports the incumbent officeholder or party when pleased with its performance and opposes it when displeased. Retrospective voting is the more common form of issue voting. When things are going poorly with the country, particularly when the economy is bad, voters are inclined to want a change in leadership. In good economic times, incumbents have less to fear. Studies have found, for example, that a weak economy in 1992 contributed greatly to the defeat of incumbent President George H. W. Bush and that a strong economy in 1996 underpinned incumbent President Bill Clinton's successful bid for a second term. The 2004 presidential election was somewhat unusual in that the top issue was not the economy but foreign policy. George W. Bush had a huge edge among voters who believed that the terrorist threat was the nation's top issue, whereas John Kerry had a decisive advantage among those who believed that the U.S. invasion of Iraq was a mistake.[15]

prospective voting
A form of electoral judgment in which voters choose the candidate whose policy positions most closely match their own preferences.

retrospective voting
A form of electoral judgment in which voters support the incumbent candidate or party when its policies are judged to have succeeded and oppose the incumbent party or candidate when its policies are judged to have failed.

ELECTORAL AND PARTY SYSTEMS

two-party system
A system in which only two political parties have a real chance of acquiring control of the government.

The United States traditionally has had a **two-party system:** Federalists versus Jeffersonian Republicans, Whigs versus Democrats, Republicans versus Democrats. These have not been the only American parties, but they have been the

How the United States Compares

Party Systems

For nearly 160 years, electoral competition in the United States has centered on the Republican and Democratic parties. By comparison, most democracies have a multiparty system, in which three or more parties receive substantial support from voters. The difference is significant. In a two-party system, the parties tend to have overlapping coalitions and programs, because each party must appeal to the middle-of-the-road voters who provide the margin of victory. In multiparty systems, particularly those with four or more strong parties, the parties tend to separate themselves as each tries to secure the enduring loyalty of voters who have a particular viewpoint.

Whether a country has a two-party or a multiparty system depends on several factors, but particularly the nature of its electoral system. The United States has a single-member, plurality district system in which only the top vote getter in a district gets elected. This system is biased against smaller parties; even if they have some support in a great many races, they win nothing unless one of their candidates places first in

an electoral district. By comparison, proportional representation systems enable smaller parties to compete; each party acquires legislative seats in proportion to its share of the total vote. All the countries in the chart that have four or more parties also have a proportional representation system of election.

NUMBER OF COMPETITIVE PARTIES

TWO	THREE	FOUR OR MORE
United States	Canada (at times)	Belgium
	Great Britain	Denmark
		France
		Germany
		Italy
		Netherlands
		Sweden

---

only ones with a realistic chance of acquiring political control. A two-party system, however, is the exception rather than the rule (see "How the United States Compares"). Most democracies have a **multiparty system,** in which three or more parties have the capacity to gain control of government, separately or in coalition. Why the difference? Why are there three or more major parties in most democracies but only two in the United States?

The Single-Member-District System of Election

America's two-party system is due largely to the fact that the nation chooses its officials through plurality voting in **single-member districts.** Each constituency elects a single member to a particular office, such as U.S. senator or representative; the candidate with the most votes (a plurality) in a district wins the office. This system discourages minor parties. Assume, for example, that a minor party received exactly 20 percent of the vote in each of the nation's 435 congressional races. Even though one in five voters nationwide backed the minor party, it would not win any seats in Congress because none of its candidates placed first in any of the 435 single-member-district races. The winning candidate in each race would be the major-party candidate who received the larger proportion of the remaining 80 percent of the vote.

By comparison, most European democracies use some form of **proportional representation,** in which seats in the legislature are allocated according to a party's share of the popular vote. This type of electoral system provides smaller

multiparty system
A system in which three or more political parties have the capacity to gain control of government separately or in coalition.

single-member districts
The form of representation in which only the candidate who gets the most votes in a district wins office.

proportional representation
A form of representation in which seats in the legislature are allocated proportionally according to each political party's share of the popular vote. This system enables smaller parties to compete successfully for seats.

Germany's electoral system allocates legislative seats on the basis of both single-district voting and the overall proportion of votes a party receives. Half the seats go to the candidates who finish first in their respective districts. The other half are allocated to the parties according to the percentage of the votes each receives. This system requires that the German voter cast two ballots in legislative races: one to choose among the candidates in the particular district and one to choose among the parties. Shown here is a ballot from a German election. The left column lists the candidates for the legislative seat in a district, and the right column lists the parties. (Note the relatively large number of parties on the ballot.)

parties an incentive to organize and compete for power. In the 2005 German elections, the Green party received 8 percent of the national vote and thereby won 51 seats in the 603-seat Bundestag, the German parliament. If the Greens had been competing under American electoral rules, they would not have won any seats.

Politics and Coalitions in the Two-Party System

The overriding goal of a major American party is to gain power by getting its candidates elected to office. Because there are only two major parties, however, the Republicans or Democrats can win consistently only by attracting majority support. In Europe's multiparty systems, a party can hope for a share of power if it has the firm backing of a minority faction. In the United States, if either party confines its support to a narrow segment of society it forfeits its chance of gaining control of government.

Seeking the Center

American parties, Clinton Rossiter said, are "creatures of compromise."[16] The two parties usually take stands that have broad appeal or at least will not alienate significant blocs of voters. Any time a party makes a pronounced shift toward either extreme, the political center is left open for the opposing party. Barry Goldwater, the Republican presidential nominee in 1964, proposed the elimination of mandatory social security and said he might consider the tactical use of small nuclear weapons in wars such as the Vietnam conflict—extreme positions that cost him many votes. Eight years later, the Democratic nominee, George McGovern, took positions on Vietnam and income security that alarmed many voters; like Goldwater, he got buried in one of the greatest landslides in presidential history.

It is impossible to understand the dynamics of the U.S. party system without recognizing that the true balance of power in American elections rests with the moderate voters in the center rather than with those who hold more extreme positions. When congressional Republicans mistook their 1994 election victory as a mandate to trim assistance programs for the elderly, the poor, and children, they alienated many of the moderate voters who had contributed to their 1994 victory. These voters wanted "less" government but not a government that neglected society's most vulnerable citizens. After weak showings in the 1996 and 1998 elections, congressional Republicans shifted course. They unseated Speaker Newt Gingrich, replacing him with a more pragmatic conservative, Dennis Hastert. "We still need to prove that we can be conservative without being mean," was how one Republican member of Congress described the change in strategy.[17] The adjustment reflects a basic truth about U.S. politics: party ideology is acceptable as long as it is tinged with moderation.

Nonetheless, the Republican and Democratic parties do offer somewhat different alternatives and, at times, a clear choice. When Roosevelt was elected president in 1932, Johnson in 1964, and Reagan in 1980, the parties were relatively far apart in their priorities and programs. Roosevelt's New Deal, for example, was an extreme alternative within the American political tradition and caused a decisive split along party lines. A lesson of these periods is that the center of the American political spectrum can be moved. Candidates risk a crushing defeat by straying too far from established ideas during normal times, but they may do so with some chance of success during turbulent times. The terrorist attacks of September 11, 2001, provided President George W. Bush with just such an opportunity. During his first term, Bush pushed major tax cuts through Congress and also sharply increased defense spending while pursuing an aggressive Middle East policy. Democrats contested these changes, but in the face of a unified Republican Congress, they were largely powerless to block them.

Party Coalitions

The groups and interests that support a party are collectively referred to as the **party coalition.** In multiparty systems, each party is supported by a relatively narrow range of interests. European parties tend to divide along class lines, with the center and right parties drawing most of their votes from the middle and upper classes and the left parties drawing most of theirs from the working class. By comparison, America's two-party system requires each party to accommodate a wide range of interests in order to gain the voting plurality necessary to win elections. The Republican and Democratic coalitions are therefore relatively broad. Each includes a substantial proportion of voters of nearly every ethnic, religious, regional, and economic grouping. Only a few groups are tightly aligned with a party. African Americans are the clearest example; they vote about 85 percent Democratic in national elections.

Although the Republican and Democratic coalitions overlap, they are hardly identical (see Figure 8–4). The party coalitions have been forged primarily through conflict over the federal government's role in solving social and economic problems. Each party has supported government action to promote economic security and social equality, but the Democrats have favored a greater level of government involvement. Virtually every major assistance program for the poor, the elderly, and low-wage workers since the 1930s has been initiated by the Democrats.

Accordingly, the Democratic coalition draws support disproportionately from society's underdogs—blacks, union members, the poor, city dwellers, Hispanics, Jews, and other "minorities."[18] For a long period, the Democratic party was also the clear choice of the nation's elderly as a result of its support for old-age assistance programs and because the basic political loyalties of the elderly were acquired during the New Deal era, a period favorable to the Democrats. Recently, however, elderly voters have split their vote about evenly between the parties.

The Democratic party's biggest gains recently have been among women, whose voting pattern traditionally was very similar to that of men. Recent elections, however, have revealed a gender gap (see Chapter 6). Women have voted disproportionately for the Democratic party, apparently as a result of its positions on issues such as abortion rights, education spending, employment policies, and gun control. The Democratic party, as a result of its leadership on civil rights issues, has also made gains among gays and lesbians, who are now the party's third most loyal voting bloc (after blacks and Jews).

Ronald Reagan's successful runs for the presidency in 1980 and 1984 illustrate that candidates with less moderate positions can win elections when Americans are seeing a change in national policy. Reagan called for large cuts in government spending except in the area of national security.

party coalition
The groups and interests that support a political party.

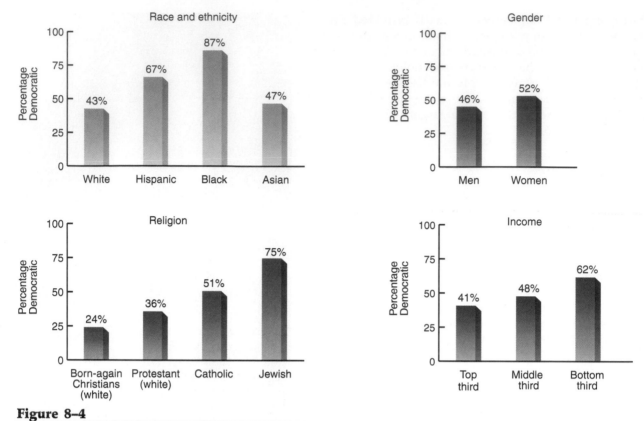

Figure 8–4

The Vote of Selected Demographic Groups in Recent Presidential Elections
Although the Democratic and Republican coalitions overlap substantially, there are important differences, as illustrated by the Democratic party's percentage of the two-party vote among some major demographic groups in recent elections.
Source: Compiled by author from NES and other surveys.

The Republican coalition consists mainly of white middle-class Protestants. The GOP has historically been the party of tax cuts and business incentives. It has also been more supportive of traditional values, as reflected, for example, in its opposition to abortion and civil unions. Not surprisingly, the GOP is strongest in the suburbs and in regions, such as the South, the Great Plains, and the Rocky Mountains, where traditional values and a desire for lower taxes and less government regulation of economic activity are most pronounced.

The Republican party has made big gains in recent decades among white fundamentalist Christians, who have been drawn to the GOP by its positions on abortion, school prayer, same-sex marriage, and other social issues.[19] In recent presidential elections, the Republican nominee has garnered the votes of roughly three-fourths of fundamentalist Christians.

Minor Parties

Although the U.S. electoral system discourages the formation of third parties, the nation has always had minor parties—more than a thousand over the nation's history.[20] Most have been short-lived, and only a few have had a lasting impact. Only one minor party, the Republican party, has ever achieved majority status.

Get Involved!

Take Sides

In high school civics classes, generations of American students have been told to "vote for the person, not the party" or to "vote on the issues, not the party." Commentators sometimes make the same pitch. On the whole, it is pretty bad advice.

To vote for the person is to assume that the individual officeholder wields singular power. But that's not true even in the case of the president. In selecting one presidential candidate over another, Americans are choosing more than the person who will sit behind the desk in the Oval Office. They are also selecting several hundred other executive officers, including the secretary of state, the attorney general of the United States, and the director of the Central Intelligence Agency. The president also nominates all federal judges and justices. The great majority of these individuals, including the judicial officers, will be of the same party as the president.

The election of a senator or a representative is also more than a decision about which individual will occupy a seat in Congress. Rarely does a single member of Congress have a decisive voice in legislation. Congress works through collective action, and power resides with the majority party in each chamber. Dozens of important legislative votes are cast in Congress each term. Typically, most Republican members are on one side of

the vote and most Democratic members are on the other side.

Accordingly, a vote based on an issue is usually short-sighted. Once in office, a successful candidate will vote on scores of policy issues, not just the one or two issues that were the cornerstone of the election campaign. And what is the best predictor of how the successful candidate will vote on these issues? In nearly every case, the best predictor is the political party to which the officeholder belongs.

An issue that dominates an election can be overtaken by events and be a secondary issue by the time the winning candidates are sworn into office. Partisanship, on the other hand, tends to endure. Today's Democratic and Republican candidates and officeholders are not all that different in their policy leanings from their partisan counterparts of a decade or two ago.

Many Americans pride themselves on "voting on the issue or the candidate rather than the party." If that's your outlook, give some thought to whether it's the most effective way to make a difference as a voter. If you are a party loyalist already, consider taking your commitment a step further. Party organizations at all levels are looking for volunteers, particularly at election time, when they are engaged in registration, canvassing, and get-out-the-vote efforts.

Minor parties in the United States have formed largely to promote policies that their followers believe are not being adequately represented by either of the two major parties. A major party is always somewhat captive to its past, which is the source of many of its ideas and most of its followers. When conditions change, major parties are often slow to respond, and a minor party can try to capitalize on neglected issues. If the minor party gains a following, one or both major parties typically awaken to the new issues, at which time the minor party usually begins to lose support. Nevertheless, the minor party will have served the purpose of making the major parties more responsive to the public's concerns.

Single-Issue Parties

Some minor parties form around a single issue of overriding interest to their supporters, such as the present-day Right-to-Life party, which was formed to oppose the legalization of abortion. Some single-issue parties have seen their policy goals enacted into law. The Prohibition party contributed to the ratification in 1919 of the Eighteenth Amendment, which prohibited the manufacture, sale, and transportation of alcoholic beverages (but which was repealed in 1933). Single-issue parties usually disband when their issue either is favorably resolved or fades in importance.[21]

Factional Parties

Although the Republican and Democratic parties are normally adept at managing internal divisions, there have been times when internal conflict has led a faction to break away and form its own party. The most successful of these factional parties at the polls was Theodore Roosevelt's Bull Moose party. In 1908, Roosevelt, after having served eight years as president, declined to seek a third term and handpicked William Howard Taft for the Republican nomination. When Taft as president showed neither Roosevelt's enthusiasm for a strong presidency nor his commitment to the goals of the Progressive movement, Roosevelt challenged Taft for the 1912 Republican nomination but lost out. Backed by Progressive Republicans, Roosevelt proceeded to form the Bull Moose party (a reference to Roosevelt's claim that he was "as strong as a bull moose"). Roosevelt won 27 percent of the presidential vote to Taft's 25 percent, but the split within Republican ranks enabled the Democratic nominee, Woodrow Wilson, to win the 1912 presidential election.

The States' Rights party in 1948 and George Wallace's American Independent party in 1968 are other examples of strong factional parties. These parties were formed by white southern Democrats angered by northern Democrats' support of civil rights for black Americans.

Deep divisions within a party give rise to factionalism and can lead eventually to a change in its coalition. The conflict over civil rights that began within the Democratic party during the late 1940s continued for the next quarter-century, leading many southern whites to shift their party loyalty to the GOP.

Ideological Parties

Other minor parties are characterized by their ideological commitment to a broad and radical philosophical position, such as redistribution of economic resources. Modern-day ideological parties include the Citizens party, the Socialist Workers party, and the Libertarian party, each of which operates on the fringes of American politics.

One of the strongest ideological parties in the nation's history was the Populist party. Its candidate in the 1892 presidential election, James B. Weaver, gained 8.5 percent of the national vote and won twenty-two electoral votes in six western states. The party began as an agrarian protest movement in response to an economic depression and the anger of small farmers over low commodity prices, tight credit, and the high rates charged by railroad monopolies to transport farm goods. The Populists' ideological platform called for government ownership of the railroads, a graduated income tax, low tariffs on imports, and elimination of the gold standard.[22]

HISTORICAL BACKGROUND

The strongest minor party today is the Green party, an ideological party that holds liberal positions on the environment, labor, taxation, social welfare, and other issues. Its 2000 presidential nominee, consumer-rights advocate Ralph Nader, received 3 percent of the national vote. According to polls, Nader (who ran as an Independent in 2004) got most of his support from voters who otherwise would have backed Democrat Al Gore, thus tipping the election to the more conservative Republican nominee, George W. Bush. In 2004, the Green party decided to compete in the presidential race, but in a way designed to reduce the chance of tipping the election to the Republicans. The Green party rejected Nader's bid for its 2004 nomination, choosing instead Green-party activist David Cobb, a little-known Texas lawyer.

Until the 2000 election, the Reform party was America's strongest minor party. It was formed by Ross Perot after he ran as an independent and garnered 19 percent of the vote in the 1992 presidential election (second only to Theodore

Roosevelt's 27 percent in 1912 among minor-party candidates). Perot's platform was based on middle-class discontent with the major parties' lack of fiscal restraint. Perot ran again in 1996, this time as the Reform party's nominee, and won 8 percent of the vote. When Perot chose not to run in 2000, a divisive fight ensued over the Reform party's nomination, which broadcaster Pat Buchanan received. His reactionary candidacy attracted only 1 percent of the general election vote and nearly wrecked the Reform party. Since then, it has been trying without much success to rebuild its base.

PARTY ORGANIZATIONS

The Democratic and Republican parties have organizational units at the national, state, and local levels. The main purpose of these **party organizations** is the contesting of elections.

A century ago, party organizations enjoyed almost complete control of nominations and elections. The party organizations still perform all the activities they formerly engaged in. They recruit candidates, raise money, develop policy positions, and canvass for votes. But they do not control these activities as completely as they once did.[23] For the most part, these activities are now directed by the candidates themselves.[24]

The Republican and Democratic parties have huge advantages over third parties. Major parties can count on the voting loyalty of their party identifiers, have an automatic place on the ballot in every state, have long-standing organizations at all levels of government, and can count on receiving millions in campaign donations. Minor parties complain particularly about campaign finance laws that work to the advantage of the major parties. Here, a protester uses a bullhorn to draw attention to a fundraiser for Senator Lincoln Chaffee (R-RI) being hosted by First Lady Laura Bush.

The Weakening of Party Organizations

Nomination refers to the selection of the individual who will run as the party's candidate in the general election. Until the early twentieth century, nominees were selected by party organizations. To be nominated, an individual had to be loyal to the party organization, a requirement that included a willingness to share with it the spoils of office—government jobs and contracts. The situation allowed party organizations to attract campaign workers and funds, but it also enabled party leaders to extort money from those seeking political favors. Reform-minded Progressives argued that the power to nominate should rest with ordinary voters rather than with the party leaders (see Chapter 2).

The result was the introduction of the **primary election** (or **direct primary**), which places nomination in the hands of the voters (see Chapters 2 and 12). Primary elections take several forms. Most states conduct closed primaries, in which participation is limited to voters registered or declared at the polls as members of the party whose primary is being held. Other states use open primaries, a form that allows independents and voters of either party to vote in a party's primary, although voters are prohibited by law from participating in both parties' primaries simultaneously. A few states have a third form of primary, known as the blanket primary. These states provide a single primary ballot listing both the Republican and Democratic candidates by office. Each voter can cast only one vote per

party organizations
The party organizational units at national, state, and local levels; their influence has decreased over time because of many factors.

nomination
The designation of a particular individual to run as a political party's candidate (its "nominee") in the general election.

primary election (direct primary)
A form of election in which voters choose a party's nominees for public office. In most primaries, eligibility to vote is limited to voters who are registered members of the party.

office but can select a candidate of either party. Louisiana has a variation on this form in which all candidates are listed on the ballot but are not identified by party.

Primaries hinder the building of strong party organizations. If primaries did not exist, candidates would have to work through party organizations in order to gain nomination, and they could be denied renomination if they were disloyal to the party's goals. Because of primaries, however, candidates have the option of seeking office on their own, and once elected (with or without the party's help), they can build a personal following that effectively places them beyond the party's direct control.

In the process of taking control of nominations, candidates also acquired control of most campaign money. At the turn of the last century, when party machines were at their peak, most campaign funds passed through the hands of party leaders. Today, most of the money goes to the candidates directly, without first passing through the parties.

Party organizations also lost capacity because of a decline in patronage. When a party won control of government a century ago, it acquired control of public jobs, which were doled out to loyal party workers. However, as government jobs in the early twentieth century shifted from patronage to the merit system (see Chapter 13), the party organizations no longer controlled many of these positions. Today, because of the large size of government, thousands of patronage jobs still exist. These government employees help staff the party organizations (along with volunteers), but most of them are indebted to an individual politician rather than to a party organization. Congressional staff members, for example, are patronage employees, but they owe their jobs and their loyalty to their senator or representative, not to their party.

In Europe, where there are no primary elections, the situation is different. Parties control their nominations, and because of this they also control campaign money and workers. A party's candidates are expected to support the national platform if elected. An officeholder who fails to do so is likely to be denied renomination in the next election.

The Structure and Role of Party Organizations

Although the influence of party organizations has declined, parties are not about to die out. Candidates and activists need an ongoing organization through which they can work together, and the party serves that purpose. Moreover, certain activities, such as get-out-the-vote efforts on election day, affect all of a party's candidates and therefore are more efficiently conducted through the party organization.[25] National and state party organizations now assist candidates with fund-raising, polling, research, and media production, all essential ingredients of a successful modern campaign.

Structurally, U.S. parties are loose associations of national, state, and local organizations (see Figure 8–5). The national party organizations cannot dictate the decisions made by the state organizations, which in turn do not control the activities of local organizations. However, there is communication between the levels because they all have a stake in the party's success.

Local Party Organizations

In a sense, U.S. parties are organized from the bottom up, not the top down. Of the roughly five hundred thousand elective offices in the United States, fewer than five hundred are contested statewide and only two—the presidency and vice presidency—are contested nationally. All the rest are local offices; not surprisingly, at least 95 percent of party activists work within local organizations.

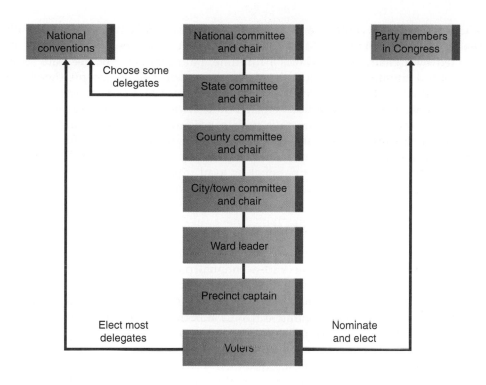

Figure 8–5

Formal Organization of the Political Party
U.S. parties are loosely structured alliances of national, state, and local organizations; most local parties are not as well organized as the chart implies.

It is difficult to generalize about local parties because they vary greatly in their structure and activities. Today only a few local party organizations, including the Democratic organizations in Albany, Philadelphia, and Chicago, bear even a faint resemblance to the fabled old-time party machines that, in return for jobs and even welfare services, were able to control the vote on election day. In many urban areas, and in most suburbs and towns, the party organizations today do not have enough activists to do organizing work outside the campaign period, at which time—to the extent their resources allow—they conduct registration drives, send mailings or hand out leaflets, and help get out the vote. These activities are not insignificant. Most local campaigns are not well funded, and the party's efforts can tip the balance in a close race.

Local parties tend to concentrate on elections that coincide with local boundaries, such as races for mayor, city council, state legislature, county offices, and the like. Local parties also take part in congressional, statewide, and presidential contests but, in these instances, their role is typically secondary to that of the candidates' personal campaign organizations, which will be discussed later in this chapter.

State Party Organizations

At the state level, each party is headed by a central committee made up of members of local party organizations and local and state

Philadelphia mayor John Street won a second term of office in 2003. A veteran of Philadelphia politics, he previously served as head of the Philadelphia City Council. Philadelphia is one of the few cities—Chicago is another—where a semblance of the old-time party machine is still found.

officeholders. State central committees do not meet regularly and provide only general policy guidance for the state organizations. Day-to-day operations are directed by a chairperson, who is a full-time, paid employee of the state party. The central committee appoints the chairperson, but it often accepts the choice of the party's leading politician, usually the governor or a U.S. senator.

The state party organizations engage in activities, such as fund-raising and voter registration, that can improve their candidates' chances of success. State party organizations concentrate on statewide races, including those for governor and U.S. senator,[26] and also focus on races for the state legislature. They play a smaller role in campaigns for national or local offices, and in most states they do not endorse candidates in statewide primary contests.

National Party Organizations

The national party organizations are structured much like those at the state level: they have a national committee and a national party chairperson. The national headquarters for the Republican and Democratic parties are located in Washington, D.C. Although in theory the national parties are run by their committees, neither the Democratic National Committee (DNC) nor the Republican National Committee (RNC) has great power. The RNC (with more than 150 members) and the DNC (with more than 300 members) are too cumbersome to act as deliberative bodies. They meet only periodically, and their power is largely confined to setting organizational policy, such as determining the site of the party's presidential nominating convention and the rules governing the selection of convention delegates. They have no power to pick nominees or to dictate candidates' policy positions.

The national party's day-to-day operations are directed by a national chairperson chosen by the national committee, although the committee defers to the president's choice when the party controls the White House. The national chairperson directs a large staff operation that seeks to build the party's base and promote its presidential and congressional candidates. The RNC and DNC, among other things, run training programs for candidates and their staffs, raise money, seek media coverage of party positions and activities, conduct issue and group research, and send field representatives to help state and local parties with their operations.

This model of the national party was created in the 1970s when Republican leaders concluded that an expanded and modernized national organization could contribute to the party's electoral success. The DNC has created a similar organization, but it is less substantial than the RNC's. Modern campaigns, as David Adamany notes, are based on "cash," and Democrats are relatively cash-poor.[27] In every recent election cycle, the Republican national party has outspent its Democratic counterpart (see Figure 8–6).

In 2005, the Democratic party chose Howard Dean as its national party chair. Most party chairs are not widely known, but Dean was familiar to voters as a result of his strong bid for the 2004 Democratic presidential nomination. The Democrats picked Dean as their chair in hopes that he could boost their fund-raising and grassroots efforts.

The Parties and Money

The parties' major role in campaigns is the raising and spending of money. The RNC and the DNC are major sources of campaign

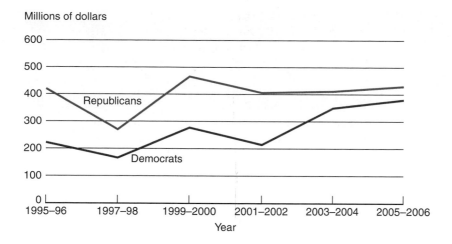

Millions of dollars

Figure 8–6

National Party Fund-raising, 1995–2006
Over the years, the Republican party has raised significantly more money than has the Democratic party. The figures include fund-raising by the DNC, RNC, DCCC, NRCC, DSCC, and NRSC. Soft-money fund-raising is not included.
Source: Federal Elections Commission. The 2005–2006 data are based on projections from incomplete cycle.

funds, as are the party campaign committees in the House and the Senate. These include the Democratic Congressional Campaign Committee (DCCC), the National Republican Congressional Committee (NRCC), the Democratic Senatorial Campaign Committee (DSCC), and the National Republican Senatorial Committee (NRSC).

In addition to providing funds, these committees have increasingly sought to persuade individuals who would make strong candidates to run for Congress. Nevertheless, the party committees have more of a **service relationship** than a power relationship with their party's candidates. Because the party nominees are chosen through primaries, and because many of the potential candidates already have a power base at the local or state level, the national committees are unable to handpick the party nominees. Accordingly, the party organizations tend to back whichever candidate wins the primary. If the candidate then wins the general election, the party at least has denied the office to the opposing party.

A party can legally give $10,000 directly to a House candidate and $37,500 to a Senate candidate. This funding, along with the money a candidate receives from individual contributors ($2,000 maximum per contributor) and interest groups ($5,000 maximum per group), is termed **hard money**; it goes directly to the candidate and can be spent as he or she chooses.

Limits on party contributions were established when the campaign finance laws were reformed in the 1970s in response to the Watergate scandal. However, a loophole in the laws was exposed when a court ruling allowed the parties to raise and spend unlimited campaign funds provided the funds were not channeled directly to a party's candidates. Thus, whereas a wealthy contributor could legally give a candidate only a limited amount, that same contributor could give an unlimited amount to the candidate's party. These contributions were termed **soft money** in that a party could not hand it over directly to a candidate. But the party could use these contributions to support party activities, such as voter registration efforts, get-out-the-vote drives, and party-centered televised ads, that could indirectly benefit its candidates. In some cases, the line between the use of hard and soft money was hard to distinguish. In 1996, for example, the Democratic party ran a $100 million ad campaign that did not directly urge voters to support Clinton but did include pictures of him and references to his accomplishments as president.

In 2002, Congress closed the loophole through enactment of the Bipartisan Campaign Reform Act (BCRA), which prohibits the national parties from raising or spending soft money. BCRA also bans the state parties from spending soft

service relationship
The situation in which party organizations assist candidates for office but have no power to require them to support the party's main policy positions.

hard money
Campaign funds given directly to candidates to spend as they choose.

#12

soft money
Campaign contributions that are not subject to legal limits and are given to parties rather than directly to candidates. (These contributions are no longer legal.)

Debating the Issues

Should There Be Limits on Campaign Contributions?

Campaign finance has been a controversial issue in the United States since at least the late nineteenth century. Millionaires literally bought their seats in the U.S. Senate through contributions to state legislators, who until ratification of the Seventeenth Amendment in 1913 appointed the Senate's members. Abuses by Richard Nixon's 1972 reelection campaign again put campaign finance in the headlines and prompted Congress to enact legislation that limited campaign contributions. However, big donors found a legal loophole that allowed them to make unrestricted contributions to political parties. More than a billion dollars of so-called soft money was donated to campaigns during the 1990s alone, prompting Congress in 2002 to enact a ban on soft-money contributions. The legislation was upheld by the Supreme Court, but the new law also had a loophole. In the 2004 campaign, tens of millions of dollars in large contributions flowed to so-called 527 groups, which used it to try to affect the election's outcome.

The regulation of campaign money has always been a contentious issue. Those favoring regulation have focused on the influence of campaign money on policy decisions. Those opposing regulation have focused on the free-speech implications of limiting political contributions.

Yes   Special interests who give large amounts of soft money to political parties do in fact achieve their objectives. They do get special access. Sitting Senate and House members have limited amounts of time, but they make time available in their schedules to meet with representatives of business and unions and wealthy individuals who gave large sums of money to their parties. These are not idle chit-chats about the philosophy of democracy. In these meetings, these special interests, often accompanied by lobbyists, press elected officials . . . to adopt their position on a matter of interest to them. [Members of Congress] are pressed by their benefac-tors to introduce legislation, to amend legislation, to block legislation, and to vote on legislation in a certain way. No one says: "We gave money so you should help us with this." No one needs to say it—it is perfectly understood by all participants in every such meeting. . . . Large soft money contributions in fact distort the legislative process. They affect what gets done and how it gets done. They affect whom Senators and House members see, whom they spend their time with, what input they get, and—make no mistake about it—this money affects outcomes as well.

—*Warren Rudman, former U.S. senator*

No   This is a sad day for the freedom of speech. Who could have imagined that the same court which, within the past four years, has sternly disapproved of restrictions upon such inconsequential forms of expression as virtual child pornography, tobacco advertising, dissemination of illegally intercepted communications, and sexually explicit cable programming would smile with favor upon a law that cuts to the heart of what the First Amendment is meant to protect: the right to criticize the government. . . . The premise of the First Amendment is that the American people are neither sheep nor fools, and hence fully capable of considering both the substance of the speech presented to them and its proximate and ultimate source. If that premise is wrong, our democracy has a much greater problem to overcome than merely the influence of amassed wealth. Given the premises of democracy, there is no such thing as too much speech. . . . The first instinct of power is the retention of power, and, under a Constitution that requires periodic elections, that is best achieved by the suppression of election-time speech. . . . It is not the proper role of those who govern us to judge which campaign speech has "substance" and "depth" (do you think it might be that which is least damaging to incumbents?) and to abridge the rest.

—*Antonin Scalia, associate justice of the Supreme Court*

money in support of candidates for federal office. The Supreme Court upheld these restrictions in a 2003 decision,[28] but a new loophole soon surfaced. The ban on soft money does not fully apply to so-called "527 groups." (Section 527 of the Internal Revenue Code defines the rules governing not-for-profit political groups.) Much of the money that before the new law would have been contributed to a party organization now finds its way into the hands of 527 groups. Although they are prohibited from attacking a candidate directly, these groups can legally engage in issue advocacy, which has enabled them to mount thinly veiled candidate attacks. During the 2004 presidential election, 527 groups spent more than $100 million. One such group, America Coming Together, spent $15 million, including $5 million provided by financier George Soros, to attack the Bush administration's economic and Iraq policies. In short, BCRA has been only partially successful in regulating campaign finance. Just as water always runs downhill, money always seems to find its way into election politics.

THE CANDIDATE-CENTERED CAMPAIGN

Although competition between the Republican and Democratic parties provides the backdrop to today's campaigns, the campaigns themselves are largely controlled by the candidates, particularly in congressional, statewide, and presidential races. Each candidate has a personal organization, created especially for the campaign and disbanded once it is over. The candidates are entrepreneurs who play what political consultant Joe Napolitan labeled "the election game."[29] The game begins with money—lots of it.

Campaign Funds: The Money Chase

Campaigns for high office are expensive, and the costs keep rising. In 1980, about $250 million was spent on all Senate and House campaigns combined. The figure had jumped to $425 million by 1990. In 2006, the figure exceeded $2 billion ($2,000 million)—roughly ten times the 1980 level. As might be expected, incumbents have a distinct advantage in fund-raising. They have contributor lists from past campaigns and have the policy influence that donors seek. House and Senate incumbents outspend their challengers by more than two to one.[30]

Because of the high cost of campaigns, candidates spend much of their time raising funds, which come primarily from individual contributors, interest groups (through PACs, discussed in Chapter 9), and political parties. The **money chase** is relentless.[31] A U.S. senator must raise $20,000 a week on average throughout the entire six-year term in order to raise the minimum $6 million it takes to run a competitive Senate campaign in most states. A Senate campaign in a large state can easily exceed that amount. In 2004, despite having a wide lead in the polls over a weak opponent, Barack Obama still spent $10 million on his Senate race in Illinois. House campaigns are less costly, but expenditures of $1 million or more are commonplace. As for presidential elections, even the nominating race is expensive. In 2004, Senator John Kerry spent more than $50 million during the competitive phase of his successful campaign for the Democratic nomination. (In presidential races, but not congressional ones, candidates are eligible to receive federal funds, a topic discussed in Chapter 12.)

money chase
A term used to describe the fact that U.S. campaigns are very expensive and candidates must spend a great amount of time raising funds in order to compete successfully.

Organization and Strategy: Hired Guns

The key operatives in today's campaigns are campaign consultants, pollsters, media producers, and fund-raising and get-out-the-vote specialists. They are **hired guns** who charge hefty fees for their services. "The new king-makers" is the way writer David Chagall characterizes these pros.[32]

hired guns
A term that refers to the professional consultants who run campaigns for high office.

States in the Nation

Public Funding of State Elections

About half the states have public funding of election campaigns. Some of them give the money to political parties, which allocate it to candidates or spend it on party activities such as get-out-the-vote efforts. Other states give funds directly to candidates, although this funding typically is limited to candidates for designated offices, such as governor.

Q: What might explain the fact that there is no clear-cut regional pattern to the public funding of state elections?

A: Public funding of elections is relatively new, so additional states may adopt it in the next decade or two, at which time a regional tendency could emerge. (If your state does not have public funding, do you think it is likely to adopt it anytime soon? Why?)

Public funding of parties

Public funding of candidates

No public funding

Source: From Thomas Patterson, *We the People*, 6th Edition. Copyright © 2006. The McGraw-Hill Companies. Reprinted by permission of The McGraw-Hill Companies.

These hired guns include campaign strategists who help the candidate to plot and execute a game plan. Over the years, some of these strategists, including James Carville, Dick Morris, and Roger Ailes, developed legendary reputations. Fund-raising specialists are also part of the new politics. They know how to tap into the networks of large donors and interest groups that contribute to election campaigns and are also adept at running targeted direct-mail fund-raising campaigns. The hired guns also include experts who conduct polls and focus groups (the latter are small groups of voters brought together to discuss at length their thoughts on the candidates and issues). Polls and focus groups enable candidates to identify issues and messages that will resonate with voters.[33] Media consultants are another staple of the modern campaign. These experts are adept at producing televised political advertising and creating the "photo-ops" and other staged events that attract news coverage.

The hired guns of the modern campaign are skilled at **packaging** a candidate—highlighting those aspects of the candidate's partisanship, policy positions, personal background, and personality that are thought most attractive to voters. Packaging is not new to politics. Andrew Jackson's self-portrayal in the nineteenth century as "the champion of the people" is an image that any modern candidate could appreciate. What is new is the need to fit the image to the requirements of a world of sound bites, thirty-second ads, and televised debates, and to do it in a persuasive way. In the old days, it was sometimes enough for candidates to drive home the point that they were a Republican or a Democrat, playing on the tendency of voters to choose a candidate on that basis. Party appeals are still critically important, but today's voters also want to know about a candidate's personality and policy positions.

Hired consultants have been a driving force for yet another characteristic of modern campaigns—the tearing down of the opponent. In one sense, negative campaigning is as old as American politics. Thomas Jefferson was the subject of a whispering campaign about his sexual life, and Abraham Lincoln was ridiculed by opponents as "a baboon" for his hairy, gangly look and his backwoods roots. But today's version of attack politics is unprecedented in its scale, ubiquity, and sophistication. Professional strategists have concluded that they can win more votes by diminishing the opponent than by building up their candidate. In the past three decades, negative televised ads have increased three-fold to the point where they now constitute the large share of political ads.[34] Most campaigns nowadays have a nasty edge, and the attacks are sometimes outright vicious. In 2002, for example, incumbent U.S. Senator Max Cleland lost his bid for reelection when his lead in the polls withered in the face of blistering attacks on his patriotism, including an ad that showed his face alternately with those of Saddam Hussein and Osama bin Laden. Cleland's patriotism would have seemed above reproach; he had lost both legs and an arm in combat in Vietnam. Yet, his

packaging
A term of modern campaigning that refers to the process of recasting a candidate's record into an appealing image.

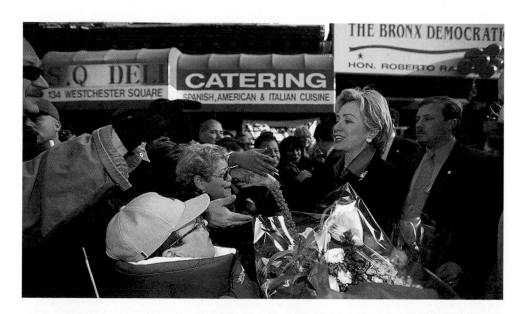

U.S. Senator Hillary Clinton is the only first lady to seek elective office. She moved to New York to compete in the state's 2000 Senate race, which she won. She ran for reelection in 2006 amidst widespread speculation that she would seek the presidency in 2008. Clinton is shown here campaigning on the streets of New York City.

opponent seized upon Cleland's vote against a Senate bill creating the Department of Homeland Security because it did not include the normal protections for civil service employees. The ad ignored Cleland's objection to the bill, portraying him instead as "soft" on terrorism.

Voter Contacts: Pitched Battle

Today's elections for high office have no historical parallel in their length and penetration. Candidates start their active campaigning much earlier—often a year in advance of election day—than they did in times past. The modern campaign is relentless. Voters are bombarded with messages that arrive by air, by land, and by web.

Air Wars

The major battleground of the modern campaign is the mass media, particularly television. Television emerged in the 1960s as the major medium of presidential and congressional politics and has remained the dominant medium ever since.

Candidates spend heavily on televised political advertising, which enables them to communicate directly—and on their own terms—with voters.[35] The production and the airing of political ads account for half or more of the expenditures in presidential campaigns and in most congressional races. Indeed, televised ads are the main reason for the high cost of U.S. campaigns. In most democracies, televised campaigning takes place through parties, which receive free air time to make their pitch. Many democracies even prohibit the purchase of televised advertising time by candidates (see Table 8–1).

air wars
A term that refers to the fact that modern campaigns are often a battle of opposing televised advertising campaigns.

Air wars is the term that political scientist Darrell West applies to candidates' use of televised ads. Candidates increasingly play off each other's ads, seeking to gain the strategic advantage.[36] Modern production techniques enable well-funded candidates to get new ads on the air within a few hours' time, which allows them to rebut attacks and exploit fast-breaking developments, a tactic known as *rapid response*.

Candidates also use the press to get their message across, although the amount of news coverage they can expect varies widely by location and office.

TABLE 8–1	**Television Campaign Practices in Selected Democracies** In many democracies, free television time is provided to political parties, and candidates are not allowed to buy advertising time. The United States provides no free time to parties and allows candidates to purchase air time. Television debates are also a feature of many U.S. campaigns.

COUNTRY	PAID TV ADS ALLOWED?	UNRESTRICTED FREE TV TIME PROVIDED?	TV DEBATES HELD?
Canada	Yes	Yes	Yes
France	No	Yes	Yes
Germany	Yes	Yes	Yes
Great Britain	No	Yes	No
Italy	No	Yes	Yes
Netherlands	No	No	Yes
United States	Yes	No	Yes

Many House candidates are nearly ignored by their local news media. The New York City media market, for example, includes more than a score of House districts in New York, New Jersey, Pennsylvania, and Connecticut, and candidates in these districts get little or no coverage from the New York media. The presidential campaign, in contrast, gets daily coverage from both national and local media. Between these extremes are Senate races, which always get some news coverage and, if hotly contested, may get heavy coverage.

Debates are also part of the modern media campaign. Debates often attract large and attentive audiences but can be risky encounters, because they give viewers a chance to compare the candidates directly. A weak or bumbling performance can hurt a candidate. Some analysts believe, for example, that Al Gore's performance in the first of the 2000 general election debates, when he grimaced and sighed loudly when George W. Bush was talking, cost him the election. Gore had been slightly ahead in the opinion polls but lost his lead immediately after the debate.

Ground Wars

Candidates' first priority in a close election is "swing voters"—those voters who conceivably could be persuaded to vote for either side. As election day nears, however, candidates concentrate on getting their supporters to the polls.

The get-out-the-vote effort traditionally has been borne by the parties and other organizations, such as labor unions. Although these groups remain the cornerstone of the effort, the candidates are also involved, and increasingly so. As partisanship has intensified in recent years, candidates have found it more difficult to persuade voters to switch sides. It has therefore become important for them to get as many of their supporters as possible to the polls on election day. Some campaign money that formerly would have been spent on televised advertising is now channeled into voter turnout efforts. In the final phase of the 2006 congressional elections, millions of potential voters were contacted by phone or in person by the Republican and Democratic campaigns.

Web Wars

New communication technology usually makes its way into campaign politics, and the Internet is no exception. Each of the nine candidates for the 2004 Democratic presidential nomination, for example, had a website dedicated to providing information, generating public support, attracting volunteers, and raising money. Howard Dean's website was by far the most successful. Through it, Dean raised more than $20 million and developed a nationwide network of a half-million supporters.

Although television is still the principal medium of election politics, some analysts believe that the Internet may eventually overtake it. E-mail is cheaper than television advertising (and both cheaper and faster than traditional mail). Because it is a targeted medium, the Internet could become the channel through which candidates reach particular voting groups. But the Internet also has some disadvantages relative to television. The most important is that the individual user has greater control over Internet messages. With television, when a political ad appears during a favorite program, most viewers will watch it. An unsolicited message on the Internet is more easily ignored or deleted. Future candidates may conclude that the Internet is the preferred medium for fund-raising and interacting with die-hard supporters and that television is the best medium for achieving public recognition and reaching less-interested voters.

Media & Politics

Fox: News with a Partisan Twist

In the nation's first century, America's newspapers were openly partisan. They sided with one party or the other and received party patronage in return. However, by the early twentieth century, most newspapers had adopted an "objective" model of reporting that emphasized facts rather than opinions and applied the same standard of newsworthiness to both parties. This model continues to dominate U.S. journalism, but there are exceptions, none more prominent than Fox News. Fox's newscasts carry the same stories as other news outlets but with a different tone and emphasis. Studies by the non-partisan firm Media Tenor show that Fox's news is pro-conservative and pro-Republican by comparison with the news presented on other television outlets.

Fox was launched in 1996 by Rupert Murdoch, an Australian-born entrepreneur and self-described conservative who has built a global media empire. Murdoch hired Roger Ailes, a longtime Republican political consultant, to run Fox News. Fox's talk-show hosts include conservatives Bill O'Reilly and Sean Hannity. When the United States invaded Iraq in 2003, one of the Fox reporters embedded with U.S. combat forces was Oliver North, a former Republican candidate for the Senate.

Fox has had remarkable success in attracting an audience. When Fox began, CNN had by far the largest audience among the cable news networks. Fox now has the largest audience, with CNN a distant second. Republican party identifiers are its core audience. Fewer than half of Fox's regular viewers identify themselves as Independents or Democrats. However, Fox has been no more successful than other news outlets in attracting young viewers; its average viewer is over 50 years of age.

Mainstream journalists are critical of Fox for its breach of the traditional norm of impartiality, claiming that it is a disservice to viewers. In particular, they point to Fox's pro-war Iraq coverage. A study found that Fox viewers had the highest percentage of mistaken facts about the Iraq situation of any news audience. The study, conducted by the University of Maryland's Program on International Policy Attitudes, asked three factual questions about Iraq and the war on terrorism. Many Americans had mistaken perceptions (see Chapter 6), but Fox viewers topped the list. Eighty percent of them had at least one false perception. (NPR listeners were at the bottom of the list, with 27 percent having at least one mistaken perception.)

Nothing in U.S. media law, however, prohibits Fox from tilting its news in a conservative direction. As a cable outlet with full First Amendment rights, Fox is free to cover politics as it chooses. And if Fox were operating in Europe, its coverage would not be controversial. Many European news outlets openly side with one party or another. In fact, some scholars argue that citizens are better off with a media system that includes a mix of partisan news outlets and straight news outlets. Partisan outlets serve to highlight the values at issue in politics, not just the facts of politics. From this perspective, the problem of the U.S. media system is not that it includes Fox but that it lacks an equivalent outlet for citizens of liberal persuasion.

PARTIES, CANDIDATES, AND THE PUBLIC'S INFLUENCE

Candidate-centered campaigns have some distinct advantages. First, they can infuse new blood into electoral politics. Candidate recruitment is normally a slow process in party-centered systems. Would-be officeholders pay their dues by working in the party and, in the process, tend to adopt the outlook of those already there. By comparison, a candidate-centered system is more open and provides opportunities for total newcomers to gain office quickly. John Edwards is a case in point. Edwards had never run for public office when, in 1997, he called a Democratic political consultant to say that he was thinking about running for the Senate. The consultant assumed that Edwards, a little-known trial lawyer, had the North Carolina state senate in mind. Edwards shocked him by saying that he was eyeing the upcoming 1998 U.S. Senate race. Edwards proceeded to gain the Democratic Senate nomination and then poured millions of his own money into a successful general-election campaign against incumbent Republican Senator

Senator Elizabeth Dole (R-N.C.) chaired the National Republican Senatorial Committee (NRSC) for the 2006 midterm election period. The chair serves a two-year term and helps Republican Senate candidates get the funds and other support they need to run successful campaigns. Dole helped GOP candidates in 2006 to raise tens of millions of dollars in campaign funds. The NRSC was established in 1916, shortly after the U.S. Constitution was amended to provide for the direct popular election of senators. The Democrats have an equivalent committee, the Democratic Senatorial Campaign Committee (DSCC).

Lauch Faircloth. In 2003, Edwards decided against seeking a second term in the Senate and entered the race for the 2004 Democratic presidential nomination. Though Edwards lost that bid, he ran so strongly in the primaries that the winner, John Kerry, picked him as his vice presidential running mate.

Candidate-centered campaigns also lend flexibility to electoral politics. When political conditions and issues change, self-directed candidates quickly adjust, bringing new ideas into the political arena. Strong party organizations are rigid by comparison. Until the early 1990s, for example, the British Labour party was controlled by old-line activists who refused to concede that changes in the British economy called for changes in the party's trade unionist and economic policies. The result was a series of humiliating defeats at the hands of the Conservative party that ended only after Tony Blair and other proponents of "New Labour" successfully recast the party's image.

Also, candidate-centered campaigns encourage national officeholders to be responsive to local interests. In building personal followings among their state and district constituents, members of Congress respond to local needs. Nearly every significant domestic program enacted by Congress is adjusted to accommodate the interests of states and localities that otherwise would be hurt by the policy. Members of Congress are not obliged to support the legislative position of their party's majority, and they often extract favors for their constituents as the price of their support. Where strong national parties exist, national interests take precedence over local concerns. In both France and Britain, for example, the pleas of representatives of underdeveloped regions have often gone unheeded by their party's majority.

In other respects, however, candidate-centered campaigns have some distinct disadvantages. Often they degenerate into mud-slinging contests, and they are fertile ground for powerful special-interest groups, which contribute much of the money that underwrites candidates' campaigns. Many groups give large

Political Culture

Parties, Political Equality, and Self-Government

Historically, political parties have given weight to the voice of ordinary citizens. Their strength is in their numbers rather than in their wealth or status, and political parties give them a means to express that strength through their votes. It is no accident that the Jacksonian Democrats created the first American grassroots party for the purpose of strengthening self-government.

As U.S. elections have changed in recent decades, the political equality reflected in the expression "one person, one vote" is being challenged. Modern campaigns run on money, and big donors and well-heeled special-interest groups often command as much, if not more, attention

from candidates as the voters themselves. Elections in the first half of the twentieth century focused on person-to-person and door-to-door campaigning by party volunteers. Elections now are centered largely on the media. The voters still matter, but they are more the target of the candidates' media messages than an integral part of the candidates' campaign organizations.

What do you make of this development? Do you think the political party as an instrument of political equality and self-government can be restored to its former position? Does the Internet show promise as a way to reinvigorate parties at the grassroots level?

sums of money to incumbents of both parties, which enables them to insulate themselves from an election's outcome: whether the Republicans win or the Democrats win, these contributors are assured of having friends in high places.

Candidate-centered campaigns also weaken accountability by making it easier for officeholders to deny personal responsibility for government's actions. If national policy goes awry, an incumbent can always say that he or she is only one vote out of many and that the real problem resides with the president or with "others" in Congress. The problem of accountability in the U.S. system is illustrated by the several trillion dollars that have been added to the national debt since 2000 because of Republican officeholders' insistence on steep tax cuts and huge increases in military spending and Democratic officeholders' refusal to accept cuts in domestic spending programs. "Running on empty" is how former cabinet secretary Peter Peterson describes the huge debt being passed along to future generations of Americans that has enabled today's members of Congress to keep their constituents happy enough to vote them back into office.[37] The problem of accountability is also illustrated by surveys that have asked Americans about their confidence in Congress. Although most citizens do not have a high opinion of Congress as a whole, most citizens also say that they have confidence in their local representative in Congress. This paradoxical attitude prevails in so many districts that the net result in most elections is a Congress whose membership is not greatly changed from the previous one (see Chapter 11). In contrast, party-centered campaigns are characterized by collective accountability. When problems occur, voters tend to hold the majority party responsible and invariably vote many of its members out of office.

In sum, candidate-centered campaigns strengthen the relationship between the voters and their individual representative while at the same time weakening the relationship between the full electorate and their representative institutions. Whether this arrangement serves the public's interest is debatable. Nevertheless, it is clear that Americans do not favor party-centered politics. Parties survived the shift to candidate-centered campaigns and will persist, but their organizational heyday has passed. (Congressional and presidential campaigns are discussed further in Chapters 11 and 12, respectively.)

Summary

Political parties serve to link the public with its elected leaders. In the United States, this linkage is provided by the two-party system; only the Republican and Democratic parties have any chance of winning control of government. The fact that the United States has only two major parties is explained by several factors: an electoral system—characterized by single-member districts—that makes it difficult for third parties to compete for power; each party's willingness to accept differing political views; and a political culture that stresses compromise and negotiation rather than ideological rigidity.

Because the United States has only two major parties, each of which seeks to gain majority support, their candidates normally tend to avoid controversial or extreme political positions. Sometimes, Democratic and Republican candidates do offer sharply contrasting policy alternatives, particularly during times of crisis. Ordinarily, however, Republican and Democratic candidates pursue moderate and somewhat overlapping policies. Each party can count on its party loyalists, but U.S. elections can hinge on swing voters, who respond to the issues of the moment either prospectively, basing their vote on what the candidates promise to do if elected, or retrospectively, basing their vote on their satisfaction or dissatisfaction with what the party in power has already done.

America's parties are decentralized, fragmented organizations. The national party organization does not control the policies and activities of the state organizations, and these in turn do not control the local organizations. Traditionally the local organizations have controlled most of the party's work force because most elections are contested at the local level. Local parties, however, vary markedly in their vitality. Whatever their level, America's party organizations are relatively weak. They lack control over nominations and elections. Candidates can bypass the party organization and win nomination through primary elections. Individual candidates also control most of the organizational structure and money necessary to win elections. The state and national party organizations have recently expanded their capacity to provide candidates with modern campaign services. Nevertheless, party organizations at all levels have few ways of controlling the candidates who run under their banners. They assist candidates with campaign technology, workers, and funds, but they cannot compel candidates' loyalty to organizational goals.

American political campaigns, particularly those for higher office, are candidate centered. Most candidates are self-starters who become adept at "the election game." They spend much of their time raising campaign funds, and they build their personal organizations around hired guns: pollsters, media producers, fund-raisers, and election consultants. Strategy and image making are key components of the modern campaign, as is televised political advertising, which accounts for half or more of all spending in presidential and congressional races.

The advantages of candidate-centered politics include a responsiveness to new leadership, new ideas, and local concerns. Yet this form of politics can result in campaigns that are personality-driven, depend on powerful interest groups, and blur responsibility for what government has done.

STUDY CORNER

Key Terms

air wars (*p. 236*)
candidate-centered politics (*p. 213*)
grassroots party (*p. 215*)
hard money (*p. 231*)
hired guns (*p. 233*)
money chase (*p. 233*)
multiparty system (*p. 221*)
nomination (*p. 227*)
packaging (of a candidate) (*p. 235*)

party-centered politics (*p. 213*)
party coalition (*p. 223*)
party competition (*p. 214*)
party organizations (*p. 227*)
party realignment (*p. 217*)
political party (*p. 213*)
primary election
   (direct primary) (*p. 227*)
proportional representation (*p. 221*)

prospective voting (*p. 220*)
retrospective voting (*p. 220*)
service relationship (*p. 231*)
single-member districts (*p. 221*)
soft money (*p. 231*)
split ticket (*p. 219*)
two-party system (*p. 220*)

Self-Test

1. The formation of political parties:
   a. acts as a support for an elitist government.
   b. makes it difficult for the public to participate in politics.
   c. can mobilize citizens to collective action to compete for power with those who have wealth and prestige.
   d. can function as an alternative to free and open media.

2. A major change in party activity in the South since the 1960s is:
   a. the emergence of a viable third party.
   b. a sharp decline in voter turnout.
   c. a decline in the level of two-party competition in state and local elections.
   d. a switch to support of Republican candidates in presidential elections.

3. The chief electoral factor supporting a two-party system in the United States is:
   a. proportional representation.
   b. multimember election districts.
   c. single-member districts with proportional voting.
   d. single-member districts with plurality voting.

4. The high cost of campaigns in the United States is largely related to:
   a. televised ads.
   b. developing a colorful website.
   c. organizing door-to-door canvassing efforts.
   d. the legal and accounting expenses related to filing information about campaign donors and expenditures with the Federal Elections Commission.

5. In recent decades state political party organizations in the United States have:
   a. become weaker and less effective.
   b. taken over control and direction of the national parties.
   c. been hurt by services provided by the national party organizations.
   d. become more professional in staffing and support of statewide races.

6. European and American political parties differ in which of the following ways?
   a. the degree to which they are party-centered as opposed to candidate-centered.
   b. the nature of their party organizations: the extent to which they are organized at the local and national levels and the amount of power that exists at each of these levels.
   c. the type of electoral system in which they elect their candidates to office.
   d. all of the above.

7. The coalitions of voters that make up the Republican and Democratic parties are virtually identical. (T/F)

8. Primary elections helped strengthen party organizations in the United States. (T/F)

9. U.S. political parties are organized from the bottom up, not the top down. (T/F)

10. Modern-day parties in the United States are described in the text as having more of a service than a power relationship with candidates. (T/F)

Critical Thinking

Why are elections conducted so differently in the United States than in European democracies? Why are the campaigns so much longer, more expensive, and more candidate-centered?

Suggested Readings

Aldrich, John H. *Why Parties? The Origin and Transformation of Political Parties in America*. Chicago: University of Chicago Press, 1995. An insightful analysis of what parties are and how they emerge and develop.

Flanigan, William H., and Nancy H. Zingale. *Political Behavior of the American Electorate*, 11th ed. Washington, D.C.: Congressional Quarterly Press, 2005. An overview of Americans' electoral behavior.

Greenberg, Stanley B. *The Two Americas: Our Current Political Deadlock and How to Break It*. New York: Thomas Dunne Books, 2004. An assessment of party politics in today's America.

Lijphardt, Arend. *Electoral Systems and Party Systems: A Study of Twenty-Seven Democracies, 1945–1990*. New York: Oxford University Press, 1994. A comprehensive study of the relationship between electoral systems and party systems.

Patterson, Kelly D. *Political Parties and the Maintenance of Liberal Democracy*. New York: Columbia University Press, 1996. A systematic look at the effects of political parties on American government and politics.

Sifreg, Micah L. *Spoiling for a Fight: Third-Party Politics in America*. New York: Routledge, 2003. An analysis of America's third parties and their impact on the two-party system.

Stonecash, Jeffrey. *Class and Party in American Politics*. Boulder, Colo.: Westview Press, 2001. An insightful analysis that argues that class is still very much a part of America's party politics.

West, Darrell M. *Air Wars: Television Advertising in Election Campaigns, 1952–2000*, 4th ed. Washington, D.C.: Congressional Quarterly Press, 2005. A thorough study of the role of televised advertising in election campaigns.

List of Websites

http://www.democrats.org/
The Democratic National Committee's site; it provides information on the party's platform, candidates, officials, and organization.

http://www.greenparties.org/
The Green party's website; it contains information on the party's philosophy and policy goals.

http://www.rnc.org/
Home page of the Republican National Committee; it offers information on Republican leaders, policy positions, and organizations.

http://www.jamescarvillesoffice.com/
The website of James Carville, one of the nation's top campaign consultants.

Participate!

Consider becoming a campaign volunteer. The opportunities are numerous. Candidates at every level from the presidency on down seek volunteers to assist in organizing, canvassing, fund-raising, and other campaign activities. As a college student, you have communication and knowledge skills that would be valuable to a campaign. You might be pleasantly surprised by the tasks you are assigned.

Extra Credit

For up-to-the-minute *New York Times* articles, interactive simulations, graphics, study tools, and more links and quizzes, visit the text's Online Learning Center at www.mhhe.com/pattersontad8.

(Self-Test Answers: 1. c   2. d   3. d   4. a   5. d   6. d   7. F   8. F   9. T   10. T)

Interest Groups:
Organizing for Influence

Chapter Outline

The Interest-Group System
Economic Groups
Citizens' Groups
A Special Category of Interest Group:
    Governments

Inside Lobbying: Seeking Influence Through Official Contacts
Acquiring Access to Officials
Webs of Influence: Groups in the Policy
    Process

Outside Lobbying: Seeking Influence Through Public Pressure
Constituency Advocacy: Grassroots
    Lobbying
Electoral Action: Votes and PAC Money

The Group System: Indispensable but Biased
The Contribution of Groups to
    Self-Government: Pluralism
Flaws in Pluralism: Interest-Group
    Liberalism and Economic Bias
A Madisonian Dilemma

CHAPTER 9

> The flaw in the pluralist heaven is that the heavenly chorus sings with
> a strong upper-class bias.
>
> —*E. E. Schattschneider*[1]

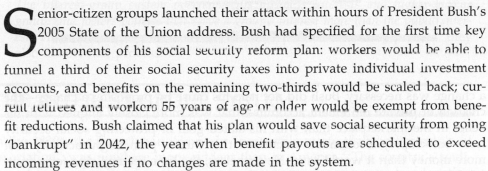

Senior-citizen groups launched their attack within hours of President Bush's 2005 State of the Union address. Bush had specified for the first time key components of his social security reform plan: workers would be able to funnel a third of their social security taxes into private individual investment accounts, and benefits on the remaining two-thirds would be scaled back; current retirees and workers 55 years of age or older would be exempt from benefit reductions. Bush claimed that his plan would save social security from going "bankrupt" in 2042, the year when benefit payouts are scheduled to exceed incoming revenues if no changes are made in the system.

Led by the American Association of Retired Persons (AARP), the seniors' lobby assailed the plan and orchestrated a campaign involving tens of thousands of angry calls, letters, telegrams, and faxes from retirees to their congressional representatives. AARP poured nearly $10 million into newspaper advertisements— "If we feel like gambling, we'll play the slots"—attacking Bush's proposal to partially privatize social security. Seniors groups found an ally in congressional Democrats. Senate minority leader Harry Reid (D-Nev.) called Bush's plan "social security roulette." "Democrats are all for giving Americans more of a say and more choices when it comes to their retirement savings," Reid declared. "But that doesn't mean taking Social Security's guarantee and gambling with it. And that's coming from a senator who represents Las Vegas." Within days, opinion polls showed declining support for Bush's plan. Over the next several months, public support for his proposal continued to fall, and by summer all but a few Republican diehards had given up on Bush's plan.

The campaign against Bush's social security initiative suggests why interest groups are both admired and feared. On one hand, groups have a legitimate right to express their views on public policy issues. It is entirely appropriate for senior citizens or other groups—whether farmers, consumers, business firms, or college students—to promote their interests through collective action. In fact, the *pluralist* theory of American politics (see Chapter 1) holds that society's interests are most effectively represented through group action.

One the other hand, groups can wield too much power. If a group gets its way at an unreasonable cost to the rest of society, the public interest is harmed. When Bush announced his intention to reform social security, most Americans felt that

How the United States Compares
Groups: "A Nation of Joiners"

"A nation of joiners" is how the Frenchman Alexis de Tocqueville described the United States during his visit to this country in the 1830s. Tocqueville was stunned by the group and community activity he saw, suggesting that Europeans would find it hard to comprehend. "The political activity that pervades the United States," said Tocqueville, "must be seen to be understood."

Today, Americans still are more actively involved in groups and community causes than are Europeans. Some observers, including Robert Putnam, believe that group activity in the United States is in decline (*Bowling Alone*, 2000). Even if that is true, Americans are more engaged in groups than citizens elsewhere. Among the reasons are the nation's tradition of free association, the prominence of religion, and the open nature of American society.

Another reason is the structure of the U.S. political system. Because of federalism and the separation of powers, the American system offers numerous points at which groups can try to influence public policy. If unsuccessful with legislators, groups can turn to executives or to the courts. If thwarted at the national level, groups can turn to state and local governments. By comparison, the governments of most other democratic nations are not organized in ways that facilitate group access and influence. France's unitary government, for example, concentrates power at the national level.

Such differences are reflected in citizens' participation rates. Americans are more likely to belong to groups than are the French, Italians, British, or Germans, as the accompanying figures from the World Values Survey indicate.

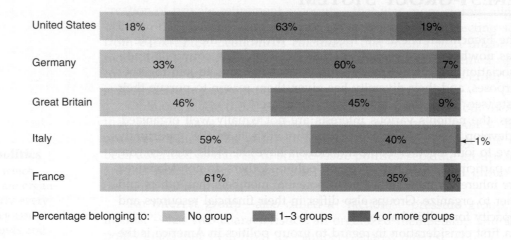

Percentage belonging to: ☐ No group ☐ 1–3 groups ☐ 4 or more groups

	No group	1–3 groups	4 or more groups
United States	18%	63%	19%
Germany	33%	60%	7%
Great Britain	46%	45%	9%
Italy	59%	40%	1%
France	61%	35%	4%

An Organizational Edge

One reason for the abundance of economic groups is their access to financial resources. Political activity does not come cheap. If a group is to make its views known, it normally must have a headquarters, an expert staff, and communication facilities. Economic groups can obtain the requisite money and expertise from their economic activities. Corporations have the greatest built-in advantage. They do not have to charge membership dues or conduct fund-raisers to support their lobbying. Their political money comes from their business income.

Some economic groups do depend on dues for their support but can offer prospective members a powerful incentive to join: **private (individual) goods,** or the benefits that a group can grant directly to the individual member. For example, workers in the state of Michigan cannot hold automobile assembly jobs unless they belong to the United Auto Workers (UAW). The UAW has a

private (individual) goods
Benefits that a group (most often an economic group) can grant directly and exclusively to individual members of the group.

material incentive—the economic lure of a high-paying job—to attract potential members.

The predominance of economic interests was predicted in *Federalist* No. 10, in which James Madison declared that property is "the most common and durable source of factions." Stated differently, nothing seems to matter quite so much to people as their economic self-interest.

Types of Economic Groups

Most economic groups are of four general types: business groups, labor groups, agricultural groups, and professional groups.

Business Groups   More than half of all groups formally registered to lobby Congress are business organizations. Virtually all large corporations and many smaller ones are politically active. They concentrate their activities on policies that touch directly on business interests, such as tax, tariff, and regulatory decisions.

Business firms are also represented through associations such as the U.S. Chamber of Commerce, which includes nearly three million businesses of all sizes. Other business associations, such as the American Petroleum Institute, are confined to a single trade or industry. Because each trade association represents a single industry, it can promote the interests of member corporations even when these interests conflict with those of business generally. Thus, while the Chamber of Commerce promotes a global free-trade policy, some trade associations seek protective tariffs because their member firms want barriers against foreign competition.

Business interests have the advantage of what economist Mancur Olson calls "the size factor."[3] It might be thought that in a democracy groups with large numbers of members would nearly always prevail over small groups when their interests conflict. However, as Olson points out, small groups are ordinarily more cohesive, and if they also have other advantages, such as lots of money, their interests can frequently win out over those of large groups. Business groups in a particular industry typically are few in number and recognize the significance of working together to influence government. Consumers, in contrast, number in the tens of millions, but most do not see any benefit in paying money to

material incentive
An economic or other tangible benefit that is used to attract group members.

Economic groups, which include business firms and labor unions, get the resources for their political activities from their economic activity. This source of support gives them an organizational advantage over citizens' groups, which depend on voluntary contributions to fund their lobbying. Shown here are leaders of Ford Motor Company and the United Auto Workers as they prepare to negotiate issues relating to their labor contract.

consumer groups that would advocate on their behalf. In 2005, these differences came together in ways that hurt consumers while helping the Big Three U.S. automakers (Chrysler, Ford, and General Motors). At issue was comprehensive legislation designed to address the nation's energy needs. With help from their friends in Congress and with an assist from a government agency that delayed issuing a report showing that little progress had been made since the 1980s in increasing the average gas mileage of automobiles, U.S. automakers worked together to keep a mandated increase in gas mileage out of the legislation. In the process, each automaker saved tens of millions of dollars they would have had to spend to design and manufacture more fuel-efficient vehicles. Their gain came at an unknown cost to new car buyers, whose autos are less fuel efficient than they would have been.

Labor Groups   Since the 1930s, organized labor has been politically active on a large scale. Its goal has been to promote policies that benefit workers in general and union members in particular. Although there are some major independent unions, such as the United Mine Workers and the Teamsters, the dominant labor group is the AFL-CIO, which has its national headquarters in Washington, D.C. The AFL-CIO has nine million members in its roughly fifty affiliated unions, which include the International Brotherhood of Electrical Workers, the Sheet Metal Workers, and the Communications Workers of America.

At one time, about a third of the U.S. work force was unionized, but today only about one in eight workers belongs to a union. Skilled and unskilled laborers have historically been the core of organized labor, but their numbers are decreasing while the numbers of professionals, technicians, and service workers are increasing. Professionals have shown little interest in union organization, perhaps because they identify with management or consider themselves economically secure. Service workers and technicians are also difficult for unions to organize because they work closely with managers and, often, in small offices.

Nevertheless, unions have made inroads in their efforts to organize service and public employees. Teachers, postal workers, police, firefighters, and social workers are among the public employee groups that have become increasingly unionized. Today, the nation's largest unions are those that represent service and public employees rather than skilled and unskilled laborers (see Table 9–1).

Agricultural Groups   Farm organizations represent another large economic lobby. The American Farm Bureau Federation is the largest of the farm groups,

TABLE 9–1	**The Largest Labor Unions, 1950 and 2000** The largest labor unions today represent service and public employees; fifty years ago, the largest unions represented skilled and unskilled workers.	
1950		**2000**
1. United Auto Workers		1. National Education Association
2. United Steel Workers		2. International Brotherhood of Teamsters
3. International Brotherhood of Teamsters		3. United Food and Commercial Workers International
4. United Brotherhood of Carpenters & Joiners		4. American Federation of State, County, & Municipal Employees
5. International Association of Machinists		5. Service Employees International

Source: U.S. Department of Labor.

with more than four million members. The National Farmers Union, the National Grange, and the National Farmers Organization are smaller farm lobbies. Agricultural groups do not always agree on policy issues. For instance, the Farm Bureau sides with agribusiness and owners of large farms, while the Farmers Union promotes the interests of smaller "family" farms.

There are also numerous specialty farm associations, including the Association of Wheat Growers, the American Soybean Association, and Associated Milk Producers. Each association acts as a separate lobby to try to secure policies beneficial to its members' specific interest.

Professional Groups   Most professions have lobbying associations. Among the most powerful of these groups is the American Medical Association (AMA), which, with nearly three hundred thousand members, represents about half the nation's physicians. The AMA has consistently opposed any government policy that would limit physicians' autonomy. Other professional groups include the American Bar Association (ABA) and the American Association of University Professors (AAUP), each of which maintains a lobbying office in Washington.

Citizens' Groups

Although economic interests are the best-organized groups, they do not have a monopoly on group activity. There are a great number and variety of other organized interests, which are referred to collectively as **citizens' groups** (or **noneconomic groups**). The members of groups in this category are drawn together not by the promise of direct economic gain but by **purposive incentives**—opportunities to promote a cause in which they believe.[4] Whether a group's purpose is to protect the environment, return prayer to the public schools, or feed the poor at home or abroad, there are citizens who are willing to participate simply because they believe the cause is a worthy one.[5]

Compared to economic groups, citizens' groups have a harder time acquiring the resources necessary for organization. These groups do not generate profits or fees as a result of economic activity. Moreover, the incentives they offer prospective members are not exclusive. As opposed to the private or individual goods provided by many economic groups, most noneconomic groups offer **collective goods** (or **public goods**) as an incentive for membership. Collective goods are, by definition, benefits that belong to all; they cannot be granted or withheld on an individual basis. The air people breathe and the national forests people visit are examples of collective goods. They are available to one and all, those who pay dues to a clean-air group or a wilderness group as well as those who do not.

The Free-Rider Problem

The shared characteristic of collective goods creates what is called the **free-rider problem**: individuals can receive the good even when they do not contribute to the group's

citizens' (noneconomic) groups
Organized interests formed by individuals drawn together by opportunities to promote a cause in which they believe but that does not provide them significant individual economic benefits.

purposive incentive
An incentive to group participation based on the cause (purpose) that the group seeks to promote.

collective (public) goods
Benefits that are offered by groups (usually citizens' groups) as an incentive for membership but that are nondivisible (e.g., a clean environment) and therefore are available to nonmembers as well as members of the particular group.

This 1873 lithograph illustrates the benefits of membership in the National Grange, an agricultural interest group.

Get Involved!

Join Up

When the Frenchman Alexis de Tocqueville came to the United States in the 1830s, he marveled at the abundance of civic and political groups and concluded that they were the underlying strength of American democracy. Little has happened in the nearly two centuries since to change this conclusion. Recent research, in fact, confirms it. In his pioneering *Making Democracy Work* (1993), Harvard University's Robert Putnam found that the more abundant a society's voluntary associations are, the more likely it is that the society's institutions will act in the public interest. Putnam uses the term *civic community* to describe a society in which voluntary associations flourish.

Democratic theorists such as Rousseau, Jefferson, Mill, and Dewey argued that communities should be constructed in ways that encourage the individual to participate as fully as possible in civic affairs. The theorists' assumption was that citizens "invest" in a community when they are an integral part of it. The theorists also assumed that participation expands the individual's vision, giving him or her the capacity, in Rousseau's words, for "seeing things in general." Said differently, civic participation enables individuals to surmount a narrowly self-interested view of what is best for society.

Putnam argues that America has undergone a long-term decline in its *social capital* (the sum of its civic relationships). In *Bowling Alone* (2000), Putnam presents evidence that indicates Americans are now less involved in community groups and other forms of social interaction. He attributes the change to television and other factors that produce social isolation. Not all scholars agree with Putnam's view of the trend (some indicators point to a rise in certain types of group membership), but no one has challenged his assumption about the importance of maintaining high levels of civic participation. The relationships fostered by this participation are a foundation of democratic life. And no democratic theorist has suggested that there can be "too much" civic participation. The higher the level of participation, the firmer the democratic base.

Citizens *should* participate in voluntary groups. By doing so, they contribute to improvements in their community, whether it be a college campus, a town, a state, or the nation. Moreover, the relationships that develop among people as a result of civic participation enable individuals to better understand the opinions and values of others. Consider joining a voluntary group. Groups of all kinds would welcome your membership.

free-rider problem

The situation in which the benefits offered by a group to its members are also available to nonmembers. The incentive to join the group and to promote its cause is reduced because nonmembers (free riders) receive the benefits (e.g., a cleaner environment) without having to pay any of the group's costs.

effort. Take the case of National Public Radio (NPR). Although NPR's programs are funded primarily through listeners' donations, those who do not contribute can hear the programs. The noncontributors are free riders: they receive the benefit without paying for it. About 90 percent of regular listeners to NPR do not contribute to their local station.

As economist Mancur Olson noted, it is not rational, in a purely economic sense, for individuals to contribute to a group when they can obtain its benefit for free.[6] Moreover, the dues paid by any single member are too small to affect the group's success one way or another. Why pay dues to an environmental group when any improvements in the air, water, or wildlife from its lobbying efforts are available to everyone and when one's individual contribution is too small to make a real difference? Although many people do join such groups anyway, the free-rider problem is a reason why citizens' groups are less fully organized than economic groups.

Citizens' groups try to surmount the free-rider problem by creating individual benefits, akin to those offered by economic groups, to make membership more attractive. Organizational newsletters and social activities are among the individual benefits that some citizens' groups offer as an incentive to membership. Computer-assisted direct mail has also helped citizens' groups attract members. Group organizers buy mailing lists and flood the mails with computer-typed "personal" letters asking recipients to pay a small annual membership fee. For some individuals, a fee of $25 to $50 annually represents no great sacrifice and offers the satisfaction of supporting a cause in which they believe. Until the computer era, citizens' groups had great difficulty identifying and contacting potential members, which is a reason why the number of such groups was so much smaller in the past than today.

The Internet has also been a boon to citizens' groups. Nearly every such group of any size has its own website and e-mail list. MoveOn is an example of the Internet's organizing capacity. MoveOn was started by a handful of liberal activists working out of a garage. By 2004, they had created an Internet network that linked hundreds of thousands of citizens who could be mobilized in support of liberal candidates and causes. MoveOn raised more than $3 million in 2006 for Democratic congressional candidates while also launching a massive get-out-the-vote effort in the election's closing days.

The Internet has made it easier for citizens' groups to organize and increase their membership. One of the most successful examples is MoveOn. It was founded by a small group of liberal activists, including Wes Boyd and Joan Blades, shown here standing outside their home in California.

On the whole, however, the organizational advantages rest with economic groups. They have an edge on citizens' groups in nearly every respect—money, solidarity, and control (see Table 9–2).

WWW.MHHE.COM/PATTERSONTAD8

Types of Citizens' Groups

Most citizens' groups are of three general types: public-interest groups, single-issue groups, and ideological groups.

Public-Interest Groups Public-interest groups are those that claim to represent the broad interests of society as a whole. Despite their label, public-interest groups are not led by people elected by the public at large, and the issues they target are ones of their own choosing, not the public's. Moreover, people often disagree on what constitutes "the public interest," which raises the issue of whether any particular viewpoint can truly be said to represent that interest. Nevertheless, there is a basis for distinguishing the so-called public-interest

TABLE 9–2	**Advantages and Disadvantages Held by Economic and Citizens' Groups** Compared with economic groups, citizens' groups have fewer advantages and more disadvantages.

ECONOMIC GROUPS	CITIZENS' GROUPS
Advantages	*Advantages*
Economic activity provides the organization with the resources necessary for political action.	Members are likely to support leaders' political efforts because they joined the group in order to influence policy.
Individuals are encouraged to join the group because of economic benefits they individually receive (e.g., wages).	*Disadvantages*
Disadvantages	The group has to raise funds, especially for its political activities.
Persons within the group may not support leaders' political efforts because they did not join the group for political reasons.	Potential members may choose not to join the group because they get collective benefits even if they do not join (the free-rider problem).

Environmental activists protest against automobile and truck emissions, which are a leading cause of air pollution. Although environmental groups have been quite successful in attracting public support, they still confront the so-called free-rider problem—the fact that people will gain the benefit of a group's effort even if they do not contribute to it.

groups from economic groups: the latter seek direct material benefits for their members, while the former seek benefits that are less tangible and more broadly shared. For example, the National Association of Manufacturers, an economic group, seeks policies favorable to large corporations, while the League of Women Voters, a public-interest group, seeks policies—such as simplified voter registration—that can benefit the public in general.

More than half of the currently active public-interest groups were established after 1960. One such organization is Common Cause, which has more than two hundred thousand members and describes itself as "a national citizens' lobby"; it concentrates on political reform in areas such as campaign finance.

Single-Issue Groups   A single-issue group is organized to influence policy in just one area. Notable current examples are the National Rifle Association and the various right-to-life and pro-choice groups that have formed around the issue of abortion. The number of single-issue groups has risen sharply in the past three decades, and these groups now pressure government on almost every conceivable issue, from nuclear arms to day care centers to drug abuse.

Environmental groups are sometimes classified as public-interest groups, but they may also be considered single-issue organizations in that most of them seek to influence public policy in a specific area, such as pollution reduction, wilderness preservation, or wildlife protection. The Sierra Club, one of the oldest environmental groups, was formed in the 1890s to promote the preservation of scenic areas. Also prominent are the National Audubon Society, the Wilderness Society, the Environmental Defense Fund, Greenpeace U.S.A., and the Izaak Walton League. Since 1960, membership in environmental groups has more than tripled as a result of the public's increased concern about the quality of the environment.[7]

Ideological Groups   Single-issue groups have an issue-specific policy agenda. In contrast, ideological groups have a broader agenda that derives from a philosophical or moral position. An example is the Christian Coalition of America, which was organized to restore "Christian values" to American life and politics. The group has addressed a wide range of issues, including school prayer, abortion, and television programming. Ideological groups on both the left and the right have increased substantially in number since the 1960s.

Groups such as the National Organization for Women (NOW) and the National Association for the Advancement of Colored People (NAACP) can also be classified generally as ideological groups. Although they represent particular demographic groups, they do so across a wide range of issues. For example, NOW addresses issues that range from jobs to reproduction to political representation.

A Special Category of Interest Group: Governments

While the vast majority of organized interests in the United States represent private concerns, a growing number of interest groups represent governments, both foreign and subnational.

The U.S. federal government makes policies that directly affect the economic development, political stability, and security of nations throughout the world. Arms sales, foreign aid, immigration, and import restrictions and other trade practices have a great impact on foreign nations. For this reason, most foreign nations supplement the political efforts made through their embassies with the services of paid lobbyists in Washington.[8] However, foreign governments are prohibited from engaging in certain lobbying activities, including contributions to U.S. election campaigns.

States, cities, and other governmental units within the United States also lobby heavily. Most major cities and two-thirds of the states have at least one Washington lobbyist. Lobbying also occurs through groups such as the Council of State Governments, the National Governors Conference, the National Association of Counties, the National League of Cities, and the U.S. Conference of Mayors. These organizations sometimes play a large role in policy debates. For example, as Congress was preparing in 2006 to renew and amend the antiterrorism legislation that had gone into effect in 2001, the National Governors Conference and the U.S. Conference of Mayors lobbied to ensure that the changes reflected state and local concerns.

LEADERS

PAT ROBERTSON

(1930–)

No one has done more in recent decades to make religion a powerful force in American politics than Pat Robertson. Through his Christian Coalition of America, formed in the late 1980s, Robertson has mobilized conservative Christians in support of a religion-based policy agenda. The Christian Coalition's website contains the phrase "America's leading grassroots organization protecting our Godly heritage." Robertson ran for public office himself in 1988, when he challenged for the Republican presidential nomination. He astonished opponents and pundits alike by placing second (ahead of George H. W. Bush but behind Robert Dole) in the Iowa caucuses, the first contest of the campaign. Although his presidential candidacy eventually faltered, Robertson's campaign inspired thousands of conservative Christians to become politically active, and many of them continued to work in Republican politics after the 1988 election.

As a young man, Robertson had planned a law career, but he failed his bar exam shortly after earning a law degree from Yale University. He underwent a religious conversion and decided to participate in ministry rather than retake the bar exam. A Southern Baptist, Robertson had an active ministry and also became involved in broadcasting. In 1960, he bought a small television station and established the Christian Broadcasting Network, which eventually grew into a worldwide organization. Robertson's own television program, *The 700 Club*, airs regularly on the network. This program has enabled Robertson to continue to promote conservative causes, although his on-the-air remarks sometimes have backfired. In 2005, Robertson suggested that the United States should consider assassinating Venezuelan president Hugo Chavez, saying it would be a lot cheaper than going to war over Venezuela's oil. Robertson later apologized for the statement.

INSIDE LOBBYING: SEEKING INFLUENCE THROUGH OFFICIAL CONTACTS

Modern government provides a supportive environment for interest groups. First, modern government is involved in so many issues—business regulation, income maintenance, urban renewal, cancer research, and energy development, to name only a few—that hardly any interest in society could fail to benefit significantly from having influence over federal policies or programs. Second, modern government is oriented toward action. Officials are inclined to respond to problems rather than let problems linger. For example, when forest fires in California, Arizona, and other western states destroyed property worth millions in 2006, Washington granted immediate assistance to residents who had incurred losses and cleanup costs.

Groups seek government's support through **lobbying,** a term that refers broadly to efforts by groups to influence public policy through contact with public officials.

lobbying
The process by which interest-group members or lobbyists attempt to influence public policy through contacts with public officials.

Inside lobbying offers groups a chance to make their policy views known. Access to public officials is critical to the inside-lobbying strategy.

Lobbying is big business in America. A section of the nation's capital, known as K Street, is populated almost completely by lobbying firms. There are more than twenty thousand Washington lobbyists, and official records indicate that roughly $1 billion is spent each year on lobbying. The actual amount is higher, but no one is quite sure by how much. Lobbying is regulated by the Lobbying Disclosure Act of 1995, which defines who must register as a lobbyist and what lobbying activities and expenditures must be reported. However, the Act's enforcement provisions are weak and its filing provisions are ambiguous, which means that some of the Washington lobbying that takes place never becomes part of the public record. Most officials and lobbyists apparently would like to keep it that way. When the Abramoff lobbying scandal rocked Washington in 2006, members of Congress vowed to amend the Lobbying Disclosure Act to put more teeth into it. That commitment quietly disappeared, as lawmakers and lobbyists had second thoughts about whether they were truly interested in bringing lobbying activities fully into the open.

Interest groups rely on two main lobbying strategies, which have been labeled "inside lobbying" and "outside lobbying."[9] Each strategy involves communication with public officials, but the strategies differ in what is communicated and who does the communicating. This section discusses **inside lobbying,** which is based on group efforts to develop and maintain close ("inside") contacts with policymakers. (Outside lobbying is described in the next section.)

inside lobbying

Direct communication between organized interests and policymakers, which is based on the assumed value of close ("inside") contacts with policymakers.

Acquiring Access to Officials

Inside lobbying is designed to give a group direct access to officials in order to influence their decisions. Access is not the same as influence, which is the capacity to affect policy decisions. But access is a critical first step in the influence process.[10] The importance of access is evident, for example, in the high salaries that former members of Congress can command when they become lobbyists. Former congressional members are prohibited for one year from lobbying Congress, but thereafter they are free to do so. They usually represent groups with which they had close ties while they were in office. Unlike other lobbyists, they have the right, as former legislators, to go directly onto the floor of the House or the Senate to speak with current members.

Lobbying once depended significantly on tangible inducements, sometimes including indirect or even outright bribes. This old form of lobbying survives, but modern lobbying generally involves subtler and more sophisticated methods than providing money or personal favors to officials. It focuses on supplying officials with information and indications of group strength that will persuade them to adopt the group's perspective.[11]

For the most part, inside lobbying is directed at policymakers who are inclined to support the group rather than at those who have opposed it in the past. This tendency reflects both the difficulty of persuading opponents to change long-held views and the advantage of having trusted allies who will work actively to promote the group's policy positions. Thus, union lobbyists work mainly with pro-labor officeholders, just as corporate lobbyists work mainly with policymakers who support business interests.

Money is the basic ingredient of inside lobbying efforts. The American Petroleum Institute, for example, with its abundant financial resources, can afford a downtown Washington office staffed by lobbyists, petroleum experts, and public relations specialists who help the oil companies maintain access to and influence with legislative and executive leaders. Many groups spend upward of $1 million annually on lobbying. The American Hospital Association (AHA), for example, spent $19 million on lobbying in 2005. Other groups get by on much less, but it is hard to lobby effectively on a small budget. Given the costs of maintaining a Washington lobby, the domination by corporations and trade associations is understandable. These groups have the money to retain high-priced lobbyists, while many other interests do not.

The targets of inside lobbying are officials of all three government branches—legislative, executive, and judicial.

Lobbying Congress

The benefits of a close relationship with members of Congress are substantial. With support in Congress, a group can obtain the legislative help it needs to achieve its policy goals. By the same token, members of Congress gain from working closely with lobbyists. The volume of legislation facing Congress is heavy, and members rely on trusted lobbyists to identify bills that deserve their attention and support. When Republican lawmakers took control of Congress in 1995, they invited corporate lobbyists to participate directly in drafting legislation affecting business. Congressional Democrats complained loudly, but Republicans said they were merely getting help from those who best understood business's needs and accused Democrats of having engaged in the same practice with organized labor when they were in power.

Lobbyists' effectiveness with members of Congress depends in part on their reputation for fair play. Lobbyists are expected to play it straight. Said one congressman: "If any [lobbyist] gives me false or misleading information, that's it— I'll never see him again."[12] Arm-twisting is another unacceptable practice. During the debate over the North American Free Trade Agreement in 1993, the AFL-CIO threatened retaliation against congressional Democrats who supported the legislation. The backlash from these Democrats was so intense that the union backed down on its threat. The safe lobbying strategy is the aboveboard approach: provide information, rely on longtime allies among members of Congress, and push steadily but not too aggressively for legislative goals.

Lobbying Executive Agencies

As the scope of the federal government has expanded, lobbying of the executive branch has increased in importance. Bureaucrats make key administrative decisions and develop policy initiatives that the legislative branch later makes into law. By working closely with executive agencies, groups can influence policy decisions at the implementation and initiation stages. In return, groups assist agencies by providing support when their programs and budgets are renewed by Congress and the president.

Nowhere is the link between groups and the bureaucracy more evident than in the regulatory agencies that oversee the nation's business sectors. For example, the Federal Communications Commission (FCC), which regulates the nation's broadcasters, uses information provided by broadcast organizations to decide many of the policies governing their activities. The FCC is sometimes cited as an example of agency capture. The capture theory suggests that regulatory agencies pass through a series of phases that constitute a life cycle. Early in an agency's existence, it regulates an industry on the public's behalf, but as the agency matures, its vigor declines until at best it protects the status quo and at worst it falls captive to the very industry it is supposed to regulate. In the mid-1990s, the FCC concluded that television broadcasts should be granted use of the new digital channels without charge. Some members of Congress and numerous citizens' groups had urged that the new channels be auctioned off to the highest bidders, a procedure that by even the lowest estimates would have netted taxpayers hundreds of millions of dollars.

Research indicates that the capture theory describes only some agencies— and then only some of the time. Agencies selectively cooperate with or oppose interest groups, depending on which strategy better suits agency purposes. Agency officials are aware that they can lose support in Congress, which controls agency funding and program authorization, if they show too much favoritism toward an interest group.[13]

Lobbying the Courts

Court rulings in areas such as education and civil rights have made interest groups recognize that the judiciary too can help them reach their goals.[14] Interest groups have several judicial lobbying options, including efforts to influence the selection of federal judges. Right-to-life groups have pressured Republican administrations to make opposition to abortion a prerequisite for nomination to the federal bench. Democratic administrations have in turn faced pressure from pro-choice groups in their judicial nominations.

Groups also rely on lawsuits in their efforts to influence the courts. For some organizations, such as the American Civil Liberties Union (ACLU), legal action is the primary means of influencing policy. The ACLU often takes on unpopular causes, such as the free speech rights of fringe groups. Such causes have little chance of success in legislative bodies but may prevail in a courtroom.

As interest groups increasingly resort to legal action, they often find themselves facing one another in court. Environmental litigation groups such as the Earthwise Legal Defense Fund and the Environmental Defense Fund have frequently sued oil, timber, and mining corporations.

Webs of Influence: Groups in the Policy Process

To get a fuller picture of how inside lobbying works, it is helpful to consider two policy processes—iron triangles and issue networks—in which many groups are enmeshed.

Iron Triangles

iron triangle
A small and informal but relatively stable group of well-positioned legislators, executives, and lobbyists who seek to promote policies beneficial to a particular interest.

An **iron triangle** consists of a small and informal but relatively stable set of bureaucrats, legislators, and lobbyists who seek to develop policies beneficial to a particular interest. The three "corners" of one such triangle are the Department of Agriculture (bureaucrats), the agriculture committees of Congress (legislators), and farm groups such as the Associated Milk Producers and the Association of Wheat Growers (lobbyists). Together they determine many of the policies affecting farmers. Of course, the support of other players, including the president and a majority in Congress, is needed to enact programs helpful to farmers. However, these players often defer to the policy views of the agricultural triangle. Its members are intimately familiar with the policy needs of farmers.

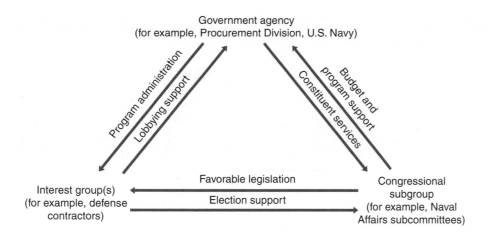

Figure 9–1

How an Iron Triangle Benefits Its Participants An iron triangle works to the advantage of each of its participants—an interest group, a congressional subgroup, and a government agency.

A group in an iron triangle has an inside track to those legislators and bureaucrats who are in the strongest position to help its cause. And because it has something of value to offer each of them, the relationships tend to be ironclad. The group provides lobbying support for the agency's funding and programs and makes campaign contributions to its congressional allies. Agricultural groups, for example, contribute millions of dollars to congressional candidates in each election. Most of this money is given to incumbents, and most of these contributions go to the campaigns of members of the House and Senate agriculture committees. Figure 9–1 summarizes the benefits that flow to each member of an iron triangle.

Issue Networks

Iron triangles represent the pattern of influence in only certain policy areas and are less common now than in the past. A more frequent pattern of influence today is the **issue network,** an informal grouping of officials, lobbyists, and policy specialists (the "network") who are brought together temporarily by their shared interest in a particular policy problem (the "issue").

Issue networks are a result of the increasing complexity of policy problems. Participants must have specialized knowledge of the issue at hand in order to participate effectively. Thus, unlike iron triangles, where a participant's position is everything, an issue network is built around specialized interests and information. On any given issue, the participants might come from a variety of executive agencies, congressional committees, interest groups, and institutions such as universities or think tanks. Compared to iron triangles, issue networks are less stable. As the issue develops, new participants may join the debate and old ones drop out. Once the issue is resolved, the network disbands.[15]

An example of an issue network is the set of participants who would come together over the issue of whether a large tract of old forest should be opened to logging. A few decades ago, that issue would have been settled in an iron triangle consisting of the timber companies, the U.S. Forest Service, and relevant members of the House and Senate agriculture committees. But as forestlands have diminished and environmental concerns have grown, such issues can no longer be contained within the cozy confines of an iron triangle. Today, an issue network would form that included logging interests, the U.S. Forest Service, House and Senate agriculture committee members, research scientists, and representatives of environmental groups, the housing industry, and animal-rights groups. Unlike the old iron triangle, which was confined to like-minded interests, this issue network would include opposing interests (for example, the loggers and the environmentalists).

issue network

An informal and relatively open network of public officials and lobbyists who have a common interest in a given area and who are brought together by a proposed policy in that area. Unlike an iron triangle, an issue network disbands after the issue is resolved.

U.S. Forest Service rangers start a controlled-burn fire to clear ground for the planting of new-growth trees. The U.S. Forest Service, which is part of the Department of Agriculture, oversees the national forests, as well as their use by logging, mining, and other industries. At an earlier time, decisions about the use of national forests typically would have been decided in an iron triangle consisting of Forest Service bureaucrats, Senate and House agricultural committee members, and industry representatives. However, ever since the environmental movement raised awareness of how the national forests are managed, decisions over their use have involved issue networks that include environmentalists, research specialists, community leaders, and others in addition to the traditional decision makers.

And unlike an iron triangle, the issue network would dissolve once the issue that brought the parties together was resolved.

Issue networks, then, differ substantially from iron triangles. In an iron triangle, a common interest brings the participants together in a stable, long-lasting, and mutually beneficial relationship. In an issue network, an immediate issue brings the participants together in a temporary network that is based on their ability to address the issue in a sophisticated way and where they play out their separate interests before disbanding once the issue is settled.

Despite these differences, iron triangles and issue networks do have one thing in common: they are arenas in which organized groups operate. The interests of the general public may be taken into account in these webs of influence, but the interests of the participating groups are paramount.

OUTSIDE LOBBYING: SEEKING INFLUENCE THROUGH PUBLIC PRESSURE

outside lobbying
A form of lobbying in which an interest group seeks to use public pressure as a means of influencing officials.

Although an interest group may rely solely on inside lobbying, this approach is not likely to be successful unless the group can demonstrate convincingly that its concerns reflect those of a vital constituency. Accordingly, groups make use of constituency connections when it is advantageous for them to do so. They engage in **outside lobbying,** which involves bringing public ("outside") pressure to bear on policymakers (see Table 9–3).[16]

TABLE 9-3	Tactics Used in Inside and Outside Lobbying Strategies Inside and outside lobbying are based on different tactics.	
INSIDE LOBBYING	**OUTSIDE LOBBYING**	
Developing contacts with legislators and executives	Encouraging group members to write, phone, or email their representatives in Congress	
Providing information and policy proposals to key officials	Seeking favorable coverage by news media	
Forming coalitions with other groups	Encouraging members to support particular candidates in elections	
	Targeting group resources on key election races	
	Making PAC contributions to candidates	

Constituency Advocacy: Grassroots Lobbying

One form of outside pressure is **grassroots lobbying**—that is, pressure designed to convince government officials that a group's policy position has popular support.

No group illustrates grassroots lobbying better than AARP (American Association of Retired Persons). With more than thirty million members and a staff of sixteen hundred, AARP is a powerful lobby on retirement issues such as social security and Medicare. When major legislation affecting retirees is pending, AARP swings into action. Congress receives more mail from members of AARP than it does from members of any other group. AARP's support was critical to passage in 2003 of a controversial prescription drug program for the elderly. Until AARP's last-minute endorsement, the program appeared to be headed for a narrow defeat in Congress.

As with other forms of lobbying, the precise impact of grassroots campaigns is often difficult to assess. Some members of Congress downplay its influence, but all congressional offices monitor letters and phone calls as a way of tracking constituents' opinions.

Electoral Action: Votes and PAC Money

An "outside" strategy can also include election campaigns. "Reward your friends and punish your enemies" is a political adage that loosely describes how interest groups view elections. The possibility of electoral opposition from a powerful group can keep an officeholder from openly obstructing the group's goals. For example, opposition from the three-million-member National Rifle Association is a major reason why the United States has lagged behind other Western societies in its handgun control laws, despite polls that show most Americans favor such laws.

Interest groups gain influence by contributing money to candidates' campaigns. As one lobbyist said, "Talking to politicians is fine, but with a little money they hear you better."[17] Members of Congress sometimes get into hot water by listening to lobbyists while also receiving favors from them. When it was alleged in 2005 that lobbyist Jack Abramoff had cheated some of his clients while also lavishing trips and money on members of Congress in return for favorable legislation, it sent a shock wave through Washington. Several members of Congress quickly returned campaign donations they had received from Abramoff in the hope that doing so would insulate them from the corruption scandal. A casualty of the Abramoff affair was Representative Tom DeLay (R-Texas), who lost his post as House majority

grassroots lobbying
A form of lobbying designed to persuade officials that a group's policy position has strong constituent support.

Lobbying in the United States rests on access, information, persuasion, and mutual support. Occasionally, lobbying is also a shadier business where favors are given that skirt the laws governing lobbying. In 2005, news broke that a prominent Washington lobbyist, Jack Abramoff, had engaged in possibly illegal deals with a number of legislative and executive officials. It did not help Abramoff's case that he had lavished expensive trips on some officials. Controversy surrounding his relationship with Abramoff prompted House majority leader Tom DeLay to resign his congressional seat. Abramoff is shown here leaving federal court in Washington in 2006.

leader when his close relationship with Abramoff became known. Abramoff had funneled hundreds of thousands of dollars to DeLay for political purposes, some of it of questionable legality.

A group's election contributions are funneled through its **political action committee (PAC).** A group cannot give organizational funds (such as corporate profits or union dues) to candidates, but through its PAC a group can solicit and donate voluntary contributions from members or employees. A PAC is legally limited in the amount it can contribute to a candidate running for federal office. The ceiling is $10,000 per candidate—$5,000 in the primary campaign and $5,000 in the general election campaign. There is no legal limit on the number of candidates a PAC can support. (These financial limits do not apply to candidates for state and local office. Their campaigns are regulated by state laws, and many states allow PACs to make unlimited campaign contributions.)

There are more than four thousand PACs, and PAC contributions account for roughly a third of total contributions to congressional campaigns. Their role is less significant in presidential campaigns, which are

political action committee (PAC)

The organization through which an interest group raises and distributes funds for election purposes. By law, the funds must be raised through voluntary contributions.

larger in scale and publicly funded in part and therefore are less dependent on PAC contributions.

More than 40 percent of all PACs are associated with corporations (see Figure 9–2). Examples include the Ford Motor Company Civic Action Fund, the Sun Oil Company Political Action Committee (Sunpac), and the Coca-Cola PAC. The next largest group of PACs consists of those linked to citizens' groups (that is, public-interest, single-issue, and ideological groups), such as the liberal People

Figure 9–2

Percentage of PACs by Category
Most PACs represent business. Corporate and trade association PACs make up 63 percent of the total.
Source: Federal Election Commission, 2006.

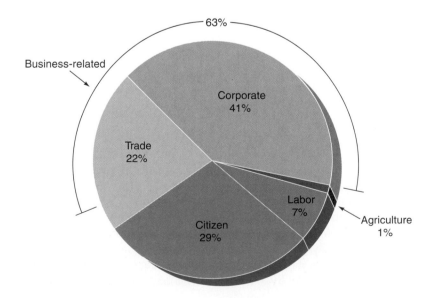

Debating the Issues

Have Interest Groups Hijacked the Initiative Process?

The initiative was pioneered by the Progressives of the early twentieth century, who saw it as a way to wrest power from the political bosses and corporate robber barons and place it in the hands of ordinary citizens. Twenty-four states allow the initiative, which requires the gathering of a sufficient number of citizens' signatures to place a legislative proposal (initiative) on the ballot. If a majority of voters approve it, the initiative becomes law, just as if it had been enacted by the legislature itself. In recent years, however, the initiative process has been used by interest groups to advance their policy agendas. These groups have the money to pay for the signature-gathering phase and to conduct a campaign in support of the initiative. To some observers, this development has corrupted the initiative process. Other observers claim that the initiative remains a bulwark of citizen-based politics.

Yes The initiative process came to the United States about 100 years ago, imported from Switzerland by populists and progressives worried about the influence of money on legislatures. The purpose was twofold: one, break the power of interest groups, and two, empower people to write the laws themselves on the ballot. The system worked pretty well [for a time]; it produced a great deal of progressive legislation. . . . [Today, however, the initiative process is] being driven very much by money. With their own political agendas, interest groups of all kinds have latched onto this device as a way of writing the law the way they would like it written without having to go through all the hoops of the normal governmental process. . . . I think it's particularly ironic that a device that was introduced into this country as a way of fighting special interest influence and the power of money now has been largely taken over by those same interest groups and by very wealthy millionaires who have the resources that it now takes to get an initiative on the ballot and to fight these campaigns to get them passed or defeated in the states.

—*David S. Broder, author and* Washington Post *columnist*

No Many of the concerns about initiatives seem unfounded, and so addressing them in turn seems unfounded as well. Political scientists have found that, whereas 40 percent of all initiatives on the California ballot from 1986 to 1996 passed, only 14 percent of initiatives promoted by special interests passed. Many people are predisposed to believe that money influences elections. But when it comes to initiative campaigns, the proof does not exist. In an era of growing government, the people need a mechanism to check government. Many claim that the people already have that check—elections. But that is a fallacy. Most people who support the initiative process and who use the process use it as a tool for addressing single issues. They want for the most part to keep a particular elected official, and so voting that official out of office for failing to deal with one specific issue is considered an extreme step, far more extreme than allowing the people to make laws occasionally. . . . Representative government and the initiative process are perfect complements to each other—two imperfect systems of government each designed to help the people and both carefully constructed to balance the weaknesses of one with the strengths of the other.

—*M. Dane Waters, president, The Initiative & Referendum Institute*

for the American Way and the conservative National Conservative Political Action Committee (NCPAC). Ranking third are PACs tied to trade and professional associations, such as AMPAC (American Medical Association) and R-PAC (National Association of Realtors). Labor unions, once the major source of group contributions, now rank fourth.

PACs contribute roughly eight times as much money to incumbents as to their challengers. PACs are well aware of the fact that incumbents are likely

States in the Nation

Limits on PAC Contributions

Elections of state officials (such as governors and state legislators) are regulated by state law rather than by federal law. In some states, there is no law limiting how much money PACs can contribute to a candidate. Of the states that limit PAC contributions, only New York and Nevada allow contributions in excess of $10,000.

Q: Why might states located to the west of the Mississippi River (which runs down the eastern borders of Minnesota, Iowa, Missouri, Arkansas, and Louisiana) place fewer limits on PAC contributions than other states?*

A: A possible explanation is that the political cultures of the westernmost states, as a result of their frontier heritage, are less accepting of government regulation of any kind.

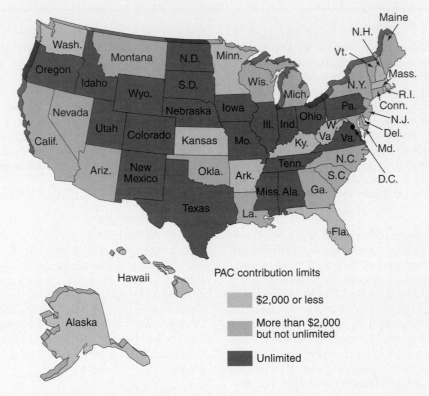

PAC contribution limits

- $2,000 or less
- More than $2,000 but not unlimited
- Unlimited

Source: Federal Elections Commission.

to win and thus to remain in a position to make policy. One PAC director, expressing a common view, said, "We always stick with the incumbent when we agree with them both."[18] The tendency of PACs to back incumbents has to some extent blurred long-standing partisan divisions in campaign funding. Business interests are especially pragmatic. Although they tend to favor Republican candidates, they are reluctant to anger Democratic incumbents. The result is that Democratic incumbents, particularly in House races, have received substantial support over the years from business-related PACs.[19] Other PACs, of course, are less pragmatic. The Christian Moral Government

Fund, for example, backs only candidates who take conservative stands on issues such as school prayer and abortion. Another example is EMILY's list (*early money is like yeast*, "it makes the dough rise"). It supports only liberal women candidates.

The influence of PACs has been the subject of intense debate. Advocates of PACs claim that groups have a right to be heard, which includes the right to express themselves with money. Because PACs raise their money from contributions by small donors, advocates also see them as a better system of campaign finance than one based on wealthy donors. On the other hand, critics complain that PACs give interest groups far too much influence with members of Congress.[20]

Although members of Congress deny they are unduly influenced by PACs, there is no question that PACs give interest groups a level of access to lawmakers that ordinary citizens do not have. Nevertheless, Congress is unlikely in the foreseeable future to pass legislation that would outlaw PACs. The fact is, most members of Congress are unwilling to eliminate a source of campaign funds that helps them to get reelected.

THE GROUP SYSTEM: INDISPENSABLE BUT BIASED

As noted in the chapter's introduction, pluralist theory holds that organized groups are a source of sound governance. On one level, this claim is beyond dispute. Without groups to carry their message, most of society's interests would find it difficult to get government's attention and support. Yet the issue of representation is also a question of whether all interests in society are fairly represented through the group system, and here the pluralist argument is less compelling.

The Contribution of Groups to Self-Government: Pluralism

Group activity is an essential part of self-government. An obstacle to popular sovereignty is the difficulty that public officials have in trying to discover what the people want from government. To discern their wishes, lawmakers consult public opinion polls, meet with constituents, and assess election results. Lobbying activities are also a clue to what people are seeking. Moreover, government does not exist simply to serve majority interests. The fact that most people are not retirees or labor union members or farmers or college students or Hispanics does not mean that the concerns of such "minorities" are unworthy of attention. And what better instrument exists for promoting their interests than organizations formed by them?

Some pluralists even question the usefulness of terms such as *the common good* and *the collective interest*. If people disagree on society's goals and priorities, as they always do, how can it be said that people have a "common" or "collective" interest? As an alternative, pluralists contend that, because society has so many interests, the common good ultimately is best served by a process that serves these many interests. Thus, if manufacturing interests prevail on one issue, environmentalists on another, farmers on a third, minorities on a fourth, and so on until many interests are served, the collective interest of society will have been promoted.

Finally, interest groups often take up issues that are neglected by the political parties. Party leaders typically shy away from issues, such as affirmative action and abortion, on which the party's voters disagree. Such issues would get less notice if not for the groups that promote them. And when groups succeed in drawing attention to these issues, the parties are nearly compelled to address them as well. In this sense, as political scientist Jack Walker noted, the party and group systems "are complementary and together constitute a more responsive and adaptive system than either would be if they somehow operated on their own."[21]

Flaws in Pluralism: Interest-Group Liberalism and Economic Bias

Although pluralist theory includes some compelling arguments, it also has some questionable aspects. Political scientist Theodore Lowi argues that there is no concept of society's collective interest in a system that gives special interests the ability to determine the policies affecting them.[22] The basis of decision in such cases is not majority (collective) rule but minority (special-interest) rule.

It is seldom safe to assume that what most people would favor is what a special-interest group wants. Consider the case of the federal law that required auto dealers to list the known defects of used cars on window stickers. The law was repealed after an extensive lobbying campaign financed by contributions of more than $1 million by the National Association of Automobile Dealers to the reelection campaigns of members of Congress.

Because lobbying groups have emerged to represent nearly every dimension of public policy, it is the rare issue that finds groups in agreement. Stem-cell research is no exception. This issue has pitted, among others, religious groups against health advocacy groups. The issue has also divided party leaders. President George W. Bush in 2006 cast the first veto of his presidency when he refused to sign a bill that would expand federal support for stem-cell research. The legislation had the backing of several prominent Republican lawmakers, including Senator Orrin Hatch (R-Utah), who is shown here with actor Michael J. Fox at a news conference to urge passage of the legislation.

Lowi uses the term **interest-group liberalism** to describe the tendency of officials to support the policy demands of the interest group or groups that have a special stake in a policy. Interest–group liberalism constitutes a partial abandonment by government of its responsibility to determine the policies by which society is governed. In practical terms, groups have as much or more say than government over the policies affecting them. One of the adverse effects is a weakening of majority rule; rather than policymaking by the majority acting through its elected representatives, interest-group liberalism involves policymaking by narrow segments of society acting on their own behalf. Another adverse effect is an inefficient use of society's resources: groups get what they want, whether or not their priorities match those of society as a whole.

Another flaw in the pluralist argument resides in its claim that the group system is representative. Pluralists recognize that better-organized interests have more influence but argue that the group process is relatively open and that few interests are at a serious disadvantage. These claims contain an element of truth, but they are far from the complete truth.

As this chapter has pointed out, organization is a political resource that is distributed unequally across society. Economic interests, particularly corporations, are the most highly organized, and some analysts argue that group politics works chiefly to the advantage of business. Of course, economic groups do not dominate everything, nor do they operate unchecked. Many of the public interest groups formed since the 1960s were deliberately created as a check against the influence of corporate lobbies. Environmental groups are an example. Although some of them, including the Sierra Club, have been in existence for the better part of a century or longer, many of them are more recent in origin and work to shield the environment from threats posed by business activity. Activist government has also brought the group system into closer balance; the government's poverty programs have spawned groups that act to protect these programs. Nevertheless, nearly two-thirds of all lobbying groups in Washington are business-related. The interest-group system is biased toward America's economically oriented groups, particularly its corporations.

The group system is also slanted toward the interests of upper-middle-class Americans. Studies indicate that individuals of higher socioeconomic status are disproportionately represented among group members and even more so among group leaders. Affluent Americans have the money, communication skills, and savvy to participate effectively in special-interest politics. The poor, minorities, women, and the young are greatly underrepresented in the group system. A lack of organization does not ensure an interest's failure, just as the existence of organization does not guarantee success. However, organized interests are obviously in a better position to promote their views.

The business and class bias of the group system is especially significant because the most highly organized interests are, in a sense, those least in need of political clout. Corporations and affluent citizens already control the largest share of society's resources. The group system magnifies their power.

A Madisonian Dilemma

James Madison recognized the dilemma inherent in group activity. Although he worried that interest groups would have too much political control, he argued in *Federalist* No. 10 that a free society is obliged to permit the advocacy of self-interest. Unless people can promote the separate opinions that stem from differences in their needs, values, and possessions, they do not have liberty.

interest-group liberalism
The tendency of public officials to support the policy demands of self-interested groups (as opposed to judging policy demands according to whether they serve a larger conception of "the public interest").

Political Culture

Interest Groups, Liberty, and Equality

Rarely is the tension between liberty and equality more evident than in the activities of interest groups. "Liberty is to faction what air is to fire," wrote James Madison in *Federalist* No. 10. Madison was lamenting the self-interested behavior of factions or, as they are called today, interest groups. Yet Madison recognized that the only way to suppress this behavior was to destroy the liberty that allows people to organize.

Interest groups tend to strengthen the already powerful and thus contribute to political inequality. As political scientist E. E. Schattschneider said, the group system "sings with a strong upper-class bias."

Numerous efforts have been made to harness the power of groups without infringing on Americans' rights of free expression, assembly, and petition. Laws have been enacted that require lobbyists to register, report their lobbying expenditures, and identify the issues on which they are working. Other laws restrict group contributions to candidates for public office. Yet nothing in the end seems to be all that effective in harnessing the self-interested actions of groups.

Do you think there is an answer to "Madison's dilemma"? Or are the excesses of group politics simply one of the costs of living in a free society?

Ironically, Madison's constitutional solution to the problem of factions has become part of the problem. The American system of checks and balances, with a separation of powers at its core, was designed primarily to prevent a majority faction from trampling on the interests of smaller groups. Indeed, throughout the nation's history, majorities have been frustrated in their efforts to exercise power by America's elaborate system of divided government, which makes it relatively easy for a determined minority to block action by the majority.

This same system, however, makes it relatively easy for minority factions—or, as they are called today, special-interest groups—to gain government support. If they can get the backing of even a small number of well-placed policymakers, as in the case of iron triangles, they are likely to get many of the benefits they seek. Because of the system's division of power, they have numerous points at which to exert influence. Often, they need only to find an ally in one place, whether that be a congressional committee or an executive agency or a federal court, to get at least some of what they seek. And once they obtain a government benefit, it is likely to persist. Benefits are hard to eliminate because concerted action by the executive branch and both houses of Congress is usually required. If a group has strong support in even a single institution, it usually can fend off attempts to terminate its benefits. Such support ordinarily is easy to acquire, because the group has resources—information, money, and votes—that officeholders want. (Chapters 11 and 13 discuss further the issue of interest-group power.)

Summary

A political interest group is composed of a set of individuals organized to promote a shared political concern. Most interest groups owe their existence to factors other than politics. These groups form for economic reasons, such as the pursuit of profit, and maintain themselves by making profits (in the case of corporations) or by providing their members with private goods, such as jobs and wages. Economic groups include corporations, trade associations, labor unions, farm organizations, and professional associations. Collectively, economic groups are by far the largest set of organized interests. The group system tends to favor interests that are already economically and socially advantaged.

Citizens' groups do not have the same organizational advantages as economic groups. They depend on voluntary contributions from potential members, who may lack interest and resources or who recognize that they will get the collective good from a group's activity even if they do not participate (the free-rider problem). Citizens' groups include public-interest, single-issue, and ideological groups. Their numbers have increased dramatically since the 1960s despite their organizational problems.

Organized interests seek influence largely by lobbying public officials and contributing to election campaigns. Using an inside strategy, lobbyists develop direct contacts with legislators, government bureaucrats, and members of the judiciary in order to persuade them to accept the group's perspective on policy. Groups also use an outside strategy, seeking to mobilize public support for their goals. This strategy relies in part on grassroots lobbying—encouraging group members and the public to communicate their policy views to officials. Outside lobbying also includes efforts to elect officeholders who will support group aims. Through political action committees (PACs), organized groups now provide nearly a third of all contributions received by congressional candidates.

The policies that emerge from the group system bring benefits to many of society's interests, and in some instances these benefits also serve the collective interest. But when groups can essentially dictate policies, the common good is not served. The majority's interest is subordinated to group (minority) interests. In most instances, the minority consists of individuals who already enjoy a substantial share of society's benefits.

STUDY CORNER

Key Terms

citizens' (noneconomic) groups (*p. 251*)
collective (public) goods (*p. 251*)
economic groups (*p. 247*)
free-rider problem (*p. 252*)
grassroots lobbying (*p. 261*)
inside lobbying (*p. 256*)

interest group (*p. 246*)
interest-group liberalism (*p. 267*)
iron triangle (*p. 258*)
issue network (*p. 259*)
lobbying (*p. 255*)
material incentive (*p. 249*)

outside lobbying (*p. 260*)
political action committee
  (PAC) (*p. 262*)
private (individual) goods (*p. 248*)
purposive incentive (*p. 251*)
single-issue politics (*p. 246*)

Self-Test

1. Interest groups tend to do all but which one of the following?
   a. try to influence the political process.
   b. pursue members' shared policy goals.
   c. contribute support to candidates and officials who favor their goals.
   d. change policy positions in order to win elections.

2. If an interest group wants to influence policy decisions at the implementation stage, efforts should be directed primarily toward the:
   a. judiciary.
   b. bureaucracy.
   c. White House.
   d. Congress.

3. Interest-group politics is aligned with the political theory of:
   a. elitism.
   b. inclusion.
   c. communitarianism.
   d. pluralism.

4. When lobbyists supply policymakers with information and indications of group strength to persuade them to adopt the group's perspective, the activity is called:
   a. arm twisting.
   b. wrangling.
   c. purposive persuasion.
   d. inside lobbying.

5. Economic interest groups have an advantage over other groups chiefly because of their:
   a. ability to muster large numbers of members.
   b. emphasis on training people to run for Congress.
   c. devotion to promoting the broad public interest.
   d. access to financial resources.

6. Political action committees:
   a. raise money for election campaigns by soliciting voluntary contributions from members or employees.
   b. have declined rapidly in number since the passage of the recent campaign finance reform legislation.
   c. are under no restrictions regarding the amount of money each PAC can give to the election campaign of a single candidate for federal office.
   d. are not an important source of funds in congressional campaigns.

7. The free-rider problem results when individuals can benefit from the activities of an interest group even if they do not contribute to the group's activities. (T/F)

8. The key tactic of outside lobbying activity is to seek influence through public pressure. (T/F)

9. Interest-group liberalism is a term used by Theodore Lowi to express the tendency of interest-group politics to favor narrow interests over majority interests. (T/F)

10. Affluent citizens and business groups dominate the interest-group system. (T/F)

Critical Thinking

Why are there so many more organized interests in the United States than elsewhere? Why are so many of these groups organized around economic interests—particularly business interests?

Suggested Readings

Berry, Jeffrey M. *The New Liberalism: The Rising Power of Citizen Groups*. Washington, D.C.: Brookings Institution Press, 2000. An exploration of the influence that citizen groups exercise.

Browne, William P. *Cultivating Congress: Constituents, Issues, and Interests in Agriculture Policymaking*. Lawrence: University Press of Kansas, 1995. An analysis of the limits of "iron triangles" as a description of congressional policymaking.

Grossman, Gene M., and Elhanan Helpman. *Interest Groups and Trade Policy*. Princeton, N.J.: Princeton University Press, 2002. An examination of the impact of groups' campaign and lobbying activities on trade policy.

Herrnson, Paul S., Ronald G. Shaiko, and Clyde Wilcox, eds. *The Interest Group Connection: Electioneering, Lobbying, and Policymaking in Washington*, 2nd ed. Washington, D.C.: CQ Press, 2004. Essays and commentaries on groups and officials and the linkages between them.

Lowery, David, and Holly Brasher. *Organized Interests and American Government*. New York: McGraw-Hill, 2004. An overview of interest-group politics.

Lowi, Theodore J. *The End of Liberalism*, 2d ed. New York: Norton, 1979. A thorough critique of interest groups' influence on American politics.

Olson, Mancur, Jr. *The Logic of Collective Action*, rev. ed. Cambridge, Mass.: Harvard University Press, 1971. A pioneering analysis of why some interests are more fully and easily organized than others.

Rozell, Mark J., and Clyde Wilcox. *Interest Groups in American Campaigns*. Washington, D.C.: Congressional Quarterly Press, 1999. An assessment of the election role of interest groups.

List of Websites

http://www.fec.gov/
The Federal Election Commission site; it offers information on elections, voting, campaign finance, parties, and PACs. It also includes a citizens' guide to campaign contributions.

http://www.pirg.org/
The Public Interest Research Group (PIRG) site; PIRG has chapters on many college campuses, and the site provides state-by-state policy and other information.

http://www.sierraclub.org/
The Sierra Club, one of the oldest environmental protection interest groups, promotes conservation; its website provides information on its activities.

http://www.townhall.com/
The website of the American Conservative Union (ACU); it includes policy and political information and has a lively chat room.

Participate!

Consider contributing to a citizens' interest group. Such groups depend on members' donations for operating funds. Citizens' groups cover the political spectrum from right to left and touch on nearly every conceivable public issue. You will not have difficulty locating a group through the Internet that has policy goals consistent with your beliefs and values.

Extra Credit

For up-to-the-minute *New York Times* articles, interactive simulations, graphics, study tools, and more links and quizzes, visit the text's Online Learning Center at www.mhhe.com/pattersontad8.

(Self-Test Answers: 1. d 2. b 3. d 4. d 5. d 6. a 7. T 8. T 9. T 10. T)

The News Media:
Communicating Political Images

Chapter Outline

Historical Development: From Partisanship to Objective Journalism

The Politics of America's News Media

Newspapers
Broadcast News
Cable Television
The Internet

The News Media as Link: Roles the Press Can and Cannot Perform Well

The Signaling Role
The Common-Carrier Role
The Watchdog Role
The Public-Representative Role

Organizing the Public in the Media Age

CHAPTER 10

> The press in America . . . determines what people will think and talk
> about—an authority that in other nations is reserved for tyrants,
> priests, parties, and mandarins.
>
> —*Theodore H. White*[1]

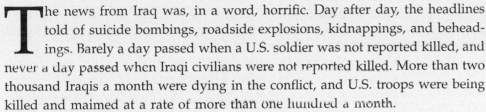

The news from Iraq was, in a word, horrific. Day after day, the headlines told of suicide bombings, roadside explosions, kidnappings, and beheadings. Barely a day passed when a U.S. soldier was not reported killed, and never a day passed when Iraqi civilians were not reported killed. More than two thousand Iraqis a month were dying in the conflict, and U.S. troops were being killed and maimed at a rate of more than one hundred a month.

Yet the situation in Iraq was not all blood and violence. Iraqi soldiers and police were being trained and equipped, schools were being built and opened, roadways were being fixed and extended, and basic services were being restored and expanded. The United States was spending billions of dollars a month on the rebuilding of Iraq, a point that Bush administration officials made repeatedly at press briefings. Nevertheless, the news from Iraq only occasionally addressed the reconstruction effort. The news from Iraq was about the fighting and dying.

Although the news has been compared to a mirror held up to society, it is instead a highly selective portrayal of reality. The **news** is mainly an account of obtruding events, particularly those that are *timely* (new or unfolding developments rather than old or static ones), *dramatic* (striking developments rather than commonplace ones), and *compelling* (developments that arouse people's emotions).[2] These tendencies have their origin in a number of factors, not the least of which is that the news organizations seek to make a profit, which leads them to prefer news stories that will attract and hold an audience. Thus, compared with the fighting in Iraq, the reconstruction effort was less newsworthy. It was a gradual process that did not lend itself to vivid storytelling in the way that the fighting did. The fighting was also the easier story for journalists to tell. It fit with the news audience's preconception of war—war is about killing, not rebuilding.

News organizations and journalists are referred to collectively as the **press** or the **news media.** The press includes broadcast networks (such as ABC and NPR), cable networks (such as CNN and Fox), newspapers (such as the *Chicago Tribune* and *Dallas Morning News*), news magazines (such as *Time* and *Newsweek*), and Internet sites that provide news and commentary (such as Instapundit and the Drudge Report). The U.S. news system has been undergoing substantial changes. For decades, the news system was virtually controlled by local daily newspapers and broadcast television. They are still the dominant players but,

news
The news media's version of reality, usually with an emphasis on timely, dramatic, and compelling events and developments.

press (news media)
Those print and broadcast organizations that are in the news-reporting business.

273

U.S. journalists covering the war in Iraq. Most of the news coverage has focused on the fighting in Iraq, as opposed to the rebuilding of that country. This focus is consistent with what journalists regard as the most newsworthy aspects of war.

during the past quarter century, they have lost audience and influence to cable news, talk radio, and Internet sites, a point that will be addressed later in the chapter.

The news media hold a privileged position in the United States. In many democracies, the press operates under substantial legal constraints. In Great Britain, for example, the news media are barred from reporting on subjects that have been designated "official secrets" by the government, and tough libel laws inhibit them from publishing weakly substantiated claims that could damage a person's reputation. U.S. libel laws, on the other hand, favor the press (see Chapter 4). It is almost impossible for a public official to meet the U.S. legal standard for a libel judgment—that a news organization was both false in its accusations and knowingly or recklessly careless in its effort to reach the truth. The American press is also free to cover politics in nearly any way it chooses. The press is protected from government by the First Amendment, which the Supreme Court has interpreted as a broad grant of immunity (see Chapter 4). Government is prohibited, for example, from blocking the publication of national-security information unless government can prove to a court that its release would pose a serious danger to the United States.

The American press also has another thing going for it: an ongoing daily relationship with the public. Like the political party and the interest group, the press is a political intermediary in the sense that it links citizens with their government. Yet the press alone has daily contact with a broad cross-section of the American people.

This chapter examines the news media's role in the American political system. The chapter will argue that the press is a key intermediary between Americans and their leaders, but it will also argue that the press is a different kind of intermediary than either the political party or the interest group.[3] They seek to represent particular interests in society. News organizations with a few exceptions do not aim to represent particular interests. They do claim, with some justification, to serve the public interest by keeping people informed about public affairs. Yet their news coverage is driven as much by a need to produce stories that will hold people's attention as it is by the goal of keeping them informed. The news media need an audience in order to sell advertising, which finances their operations. News coverage tends to focus on sensational events that will catch people's attention rather than on ordinary developments that can be far more important in people's lives. This chapter will explore this and other aspects of the press and its news coverage. The main ideas presented in the chapter are these:

- *The American press initially was tied to the nation's political party system (the partisan press) but gradually developed an independent position (the objective press). In the process, the news shifted from a political orientation, which emphasizes political values and ideas, to a journalistic orientation, which stresses newsworthy information and events.*

- *In recent years, traditional news organizations have faced increased competition for people's attention. Cable and the Internet have contributed to a fragmenting of the news audience and, to a lesser extent, to the rise of opinionated journalism.*

- *In fulfilling their responsibility to the public, the news media play several roles— the signaling role (the press brings relevant events and problems into public view), the common-carrier role (the press serves as a channel through which leaders and citizens can communicate), the watchdog role (the press scrutinizes official behavior for evidence of deceitful, careless, or corrupt acts), and the representative role (the press promotes particular interests and values). The American press is better equipped to handle the first three of these roles than the last one.*

HISTORICAL DEVELOPMENT: FROM PARTISANSHIP TO OBJECTIVE JOURNALISM

Democracy thrives on a free flow of information. Communication enables a free people to keep in touch with one another and with officials, a fact not lost on America's early leaders. Alexander Hamilton persuaded John Fenno to start a newspaper, the *Gazette of the United States,* in order to publicize the policies of George Washington's administration. In return, Hamilton, as secretary of the treasury, granted Treasury Department printing contracts to Fenno's paper. Hamilton's political adversary, Thomas Jefferson, dismissed the *Gazette*'s reporting as "pure Toryism" and convinced Philip Freneau to start the *National Gazette* as an opposition paper. Jefferson was secretary of state and gave Freneau the authority to print State Department documents.

Early newspapers were printed on flat presses, a process that limited production and kept the cost of each copy beyond the reach of ordinary citizens—many of whom were illiterate anyway. Leading papers such as the *Gazette of the United States* had fewer than fifteen hundred subscribers and could not have survived without party support. Not surprisingly, the "news" they printed was a form of party propaganda.[4] In this era of the **partisan press,** publishers openly backed one party or the other.[5]

Technological innovation in the early decades of the 1800s helped bring about the gradual decline of the partisan newspaper. Invention of the telegraph provided editors with timely information on events outside the local area, which led them to substitute news stories for opinion commentary.[6] Creation of the hand-cranked rotary press was equally important because it enabled publishers to print their newspapers more cheaply and quickly. The *New York Sun* was the first paper to pass on the benefit of higher-speed printing to subscribers by reducing the price of a daily copy from six cents to a penny. The *Sun*'s circulation rose from one thousand to ten thousand in less than a year.[7] Increased circulation meant increased advertising revenue, which helped to free newspapers of their dependence on government printing contracts.

By the late nineteenth century, helped along by the invention of newsprint and power-driven presses, many American newspapers were printing fifty thousand or more copies a day, and their large circulations enabled them to charge high prices for advertising. The period marked the height of newspapers' power and the low point in their sense of public responsibility. A new style of reporting— "yellow journalism"—had emerged as a way of boosting circulation.[8] It was "a shrieking, gaudy, sensation-loving, devil-may-care kind of journalism which lured the reader by any possible means."[9] A circulation battle between William Randolph Hearst's *New York Journal* and Joseph Pulitzer's *New York World* is believed to have contributed to the outbreak of the Spanish-American War through sensational (and largely inaccurate) reports on the cruelty of Spanish rule in Cuba. A young Frederic Remington (who later became a noted painter and sculptor), working as a news artist for Hearst, planned to return home because

partisan press

Newspapers and other communication media that openly support a political party and whose news in significant part follows the party line.

Yellow journalism was characterized by its sensationalism. William Randolph Hearst's *New York Journal* whipped up public support for a war in Cuba against Spain through inflammatory reporting on the sinking of the battleship *Maine* in Havana Harbor in 1898.

Cuba appeared calm and safe, but Hearst cabled back: "Please remain. You furnish the pictures and I'll furnish the war."[10]

The excesses of yellow journalism led some publishers to consider ways of reporting the news more responsibly. One step was to separate the newspaper's advertising department from its news department, thus reducing the influence of advertisers on news content. A second development was a new model of reporting called **objective journalism,** which was based on the reporting of "facts" rather than opinions and was "fair" in that it presented both sides of partisan debate.[11]

A chief advocate of this new form of journalism was Adolph Ochs of the *New York Times*. Ochs bought the *Times* in 1896, when its circulation was 9,000; four years later, its readership had grown to 82,000. Ochs told his reporters that he "wanted as little partisanship as possible . . . as few judgments as possible."[12] The *Times* gradually acquired a reputation as the country's best newspaper. Objective reporting was also promoted through newly formed journalism schools. Among the first of these professional schools were those at Columbia University and the University of Missouri.

objective journalism
A model of news reporting that is based on the communication of "facts" rather than opinions and that is "fair" in that it presents all sides of partisan debate.

THE POLITICS OF AMERICA'S NEWS MEDIA

Objective journalism is still the defining norm of American reporting, but it does not dictate what news organizations and journalists must do, nor does it govern all news mediums equally. Its influence varies, as the following discussion will indicate.

Newspapers

The United States has roughly fifteen hundred daily newspapers. Most of them side with one political party or the other on their editorial and opinion pages. However, it is usually difficult to tell from their news pages which party they back editorially. In their news coverage, they tend to highlight the same national stories each day and, if a high-ranking public official gets caught in a scandal or makes a policy mistake, they will play it up, whether that official is a Republican or a Democrat. As developments in Iraq soured, President George W. Bush received reams of bad press in nearly all U.S. newspapers. During low periods of his presidency, Bill Clinton received the same rough treatment from reporters.

Even the editorial and opinion pages of most American newspapers are not completely one-sided. They usually include at least one columnist of opposing opinion among their regular columnists. Since the early 1970s, for example, the *New York Times* has always had at least one conservative columnist—William Safire, a Nixon speechwriter, was the first—to serve as a counterweight to its liberal columnists.

Of course, America's newspapers differ in their reporting styles. Some thrive on sensationalism. The top story on the front page of the staid *Denver Post*, for example, will compete for readers' attention with a half-dozen other front-page stories. That same story in the tabloid *Rocky Mountain News* might be splashed across the entire front page. Such differences in approach, however, do not disguise the fact that most news organizations, regardless of their editorial position, tell their various audiences the same top stories each day. In U.S. newspapers, there is not a Republican version of the news and an opposing Democratic version.

The evenhandedness of America's newspapers is buttressed by their dependence on wire services.[13] Most U.S. newspapers lack the resources to gather substantial amounts of news outside their own localities and thus depend for their national coverage on the wire services, particularly the Associated Press (AP).

The AP has three hundred full-time reporters stationed throughout the country and the world to gather news stories, which are then relayed to subscribing newspapers. More than 95 percent of the nation's dailies (as well as most broadcast stations) subscribe to the AP, which, because it serves the full range of American newspapers, studiously avoids partisanship.

A few U.S. newspapers—including the *New York Times, Wall Street Journal, Los Angeles Times, Washington Post,* and *Chicago Tribune*—have large enough reporting staffs to generate their own national coverage. Although these papers, too, usually cover the same top stories in pretty much the same way each day, they diverge in their feature, follow-up, and investigative reporting. It is here that their partisan leanings are most evident. For example, the *New York Times* devotes more news space to America's social problems than does the *Wall Street Journal,* an editorially conservative paper. Conversely, the *Journal* devotes more space to the problems of corporate America than does the *Times.* Nevertheless, differences of this kind are a far cry from the robust partisanship that characterized nineteenth-century American newspapers or that is found today in some European newspapers (see How the United States Compares).

Broadcast News

Until the early twentieth century, the print media were the only form of mass communication. Within a few decades, however, hundreds of radio stations were broadcasting throughout the nation. Broadcasting was the first truly *national* mass medium. Newspapers had local readerships, whereas radio could reach millions of Americans across the country simultaneously.

Television followed radio, and by the late 1950s more than 90 percent of American homes had a television set. However, television newscasts of the 1950s were brief, lasting no more than fifteen minutes, and relied on news gathered by other organizations, particularly the Associated Press and other wire services. In the early 1960s, the three commercial networks—CBS, NBC, and ABC expanded their evening newscasts to thirty minutes, and their audience ratings increased. Simultaneously, they increased the size of their news divisions, and television soon became the leading medium of national politics.

Today, television provides a twenty-four-hour forum of political news and information. The creation of the Cable News Network (CNN) and C-SPAN in the late 1970s brought Americans round-the-clock public-affairs coverage. Television talk shows, such as *The O'Reilly Factor* and *Larry King Live,* have broadened the range of choices available to politically interested viewers. A parallel development is the emergence of radio talk shows. Nearly a sixth of the American public claim to listen regularly to politically oriented radio talk shows, most of which have a conservative slant. The best known of the radio talk-show hosts is Rush Limbaugh, whose blistering attacks on Democratic politicians and policies has gained him a devoted following among conservative listeners.

Radio Talk Shows

Partisan programs like Limbaugh's talk show were virtually nonexistent until two decades ago. In 1934, Congress passed the Communications Act, which regulated broadcasting and created the Federal Communications Commission (FCC) to oversee the regulation. Broadcasters are required to be licensed by the federal government, and, because the number of available broadcasting frequencies is limited, those few individuals who are awarded a broadcasting license are

How the United States Compares
Partisan Neutrality as a News Value

In the nineteenth century, the United States had a partisan press. Journalists were partisan actors, and news was a blend of reporting and advocacy. Facts and opinions were freely intermixed in news stories. This type of reporting gradually gave way to a model of journalism that emphasizes the "facts" and covers the two major parties more or less equally. American journalists are fairly evenhanded in their daily news reporting. For example, a political scandal, whether it involves a Democrat or a Republican, is a big story for any major U.S. news organization.

European news organizations are less committed to political neutrality. Many European newspapers are aligned with a party, and although they focus on events, their coverage has a partisan component. In Great Britain, for example, the *Daily Telegraph* often serves as a voice of the Conservative party, while the *Guardian* favors the liberals. Broadcasters in most European countries are politically neutral by law and practice, but there are exceptions, as in the case of French and Italian broadcasters.

The difference between the U.S. and European media is evident in a five-country survey that asked reporters whether they thought journalists should remain neutral in reporting on political parties. Compared with their counterparts in Great Britain, Germany, Sweden, and Italy, U.S. journalists were more likely to believe in partisan neutrality.

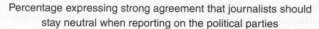

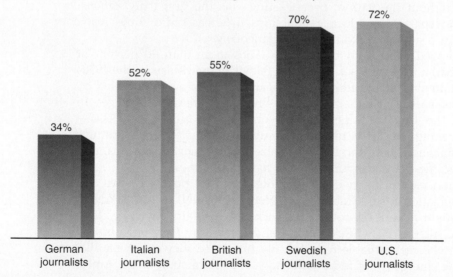

Percentage expressing strong agreement that journalists should stay neutral when reporting on the political parties

German journalists: 34%
Italian journalists: 52%
British journalists: 55%
Swedish journalists: 70%
U.S. journalists: 72%

Source: Thomas E. Patterson, Media and Democracy Project, in progress. Reprinted by permission of the author.

expected to serve the public interest in addition to their own. Section 315 of the Communications Act, for example, imposes on broadcasters an "equal time" restriction, which means that they cannot sell or give air time to a political candidate without offering to sell or give an equal amount of air time to other candidates running for the same office. (Election debates are an exception; broadcasters can televise them even if participation is limited to the Republican and Democratic nominees, excluding third-party candidates.)

Media & Politics

Rush Limbaugh, the King of Talk Radio

In 1967, the teen-age son of a judge and radio station owner did his first radio show under the name of Rusty Sharp. After dropping out of Southeast Missouri State University, he went to Pittsburgh and took another radio job, this time as a disk jockey under the name Jeff Christie. Today, that individual, under his real name, hosts America's biggest political talk radio program, *The Rush Limbaugh Show*.

Broadcasting deregulation in the late 1980s enabled Limbaugh to build an audience for his mix of news headlines and stinging attacks on Democrats. Earlier, a station that aired Limbaugh's show would have had to balance it with an opposing program. With deregulation, station owners could schedule talk shows of their choosing. Limbaugh's program was picked up by hundreds of stations nationwide, and it grew to more than twenty million listeners a week. His syndicated half-hour television show (produced by Republican campaign consultant Roger Ailes, who then went on to head Fox News) was less successful; it folded in 1996 after a four-year run.

The Clintons are Limbaugh's favorite target. As a candidate and as president, Bill Clinton was variously characterized by Limbaugh as a draft-dodger, womanizer, and wimp. When Clinton said Limbaugh was polluting the public debate, Limbaugh shot back: "Oh, dissent and disagreement are not good for the United States of America. We're so sorry Mr. President." Hillary Clinton became his

prime target after beginning her own career in elective politics in 2000. At one point, Limbaugh ridiculed the Clintons' then teen-aged daughter, Chelsea, calling her an ugly child, but backed off when his listeners complained.

Limbaugh's audience dwarfs that of any, and all, of the liberal talk shows. In the top twenty-five radio markets, Limbaugh's show in 2006 had more listeners, in all age groups, than the Al Franken, Ed Schultz, and Jerry Springer shows combined. Limbaugh took particular satisfaction in outdrawing Franken. In 1996, after Limbaugh published his best seller, *See, I Told You So*, Franken wrote a best seller titled *Rush Limbaugh Is a Big Fat Idiot and Other Observations*. (After publication of Franken's book, Limbaugh went on a year-long diet, announcing at the end that he had shed one hundred pounds, a third of his weight.)

Limbaugh's finest hour came in the 1994 midterm elections when the Republicans, for the first time in four decades, won control of the Senate and the House of Representatives. Limbaugh's attacks on President Clinton and his praise for the Republicans' "Contract With America" were regarded as decisive contributions. "Operation Restore Democracy" was Limbaugh's label for his months-long radio campaign to get GOP candidates elected. Conservatives turned out to vote in unusually high numbers, prompting journalists to call Limbaugh the Republicans' "electronic precinct captain."

Until the late 1980s, broadcasters also were bound by the Fairness Doctrine, which required their news programming to treat fairly all sides of the debate on controversial public issues. In practice, this meant that the objective-reporting model practiced voluntarily by the newspapers was also the model that broadcasters by law were required to practice. The Fairness Doctrine was rescinded in the late 1980s on grounds that cable television, which is not subject to broadcasting regulation because it does not use public airways, had expanded the number of television news channels available to viewers.

Broadcasters no longer had to balance their public affairs programming. They previously had to air a liberal talk show if they aired a conservative one. Free of this constraint, a number of local radio stations switched from playing music to airing political talk shows. They soon discovered that talk radio appealed mostly to conservative listeners. Limbaugh was among the conservative talk-show hosts who quickly gained a wide following. Limbaugh's show alone was being heard by twenty million listeners a week by the early 1990s. The only radio competitor with a comparably sized audience was National Public Radio (NPR) with its mix of news and talk shows. NPR's reporting model is nonpartisan; it balances the time given to Republican and Democratic leaders. NPR's talk shows, however, typically address topics that have greater appeal to liberal listeners, who make up a disproportionate share of its audience.

Franklin D. Roosevelt was the first president to make effective use of broadcasting to communicate directly with the American people. He broadcast a series of fireside chats that reached millions of listeners across the country. Radio was eclipsed by television as a political medium during the 1950s.

Television Network News

Television production is vastly more expensive than radio production, which limits the ability of local television stations to produce anything other than local news. As a consequence, broadcast production of televised national and international news is almost totally dominated by the three major networks—ABC, CBS, and NBC. For news of the nation and the world, America's nearly nine hundred local television stations depend on video transmissions fed to them by the three broadcast networks.

In their heyday, the ABC, CBS, and NBC nightly national newscasts were the envy of the news industry. Each evening at the dinner hour, these newscasts attracted 80 percent of television viewers. They now attract about 40 percent of the viewers—more than twenty million people each night. These viewers divide somewhat evenly between the three networks; thus, each network even today has a daily audience much larger than that of any other U.S. news organization.

The three networks attract audiences of roughly equal size in part because their newscasts are similar in content. Ten minutes of these half-hour newscasts are taken up by advertising. With so little time for news, the day's top stories tend to dominate the newscasts of all three networks. In addition, network correspondents cover the same beats, rely on the same sources, and employ the same techniques. Long practice at television reporting leads network correspondents to develop a common understanding of what makes for a good story.[14] After filming a congressional hearing, for example, network correspondents are likely to agree on what was most newsworthy about it—often a testy exchange between a witness and one of the committee members. Similarly, the live "stand-ups" that the networks' White House correspondents do each evening from the lawn outside the Oval Office are nearly indistinguishable from each other. Rarely are they much more than a review of the day's major development at the White House.

Despite the emphasis on top stories, the networks are frequently accused of partisan bias, usually by conservatives. In a best-selling recent book, a former

Broadcast news dominated television until the advent of cable. Today, the ABC, CBS, and NBC newscasts compete for viewers with those of Fox News, CNN, and MSNBC. Cable news organizations have also developed new models of journalism. For example, CNN specializes in live coverage of events while Fox News pursues a politically conservative news agenda. Shown here is Vice President Dick Cheney appearing on Fox News.

network correspondent, Bernard Goldberg, accused the networks of having a liberal agenda.[15] Such allegations are not completely baseless. Until recently, for example, the concerns of evangelical Christians were rarely a subject of broadcast news except in the context of divisive issues like creationism and abortion. There is also the fact that most broadcast news journalists, as well as most journalists generally, lean Democratic in their personal beliefs.[16]

Content analysis studies, however, have not revealed a large and consistent liberal bias on the evening newscasts. In fact, the television-age president who was found to have received the worst coverage is a Democrat, Bill Clinton. The Center for Media and Public Affairs found that Clinton's negative coverage exceeded his positive coverage in every quarter of every year of his two-term presidency—a dubious record that no president before or since has equaled.[17] Instead of a partisan bias, scholars have highlighted a different tendency—the networks' preference for the negative. Michael Robinson concluded that broadcast journalists have a "negativist, contentious" outlook on politics.[18] The networks' preference for "bad news" can be seen, for example, in their coverage of presidential candidates. Virtually every nominee since the 1980s has received mostly negative coverage during the course of the campaign. "Bad news" has characterized network coverage of Democratic and Republican nominees alike. In any given election, one of the nominees gets more favorable coverage than the other, but not by much and not with any partisan regularity. Compared with his Democratic rivals, for example, George W. Bush received more favorable coverage during the 2000 presidential campaign but less favorable coverage during the 2004 campaign.[19]

Objective journalism dictates that the opposing parties be treated equally, not that they be treated well. There is no rule of journalism that limits criticism, and the networks take it to the extreme. Network coverage of the Democratic-controlled Congress of 1993–94 was nearly 70 percent negative. It was derided as a "do-nothing" Congress. When Republicans had control of Congress in

1995–96, network coverage was again nearly 70 percent negative. That particular Congress was criticized for trying to do too much.[20] Such evidence suggests that the consistent bias of the networks is not a liberal as opposed to a conservative bias, but a pronounced tendency to report what might be wrong with politics and politicians as opposed to what might be right.

The networks' unbridled negativity helps to explain why they are widely perceived as biased. Research has found that negative news is perceived differently by those who support and those who oppose the official being criticized. Opponents tend to see the criticism as valid while supporters tend to see it as unjustified. This reaction is heightened when people see an attack on television as opposed to reading about it in a newspaper.[21] It is not surprising, then, that Democrats during the Clinton presidency tended to think the networks favored the Republicans while Republicans during the two Bush presidencies tended to think the networks favored the Democrats. Such findings do not mean that the networks are unbiased, but they do indicate that some of the perceived bias is in the eye of the beholder.

Cable Television

Because cable television is transmitted by wire rather than through the air waves, it was not governed by the Fairness Doctrine. Thus, cable news organizations have always been free to cover politics in a manner of their choosing. Nevertheless, when the media mogul Ted Turner started CNN in 1980, he chose to abide by the Fairness Doctrine, instructing his correspondents to pursue a path of partisan neutrality. He sought to make his mark by delivering the news around the clock and through live on-the-scene coverage. Turner's marketing idea worked. CNN's audience and reputation ballooned whenever a major event occurred. In 1991, for example, Americans were riveted to CNN's live coverage from Baghdad as the first American bombs of the Persian Gulf War began falling on that city.

When the billionaire media owner Rupert Murdoch started Fox News in 1996, he had a different marketing model in mind. Murdoch hired a Republican consultant, Roger Ailes, to run Fox News, instructing him to devise a format that would appeal to political conservatives. Ailes hired a number of conservative talk-show hosts, including Bill O'Reilly, and developed a news division that, though it concentrates on top stories, reports them through a conservative lens. During the period of the 2004 presidential debates, for example, Fox did not ignore the post-debate polls that indicated most Americans thought John Kerry had outdebated George W. Bush. However, according to a study by the Project for Excellence in Journalism, Fox News did fewer debate stories than the other networks and was the only network during the debate period to cover Bush more favorably than Kerry.[22]

Murdoch's market strategy has paid off. Fox News is the most highly rated cable news network, a position it has held for more than five years. The Fox News audience at a given time averages about one million viewers compared with CNN's seven hundred thousand viewers. Moreover, as Murdoch anticipated, Fox's audience is heavily Republican (see Figure 10–1). Compared with Democrats, Republicans are more than twice as likely to be regular viewers of Fox News. CNN's audience, which was rather evenly balanced between Republicans and Democrats until Fox News came along, now includes a disproportionate number of Democrats, largely because of the exodus of Republican viewers to Fox. The third-rated cable news network, MSNBC, is closer to CNN than Fox News both in its audience and in its news practices.

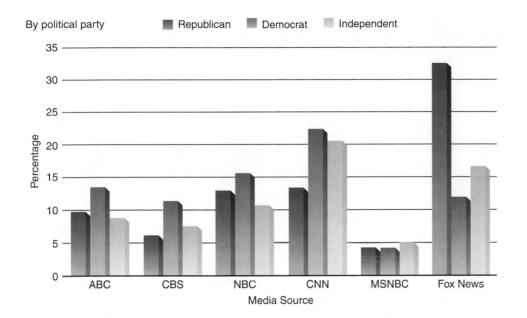

By political party   ■ Republican   ■ Democrat   □ Independent

Figure 10–1

Television Campaign News Source, by Party Identification
As indicated by where people said they got most of their news about the 2004 presidential election campaign, Fox News is far and away the preferred choice of Republican voters.
Source: The Pew Research Center for the People & the Press report, September 16, 2004.

Traditional journalists are critical of Fox News, claiming that partisanship should play no part in political reporting. Their view, while defensible from a professional perspective, has no basis in law, in audience preference, or in history. Objective reporting is a professional code, not a legal one. Moreover, judged by Fox's success in attracting Republicans, some Americans prefer news that has a partisan slant. Finally, Fox News *is* part of an age-old journalism tradition, although not the one dominant at the moment in the United States. Partisan journalism was once the mainstay of the American press and is still widely practiced in Europe. It is also a type of journalism that is found with some frequency on the Internet, the medium to which we now turn.

The Internet

Although the First Amendment protects each individual's right to press freedom, in practice the right has been reserved for a tiny few. Journalist A. J. Liebling wrote that freedom of the press belongs to those with the money to own a broadcast station or newspaper.[23] Even a small broadcast station or daily newspaper costs millions to buy; larger ones are worth hundreds of millions.

Access to the Internet is no substitute for owning a newspaper or a television station, but it does provide ordinary citizens with an opportunity to exercise their free-press rights. By creating a website, the citizen can post news and information about public affairs, harangue officials, argue for public policies, and mobilize the support of others. The Internet has reduced the barriers to public communication to a level not seen since colonial days, when pamphlets, some of them hand written, were the primary medium of politics. The Internet has also been a boon to political organizers. During the 2004 presidential campaign, Vermont governor Howard Dean used his opposition to the Iraq war and the power of the Internet to go from relative obscurity to a strong early presence in the race for the Democratic presidential nomination. Dean's campaign raised more than $50 million, mostly through Internet contributions of less than $100. The Internet was also the medium for one of the most successful citizen-led efforts in history—a global movement that succeeded in getting nearly one hundred countries to sign an international treaty banning the use of land mines. Its organizer, Jody Williams, was awarded the Nobel Peace Prize.

The Internet has opened up the media system, allowing citizens, groups, and leaders to communicate more powerfully than was possible during the not-so-distant era when news organizations almost totally controlled the instruments of mass communication. Shown here is a web page of Rock the Vote, an organization dedicated to helping young adults to register and vote.

LEADERS

JODY WILLIAMS

(1950–   )

In 1992, Jody Williams launched a global Internet campaign that aimed to get countries around the world to ban the use of antipersonnel land mines. Each year, more than ten thousand civilians—mostly peasant farmers and children—are killed when they accidentally detonate an abandoned land mine while working or playing in areas that once were war zones. Working out of her home, Williams relentlessly sought allies in her effort to convince countries not to place additional antipersonnel mines and to remove those already in place. Williams gained a key supporter when the Canadian government joined the effort. In 1997, she achieved her goal when an international treaty banning antipersonnel mines was signed in Ottawa, Canada, by scores of countries. For her efforts, she received the Nobel Peace Prize, which was awarded jointly to her and to the International Campaign to Ban Landmines (ICBL), a coalition of nongovernmental organizations (NGOs) that she headed. Since then, Williams has tried to convince nonsignatory countries, including the United States, to sign the treaty. Before dedicating herself to land-mine eradication, Williams worked for a decade on humanitarian issues affecting Central America, including medical and food relief.

When it comes to news, however, the Internet's significance is harder to assess. Because the cost of entry is low, there are literally thousands of websites where news is regularly posted and examined. However, Internet news is characterized by what analysts call "the long tail." When news-based websites are arrayed by the number of visitors to each site, there are a few heavily visited sites on one end and many lightly visited sites on the other end—"the long tail." As it happens, most of the heavily visited sites are those of the traditional media, including CNN.com, newyorktimes.com, and MSNBC.com. In addition, most of the other heavily visited sites, such as Google News, simply republish news gathered and reported first by the established media. In other words, most Americans who go to the Internet for news are seeing news generated by the same sources they otherwise rely on for news.

Of course, a news outlet's influence is not measured merely by the size of its audience. For example, the *New York Times*, with a daily circulation of roughly a million readers, has been rightly called "the bulletin board" for the network evening newscasts with their combined

Get Involved!

Communicate

Before the Internet opened new channels of communication, freedom of the press, which is granted by the First Amendment to all Americans, was enjoyed for the most part only by the very few who owned or worked in the news media. With the Internet, the opportunity for citizen communication, though not unlimited, is greater than at any time in the nation's history.

Take advantage of the opportunity. Meetup.com is one of literally thousands of Internet sites where you can participate in discussion forums about politics and issues.

A more ambitious alternative is to start your own web log. Blogging is time consuming but allows you to create an agenda of news, information, and opinion—an activity previously reserved for newspaper editors and broadcast producers.

Either of these options will enable you to make your voice heard and also help you to hone your citizenship skills—the ability to communicate, to defend your own views, and to learn what others think.

audience of twenty-five million viewers. When network executives gather in the morning to plan the evening newscast, one of the first things they do is review the stories in that day's *New York Times*. In a similar vein, Internet-based news outlets have broken some important stories, most famously the Drudge Report's revelation of President Clinton's affair with a White House intern, Monica Lewinsky.

The Drudge Report was started in 1995 by Matt Drudge and for a time was the most popular Internet-specific news site. Its visitors now number fewer than those of several other websites including Instapundit, Daily Kos, and Boing Boing. Known as "blogs," such sites are often closer in kind to political talk-radio than to news pages or newscasts in that they freely mix news and opinion. Unlike most of the successful talk radio programs, however, most of the successful blogs have a liberal bias. (The Drudge Report is an exception.) Liberal blogs tend to be less narrowly partisan, however, than conservative talk shows. In their criticism of the war in Iraq, for example, liberal blogs are nearly as scathing in their denunciation of Democratic leaders who support the war as they are of the Bush administration's pursuit of the war.

Many liberal and conservative blogs have one thing in common. Neither has much respect for the mainstream press, which they accuse of everything from bias to irrelevance. Many traditional journalists have a similarly low opinion of blogs, saying that because they do little original reporting, they ought to be regarded as nothing more than places where opinions are aired.

The Internet is in its early years as a news medium, so it is hazardous to guess whether initial tendencies will continue. But with Americans increasingly looking to the Internet for information, including news, it is safe to say that the Internet's importance will continue to grow. Another prediction also seems safe. Economics will drive much of what happens on the Internet, just as it helped shape the development of older media. News is expensive to produce, and reputations take time to develop, which is a reason why traditional media have been successful in attracting visitors to their web sites. A major question is whether relative newcomers to the news business will be able to overcome the huge head start that established media got on the Internet because they are known brands with a substantial capacity for original reporting.

THE NEWS MEDIA AS LINK: ROLES THE PRESS CAN AND CANNOT PERFORM WELL

When the objective model of reporting came to dominate American news coverage, the relationship between the press and the public was fundamentally altered. The nineteenth-century partisan press gave its readers clear-cut cues as to how to evaluate political issues and leaders. In the presidential election campaign of 1896, the *San Francisco Call* devoted 1,075 column-inches of photographs to the Republican ticket of McKinley-Hobart and only 11 inches to the Democrats, Bryan and Sewell.[24] Many European newspapers still function in this way, guiding their readers by applying partisan or ideological values to current events. The *Daily Telegraph,* for example, is an unofficial but fiercely loyal mouthpiece of Britain's Conservative party.

The modern American press operates by a different standard. Partisanship is accepted on talk shows and editorial pages but is discouraged in news reporting. Journalists are expected to concentrate on describing and explaining events and developments. The media thus are very different from political parties and interest groups, the other major links between the public and its leaders. Parties and groups exist to promote political positions. The media are driven by the search for interesting and important stories.

This distinction provides a basis for determining what roles the media can and cannot be expected to fulfill. The press is adept at fulfilling those public responsibilities that are compatible with journalistic values: the signaling role, the common-carrier role, and the watchdog role. The media are less successful in their attempts to perform a fourth and more politically oriented role: public representative.

The Signaling Role

signaling (signaler) role
The accepted responsibility of the media to alert the public to important developments as soon as possible after they happen or are discovered.

As journalists see it, their responsibilities include a **signaling role.** They seek to alert the public to important developments as soon as possible after they happen—a state visit to Washington by a foreign leader, a bill that has just been passed by Congress, a change in the nation's unemployment level, a terrorist bombing in a foreign capital.

The U.S. media are well equipped to play a signaling role (also known as the signaler role). They are poised to converge on any major news event anywhere in the nation and nearly anywhere in the world. For instance, as the United States prepared to attack Iraq in 2003, hundreds of U.S. journalists descended on that part of the world. Many of them were "embedded" in U.S. combat units. When the attack began, they traveled into battle with the troops. Their news stories kept Americans abreast of the war and the subsequent struggle to form a stable government in Iraq.

The media are particularly well suited to signal developments from Washington. More than half of all national news coverage emanates from the nation's capital, most of it from the White House and Congress. Altogether, more than ten thousand people in Washington work in the news business. The key players are the leading correspondents of the television networks and the major newspapers, the heads of the Washington news bureaus, and a few top editors.

agenda setting
The power of the media through news coverage to focus the public's attention and concern on particular events, problems, issues, personalities, and so on.

The press, in its capacity as signaler, has the power to focus the public's attention. The term **agenda setting** has been used to describe the media's ability

States in the Nation

In the News, or Out?

Most of the news that reaches Americans no matter where they might live originates with a handful of news outlets, such as NBC News. This coverage, however, concentrates on events in a few places. The map shows the relative frequency with which each of the fifty states was mentioned on NBC News during a recent one-year period.

Q: Why do some states get more coverage than other states?

A: The heavily covered states are the more populous ones, which increases the likelihood that a newsworthy event will occur. In NBC's case, coverage is also heavier in states where one of its news bureaus is located. NBC has bureaus in New York, Washington, Los Angeles, Dallas, Atlanta, Chicago, and Boston.

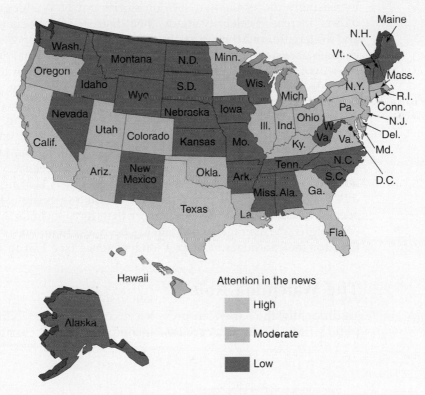

Source: Data compiled by author from Nexis.

to influence what is on people's minds.[25] By covering the same events, problems, issues, and leaders—simply by giving them space or time in the news—the media place them on the public agenda. The press, as Bernard Cohen notes, "may not be successful much of the time in telling people what to think, but it is stunningly successful in telling them what to think about."[26] This influence is most obvious in situations such as the U.S. war in Iraq, a development that continues to occupy Americans' attention.

The Common-Carrier Role

common-carrier role
The media's function as an open channel through which political leaders can communicate with the public.

The press also plays a **common-carrier role** in that it provides political leaders a channel through which to communicate with the public. The importance of this role to officials and citizens alike is obvious. Citizens cannot very well support or oppose a leader's plans and actions if they do not know about them, and leaders need news coverage if they are to get the public's attention. Indeed, national news is mainly about the actions of political leaders and institutions, as reflected in the hundreds of reporters who station themselves regularly at the Capitol and the White House.

Officials try to get the most favorable news coverage they can. For example, the White House Press Office and the White House Office of Communications try to shape information in a way favorable to the president. Sometimes they succeed in placing their spin (that is, the president's interpretation) on the media's coverage of events.

Even though the president and Congress can expect wide coverage, the press increasingly places its own spin on stories out of Washington. Because of journalists' increased celebrity status, their distrust of politicians ever since Vietnam and Watergate, and their greater need to draw the audience's attention, they have become accustomed not only to covering what newsmakers say but to having their own say as well. In fact, the news today, at least on television, is as much journalist-centered as it is newsmaker-centered. For every minute the presidential candidates spoke on the network newscasts during recent presidential campaigns, for example, the journalists who were covering them spoke for six minutes.[27] Most of the time a candidate could be seen on television with his mouth moving, his voice could not be heard; it was the journalist's voice that was audible. At these times, it was the journalist's version of the day's events—not the candidate's—that the viewing audience was hearing. In the 1960s, a candidate's sound bite (the length of time within a television story that a candidate speaks without interruption) was more than forty seconds on average.[28] In recent campaigns, the average sound bite has been less than ten seconds, barely enough time for the candidate to utter a long sentence (see Figure 10–2).

The Watchdog Role

Traditionally, the American press has accepted responsibility for protecting the public from deceitful, careless, incompetent, and corrupt officials. In this

Figure 10–2

The Shrinking Sound Bite of Television Campaign Coverage
The average length of time that presidential candidates are shown speaking without interruption on broadcast television newscasts has declined sharply in recent elections.
Source: Adapted from Daniel C. Hallin, "Sound Bite News: Television Coverage of Elections 1968–1988." *Journal of Communication* 42 (Spring 1992): 6. The 1992–2004 data are from the Center for Media and Public Affairs.

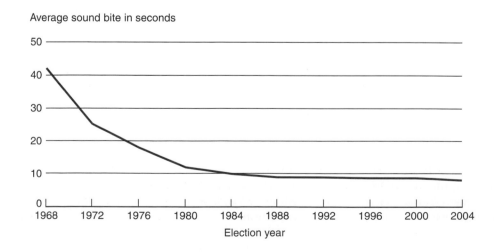

Average sound bite in seconds

Election year

watchdog role, the press stands ready to expose any official who violates accepted legal, ethical, or performance standards.

The press was acting in its watchdog role in 2004 when it reported the abuse of prisoners by U.S. soldiers in Iraq. Graphic photos of naked Iraqi prisoners forced into humiliating sexual poses and acts shocked the nation and the world. Allegations of abuse in U.S. military prisons in Iraq had been circulating for months, but publication of the photos brought the issue into the open. High-ranking U.S. officials, including Secretary of Defense Donald Rumsfeld, had learned of the photos months earlier but had not shared their discovery with President Bush or Congress. After the photos were aired on television and published in newspapers, Congress launched hearings to discover why U.S. troops had violated laws governing the treatment of war prisoners and who should be held responsible.

Acting in its watchdog role, the press in recent decades has vigorously pursued allegations of official wrongdoing. The Watergate scandal is the most renowned example. Led by the *Washington Post*, the press uncovered evidence that high-ranking officials in the Nixon administration had lied about their role in the burglary of the Democratic National Committee's headquarters and the subsequent cover-up. President Richard Nixon was forced to resign, as was his attorney general, John Mitchell. The press also exposed illegal government activity (the Iran-Contra connection) during the Reagan presidency; illicit personal behavior (the Monica Lewinsky scandal) during the Clinton presidency; and unauthorized wiretapping (the NSA flap) during the George W. Bush presidency. These examples indicate that the press, as watchdog, is a vital part of the American system of checks on those who hold positions of power.

There is an inherent tension between the watchdog role and the common-carrier role. The watchdog role demands that the journalist maintain a skeptical view of government and keep it at a distance. The common-carrier role requires the journalist to maintain close ties with government officials. In the period before Watergate, the common-carrier role was clearly the dominant orientation. It perhaps still is, but journalists have become increasingly critical of political leaders and institutions.

The press's watchdog role is especially controversial when issues of national security are involved. In 1970, the *New York Times* published the so-called Pentagon Papers—classified documents that revealed the government had deceived the public by claiming that the war in Vietnam was going well when in fact it knew the war was going badly. The Nixon administration tried to block the publication but was overruled by the Supreme Court (see Chapter 4). After the *Times* published the story, the Nixon administration had the option of charging the *Times* with transmitting classified information but decided that to do so would only compound an embarrassing situation. The *Times* found itself enmeshed in a similar controversy in late 2005 when it revealed that President George W. Bush, without judicial authorization, had ordered National Security Agency (NSA) wiretapping of communication originating in the United States and connecting to parties overseas. The Bush White House claimed that the story reported in the *Times* had damaged the U.S. government's ability to discover in advance whether terrorist groups were planning attacks on the United States. However, the *Times'* story put the White House on the defensive because a 1978 law expressly prohibits the type of surveillance that NSA was conducting unless authorized by a judge. Even some congressional Republicans viewed the Bush wiretaps as illegal.

watchdog role
The accepted responsibility of the media to protect the public from deceitful, careless, incompetent, and corrupt officials by standing ready to expose any official who violates accepted legal, ethical, or performance standards.

WWW.MHHE.COM/PATTERSONTAD8

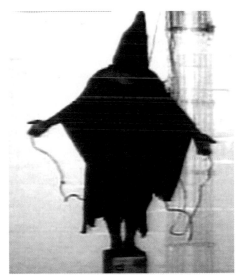

The publication of photos showing the abuse of Iraqi prisoners by U.S. soldiers undermined the U.S. government's claim that allegations about prisoner abuse were exaggerated. The press was acting in its watchdog role when it published the photos and reported on conditions in U.S. military prisons in Iraq. The news coverage led to a congressional investigation.

Political Culture

Liberty, Self-Government, and a Free Press

In democracies, press freedom is seen as a necessary condition of liberty and of self-government. Information that can help people freely decide their policies and leaders flows through the media. Nevertheless, news organizations do not have license to say anything they please. Press freedom in every democracy is balanced against other rights and interests. In some democracies, for example, the press is prohibited from reporting crime in a way that would jeopardize the fair-trial rights of the criminally accused.

The United States has one of the freest media in the world. The U.S. government has limited power to block the press from reporting information that could damage national security. The principle of "no prior restraint" holds that government cannot stop a publication or broadcast program unless it can convince a court that grave harm to the nation would result from release of the information. The U.S. press is also protected, as explained in Chapter 4, by an imposing legal standard for libel. It is nearly impossible for a U.S. official to win a libel suit against a newspaper, magazine, or broadcast organization even in situations

where his or her reputation has been destroyed by false allegations.

By comparison, Britain's government has the power to prevent news organizations from reporting on national security issues. For example, there was a long period during which British journalists were prohibited from reporting stories on the Irish separatist issue that presented the conflict from the viewpoint of separatists who advocated violence. British libel law also differs from American law when it comes to libel. Although libel judgments in Britain typically result in relatively small monetary awards, the standard of proof in British courts is such that a person whose reputation has been unfairly tarnished by a news reporter or organization has a reasonable chance of winning a libel judgment.

What arguments would you make for and against each model? Would it surprise you to learn that in opinion surveys a sizable minority of Americans believe the press has too much freedom? What's your view on the amount of freedom afforded the U.S. media?

The *Times* had less backing in 2006 when it revealed that President Bush had ordered the secret monitoring of international banking transactions as a means of detecting the flow of money to terrorist organizations. This surveillance program appeared to be within the law, and the White House immediately struck back at the *Times*. Bush called its revelation "disgraceful," saying further: "We're at war with a bunch of people who want to hurt the United States of America, and for people to leak that program, and for a newspaper to publish it, does great harm to the United States of America." Vice President Dick Cheney added: "Some of the press, in particular the *New York Times*, have made the job of defending against further terrorist attacks more difficult by insisting on publishing detailed information about vital national security programs." Congressman Peter King called the *Times'* action "treasonous." House Republicans, backed by seventeen Democrats, passed a nonbinding congressional resolution that said the revelation "may have placed the lives of Americans in danger."

The *Times* called its decision to publish the banking story "a close call," saying that it chose to reveal the secret program because it was possibly connected to other programs that were unlawful. It was an argument that resonated with other news organizations. Journalists subscribe to the view that the American people are best served when the press errs on the side of making public what the government is doing, even if that opens the press to attack from those in power. As CNN correspondent Bob Franken put it: "We historically are not supposed to be popular, and it's almost our role to be the bearer of bad news."[29]

The Public-Representative Role

Traditionally, the **public-representative role**—that of spokesperson for and advocate of the public—has belonged to political leaders, political institutions, and political organizations. Today, however, many reporters believe they also have a mandate to represent the public. "[Our] chief duty," said a prominent newscaster, "is to put before the nation its unfinished business."[30]

Although the press has to some degree always acted as a stand-in for the people, the desire of journalists to play the role of public advocate increased significantly after the 1960s. As journalists' status rose, they became more assertive, a tendency sharpened by the trend toward interpretive reporting. Vietnam and Watergate also contributed to the change by convincing many journalists that their judgments were superior to those of political leaders. James Reston of the *New York Times* said of Vietnam, "Maybe the historians will agree that the reporters and cameras were decisive in the end. They brought the issue of the war to the people, before the Congress and the courts, and forced the withdrawal of American power from Vietnam."[31]

Nevertheless, there are at least two basic reasons for concluding that journalists are not nearly as well suited as political leaders to the role of public representative. First, the news media are not subject to the level of public accountability required of a public representative. Political institutions are made responsible to the public by a formal mechanism of accountability—elections. The vote gives officeholders a reason to act in the majority's interest, and it offers citizens an opportunity to boot from office anyone they feel has failed them. Thousands of elected officials have lost their jobs this way. The public has no comparable hold over the press. Journalists are neither chosen by nor removable by the people.

A second obstacle to journalists' attempts to play the role of public representative is that representation requires a point of view. Politics is essentially the mobilization of bias—that is, it involves the representation of particular values and interests. Political parties and interest groups, as explained in Chapters 8 and 9, exist to represent particular interests in society. But what political interests do the media represent? A few news outlets, such as Fox News, consciously promote a point of view, but the vast majority do not. As a television executive

public-representative role

A role whereby the media attempt to act as the public's representatives.

Whenever a high-ranking official becomes enmeshed in an uncomfortable episode, a media feeding frenzy erupts that momentarily disrupts the ordinary flow of life in Washington. One such episode was the accidental shooting of a hunting companion by Vice President Dick Cheney. For a week, it was the nation's top story, eclipsing even what was happening in Iraq. Shown here is attorney Harry Wittington meeting with members of the press outside the Corpus Christi hospital where he was taken after being shot by Cheney.

Debating the Issues

Should Reporters Be Protected Against Having to Reveal Sources of National Secrets?

Journalists in the nation's capital would have trouble doing their jobs if they were barred from reporting information that is given to them "off the record." Insiders who disagree with what other officials are doing or who are aware of wrongdoing are often reluctant to make that information public through the press unless their identity is shielded. In news stories, they are identified simply as "high-ranking government officials" or "anonymous sources." But what if the information they leak is classified? The leaking of classified information is a federal crime, although the reporting of it ordinarily is not. In cases where the government believes national security has been seriously harmed by a leak, should the reporter involved be required to reveal the source of the information? This question has featured prominently in public debate about two recent controversies involving the *New York Times*, whose reporters were involved in leaks surrounding the outing of a CIA covert agent (Valerie Plame) and the

revelation that President George W. Bush without judicial approval had authorized the wiretapping of overseas messages originating in the United States as part of a top-secret terrorist surveillance program. In each case, the government sought to force *Times* reporters to divulge their source. Each time, the *Times* resisted, saying that if reporters reveal a confidential source they will not in the future be able to get sources to give them sensitive information the public needs access to.

The following statements are part of the testimony heard by the Senate Judiciary Committee when it was considering the desirability of a law that, in some circumstances, would protect journalists against having to reveal their sources. One statement is an argument in favor of such a law, while the other is in opposition to it. Where do you stand on this issue? Where would you draw the line in terms of when, if ever, journalists should be protected against having to reveal the identity of a source of classified information?

Yes

The Justice Department has told you this bill is bad policy and a threat to law enforcement and national security. The implication is that when the press tells its readers, as the *Inquirer* recently did, for example—that nearby refineries are vulnerable to attack and accidents that would imperil hundreds of thousands, it is threatening national security. The threat comes not from inadequate protection of these sites; the Justice Department seems to reason, but from the use of confidential sources to reveal these types of stories. In fact, NOT publishing this material threatens national security. . . . Some of the information needed to tell such stories does indeed come from confidential sources—sources that would not speak out, leak documents, and point the way to change if it were not for the assurance of the *Inquirer*'s journalists that they will be protected from reprisals. . . . Last year, in the United States, more than two dozen reporters have been subpoenaed or questioned about their confidential sources in federal court cases. Six journalists from across the country were jailed or fined for

refusing to disclose a source. That number may seem small to you, but consider that action against these six individuals sent doubt into the minds and spines of whistleblowers and journalists alike. . . . In sum, we can all—each of us—understand why a promise of confidentiality is crucial to disclosure. . . . What is most important here is that the wrongdoing was exposed. Wrongdoers were punished. . . . I could give you a hundred examples. But I don't need to. You read about them every day in the newspaper. You see them on TV and hear about these promises on the radio—but you may not know that what you are hearing about is the promise of confidentiality that one journalist made to a man or woman who had a story to tell. When we hear, as a nation, about Watergate, or the fact that tobacco companies worked to make cigarettes more addictive, or that Enron was a financial nightmare, we are hearing about promises made and kept—about a pact with our forefathers that this nation would respect a free press.

—*Anne Gordon, Managing Editor,* Philadelphia Inquirer

No

Even in cases involving harm to the national security, [the proposed bill would provide to the Government] information about media sources only if it were necessary to prevent imminent and actual harm to the national security. If harm to the national security already had been done, the Government

would not be able to obtain the information. This may make it difficult, if not impossible, to obtain vital information on how national security information was disclosed and to whom it was disclosed. For instance, in the case of the analysis and assessment of damage to national security, where information revealed through unauthorized disclosure originated can be important in determining what has been put at risk. Not all material "leaked" in a given unauthorized disclosure may be published, but nonetheless [it] may be shared with additional parties, further compounding the damage to national security. Damage also is not always temporally confined to a given point in time; sometimes repeated disclosures magnify the impact by serving as corroboration, especially if they come from different sources. . . . [The bill has] such an expansive definition of "covered person" [i.e., journalist] [that it] could unintentionally offer a safe haven for criminals. As drafted, the definition invites criminals to cloak their activities under the guise of a "covered person," so as to avoid investigation by the Federal government. The overbroad definition of a "covered person" could be read to include any person or corporate entity whose employees or corporate subsidiaries publish a book, newspaper, or magazine; operate a radio or television broadcast station; or operate a news or wire service. Additionally, the definition arguably could include any person who sets up an Internet "blog.". . . More generally, the [Justice] Department does not believe that legislation is necessary because there is no evidence that the subpoena power is being abused by the Department in this context. The Department prides itself on its record of objectivity in reviewing press subpoenas, and any legislation that would impair the discretion of the Attorney General to issue press subpoenas—or to exercise any other investigative options in the exercise of the President's constitutional powers—is unwarranted.

—*Chuck Rosenberg, U.S. Attorney on behalf of the Justice Department*

once said, journalists cover news "from nobody's point of view."[32] What he was saying, in effect, was that journalists do not consistently represent the political concerns of any segment of society. They respond to news opportunities, not to political interests. Above all, they prize good stories.[33]

The 2004 criminal trials of Michael Jackson, Kobe Bryant, Scott Peterson, and Martha Stewart are prime examples. These trials, and the hoopla surrounding them, received far more news coverage in 2004 than health care, unemployment, drug abuse, education, and every other domestic policy problem.

Underlying the press's obsession with the dramatic story is its quest for profits. The bottom line, rather than the public interest, increasingly drives news coverage. Audience competition has intensified with the spread of cable and satellite television, and the news has become increasingly sensational. During the 2004 campaign, as the public was expressing concern over Iraq and the economy, the press spent weeks on end rehashing events of thirty years earlier: whether George W. Bush had fulfilled his National Guard duties and whether the heroic portrayal of John Kerry's Vietnam service was fully accurate.

Even when the media cover policy developments, the reporting can be distorted by the quest for higher ratings. The U.S. invasion of Iraq in March of 2003, for example, was accompanied by audience-pleasing reports from the battlefield, while other important aspects were underplayed, including reactions elsewhere in the world to the invasion. This balance affected Americans' perceptions of the war. Many Americans wrongly believed, for example, that the U.S. invasion had the support of most other countries.[34]

The relentless search for attention-getting stories weakens the press's ability to provide citizens with a clear understanding of what is broadly at issue in politics. Journalist Walter Lippmann put it plainly when he said:

> The press is no substitute for [political] institutions. It is like the beam of a searchlight that moves restlessly about, bringing one episode and then another out of darkness into vision. Men cannot do the work of the world by this light alone. They cannot govern society by episodes, incidents, and interruptions.[35]

ORGANIZING THE PUBLIC IN THE MEDIA AGE

Lippmann's point was not that news organizations are somehow inferior to political organizations but that each has a different role and responsibility in society. Democracy cannot function properly unless the news media carry out their signaling, common-carrier, and watchdog roles effectively. Citizens must have access to timely and uncensored news about public affairs. However, the media cannot also be expected to do the job of political institutions.

As previous chapters have emphasized, the challenge of democracy lies in organizing the public so that people can act together effectively. The news media merely appear to meet this challenge. The fact that millions of people each day receive the same news about their government does not mold them into an organized community. The news creates a pseudo-community: citizens who feel they are part of a functioning whole until they try to act on their news awareness. The futility of media-centered democracy was dramatized in the movie *Network* when its central character, a television anchorman, became enraged at the nation's political leadership and urged his viewers to go to their windows and yell "I'm mad as hell and I'm not going to take it anymore!" Citizens heeded his instructions, but the main effect was to raise the network's ratings. It was not clear what officials in Washington were expected to do about several million people leaning out their windows and shouting a vague slogan. The film vividly illustrated the fact that the news can raise public consciousness as a prelude to action but cannot itself organize the public to take action, a task for which other organizations—political parties and interest groups—are much better suited.

Whether the press in the future will be in a better or worse position to give order and direction to public opinion is unclear. By certain indicators, the American media are in trouble. Newspaper circulations are declining, as are television news audiences. As their profits have shrunk, news organizations have cut back on their news budgets and hyped their coverage—actions that

The audience reach of the U.S. news media is truly substantial. More than twenty million Americans each evening watch a network newscast, and about twice that number read a daily paper. However, the news audience is shrinking, which has caused alarm among those in the news industry and those who believe that attention to the news is critical to an informed citizenry.

serve to reduce the quality of news. At the same time, however, cable television and the Internet have increased the number of news outlets, including some like blogs and Fox News that bring politics more clearly into the news. An uncertain factor in the equation is the public's appetite for news, whatever its form. Today's young adults evince less interest in news than their predecessors, a disturbing development regardless of the news model—objective or partisan—that one prefers. For if citizens cannot be prompted to follow public affairs, the nation will one day face the larger challenge of how to maintain self-government when most citizens know little to nothing about the policy problems and choices they face.

Summary

 Self-Test www.mhhe.com/pattersontad8

In the nation's first century, the press was allied closely with the political parties and helped the parties mobilize public opinion. Gradually the press freed itself from this partisan relationship and developed a form of reporting, known as objective journalism, that emphasizes the fair and accurate reporting of newsworthy developments. The foundation of modern American news rests on the presentation and evaluation of significant events, not on the advocacy of partisan ideas. The nation's news organizations do not differ greatly in their daily reporting; broadcast stations and newspapers throughout the country emphasize many of the same events, issues, and personalities, following the lead of the major broadcast networks, a few elite newspapers, and the wire services.

The press performs four basic roles in a free society. First, in their signaling role, journalists communicate information to the public about events and problems that they consider important, relevant, and therefore newsworthy. Second, the press serves as a common carrier in that it provides political leaders with a channel for addressing the public. Third, the press acts as a public protector, or watchdog, by exposing deceitful, careless, or corrupt officials. The American media can and, to a significant degree, do perform these roles adequately.

The press is less well suited, however, to the fourth role it plays, that of public representative. This role requires a consistent political viewpoint and public accountability, neither of which the press possesses. The media are not a substitute for effective political institutions. The press's strength lies ultimately in its capacity to inform the public, not in its attempt to serve as the public's representative.

STUDY CORNER

Key Terms

agenda setting (*p. 286*)
common-carrier role (*p. 288*)
news (*p. 273*)

objective journalism (*p. 276*)
partisan press (*p. 275*)
press (news media) (*p. 273*)

public-representative
  role (*p. 291*)
signaling (signaler) role (*p. 286*)
watchdog role (*p. 289*)

Self-Test

1. Recent trends in news reporting include:
   a. presenting liberal rather than conservative columnists.
   b. combining the activities of the news and advertising departments.
   c. a more aggressive style of reporting.
   d. an increase in the readership of newspaper reporting.

2. When the media are playing the role of watchdog, they are primarily:
   a. protecting the public from deceitful, careless, incompetent, or corrupt public officials.
   b. conveying objective information about an event and minimizing reporting bias.
   c. trying to get their audience more interested in issues of animal rights.
   d. trying to help their favorite political party at the expense of the other.

3. The news is said to provide a selective depiction of reality because it:
   a. emphasizes dramatic events rather than the slow and steady social, economic, and political developments that typically have a larger impact on the nation.
   b. is biased in favor of a Democratic point of view.
   c. emphasizes the daily lives of ordinary Americans rather than the actions of public officials.
   d. places more emphasis on international affairs than these developments deserve.

4. Broadcasting revolutionized the American media because it:

a. was the first truly national mass medium.
b. opened a direct, instantaneous channel between a leader and the people.
c. reached millions of people simultaneously.
d. all of the above.

5. The news media have grown more visible and powerful in recent decades and, in the process, have shown that they can do the job of:
   a. political parties.
   b. interest groups.
   c. elected representatives.
   d. none of the above.

6. Desire for profit making and an increased share of the audience market encourage the media to:
   a. prefer dramatic news stories.
   b. keep public policy issues at the top of the news coverage agenda.
   c. shun sensational stories.
   d. provide the public with a clear understanding of what is broadly at issue in politics.

7. Objective journalism is based on the reporting of opinions in preference to "facts." (T/F)

8. The United States' libel laws strongly favor the press. (T/F)

9. Studies reveal that much of the perceived bias in television news is due to the viewers' partisanship as opposed to slanted news coverage. (T/F)

10. Liberals tend to prefer talk radio while conservatives tend to prefer bloggers. (T/F)

Critical Thinking

Why does almost every U.S. news outlet, despite having the freedom to say nearly anything it wants, cover virtually the same national stories in virtually the same way as other news organizations?

Suggested Readings

Bagdikian, Ben H. *The New Media Monopoly*. Boston: Beacon Press, 2004. An examination of the growing power of the press, including tendencies toward monopolies of ownership and news production.

Baum, Matthew. *Soft News Goes to War*. Princeton, N.J.: Princeton University Press, 2003. A study of the impact of soft-news coverage of war.

Hamilton, James T. *All the News That's Fit to Sell*. Princeton, N.J.: Princeton University Press, 2004. A careful study of the economic influences on news content.

Kovach, Bill, and Tom Rosenstiel, *The Elements of Journalism*. New York: Three Rivers Press, 2001. An insightful look at the values of American journalism.

Maltese, John Anthony. *Spin Control: The White House Office of Communications and the Management of Presidential News.*

Chapel Hill: University of North Carolina Press, 1994. An assessment of how presidents attempt to manage news coverage.

Overholser, Geneva, and Kathleen Hall Jamieson. *The Press*. New York: Oxford University Press, 2005. A comprehensive survey of U.S. journalism and news.

Patterson, Thomas E. *Out of Order*. New York: Vintage Books, 1994. An analysis of how election news coverage has changed in recent decades.

Sparrow, Bartholomew H. *Uncertain Guardians*. Baltimore, Md.: Johns Hopkins University Press, 1999. A systematic assessment of the news media's political role and tendencies.

List of Websites

http://www.cmpa.com/
The website for the Center for Media and Public Affairs (CMPA), a nonpartisan organization that analyzes news coverage on a continuing basis, provides analyses of news content that are useful to anyone interested in the media's political coverage.

http://www.drudgereport.com/
The website through which Matt Drudge (The Drudge Report) has challenged the traditional media's control of the news.

http://www.fcc.gov/
The Federal Communications Commission (FCC) website, which provides information on broadcasting regulation and current issues.

http://www.newslink.org/
Provides access to more than a thousand news organizations, including most U.S. daily newspapers.

Participate!

If you are like most citizens, news consumption is the politically related activity that takes up most of your time. And if you are like most citizens, you will spend this time without thinking critically about what you are seeing and hearing. The next time you watch a television newscast or read a newspaper, pay attention to how a story is constructed. Is it framed in terms of conflict? Does it sensationalize the material? Is it framed critically—that is, does it present a negative view of a development, institution, or leader? How else might the same factual information have been presented? Do significant items of information or points of view seem to be missing from the story?

Extra Credit
For up-to-the-minute *New York Times* articles, interactive simulations, graphics, study tools, and more links and quizzes, visit the text's Online Learning Center at www.mhhe.com/pattersontad8.

(Self-Test Answers: 1. c   2. a   3. a   4. d   5. d   6. a   7. F   8. T   9. T   10. F)

PART 3

GOVERNING INSTITUTIONS

American democracy is often described as government by the people. But direct democracy is a practical impossibility in a nation the size of the United States. Americans are governed largely through institutions.

A debate has long raged over the proper relationship between a people and their representatives. One view holds that representatives should follow the expressed opinions of the governed; if they do not, they will promote their own narrow interests. Another view, first elaborated by the English theorist Edmund Burke, holds that representatives should exercise their best judgment in deciding policy; if they listen too closely to those who elected them, they will serve parochial interests rather than the general interests of society.

The governing system of the United States embodies both conceptions of representation. The presidency is a truly national office that, as Chapter 12 will describe, encourages its incumbent to take a national view of issues. On the other hand, Congress, as Chapter 11 will show, is both a national institution and a body subject to powerful local influences.

Americans are also governed through unelected bureaucrats and appointed judges whose decisions, as Chapters 13 and 14 will describe, can in some instances be as far-reaching as those made by the people's elected representatives.

PART THREE OUTLINE

11 Congress: Balancing National Goals and Local Interests 300

12 The Presidency: Leading the Nation 336

13 The Federal Bureaucracy: Administering the Government 372

14 The Federal Judicial System: Applying the Law 402

Congress:
Balancing National Goals and Local Interests

Chapter Outline

Congress as a Career: Election to Congress
Using Incumbency to Stay in Congress
Pitfalls of Incumbency
Safe Incumbency and Representation
Who Are the Winners in Congressional Elections?

Congressional Leadership
Party Leadership in Congress
Committee Chairs: The Seniority Principle
Oligarchy or Democracy: Which Principle Should Govern?

The Committee System
Committee Membership
Committee Jurisdiction

How a Bill Becomes Law
Committee Hearings and Decisions
From Committee to the Floor
Leadership and Floor Action
Conference Committees and the President

Congress's Policymaking Role
The Lawmaking Function of Congress
The Representation Function of Congress
The Oversight Function of Congress

Congress: Too Much Pluralism?

CHAPTER 11

There are two Congresses. . . . The tight-knit complex world of
Capitol Hill is a long way from [the member's district], in perspective
and outlook as well as in miles.

—*Roger Davidson and Walter Oleszek*[1]

In September 2005, Congress faced the question of how to come up with the
billions of dollars that would be required to rebuild New Orleans and the
other Gulf Coast communities devastated by hurricane Katrina.

One option was to trim the $286 billion transportation bill that Congress had
enacted a little more than a month earlier. In it were hundreds of pork-barrel
projects that members of Congress had secured for their home states and districts. One such project was a bridge that came to be known as "the bridge to
nowhere." Nearly the length of the Golden Gate Bridge, it would link the town
of Ketchikan, Alaska (population 9,000) to Gravina Island (population 50). Its
inclusion in the transportation bill was due to the power of its sponsor, Representative Don Young (R-Alaska), who chaired the House Transportation and
Infrastructure Committee that oversaw the legislation. Congressman Young's
project was only the most salient example. Virtually every member of Congress,
House and Senate alike, had put something into the transportation bill that
served constituent interests.

When commentators proposed that the projects be cancelled and the money
spent instead on Katrina relief, the response from Congress was a deafening no.
Almost no member stepped forward to say that his or her pet project should be
shelved. When a reporter asked Representative Young whether he was willing
to cancel the Ketchikan-Gravina bridge, he replied, "They can kiss my ear! That's
the dumbest thing I've ever heard." Young later relented, but the money for the
bridge, rather than being spent in the Gulf Coast area, was shuttled to Alaska
transportation officials to use on other projects in their state.

The story of Katrina and the 2005 transportation bill illustrates the dual
nature of Congress. It is both a lawmaking institution for the country and a
representative assembly for states and districts.[2] Members of Congress have a
duty to serve both the interests of their constituencies and the interests of the
nation as a whole. The nation's needs sometimes come first, but not always.
Senators and representatives depend on the voters back home to win reelection, and they seldom miss an opportunity to serve their interests.[3]

The Framers of the Constitution established Congress as the leading branch
of the national government. Congress is the first institution defined in the Constitution. Moreover, Article I does not simply give to Congress the lawmaking

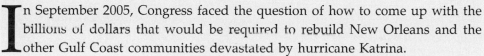

The U.S. Capitol in Washington, D.C., with the House wing in the foreground. The Senate meets in the wing at the right of the central rotunda (under the dome). The offices of the House and Senate party leaders—Speaker, vice president, majority and minority leaders and whips—are located in the Capitol. Other members of Congress have their offices in nearby buildings.

powers of government. It grants Congress, and Congress alone, this power: "All legislative powers herein granted shall be invested in a Congress, which shall consist of a Senate and House of Representatives." Congress is granted the authority even to decide the form and function of the executive departments and the lower courts. No executive agency or lower court can exist except as authorized by Congress.

The positioning of Congress as the first among equals in a system of divided powers reflected the Framers' trust in representative institutions. Congress was to be the branch where the interests of the people, through the House of Representatives, and the interests of the states, through the Senate, found their fullest expression, a rejection of the European monarchical model of executive supremacy. Of course, the Framers had an innate mistrust of political power and were not about to give Congress free rein. The president and the courts were granted significant checks on legislative power. Yet, the government's lawmaking and representation functions, which are in combination the signature functions of a republic, were granted to Congress.

The Framers' vision of how the federal branches would operate has not withstood fully the test of time, as this chapter and subsequent chapters on the presidency and the judiciary will show. Nevertheless, an accounting of the U.S. political institutions starts naturally with Congress. This chapter examines that institution, beginning with congressional election and organization and concluding with congressional policymaking. The points emphasized in the chapter are these:

- *Congressional elections tend to have a strong local orientation and to favor incumbents.* Congressional office provides incumbents with substantial resources (free publicity, staff, and legislative influence) that give them (particularly House members) a major advantage in election campaigns. However, incumbency also has some liabilities that contribute to turnover in congressional membership.

- *Leadership in Congress is provided by party leaders, including the Speaker of the House and the Senate majority leader.* Party leaders are in a more powerful position today than a few decades ago because the party caucuses have become more cohesive.

- *The work of Congress is done mainly through its committees and subcommittees, each of which has its separate leadership and policy jurisdiction.* The committee system of Congress allows a broad sharing of power and leadership, which serves the power and reelection needs of Congress's members but fragments the institution.

- *Congress lacks the direction and organization required to provide consistent leadership on major national policies, but it is well organized to handle policies of relatively narrow scope.* At times, Congress takes the lead on broad national issues, but ordinarily it does not do so.

- *Congress's policymaking role is based on three major functions: lawmaking, representation, and oversight.*

CONGRESS AS A CAREER: ELECTION TO CONGRESS

In the nation's first century, service in Congress was not a career for most of its members. Before 1900, at least a third of the seats in Congress changed hands at each election. Most members left voluntarily. Because travel was slow and arduous, serving in the nation's capital meant spending months away from one's family. Moreover, the national government was not the center of power that it is today; many politicians preferred to serve in state capitals.

The modern Congress is a different kind of institution. Most of its members are professional politicians, and a seat in the U.S. Senate or House is as high as most of them can expect to rise in politics. The pay (about $165,000 a year) is reasonably good, and the prestige of their office is substantial, particularly if they serve in the Senate. A lengthy career in Congress is the goal of most of its members.

The chances of sustaining a career in Congress are high. Getting elected to Congress is difficult, but staying there is relatively easy. In recent decades, roughly 95 percent of House incumbents and about 90 percent of Senate incumbents seeking another term have been reelected (see Figure 11–1). These figures slightly overestimate incumbents' success rate. A few incumbents each term retire from Congress rather than face a challenger they fear will beat them. On balance, however, incumbents have a commanding edge over their opponents. Most of them, particularly those in the House, win reelection by a margin of 20 percentage points or higher.

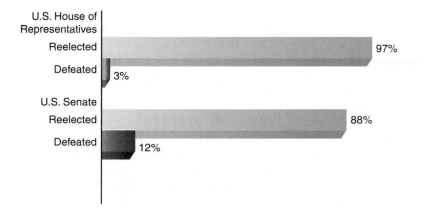

U.S. House of Representatives
Reelected — 97%
Defeated — 3%

U.S. Senate
Reelected — 88%
Defeated — 12%

Figure 11–1

Recent Reelection Rates of House and Senate Incumbents
Congressional incumbents have a very good chance of winning another term, as indicated by the reelection rates of U.S. representatives and senators who sought reelection during the five congressional elections from 1996 to 2004.

Using Incumbency to Stay in Congress

One reason incumbents run so strongly is that many congressional districts and some states are so lopsidedly Democratic or Republican that candidates of the stronger party seldom lose. In Utah and Kansas, for example, residents who identify themselves as Republicans outnumber by a wide margin residents who identify themselves as Democrats. Massachusetts and California are examples of states where the Democrats hold a commanding majority. However, whether their constituency is lopsided or competitive, incumbents have several built-in advantages over their challengers.

The Service Strategy: Taking Care of Constituents

An incumbent promotes his or her reelection prospects by catering to the **constituency:** the body of citizens eligible to vote in the incumbent's state or district. Members of Congress pay attention to constituency opinions when choosing positions on legislation, and they work hard to get their share of **pork-barrel projects** (a term referring to legislation that funds a special project for a particular locale, such as a new highway or hospital). They also respond to their constituents' individual needs, a practice known as the **service strategy.** Whether a constituent is seeking information about a government program, expressing an opinion about pending legislation, or looking for help in obtaining a federal benefit, the representative's staff is ready to assist.

Congressional staffers spend most of their time not on legislative matters but on constituency service and public relations—efforts that pay off on election day.[4] Each House member receives an office allowance of roughly $800,000 a year with which to hire no more than eighteen permanent staff members.[5] Senators receive allowances that range between two and four million dollars a year, depending on the population size of the state they represent. Smaller-state senators tend to have staffs in the range of thirty people while larger-state senators have staffs closer in number to fifty people.[6] Each member of Congress is also permitted several free mailings annually to constituent households, a privilege known as the frank. These mailings, along with press releases and other public relations efforts, help incumbents build name recognition and constituent support—major advantages in their reelection campaigns.

Campaign Fund-Raising: Raking in the Money

Incumbents also have a decided advantage when it comes to raising campaign funds. Congressional elections are expensive because of the high cost of polling, televised advertising, and other modern techniques (see Figure 11–2). Today a successful House campaign in a competitive district costs more than a million dollars. The price of victory in competitive Senate races is much higher, ranging from several million dollars in small states to $20 million or more in larger states. Rarely do incumbents say they had trouble raising enough money to conduct an effective campaign. Challengers, however, usually say their fund-raising fell far short of what they needed.[7] However, challengers, though they still trail incumbents, find it easier to attract funds when they have a chance of winning. In the 2006 midterm election, with political conditions working in their favor, Democratic challengers had a much easier time raising money than they did in the 2002 midterms, when the issues favored the Republicans.

Incumbents' past campaigns and constituent service enable them to develop mailing lists of potential contributors. Individual contributions, most of which are

---

constituency

The individuals who live within the geographical area represented by an elected official. More narrowly, the body of citizens eligible to vote for a particular representative.

pork-barrel projects

Legislation whose tangible benefits are targeted at a particular legislator's constituency.

service strategy

Use of personal staff by members of Congress to perform services for constituents in order to gain their support in future elections.

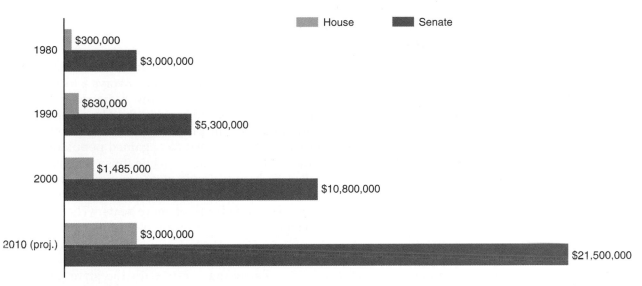

Figure 11–2

Congressional Campaign Expenditures, by Decade
Each decade, the cost of running for congressional office has risen sharply as campaign techniques—television advertising, opinion polling, and so on—have become more elaborate and sophisticated. The increase in spending can be seen from a comparison of the approximate average spending by both candidates per House or Senate seat at ten-year intervals, beginning in 1980. Roughly speaking, the cost has doubled each decade, which is the basis for the 2010 projection.
Source: Federal Election Commission.

$100 or less, account for about 60 percent of all funds raised by congressional candidates and are obtained mainly through fund-raising events and direct-mail solicitation. Incumbents also have an edge with political action committees, or PACs, which are the fund-raising arm of interest groups (see Chapter 9). Most PACs are reluctant to oppose an incumbent unless it is clear that the candidate is vulnerable. More than 85 percent of PAC contributions in recent elections have been given to incumbents; their challengers received less than 15 percent (see Figure 11–3). "Anytime you go against an incumbent, you take a minute and think long and hard about what your rationale is," said Desiree Anderson, director of the Realtors PAC.[8] (A race without an incumbent—called an **open-seat election**—usually brings out a strong candidate from each party and involves heavy spending, especially when the parties are closely matched in the state or district.)

open-seat election
An election in which there is no incumbent in the race.

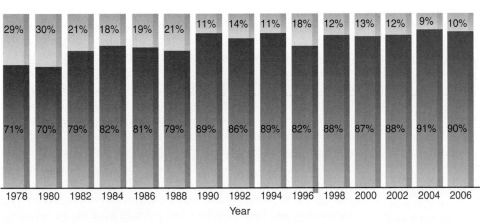

Figure 11–3

Allocation of PAC Contributions Between Incumbents and Challengers in Congressional Races That Included an Incumbent, 1978–2006.
In allocating campaign contributions, PACs favor incumbent members of Congress over their challengers by a wide margin.
Source: Federal Elections Commission. Figures for 2006 based on preliminary data.

Redistricting: Favorable Boundaries for House Incumbents

House members, but not senators, have a final advantage in winning reelection. Because incumbents are hard to unseat, they are always a force to be reckoned with, a fact that is blatantly apparent during redistricting. Every ten years, after each population census, the 435 seats in the House of Representatives are reallocated among the states in proportion to their population. This process is called **reapportionment.** States that have gained population since the last census may acquire additional House seats, while those that have lost population may lose seats. New York and Illinois were among the states that lost one or more House seats as a result of the 2000 census; Arizona and Washington were among the states that gained one or more seats. (The Senate is not affected by population change, because each state has two senators regardless of its size.)

The responsibility for redrawing House election districts after a reapportionment—a process called **redistricting**—rests with the state governments. States are required by law to make their districts as nearly equal in population as possible. There are many ways, however, to divide a state into districts of nearly equal size, and the party in power in the state legislature will draw the new district boundaries in ways that favor candidates of its party—a process called **gerrymandering.** The party's incumbents will be given districts packed with enough of the party's voters to ensure their reelection. What of the other party's incumbents? The safest tactic in this case is to place them in districts with overwhelming numbers of voters of their own party, assuring them of an easy victory but also reducing the number of voters of that party in other districts and placing that party at a disadvantage in these races.

For a small number of House incumbents, redistricting threatens their reelection. When a state loses a congressional seat or seats, there may be fewer seats than there are incumbents who plan to seek another term. In this case, incumbents can end up running against each other. Moreover, the party in control of the state legislature might conclude that a particular incumbent of the opposite party can be beaten and will redraw the boundaries of the incumbent's district to the incumbent's disadvantage. Turnover in House seats typically is higher in the first election after redistricting than in subsequent elections. The newly redrawn districts include some voters who are unfamiliar with the incumbent, diminishing one advantage incumbents ordinarily enjoy over their challengers. By and large, however, incumbents do not suffer greatly from redistricting, and the great majority of them wind up in districts that virtually assure their reelection. After the 2000 census, no more than 50 of the 435 House districts were competitive in the sense that they had a relatively close balance of Republican and Democratic voters. The rest were heavily Republican or heavily Democratic. In the 2002 midterm election, the first election after the 2000 census, four incumbents lost their seats by virtue of losing a primary to another incumbent, and eight incumbents lost in the general election. Most of the other incumbents breezed to victory, many of them running unopposed and many winning 65 percent or more of the vote.

reapportionment

The reallocation of House seats among states after each census as a result of population changes.

redistricting

The process of altering election districts in order to make them as nearly equal in population as possible. Redistricting takes place every ten years, after each population census.

gerrymandering

The process by which the party in power draws election district boundaries in a way that is to the advantage of its candidates.

When Massachusetts was redistricted in 1812, Governor Elbridge Gerry had the lines of one district redrawn in order to ensure that a candidate of his party would be elected. Cartoonist Elkanah Tinsdale, noting that the strangely shaped district resembled a salamander, called it a "Gerry-mander."

Debating the Issues

Should Partisan Gerrymandering Be Abolished?

Elections to the U.S. House of Representatives are uncompetitive and have been made so deliberately through a process of partisan gerrymandering. In redrawing election-district boundaries after the census, the states tend to draw the lines in ways designed to create safe Democratic or Republican districts. Of the 435 House districts today, roughly 400 are safely in the hands of one party. An issue is whether partisan gerrymandering puts election of House members in the hands of the states rather than in the hands of the voters. In *Vieth v. Jubelirer* (2004), the Supreme Court by a 5-4 vote refused to overturn Pennsylvania's redistricting arrangement, saying that, although there might be constitutional limits on partisan redistricting, workable standards for determining fairness in redistricting do not exist. Following are excerpts from two amicus curiae briefs (see Chapter 14) filed in the Pennsylvania case.

Challengers to incumbents and third party voters and candidates are disadvantaged when the two political parties create safe seats for themselves. '[Partisan]' gerrymandering violates the Constitution's Equal Protection Clause by intentionally discriminating against identifiable groups and diminishing those groups' political power. Congressional elections are becoming less competitive every year. . . . Over ninety percent of Americans live in congressional districts that are essentially one-party monopolies. The situation is even worse in some states. For example, in California, 50 out of 53 races were decided by margins of greater than 20 percent. In a related phenomenon, incumbents are now more than ever, nearly guaranteed reelection. . . . This situation is not mere happenstance, but rather the result of carefully orchestrated political gerrymandering—sometimes by one of the major political parties to the disadvantage of the other, and sometimes by the two parties colluding to protect their seats and their incumbents. . . . [E]ven though most states are close to evenly divided between the two major political parties, the vast majority of districts for the U.S. House of Representatives are drawn so as to prevent any real competition.

—*Center for Voting and Democracy*

Fairness in the redistricting process [has evaded] resolution for generations. Scholars cannot even agree on such foundational points as (1) whether there is a problem at all with respect to the ability of Republicans and Democrats to compete for control of the legislature; (2) if there is a problem, whether redistricting is to blame for it; (3) whether creation of safe seats is a bad thing, and, if so, whether it can be avoided; and (4) whether neutral, nonpartisan redistricting standards are either theoretically or practically possible. . . . Justice White [once] cited the work of the late Robert G. Dixon, Jr., "one of the foremost scholars of reapportionment," for the proposition "that there are no neutral lines for legislative districts . . . every line drawn aligns partisans and interest blocs in a particular way different from the alignment that would result from putting the line in some other place." Elsewhere, Professor Dixon rebuked those of his colleagues who aspire to discover universal principles of fair representation: "My own experience tells me that although I may find nonpartisanship in heaven, in the real world, and especially in academia, there are no nonpartisans, although there may be noncombatants."

—*Leadership of the Alabama Senate and House of Representatives*

Pitfalls of Incumbency

Incumbency is not without its risks. In addition to the outside possibility that a House member will be placed in an unfavorable district as a result of reapportionment, potential pitfalls for Senate and House members alike include disruptive issues, personal misconduct, and variation in turnout.

Disruptive Issues

Most elections are not waged in the context of disruptive issues, but when they are, incumbents are at greater risk. When voters are angry about existing political conditions, they are more likely to believe that those in power should be tossed out of office. In the 1994 midterm elections, when the public was upset over the economy and Democratic president Bill Clinton's leadership, more than 10 percent of congressional incumbents—more than twice the usual percentage and virtually all of them Democrats—were defeated. The 2006 midterm election, which was waged in the context of Republican President George W. Bush's leadership of an unpopular war in Iraq, also saw the defeat of more than twice the usual number of incumbents; this time, virtually all of them were Republicans. A prominent victim was Pennsylvania Senator Rick Santorum, who as chair of the Republican Senate Conference, was the third-ranking member of the Republican Senate leadership. Easily reelected six years earlier, Santorum was defeated by Bob Casey, Pennsylvania's state treasurer.

Personal Misconduct

Members of Congress can also fall prey to scandal. Life in Washington can be fast paced, glamorous, and expensive, and some members of Congress get caught up in influence peddling, sex scandals, and other forms of misconduct. Roughly a fourth of House incumbents who lost their bid for reelection in the past two decades were shadowed by ethical questions. "The first thing to being reelected is to stay away from scandal, even minor scandal," says political scientist John Hibbing.[9] Even top congressional leaders are not immune to the effects of scandal, as illustrated by the experience of former House majority leader Tom DeLay. Accused of questionable fund-raising and deal making, DeLay resigned his House seat in 2006. Another House Republican, Florida's Mark Foley, also resigned in 2006. He was discovered to have sent sexually explicit email messages to underage congressional interns. The Foley scandal was particularly damaging to his party because it occurred within weeks of the November election, placing the GOP on the defensive at an inopportune time.

Turnout Variation: The Midterm Election Problem

Typically, the party holding the presidency loses seats in the midterm congressional elections, particularly in the House of Representatives. In only four of the last twenty-five midterm elections (including those in 1998 and 2004) has the president's party gained seats. The 2006 midterm election, when the Republicans lost seats, fit the typical pattern.

   The tendency is attributable partly to the drop-off in turnout that accompanies a midterm election. The electorate in a presidential election is substantially larger than the midterm electorate. People who vote only in the presidential election tend to have weaker party affiliation and to be more responsive to the issues of the moment. These issues are likely to favor one party, which contributes to the success not only of its presidential candidate but also of its congressional candidates. In the midterm election, those who turn out tend to vote along party lines. Accordingly, the congressional candidates of the president's party do not get the boost they enjoyed in the previous election, and House seats are lost as a result.[10] The pattern also can be explained by the tendency of voters to view national politics through their opinion of the president's performance. Presidents usually lose popularity after taking office as a result of tough policy choices or the emergence of new problems. As the president's support declines, so does the voters' inclination to support congressional candidates from the president's party.[11]

Strong Challengers: A Particular Problem for Senators

Incumbents are also vulnerable to strong challengers. Senators are particularly likely to face formidable opponents: after the presidency, the Senate is the highest rung of the political ladder. Governors and House members are frequent challengers for Senate seats, and they have the electoral base, reputation, and experience to compete effectively. Moreover, the U.S. Senate lures wealthy challengers. Maria Cantwell spent $10 million of her own money to defeat Senator Slade Gorton in the state of Washington's Senate race in 2000. Cantwell made her fortune as an executive with RealNetworks, a high-tech company. Running again in 2006, Cantwell found herself in a tight race, partly because her opponent, Mike McGavick, was himself a millionaire executive.

House incumbents have less reason to fear strong challengers. A House seat often is not attractive enough to induce prominent local politicians, such as mayors or state legislators, to risk their political careers in a challenge to an incumbent.[12] This situation leaves the field open to weak opponents with little or no government or political experience. However, the dynamic changes somewhat when the electorate is angry and wants a change in leadership. Then the party not in power has an easier time

LEADERS

JOHN McCAIN

(1936–   )

There have always been a few members of Congress who have stood out in the public's mind. Arizona Senator John McCain is one of those members today. McCain comes from a Navy family. His grandfather and his father both attained the rank of admiral, and McCain followed them into the Navy. Although his career got off to a rocky start—McCain placed near the bottom of his Naval Academy class and crashed his jet into the sea while in training—he served with distinction in Vietnam before his jet was shot down over North Vietnam. After more than five years of imprisonment, McCain was released along with other American POWs and resumed his naval career. He retired in 1980, but his retirement was short-lived. In 1982, he ran successfully for a seat in the U.S. House and four years later won the Senate seat being vacated by the retiring Barry Goldwater, the Republicans' 1964 presidential nominee.

McCain soon gained a reputation as a maverick, backing his party on national defense and abortion but breaking with it frequently over tax and spending policy. In 2000, he campaigned for the Republican presidential nomination. Although he won New Hampshire's opening primary, McCain lacked the financial and organizational support to defeat George W. Bush. In 2004, he was offered the second spot on the Democratic ticket by John Kerry, a close Senate colleague, but chose instead to work for Bush's reelection. McCain makes no secret of his desire to become president and is positioned for a run in 2008. McCain's reputation as a straight-talker has gained him a devoted following. In 2005, to the chagrin of many Republicans, he pressured the Bush administration to accept legislation that would ban the use of torture by U.S. personnel. Exposés of the torture of prisoners held in U.S. custody had outraged McCain, and he rejected the White House's claim that it was not bound by the Geneva Convention in its handling of terrorist suspects. Drawing on his experiences as a POW, during which he himself was tortured, McCain said that America must uphold a higher standard than that of its enemies.

convincing potentially strong challengers to run. In 1994, when the political mood favored the Republicans, the GOP fielded a relatively strong slate of challengers, which contributed to its success in unseating Democratic incumbents. In 2006, the parties' roles were reversed. The Democrats were able to field a relatively strong group of challengers and thereby gain congressional seats.

Safe Incumbency and Representation

Although incumbents can and do lose their reelection bids, they normally win easily. An effect is to reduce Congress's responsiveness to political change. Research indicates that incumbents tend to hold relatively stable policy positions during their time in office.[13] Thus, because few congressional seats normally change hands during an election, Congress normally does not change its direction all that much from election to election. Even when people are dissatisfied with national conditions, congressional elections sometimes produce only a small turnover in congressional membership.

Safe incumbency weakens the public's influence on Congress. Democracy depends on periodic shifts in power between the parties to bring public policy into closer alignment with public opinion. In European democracies, incumbents tend to win or lose depending on their political party's popularity, which can change markedly from one election to the next; shifts in popularity can produce huge shifts in the number of legislative seats controlled by the various parties. In the United States, incumbents often are able to overcome an adverse political climate through constituency service and other advantages of their office. In 1980, for example, the U.S. economy was mired in double-digit inflation and unemployment. A similar situation in a European democracy would result in huge losses for the party in power. In the 1980 U.S. election, however, the Democratic party held onto its majority in the House of Representatives, largely because most Democratic incumbents had enough cushion to win despite the public mood.

It is worth noting that national legislators in other democracies do not have the large personal staffs or the travel and publicity budgets that members of Congress have. Nor do national legislators elsewhere enjoy anywhere near the inside track to campaign funding that members of Congress enjoy.

Who Are the Winners in Congressional Elections?

The Constitution places only a few restrictions on who can be elected to Congress. House members must be at least twenty-five years of age and have been a citizen for at least seven years. For senators, the age and citizenship requirements are thirty years and nine years, respectively. Senators and representatives alike must be residents of the state from which they are elected.

But if the formal restrictions are minimal, the informal limits are substantial. Members of Congress are in no way a microcosm of the people they are elected to serve. For example, although lawyers constitute less than 1 percent of the population, they make up a third of Congress. Attorneys enter politics in large numbers in part because of the central place of law in government and also because seeking elective office is a good way—even if a candidate loses—to build up a law practice. Along with lawyers, professionals such as business executives, educators, bankers, and journalists account for more than 90 percent of congressional membership.[14] Blue-collar workers, clerical employees, and homemakers are seldom elected to Congress. Farmers and ranchers are not as rare; a fair number of House members from rural districts have agricultural backgrounds.

Finally, members of Congress are disproportionately white and male. Minority-group members and women each account for less than 15 percent of the Congress (see Chapter 5). This proportion, however, is twice that of a decade ago.

Safe incumbency is a major obstacle to the election to Congress of more women and minorities.[15] In open-seat races in which they have run, they have won about half the time. However, they have been no more successful than other challengers in dislodging congressional incumbents. In elections to state and local office, where incumbency is less important, women and minority candidates have made greater inroads (see "States in the Nation").

States in the Nation

Women in the State Legislatures

More than one in five state legislators are women, a four-fold increase since 1970. The state of Maryland, with more than 35 percent, has the highest proportion of women legislators. South Carolina, with fewer than 10 percent, has the lowest.

Q: Why do the northeastern and western regions have the most women legislators?

A: The northeastern and western regions have a higher proportion of college-educated women in the work force than do other regions. College-educated women are more likely to run for public office and to actively support those who do run.

Women in state legislature

Less than 20%

20–29.9%

30% or more

Source: Created from data gathered by the Center for the American Woman and Politics (CAWP). National Information Bank on Women in Public Office. Eagleton Institute of Politics, Rutgers University, 2006.

CONGRESSIONAL LEADERSHIP

The way Congress functions is related to the way its members win election. Because each of them has an independent power base in their state or district, members of Congress have substantial independence within the institution. The Speaker of the House and other top leaders in Congress are crucial to its operation, but unlike their counterparts in European legislatures, they cannot force their members to follow their lead. There is an inherent tension in Congress between the institution's need for strong leadership at the top and the individual

TABLE 11–1	Number of Democrats and Republicans in the House of Representatives and Senate, 1987–2008										
	87–88	89–90	91–92	93–94	95–96	97–98	99–00	01–02	03–04	05–06	07–08
House											
Democrats	258*	262*	268*	259	205*	207*	212*	213	208	203	235*
Republicans	177	173	167	176	230	228	223	222	227	232	200
Senate											
Democrats	54*	55*	56*	56	46*	45*	45*	51*	49	45	51*
Republicans	46	45	44	44	54	55	55	49	51	55	49

*Chamber not controlled by the president's party. Independents are included in the total for the party with which they caucused.

members' need to exercise power on behalf of their constituents and to protect their reelection prospects. The result is an institution in which the power of the top leaders rests on the willingness of other members to back them.

party caucus
A group that consists of a party's members in the House or Senate and that serves to elect the party's leadership, set policy goals, and determine party strategy.

Party Leadership in Congress

The House and Senate are organized along party lines. When members of Congress are sworn in at the start of a new two-year session, they automatically are members of either the Republican or the Democratic **party caucus** in their chamber. Through the caucuses, the Democrats and Republicans in each chamber meet periodically to plan strategy and discuss their differences in the process of settling on the party's legislative program. The caucuses also select the **party leaders** who represent the party's interests in the chamber and give direction to the party's goals.

The House Leadership

The Constitution specifies that the House of Representatives will be presided over by a Speaker, elected by its members. In practice this means the Speaker will be a member of the majority party, because it has enough votes to elect one of its own to the post. Thus, when the Democrats took control of the House after the 2006 election, Nancy Pelosi, the Democrats' leader in the chamber, replaced Republican Dennis Hastert as Speaker. (Table 11–1 shows the party composition in Congress during the past two decades.)

The Speaker is sometimes said to be the second most powerful official in Washington, after the president. The Speaker is active in developing the party's positions on issues and in persuading party members in the House to support these positions.[16] Although the Speaker cannot force party members to support the party's program, they look to the Speaker for leadership. The Speaker also has certain formal powers, including the right to speak first during House debate on legislation and the power to recognize members—that is, give them permission to speak from the floor. Because the House places a time limit on floor debate, not everyone has a chance to speak on a given bill, and the Speaker can sometimes influence legislation simply by exercising the power to decide who will speak and when. The Speaker also chooses the chairperson and the majority-party members of the powerful House Rules Committee, which controls the scheduling of bills for debate. Legislation that the Speaker wants passed is likely to reach the floor under conditions favorable to its enactment; for example, the

Former House majority leader Tom DeLay (R-Texas) speaking to the press. DeLay was known as the "hammer" for his ability to round up the votes necessary to drive home Republican-sponsored legislation. In 2006, months after quitting his House leadership post following accusations of wrongdoing, DeLay resigned his House seat.

Speaker may ask the Rules Committee to delay sending a bill to the floor until there is enough support for its passage. The Speaker has other ways of influencing the work of the House. The Speaker assigns bills to committees, places time limits on the reporting of bills out of committees, and assigns members to conference committees. (The importance of these powers over committee action will become apparent later in this chapter.)

The Speaker is assisted by the House majority leader and the House majority whip, who are also chosen by the majority party's members. The majority leader acts as the party's floor leader, organizing the debate on bills and working to line up legislative support. The whip has the job of informing party members when critical votes are scheduled. As voting is getting under way on the House floor, the whip will sometimes stand at a location that is easily seen by party members and let them know where the leadership stands on the bill by giving them a thumbs-up or thumbs-down signal.

The minority party has its own leaders in the House. The House minority leader heads the party's caucus and its policy committee and plays the leading role in developing the party's legislative positions. The minority leader is assisted by a minority whip.

The Senate Leadership

In the Senate, the most important party leadership position is that of the majority leader, who heads the majority-party caucus. The majority leader's role is much like that of the Speaker of the House in that the Senate majority leader formulates the majority party's legislative agenda and encourages party members to support it. Like the Speaker, the Senate majority leader chairs the party's policy committee and acts as the party's voice in the chamber. The majority leader is assisted by the majority whip, who sees to it that members know when important votes are scheduled and ensures that the party's strongest advocates on a legislative measure are present for the debate. The Senate also has a minority leader and a minority whip, whose roles are comparable to those performed by their counterparts in the House.

Unlike the Speaker of the House, the Senate majority leader is not the chamber's presiding officer. The Constitution assigns this responsibility to the vice president of the United States. However, because the vice president is allowed to vote in the Senate only to break a tie, the vice president normally is not in the Senate chamber unless support for a bill is so closely divided that a tie vote appears possible. The Senate has a president pro tempore, who, in the absence of the vice president, has the right to preside over the Senate. President pro tempore is largely an honorary position that by tradition is usually held by the majority party's senior member. The presiding official has limited power, because each senator has the right to speak at any length on bills under consideration.

The Senate's tradition of unlimited debate stems mainly from its small size (only 100 members, compared with the House's 435 members). Senators like to view themselves as the equals of all others in their chamber and thus are reluctant to take orders from their leadership. For these reasons, the Senate majority leader's position is weaker than that of the House Speaker.

The Power of Party Leaders

The power of all party leaders, in the Senate and House alike, rests substantially on the trust placed in them by the members of their party. They do not have the strong formal powers of parliamentary leaders (see "How the United States Compares"), but they are expected to lead. If they are adept at promoting ideas

party leaders
Members of the House and Senate who are chosen by the Democratic or Republican caucus in each chamber to represent the party's interests in that chamber and who give some central direction to the chamber's deliberations.

How the United States Compares

Legislative Leadership and Authority

The U.S. House and Senate are separate and coequal chambers, each with its own leadership and rules. This type of legislative structure is not found in most democracies. Many democracies, for example, have a single legislative chamber, which is apportioned by population. If the United States had an equivalent legislature, it would consist only of the House of Representatives.

Even most of the democracies that have a bicameral (two-chamber) legislature organize it differently from how the U.S. Congress is organized. The U.S. Senate is apportioned strictly by geography: there are two senators from each state. Germany is among the democracies that have a chamber organized along geographical lines, but Germany's upper house (the Bundesrat) differs from the U.S. Senate. Each of the German states (known as Länder) has at least three representatives in the Bundesrat, but the more populous states have more than three representatives.

Moreover, in most bicameral legislatures, one legislative chamber has substantially less power than the other. In the British Parliament, for example, the House of Lords is far weaker than the House of Commons; the House of Lords can delay legislation in some instances but cannot kill it. In the German Parliament, the Bundesrat has a voice on constitutional policy issues but not on most national policy issues, and its vote can in some cases be overridden by the population-based chamber (the Bundestag). In the United States, the Senate and House are equal in their legislative powers; without their joint agreement, a law cannot be enacted.

The U.S. Congress is fragmented in other ways as well: it has elected leaders with limited formal powers, a network of relatively independent and powerful committees, and members who are free to follow or ignore other members of their party. It is not uncommon for a fourth or more of a party's legislators to vote against their party's position on important legislative issues. In contrast, European legislatures have a centralized power structure: top leaders have substantial authority, the committees are weak, and the parties are unified. European legislators are expected to support their party unless granted permission to vote otherwise on a particular bill. Legislative leadership is much easier to exercise in Europe's hierarchical parliaments than in America's "stratarchical" Congress.

COUNTRY	FORM OF LEGISLATURE
Canada	One house dominant
France	One house dominant
Germany	One house dominant (except on certain issues)
Great Britain	One house dominant
Israel	One house only
Japan	One house dominant
Mexico	Two equal houses
Sweden	One house only
United States	Two equal houses

and building coalitions, they can exercise considerable power within their chamber. By the same token, their power can evaporate if they make a mistake that hurts their party. In 2002, Republican Senate leader Trent Lott of Mississippi resigned his post after he placed his party at the center of an unwanted controversy by publicly praising the South's segregated past.

Party leaders are in a more powerful position today than they were a few decades ago as a result of changes in the composition of the congressional parties. The GOP once had a substantial progressive faction within it, but this faction has been eclipsed by its conservative wing. At the same time, the Democratic party's conservative wing, represented by its southern lawmakers, has withered away almost entirely. As congressional Republicans have become more alike in their thinking and more different from congressional Democrats, each group has found it easier to band together and stand against the opposing party. Accordingly, the party leaders through the party caucus have found it easier to bring their party's lawmakers together on legislative issues.

The party leadership has also been strengthened by the high cost of election campaigns. Party leaders acquire loyalty from their members by making

WWW.MHHE.COM/PATTERSONTAD8

fund-raising appearances on behalf of vulnerable candidates and by organizing large-scale fund-raising efforts that benefit all party members. Party leaders also are positioned to steer pork-barrel money to party loyalists.

These sources of influence are not total, however. Most party members are secure in their reelection prospects and thus have some leeway in accepting party leadership. Also, members of Congress have their own policy goals, which do not always accord with those of the party leadership. Moreover, some members have close ties to the special interests that back their campaigns and feel an obligation to help them out, an outlook not shared in every instance by the party leadership. Some members of Congress, particularly those in the Senate, have personal ambitions—such as a desire to become president or to attain national recognition—that put them at odds with party leaders or cause them to compete with the leadership for media attention.

Despite these factors that pull congressional members away from the direction of their leadership, adept party leaders are able to wield considerable influence over party members. Party leaders act as agents for party members and are effective to the degree to which they pursue collective tasks well, allowing the party's members to devote their time to their own pursuits. The challenge for the leader is to create harmony among members by catering to their needs and by forging party positions that are agreeable enough to the members so that they act in concert. If the party leaders can get them working as one and keep them together, both the party and its leaders will benefit. If leaders fail at this task, their leadership will falter, as will the party's ability to influence legislation.[17]

Recent party leaders have been fairly adept at managing their party's caucus, primarily because party members are increasingly like-minded. Congress today has fewer liberal Republicans and fewer conservative Democrats. Moreover, those who are somewhat outside the party mainstream usually have more in common with the other members of their party than with members of the opposing party. Finally, those who are further removed from the party mainstream must conform to it to a large degree if they want to enjoy the perks of office, as Senator Arlen Specter (R-Penn.) discovered after the 2004 election. Specter was in line to become chair of the powerful Senate Judiciary Committee when he publicly cautioned against appointing judges that would overturn *Roe v. Wade*, a goal of many Republicans. As a condition of granting him the chairmanship, the GOP's Senate caucus forced Specter to agree that he would not use the position to block antiabortion judicial nominees. A more systematic indicator of heightened party leadership and discipline in Congress is the pattern of *roll-call votes* (votes on which each member's vote is officially recorded, as

LEADERS

NANCY PELOSI

(1940–)

Nancy Pelosi, House Democratic leader since 2002, is the first woman in U.S. history to lead a major political party in Congress. Pelosi comes from a politically active family. Her father was in the House of Representatives and later served five terms as Baltimore's mayor. A brother subsequently served as that city's mayor as well. A graduate of Trinity College in Washington, D.C., she moved west with her husband, a native of San Francisco. She was first elected to Congress in 1987 from a northern California district in a special election to fill the vacancy created by the death of the incumbent. Once in Congress, she quickly made a reputation for herself as a tenacious legislator. As a member of the House Appropriations Committee, she became a leading advocate of improving the nation's health-care policies. She was serving on the House Permanent Select Committee on Intelligence when the terrorist attacks of September 11, 2001, occurred. In this position, she was a key congressional player in efforts to strengthen the country's intelligence agencies. She was elected House minority leader when Missouri's Dick Gephardt voluntarily stepped down and became Speaker when the Democrats took control of the House in the 2006 election.

Figure 11–4

Percentage of Roll-Call Votes in House and Senate in Which a Majority of Democrats Voted Against a Majority of Republicans
Democrats and Republicans in Congress are often on opposite sides of issues; party-line voting has been relatively high since the 1980s.
Source: *Congressional Quarterly Weekly,* various dates.

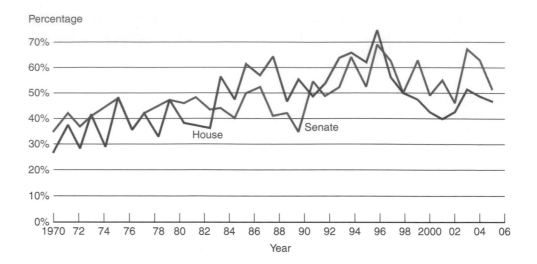

opposed to voice votes, where the members simply say "aye" or "nay" in unison and the presiding officer indicates which side prevails without tallying individual members' positions). Over the past three decades, party-line voting on roll calls has increased considerably (see Figure 11–4). In the 1970s, roll-call votes generally did not pit most Republicans against most Democrats. More recently, most roll-call votes have divided along party lines.

Committee Chairs: The Seniority Principle

Party leaders are not the only important leaders in Congress. Most of the work of Congress takes place in the meetings of its thirty-five standing (permanent) committees and their numerous subcommittees, each of which is headed by a chairperson. A committee chair schedules committee meetings, determines the order in which committee bills are considered, presides over committee discussions, directs the committee's majority staff, and can choose to lead the debate when a committee bill reaches the floor of the chamber for a vote by the full membership.

seniority
A member of Congress's consecutive years of service on a particular committee.

Committee chairs are always members of the majority party, and they usually have the most **seniority** (the most consecutive years of service on a particular committee). Seniority is based strictly on time served on a committee, not on time spent in Congress. If a member switches committees, the years spent on the first committee do not count toward seniority on the second one.

The seniority system has advantages: it reduces the number of power struggles that would occur if the chairs were decided each time by open competition, it provides experienced and knowledgeable committee leadership, and it enables members to look forward to the reward of a position as chair after years of service on the same committee. However, a strict seniority system can place committee chairs beyond any control by the House and

U.S. senators Orrin Hatch (R-Utah) and Patrick Leahy (D-Vt.) confer at a Judiciary Committee hearing. Most of the legislative work of Congress is done in committees and their subcommittees.

Senate's elected leaders. To counter this problem, Senate and House Republicans, but not Democrats, place term limits on committee chairs. After a set number of years, a chair must relinquish the post, which then usually goes to the next most senior GOP committee member.

Congressional organization and leadership extend into subcommittees, smaller units within each committee formed to conduct specific aspects of the committee's business. Altogether there are about two hundred subcommittees in the House and Senate, each with a chairperson who decides its order of business, presides over its meetings, and coordinates its staff. In both chambers, a subcommittee chair is often the most senior member on the panel, but seniority is not as important in these appointments as it is in the designation of committee chairs.

Oligarchy or Democracy: Which Principle Should Govern?

In 1995, House Republicans gave committee chairs the power to select the chairs of their subcommittees and granted them the authority to appoint all majority-party staff members, including those who work for the subcommittees. Each committee chair was to use this power to promote the Republican party's policy goals as opposed to those of committee members. The changes reversed House reforms of the 1970s that gave subcommittees greater authority in order to spread power more widely among House members.

The opposing ideas embodied in the 1970s and 1995 reforms have played themselves out many times in the history of Congress. The institution is at once a place for conducting the nation's business and a venue for promoting constituency interests. At times, the power of top party leaders has been increased. At other times, the power of rank-and-file members has been enlarged. At all times, there has been an attempt to achieve a workable balance of the two. The result is an institution very different from European parliaments, where power is always concentrated at the top (an arrangement reflected even in the name for rank-and-file members: "backbenchers"). The distinguishing feature of congressional power is its division among the membership, with provision for added power—sometimes more and sometimes less—at the top.

THE COMMITTEE SYSTEM

As indicated earlier, most of the work in Congress is conducted through **standing committees,** permanent committees with responsibility for a particular area of public policy. At present there are twenty standing committees in the House and sixteen in the Senate (see Table 11–2). Both the House and the Senate, for example, have a standing committee that handles foreign policy issues. Other important standing committees are those that deal with agriculture, commerce, the interior (natural resources and public lands), defense, government spending, labor, the judiciary, and taxation. House committees, which average about thirty-five to forty members each, are about twice the size of Senate committees. Each standing committee has legislative authority in that it can draft and rewrite proposed legislation and can recommend to the full chamber the passage or defeat of the legislation it considers.

Each standing committee in Congress has its own staff. Unlike the members' personal staffs, which concentrate on constituency relations, the committee staffs perform an almost entirely legislative function. They help draft legislation, organize hearings, and participate in altering bills within the committee.

standing committees
Permanent congressional committees with responsibility for a particular area of public policy. An example is the Senate Foreign Relations Committee.

| TABLE 11-2 | The Standing Committees of Congress |

HOUSE OF REPRESENTATIVES	SENATE
Agriculture	Agriculture, Nutrition, and Forestry
Appropriations	Appropriations
Armed Services	Armed Services
Budget	Banking, Housing, and Urban Affairs
Education and the Workforce	Budget
Energy and Commerce	Commerce, Science, and Transportation
Financial Services	Energy and Natural Resources
Government Reform	Environment and Public Works
Homeland Security	Finance
House Administration	Foreign Relations
International Relations	Health, Education, Labor, and Pensions
Judiciary	Homeland Security and Governmental Affairs
Resources	Judiciary
Rules	Rules and Administration
Science	Small Business and Entrepreneurship
Small Business	Veterans' Affairs
Standards of Official Conduct	
Transportation and Infrastructure	
Veterans' Affairs	
Ways and Means	

conference committees
Temporary committees formed to bargain over the differences in the House and Senate versions of a bill. A conference committee's members are usually appointed from the House and Senate standing committees that originally worked on the bill.

In addition to its standing committees, Congress also has a number of *select committees,* which are created to perform specific tasks. An example is the Senate Select Committee on Intelligence, which oversees the work of intelligence agencies, such as the CIA. Congress also has *joint committees,* composed of members of both houses, that perform advisory functions. The Joint Committee on the Library, for example, oversees the Library of Congress, the largest library in the world. Finally, Congress has **conference committees,** joint committees formed temporarily to work out differences in House and Senate versions of a particular bill. The role of conference committees is discussed more fully later in the chapter.

Congress could not possibly handle its workload without the help of its committee system. About ten thousand bills are introduced during each two-year session of Congress. The sheer volume of legislation would paralyze the institution if it did not have a division of labor. Yet the very existence of committees and subcommittees helps fragment Congress: each of these units is relatively secure in its power, jurisdiction, and membership.

Committee Membership

Each committee includes Republicans and Democrats, but the majority party holds the majority of seats. The ratio of Democrats to Republicans on each committee is approximately the same as the ratio in the full House or Senate, but there is no fixed rule on this matter, and the majority party decides what the ratio will be (mindful that at the next election it could become the chamber's minority party). Members of the House typically serve on only two committees.

There are dozens of informal caucuses in Congress that aim to represent the concerns of particular constituencies. Pictured here is U.S. Representative Loretta Sanchez (D-Calif.), a member of the Hispanic caucus.

Senators often serve on four, although they can sit on only two major committees, such as Foreign Relations and Finance.

Each standing committee has a fixed number of members, and a committee must have a vacancy before a new member can be appointed. Most vacancies occur after an election as a result of the retirement or defeat of committee members. Each party has a special committee in each chamber that decides who will fill committee vacancies. Several factors influence these decisions, including the preferences of the legislators themselves. Most newly elected members of Congress ask for and receive assignment to a committee on which they can serve their constituents' interests and at the same time enhance their reelection prospects. For example, when Barack Obama was elected to the Senate in 2004 from Illinois, a state that depends heavily on transportation and other public works, he asked for and received an appointment on the Senate Environment and Public Works Committee that oversees these policy areas.

Members of Congress also prefer membership on one of the more prominent committees, such as Foreign Relations or Finance in the Senate and Appropriations or Ways and Means in the House. A seat on these committees is coveted because they deal with vital issues, such as taxation and international affairs. Factors such as members' work habits, party loyalty, and length of congressional service weigh heavily in the determination of appointments to these prestigious committees.[18]

Subcommittee assignments are handled differently. The members of each party on a committee decide who among them will serve on each of its subcommittees. The members' preferences and seniority, as well as the interests of their constituencies, are key influences on subcommittee assignments.

Committee Jurisdiction

The 1946 Legislative Reorganization Act requires that each bill introduced in Congress be referred to the proper committee. An agricultural bill introduced in the Senate must be assigned to the Senate Agriculture Committee, a bill dealing with foreign affairs must be sent to the Senate Foreign Relations Committee, and

jurisdiction (of a congressional committee)

The policy area in which a particular congressional committee is authorized to act.

so on. This requirement is a major source of each committee's power. Even if its members are known to oppose certain types of legislation, bills clearly within its jurisdiction—the policy area in which it is authorized to act—must be sent to it for deliberation.

However, policy problems are increasingly complex, and jurisdiction accordingly has become an increasingly contentious issue, particularly with regard to major bills. Which House committee, for example, should handle a major bill addressing the role of financial institutions in global trade? The Financial Services Committee? The Commerce Committee? The International Relations Committee? All committees seek legislative influence and each is jealous of its jurisdiction, so bills that overlap committee boundaries provoke "turf wars."[19] Party leaders can take advantage of these situations by shuttling a bill to the committee that is most likely to handle it in the way they would like. But because party leaders depend on the committee chairs for support, they cannot regularly ignore a committee that has a strong claim to a bill. At times, party leaders have responded by dividing up a bill, handing over some of its provisions to one committee and other provisions to a second committee.

House and Senate subcommittees also have defined jurisdictions. The House International Relations Committee, for instance, has seven subcommittees: Europe and Emerging Threats; Middle East and Central Asia; Asia and the Pacific; Western Hemisphere; Africa, Global Human Rights, and International Operations; International Terrorism and Nonproliferation; and Oversight and Investigations. Each subcommittee has about a dozen members, and these few individuals do most of the work and have the major voice in the disposition of most bills in their policy area.

HOW A BILL BECOMES LAW

Parties, party leaders, and committees are critical actors in the legislative process. Their roles and influence, however, vary with the nature of the legislation under consideration.

Committee Hearings and Decisions

bill

A proposed law (legislative act) within Congress or another legislature.

The formal process by which bills become law is shown in Figure 11–5. A **bill** is a proposed legislative act. Many bills are prepared by executive agencies, interest groups, or other outside parties, but members of Congress also draft bills, and only they can formally submit a bill for consideration by their chamber. Once a bill is introduced by a member of the House or Senate, it is given a number and a title and is then sent to the appropriate committee, which assigns it to one of its subcommittees. Less than 10 percent of the bills that committees consider reach the floor for a vote; the others are "killed" when committees decide that they do not warrant further consideration and table them. The full House or Senate can overrule committee decisions, but this rarely occurs.

The fact that committees kill more than 90 percent of the bills submitted in Congress does not mean that committees exercise 90 percent of the power in Congress. A committee rarely decides fully the fate of legislation that is important to the majority party or its leadership. Most bills die in committee because they are of little interest to anyone other than a few members of Congress or are so poorly conceived that they lack merit. Some bills are not

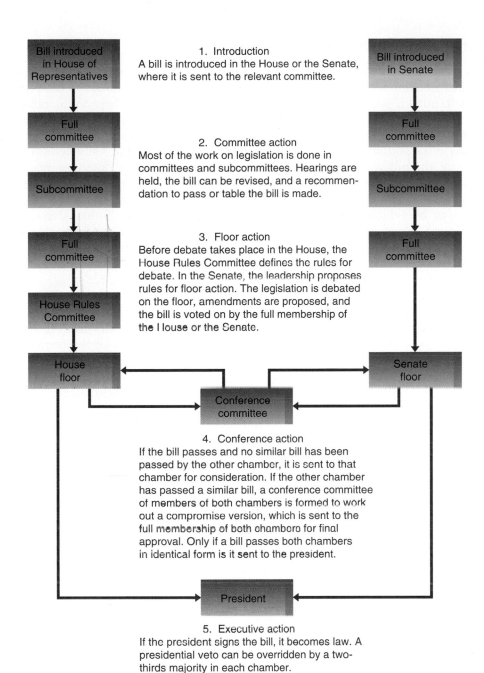

1. Introduction
A bill is introduced in the House or the Senate, where it is sent to the relevant committee.

2. Committee action
Most of the work on legislation is done in committees and subcommittees. Hearings are held, the bill can be revised, and a recommendation to pass or table the bill is made.

3. Floor action
Before debate takes place in the House, the House Rules Committee defines the rules for debate. In the Senate, the leadership proposes rules for floor action. The legislation is debated on the floor, amendments are proposed, and the bill is voted on by the full membership of the House or the Senate.

4. Conference action
If the bill passes and no similar bill has been passed by the other chamber, it is sent to that chamber for consideration. If the other chamber has passed a similar bill, a conference committee of members of both chambers is formed to work out a compromise version, which is sent to the full membership of both chambers for final approval. Only if a bill passes both chambers in identical form is it sent to the president.

5. Executive action
If the president signs the bill, it becomes law. A presidential veto can be overridden by a two-thirds majority in each chamber.

Figure 11–5
How a Bill Becomes Law
Although the legislative process can be short-circuited in many ways, this diagram describes a normal way a bill becomes law.

even supported by the members who introduce them. A member may submit a bill to appease a powerful constituent group and then quietly inform the committee to ignore it.

If a bill seems to have merit, the subcommittee will schedule hearings on it. The subcommittee invites testimony on the proposed legislation from lobbyists, administrators, and experts. After the hearings, if the subcommittee still feels that the legislation is warranted, members recommend the bill to the full committee, which can hold additional hearings. In the House, both the full committee and a subcommittee can "mark up," or revise, a bill. In the Senate, markup usually is reserved for the full committee.

From Committee to the Floor

If a majority of the committee vote to recommend passage of the bill, it is referred to the full chamber for action. In the House, the Rules Committee has the power to determine when the bill will be voted on, how long the debate on the bill will last, and whether the bill will receive a "closed rule" (no amendments will be permitted), an "open rule" (members can propose amendments relevant to any of the bill's sections), or something in between (for example, only certain sections of the bill will be subject to amendment). The Rules Committee has this scheduling power because the House is too large to operate effectively without strict rules for the handling of legislation by the full chamber. The rules are also a means by which the majority party controls legislation. House Democrats employed closed rules to prevent Republicans from proposing amendments to major bills, a tactic House Republicans said they would forgo when they took control in 1995. Once in control, however, the Republicans applied closed rules to a number of major bills. The tactic was too effective to ignore.

On most House bills, only a small number of legislators are granted the opportunity to speak on the floor. In most cases, the decision as to who will speak is delegated to the bill's chief sponsor and one of the bill's leading opponents. Typically, both of these House members are members of the committee that handled the bill.

The Senate also has a rules committee, but it has much less power than in the House. In the Senate, the majority leader, usually in consultation with the minority leaders, schedules bills. All Senate bills are subject to unlimited debate unless a three-fifths majority of the full Senate votes for **cloture,** which limits debate to thirty hours. Cloture is a way of defeating a Senate **filibuster,** which is a procedural tactic whereby a minority of senators prevent a bill from coming to a vote by holding the floor and talking until other senators give in and the bill is withdrawn from consideration. In late 2005, Senate Democrats used the filibuster to block a vote on renewal of the USA Patriot Act, saying that they would allow it to come to a vote only if Republicans agreed to add protections of privacy rights. Three months later, Senate Democrats got the changes they wanted, and the bill passed by an overwhelming majority.

The Senate also differs from the House in that its members can propose any amendment to any bill. Unlike House amendments, those in the Senate do not have to be germane to a bill's content. For example, a senator may propose an antiabortion amendment to a bill dealing with defense expenditures. Such an amendment is called a **rider,** and riders are frequently introduced.

Leadership and Floor Action

Committee action is usually decisive on bills that address small issues. If a majority of committee members favor such a bill, it normally is passed by the full chamber, often without amendment. In a sense, the full chamber merely votes to confirm or modify decisions made previously by committees and subcommittees. Of course, these units do not operate in a vacuum. In making its decisions, a committee takes into account the fact that its action can be reversed by the full chamber, just as a subcommittee recognizes that the full committee can overrule its decision.[20] Partisanship also serves as a check on committee action. When a committee's vote is sharply divided along party lines, other members may conclude that they need to look more closely at the bill before deciding whether to vote for it.

On major bills, the party leaders are the key players. They will have worked closely with the committee during its deliberations and may assume leadership

cloture
A parliamentary maneuver that, if a three-fifths majority votes for it, limits Senate debate to thirty hours and has the effect of defeating a filibuster.

filibuster
A procedural tactic in the U.S. Senate whereby a minority of legislators prevent a bill from coming to a vote by holding the floor and talking until the majority gives in and the bill is withdrawn from consideration.

rider
An amendment to a bill that deals with an issue unrelated to the content of the bill. Riders are permitted in the Senate but not in the House.

Get Involved!

Working on the Inside

Each year, thousands of college students serve as interns in Congress or state legislatures. Many internships are unpaid, but students can receive college credit for the experience.

Internships provide an opportunity to see the political process firsthand. For most citizens, politics is a second-hand world seen largely through the window on that world provided by the news media. An internship offers an opportunity to see how institutions work on a daily basis from the inside. Internships are not always a great adventure. Many legislative interns envision themselves contributing ideas and research that might influence public policy only to find that they are answering letters, developing mailing lists, or duplicating materials. Nevertheless, few interns conclude that their experience has been a waste of time. Most find it rewarding and, ultimately, memorable.

Many executive agencies at the federal and state levels also accept interns, and some have well-organized internship programs. The Department of State has one of the best internship programs, but it is in heavy demand and has an early application deadline. The internships offered by exec-

utive agencies typically are more challenging than those provided by legislative offices. Legislators dedicate a lot of their staff time to constituency service, whereas agencies concentrate on the administration of policies and programs. On the other hand, legislative offices are usually more spirited, and interns in these offices are more likely to strike up friendships with other interns in the same office or in nearby offices.

Information about internships can be obtained from the American Political Science Association (www.apsa.org). In addition, there are organizations in Washington that arrange internships in Congress and the executive agencies. These organizations frequently charge a fee for their services, so you might want to contact a legislative office or executive agency directly. It is important to make your request as early as possible in the college year, because some internship programs have deadlines and nearly all offices receive more requests than they can accommodate. You could also check with the student services office at your college or university. Some of these offices have information on internship programs and can be of assistance.

---

of the bill when it clears the committee. (In the case of "minor" bills, leadership during floor debate normally is provided by committee members.)

The majority party's leaders (particularly in the House) have increasingly set the legislative agenda and defined the debate on major bills.[21] They shape the bills' broad outlines and set the boundaries of the floor debate. In these efforts, they depend on the support of their party's members. To obtain it, they consult their members informally and through the party caucus. **Party discipline**—the willingness of a party's House or Senate members to act as a unified group—is increasingly important in congressional action and is the key to party leaders' ability to shape major legislation. (The role of parties in Congress is discussed further in the section on Congress's representation function.)

party discipline
The willingness of a party's House or Senate members to act as a unified group and thus exert collective control over legislative action.

Conference Committees and the President

For a bill to pass, it must have the support of a simple majority (50 percent plus one) of the House or Senate members voting on it. To become law, however, a bill must be passed in identical form by both the House and the Senate. About 10 percent of all bills that pass both chambers—the proportion is larger for major bills—differ in important respects in their House and Senate versions. These bills are referred to conference committees to resolve the differences. Each conference committee is formed temporarily for the sole purpose of handling a particular bill; its members are usually appointed from the House and Senate standing committees that drafted the bill. The conference committee's job is to develop a compromise version, which then goes back to the House and Senate floors for a

WWW.MHHE.COM/PATTERSONTAD8

law (as enacted by Congress)

A legislative proposal, or bill, that is passed by both the House and the Senate and is not vetoed by the president.

veto

The president's rejection of a bill, thereby keeping it from becoming law unless Congress overrides the veto.

vote. There it can be passed, defeated, or returned to conference, but not amended.

A bill that is passed in identical form by the House and the Senate is not yet a law. The president also plays a role. If the president signs the bill, it becomes **law.** If the president exercises the **veto,** the bill is sent back to Congress with the president's reasons for rejecting it. Congress can override a veto by a two-thirds vote of each chamber; the bill then becomes law.

If the president fails to sign a bill within ten days (Sundays excepted) and Congress is still in session, the bill automatically becomes law anyway. If the president fails to sign within ten days and Congress has concluded its term, the bill does not become law. This last situation, called a pocket veto, forces Congress in its next term to start over from the beginning: the bill again must pass both chambers and again is subject to presidential veto.

CONGRESS'S POLICYMAKING ROLE

The Framers of the Constitution expected that Congress, as the embodiment of representative government, would be the institution to which the people looked for policy leadership. During most of the nineteenth century, Congress had that stature. Aside from a few strong leaders such as Jackson and Lincoln, presidents did not play a major legislative role (see Chapter 12). However, as national and international forces combined to place greater leadership and policy demands on the federal government, the president became a vital part of the national legislative process. Today Congress and the president substantially share the legislative effort, although their roles differ greatly.[22]

Congress's policymaking role revolves around its three major functions: lawmaking, representation, and oversight (see Table 11–3). In practice, the three functions overlap, but they are conceptually distinct.

The Lawmaking Function of Congress

lawmaking function

The authority (of a legislature) to make the laws necessary to carry out the government's powers.

Under the Constitution, Congress is granted the **lawmaking function:** the authority to make the laws necessary to carry out the powers granted to the national government. The constitutional powers of Congress are substantial; they include the power to tax, to spend, to regulate commerce, and to declare war. However, whether Congress takes the lead in the making of laws depends heavily on the type of policy at issue.

TABLE 11–3	The Major Functions of Congress
FUNCTION	**BASIS AND ACTIVITY**
Lawmaking	Through its constitutional grant to enact law, Congress makes the laws authorizing federal programs and appropriating the funds necessary to carry them out.
Representation	Through its elected constitutional officers—U.S. senators and representatives—Congress represents the interests of constituents and the nation in its deliberations and its lawmaking.
Oversight	Through its constitutional responsibility to see that the executive branch carries out the laws faithfully and spends appropriations properly, Congress oversees and sometimes investigates executive action.

Kay Bailey Hutchison was elected to the U.S. Senate from Texas in 1993 to fill the seat vacated by Lloyd Bentsen, who had resigned to become secretary of the treasury. Hutchison is among the growing number of women who sit in the U.S. Congress. Hutchison easily won her race for a third Senate term in 2006.

Broad Issues: Fragmentation as a Limit on Congress's Role

Congress is structured in a way that can make agreement on large issues difficult to obtain. Congress is not one house but two, each with its own authority and constituency base. Neither the House nor the Senate can enact legislation without the other's approval, and the two chambers are hardly two versions of the same thing. California and North Dakota have exactly the same representation in the Senate, but in the House, which is apportioned by population, California has fifty-three seats compared to North Dakota's one.

Congress also includes a lot of people: 100 members of the Senate and 435 members of the House. They come from different constituencies and represent different and sometimes opposing interests, which leads to disagreements. Nearly every member of Congress, for example, supports the principle of global free trade. Yet when it comes to specific trade provisions members often disagree. Foreign competition means different things to manufacturers who produce automobiles, computer chips, or underwear; it means different things to farmers who produce corn, sugar, or grapes; and it means different things to firms that deal in international finance, home insurance, or student loans. And because it means different things to different people in different parts of the country, members of Congress who represent these areas have conflicting views on when free trade makes sense.

For such reasons, Congress often has difficulty taking the lead on broad issues of national policy. A legislative institution can easily lead on such issues only if it grants this authority to its top leader. But Congress does not have such a leader. The House has its separate leaders, as does the Senate. Moreover, although the rise in party discipline in Congress has strengthened the role of the chambers' leaders, the fact remains that House and Senate members of the same party are still literally free to go their separate ways if they so choose. As a result, Congress sometimes struggles when faced with the task of developing a comprehensive policy response to broad national issues. Few recent controversies illustrate this fact more clearly than does immigration reform. House Republicans, in part because elections in their districts seldom hinge on the Hispanic vote, held firm in 2006 to their opposition to a guest-worker program. Senate Republicans were warier of alienating Hispanic voters, who in some parts of the country have the votes to tip the balance in a statewide race. Enough Senate Republicans sided with their Democratic colleagues in support of a guest-worker program that a deadlock with the House was the result.

As an institution, the presidency is better suited to the task of providing leadership on major national issues. First, whereas Congress's authority is divided, the presidency's authority is not. Executive power is vested constitutionally in the hands of a single individual—the president. Unlike congressional leaders, who must negotiate with their members when taking a stand on legislation, the president does not have to consult with other executive officials when taking a position. Second, whereas members of Congress tend to see issues mainly from the perspective of their state or district, the president tends to see them from a national perspective.

Presidential leadership means that Congress normally will pay attention to White House proposals, not that it will adopt them. Congress typically accepts a presidential initiative only as a starting point in its deliberations. It may reject the proposal outright—particularly when the president is from the opposing party—but any such proposal provides Congress with a tangible bill to focus on. If the proposal is at all close to what a congressional majority would regard as acceptable, Congress will use it as a baseline from which to make changes that will bring it in line with the thinking of a congressional majority. (The legislative roles of Congress and the president are discussed further in Chapter 12.)

In its lawmaking activities, Congress has the support of three congressional agencies. One is the Congressional Budget Office (CBO), which was created as part of the Budget Impoundment and Control Act of 1974. Its two hundred fifty employees provide Congress with general economic projections, overall estimates of government expenditures and revenues, and specific estimates of the costs of proposed programs. (The budgetary process is described more fully in later chapters.)

A second congressional agency is the Government Accountability Office (GAO). With three thousand employees, the GAO is the largest congressional agency. Formed in 1921, it has primary responsibility for overseeing executive agencies' spending of money that has been appropriated by Congress. The programs that the executive agencies administer are authorized and funded by Congress. The GAO's responsibility is to ensure that executive agencies operate in the manner prescribed by Congress.

The third and oldest congressional agency is the Congressional Research Service (CRS). It has a staff of one thousand employees and operates as a nonpartisan reference agency. It conducts research and responds to information requests from congressional committees and members.

Congress in the Lead: Fragmentation as a Policymaking Strength

Congress occasionally does take the lead on large issues. Except during Roosevelt's New Deal, Congress has been a chief source of major labor legislation. Environmental legislation, federal aid to education, and urban development are other areas in which Congress has played an initiating role.[23] The Republicans' Contract with America, introduced during the 1994 election, is yet another example of congressional policy leadership. The contract included broad fiscal, regulatory, and social initiatives. In 1996, for example, the Republican-controlled Congress led the way on legislation that fundamentally changed the nation's welfare system. Nevertheless, Congress does not routinely develop broad policy programs and carry them through to passage. "Congress remains organized," James Sundquist notes, "to deal with narrow problems but not with broad ones."[24]

Newt Gingrich and three hundred Republican congressional candidates stand in front of the Capitol to dramatize their Contract with America. After their stunning victory in the 1994 elections, they launched an aggressive attempt to reduce the scope of the federal government, illustrating that, in some instances, Congress can take the lead on broad national issues.

As it happens, the great majority of the hundreds of bills that Congress considers each session deal with narrow issues. The leading role in the disposition of these bills falls not on the president but on Congress and, in each case, on the relatively small number of its members that sit on the committee responsible for it. The same fragmentation that makes it difficult for Congress to take the lead on broad issues makes it easy for Congress to tackle scores of narrow issues simultaneously. Most of the legislation passed by Congress is "distributive"—that is, it distributes benefits to a particular group while spreading the costs across the taxpaying public. Veterans' benefits are one example.

Such legislation, because it directly benefits a constituent group, is a type of policy that members of Congress like to support. It is also a type of policy that Congress, through its committee system, is organizationally best suited to handle. Most committees parallel a major constituent interest, such as agriculture, commerce, labor, or veterans.

The Representation Function of Congress

In the process of making laws, the members of Congress represent various interests within American society, giving them a voice in the national legislature. The proper approach to the **representation function** has been debated since the nation's founding. A recurrent issue has been whether the main concern of a representative should be the interests of the nation as a whole or those of his or her own constituency. These interests overlap to some degree but rarely coincide exactly. Policies that are of benefit to the full society are not always equally advantageous to particular localities and can even cause harm to some constituencies.

representation function
The responsibility of a legislature to represent various interests in society.

Representation of States and Districts

The choice between national and local interests is not a simple one, even for a legislator who is inclined toward either orientation. To be fully effective, members of Congress must be reelected time and again, a necessity that compels them to pay attention to local demands. Yet, as part of the nation's legislative body,

Members of Congress are keenly sensitive to local opinion on issues of personal interest to their constituents. Representatives from urban areas are more supportive of gun control than are those from rural areas, where sport hunting is widespread.

no member can easily put aside his or her judgment as to the nation's needs. In making the choice, most members of Congress, on narrow issues at least, tend toward a local orientation. Opposition to gun control legislation, for example, has always been much higher among members of Congress representing rural areas where hunting weapons are part of the fabric of everyday life.

Local representation also occurs through the committee system. Although studies indicate that the views of committee members are not radically different from the views of the full House or Senate membership,[25] senators and representatives typically sit on committees and subcommittees with policy jurisdictions that coincide with their constituents' interests. For example, farm-state legislators dominate the membership of the House and Senate Agriculture Committees, and westerners dominate the Interior Committees (which deal with federal lands and natural resources, most of which are concentrated in the West). Committees are also the site of most of the congressional **logrolling**, the practice of trading one's vote with another member so that both get what they want. It is not uncommon, for example, for Agriculture Committee members from livestock-producing states of the North to trade votes with committee members from the South, where crops such as cotton, tobacco, and peanuts are grown.

Nevertheless, representation of constituency interests has its limits. A representative's constituents have little interest in most issues that come before Congress. Whether the government should appropriate a few million dollars in foreign aid for Bolivia is not the sort of issue that local constituent groups are likely to know or care about. Moreover, members of Congress often have no choice but to go against the wishes of a significant portion of their constituency. The interests of workers and employers in a district or state, for example, can differ considerably.

Of course, constituent groups are not the only groups that get legislators' support. The nation's capital is filled with powerful lobbies that contribute funds to congressional campaigns. These lobbying groups sometimes have as much influence with a member of Congress as do interest groups in the member's home district or state.

logrolling
The trading of votes between legislators so that each gets what he or she most wants.

Representation of the Nation Through Parties

When a clear-cut and vital national interest is at stake, members of Congress can be expected to respond to that interest. The difficulty of using the common good as a routine basis for thinking about representation, however, is that Americans often disagree on what constitutes the common good and what government should do to further it.

Most Americans believe, for example, that the nation's education system requires strengthening. The test scores of American schoolchildren on standardized reading, math, and science examinations are significantly below those of children in many other industrial democracies. This situation creates pressure for political action. But what action is necessary and desirable? Does more money have to be funneled into public schools, and, if so, which level of government—federal, state, or local—should provide it? Or does the problem rest with teachers? Should they be subject to higher certification and performance standards? Or is the problem a lack of competition for excellence? Should schools be required to compete for students and the tax dollars they represent? Should private schools be part of any such competition, or would their participation wreck the public school system? There is no general agreement on such issues. The quality of America's schools is of vital national interest, and quality schools would serve the common good. But the means to that end are the subject of endless dispute.

In Congress, debates over national goals occur primarily along party lines. Republicans and Democrats have different perspectives on national issues because their parties differ philosophically and politically. In the end-of-the-year budget negotiations in 1998 and 1999, for example, Republicans and Democrats were deadlocked on the issue of new funding to hire thousands of public school teachers. The initiative had come from President Clinton and was supported by congressional Democrats. But it was opposed by congressional Republicans, who objected to spending federal (as opposed to state and local) funds for that purpose and who also objected to the proposed placement of the new teachers (most of whom would be placed in overcrowded schools, most of which are in Democratic constituencies). Democrats and Republicans alike agreed that more teachers were needed, but they disagreed on how that goal should be reached. In the end, through concessions in other areas, Clinton and the congressional Democrats obtained federal funding for new teachers, but it was obtained through an intensely partisan process.

Partisanship also affects the president's relationship with Congress. Presidents serve as legislative leaders not so much for the whole Congress as for members of their own party. Opposition and support for presidential initiatives usually divides along party lines. Accordingly, the president's legislative success typically has depended on which party controls Congress (see Chapter 12).

In short, any accounting of representation in Congress that minimizes the influence of party is faulty. If constituency interests drive the thinking of many members of Congress, so do partisan values. In fact, constituent and partisan influences are often difficult to separate in practice. In the case of conflicting interests within their constituencies, members of Congress naturally side with those that align with their party. When local business and labor groups take opposing sides on issues before Congress, for example, Republican members tend to back business's position, while Democratic members tend to line up with labor.

The Oversight Function of Congress

Although Congress enacts the nation's laws and appropriates the money to implement them, the administration of these laws is entrusted to the executive branch. Congress has the responsibility to see that the executive branch carries

Political Culture

Congress and Self-Government

To the Framers of the Constitution, Congress was the first branch of government. It was through their representatives in Congress that the people would have their say on national policy. Congress was expected to be at once the symbol and the instrument of self-government. As Alexander Hamilton expressed it, "Here, sir, the people govern!"

Some analysts wonder whether that claim is as valid today as it has been in the past. The modern Congress is filled with careerists, who have the capacity to hold onto their offices indefinitely. This diminishes the ability of citizens, through their votes, to change the direction of Congress. Moreover, today's election campaigns run more on money than on citizen volunteers. While most congressional campaign money comes from small citizen contributions, significant amounts come from groups that have more access to members of Congress than do ordinary citizens. When in office, members of Congress work closely—some say too closely—with powerful lobbies.

Political scientists have not studied representative-constituency relations closely enough over a long enough period of time to say whether the public's influence on Congress has been declining. There is observational evidence to suggest that it has declined, but there is also evidence to the contrary, such as the increased use of polls by members of Congress as a means of determining where their constituents stand on issues of policy.

What's your sense of Congress? Do you feel its members are sufficiently in tune with constituent opinion? Regardless of how you feel, can you think of ways to bring members of Congress into closer alignment with the people they serve? How desirable is it to have a close alignment of public sentiment and congressional action? (You might find it helpful to review the distinction made in Chapter 2 between representatives as the public's trustees and representatives as the public's delegates.)

---

oversight function

A supervisory activity of Congress that centers on its constitutional responsibility to see that the executive branch carries out the laws faithfully and spends appropriations properly.

out the laws faithfully and spends the money properly, a supervisory activity referred to as the **oversight function** of Congress.[26]

Oversight is carried out largely through the committee system of Congress and is facilitated by the parallel structure of the committees and the executive bureaucracy: the House International Relations Committee and Senate Foreign Relations Committee oversee the work of the State Department, the House and Senate Agriculture Committees monitor the Department of Agriculture, and so on. The Legislative Reorganization Act of 1970 spells out each committee's responsibility for overseeing its parallel agency:

> Each standing committee shall review and study, on a continuing basis, the application, administration, and execution of those laws, or parts of laws, the subject matter of which is within the jurisdiction of that committee.

Most federal programs must have their funding renewed every year, a requirement that gives Congress leverage in its ongoing oversight function. If an agency has acted improperly, Congress may reduce the agency's appropriation or tighten the restrictions on the way its funds can be spent. A major difficulty is that the House and Senate Appropriations Committees must review nearly the entire federal budget, a task that limits the amount of attention they can give any particular program.

Oversight is a challenging task. If congressional committees were to try to monitor all the federal bureaucracy's activities, they would have no time to do anything else. Although Congress is required by law to maintain "continuous watchfulness" over programs, oversight normally is not pursued aggressively unless members of Congress are annoyed with an agency, have discovered that

Media & Politics

C-SPAN

Former Speaker of the House Thomas P. "Tip" O'Neill once said if there was only one thing he could accomplish as Speaker it would be to persuade the news media that Congress is a branch of government coequal with the president. O'Neill's gripe was that the news media fawn over the White House while giving short shrift to Congress, an observation supported by scholarly studies. Congress gets only about half as much attention as the presidency, and congressional coverage often occurs in the context of its reaction to presidential initiatives.

In 1979, Congress acted on its own to bring its work into full public view. Previously, television had been barred from the floors of Congress except for special joint sessions, such as the president's annual State of the Union message. Congressional leaders objected to television on the grounds that some members would grandstand, playing to the voters rather than engaging in serious debate. But House members decided on a seven-month trial period of a closed-circuit television system to see whether the quality of debate would be affected. Judging the trial a success, the House began to transmit its proceedings to the outside world through C-SPAN, which is carried by nearly all the nation's cable systems. Television broadcasters are also authorized to use the material as news content.

The Senate refused for nearly a decade to follow the House's lead, convinced that television would likely disrupt the chamber's tradition of reasoned debate. In 1986, the Senate changed its position. Like the House, the Senate operates the cameras and allows broadcasters to use the telecast material as they see fit.

The worst fears have not materialized—most analysts conclude that the quality of House and Senate debate has not been substantially affected by the presence of television cameras. Yet the highest hopes for congressional television also have not been realized. Washington journalists continue to look first to the White House for their news stories. Nevertheless, C-SPAN has brought the workings of Congress to the viewing public. Although the C-SPAN audience is not large, several million Americans say they pay attention to it, some of them regularly. After heated floor debate on a major issue, congressional phone lines and e-mail typically are jammed with messages from C-SPAN viewers expressing their opinion.

a legislative authorization is being grossly abused, or are reviewing a program for possible major changes.

The biggest obstacle to effective oversight is the sheer magnitude of the task. With its hundreds of agencies and thousands of programs, the bureaucracy is beyond comprehensive scrutiny. Even some of Congress's most publicized oversight activities are relatively trivial when viewed against the extensive scope of the bureaucracy. For example, congressional investigations into the Defense Department's purchase of small hardware items, such as wrenches and hammers, at many times their market value do not begin to address the issue of whether the country is overspending on the military. Overpriced hand tools represent pocket change in a defense budget of hundreds of billions of dollars. The real oversight question is whether the defense budget as a whole provides cost-effective national security. It is a question that Congress has neither the capacity nor the determination to investigate fully.

When an agency is suspected of serious abuses, a committee is likely to hold hearings. Except in cases involving *executive privilege* (the right to withhold confidential information affecting national security), executive-branch officials must testify at these hearings if asked to do so. If they refuse, they can be cited for contempt of Congress, a criminal offense. Congress's investigative power is not listed in the Constitution, but the judiciary has not challenged that power, and Congress has used it extensively.

Congress's zeal for oversight increases substantially when the White House is the target, particularly if the presidency is in the hands of the other party. Republican-controlled committees scheduled numerous hearings to grill President Bill Clinton's appointees on allegations of presidential wrongdoing and, in the case of the Lewinsky scandal, even sought to remove the president from office. Republican-controlled committees were less inclined to schedule hearings in response to allegations of wrongdoing by President George W. Bush. When hearings were held, such as the 2006 hearings on the issue of National Security Agency (NSA) wiretapping without judicial permission, their scope and testimony were tightly controlled. Republicans were determined not to stage hearings that day after day would produce headlines damaging to the Bush presidency. However, after Republicans in the 2006 election lost their hold on congress, they were powerless to prevent Congressional Democrats from holding such hearings. Congressional Democrats mimicked the strategy congressional Republicans had used earlier against Clinton—scheduling hearings as a means of embarrassing President Bush and his party.

CONGRESS: TOO MUCH PLURALISM?

Congress is an institution divided between service to the nation and service to the separate constituencies within it. Its members have responsibility for the nation's laws, yet for reelection they depend on the voters of their states and districts and are highly responsive to constituency interests. This latter focus is facilitated by the committee system, which is organized around particular interests. Agriculture, labor, education, banking, and commerce are among the interests represented through this system. It is hard to conceive of a national legislature structured to respond to special interests more closely than is the Congress of the United States.

Pluralists admire this feature of Congress. They argue that the United States has a majoritarian institution in the presidency and that Congress is a place where a *diversity* of interests is represented. Critics of this view say that Congress sometimes is so responsive to particular interests that it neglects the overall national interest. This criticism is blunted from time to time by a strong majoritarian impulse in Congress. The current period is one of those moments. The high level of party discipline in recent years, coupled with a widening ideological gap between the parties, has placed Congress at the center of many national policy debates.

Yet Congress cannot easily be an institution that is highly responsive both to diverse interests and to the national interest. These interests often conflict, as the rise and fall of former Speaker Newt Gingrich illustrate. He sought to make the Republican congressional majority into the driving force in American national politics, but he was ousted from his position when the conflicts generated by his uncompromising pursuit of conservative policy goals weakened the GOP's support in the states and districts, threatening the reelection chances of Republican incumbents. This inherent tension between Congress's national role and its local base has been replayed many times in U.S. history. In a real sense, the strengths of Congress are also its weaknesses. Those features of congressional election and organization that make Congress responsive to separate constituencies are often the very ones that make it difficult for Congress to act as a strong instrument of a national majority. The perennial challenge for members of Congress is to find a workable balance between what Roger Davidson and Walter Oleszek call the "two Congresses": one embodied by the Capitol in Washington and the other embodied by the members' separate districts and states.[27]

Summary

Self-Test www.mhhe.com/pattersontad8

Members of Congress, once elected, are likely to be reelected. Members of Congress can use their office to publicize themselves, pursue a service strategy of responding to the needs of individual constituents, and secure pork-barrel projects for their states or districts. House members gain a greater advantage from these activities than do senators, whose larger constituencies make it harder for them to build close personal relations with voters and whose office is more likely to attract strong challengers. Incumbency does have some disadvantages. Members of Congress must take positions on controversial issues, may blunder into political scandal or indiscretion, must deal with changes in the electorate, or may face strong challengers; any of these conditions can reduce members' reelection chances. By and large, however, the advantages of incumbency far outweigh the disadvantages. Incumbents' advantages extend into their reelection campaigns: their influential positions in Congress make it easier for them to raise campaign funds from PACs and individual contributors.

Congress is a fragmented institution. It has no single leader; rather, the House and Senate have separate leaders, neither of whom can presume to speak for the other chamber. The principal party leaders of Congress are the Speaker of the House and the Senate majority leader. They share leadership power with committee and subcommittee chairpersons, who have influence on the policy decisions of their committee or subcommittee.

It is in the committees that most of the day-to-day work of Congress is conducted. Each standing committee of the House or the Senate has jurisdiction over congressional policy in a particular area (such as agriculture or foreign relations), as does each of its subcommittees. In most cases, the full House and Senate accept committee recommendations about the passage of bills, although amendments to bills are quite common and committees are careful to take other members of Congress into account when making legislative decisions. Congress is a legislative system in which influence is widely dispersed, an arrangement that suits the power and reelection needs of its individual members. However, partisanship is a strong and binding force in Congress. It is the basis on which party leaders are able to build support for major legislative initiatives. On this type of legislation, party leaders and caucuses, rather than committees, are the central actors.

The major function of Congress is to enact legislation. Yet the role it plays in developing legislation depends on the type of policy involved. Because of its divided chambers and committee structure, as well as the concern of its members with state and district interests, Congress, through its party leaders and caucuses, only occasionally takes the lead on broad national issues; Congress instead typically looks to the president for this leadership. Nevertheless, presidential initiatives are passed by Congress only if they meet its members' expectations and usually only after a lengthy process of compromise and negotiation. Congress is more adept at handling legislation that deals with problems of narrow interest. Legislation of this sort is decided mainly in congressional committees, where interested legislators, bureaucrats, and groups concentrate their efforts on issues of mutual concern.

A second function of Congress is the representation of various interests. Members of Congress are highly sensitive to the state or district they depend on for reelection. They do respond to overriding national interests, but for most of them local concerns generally come first. National or local representation often operates through party representation, particularly on issues that divide the Democratic and Republican parties and their constituent groups.

Congress's third function is oversight, the supervision and investigation of the way the bureaucracy is implementing legislatively mandated programs. Although oversight is a difficult process, it is an important means of legislative control over the actions of the executive branch.

STUDY CORNER

Key Terms

bill (*p. 320*)
cloture (*p. 322*)
conference committees (*p. 318*)
constituency (*p. 304*)
filibuster (*p. 322*)
gerrymandering (*p. 306*)
jurisdiction (of a congressional committee) (*p. 320*)
law (as enacted by Congress) (*p. 324*)

lawmaking function (*p. 324*)
logrolling (*p. 328*)
open-seat election (*p. 305*)
oversight function (*p. 330*)
party caucus (*p. 312*)
party discipline (*p. 323*)
party leaders (*p. 313*)
pork-barrel projects (*p. 304*)
reapportionment (*p. 306*)

redistricting (*p. 306*)
representation function (*p. 327*)
rider (*p. 322*)
seniority (*p. 316*)
service strategy (*p. 304*)
standing committees (*p. 317*)
veto (*p. 324*)

Self-Test

1. General characteristics of the U.S. Congress include all **except** which one of the following?
   a. Congress is a fragmented institution.
   b. Influence in Congress is widely dispersed.
   c. Congress rather than the president usually takes the lead in addressing broad national issues.
   d. Both the House and the Senate are directly elected by the voters.

2. In Congress, the role of representation of the nation through political parties is illustrated by all **except** which one of the following?
   a. conflicts over national goals primarily along party lines.
   b. the emphasis that members of Congress place on pork-barrel legislation.
   c. a common division of votes along party lines in committee voting.
   d. Republicans aligned against Democrats on roll-call votes.

3. Which of the following give(s) the president a policymaking advantage over Congress on broad national issues?
   a. the public's expectation that the president will take the lead on such issues.
   b. the fragmented leadership structure of Congress.
   c. the president's position as the sole chief executive and thus the authoritative voice of the executive branch.
   d. all of the above.

4. Which of the following factors usually plays the largest role in the reelection of members of Congress?
   a. incumbency.
   b. positions taken on issues.
   c. popularity with the president.
   d. gender.

5. Most bills that are introduced in Congress:
   a. are defeated in committee.
   b. are passed in committee and defeated on the floor.
   c. are passed and become law.
   d. are sent to executive agencies for review.

6. The most important party leadership position in the U.S. Senate is that of:
   a. Speaker.
   b. majority leader.
   c. president pro tempore.
   d. vice president of the United States.

7. Congressional incumbents receive fewer campaign contributions from PACs than their opponents do. (T/F)

8. The Speaker is the only officer of the House of Representatives provided for in the Constitution. (T/F)

9. Most of the work done in Congress is conducted through standing committees. (T/F)

10. A bill must be passed in identical form by both chambers of Congress before it can be sent to the president for approval or veto. (T/F)

Critical Thinking

How does the structure of Congress (for example, its two chambers and its committee system) affect its policymaking role?

Suggested Readings

Dwyre, Diana, and Victoria Farrar-Myers. *Legislative Labyrinth: Congress and Campaign Finance Reform.* Washington, D.C.: Congressional Quarterly Press, 2001. An inside look at the mix of Congress and campaign money.

Herrnson, Paul S. *Congressional Elections: Campaigning at Home and in Washington,* 4th ed. Washington, D.C.: Congressional Quarterly Press, 2003. A study that argues that members of Congress run two campaigns, one at home and one in Washington.

Hibbing, John R., and Elizabeth Theiss-Morse. *Congress as Public Enemy: Public Attitudes Toward American Political Institutions.* New York: Cambridge University Press, 1995. An analysis through survey and focus group data of Americans' attitudes toward Congress.

Jacobson, Gary C. *The Politics of Congressional Elections,* 6th ed. New York: Longman, 2003. An overview of the congressional election process and its impact on policy and representation.

Quirk, Paul J., and Sarah A. Binder, eds. *The Legislative Branch.* New York: Oxford University Press, 2005. A comprehensive set of essays on Congress by many of the best congressional scholars.

Sidlow, Edward. *Challenging the Incumbent: An Underdog's Undertaking.* Washington, D.C.: Congressional Quarterly Press, 2003. A fascinating case study of the difficulties faced by those who dare to challenge an incumbent.

Sinclair, Barbara. *Unorthodox Lawmaking: New Legislative Processes in the U.S. Congress,* 2nd ed. Washington, D.C.: Congressional Quarterly Press, 2000. A detailed analysis of the American legislative process.

List of Websites

http://www.usafmc.org/default.asp?pagenumber=8

The website of the United States Association of Former Members of Congress, which has a "Congress to Campus" program that upon request brings former congressional members to campuses for talks.

http://thomas.loc.gov/

The Library of Congress site, named after Thomas Jefferson, that provides information about the congressional process, including the status of pending legislation.

http://www.house.gov/

The U.S. House of Representatives' website; it has information on party leaders, pending legislation, and committee hearings, as well as links to each House member's office and website.

http://www.senate.gov/

The U.S. Senate's website, which is similar to that of the House and provides links to each senator's website.

Participate!

Congressional offices get thousands of letters and emails every day from Americans voicing opinions on the issues of the moment. Consider writing to the House member from your congressional district (the address can be found at www.house.gov) or to one of your state's two U.S. senators (www.senate.gov) expressing your thoughts on a public policy problem. Your letter or email is almost certain to draw a response and to be included in a file that will help the member to judge what constituents are saying about the issue in question. These letters occasionally affect a member's thinking about an issue.

Extra Credit

For up-to-the-minute *New York Times* articles, interactive simulations, graphics, study tools, and more links and quizzes, visit the text's Online Learning Center at www.mhhe.com/pattersontad8.

(Self-Test Answers: 1. c   2. b   3. d   4. a   5. a   6. b   7. F   8. T   9. T   10. T)

The Presidency:
Leading the Nation

Chapter Outline

Foundations of the Modern Presidency
  Asserting a Claim to National Leadership
  The Need for Presidential Leadership of an
    Activist Government

Choosing the President
  The Primary Elections
  The National Party Conventions
  The Campaign for Election

Staffing the Presidency
  Presidential Appointees
  The Problem of Control

Factors in Presidential Leadership
  The Force of Circumstance
  The Stage of the President's Term
  The Nature of the Issue: Foreign or
    Domestic
  Relations with Congress
  Public Support

CHAPTER 12

[The president's] is the only voice in national affairs. Let him once
win the admiration and confidence of the people, and no other single
voice will easily overpower him.

—*Woodrow Wilson*[1]

George W. Bush was sinking in the polls. The economy was weakening,
and the newly elected president was being criticized for not doing
enough to reverse the downturn. Bush was also getting heat for the
defection of Senator James Jeffords of Vermont, which cost Republicans control
of the Senate. The news media had given him the honeymoon period traditionally accorded a new president, but they were now turning on him.

Everything changed on September 11, 2001. After the terrorist attacks on the
World Trade Center and the Pentagon, Americans rallied around their president.
Bush vowed that America would not rest until the terrorists were brought to justice and the international network of which they were a part was destroyed. His
presidential approval rating reached 96 percent, the highest level ever recorded.
Not even Franklin Roosevelt and Harry Truman had received approval ratings
that high during the Second World War. During the next two years, buoyed by
public support, Bush led the nation into wars in Afghanistan and Iraq as part of
his "war on terrorism."

By 2005, everything had changed again for President Bush. The U.S. invasion of Iraq was followed by problems the Bush administration had not anticipated. Continued attacks on U.S. forces, a failure to find weapons of mass
destruction, abuses of Iraqi prisoners by U.S. soldiers, and the escalating financial cost of Iraq's reconstruction were eroding his public support. Bush was able
to win reelection in 2004, but his victory was by the smallest margin for an
incumbent since Harry Truman's victory in 1948. Bush's reelection gave him a
boost in the opinion polls, but it was short-lived. By early 2005, his approval
rating was dropping again, and it eventually fell below 40 percent.

The Bush story is but one in the saga of the ups and downs of the modern
presidency. Lyndon Johnson's and Richard Nixon's dogged pursuit of the
Vietnam War led to talk of "the imperial presidency," an office so powerful that
constitutional checks and balances were no longer an effective constraint on it.
Within a few years, because of the undermining effects of Watergate and of
changing international conditions during the Ford and Carter presidencies, the
watchword became "the imperiled presidency," an office too weak to meet the
nation's demands for executive leadership. Ronald Reagan's policy successes
before 1986 renewed talk heard in the Roosevelt and Kennedy years of "a heroic

President George W. Bush gestures as he responds to reporters' questions in 2006 as part of a White House effort to revive public support for his presidency. In 2001, his presidential approval rating soared above 90 percent. By 2006, it had fallen below 40 percent and was hurting his ability to lead Congress and the public.

presidency," an office that is the inspirational center of American politics. After the Iran-Contra scandal in 1986, Reagan was more often called a lame duck. The first George Bush's handling of the Gulf crisis—leading the nation in 1991 into a major war and emerging from it with a stratospheric public approval rating—bolstered the heroic conception of the office. A year later, Bush was on his way to being removed from office by the voters. Bill Clinton overcame a fitful start to his presidency to become the first Democrat since Franklin D. Roosevelt in the 1930s to win reelection. As Clinton was launching an aggressive second-term policy agenda, however, he got entangled in an affair with a White House intern, Monica Lewinsky, that led to his impeachment by the House of Representatives and weakened his claim to national leadership.

No other political institution has been subject to such varying characterizations as the modern presidency. One reason is that the formal powers of the office are somewhat limited and thus presidential power changes with national conditions, political circumstances, and the personal capacity of the office's occupant.[2] The American presidency is always a central office in that its occupant is a focus of national attention. Yet the presidency is not an inherently powerful office, in the sense that presidents routinely get what they want. Presidential power is conditional. It depends on the president's own abilities but even more on circumstances—on whether the situation demands strong leadership and whether the political support for that leadership exists. When conditions are favorable, the president will look powerful. When conditions are adverse, the president will appear vulnerable.

This chapter examines the roots of presidential power, the presidential selection process, the staffing of the presidency, and the factors associated with the success and failure of presidential leadership. The main ideas of this chapter are these:

- *Public expectations, national crises, and changing national and world conditions have required the presidency to become a strong office.* Underlying this development is the public support the president acquires from being the only nationally elected official.

- *The modern presidential election campaign is a marathon affair in which self-selected candidates must plan for a strong start in the nominating contests and center their general-election strategies on media, issues, and a baseline of support.* The lengthy campaign process heightens the public's sense that the presidency is at the center of the U.S. political system.

- *The modern presidency could not operate without a large staff of assistants, experts, and high-level managers, but the sheer size of this staff makes it impossible for the president to exercise complete control over it.*

- *The president's election by national vote and position as sole chief executive ensure that others will listen to the president's ideas; but to lead effectively, the president must have the help of other officials and, to get their help, must respond to their interests as they respond to the president's.*

- *Presidential influence on national policy is highly variable.* Whether presidents succeed or fail in getting their policies enacted depends heavily on the force of circumstance, the stage of their presidency, partisan support in Congress, and the foreign or domestic nature of the policy issue.

FOUNDATIONS OF THE MODERN PRESIDENCY

The writers of the Constitution knew what they wanted from a president—national leadership, statesmanship in foreign affairs, command in time of war or insurgency, enforcement of the laws—but they could devise only general phrases to describe the president's constitutional authority. Compared with Article I, which enumerates Congress's specific powers, Article II of the Constitution contains relatively general statements on the president's powers (see Table 12–1).[3]

Over the course of American history, each of the president's constitutional powers has been extended in practice beyond the Framers' intention. For example, the Constitution grants the president command of the nation's military, but only Congress can declare war. In *Federalist* No. 69, Alexander Hamilton wrote that a surprise attack on the United States was the only justification for war by presidential action. Nevertheless, the nation's presidents have sent troops into military action abroad more than two hundred times. Of the more than a dozen wars included in that figure, only five were declared by Congress.[4] All of America's most recent wars—the Korean, Vietnam, Persian Gulf, Balkans, Afghanistan, and Iraq conflicts—have been undeclared.

The Constitution also empowers the president to act as diplomatic leader with the authority to appoint ambassadors and to negotiate treaties with other countries, subject to approval by a two-thirds vote of the Senate. The Framers

TABLE 12–1	**The Constitutional Authority for the President's Roles** Unlike Congress's powers, which are specifically enumerated in the Constitution, the president's powers are provided through relatively general clauses. This openness has facilitated an expansion of presidential power over the course of the nation's history.

Commander in chief: Article II, Section 2: "The President shall be commander in chief of the Army and Navy of the United States, and of the militia of the several states."

Chief executive: Article II, Section 2: "He may require the opinion, in writing, of the principal officer in each of the executive departments, upon any subject relating to the duties of their respective offices, and he shall have power to grant reprieves and pardons for offences against the United States, except in cases of impeachment."

Article II, Section 2: "He shall have power, by and with the advice and consent of the Senate, to make treaties, provided two thirds of the senators present concur; and he shall nominate, and by and with the advice and consent of the Senate, shall appoint ambassadors, other public ministers and consuls, judges of the Supreme Court, and all other officers of the United States, whose appointments are not herein otherwise provided for, and which shall be established by law."

Article II, Section 2: "The President shall have power to fill up all vacancies that may happen during the recess of the Senate, by granting commissions which shall expire at the end of their next session."

Article II, Section 3: "He shall take care that the laws be faithfully executed, and shall commission all the officers of the United States."

Chief diplomat: Article II, Section 2: "He shall have power, and with the advice and consent of the Senate, to make treaties, provided two thirds of the senators present concur."

Article II, Section 3: "He shall receive ambassadors and other public ministers."

Legislative leader: Article II, Section 3: "He shall from time to time give to the Congress information of the state of the Union, and recommend to their consideration such measures as he shall judge necessary and expedient; he may, on extraordinary occasions, convene both houses, or either of them, and in case of disagreement between them, with respect to the time of adjournment, he may adjourn them to such time as he shall think proper." (Article I, Section 7, which defines the president's veto power, is also part of his legislative authority.)

anticipated that Congress would define the nation's foreign policy objectives, while the president would oversee their implementation. However, the president has become the principal architect of U.S. foreign policy and has even acquired the power to make treaty-like arrangements with other nations, in the form of executive agreements. In 1937, the Supreme Court ruled that such agreements, signed and approved only by the president, have the same legal status as treaties, although Congress can cancel executive agreements with which it disagrees.[5] Since World War II, presidents have negotiated more than ten thousand executive agreements, compared to fewer than one thousand treaties ratified by the Senate.[6]

The Constitution also vests "executive power" in the president. This power includes the responsibility to execute the laws faithfully and to appoint major administrators, such as heads of the various departments of the executive branch. In *Federalist* No. 76, Hamilton indicated that the president's real authority as chief executive was to be found in this appointive capacity. Presidents have indeed exercised substantial power through their appointments, but they have found their administrative authority—the power to execute the laws—to be of even greater value, because it enables them to determine how laws will be interpreted and applied. President Ronald Reagan used his executive power to *prohibit* the use of federal funds by family-planning clinics that offered abortion counseling. President Bill Clinton exerted the same power to *permit* the use of federal funds for this purpose. The same act of Congress was the basis for each of these actions. The act authorizes the use of federal funds for family-planning services, but it neither requires nor prohibits their use for abortion counseling, enabling the president to decide this issue.

Finally, the Constitution provides the president with legislative authority, including use of the veto and the opportunity to recommend proposals to Congress. The Framers expected this authority to be used in a limited way. George Washington acted as the Framers anticipated: he proposed only three legislative measures and vetoed only two acts of Congress. Modern presidents have assumed a more active legislative role. They regularly submit proposals to Congress and most of them have not hesitated to veto legislation they find disagreeable.

The presidency is a more powerful office than the Framers envisioned, for many reasons. But two features of the office in particular—*national election* and *singular authority*—have enabled presidents to make use of changing demands on government to claim the position of leader of the American people. It is a claim that no other elected official can routinely make, and it is a key to understanding the role and power of the president.

Asserting a Claim to National Leadership

The first president to forcefully assert a claim to popular leadership was Andrew Jackson, who had been swept into office in 1828 on a tide of public support that broke the hold of the upper classes on the presidency. Jackson used his popular backing to challenge Congress's claim to national policy leadership, contending that he was "the people's tribune."

However, Jackson's view was not shared by most of his successors during the nineteenth century, because national conditions did not routinely call for strong presidential leadership. The prevailing conception was the **Whig theory,** which held that the presidency was a limited or constrained office whose occupant was confined to the exercise of expressly granted constitutional authority.

HISTORICAL BACKGROUND

Whig theory
A theory that prevailed in the nineteenth century and held that the presidency was a limited or restrained office whose occupant was confined to expressly granted constitutional authority.

The president had no implicit powers for dealing with national problems but was primarily an administrator, charged with carrying out the will of Congress. "My duty," said President James Buchanan, a Whig adherent, "is to execute the laws . . . and not my individual opinions."[7]

Theodore Roosevelt rejected the Whig tradition upon taking office in 1901. He attacked the business trusts, pursued an aggressive foreign policy, and pressured Congress to adopt progressive domestic policies. Roosevelt embraced the **stewardship theory,** which calls for an assertive presidency that is confined only at points specifically prohibited by law. As "steward of the people," Roosevelt said, he was permitted "to do anything that the needs of the Nation demanded unless such action was forbidden by the Constitution or by the laws."[8]

Roosevelt's image of a strong presidency was shared by Woodrow Wilson, but his other immediate successors reverted to the Whig notion of the limited presidency.[9] Herbert Hoover's restrained conception of the presidency prevented him from acting decisively during the devastation of the Great Depression. Hoover said that he lacked the constitutional authority to establish public relief programs for jobless Americans. However, Hoover's successor, Franklin D. Roosevelt, shared the stewardship theory of his distant cousin Theodore Roosevelt, and FDR's New Deal signaled the end of the limited presidency. As FDR's successor, Harry Truman, wrote in his memoirs: "The power of the President should be used in the interest of the people and in order to do that the President must use whatever power the Constitution does not expressly deny him."[10]

Today the presidency is an inherently strong office.[11] The modern presidency becomes a more substantial office in the hands of a confident individual like George W. Bush, but even a less forceful person like Jimmy Carter is expected to act assertively. This expectation not only is the legacy of former strong presidents but also stems from changes that have occurred in the federal government's national and international policy responsibilities.

stewardship theory
A theory that argues for a strong, assertive presidential role, with presidential authority limited only at points specifically prohibited by law.

LEADERS

GEORGE WASHINGTON

(1732–99)

George Washington, the nation's first president and its greatest in the minds of some historians, was born into a Virginia planter family. As a child, he excelled as a horseman, a skill that along with family connections earned him an officer's commission. He was involved in the first major skirmish of the French and Indian War. His daring and bravery under fire—two horses were shot out from under him as he rallied troops who had fled in the face of the enemy—made him a national hero. When the American colonies a decade later declared their independence from Britain, he was the natural choice to lead the Continental Army. Throughout the six-year Revolutionary War, Washington avoided pitched battles, knowing that his poorly equipped soldiers were no match for British regulars. Finally, in 1781, his forces trapped the British army at Yorktown and with the help of French naval vessels scored a decisive victory that ended the war. Some of his countrymen thought Washington should be named king, but he dismissed the idea, saying America would instead be a new type of nation. He retired to his Mount Vernon plantation, only to grow increasingly worried by the growing discord among the states and the inability of Congress to govern effectively.

In 1787, Washington presided over the Philadelphia convention that drafted a constitution that became the basis for a stronger central government. Following ratification of the Constitution, Washington was elected president by unanimous vote of the Electoral College. He recognized that his presidency would define future ones. In a letter to James Madison, Washington wrote, "It is devoutly wished on my part that these precedents may be fixed on true principles." Washington pushed for a strong national government, believing that it could keep the nation from devolving into sectional rivalries. He also kept the United States out of foreign affairs, believing the new country was too weak militarily to play such a role. Washington could have been elected to a third term, but he stepped down after two terms, stating that the presidency was a citizen's office, not a monarchal one. It was a precedent that all presidents adhered to until Franklin Roosevelt ran for and won a third term in 1940 at a time when the country was confronting the twin threats of economic depression and war. Roosevelt's presidency prompted Congress to initiate the Twenty-Second Amendment to the Constitution, which limits a president to two terms in office.

The Need for Presidential Leadership of an Activist Government

During most of the nineteenth century (the Civil War being the notable exception), the United States did not need a strong president. The federal government's policymaking role was small, as was its bureaucracy. Moreover, the nation's major issues were of a sectional nature (especially the North-South split over slavery) and thus were suited to action by Congress, which represented state interests. The U.S. government's role in world affairs was also small. As these conditions changed, however, the presidency also changed.

Foreign Policy Leadership

The president has always been the nation's foreign policy leader, but the role was initially a rather undemanding one. The United States avoided entanglement in the turbulent affairs of Europe and was preoccupied with westward expansion. By the end of the nineteenth century, however, the nation was seeking a world market for its goods. President Theodore Roosevelt advocated an American economic empire and looked south toward Latin America and west toward Hawaii, the Philippines, and China for new markets (the "Open Door" policy). However, the United States' tradition of isolationism remained a powerful influence on national policy. The United States fought in World War I but immediately thereafter demobilized its armed forces. Over President Woodrow Wilson's objections, Congress then voted against the entry of the United States into the League of Nations.

World War II fundamentally changed the nation's international role and the president's role in foreign policy. In 1945, the United States emerged as a global superpower, a giant in world trade, and the recognized leader of the noncommunist world. The United States today has a military presence in nearly every part of the globe and an unprecedented interest in trade balances, energy supplies, and other international issues affecting the nation.

The effect of these developments on America's political institutions has been one-sided. Because of the president's constitutional authority as chief diplomat and military commander and the special demands of foreign policy leadership, the president, not Congress, has taken the lead in addressing the nation's increased responsibilities in the world. Foreign policy requires singleness of purpose and, at times, fast action. Congress—a large, divided, and unwieldy institution—is poorly suited to such a response. In contrast, the president, as sole head of the executive branch, can act quickly and speak authoritatively for the nation as a whole in its relations with other nations.

This capacity has rarely been more evident than after the terrorist attacks of September 11, 2001. The initiative in the war on terrorism rested squarely with the White House. President Bush decided on the U.S. response to the attacks and took the lead in

Harry S Truman's presidency was characterized by bold foreign policy initiatives. He authorized the use of nuclear weapons against Japan in 1945, created the Marshall Plan as the basis for the economic reconstruction of postwar Europe, and sent U.S. troops to fight in Korea in 1950. Truman is shown here greeting British Prime Minister Winston Churchill at a Washington airport in early 1952.

The White House contains, on the first floor, the president's Oval Office, other offices, and ceremonial rooms. The First Family's living quarters are on the second floor.

obtaining international support for U.S. military, intelligence, and diplomatic initiatives. Congress backed these actions enthusiastically. The joint resolution that endorsed Bush's decision to attack the Taliban government in Afghanistan passed unanimously in the Senate and with only a single dissenting vote in the House. In reality, however, Congress had little choice but to support whatever policies Bush chose. Americans wanted decisive action and were looking to the president, not to Congress, for leadership.

In other situations, of course, Congress is less compliant. In recent decades, it has contested presidential positions on issues such as global trade and international human rights. Nevertheless, the president is clearly the leading voice in U.S. foreign policy. (The changing shape of the world and its implications for presidential power and leadership are discussed more fully later in the chapter.)

Domestic Policy Leadership

The change in the president's domestic leadership role has also been substantial. Throughout most of the nineteenth century Congress jealously guarded its constitutional powers, making it clear that it was in charge of domestic policy. James Bryce wrote in the 1880s that Congress paid no more attention to the president's views on legislation than it did to the editorial positions of newspaper publishers.[12]

By the early twentieth century, however, the national government was taking on regulatory and policy responsibilities imposed by the nation's transition from an agrarian to an industrial society, and the executive branch was growing ever larger. In 1921, Congress conceded that it lacked the centralized authority to coordinate the growing national budget and enacted the Budget and Accounting Act, which provided for an executive budget. Federal departments and agencies would no longer submit their annual budget requests directly to Congress. Instead, the president would develop the various agencies' requests into a comprehensive budgetary proposal, which then would be submitted to Congress as a starting point for its deliberations.

HISTORICAL BACKGROUND

During the Great Depression of the 1930s, Franklin D. Roosevelt's New Deal responded to the public's demand for economic relief with a broad program that required a level of policy planning and coordination beyond the capacity of Congress. In addition to public works projects and social welfare programs, the New Deal made the government a partner in nearly every aspect of the nation's economy. If economic regulation was to work, unified and continuous policy leadership was needed, and only the president could routinely provide it.

Presidential authority has continued to grow since Roosevelt's time. In response to pressures from the public, the national government's role in areas such as education, health, welfare, safety, and protection of the environment has expanded greatly, which in turn has created additional demands for presidential leadership.[13] Big government, with its emphasis on comprehensive planning and program coordination, has favored executive authority at the expense of legislative authority. All democracies have seen a shift in power from their legislature to their executive. In Britain, for example, the prime minister has taken on responsibilities that once belonged to the cabinet or to Parliament.

CHOOSING THE PRESIDENT

As the president's policy and leadership responsibilities changed during the nation's history, so did the process of electing presidents. The changes do not parallel each other exactly, but they are related both politically and philosophically. As the presidency drew ever closer to the people, their role in selecting the president grew ever more important.[14] The United States in its history has had four systems of presidential selection, each more "democratic" than its predecessor (see Table 12–2).

TABLE 12–2	The Four Systems of Presidential Selection	
SELECTION SYSTEM	PERIOD	FEATURES
1. Original	1788–1828	Party nominees are chosen in congressional caucuses. Electoral College members act somewhat independently in their presidential voting.
2. Party convention	1832–1900	Party nominees are chosen in national party conventions by delegates selected by state and local party organizations. Electoral College members cast their ballots for the popular-vote winner in their respective states.
3. Party convention, primary	1904–68	As in system 2, except that a *minority* of national convention delegates are chosen through primary elections (the majority still being chosen by party organizations).
4. Party primary, open caucus	1972–present	As in system 2, except that a *majority* of national convention delegates are chosen through primary elections.

The delegates to the constitutional convention of 1787 feared that popular election of the president would make the office too powerful and accordingly devised an electoral vote system (the so-called Electoral College). The president was to be chosen by electors picked by the states with each state being entitled to one elector for each of its members of Congress (House and Senate combined). This system was changed after the election in 1828 of Andrew Jackson, who believed the people's will had been denied four years earlier when he got the most popular votes but failed to gain an electoral majority. Jackson was unable to persuade Congress to support a constitutional amendment that would have eliminated the Electoral College, but he did obtain the next-best alternative: he persuaded the states to link their electoral votes to the popular vote. Under Jackson's reform, which is still in effect today, each party in a state has a separate slate of electors who gain the right to cast a state's electoral votes if their party's candidate places first in the state's popular voting. Thus, the popular vote for the candidates directly affects their electoral vote, and one candidate is likely to win both forms of the presidential vote. Since Jackson's time, only Rutherford B. Hayes (in 1876), Benjamin Harrison (in 1888), and George W. Bush (in 2000) have won the presidency after having lost the popular vote.

Jackson also championed the national convention as a means of nominating the party's presidential candidate (before this time, nominations were made by party caucuses in Congress and in state legislatures). The parties' strength was at the grass roots, among the people, and Jackson saw the convention process as a means of bringing the citizenry and the presidency closer together. Since Jackson's time, presidential nominees have been formally chosen at national party conventions. Each state party sends delegates to the national convention, and these delegates select the party's nominee.

Jackson's system of presidential nomination remained fully intact until the early twentieth century, when the Progressives devised the primary election as a means of curbing the power of the party bosses (see Chapter 2). State party leaders had taken control of the nominating process by handpicking their states' convention delegates. The Progressives sought to give voters the power to select the delegates. Such a process is called an *indirect primary*, because the voters are not choosing the nominees directly (as they do in House and Senate races) but rather are choosing delegates who in turn select the nominees.

However, the Progressives were unable to persuade most states to adopt presidential primaries, which meant that party leaders continued to control enough of the delegates to pick the nominees. That arrangement held until 1968 when Democratic party leaders ignored the strength of anti-Vietnam war sentiment in the primaries and nominated Vice President Hubert Humphrey, who had not entered a single primary and was closely identified with the Johnson administration's Vietnam policy. After Humphrey narrowly lost the 1968 general election to Richard Nixon, reform-minded Democrats forced changes in the nominating process. The new rules gave rank-and-file party voters more control by requiring states to choose their delegates through either primary elections or **open party caucuses** (meetings open to any registered party voter who wants to attend). Although the Democrats initiated the change, the Republicans were also affected by it. Most states that adopted a presidential primary in order to comply with the Democrats' new rules also required Republicans to select their convention delegates through a primary.

Today it is the voters in state primaries and open caucuses who play the decisive role in the selection of the Democratic and Republican presidential nominees.[15] A state's delegates are awarded to candidates in accordance with how

open party caucuses
Meetings at which a party's candidates for nomination are voted on and that are open to all the party's rank-and-file voters who want to attend.

Debating the Issues

Should the Electoral College Be Abolished?

As the votes in the 2000 election were counted, the country was thrown into turmoil by the electoral vote system. The president is chosen by an indirect system of election. Voters cast ballots for candidates, but their votes choose only each state's electors, whose subsequent ballots result in the actual selection of the president. Electoral votes are apportioned by states based on their representation in Congress, which creates the possibility that the candidate who receives the most popular votes will not receive the most electoral votes and thus will not be elected president. The 2000 election was of this type, and it renewed the debate about retaining the electoral vote system.

It's time to abolish the Electoral College and to count the votes of all Americans in presidential elections. . . . Two centuries ago the Constitutional Convention considered many ways to select the president of the emerging republic, from popular election to assigning the decision to the Congress. The Electoral College was a compromise that reflected a basic mistrust of the electorate—the same mistrust that denied the vote to women, African-Americans, and people who did not own property. The Electoral College may or may not have made sense in 1787. But through 21st-century eyes it is as anachronistic as the limitations on suffrage itself. Whether or not you like the results of a particular election . . . your vote should count. . . . If the Electoral College merely echoes the election results, then it is superfluous. If it contradicts the voting majority, then why tolerate it? It is a remarkable and enduring virtue of our political system that our elections are credible and decisive—and that power changes hands in a coherent and dignified manner. . . . Every other public official is chosen by majority vote. That's the way it's supposed to work in a democracy. For reasons both philosophical and practical, that's also how we should elect the president.

—*William D. Delahunt, U.S. representative (D-Mass.)*

The pundits will argue that it is not fair to deny the presidency to the man who received the most total votes. After all, to do so would be "undemocratic." This argument ignores the fundamental nature of our constitutional system. The Founding Fathers sought to create a loose confederacy of states, joined together by a federal government with very little power. They created a constitutionally limited republic, not a direct democracy. They did so to protect fundamental liberties against the whims of the masses. The Electoral College likewise was created in the Constitution to guard against majority tyranny in federal elections. The President was to be elected by the states rather than the citizenry as a whole, with votes apportioned to states according to their representation in Congress. The will of the people was to be tempered by the wisdom of the Electoral College. By contrast, election of the President by pure popular vote totals would damage statehood. Populated areas on both coasts would have increasing influence on national elections, to the detriment of less populated southern and western states. A candidate receiving a large percentage of the popular vote in California and New York could win a national election with very little support in dozens of other states! A popular vote system simply would intensify the populist pandering which already dominates national campaigns.

—*Ron Paul, U.S. representative (R-Texas)*

---

well they do in the state's primary or caucus. Thus, to win the majority of national convention delegates necessary for nomination, a candidate must place first in a lot of states and do at least reasonably well in most of the rest. (About forty states choose their delegates through a primary election; the others use the caucus system.)

In sum, the presidential election system has changed from an elite-dominated process to one based on voter support. This arrangement has strengthened the presidency by providing the office with the reserve of power that popular election confers on democratic leadership.

The Primary Elections

The fact that voters pick the party nominees has opened the nominating races to any politician with the energy and resources to run a major national campaign. Nominating campaigns, except those in which an incumbent president is seeking reelection, typically attract a half-dozen contenders. The 2004 Democratic race drew an even larger number—nine candidates.

In early 2007, almost two years before Americans would choose their next president, nearly two dozen presidential hopefuls were positioning themselves for a possible run by raising funds, sounding out party leaders, visiting key states, and seeking media attention. The list of hopefuls was so long that not even seasoned pundits could rattle off the names of all of them. Among the possible contenders on the Democratic side were Evan Bayh, Joe Biden, Hillary Clinton, Christopher Dodd, John Edwards, Russ Feingold, Al Gore, John Kerry, Barack Obama, Bill Richardson, Tom Vilsack, and Mark Warner. Among those mentioned as Republican possibilities were George Allen, Sam Brownback, Bill Frist, Newt Gingrich, Rudy Giuliani, Chuck Hagel, Mike Huckabee, John McCain, George Pataki, Condoleeza Rice, and Mitt Romney.

Candidates have no choice but to start early and campaign hard. A key to success in the nominating campaign is **momentum**—a strong showing in the early contests that leads to a buildup of public support in subsequent ones. Nobody—not the press, not donors, not the voters—has time for an also ran. No candidate in recent decades has got off to a lousy start in the first few contests and then picked up enough steam to come anywhere near to winning the nomination. All the advantages rest with the fast starters. They get more attention from the press, more money from contributors, and get more consideration by the voters. Not surprisingly, presidential contenders strive to do well in the early contests, particularly the first caucuses in Iowa and the first primary in New Hampshire.

Money, always a critical factor in elections, has become increasingly important in the last three decades because states have moved their primaries and caucuses to the early weeks of the nominating period in order to increase their influence on the outcome. To compete effectively in so many contests over such a short period, candidates need money—lots of it. A candidate can be in only one place at a time, so the campaign must be carried to other voters through costly televised political advertising. Observers estimate it takes at least $40 million to run a strong nominating campaign, and possibly a lot more than that for a candidate who does not have substantial name

The modern presidential campaign is a marathon event that formally lasts nearly a year and speculatively is always under way. Two years before the 2008 election, nearly two dozen presidential possibilities—about half of them Republicans and half of them Democrats—were traveling around the country in hopes of gathering enough support to make a run for their party's nomination. Pundits picked Senator Hillary Clinton on the Democratic side and Senator John McCain on the Republican side as two of the early favorites for nomination. Clinton and McCain are shown here while visiting Norway as part of a Senate delegation studying global environmental issues.

momentum (in campaigns)
A strong showing by a candidate in early presidential nominating contests, which leads to a buildup of public support for the candidate.

Get Involved!

Every Four Years

No event over the years has lured more young people into politics than has the presidential campaign. It is to American politics what the Super Bowl is to professional football or what the World Series is to professional baseball. On election day, the number of voters who go to the polls is nearly 50 percent greater than in a midterm election.

A presidential election is also an occasion for more active political participation. There is no exact tally of the number of Americans who contribute time or money to a presidential campaign, but it is in the millions.

The points of entry for a campaign volunteer are many and start early. Residents of Iowa, Nevada, New Hampshire, and South Carolina—the states with the first nominating contests—get the first shot at helping candidates of their choice. From there, the campaign unfolds state by state, although the nominating race usually is over in March, when

it reaches the point at which one candidate's lead is so substantial that the other contenders drop out. (Information on the presidential nominating contests, including the date for the contest in your state, can be found online at http://www.thegreenpapers. com/P08.)

After the nominating races end, months remain in the presidential campaign, and there is still much to do. Volunteers are needed to staff phone banks, knock on doors, and do the many other things that comprise a presidential campaign. Sending e-mail messages to family and friends promoting one's candidate is another way to get involved. And for those with little or no spare time, a small monetary donation to the candidate of choice is always an option. Consider getting involved. Millions of other Americans in one way or another will be taking part in the presidential campaign.

recognition and public support before the campaign begins. In every nominating race but one from 1984 to 2004, the winner was the candidate who had raised the most money before the start of the primaries. (The exception was the 2004 race, when Howard Dean was the top Democratic fund-raiser in advance of the Iowa caucuses.)

Candidates in primary elections receive federal funding if they meet the eligibility criteria. The Federal Election Campaign Act of 1974 (as amended in 1979) provides for federal matching funds. Under the program, the government matches the first $250 of each private donation received by a primary election candidate, provided the candidate raises at least $5,000 in individual contributions of up to $250 in at least twenty states. This provision is designed to restrict matching funds to candidates who can show they have a reasonable amount of public support. In addition, any candidate who receives matching funds must agree to limit expenditures for the nominating phase to a set amount overall (roughly $50 million in 2008) and in particular states (the 2008 limits in Iowa and New Hampshire, for example, are roughly $1.4 million and $800,000, respectively). The limits are adjusted upward each election year to account for inflation. Taxpayers fund the matching program by checking a box on their income-tax return allocating $3 of their taxes to it.

Until the 2000 election, when George Bush declined matching funds so that he could raise unrestricted amounts of money for his nominating campaign, candidates had routinely accepted matching funds, which meant they were willing to abide by the spending limit. In 2004, Bush again turned down matching funds, raising more than $200 million for a nominating campaign in which he faced no Republican opponent. He spent the money to improve his standing with the voters—a perfectly legal tactic as long as the candidate spends the money before the party's summertime nominating convention. On the

Democratic side in 2004, Kerry and Dean chose not to accept matching funds, which enabled them to outspend their Democratic rivals in Iowa, New Hampshire, and other early contests.

As candidates have increasingly declined public funding, there have been calls to raise the allowable spending limit under public financing, perhaps to as high as $100 million. Otherwise, observers say, the only candidates who will accept matching funds will be those with no chance of victory. This development would defeat the purpose of public funding, which is to free candidates from the obligations that come from accepting large sums of money from private groups and individuals.

The National Party Conventions

The summertime national party conventions mark the end of the nominating campaign. In an earlier era, the convention was where the nomination was actually decided. State party delegations would come together at their convention to bargain and choose among potential nominees. Since 1972, when the delegate-selection process was changed, the leading candidate in every case has acquired enough delegates in the primaries to lock up the nomination before the convention begins. Nevertheless, the convention is a major event. It brings together the delegates elected in the state caucuses and primaries, who then approve a party platform and formally nominate the party's presidential and vice presidential candidates.

By tradition, the choice of the vice presidential nominee rests with the presidential nominee. In 2004, Kerry alone decided upon John Edwards as his running mate. Critics say the vice presidential nomination should be decided in open competition, because the vice president could become president someday (see Table 12–3). The chief argument for the existing method is that the president needs a trusted and like-minded vice president.

The Campaign for Election

The winner in the November general election is certain to be either the Republican or the Democratic candidate. Two-thirds of the nation's voters identify with the Republican or Democratic party, and most Independents lean toward one or the other of them. As a result, the major-party presidential nominees have a built-in source of votes. Even Democrat George McGovern, who had the lowest level of party support in the past half-century, was backed in 1972 by 60 percent of his party's identifiers. The level of party support for a major-party nominee can be quite high. In 2004, Bush was backed by 93 percent of Republicans, while Kerry was supported by 89 percent of Democrats.

Because the Democratic and Republican nominees have this huge advantage, a third-party candidate has no realistic hope of victory. Even Ross Perot, who in 1992 ran the most successful third-party campaign in nearly a century, was able to garner only a fifth of the vote. On the other hand, third-party candidates have sometimes caused problems for a major party by siphoning votes away from its nominee. In 2000 and again in 2004, third-party candidate Ralph Nader drew the bulk of his support from voters who indicated they otherwise would have backed the Democratic nominee.

Election Strategy

The candidates' strategies in the general election are shaped by many considerations, including the constitutional provision that each state shall have

TABLE 12–3	The Path to the White House		
PRESIDENT	**YEARS IN OFFICE**	**HIGHEST PREVIOUS OFFICE**	**SECOND-HIGHEST OFFICE**
Theodore Roosevelt	1901–8	Vice president*	Governor
William Howard Taft	1909–12	Secretary of war	Federal judge
Woodrow Wilson	1913–20	Governor	None
Warren G. Harding	1921–24	U.S. senator	Lieutenant governor
Calvin Coolidge	1925–28	Vice president*	Governor
Herbert Hoover	1929–32	Secretary of commerce	War relief administrator
Franklin D. Roosevelt	1933–45	Governor	Assistant secretary of Navy
Harry S Truman	1945–52	Vice president*	U.S. senator
Dwight D. Eisenhower	1953–60	None (Army general)	None
John F. Kennedy	1961–63	U.S. senator	U.S. representative
Lyndon Johnson	1963–68	Vice president*	U.S. senator
Richard Nixon	1969–74	Vice president	U.S. senator
Gerald Ford	1974–76	Vice president*	U.S. representative
Jimmy Carter	1977–80	Governor	State senator
Ronald Reagan	1981–88	Governor	None
George Bush	1989–92	Vice president	Director, CIA
Bill Clinton	1993–2000	Governor	State attorney general
George W. Bush	2001–	Governor	None

*Became president on death or resignation of incumbent.

unit rule

The rule that grants all of a state's electoral votes to the candidate who receives the most popular votes in the state.

electoral votes equal in number to its representation in Congress. Each state thus gets two electoral votes for its Senate representation and a varying number of electoral votes depending on its House representation. Altogether, there are 538 electoral votes (including 3 for the District of Columbia, even though it has no voting representatives in Congress). To win the presidency, a candidate must receive at least 270 votes, an electoral majority. (If no candidate receives a majority, the election is decided in the House of Representatives. No president since John Quincy Adams in 1824 has been elected in this way. The procedure is defined by the Constitution's Twelfth Amendment, which is reprinted in the appendixes.)

The importance of the electoral votes is magnified by the existence of the **unit rule:** all the states except Maine and Nebraska grant all their electoral votes as a unit to the candidate who wins the state's popular vote. For this reason, candidates are concerned with winning the most populous states, such as California (with 55 electoral votes), Texas (34), New York (31), Florida (27), Pennsylvania (21), Illinois (21), Ohio (20), Michigan (17), and Georgia, New Jersey, and North Carolina (15 each).

Even more so than a state's size, however, the closeness of the vote in a state dictates how much attention it will get from the candidates. Because of the unit rule, a state that is lopsidedly Democratic or Republican will be ignored. Its electoral votes are already locked up. Thus, the fall campaign becomes a fight over the toss-up states or, as they have come to be called, the battleground states. In 2004, only one-third of the states—many of them in a band that stretched west from Pennsylvania through Iowa and Minnesota—were seen by

States in the Nation

Electoral Votes in the 2004 Election

There are a total of 538 electoral votes, and a candidate must receive a majority to win the presidency. In 2004, George W. Bush was elected to a second term with 286 electoral votes—sixteen more than required. If John Kerry had gathered roughly 150,000 more popular votes in Ohio, he would have had an electoral vote majority and become president, even though he trailed Bush by 3.5 million popular votes nationwide. Because electoral votes are allocated on a state-by-state basis, the loser of the national popular vote can gain an electoral-vote victory. In 2000, Bush trailed Democratic nominee Al Gore by half a million popular votes nationwide but became president by virtue of a 537-vote popular margin in Florida. Bush was the first president since Benjamin Harrison in 1898 to win the presidency while losing the national popular vote.

States can determine for themselves how their electors will be chosen. Today, all states except two (Maine and Nebraska, which give one electoral vote to the winner of each congressional district and two electoral votes to the statewide winner), give all of their electoral votes to the popular-vote winner in the state.

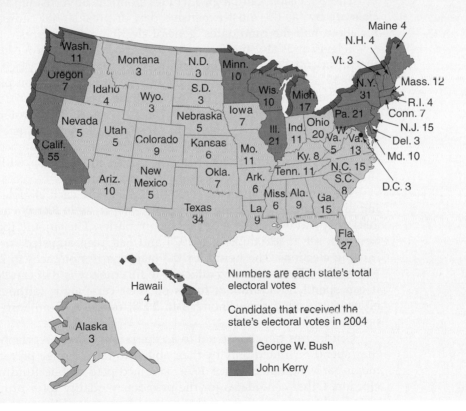

Numbers are each state's total electoral votes

Candidate that received the state's electoral votes in 2004

George W. Bush

John Kerry

the Bush and Kerry campaigns as states that realistically could be won by either candidate. The two candidates spent nearly all their money and time in the battleground states during the closing months of the campaign. Other states might just as well have been located in Canada for the attention they received from the candidates.

At campaign's end, electoral votes and not popular votes determine the winner (see "States in the Nation"). In 2000, Bush was elected with 271 electoral votes, two more than required, even though he received 550,000 fewer popular votes than Al Gore. Bush was the first president since Harrison in 1888 to win the presidency despite losing the popular vote. In 2004, Bush won with 286 electoral votes. His popular margin exceeded 3 million votes, but he would have lost if Kerry had attracted 150,000 more votes in Ohio, which would have earned him Ohio's 20 electoral votes—enough for an electoral college victory.

Media and Money

The modern presidential campaign is a media campaign. At one time, candidates relied heavily on party organization and rallies to carry their messages to the voters, but now they rely on the media, particularly television. Candidates strive to produce the pithy ten-second sound bites that the television networks prefer to highlight on the evening newscasts. They also rely on the power of the "new media," making frequent appearances on programs such as *Larry King Live* and creating their own Internet websites.

The television campaign includes political advertising. Televised commercials are by far the most expensive part of presidential campaigns, accounting for about half the candidates' general election expenditures.

Television is also the forum for the major confrontation of the fall campaign: the presidential debates. The first televised debate took place in 1960 between Kennedy and Nixon, and an estimated one hundred million people saw at least one of their four debates.[16] Televised debates resumed in 1976 and have become a fixture of presidential campaigns. Debates can influence voters' assessments of the candidates. In 2004, George W. Bush's weak performance in the debates— polls indicate that viewers felt John Kerry won all three encounters—hurt his candidacy. Before the first debate, the polls showed Bush with a clear lead. By the last debate, the race was nearly a dead heat.

The Republican and Democratic nominees are each eligible for federal funding of their general election campaigns even if, as in Kerry's and Bush's case in 2004, they did not accept it during the primaries. The amount for the general election was set at $20 million in 1975 and has been adjusted for inflation in succeeding elections. The figure for the major-party nominees in 2008 is more than $80 million. The only string attached to this money is that candidates who accept it can spend no additional funds on their campaigns (although each party is allowed to spend some money—in 2008, roughly $5 million—on behalf of its nominee).

Candidates can choose not to accept public funds, in which case the amount they spend is limited only by their ability to raise money privately. However, all major-party nominees since 1976 have accepted public funding in the general election. Other candidates for the presidency qualify for a proportional amount of federal funding if they receive at least 5 percent of the vote and do not spend more than $50,000 of their own money on the campaign. In 1992, Perot spent over $60 million of his own money and thus was ineligible for federal funding. He accepted $29 million in federal funding in 1996, receiving about half as much as the major-party nominees because his 1992 vote total was roughly half that averaged by the two major-party candidates.

The Winners

The Constitution specifies only that the president must be at least thirty-five years old, a natural-born U.S. citizen, and a U.S. resident for at least fourteen years. Yet the holding of high public office is nearly a prerequisite for gaining

TABLE 12–4	**Ranking America's Presidents** Historian Arthur Schlesinger, Sr., began the game of ranking U.S. presidents when he sought the opinions of other historians in a 1948 article for *Life* magazine. Since then, a great many scholars and analysts, including historian Arthur Schlesinger, Jr., have tried their hand at it. Here is the list from a survey in 2000 of seventy-eight history, political science, and law professors that was conducted by the Federalist Society and the *Wall Street Journal*. Unlike many such lists, this list ranks Abraham Lincoln second rather than first.

Great

1	George Washington
2	Abraham Lincoln
3	Franklin Roosevelt

Near Great

4	Thomas Jefferson
5	Theodore Roosevelt
6	Andrew Jackson
7	Harry Truman
8	Ronald Reagan
9	Dwight Eisenhower
10	James Polk
11	Woodrow Wilson

Above Average

12	Grover Cleveland
13	John Adams
14	William McKinley
15	James Madison
16	James Monroe
17	Lyndon Johnson
18	John Kennedy

Average

19	William Taft
20	John Quincy Adams
21	George H. W. Bush
22	Rutherford Hayes
23	Martin Van Buren
24	William Clinton
25	Calvin Coolidge
26	Chester Arthur

Below Average

27	Benjamin Harrison
28	Gerald Ford
29	Herbert Hoover
30	Jimmy Carter
31	Zachary Taylor
32	Ulysses Grant
33	Richard Nixon
34	John Tyler
35	Millard Filmore

Failure

36	Andrew Johnson
37T	Franklin Pierce
37T	Warren Harding
39	James Buchanan

the presidency. Except for four army generals, all presidents to date have served previously as vice presidents, members of Congress, state governors, or top federal executives.

All presidents have been white and male, but it is likely only a matter of time before the nation has its first minority-group president or its first woman president. Until the early 1950s, a majority of Americans polled said they would not vote for a woman for president. Today, fewer than 10 percent hold this view. A similar change of opinion preceded John Kennedy's election to the presidency in 1960. Kennedy was the nation's first Catholic president and only the second Catholic to receive a major party's nomination.

WWW.MHHE.COM/PATTERSONTAD8

Historians have developed rankings of the presidents (see Table 12–4), and, if one thing is clear from their effort, it is that there is no template for the successful president. The nation's stronger presidents—and also its weaker ones—have included former governors, army generals, members of Congress, and cabinet officers.

STAFFING THE PRESIDENCY

When Americans go to the polls on election day, they have in mind the choice between two individuals, the Democratic and the Republican presidential nominees. In effect, however, they are choosing a lot more than a single executive leader. They are also picking a secretary of state, the director of the FBI, the chair of the Federal Reserve Board, and a host of other executives. Each of these is a presidential appointee.

Presidents rely heavily on trusted cabinet officers and personal assistants in making critical policy decisions. During the Cuban missile crisis in 1962, this group of advisers to President John F. Kennedy helped him decide on a naval blockade as a means of forcing the Soviet Union to withdraw its missiles from Cuba.

Presidential Appointees

A president's ability to make executive appointments is a significant source of power. For one thing, modern policymaking rests on a deep understanding of policy issues and also on knowing how to successfully guide proposals through policy channels. Many presidential appointees have these skills. Further, the president cannot be in a hundred different places at once—but the president's appointees can be. They extend the president's influence into the huge federal bureaucracy by overseeing those agencies they are appointed to head. Not surprisingly, the president seeks to appoint individuals who are members of the same political party and are committed to the Administration's policy goals.

The Executive Office of the President

The key staff organization is the Executive Office of the President (EOP), created by Congress in 1939 to provide the president with the staff necessary to coordinate the activities of the executive branch.[17] The EOP has since become the command center of the presidency. Its configuration is determined by the president, and it currently consists of the Office of the Vice President and eighteen other organizations (see Figure 12–1). These include the White House Office (WHO), which consists of the president's closest personal advisers; the Office of Management and Budget (OMB), which consists of experts who formulate and administer the federal budget; and the National Security Council (NSC), which advises the president on foreign and military affairs.

The Vice President   The Constitution assigns all executive authority to the president, none to the vice president. Earlier presidents often refused to delegate significant duties to their vice presidents, which diminished the office's appeal. Nomination to the vice presidency was refused by many leading politicians, including Daniel Webster and Henry Clay. Said Webster, "I do not propose to be buried until I am really dead."[18] Recent presidents, however, have assigned important duties to their vice presidents. George W. Bush, for example, chose Dick Cheney as his running mate in part because of Cheney's

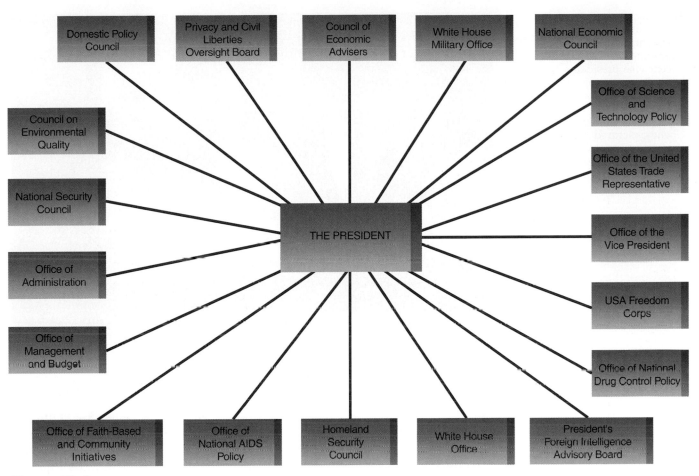

Figure 12–1

Executive Office of the President (EOP)
The EOP helps the president manage the rest of the executive branch and promotes the president's policy and political goals.
Source: White House, 2007.

experience as White House chief of staff and secretary of defense during previous Republican administrations. Cheney played such a large role in setting the policies of the Bush administration, including the decision to invade Iraq, that seasoned Washington observers questioned whether he had too much influence, a claim that would have baffled Daniel Webster. The vice president is supported by an administrative staff (the Office of the Vice President) of a dozen people, including a domestic policy adviser and a national security policy adviser.

The White House Office   Of the EOP's eighteen other organizations, the White House Office serves the president most directly and personally. The units within the WHO include the Communications Office, the Office of the Press Secretary, the Office of the Counsel to the President, and the Office of Legislative Affairs. As these names suggest, the WHO consists of the president's personal assistants, including close personal advisers, press agents, legislative and group liaison aides, and special assistants for domestic and international policy. They work in the White House, and the president can hire and fire them at will. The personal assistants do much of the legwork for the

The Constitution assigns no policy authority to the vice president, whose role is determined by the president. Recent vice presidents have been assigned major policy responsibilities. Earlier vice presidents played smaller roles. Vice President Dick Cheney, pictured here with President George W. Bush, is reputedly the most powerful vice president in history.

president and serve as a main source of advice. Most of them are skilled at developing political strategy and communicating with the public, Congress, state and local governments, key groups, and the news media. Because of their proximity to the president, they are among the most powerful individuals in Washington.

Policy Experts   The president is also served by the policy experts in the EOP's other organizations. These include economists, legal analysts, national security specialists, and others. The president is advised on economic issues, for example, by the National Economic Council (NEC). The NEC gathers information to develop indicators of the economy's strength and applies economic theories to various policy alternatives. Modern policymaking cannot be conducted in the absence of such expert knowledge and advice.

The President's Cabinet

cabinet

A group consisting of the heads of the executive (cabinet) departments, who are appointed by the president, subject to confirmation by the Senate. The cabinet was once the main advisory body to the president but it no longer plays this role.

The heads of the fifteen executive departments, such as the Department of Defense and the Department of Agriculture, constitute the president's **cabinet.** They are appointed by the president, subject to confirmation by the Senate. Although the cabinet once served as the president's main advisory group, it has not played this role since Herbert Hoover's administration. As national issues have become increasingly complex, the cabinet has become outmoded as a policymaking forum: department heads are likely to be well informed only about issues in their areas.[19] Accordingly, cabinet meetings are no longer a forum for deciding on policy. Nevertheless, cabinet members, as individuals who head major departments, are important figures in any administration. The president chooses them for their prominence in politics, business, government, or the professions.[20] The office of secretary of state is generally regarded as the most prestigious of the cabinet posts.

States in the Nation

Divided Power in the Executive

The president operates in a system of divided power in which joint action by Congress is often required for the president's programs to be adopted. The chief executives in the states are the governors, nearly all of whom must contend with a further division: a separation of power within the executive itself. Maine and New Jersey are the only states in which executive power is vested solely in a governor. Five other states have separately elected and (unlike the vice president) constitutionally empowered lieutenant governors. In most of the other states, other major executive officials, such as the attorney general and the secretary of state, are also elected. Finally, there are twelve states in which even minor executive officials, such as commissioner of education, are chosen by the voters. In the case of the federal government, these other major and minor officials are appointed by the president.

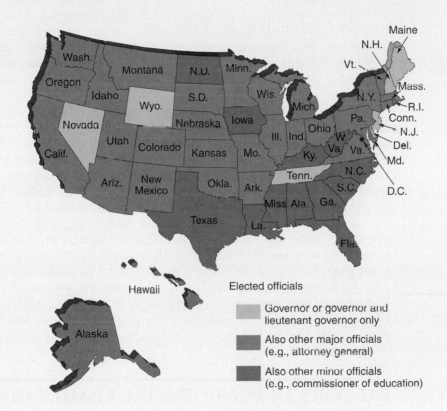

Elected officials

■ Governor or governor and lieutenant governor only

■ Also other major officials (e.g., attorney general)

■ Also other minor officials (e.g., commissioner of education)

Other Presidential Appointees

In addition to cabinet secretaries, the president appoints the heads and top deputies of federal agencies and commissions. Altogether, the president appoints a few thousand executive officials. However, most of these appointees are selected at the agency level or are part-time workers. This still leaves nearly seven hundred full-time appointees who serve the president more or less directly, a much larger number than are appointed by the chief executive of any other democracy.[21]

The Problem of Control

Although the president's appointees are a valuable asset, they also pose a problem: because they are so numerous, the president has difficulty controlling them. President Truman had a wall chart in the Oval Office listing more than one hundred officials who reported directly to him; he often told visitors, "I cannot even see all of these men, let alone actually study what they are doing."[22] Since Truman's time, the number of bureaucratic agencies has more than doubled, compounding the problem of presidential control over subordinates.[23]

The problem of presidential control is most severe in the case of appointees who work outside the White House, in the departments and agencies. The loyalty of agency heads and cabinet secretaries often is split between a desire to promote the president's goals and an interest in boosting themselves or the agencies they lead. In late 2002, Harvey Pitt, appointed by President Bush to chair the Securities and Exchange Commission (SEC), resigned amid charges that he had not aggressively pursued corporate accounting irregularities. The Enron, WorldCom, and other corporate scandals had put regulatory action in the spotlight, and Pitt's apparent favoritism toward accounting firms, which he had represented as a lawyer before his appointment to the SEC, was an embarrassment to the Bush administration.

Lower-level appointees within the departments and agencies pose a different type of problem. The president rarely, if ever, sees them, and they typically are political novices (most have fewer than two years of government experience) and are not very knowledgeable about policy. These appointees are often "captured" by the agency in which they work because they depend on the agency's career bureaucrats for advice. (Chapter 13 examines further the relationship between presidential appointees and career bureaucrats.)

In sum, the modern presidential office is a double-edged sword. Presidents today have greater responsibilities than their predecessors, and this increase in responsibilities expands their opportunities to exert power. At the same time, the range of these responsibilities is so broad that presidents must rely on staffers who may or may not act in the president's best interests. The modern president's recurring problem is to find some way of making sure that appointees serve the interests of the presidency above all others. (The subject of presidential control of the executive branch is discussed further in Chapter 13.)

FACTORS IN PRESIDENTIAL LEADERSHIP

The president operates within a system of separate institutions that share power (see "How the United States Compares"). Significant presidential action normally depends on the approval of Congress, the cooperation of the bureaucracy, and sometimes the acceptance of the judiciary. Because other officials have their own priorities, presidents do not always get their way. Congress in particular—more than the courts or the bureaucracy—holds the key to presidential success. Without congressional authorization and funding, most presidential proposals are nothing but ideas, empty of action.

Whether a president's initiatives succeed or fail depends substantially on several factors, including the force of circumstance, the stage of the president's term, the nature of the particular issue, the president's support in Congress, and the level of public support for the president's leadership. The remainder of this chapter examines each of these factors.

How the United States Compares

Systems of Executive Policy Leadership

The United States instituted a presidential system in 1789 as part of its constitutional checks and balances. This form of executive leadership was copied in Latin America but not in Europe. European democracies adopted parliamentary systems, in which executive leadership is provided by a prime minister, who is a member of the legislature. In recent years, some European prime ministers have campaigned and governed as if they were a singular authority rather than the head of a collective institution. France in the 1960s created a separate chief executive office but retained its parliamentary form of legislature.

The policy leadership of a president can differ substantially from that of a prime minister. As a singular head of an independent branch of government, a president does not have to share executive authority but nevertheless depends on the legislative branch for support. By comparison, a prime minister shares executive leadership with a cabinet, but once agreement within the cabinet is reached, he or she is almost assured of the legislative support necessary to carry out policy initiatives.

PRESIDENTIAL SYSTEM	PRESIDENTIAL/ PARLIAMENTARY SYSTEM	PARLIAMENTARY SYSTEM
Mexico	Finland	Australia
United States	France	Belgium
Venezuela		Canada
		Germany
		Great Britain
		Israel
		Italy
		Japan
		Netherlands
		Sweden

The Force of Circumstance

During his first months in office and in the midst of the Great Depression, Franklin D. Roosevelt accomplished the most sweeping changes in domestic policy in the nation's history. Congress moved quickly to pass nearly every New Deal initiative he proposed. In 1964 and 1965, Lyndon Johnson pushed landmark civil rights and social welfare legislation through Congress on the strength of the civil rights movement, the legacy of the assassinated President Kennedy, and large Democratic majorities in the House and Senate. When Ronald Reagan assumed the presidency in 1981, high unemployment and inflation had greatly weakened the national economy and created a mood for significant change, enabling Reagan to persuade Congress to support some of the most substantial taxing and spending changes in history.

From such presidencies has come the popular impression that presidents single-handedly decide national policy. However, each of these periods of presidential dominance was marked by a special set of circumstances: a decisive election victory that gave added force to the president's leadership, a compelling national problem that convinced Congress and the public that bold presidential action was needed, and a president who was mindful of what was expected and who vigorously advocated policies consistent with those expectations.

When conditions are favorable, the power of the presidency is remarkable. The problem for most presidents is that conditions normally are not conducive to strong leadership. Political scientist Erwin Hargrove suggests that presidential influence depends largely on circumstance.[24] Some presidents serve in periods

President Lyndon Johnson addresses a joint session of Congress in 1965. Johnson had an extraordinary record of success with Congress, which adopted the great majority of his legislative proposals. Johnson had the good fortune of working with a Congress controlled—by a wide margin—by his own party.

when resources are scarce or when important problems are surfacing in American society but have not yet become critical. Such a situation, Hargrove contends, works against the president's efforts to accomplish significant policy change. In 1994, reflecting on the constraints of budget deficits and other factors beyond his control, President Clinton said he had no choice but "to play the hand that history had dealt" him.

The Stage of the President's Term

If conditions conducive to great accomplishments occur infrequently, it is nonetheless the case that nearly every president has favorable moments. Such moments often come during the first months in office. Most newly elected presidents enjoy a **honeymoon period** during which Congress, the press, and the public anticipate initiatives from the Oval Office and are more predisposed than usual to support these initiatives.

Not surprisingly, presidents have put forth more new programs in their first year in office than in any subsequent year. James Pfiffner uses the term *strategic presidency* to refer to a president's need to move quickly on priority items in order to take advantage of the policy momentum gained from the election.[25] Later in their terms, presidents tend to be less successful in presenting initiatives and getting them enacted. They may run out of good ideas, get caught up in scandal, or exhaust their political resources; the momentum of their election is gone and sources of opposition have

honeymoon period
The president's first months in office, a time when Congress, the press, and the public are more inclined than usual to support presidential initiatives.

emerged. Even highly successful presidents like Johnson and Reagan tended to have weak records in their final years. Franklin Roosevelt began his presidency with a remarkable period of achievement—the celebrated "Hundred Days"—but during his last six years in office, few of his major domestic proposals were enacted.

An irony of the presidency, then, is that presidents are usually most powerful when they are least knowledgeable—during their first months in office. These months can, as a result, be times of risk as well as times of opportunity. An example is the Bay of Pigs fiasco during the first year of John Kennedy's presidency, in which a U.S.-backed invasion force of anticommunist Cubans was easily defeated by Fidel Castro's army.

The Nature of the Issue: Foreign or Domestic

In the 1960s, political scientist Aaron Wildavsky wrote that although the nation has only one president, it has two presidencies: one domestic and one foreign.[26] Wildavsky was referring to Congress's greater tendency to defer to presidential leadership on foreign policy issues than on domestic policy issues. He had in mind the broad leeway Congress had granted Truman, Eisenhower, Kennedy, and Johnson in their foreign policies. Wildavsky's thesis is now regarded as a somewhat time-bound conception of presidential influence. Today, many of the same factors that affect a president's domestic policy success, such as the partisan composition of Congress, also affect foreign policy success.

Political Culture

Executive Power and Liberty

When the Constitution was written, fear of executive power was widespread. The American Revolution had been fought to overthrow the punitive policies of the British king, who was far less tyrannical than most monarchs of the period.

The Framers, worried that a too-powerful executive would threaten Americans' hard-won liberty, placed executive power within a system of divided power. Each branch would act as a check on the others. The Framers also chose an indirect method of electing the president, fearing that direct popular election would make it too easy for the president to harness the power of popular majorities in pursuit of policies destructive of the rights and interests of minorities.

American history can be read as a refutation of the Framers' concerns. Presidents often have been in the forefront of efforts to expand Americans' liberty. Thomas Jefferson, Abraham Lincoln, and Lyndon Johnson are among the presidents whose names are linked to such efforts. Johnson's leadership, for example, was instrumental in passage of the 1964 Civil Rights Act and the 1965 Voting Rights Act.

On the other hand, U.S. history also contains examples of presidents who have used their power to shrink personal liberty. During the Wilson administration, for example, antiwar dissenters were harassed and more than two thousand jailed for actions such as the distribution of antiwar leaflets. During Franklin Roosevelt's administration, Japanese Americans were uprooted from their West Coast homes and placed in internment camps. During the Nixon administration, antiwar activists were spied upon by the FBI, had their tax returns audited by the IRS, and had their homes and offices burglarized by White House hirelings. In each case, the president argued that a larger issue of liberty—the nation's survival—was at stake and that intrusions on individual liberty were an unfortunate but necessary consequence of the threat. By and large, public opinion supported these presidential actions, although in Nixon's case it eventually turned against the president.

How do you read American history on the issue of executive power and liberty? Where do you think the balance between personal liberty and national security should be struck? What is your opinion of executive action in the context of the war on terrorism? Do you think actions such as expanded wiretapping and detention are necessary if America is to counter the threat of terrorist groups? Or do you think these actions constitute an unwarranted intrusion on personal liberty?

Nevertheless, presidents still have somewhat of an advantage when the issue is foreign policy, because they have more authority to act on their own and are more likely to receive support from Congress.[27] The clash between powerful interest groups that occurs over many domestic issues is less prevalent in the foreign policy area. Additionally, the president is recognized by other nations as America's voice in world affairs, and members of Congress sometimes will defer to the president in order to maintain America's credibility abroad. In some cases, Congress effectively has no choice but to accept presidential leadership. When President Bush in 2002 sought a congressional resolution authorizing him to use force if necessary against Iraq, even some members of Congress who questioned the wisdom of giving the president a blank check to wage war chose to back the resolution. They were reluctant to give Iraqi president Saddam Hussein a reason to believe that America lacked unity in its determination to force him to disarm.

Presidents also have leverage in foreign and defense policy because of their special relationship with the defense, diplomatic, and intelligence agencies, sometimes called "presidential agencies." Other agencies that are responsive to the president are sometimes even more receptive to Congress; the Department of Agriculture, for example, often is more concerned with having the support of farm-state senators and representatives than with having the president's backing. The defense, diplomatic, and intelligence agencies, however, are different in that their missions are closely tied to the president's constitutional authority as commander-in-chief and chief diplomat. In the buildup to the Iraq war, for example, the defense and intelligence agencies operated in ways that promoted President Bush's stand on the need to confront Saddam Hussein militarily. Only later did Congress discover that the intelligence information it was provided, as well as the assessments it was given by the Defense Department on the level of military force required to invade and pacify Iraq, had been tailored to suit President Bush's plans.

Relations with Congress

Although the presidency is not nearly as powerful as most Americans assume, presidents' ability to influence the agenda of national debate is unrivaled, reflecting their unique claim to represent the whole country. Whenever the president directs attention to a particular issue, members of Congress take notice. But will they take action? The answer is sometimes yes and sometimes no, depending in part on whether the president takes their concerns into account.

Seeking Cooperation from Congress

As the center of national attention, presidents can start to believe that their ideas should prevail over those of Congress. This reasoning invariably gets any president into trouble. Jimmy Carter had not held national office before he was elected president in 1976 and thus had no clear understanding of how Washington operates.[28] Soon after taking office, Carter deleted from his budget nineteen public works projects that he believed were a waste of taxpayers' money, ignoring the determination of members of Congress to obtain federally funded projects for their constituents. Carter's action set the tone for a conflict-ridden relationship with Congress.

In order to get the help of members of Congress, the president must respond to their interests as they respond to those of the president.[29] The most basic fact about presidential leadership is that it takes place in the context of a system of divided powers. Although the president gets most of the attention, Congress has most of the constitutional authority in the American system. The powers of the presidential office are by themselves insufficient to sustain the president in a strong position.

Even the president's most direct legislative tool, the veto, has limits. Congress can seldom muster the two-thirds majority in each chamber required to override a presidential veto, so the threat of a veto can make Congress bend to the president's demands. Yet, as presidential scholar Richard Neustadt argued, the veto is as much a sign of presidential weakness as it is a sign of strength, because it arises when Congress refuses to go along with the president's ideas.[30] An example is the first veto cast by George W. Bush. Until then, Bush was on track to join Thomas Jefferson as the only two-term president not to veto a bill. In 2006, however, Bush vetoed a bill that would have expanded federal support for embryonic stem cell research. He had announced his opposition to such research early in his presidency and was successful for a time in getting congressional Republicans to back him. As Bush's popularity plummeted in 2005, however, some congressional Republicans separated themselves from the president out of concern for their reelection chances. Enough Republicans defected on the stem-cell bill to get it through Congress, setting the stage for Bush's veto.

Congress is a constituency that all presidents must serve if they expect to have its support. Neustadt concludes that presidential power, at base, is "the power to persuade."[31] Like any singular notion of presidential power, Neustadt's has limitations. Presidents at times have the power to command and to threaten. They can also appeal directly to the American people as a means of pressuring Congress. But Congress can never be taken for granted. Theodore Roosevelt expressed the wish that he could "be the president and Congress, too," if only for a day, so that he would have the power to enact as well as to propose laws.

Benefiting from Partisan Support in Congress

For most presidents, the next best thing to being "Congress, too" is to have a Congress filled with members of their own party. The sources of division within Congress are many. Legislators from urban and rural areas, wealthier and poorer constituencies, and different regions of the country often

Secretary of State Condoleezza Rice testifies in 2006 before the Senate Foreign Relations Committee on the subject of atomic energy cooperation with India. The secretary of state is always a prominent member of the Administration, a reflection of the president's constitutional authority in the realm of foreign affairs.

have very different views of the national interest. To obtain majority support in Congress, the president must find ways to overcome these differences.

No source of unity is more important to presidential success than partisanship. Presidents are more likely to succeed when their own party controls Congress (see Figure 12–2). Between 1954 and 1992, each Republican

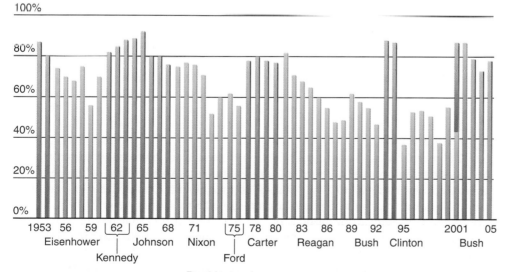

Percentage of bills on which Congress supported president's position

Control of Congress

■ President's party

■ Other party (one or both houses)

Figure 12–2

Percentage of Bills Passed by Congress on Which the President Announced a Position, 1953–2005

In most years, presidents have been supported by Congress on a majority of policy issues on which they have taken a stand. Presidents fare better when their party controls Congress.

Source: *Congressional Quarterly Weekly Report.* Copyright © 1999 by Congressional Quarterly Inc. Reproduced with permission of Congressional Quarterly Inc. in the format textbook via Copyright Clearance Center.

president—Eisenhower, Nixon, Ford, Reagan, and Bush—had to contend with a Democratic majority in one or both houses of Congress. Congress passed a smaller percentage of the initiatives supported by each of these presidents than those supported by any Democratic president of the period: Kennedy, Johnson, or Carter. In his first two years in office, backed by Democratic majorities in the House and Senate, more than 85 percent of the bills Clinton supported were enacted into law. After Republicans took control of Congress in 1995, Clinton's legislative success rate sank below 40 percent, a dramatic illustration of the way presidential power is affected by whether the president's party controls Congress.

Colliding with Congress

On rare occasions, presidents have pursued their goals so zealously that Congress has been compelled to take steps to curb their use of power.

The ultimate sanction of Congress is its constitutional power to impeach and remove the president from office. The House of Representatives decides by majority vote whether the president should be impeached (placed on trial), and the Senate conducts the trial and then votes on the president's case, with a two-thirds vote required for removal from office. In 1868, Andrew Johnson came within one Senate vote of being removed from office for his opposition to Congress's harsh Reconstruction policies after the Civil War. In 1974, Richard Nixon's resignation halted congressional proceedings on the Watergate affair that almost certainly would have ended in his impeachment and removal from office.

The specter of impeachment arose again in 1998 when the House of Representatives by a vote of 258 to 176 authorized an investigation of President Clinton's conduct. He was accused of lying under oath about his relationship with intern Monica Lewinsky and of obstructing justice by trying to conceal the affair. The gravity of the allegations was leavened by the circumstances. The charges had grown out of an extramarital affair rather than a gross abuse of executive power and were tied to a controversial five-year, $40 million investigation by independent counsel Kenneth Starr. For its part, the public was ambivalent about the whole issue. Most Americans disapproved of Clinton's behavior but did not think it constituted "treason, bribery, or other high crimes and misdemeanors," the Constitution's basis for impeachment and removal from office. Not surprisingly, congressional Republicans and Democrats differed sharply on the impeachment issue. At all formal stages of the process—the House vote to authorize an inquiry, the House vote on the articles of impeachment, and the Senate vote on whether to remove the president—the vote was divided largely along party lines. In the end, Clinton was acquitted by the Senate, but his legacy will forever be tarnished by his impeachment by the House.

The gravity of an impeachment action makes it an unsuitable basis for curbing presidential power except in rare instances. More often, Congress has responded legislatively to what it sees as unwarranted assertions of executive power. An example is the Budget Impoundment and Control Act of 1974, which prohibits a president from indefinitely withholding funds that have been appropriated by Congress. The legislation was enacted in response to President Nixon's practice of withholding funds from programs he disliked.

A similar controversy erupted in 2006 when it was revealed that President Bush had used so-called signing statements to challenge the constitutionality of more than seven hundred bills. These statements, appended to a bill when the president signs it, are meant to indicate that the president does

WWW.MHHE.COM/PATTERSONTAD8

not necessary intend to abide by particular provisions of a law. Although Bush was not the first president to use this device, he had attached signing statements to more bills than all of his predecessors combined and had done so in secrecy. Even congressional Republicans expressed concerned about the practice. At Senate Judiciary Committee hearings, Senate Arlen Specter (R-Penn.), chair of the committee, argued: "There's a real issue here as to whether the president may, in effect, cherry-pick the provisions he likes, excluding the provisions he doesn't like. . . . The president has the option under the Constitution to veto or not." Not unexpectedly, Senate Democrats had harsher words for the president. Said Russ Feingold (D-Wisc.): "[The executive has] assigned itself the sole responsibility for deciding which laws it will comply with, and in the process has taken upon itself the powers of all three branches of government."[32]

Congress's most significant historical effort to curb presidential power is the War Powers Act. During the Vietnam War, Presidents Johnson and Nixon repeatedly misled Congress, supplying it with intelligence estimates that painted a falsely optimistic picture of the military situation. Believing the war was being won, Congress regularly voted to provide the money necessary to keep it going. However, congressional support changed abruptly in 1971 with publication in the *New York Times* of classified documents (the so-called Pentagon Papers) that revealed the Vietnam situation to be much worse than portrayed by Johnson and Nixon.

To prevent future presidential wars, Congress in 1973 passed the War Powers Act. Nixon vetoed the measure, but Congress overrode his veto. The act does not prohibit the president from sending troops into combat, but it does require the president to notify Congress of the reason for committing combat troops within forty-eight hours of their deployment. The act also specifies that hostilities must end within sixty days unless Congress extends the period; gives the president an additional thirty days to withdraw the troops from hostile territory, although Congress can shorten this period; and requires the president to consult with Congress whenever feasible before sending troops into a hostile situation.

Every president since Nixon has claimed that the War Powers Act infringes on his constitutional power as commander in chief, and each has refused to accept it fully. Nevertheless, the War Powers Act is a potentially significant constraint on the president's war-making powers.

Thus, the effect of executive efforts to circumvent congressional authority has been heightened congressional opposition. Even if presidents gain in the short run by acting on their own, they undermine their capacity to lead in the long run if they fail to keep in mind that Congress is a coequal branch of the American governing system.

Public Support

Every recent president has had the public's confidence at the start of his term of office. When asked in polls whether they "approve or disapprove of how the president is doing his job," a majority of Americans have expressed approval during the first months of the president's term. Sooner or later, however, all **presidential approval ratings** have slipped below this high point, and several recent presidents have left office with a rating below 50 percent (see Table 12–5).

Public support affects a president's ability to achieve policy goals. Presidential power rests in part on a claim to national leadership, and the legitimacy of that claim is roughly proportional to the president's public

presidential approval ratings
A measure of the degree to which the public approves or disapproves of the president's performance in office.

TABLE 12–5	Percentage of Public Expressing Approval of President's Performance Presidential approval ratings generally are higher at the beginning of the term than at the end.

PRESIDENT	YEARS IN OFFICE	AVERAGE DURING PRESIDENCY	FIRST-YEAR AVERAGE	FINAL-YEAR AVERAGE
Harry Truman	1945–52	41%	63%	35%
Dwight Eisenhower	1953–60	64	74	62
John Kennedy	1961–63	70	76	62
Lyndon Johnson	1963–68	55	78	40
Richard Nixon	1969–74	49	63	24
Gerald Ford	1974–76	46	75	48
Jimmy Carter	1977–80	47	68	46
Ronald Reagan	1981–88	53	58	57
George H. W. Bush	1989–92	61	65	40
Bill Clinton	1993–2000	57	50	60
George W. Bush	2001–	—	68	—

Source: Averages compiled from Gallup polls.

support. With public backing, the president's leadership cannot easily be dismissed by other Washington officials. If the president's public support sinks, officials are less inclined to accept presidential leadership.

Congress's response to George W. Bush's leadership illustrates the pattern. In the early years of his presidency, Bush got from the Congress nearly everything he asked for, a reason that five years elapsed before he cast his first veto. As his popularity declined, however, congressional inaction on his major proposals became nearly the rule. Among the casualties were major components of Bush's social security, energy, and immigration reform proposals.

Events and Issues

The public's support for the president is affected by national and international conditions. Threats from abroad tend to produce a patriotic "rally 'round the flag" reaction that initially creates widespread support for the president. Every foreign policy crisis in the past four decades has followed this pattern. Americans were deeply divided in 2003 over the wisdom of war with Iraq, but, when the fighting began, President Bush's approval rating immediately increased.

Ongoing crises, however, can erode a president's support if they are not resolved successfully. George W. Bush's approval rating rose above 70 percent with the attack on Iraq in 2003 but then fell steadily as U.S. casualties mounted. By 2006, his approval rating had fallen below 40 percent and his party suffered losses in that year's midterm election.

Historically, the economy has had the greatest influence on presidents' public support. Economic downswings reduce the public's confidence in the president.[33] Ford, Carter, and the first President Bush lost their reelection bids when their popularity plummeted after the economy swooned. In contrast, Clinton's popularity rose in 1995 and 1996 as the economy strengthened, contributing to his reelection in 1996. In 2004, an improving economy contributed to George W. Bush's reelection. Of course, the irony is that presidents do not actually have that much control over the economy. If they did, it would always be strong.

The Televised Presidency

A major advantage that presidents enjoy in their efforts to nurture public support is their access to the media, particularly television. Only the president can expect the television networks to provide free air time on occasion, and in terms of the amount of news coverage, the president and top presidential advisers receive half again as much coverage as all members of Congress combined.

Political scientist Samuel Kernell calls it "going public" when the president bypasses inside bargaining with Congress and promotes "himself and his policies by appealing to the American public for support."[34] Such appeals are at least as old as Theodore Roosevelt's use of the presidency as a "bully pulpit," but they have increased substantially in recent years. As the president's role has moved from administrative leader to policy advocate and agenda setter, public support has become increasingly important to presidential success. Television has made it easier for presidents to go public with their programs. Ronald Reagan was called "the Great Communicator" in part because of his ability to use television to generate public support for his initiatives.

On the other hand, the press is adept at putting its own spin on events and tends to play up adverse developments. For example, although presidents get some credit in the press when the economy is doing well, they get mounds of negative coverage when the economy is doing poorly. Scandal is the biggest threat to a president's ability to influence news coverage. When the whiff of a possible scandal is detected, a media "feeding frenzy" ensues, and power shifts from the White House to the press and the president's political opponents. In 2004, for example, informed sources claimed that the Bush administration had targeted Iraq long before it ordered an invasion of that country. Secretary of Defense Donald Rumsfeld

White House press secretary Tony Snow briefs reporters in the cramped space of the White House briefing room. Effective communication is an essential part of the modern presidency.

reportedly wanted to bomb Iraq immediately after the terrorist attacks of September 11, 2001, even though there was no evidence linking Iraq to the attacks. Rumsfeld was quoted by a White House insider as saying "There aren't any good targets in Afghanistan and there are lots of good targets in Iraq." The allegations were front-page news for days on end and placed the Bush administration on the defensive.

The Illusion of Presidential Government

Presidents have no choice but to try to counter negative press coverage with their own version of events. President George W. Bush did exactly that by scheduling blocks of interviews with journalists from local and regional news outlets to say that the real story of the Iraq effort—the success story of reopened schools, restored oil production, and renewed hope for the Iraqi people—was not being told by the Washington press corps. Bush accused national reporters of focusing only on the death and destruction in Iraq.

Such efforts can carry a president only so far, however. No president can fully control his communicated image, and national conditions ultimately have the largest impact on a president's public support. No amount of public relations can disguise adverse developments at home or abroad. Indeed, presidents run a risk by building up their images through public relations. By thrusting themselves into the limelight, presidents contribute to the public's belief that the president is in charge of the national government, a perception political scientist Hugh Heclo calls "the illusion of presidential government."[35] If they are as powerful as they project themselves to be, they will be held responsible for policy failures as well as policy successes.

WWW.MHHE.COM/PATTERSONTAD8

Because the public expects so much from its presidents, they get too much credit when things go well and too much blame when things go badly. Therein lies an irony of the presidential office. More than from any constitutional grant, more than from any statute, and more than from any crisis, presidential power derives from the president's position as the sole official who can claim to represent the entire American public. Yet because presidential power rests on a popular base, it erodes when public support declines. The irony is that the presidential office typically grows weaker as problems mount. Just when the country most needs effective leadership, strong leadership often is hardest to achieve.[36]

Summary

Self-Test www.mhhe.com/pattersontad8

The presidency has become a much stronger office than the Framers envisioned. The Constitution grants the president substantial military, diplomatic, legislative, and executive powers, and in each case the president's authority has increased measurably over the nation's history. Underlying this change is the president's position as the one leader chosen by the whole nation and as the sole head of the executive branch. These features of the office have enabled presidents to claim broad authority in response to the increased demands placed on the federal government by changing world and national conditions.

During the course of American history, the presidential selection process has been altered in ways intended to make it more responsive to the preferences of ordinary people. Today, the electorate has a vote not only in the general election, but also in the selection of party nominees. To gain nomination, a presidential hopeful must gain the support of the electorate in state primaries and open caucuses. Once nominated, the candidates receive federal funds for their general election campaigns, which today are based on televised appeals.

Although the campaign tends to personalize the presidency, the responsibilities of the modern presidency far exceed any president's personal capacities. To meet their obligations, presidents have surrounded themselves with large staffs of advisers, policy experts, and managers. These staff members enable the president to extend control over the executive branch while at the same time providing the information necessary for policymaking. All recent presidents have discovered, however, that their control of staff resources is incomplete and that some things others do on their behalf can work against what they are trying to accomplish.

As sole chief executive and the nation's top elected leader, presidents can always expect that their policy and leadership efforts will receive attention. However, other institutions, particularly Congress, have the authority to make presidential leadership effective. No president has come close to winning approval of all the programs he has placed before Congress, and the presidents' records of success have varied considerably. The factors in a president's success include whether national conditions that require strong leadership from the White House are present and whether the president's party has a majority in Congress.

To hold onto an effective leadership position, the president depends on the backing of the American people. Recent presidents have made extensive use of the media to build support for their programs, yet they have had difficulty maintaining that support throughout their terms of office. A major reason is that the public expects far more from its presidents than they can deliver.

STUDY CORNER

Key Terms

cabinet (*p. 356*)
honeymoon period (*p. 360*)
momentum (in campaigns) (*p. 347*)

open party caucuses (*p. 345*)
presidential approval ratings (*p. 365*)
stewardship theory (*p. 341*)

unit rule (*p. 350*)
Whig theory (*p. 340*)

Self-Test

1. Which two features of the presidency have enabled it to become more powerful than the Framers envisioned?
   a. power to disregard the Supreme Court and also Congress during national emergencies.
   b. power to use presidential resources to defeat members of Congress and power to veto acts of Congress.
   c. election by national vote and president's position as sole chief executive.
   d. power to appoint federal judges and to appoint high-ranking executives.

2. Key presidential appointees who are responsible for coordinating the activities of the executive branch are located in the:
   a. Office of the General Counsel.
   b. Attorney General's Office.
   c. General Accounting Office.
   d. Executive Office of the President.

3. A president is most successful passing legislative initiatives when Congress is:
   a. in recess.
   b. acting in an election year as opposed to a year when no federal election is scheduled to be held.
   c. controlled by the president's own party.
   d. concentrating on domestic policy issues as opposed to foreign policy issues.

4. Which of the following is **not** an important factor in the success that presidents have had in getting their policy proposals enacted into law?
   a. a force of circumstance, such as war or economic stability.
   b. stage of the president's term.
   c. level of public support for the president's leadership.
   d. ability to raise campaign funds.

5. Systems that have been used in the United States for presidential selection include all **except** which one of the following?
   a. congressional caucus.
   b. national party convention.
   c. direct election by popular vote.
   d. combination of national convention and primary elections.
   e. party primary and open party caucus.

6. Advantages that newly elected presidents gain from their appointment powers include all **except** which one of the following?
   a. gain a source of information for policymaking.
   b. can force Congress to confirm the appointment even of nominees Congress judges as unfit to hold executive office.
   c. can extend the president's authority into the federal bureaucracy.
   d. can make sure that some people in key positions share the president's political and policy goals.

7. A candidate running for president has to accept federal campaign funding. (T/F)

8. Under the War Powers Act, the president must have the formal consent of Congress to send U.S. troops into combat. (T/F)

9. National conditions, such as the state of the economy, rarely affect the level of public confidence in the president. (T/F)

10. Big government after the Roosevelt era has favored the growth of legislative authority at the expense of executive authority. (T/F)

Critical Thinking

Why is presidential power "conditional"—that is, why is it affected so substantially by circumstance, the makeup of Congress, and popular support? (The separation of powers should be part of your answer.)

Suggested Readings

Cohen, Jeffrey, and David Nice. *The Presidency.* New York: McGraw-Hill, 2002. A comprehensive overview of the presidency.

Eisinger, Robert M. *The Evolution of Presidential Polling.* New York: Cambridge University Press, 2003. A close look at the use of opinion polls by the White House and how their use has changed since Franklin Roosevelt.

Entman, Robert M. *Projections of Power: Framing News, Public Opinion, and U.S. Foreign Policy.* Chicago: University of Chicago Press, 2003. An assessment of the president's power to set the news agenda.

Jackson, John S., and William J. Crotty. *The Politics of Presidential Selection.* New York: Longman, 2001. A careful look at the presidential election process by two of its best analysts.

Milkis, Sidney, and Michael Nelson. *The American Presidency: Origins and Development, 1776–2002,* 4th ed. Washington, D.C.: Congressional Quarterly Press, 2003. A thoughtful assessment of the factors and conditions that have molded the presidential office.

Neustadt, Richard E. *Presidential Power and the Modern Presidents: The Politics of Leadership from Roosevelt to Reagan.* New York: Free Press, 1990. The classic analysis of the limitations on presidential power.

Pika, Joseph A., and John Anthony Maltese. *The Politics of the Presidency,* 6th ed. Washington, D.C.: Congressional Quarterly Press, 2004. An insightful look at the leadership skills demanded of presidents.

Schlesinger, Arthur M., Jr. *The Imperial Presidency.* Boston: Mariner Books, 2004. An assessment of the modern presidency by a Pulitzer Prize–winning historian.

List of Websites

http://www.ibiblio.org/lia/president
A site with general information on specific presidents and links to the presidential libraries.

http://www.ipl.org/ref/POTUS
Profiles of the nation's presidents, their cabinet officers, and key events during their time in office.

http://www.firstgov.gov/Agencies/Federal/Executive.shtml
Information on the presidency and the Executive Office of the President as well as links to key executive agencies and organizations.

http://www.whitehouse.gov/
The White House's home page; it has an e-mail guest book and includes information on the president, the vice president, and current White House activities.

Participate!

Consider writing a letter or sending an e-mail to the president or a top presidential appointee that expresses your opinion on an issue that is currently the object of executive action. You can inform yourself about the administration's policy or stance on the issue through the website of the White House (www.whitehouse.gov) or of the agency in question (for example, the State Department's site, www.state.gov).

Extra Credit
For up-to-the-minute *New York Times* articles, interactive simulations, graphics, study tools, and more links and quizzes, visit the text's Online Learning Center at www.mhhe.com/pattersontad8.

(Self-Test Answers: 1. c   2. d   3. c   4. d   5. c   6. b   7. F   8. F   9. F   10. F)

The Federal Bureaucracy:
Administering the Government

Chapter Outline

Federal Administration: Form, Personnel, and Activities
- The Federal Bureaucracy in Americans' Daily Lives
- Types of Administrative Organizations
- Federal Employment
- The Federal Bureaucracy's Policy Responsibilities

Development of the Federal Bureaucracy: Politics and Administration
- Small Government and the Patronage System
- Growth in Government and the Merit System
- Big Government and the Executive Leadership System

The Bureaucracy's Power Imperative
- The Agency Point of View
- Sources of Bureaucratic Power

Bureaucratic Accountability
- Accountability Through the Presidency
- Accountability Through Congress
- Accountability Through the Courts
- Accountability Within the Bureaucracy Itself

Reinventing Government?

CHAPTER 13

[No] industrial society could manage the daily operations of its public affairs without bureaucratic organizations in which officials play a major policymaking role.

—Norman Thomas[1]

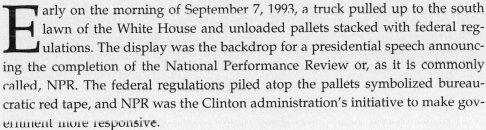

arly on the morning of September 7, 1993, a truck pulled up to the south lawn of the White House and unloaded pallets stacked with federal regulations. The display was the backdrop for a presidential speech announcing the completion of the National Performance Review or, as it is commonly called, NPR. The federal regulations piled atop the pallets symbolized bureaucratic red tape, and NPR was the Clinton administration's initiative to make government more responsive.

The origins of the National Performance Review were plain enough. For years, the federal bureaucracy had been derided as being too big, too expensive, and too intrusive. These charges gained strength as federal budget deficits increased and the public became increasingly dissatisfied with the performance of the government in Washington. Reform attempts in the 1970s and 1980s had not stemmed the tide of federal deficits or markedly improved the bureaucracy's performance. Clinton campaigned on the issue of "reinventing government" and acted swiftly on the promise. Vice President–elect Al Gore was placed in charge of the National Performance Review. He assembled more than two hundred career bureaucrats, who knew firsthand how the bureaucracy operated, and organized them into "reinventing teams." NPR's report included 384 specific recommendations grouped into four broad imperatives: reducing red tape, putting customers first, empowering administrators, and cutting government back to basic services.[2]

NPR was the most recent in a lengthy list of major efforts to remake the federal bureaucracy. NPR was different in its particulars, but its claim to improve administration while saving money was consistent with the claims of earlier reform panels, including the Brownlow, Hoover, and Volcker commissions.[3] Like those efforts, NPR addressed an enduring issue of American politics: the bureaucracy's efficiency, responsiveness, and accountability.

Modern government would be impossible without a large bureaucracy. It is the government's enormous administrative capacity that makes it possible for the United States to have ambitious programs such as space exploration, social security, interstate highways, and universal postal service. Yet the bureaucracy also poses special problems. Even those who work in federal agencies agree that the bureaucracy can be unresponsive, wasteful, and self-serving.

This chapter examines both the need for bureaucracy and the problems associated with it. The chapter describes the bureaucracy's responsibilities,

As one of thousands of services provided by the federal bureaucracy, the National Hurricane Service monitors hurricane activity and provides early warning to affected coastal areas.

organizational structure, and management practices and explains the "politics" of the bureaucracy. The three constitutional branches of government impose a degree of accountability on the bureaucracy, but its sheer size and fragmented nature confound efforts to control it completely. The main points discussed in this chapter are these:

- *Bureaucracy is an inevitable consequence of complexity and scale.* Modern government could not function without a large bureaucracy. Through authority, specialization, and rules, bureaucracy provides a means of managing thousands of tasks and employees.

- *The bureaucracy is expected simultaneously to respond to the direction of partisan officials and to administer programs fairly and competently.* These conflicting demands are addressed through a combination of personnel management systems—the patronage, merit, and executive leadership systems.

- *Bureaucrats naturally take an "agency point of view." They seek to promote their agency's programs and power.* They do this through their expert knowledge, support from clientele groups, and backing by Congress or the president.

- *Although agencies are subject to oversight by the president, Congress, and the judiciary, bureaucrats are able to exercise power in their own right.*

bureaucracy

A system of organization and control based on the principles of hierarchical authority, job specialization, and formalized rules.

hierarchical authority

A basic principle of bureaucracy that refers to the chain of command within an organization whereby officials and units have control over those below them.

job specialization

A basic principle of bureaucracy that holds that the responsibilities of each job position should be explicitly defined and that a precise division of labor within the organization should be maintained.

formalized rules

A basic principle of bureaucracy that refers to the standardized procedures and established regulations by which a bureaucracy conducts its operations.

FEDERAL ADMINISTRATION: FORM, PERSONNEL, AND ACTIVITIES

For many Americans, the word *bureaucracy* brings to mind waste, mindless rules, and rigidity. This image is not unfounded, but it is one-sided. Bureaucracy is also an efficient and effective method of organization. Although Americans tend to equate bureaucracy with the federal government, bureaucracy is found wherever there is a need to manage large numbers of people and tasks. All large-scale, task-oriented organizations—public and private—are bureaucratic in form.[4] General Motors is a bureaucracy, as is every university. The state governments are also every bit as "bureaucratic" as the federal government (see "States in the Nation").

In formal terms, **bureaucracy** is a system of organization and control that is based on three principles: hierarchical authority, job specialization, and formalized rules. **Hierarchical authority** refers to a chain of command whereby the officials and units at the top of a bureaucracy have authority over those in the middle, who in turn control those at the bottom. In a system of **job specialization,** the responsibilities of each job position are explicitly defined, and there is a precise division of labor within the organization. **Formalized rules** are the standardized procedures and established regulations by which a bureaucracy conducts its operations.

These features are the reason why bureaucracy, as a form of organization, is the most efficient means of getting people to work together on tasks of great magnitude. Hierarchy speeds action by reducing conflict over the power to make decisions: those higher in the organization have authority over those below them. Specialization yields efficiency because each individual is required to concentrate on a particular job: workers acquire specialized skills and knowledge. Formalized

States in the Nation

The Size of State Bureaucracies

Although the federal bureaucracy is often criticized as being "too big," it is actually smaller on a per capita basis than even the smallest state bureaucracy. There is 0.91 federal employee for every 100 Americans. Illinois, with 1.04 state employees for every 100 residents, has the smallest state bureaucracy on a per capita basis. Hawaii has the largest—4.48 state employees per 100 residents.

Q: What do the states with larger per capita bureaucracies have in common?

A: In general, the least populous states, especially those that are larger geographically, have larger bureaucracies on a per capita basis. This pattern reflects the fact that a state, whatever its population, has basic functions (such as highway maintenance and policing) that it must perform.

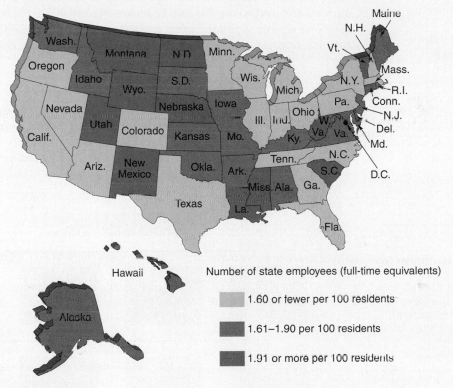

Number of state employees (full-time equivalents)

- 1.60 or fewer per 100 residents
- 1.61–1.90 per 100 residents
- 1.91 or more per 100 residents

Source: U.S. Bureau of the Census, 2004.

rules enable workers to make quick and consistent judgments because decisions are based on preestablished rules rather than on a case-by-case basis.

These organizational characteristics are also the source of bureaucracy's pathologies. Administrators perform not as whole persons but as parts of an organizational entity. Their behavior is governed by position, specialty, and rule. At its worst, bureaucracy grinds on, heedless of the interests of its members or their clients. Fixed rules become an end unto themselves, as anyone who has applied for a driver's license or a student loan knows all too well.

If bureaucracy is an indispensable condition of large-scale organization, gross bureaucratic inefficiency and unresponsiveness are not. At least that is the assumption underlying efforts to strengthen the administration of government, a topic examined later in this chapter.

The Federal Bureaucracy in Americans' Daily Lives

The U.S. federal bureaucracy has roughly 2.5 million employees, who have the responsibility for administering thousands of programs. The president and Congress get far more attention in the news, but it is the bureaucracy that has the more immediate impact on Americans' daily lives. The federal bureaucracy performs a wide range of functions; for example, it delivers the daily mail, maintains the national forests, administers social security, enforces environmental protection laws, develops the country's defense systems, provides foodstuffs for school lunch programs, and regulates the stock markets.

Types of Administrative Organizations

cabinet (executive) departments
The major administrative organizations within the federal executive bureaucracy, each of which is headed by a secretary or, in the case of Justice, the attorney general. Each department has responsibility for a major function of the federal government, such as defense, agriculture, or justice.

The U.S. federal bureaucracy is organized along policy lines. One agency handles veterans' affairs, another specializes in education, a third is responsible for agriculture, and so on. No two units are exactly alike. Nevertheless, most of them take one of five general forms: cabinet department, independent agency, regulatory agency, government corporation, or presidential commission.

Cabinet Departments

The major administrative units are the fifteen **cabinet** (or **executive**) **departments** (see Figure 13–1). Except for the Department of Justice, which is led by the attorney general, the head of each department is its secretary (for example, the secretary of defense), who also serves as a member of the president's cabinet.

Figure 13–1

Cabinet (Executive) Departments
Each executive department is responsible for a general policy area and is headed by a secretary or, in the case of Justice, the attorney general, who serves as a member of the president's cabinet. Shown are each department's year of origin (above the title) and annual budget in billions of dollars (below the title). (The Office of the Attorney General was created in 1789 and became the Justice Department in 1870.)
Source: White House Office of Management and Budget, FY2007.

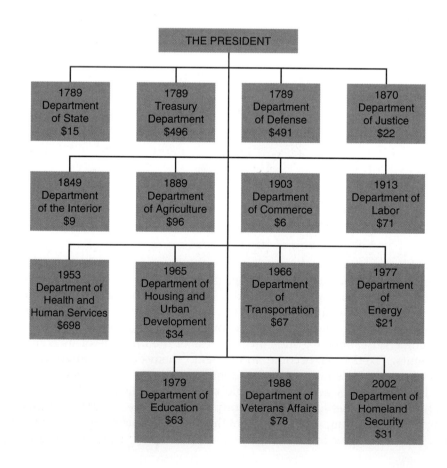

Cabinet departments vary greatly in their visibility, size, and importance. The Department of State, one of the oldest and most prestigious departments, is also one of the smallest, with approximately twenty-five thousand employees. The Department of Defense has the largest work force, with more than six hundred thousand civilian employees (apart from the more than 1.4 million uniformed active service members). The Department of Health and Human Services has the largest budget; its activities account for more than a fourth of all federal spending, much of it in the form of social security benefits. The Department of Homeland Security is the newest department, dating from 2002.

Each cabinet department has responsibility for a general policy area, such as defense or law enforcement. This responsibility is carried out by semiautonomous operating units that typically carry the label "bureau," "agency," "division," or "service." The Department of Justice, for example, has thirteen such operating units, including the Federal Bureau of Investigation (FBI), the Civil Rights Division, the Tax Division, and the Drug Enforcement Administration (DEA). In short, the Department of Justice is itself a large bureaucracy.

WWW.MHHE.COM/PATTERSONTAD8

Independent Agencies

Independent agencies resemble the cabinet departments, but most of them have a narrower area of responsibility. They include organizations such as the Central Intelligence Agency (CIA) and the National Aeronautics and Space Administration (NASA). The heads of these agencies are appointed by and report to the president but are not members of the cabinet. In general, the independent agencies exist apart from cabinet departments because their placement within a department would pose symbolic or practical policy problems. NASA, for example, could conceivably be located in the Department of Defense, but such positioning would suggest that the space program exists solely for military purposes and not also for civilian purposes such as space exploration and satellite communication.

independent agencies
Bureaucratic agencies that are similar to cabinet departments but usually have a narrower area of responsibility. Each such agency is headed by a presidential appointee who is not a cabinet member. An example is the National Aeronautics and Space Administration.

Regulatory Agencies

Regulatory agencies are created when Congress recognizes the importance of close and continuous regulation of an economic activity. Because such regulation requires more time and expertise than Congress can provide, the responsibility is delegated to a regulatory agency. The Securities and Exchange Commission (SEC), which oversees the stock and bond markets, is a regulatory agency. So is the Environmental Protection Agency (EPA), which monitors and prevents industrial pollution. Table 13–1 lists some of the regulatory agencies and other noncabinet units of the federal bureaucracy.

Beyond their executive functions, regulatory agencies have legislative and judicial functions. They issue regulations and judge whether individuals or organizations have complied with them. The SEC, for example, can impose fines and other penalties on business firms that violate regulations pertaining to the trading of stocks and bonds.

Some regulatory agencies, particularly the older ones (such as the SEC), are "independent" by virtue of their relative freedom from ongoing political control. They are headed by a commission of several members who are appointed by the president and confirmed by Congress but who are not subject to removal by the president. Commissioners serve for a fixed number of years, a legal stipulation intended to free them and thereby their agencies from political interference. The newer regulatory agencies (such as the EPA) lack such autonomy. They are headed by a presidential appointee who can be removed at the president's discretion.

regulatory agencies
Administrative units, such as the Federal Communications Commission and the Environmental Protection Agency, that have responsibility for the monitoring and regulation of ongoing economic activities.

TABLE 13–1	Selected U.S. Regulatory Agencies, Independent Agencies, Government Corporations, and Presidential Commissions
Central Intelligence Agency	National Foundation on the Arts and the Humanities
Commission on Civil Rights	National Labor Relations Board
Consumer Product Safety Commission	National Railroad Passenger Corporation (Amtrak)
Environmental Protection Agency	National Science Foundation
Equal Employment Opportunity Commission	National Transportation Safety Board
Export-Import Bank of the United States	Nuclear Regulatory Commission
Farm Credit Administration	Occupational Safety and Health Review Commission
Federal Communications Commission	Office of Personnel Management
Federal Deposit Insurance Corporation	Peace Corps
Federal Election Commission	Securities and Exchange Commission
Federal Maritime Commission	Selective Service System
Federal Reserve System, Board of Governors	Small Business Administration
Federal Trade Commission	U.S. Arms Control and Disarmament Agency
General Services Administration	U.S. Information Agency
National Aeronautics and Space Administration	U.S. International Trade Commission
National Archives and Records Administration	U.S. Postal Service

Source: *The U.S. Government Manual.*

Government Corporations

government corporations
Bodies, such as the U.S. Postal Service and Amtrak, that are similar to private corporations in that they charge for their services but differ in that they receive federal funding to help defray expenses. Their directors are appointed by the president with Senate approval.

Government corporations are similar to private corporations in that they charge clients for their services and are governed by a board of directors. However, government corporations receive federal funding to help defray operating expenses, and their directors are appointed by the president with Senate approval. The largest government corporation is the U.S. Postal Service, with roughly seven hundred thousand employees. Other government corporations include the Federal Deposit Insurance Corporation (FDIC), which insures savings accounts against bank failures, and the National Railroad Passenger Corporation (Amtrak), which provides passenger rail service.

Presidential Commissions

presidential commissions
Advisory organizations within the bureaucracy that are headed by commissioners appointed by the president. An example is the Commission on Civil Rights.

Presidential commissions provide advice to the president. Some of them are permanent bodies; examples are the Commission on Civil Rights and the Commission on Fine Arts. Other presidential commissions are temporary and disband after making recommendations on specific issues. An example is the President's Commission to Strengthen Social Security, which was established by President Bush in 2001 to study possible ways of reforming social security.

Federal Employment

The roughly 2.5 million civilian employees of the federal government include professionals who bring their expertise to the problems involved in governing a large and complex society, service workers who perform such tasks as the typing of correspondence and the delivery of mail, and middle and top managers who supervise the work of the various federal agencies.

More than 90 percent of federal employees are hired by merit criteria, which include educational attainment (in the case, for example, of lawyers and engineers), employment experience, and performance on competitive tests (such as the civil service and foreign service examinations). The merit system is intended to protect the public from inept or biased administrative practices that could result if partisanship were the employment criterion.

Federal employees are underpaid in comparison with their counterparts in the private sector. The large majority of federal employees have a GS (Graded Service) job ranking. The rankings range from GS-1 (the lowest rank) to GS-18 (the highest). College graduates who enter the federal service usually start at the GS-5 level, which provides a salary of about $30,000 for a beginning employee. With a master's degree, employees begin at level GS-9 with a salary of $45,000. Federal employees' salaries increase with rank and length of service. Public employees receive substantial fringe benefits, including full health insurance, secure retirement plans, and generous vacation time and sick leave.

Get Involved!

Serve

President John F. Kennedy said that government is "the highest calling." Most Americans today do not share that belief. They prefer a career in the private sector, and many believe government to be staffed by people who are not particularly talented and who do not work all that hard.

These stereotypes have some basis. There is waste in federal programs, and some civil servants do take advantage of the job security provided by a civil service appointment. However, these problems are not as large as many people think. As former New York governor Mario Cuomo pointed out, fairness rather than efficiency is the goal of many federal programs. Loans to college students, for example, are awarded on the basis of need rather than simply handed out in equal amounts to anyone who applies. The latter approach would be much less expensive to administer; a need-based program requires a detailed application process and a case-by-case assessment of the applicants.

Some deadbeats work in the federal bureaucracy, which is not surprising in view of the fact that it has more than two million employees. Interestingly, when people are asked about their direct experiences with federal employees, they usually express satisfaction with the service they personally have received from postal workers, social security administrators, National Park Service rangers, and other civil servants.

However, the federal bureaucracy has had difficulty attracting top-notch employees. As the gap has widened between the pay and benefits in the public sector relative to the private sector, college graduates have shown less interest in careers in government. A 2001 survey found

that only one in ten graduates was considering such a career path.

A government career is not without its frustrations. A 2002 study by Harvard's Kennedy School of Government found that management-level public-sector employees have less opportunity than comparable private-sector employees to pursue initiatives. Their work is more constrained because the operating rules and budget allocations are less flexible than in the private sector. However, the Kennedy School's study also found that public-sector managers get more intrinsic satisfaction from their work, which focuses on improving public life, than do private-sector managers.

The quality of the nation's public servants affects the quality of governance. Ultimately, an organization is no better than the people who staff it. What would it take for you to consider a career in government? What agency could you envision working in? For people who want to pursue a government career, a first step is often a master's degree program in public administration or public policy. Many of these programs require only a year of study after the bachelor's degree. For an entry-level employee with a master's degree rather than a bachelor's degree, the initial salary is 50 percent higher. Appointees with master's degrees enter the civil service at a higher rank (GS-9 rather than GS-5) and are placed in positions that entail greater responsibility than those assigned to newly hired appointees with bachelor's degrees. Those who enter the civil service at the higher rank also are more likely to advance to top positions as their careers develop.

Public service has its drawbacks. Federal employees can form labor unions, but their unions by law have limited authority: the government maintains full control of job assignments, compensation, and promotion. Moreover, the Taft-Hartley Act of 1947 prohibits strikes by federal employees and permits the firing of striking workers. When federal air traffic controllers went on strike anyway in 1981, they were fired by President Reagan. There are also limits on the partisan activities of civil servants. The Hatch Act of 1939 prohibited them from holding key positions in election campaigns. In 1993, Congress relaxed this prohibition but retained it for certain high-ranking career bureaucrats.

Government employment is overseen by two independent agencies. The Merit Service Protection Board handles appeals of career civil servants who have been fired or who face other disciplinary action. The office of Personnel Management supervises the hiring and classification of federal employees.

policy implementation
The primary function of the bureaucracy; it refers to the process of carrying out the authoritative decisions of Congress, the president, and the courts.

The Federal Bureaucracy's Policy Responsibilities

The Constitution mentions executive departments but does not grant them any powers. Their authority derives from grants of power to the three constitutional branches: Congress, the president, and the courts. Nevertheless, the bureaucracy is far more than an administrative extension of the three branches. It never merely follows orders.

The primary function of administrative agencies is **policy implementation,** that is, carrying out decisions made by Congress, the president, and the courts. Although implementation is sometimes described as "mere administration," it is a creative activity. In the course of their work, administrators come up with policy ideas that are then brought to the attention of the president or members of Congress. Administrative agencies also make policy in the process of determining how to implement congressional, presidential, and judicial decisions. The Telecommunications Act of 1996, for example, had as its stated goal "to promote competition and reduce regulation in order to secure lower prices and higher quality services for American telecommunication consumers and encourage the rapid deployment of new telecommunications technologies." Although the act included specific provisions, its implementation was determined in large part by the Federal Communications Commission (FCC). The FCC decided, for example, that regional telephone companies (the Bell companies) had to open their networks to AT&T and other competitors at wholesale rates far below what they were charging their retail customers. The purpose was to enable AT&T and other carriers to compete with the Bell companies for local phone customers; in other words, the FCC was responding to its legislative mandate "to promote competition." But it was the FCC, not Congress, that determined the wholesale rates and many of the interconnection rules. This development of policy—through *rulemaking* that determines how laws will work in practice—is perhaps the chief way administrative agencies exercise real power.[5]

The U.S. Postal Service is one of the most efficient in the world, delivering hundreds of millions of pieces of mail each day, inexpensively and without undue delay. Yet, like many other government agencies, it is often criticized for its inefficiency and ineptness.

Agencies also are charged with the delivery of services—carrying the mail, processing welfare applications, approving government loans, and the like. Such activities are governed by rules, and in most instances the rules determine what gets done. But some services allow agency employees enough discretion that laws end up being applied arbitrarily, a situation that Michael Lipsky describes as "street-level bureaucracy."[6] For example, FBI agents more diligently pursue organized crime than they do white-collar crime, even though the laws do not say that white-collar crime should somehow be pursued less aggressively.

In sum, administrators exercise discretion in carrying out their responsibilities. They initiate policy, develop it, evaluate it, apply it, and determine whether others are complying with it. The bureaucracy does not simply administer policy; it also *makes policy.*

DEVELOPMENT OF THE FEDERAL BUREAUCRACY: POLITICS AND ADMINISTRATION

Agencies are responsible for programs that serve society, yet each agency was created and is maintained in response to partisan interests. Each agency thus confronts two simultaneous but incompatible demands: that it administer programs fairly and competently and that it respond to partisan demands.

Historically, this conflict has worked itself out in ways that have made the organization of the modern bureaucracy a blend of the political and the administrative. This dual line of development is reflected in the mix of management systems that characterizes the bureaucracy today—the *patronage, merit,* and *executive leadership* systems.

Small Government and the Patronage System

The federal bureaucracy originally was small (three thousand employees in 1800, for instance). The federal government's role was confined mainly to defense and foreign affairs, currency and interstate commerce, and the delivery of the mail. The nation's first six presidents, from George Washington through John Quincy Adams, believed that only distinguished men should be entrusted with the management of the national government. Nearly all top presidential appointees were men of education and political experience, and many of them were members of socially prominent families. They often remained in their jobs year after year.

The nation's seventh president, Andrew Jackson, did not share his predecessors' admiration for the social elite. In Jackson's view, government would be more responsive to the public if it were administered by ordinary

The Central Intelligence Agency (CIA) is located in Langley, Virginia, which is roughly ten miles from the nation's capital. The CIA is an independent federal agency that gathers intelligence used in deciding national security policy. The internal workings of the normally secretive agency came into public view in 2004 as a result of its faulty assessments of Iraqi weapon systems.

patronage system
An approach to managing the bureaucracy whereby people are appointed to important government positions as a reward for political services they have rendered and because of their partisan loyalty.

spoils system
The practice of granting public office to individuals in return for political favors they have rendered.

HISTORICAL
BACKGROUND

merit (civil service) system
An approach to managing the bureaucracy whereby people are appointed to government positions on the basis of either competitive examinations or special qualifications, such as professional training.

people of good sense.[7] Jackson also believed that top administrators should remain in office only for short periods to ensure a steady influx of fresh ideas.

Jackson's version of the **patronage system** was popular with the public, but critics labeled it a **spoils system**—a device for placing political cronies in government office as a reward for partisan support. Although Jackson was motivated as much by a concern for responsive government as by his desire to reward loyal partisans, later presidents were often more interested in giving the spoils of victory to friends and supporters. Jackson's successors extended patronage to all levels of administration.

Growth in Government and the Merit System

Because the government of the early nineteenth century was relatively small and limited in scope, it could be managed by employees who had little or no administrative training or experience. As the century advanced, however, the nature of the country changed rapidly, and the bureaucracy changed along with it. The Industrial Revolution brought with it massive economic shifts, which prompted groups to look to government for assistance. Farmers were among these groups, and in 1889 Congress created the Department of Agriculture. Business and labor interests also pressed their claims, and in 1903 Congress established the Department of Commerce and Labor to "promote the mutual interest" of the nation's firms and workers. (The separate interests of business and labor proved stronger than their shared concerns, and thus in 1913 Labor became a separate department.)

By 1930, federal employment had reached six hundred thousand, a sixfold increase over the level of the 1880s (see Figure 13–2). During the 1930s, as a result of President Franklin Roosevelt's New Deal, the federal work force again expanded, climbing to 1.2 million. Public demand for relief from the economic hardship and uncertainty of the Great Depression led to the formation of economic and social welfare agencies such as the Securities and Exchange Commission and the Social Security Board. An effect was to give the federal government an ongoing role in promoting Americans' economic well-being.

A large and active government requires skilled and experienced personnel. In 1883, Congress passed the Pendleton Act, which established a **merit** (or **civil service**) **system** whereby certain federal employees were hired through competitive examinations or by virtue of having special qualifications, such as an advanced degree in a particular field. The transition to a career civil service was gradual. Only 10 percent of federal positions in 1885 were filled on the basis of merit. But the pace accelerated when the Progressives (see Chapter 2) championed the merit system as

Figure 13–2

Number of Persons Employed by the Federal Government
The federal bureaucracy grew slowly until the 1930s, when an explosive growth began in the number of programs that required ongoing administration by the federal government.
Source: Historical Statistics of the United States and Statistical Abstract of the United States, 1986, 322; recent figures from U.S. Office of Personnel Management.

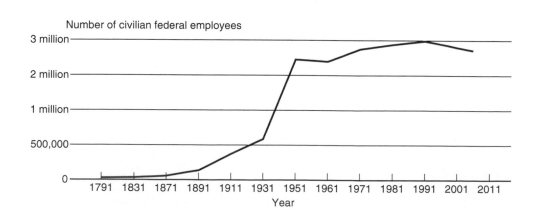

a way of eliminating partisan graft and corruption in the administration of government. By 1920, as the Progressive era was concluding, more than 70 percent of federal employees were merit appointees. Since 1950, the proportion of merit employees has never dipped below 80 percent.[8]

The administrative objective of the merit system is **neutral competence.**[9] A merit-based bureaucracy is "competent" in the sense that employees are hired and retained on the basis of their skills, and it is "neutral" in the sense that employees are not partisan appointees and thus are expected to do their work on behalf of everyone, not just those who support the incumbent president.

Although the merit system contributes to the impartial and proficient administration of government programs, it has its own sources of bias and inefficiency. Career bureaucrats tend to place their agency's interests ahead of those of other agencies and typically oppose substantial efforts to trim their agency's activities. They are not partisans in the sense of Democratic or Republican politics, but they are partisans when it comes to protecting their own positions and agencies, as explained more fully later in the chapter.

The assassination of President James A. Garfield in 1881 by Charles Guiteau, a disappointed officeseeker, did much to end the spoils system of distributing government jobs.

Big Government and the Executive Leadership System

As problems with the merit system surfaced after the early years of the twentieth century, reformers looked to a strengthened presidency—an **executive leadership system**—as a means of coordinating the bureaucracy's activities to increase its efficiency and responsiveness.[10] The president was to provide the general leadership that would overcome agency boundaries. As Chapter 12 describes, Congress in 1939 provided the president with some of the tools needed for improved coordination of the bureaucracy. The Office of Management and Budget (OMB) was created to give the president the authority to coordinate the annual budgetary process. Agencies would be required to prepare their budget proposals under the direction of the president, who would then submit the overall budget to Congress for its approval and modification. The president was also authorized to develop the Executive Office of the President, which oversees the agencies' activities on the president's behalf.

Like the merit and patronage systems, the executive leadership system has brought problems as well as improvements to the administration of government. In practice, the executive leadership concept can give the president too much leverage over the bureaucracy and thereby weaken Congress's ability to act as a check on presidential power. A case in point is the intelligence estimates the Bush administration gave Congress while seeking a congressional resolution authorizing a military attack on Iraq. The Bush administration claimed that the CIA had evidence that Iraq's Saddam Hussein was accumulating weapons of mass destruction (WMDs) that threatened the security of the United States. Bush also used this argument in the effort to generate public and international support for the war. In his 2003 State of the Union address, President Bush said, "The dictator of Iraq is not disarming. To the contrary, he is deceiving." In a speech to the United Nations, Secretary of State Colin Powell claimed, "The facts on Iraq's behavior demonstrate . . . that Saddam Hussein and his regime are concealing their efforts to produce more weapons of mass destruction."

neutral competence

The administrative objective of a merit-based bureaucracy. Such a bureaucracy should be "competent" in the sense that its employees are hired and retained on the basis of their expertise and "neutral" in the sense that it operates by objective standards rather than partisan ones.

executive leadership system

An approach to managing the bureaucracy that is based on presidential leadership and presidential management tools, such as the president's annual budget proposal.

Debating the Issues

The Case of Iraq's Weapons of Mass Destruction: Did the CIA Play Politics?

The federal bureaucracy is a storehouse of knowledge that informs national policy. Though major policy decisions are made primarily by elected officials, these officials rely on agencies for policy-related information. Seldom has this relationship created more controversy than in the case of Iraq's weapons programs. The Bush administration justified its attack on Iraq in 2003 by saying that intelligence agencies had confirmed Iraq's possession of large stockpiles of weapons of mass destruction and its willingness to use them. After U.S. military forces took over Iraq, investigators could not find evidence of an Iraqi weapons program anywhere near the scale portrayed by the Administration. Suddenly the intelligence agencies themselves were on the spot. Had they misread their intelligence or slanted it to fit the Bush administration's agenda? Or had they offered their best judgment based on the intelligence they had? There were sharply conflicting views on this issue, including those of Senator Carl Levin, a member of the Senate Select Committee on Intelligence, and George Tenet, the director of central intelligence.

Yes
There is now confirmation from the administration's own leading weapons inspector that the intelligence community produced greatly flawed assessments about Iraq's weapons of mass destruction in the months leading up to the invasion of Iraq. It is my opinion that flawed intelligence and the administration's exaggerations concerning Iraq's weapons of mass destruction resulted from an effort to make the threat appear more imminent and the case for military action against Iraq appear more urgent than they were. . . . Director Tenet, after 12 months of indefensible stonewalling, recently relented and declassified the material that I requested, which makes clear that his public testimony before the Congress on the extent to which the United States shared intelligence with the United Nations on Iraq's weapons of mass destruction programs was false. . . . In other words, honest answers by Director Tenet might have undermined the false sense of urgency for proceeding to war and could have contributed to delay, neither of which fit the administration's policy goals. . . . We rely on our intelligence agencies to give us the facts, not to give us the spin on the facts. The accuracy and objectivity of intelligence should never be tainted or slanted to support a particular policy.

—*Carl Levin, U.S. senator (D-Mich.)*

No
Much of the current controversy centers on our prewar intelligence on Iraq, summarized in the National Intelligence Estimate of October 2002. . . . This Estimate asked if Iraq had chemical, biological, and nuclear weapons and the means to deliver them. We concluded that in some of these categories, Iraq had weapons. And that in others—where it did not have them—it was trying to develop them. Let me be clear: analysts differed on several important aspects of these programs and those debates were spelled out in the Estimate. They never said there was an "imminent" threat. Rather, they painted an objective assessment for our policymakers of a brutal dictator who was continuing his efforts to deceive and build programs that might constantly surprise us and threaten our interests. No one told us what to say or how to say it. . . . Did these strands of information weave into a perfect picture—could they answer every question? No—far from it. But, taken together, this information provided a solid basis on which to *estimate* whether Iraq did or did not have weapons of mass destruction and the means to deliver them. It is important to underline the word *estimate*. Because not everything we analyze can be known to a standard of absolute proof.

—*George J. Tenet, director of central intelligence*

Yet the facts proved different. In testimony before Congress in 2004, the chief U.S. weapons inspector in Iraq, David Kay, said that his team had failed to uncover evidence of an Iraq weapons program on the scale claimed by the Bush administration. This and other revelations produced heated debate over who was to blame for the faulty claim. Did the blame rest largely with the White House,

TABLE 13–2	Strengths and Weaknesses of Major Systems for Managing the Bureaucracy	
SYSTEM	**STRENGTHS**	**WEAKNESSES**
Patronage	Makes the bureaucracy more responsive to election outcomes by allowing the president to appoint some executive officials.	Gives executive authority to individuals chosen for their partisan loyalty rather than for their administrative or policy expertise; can favor interests that supported the president's election.
Merit	Provides for *competent* administration in that employees are hired on the basis of ability and allowed to remain on the job and thereby become proficient, and provides for *neutral* administration in that civil servants are not partisan appointees and are expected to work in an evenhanded way.	Can result in fragmented, unresponsive administration because career bureaucrats are secure in their jobs and tend to place the interests of their particular agency ahead of those of other agencies or the nation's interests as a whole.
Executive leadership	Provides for presidential leadership of the bureaucracy in order to make it more responsive and to coordinate and direct it (left alone, the bureaucracy tends toward fragmentation).	Can upset the balance between executive and legislative power and can make the president's priorities, not fairness or effective management, the basis for administrative action.

which had pressured the intelligence agencies to make the strongest case possible for war with Iraq, or did the blame rest largely with the intelligence agencies themselves? Many observers blamed both, concluding that the White House had overstated its case and that the intelligence agencies had been too eager to tell the White House what it wanted to hear.

Thus, the executive leadership system, like the patronage and merit systems, is not foolproof. It can make bureaucratic agencies overly dependent on the presidency, thereby distorting their activities and reducing congressional checks on executive power. Nevertheless, the executive leadership system is a necessary part of an overall strategy for the effective handling of the bureaucracy. At its best, the system imposes principles of effective management—such as eliminating wasteful duplication—on the work of government agencies.

The federal bureaucracy today embodies aspects of all three systems—patronage, merit, and executive leadership—a situation that reflects the tensions inherent in governmental administration. The bureaucracy is expected to carry out programs fairly and competently (the merit system), but it is also expected to respond to political forces (the patronage system) and to operate efficiently (the executive management system). Table 13–2 summarizes the strengths and weaknesses of each of these administrative systems.

THE BUREAUCRACY'S POWER IMPERATIVE

A common misperception is that the president, as the chief executive, has the sole claim on the bureaucracy's loyalty. In fact, each of the elected institutions has reason to claim ownership: the president as chief executive and Congress as the source of the bureaucracy's programs and funding. One presidential appointee asked a congressional committee whether it had any problem with his plans to reduce one of his agency's programs. The committee chairman replied, "No, you have the problem, because if you touch that bureau I'll cut your job out of the budget."[11]

The U.S. system of separate institutions sharing power results in a natural tendency for each institution to guard its turf. In addition, the president and members of Congress differ in their constituencies and thus in the interests to which they are most responsive. For example, although the agricultural sector is just one of many concerns of the president, it is of vital interest to senators and representatives from farm states. Finally, because the president and Congress are elected separately, the White House and one or both houses of Congress may be in the hands of opposing parties. Since 1968, this source of executive-legislative conflict has been as much the rule as the exception.

If agencies are to operate successfully in this system, they must seek support where they can find it—if not from the president, then from Congress. In other words, agencies have no choice but to play politics.[12] Any agency that sits by idly while other agencies fight for their programs is certain to lose out.

The Agency Point of View

agency point of view
The tendency of bureaucrats to place the interests of their agency ahead of other interests and ahead of the priorities sought by the president or Congress.

Administrators tend to look out for their agency's interests, a perspective that is called the **agency point of view.** This perspective comes naturally to most high-ranking civil servants. More than 80 percent of top bureaucrats reach their high-level positions by rising through the ranks of the same agency.[13] As one top administrator said when testifying before the House Appropriations Committee, "Mr. Chairman, you would not think it proper for me to be in charge of this work and not be enthusiastic about it . . . would you? I have been in it for thirty years, and I believe in it."[14] Studies confirm that bureaucrats believe in the importance of their agency's work. One study found that social welfare administrators are three times as likely as other civil servants to believe that social welfare programs should be a high policy priority.[15]

Professionalism also cements agency loyalties. High-level administrative positions have increasingly been filled by scientists, engineers, lawyers, educators, physicians, and other professionals. Most of them take jobs in an agency whose mission they support, as in the case of the aeronautical engineers who work for NASA.

Sources of Bureaucratic Power

In promoting their agency's interests, bureaucrats rely on their specialized knowledge, the support of interests that benefit from the programs they run, and the backing of the president and Congress.

The Power of Expertise

Most of the policy problems that the federal government confronts do not lend themselves to simple solutions. Whether the issue is space travel or hunger in America, expert knowledge is essential to the development of effective public policy. Much of this expertise is held by bureaucrats. They spend their careers working in a particular policy area, and many of them have had scientific, technical, or other specialized training.[16]

By comparison, elected officials are generalists. To some degree, members of Congress do specialize through their committee work, but they rarely have the time or the inclination to acquire a commanding knowledge of a particular issue. The president's understanding of policy issues is even more general. Not surprisingly, the president and members of Congress rely on the bureaucracy for policy advice and guidance.

All agencies acquire some power through their careerists' expertise. No matter how simple a policy issue may appear at first, it invariably involves more

How the United States Compares

Educational Backgrounds of Bureaucrats

To staff its bureaucracy, the U.S. government tends to hire persons with specialized educations to hold specialized jobs. This approach heightens the tendency of bureaucrats to take the agency point of view. By comparison, Great Britain tends to recruit its bureaucrats from the arts and humanities, on the assumption that general aptitude is the best qualification for detached professionalism. The continental European democracies also emphasize detached professionalism, but in the context of the supposedly impartial application of rules. As a consequence, high-ranking civil servants in Europe tend to have legal educations. The college majors of senior civil servants in the United States and other democracies reflect these tendencies.

COLLEGE MAJOR OF SENIOR CIVIL SERVANTS	NORWAY	GERMANY	GREAT BRITAIN	ITALY	BELGIUM	UNITED STATES
Natural science/engineering	8%	8%	26%	10%	20%	32%
Social science/humanities/business	38	18	52	37	40	50
Law	38	63	3	53	35	18
Other	16	11	19	—	5	—
	100%	100%	100%	100%	100%	100%

Adapted from *The Politics of Bureaucracy*, 5th ed. By B. Guy Peters. Copyright © 2001 by Routledge. Printed by permission of Thomsen Publishing Services.

complexity than meets the eye. A recognition that the United States has a trade deficit with China, for example, can be the premise for policy change, but this recognition does not begin to address basic issues such as the form the new policy might take, its probable cost and effectiveness, and its links to other issues, such as America's standing in Asia. Among the officials most likely to understand these issues are the career bureaucrats in the Commerce Department and the Federal Trade Commission.

The Power of Clientele Groups

Most agencies have **clientele groups,** special interests that benefit directly from an agency's programs. Clientele groups assist agencies by placing pressure on Congress and the president to support those programs from which they benefit.[17] For example, when House Speaker Newt Gingrich threatened in 1995 to "zero out" funding for the Corporation for Public Broadcasting, audience members and groups such as the Children's Television Workshop wrote, called, faxed, and cajoled members of Congress, saying that programs like *Sesame Street* and *All Things Considered* were irreplaceable. Within a few weeks, Gingrich had retreated from his position, saying that a complete cessation of funding was not what he had in mind.

In general, agencies both assist and are assisted by the clientele groups that depend on the programs they administer.[18] Many agencies were created for the purpose of promoting particular interests in society. For example, the Department of Agriculture's career bureaucrats are dependable allies of farm interests year after

clientele groups
Special interest groups that benefit directly from the activities of a particular bureaucratic agency and therefore are strong advocates of the agency.

The popular children's program *Sesame Street* is produced through the Corporation for Public Broadcasting, a government agency that gains leverage in budgetary deliberations from its public support. Singer Garth Brooks is shown here with two muppets during his appearance on *Sesame Street*.

year. The same cannot be said of the president, Congress as a whole, or either political party, all of whom must balance farmers' demands against those of other interests.

The Power of Friends in High Places

Although members of Congress and the president sometimes appear to be at war with the bureaucracy, they need it as much as it needs them. An agency's resources—its programs, expertise, and group support—can assist elected officials in their efforts to achieve their goals. When President George W. Bush in 2001 announced plans for a war on terrorism, he needed the help of careerists in the Central Intelligence Agency and the Department of Defense to make his efforts successful. At a time when other agencies were feeling the pinch of a tight federal budget, these agencies received substantial new funding.

Bureaucrats also seek favorable relations with members of Congress. Congressional support is vital because agencies' funding and programs are established through legislation. Agencies that offer benefits to major constituency interests are particularly likely to have close ties to Congress. In some policy areas, more or less permanent alliances—iron triangles—form among agencies, clientele groups, and congressional subcommittees. In other policy areas, temporary issue networks form among bureaucrats, lobbyists, and members of Congress. As explained in Chapters 9 and 11, these alliances are a means by which an agency can gain support from key legislators and groups.

BUREAUCRATIC ACCOUNTABILITY

Even though most Americans say that they have a favorable impression of their most recent personal experience with the bureaucracy (as, say, when a senior citizen applies for social security), they have an unfavorable impression of the bureaucracy as a whole (see Figure 13–3). Along with citizens of other democracies, they see the programs of government bureaucracies as wasteful and inefficient. This view is somewhat unfair. In areas such as health care and retirement insurance, government bureaucracies are actually more efficient than private organizations. In other areas, efficiency is an inappropriate standard for government programs. The most efficient way to administer government loans to college students, for example, would be to give money to the first students who apply and then close down the program when the money runs out. However, college loan programs, like many other government programs, operate on the principles of fairness and need, which require that each application be judged on its merits.

Studies indicate that the U.S. bureaucracy compares favorably to government bureaucracies elsewhere. "Some national bureaucracies," writes Charles Goodsell, "May be roughly the same [as the U.S. bureaucracy] in quality of overall performance, but they are few in number."[19] Of course, not all U.S. agencies have strong performance records (see Figure 13–4). The Immigration and Naturalization

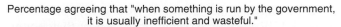

Percentage agreeing that "when something is run by the government, it is usually inefficient and wasteful."

Canada	61%
France	70%
Germany	65%
Great Britain	66%
Italy	82%
Japan	74%
Mexico	66%
United States	63%

Figure 13–3
Opinions on Bureaucratic Inefficiency and Waste
Although Americans believe that government programs are inefficient and wasteful, they are not alone in their belief. Public opinion on this issue is remarkably consistent across democratic nations.
Source: Global Attitudes Survey, Pew Research Center on the People and the Press, 2002.

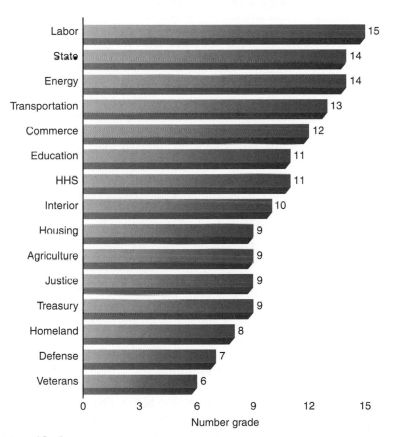

Department	Number grade
Labor	15
State	14
Energy	14
Transportation	13
Commerce	12
Education	11
HHS	11
Interior	10
Housing	9
Agriculture	9
Justice	9
Treasury	9
Homeland	8
Defense	7
Veterans	6

Number grade

Figure 13–4
Ranking the Cabinet Departments by Managerial Performance
Through its Executive Branch Management Scorecard, OMB evaluates federal agencies by five managerial reform criteria: human capital, competitive sourcing, financial management, e-government, and budget and performance integration. By these criteria, the Department of Labor ranks as the best managed cabinet department and the Veterans Administration ranks as the worst.
Source: Office of Management and Budget, 2006. OMB has three levels of performance in each of its five categories. Author derived the scores in figure by assigning the numbers 3, 2, and 1 for an agency's score in each category, with a "3" representing the highest level of performance.

Service (INS) is one agency that has been chronically mismanaged. Yet the performance of many U.S. agencies is superior to that of their counterparts in other industrialized democracies. The U.S. postal service, for example, has an on-time and low-cost record that few postal services can match.

Nevertheless, it is easy to see why most Americans hold a relatively unfavorable opinion of the federal bureaucracy. Americans have traditionally mistrusted political power, and the bureaucracy is the symbol of "big government." It is also a convenient target for politicians who claim that "Washington bureaucrats" are wasting taxpayer money. (The irony is that the bureaucracy has no power to create programs or authorize spending; these decisions are made by Congress and the president.) It is no surprise that Americans have qualms about the federal bureaucracy and want it to be more closely supervised.

Adapting the requirements of the bureaucracy to those of democracy is challenging. Bureaucracy is the antithesis of democracy. Bureaucrats are unelected and hold office indefinitely, and they make decisions based on fixed rules rather than on debate and deliberation. This situation raises the question of **bureaucratic accountability**—the degree to which bureaucrats are held accountable for the power they exercise. Bureaucratic accountability occurs primarily through oversight by the president, Congress, and the courts.[20]

bureaucratic accountability
The degree to which bureaucrats are held accountable for the power they exercise.

Accountability Through the Presidency

The president can only broadly influence, not directly control, the bureaucracy. "We can outlast any president" is a maxim of bureaucratic politics. Each agency has its clientele and its congressional supporters as well as statutory authority for its existence and activities. No president can unilaterally eliminate an agency or its funding and programs. Nor can the president be indifferent to the opinions of career civil servants—not without losing their support and expertise in developing and implementing presidential policy objectives.

To encourage the bureaucracy to act responsibly, the president can apply management tools that have developed out of the "executive leadership" concept discussed earlier in this chapter. These tools include reorganization, presidential appointments, and the executive budget.

Reorganization

The bureaucracy's extreme fragmentation—its hundreds of separate agencies—makes presidential coordination of its activities difficult. Agencies pursue independent and even contradictory paths, resulting in an undetermined amount of waste and duplication of effort. For example, more than one hundred governmental units are responsible for different pieces of federal education policy.

All recent presidents have tried to streamline the bureaucracy and make it more accountable.[21] Such changes seldom greatly improve things, but they can produce marginal gains.[22] For George W. Bush, the challenge came after the terrorist attacks on the World Trade Center and the Pentagon. Breakdowns in the FBI and CIA had undermined whatever chance there might have been to prevent the attacks. These agencies had neither shared nor vigorously pursued the intelligence information they had gathered. Bush concluded, and Congress agreed, that a reorganization of the FBI and CIA, as well as the creation of the Department of Homeland Security (DHS), was necessary. Nevertheless, neither the White House nor Congress was under the illusion that this reorganization would fully correct the coordination problems plaguing the agencies accountable for responding to external and internal threats to Americans' safety.

Political Culture

Bureaucracy, Liberty, and Self-Government

Americans are distrustful of bureaucracy, associating it with big government, which they historically have seen as a threat to liberty. This opinion may be based more on cultural bias than on personal experience, but it is not without foundation. Bureaucrats in agencies charged with law enforcement and national security, like bureaucrats in other agencies, can become insular in their thinking. A narrow-minded pursuit of their mission can override their dedication to the nation's governing principles. Abuses of individual rights, of intelligence gathering, and of the use of military force are a part of America's history, just as they are a part of the history of other democracies.

At times the power of the bureaucracy is also difficult to reconcile with the principle of self-government. Bureaucracy entails hierarchy, command, permanence of office, appointment to office, and fixed rules, whereas self-government involves equality, consent, rotation of office, election to office, and open decision making. At base, the conflict between bureaucracy and self-government centers on the degree of power held by officials who are not elected by vote of the people.

The answer to such dilemmas is not found in making the bureaucracy more efficient. Often, those bureaucratic decisions made in the name of efficiency are the very ones that run counter to the principles of self-government and

liberty. When some U.S. soldiers and intelligence agents were charged recently with using interrogation techniques in Iraq and Afghanistan that are banned under the Geneva Conventions, they defended their actions by saying it was the quickest way to get the information they were seeking.

The United States, like any large-scale society, has no choice but to accept bureaucracy as a fact of life. Indeed, the United States could not possibly operate as a nation without its defense establishment, its education and welfare programs, the regulation of business, its transportation system, and the hundreds of other undertakings of the federal government.

The challenge, then, is to make the bureaucracy work in ways that are compatible with the principles of liberty and self-government. America's approach to this challenge has been to entrust oversight to Congress, the president, and the judiciary. Can you think of ways this oversight might be made more effective? Can you also think of ways of reorganizing the bureaucracy that would enhance accountability? For example, do you think the bureaucracy would be more accountable if civil servants rotated from one agency to another every few years, much as military personnel rotate in their assignments? What would be the disadvantages of such a personnel system?

Indeed, DHS failed miserably in its first big test after the reorganization. That test came not from terrorists but from hurricane Katrina, which slammed into the Gulf Coast in 2005, killing hundreds of Americans and displacing tens of thousands. One of DHS's agencies, the Federal Emergency Management Agency (FEMA), has responsibility for coordinating disaster response efforts, and its response by all accounts was disorganized and inadequate. At times, FEMA appeared to know less than the news media about what was happening in the Gulf area. Its communication and transportation systems broke down, resulting in long delays in providing relief assistance. FEMA's director, Michael Brown, did not even keep his boss, DHS secretary Michael Chertoff, informed of his actions, telling Congress months later that doing so would have been "a waste of time" because DHS did not have the needed resources. Brown was fired two weeks into the relief effort, and some observers felt that Chertoff's job was saved only to avoid the appearance that the entire department was in disarray.

Presidential Appointments

Although there is almost no direct confrontation with a bureaucrat that a president cannot win, the president does not have time to deal personally with every troublesome careerist or to make sure that the bureaucracy has complied with

The Old Executive Office Building is adjacent to the West Wing of the White House. Its occupants are part of the Executive Office of the President (EOP) and serve as contacts between the president and agency bureaucrats.

every presidential order. The president relies on political appointees in federal agencies to ensure that directives are followed.

The power of presidential appointees is greater in those agencies where wide latitude exists in the making of decisions. Although the Social Security Administration (SSA) has a huge budget and makes monthly payments to more than forty million Americans, the eligibility of recipients is determined by relatively fixed rules. The head of the SSA does not have the option, say, of granting a retiree an extra $100 a month because the retiree is facing financial hardship. In contrast, most regulatory agencies have broad discretion over regulatory policy, and the heads of these agencies have wide latitude in their decisions. For example, President Reagan's appointee to chair the Federal Trade Commission (FTC), James Miller III, was a strong-willed economist who shared Reagan's belief that consumer protection policy had gone too far and was adversely affecting business interests. In Miller's first year as head of the FTC, the commission dropped one-fourth of its pending cases against business firms.[23] Overall, enforcement actions declined by about 50 percent during Miller's tenure compared with the previous period.

However, as noted in Chapter 12, there are limits to what a president can accomplish through appointments. High-level presidential appointees number in the hundreds, and their turnover rate is high: the average appointee remains in the Administration for less than two years before moving on to other employment.[24] No president can keep track of all appointees, much less instruct them in detail on all intended policies. Moreover, many presidential appointees have little knowledge of the agencies they head, which makes it difficult for them to exercise control. FEMA's fired director, Michael Brown, was appointed to head the agency because of his political connections. He had little management experience and virtually no disaster relief experience before taking up his post at FEMA.

The Executive Budget

Faced with the difficulty of controlling the bureaucracy, presidents have come to rely heavily on their personal bureaucracy, the Executive Office of the President (EOP).

In terms of presidential management, the key unit within the EOP is the Office of Management and Budget (OMB). Funding, programs, and regulations are the mainstays of every agency, and the OMB has substantial influence on each of these areas. No agency can issue a major regulation without the OMB's verification that the regulation's benefits outweigh its costs, and no agency can propose legislation to Congress without the OMB's approval. However, the OMB's greatest influence over agencies derives from its budgetary role. At the start of the annual budget cycle, the OMB assigns each agency a budget limit in accord with the president's directives. The agency's tentative allocation requests are sent back to the OMB, which then conducts a final review of all requests before sending the full budget to Congress in the president's name (see Table 13–3).

In most cases, an agency's overall budget does not change much from year to year, indicating that a significant portion of the bureaucracy's activities persist regardless of who sits in the White House or Congress. It must be noted, however, that the bulk of federal spending is for programs such as social security that, although enacted in the past, enjoy the continuing support of the president, Congress, and the public.

TABLE 13–3

The Budgetary Process Bureaucratic agencies are funded through a process that assigns significant roles to the president and Congress, as well as to the agencies themselves. The annual federal budget allocates the hundreds of billions of dollars that support federal agencies and programs. This table gives a simplified step-by-step summary of the process.

1. In the calendar year preceding enactment of the budget, the Office of Management and Budget (OMB) instructs each agency to prepare its budget request within guidelines established by the White House.

2. Agencies work out their budget proposals in line with White House guidelines and their own goals. Once completed, agency proposals are sent to the OMB for review and adjustment to fit the president's goals.

3. In January, the president submits the adjusted budget to Congress.

4. The president's budget is reviewed by the Congressional Budget Office (CBO) and is referred to the House and Senate budget and appropriations committees. The budget committees in each chamber then set expenditure ceilings in particular areas, which are voted upon by the members of Congress. Once set (usually in April), the budget ceilings establish temporary limits within which the appropriations committees must act.

5. Through subcommittee hearings, the House and Senate appropriations committees meet with agency heads and adjust the president's budgetary recommendations to fit congressional goals. Once the appropriations committees have completed their work, the proposals are submitted to the full House and Senate for a vote. Differences in the House and Senate versions are reconciled in conference committee.

6. The legislation is sent to the president for approval or veto. Before this point, the White House and Congress will have engaged in intense negotiations to resolve differences in their priorities. If the White House is satisfied with the outcome of the bargaining, the president can be expected to sign the legislation.

7. The new budget takes effect October 1, unless Congress has not completed its work by then or the president exercises the veto. If agreement has not been reached by this date, temporary funding (authorized by Congress and approved by the president) is required to keep the government in operation until a permanent budget can be enacted. If temporary funding is not provided, a shutdown of nonessential government services occurs.

Accountability Through Congress

Congress has powerful means of influencing the bureaucracy. All agencies depend on Congress for their existence, authority, programs, and funding.

The most substantial control that Congress exerts on the bureaucracy is through its power to authorize and fund programs. Without authorization and funding, a program simply does not exist, regardless of the priority an agency claims it deserves. Congress can also void an administrative decision through legislation that instructs the agency to follow a different course of action. However, Congress lacks the time and expertise to work out complex policies down to the last detail.[25] The government would grind to a halt if Congress tried to define fully how federal programs will be designed and run.

Congress also exerts some control through its oversight function, which involves monitoring the bureaucracy's work to ensure its compliance with legislative intent.[26] However, as noted in Chapter 11, oversight is a difficult and relatively unrewarding task, and members of Congress ordinarily place less emphasis on oversight than on their other major duties. Only when an agency has clearly stepped out of line is Congress likely to take decisive corrective action by holding hearings to ask tough questions and to warn of legislative punishment.

Because oversight is burdensome, Congress has shifted much of the responsibility to the Government Accountability Office (GAO). The GAO's primary function once was to keep track of the funds spent within the bureaucracy; it now also monitors whether policies are being implemented as Congress intended. The Congressional Budget Office (CBO) also carries out oversight studies. When the GAO or CBO uncovers a major problem with an agency's handling of a program, it notifies Congress, which can then take remedial action.

Bureaucrats generally are kept in check by an awareness that misbehavior can trigger a response from Congress. Nevertheless, oversight cannot correct

LEADERS

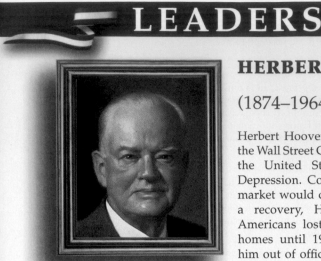

HERBERT HOOVER

(1874–1964)

Herbert Hoover was president when the Wall Street Crash of 1929 propelled the United States into the Great Depression. Convinced that the free market would correct itself and bring a recovery, Hoover stood by as Americans lost their jobs and their homes until 1932 when they voted him out of office. If Hoover is not regarded as a great president, he is believed to be the finest bureaucrat America has produced. He was in China during the Boxer Rebellion and used the engineering skills he had been taught at Stanford to build barricades that protected his work crew from marauding gangs. He was in London when World War I broke out and was asked to head a relief effort to help ten million food-starved Belgians. Although Belgium was sandwiched between the British and German armies, Hoover's organizing skills enabled him to dispatch the food, trucks, and ships to get the job done. When the United States entered the war in 1917, Hoover became U.S. Food Administrator, charged with supplying food to the U.S. military and its allies without starving the American public in the process. Hoover developed a campaign—"Food Will Win the War"—that asked Americans to eat less. "Meatless Mondays" was part of it. Domestic food consumption declined by a sixth, enabling the United States to triple its shipments abroad. After the war, Hoover headed the American Relief Organization that was the main supplier of food for more than 300 million people in nearly two dozen countries. Hoover's food packets were the origin of the CARE packages.

When Warren Harding was elected president in 1920, Hoover was appointed to head the Commerce Department, which took on the task of eliminating waste and duplication in industry—for example, through standardizing the size of nuts, bolts, and other parts. He brought statistical analysis into the department, arguing that policy decisions should be based on precise information, not guesswork. In 1927, Hoover oversaw the nation's response to a devastating Mississippi River flood. A year later, Hoover was elected to the presidency. After his White House years, Hoover stayed active in public life. Presidents Roosevelt and Truman placed him in charge of food and famine relief efforts during and after World War II. In the 1950s, at the request of President Eisenhower, he chaired the first and second Hoover Commissions, which proposed ways to improve the bureaucracy.

sunset law
A law containing a provision that fixes a date on which a program will end unless the program's life is extended by Congress.

mistakes or abuses that have already occurred. Recognizing this limit on oversight, Congress has devised ways to constrain the bureaucracy *before* it acts. The simplest method is to draft laws that contain very specific provisions that limit bureaucrats' options in implementing policy. Another restrictive device is the **sunset law,** which establishes a specific date when a law will expire unless it is reenacted by Congress. Advocates of sunset laws see them as a means to counter the bureaucracy's reluctance to give up programs that have outlived their usefulness. Because members of Congress usually want the programs they create to last far into the future, however, most legislation does not include a sunset provision.

Accountability Through the Courts

The judiciary's influence on agencies is less direct than that of the elected branches, but the courts too can and do act to ensure the bureaucracy's compliance with Congress's directives. Legally, the bureaucracy derives its authority from acts of Congress, and an injured party can bring suit against an agency on the grounds that it has failed to carry out a law properly. Judges can then order an agency to change its application of the law.[27]

However, the courts have tended to support administrators if their actions seem at all consistent with the laws they are administering. The Supreme Court has held that agencies can apply any reasonable interpretation of statutes unless Congress has specifically stated something to the contrary and that agencies in many instances have wide discretion in deciding whether to enforce statutes.[28]

These positions reflect the need for flexibility in administration. The bureaucracy and the courts would both grind to a halt if judges regularly second-guessed bureaucrats' decisions. The judiciary promotes bureaucratic accountability primarily by encouraging administrators to act responsibly in their dealings with the public and by protecting individuals from the bureaucracy's worst abuses. In 1999, for example, a federal court approved a settlement in favor of African American farmers who demonstrated that the Department of Agriculture had systematically favored white farmers in granting federal farm loans.[29]

Accountability Within the Bureaucracy Itself

A recognition of the difficulty of ensuring adequate accountability of the bureaucracy through the presidency, Congress, and the courts has led to the development of mechanisms of accountability within the bureaucracy itself. Two measures, whistle-blowing and demographic representativeness, are particularly noteworthy.

Whistle-Blowing

Although the bureaucratic corruption that is rampant in some countries is relatively uncommon in the United States, a certain amount of waste, fraud, and abuse is inevitable in a bureaucracy as big as that of the federal government. **Whistle-blowing,** the act of reporting instances of official mismanagement, is a potentially effective internal check. To encourage whistle-blowers to come forward with their information, Congress enacted the Whistle Blower Protection Act to protect them against retaliation. Federal law also provides whistle blowers with financial rewards in some cases.

Nevertheless, whistle-blowing is not for the faint-hearted. Many federal employees are reluctant to report instances of mismanagement because they fear retaliation. Their superiors might claim that they are malcontents or find subtle ways to punish them. Even their fellow employees are unlikely to think highly of "tattletales."

Accordingly, whistle-blowing sometimes does not occur until an employee has left an agency or quit government service entirely. A case in point is Richard Clarke, the former chief terrorist adviser in the Bush administration. In 2004, Clarke accused President Bush and other top White House officials of downplaying the terrorist threat and being preoccupied with Iraq in the period leading up to the September 11, 2001, terrorist attacks. "I believe the Bush administration in the first eight months considered terrorism an important issue, but not an urgent issue," Clarke told the 9/11 Commission, a bipartisan commission formed by Congress to investigate the attacks. The White House countered with accusations that Clarke was exaggerating his claims in order to boost sales of his recently published book. Vice President Dick Cheney claimed that Clarke "wasn't in the loop" and could not possibly have known what was going on in the Bush administration's inner circle. The White House slowed its attack on Clarke only after documents surfaced supporting some of his allegations. In a pre-9/11 memo prepared for Bush's national security advisor Condoleezza Rice, Clarke had expressed alarm at the slow pace of the Administration's antiterrorism planning, saying "Imagine a day after hundreds of Americans lay dead at home or abroad after a terrorist attack."[30]

Demographic Representativeness

Although the bureaucracy is an unrepresentative institution in the sense that its officials are not elected by the people, it can be representative in the demographic sense. If bureaucrats were a demographic microcosm of the general public, they presumably would treat the various groups and interests in society more fairly.[31]

Whistle-blower Richard Clarke testifies about Bush administration antiterrorism policies in the months before the September 11, 2001, attacks on the World Trade Center and the Pentagon. In high-profile appearances before Congress and the 9/11 Commission, Clarke accused the Bush administration, in which he had served as the top terrorist adviser, of ignoring warnings of a possible large-scale terrorist attack on the United States.

whistle-blowing
An internal check on the bureaucracy whereby employees report instances of mismanagement that they observe.

TABLE 13–4	**Federal Job Rankings (GS) of Various Demographic Groups** Women and minority-group members are underrepresented in the top jobs of the federal bureaucracy, but their representation has been increasing.					
	WOMEN'S SHARE		**BLACKS' SHARE**		**HISPANICS' SHARE**	
GRADE LEVEL*	1982	2002	1982	2002	1982	2002
GS 13–15 (highest ranks)	5%	32%	5%	10%	2%	4%
GS 9–12	20	46	10	16	4	7
GS 5–8	60	67	19	26	4	9
GS 1–4 (lowest ranks)	78	69	23	28	5	8

*In general, the higher-numbered grades are managerial and professional positions, and the lower-numbered grades are clerical and manual labor positions.
Source: Office of Personnel Management, 2006.

At present, the bureaucracy is not demographically representative at its top levels (see Table 13–4). Roughly 60 percent of managerial and professional positions are held by white males. However, the employment status of women and, to a lesser extent, minorities has improved in recent decades, and top officials in the bureaucracy include a greater proportion of women and minorities than is found in Congress or the judiciary. Moreover, if all employees are considered, the federal bureaucracy comes reasonably close to being representative of the nation's population.[32]

demographic representativeness
The idea that the bureaucracy will be more responsive to the public if its employees at all levels are demographically representative of the population as a whole.

Demographic representativeness is only a partial answer to the problem of bureaucratic accountability. A fully representative civil service would still be required to play agency politics. The careerists in, say, defense agencies and welfare agencies are similar in their demographic backgrounds, but they differ markedly in their opinions about policy. Each group believes that the goals of its agency should take priority. The inevitability of an agency point of view is the most significant of all political facts about the U.S. federal bureaucracy.

REINVENTING GOVERNMENT?

In *Reinventing Government*, David Osborne and Ted Gaebler argue that the bureaucracy of today was created in response to earlier problems, particularly those spawned by the Industrial Revolution and a rampant spoils system. They claim that the information age requires a different kind of administrative structure, one that is leaner and more responsive. Osborne and Gaebler argue that government should set program standards but should not necessarily take on all program responsibilities. If, for example, a private firm can furnish meals to soldiers at U.S. army posts at a lower cost than the military can provide them, it should be contracted to provide the meals. Osborne and Gaebler also say that administrative judgments should be made at the lowest bureaucratic level feasible. If, for example, Department of Agriculture field agents have the required knowledge to make a certain type of decision, they should be empowered to make it rather than being required to get permission from superiors. Finally, Osborne and Gaebler argue that the bureaucracy should focus on outputs (results) rather than inputs (dollars spent). Federal

Media & Politics

National Public Radio and the Corporation for Public Broadcasting

The Corporation for Public Broadcasting (CPB), established by Congress in 1967, is a nonprofit corporation rather than a government agency. Congress provides an annual appropriation to CPB, but most of its funds come from contributions by audience members, corporate sponsors, and foundations. Like a government agency, the CPB is directed by political appointees. Members of the CPB governing board are appointed to six-year terms by the president, subject to confirmation by the Senate. Unlike agency heads, however, the CPB governors do not direct the day-to-day operations of public broadcasting.

Public broadcasting got off to a slow start in the United States. Unlike the case in Europe, where public broadcasting networks (such as Britain's BBC) were created at the start of the radio age, the U.S. government handed control of broadcasting to commercial networks, such as NBC and CBS. By the time Congress decided in the 1960s that public broadcasting was needed, the commercial networks were so powerful that they convinced Congress to assign it second-class status. Public broadcasting was poorly funded and was denied access to the most powerful broadcast frequencies. Most television sets in the 1960s had tuners that could not dial in the stations on which public broadcast programs were aired. Not surprisingly, public broadcasting faltered at the beginning and still operates in the shadow of commercial broadcasting.

Nevertheless, public broadcasting does have a success story—National Public Radio (NPR). During the past two decades, NPR's audience has quadrupled. Each week, more than 20 million Americans listen to NPR, many of them on a regular basis. NPR's growth is a stark contrast to what has happened to commercial newscasts during the same period. The combined audience of the ABC, CBS, and NBC evening newscasts is now half that of the early 1980s.

NPR has built its audience through a strategy opposite to that of the commercial networks. As the news audiences of these networks declined in the face of widening competition from cable television, they "softened" their newscasts—boosting entertainment content in the hope of luring viewers away from cable programs. Former Federal Communication Commission chairman Newton Minow derided the change as "pretty close to tabloid." In contrast, NPR has held to the notion that news is news and not also entertainment. Although NPR carries features, they are typically tied to news developments. Studies indicate that NPR's audience is more politically interested and informed than any other broadcast news audience. Many of its listeners are refugees from the broadcast network news they used to watch but now find lacking in substance. Informative news is not the sole reason for NPR's success. Americans spend more time now in their cars commuting to and from work; radio listening has increased overall for this reason. Nevertheless, NPR has shown that there is still a market in America for serious broadcast news.

loans to college students, for example, should be judged by how many students stay in college as a result of these loans rather than by how much money they receive.[33]

These ideas informed the Clinton administration's National Performance Review (described in this chapter's introduction). Even though the Bush administration decided not to continue the initiative, NPR's impact is felt through laws and administrative practices established during its tenure. An example is a law that requires agencies to systematically measure their performance by standards such as efficiency, responsiveness, and outcomes.

Some analysts question whether government bureaucracy can or even should be reinvented. They have asked, for example, whether the principles of decentralized management and market-oriented programs are as sound as their advocates claim. A reason for hierarchy is to ensure that decisions made at the bottom of the bureaucracy are faithful to the laws enacted by Congress. Free to act on their own, lower-level administrators, as they did under the spoils system, might favor certain people and interests over others.[34] There is also the issue of the identity of the "customers" in a market-oriented administration.[35] Who are the Security and Exchange Commission's customers-firms, brokerage houses, or shareholders? Won't some agencies inevitably favor their more powerful customers at the expense of their less powerful ones?

Furthermore, there are practical limits on how much the federal bureaucracy can be trimmed. While some activities can be delegated to states and localities and others can be privatized, most of Washington's programs cannot be reassigned. National defense, social security, and Medicare are but three examples, and they alone account for well over half of all federal spending. In addition, the outsourcing of tasks to private contractors does not necessarily result in smaller government or reduced waste. Many contracts are a better deal for the private firms awarded them than for taxpayers. In one case, the GAO found that a contractor was charging the government $86 per sheet for plywood that normally sold for $14 a sheet. Nor does outsourcing necessarily result in better performance. When the space shuttle Columbia disintegrated upon reentry in 2003, some analysts suggested that the tragedy was rooted in NASA's decision to assign many of the shuttle program's safety checks to private contractors in order to cut costs.

Thus, although the current debate over the functioning of the federal bureaucracy is unique in its specific elements, it involves long-standing issues. How can the federal government be made more efficient and yet accomplish all that Americans expect of it? How can it be made more responsive and yet act fairly? How can it be made more creative and yet be held accountable? As history makes clear, there are no easy or final answers to these questions.

Summary

Self-Test: www.mhhe.com/pattersontad8

Bureaucracy is a method of organizing people and work, based on the principles of hierarchical authority, job specialization, and formalized rules. As a form of organization, bureaucracy is the most efficient means of getting people to work together on tasks of great magnitude and complexity. It is also a form of organization that is prone to waste and rigidity, which is why efforts are always being made to "reinvent" it.

The United States could not be governed without a large federal bureaucracy. The day-to-day work of the federal government, from mail delivery to provision of social security to international diplomacy, is done by the bureaucracy. Federal employees work in roughly four hundred major agencies, including cabinet departments, independent agencies, regulatory agencies, government corporations, and presidential commissions. Yet the bureaucracy is more than simply an administrative giant. Administrators exercise considerable discretion in their policy decisions. In the process of implementing policy, they make important policy and political choices.

Each agency of the federal government was created in response to political demands on national officials. Because of its origins in political demands, the administration of government is necessarily political. An inherent conflict results from two simultaneous but incompatible demands on the bureaucracy: that it respond to the prefer-

ences of partisan officials and that it administer programs fairly and competently. This tension is evident in the three concurrent personnel management systems under which the bureaucracy operates: patronage, merit, and executive leadership.

Administrators are actively engaged in politics and policymaking. The fragmentation of power and the pluralism of the American political system result in a policy process that is continually subject to conflict and contention. There is no clear policy or leadership mandate in the American system, and hence government agencies must compete for the power required to administer their programs effectively. Accordingly, civil servants tend to have an agency point of view: they seek to advance their agency's programs and to repel attempts by others to weaken their position. In promoting their agency, civil servants rely on their policy expertise, the backing of their clientele groups, and the support of the president and Congress.

Administrators are not elected by the people they serve, yet they wield substantial independent power. Because of this, the bureaucracy's accountability is a central issue. The major checks on the bureaucracy are provided by the president, Congress, and the courts. The president has some power to reorganize the bureaucracy and the authority to appoint the political head of each agency. The president also has management tools (such as the executive budget) that can be used to limit administrators' discretion. Congress has influence on bureaucratic agencies through its authorization and funding powers and through various devices (including sunset laws and oversight hearings) that hold administrators accountable for their actions. The judiciary's role in ensuring the bureaucracy's accountability is smaller than that of the elected branches, but the courts do have the authority to force agencies to act in accordance with legislative intent, established procedures, and constitutionally guaranteed rights.

Nevertheless, administrators are not fully accountable. They exercise substantial independent power, a situation not easily reconciled with democratic values. Because of this, and also because of the desire to make the bureaucracy more efficient, there have been numerous efforts over time to reform the bureaucracy. The most recent such effort includes contracting out the work of government to private firms. Like all such efforts, this latest reinvention has solved some problems while creating new ones—an indication of the immensity of the challenge.

STUDY CORNER

Key Terms

agency point of view (*p. 386*)
bureaucracy (*p. 374*)
bureaucratic accountability (*p. 390*)
cabinet (executive) departments (*p. 376*)
clientele groups (*p. 387*)
demographic representativeness (*p. 396*)

executive leadership system (*p. 383*)
formalized rules (*p. 374*)
government corporations (*p. 378*)
hierarchical authority (*p. 374*)
independent agencies (*p. 377*)
job specialization (*p. 374*)
merit (civil service) system (*p. 382*)

neutral competence (*p. 383*)
patronage system (*p. 382*)
policy implementation (*p. 380*)
presidential commissions (*p. 378*)
regulatory agencies (*p. 377*)
spoils system (*p. 382*)
sunset law (*p. 394*)
whistle-blowing (*p. 395*)

Self-Test

1. America's governmental bureaucracy operates under which three personnel management systems?
   a. merit, patronage, civil service
   b. executive leadership, exchange theory, streamlined management
   c. patronage, merit, executive leadership
   d. executive agreements, civil service, merit

2. The strength of bureaucracy as a form of organization is that it:
   a. leads to flexibility in the completion of tasks.
   b. can only be used in the public sector.
   c. is the most efficient means of getting people to work together on tasks of great magnitude.
   d. allows individuals great latitude in making decisions.

3. Bureaucratic accountability through the president includes all of the following **except:**
   a. appointment of agency heads.
   b. budgetary oversight through the Office of Management and Budget.
   c. the power to fire at will any civil servant the president chooses to fire.
   d. the president's authority to recommend the reorganization of federal agencies.

4. Merit hiring has provided all **except** which one of the following advantages?
   a. a more competent work force through use of competitive exams
   b. ability to hire people with special qualifications
   c. greater responsiveness to presidential leadership

   d. employees who are likely to treat clients and customers the same whether they are Republicans or Democrats

5. Sources of bureaucratic power in the federal bureaucracy include all of the following **except:**
   a. power of broad public support and esteem.
   b. power of expertise.
   c. power of clientele groups.
   d. power of friends in Congress and the White House.

6. The primary function of America's federal bureaucracy is:
   a. oversight of the executive branch.
   b. developing laws for review by Congress.
   c. bringing cases for trial before the Supreme Court.
   d. policy implementation.

7. Bureaucracies are found only in the governmental sector of society and not in the private and corporate sectors. (T/F)

8. Regulatory agencies such as the Securities and Exchange Commission are permitted only to issue advisory opinions to the firms they regulate. Only the judiciary and Congress are allowed to take more decisive action if a firm disregards the law. (T/F)

9. Congress holds the bureaucracy accountable in part through its power to authorize and fund agency programs. (T/F)

10. Once they are in place, federal programs are often terminated at the request of their clientele groups. (T/F)

Critical Thinking

What are the major sources of bureaucrats' power? What mechanisms for controlling that power are available to the president and Congress?

Suggested Readings

Aberbach, Joel D., and Bert A. Rockman. *In the Web of Politics: Two Decades of the U.S. Federal Executive.* Washington, D.C.: Brookings Institution, 2000. An evaluation of the federal bureaucracy and its evolving nature.

Du Gay, Paul. *The Values of Bureaucracy.* New York: Oxford University Press, 2005. An insightful analysis of how bureaucracies work and the values they embody.

Kerwin, Cornelius M. *Rulemaking: How Government Agencies Write Law and Make Policy,* 3d ed. Washington, D.C.: Congressional Quarterly Press, 2003. An analysis of rulemaking in the federal bureaucracy.

Meier, Kenneth J., and Laurence J. O'Toole Jr. *Bureaucracy in a Democratic State.* Baltimore, Md.: Johns Hopkins University Press, 2006. A careful assessment of the relationship between bureaucracy and democracy.

Osborne, David, and Ted Gaebler. *Reinventing Government: How the Entrepreneurial Spirit Is Transforming the Public Sector.* New York: Addison-Wesley, 1992. The book that Washington policymakers in the 1990s regarded as the guide to transforming the bureaucracy.

Page, Edward C., and Bill Jenkins. *Policy Bureaucracy: Government with a Cast of Thousands.* New York: Oxford University Press, 2005. An assessment of the bureaucracy as a policymaking institution.

Sagini, Meshack M. *Organizational Behavior: The Challenges of the New Millennium.* Lanham, Md.: University Press of America, 2001. A comprehensive assessment of bureaucratic structures and behaviors.

List of Websites

http://www.census.gov/
Website of the Census Bureau; the bureau is the best source of statistical information on Americans and the government agencies that administer programs affecting them.

http://www.whistleblower.org/
The Government Accountability Project's website; this project is designed to protect and encourage whistle-blowers by providing information and support to federal employees.

http://www.whitehouse.gov/government/cabinet.html
Lists the cabinet secretaries and provides links to each cabinet-level department.

Participate!

If you are considering a semester or summer internship, you might want to look into working for a federal, state, or local agency. Compared with legislative interns, executive interns are more likely to get paid and to be given significant duties. (Many legislative interns spend the bulk of their time answering phones or responding to mail.) Internship information can often be obtained through an agency's website. You should apply as early as possible; some agencies have application deadlines.

Extra Credit

For up-to-the-minute *New York Times* articles, interactive simulations, graphics, study tools, and more links and quizzes, visit the text's Online Learning Center at www.mhhe.com/pattersontad8.

(Self-Test Answers: 1. c   2. c   3. c   4. c   5. a   6. d   7. F   8. F   9. T   10. F)

The Federal Judicial System:
Applying the Law

Chapter Outline

The Federal Judicial System
The Supreme Court of the United States
Other Federal Courts
The State Courts

Federal Court Appointees
The Selection of Supreme Court Justices
and Federal Judges
Justices and Judges as Political Officials

The Nature of Judicial Decision Making
The Constraints of the Facts
The Constraints of the Law

Political Influences on Judicial Decisions
Outside Influences on Court Decisions
Inside Influences: The Justices' Own
Political Beliefs

Judicial Power and Democratic Government
The Debate over the Proper Role of the
Judiciary
The Judiciary's Proper Role: A Question of
Competing Values

CHAPTER 14

It is emphatically the province and duty of the judicial department to say what the law is. Those who apply the rule to particular cases, must of necessity expound and interpret that rule. If two laws conflict with each other, the courts must decide on the operation of each.

—*John Marshall*[1]

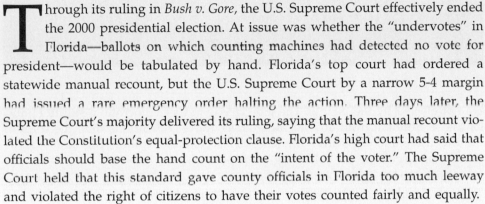

hrough its ruling in *Bush v. Gore*, the U.S. Supreme Court effectively ended the 2000 presidential election. At issue was whether the "undervotes" in Florida—ballots on which counting machines had detected no vote for president—would be tabulated by hand. Florida's top court had ordered a statewide manual recount, but the U.S. Supreme Court by a narrow 5-4 margin had issued a rare emergency order halting the action. Three days later, the Supreme Court's majority delivered its ruling, saying that the manual recount violated the Constitution's equal-protection clause. Florida's high court had said that officials should base the hand count on the "intent of the voter." The Supreme Court held that this standard gave county officials in Florida too much leeway and violated the right of citizens to have their votes counted fairly and equally.

The ruling brought charges that the Supreme Court had acted politically rather than on any strict interpretation of the law. In issuing a halt to the recount, the Court had divided sharply along ideological lines. The majority consisted of its most conservative members, all of whom were Republican appointees: Chief Justice William Rehnquist and associate justices Sandra Day O'Connor, Anthony Kennedy, Antonin Scalia, and Clarence Thomas. In a dissenting opinion, Justice John Paul Stevens said, "Preventing the recount from being completed will inevitably cast a doubt upon the legitimacy of the election." Stevens argued that the Supreme Court's majority had ignored "the basic principle, inherent in our Constitution and our democracy, that every legal vote should be counted."[2]

Bush v. Gore illustrates three key points about court decisions. First, the judiciary is an extremely important policymaking body. Some of its rulings are as consequential as a law of Congress or an executive order of the president. Second, the judiciary has considerable discretion in its rulings. The *Bush v. Gore* ruling was not based on any literal reading of the law: the justices invoked their individual interpretations of the law. Third, the judiciary is a political as well as legal institution. The *Bush v. Gore* case was a product of contending political forces, was developed through a political process, had political content, and was decided by political appointees.

This chapter describes the federal judiciary and the work of its judges and justices. Like the executive and legislative branches, the judiciary is an independent branch of the U.S. government, but unlike the two other branches, its top officials

Demonstrators rally outside the U.S. Supreme Court building during hearings on the *Bush v. Gore* case that effectively brought the 2000 presidential election to an end. At times, the policy rulings of the judiciary are as significant as the decisions of the president or Congress.

are not elected by the people. The judiciary is not a democratic institution, and its role is different from and, in some areas, more contentious than the roles of the executive and legislative branches. This chapter explores this issue in the process of discussing the following main points:

- *The federal judiciary includes the Supreme Court of the United States, which functions mainly as an appellate court; courts of appeals, which hear appeals; and district courts, which hold trials.* Each state has a court system of its own, which for the most part is independent of supervision by the federal courts.

- *Judicial decisions are constrained by applicable constitutional law, statutory and administrative law, and precedent.* Nevertheless, political factors have a major influence on judicial appointments and decisions; judges are political officials as well as legal ones.

- *The judiciary has become an increasingly powerful policymaking body in recent decades, raising the question of the judiciary's proper role in a democracy.* The philosophies of judicial restraint and judicial activism provide different answers to this question.

THE FEDERAL JUDICIAL SYSTEM

The Constitution establishes the judiciary as a separate and independent branch of the federal government. The Constitution provides for the Supreme Court of the United States but gives Congress the power to determine the number and types of lower federal courts.

Federal judges are nominated and appointed to office by the president, subject to confirmation by a majority vote in the Senate. Unlike the case for the president, senators, and representatives, the Constitution places no age, residency, or citizenship requirements on federal judicial officers. Nor does the Constitution require judges to have legal training, though by tradition they do. Once seated on the bench, as specified in the Constitution, they "hold their offices during good behavior." This has meant, in effect, that federal judges serve until they die or voluntarily retire. No Supreme Court justice and only a handful of lower-court

Debating the Issues

Should All the Florida Ballots Have Been Counted?

In *Colegrove v. Green* (1946), Justice Felix Frankfurter warned the Supreme Court about getting involved in election politics, saying that it "ought not to enter this political thicket." In 2000, the Court thrust itself into the thorniest political thicket of all—a presidential campaign. In *Bush v. Gore*, the Court by a narrow majority blocked a statewide manual recount of uncounted ballots in Florida, thereby settling the election in favor of Republican George W. Bush. His Democratic opponent, Al Gore, had argued that all the Florida votes—not just those that could be read by machine—should count. Bush supporters retorted that a manual recount would be inherently subjective and open to mischief. These opposing views also existed within the Supreme Court, as the following opinions show.

Yes   Florida law holds that all ballots that reveal the intent of the voter constitute valid votes. . . . [The Florida Supreme Court] decided the case before it in light of the legislature's intent to leave no legally cast vote uncounted. In so doing, it relied on the sufficiency of the general "intent of the voter" standard articulated by the state legislature, coupled with a procedure for ultimate review by an impartial judge, to resolve the concern about disparate evaluations of contested ballots. If we assume—as I do—that the members of that court and the judges who would have carried out its mandate are impartial, its decision does not even raise a colorable federal question. . . . What must underlie petitioners' entire federal assault on the Florida election procedures is an unstated lack of confidence in the impartiality and capacity of the state judges who would make the critical decisions if the vote count were to proceed. Otherwise, their position is wholly without merit. . . . Although we may never know with complete certainty the identity of the winner of this year's Presidential election, the identity of the loser is perfectly clear. It is the Nation's confidence in the judge as an impartial guardian of the rule of law.

—*John Paul Stevens, associate justice of the Supreme Court*

No   The standards for accepting or rejecting contested ballots might vary not only from county to county but indeed within a single county from one recount team to another. . . . The question before the Court is not whether local entities, in the exercise of their expertise, may develop different systems for implementing elections. Instead, we are presented with a situation where a state court with the power to assure uniformity has ordered a statewide recount with minimal procedural safeguards. . . . It is obvious that the recount cannot be conducted in compliance with the requirements of equal protection and due process without substantial additional work. It would require not only the adoption (after opportunity for argument) of adequate statewide standards for determining what is a legal vote, and practicable procedures to implement them, but also orderly judicial review of any disputed matters that might arise. . . . The Supreme Court of Florida has said that the legislature intended the State's electors to "participat[e] fully in the federal electoral process." That statute, in turn, requires that any controversy or contest that is designed to lead to a conclusive selection of electors be completed by December 12. That date is upon us, and there is no recount procedure in place under the State Supreme Court's order that comports with minimal constitutional standards.

—*Supreme Court's majority opinion*

judges have been removed through impeachment and conviction by Congress, the method of early removal provided for by the Constitution.

The Supreme Court of the United States

The Supreme Court of the United States is the nation's highest court. The chief justice of the United States presides over the Supreme Court and, like the eight associate justices, is nominated by the president and is subject to Senate confirmation.

jurisdiction (of a court)
A given court's authority to hear cases of a particular kind. Jurisdiction may be original or appellate.

original jurisdiction
The authority of a given court to be the first court to hear a case.

appellate jurisdiction
The authority of a given court to review cases that have already been tried in lower courts and are appealed to it by the losing party; such a court is called an appeals court or appellate court.

precedent
A judicial decision that serves as a rule for settling subsequent cases of a similar nature.

writ of certiorari
Permission granted by a higher court to allow a losing party in a legal case to bring the case before it for a ruling; when such a writ is requested of the U.S. Supreme Court, four of the Court's nine justices must agree to accept the case before it is granted certiorari.

solicitor general
The high-ranking Justice Department official who serves as the government's lawyer in Supreme Court cases.

The chief justice has the same voting power as the other justices but usually has exercised additional influence because of the position's leadership role.

The Constitution grants the Supreme Court both original and appellate jurisdiction. A court's **jurisdiction** is its authority to hear cases of a particular type. **Original jurisdiction** is the authority to be the first court to hear a case. The Supreme Court's original jurisdiction includes legal disputes involving foreign diplomats and cases in which the opposing parties are state governments. The Court in its history has convened as a court of original jurisdiction only a few hundred times and has rarely done so in recent decades.

The Supreme Court does its most important work as an appellate court. **Appellate jurisdiction** is the authority to review cases that have already been heard in lower courts and are appealed to a higher court by the losing party; these higher courts are called appeals courts or appellate courts. The Supreme Court's appellate jurisdiction extends to cases arising under the Constitution, federal law and regulations, and treaties. The Court also hears appeals involving legal controversies that cross state or national boundaries. Appellate courts, including the Supreme Court, do not retry cases; rather, they determine whether a trial court acted in accord with applicable law.

Selecting and Deciding Cases

The primary function of the judiciary is to interpret the law in such a way that rules made in the past (for example, the Constitution or legislation) can be applied reasonably in the present. This function gives the courts—all courts—a role in policymaking. Antitrust legislation, for example, is designed to prevent uncompetitive business practices, but like all such legislation, it is not self-enforcing. It is up to the courts to decide whether and how the laws apply to the case at hand.

As the nation's highest court, the Supreme Court is particularly important in establishing legal precedents that guide lower courts. A **precedent** is a judicial decision that serves as a rule for settling subsequent cases of a similar nature. Lower courts are expected to follow precedent—that is, to resolve cases of a like nature in ways consistent with upper-court rulings. However, for reasons that will be explained later in this chapter, they do not always do so.

The Supreme Court's ability to set legal precedent is strengthened by its nearly complete discretion in choosing the cases it will hear. Nearly all cases that reach the Supreme Court do so through a **writ of certiorari**, in which the losing party in a lower-court case explains in writing why its case should be heard by the Court. Four of the nine justices must agree to accept a particular case before it is granted a writ. Each year roughly seven thousand parties apply for certiorari, but the Court accepts only about a hundred cases for a full hearing and signed ruling (see Figure 14–1). The Court issues another fifty or so per curiam ("by the court") decisions each year. Typically, these decisions are very brief, are issued without a hearing, and are a response to relatively noncontroversial issues. They are issued in the name of the full Court rather than signed by the particular justices who wrote the opinion.

The Court is most likely to grant certiorari when the U.S. government through the **solicitor general** (the high-ranking Justice Department official who serves as the government's lawyer in Supreme Court cases) requests it.[3] The solicitor general tracks cases in which the federal government is a party. When the government loses a case in a lower court, the solicitor general decides whether to appeal it to the Supreme Court. Such cases often make up half or more of the cases the Court hears in a term.

The Court seldom accepts a routine case, even if the justices believe that a lower court has made a mistake. The Supreme Court's job is not to correct the

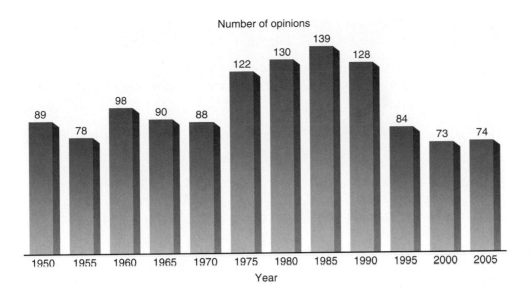

Number of opinions

89 78 98 90 88 122 130 139 128 84 73 74

1950 1955 1960 1965 1970 1975 1980 1985 1990 1995 2000 2005

Year

Figure 14-1

Supreme Court Opinions, 1950–2005
The number of signed Supreme Court opinions each term is relatively small. The Court has considerable control over the cases it selects. The cases that are heard by the Supreme Court tend to be ones that have legal significance beyond the particular case itself. The Court's term runs from October 1 to June 30; the year indicated is the closing year of the term.
Source: Supreme Court of the United States.

errors of other courts but to resolve substantial legal issues. This vague criterion essentially means that a case must center on an issue of significance not merely to the parties involved but to the nation. As a result, most cases heard by the Court raise major constitutional issues, affect the lives of many Americans, address issues that are being decided inconsistently by the lower courts, or involve rulings that conflict with a previous Supreme Court decision.[4] When the Court does accept a case, chances are that most of the justices disagree with the lower court's ruling. About three-fourths of the Supreme Court's decisions have reversed the judgments of lower courts.[5]

Once the Supreme Court accepts a case, it sets a date on which the attorneys for the two sides will present their oral arguments. Strict time limits, usually thirty minutes per side, are imposed on these presentations. However, the oral arguments are less important than the lengthy written **brief** submitted earlier by each side, which contains the side's complete argument.

The oral session is also far less important than the **judicial conference** that follows, which is attended only by the nine justices and in which they discuss and vote on the case. The conference's proceedings are kept strictly confidential. This secrecy allows the justices to speak freely about a case and to change their minds as the discussion unfolds.[6]

Issuing Decisions and Opinions

After a case has been decided on in conference, the Court prepares and issues its ruling, which consists of a decision and one or more opinions. The **decision** indicates which party the Court supports and by how large a margin. The **opinion** explains the reasons behind the decision. The opinion is the most important part of a Supreme Court ruling because it contains the justices' legal reasoning. For example, in the landmark *Brown v. Board of Education of Topeka* (1954) opinion, the Court held that government-sponsored school segregation was unconstitutional because it violated the Fourteenth Amendment provision that guarantees equal protection under the law to all citizens. This opinion became the legal basis by which communities throughout the southern states were ordered by lower courts to end their policy of segregating public school students by race.

brief
A written statement by a party in a court case that details its argument.

judicial conference
A closed meeting of the justices of the U.S. Supreme Court to discuss and vote on the cases before them; the justices are not supposed to discuss conference proceedings with outsiders.

decision
A vote of the Supreme Court in a particular case that indicates which party the justices side with and by how large a margin.

opinion (of a court)
A court's written explanation of its decision, which serves to inform others of the legal basis for the decision. Supreme Court opinions are expected to guide the decisions of other courts.

The Supreme Court building is located across from the Capitol in Washington, D.C. Sixteen marble columns support the pediment. Two bronze doors, each weighing more than six tons, lead into the building. The courtroom, the justices' offices, and the conference room are on the first floor. Administrative staff offices and the Court's records and reference materials occupy the other floors.

majority opinion

A court opinion that results when a majority of the justices are in agreement on the legal basis of the decision.

plurality opinion

A court opinion that results when a majority of justices agree on a decision in a case but do not agree on the legal basis for the decision. In this instance, the legal position held by most of the justices on the winning side is called a plurality opinion.

concurring opinion

A separate opinion written by one or more Supreme Court justices who vote with the majority in the decision on a case but who disagree with their reasoning.

When a majority of the justices agree on the legal basis of a decision, the result is a **majority opinion** (see Table 14–1). In some cases there is no majority opinion because a majority of the justices agree on the decision but cannot agree on the legal basis for it. The result in such cases is a **plurality opinion,** which presents the view held by most of the justices who side with the winning party. Another type of opinion is a **concurring opinion,** a separate view written by a justice who votes with the majority but disagrees with its reasoning.

TABLE 14–1	**Types of Supreme Court Opinions** Supreme Court opinions vary by type, depending on how many justices agree with the opinion and whether the opinion is on the winning or losing side of the decision.

Per curiam: Unsigned decision of the Court that states the facts of the case and the Court's ruling.

Majority opinion: A written opinion of the majority of the Court's justices stating the reasoning underlying their decision on a case.

Plurality opinion: A written opinion that in the absence of a majority opinion presents the reasoning of most of the justices who side with the winning party.

Concurring opinion: A written opinion of one or more justices who support the majority position but disagree with the majority's reasoning on a case. This opinion expresses the reasoning of the concurring justices.

Dissenting opinion: A written opinion of one or more justices who disagree with the majority's decision and opinion. This opinion provides the reasoning underlying the dissent.

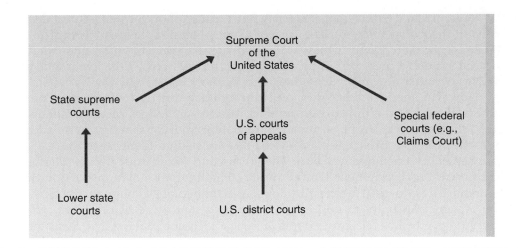

Figure 14–2
The Federal Judicial System
The simplified diagram shows the relationships among the various levels of federal courts and between state and federal courts. The losing party in a case can appeal a lower-court decision to the court at the next-highest level, as the arrows indicate. Decisions normally can be moved from state courts to federal courts only if they raise a constitutional question.

Justices on the losing side can write a **dissenting opinion** to explain their reasons for disagreeing with the majority position. Sometimes these dissenting arguments become the foundation of subsequent decisions. In a 1942 dissenting opinion, Justice Hugo Black wrote that defendants in state felony trials should have legal counsel even if they could not afford to pay for it. Two decades later, in *Gideon v. Wainwright* (1963), the Court adopted Justice Black's position.[7]

When part of the majority, the chief justice decides which justice will write the majority opinion. Otherwise, the senior justice in the majority determines the author. Chief justices have often given themselves the task of writing the majority opinion in important cases. John Marshall did so often; *Marbury v. Madison* (1802) and *McCulloch v. Maryland* (1819) were among the opinions he wrote. The justice who writes the Court's majority opinion has the responsibility to express accurately the majority's reasoning. The vote on a case is not considered final until the opinion is written and agreed upon, so plenty of give-and-take can occur during the writing stage.

dissenting opinion
The opinion of a justice in a Supreme Court case that explains his or her reasons for disagreeing with the majority's decision.

Other Federal Courts

There are more than one hundred federal courts but only one Supreme Court, and its position at the top of the judicial system gives the Supreme Court unparalleled importance. It is a mistake, however, to conclude that the Supreme Court is the only court that matters. Judge Jerome Frank once wrote of the "upper-court myth," which is the view that appellate courts, and in particular the Supreme Court, are the only truly significant judicial arena and that lower courts just dutifully follow the rulings handed down by courts at the appellate level.[8] The reality is very different, as the following discussion explains.

U.S. District Courts

The lowest federal courts are the district courts (see Figure 14–2). There are more than ninety federal district courts altogether—at least one in every state and as many as four in some states. District court judges, who number about seven hundred in all, are appointed by the president with the consent of the Senate. Federal cases usually originate in district courts, which are trial courts where the parties argue their sides. District courts are the only courts in the federal system in which juries hear testimony. Most cases at this level are presented before a single judge.

Lower federal courts unquestionably rely on and follow Supreme Court decisions in their own rulings. The Supreme Court reiterated this requirement in a 1982 case, *Hutto v. Davis:* "Unless we wish anarchy to prevail within the federal judicial system, a precedent of this Court must be followed by the lower federal courts no matter how misguided the judges of those courts may think it to be."[9]

However, the idea that lower courts are guided strictly by Supreme Court rulings is part of the upper-court myth. District court judges might misunderstand the Supreme Court's position and deviate from it for that reason. In addition, the facts of a case before a district court are seldom identical to those of a case settled by the Supreme Court. The lower-court judge must decide whether a different legal judgment is appropriate. Finally, it is not unusual for the Supreme Court to issue a general ruling that is ambiguous enough to give lower courts some flexibility in deciding similar cases that come before them. Trial court judges then have a creative role in judicial decision making that rivals that of appellate court judges.

Most federal cases end with the district court's decision; the losing party does not appeal the decision to a higher court. This fact is another indication of the highly significant role of district court judges.

U.S. Courts of Appeals

When cases are appealed from district courts, they go to a federal court of appeals. These appellate courts are the second level of the federal court system. Courts of appeals do not use juries. Ordinarily, no new evidence is submitted in an appealed case; rather, appellate courts base their decisions on a review of lower-court records. Appellate judges act as supervisors in the legal system, reviewing trial court decisions and correcting what they consider to be legal errors. Facts (i.e., the circumstances of a case) found by district courts are ordinarily presumed to be correct.

The United States has thirteen courts of appeals, each of which serves a "circuit" comprised of between three and nine states, except for the circuit that serves the District of Columbia only and the U.S. Court of Appeals for the Federal Circuit, which specializes in appeals involving patents and international trade (see Figure 14–3). Between four and twenty-six judges sit on each court of appeals, but each case usually is heard by a panel of three judges. On rare occasions, all the judges of a court of appeals sit as a body (*en banc*) in order to resolve difficult controversies, typically ones that have resulted in conflicting decisions within the same circuit. Each circuit is monitored by a Supreme Court justice, who normally takes the lead in reviewing appeals originating in that circuit.

Courts of appeals offer the only real hope of reversal for many appellants, because the Supreme Court hears so few cases. The Supreme Court reviews less than 1 percent of the cases heard by federal appeals courts.

Special U.S. Courts

In addition to the Supreme Court, the courts of appeals, and the district courts, the federal judiciary includes a few specialty courts. Among them are the U.S. Claims Court, which hears cases in which the U.S. government is being sued for damages; the U.S. Court of International Trade, which handles cases involving appeals of U.S. Customs Office rulings; and the U.S. Court of Military Appeals, which hears appeals of military courts-martial. Some federal agencies and commissions also have judicial powers (for example, the issuing of fines), and their decisions can be appealed to a federal court of appeals.

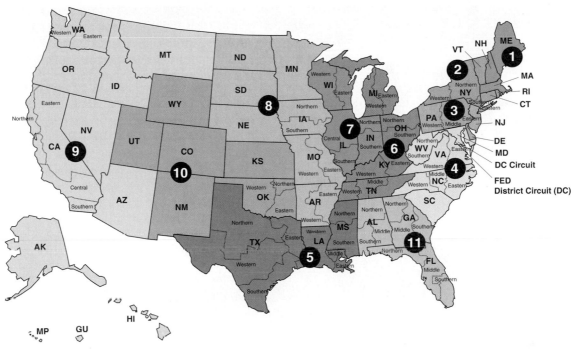

Figure 14-3

Geographic Boundaries of U.S. Courts of Appeals
The United States has thirteen courts of appeals, each of which serves a "circuit." Eleven of these circuit courts serve anywhere from three to nine states, as the map shows. The other two are located in the District of Columbia: the Court of Appeals for the District of Columbia and the Court of Appeals for the Federal Circuit, which specializes in appeals involving patents and international trade. Within each circuit are federal trial courts, most of which are district courts. Each state has at least one district court within its boundaries. Larger states like California (which has four district courts, as can be seen on the map) have more than one.
Source: Administrative Office of the U.S. Courts.

The State Courts

The American states are separate governments within the U.S. political system. The Tenth Amendment protects each state in its sovereignty, and each state has its own court system. Like the federal courts, state court systems have trial courts at the bottom level and appellate courts at the top.

Each state decides for itself the structure of its courts and the method of judicial appointment. In some states judges are appointed by the governor, but in most states judgeships are *elective offices*. The most common form involves competitive elections of either a partisan or a nonpartisan nature. Other states appoint their judges. Some of them use a mixed system called the *merit plan* (also called the "Missouri Plan" because Missouri was the first state to use it) under which the governor appoints a judge from a short list of acceptable candidates provided by a judicial selection commission. The judge selected must then periodically be reviewed by the voters, who, rather than choosing between the judge and an opponent, simply decide by a "yes" or "no" vote whether the judge should be allowed to stay in office (see "States in the Nation").

Besides the upper-court myth, there exists a "federal court myth," which holds that the federal judiciary is the most significant part of the judicial system and that state courts play a subordinate role. This view also is inaccurate. More than 95 percent of the nation's legal cases are decided in state courts. Most crimes

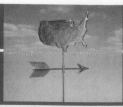

States in the Nation

Principal Methods of Selecting State Judges

The states use a variety of methods for selecting the judges on their highest court, including the merit plan, election, and political appointment. The states that appoint judges grant this power to the governor, except in Virginia, Connecticut, and South Carolina, where the legislature makes the choice.

Q: What might explain why several states in the middle of the nation use the merit plan for selecting judges?

A: The merit plan originated in the state of Missouri. Innovations in one state sometimes spread to adjacent states that have similar political cultures.

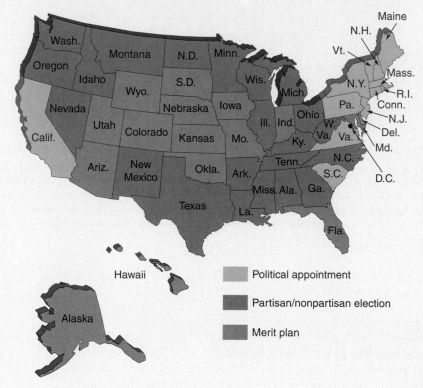

Political appointment

Partisan/nonpartisan election

Merit plan

Source: Council of State Governments.

(from shoplifting to murder) and most civil controversies (such as divorces and business disputes) are defined by state or local law. Moreover, nearly all cases that originate in state courts end there. The federal courts don't come into the picture because the case does not involve a federal issue.

In state criminal cases, after a person has been convicted and after all avenues of appeal in the state court system have been exhausted, the defendant can seek a writ of habeas corpus from a federal district court on grounds that constitutional rights were violated—as, for example, in a claim that local police failed to inform the suspect of the right to remain silent (see Chapter 4). If the federal court accepts such an appeal, it ordinarily confines itself to the federal aspects of the matter, such as whether the defendant's constitutional rights were in fact violated. In addition, the federal court accepts the facts determined by the

Texas solicitor general Ted Cruz presents a case before the Supreme Court of Texas. It is one of two high courts in the state and has final say in civil and juvenile cases. The other high court in Texas is the Court of Criminal Appeals, which hears appeals of criminal cases. Each court has nine judges, elected to staggered six-year terms. More than 95 percent of the nation's legal cases are decided entirely by state courts, a refutation of the federal court myth, which wrongly holds that the federal courts are all that matter in the end. The United States has a federal system of government, and the division of power between the national and state governments affects the courts as well as other governing institutions.

state court unless such findings are clearly in error. In short, legal and factual determinations of state courts can bind the federal courts—a clear contradiction of the federal court myth.

However, issues traditionally within the jurisdiction of the states can become federal issues through the rulings of federal courts. In its *Lawrence v. Texas* decision in 2003, for example, the Supreme Court invalidated state laws that made it illegal for consenting adults of the same sex to engage in private sexual relations.[10] Earlier, the Court had held that states had the authority to decide for themselves whether to prohibit such acts.[11]

FEDERAL COURT APPOINTEES

The quiet dignity of the courtroom and the lack of fanfare with which a court delivers its decisions give the impression that the judiciary is as far removed from the world of politics as a governmental institution can possibly be. In reality, federal judges and justices are political officials who exercise the authority of a separate and powerful branch of government. All federal jurists bring their political views with them to the courtroom and have regular opportunities to promote their political beliefs through the cases they decide. Not surprisingly, the process by which federal judges are appointed is a partisan one.

The Selection of Supreme Court Justices and Federal Judges

The formal method for appointments to the Supreme Court and to the lower federal courts is the same: the president nominates, and the Senate confirms or rejects. Beyond that basic similarity, however, lie significant differences.

The justices of the U.S. Supreme Court pose for a photo. From left, they are: Anthony Kennedy, Stephen Breyer, John Paul Stevens, Clarence Thomas, Chief Justice John Roberts, Ruth Bader Ginsburg, Antonin Scalia, Samuel Alito, David Souter.

Supreme Court Nominees

A Supreme Court appointment is a major opportunity for a president.[12] Most justices retain their positions for many years, enabling presidents to influence judicial policy through their appointments long after they have left office. The careers of some Supreme Court justices provide dramatic testimony to the enduring effects of judicial appointments. Franklin D. Roosevelt appointed William O. Douglas to the Supreme Court in 1939, and for thirty years after Roosevelt's death in 1945, Douglas remained a strong liberal influence on the Court.

Presidents invariably seek nominees who share their political philosophy, but they also must take into account a nominee's acceptability to others. Every nominee is closely scrutinized by the legal community, interested groups, and the media; must undergo an extensive background check by the FBI; and then must gain the approval of a Senate majority. Within the Senate, the key body is the Judiciary Committee, whose members have responsibility for conducting hearings on judicial nominees and recommending their confirmation or rejection by the full Senate.

Nearly 20 percent of presidential nominees to the Supreme Court have been rejected by the Senate on grounds of judicial qualification, political views, personal ethics, or partisanship. Most of these rejections occurred before 1900, and partisan politics was the main reason. Today a nominee with strong professional and ethical credentials is less likely to be blocked for partisan reasons alone. An exception was Robert Bork, whose 1987 nomination by President Reagan was rejected primarily because of intense opposition to his judicial philosophy from Senate Democrats.

On the other hand, nominees can expect confirmation if they have personal integrity and a solid legal record and also show during Senate confirmation hearings the temperament and reasoning expected of a Supreme Court justice. The nomination of John Roberts in 2005 to be chief justice is a case in point. He faced tough questioning during Senate hearings, but nothing startlingly new or disturbing came out, and he was confirmed by a 78-22 vote. Senate hearings held a few months later on the nomination of Samuel Alito, whose past record raised more issues than did that of Roberts, went less smoothly, but he nonetheless was confirmed by a 58-42 vote.

Lower-Court Nominees

The president normally delegates to the deputy attorney general the task of screening potential nominees for lower-court judgeships. **Senatorial courtesy** is also a consideration in these appointments; this tradition, which dates back to the 1840s, holds that a senator from the state in which a vacancy has arisen should be given a say in the nomination if the senator is of the same party as the president.[13] If not consulted, the senator involved can request that confirmation be denied, and other senators will normally grant the request as a "courtesy" to their colleague.

Although the president does not become as personally involved in selecting lower-court nominees as in naming potential Supreme Court justices, lower-court appointments are collectively a significant factor in the impact of a president's Administration. Recent presidents have appointed on average more than one hundred judges during a four-year term of office.

President Dwight D. Eisenhower shakes hands with William Brennan in the Oval Office after selecting Brennan to be an associate justice of the Supreme Court. Eisenhower would later say that he made a mistake in appointing Brennan to the Court. Brennan's decisions were more liberal than Eisenhower had expected.

senatorial courtesy
The tradition that a U.S. senator from the state in which a federal judicial vacancy has arisen should have a say in the president's nomination of the new judge if the senator is of the same party as the president.

Justices and Judges as Political Officials

Presidents generally manage to appoint jurists who have a similar political philosophy. Although Supreme Court justices are free to make their own decisions, their legal positions usually can be predicted from their prior work. A study by judicial scholar Robert Scigliano found that about three of every four appointees have behaved on the Supreme Court approximately as presidents could have expected.[14] Of course, a president has no guarantee that a nominee will fulfill his hopes. Justices Earl Warren and William Brennan proved to be more liberal than President Dwight D. Eisenhower had anticipated. Asked whether he had made any mistakes as president, Eisenhower replied, "Yes, two, and they are both sitting on the Supreme Court."[15]

The Role of Partisanship

In nearly every instance, presidents choose members of their own party as Supreme Court nominees. Partisanship is also decisive in nominations to lower-court judgeships. More than 90 percent of recent district and appeals court nominees have been members of the president's own party.[16]

This fact should not be interpreted to mean that federal judges and justices engage in blatant partisanship while on the bench. They are officers of a separate branch and prize their judicial independence. All Republican appointees do not vote the same way on cases, nor do all Democratic appointees. Nevertheless, partisanship influences judicial decisions. A study of the voting records of appellate court judges, for example, found that Democratic appointees are more likely

TABLE 14–2	Justices of the Supreme Court Most recent appointees held an appellate court position before being nominated to the Supreme Court.		
JUSTICE	**YEAR OF APPOINTMENT**	**NOMINATING PRESIDENT**	**POSITION BEFORE APPOINTMENT**
John Paul Stevens	1975	Ford	Judge, U.S. Court of Appeals
Antonin Scalia	1986	Reagan	Judge, U.S. Court of Appeals
Anthony Kennedy	1988	Reagan	Judge, U.S. Court of Appeals
David Souter	1990	G. H. W. Bush	Judge, U.S. Court of Appeals
Clarence Thomas	1991	G. H. W. Bush	Judge, U.S. Court of Appeals
Ruth Bader Ginsburg	1993	Clinton	Judge, U.S. Court of Appeals
Stephen Breyer	1994	Clinton	Judge, U.S. Court of Appeals
John Roberts, Jr.*	2005	G. W. Bush	Judge, U.S. Court of Appeals
Samuel Alito, Jr.	2006	G. W. Bush	Judge, U.S. Court of Appeals

*Chief justice.

than Republican appointees to side with parties that claim their civil rights or civil liberties have been violated.[17]

Other Characteristics of Judicial Appointees

In recent years, increasing numbers of federal justices and judges have had prior judicial experience; the assumption is that such individuals are best qualified for appointment to the federal bench. Most recent appellate court appointees have been district or state judges or have worked in the office of the attorney general.[18] Elective office (particularly a seat in the U.S. Senate) was once a common route to the Supreme Court,[19] but recent justices have typically held an appellate court judgeship before their appointment (see Table 14–2).

White males are greatly overrepresented on the federal bench, just as they dominate in Congress and at the top levels of the executive branch. However, the number of women and minority-group members appointed to federal judge-ships has increased significantly in recent decades. The number of such appointees has varied according to which party controls the presidency. Women and minority-group members are key constituencies of the Democratic party; not surprisingly, Democratic presidents have appointed more judges from these groups than have Republican presidents (see Figure 14–4). Of President Bill Clinton's appointees, for example, 30 percent were women and 25 percent were members of racial or ethnic minority groups. For President George W. Bush, the figures are 21 percent and 19 percent, respectively.

The Supreme Court is less demographically representative than are the lower courts. Of the nine current justices, only one (Ruth Bader Ginsburg) is a woman, and only one (Clarence Thomas) is a minority-group member. The historical pattern is even more one-sided. Until 1916, when Louis D. Brandeis was appointed to the Court, no Jewish justice had ever served. At least one Catholic, but at most times only one, has sat on the Court almost continuously for nearly a century. Thurgood Marshall in 1967 was the first black justice, and Sandra Day O'Connor in 1981 was the first woman justice. Antonin Scalia in 1986 was the Court's first justice of Italian descent. No person of Hispanic or Asian descent has ever been a member of the Supreme Court.

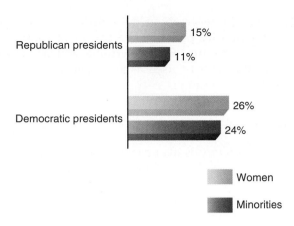

Figure 14–4

Political Parties, Presidents, and Women and Minority Judicial Appointees
Reflecting differences in their parties' coalitions, recent Republican and Democratic presidents have quite different records in terms of the percentage of their judicial appointees who have been women or minority-group members.
Source: Various sources. Data based on appointees of Presidents Carter, Reagan, G. H. W. Bush, Clinton, and G. W. Bush.

THE NATURE OF JUDICIAL DECISION MAKING

Federal judges and justices are political officials: they constitute one of three coequal branches of the national government. Yet, unlike members of Congress or the president, judges make their decisions within the context of a legal process. As a consequence, their discretionary power is less than that of elected officials. Article III of the Constitution bars a federal court from issuing a decision except in response to an actual case presented to it. As federal judge David Bazelon noted, a judge "can't wake up one morning and simply decide to give a helpful little push to a school system, a mental hospital, or the local housing agency."[20]

Judicial decisions are also restricted in scope. Technically, a court ruling is binding only on the parties involved. Its broader impact depends on the willingness of others to follow its lead. For example, if a court should decide that a school is bound by law to spend more on programs for the learning-disabled, the ruling would extend to other schools in the same situation only if those schools voluntarily responded or were forced by subsequent court action to do so. By comparison, if Congress were to pass legislation granting funds for programs for the learning-disabled, all eligible schools would receive the funding.

Another major restriction on the courts is the law itself. Although a president or Congress can make almost any decision that is politically acceptable, the judiciary must justify its decisions in terms of existing provisions of the law. When asked by a friend to "do justice," Justice Oliver Wendell Holmes Jr. said that the law, rather than his inclination, was his guide.[21] In applying the law, judges engage in a creative legal process that requires them to identify the facts of the case, determine and sometimes formulate the relevant legal principles or rules, and then apply these to the case at hand.

The Constraints of the Facts

A basic distinction in any legal case is between "the facts" and "the laws." The **facts** of a case, as determined by trial courts, are the relevant circumstances of a legal dispute or offense. In the case of a person accused of murder, for example,

facts (of a court case)
The relevant circumstances of a legal dispute or offense as determined by a trial court. The facts of a case are crucial because they help determine which law or laws are applicable in the case.

key facts would include evidence about the murder and whether the rights of the accused were respected by police in the course of their investigation. The facts of a case are crucial because they determine which law or laws apply to the case. A murder case cannot be used as an occasion to pronounce judgment on freedom of religion, for example.

The Constraints of the Law

laws (of a court case)
The constitutional provisions, legislative statutes, or judicial precedents that apply to a court case.

In deciding cases, the judiciary is also constrained by existing **laws.** To use an obvious comparison, the laws that apply to a case of alleged murder differ from those that apply to a case of alleged shoplifting. A judge must treat a murder case as a murder case, applying to it the laws that define murder and the penalties that can be imposed when someone is found guilty of that crime.

Laws fall into three broad categories—civil, criminal, and procedural. **Civil law** governs relations between private parties. Marriage, divorce, business contracts, and property ownership are examples of relations covered by civil law. In all states but Massachusetts, for example, civil law limits marriage to a man and a woman; same-sex couples in these states are prohibited by law from marrying. In this example, civil law defines the basis for a legally binding contract. Civil law also applies to disputes between private parties. The courts ordinarily do not get involved in such disputes unless the parties themselves cannot resolve their differences. For example, a dispute in which a homeowner alleges that an insurance company has failed to pay a policy claim could end up in court if they cannot settle it themselves. The losing party in a civil suit might be ordered to pay or otherwise compensate the other party but would not face jail unless he or she refuses to comply with a court order, which can be a punishable offense.

civil law
Laws governing relations between private parties where no criminal act is alleged and where the parties are making conflicting claims or are seeking to establish a legal relationship.

criminal law
Laws governing acts deemed illegal and punishable by government, such as robbery. Government is always a party to a criminal law case; the other party is the individual accused of breaking the law.

Criminal law deals with acts that government defines as illegal and which can result in a fine, imprisonment, or other punishment. Murder, assault, shoplifting, and drunk driving are examples of acts that are covered by criminal law. The government is always a party to a criminal law case; the other party is the individual alleged to have broken the law.

Procedural law refers to rules that govern the legal process. In some cases, these rules apply to government, as in the example of the obligation of police to inform suspects of their right to an attorney and to remain silent. In other cases, the rules apply to private parties. For example, in some states, a homeowner cannot take an insurance company to court over a policy claim without first having that claim heard, and possibly resolved, by an arbitration board.

procedural law
Laws governing the legal process that define proper courses of action by government or private parties.

There are three sources of law that constrain the courts: the Constitution, legislative statutes (and the administrative regulations derived from them), and precedents established by previous court rulings (see Table 14–3).

The Constitution and Its Interpretation

The Constitution of the United States is the nation's highest law, and judges and justices are sworn to uphold it. When a case raises a constitutional issue, a court has the duty to apply the Constitution to the case. For example, the Constitution prohibits the states from printing their own currency. If a state decided that it would do so anyway, a federal judge would be obligated to rule against the practice.

Nevertheless, constitutional provisions are open to interpretation in some cases. For example, the Fourth Amendment of the Constitution protects individuals against "unreasonable searches and seizures," but the meaning of "unreasonable" is not specified. Judges must decide upon its meaning in particular

	Sources of Law That Constrain the Decisions of the Federal Judiciary Federal judges make their
TABLE 14-3	decisions in the context of law, which limits their discretion. The Constitution, statutes, and precedents are major constraints on the judiciary.

U.S. Constitution: The federal courts are bound by the provisions of the U.S. Constitution. The sparseness of its wording, however, requires the Constitution to be applied in the light of present circumstances. Thus, judges are accorded some degree of discretion in their constitutional judgments.

Statutory law: The federal courts are constrained by statutes and by administrative regulations derived from the provisions of statutes. Most laws, however, are somewhat vague in their provisions and often have unanticipated applications. As a result, judges have some freedom in deciding cases based on statutes.

Precedent: Federal courts tend to follow precedent (or stare decisis), which is a legal principle developed through earlier court decisions. Because times change and not all cases have a clear precedent, judges have some discretion in their evaluation of the way earlier cases apply to a current case.

situations. Take, for example, the question of whether wiretapping, which was not invented until 150 years after ratification of the Fourth Amendment, is included in the prohibition on unreasonable searches and seizures. Reasoning that the Fourth Amendment was intended to protect individuals from government snooping into their private lives, judges have ruled that indiscriminate wiretapping is unconstitutional.

Statutes and Administrative Laws, and Their Interpretation

The vast majority of cases that arise in courts involve issues of statutory and administrative law rather than constitutional law. Statutory law is legislative (statute) law. Administrative law is derived from statutory law but is set by government agencies rather than by legislatures. Administrative law consists of the rules, regulations, and judgments that agencies make in the process of implementing and enforcing statutes.

All federal courts are bound by federal statutes (laws passed by Congress) and by federal administrative regulations, as well as by treaties. When hearing a case involving statutory law or administrative regulation, judges must work within the limits of the applicable law or regulation. A company that is charged with violating an air-pollution law will be judged within the context of that law—what it permits and what it prohibits, and the penalties that apply if the company is found to have broken the law.

When hearing such a case, judges will often try to determine whether the meaning of the statute or regulation can be determined by common sense (the "plain meaning rule"). The question for the judge is what the law or regulation was intended to safeguard (such as clean air). The law or regulation in most cases is clear enough that when the facts of the case are considered, the decision is fairly predictable. Not all cases, however, are clear-cut in their facts or in the applicable law or laws. Where, for example, do college admissions programs that take race into account cross the line from legal to illegal by placing too much weight on race? In such instances, courts have no choice but to exercise their judgment.

Legal Precedents (Previous Rulings) and Their Interpretation

The U.S. legal system developed from the English common-law tradition, which includes the principle that a court's decision on a case should be consistent with previous judicial rulings. This principle, known as precedent, reflects the philosophy of stare decisis (Latin for "to stand by things that have been settled"). Precedent holds that principles of law, once established, should be applied in subsequent similar cases. Judges and justices often cite past rulings as justification for their decisions in the cases before them.

Precedent is important because it gives predictability to the application of law. Government has an obligation to make clear what its laws are and how they are being applied. If courts routinely ignored how similar cases had been decided in the past, they would create confusion and uncertainty about what is lawful and what is not. A business firm that is seeking to comply with environmental protection laws, for example, can develop company policies that will keep the company safely within the law if court decisions in this area are consistent. If courts routinely ignored precedent, a firm could unintentionally engage in an activity that a court might conclude was unlawful.

POLITICAL INFLUENCES ON JUDICIAL DECISIONS

Although judicial rulings are constrained by existing laws, judges nearly always have some degree of discretion in their decisions.[22] The Constitution is a sparsely worded document and must be adapted to new and changing situations. The judiciary also has no choice at times but to apply its own judgment to statutory law. Congress often cannot anticipate or reach agreement on all the specific applications of a legislative act and therefore uses general language to state the act's purpose. It is left to the judiciary to decide what this language means in the context of a specific case arising under the act. Precedent is even less precise as a guide to decisions. Precedent must be considered in the context of the changes that have occurred since it was established. In the words of Justice Oliver Wendell Holmes Jr., precedent must be judged against the "felt necessities of the time."

The Supreme Court's ruling in a 1998 case (*Faragher v. City of Boca Raton*) involving sexual harassment in the workplace illustrates the ambiguity that can occur in existing law. The Court developed its ruling in the context of the antidiscrimination provisions of the Civil Rights Act of 1964. However, the act itself contains no description of, or even reference to, job-related sexual harassment. Nevertheless, the act does prohibit workplace discrimination, and the Court was unwilling to dismiss sexual harassment as an irrelevant form of job-related discrimination. In judging the case, the Court had to determine for itself which actions in the workplace are instances of harassment and which are not. In this sense, the Court was "making" law; it was deciding how legislation enacted by Congress applied to behavior that Congress had not specifically addressed when it wrote the legislation.[23]

In sum, judges have leeway in their decisions. As a consequence, their rulings reflect not only legal influences but political ones. Political influences can come from both outside and inside the judicial system.

Outside Influences on Court Decisions

The courts can and do make unpopular choices, but in the long run judicial decisions must be seen as fair if they are to be obeyed. In other words, the judiciary cannot ignore the expectations of the general public, interest groups, and elected representatives.

The judicial branch is increasingly an arena in which interest groups contend for influence. Many such disputes have pitted environmental groups against economic interests. Shown here are demonstrators expressing their views on the issue of whether the Maine Atlantic salmon should be declared an endangered species and placed off-limits to commercial fishing.

Public Opinion and Interest Groups

Judges are responsive to public opinion, although much less so than are elected officials. In some cases, for example, the Supreme Court has tailored its rulings in an effort to gain public support or reduce public resistance. In the *Brown* case, the justices, recognizing that school desegregation would be an explosive issue in the South, required only that desegregation take place "with all deliberate speed" rather than immediately or on a fixed timetable. The Supreme Court typically has stayed close enough to public opinion to avoid massive public resistance to its decisions.[24]

The courts also respond to interest groups, primarily through rulings in the lawsuits filed by them. Some groups rely on lawsuits as their primary political strategy because their issues are more likely to be decided favorably in a court than through an elected institution. An example is the American Civil Liberties Union (ACLU), which has filed hundred of lawsuits over the years on issues of individual rights. In 2006, for example, the ACLU filed suit against the Bush administration over its wiretapping of individuals' phone and e-mail messages without obtaining a court order, claiming such action to be a violation of the First and Fourth Amendments. A group can also try to influence the courts by filing an amicus curiae ("friend of the court") brief in which it presents its views on a case in which it is not one of the parties directly involved (see Chapter 9). Groups' influence on the courts has increased in recent decades as a result of both a sharp rise in group activity and the use of more sophisticated judicial strategies. Groups carefully select the cases they pursue, choosing those with the greatest chance of success. They also carefully pick the courts in which they file, because some judges are more sympathetic than others to their particular issue.

Get Involved!

Sit, When Called

The right to a jury trial is one of the oldest features—dating to the colonial period—of the American political experience. Jury trials also offer the average citizen a rare opportunity to be part of the governing structure. Yet Americans increasingly shirk jury duty. When summoned, many of them find all sorts of reasons why they should be excused from jury duty. In some areas of the country, the avoidance rate exceeds 50 percent. Some citizens even give up their right to vote because they know that jurors in their area are selected from names on voter registration lists.

There are reasons, however, to look upon jury duty as an opportunity as well as a responsibility. Studies indicate that citizens come away from the jury experience with a fuller appreciation of the justice system. Jurors acquire an understanding of the serious responsibility handed to them when asked to decide upon someone's guilt or innocence. The legal standard in American courts—"guilty beyond a reasonable doubt"—is a solemn one. No wonder that jurors

in difficult cases often take hours or even days to reach a verdict. The fairness of the jury system also requires full participation by the community. Studies show that jurors' life experiences can affect the decisions they reach. If everyone on a jury is from the same background and one that is different from the defendant's, the odds of a wrongful verdict increase. "A jury of one's peers" should mean just that—a jury of individuals who, collectively, represent the range of groups in the community.

A test that can be applied to any political arrangement is whether one is willing to abide by it not knowing one's role in that arrangement. As alluring as it might be to be an absolute dictator, would anyone freely choose to be governed by such a system if the odds of being the dictator were a million to one? So it should be with jury duty. If you are called to serve, you should answer the call. You would want nothing less from others if you or one of your friends or family members were the person on trial.

Congress and the President

Groups and the general public also make an impact on the judiciary indirectly, through their elected representatives. Both Congress and the president have powerful means of influencing the federal judiciary.

Congress is constitutionally empowered to establish the Supreme Court's size and appellate jurisdiction and can rewrite legislation that it feels the judiciary has misinterpreted. Although Congress seldom threatens the judiciary directly, its members often express displeasure with judicial action. In a 1998 Senate speech, the chair of the Judiciary Committee, Orrin Hatch (R-Utah), lashed out at judges who he claimed were "making laws instead of interpreting the law."[25] Hatch argued that judges should be "strict constructionists." (*Strict constructionism* holds that a judicial officer should apply a narrow interpretation of the law, whereas *loose constructionism* holds that a judicial officer can apply an expansive interpretation.)

The president too has ways of influencing the judiciary. The president is responsible for enforcing court decisions and has some influence over the issues that come before the courts. Under President Ronald Reagan, for instance, the Justice Department pushed lawsuits that challenged the legality of affirmative action. Judicial appointments also provide the president with opportunities to influence the judiciary's direction. When Democrat Bill Clinton took office in 1993, more than a hundred federal judgeships were vacant. The first President Bush had expected to win reelection and had not moved quickly to fill vacancies as they arose. As it became apparent that he might lose the election, the Democrat-controlled Congress delayed action on his appointments. This enabled Clinton to fill many of the positions with loyal Democrats. The tables were turned in 2001.

Senate Republicans had slowed action on Clinton nominees, enabling George W. Bush to appoint Republicans to existing vacancies when he took office.

In recent decades, the judicial appointment process has been unusually contentious, reflecting both the growing partisanship in Congress (see Chapter 11) and the widening range of issues (everything from abortion to the environment) being fought out in the courts. Nevertheless, the influence of elected officials on the judiciary is never total. Judges prize their independence. The fact that they are not popularly elected and hold their appointments indefinitely allows them to resist undue pressure from the elected branches of government. In 2004, for example, the Supreme Court rejected the Bush administration's claim that U.S. citizens charged with terrorism can be jailed indefinitely without a judicial hearing (see Chapter 4).

Inside Influences: The Justices' Own Political Beliefs

Although the judiciary symbolizes John Adams's characterization of the U.S. political system as "a government of laws, and not of men," judicial rulings are affected by the political beliefs of the men and women who sit on the courts.[26] Decisions of the Supreme Court often divide along political lines. In more than two-thirds of recent nonunanimous Supreme Court decisions, for example, justices Antonin Scalia and Clarence Thomas, each of whom was a Republican appointee, were opposed by justices Stephen Breyer and Ruth Bader Ginsburg, the two Democratic appointees on the Court.[27]

Arguably, partisanship was never more evident than in the Supreme Court's Bush v. Gore (2000) decision.[28] The five justices in the majority were the same justices who in previous decisions had upheld states' rights and had opposed new applications of the Fourteenth Amendment's equal protection clause. Yet they used the equal protection clause to block the statewide manual recount that had been ordered by Florida's high court because no uniform standard for counting the ballots existed. When the Court issued a rare stay order to stop the recount, Justice Antonin Scalia claimed that it was justified because the recount could cast doubt on the legitimacy of Bush's victory even though Bush had not yet been elected. Some observers suggested that if Bush had been trailing in the Florida vote, the Court's majority would have allowed the recount to continue. Justice John Paul Stevens, who thought the Florida high court had acted properly in ordering a manual count, accused the Court's majority of devising a ruling based on their partisan desires rather than on the law. Stevens noted that different standards for casting and counting ballots are used throughout the country, even within the same state.[29]

Most Supreme Court justices do not change their views greatly during their tenure. As a result, major shifts in the Supreme Court's positions usually occur when its membership changes. Such shifts are related to political changes. When the Court in the 1980s watered down the criminal justice rulings of the 1960s, for instance, it was largely because the more recently appointed justices, like the presidents who had nominated them, believed that government should have more leeway in its efforts to fight crime.

JUDICIAL POWER AND DEMOCRATIC GOVERNMENT

The issue of judicial power is heightened by the fact that federal judges are not elected. The principle of self-government asserts that lawmaking majorities have the power to decide society's policies. Because the United States has a constitutional system that places checks on the will of the majority, there is obviously an

TABLE 14–4	**Significant Supreme Court Cases** Included are a few of the most significant cases decided by the U.S. Supreme Court.
Marbury v. Madison (1803)	Established principle of judicial review (Chapter 2)
McCulloch v. Maryland (1819)	Strengthened national power over states (Chapter 3)
Dred Scott v. Sanford (1857)	Decided that slaves were property and not citizens (Chapter 3)
Plessy v. Ferguson (1896)	Established the "separate but equal" doctrine (Chapter 5)
Gitlow v. New York (1925)	Protected free expression from state action through Fourteenth Amendment (Chapter 4)
Brown v. Board of Education of Topeka (1954)	Abolished the "separate but equal" doctrine and banned segregation in public schools (Chapter 5)
Gideon v. Wainwright (1963)	Decided that states must provide an attorney for poor defendants accused of committing felonies (Chapter 4)
Roe v. Wade (1973)	Decided that women have full freedom to choose abortion during the first three months of pregnancy under the right of privacy (Chapter 4)
Bush v. Gore (2000)	Decided that a hand count of disputed Florida ballots would violate equal protection, thereby deciding the 2000 election in George W. Bush's favor (Chapter 12)

important role in the system for an institution such as the judiciary to play (see Table 14–4). Yet court decisions often reflect the political philosophy of the judges, who constitute a tiny political elite that wields significant power.[30] A critical question is how far unelected judges ought to go in substituting their policy judgments for those of the legislative and executive officials who are elected by the people.

The judiciary's power is most evident when it declares executive or legislative action to be unconstitutional. The power of the courts to make such determinations, called **judicial review,** was first asserted in the landmark *Marbury v. Madison* case of 1803, when the Supreme Court rebuked both the president and Congress (see Chapter 2). Without judicial review, the federal courts would be unable to restrain an elected official or institution that has gone out of control.

Yet judicial review places the judgment of the courts above that of elected officials when interpretation of the Constitution is at issue, creating the possibility of conflict between the courts and the elected branches. The imposing nature of judicial review has led the courts to apply it judiciously, but the Supreme Court alone has invoked it in more than a thousand cases. Only a small percentage of these cases have involved action by Congress or the president, an indication that the Supreme Court normally prefers to avoid showdowns with the other branches of the federal government. The state and local governments are an entirely different matter. More than 90 percent of rulings involving judicial review have been directed at states and localities. A prime example is the 1954 *Brown v. Board of Education* decision, which employed the Fourteenth Amendment to invalidate state laws prohibiting black children from attending the same local public schools as white children.

The Debate over the Proper Role of the Judiciary

The question of judicial power centers on the basic issue of **legitimacy**—the proper authority of the judiciary in a political system based in part on the principle of majority rule. The judiciary's policymaking significance and discretion

judicial review
The power of courts to decide whether a governmental institution has acted within its constitutional powers and, if not, to declare its action null and void.

legitimacy (of judicial power)
The issue of the proper limits of judicial authority in a political system based in part on the principle of majority rule.

Political Culture

Judicial Review and Liberty

The French writer Alexis de Tocqueville observed that there is barely a political controversy in America that sooner or later does not become also a judicial issue. Abortion, age-related discrimination, and Internet content are but a few of the recent examples.

Americans know less about the judiciary than about the elected branches of their government, Congress and the presidency. Nevertheless, when it comes to the protection of their liberty, the judiciary is key. Its power to protect personal freedom is most evident when the Supreme Court strikes down action taken by elected officials. In most cases, the target of Supreme Court action is not the Congress or the president, but state and local officials. The Supreme Court has struck down well over a thousand state laws and local ordinances, most of which have

involved issues of personal freedom, as in *Near v. Minnesota* (freedom of the press) and *Gideon v. Wainwright* (the right to an attorney, even if the defendant is too poor to hire one). That the actions of state and local governments would more often prompt judicial review is hardly surprising. There are fifty state governments and thousands of local governments, compared with a single federal government. Moreover, state and local governments have most of the responsibility for law enforcement and public order, which is where individual rights most frequently collide with authority.

Imagine, as was originally the case, that the Supreme Court had no authority to rule on Bill of Rights issues arising from state and local action. Do you think you would have less liberty in that situation? Why or why not?

have been sources of controversy throughout the country's history, but the controversies have seldom been livelier than during recent decades.

The judiciary at times has acted almost legislatively by defining broad social policies, such as abortion, busing, affirmative action, church-state relations, and prison reform. During the 1990s, for example, the prison systems in forty-two states were operating under federal court orders that mandated improvements in health care or overcrowding. Through such actions the judiciary has restricted the policymaking authority of the states, has narrowed legislative discretion, and has made judicial action an effective political strategy for certain interests.[31]

The judiciary has become more extensively involved in policymaking for many of the same reasons that Congress and the president have been thrust into new policy areas and become more deeply involved in old ones. Social and economic changes have required government to play a larger role in society, and this development has generated a seemingly endless series of new legal controversies. Environmental pollution, for example, was not a major issue until the 1960s; since then, it has been the subject of numerous court cases.

Judicial action raises an important question: How far should the judiciary go in asserting its authority when that authority conflicts with or goes beyond the action of elected institutions? There are two schools of thought on this question: judicial activism and judicial restraint. Although these terms are somewhat imprecise and not fully consistent, they provide a lens through which to examine the judiciary's proper role.[32]

Judicial Restraint Versus Judicial Activism

The doctrine of **judicial restraint** holds that judges should work closely within the wording of the law, be respectful of precedent, and generally defer to decisions made by legislatures. The restraint doctrine holds that in nearly all cases

judicial restraint
The doctrine that the judiciary should closely follow the wording of the law, be highly respectful of precedent, and defer to the judgment of legislatures. The doctrine claims that the job of judges is to work within the confines of laws set down by tradition and lawmaking majorities.

public issues should be decided by elected lawmakers and not appointed judges. The role of judges is to determine how the Constitution, statutes, and precedents apply to specific cases rather than to find new meanings that create new law or substantially modify existing law.

Advocates of judicial restraint say that when judges substitute their views for those of elected institutions, they undermine the fundamental principle of self-government—the right of the majority, through its elected representatives, to decide the policies by which they will be governed.[33] Advocates also claim that restraint serves to maintain public confidence in the judiciary, thereby increasing the likelihood of **compliance** with its decisions, that is, whether people will respect and obey court rulings.[34] Advocates of judicial restraint acknowledge that established law is not precise enough to provide exact answers to every question raised by every case and that judges therefore must exercise some degree of discretion. They also acknowledge that in some instances judges have little choice but to override the decisions of elected institutions, as in cases where lawmakers have overstepped their constitutional authority. Nevertheless, the judicial restraint philosophy broadly holds that the role of judges is to review the law, not make the law.

Contrasting the judicial restraint doctrine is the doctrine of **judicial activism,** which holds that judges should actively interpret the Constitution, statutes, and precedents in light of established principles when the elected branches ignore or trample on these principles. Although advocates of judicial activism acknowledge the importance of precedent and majority rule, they claim that the courts should not be wholly subservient to past rulings or to the decisions of elected officials when core principles are at issue.

Advocates of judicial activism argue that law is not simply a narrow reading of the exact words in a statute or constitution but must take into account the larger meaning of the words. What is it that a constitution is designed to protect or that a statute is intended to promote? Judicial activist proponents argue that judges should be especially vigilant on questions of constitutional rights and the democratic process. They claim that the judiciary must prevent majorities, acting through lawmakers, from violating or ignoring the legitimate rights of the

compliance

The issue of whether judicial decisions will be respected and obeyed.

judicial activism

The doctrine that the courts should develop new legal principles when judges see a compelling need, even if this action places them in conflict with the policy decisions of elected officials.

The Supreme Court's power is never more evident than when it strikes down a law passed by Congress or a state legislature on grounds that it violates the Constitution. Over the years, the Court has invalidated a number of state laws that sought to promote religion in public schools. The Court considers the issue of religion in the schools to be an issue of individual rights rather than of majority rule.

minority or rigging the political process in ways that deprive certain classes of citizens of a meaningful voice. They view the Constitution as designed chiefly to protect individuals from unresponsive or repressive government, a goal that can be accomplished only by a judiciary willing to act when lawmaking majorities perpetrate or fail to correct injustice.[35]

A classic example of the conflict between the opposing judicial philosophies of restraint and activism was the malapportionment issue. Until the 1960s, the legislative districts in many states varied greatly in the number of voters they encompassed. Rural legislators controlled the state legislatures, and as the urban population grew, they refused to adjust election districts to increase the number of urban districts. Each such district accordingly was packed with voters, while each rural district had relatively few. By this means, rural areas maintained control of state legislatures and used that control to enact policies disadvantageous to the cities. Legal challenges to this situation initially were denied under the philosophy of judicial restraint. Redistricting was regarded as a "political" issue, not a legal one, properly decided by legislatures rather than courts. In *Colegrove v. Green* (1946), the Supreme Court rejected a malapportionment claim; in a classic statement of judicial restraint, Justice Felix Frankfurter argued that, "courts ought not to enter this political thicket."[36] Nearly two decades later, the Supreme Court changed its stand. In *Baker v. Carr* (1962), the Court by a 6-2 vote took an activist position, holding that state legislative districts must be apportioned on the principle of "one person, one vote." The Court's majority said that any other apportionment system violated the equal protection clause of the Fourteenth Amendment. Justice William Brennan wrote for the majority: "The political question doctrine, a tool for maintenance of governmental order, will not be so applied as to promote only disorder." Justice John Harlan, in a dissent that was joined by Justice Frankfurter, argued for judicial restraint: "I can find nothing in the Equal Protection Clause or elsewhere in the Federal Constitution which expressly or impliedly supports the view that state legislatures must be so structured as to reflect with approximate equality the voice of every voter. . . . Its acceptance would require us to turn our backs on the regard which this Court has always shown for the judgment of state legislatures and courts on matters of basically local concern."[37]

Restraint Versus Activism in Practice

Just as presidential and congressional politics in recent years have become more intensely partisan (see Chapters 11 and 12), so too has the judiciary. Judicial appointments and rulings have been increasingly contentious, and judicial restraint and activism have become part of the vocabulary of these fights. Republicans, who have controlled the U.S. Senate for most of the past decade, have demanded that judicial appointees adhere to the principle of judicial restraint. A leading Republican member of the Senate Judiciary Committee, Orren Hatch of Utah, has said repeatedly that judges "should not legislate from the bench" and that "activist judges" should step down from the bench and run for public office if they are intent on promoting their policy views.

However, judicial restraint does not precisely describe the legal rulings of Republican appointees, just as judicial activism does not precisely describe those of Democratic appointees. Supreme Court justices appointed by both parties have variously tended toward restraint or activism at different points in history and on different issues. The Republican-dominated Supreme Court in the period between the Civil War and the Great Depression was an activist judiciary, striking down most state and congressional legislation aimed at economic regulation (see Chapter 3).

How the United States Compares

Judicial Power

U.S. courts are highly political compared to the courts of most other democracies. First, U.S. courts operate within a common-law tradition, in which judge-made law becomes (through precedent) a part of the legal code. Many democracies have a civil-law tradition, in which nearly all law is defined by legislative statutes. Second, because U.S. courts operate in a constitutional system of divided powers, they are required to rule on conflicts between state and nation or between the executive and the legislative branches, which thrusts the judiciary into the middle of political conflicts. It should not be surprising, then, that federal judges and justices are appointed through an overtly political process in which partisan views and activities are major considerations. Many federal judges, particularly at the district level, have no significant prior judicial experience. In fact, the United States is one of the few countries that does not mandate formal training for judges.

The pattern is different in most European democracies, where judgeships tend to be career positions. Individuals are appointed to the judiciary at an early age and then work their way up the judicial ladder largely on the basis of seniority. Partisan politics does not play a large role in appointment and promotion. By tradition, European judges see their job as the strict interpretation of statutes, not the creative application of them.

The power of U.S. courts is nowhere more evident than in the exercise of judicial review—the voiding of a legislative or executive action on the grounds that it violates the Constitution. Judicial review had its origins in European experience and thought, but it was first formally applied in the United States when, in *Marbury v. Madison* (1803), the Supreme Court declared an act of Congress unconstitutional. Some democracies, including Great Britain, still do not allow broad-scale judicial review, but most democracies now provide for it.

In the so-called American system of judicial review, all judges can evaluate the applicability of constitutional law to particular cases and can declare ordinary law invalid when it conflicts with constitutional law. By comparison, the so-called Austrian system restricts judicial review to a special constitutional court. Judges in other courts cannot declare a law void on the grounds that it is unconstitutional: they must apply ordinary law as it is written. In the Austrian system, moreover, constitutional decisions can be made in response to requests for judicial review by elected officials when they are considering legislation. In the American case, judges can act only within the framework of actual legal cases; thus, their rulings are made only after laws have been enacted.

It did not defer to laws passed by elected representatives. By the same token, the Democratic-dominated Supreme Court in the period after World War II was also an activist judiciary, expanding the civil rights of black Americans (see Chapter 5) and the civil liberties of the criminally accused (see Chapter 4). It vigorously asserted its authority against that of local and state elected officials.

Even today, it is difficult on the basis of their partisan backgrounds to neatly assign judges and justices to the activist or restraint category. A study of Supreme Court decisions found that, as measured by a willingness to invalidate acts of Congress, all recent Supreme Court justices have been activists to some degree. Republican appointees have been just as likely as Democratic appointees to reject laws enacted by Congress—in other words, to place their judgments ahead of those of the people's elected representatives.[38] The Republican-dominated Supreme Court has struck down more acts of Congress in the past decade than were invalidated during the entire previous half-century. Although Chief Justice William Rehnquist has often been described as a proponent of judicial restraint, the Court he led until his death in 2005 had an agenda that, if not entirely activist, was not entirely restrained. Rehnquist led a federalist revolution, with the goal of increasing state sovereignty and diminishing Congress's power to enact laws binding on state governments (see Chapter 3). It could be argued that the Rehnquist Court was establishing a balance of federal-state power more

I was sentenced to the State Penitentiary by The Circuit Court of Bay County, State of Florida. The present proceeding was commenced on a ~~w~~ petition for a Writ of Habeus Corpus To The Supreme Court of The State of Florida to vacate the sentence, on the grounds that I was made to stand Trial without the aid of counsel, and, at all times of my incarseration. The said Court refused To appoint counsel and therefore deprived me of Due process of law, and violate my rights in The Bill of Rights and the constitution of the United States.

5th day of Jan 1962 Petitioner

Notary Public

Notary Public
My Comm. at   Jan. 1st, 1962
Bonded by American Surety Co. of N. Y.

Gideon's Letter to the Supreme Court
John F. Davis, Clerk, Supreme Court of the United States

The handwritten letter that Clarence Gideon (insert) sent to the Supreme Court in 1962. The letter led eventually to the *Gideon* decision, in which the Court held that states must provide poor defendants with legal counsel (see Chapter 4). Seen by many people at the time as judicial activism, the ruling is now fully accepted.

consistent with the original intent of the Constitution than was the balance that emerged from the New Deal; in this sense, the Court could be seen as having acted with restraint.[39] On the other hand, the Rehnquist Court was repudiating precedent and laws of Congress—actions consistent with judicial activism. Walter Dellinger, a former U.S. Solicitor General, said of the Rehnquist court: "[It] doesn't defer to government at any level. [It] is confident it can come up with the right decisions, and it believes it is constitutionally charged with doing so.[40]

One reason why justices' decisions do not neatly align with specific judicial philosophies is that disputes that reach the Supreme Court are anything but clear-cut. If they were, they would have been settled in the lower federal courts. Also, the justices are political appointees and political actors as well as legal ones. Studies indicate that, in cases that reasonably could be decided for either side, justices tend toward the side that suits their political ideology.[41] On the liberal side, this leads to the active promotion of social justice for the disadvantaged; on the conservative side, it leads to the protection of property claims and the upholding of preferred forms of authority, such as state government.

Thus, all justices are activists in the sense that they are willing to pit their judgment against the judgment of elected officials. The law as expressed through the Constitution, statutes, and precedent is not precise enough to provide an automatic answer to every court case. Judges and justices must exercise their judgment when the text of the law is inexact. And all judges and justices are restrained in the sense that their decisions must be rooted in the law. Judges cannot simply make any decision they might choose but rather are confined by the facts of the case and the laws that might reasonably be applied to it.

Nonetheless, judges and justices vary in the degree to which they are willing to contest the judgment of elected officials as well as in the degree to which they are willing to depart from the wording of the law. These differences do, on some issues, coincide with judges' and justices' partisan backgrounds. In *Vieth v. Jubelirer* (2004), for example, the Supreme Court was split over a case that had

LEADERS

JOHN MARSHALL

(1755–1835)

John Marshall served thirty-four years as chief justice of the Supreme Court, the longest tenure in that position in U.S. history. Marshall had served for a time as John Adams's secretary of state and in the House of Representatives before being appointed chief justice by Adams. Before Marshall's tenure, the Supreme Court was perceived as a feeble branch of the federal government. Marshall changed that notion. An ardent nationalist who saw himself as a guardian of federal authority, Marshall steered the Court through a series of decisions that established it as a powerful institution and helped lay the foundation for a strong Union. The Supreme Court's ruling in *McCulloch v. Maryland* (1819) affirmed the claims that national law was supreme over conflicting state law and that the federal government's powers were not narrowly constrained by the Constitution.

Despite philosophical differences with the presidents who succeeded Adams, Marshall dominated the Court throughout his long tenure, persuading newly appointed justices to back him on key constitutional issues. Marshall saw himself as a Framer of the Constitution, acting as the ongoing architect of the work begun in Philadelphia during the summer of 1787. Although Marshall was a distant cousin of Thomas Jefferson, the two men were bitter opponents. Marshall's first landmark decision, *Marbury v. Madison* (1803), which established the principle of judicial review, was a rebuke to President Jefferson's executive authority. Their ongoing dispute peaked in 1807 at the trial of Aaron Burr, who was justly accused of treason by the Jefferson administration. Marshall presided over the trial and acquitted Burr, ruling that the word of a single eyewitness was insufficient grounds for conviction.

some similarities to the *Baker v. Carr* case of forty years earlier. At issue was whether partisan gerrymandering, in which state legislatures stack election districts with voters of one party when they redraw election district boundaries after a census, is a violation of the voters' right to equal protection under the Fourteenth Amendment. The Court's three most conservative justices, all of them Republican appointees, were joined by the more moderate Justice Sandra Day O'Connor in concluding that the partisan gerrymandering issue is for the legislatures, not the courts, to decide. The Court's four most liberal justices, two of them Democratic appointees, said that the Court should be open to ruling on such cases. The deciding vote was cast by Justice Anthony Kennedy, a relative moderate, who wrote that in some future case—but not in this particular one—the abuse of redistricting power might be so extreme as to warrant judicial involvement.[42]

Over its history, the Supreme Court has had many great (as well as many mediocre) justices who have been proponents of each philosophy. Chief Justice John Marshall was an activist who used the Court to enlarge the judiciary's power and to promote the national government (see Chapters 2 and 3). Judicial review—the most substantial form of judicial power—is not explicitly granted by the Constitution but was claimed through Marshall's opinion in *Marbury v. Madison*. Associate Justice Oliver Wendell Holmes Jr. was Marshall's philosophical opposite, favoring judicial restraint. In the court opinions he wrote, as well as in his other writings, Holmes spoke of the need for the judiciary to work within the tight confines of the law: "My job is to play the game according to the rules."[43] But he too left an indelible mark on jurisprudence, particularly in the area of free expression (see Chapter 4). Looking back on history, an observer could conclude that the nation has been well served by the fact that its judges and justices have not all been advocates of judicial restraint or advocates of judicial activism—both the nation and the judiciary are stronger for having had jurists of each persuasion.

The Judiciary's Proper Role: A Question of Competing Values

The dispute between advocates of judicial activism and advocates of judicial restraint is a philosophical one that involves opposing values. The debate is important because it addresses the normative question of what role the judiciary ought to play in American democracy. Should unelected judges involve themselves deeply in policy by adopting a broad conception of their power, or should they grant wide discretion to elective institutions? Should judges defer to precedent, or should they be willing to change course, even at the risk of sending the law down uncharted paths? These questions cannot be answered simply on the basis of whether one personally agrees or disagrees with a particular judicial decision. The answer necessarily depends on a value judgment about the role the judiciary should play in a governing system based on the often-conflicting concepts of majority rule and individual rights.

The United States is a constitutional democracy that recognizes both the power of the majority to rule and the claim of the minority to protection of its rights. The judiciary was not established as the nation's moral conscience and does not have a monopoly on the issue of minority interests and rights. Yet the judiciary was established as a coequal branch of government charged with the responsibility of protecting individual rights and minority interests. In short, the constitutional question of how far the courts should be allowed to go in substituting their judgment for that of elected institutions and established law is open to interpretation. The trade-off is significant on all issues: minority rights versus majority rule, states' rights versus federal power, legislative authority versus judicial authority.

Summary

Self-Test www.mhhe.com/pattersontad8

At the lowest level of the federal judicial system are the district courts, where most federal cases begin. Above them are the federal courts of appeals, which review cases appealed from the lower courts. The U.S. Supreme Court is the nation's highest court. Each state has its own court system, consisting of trial courts at the bottom and one or two appellate levels at the top. Cases originating in state courts ordinarily cannot be appealed to the federal courts unless a federal issue is involved, and then the federal courts can choose to rule only on the federal aspects of the case. Federal judges at all levels are nominated by the president, and if confirmed by the Senate they are appointed by the president to the office. Once on the federal bench, they serve until they die, retire, or are removed by impeachment and conviction.

The Supreme Court is unquestionably the most important court in the country. The legal principles it establishes are binding on lower courts, and its capacity to define the law is enhanced by the control it exercises over the cases it hears. However, it is inaccurate to assume that lower courts are inconsequential (the upper-court myth). Lower courts have considerable discretion, and the great majority of their decisions are not reviewed by a higher court. It is also inaccurate to assume that federal courts are far more significant than state courts (the federal court myth).

The courts have less discretionary authority than elected institutions do. The judiciary's positions are constrained by the facts of a case and by the laws as defined through the Constitution, statutes and government regulations, and legal precedent. Yet existing legal guidelines are seldom so precise that judges have no choice in their decisions. As a result, political influences have a strong impact on the judiciary. It responds to national conditions, public opinion, interest groups, and elected officials, particularly the president and members of Congress. Another political influence on the judiciary is the personal beliefs of judges, who have individual preferences that are evident in the way they decide issues that come before the courts. Not surprisingly, partisan politics plays a significant role in judicial appointments.

In recent decades, the Supreme Court has issued broad rulings on individual rights, some of which have required governments to take positive action on behalf of minority interests. As the Court has crossed into areas traditionally left to lawmaking majorities, the legitimacy of its policies has been questioned. Advocates of judicial restraint claim that the justices' personal values are inadequate justification for exceeding the proper judicial role; they argue that the Constitution entrusts broad issues of the public good to elective institutions and that judicial activism ultimately undermines public respect for the judiciary. Judicial activists counter that the courts were established as an independent branch and should not hesitate to promote new principles when they see a need, even if this action brings them into conflict with elected officials.

STUDY CORNER

Key Terms

appellate jurisdiction (*p. 406*)
brief (*p. 407*)
civil law (*p. 418*)
compliance (*p. 426*)
concurring opinion (*p. 408*)
criminal law (*p. 418*)
decision (*p. 407*)
dissenting opinion (*p. 409*)
facts (of a court case) (*p. 417*)

judicial activism (*p. 426*)
judicial conference (*p. 407*)
judicial restraint (*p. 425*)
judicial review (*p. 424*)
jurisdiction (of a court) (*p. 406*)
laws (of a court case) (*p. 418*)
legitimacy (of judicial power) (*p. 424*)
majority opinion (*p. 408*)
opinion (of a court) (*p. 407*)

original jurisdiction (*p. 406*)
plurality opinion (*p. 408*)
precedent (*p. 406*)
procedural law (*p. 418*)
senatorial courtesy (*p. 415*)
solicitor general (*p. 406*)
writ of certiorari (*p. 406*)

Self-Test

1. When nominating a justice to the U.S. Supreme Court, presidents:
   a. are required by law to consult with the American Bar Association.
   b. in accordance with senatorial courtesy have usually decided the choice by finding out who a majority of the senators in their party would like the nominee to be.
   c. tend to select a nominee who shares their political philosophy.
   d. get their nominee confirmed by the Senate only about half the time.

2. Judges in the U.S. judiciary:
   a. after issuing a ruling are personally responsible for seeing that the ruling is carried out by other officials.
   b. by law must attend public meetings from time to time and, while at these meetings, advise the public on judicial matters.
   c. are prohibited from issuing decisions except on actual cases that come to their court.
   d. have greater freedom than legislators or executives to choose the issues they will address.

3. The federal district courts are:
   a. courts of original jurisdiction.
   b. the only federal courts that regularly use juries to determine the outcome of cases.
   c. the courts that, in practice, make the final decision in most federal cases.
   d. the lowest level of federal courts.
   e. all of the above.

4. Most cases reach the U.S. Supreme Court through:
   a. appeal of cases that the court is bound by the Constitution or by act of Congress to hear even if it would prefer not to hear them.

   b. grant of a writ of certiorari.
   c. plea bargaining.
   d. its power of original jurisdiction.

5. Which constitutional power does Congress have in relation to the Supreme Court?
   a. Congress can change the number of justices on the Supreme Court.
   b. Congress can change the Supreme Court's original jurisdiction.
   c. By two-thirds vote of both chambers, Congress determines which justice will become Chief Justice when that office becomes vacant.
   d. Congress can refuse to implement Supreme Court decisions when it disagrees with those decisions.

6. A court exercising judicial activism would likely:
   a. totally disregard judicial precedent.
   b. totally disregard legislative and executive action.
   c. not hesitate to act when it thought an important constitutional principle was at issue, even if such action would bring the court into conflict with public opinion or the elected branches.
   d. none of the above.

7. State court systems in the United States are lower-level administrative units of the federal court system and not independent judicial units. (T/F)

8. The U.S. judiciary is not influenced by either public opinion or the actions of interest groups. (T/F)

9. The "federal court myth" implies that the federal courts are far more important than state courts. (T/F)

10. According to the text, social and economic changes have required the government, including the judiciary, to play a larger role in settling societal problems and conflicts. (T/F)

Critical Thinking

Which philosophy—judicial restraint or judicial activism—comes closer to your own thinking about the proper role of the courts? Does your support for restraint or activism depend on whether a judicial decision conforms to your own preference on the issue in question?

Suggested Readings

Carp, Robert, and Ronald Stidham. *The Federal Courts*, 4th ed. Washington, D.C.: Congressional Quarterly Press, 2001. An overview of the federal judiciary system.

Davis, Richard. *Electing Justices: Fixing the Supreme Court Nomination Process*. New York: Oxford University Press, 2005. An examination of the now contentious process through which Supreme Court justices are nominated and confirmed.

Gillman, Howard. *Votes That Counted: How the Court Decided the 2000 Presidential Election*. Chicago: University of Chicago Press, 2001. An accounting of the *Bush v. Gore* ruling.

Hansford, Thomas G., and James F. Spriggs II. *The Politics of Precedent on the Supreme Court*. Princeton, N.J.: Princeton University Press, 2006. An examination of how the Court interprets precedent to suit new situations and goals.

McGuire, Kevin T. *Understanding the Supreme Court: Cases and Controversies*. New York: McGraw-Hill, 2002. An overview of Supreme Court decisions and approaches to legal disputes.

O'Brien, David M. *Storm Center: The Supreme Court in American Politics*, 7th ed. New York: Norton, 2005. A thorough assessment of the Supreme Court.

Sandler, Ross, and David Schoenbord. *Democracy by Decree: What Happens When Courts Run Government*. New Haven, Conn.: Yale University Press, 2003. A critical evaluation of the courts' growing policy role.

Seidman, Louis Michael. *Our Unsettled Constitution*. New Haven, Conn.: Yale University Press, 2002. A defense of constitutionalism and judicial review.

List of Websites

http://www.courttv.com/cases
A website that allows you to take the facts of actual court cases, examine the law and the arguments, and then decide each case for yourself.

http://www.fjc.gov/
The home page of the Federal Judicial Center, an agency created by Congress to conduct research and provide education on the federal judicial system.

http://www.lib.umich.edu/govdocs/fedjudi.html
A University of Michigan web page that provides detailed information on the federal judicial system.

http://www.rominger.com/supreme.htm
A vast site that provides links to the Supreme Court, pending cases, the state court systems, and other subjects.

Participate!

The right to a fair and open trial decided by a jury is one of the oldest hallmarks of the American justice system. If you have never done so, you might want to attend a trial at your local courthouse to see how the process works. If you live in or near Washington, D.C., or a state capital, you might choose instead to observe a session of a supreme court. Such courts are appellate courts, so there is no jury, but you are more likely to hear arguments on cases of broad significance. Finally, if you have the opportunity to serve on a jury, you should welcome the chance to participate in a decision that is important to society as well as to the parties directly involved. Too many Americans today see jury duty as a responsibility to be shirked.

Extra Credit

For up-to-the-minute *New York Times* articles, interactive simulations, graphics, study tools, and more links and quizzes, visit the text's Online Learning Center at www.mhhe.com/pattersontad8.

(Self-Test Answers: 1. c　2. c　3. e　4. b　5. a　6. c　7. F　8. F　9. T　10. T)

PART 4

PUBLIC POLICY

Politics, said Harold Lasswell, is the struggle over "who gets what, when, and how." Americans differ in many of their interests, and they also disagree over policy. Yet they are often able to find common ground. The typical response when a policy question arises is not only to fight over it but also to resolve it. This philosophy speaks volumes about the nature of American governance.

The four chapters in this section are designed mainly to address broad policy issue areas: the economy and the environment (Chapter 15); welfare, education, and health (Chapter 16); foreign and defense policy (Chapter 17); and state and local politics and policy (Chapter 18).

There is a common pattern to policy action in these areas—it tends to be piecemeal and reactive. The nation's diversity and fragmented governing structure make it difficult for policymakers to deal with issues except in small parts and until they have reached the problem stage. This tendency increases the likelihood that major errors of policy will be avoided, but it also increases the chance that problems will be left to grow to the point where solutions are harder to find and more costly to implement.

Regardless, a democratic nation's policies reflect the nature of its political system and its people. They reveal the way a society has chosen to govern itself.

PART FOUR OUTLINE

15 Economic and Environmental Policy: Contributing to Prosperity 436

16 Welfare and Education Policy: Providing for Personal Security and Need 472

17 Foreign and Defense Policy: Protecting the American Way 498

18 State and Local Politics: Maintaining Our Differences 526

Economic and Environmental Policy:
Contributing to Prosperity

Chapter Outline

The Public Policy Process
Emergence of Policy Issues
Resolution of Policy Issues

Government as Regulator of the Economy
Efficiency Through Government Intervention
Equity Through Government Intervention
The Politics of Regulatory Policy

Government as Protector of the Environment
Conservationism: The Older Wave
Environmentalism: The Newer Wave

Government as Promoter of Economic Interests
Promoting Business
Promoting Labor
Promoting Agriculture

Fiscal Policy: Government as Manager of the Economy, I
Taxing and Spending Policy
The Process and Politics of Fiscal Policy

Monetary Policy: Government as Manager of the Economy, II
The Fed
The Politics of the Fed

CHAPTER 15

We the people of the United States, in order to . . .
insure domestic tranquility . . .

—*Preamble, U.S. Constitution*

The stock market was downright scary. The Dow Jones and Nasdaq indexes had dropped steadily for two years, knocking trillions of dollars off the value of stocks. Stocks that sold on the technology-heavy Nasdaq index were particularly hard hit. By 2003, it had fallen 75 percent—a steeper decline over the same length of time than had occurred at the onset of the Great Depression. Was history about to repeat itself? Was the U.S. economy in danger of collapse?

In fact, Wall Street and the rest of America reacted rather calmly to the market downturn. Institutional and individual investors were unhappy with the drop in the value of their stocks, but they did not panic. Among the reasons was the existence of substantial government programs designed to stabilize and stimulate the U.S. economy. When the Great Depression struck, no such programs existed. Moreover, the response to the 1929–31 drop in stock prices made matters worse: businesses cut back on production, investors fled the stock market, depositors withdrew their bank savings, and consumers slowed their spending. All these actions accelerated the downward spiral. In 2003, however, government programs were in place to protect depositors' savings, slow the drop in stock prices, and steady the economy through adjustments in interest rates and spending programs. By 2004, the economy was already showing signs of strengthening.

This chapter examines economic policy. As was discussed in the first chapter, public policy is a decision by government to follow a course of action designed to produce a particular result. In this vein, economic policy centers on the promotion and regulation of economic interests and, through fiscal and monetary actions, on economic growth and stability. Directly or indirectly, the federal government is a party to almost every economic transaction in which Americans engage. Although the private decisions of firms and individuals are the main force in the American economic system, these decisions are influenced by government policy. Washington seeks to maintain high productivity, employment, and purchasing power; regulates business practices that otherwise would harm the environment or result in economic inefficiencies and inequities; and promotes economic interests. The main ideas presented in this chapter are these:

- *Through regulation, the U.S. government imposes restraints on business activity that are designed to promote economic efficiency and equity.* This regulation is often the cause of political conflict, which is both ideological and group-centered.

- *Through regulatory and conservation policies, the U.S. government seeks to protect and preserve the environment from the effects of business firms and consumers.*

- *Through promotion, the U.S. government helps private interests achieve their economic goals.* Business in particular benefits from the government's promotional efforts, which take place largely in the context of group politics.

- *Through its taxing and spending decisions (fiscal policy), the U.S. government seeks to maintain a level of economic supply and demand that will keep the economy prosperous.* The condition of the economy is generally the leading issue in American electoral politics and has a major influence on each party's success.

- *Through its money-supply decisions (monetary policy), the U.S. government— through the Fed—seeks to maintain a level of inflation consistent with sustained, controllable economic growth.*

THE PUBLIC POLICY PROCESS

public policy process
The political interactions that lead to the emergence and resolution of public policy issues.

Government action in the economic sector is part of the **public policy process**— the political interactions that lead to the emergence and resolution of public policy issues. Before examining economic policy, it is helpful to describe the process through which it and other types of policy are developed.

Political scientists have identified six stages that together make up the policy process (see Figure 15–1). The first two stages—problem recognition and problem transformation—refer to the emergence of issues and the last four stages—policy formulation, policy adoption, policy implementation, and policy evaluation— refer to their resolution.

Emergence of Policy Issues

Policy problems stem from conditions of society—the employment rate, the quality of the schools, the security of the nation, the safety of the streets, and so on. Yet only certain conditions will be seen as problems of a *public* nature. Even conditions that are life threatening can intensify for years without people thinking

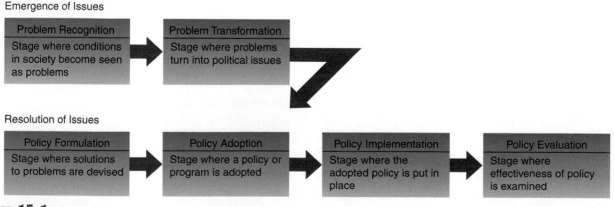

Figure 15–1

The Public Policy Process
The public policy process refers to the political interactions that lead to the emergence and resolution of public policy issues. The process includes six stages, although not every issue goes through all stages or necessarily in the exact order that the stages are shown here.

of them as anything but a personal problem. Obesity is an example. Americans did not suddenly wake up one day to discover that they had gained dozens of pounds during the course of a night's sleep. Yet they had slowly gotten heavier to the point where obesity was a leading cause of poor health. Only recently, after research studies revealed the extent of the problem, did Americans begin to think of obesity as a public policy problem.

In some cases *problem recognition* happens suddenly, even shockingly, as in the case of the terrorist attacks of September 11, 2001, when hatred of the United States by extremist elements abroad—a condition—erupted into a threat to America's long-term security—a policy problem. Yet, it ordinarily takes time for people to realize that they have a problem requiring attention. During World War II, Americans of all races fought together against the Nazis and their racist ideology. But when the war ended, white Americans acted at first as if nothing in their own society needed correcting. Black Americans knew better. They were still by law shuttled off to separate and inferior public schools and denied entry to white hospitals, restaurants, and theaters. The contradiction was simply too large to be ignored. Within a decade, America had begun to dismantle its system of government-imposed racial segregation.

Problem transformation is the second stage in the policy process. It is here that policy problems get turned into political issues. Not all problems make the transition. In many American neighborhoods, residents are resigned to unsightly streets and yards. They complain about how things look, but that is as far as it goes.

Leadership is a vital part of this stage in the policy process. Leadership can sometimes transform even a small problem into a leading issue. Although the estate tax has been a fact of death ever since the Progressive era, it bothered only the very rich until the 1990s when conservative groups decided to make it an issue. They even relabeled it, believing that Americans would more readily oppose a tax known as the "death tax." Through public forums, media appearances, and op-ed pieces, they sought to change how Americans thought about the tax. Their campaign was remarkably successful. In a 2006 NBC News/Wall Street Journal Poll, more than twice as many respondents said they would support a candidate who favors repeal of the estate tax as said they would oppose such a candidate.

Interests do not always seek to publicize their issue. The political scientist E.E. Schattschneider noted that the "scope of conflict" affects the outcome of issues.[1] As a conflict widens, an ever larger number of interests join the fight, forcing concessions from those already part of it. Accordingly, if a group can somehow manage to limit the scope of conflict—that is, to keep an issue to itself—it improves its chances of getting what it wants. Iron triangles are an arrangement of this type (see Chapter 9). Through close and ongoing relationships with relevant executive agencies and congressional committees, well-placed interest groups are able to exert considerable influence over issues affecting them.

Interest groups are not the only actors that help set the issue agenda. Members of Congress, political parties, and the news media do so as well. The media, for example, have the power to focus public attention. By highlighting a problem day after day, the media can lead people to think that something needs to be done about it. No agenda setter, however, has more influence than does the president. Even a single presidential pronouncement will sometimes trigger a policy response. The AIDS crisis in Africa was far from Americans' minds until January 28, 2003. That evening in his State of the Union Address, President George W. Bush declared that Africa's problem could no longer be ignored. Within months, Congress had appropriated $1.4 billion to fight AIDS in Africa.

Resolution of Policy Issues

An occasional policy proposal is so straightforward that almost anyone could draft it. As the 2006 midterm elections approached, congressional Republicans revived an old issue—flag burning—as a means of energizing their conservative base. Their proposed constitutional amendment, which came within a single Senate vote of passage, contained just seventeen words: "The Congress shall have power to prohibit the physical desecration of the flag of the United States."

Most policy proposals, however, are as intricate as the problems they address. Because of the complexity of modern society, almost no problem exists by itself. Problems are invariably connected to other problems, which means that they cannot be addressed in isolation. Consider, for example, the question of whether government price-supports for corn should be increased as a way of easing the problems of corn farmers. Although a subsidy would clearly help corn growers, there are other interests that may or may not be helped by it. How would a subsidy impact on consumers, on farmers' decisions about which crops to plant, on Ethanol production, and on the federal deficit? How might such a subsidy affect even foreign policy? Other countries have corn growers who compete in the world market with America's farmers. If U.S. growers are provided a subsidy, they can sell their corn at a lower price, giving them an advantage over other sellers in the world market. Faced with that prospect, foreign governments might decide to subsidize their own corn growers, possibly triggering a trade war. As far-fetched as this example might seem, it approximates what happened in 2006 at the international round of trade talks. After five years of negotiation among scores of countries, the talks collapsed, partly because the United States refused to reduce its hefty farm subsidies.

The complexity of modern policymaking has created an entire industry—that of the policy analyst. Thousands of scholars, consultants, and policy specialists are engaged in *policy formulation*. Most economic policy, for example, is designed by trained economists. Their ideas do not always work but the success rate is far higher than that of economic proposals set forth by non-economists.

Politicians also formulate policy. They lack the analytic tools of the policy specialists but have their own strength: they have a sense of what other politicians will support. The best crafted policy proposal in the world is worth nothing if lawmakers will not vote for it. When President Lyndon Johnson decided in 1965 to tackle the issue of public health, some of his advisors wanted him to propose to Congress a government-paid universal health care system like those of Europe. Knowing that Congress would not enact such a program, Johnson opted for a medical-care amendment to the social security act. The result was Medicare, which today serves the medical needs of nearly forty million American retirees.

Policies on the scale of the Medicare program are rare. *Policy adoption* in the United States takes place through a system of divided powers that is a barrier to enactment of ambitious programs. To become law, a bill must get majority support in the House and in the Senate and be signed by the president. Unless there is solid support in each place for substantial change, it is unlikely to happen. A Senate filibuster by itself is sometimes enough to deter further action. As a result of the obstacles, most policies enacted by Congress are modest in scope. As the political scientist Aaron Wildavsky noted, incremental policies—

Striking janitors parade in Beverly Hills, California. Citizen action has the potential to influence several stages of the policy process. A protest march ordinarily would be part of the political transformation stage—the point at which problems turn into issues.

those that depart only slightly from existing policies—are the characteristic output of the U.S. policy process.[2]

Political scientist John Kingdon found that major policy breakthroughs tend to occur only when several aspects of the policy process converge.[3] When a problem is compelling, when political leaders are ready to tackle it, and when policy analysts think they have an answer to it, decisive action can result. Kingdon's analysis describes rather accurately the circumstances that led in 2001 to enactment of President Bush's ambitious tax cut plan. At the time, the economy needed a boost, Republicans were empowered by their victory in the presidential election, and GOP policy analysts had amassed an array of tax-cutting proposals. Bush got nearly all that he asked for, including a reduction nearly by half of the capital gains tax.

After policy is adopted, *policy implementation* occurs. Responsibility for implementation rests mostly with bureaucrats and judges. Bureaucrats are charged with administering the law, and judges are responsible for applying it in specific cases. As was explained in Chapters 13 and 14, administrators and judges often have considerable latitude in carrying out the law.

Bureaucrats and judges often take the blame when implementation goes astray. Frequently, however, the problem rests with the lawmakers. Federal bureaucrats had the unenviable task in 2006 of implementing a prescription drug benefit for the elderly that was based on poorly drafted legislation. It had so many exceptions, thresholds, and exclusions that many senior citizens were baffled by their options. And when they asked for help, they often found that there was none to be had. Congress had neglected to appropriate enough money to staff the program fully. At one point during implementation, fewer than half as many retirees were enrolled in the program as had been projected to be enrolled by then.

Policy evaluation is the final stage of the policy process. At this point, the basic question is whether a program is working as intended. Sometimes the question can be answered in specific terms, such as whether the construction of a new stretch of federal highway is on time and within budget. Many policies, however, are hard to evaluate. An example is foreign economic aid. Economic development in poor countries is subject to so many factors that it is difficult to assess the effect of assistance grants. In such cases, policy evaluation usually centers on how well the program is being administered—for example, whether the money is being channeled to the right places or is finding its way into the pockets of corrupt officials.

Policy evaluation is a substantial part of the policy process. Nearly every government agency has an evaluation unit. In addition, broad oversight is provided by agencies such as the Government Accountability Office (GAO) within Congress and the Office of Management and Budget within the executive branch (see Chapters 11–13). The GAO alone has a budget of nearly $500 million.

On occasion, the public has had the final say in policy evaluation. Some programs have been terminated because of public opposition. In 1989, for example, Congress rescinded a law that it had passed less than a year earlier. The law was intended to protect Medicare recipients from the financial ruin of catastrophic illness. Retirees afflicted with such illness would pay only the first $1,000 in medical costs; the federal government would pay the rest. In formulating the policy, Congress decided to require all Medicare recipients to pay an insurance premium to help defray program costs. The outcry from seniors was deafening. They liked the benefit but were deadset against paying the premium. When Dan Rostenkowsky (D-Ill), chair of the House committee that drafted the legislation, was leaving a meeting in Chicago where he had tried to explain the logic of the program, irate senior citizens followed him to his car, beating it with canes and yelling "Rottenkowski" at him. Feeling trapped, Rostenkowsky broke through the crowd and raced down the street on foot.[4]

In summary, the public policy process is a set of stages that problems go through on their way to some sort of resolution. In practice, the stages sometimes merge or reverse their order. Policy formulation, for example, sometimes goes hand in hand with problem transformation. Interested parties may conclude they can strengthen their case by offering a solution at the same time that they highlight the problem. Nevertheless, the stages are analytically distinct. The problem recognition stage is when conditions in society become seen as public problems; the problem transformation stage is when these problems turn into political issues; the policy formulation stage is when solutions to problems are devised; the policy adoption stage is when a solution is settled upon in the form of a policy or program; the policy implementation stage is when the adopted policy is put into place; and the policy evaluation stage is when the effectiveness of the policy is examined.

We turn now to a particular area of policy—the economy. The discussion will start with regulatory policy and conclude with an explanation of government's efforts to maintain a stable economy.

economy
A system of production and consumption of goods and services that are allocated through exchange among producers and consumers.

laissez-faire doctrine
A classic economic philosophy that holds that owners of business should be allowed to make their own production and distribution decisions without government regulation or control.

GOVERNMENT AS REGULATOR OF THE ECONOMY

An **economy** is a system of production and consumption of goods and services that are allocated through exchange. When a shopper chooses groceries at a store and pays money for them, that transaction is one of the millions of economic exchanges that make up the economy. In *The Wealth of Nations* (1776), Adam Smith presented the case for the **laissez-faire doctrine,** which holds that private individuals and firms should be left alone to make their own production and distribution decisions. Smith reasoned that when there is a demand for a good (that is, when people are willing and able to buy a good), private entrepreneurs will respond by producing the good and distributing it to those places where demand exists. Smith argued that the desire for profit is the "invisible hand" that guides the system of demand and supply toward the greatest benefit for all.

Smith acknowledged that the doctrine of laissez-faire capitalism has limits. Certain areas of the economy, such as roadways, are natural monopolies and are better run by government than by private firms. In addition, by regulating banking, currency, and contracts, government can give stability to private transactions. Otherwise, Smith argued, the economy is best left in private hands.

For a period in the twentieth century, an alternative way of thinking about the economy, Marxism, held sway in the Communist bloc countries, although their economies were not precisely what Karl

LEADERS

ADAM SMITH

(1723–90)

Born in Scotland, Adam Smith was a moral philosopher who first came to public attention with his 1759 book *Theory of Moral Sentiments*. A shy man, Smith was nonetheless a spellbinding lecturer and a favorite of students at Oxford. Smith was nearly fifty when his interests turned to political economy. Among those with whom he discussed economic ideas was Benjamin Franklin, whom he met in France while Franklin was serving as an American diplomat. The work for which Smith is best know and that has made him one of the most widely recognized economic theorists in history is *The Wealth of Nations,* a treatise on the moral and economic superiority of the free-market system. In it, Smith claimed that government policies and personal efforts to promote the common good were of little consequence compared with the effects of an unrestricted marketplace. However, *The Wealth of Nations* is critical of monopolistic markets, whether in the hands of merchants or of a king. In its time, it was a democratic treatise, concerned with the wealth of the nation as a whole—and thus the wealth of all—as opposed to the economic well-being of a particular interest or class.

Marx intended. In *Das Kapital* (*Capital*, 1867), Marx argued that a free-market system is exploitative because producers, through their control of markets, can compel workers to labor at a wage below the value they add to production. Marx proposed a collective economy in which workers own the means of production. In the former Soviet Union and its satellite countries, even though the economy was collectivized, ordinary workers had little say in its operation. The Soviet model collapsed because it proved to be an inefficient method for allocating capital and labor and for coordinating the supply of goods with the demand for them.

Today, free-market systems dominate the world economy, although they are not the laissez-faire systems that Smith envisioned. All economies assign a substantial role to government. However, the level of government involvement varies widely. In the partially socialized economies of the Scandinavian countries, for example, the government owns some industry (for example, the airline and energy companies) and redistributes wealth through relatively steep progressive tax systems and through the broad provision of welfare services, such as government-provided health care for all. In these economies, business and labor are also closely regulated by government, but the free market determines most supply and demand decisions.

The U.S. economy is also a "mixed" system in that it contains elements of both public and private control. Indeed, the U.S. government owns some industry (for example, the Tennessee Valley Authority, which produces electricity) and provides some welfare services (for example, its Medicare and Medicaid programs furnish health care for the elderly and the poor, respectively). In comparison with the partially socialized Scandinavian countries, however, the U.S. economy tilts more toward the free-market end of the continuum than toward the government-control end. Even by comparison with most democracies, the United States relies more heavily on the free market to make its production, distribution, and consumption decisions.

Nevertheless, the U.S. government plays a substantial economic role through the **regulation** of privately owned businesses. U.S. firms are not free to act as they please but rather must operate within production and distribution rules set by federal regulations. Regulatory policy is generally intended to promote either economic *efficiency* or *equity* (see Table 15–1).

regulation
A term that refers to government restrictions on the economic practices of private firms.

efficiency
An economic principle that holds that firms should fulfill as many of society's needs as possible while using as few of its resources as possible. The greater the output (production) for a given input (for example, an hour of labor), the more efficient the process.

Efficiency Through Government Intervention

Economic efficiency results when firms fulfill as many of society's needs as possible while using as few of its resources as possible.[5] **Efficiency** refers to the relationship of inputs (the labor and material that go into making a product or service) to outputs (the product or service itself). The greater the output for a given input, the more efficient the production process.

TABLE 15–1	The Main Objectives of Regulatory Policy The government intervenes in the economy to promote efficiency and equity.	
OBJECTIVE	DEFINITION	REPRESENTATIVE ACTIONS BY GOVERNMENT
Efficiency	Fulfillment of as many of society's needs as possible at the cost of as few of its resources as possible. The greater the output for a given input, the more efficient the process.	Preventing restraint of trade; requiring producers to pay the costs of damage to the environment; reducing restrictions on business that cannot be justified on a cost-benefit basis.
Equity	When the outcome of an economic transaction is fair to each party.	Requiring firms to bargain in good faith with labor; protecting consumers in their purchases; protecting workers' safety and health.

Preventing Restraint of Trade

Adam Smith and other classical economists argued that the free market is the optimal means of achieving efficiency. Producers will try to use as few resources as possible in order to keep their prices low so as to attract customers. To compete, less efficient producers will then either have to find a way to cut their production costs or be forced out of business. However, the assumption that the market always determines price is flawed. The same incentive—the profit motive—that drives producers to keep prices low can drive them to seek a monopoly on a good or to conspire with other producers to fix its price. If they succeed in their effort to restrain trade, consumers who want or need a good have no choice but to buy it at the price the monopolist is charging. A monopoly does not have to worry about efficiency because it has no competitors.

Restraint of trade was prevalent in the United States in the late nineteenth century when large trusts came to dominate many areas of the economy, including the oil, steel, railroad, and sugar markets. Railroad companies, for example, had no competition on short routes and charged such high rates that many farmers went broke because they could not afford to ship their crops to markets. In 1887, Congress took its first step toward regulating the trusts by enacting the Interstate Commerce Act. The legislation created the Interstate Commerce Commission (ICC), which was charged with regulating railroad practices and fares.

Business competition today is regulated by a wide range of federal agencies, including, for example, the Federal Trade Commission (FTC), the Food and Drug Administration (FDA), and the Antitrust Division of the Justice Department. The goal of regulatory activity is to protect consumers while preserving the market incentives that create a dynamic economy. In some cases, the government has prohibited mergers in order to increase competition. In 1999, for example, the Federal Communications Commission (FCC) voided a proposed merger of Bell Atlantic and GTE, ruling that the companies had failed to show that the merger would not hurt phone customers.

In most cases, however, the government tolerates mergers on the assumption that larger firms can take advantage of economies of scale, thereby operating more efficiently and passing on the lower costs to consumers. The government is particularly inclined to accept concentrated ownership in the oil, automobile, and other industries where the capital costs are so high that it is difficult for small firms to operate, much less compete.[6] Government acceptance of corporate giants also reflects the realization that market competition is no longer simply an issue of domestic firms. U.S. automakers, for example, compete for customers not only with each other but with Asian and European auto manufacturers. Indeed, the best selling car in America during the past decade is a Japanese brand, the Toyota Camry.

The U.S. government's general policy toward corporate giants that act in restraint of trade has been to penalize them financially. In 1993, for example, a number of air carriers (including American, Delta, United, Northwest, and US Air) were found to have engaged in price fixing and were ordered to award hundreds of millions of dollars in certificates to travelers who could prove they had flown on these carriers during the period in question. More than four million individuals, organizations, and businesses filed claims.

Making Business Pay for Indirect Costs

Economic inefficiencies can result not only from restraint of trade but from the failure of businesses or consumers to pay the full costs of resources used in production. Consider companies whose industrial wastes seep into nearby lakes and

Microsoft's Bill Gates speaks to an audience about his firm's international scope. Microsoft's large market share and aggressive practices have made it a target of antitrust action.

rivers. The price of these companies' products does not reflect the resulting water pollution, and hence customers do not pay all the costs that society has incurred in the making of the products. Economists label these unpaid costs **externalities.**

Until the 1960s, the federal government did not require firms to pay such costs. The impetus to begin doing so came not only from lawmakers but also from the scientific community and environmental groups. The Clean Air Act of 1963 and the Water Quality Act of 1965 required industry to install antipollution devices to keep the discharge of air and water pollutants within specified limits. In 1970, Congress created the Environmental Protection Agency (EPA) to monitor firms and ensure their compliance with federal regulations governing air and water quality and the disposal of toxic wastes. (Environmental policy is discussed more fully later in the chapter.)

externalities
Burdens that society incurs when firms fail to pay the full costs of production. An example of an externality is the pollution that results when corporations dump industrial wastes into lakes and rivers.

Overregulation

Although government regulation is intended to increase economic efficiency, it can have the opposite effect by raising the cost of doing business. Firms have to expend work hours to monitor and implement government regulations, which in some instances (for example, pollution control) also require companies to buy and install expensive equipment. These costs are efficient to the degree that they produce commensurate benefits. Yet if government places excessive regulatory burdens on firms, they waste resources in the process of complying. The result is higher-priced goods that are more expensive for consumers and less competitive in the domestic and global markets (see "How the United States Compares").

Overregulation can also be costly to governments. An example is a provision of the Safe Drinking Water Act that required communities to reduce contaminants in their water supply from the current level, whatever that level happened to be. In most communities, the effect was to improve the quality of the water supply. But in Anchorage, Alaska, the result was an absurd remedy. The city's water supply was already so clean that officials had to ask local fish-processing plants to dump their wastes into the sewer system so that Anchorage would have impurities to remove from its water.[7]

How the United States Compares
Global Economic Competitiveness

The United States ranked second only to Finland in the World Economic Forum's 2005 economic growth competitiveness survey. The World Economic Forum (WEF) is a private economic research organization based in Switzerland.

To determine its rankings, the WEF takes into account factors such as a nation's corporate management, finance, institutional openness, government regulation, public infrastructure, science and technology, and labor. The United States ranks particularly high on its technology, management, and finance. A weakness is its labor practices. U.S. workers enjoy fewer protections and benefits (such as health care coverage) than do their counterparts in many other industrialized societies.

The United States has been at or near the top of the WEF's rankings for a number of years. It has ranked substantially higher than some of its major economic rivals, such as Germany and Japan. These countries rank lower because their management, regulation, and finance systems are comparatively rigid, reducing their ability to respond flexibly to the global marketplace.

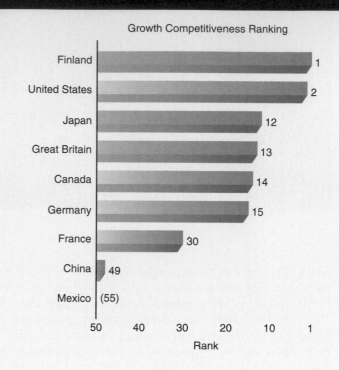

Situations of this kind led to regulatory reform.[8] In 1995, Congress enacted legislation to tighten the regulatory process by requiring cost-benefit analysis and risk assessment (determining the severity of the problem) to be taken into account in certain regulatory decisions.

Deregulation

deregulation

The rescinding of excessive government regulations for the purpose of improving economic efficiency.

Another response to regulatory excess is the policy of **deregulation**—the rescinding of regulations already in force for the purpose of improving efficiency. This process began in 1977 with passage of the Airlines Deregulation Act, which eliminated government-set airfares and, in some instances, government-mandated air routes. The change had the intended effect: airfares declined, and competition between airlines increased on most routes. Congress followed airline deregulation with partial deregulation of the trucking, banking, energy, and communications industries, among others.

Reductions in regulation, however, can be carried too far.[9] Underregulation can result in harmful business practices. The profit motive can lead firms and their executives to manipulate the market illegally. Companies are more likely to try unlawful schemes when weak regulation leads them to believe they can escape detection. Such was the case with top executives of the Enron Corporation. They employed illegal maneuvers that falsely inflated the firm's earnings, which drove up the price of its stock. Only after the schemes failed and the firm went bankrupt were the deceptions exposed. It was too late to help the

The collapse of Enron Corporation, which had been America's seventh-largest firm, cost investors and Enron employees (through the loss of retirement accounts) billions of dollars. The debacle brought calls for closer government regulation of corporations, accounting firms, and pension plans. Shown here is Enron founder Kenneth Lay as he leaves the courthouse during his trial in 2006 for fraud and conspiracy. Lay was convicted but died of a heart attack while awaiting sentencing.

stockholders who lost billions of dollars and the low-level Enron employees who lost their jobs as well as their company-based retirement savings.

The Enron scandal demonstrates that the issue of business regulation is not a simple question of whether or not to regulate. On one hand, too much regulation can burden firms with bureaucratic red tape, costly implementation procedures, and limited options. On the other hand, too little regulation can give firms the leeway to exploit the public unfairly or recklessly. Either too little or too much regulation can result in economic inefficiency. The challenge for policymakers is to strike the proper balance between regulatory measures and free-market mechanisms.

Equity Through Government Intervention

The government intervenes in the economy to bring equity as well as efficiency to the marketplace. **Equity** occurs when an economic transaction is fair to each party.[10] Equity is judged by *outcomes*—whether they are reasonable and mutually acceptable to the parties involved. A transaction can be considered fair if each party enters into it freely and is not unknowingly at a disadvantage (for example, if the seller knows a product is defective, equity requires that the buyer also know of the defect).

An early equity measure was the creation of the Food and Drug Administration (FDA) in 1907. Because consumers often are unable to tell whether foods and drugs are safe to use, the FDA works to keep adulterated foods and dangerous or ineffective drugs off the market. In the 1930s, financial reforms were among the equity measures enacted under the New Deal. The Securities and Exchange Act of 1934 and the Banking Act of 1934 were designed in part to protect investors and savers from dishonest or imprudent brokers and bankers. The New Deal also provided greater equity for organized labor, which previously had been in a weak position in its dealings with management. The Fair Labor Standards Act of 1938, for example, established minimum wages, maximum working hours, and constraints on the use of child labor.

equity (in relation to economic policy)
The situation in which the outcome of an economic transaction is fair to each party. An outcome can usually be considered fair if each party enters into a transaction freely and is not unknowingly at a disadvantage.

HISTORICAL BACKGROUND

Shown here are demonstrators protesting the practices of health maintenance organizations (HMOs). The central issue of business regulation is the proper balance of regulatory and free-market mechanisms. Critics of HMOs say the organizations are more interested in profits than in patients' health and that more regulation of their activities is warranted.

The 1960s and 1970s produced the greatest number of equity reforms. Ten federal agencies, including the Consumer Product Safety Commission, were established to protect consumers, workers, and the public from harmful effects of business activity. Among the products declared to be unsafe in the 1960s and 1970s were the insecticide DDT, cigarettes, and leaded gasoline. The benefits have been substantial. Lead, for example, can cause brain damage in children. Since regulation went into effect, the average level of lead in children's blood has decreased by 75 percent.[11]

The Politics of Regulatory Policy

Economic regulation has come in waves, as changes in national conditions have produced intermittent bursts of social consciousness. The first wave came during the Progressive Era, when reformers sought to stop the unfair business practices of the new monopolies. The second wave came during the Great Depression, when reformers sought to stimulate economic recovery through regulatory policies that were designed as much to save business as to restrain it.

Although business fought the Progressive and New Deal reforms, long-term opposition was lessened by the fact that most of the resulting regulation applied to a particular industry rather than to firms of all types. This pattern makes it possible for a regulated industry to gain influence with those officials responsible for regulating it. By cultivating close ties to the FCC, for example, the broadcast networks have managed to obtain policies that protect their near monopoly on broadcasting and give them high and sustained profits.[12] Although not all industries have as much leverage with their regulators as broadcasting has, it is generally true that industries have not been greatly hampered by the older form of regulation and in many cases have benefited from it.

The third wave of regulatory reform, in the 1960s and 1970s, differed from the Progressive and New Deal phases in both its form and its politics. This third wave has been called the era of "new social regulation" because of the social goals it addressed in its three major policy areas: environmental protection, consumer protection, and worker safety.

Political Culture

Liberty and Equality Through the Economy

The U.S. economy is based on free-market principles. Producers and consumers are more or less free to act as they please, subject of course to their financial resources.

Few Americans would trade their free-enterprise system for a socialist system that would put more constraints on their economic activity in return for greater economic security (see Chapter 1). In fact, Americans' notions of liberty and economic freedom are closely connected. Americans want the liberty that attends economic freedom, even if it means that in the end only some of them will do well economically.

Paradoxically, a minimum of economic security ordinarily is required for people to exercise their liberty. If people have to scrape to make a living, they will have neither the energy nor the financial means to enjoy fully the fruits of liberty. The Framers of the Constitution saw economic well-being as a precondition of liberty, which is why the Fifth (and later the Fourteenth) Amendment speaks at once of "life, liberty, or property." The Framers believed that America, in its abundance of land, offered a natural basis for the widespread prosperity that would bring meaningful liberty to all, as well as a greater measure of equality. Twenty-first-century America is a different kind of nation, vastly more affluent on one level but offering less economic opportunity on another. Studies show a widening gap between rich and poor in America, raising the issue of whether wealth in the United States is properly distributed across the society. In your opinion, is wealth distributed widely enough to allow nearly all Americans to enjoy the type of liberty the economic marketplace can supply? Or do you believe that too many Americans lack the economic means to attain the full measure of their liberty?

Economic equity (as opposed to economic equality) is also tied to liberty. The issue of equity addresses whether economic transactions are free and fair to each party or whether, instead, one party in the relationship is exploited because he or she lacks any real choice in the transaction. U.S. history is replete with examples of people who lacked the freedom to reject their own exploitation. Many of the millions of Irish, Italians, and Chinese who came to America in the nineteenth and early twentieth centuries, for example, had no power to bargain with their employers and virtually no choice—short of returning home or turning to a life of crime—but to work for long hours under adverse conditions for low pay. From your own experience and observations, do you think many people today are in a similar situation? Or do you think almost everyone now enjoys the marketplace freedom that will assure them of equity in economic relationships?

Most of the regulatory agencies established during the third wave have broader mandates than those created earlier. They have responsibility not for a single industry but for firms of all types, and their policy scope covers a wide range of activities. The Environmental Protection Agency (EPA), for example, is charged with regulating environmental pollution of almost any kind by almost any firm. Unlike the older agencies that are run by a commission whose members serve for fixed terms, some of the newer agencies, including the EPA, are headed by a single director who is appointed by the president with Senate approval and is subject to immediate removal by the president.

Because newer agencies such as the EPA have a wide-ranging clientele, no one firm or industry can easily influence agency policy to a great extent. There is also strong group competition within some of the newer regulatory spheres. For example, business lobbies must compete with environmental groups such as the Sierra Club and Greenpeace for influence with the EPA.[13] The firms regulated by the older agencies, in contrast, face no powerful competition in their lobbying activities. Broadcasters, for example, are largely unopposed in their efforts to influence the FCC. Although television viewers and radio listeners have a stake in FCC decisions, they are not well enough organized to petition it effectively.

GOVERNMENT AS PROTECTOR OF THE ENVIRONMENT

Few changes in public opinion and policy during recent decades have been as dramatic as those relating to the environment. Most Americans today recycle some of their garbage, and roughly two-thirds say they are either an active environmentalist or sympathetic to environmental concerns. In the 1960s, few Americans sorted their trash, and few could have answered a polling question that asked them whether they were an "environmentalist." The term was not commonly used, and most people would not have understood its meaning.

The publication in 1962 of Rachel Carson's *The Silent Spring* helped launch the environmental movement.[14] Written at a time when the author was dying of breast cancer, *Silent Spring* revealed the threat of harmful pesticides such as DDT and challenged the notion that scientific breakthroughs were an unqualified benefit to society. Carson's appearance at a Senate hearing contributed to legislative action that produced the 1963 Clean Air Act and the 1965 Water Quality Act. They were the first major federal laws designed to protect the nation's air, water, and ground from pollution. Today, environmental protection extends to nearly two hundred harmful forms of emission.

Conservationism: The Older Wave

Although government policy aimed at reducing pollution is relatively new, the government has been involved in land conservation for more than a century.[15] The first national park was created at Yellowstone in 1872 and, like the later ones, was established to preserve the nation's natural heritage for generations to come. The national park system serves more than one hundred million visitors each year and includes a total of eighty million acres, an area larger than every state except Alaska, Texas, California, and Montana.

The national parks are run by the National Park Service, an agency within the Department of Interior. Another agency, the U.S. Forest Service, located within the Department of Agriculture, manages the national forests, which cover an area more than twice the size of the national parks. They too have been preserved in part to protect America's natural heritage.

LEADERS

RACHEL CARSON

(1907–64)

Born on a farm near Pittsburgh, Rachel Carson had hoped to become a writer but switched to biology as an undergraduate and went on to earn a master's degree in zoology at Johns Hopkins University. She then started work on a doctorate, but the untimely death of her father and the need to take care of her mother ended this pursuit. In 1936, while working part-time at the U.S. Bureau of Fisheries (later the U.S. Fish and Wildlife Services), she learned of a full-time position that was opening up and decided to take the civil service exam, a rare ambition at the time for a woman. Carson outscored all the men who took the exam with her and was given the position.

In her job, Carson worked on scientific journals, but she wanted to reach a wider audience. She astonished even herself when *Atlantic Monthly* accepted an article she had submitted. The article's publication led to a book contract with Simon and Schuster, but the resulting book sold hardly any copies. Undeterred, she continued to publish articles in popular magazines, and her second book, *The Sea Around Us*, won the 1952 National Book Award. But it was *The Silent Spring*, published in 1962, that brought her lasting fame. Even before the book was released, chemical companies were threatening lawsuits and conducting a public relations campaign that portrayed her as unstable and lacking in scientific expertise. Even the Department of Agriculture came out against her, labeling as false the book's charge that the insecticide DDT was a carcinogen and was destroying natural diversity. *The Silent Spring* was a huge best-seller, however, and led to invitations for Carson to testify before Congress. Her book and her widely publicized congressional testimony contributed to passage of the first federal safe air and water legislation. At the height of her fame, Carson was fatally stricken with breast cancer. In 1981, she was posthumously awarded the Presidential Medal of Freedom, the nation's highest civilian award.

The federal government's environmental efforts include programs designed to conserve nature through the protection of forests and other natural assets. Shown here is a scene from Yellowstone National Park.

However, the nation's parks and forests are subject to a "dual use" policy. They are nature preserves and recreation areas, but they are also rich in natural resources—minerals, trees, and grazing lands. The federal government sells permits to ranchers, timber companies, and mining firms that give them the right to take some of these resources, a policy that can place their interests in conflict with those of conservationists. A case in point is Alaska's Arctic National Wildlife Refuge. The refuge is home to numerous species, including caribou and moose, but it also contains oil and natural gas. Oil companies have long wanted to drill in this wilderness area, while environmental groups have sought to prohibit drilling. Over the past few decades, the Arctic National Wildlife Refuge has periodically been the focus of intense political debate and lobbying. President Clinton threatened to veto any bill that would open the area to drilling. President Bush, in contrast, proposed to open the area to drilling as part of his program to increase the nation's energy supplies.

As the debate over Alaska's Arctic National Wildlife Refuge reveals, conservation is more than an issue of protecting nature's unspoiled beauty. Also involved is the protection of species that need their natural habitat to survive. Some species, such as the deer and the raccoon, adapt easily to human encroachment. Other species are threatened by it. These species are covered by the Endangered Species Act (ESA) of 1973; it directs federal agencies to protect threatened and endangered species and authorizes programs that will preserve natural habitats. Hundreds of mammals, birds, fishes, insects, and plants are currently on ESA's protection list.

Disputes have arisen between ESA administrators and those individuals and firms that depend on natural resources for their jobs and profits. The northern spotted owl, which inhabits the forests of Oregon and Washington, was at the center of one of these controversies. The spotted owl nests in old-growth trees that are prized by the logging industry. Federal administrators, citing the ESA, banned logging in the owl's habitat. The ensuing legal battle ended with a compromise in which logging was permitted in some old-growth timber areas and prohibited in others. Although this outcome left neither side fully satisfied, it is typical of how most such disputes are settled. More recently, federal officials

Get Involved!

Do Your Part

The environment is a policy area where individual citizens can make a difference by reducing the natural resources they use and the pollution they cause. In the United States, the largest polluter is the personal automobile. Car owners are understandably unwilling to sell their vehicles and rely entirely on public transporation. However, some simple steps can reduce the environmental impact of owning a car. By accelerating and driving more slowly, you will burn significantly less fuel, reducing the stress on your pocketbook as well as on the environment. Choosing a fuel-efficient car, keeping your car properly tuned, walking rather than driving short distances to stores, and living closer to work or school are other ways to cut gas consumption.

At home, the simplest steps are to turn off lights as you leave the room and to set the thermostat lower during cold periods and higher during hot periods. Smaller but meaningful savings can be achieved through simple things such as using low-flow shower heads and replacing incandescent

bulbs with fluorescent lights, which require less energy and last longer.

Even a change in eating habits will make a difference. Frozen convenience foods are wasteful of energy. They are cooked, frozen, and then cooked again—not to mention the resources used up in packaging. Fresh foods are more nutritious and less wasteful. And if you prefer bottled water to tap water, consider using a water filter system instead. Nearly all of the cost of bottled water is due to the plastic container, which is a non-biodegradable petroleum product.

The recycling of paper, plastics, and bottles also conserves natural resources. However, the recycling process itself requires the use of energy. By cutting back on your use of recyclables and by recycling those you do use, you will contribute twice over to a better environment.

You can find additional environmentally friendly tips on the Internet. Most of them have the added benefit of saving you money because you'll be using fewer natural resources in your daily life.

have emphasized cooperative relationships with private parties. They are eligible for grants if they act to protect threatened and endangered species. In 2006, for example, a Wyoming association was given a $120,000 grant to dredge a creek that a rare species of trout travels to get to its traditional spawning area.

Environmentalism: The Newer Wave

The pivotal decade in the federal government's realization that Americans needed protection from the harmful effects of air, water, and ground pollutants was the 1960s. The period was capped by the first Earth Day. Held in the spring of 1970, it was the brainchild of Senator Gaylord Nelson (D-Wis.), who had devoted nearly ten years to finding ways to increase public interest in environmental issues. With Earth Day, Nelson succeeded to a degree not even he could have imagined: ten thousand grade schools and high schools, two thousand colleges, and one thousand communities participated in the event, which included public rallies and environmental cleanup efforts. Earth Day has been held every year since 1970 and is now a worldwide event.

Environmental Protection

The year 1970 also marked the creation of the Environmental Protection Agency. Within a few months, the EPA was issuing new regulations at such a rapid pace that business firms had difficulty keeping track of all the mandates, much less complying fully with them. Corporations eventually found an ally in President

Demonstrators outside the U.S. Capitol in Washington urge Congress to keep the Arctic National Wildlife Refuge off-limits to oil drilling. The dispute over the wildlife refuge reflects the intense conflict that can ensue when environmental interests clash with energy concerns.

Gerald Ford, who in a 1975 speech claimed that business regulation was costing $150 billion annually, or $2,000 for every American family.[16] Although Ford's estimate exceeded that of economic analysts, his point was not lost on policymakers or the public. The economy was in a slump, and the costs of complying with the new regulations were slowing an economic recovery. Polls indicated a decline in public support for regulatory action.

Since then, environmental protection policy has not greatly expanded, but neither has it greatly contracted. The emphasis has been on administering and amending the laws put into effect in the 1960s and 1970s. Nevertheless, the EPA has a broad mandate to protect America's air and water. In a 2001 decision, for example, the Supreme Court ruled unanimously that the EPA is to consider only public health and not industry costs in setting air quality standards.[17]

Environmental regulation has led to dramatic improvements in air and water quality. Pollution levels today are far below their levels of the 1960s, when yellowish-gray fog ("smog") hung over cities like Los Angeles and New York and when bodies of water like the Potomac River and Lake Erie were open sewers. In the past four decades, toxic waste emissions have been cut by half, hundreds of polluted lakes and rivers have been revitalized, energy efficiency has increased, food supplies have been made safer, and urban air pollution has decreased by more than 60 percent.[18]

Progress has been slower in cleaning up badly contaminated toxic-waste sites. These sites can contaminate area water supplies and become a health hazard. Abnormally high cancer rates have been found in the vicinity of some of these sites. In the 1980s, Congress established the so-called Superfund program to rid these sites of their contaminants. However, the cleanup process has been slow and contentious. Firms that caused the pollution are liable for some of the cleanup costs, but many of these firms are no longer in business, have since been purchased by other companies, or lack the money. Firms that could pay have often chosen instead to fight the issue in court, further delaying the cleanup. To date, only about half of the sites targeted by the Superfund program as posing serious hazards have been cleaned up.

Debating the Issues

Should the United States Have Supported the Kyoto Agreement?

At a conference in Kyoto, Japan, representatives of the United States and other nations came together to address the problem of climate change as a result of the emission of greenhouse gases. The resulting accord, called the Kyoto Agreement, established targets that countries would meet to help reduce the carbon emissions contributing to global warming. In 2002, President George W. Bush announced that the United States would not sign the agreement, citing objections to it from U.S. firms and a majority in Congress. His decision provoked criticism from European countries, environmental groups, and some members of Congress, including Senator John McCain. Bush's rejection effectively doomed the Kyoto Agreement. The United States is the largest single producer of greenhouse emissions, and any comprehensive global agreement would virtually require its participation.

Yes
Given the fact that the United States produces approximately 25 percent of the total greenhouse gases emissions, the United States has a responsibility to cut its emissions of greenhouse gases. The United States must realize that when it comes to the climate, there are no boundaries. Therefore, climate change is a global problem and must be resolved globally. The current situation demands leadership from the United States. . . . There is going to be a world marketplace for carbon reductions, a marketplace that rewards improvements in energy efficiency, advances in energy technologies, and improvements in land-use practices—and we are running the risk that America is not going to be part of it. The risks that climate change poses for businesses have now increased. . . . While U.S. businesses are gaining experience with voluntary programs and are recognized as the world's experts in this area, they are increasingly recognizing that purely voluntary approaches will not be enough to meet the goal of preventing dangerous effects on the climate system. . . . As usual, industry is ahead of government in this area. . . . Deploying the power of a marketplace to pursue the least expensive answers is a unique and powerful American approach to the threat of climate change.

—*John McCain, U.S. senator (R-Ariz.)*

No
We do not know how much effect natural fluctuations in climate may have had on warming. We do not know how much our climate could, or will, change in the future. We do not know how fast change will occur, or even how some of our actions could impact it. Our country, the United States, is the world's largest emitter of man-made greenhouse gases. We account for almost 20 percent of the world's man-made greenhouse emissions. We also account for about one-quarter of the world's economic output. We recognize the responsibility to reduce our emissions. We also recognize the other part of the story—that the rest of the world emits 80 percent of all greenhouse gases. . . . Kyoto is, in many ways, unrealistic. Many countries cannot meet their Kyoto targets. The targets themselves were arbitrary and not based upon science. For America, complying with those mandates would have a negative economic impact, with layoffs of workers and price increases for consumers. And when you evaluate all these flaws, most reasonable people will understand that it's not sound public policy. . . . Yet, America's unwillingness to embrace a flawed treaty should not be read by our friends and allies as any abdication of responsibility. To the contrary, my administration is committed to a leadership role on the issue of climate change.

—*George W. Bush, president of the United States*

Global Warming and Energy Policy

No environmental issue has received more attention recently than has global warming. The scientific community has been warning for more than a decade that carbon emissions are creating a "greenhouse effect" (the trapping of heat in the atmosphere). The result has been a rise in the earth's temperatures and in ocean levels, as a result of melting of the polar ice caps. Until recently, many politicians dismissed this evidence, saying that "more research was needed." Today, few politicians doubt the existence of global warming.

However, they disagree sharply on what should be done about it. Global warming can be retarded only by carbon-emission reductions that in some cases require costly technological innovations and would slow economic growth. So far in the United States, the pro-growth side has had the upper hand. The United States is the single largest source of worldwide carbon emissions, and U.S. policymakers have resisted demands at home and from abroad for substantial new restrictions on air pollution. In 2002, for example, President George W. Bush declared that the United States would not participate in the Kyoto agreement, a multinational effort to reduce the emission of greenhouse gases (see "Debating the Issues").

Even critics of Bush's action acknowledged that the Kyoto agreement was problematic. It imposed light burdens on some countries and heavy burdens on others, including the United States. Nevertheless, support is growing among Republican and Democratic leaders alike for a substantial response to the problem of global warming. The form of that response is as yet unclear. Virtually every possibility has large drawbacks. Wind-powered generators are increasingly used, but they do not produce enough electricity to keep up even with new demand. Nuclear power plants generate large amounts of electricity, but they are the costliest source of energy and are thought by many to be unsafe. Hydrogen fuel cells have promise but this technology is not anywhere near the point of wide commercial application.

Energy conservation through a steep hike in the tax on gasoline would be a short-term answer, but it is unlikely that America's consumers would embrace it or that officeholders would risk their political careers by voting for it. The price of gasoline is already a hot issue because of the rise in the world price of oil. Instability in the Middle East and increased demand for oil in China and India helped push oil prices in 2006 above seventy-five dollars a barrel—five times the price of a few years earlier. And as the price of oil rose, so did the price of gasoline; it topped three dollars a gallon, far more than Americans were accustomed to paying.

In addition to its impact on oil prices, worldwide economic growth is accelerating the rate at which carbon emissions are being spewed into the atmosphere, exacerbating the problem of global warming. In the years ahead, Americans will increasingly have to make trade-offs between environmental protection, energy costs, and economic growth. To a degree, they are already prepared to make them. Polls indicate that a majority of Americans would support further environmental regulation even if slower economic growth and some job loss result. However, in part because of their greater resistance to government regulation and to taxes (including the gas tax), Americans are less willing to make the trade-offs than are Canadians, the Japanese, or Western Europeans (see Figure 15–2).

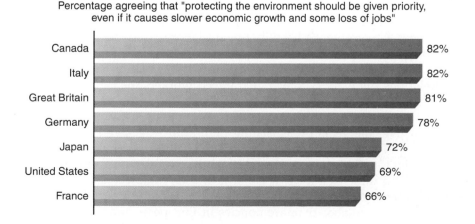

Percentage agreeing that "protecting the environment should be given priority, even if it causes slower economic growth and some loss of jobs"

Canada	82%
Italy	82%
Great Britain	81%
Germany	78%
Japan	72%
United States	69%
France	66%

Figure 15–2

Opinions on the Environment and Economic Growth Majorities in industrialized democracies support environmental protection, even if it means somewhat slower economic growth. However, Americans are somewhat less likely than citizens elsewhere to accept this trade-off.
Source: The Pew Research Center for the People and the Press, Global Attitudes Survey, 2002.

GOVERNMENT AS PROMOTER OF ECONOMIC INTERESTS

The U.S. government has always made important contributions to the nation's economy. Congress in 1789 gave a boost to the nation's shipping industry by placing a tariff on imported goods carried by foreign ships. Since that first favor, the U.S. government has provided thousands of direct benefits to economic interests. The following sections provide brief examples of a few of these benefits.

Promoting Business

American business is not opposed to government regulation as such. Corporations object only to regulatory policies that hurt their interests. At various times and in different ways, as in the case of the FCC and broadcasters, some regulatory agencies have promoted the interests of the very industries they are supposed to regulate in the public interest.

Providing loans and tax breaks is another way that government promotes business. Firms receive loan guarantees, direct loans, tax credits for capital investments, and tax deductions for capital depreciation. Over the past forty years, the burden of federal taxation has shifted dramatically from corporations to individuals. A few decades ago, the revenues raised from taxes on corporate income were roughly the same as the revenues raised from taxes on individual income. Today, individual taxpayers carry the heavier burden by a five-to-one ratio. Some analysts do not regard the change as particularly significant, arguing that higher corporate taxes would be passed along to the public anyway in the form of higher prices for goods and services.

The most significant contribution that government makes to business is the traditional services it provides, such as education, transportation, and defense. Colleges and universities, which are funded primarily by governments, furnish business with most of its professional and technical work force and with much of the basic research that goes into product development. The nation's roadways, waterways, and airports are other public-sector contributions without which business could not operate. In short, America's business has no bigger booster than government.

Promoting Labor

Laissez-faire thinking dominated government's approach to labor well into the twentieth century. The governing principle, developed by the courts a century earlier, held that workers had limited rights of collective action. Union activity was regarded as interference with the natural supply of labor and the free setting of wages. Government's hostility toward labor was evident, for example, in the use of police and soldiers during the late 1800s to break up strikes.

The 1930s brought major changes. The key legislation was the National Labor Relations Act of 1935, which guaranteed workers the right to bargain collectively and prohibited business from discriminating against union employees and from unreasonably interfering with union activities. Government has also aided labor over the years by legislating minimum wages and maximum work hours, unemployment benefits, safer and more healthful working conditions, and nondiscriminatory hiring practices. Although government support for labor extends beyond these examples, it is not nearly as extensive as its assistance to business. America's culture of individualism has resulted in public policies that are less favorable to labor than are policies in European countries.

Promoting Agriculture

Until well into the twentieth century, most Americans still lived on farms and in small rural communities. Agriculture was America's dominant business and was assisted by the government's land policies. The Homestead Act of 1862, for example, opened government-owned lands to settlement, creating spectacular "land rushes" by offering 160 acres of government land free to each family that staked a claim, built a house, and farmed the land for five years.

Farm programs today provide assistance to both small farmers and large commercial enterprises (agribusinesses) and cost the federal government billions of dollars annually. A major goal of this spending is to eliminate some of the risks associated with farming. Weather, world markets, and other factors can radically affect crop and livestock prices, and federal programs are designed to protect farmers from adverse developments.

Experience has shown that the agricultural sector benefits from government intervention. In 1996, Congress passed legislation that trimmed long-standing crop subsidy and crop allocation programs. The goal was to let the free market largely determine the prices farmers would get for their crops and to let farmers themselves decide on the crops they would plant. The result was a depressed farm economy—prices fell sharply because of the surplus production of particular crops. In 2002, Congress abandoned the free-market approach. Crop subsidies were increased and expanded to include more crops, and quotas were established for the planting of particular crops. The 2002 Farm Bill put farmers in line for hundreds of billions of dollars in government assistance in future years. At present, federal subsidies account for more than a third of net farm income.

FISCAL POLICY: GOVERNMENT AS MANAGER OF THE ECONOMY, I

Until the 1930s, the U.S. government adhered to the prevailing free-market theory and made no attempt to regulate the economy as a whole. The economy, which was regarded as largely self-regulating, was fairly prosperous, but it collapsed periodically, resulting in widespread unemployment.

The greatest economic collapse in the nation's history—the Great Depression of the 1930s—finally brought an end to traditional economics. Franklin D. Roosevelt's government spending and job programs, designed to stimulate the economy and put Americans back to work, heralded the change. Although Roosevelt's use of government policy as an economic stimulus was highly controversial, today it is accepted practice. Government is expected to pursue policies that will foster economic growth and stability.

Taxing and Spending Policy

The government's efforts to maintain a thriving economy are made mainly through its taxing and spending decisions, which together are referred to as its **fiscal policy** (see Table 15–2).

The annual federal budget is the basis of fiscal policy. Thousands of pages in length, the budget allocates federal expenditures among government programs and identifies the revenues—taxes, social insurance receipts, and borrowed funds—that will be used to pay for these programs (see Figure 15–3). From one perspective, the budget is the national government's allocation of costs and benefits. Every federal program benefits some interest, whether it be farmers who get price supports, defense firms that obtain military contracts, or

fiscal policy
A tool of economic management by which government attempts to maintain a stable economy through its taxing and spending policies.

TABLE 15–2	Fiscal Policy: A Summary Taxing and spending levels can be adjusted in order to affect economic conditions.	
PROBLEM		**FISCAL POLICY ACTIONS**
Low productivity and high unemployment		Demand side: increase spending
		Supply side: cut business taxes
Excess production and high inflation		Decrease spending
		Increase taxes

deficit spending

When the government spends more than it collects in taxes and other revenues.

economic depression

A very severe and sustained economic downturn. Depressions are rare in the United States; the last one was in the 1930s.

economic recession

A moderate but sustained downturn in the economy. Recessions are part of the economy's normal cycle of ups and downs.

demand-side economics

A form of fiscal policy that emphasizes "demand" (consumer spending). Government can use increased spending or tax cuts to place more money in consumers' hands and thereby increase demand.

retirees who receive monthly social security checks. From another standpoint, that of fiscal policy, the budget is a device for stimulating or dampening economic growth. Through changes in overall levels of spending and taxing, government can help keep the economy running smoothly.

Fiscal policy has origins in the economic theories of John Maynard Keynes. In *The General Theory of Employment, Interest, and Money* (1936), Keynes noted that employers naturally become cautious during a depression and cut back on production and the number of workers. Challenging the traditional idea that government should also cut back during depressions, Keynes claimed that severe economic downturns can be shortened only by increased government spending. Keynes said that government should engage in **deficit spending**—spending more than it gets from taxes, which can be accomplished through the borrowing and printing of money. By placing additional money in the hands of consumers, government can stimulate spending, which in turn will stimulate production and create jobs, thereby promoting an economic recovery.[19]

According to Keynesian theory, the level of the government's response should be commensurate with the severity of the problem. During an **economic depression**—an exceptionally steep and sustained downturn in the economy— the government should engage in massive new spending programs to hasten the recovery. During an **economic recession,** which is a less severe downturn, government spending should also be increased but by a smaller amount.

Demand-Side Stimulation

Keynes's theory focused on government's efforts to stimulate consumer spending. This **demand-side economics** emphasizes the consumer "demand" component of the supply-demand equation. When the economy is sluggish, the

Figure 15–3

The Federal Budget Dollar, Fiscal Year 2007
Source: Office of Management and Budget.

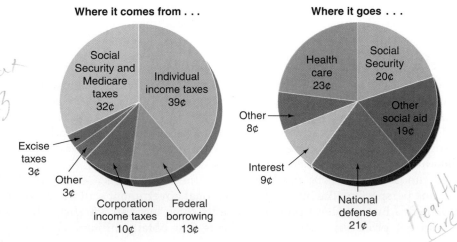

Where it comes from . . .

Social Security and Medicare taxes 32¢

Individual income taxes 39¢

Excise taxes 3¢

Other 3¢

Corporation income taxes 10¢

Federal borrowing 13¢

Where it goes . . .

Health care 23¢

Social Security 20¢

Other social aid 19¢

Other 8¢

Interest 9¢

National defense 21¢

government can increase its spending, thus placing more money in consumers' hands. With additional money to spend, consumers buy more goods and services. This increased demand, in turn, stimulates businesses to produce more goods and hire more workers. In this way, government spending contributes to economic recovery.

Although increased spending is a tool that government can employ during a severe economic crisis, it is not a sensible response to every economic dip. Its application is affected by government's overall financial situation. In the early 1990s, for example, the U.S. economy was in its longest downturn since World War II, but policymakers chose not to boost federal spending temporarily as a means of blunting the recession. The reason was simple enough. During the previous two decades, there had been a **budget deficit**—each year, the federal government had spent more than it had received in tax and other revenues. The result was a huge **national debt,** which is the total cumulative amount that the U.S. government owes to creditors. By the early 1990s, the national debt had reached $4 trillion, and an enormous sum of money was required each year just to pay the interest on it. Interest payments were roughly the total of all federal income taxes paid by Americans living west of the Mississippi River. This ongoing drain on the government's resources made it politically difficult for policymakers to increase government spending in order to stimulate the economy.

The situation changed dramatically in the late 1990s. In 1998, for the first time since 1969, the U.S. government had a **balanced budget**—revenues were equal to government expenditures. Thereafter, there was a **budget surplus**—the federal government received more in tax and other revenues than it spent. The surplus was attributable to a surging U.S. economy that was in the midst of its longest period of sustained growth in the country's history. With more people working and with the stock market climbing, tax revenues had increased and government welfare expenditures had declined. The rosy budget picture also reflected the fiscal discipline of the Clinton administration and the Republican Congress, which had slowed the growth in federal spending.

The turnaround was short-lived. A slowdown in the economy, steep tax cuts, and a sharp increase in defense spending contributed by 2002 to a budget shortfall. Deficits are now projected to persist for years to come (see Figure 15–4). The severity of the deficit is a constraint on policymakers' ability to apply demand-side measures as a means of boosting the economy. Even though a large tax cut or a major spending increase would contribute to economic growth, it would also increase the deficit.

The impact of demand-side fiscal policy, however, cannot be measured only by its effect during economic downturns. Although the United States has had

budget deficit
The situation when the government's expenditures exceed its tax and other revenues.

national debt
The total cumulative amount that the U.S. government owes to creditors.

balanced budget
Situation when the government's tax and other revenues for the year are roughly equal to its expenditures.

budget surplus
Situation when the government's tax and other revenues exceed its expenditures.

Annual federal budget deficit/surplus
(in billions of dollars)

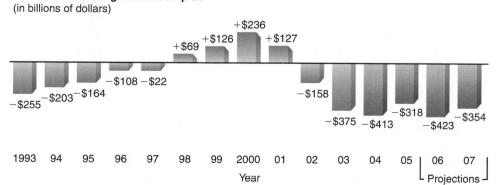

Figure 15–4

The Federal Budget Deficit/Surplus
The federal government ran a budget deficit until 1998, at which time a surplus that was expected to last for years emerged. In 2001, however, the surplus quickly disappeared as a result of an economic downturn, costs associated with the war on terrorism, and a cut in federal taxes.
Source: Office of Management and Budget, 2006.

recessionary periods since the 1930s, none of these downturns has come anywhere near the severity of the Great Depression. One reason is that government spending is now at permanently high levels. Each month, for example, roughly forty million Americans receive a social security check from the government. In turn, they spend it on food, clothing, housing, entertainment, and other goods and services. They pump billions of dollars each month into the U.S. economy, which creates jobs and income for millions of other Americans. And social security is only one—albeit the largest—of numerous federal spending programs. Every day, the federal government spends about $4 billion, more than the typical large corporation pumps into the economy during an entire year. The U.S. economy thus has a constant demand-side stimulus: government spending on an ongoing and massive scale.

Supply-Side Stimulation   *trickle down*

supply-side economics
A form of fiscal policy that emphasizes "supply" (production). An example of supply-side economics is a tax cut for business.

A fiscal policy alternative to demand-side stimulation is **supply-side economics,** which emphasizes the business (supply) component of the supply-demand equation. Supply-side theory was a cornerstone of President Reagan's economic program. He believed that economic growth could occur as easily from stimulation of the business sector as from stimulation of consumer demand. "Reaganomics" included substantial tax breaks for businesses and upper-income individuals.[20]

The Reagan administration overestimated the stimulus effect of its tax-cuts policy. It had estimated that the increased tax revenues from increased business activity would soon offset the loss of revenue from reduced tax rates. However, the loss in tax revenues was much greater than the gain in revenues from the economic growth that followed. As a result, the tax cuts contributed to a growing budget deficit. Despite this discouraging result, Reagan's supply-side measures contributed to the economic growth in the United States during the 1990s. The Reagan tax cuts allowed business firms to spend more on capital investments and enabled higher-income Americans to place more money into the stock markets, providing additional funds for business investment.

Supply-side theory was also the basis of President George W. Bush's economic program. Although his Economic Growth and Tax Reconciliation Act of 2001 included a demand-side component (an immediate cash rebate to taxpayers), supply-side measures were its signature: sharp cuts in the tax rate on individuals, with most of the gains going to high-income taxpayers, and a reduction in the **capital-gains tax,** the tax that individuals pay on gains in capital investments such as property and stocks. A reduction in the capital-gains tax increases the incentive for individuals to invest their money in capital markets. In turn, firms use this money to expand their operations and markets. The subsequent job creation and increased supply of goods can stimulate consumer demand and contribute to economic growth.

capital-gains tax
The tax that individuals pay on money gained from the sale of a capital asset, such as property or stocks.

When Bush's tax bill was enacted in 2001, he had agreed—in order to get the congressional support necessary for its passage—to a phase-in of the individual and capital-gains tax cuts. In 2003, he went back to Congress and asked for a speeded-up timetable as a means of boosting the economy. Bush got what he requested. The capital-gains tax rate, which had been 28 percent in 2001, fell to 15 percent, as did the tax rate for dividend income. Meanwhile, the highest marginal rate assessed on individual income fell to 35 percent, down from 39 percent in 2001. The larger share of the tax savings resulting from Bush's policies went to high-income taxpayers—precisely those people who, according to supply-side economics, are the key to economic growth.

However, as indicated previously, the Bush tax cuts, combined with large increases in defense spending, drove the U.S. budget deficit to record highs, threatening to cancel any long-term contribution the tax cuts might make to economic growth.[21] During congressional testimony in 2005, outgoing Federal Reserve chairman Alan Greenspan warned that the budget deficits were "unsustainable" and posed a severe threat to the continued health of the U.S. economy. The Fed chairman said he would prefer to see the deficit reduced through spending cuts rather than increased taxes, but he argued that both should occur. Deficit reduction, said Greenspan, must be "the overriding principle." (Bush's tax cuts are discussed further in Chapter 16.)

Controlling Inflation

High unemployment and low productivity are only two of the economic problems that government is called on to solve. Another is **inflation,** an increase in the average level of prices of goods and services. Before the late 1960s, inflation was a minor problem: prices rose by less than 4 percent annually. But inflation rose sharply during the last years of the Vietnam War and remained high throughout the 1970s, reaching a postwar record rate of 13 percent in 1979 (see Figure 15–5). Since then, the annual inflation rate has averaged about 4 percent, and concern about inflation has lessened significantly.

To fight inflation, government can apply remedies exactly the opposite of those used to fight unemployment and low productivity. Inflation normally occurs when jobs are plentiful and people have extra money to spend. Demand is high in such periods, and prices go up. By cutting spending or raising personal income taxes, government takes money from consumers, thus reducing demand and dampening prices. (The main policy tool for addressing inflation is monetary policy, which is discussed later in the chapter.)

inflation
A general increase in the average level of prices of goods and services.

The Process and Politics of Fiscal Policy → taxing and spending policies

The president and Congress jointly determine fiscal policy, mainly through the annual budgetary process. The Constitution grants Congress the power to tax and spend, but the president, as chief executive, plays a major role in shaping the budget (see Chapter 12). In reality, the budgetary process involves give-and-take between Congress and the president as each tries to exert influence over the final budget.[22]

Inflation rate since 1979 (Consumer Price Index)

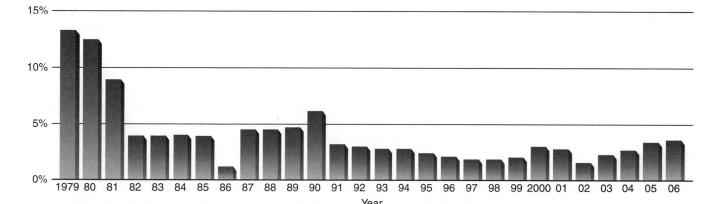

Figure 15–5

The Annual Rate of Inflation, 1979–2006
Price increases have declined in the last decade compared to the late 1970s.
Source: U.S. Department of Labor, 2006.

Figure 15–6

Federal Budgetary Process
The budget begins with the president's instructions to the agencies and ends when Congress enacts the budget. The entire process spans about eighteen months.

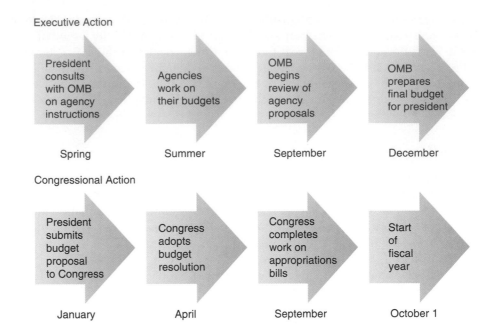

Executive Action

President consults with OMB on agency instructions	Agencies work on their budgets	OMB begins review of agency proposals	OMB prepares final budget for president
Spring	Summer	September	December

Congressional Action

President submits budget proposal to Congress	Congress adopts budget resolution	Congress completes work on appropriations bills	Start of fiscal year
January	April	September	October 1

The Budgetary Process

The budgetary process is an elaborate one, as could be expected when billions of dollars in federal spending are at issue. From beginning to end, the process lasts a year and a half (see Figure 15–6). The process begins in the executive branch when the president, in consultation with the Office of Management and Budget (OMB), establishes general budget guidelines. The OMB is part of the Executive Office of the President (see Chapter 12) and takes its directives from the president. Hundreds of agencies and thousands of programs are covered by the budget, and the OMB uses the president's directives to issue the instructions that will guide each agency's budget preparations. For example, each agency is assigned a budget ceiling within which it must work.

The agencies receive these instructions in the spring and then work through the summer to develop a detailed agency budget, taking into account their existing programs and any new proposals. These agency budgets then go to the OMB in September for a full review that invariably includes further consultation with each agency. The agency budgets are then finalized and combined into the full budget. Throughout, the OMB stays in touch with the White House to ensure that the budget items conform to the president's objectives.

The agencies naturally tend to want more money, whereas the OMB has the job of matching the budget to the president's priorities. In fact, however, the president does not have any real say over most of the budget, about two-thirds of which involves mandatory spending. This spending is authorized by current law, and the government must allocate and spend the money unless the law itself is rescinded, an unlikely occurrence. Examples are social security and Medicare, which provide benefits to the elderly. The president does not have the authority to suspend or reduce these programs. Interest on the national debt is also part of the budget, and here too the president has no real option. The federal government is obligated to pay interest on the money it has borrowed.

The OMB focuses on the one-third of the budget that involves discretionary spending, which includes areas such as defense, foreign aid, education, national parks, space exploration, public broadcasting, and highways. In reality, even a large part of this spending is not truly discretionary. No president would even consider slashing defense spending to almost nothing or closing the national parks, and even modest cuts in a discretionary program may encounter resistance in Congress.

The president, then, works on the margins of the budget, trying to push it in directions that are consistent with administration goals. The effort in many policy areas consists of a modest increase or decrease in spending compared with the previous year. There are always a few areas, however, where the president will attempt a more dramatic adjustment. In each of his budgets, for example, President Bush asked for large increases in defense spending to assist in the war on terrorism and to pay for the Iraq war and reconstruction.

In January, the president transmits the full budget to Congress. This budget is just a proposal, because Congress alone has the constitutional power to appropriate funds. In reviewing the president's proposed budget, Congress relies heavily on the Congressional Budget Office (CBO), which, as discussed in Chapter 11, is the congressional equivalent of the OMB. If the CBO believes that an agency has misjudged the amount of money needed to meet its legislatively required programs, it will bring this information to the attention of the appropriate committees of Congress. Similarly, if the CBO concludes that the OMB has miscalculated how much the government can be expected to receive in taxes and other revenues, committees will be notified of the discrepancy.

The key congressional committees in the budgetary process are the budget committees and the appropriations committees. The House and Senate Budget Committees are responsible for drafting a "budget resolution," which includes guidelines on total spending, total revenues, and allocations between the mandatory and discretionary spending categories. These guidelines then go to the full House and Senate for approval. The budget ceilings that are part of the resolution place a tentative limit on how much money will be allocated for each spending area.

The House Appropriations Committee through its subcommittees then takes on the primary task of reviewing the budget items, a review that includes hearings with each federal agency. There are ten such subcommittees, each of which has responsibility for a substantive area, such as defense or agriculture. Agency budgets invariably are changed at this stage. A subcommittee may cut an agency's budget because it believes that the agency's work is not a priority or that the agency has asked for more funds than it needs. Or the subcommittee may decide to increase an agency's budget beyond what the president has requested. The subcommittees' recommendations are then submitted to the House Appropriations Committee for final review and submission to the full House for a vote. The Senate Appropriations Committee and its subcommittees conduct a similar review, but the Senate is a smaller body and its review of agency requests is normally less thorough. To some degree, the Senate committee and its subcommittees serve as a "court of appeals" for agencies that have had their budget requests reduced by the House.

During Congress's work on the budget, the president's recommendations undergo varying degrees of change. The priorities of a majority in Congress are never exactly those of the president, even when they are members of the same party. When they are members of opposite parties, their priorities may differ greatly.

After the work of the appropriations committees has been completed and is approved by the full House and Senate, differences in the Senate and House versions of the appropriations bill are reconciled in conference committee (see Chapter 11). The legislation is then sent to the president for approval or veto. The threat of a presidential veto often is enough to persuade Congress to accept many of the president's recommendations. In the end, the budget inevitably reflects both presidential and congressional priorities. Neither branch ever gets everything it wants, but each branch always gets some of what it wants.

Once the budget has been passed by both the House and the Senate and is signed by the president, it takes effect on October 1, the starting date of the

States in the Nation

Federal Taxing and Spending: Winners and Losers

Fiscal policy (the federal government's taxing and spending policies) varies in its effect on the states. The residents of some states pay a lot more in federal taxes than they receive in benefits. The biggest loser is New Jersey, whose taxpayers get back in federal spending in their state only $0.62 for every dollar they pay in federal taxes. Connecticut taxpayers ($0.65 for every dollar) are the next-biggest losers. In contrast, the residents of some states get back more from federal spending programs than they contribute in taxes. The biggest winners are New Mexico and North Dakota, whose taxpayers get back $2.37 and $2.07, respectively, in federal spending in their states for every dollar they pay in federal taxes.

Q: Why are most of the "losers" in the northeastern section of the country?

A: The federal taxes that originate in a state reflect its wealth, and the northeastern states are generally the wealthier ones. Because they are wealthier, they also get less federal assistance for programs designed to help lower-income people and areas. Finally, most federal lands and military installations—sources of federal money—lie outside the northeastern region.

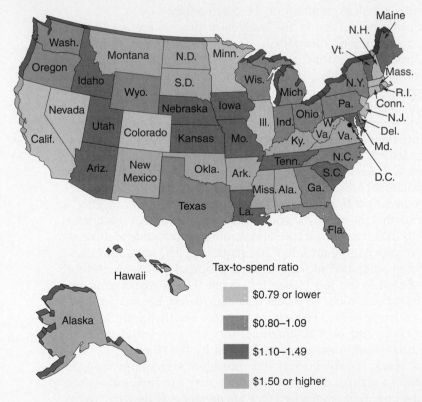

Tax-to-spend ratio

- $0.79 or lower
- $0.80–1.09
- $1.10–1.49
- $1.50 or higher

Source: From Thomas Patterson, *We the People*, 5th ed. Copyright © 2006. The McGraw-Hill Companies. Reprinted by permission of The McGraw-Hill Companies.

federal government's fiscal year. If agreement on the budget has not been reached by October 1, temporary funding is required in order to maintain government operations. In late 1995, President Clinton and the Republican Congress deadlocked on budgetary issues to such an extent that they could not even agree on temporary funding. Their standoff twice forced a brief shutdown of nonessential government activities.

Partisan Differences

Partisan politics is a component of fiscal policy. The Democratic coalition has traditionally included the majority of lower-income and working-class Americans. Accordingly, the party's leaders are sensitive to rising unemployment because blue-collar workers are often the first and most deeply affected. Democrats in Washington have usually responded to a sluggish economy with increased government spending (demand-side fiscal policy), which offers direct help to the unemployed and stimulates consumption. Virtually every increase in federal unemployment benefits during the past fifty years, for example, has been initiated by Democratic officeholders.

Republican leaders are more likely to see an economic downturn through the eyes of business firms. Republicans in Washington typically have sought ways to stimulate business activity as a means of economic recovery. Thus, in most cases, Republicans have resisted large increases in government spending (with the exception of defense spending) as a response to a sluggish economy. Such spending requires government to borrow money, which leads to upward pressure on interest rates. This pressure in turn raises business costs, because firms must pay higher interest rates for the money they borrow.

Tax policy also has partisan dimensions. Democratic policymakers have typically sought tax policies that help working-class and lower-middle-class Americans. Democrats have favored a **graduated** (or progressive) **personal income tax,** in which the tax rate goes up substantially as income rises. Republicans have preferred to keep taxes on upper incomes at a relatively low level, contending that this policy encourages the savings and investment that foster economic growth (supply-side fiscal policy). These differences were evident, for example, in the battle over the Economic Growth and Tax Relief Reconciliation Act of 2001. Proposed by President Bush, the legislation contained the largest tax cut since 1981. The chief beneficiaries were upper-income taxpayers. In both the Senate and the House of Representatives, the bill had the overwhelming support of Republicans and very little support from Democrats. In the Senate, for example, about 90 percent of Republicans voted for it, whereas about 80 percent of Democrats voted against it.[20] (Tax policy is discussed further in Chapter 16.)

graduated personal income tax

A tax on personal income in which the tax rate increases as income increases; in other words, the tax rate is higher for higher income levels.

MONETARY POLICY: GOVERNMENT AS MANAGER OF THE ECONOMY, II

Fiscal policy is not the only instrument of economic management available to government; another is **monetary policy,** which is based on manipulation of the amount of money in circulation (see Table 15–3). Monetarists such as

monetary policy

A tool of economic management, available to government, based on manipulation of the amount of money in circulation.

TABLE 15–3	**Monetary Policy: A Summary of the Fed's Role** The money supply can be adjusted in order to affect economic conditions.	
PROBLEM	**MONETARY POLICY ACTIONS BY FEDERAL RESERVE**	
Low productivity and high unemployment (require an increase in the money supply)	Decrease interest rate on loans to member banks	
	Decrease cash reserve that member banks must deposit in Federal Reserve System	
Excess productivity and high inflation (require a decrease in the money supply)	Increase interest rate on loans to member banks	
	Increase cash reserve that member banks must deposit in Federal Reserve System	

LEADERS

ALAN GREENSPAN

(1926–   )

During the nearly nineteen years that he headed the Federal Reserve, Alan Greenspan was at times called "the most powerful man in America" because of his influence on markets through the Fed's interest-rate policies. Some of his projections proved faulty, but others were astute. As stock prices rose ever higher in the late 1990s, Greenspan warned against what he called "irrational exuberance"—investing based on a belief that the stock markets would continue to go higher. As Greenspan predicted, the markets turned sharply downward, at great cost to many investors. Shortly before leaving office in early 2006, Greenspan issued another warning, saying that U.S. budget deficits were "unsustainable" and posed a serious threat to the future health of the U.S. economy.

economist Milton Friedman hold that control of the money supply is the key to sustaining a healthy economy. Friedman was not convinced that government spending of the type advocated by Keynes was all that helpful and argued instead for a marketplace mechanism, letting the money supply drive demand and production decisions. Too much money in circulation contributes to inflation because too many dollars are chasing too few goods, which drives up prices. Too little money in circulation results in a slowing economy and rising unemployment, because consumers lack the ready cash and easy credit required to push up spending levels. Monetarists believe in increasing the money supply as a way of boosting the economy and decreasing the supply to slow it down.

The Fed

Control over the money supply rests not with the president or Congress but with the Federal Reserve System (known as "the Fed"). Created by the Federal Reserve Act of 1913, the Fed has a board of governors whose seven members serve for fourteen years, except for the chair and vice chair, who serve for four years. All members are appointed by the president, subject to Senate approval. The Fed regulates all national banks and those state banks that meet certain standards and choose to become members of the Federal Reserve System.

The Fed decides how much money to add to or subtract from the economy, seeking a balance that will permit steady growth without causing an unacceptable level of inflation. One way the Fed affects the money supply is by raising or lowering the cash reserve that member banks are required to deposit with the Federal Reserve. This reserve is a proportion of each member's total deposits. By increasing the reserve rate, the Fed takes money from member banks and thereby takes it out of circulation. When the Fed lowers the reserve rate, banks have more money available to loan to consumers and investors.

A second and more visible way the Fed affects the money supply is by lowering or raising the interest rate that member banks are charged when they borrow from the Federal Reserve. When the Fed raises the interest rate, banks also tend to raise the rate they charge for new loans, which discourages borrowing and thus reduces the amount of money entering the economy. Conversely, by lowering the interest rate, the Fed encourages firms and individuals to borrow from banks, which increases the money supply.

The Fed's interest-rate adjustments are often front-page news because they are a signal of the strength of the economy and thus affect the decisions of consumers and firms. As the economy accelerated in 2004, for example, the Fed began a series of adjustments that by 2006 had raised the interest rate by more than four percentage points. As the rate increased, home buying and refinancing slowed, as did other loan activity, including credit card borrowing. As

slowed, as did other loan activity, including credit card borrowing. As demand weakened, so did the threat of inflation that accompanies a period of economic growth.

Economists debate the relative effectiveness of monetary policy and fiscal policy, but monetary policy has one obvious advantage: it can be implemented more quickly than fiscal policy. The Fed can adjust interest and reserve rates on short notice, thus providing the economy with a psychological boost to go along with the financial effect of a change in the money supply. In contrast, changes in fiscal policy usually take much longer to implement. Congress is normally a slow-acting institution, and new taxing and spending programs ordinarily require a substantial preparation period before they can be put into effect. Moreover, Republicans and Democrats are often divided over which fiscal policy tool to use—taxing or spending—and may not be able to reach agreement on how to respond to a faltering economy.

The Politics of the Fed

The greater flexibility of monetary policy has positioned the Fed as the institution with primary policy responsibility for keeping the U.S. economy on a steady course. The Fed's power can easily be exaggerated. The U.S. economy is subject to a lot of influences, of which the money supply is only one. Nevertheless, the Fed is a vital component of U.S. economic policy.[24]

The power of the Fed raises important questions. One is the issue of representation: whose interests does the Fed serve, those of the public as a whole or those of the banking sector? The Fed is not a wholly impartial body. Although it makes decisions in the context of economic theories and projections, it is "the bankers' bank" and as such is protective of monied interests. The Fed typically is more concerned with rising inflation, which erodes the value of money, than with rising unemployment, which has its greatest impact on people at the bottom of the economic ladder. The Fed tends to hike interest rates when signs of rising inflation appear. Higher rates have the effect of slowing inflation, but they also slow job and income growth.

A related issue is one of accountability: should the Fed, an unelected body, have so much power? Though appointed by the president, members of the Federal Reserve Board are not subject to removal. They serve for fixed terms and are relatively insulated from political pressures, including the changes that take place through elections. Of course, the Fed, as a banking institution, has a vested interest in a healthy economy (too much inflation erodes banks' returns on loans; too much unemployment decreases demand for loans) and thus operates within its own system of checks and balances. Nevertheless, the restraints on the Fed are much weaker than those on popularly elected institutions. The Fed is a preeminent example of *elitist* politics at work.

At the time the Fed was created in 1913, economists had not yet "invented" the theory of monetary policy, and the Fed had no role in the management of the nation's economy. If the Fed were being created today, it would likely have a different structure, although there is general agreement among policymakers that some degree of independence is desirable. Congress at some future point may decide that an overly independent Fed can no longer be tolerated and may bring monetary policy more closely under the control of elected institutions. Whether this happens will likely hinge on the Fed's willingness to exercise power sparingly and in the broad interests of society.

Regardless, the Fed is part of the new way of thinking about the federal government and the economy that emerged during the Great Depression of the

1930s. Until then, the federal government's economic role was largely confined to the provision of a limited number of public services, such as the postal service and the currency. Roosevelt's New Deal permanently changed policymakers' thinking. Through economic management and regulatory activities, the government would have an ongoing influence on the economy, contributing to its stability and efficiency.

The results nearly speak for themselves. In the roughly three-quarters of a century that the U.S. government has played a significant policy role, the American economy has prospered. The economic depressions that periodically wreaked havoc with firms and workers have disappeared. The cycle of economic ups and downs has remained but the cycle no longer consists of booms and busts, a testimony to the soundness of economic theory and of its use by policymakers. History has shown that the economy can be managed and regulated through government action, and that the nation is better off because of it.

Economic theory does not always give policymakers the answers they need. In the late 1970s, an unusual combination of circumstances created an economic condition that came to be known as "stagflation." Inflation, as was noted earlier in the chapter, was at a postwar high. Ordinarily, when inflation is high, so is economic growth. The late 1970s was a stark exception—the economy was stagnant. Economists had no theory to apply. Actions that would normally be taken to stimulate the economy would worsen the inflation problem. Actions that would normally be taken to bring down inflation would worsen the stagnation problem. Policymakers were stymied and had little choice but to let the economy work itself out, which it eventually did.

Nevertheless, economic theories have given U.S. policymakers a set of powerful tools for addressing problems such as jobs, productivity, and inflation. Most Americans appear to have little understanding of this fact. Many citizens continue to believe that the economy would work better if the government's economic role was curtailed. Moreover, most citizens are largely unaware of how federal economic policy works. A Harris poll found that, whereas Americans are relatively savvy consumers, only one in eight has a reasonable understanding of government's contribution to a sound economy. But even if they are not aware of it, Americans are indebted to the economists who devised the theories and to the federal policymakers who have had the skill to apply the theories effectively. (The economic policies of the federal government in the areas of social welfare and national security are discussed in the next two chapters.)

Summary

Self-Test www.mhhe.com/pattersontad8

Although private enterprise is the main force in the American economic system, the federal government plays a significant role through its policies to regulate, promote, and stimulate the economy.

Regulatory policy is designed to achieve efficiency and equity, which require government to intervene, for example, to maintain competitive trade practices (an efficiency goal) and to protect vulnerable parties in economic transactions (an equity goal). Many of the regulatory decisions of the federal government, particularly those of older agencies (such as the Federal Communication Commission), are made largely in the context of group politics. Business lobbies have an especially

strong influence on the regulatory policies that affect them. In general, newer regulatory agencies (such as the Environmental Protection Agency) have policy responsibilities that are broader in scope and apply to a larger number of firms than those of the older agencies. As a result, the policy decisions of newer agencies are more often made in the context of party politics. Republican administrations are less vigorous in their regulation of business than are Democratic administrations.

Business is the major beneficiary of the federal government's efforts to promote economic interests. A large number of programs, including those that provide loans and research grants, are designed to assist businesses, which are also protected from failure through measures such as tariffs and favorable tax laws. Labor, for its part, obtains government assistance through laws concerning matters such as worker safety, the minimum wage, and collective bargaining. Yet America's individualistic culture tends to put labor at a disadvantage, keeping it less powerful than business in its dealings with the government. Agriculture is another economic sector that depends substantially on government's help, particularly in the form of income stabilization programs such as those that provide crop subsidies.

The U.S. government pursues policies that are designed to protect and conserve the environment. A few decades ago, the environment was not a policy priority. Today, there are many programs in this area, and the public has become an active participant in efforts to conserve resources and prevent exploitation of the environment.

Through its fiscal and monetary policies, Washington attempts to maintain a strong and stable economy—one characterized by high productivity, high employment, and low inflation. Fiscal policy is based on government decisions in regard to spending and taxing, which are aimed at either stimulating a weak economy or dampening an overheated (inflationary) economy. Fiscal policy is worked out through Congress and the president and consequently is responsive to political pressures. However, because it is difficult to raise taxes or cut programs, the government's ability to apply fiscal policy as an economic remedy is limited. Monetary policy is based on the money supply and works through the Federal Reserve System, which is headed by a board whose members hold office for fixed terms. The Fed is a relatively independent body, a fact that has given rise to questions as to whether it should have such a large role in influencing national economic policy.

STUDY CORNER

Key Terms

balanced budget (*p. 459*)
budget deficit (*p. 459*)
budget surplus (*p. 459*)
capital-gains tax (*p. 460*)
deficit spending (*p. 458*)
demand-side economics (*p. 458*)
deregulation (*p. 446*)
economic depression (*p. 458*)

economic recession (*p. 458*)
economy (*p. 442*)
efficiency (*p. 443*)
equity (in relation to economic
    policy) (*p. 447*)
externalities (*p. 445*)
fiscal policy (*p. 457*)
graduated personal income tax (*p. 465*)

inflation (*p. 461*)
laissez-faire doctrine (*p. 442*)
monetary policy (*p. 465*)
national debt (*p. 459*)
public policy process (*p. 438*)
regulation (*p. 443*)
supply-side economics (*p. 460*)

Self-Test

1. Which of the following steps in the U.S. budget process is not in its proper sequential order?
   a. Office of Management and Budget compiles budget.
   b. Proposed budget is studied in the House and Senate Budget and Appropriations Committees.
   c. President sends budget proposal to Congress.
   d. Budget is approved by Congress and presented to the president to be signed.

2. The challenge for policymakers in devising and implementing regulatory and deregulatory policies is to:
   a. simply remove all regulations.
   b. not be concerned about economic inefficiency in protecting the public interest.
   c. favor equity at the expense of efficiency.
   d. strike a proper balance between regulatory measures and free-market mechanisms.

3. The institutions of the U.S. government involved in determining fiscal policy are:
   a. the executive and legislative branches.
   b. the Fed and the regulatory agencies.
   c. the judicial branch and the states.
   d. the legislative branch and the Fed.

4. The era of new social regulation in the 1960s and 1970s differed from that of previous eras in:
   a. narrowing the scope and range of activities regulated.
   b. concentrating on reforms of labor practices.
   c. expanding social goals to the areas of environment and consumer protection as well as worker safety.
   d. reducing the amount of lobbying by regulated firms.

5. Examples of services provided by government that aid business include:
   a. loan guarantees and direct loans to business.
   b. funding of public colleges and universities.
   c. subsidizing the building of roads, waterways, and airports.
   d. all of the above.

6. The Federal Reserve Board affects the economy by taking all **except** which one of the following actions?
   a. meeting periodically to evaluate the economy and to decide on a proper response.
   b. lowering or raising interest charged on money borrowed by banks.
   c. raising or lowering the cash reserve that member banks are required to deposit with regional Federal Reserve banks.
   d. submitting monetary strategies to Congress for a vote.

7. Early in the development of America's economy, there was hostility toward labor union activity. (T/F)

8. In times when the economy needs a quick fix, one would be better off to use fiscal policy than monetary policy because fiscal policy can be implemented within a faster time frame. (T/F)

9. Rachel Carson's *Silent Spring* encouraged the growth of the modern environmental movement. (T/F)

10. Fiscal policy has its origins in the economic theories of John Maynard Keynes. (T/F)

Critical Thinking

What are the tools of fiscal policy and monetary policy? What are the advantages and disadvantages of each of these two approaches to managing the economy?

Suggested Readings

Duncan, Richard. *The Dollar Crisis: Causes, Consequences, Cures*, rev. ed. New York: John Wiley & Sons, 2005. A look at the problem of budget and trade deficits.

Keith, Robert, and Allen Schick. *The Federal Budget Process*. Hauppauge, N.Y.: Now Science Publishers, 2003. An explanation of the federal budgetary process.

Lindbloom, Charles E. *The Market System: What It Is, How It Works, and What to Make of It*. New Haven, Conn.: Yale University Press, 2001. A clear analysis of the advantages and disadvantages of the market system.

Mayer, Martin. *FED: The Inside Story of How the World's Most Powerful Financial Institution Drives the Markets*. New York: Free Press, 2001. A look at the Fed's impact on the economy and politics.

McChesney, Robert. *The Problem of the Media*. New York: Monthly Review Press, 2004. A scathing critique of media regulation.

Rosenbaum, Walter A. *Environmental Politics and Policy*, 6th ed. Washington, D.C.: Congressional Quarterly Press, 2004. A comprehensive examination of the politics of environmental policy.

Shaiko, Ronald G. *Voices and Echoes for the Environment*. New York: Columbia University Press, 1999. The representation and communication of environmental groups.

Sheingate, Adam D. *The Rise of the Agricultural Welfare State*. Princeton, N.J.: Princeton University Press, 2003. A penetrating analysis of farm policy in the United States, France, and Japan.

List of Websites

http://www.federalreserve.gov/default.htm
The Federal Reserve System website; it describes the Fed, provides information about its current activities, and has links to some of the Fed's national and international information sources.

http://www.epa.gov/
The Environmental Protection Agency (EPA) website; it has information on environmental policy and regulations, EPA projects, and related subjects.

http://www.ftc.gov/
The website of the Federal Trade Commission, one of the older regulatory agencies; it describes the range of the FTC's activities.

http://www.whitehouse.gov/OMB
The home page of the Office of Management and Budget; it contains a summary of the annual federal budget and describes the OMB's operations and responsibilities.

Participate!

All states and many communities have roadway beautification programs. The "Adopt a Highway" program is one of the better known. Many of these programs depend on volunteers. Consider joining such an effort in your local or college community. You will be contributing to the scenic beauty of your area. You will also be helping to reduce littering; drivers are less likely to toss trash from their cars when the roadway on which they are driving is free of debris.

Extra Credit

For up-to-the-minute *New York Times* articles, interactive simulations, graphics, study tools, and more links and quizzes, visit the text's Online Learning Center at www.mhhe.com/pattersontad8.

(Self-Test Answers: 1. c   2. d   3. a   4. c   5. d   6. d   7. T   8. F   9. T   10. T)

Welfare and Education Policy:
Providing for Personal Security and Need

Chapter Outline

Poverty in America: The Nature of the Problem
The Poor: Who and How Many?
Living in Poverty: By Choice or Chance?

The Politics and Policies of Social Welfare
Social Insurance Programs
Public Assistance Programs
Culture, Welfare, and Income

Education as Equality of Opportunity
Public Education: Leveling Through the Schools
Public School Issues
The Federal Role in Education: Political Differences

The American Way of Promoting the General Welfare

CHAPTER 16

We the people of the United States, in order to . . .
promote the general welfare . . .

—*Preamble, U.S. Constitution*

As the Welfare Reform Act came up for renewal in 2002, there was cause for both hope and fear. The original legislation had been a stunning success. In the latter part of the 1990s, the number of people on the welfare rolls had been cut almost in half. In only three states—Hawaii, Rhode Island, and New Mexico—was the drop less than 20 percent (see "States in the Nation"). The trend defied what had been called welfare policy's "reverse gravity" law: welfare rolls that went up but never came down. Two factors accounted for the change. One was the booming national economy. As more Americans got jobs, the demand for welfare decreased. The second factor was the 1996 Welfare Reform Act, which shortened the length of eligibility and required that able-bodied recipients find work or risk loss of benefits.

The situation in 2002 was starkly different. Those welfare recipients who had found work were the ones easiest to place in jobs. Many of those still unemployed lacked the education, skill, or temperament to find and hold a job. Moreover, the economy had weakened, and welfare rolls were starting to rise while government revenues were declining. "At the beginning of welfare reform, we had the happy circumstance of a booming economy, low unemployment, falling welfare caseloads, and the states having the money to give more help to the poor, especially the working poor," said Sharon Parrott of the Center on Budget and Policy Priorities. "Now, everything is going the other way. Caseloads are rising, the value of the federal block grant is down, and state budgets are in catastrophic shape."[1]

The 2002 debate in Congress reflected these new realities. Yet it also brought out old differences. Congressional Republicans wanted to increase pressure on the states to move more people off welfare and into work; they also argued for strict adherence to the eligibility rules, tight controls on federal spending, and increased work hours for welfare recipients. Congressional Democrats sought more funding for day care, education, and job-training programs; they also wanted to give the states more latitude in their administration of the welfare program. The differences were substantial enough to create a months-long deadlock between the Republican-controlled House and the Democratic-controlled Senate. "By stalling on . . . welfare reform," said Bill Thomas (R-Calif.) of the House Committee on Ways and Means, "the Senate is shaping their legacy—inaction."

LEADERS

FRANKLIN D. ROOSEVELT

(1882–1945)

Franklin D. Roosevelt won the presidency in 1932 during the depths of the Great Depression. FDR's job programs put Americans back to work, and his social programs met their immediate and long-term economic needs. His greatest domestic policy legacy is the Social Security Act of 1935, which for nearly eight decades has been the foundation of elderly Americans' financial security. Roosevelt's New Deal also changed Americans' conception of government—it could be an instrument for protecting citizens against economic adversity. A distant cousin of President Theodore Roosevelt, FDR had a passion for politics even as a youth. After graduating from Harvard and Columbia Law School, he won a seat in the New York State Senate. During World War I, he served as assistant secretary of the Navy, and in 1920, when he was still in his thirties, he was chosen as the Democratic party's vice-presidential nominee. A year later, he contracted polio and lost full use of his legs, a fact that he kept largely hidden from the public. He fought to regain his health and was elected governor of New York before winning election to the presidency. In 1940, Roosevelt broke with tradition and announced that he would seek a third presidential term. Against the backdrop of war in Europe and continuing economic problems at home, he won the election—though by a narrower margin than in his two previous campaigns. Roosevelt was in office when the Japanese attacked Pearl Harbor, and he oversaw the mobilization of the greatest military power the world had yet known. America's industrial might and its armed forces were critical weapons in the Allies' defeat of the Axis powers. FDR won a fourth term in 1944 but died in office of a cerebral hemorrhage as the war was concluding.

adequately addressed by them, even though they did not offer substantial welfare services. Individuals were expected to fend for themselves, and those unable to do so were usually supported by relatives and friends. This approach reflected the idea of **negative government,** which holds that government governs best by staying out of people's lives, giving them as much freedom as possible to determine their own pursuits and encouraging them to become self-reliant.

The Great Depression changed that outlook. The unemployment level reached 25 percent, and many of those with jobs were working for pennies. Americans looked to the federal government for help. Franklin D. Roosevelt's New Deal brought economic relief in the form of public jobs and assistance programs and changed opinions about the federal government's welfare role.[7] This new attitude reflected a faith in **positive government,** the idea that government intervention is necessary in order to enhance personal liberty and security when individuals are buffeted by economic and social forces beyond their control.

Not all Americans of the 1930s embraced the new philosophy. Most Republican leaders and loyalists clung to traditional ideas about self-reliance and free markets. Democrats spearheaded the change. The key vote in the House of Representatives on the Social Security Act of 1935, for example, had 85 percent of Democrats voting in favor of it and 99 percent of Republicans voting against it.[8]

negative government
The philosophical belief that government governs best by staying out of people's lives, giving individuals as much freedom as possible to determine their own pursuits.

positive government
The philosophical belief that government intervention is necessary in order to enhance personal liberty and security when individuals are buffeted by economic and social forces beyond their control.

Republicans gradually came to accept the idea that the federal government has a role in social welfare but argued that the role should be kept as small as practicable. Thus, in the 1960s, Republican opposition to President Lyndon Johnson's Great Society was substantial. His programs included federal initiatives in health care, education, public housing, nutrition, and other areas traditionally dominated by state and local governments. More than 70 percent of congressional Republicans voted against the 1965 Medicare and Medicaid programs, which provide government-paid medical assistance for the elderly and the poor. In contrast, the 1996 Welfare Reform Act, which was designed to cut welfare rolls and costs, had the overwhelming support of congressional Republicans, while a majority of congressional Democrats voted against it.

Although the Republican and Democratic parties have been at odds on social welfare issues, they have also had reason to work together. Millions of Americans depend on the federal government to provide benefits to ease the loss of income caused by retirement, disability, unemployment, and the like. These benefit programs differ in whom they serve, what they provide, and how eligibility is acquired. In broad terms, they fall into two general categories: social insurance

Get Involved!

Lend a Hand

When it comes to partisan politics, poverty is a contentious issue. Republicans and Democrats disagree mightily on the question of how far government should go in helping the poor.

On the other hand, virtually all Americans—on the right and on the left—support private efforts to help the poor. Numerous local religious, civic, social, and economic groups run programs for the poor, such as food kitchens and clothing drives. Also, many national organizations work locally to assist the poor. An example is Habitat for

Humanity, which builds modest houses with volunteer labor and then makes them available to low-income families, which assist in the construction and receive low-interest or no-interest mortgages to pay for the cost of construction materials.

Consider volunteering some of your time to a group that gives a helping hand to those in need—whether a church or a community group or a nonprofit organization like Habitat for Humanity. Habitat for Humanity has a website that makes it easy for you to volunteer.

and public assistance. Programs in the first category enjoy broader public support, are more heavily funded, and provide benefits to individuals of all income levels. Programs in the second category have less public support, receive less funding, and are restricted to people of low income.

Programs in both categories involve **transfer payments,** government benefits given directly to individual recipients, such as the monthly social security checks that retirees receive. Some social welfare spending, such as federal grants for health research, is not in the form of a transfer payment because the money does not go to individual recipients. Most programs that support individuals directly are **entitlement programs,** meaning that any individual who meets the criteria for eligibility is entitled to the benefit. For example, upon reaching the legal retirement age, any senior citizen who has paid social security taxes for the required amount of time is entitled to receive social security benefits. In this sense, entitlement programs have the same force of law as taxes. Just as individuals are required by law to pay taxes on the income they earn, they are entitled by law to receive government benefits for which they qualify.

WWW.MHHE.COM/PATTERSONTAD8

transfer payments
Government benefits that are given directly to individuals, as in the case of social security payments to retirees.

Social security benefits make it possible for many elderly Americans to maintain a secure, independent retirement.

entitlement programs
Any of a number of individual-benefit programs, such as social security, that require government to provide a designated benefit to any person who meets the legally defined criteria for eligibility.

social insurance
Social welfare programs based on the "insurance" concept, requiring that individuals pay into the program in order to be eligible to receive funds from it. An example is social security for retired people.

As indicated, individual-benefit programs fall into two broad groups: social insurance programs and public assistance programs. The next two sections discuss these two types of programs.

Social Insurance Programs

More than forty million Americans receive monthly benefits from social insurance programs—including social security, Medicare, unemployment insurance, and workers' compensation. The two major programs, social security and Medicare, cost the federal government more than $800 billion per year. Such programs are labeled **social insurance** because only those individuals who paid special payroll taxes when they were employed are eligible for these benefits.

Social Security

The leading social insurance program is social security for retirees. The program began with passage of the Social Security Act of 1935 and is funded through payroll taxes on employees and employers (currently set at 6.2 percent). Franklin D. Roosevelt emphasized that retiring workers would receive an insurance benefit that they had earned through their payroll taxes, not a handout from the government. In part because of this method of financing the social security program has broad public support.[9] Opinion polls indicate that the large majority of Americans favor current or higher levels of social security benefits for the elderly. Social security is one of the few welfare programs run entirely by the federal government. Washington collects the payroll taxes that fund the program and sends monthly checks directly to the nearly forty million social security recipients, who receive on average about $900 a month.

Although people qualify for social security by paying payroll taxes during their working years, the money they receive upon retirement is funded by payroll taxes on current workers' salaries. This arrangement poses a long-term threat to the viability of the social security program because people are living longer than they once did. Three decades from now, about one in five Americans will be over age sixty-five, at which time—unless changes are made in the social security program—there will not be enough workers to pay for retiree benefits.

In 2005, President George W. Bush proposed a partial privatization of social security as an answer to the long-term problem. Workers would have been allowed to place roughly a third of social security tax payments into private individual stock accounts. Bush claimed that individuals would get a greater return on their money through the stock market, thereby reducing what government would need to pay when workers retired. Bush's proposal was attacked by congressional Democrats and by powerful groups including the American Association of Retired Persons (AARP), who argued that Bush's proposal would expose retirees to the risks of the stock market. Critics also said that the Bush plan would make the solvency problem worse, not better. Payroll taxes that otherwise would have been used to offset payments to retirees would be diverted into private accounts. Bush's plan failed to win congressional approval, but a need to overhaul social security remains. At some point, as happened in the 1980s, a bipartisan commission is likely to be formed to develop a compromise solution that will preserve America's commitment to its elderly retirees.

Unemployment Insurance

The 1935 Social Security Act provides for unemployment benefits for workers who lose their jobs involuntarily. Unemployment insurance is a joint federal-state program. The federal government collects the payroll taxes that fund unemployment benefits, but states have the option of deciding whether the taxes will be paid by both employees and employers or by employers only (most states use the latter option). Individual states also set the tax rate, conditions of eligibility, and benefit level, subject to minimum standards established by the federal government. Although unemployment benefits vary widely among states, they average $350 a week, somewhat more than a third of what an average worker makes while employed. The benefits in most cases are terminated after twenty-six to thirty-nine weeks.

The unemployment program does not have the broad public support that social security enjoys. This situation reflects the widespread assumption that the loss of a job, or the failure to find a new one right away, is typically a personal failing. Unemployment statistics indicate otherwise. For example, U.S. Bureau of Labor statistics reveal that of those workers who lost their jobs in 2001, only 13 percent were fired or quit voluntarily. The rest became unemployed because of either a temporary layoff or the permanent elimination of a job position.

Medicare

After World War II, most European democracies created government-paid health care systems, and President Harry Truman, a Democrat, proposed a similar program for Americans. The American Medical Association (AMA) called Truman's plan "un-American" and vowed to mobilize local physicians to campaign against members of Congress who supported "socialized medicine." Truman's proposal never came to a vote in Congress. In 1961, President John F. Kennedy, also a Democrat, proposed a health care program restricted to social security recipients, but the AMA, the insurance industry, and congressional conservatives succeeded in blocking the plan.[10]

The 1964 elections swept a tide of liberal Democrats into Congress, and the result was Medicare. Enacted in 1965, the program provides medical assistance to retirees and is funded primarily through payroll taxes. Medicare is based on the insurance principle and because of this has gained as much public support as social security has. Medicare does not cover all hospital, nursing home, or physicians' fees, but enrollees in the program have the option of paying an insurance premium for fuller coverage of these fees. Enrollees who cannot afford the additional premium can apply to have the government pay it.

In 2006, a prescription drug benefit as part of the Medicare program went into effect. The program includes a recipient contribution and primarily benefits retirees who either are too poor to afford prescription drugs or have very high prescription drug costs. Retirees not in these categories receive a small benefit from the program but are required to pay most of the cost of their prescription drugs. The program's complicated rules have led to numerous complaints from senior citizens.

At some point soon, Congress will have to overhaul the Medicare program as a whole. The rising cost of medical care and the growing number of elderly have combined to threaten the solvency of the program; it is projected to run out of money within a decade unless new revenues and cost-cutting measures are devised. Among the options under consideration are increased payroll taxes, more cost-sharing by recipients, more use of managed care options, and further limits on government payments to doctors and hospitals.

Public Assistance Programs

Unlike social insurance programs, **public assistance** programs are funded through general tax revenues and are available only to the financially needy.

public assistance
A term that refers to social welfare programs funded through general tax revenues and available only to the financially needy. Eligibility for such a program is established by a means test.

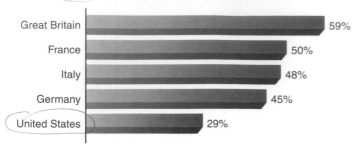

Percentage saying they "completely agree" that it is "the responsibility of the government to take care of very poor people who can't take care of themselves"

Great Britain	59%
France	50%
Italy	48%
Germany	45%
United States	29%

Figure 16–2

Opinions on Government's Responsibility for the Poor
Compared to Europeans, Americans are much less likely to believe that government has a responsibility for the poor.
Source: The Pew Research Center for the People and the Press, Global Attitudes Survey, 2002.

means test
The requirement that applicants for public assistance must demonstrate that they are poor in order to be eligible for the assistance.

Eligibility for these programs is established by a **means test;** applicants must prove that they are poor enough to qualify for the benefit. Once they have done so, they are entitled to the benefit, unless their personal situation changes or government legislates different eligibility criteria. These programs often are referred to as "welfare" and the recipients as "welfare cases."

Americans are much less supportive of public assistance programs than they are of social insurance programs. Americans tend to look upon social insurance benefits as having been "earned" by the recipient, while they see public assistance benefits as "handouts." Because of their individualistic culture, Americans are less inclined than Europeans to believe that government should provide substantial help to the poor (see Figure 16–2). Support for public assistance programs also is weakened by Americans' perception that the government is already spending vast amounts on welfare. A poll found that Americans believe public assistance programs to be the second costliest item in the federal budget. These programs actually rank much farther down the list. In fact, the federal government spends hundreds of billions of dollars more on its two major social insurance programs, social security and Medicare, than it does on all public assistance programs combined.

Supplemental Security Income

A major public assistance program is Supplemental Security Income (SSI), which originated as federal assistance to the blind and elderly poor as part of the Social Security Act of 1935. By the 1930s, most states had begun or were considering such programs. Although the federal legislation was designed to replace their efforts, the states have retained a measure of control over benefits and eligibility and are required to provide some of the funding. Because SSI recipients (who now include the disabled in addition to the blind and elderly poor) have obvious reasons for their inability to provide fully for themselves, this public assistance program is not widely criticized.

Temporary Assistance for Needy Families (TANF)

Before passage of the 1996 Welfare Reform Act (discussed in the chapter's introduction), needy American families had an open-ended guarantee of cash assistance. As long as their income was below a certain level, they were assured of government support. The program (Aid for Families with Dependent Children, or AFDC for short) was created in the 1930s as survivors' insurance to assist children whose fathers had died prematurely. Relatively small at the outset, it became controversial as Americans increasingly linked it to welfare dependency and irresponsibility. AFDC was an entitlement program, which

Supplemental Security Income (SSI) is a combined federal-state program that provides public assistance to blind and disabled people.

meant that any single parent (and in some states two parents) living in poverty could claim the benefit and keep it for as long as a dependent child was in the household. Some AFDC recipients were content to live on this assistance, and in some cases their children also grew up to become AFDC recipients, creating what was called "a vicious cycle of poverty." By 1995, AFDC was supporting fourteen million Americans at an annual cost of more than $15 billion.

The 1996 Welfare Reform Act abolished AFDC, replacing it with the program titled Temporary Assistance for Needy Families (TANF). TANF's goal is to reduce long-term welfare dependency by limiting the length of time recipients can receive assistance and by giving the states an incentive to get welfare recipients into jobs. Each state is given an annual federal bloc grant that it uses to help poor families meet their subsistence needs and to develop programs that will help the parents to find employment. The state programs operate within strict federal guidelines, including the following:

- Americans' eligibility for federal cash assistance is limited to no more than five years in their lifetime.

- Within two years, the head of most families on welfare will have to find work or risk the loss of benefits.

- Unmarried teenage mothers are qualified for welfare benefits only if they remain in school and live with a parent or legal guardian.

- Single mothers will lose a portion of their benefits if they refuse to cooperate in identifying for child-support purposes the father of their children.

Although states are allowed to make exceptions to some of the rules (for example, an unmarried teenage mother who faces sexual abuse at home is permitted to live elsewhere), the exceptions are limited. States can even choose

A New Beginning

Welfare to Work

President Clinton signs into law the 1996 welfare reform bill that ended the sixty-one-year-old federal guarantee of aid to the poor. The new legislation limits federal welfare assistance to a period of five years.

LEADERS

MARIAN WRIGHT EDELMAN

(1939–   )

As a child in segregated South Carolina, Marian Wright Edelman saw firsthand the effects of racial discrimination and abject poverty. In her hometown of Bennettsville, black children were not allowed to play in the local park and often went to bed hungry. Upon graduating from Yale Law School in 1963, she went to Mississippi, where she became the first black woman to pass the state's bar exam. She was active in poverty and education issues, contributing to the launching of Head Start in Mississippi. She later moved to Washington, D.C., where she started the Children's Defense Fund, which became the country's most powerful advocacy group on behalf of poor children. For more than three decades, the fund has lobbied and organized to improve the nutrition, education, and health care of America's children. Edelman is one in a long line of women who have made substantial contributions to the welfare of America's disadvantaged. Many of these women—such as Dorothea Dix, Clara Barton, and Jane Addams—made their contributions during the period when federal, state, and local governments had few social welfare programs. In that earlier time, women were denied opportunities to contribute to society by holding high public office. Dix, Barton, and Addams were pioneering reformers whose dedication improved the lives of countless Americans.

to impose more restrictive rules in some areas. For example, states have the option of denying increased benefits to unwed mothers who give birth to another child.

The long-term effectiveness of TANF is not yet known. The trend so far is cause for mild optimism. The number of families on public assistance has declined sharply since passage of the 1996 Welfare Reform Act. The biggest challenge facing the states is developing welfare-to-work programs that will qualify people for jobs secure enough to free them from welfare dependency. Most welfare recipients who have found employment since 1996 had enough skills that they required little or no job training from their state. In contrast, most of those who have been unable to find long-term employment have limited education and few job-related skills. States are trying innovative ways to train these individuals for work; whether these programs will succeed is unclear.[11]

Food Stamps

The food stamp program, which took its present form in 1961, is fully funded by the federal government. The program provides an **in-kind benefit**—not cash, but food stamps that can be spent only on grocery items.

in-kind benefit
A government benefit that is a cash equivalent, such as food stamps or rent vouchers. This form of benefit ensures that recipients will use public assistance in a specified way.

Food stamps are available only to people who qualify on the basis of low income. The program is intended to improve the nutrition of poor families by enabling them to purchase qualified items—mainly foodstuffs—with food stamps. Some critics say that food stamps stigmatize their users by making it obvious to onlookers in the checkout line that they are "welfare cases." More prevalent criticisms are that the program is too costly and that too many undeserving people receive food stamps.

Subsidized Housing

Low-income persons are also eligible for subsidized housing. Most of the federal spending in this area is on rent vouchers, an in-kind benefit. The government gives the individual a monthly rent-payment voucher, which the individual then gives in lieu of cash to the landlord, who then hands the voucher over to the government in exchange for cash. About five million households annually receive a federal housing subsidy.

The U.S. government spends much less on public housing than on tax breaks for homeowners, most of whom are middle- and upper-income Americans. Homeowners are allowed tax deductions for their mortgage interest payments and their local property tax payments. The total of these tax concessions is three times as much as is spent by the federal government on housing for low-income families.

Medicaid

When Medicare, the health care program for the elderly, was created in 1965, Congress also established Medicaid, which provides health care for poor people who are already on welfare. It is considered a public assistance program, rather than a social insurance program like Medicare, because it is based on need and funded by general tax revenues. Roughly 60 percent of Medicaid funding is provided by the federal government, and about 40 percent by the states. More than twenty million Americans receive Medicaid assistance.

Medicaid is controversial because of its costs. As health care costs have spiraled far ahead of the inflation rate, so have the costs of Medicaid. It absorbs roughly half of all public assistance dollars spent by the U.S. government and has forced state and local governments to cut other services to meet their share of the costs. "It's killing us," is how one local official described the impact of Medicaid on his community's budget.[12] As is true of other public assistance programs, Medicaid has been criticized for supposedly helping too many people who could take care of themselves if they tried harder. This belief is contradicted, ironically, by the situation faced by many working Americans. There are roughly forty-five million Americans living in families with incomes that are too high to qualify them for Medicaid but too low to cover the cost of health insurance.[13]

Culture, Welfare, and Income

Surveys repeatedly show that most Americans are convinced people on welfare could get along without if they tried. As a consequence, there is constant political pressure to reduce welfare expenditures and to weed out undeserving recipients. The result is a welfare system that is both *inefficient*, in that much of the money spent on welfare never reaches the intended recipients, and *inequitable*, in that less than half of social welfare spending goes to the people who need it the most.

Inefficiency and Inequity

The United States has the most inefficient welfare system in the Western world. Because of the unwritten principle that the individual must somehow earn or be in absolute need of assistance, the U.S. welfare system is heavily bureaucratic. For example, the 1996 welfare reform bill—which limits eligibility to families with incomes below a certain level and, in most instances, to families with a single parent living in the home—requires that the eligibility of each applicant be checked periodically by a caseworker. This procedure makes such programs doubly expensive; in addition to payments to the recipients, the programs must pay local caseworkers, supervisors, and support staffs (see Figure 16–3). These costs do not include the costs of the state and federal agencies that oversee the programs.

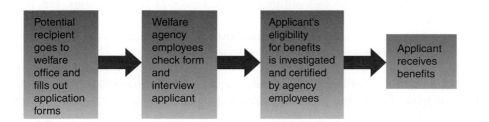

Figure 16–3

The cumbersome administrative process by which welfare recipients receive their benefits

One of the many ironies of U.S. social welfare policy is that tax deductions for home mortgages for the middle and upper classes are government subsidies, just as are rent vouchers for the poor, but only the latter are stigmatized as a government "handout."

The bureaucratic costs of welfare are substantially lower in Europe because most European countries have unitary rather than federal systems, which eliminates a layer of government, and also because eligibility is more often universal, as in the case of government-paid health care. Caseworkers do not have to pore over records to determine who is and who is not eligible for medical treatment—everyone is.[14]

European welfare programs are also more equitable in the sense that the major beneficiaries are those individuals most in need, unlike the case in the United States. The federal government spends far more on social security and Medicare, which assist rich and poor alike, than it spends in total on all public assistance programs, which help only the needy. Of course, social insurance programs do help some who are needy. Monthly social security checks keep millions of Americans, mostly widows, out of poverty; about one-fourth of America's elderly have no significant monthly income aside from what they receive from social security. Nevertheless, families in the top fifth of the income population receive more in federal social insurance benefits than is spent on TANF, food stamps, and housing subsidies combined.

Income and Tax Measures

The American political culture's emphasis on individualism is also evident in its tax and income policies. Economic redistribution—the shifting of money from the more affluent to the less affluent—is an aspect of these policies, but it is a relatively small component.

The United States has substantial income inequality (see Figure 16–4). Americans in the top fifth by income receive half of total U.S. income, while those in the bottom fifth get less than a twentieth. The imbalance is greater than that in any other industrialized democracy. One reason is that income taxes are not used for economic redistribution to the extent that they are in other

#8, One Reason

democracies. In 2007, the top tax rate in the United States was 35 percent and applied to net income above $335,000. Income below that level is taxed at lower rates. Thus, a taxpayer with a net income of $500,000 pays the 35 percent rate on the amount above $335,000 and lower rates on the rest. In Europe, a top rate of 50 percent is not uncommon, and the top rate starts at a lower income level than in the United States.

The U.S. tax code also includes numerous tax deductions for upper-income individuals, such as the deduction for mortgage interest on a vacation home. Moreover, the well-to-do escape social security taxes on a large part of their income. The social security tax is a flat rate of about 6 percent that begins with the first dollar earned and stops completely after roughly $95,000 in earnings is reached. Thus, individuals earning less than $95,000 pay social security taxes on every dollar they make, while those earning more than $95,000 pay no social security taxes on the dollars they make over this amount.

The net result is that the **effective tax rate** (the actual percentage of a person's income spent to pay taxes) of high- and middle-income Americans is not greatly different. When all taxes (including personal income taxes, social security taxes, state sales taxes, and local property taxes) are combined, the average American family's effective tax rate is about three-fourths that of a family with an income over a million dollars. In Europe, where tax breaks for the well-to-do are few, the effective tax rate for high-income taxpayers is substantially greater than that for average taxpayers.[15]

#8, 2 Reason

Of course, although well-to-do Americans pay relatively low taxes, the fact that they earn a lot of money means that they contribute the large share of tax revenues in absolute dollars. The top 10 percent of U.S. earners pay about half the personal income taxes received by the federal government. On the other hand, they keep much more of what they earn than do high-income taxpayers elsewhere.

Over the past few decades, the trend has been toward reducing taxes on the wealthy, a development that began during the Reagan administration and continued under George W. Bush. Arguing that high taxes on the wealthy hurt economic growth (see Chapter 15), Bush persuaded Congress to enact phased-in tax cuts that sharply reduced taxes on high incomes. Capital gains taxes were slashed, and marginal tax rates on personal income were reduced. The savings to Americans in the top 1 percent of income is $54,493 per year, compared with an average of $67 for those in the bottom 20 percent and $611 for those in the middle 20 percent. In terms of total dollars, less than 1 percent of the cuts are for those in the bottom fifth by income, while those in the middle fifth get 8 percent of the cuts and those in the top fifth receive 75 percent of the cuts.[16]

However, America's poorest working families have also received tax relief in recent decades. The vehicle for this relief is the Earned Income Tax Credit (EITC). About ten million low-income American families each year receive an EITC payment. The maximum yearly payment to any family is roughly $4,500, and eligibility is limited to families that include a wage earner. EITC payments result when individuals file their personal income taxes. The payment declines in amount as income rises and phases out entirely at a specified income level. The EITC program was started in 1975 and has been expanded to become the

#9

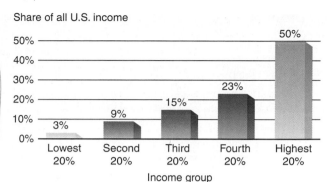

Share of all U.S. income

Figure 16–4

Income Inequality in the United States
The United States has the highest degree of income inequality of any industrialized democracy. Citizens in the top fifth by income get half of all income; those in the bottom fifth get less than a twentieth of all income.
Source: U.S. Bureau of the Census, 2006.

effective tax rate
The actual percentage of a person's income that is spent to pay taxes.

Debating the Issues

Are Tax Cuts for High-Income Taxpayers Good for America?

Few issues spark more controversy than taxes. When a tax cut is at issue, the debate is usually over how the cut is to be divided. Supply-side economists have a unique answer to the question: those taxpayers who are personally least in need of tax relief are the ones who should get the largest share of the cut. Supply-side theory holds that high-income taxpayers will invest their extra income, thus boosting the economy and, along with the economy, the fortunes of everyone else. It is this argument that the Heritage Foundation's

Daniel Mitchell makes below in support of President George W. Bush's supply-side tax initiatives, which substantially cut taxes for America's wealthier individuals. Among the critics of the Bush tax program was Warren Buffett, one of America's richest people. Buffett called Bush's tax program "voodoo economics"—a term he borrowed from debates over the same issue in the 1980s. In his argument below, Buffett rejects both the logic and the symbolism of supply-side economics.

Yes

Pro-growth tax cuts are an important part of fiscal discipline. They take money out of Washington, thereby removing the temptation to spend tax dollars on programs that are wasteful, duplicative, or counterproductive. . . . Any money the government gives to one person must first be taken from someone else. This Keynesian approach—attempting to boost the economy by giving people more money to spend—makes sense only if one assumes that the money distributed by the government for tax relief or new spending materializes out of thin air. The essential insight of supply-side economics is that the right kind of tax cuts will help an economy by increasing incentives to work, save, and invest. This relationship is the reason why President Reagan's across-the-board reductions in marginal tax rates resulted in nearly 20 years of above-average economic performance. President Bush's . . . tax cut package seeks to reduce the tax penalty on productive behavior, so there is every reason to think it would yield significant benefits as well. . . . People invest in the expectation of earning after-tax income. . . . The argument for supply-side tax policy is simple: Lowering tax rates on productive behavior will improve the incentives to work, save, and invest.

—*Daniel J. Mitchell, senior fellow, the Heritage Foundation*

No

[These tax cuts] supply major aid to the rich in their pursuit of even greater wealth. . . . Administration officials say that the $310 million suddenly added to my wallet would stimulate the economy because I would invest it and thereby create jobs. But they conveniently forget that if Berkshire [Buffett's investment company] kept the money, it would invest that same amount, creating jobs as well. . . . Instead, give reductions to those who both need and will spend the money gained. Enact a Social Security tax "holiday" or give a flat-sum rebate to people with low incomes. Putting $1,000 in the pockets of 310,000 families with urgent needs is going to provide far more stimulus to the economy than putting the same $310 million in my pockets. When you listen to tax-cut rhetoric, remember that giving one class of taxpayer a "break" requires—now or down the line—that an equivalent burden be imposed on other parties. In other words, if I get a break, someone else pays. Government can't deliver a free lunch to the country as a whole. It can, however, determine who pays for lunch. And last week the [government] handed the bill to the wrong party.

—*Warren Buffett, chief executive officer, Berkshire Hathaway, Inc.*

federal government's largest means-tested cash assistance program. According to U.S. Census Bureau calculations, EITC lifts about a third of low-income Americans above the poverty line. Moreover, because EITC payments are based on income tax returns, the program does not require a costly bureaucracy of caseworkers. EITC payments are processed at the same time and in the same way as tax refunds for employees who have paid too much in withholding.

EDUCATION AS EQUALITY OF OPPORTUNITY

Although the Earned Income Tax Credit is subject to budgetary and political pressures, it enjoys more support than most assistance programs. The reason is simple: EITC is tied to jobs. Only those who work are eligible to receive the payment. Polls that span more than a half century reveal that Americans have consistently favored work-based assistance to welfare payments as the answer to poverty. Work is believed to foster initiative and accountability; welfare "handouts" are believed to breed dependency and irresponsibility.

At the same time, Americans believe that people should have a fighting chance to succeed in the job market. Although few Americans would support economic equality for all, most Americans endorse the principle of **equality of opportunity**—the idea that people should have a reasonable chance to succeed if they make the effort. The concept includes a commitment to equality in the narrow sense that everyone should have a fair chance to get ahead. But it is a form of equality shaped by liberty because the outcome—personal success or personal failure—depends on what individuals do with that opportunity. The expectation is that people will end up differently—some will make a good living and some will be poor. It is sometimes said that equality of opportunity gives individuals an equal chance to become unequal.

Equality of opportunity is an ideal. Americans obviously do not start life on an equal footing. It was said of one successful American politician, whose father before him was a successful politician and a millionaire, that "he was born on third base and thought he hit a triple."[17] Some Americans are born into privilege, and others start life in such abject poverty that they realistically have no chance of escaping it. Nonetheless, equality of opportunity is more than a catch phrase. It is the philosophical basis for a number of government programs, none more so than public education.

equality of opportunity
The idea that all individuals should be given an equal chance to succeed on their own.

Public Education: Leveling through the Schools

During the nation's first century, the question of a free education for all children was a divisive issue. Wealthy interests feared that an educated public would challenge their power. Egalitarians, on the other hand, saw education as a means of enabling ordinary people to get ahead. The egalitarians won out. Public schools sprang up in nearly every community and were open free of charge to children who could attend.

Today, as discussed in Chapter 1, the United States invests more heavily in public education at all levels than does any other country. The curriculum in American schools is also relatively standardized. Unlike those countries that divide children even at the grade school level into different tracks that lead ultimately to different occupations, the United States aims to educate all children in essentially the same way. Of course, public education is not a uniform experience for American children. The quality of education depends significantly on the wealth of the community in which a child resides. The Supreme Court has upheld this arrangement, saying that states are obliged to give all children an "adequate" education as opposed to an "equal" one across all communities.

The United States does have a federal education program, Head Start, dedicated to helping poor children. Established in the 1960s during the Johnson administration, it provides preschool education to low-income children in order to help them succeed when they begin kindergarten. At no time in its

The Head Start education program is designed to give preschool children from poorer homes a better chance to succeed when they enter kindergarten. Shown here is a teacher reading to a Head Start class in Austin, Texas.

history, however, has the Head Start program been funded at a level that would allow all eligible children to participate. The low point was reached in the 1980s when there was only enough money to allow the enrollment of one in ten of those eligible. Today, less than half of all eligible children get to participate.

Nevertheless, the United States through its public schools educates a broad segment of the population. Arguably, no country in the world has made an equivalent effort to give children, whatever their parents' background, an equal opportunity in life through education. Per-pupil spending on public elementary and secondary schools is roughly twice as high in the United States as it is in Western Europe. America's commitment to broad-based education extends to college. The United States is far and away the world leader in terms of the proportion of adults receiving a college education.[18]

The nation's education system preserves both the myth and the reality of an equal-opportunity society. The belief that success can be had by anyone who works for it could not be sustained if the education system were tailored for a privileged elite. And educational attainment is related to personal success, at least as measured by annual incomes. In fact, the gap in income between those with and those without a college education is greater now than at any time in the country's history.

Public School Issues

Because America's public schools play such a key role in creating an equal-opportunity society, they are closely scrutinized. Parents of schoolchildren are not shy about saying what they think of their local schools. Interestingly, parents tend to rate their own children's schools more highly than they rate other schools. A national survey found that two-thirds of parents gave their children's schools a grade of A or B but only a fourth gave the nation's schools as a whole a grade that high.[19]

Political Culture
Education and Equality

Public education has never been a uniform experience for American children. Cities in the late nineteenth century neglected the education of many immigrant children, who were thereby placed at a permanent disadvantage. During the first half of the twentieth century, southern public schools for black children were designed to keep them down, not lift them up. Today, many children in poorer neighborhoods attend overcrowded and understaffed public schools.

Nevertheless, the nation's public schools have been the primary means by which Americans of all nationalities, colors, creeds, and income levels have been brought together. At no time in most Americans' lives are they as thoroughly immersed in a socially diverse environment as when, as children and adolescents, they attend public schools.

America's broad-based system of public education stems from a melding of its egalitarian and individualistic traditions. Leon Sampson, a nineteenth-century socialist, noted the stark difference between the philosophy of public education in the United States and that in Europe. "The European ruling classes," he wrote, "were open in their contempt for the proletariat. But in the United States equality, and even classlessness, the creation of wealth for all and political liberty were extolled in the public schools." Sampson concluded that American schools embodied a unique conception of equality. Everyone was being trained in much the same way so that each person would have the opportunity to succeed. "It is," he said, "a socialist conception of capitalism."

The making of one people out of many is fostered by the general philosophy of public education in America, which holds that students should share a common curriculum. A system that would seek instead to enhance the education of top students would work to the disadvantage of poor students and others who, for reasons of language or life circumstances, are less prepared to do well when they enter school. An elite-centered school system of the type found in some European societies would serve to widen the gap between the country's richer and poorer groups and to slow the assimilation into American society of its newer arrivals.

Of course, other institutions also contribute to the integration of American society, but no institution does it as well or as thoroughly as the public schools. This is not to say that the schools are mirrors of America's diversity. A great deal of ethnic, racial, and class segregation still exists in the schools. For example, in some suburban schools few of the children come from families earning less than $75,000 a year. And in some urban schools few of the children come from families earning more than $25,000 a year. Yet, were it not for public schools, America would be a substantially more stratified society, both in terms of one's classmates while in school and in terms of one's prospects for success after leaving school.

Public education in America was called "the great leveler" when it began in the early nineteenth century. Since then it has earned that label. Rarely has a public institution served so many so well for such a long period.

The issues facing public schools are far-ranging. Disorder in the schools is a major issue in some communities, as is student performance on standardized tests. American students do not even score in the top ten internationally on tests in science or math. Nevertheless, the most controversial policy issues involve proposals to reallocate money among schools. School choice is one such issue. Under this policy, the public schools compete for students, and schools that attract the most students are rewarded with the largest budgets. Advocates of the policy claim that it forces school administrators and teachers to do a better job and gives students the option of leaving a school that is performing poorly.[20] Parents favor such a policy by a wide margin, unless their children are harmed by it. Poor children in particular often have little choice but to attend the nearest school because their parents are unable to transport them to a better but more distant school.[21]

School vouchers are a related issue. A voucher system allows parents to use tax dollars to keep their children out of the public schools entirely. Parents receive a voucher from the government that they can give to a private or parochial school to cover part of the cost of their child's tuition. Proponents say that vouchers force failing public schools to improve their instructional programs or face a permanent loss of revenue. Opponents, however, argue that vouchers weaken the public schools by siphoning off revenue and say that vouchers subsidize many families that would have sent their children to private or parochial schools anyway. They note that vouchers are of little use to students from poor families because they lack the additional money required to pay the full tuition costs at a nonpublic school.

Although the courts have upheld the constitutionality of vouchers in some circumstances, polls indicate that Americans are divided over whether they would like to see a universal voucher system.[22] The question gets majority support when it is framed in the context of choice among public schools but is opposed by the majority when private and parochial schools are included among the choices. The issue of vouchers reflects the tensions inherent in the concept of equal opportunity. Vouchers expand opportunity the number of choices available to students. Yet, not all students are able to take advantage of the choices, and not all taxpayers want their tax dollars used to support private and parochial schools. (Another public school issue—uniform testing of all schoolchildren—is discussed in the next section.)

The Federal Role in Education: Political Differences

Education has traditionally been a state and local responsibility. Most school policies—from length of the school year to teachers' qualifications—are set by state legislatures and local school boards. Over 90 percent of the funds spent on schools are provided through state and local tax revenues.

Federal intervention in school policy has often been resisted by states and localities, as exemplified by their response to desegregation and busing directives (see Chapter 5). State and local governments have been less hesitant when it comes to federal education grants, but it is difficult to get congressional support for grant programs targeted at those schools that are most in need. Few members of Congress are willing to support large appropriations for education that do not benefit their constituents, a situation that has reduced Washington's contribution to a goal—quality education for every American child—that nearly every official endorses, at least in principle.

The Supreme Court has held that American children are entitled to an "adequate" education but do not have a right to an "equal" education. America's public schools differ greatly in quality primarily as a result of differences in the wealth of the communities they serve. Some public schools are overcrowded and have few facilities and little equipment. Others are very well equipped, have spacious facilities, and offer small class sizes.

Indeed, not until 1965, with passage of the Higher Education Act and the Elementary and Secondary Education Act (part of President Johnson's Great Society initiatives), did the federal government become involved in public education in a comprehensive way. Earlier federal efforts in the area of education had been either one-time or targeted interventions. In 1862, for example, Congress passed the Morrill Act, which provided states with free tracts of land if they used the land to establish colleges—the nation's great "land-grant" universities are the product of that legislation. Another one-time federal program was the G.I. Bill, enacted after World War II, giving financial assistance to enable military veterans to attend college or vocational school.

With passage of the 1965 federal legislation, the federal government assumed an ongoing role in public education. Federal grants to public schools and colleges became a regular part of their funding, though still a smaller part than that provided by state and local governments (see Chapters 3 and 18). The Higher Education Act became the foundation for Pell Grants, federal loans to college students, and federally subsidized college work-study programs. The Elementary and Secondary Education Act provides funding for items such as school construction, textbooks, special education, and teacher training. Federal funding is split almost evenly between support for colleges and support for elementary and secondary schools.

In recent years, education has increasingly become an issue of national debate, involving Washington officials ever more deeply in the issues. President Bill Clinton rejected the idea of unrestricted school choice, arguing that it would weaken the nation's public schools and make them a repository of America's poorest children. Clinton persuaded Congress instead to appropriate billions in new funding to enable overcrowded schools to hire tens of thousands of new teachers.

President George W. Bush brought a different education agenda to the White House, persuading Congress in 2001 to enact the No Child Left Behind Act. The legislation requires national testing in reading, math, and science and ties federal funding to the test results. Schools that show no improvement in students' test scores after years receive an increased amount of federal aid. If these schools show no improvement by the end of the third year, however, their students become eligible to transfer elsewhere and their federal assistance is reduced.

Few federal education policies have provoked as much controversy as the No Child Left Behind Act. The National Education Association (NEA) claims that the law has forced teachers to teach to the national tests and thus has interfered with real learning in the classroom. Congressional Democrats say that the program has failed to provide struggling schools with enough funds to improve the quality of classroom education and has encouraged the flight of students from public to private schools. For their part, congressional Republicans have applauded the law, saying that it holds teachers and schools accountable for their students' performance. Congressman John Boehner (R-Ohio) said in 2003, "Money alone is not the answer to the problems facing our children's schools. High standards and accountability for results—not just spending—are the key to erasing the achievement gap in education."[23]

Some states and localities have embraced the No Child Left Behind Act as an answer to underperforming schools. Some schools have, in fact, improved in terms of their performance on the national tests. Other states and localities have opposed the act, saying that the federal government has not provided the funds necessary to fully implement the testing program and that penalizing schools for this failure is unfair. They also say that the legislation fails to account for the testing difficulties faced by special education children. Opinion polls show that Americans are split nearly 50-50 on the new law, with Democrats generally more opposed to it and Republicans more supportive of it.[24]

HISTORICAL BACKGROUND

Thus, many of the partisan and philosophical differences that affect federal welfare policy also affect federal education policy. Democrats are more inclined to find the answer to how to improve schools in increased federal spending on education, particularly in less affluent communities, while Republicans are more inclined to look to marketlike mechanisms such as school choice and achievement tests.

THE AMERICAN WAY OF PROMOTING THE GENERAL WELFARE

All democratic societies promote economic security, but they do so in different ways and degrees. Economic security has a higher priority in European democracies than in the United States. European democracies have instituted programs such as government-paid health care for all citizens, compensation for all unemployed workers, and retirement benefits for all elderly citizens. As this chapter shows, the United States provides these benefits only to some citizens in each category. On the other hand, the American system of public education dwarfs those in Europe.

Such policy differences stem from historical and cultural differences. Democracy in Europe developed in reaction to centuries of aristocratic rule, which brought the issue of economic privilege to the forefront. When strong labor and socialist parties then emerged as a consequence of industrialization, European democracies initiated sweeping social welfare programs designed to bring about greater economic equality. Social inequality was harder to root out because it was thoroughly embedded in European society, shaping everything from social manners to education. Private schools and university training were the preserve of the elite, a tradition that, though now past, continues to affect how Europeans think about educational opportunity.

The American historical experience is a different one. Democracy in America grew out of a tradition of limited government that emphasized personal liberty, which included a belief in self-reliance. This belief contributed to Americans' strong support for public education and their weak support for public assistance. Unlike political equality, the idea of economic equality never captured Americans' imagination. Try as they might during America's Industrial Age, labor and socialist parties were unable to gain large and loyal followings. Even today, when Americans think of the plight of poorer people, they are as likely to make moral judgments as political ones. Political scientists Stanley Feldman and John Zaller found that Americans' support for public assistance programs rests more on compassion for the poor than on an ideological belief in economic sharing.[25] Or, as the political scientist Robert Lane expressed it, Americans have a preference for market justice, meaning that they prefer that society's material benefits be allocated through the economic marketplace rather than through government policies.[26]

Summary

Self-Test www.mhhe.com/pattersontad8

The United States has a complex social welfare system of multiple programs addressing specific welfare needs. Each program applies only to those individuals who qualify for benefits by meeting the specific eligibility criteria. In general, these criteria are designed to encourage self-reliance or, when help is necessary, to ensure that laziness is not rewarded or fostered. This approach to social welfare reflects Americans' traditional belief in individualism.

Poverty is a large and persistent problem in the United States. About one in nine Americans falls below the government-defined poverty line, including a disproportionate number of children, female-headed families, minority-group members, and   nd inner-city dwellers. The ranks of the poor are increa   economic recessions and are reduced through governu   ssistance programs.

Welfare polic   s been a partisan issue, with Democrats taking the lea   n government programs to alleviate economic insecurity an   Republicans acting to slow down or decentralize these initiatives. Changes in social welfare have usually occurred through presidential leadership in the context of majority support for the change. Welfare policy has been worked out through programs to provide jobs and job training, education programs, income measures, and especially transfer payments through individual-benefit programs.

Individual-benefit programs fall into two broad categories: social insurance and public assistance. The former includes programs such as social security for retired workers and Medicare for the elderly. Social insurance programs are funded by payroll taxes paid by potential recipients, who thus, in a sense, earn the benefits they later receive. Because of this arrangement, social insurance programs have broad public support. Public assistance programs, in contrast, are funded by general tax revenues and are targeted toward needy individuals and families. These programs are not controversial in principle; most Americans believe that government should assist the truly needy. However, because of a widespread belief that most welfare recipients could get along without assistance if they tried, these programs do not have universal public support, are only modestly funded, and are politically vulnerable.

Social welfare is a contentious issue. In one view, social welfare is too costly and assists too many people who could help themselves; another view holds that social welfare is not broad enough and that too many disadvantaged Americans live in poverty. Because of these irreconcilable differences and because of federalism and the widely shared view that welfare programs should target specific problems, the existing system of multiple programs, despite its administrative complexity and inefficiency, has been the only politically feasible solution.

The balance between economic equality and individualism tilts more heavily toward individualism in the United States than in other advanced industrialized democracies. Other democracies, for example, have government-paid health care for all citizens where as the United States does not. Compared to other democracies, however, the United States attempts to more equally educate its children, a policy consistent with its cultural emphasis on equality of opportunity. Like social welfare, however, education is a contentious issue involving disputes over the federal government's role, school choice, spending levels, and mandatory testing.

STUDY CORNER

Key Terms

effective tax rate (*p. 487*)
entitlement programs (*p. 480*)
equality of opportunity (*p. 489*)
in-kind benefit (*p. 484*)

means test (*p. 482*)
negative government (*p. 478*)
positive government (*p. 478*)
poverty line (*p. 475*)

public assistance (*p. 481*)
social insurance (*p. 480*)
transfer payments (*p. 479*)

Self-Test

1. The shape of the U.S. welfare policy system has been strongly influenced by:
   a. the cultural emphasis placed on economic equality.
   b. the fact that the United States has a federal system of government.
   c. the fact that the United States is the wealthiest nation on earth and thus can afford the most generous benefit system.
   d. a and b only.

2. The 1996 Welfare Reform Act that Congress passed provides:
   a. an end to the federal guarantee of cash assistance to needy families.
   b. a limitation of five years in most cases for a person to receive assistance.
   c. that states must train and help welfare recipients find employment.
   d. all of the above.

3. Public assistance programs include all of the following **except:**
   a. subsidized housing.
   b. unemployment insurance.
   c. Medicaid.
   d. food stamps.

4. Regarding American education, all **except** which one of the following statements are true?
   a. The U.S. invests more heavily in public education than any other nation.
   b. U.S. law requires states to spend roughly equal amounts on each public school student, regardless of whether that student is going to school in a city, suburb, or rural area.
   c. Free public education provides a way that more people can gain the foundation for economic advantage.
   d. The curriculum in U.S. schools is relatively standardized on the assumption that children should be given an equal opportunity to get ahead in life.

5. Administrative costs of welfare are substantially lower in Europe than in the United States because:
   a. European eligibility is universal for certain programs, such as health care, and thus money does not have to be spent on the paperwork necessary to determine eligibility, which is the case in the United States.
   b. European eligibility for most programs is restricted to providing services to only the poorest 5 percent of the population.
   c. Europe has primarily unitary governments, which means they have to administer only one set of rules, rather than fifty different sets as is the case in the United States because of state involvement in social welfare programs.
   d. a and c.

6. Regarding unemployment:
   a. according to research, the loss of a job or failure to immediately find a new job is in most cases the fault of the individual.
   b. U.S. Bureau of Labor statistics indicate that of those who have lost jobs, the large majority made the decision on their own to stop working rather than being terminated as part of a larger job layoff.
   c. government unemployment programs enjoy high levels of public support.
   d. none of the above.

7. The United States has one of the lowest poverty rates of any Western democracy. (T/F)

8. The Republican party has initiated nearly all major federal welfare programs. (T/F)

9. Social security and Medicare have widespread public support because they cost less than other welfare programs. (T/F)

10. There is a considerable gap in income levels between the top and bottom fifth of the American population. (T/F)

Critical Thinking

How has U.S. policy on welfare and education been influenced by Americans' belief in individualism? By America's federal system of government?

Suggested Readings

Alesina, Alberto, and Edward Glaeser. *Fighting Poverty in the U.S. and Europe: A World of Difference.* New York: Oxford University Press, 2006. A comparison of poverty policies in the United States and Europe.

Diamond, Peter A. *Social Security Reform.* New York: Oxford University Press, 2002. A comprehensive look at the issue of social security reform.

Melnick, R. Shep. *Between the Lines: Interpreting Welfare Rights.* Washington, D.C.: Brookings Institution Press, 1994. An analysis of the intricate relationship between social welfare legislation and its interpretation in the courts.

Patterson, James T. *America's Struggle Against Poverty in the Twentieth Century.* Cambridge, Mass.: Harvard University Press, 2000. A careful study of poverty and its history.

Quadagno, Jill. *One Nation, Uninsured: Why the United States Has No National Health Insurance.* New York: Oxford University Press, 2005. A look at the politics of U.S. health care policy.

Reed, Douglas S. *On Equal Terms: The Constitutional Politics of Educational Opportunity.* Princeton, N.J.: Princeton University Press, 2003. An insightful analysis of school reform issues.

Reese, William J. *America's Public Schools: From the Common School to "No Child Left Behind."* Baltimore, Maryland: Johns Hopkins University Press, 2005. A history of U.S. public schools.

Van Dunk, Emily, and Anneliese M. Dickman, *School Choice and the Question of Accountability.* New Haven, Conn.: Yale University Press, 2003. A careful look at the voucher system as applied in the Milwaukee school system.

List of Websites

http://www.doleta.gov/
The U.S. Department of Labor's website on the status of the welfare-to-work program, including state-by-state assessments.

http://www.nea.org/
The home page of the National Education Association; it provides information on the organization's membership and policy goals.

http://www.os.dhhs.gov/
The website of the Department of Health and Human Services—the agency responsible for most federal social welfare programs.

http://www.fordschool.umich.edu/poverty
The website of the University of Michigan's Program on Poverty and Social Welfare Policy; the program seeks to stimulate interest in policy issues and to transmit research findings to policymakers.

Participate!

Although social security might seem remote at this stage in your life, it is America's premier economic security program. Today, millions of retirees' lives are greatly eased by the monthly arrival of a social security check. Yet a social security crisis is looming because the number of retirees is increasing faster than the number of workers who pay taxes to fund the program. U.S. policymakers soon will have to address the issue of the program's solvency. Your voice can be part of that debate. Consider writing to a U.S. senator or representative expressing your opinion on the future of social security—for example, whether private individual accounts should be made a part of the program.

Extra Credit

For up-to-the-minute *New York Times* articles, interactive simulations, graphics, study tools, and more links and quizzes, visit the text's Online Learning Center at www.mhhe.com/pattersontad8.

Foreign and Defense Policy:
Protecting the American Way

Chapter Outline

The Roots of U.S. Foreign and Defense Policy

The United States as Global Superpower

The Cold War and Vietnam

Disintegration of the "Evil Empire"

A New World Order

The War on Terrorism

The Iraq War

The Military Dimension of National Security Policy

Military Power, Uses, and Capabilities

The Politics of National Defense

The Economic Dimension of National Security Policy

A Changing World Economy

America's Global Economic Goals

A New World

CHAPTER 17

We the people of the United States, in order to . . .
provide for the common defense . . .

—Preamble, U.S. Constitution

As the sectarian violence continued in Iraq in 2007, U.S. policymakers worried that it was jeopardizing all that America had sacrificed during its four-year occupation of that country. Nearly three thousand U.S. soldiers had lost their lives and hundreds of billions of dollars had been spent, but Iraq nonetheless seemed to have devolved into civil war. But if the military situation in Iraq was foremost in U.S. policymakers' minds, they also had their eye on a second issue: the economic consequences of the Iraq conflict. The war had raised tensions throughout the Middle East, leading to fears of a disruption in the flow of the region's oil, which could destabilize world markets. The price of oil had already reached record heights, and a sharp reduction in Middle East oil production could send the costs skyrocketing with devastating consequences for the U.S. economy.

As America's involvement in Iraq illustrates, national security is an issue that ranges from military strength to economic vitality. The primary goal of U.S. foreign policy is protection of the American state. This objective requires military readiness in order to safeguard the territorial integrity of the United States, and it rises to the fore with every immediate threat, such as the terrorist attacks of September 11, 2001. But the American state also represents a society of 300 million people whose livelihood depends in significant part on the nation's position in the global economy. Through participation in economic policies that foster economic growth and international stability, the United States can secure the jobs and trade that contribute to the maintenance of a high standard of living.

National security, unlike other areas of government policy, rests on relations with actors outside rather than within the country. As a result, the chief instruments of national security policy differ substantially from those of domestic policy. One of these instruments is diplomacy, the process of negotiation between countries. The lead agency in U.S. diplomatic efforts is the Department of State, which is headed by the secretary of state and coordinates the efforts of U.S. embassies abroad, each of which is directed by a U.S. ambassador. American diplomacy also takes place through international organizations—such as the United Nations—to which the United States belongs. A second instrument of foreign policy is military power. The lead agency in military affairs is the Department of Defense, which is headed by the secretary of defense and oversees the three U.S. military branches—the Army, Navy, and Air Force. Here, too, the United States sometimes works through

President George W. Bush talks with firefighters and police on the site of the collapsed World Trade Center buildings. The terrorist attacks of September 11, 2001, produced a fundamental change in U.S. foreign policy and public opinion.

alliances, the most important of which is the North Atlantic Treaty Organization (NATO). NATO has twenty-six member nations, including the United States, Canada, and most Western and Eastern European countries. A third instrument of world politics is intelligence gathering, or the process of monitoring other countries' activities. For many reasons, but primarily because all countries pursue their own self-interest, each nation keeps a watchful eye on other nations. In the United States, the task of intelligence gathering falls to specialized federal agencies including the Central Intelligence Agency (CIA) and the National Security Agency (NSA). Because the intelligence budget is classified, the exact amount the United States spends annually in this area is unknown; it is estimated to be in the range of $40 billion to $50 billion. Economic exchange, the fourth instrument of foreign affairs, involves both international trade and foreign aid. U.S. interests in this area are promoted by a range of U.S. agencies, such as the Agriculture, Commerce, Labor, and Treasury Departments, as well as specialty agencies such as the Federal Trade Commission. The United States also pursues its economic goals through international organizations of which it is a member, including the World Trade Organization (WTO), the World Bank, and the International Monetary Fund (IMF).

The president is at the center of these activities. Although the president shares power and responsibility in the area of foreign and defense policy with Congress, the president's constitutional authority as commander-in-chief, chief diplomat, chief of state, and chief executive puts that office in the lead (see Chapter 12). For example, although President George W. Bush briefed congressional leaders on his plans for war with Iraq, they did not have full access to his intelligence reports, did not participate in strategic planning for the war, and did not have a say in how the war plan was executed.

The national security policies of the United States include an extraordinary array of activities—so many, in fact, that they could not possibly be addressed adequately in an entire book, much less a single chapter. There are roughly two hundred countries in the world, and the United States has relations of one kind or another—military, diplomatic, economic—with all of them. This chapter narrows the subject by concentrating on a few main ideas:

- *Since World War II, the United States has acted in the role of world leader, which has substantially affected its military, diplomatic, and economic policies.*

- *The United States maintains a high degree of defense preparedness, which mandates a substantial level of defense spending and a worldwide deployment of U.S. conventional and strategic forces.*

- *Changes in the international marketplace have led to increased economic interdependence among nations, which has had a marked influence on the U.S. economy and on America's security planning.*

THE ROOTS OF U.S. FOREIGN AND DEFENSE POLICY

HISTORICAL BACKGROUND

For nearly half a century, U.S. defense policy was defined by conflict with the Soviet Union. From the Berlin airlift in 1948 to the Vietnam escalation in 1965 to the Star Wars initiative in 1983, the United States seemed willing to pay any price to halt the spread of Soviet influence. Then, in the late 1980s, the Soviet empire dramatically began to fall apart. In December 1991, the Soviet Union itself ceased to exist. For decades, there had been two superpowers, the Soviet Union and the United States. Now there is only one.

Since the fall of the Soviet Union, the United States has redefined its foreign and defense policies. The country is still at the center of world politics, but its challenges have changed. The terrorist attacks on the World Trade Center and the Pentagon in 2001 revealed to all what some analysts had been warning: the biggest threat to the physical security of the American people is not other nations but international terrorists who fight on behalf of causes. Developments in the previous decade had made another fact abundantly clear: a strong domestic base is the key to success in the increasingly important global economy.[1]

Although the age of superpower conflict is over, America's role in world affairs was shaped by that era. Accordingly, an understanding of the nation's foreign and defense policies and capabilities necessarily begins with an awareness of key developments during that period.

The United States as Global Superpower

Before World War II, the United States was an **isolationist** country, deliberately avoiding a large role in world affairs. A different America emerged from the war. It had more land, sea, and air power than any other country in the world, a huge military-industrial base, and several hundred overseas military bases. The United States had become an **internationalist** country, deeply involved in the affairs of other nations.

The shift away from isolationism was evident in Americans' attitude toward international organizations. After World War I, the United States refused to join the League of Nations, virtually guaranteeing that the League would be too weak to broker conflicts between the European powers. After World War II, the United States was the leading advocate of the United Nations, even granting it land in New York City for its headquarters. The UN Security Council, with the United States, France, Britain, the Soviet Union, and the Republic of China as its permanent members, was expected to create a new era of international cooperation.

This hope was derailed when the Soviet Union helped the communist parties in Eastern Europe capture state power, usually by coercive

isolationist
Describes the view that the country should deliberately avoid a large role in world affairs and instead concentrate on domestic concerns.

internationalist
Describes the view that the country should involve itself deeply in world affairs.

AMERICA UNDER COMMUNISM!

Cold war propaganda, like this poster warning of the danger of communism, contributed to a climate of opinion in the United States that led to public support for efforts to contain Soviet power.

means. Poland, Hungary, and the other Eastern European countries were dragged into the Soviet orbit. The British wartime prime minister, Winston Churchill, said that an "iron curtain" had fallen across Europe.

U.S. security policy thereafter was designed to contain Soviet power. President Harry Truman regarded the Soviet Union as an implacable ideological foe bent on global domination that could be stopped only by the forceful use of U.S. power. Truman's view was based on assumptions derived from territorial concessions made to Germany's Adolf Hitler by Britain and France at a conference in Munich in 1938; rather than appeasing Hitler, these concessions convinced him that Germany could bully its way to further gains. The idea that appeasement only encourages further aggression was the *lesson of Munich,* and it became the dominant view of U.S. policymakers in the postwar period. It contributed to the formulation of the doctrine of **containment,** which was based on the idea that the Soviet Union was an aggressor nation that had to be stopped from achieving its global ambitions.[2]

The Cold War and Vietnam

Developments in the late 1940s embroiled the United States in a **cold war** with the Soviet Union. The term refers to the fact that the two countries were not directly engaged in actual combat (a "hot war") but were locked in a deep-seated hostility that lasted forty-five years. The structure of international power was **bipolar:** the United States against the Soviet Union. Each side was supreme in its sphere and was blocked from expanding its influence by the power of the other.

The cold war included U.S. support for governments threatened by communist takeovers. In China, the United States backed the Nationalist government, which nevertheless was defeated in 1949 by the Soviet-supplied communist forces of Mao Zedong. In June 1950, when the Soviet-backed North Koreans invaded South Korea, President Truman sent troops into the conflict, which ended in stalemate and resulted in the death of thirty-five thousand U.S. soldiers.

A major turning point in U.S. foreign policy was the Vietnam War. Responding to the threat of a communist takeover, the United States became ever more deeply involved in the civil war in Vietnam. By the late 1960s, 550,000 Americans were stationed in South Vietnam. U.S. forces were technically superior in combat to the communist fighters, but they were fighting an enemy they could not easily identify in a society they did not fully understand.[3] Vietnam was a guerrilla war, with no front lines and few set battles. As the conflict dragged on, American public opinion, most visibly among the young, turned against the war, contributing to President Lyndon Johnson's decision not to run for reelection in 1968. Public opinion forced Richard Nixon, who became president in 1969, to aim not for victory but for a gradual disengagement. U.S. combat troops left Vietnam in 1973, and two years later North Vietnamese forces concluded their takeover of the country. Vietnam was the most painful and costly application of the containment doctrine: fifty-eight thousand American soldiers lost their lives in the fighting.

Disintegration of the "Evil Empire"

America's defeat in Vietnam forced U.S. policymakers to reconsider the country's international role. The *lesson of Vietnam* was that there were limits to the country's ability to assert its will in the world. Nixon claimed that the United States could no longer act as the "Lone Ranger" for the free world, and he sought

containment

A doctrine, developed after World War II, based on assumptions that the Soviet Union was an aggressor nation and that only a determined United States could block Soviet territorial ambitions.

cold war

The lengthy period after World War II when the United States and the Soviet Union were not engaged in actual combat (a "hot war") but were locked in a state of deep-seated hostility.

bipolar (power structure)

A power structure dominated by two powers only, as in the case of the United States and the Soviet Union during the cold war.

In the jungle warfare of Vietnam, American soldiers had difficulty finding the enemy and adapting to guerrilla tactics.

to reduce tensions with communist countries. In 1972, Nixon took a historic journey to the People's Republic of China, the first official contact with that country since the communists seized power in 1949. Nixon also initiated the Strategic Arms Limitation Talks (SALT), which presumed that the United States and the Soviet Union each had an interest in retaining enough nuclear weapons to deter the other from an attack but that neither side had an interest in an arms race that could lead to their mutual destruction. This spirit of cooperation did not last. The Soviet invasion of Afghanistan in 1979 convinced U.S. leaders that the USSR was still bent on expansion and threatened Western interests in the oil-rich Middle East. Ronald Reagan, elected president in 1980, called for a renewed hard line toward the Soviet Union, which he described as the "evil empire."

Although U.S. policymakers did not fully realize it at the time, the Soviet Union was collapsing under its heavy defense expenditures, its isolation from Western technology and markets, and its inefficient centralized economy. In 1985, Mikhail Gorbachev became the Soviet leader and sought to restructure Soviet society, an initiative known as *perestroika*. He also ordered a Soviet withdrawal from Afghanistan (which had become his country's Vietnam).

Gorbachev's efforts came too late to save the Soviet Union. In 1989, the withdrawal of Soviet troops from Eastern Europe accelerated a pro-democracy movement that was already under way in the region. Poland initiated major reforms. Hungary dismantled the "iron curtain" that had blocked free travel to Austria. Then, in November, the Berlin Wall between East and West Germany—the most visible symbol of the separation of East and West—came down. The Soviet Union itself was also disintegrating. On December 8, 1991, the leaders of the Russian, Belarus, and Ukrainian republics declared that the Soviet Union no longer existed. The bipolar power structure that had dominated world politics since the end of World War II had collapsed. The new structure was **unipolar**—the United States was now the unchallenged world power.

A New World Order

The end of the cold war prompted the first President Bush in 1990 to call for a "new world order." His formulation abandoned the assumption that world affairs are a zero-sum game, in which for one nation to gain something, another

unipolar (power structure)
A power structure dominated by a single powerful actor, as in the case of the United States after the collapse of the Soviet Union.

multilateralism

The situation in which nations act together in response to problems and crises.

nation has to lose. Bush championed **multilateralism**—the idea that major nations should act together in response to problems and crises. Included in Bush's plan was an enhanced status for the United Nations, which would assume a pivotal international role.

Multilateralism defined America's response to the Iraqi invasion of Kuwait in August 1990. President Bush obtained a UN resolution that imposed economic sanctions on Iraq and demanded its withdrawal from Kuwait. When Iraqi president Saddam Hussein did not comply, the UN authorized a military buildup in the Gulf. A half million troops, mostly American but including contingents from nearly two dozen other nations, were moved into positions facing the Iraqi army. When Iraq still refused to withdraw, the UN force attacked, first with an aerial bombardment and then with ground troops. The ground assault was spearheaded by U.S. Army and Marine units, flanked by French and British armored divisions. Four days into the ground fighting, Iraqi units fled the battlefield, ending the war.

The Gulf operation was a military triumph, prompting President Bush to declare that the United States had "kicked the Vietnam syndrome [the legacy of America's defeat in Vietnam] once and for all." The Gulf War, however, was in another way less successful. Believing that an overthrow of Hussein's regime would destabilize Iraq, President Bush ordered a halt to the hostilities after Iraqi forces retreated. Hussein remained in power but was ordered by a UN resolution to dismantle his weapons programs, subject to UN inspections. However, Hussein constantly interfered with UN inspectors' attempts to verify the status of his weapons programs, raising concerns about his plans.

President Bush's multilateral approach to foreign affairs carried over into the Clinton administration. Confronting Serb atrocities in Bosnia—where tens of thousands of Muslims and Croats were murdered, raped, and driven from their homes—President Clinton pursued UN economic sanctions as a means of halting the slaughter. When sanctions failed, the United States and its NATO allies attacked Serb forces with air power. The result was a U.S.-negotiated peace agreement (the Dayton Accords) that included the deployment to Bosnia of nearly sixty thousand peacekeeping troops, including twenty thousand Americans. War in the Balkans flared again in 1999 when the Serbs undertook a campaign of "ethnic cleansing" in the Serbian province of Kosovo, whose population was 90 percent Albanian. When attempts at a negotiated settlement failed, NATO planes, including U.S. aircraft, attacked Serbia. After weeks of intensive bombing, Yugoslav president Slobodan Milosevic (who died in 2006 while on trial for war crimes) pulled his troops out of Kosovo. Ethnic Albanians moved back in and, despite the presence of UN peacekeeping troops, commenced revenge attacks on some of the Serbs who remained.

As these examples indicate, multilateralism has been only partly successful as a strategy for resolving international conflicts. With the deployment of enough resources, the world's major powers can intervene with some success in many parts of the developing world. However, these interventions offer no guarantee of long-term success. Regional and internal conflicts typically stem from enduring ethnic, religious, factional, or national hatreds or from chronic problems such as famine, overcrowding, or government corruption. Even if these hatreds or problems can be momentarily eased, they are often too deep-seated to be permanently resolved.

The War on Terrorism

When he assumed the presidency in 2001, George W. Bush made it clear that he would not follow the national security policy of his father. Bush declared that he had no plans to engage in "nation building" and that he would reduce America's

Media & Politics

Global Television and Foreign Policy

In just the past few decades, global television networks such as CNN have developed the capacity to provide live television coverage from almost anywhere in the world. Americans have been eyewitnesses to fighting in places such as Iraq, Somalia, Bosnia, Kosovo, and Afghanistan. Global television has broken down the boundaries of space and time that once formed a buffer between Americans and warfare in distant areas of the globe.

Some analysts believe that television coverage has affected U. S. foreign policy. They point, for example, to U.S. intervention in Somalia in the early 1990s. CNN's pictures of long lines of starving refugees touched a responsive chord in the United States and other countries, and the United Nations sent a humanitarian mission to Somalia that included American soldiers. This intervention turned sour when warring Somalian clans threatened the mission. An American military unit was ambushed, and several dozen U.S. soldiers died. Television captured the haunting image of one of the dead soldiers being dragged by a mob through the streets of the Somalian capital, and public opinion quickly shifted. Americans had supported the humanitarian mission, but they now wanted U.S. troops pulled out of Somalia as rapidly as possible. Within a short period, the troops were withdrawn.

With its preference for action and drama, television in its war coverage tends to play up conflict and death rather than cooperation and progress. The compelling news story out of Iraq after the active combat phase was not the reopening of schools or the rebuilding of the oil industry. The coverage concentrated instead on the deaths of U.S. soldiers, the frustrating search for weapons of mass destruction, and the abuse of Iraqi prisoners, contributing to declining public support for a protracted stay in Iraq.

Some analysts see this type of coverage as a positive development because it mobilizes public opinion and makes leaders more sensitive to it. They claim that this makes it harder for leaders to paint rosy scenarios that gain support simply because leaders present them as the proper course of action. Other analysts are critical of the development. They argue that television's pictures tend to reflect only the most incendiary aspects of a situation and thus serve to distort both the situation and the public's response to it, possibly forcing policymakers to base policy choices on short-term political considerations rather than on long-term policy objectives. What's your view? Do television pictures of conflict abroad help or hurt in the making of foreign policy?

---

military presence abroad as well as its reliance on the United Nations. He also announced that the United States would not participate in either the Kyoto Accord (a global climate treaty) or the International Criminal Court (the ICC, a permanent tribunal with jurisdiction over war crimes).

The terrorist attacks of September 11, 2001, on the World Trade Center and the Pentagon forced Bush to reverse course. Although he did not change his position on the ICC or the Kyoto Accord, he called upon the other nations of the world to join the United States in a global "war on terrorism." Unlike past wars, it targets not nations but groups engaged in terrorism that is aimed at U.S. interests at home and abroad. A war without sharply defined battlefronts, it is being waged through a wide variety of instruments, including military force, intelligence gathering, law enforcement, foreign aid, international cooperation, and immigration control. The tactics are also unusual. The rooting out of terrorist cells in the United States and Europe, for example, is entrusted to law enforcement agencies rather than to military units.

The war on terrorism resulted in the first major reorganization of the U.S. national security bureaucracy since the Department of Defense was formed after World War II to combine the previously separate War and Navy Departments. The new agency this time was the Department of Homeland Security (DHS), which was created in 2002 to coordinate domestic efforts to protect the United States against terrorist threats. The responsibilities of the homeland security agency include securing the nation's borders, enhancing defense against biological attacks, preparing emergency personnel (police, firefighters, and rescue workers) for their roles in responding to terrorist attacks, and coordinating efforts to stop domestic terrorism.[4]

The first U.S. military action in the war on terrorism was an attack on Afghanistan. Its Taliban-led government had provided training sites and protection to the Al Qaeda terrorist network, which had carried out the September 11 attacks. Backed by a UN resolution authorizing the use of force and supported by other NATO member countries, the United States toppled the Taliban government in early 2002; however, Al Qaeda leader Osama bin Laden and most of his top lieutenants evaded capture.

In 2002, President Bush labeled Iraq, Iran, and North Korea an "axis of evil," thereby signaling a widening of the war on terrorism. Shortly thereafter, he announced a new national security doctrine: the **preemptive war doctrine.** Speaking at West Point, President Bush said that the threat of international terrorism meant that the United States could not afford to wait until it was attacked by hostile nations. Bush declared that America was prepared to take "preemptive action."[5] This concept was not entirely new—U.S. officials had long maintained a right to strike first if faced with a serious and immediate threat. What was new about the Bush doctrine was that it extended the option to include military action against remotely threatening countries.

preemptive war doctrine

The idea, espoused by President George W. Bush, that the United States could attack a potentially threatening nation even if the threat had not yet reached a serious and immediate level.

unilateralism

The situation in which one nation takes action against another state or states.

The Iraq War

In the summer of 2002, Bush targeted the regime of Iraq's Saddam Hussein, claiming that it had weapons of mass destruction (WMDs)—chemical and biological weapons, and possibly even nuclear weapons. Bush asked Congress for a resolution authorizing the use of military force against Iraq if it did not fully and rapidly disarm. In October, Congress passed the resolution.

Facing the possibility of a Middle Eastern war, America's European allies urged the disarmament of Iraq through UN weapons inspectors. In late 2002, the United Nations passed a resolution that required Iraq to accept weapons inspections. A two-track policy ensued. UN weapons inspectors entered Iraq in search of WMDs, while at the same time the United States deployed combat units to the Middle East.

Over the strenuous objections of the French, German, and Russian governments and despite a failure to get UN authorization for military action, President Bush in March 2003 ordered U.S. forces to attack Iraq. Although British units were also involved, the assault was essentially an act of **unilateralism**—the situation in which one nation takes action against another state or states. The Iraqi regime quickly collapsed— Hussein was deposed after less than a month of fighting. However, the post-combat phase proved deadlier than the Bush administration had anticipated. Roadside mines and

In March 2003, by order of President George W. Bush, U.S. troops attacked Iraq. The intense combat phase was relatively short, ending in the defeat of Iraqi forces. However, the reconstruction phase that followed was marked by continuing U.S. casualties and questions about the validity of the intelligence estimates that had been used to justify the attack.

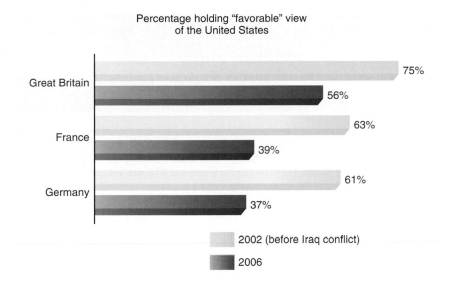

Percentage holding "favorable" view
of the United States

Great Britain — 75%, 56%

France — 63%, 39%

Germany — 61%, 37%

2002 (before Iraq conflict)
2006

Figure 17–1

Impact of Iraq Conflict on Europeans' Opinion of the United States
The Iraq conflict has led to a sharp decline in Europeans' opinion of the United States.
Source: The Pew Research Center for the People and the Press surveys.

suicide bombers took a heavy toll on U.S. soldiers, and the cost of rebuilding Iraq soon rose above $100 billion. Moreover, the WMDs that Bush had stated were the reason for the war could not be found. In early 2004, the chief U.S. weapons inspector, David Kay, testified before Congress that U.S. intelligence agencies had grossly exaggerated the extent of Iraq's weapons program.

The American public, which had strongly backed the invasion of Iraq, came to question the war. Americans also expressed doubts about Bush's pre-emptive war doctrine. One poll found that only 34 percent agreed that the "United States has the right and even the responsibility to overthrow dictatorships and help their people build a democracy."[6] Opinion elsewhere was more critical. For the first time since World War II, Western Europeans held that the United States should not be entrusted with world leadership. A year before the war, roughly 65 percent of Western Europeans had expressed a favorable opinion of the United States; fewer than 50 percent held that view afterward (see Figure 17–1).

Public opinion in Europe hampered the postwar reconstruction of Iraq. America's request for assistance in rebuilding Iraq was not ignored by European governments, but they hardly jumped at the opportunity. Although some assistance was offered, it was limited by public opposition to what was seen as "America's war." Negative public opinion also led the Dutch and Spanish governments, which had backed the invasion, to withdraw their small troop units from Iraq.

Postwar reconstruction was also hampered by instability in Iraq. Age-old animosities between Sunni, Shiite, and Kurdish groups within Iraq blocked political compromise and fueled violence. As the sectarian killings escalated, the animosities deepened. Foreign-born fighters compounded the problem. Iraq's lengthy border with Iran and Syria—countries antagonistic to the United States—allowed Islamic militants from other countries to join the fighting in Iraq.

During White House deliberations before the war, Secretary of State Colin Powell had invoked what he called "the Pottery Barn rule." Powell warned that officials who believed Iraqis would welcome U.S. troops with open arms were engaging in wishful thinking. Foreseeing a difficult post-invasion phase, Powell said, "If you break it, you own it." Indeed, the United States has been forced to go it nearly alone in the reconstruction of Iraq, at considerable cost in terms of

Debating the Issues

Should U.S. Forces Stay in Iraq?

In 2003, at the order of President George W. Bush, U.S. forces attacked Iraq. Within a few weeks, the regime of Saddam Hussein had been toppled. The reconstruction phase, however, proved far more difficult than the White House had promised. Continuing attacks on U.S. forces and Iraqi civilians slowed the rebuilding of Iraq's infrastructure and the creation of an effective Iraqi government. Two years after the invasion, a majority of Americans had come to believe that the invasion of Iraq was a mistake. Most, however, felt that the United States had no choice but to complete the task of stabilizing Iraq before withdrawing U.S. troops. For his part, President Bush remained unwavering in his belief in the need for the continuing presence of U.S. forces in Iraq. One of the first prominent congressional critics of Bush's position was Representative John Murtha of Pennsylvania, a former Marine who received the Bronze Star and two Purple Hearts for service in Vietnam. Murtha drew national attention when he called for a withdrawal of U.S. forces. Murtha had supported the congressional resolution authorizing the invasion but came to conclude that President Bush had misled the nation. What's your view on the U.S. occupation of Iraq? Should American troops stay, or should they be withdrawn? What is your opinion based on?

Yes A secure and free Iraq is an historic opportunity to change the world and make America more secure. A free Iraq in the midst of the Middle East will have incredible change. It's hard—freedom is not easy to achieve. . . . We're changing the world. And the world will be better off and America will be more secure as a result of the actions we're taking. . . . Saddam Hussein was a threat. He was a threat because he had used weapons of mass destruction on his own people. He was a threat because he coddled terrorists. He was a threat because he funded suiciders. He was a threat to the region. He was a threat to the United States. . . . The Iraqis are really pleased we got rid of Saddam Hussein. And you can understand why. This is a guy who . . . [made them] fearful of making decisions toward liberty. That's what we've seen recently. Some citizens are fearful of stepping up. . . . They're not happy they're occupied. I wouldn't be happy if I were occupied either. They do want us there to help with security, and that's why this transfer of sovereignty is an important signal to send, and it's why it's also important for them to hear we will stand with them until they become a free country.

—*George W. Bush, president of the United States*

No The war in Iraq is not going as advertised. It is a flawed policy wrapped in illusion. The American public is way ahead of us. The United States and coalition troops have done all they can in Iraq, but it is time for a change in direction. Our military is suffering. The future of our country is at risk. We can not continue on the present course. It is evident that continued military action in Iraq is not in the best interest of the United States of America, the Iraqi people or the Persian Gulf Region. General Casey said in a September 2005 hearing, "the perception of occupation in Iraq is a major driving force behind the insurgency.". . . We spend more money on Intelligence than all the countries in the world together, and more on Intelligence than most countries' GDP. But the intelligence concerning Iraq was wrong. It is not a world intelligence failure. It is a U.S. intelligence failure and the way that intelligence was misused. . . . Our troops have become the primary target of the insurgency. They are united against U.S. forces and we have become a catalyst for violence. U.S. troops are the common enemy of the Sunnis, Saddamists and foreign jihadists. I believe with a U.S. troop redeployment, the Iraqi security forces will be incentivized to take control. A poll recently conducted shows that over 80% of Iraqis are strongly opposed to the presence of coalition troops, and about 45% of the Iraqi population believe attacks against American troops are justified. I believe we need to turn Iraq over to the Iraqis. . . . Because we in Congress are charged with sending our sons and daughters into battle, it is our responsibility, our obligation to speak out for them. That's why I am speaking out. Our military has done everything that has been asked of them; the U.S. can not accomplish anything further in Iraq militarily. It is time to bring them home.

—*John P. Murtha, U.S. representative (D-Pa.)*

American lives and dollars. An indicator of the price of unilateralism in Iraq is the fact that 90 percent of the casualties and the monetary costs have been borne by the United States. Nevertheless, most U.S. officials—Democrats and Republicans alike—believe there is little choice but to stay in Iraq until its government and security forces are stronger.

The difficulty of the reconstruction phase in Iraq has limited America's ability to respond to other fronts in the war on terrorism. Since the U.S. invasion, North Korea has acquired nuclear weapons, Iran is developing the technology that could lead to the acquisition of such weapons, and Taliban forces in Afghanistan have regrouped and are expanding the fighting in that country. Thus, as was true of multilateralism, unilateralism has been shown to have its limits. Even with the world's most powerful military, the United States has found it difficult to go it alone in Iraq. Wars like those in Iraq and Vietnam do not lend themselves to quick and tidy battlefield solutions. It is one thing to defeat a conventional army in open warfare and quite another to prevail in a conflict in which the fight is not for territory but for people's hearts and minds, especially when the people are not of one heart and one mind but instead are at each other's throats.

THE MILITARY DIMENSION OF NATIONAL SECURITY POLICY

The launching of the war on terrorism brought about the first major increase—tens of billions of dollars—in U.S. defense spending since the 1980s. The United States spends far more on defense, in both relative and absolute terms, than its allies do. On a per capita basis, U.S. military spending is more than twice that of other nations in the NATO alliance (see "How the United States Compares"). The U.S. defense budget is second to none in the world, but so is the military power it buys.

Military Power, Uses, and Capabilities

U.S. military forces are trained or called on for different types of military action, ranging from nuclear conflict to guerrilla warfare.

Nuclear War Capability

Although the possibility of all-out nuclear war with Russia declined dramatically with the end of the cold war, the United States retains a nuclear arsenal designed to prevent such a war from ever happening. **Deterrence policy** is based on the notion that any nation would be deterred from launching a full-scale nuclear attack on the United States by the knowledge that, even if it obliterated the country, it would be destroyed as well. America's nuclear weapons are deployed in what is called the "nuclear triad." This term refers to the three ways nuclear weapons can be launched: by land-based missiles, by submarine-based missiles, and by bombers. The triad provides a second-strike capability, that is, the ability to absorb a first-strike nuclear attack and survive with enough nuclear punch for a massive retaliation (second strike). Since the end of the cold war, the United States and Russia have negotiated reductions in their nuclear arsenals and have created monitoring systems designed to reduce the possibility that either side, by mistake or by design, could launch a surprise attack with its remaining warheads.

deterrence policy
The idea that nuclear war can be discouraged if each side in a conflict has the capacity to destroy the other with nuclear weapons.

How the United States Compares

The Burden of Military Spending

The United States bears a disproportionate share of the defense costs of the NATO alliance. The U.S. military establishment is huge and is deployed all over the world, and taxpayers spend more than $400 billion per year to maintain it. These expenditures directly account for roughly 5 percent of the U.S. gross national product (GNP). By comparison, defense spending by Germany, Italy, and Canada accounts for 3 percent or less of their GNPs. The percentages for Britain and France are higher but not as high as for the United States. Japan, which is not part of NATO, spends only 1 percent of its GNP on defense. Japan's small military force is confined by World War II peace agreements to the country's islands and the adjoining waters.

The United States has pressured its allies to carry a larger share of the defense burden, but these countries have resisted, contending that the cost would be too high and that their security would not be substantially improved. A partial exception to this situation was the Persian Gulf War of the early 1990s. U.S. troops accounted for the bulk of the military strength arrayed against Iraq, but the financial cost of the war effort was borne by other countries. Germany, Japan, Saudi Arabia, and Kuwait were among those that helped fund the war. In fact, other countries gave the United States $20 billion more than it spent on the war.

The war on terrorism has forced an increase in U.S. military spending that, except for Great Britain, has not been matched by increased spending by America's allies. However, some U.S. officials prefer the imbalance because it gives the United States more freedom to act on its own when it prefers to do so.

The United States accounts for nearly half of the total defense spending worldwide.

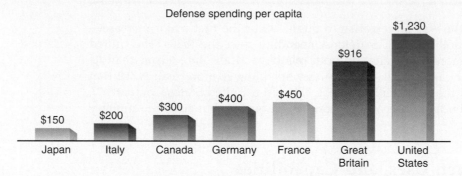

Defense spending per capita

Japan	Italy	Canada	Germany	France	Great Britain	United States
$150	$200	$300	$400	$450	$916	$1,230

Source: OECD (Organization for Economic Cooperation and Development) and U.S. and British government statistics.

A greater fear today than nuclear war with Russia is the possibility that a terrorist group or rogue nation could smuggle a nuclear device into the United States and detonate it. The technology and materials necessary to build a nuclear weapon (or to buy one clandestinely) are more readily available than ever before. Accordingly, the United States, Russia, and other nations are cooperating to halt the spread of nuclear weapons. This effort has had some success, but North Korea has recently acquired nuclear weapons and Iran could be moving in the same direction. Both nations have hostile relations with the United States.

Conventional and Guerrilla War Capability

Nuclear preparedness is just one part of America's combat readiness. A second is conventional-force preparedness. Not since World War II has the United States fought an all-out conventional war, nor does it at present have the capacity to fight one. That type of war would require a reinstatement of the military draft

States in the Nation

The All-Volunteer Military's Recruits

Until 1973, the United States had an active military draft. Upon reaching the age of eighteen, males were required to register for the draft. Local draft boards would then pick the draftees based on quotas that varied with the size of the local population. Accordingly, each state contributed equally to the military's manpower needs relative to its population size. Today's military is an all-volunteer force, and the states' contributions vary significantly. The map below indicates the degree to which each state is over- and underrepresented in the military as indicated by the ratio of military recruits from a state to the number of males ages eighteen to thirty-four in that state's population. Montana has the largest number of recruits relative to its population, followed in order by Alaska, Wyoming, and Maine. Utah, Rhode Island, and Massachusetts rank lowest, in that order.

Q: What might explain why military recruits come disproportionately from states like Montana, Alaska, Wyoming, and Maine as well as from the southern states?

A: According to Department of Defense data, recruits are more likely to come from rural areas, particularly areas where few well-paying jobs are available to young adults. The four states with the highest recruitment ratios have these characteristics. As for the South, higher recruitment levels there have been explained in terms of its stronger military tradition and its numerous military installations. Individuals from areas near these installations, as well as the sons and daughters of military personnel, are more likely to enlist in the military.

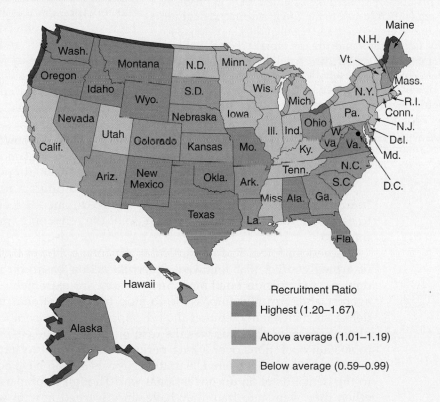

Recruitment Ratio

Highest (1.20–1.67)

Above average (1.01–1.19)

Below average (0.59–0.99)

Source: Adapted from Tim Kane, "Who Bears the Burden? Demographic Characteristics of U.S. Military Recruits Before and After 9/11," Heritage Foundation, Center for Data Analysis Report #05-08, November 7, 2005.

LEADERS

MARY EDWARDS WALKER

(1832–1919)

The Congressional Medal of Honor is the nation's highest award. Only one woman, Mary Edwards Walker, has received it. Born in upstate New York, she attended Syracuse Medical College, the first such college to accept women as students. When the Civil War broke out, she joined the Union Army as a nurse because the Army would not accept women physicians. Later she worked as a surgeon, although the Army classified her as a civilian rather than as a soldier. She treated the wounded at numerous battlefronts and would sometimes cross enemy lines to help victims on the Confederate side. In 1864, while doing just that, she was taken prisoner by Confederate soldiers. Sent to prison in Richmond, she was subsequently returned to the Union side in exchange for a captured Confederate officer. Once freed, she rejoined the Union forces as a surgeon. Impressed by her fearless and tireless work, General William Tecumseh Sherman recommended her for the Medal of Honor, which she was awarded by President Andrew Johnson. Fifty years later, Dr. Walker's medal and a number of others were rescinded by Congress on grounds that the actions were not heroic enough. However, she refused to return the medal, believing that her support of women's suffrage was the reason Congress had included her in the group. Six decades later, Congress reinstated Mary Edwards Walker's Congressional Medal of Honor.

and a full-scale mobilization of the nation's industrial capacity. Instead, the United States today has an all-volunteer military force with the training and armament needed to overwhelm any foe that would engage it in pitched battle (see "States in the Nation"). The U.S. Navy has a dozen aircraft carriers, scores of attack submarines, and hundreds of fighting and supply ships. The U.S. Air Force has thousands of high-performance aircraft, ranging from fighter jets to jumbo supply planes. The U.S. Army has roughly five hundred thousand regular troops and more than three hundred thousand Reserve and National Guard soldiers who are supplied with state-of-the-art tanks, artillery pieces, armored personnel carriers, and attack helicopters.

What makes these planes, tanks, and other weapons doubly lethal are the high-tech systems that support them. Surveillance devices (such as satellites), high-speed computers, and sophisticated software give U.S. military commanders an unrivaled ability to gather, process, and disseminate tactical information. No other nation has anywhere near the advanced weapons systems that the United States possesses. The full combat phases of the Afghanistan and Iraq wars demonstrated that modern warfare rests both on sheer firepower and on the capacity to direct it for maximum effect. In Iraq, U.S. forces were outnumbered by three to one yet took only three weeks to seize control of Baghdad, at which point the remaining Iraqi army units quit the field.

American forces had no particular advantage, however, in waging the type of armed conflict that followed—guerrilla action based on roadside explosive devices and suicide bombings. Such tactics are extremely difficult to defend against and virtually impossible to stop by conventional military means. To defeat such an enemy requires the full support and cooperation of the local population. Without them, as was the case in Vietnam, the enemy has the capacity to sustain operations over a long period in an attempt to force a withdrawal of U.S. forces. As in Vietnam, U.S. military forces in Iraq have adapted their tactics to the demands of an unconventional war. Though unprepared for such combat when they went into Iraq, they have since learned how to wage it more effectively. But such conflicts are not settled by the standards of conventional war. There is no visible enemy army to destroy or territory to be conquered. In some cases—some analysts believe Iraq is one of them—the mere presence of foreign troops in a country can be a reason why some in the local populace take up arms against them.

Such situations require a political solution, not a military one, and political solutions are never as decisive as battlefield encounters. They require compromise and concessions from both sides. An occupying power, such as the United States, often is at a disadvantage in these negotiations because its interests include the withdrawal of its forces. If the occupier is dealing with a determined enemy that has the will and the capacity to continue the fight indefinitely, as was the case in Vietnam and might be the situation in Iraq, at some point it can be forced to accept an arrangement that is far less satisfying than the outcome that was anticipated upon entering into war.

The Politics of National Defense

Policy elites, public opinion, and special interests all play significant roles in national defense policy. The U.S. public typically supports the judgments of its political leaders on the use of military force. In virtually every conflict of the past half-century in which U.S. troops have been sent into battle, Americans have endorsed the action. When U.S. forces invaded Iraq in 2003 upon order of President George W. Bush, roughly 75 percent of Americans said they supported his decision. Such support invariably remains strong if the conflict is brief and not too costly. Public support might even hold up for years, as was the case during the first six years of the Vietnam War. However, if a conflict seems endless and if the human and financial toll keeps rising, public support eventually declines. A swing in public opinion against the Vietnam War forced U.S. policymakers to withdraw American troops in 1973. Public opinion on the Iraq War soured more quickly, partly because of indications that the stated justification for the war—to rid Iraq of its weapons of mass destruction—was not the full reason for the military action. As public opinion turned negative, the Bush administration's options narrowed. In 2004, for example, President Bush, who had planned to keep a U.S. administrator in charge of Iraq, concluded that he had no choice but to accelerate the timetable for turning the government over to Iraqis.

Even though public opinion places boundaries on what political leaders can do militarily, leaders have considerable latitude within these boundaries.[7] Policy debates and planning in the area of national security typically take place among political and policy elites. Most citizens are not informed enough about national security issues to contribute to the debate, particularly at the formative stage when critical first decisions are made. Moreover, early debates on critical issues— for example, whether to take the nation to war in the absence of a clear-cut and direct threat to the United States—take place behind closed doors in the Pentagon and the White House. The American people ordinarily trust their leaders to make the right decisions in such cases and will back them unless the decisions turn out badly.

The U.S. public assumes that great decisions about war and military might are driven by considerations of national security—doing what is necessary to protect and preserve the American nation and its interests. This view is not unwarranted, but it also is not the full picture. National defense is big business, involving the annual expenditure of hundreds of billions of dollars, and self-interested parties have a stake in maintaining permanently high levels of military spending and readiness.[8] In his 1961 farewell address, President Dwight D. Eisenhower, who had commanded U.S. forces in Europe during World War II, warned Americans against "the unwarranted influence" and "misplaced power" of what he termed "the military-industrial complex." The **military-industrial complex** has three components: the military establishment, the arms industry, and the members of Congress from states and districts that depend heavily on the arms industry. None of the three is predisposed to war, but neither are they, if the issue of war arises, adverse to it. If a president signals the likelihood of war, all three can be expected to endorse it. And all three benefit from a high level of defense spending,

military-industrial complex
The three components (the military establishment, the industries that manufacture weapons, and the members of Congress from states and districts that depend heavily on the arms industry) that mutually benefit from a high level of defense spending.

LEADERS

DWIGHT D. EISENHOWER

(1890–1969)

One of four army generals to be elected to the presidency, Dwight D. Eisenhower left his mark on war and peace. Born in Abilene, Texas, Eisenhower was an accomplished athlete and student, and in his senior year of high school he received an appointment to West Point. During World War II, he commanded the Allied Forces that landed in North Africa and drove the German army back to the European mainland. He was Supreme Commander of the multinational force that on June 6, 1944 (D-Day) landed at Normandy, initiating the drive across Europe that eventually would force Germany to surrender. He declined an opportunity to run for the presidency in 1948 but accepted a Republican draft to run in 1952. Given his stature as the most popular figure in America, Eisenhower won easily.

Though trained in the art of war, Eisenhower sought throughout his presidency to reduce cold war tensions. He signed the truce that led to the end of the Korean conflict. Although he was unsuccessful in negotiating a thaw in the nuclear arms race with Soviet leaders, he convinced them that the United States was not seeking their country's destruction. In 1956, after Egypt nationalized the Suez Canal, a plan by the governments of Britain, France, and Israel to take it back by force was aborted when Eisenhower refused to support it, saying that Egypt had a right to self-determination and that the United Nations, not the force of arms, was the proper avenue for settling the dispute. As he was leaving the presidency, he used his farewell address to warn of the dangers of the military-industrial complex, arguing that sustained high levels of military expenditure and secrecy would only weaken America in the long run.

WWW.MHHE.COM/PATTERSONTAD8

HISTORICAL BACKGROUND

regardless of whether the expenditures are necessary. Without doubt, as Eisenhower knew, some proportion of U.S. defense strategy and spending reflects the power of the military-industrial complex rather than what is required to keep America safe. The problem is that no one knows exactly what that proportion is.

THE ECONOMIC DIMENSION OF NATIONAL SECURITY POLICY

Economic considerations are a vital component of national security policy. In the simplest sense, economic strength is a prerequisite of military strength—a powerful defense establishment can be maintained only by a country that is economically well off. In a broader and more important sense, economic prosperity enables a people to "secure" their way of life. As President Eisenhower said, it is folly to weaken at home what one is trying to strengthen abroad.

A Changing World Economy

Some aspects of the U.S. superpower policy have economic benefits. The clearest example is the European Recovery Plan, better known as the Marshall Plan. Proposed in 1947 and named after one of its chief architects, the widely respected General George Marshall, it is perhaps the boldest and most successful U.S. foreign policy initiative of the twentieth century. It called for $3 billion in immediate aid for the postwar rebuilding of Europe, with an additional $10 billion or so to follow. The Marshall Plan was unprecedented both in its scope (today, the equivalent cost would exceed $100 billion) and in its implications—for the first time, the United States had committed itself to an ongoing role in European affairs.

Apart from enabling the countries of Western Europe to better confront the perceived Soviet threat, the Marshall Plan was also designed to meet the economic needs of the United States. Wartime production had lifted the country out of the Great Depression, but the end of the war in 1945 brought a recession and renewed fears of hard times. A rejuvenated Western Europe furnished a market for U.S. goods. In effect, Western Europe became a junior partner within a system of global trade that worked to the advantage of the United States. Since then, major changes have taken place in the world economy. Germany has become an economic rival of the United States, and trade with Germany now results in a deficit for the United States. In addition, Western Europe, including Germany, has become a less receptive market for U.S. goods. European countries are now each other's best customers, trading among themselves through the European Union (EU).

In economic terms, the world today is tripolar—power is concentrated in three centers. One center is the United States, which produces roughly 20 percent of the world's goods and services. Another center is Japan and China, which account for more than 15 percent of the world's economy. The third and largest center, responsible for more than 25 percent of the world's economy, is the twenty-five-country EU. The EU is dominated by Germany, Britain, and France, which together account for more than half its economy.

By a few indicators, the United States is the weakest of the three economic centers. For example, it has the worst trade imbalance. Although the United States exports roughly $1 trillion annually in goods and services, the country imports an even larger amount. The result is a huge trade deficit that is easily the world's largest. The United States has not had a trade surplus since 1975 and in recent years has run deficits exceeding $500 billion (see Figure 17–2).

In other ways, however, the United States is the strongest of the three economic powers. For one thing, the American economy is the best balanced. Like the other economic powers, the United States has a strong industrial base, but it has a stronger agricultural sector and more abundant natural resources. Its vast fertile plains have made it the world's leading agricultural producer. The United States ranks among the top three countries worldwide in production of wheat, corn, potatoes, peanuts, cotton, eggs, cattle, and pigs. As for natural resources, the United States ranks among the top five nations in deposits of copper, uranium, lead, sulfur, zinc, coal, gold, iron ore, natural gas, silver, and magnesium.[9]

Some U.S. firms are now as recognizable in other countries as they are in the United States. A Pepsi sign adorns the front of this small shop in Vietnam's Ho Chi Minh City (formerly Saigon).

According to the Switzerland-based World Economic Forum, the United States also is more economically competitive than are its major trading rivals (see Chapter 15). The United States owes this position to factors such as the strength of its domestic economy and its technological know-how.[10] This competitive advantage has been evident since the early 1990s. As Japan and parts of Europe have at times struggled with slow growth rates, the United States has enjoyed economic growth without the accelerated inflation that normally accompanies such a period. The slowdown in the U.S. economy that began in 2000 tempered the belief that technological know-how had unleashed unstoppable growth. Nevertheless, other countries have looked to the United States, particularly its technology sector, for policy and market innovations that might spark their own economic expansion.

America's Global Economic Goals

The United States depends on other countries for raw materials, finished goods, and capital to meet Americans' production and consumption demands. Meeting this objective requires the United States to exert influence on world markets. The broad goals of the United States in the world economy include the following:[11]

- Maintaining access to energy and other natural resources vital to the strength of the U.S. economy

- Sustaining a stable and open system of trade that will promote prosperity at home

- Keeping the widening gap between the rich and poor countries from destabilizing the world economy

WWW.MHHE.COM/PATTERSONTAD8

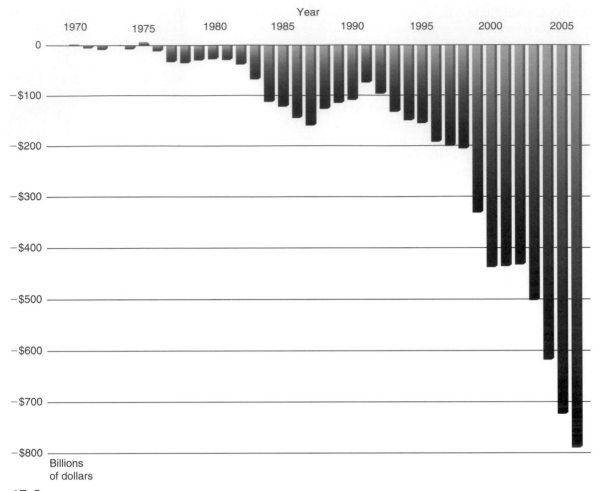

Figure 17–2

The U.S. Trade Deficit
Not since 1975 has the United States had a trade surplus; the deficit reached a record level in 2006.
Source: U.S. Bureau of the Census, Trade Data Services, 2006. The 2006 figure is based on preliminary projections.

Access to Natural Resources

Although the United States is rich in natural resources, it is not self-sufficient. Oil is the main problem; domestic production provides only about half the nation's needs. Oil has been called "black gold," and even that description understates its significance. Oil is the engine of American society, powering the economy and providing fuel for automobiles and heat for homes and offices. For decades, the United States has used its economic and military power to protect its access to oil.

Outside the United States, most of the world's oil is found in the Middle East, Latin America, Africa, and Russia. Access to oil occurs through the world market for it. After World War II, the United States acquired a foothold in that market when its leading oil companies, with their technical expertise and huge amounts of capital, acquired a stake in Middle Eastern oil fields. Since then, U.S. firms have been leaders in worldwide oil exploration and production. Underpinning their activities is the military might of the United States. For example, the U.S. Navy patrols the world's shipping routes to ensure that oil tankers reach their destinations safely. The United States has also used its

After Saddam Hussein's regime in Iraq was toppled, the United States began the task of reconstructing Iraqi oil operations, schools, hospitals, roads, and other facilities. The reconstruction costs were far higher than policymakers had anticipated and pushed total U.S. foreign assistance spending to new heights.

power to try to prevent oil-rich countries from being taken over by hostile interests. In 1951, for example, the Iranian government voted to nationalize its oil fields, threatening Western influence over that country's production and distribution. Two years later, the CIA helped orchestrate a coup that placed the pro-Western Shah of Iran, Mohammad Reza Pahlavi, in charge. The 1991 Gulf War was driven largely by a concern with oil. Iraq's invasion of Kuwait threatened access not only to Kuwait's oil fields but also to those of its neighbors, which is why Saudi Arabia and other Arab countries backed the use of force to drive Iraq from Kuwait. Some observers believe that oil was also a factor in President George W. Bush's decision to invade Iraq in 2003. Iraq's proven oil reserves of more than 100 billion barrels are second only to those of Saudi Arabia.

The issue of oil will grow in significance in coming years. Oil production may be nearing peak capacity. New oil fields are still being developed, but the world's major oil reserves are being depleted. Meanwhile, the demand for oil is rising as a result of the rapid economic growth of China, India, and other emerging industrialized countries. Oil topped seventy-five dollars a barrel for the first time in 2006. If a major disruption in the world's oil supply were to occur, oil prices would skyrocket, possibly causing a global recession and perhaps even triggering a regional war.

Promoting Global Trade

The American economy today depends more heavily on international commerce than at any time in the past. The domestic manufacturing sector that once was the source, directly or indirectly, of most U.S. jobs has shrunk, and many of the goods Americans buy, from their television sets to their automobiles, are produced by foreign firms. Indeed, nearly all large U.S. firms are themselves **multinational corporations,** with operations in more than one country. From a

multinational corporations
Business firms with major operations in more than one country.

headquarters in New York City, a firm has no difficulty directing a production facility in Thailand that is filling orders for markets in Europe and South America. Money, goods, and services today flow freely and quickly across national borders, and large firms increasingly think about markets in global rather than national terms.

economic globalization

The increased interdependence of nations' economies. The change is a result of technological, transportation, and communication advances that have enabled firms to deploy their resources around the globe.

Economic globalization is a term that describes the increased interdependence of nations' economies. This development is both an opportunity and a threat to U.S. economic interests. The opportunity rests with the possibility of increased demand abroad for U.S. products and lower prices to U.S. consumers as a result of inexpensive imports. The threat lies in the fact that foreign firms also compete in the global marketplace and may use their competitive advantages, such as cheaper labor, to outposition U.S. firms.[12]

In general, international commerce works best when countries trade freely with one another. This situation keeps the prices of traded items, whether finished goods or raw materials, at their lowest level, resulting in economic efficiency (see Chapter 15). However, global trade is a political issue as well as an economic one, and different countries and interests have different views on how trade among nations should be conducted. The **free-trade position** holds that the long-term economic interests of all countries are advanced when tariffs and other trade barriers are kept to a minimum. Most free-trade advocates couple their advocacy with fair-trade demands, but they are committed philosophically and in practice to the idea that free trade fuels economic growth, results in a net gain for business, and provides consumers with lower-priced goods.

free-trade position

The view that the long-term economic interests of all countries are advanced when tariffs and other trade barriers are kept to a minimum.

Recent U.S. presidents have been free-trade advocates. Large U.S. firms generally seek access to markets around the globe, and a president would have difficulty insisting that other countries open their markets to U.S. firms while simultaneously denying foreign firms open access to U.S. markets. Moreover, free trade can stimulate economic growth, which is always a presidential concern. The American people, when judging a president, base their judgment on whether the U.S. economy as a whole is doing well or poorly rather than on the basis of particular economic policies.

From a congressional perspective, free trade often is more appealing in theory than in practice. Although most members of Congress say they support free trade and some are unabashed advocates of it, many of them act differently when their state or district is threatened by foreign competition. Then they often try to protect their constituents' interests through measures such as favorable treatment of U.S. goods or tariffs on the goods of foreign competitors.

protectionism

The view that the immediate interests of domestic producers should have a higher priority (through, for example, protective tariffs) than should free trade between nations.

Protectionism, as opposed to the free-trade position, emphasizes the immediate interests of domestic producers and includes measures designed to enable them to compete successfully with foreign competitors in the domestic market. For some protectionists, the issue is simply a matter of defending domestic firms against the actions of their foreign competitors. For others, the issue is one of fair trade; they are protectionists in those instances where foreign firms have an unfair competitive advantage, as, for example, when government subsidies allow them to market their goods at an artificially low price.

During the past two decades, the free-trade position usually has prevailed in U.S. policy disputes. In 1993, for example, Congress ratified the North American Free Trade Agreement (NAFTA), which creates a mostly free market among the United States, Canada, and Mexico. Although NAFTA was opposed by most congressional Democrats and by environmental and labor groups that objected to its weak protection of their interests, proponents prevailed due to the backing of President Bill Clinton and most congressional Republicans. The final votes needed for passage were gained by promises of trade protection for Florida citrus and vegetable growers. Another example of support for free trade is U.S.

membership in the World Trade Organization (WTO). The WTO, created in 1995, is the formal institution through which most nations negotiate general rules of international trade. The WTO's mission is to promote a global free market through reductions in tariffs, protections for intellectual property (copyrights and patents), and similar policies. WTO members (roughly one hundred thirty in number) are committed to an open trade policy buttressed by regulations designed to ensure fair play among participating nations. Trade disputes among WTO members are settled by arbitration panels, which consist of representatives from the member nations. In 2003, for example, the WTO held that U.S. tariffs on imported steel, which were intended to protect U.S. steelmakers, were illegal under WTO trade rules and had to be rescinded.

More recently, protectionist sentiment has gained strength in the United States. The WTO, for example, has been criticized for placing trade ahead of environmental protection and human rights. Some countries have gained a trade advantage through production processes that degrade the environment and exploit workers, including child laborers. Loss of jobs has also been an issue. Employment in U.S. textile factories, for example, has fallen sharply in the face of foreign competition. Even some high-tech jobs have been shipped abroad. Telephone-based technical services, for example, often can be provided at lower cost by hiring educated English-speaking technicians in India instead of their American counterparts.

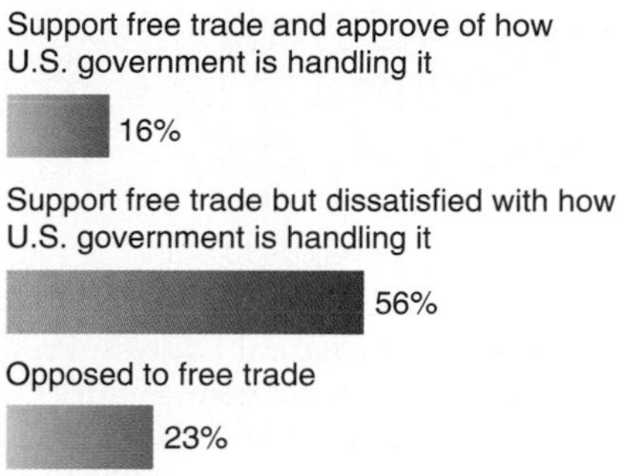

The jobs issue did not receive much attention during the late 1990s, when the overall U.S. economy was growing at a rapid pace. However, in the economic downturn that began in 2000, nearly three million U.S. manufacturing jobs were lost, thrusting the issue into prominence and dramatically changing opinions on global trade. In polls taken during the late 1990s, a majority of respondents favored global trade, believing that it was good both for them and for the country as a whole. By 2005, Americans were of the opinion that international trade was hurting the country (see Figure 17–3).

U.S. officials have struggled to find an effective response to this development. Economists argue that the job losses are simply part of the "creative destruction" that occurs naturally in free markets. Firms have no choice but to adapt if they are to survive. Public officials, however, cannot so easily take such a long-range view, because they face immediate pressures from constituents who have lost jobs and from communities that have lost firms. In response to these pressures, U.S. officials have sought to preserve free trade by insisting that foreign governments improve their labor and environmental practices and end whatever protectionist policies they still promote. The stated goal is to make global trade work in ways that will allow U.S. goods to compete on an even playing field. However, other countries are not always convinced that the United States itself plays fair. In 2006, WTO trade talks collapsed in part because the United States refused to reduce its hefty farm subsidies, which enable U.S. agricultural producers to keep their prices low, thereby giving them an advantage in world commodity markets.

Trade with China is an issue that looms ever larger with U.S. policymakers. In the past decade, America's trade deficit with China has increased more than thirty-fold and now exceeds $200 billion annually. The United States has provided China with a marketplace for its goods, which has helped fuel China's economic growth. China in turn has provided the United States with inexpensive goods, which has satisfied America's consumers and helped keep inflation in check. But Congress is increasingly signaling concern with the trade deficit. Many members of Congress from both parties would like to see China increase the value of its currency, which would raise the price of its goods and thereby

Support free trade and approve of how U.S. government is handling it

 16%

Support free trade but dissatisfied with how U.S. government is handling it

 56%

Opposed to free trade

 23%

Figure 17–3

Americans' Opinion of Free Trade
Most Americans support free trade, but most of them also are dissatisfied with how the U.S. government is handling issues of job loss, the environment, and the exploitation of foreign workers.
Source: PIPA-Knowledge Networks survey, June 2005.

Get Involved!

Serve Your Country

In his 1961 inaugural address, President John F. Kennedy said, "Ask not what your country can do for you. Ask what you can do for your country." Kennedy called America's young people to service on behalf of their country. His call was not just a call to military service. One of Kennedy's early initiatives, the Peace Corps, offered Americans the opportunity to apply their skills to development projects in other countries. Under Kennedy's successor, President Lyndon Johnson, a domestic version of the Peace Corps—Volunteers in Service to America (VISTA)—was established.

Before the military draft ended in 1973, male Americans expected to serve their country. Not all did so, but millions served in the Army, Navy, Air Force, or Marines. Some gave their lives for their country. There was a shared sense of duty and sacrifice.

Since the end of the draft, Congress has from time to time considered establishing a National Service that would require every young American man and woman to serve the country in one way or another for a set period of time. However, you do not need an act of Congress if you want to serve your country. There are a range of alternatives. America's all-volunteer military seeks educated recruits for its enlisted and its officer ranks. The Peace Corps, now four decades old, continues to send Americans to countries where their skills are needed. AmeriCorps, a network of local, state, and national service programs, places more than seventy thousand Americans each year in service positions in the areas of education, public safety, health, and the environment. These are just some of the numerous government programs to which you could apply.

---

dampen consumer demand in the United States. Such a step would make U.S. goods more competitive with those produced in China and offer some protection to U.S. firms and workers. One thing is certain—trade between the United States and China is sure to remain a pressing political issue. China is the emerging giant in international trade.[13]

Relations with the Developing World

Although political instability in the less developed countries can disrupt world markets, less developed countries also offer marketplace opportunities. In order to develop further, they need to acquire the goods and services that more industrialized countries can provide. To foster this demand, the United States and the other industrialized countries provide developmental assistance to poorer countries. Contributions include direct foreign aid and also indirect assistance through international organizations, such as the International Monetary Fund (IMF) and the World Bank. These two organizations were created by the United States and Great Britain at the Bretton Woods Conference near the end of World

In terms of its trade deficit, the United States' most significant trading partner is China. Shown here is China's president, Hu Jintao, on the South Lawn of the White House during his visit to the United States in 2006. Presidents Hu and Bush discussed U.S.–China relations during the visit.

War II. The IMF makes short-term loans to prevent countries experiencing temporary problems from collapsing economically or resorting to destructive practices such as the unrestricted printing of paper money. The World Bank, on the other hand, makes long-term development loans to poor countries for capital investment projects such as dams, highways, and factories.

Since World War II, the United States has been the leading source of aid to developing countries. Although the United States still contributes the most in terms of total dollars, Canada, Japan, and the European countries spend more on a per capita basis than does the United States (see Figure 17–4). The United States has narrowed the gap since the events of September 11, 2001, which awakened some policymakers to the fact that global poverty generates resentment of the United States.[14] In the past few years, U.S. foreign aid spending has increased significantly.[15]

Public opinion is an obstacle to higher levels of spending on foreign aid. Polls show that most Americans believe the United States is already spending huge amounts on foreign aid. In a poll that asked Americans to name the largest federal programs, foreign aid topped the list, with 27 percent identifying it as the most expensive program.[16] In fact, foreign aid is far from the top. Nevertheless, Americans' perception makes foreign aid a potent political issue for politicians who would like to decrease it. Jesse Helms (R-N.C.), a past chair of the Senate Foreign Relations Committee, liked to say that foreign aid was nothing more than pouring billions of dollars "down foreign ratholes."[17]

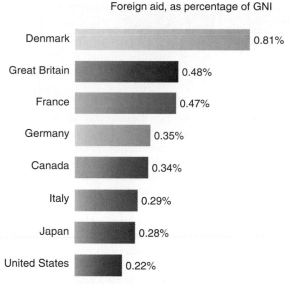

Foreign aid, as percentage of GNI

Denmark	0.81%
Great Britain	0.48%
France	0.47%
Germany	0.35%
Canada	0.34%
Italy	0.29%
Japan	0.28%
United States	0.22%

Figure 17–4

Assistance to Developing Countries, as Percentage of Gross National Income
The United States ranks highest in terms of total amount spent on foreign aid to developing countries but ranks lower in terms of percentage of gross national income (GNI). Data exclude Iraq reconstruction spending.
Source: OECD (Organization for Economic Cooperation and Development), 2006.

A NEW WORLD

Although economic interests are a driving force in U.S. foreign policy, global terrorism has become America's top priority. "The world will never again be the same" became a common refrain after September 11, 2001. Subsequent developments have confirmed that judgment. Stopping terrorism has become the nation's most urgent policy goal, leading to massive increases in federal spending to combat the terrorist threat at home and abroad. The nation's intelligence and law-enforcement agencies have been reorganized to increase their capacity to blunt the threat. Shifts in policy toward the Middle East and South Asia have occurred. The U.S. attack on Iraq in 2003 was premised on the assumption that Iraq had chemical and biological weapons that could be funneled into the hands of anti-American terrorists. These are only a few examples of the changes brought about by the events of September 11. Virtually no area of U.S. foreign and defense policy has been unaffected.

One of the largest changes has been in a direction the terrorists had not predicted. With the September 11 attacks, they sought to force the United States to reduce its presence in the Middle East and in the Arab world generally. The effect has been the opposite. Just as Pearl Harbor ended Americans' isolationism, September 11 blunted a movement by some U.S. officials to reduce America's involvement in international affairs. As security analyst Philip Gordon noted, "The result of the September 11 attacks has not been an American return to isolationism, but a reinvigoration of engagement."[18]

Political Culture

Foreign Policy and America's Ideals

During the 1950s, when the cold war was at a peak, President Dwight D. Eisenhower warned against actions that undermined the principles America stood for. He worried that threats originating abroad would lead Americans to support policies that compromised the ideals upon which the nation had been founded. Eisenhower believed that excessive government secrecy—justified in the name of national security—threatened liberty. He worried that a huge permanent military and the industrial firms that benefited from it would sap America of its resources and encourage the country to seek military solutions to international problems. If America was to remain a beacon of freedom for the world, it had to remain steadfast in its ideals.

Similar concerns have been raised in the context of the war on terrorism. Nearly all Americans agree that the terrorist threat cannot be met without making some adjustments in how government operates. However, disagreement has arisen over specific policies, such as the prolonged detention of noncitizens, the preemptive invasion of Iraq, and the wiretapping of phone calls without a judicial warrant.

How much leeway do you think policymakers should have in their pursuit of the war on terrorism? What compromises of principle do you find acceptable? Do you think noncitizens deserve the same constitutional protections as citizens? Do you think military force should be the nation's first response to terrorist threats? If not, what are the alternatives, and how, if at all, are they more consistent with America's founding ideals?

However, the United States is struggling in its attempt to engage with the world in the aftermath of September 11, 2001. The global support that the United States received as a result of the terrorist attacks on the World Trade Center and the Pentagon suddenly evaporated eighteen months later when the United States invaded Iraq. The conflict there has also raised the risks for America. According to the National Intelligence Estimate that U.S. intelligence agencies compiled in 2006, the terrorist threat has worsened in the past few years, largely because the Iraq conflict has mobilized and united Islamic extremists around the globe. What analysts disagree about is the length of America's struggle with radical Islamists. Some analysts predict that the conflict will unwind within a decade or so. Others see it stretching across a far longer period, much like the religiously motivated Thirty Years War that consumed the first half of the seventeenth century in Europe. The challenge for Americans in the coming years is to discover how to navigate this conflict in a way that preserves the integrity of the United States as a territorial state and as a vibrant democracy. It is the same challenge that President Dwight D. Eisenhower set forth near the start of the Cold War: "The problem in defense is how far you can go without destroying from within what you are trying to defend from without."

Summary

Self-Test www.mhhe.com/pattersontad8

The chief instruments of national security policy are diplomacy, military force, economic exchange, and intelligence gathering. These are exercised through specialized agencies of the U.S. government, such as the Departments of State and Defense, that are largely responsive to presidential leadership. National security policy has also relied on international organizations, such as the United Nations and the World Trade Organization, that are responsive to the global concerns of major nations.

From 1945 to 1990, U.S. foreign and defense policies were dominated by a concern with the Soviet Union. During most of this period, the United States pursued a policy of containment based on the premise that the Soviet Union was an aggressor nation bent on global conquest. Containment policy led the United States to enter into wars in Korea and Vietnam and to maintain a large defense establishment. U.S. military forces are deployed around the globe, and the nation maintains a large nuclear arsenal. The end of the cold war, however, made some of this weaponry and strategic planning less relevant to America's national security.

A first response to the post–cold-war world was multilateralism, the idea that major nations could achieve common goals by working together, including using force as a means of arresting regional conflicts. The interventions in the Persian Gulf and the Balkans during the 1990s are examples. They demonstrated that major nations can intervene with some success in global hot spots but also showed that the ethnic, religious, and national conflicts that fuel these flashes are not easily resolved.

The terrorist attacks on the World Trade Center and the Pentagon in 2001 led to broad changes in national security organization and strategy. Increased spending on defense and homeland security have been coupled with a partial reorganization of U.S. intelligence, law-enforcement, and immigration agencies, as well as new laws affecting the scope of their activities. However, the defining moment of the post–September 11 period was America's invasion of Iraq in 2003, which was rooted in President George W. Bush's preemptive war doctrine and his willingness to commit the United States to unilateral action. Iraq has largely been America's war—90 percent of the coalition casualties and monetary costs have been borne by the United States. Public support for the Iraq intervention has declined sharply, but most American citizens, as well as most of their leaders, have concluded that the United States has little choice but to remain in Iraq until a greater level of stability is attained there.

In recent decades, the United States has increasingly taken economic factors into account in its national security considerations, which has meant, for example, that trade has played a larger part in defining its relationships with other countries. The trading system that the United States helped erect after World War II has given way to one that is more global in scale and more competitive. Changes in communication, transportation, and computing have altered the way large corporations operate, and as businesses have changed their practices, nations have had to adapt. The changes include the emergence of regional and international economic structures, such as the European Union, NAFTA, and the WTO. Nevertheless, nations naturally compete for economic advantage, including access to natural resources; accordingly, trade is a source of conflict as well as a source of cooperation. In the coming years, oil is likely to be at the center of the conflict.

STUDY CORNER

Key Terms

bipolar (power structure) (*p. 502*)

cold war (*p. 502*)

containment (*p. 502*)

deterrence policy (*p. 509*)

economic globalization (*p. 518*)

free-trade position (*p. 518*)

internationalist (*p. 501*)

isolationist (*p. 501*)

military-industrial complex (*p. 513*)

multilateralism (*p. 504*)

multinational corporations (*p. 517*)

preemptive war doctrine (*p. 506*)

protectionism (*p. 518*)

unilateralism (*p. 506*)

unipolar (power structure) (*p. 503*)

Self-Test

1. Diplomacy is distinct from military power as a foreign policymaking instrument in that diplomacy:
   a. is effective only when used in conjunction with other instruments.
   b. requires a bilateral relationship; it cannot be employed unilaterally.
   c. is subject to direction by the president.
   d. is sometimes applied through an international intermediary, such as the United Nations.

2. Economic exchange primarily takes place through:
   a. entering into military alliances that then turn into trading alliances.
   b. monitoring other countries' economic activities and enacting tariffs if necessary.
   c. developing trade relations with nations that are premised on the assumption that these relations will benefit both sides.
   d. military takeovers of countries that have raw materials of value.

3. Drawbacks to the pursuit of a policy of multilateralism include which of the following?
   a. Multilateral interventions are almost always less successful than when the United States acts unilaterally.
   b. Multilateral intervention does not guarantee long-term success in solving situations.
   c. Multilateral interventions abroad almost always reduce the president's popularity at home.
   d. All of the above.

4. The formal organization through which nations administer and negotiate the general rules governing international trade is called:
   a. UN.
   b. NATO.
   c. World Bank.
   d. WTO.

5. The *lesson of Vietnam* for the United States was that:
   a. there are limits to America's ability to assert its will in the world alone.
   b. America's military arsenal was obsolete and needed updating.
   c. appeasement only encourages further aggression.
   d. an isolationist foreign policy is the only safe direction for U.S. policy.

6. After World War II, the United States emerged as:
   a. an economically impoverished country.
   b. the major country with the least amount of domestic oil reserves.
   c. an internationalist country.
   d. the world's only superpower.

7. The main threat to the physical security of the United States after the attacks on the World Trade Center and the Pentagon is international terrorists who fight on behalf of causes. (T/F)

8. High levels of congressional support for an expensive weapons program are sometimes linked more to the jobs it creates than to its overall usefulness to the U.S. arsenal. (T/F)

9. The United States spends more on foreign aid as a percentage of its total national budget than do most Western democracies. (T/F)

10. U.S. military intervention both in the Persian Gulf and in Kosovo not only punished the aggressor party in each case but also settled the underlying dispute once and for all. (T/F)

Critical Thinking

What are the major objectives of U.S. foreign and defense policy? What are the mechanisms for pursuing those objectives?

Suggested Readings

Clarke, Richard A. *Against All Enemies: Inside America's War on Terror.* New York: Free Press, 2004. A best-selling book by the nation's former top-ranking presidential advisor on terrorism.

Fishman, Ted C. *China, Inc.: How the Rise of the Next Superpower Challenges America and the World.* New York: Scribner, 2005. A look at China's rapid economic growth and its implications.

Kegley, Charles W., and Gregory A. Raymond. *The Imperiled Imperium: America and the Erosion of Global Security.* New York: Oxford University Press, 2006. A pessimistic view of U.S. national security policy.

Lind, Michael. *The American Way of Strategy.* New York: Oxford University Press, 2006. An analysis that claims U.S. foreign policy works best when conducted in the context of America's ideals.

Nye, Joseph S. *Soft Power: The Means to Success in World Politics.* New York: PublicAffairs, 2004. An argument for making diplomacy, assistance, and other forms of "soft power" the basis of U.S. foreign policy.

Odom, William E. *Fixing Intelligence.* New Haven, Conn.: Yale University Press, 2003. A detailed critique of U.S. intelligence efforts by a former military intelligence officer.

Sobel, Richard. The Impact of Public Opinion on U.S. Foreign Policy Since Vietnam. New York: Oxford University Press, 2001. An account of public opinion's impact on foreign policy.

Woodward, Bob. *Plan of Attack.* New York: Simon & Schuster, 2004. An inside look at the Bush administration's decision to go to war in Iraq.

List of Websites

http://www.defenselink.mil/
The U.S. Department of Defense website; it provides information on each of the armed services, daily news from the American Forces Information Service, and other material.

http://www.cfr.org/
A website that includes reports and assessments of the Council of Foreign Relations and transcripts of speeches by U.S. and world political leaders on topics of international interest.

http://www.igc.org/igc
Website of the Institute for Global Communications (IGC); it provides information and services to organizations and activists on a broad range of international issues, including human rights.

http://www.wto.org/
The World Trade Organization (WTO) website; it contains information on the organization's activities and has links to related sites.

Participate!

International conflicts stem from real causes but also have roots in cultural misunderstandings. American are thought to be more prone than most peoples to such misunderstandings because they have not been forced by geography to take different cultures, languages, and national identities fully into account. British social scientist Harold Lasswell remarked that Americans tend to view the world through the lens of their own experiences. This perspective has become a greater handicap as trade and communication have made the countries of the world ever more interdependent. Even the war on terrorism will depend for its success on a greater sensitivity to the beliefs and aspirations of other peoples. Individual Americans can do their part by educating themselves about the world. Consider taking a college course in history, political science, language and culture, geography, religion, or any other subject that will introduce you to a part of the world you have not previously studied. Close attention to the foreign affairs coverage in a quality newspaper or periodical can also deepen your understanding of other peoples and cultures.

Extra Credit
For up-to-the-minute *New York Times* articles, interactive simulations, graphics, study tools, and more links and quizzes, visit the text's Online Learning Center at **www.mhhe.com/pattersontad8.**

(Self-Test Answers: 1. b   2. c   3. b   4. d   5. a   6. c   7. T   8. T   9. F   10. F)

PART 5

TEXAS GOVERNMENT AND POLITICS

A lthough these chapters are primarily about the government and politics of Texas, they also are a study of other state governments. It is important to understand Texas government in the context of the governments of other states. This part of the book will explain how and why Texas is different from other states and also how and why Texas is similar to the other forty-nine states. While there are many similarities, each state has a unique history that influences its government and politics. Regional differences within the United States also affect state policies. Texas's history and its southern heritage strongly influence its government, politics, and policies.

PART FIVE OUTLINE

18 Introduction to Texas Government 528

19 The State Constitution 546

20 Participation Politics and Interest Groups in Texas Politics 564

21 Political Parties and Elections in Texas 586

22 The Texas Legislature 618

23 The Office of Governor and State Agencies in Texas 660

24 The Court System in Texas 696

25 Local Governments in Texas 724

Introduction to Texas Government

Chapter Outline

Texas: A Land of Contrasts

Settlement Patterns in Texas History
    The Tejanos or Mexican Settlers
    Anglo Settlers
    German Immigrants

Urban and Rural Contrasts

Population Growth and the Changing Climate of Texas Politics

Minority Groups
    Hispanic Americans
    African Americans
    Asian Americans

The Political Culture of Texas

The Economy of Texas

CHAPTER 18

Texas is a state of mind. Texas is an obsession. Above all, Texas is a nation in every sense of the word. . . . A Texan outside of Texas is a foreigner.

—*John Steinbeck*[1]

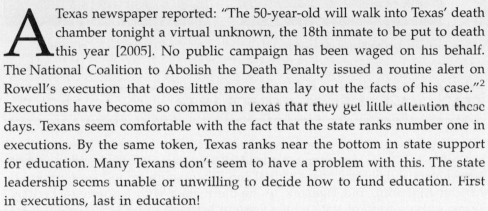

A Texas newspaper reported: "The 50-year-old will walk into Texas' death chamber tonight a virtual unknown, the 18th inmate to be put to death this year [2005]. No public campaign has been waged on his behalf. The National Coalition to Abolish the Death Penalty issued a routine alert on Rowell's execution that does little more than lay out the facts of his case."[2] Executions have become so common in Texas that they get little attention these days. Texans seem comfortable with the fact that the state ranks number one in executions. By the same token, Texas ranks near the bottom in state support for education. Many Texans don't seem to have a problem with this. The state leadership seems unable or unwilling to decide how to fund education. First in executions, last in education!

A **comparative approach** will give a better understanding of Texas government by showing that Texas is very much influenced by the actions of other states and at the same time influences what other states do. As the second most populous state, Texas is also a leader in influencing national policy. A broad comparative perspective is important to understanding the government and politics of the Lone Star State.

comparative approach
A study of state government by comparing Texas with other states.

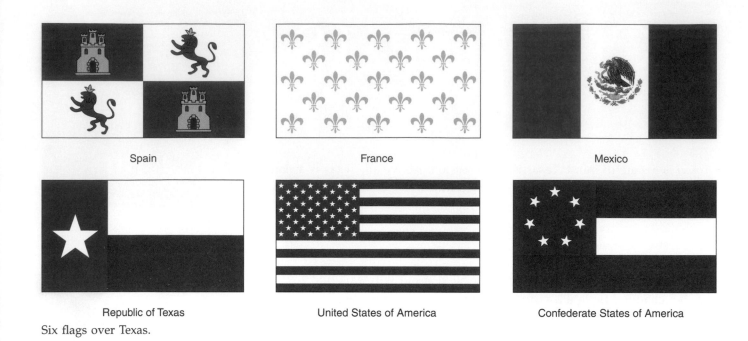

Spain

France

Mexico

Republic of Texas

United States of America

Confederate States of America

Six flags over Texas.

TEXAS: A LAND OF CONTRASTS

Several years ago, Texas state tourism literature used the theme "Texas, a Land of Contrasts." Texas is very much a land of contrasts, and this is reflected in its government and politics. Texas is rural and urban; southern and western; Anglo, African American, and Hispanic. A southern state with a southern heritage, Texas is also a western state with a western heritage and a strong Spanish and Mexican heritage. The southern culture of East Texas is different from the western culture of the Lower Plains and High Plains regions, and both are different from the Hispanic culture of the Rio Grande Valley and the San Antonio area.

The diversity of Texas history is reflected in the name of a popular theme park in the Dallas–Fort Worth area, Six Flags over Texas. Texas has been a Spanish colony partially under French control, a Mexican state, an independent republic, a state in the United States, and a Confederate state. Each period of its history has influenced the culture of the state today.

SETTLEMENT PATTERNS IN TEXAS HISTORY

The contrasts are better understood and take on clearer meaning with an examination of the history of settlement patterns in the state. This large state (268,601 square miles) has been a crossroads where the cultures of Spain, Mexico, the Old South, the West, and the Midwest have met and clashed (see Figure 18–1). Texas had four distinct and contrasting settlement periods and regions: Spanish South Texas, antebellum East Texas, frontier West Texas, and the German Fredericksburg Hill Country area. As will be seen in later sections, these regional differences continue to influence Texas politics today.

HISTORICAL BACKGROUND

The Tejanos or Mexican Settlers

The Rio Grande Valley was the first area of the state to be settled by Europeans. In the late 1600s, Spaniards developed settlements along the Rio Grande and as far

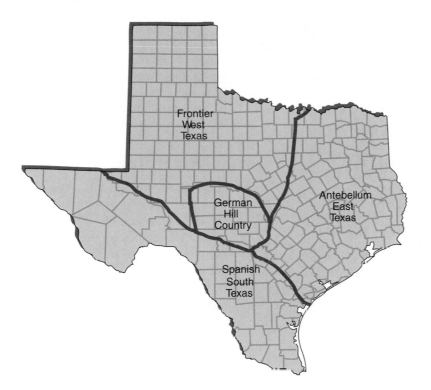

Figure 18–1
Settlement Patterns in Texas
Source: D. W. Meining, *Imperial Texas: An Interpretive Essay in Cultural Geography* (Austin: University of Texas Press, 1969).

north and east as San Antonio. Of the Spanish settlements in other parts of the state, only Nacogdoches lasted more than a few years. Although permanent Spanish settlements did not penetrate much beyond San Antonio, the influence of Spain extends throughout the state. Most major rivers have Spanish names; for example, the Rio Grande, Pecos, Nueces, Frio, San Antonio, Guadalupe, Lavaca, Colorado, Brazos, and San Jacinto. Many other geographic features as well as a number of cities and counties also have Spanish names. Texas state laws are still very much influenced by early Spanish law, especially laws on land ownership and rights.

Anglo Settlers

Southern Anglos and African Americans began settling East Texas in the 1820s. The southern white Protestant settlers were decidedly different from the resident Spanish Catholic settlers. These two groups clashed in 1836 during the Texas Revolutionary War (1836–45), with many of the Spanish remaining loyal to Mexico as the Anglos formed the Republic of Texas.

The settlements of Anglo southerners did not extend much farther west than a line running from the Red River to present-day Fort Worth and south through Waco and Austin to San Antonio. This line is a natural geological feature, known as the Balcones Escarpment, that separates the Coastal Plain and pine forest regions of Texas from the middle and High Plains regions of the state. For two reasons, most of the area west of this line was not settled until after the Civil War. First, Comanche, Lipan Apache, Kiowa, and Tonkawa Native Americans inhabited this region. The second reason for the lack of settlement was that the southern wood, water, and plantation culture was not adaptable to the dry, arid, treeless plains west of the Balcones Escarpment.

Texas's rich Spanish heritage is exemplified by this Spanish mission in the San Antonio area.

LEADERS

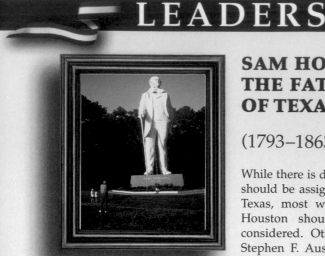

SAM HOUSTON: THE FATHER OF TEXAS

(1793–1863)

While there is disagreement over who should be assigned the title Father of Texas, most would agree that Sam Houston should be among those considered. Others might nominate Stephen F. Austin, who successfully began the Anglo immigration to Texas, although his early death at the end of the war that freed Texas from Mexico limited his impact on the formation of the Republic.

Sam Houston was one of the most colorful and controversial figures in Texas politics. He was born in Virginia in 1793 and moved to Tennessee with his family when he was very young. He served as a congressman from Tennessee for two terms and as governor of the state from 1827 to 1830. He resigned as governor and moved to Texas in 1832. By 1833 he was heavily involved in Texas politics and helped write and sign Texas's Declaration of Independence at Washington on the Brazos. Elected commander in chief of the Texas army, he successfully led the army that defeated Mexican General Santa Anna and held him hostage, forcing Mexico to agree to the independence of Texas from Mexico.

Houston served as the first president of the Republic of Texas, serving from 1839 to 1841. After Texas became a state, he served in the United States Senate and as governor of Texas. In 1861, after narrowly losing the Democratic nomination for president of the United States, he opposed the secession of Texas from the Union and was forced to resign as governor, ending his political career. He died in Huntsville, Texas, in 1863 and is buried there.

For a popular biography of this early Texan, see *The Raven*, by Marquis James, a Pulitzer Prize–winning novel that has been in print for over seventy years (available at http://www.texasindians.com/store/raven.htm).

Settlement in this area increased after 1875, taking the form of large ranches and, later, small farms. Many of these settlers migrated from northern states, mostly in the Midwest, and from foreign countries. These settlers lacked the southern culture and traditions that dominated East Texas.

German Immigrants

One other early immigrant group also contributed to the character of Texas politics. Due to the efforts of the Adelsverein Society (established to promote German immigration to Texas), Germans began to immigrate to Texas in the 1840s. By 1847, the society had brought more than seven thousand Germans to Texas, most settling in and around the town of Fredericksburg.[3] By 1850, German settlers made up 5.4 percent of the state's population.[4]

These German immigrants were not slave owners and objected to the institution of slavery. They lived apart from—and often shunned contact with—non-Germans. During the Civil War, many young German men refused to fight, and some fled to Mexico. From Reconstruction until the 1960s, a majority of the votes for Republicans cast in Texas were cast in areas settled by Germans.

URBAN AND RURAL CONTRASTS

HISTORICAL BACKGROUND

Texas is the second most populous state in the United States, and over 80 percent of its 20.9 million people live in 53 metropolitan counties. The remaining 20 percent live in the other 201 counties. Texas has three of the ten largest cities in the United States (Houston, Dallas, and San Antonio). But Texas is also a rural state. In 2002, Texas had the largest nonmetropolitan population (3,160,000) of any state.

You don't have to travel far from an urban center to see the contrast. A young urban professional living in Dallas has very little in common with a person working in a sawmill in Diboll. If the urban professional and the mill worker were to meet, they might have little to talk about other than the Dallas Cowboys football team.

These contrasts often frame the conflicts of Texas politics. East Texas Anglos demanding English-only amendments to the state constitution view demands for bilingual education by South Texas Hispanics with contempt. High Plains Republicans from Amarillo often clash with East Texas traditional Democrats. The urban legislator from Austin likely sees things quite differently than does a colleague from Muleshoe in West Texas.

POPULATION GROWTH AND THE CHANGING CLIMATE OF TEXAS POLITICS

For the last thirty years, Texas has experienced a migration of people from other states, due partly to its strategic location in the Sunbelt and its proximity to Mexico. The 1970s Texas oil boom and economic decline in the industrial Midwest also contributed to the migration. Some people migrated out of the state between 1987 and 1989, but by 1990 the population had increased to almost 17 million, up from 11.2 million in 1970. In 1996, the population of Texas was estimated to be 18.6 million, and by 2000 the population had reached 20.9 million (see "How Texas Compares").

Many of these newcomers to Texas changed the political landscape in significant ways. From the end of Reconstruction until the mid-1970s, the Democratic party dominated Texas politics, with only one person (Senator John Tower) winning statewide office as a Republican.

MINORITY GROUPS

Minority groups play a significant role in Texas politics today. Higher birthrates for minorities and migration to urban areas, coupled with white migration to suburban areas, have contributed to the concentration of minority groups in major cities of the state. Corpus Christi, Dallas, El Paso, Houston, and San Antonio have **majority-minority** populations.

Official estimates project that by the early twenty-first century the majority of the state's population will be Mexican American and African American and that Anglos will be a minority (see Table 18–1). School enrollments are already majority-minority, according to the Texas Education Agency. In 1987, Anglos made up 52.5 percent of all school attendees in Texas. In 2000, Anglos made up 43 percent of the school population. These changes in majority and minority status will have many implications for the politics of the state and for public policy decisions.

majority-minority
Minority groups now make up a majority of the population of the state. Anglos are no longer a majority.

A midwestern family, early settlers in the High Plains region of Texas.

How Texas Compares

Comparison of Growth Rates of the Fifteen Most Populous States

In the past thirty years, Texas has experienced tremendous growth in its population. This growth is due both to birthrates and to immigration of citizens from other states and countries. The largest-growing segment of the population is Mexican Americans. The growth in Texas population is also due to a movement of population from the northeastern states to the southern states.

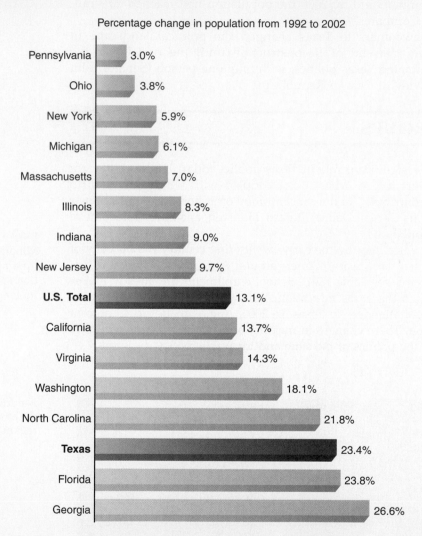

Percentage change in population from 1992 to 2002

State	Percentage
Pennsylvania	3.0%
Ohio	3.8%
New York	5.9%
Michigan	6.1%
Massachusetts	7.0%
Illinois	8.3%
Indiana	9.0%
New Jersey	9.7%
U.S. Total	13.1%
California	13.7%
Virginia	14.3%
Washington	18.1%
North Carolina	21.8%
Texas	23.4%
Florida	23.8%
Georgia	26.6%

Source: Legislative Budget Board, *Texas Fact Book* (2004), 30.

Hispanic Americans

Hispanic immigration from Mexico to Texas has been a factor in both population increases and state politics. In 1960, Hispanics made up 15 percent of the total population of Texas. Their percentage increased to 18 percent by 1970, 21 percent in 1980, 25 percent in 1990, and 32 percent in 2000. Liberalized voter

TABLE 18–1	Historical and Projected Population Changes in Texas, 1980 to 2030, as Percentage of Total Population			
YEAR	ANGLO	AFRICAN AMERICAN	MEXICAN AMERICAN	OTHER
1980	65.7%	11.9%	21.0%	1.4%
1990	60.7	11.8	25.4	2.1
2000	53.1	11.6	32.0	3.3
2010	48.4	10.9	36.3	4.4
2020	42.3	10.3	41.4	6.0
2030	36.4	9.5	46.2	7.9

Source: Steve H. Murdock, *Projections of Texas and Counties in Texas by Age, Sex, and Race/Ethnicity for 1980 to 2030*, Department of Rural Sociology, Texas Agricultural Experiment Station, Texas A&M University System, February 1992.

registration procedures have enabled Hispanics to begin to dominate politics in the border areas, in some sections of the Gulf Coast, and in the San Antonio area, where they have been successful in electing local officials to city and county government and school boards, to the state legislature, and to Congress. For example, Dan Morales was elected state attorney general in 1990 and served until 1999. Raul Gonzales was appointed by Governor Mark White to serve on the Texas Supreme Court in 1984 and served until 1999, winning election twice. Victor Morales, a newcomer to politics, won the Democratic party nomination for the U.S. Senate in April 1996 to oppose Senator Phil Gramm. The Hispanic vote will continue to be a major force in state politics in the future. What form that force will take is uncertain.

African Americans

Unlike the Hispanic population, which has increased steadily as a percentage of total state population since the 1960s, the African American population has remained constant at about 12 percent since 1950. African Americans tend to be concentrated in three metropolitan areas: Houston, Dallas–Fort Worth, and Austin. They have had some political success in electing officials to local offices (school boards, city councils, and county offices), to the state legislature, and to a few seats in the U.S. Congress. Only one African American, Morris Overstreet, has been elected to statewide office. From 1990 to 1999, Judge Overstreet served on the Texas Court of Criminal Appeals, the Supreme Court for criminal matters in the state. In 2002, Ron Kirk, a popular Dallas mayor, ran for the U.S. Senate. While polls showed Kirk to be in a dead heat with John Cornyn, he lost the race. Voter turnout among African Americans was low, and some Anglos who normally support Democrats voted for the Republican, Cornyn.

Asian Americans

Asian Americans constituted less than 1 percent of the population of Texas in 1980; by 1990, they made up 1.9 percent of state population. Projections are that by the year 2020 the Asian American population of Texas will increase to 4.5 percent. Most Asian Americans are concentrated in the Houston area. One section of Houston has such a large concentration of Chinese Americans that

Political Culture

Texas as a Majority-Minority State

A majority of Texans are now members of officially recognized minority groups, and Anglos are now a minority of the total population (see Table 18–1). Hispanics are the largest minority in the state and continue to grow as a percentage of the total population. At some point in the next decade, Hispanics will be the dominant population group in the state. African Americans, while growing in number, are not increasing as a percentage of the population.

What are the implications for the future of Texas and politics in the state? As later chapters will show, Hispanics are underrepresented in the state legislature and state court systems. Hispanics also have lower education and income levels and attend college at a much lower rate than Anglos.

By 2030, Hispanics might be the dominant force in Texas politics. They might be able to elect many statewide officeholders and become, perhaps in coalition with other minority groups, the majority in the Texas legislature. What will this mean in terms of party control? Will Hispanics continue to give most of their votes to Democrats, or will they switch to a majority supporting Republicans? Most state universities today are overwhelmingly Anglo. How will state universities fare in terms of appropriations of money? Will a Hispanic majority in the legislature shift appropriations to the universities in South Texas with majority Hispanic student bodies?

These questions are the great unknowns in Texas politics. What is not in doubt is that a Hispanic majority will change the face of Texas policies and public policy in the twenty-first century.

some of the street signs have Chinese writing. Asian Americans in the Houston area have had some success in electing local officials, including one city council member and a county judge. In 2002 the voters of Houston elected Martha Wong to the Texas statehouse, and in 2004 they elected Hubert Vo over twenty-year veteran Talmadge Heflin.

THE POLITICAL CULTURE OF TEXAS

Thus far we have discussed the historical settlement patterns, the changing makeup of the current population, and the ethnic mix of the population in the state. These factors all contribute to what is called "political culture." To understand politics, it is necessary to understand political culture. Government is the process by which values in a society are authoritatively allocated.[5] In the political process, government decides which of the competing values regarding the role of government will be upheld. The predominant values that government supports are the values held by most citizens. These dominant values are called the political culture. Thus, a state's **political culture** is the attitudes, values, and beliefs about the proper role of government held by most people in a state. Most people might not know much about government or how it works, but most do have views and values, sometimes poorly defined, about what government should and should not do.

Daniel J. Elazar, in his book *American Federalism: A View from the States*, developed a system for applying the idea of political culture to the fifty states.[6] Elazar found that there were three distinctive political subcultures in the United States: moralistic, individualistic, and traditionalistic (see "How Texas Compares").

In the **moralistic subculture,** politics "is considered one of the great activities of [people in their] search for the good society . . . an effort to exercise power for

political culture

A system of beliefs and values that defines the role of government and the role of citizens in that government.

moralistic subculture

Political culture in which government is seen as a positive force to achieve a common good for all citizens.

How Texas Compares

Political Subcultures

The map below shows how the states compare based on the concept of political culture. Note that the South is dominated by traditionalistic culture, the states in the Great Lakes region and some states in the West by moralistic culture, and the Midwest by individualistic culture. Compare this map with the map of the United States in Chapter 6, page 177, showing liberal and conservative states. How closely do the two maps compare? Are southern states the most conservative? Are states with a moralistic political subculture classified as liberal or conservative?

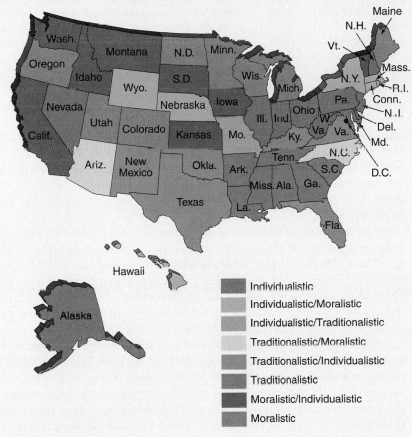

Individualistic

Individualistic/Moralistic

Individualistic/Traditionalistic

Traditionalistic/Moralistic

Traditionalistic/Individualistic

Traditionalistic

Moralistic/Individualistic

Moralistic

Source: Daniel J. Elazar, *American Federalism: A View from the States* (New York: HarperCollins, 1984), 124–25.

the betterment of the commonwealth."[7] Government is a positive instrument for change and a means of promoting the general welfare of all citizens. Politics becomes the responsibility of all citizens, who have an obligation to participate in government. People serve in government not for personal gain but out of a sense of serving the public. The government has a right and an obligation to intervene in the private affairs of citizens when it is necessary for the "public good or the well-being of the community."[8]

The **individualistic subculture** "emphasizes the conception of the democratic order as a marketplace. In its view, a government is created for strictly utilitarian

individualistic subculture

Political culture that sees the role of government as benefiting the individual rather than society generally.

Get Involved!

Who Governs?

Many years ago, Robert Dahl wrote a famous book titled *Who Rules?* about New Haven, Connecticut, in which he pointed out that democratic institutions worked in this city in much the same way moralistic political culture says they work. By contrast, Floyd Hunter wrote an equally famous book about Atlanta, Georgia, titled *Who Governs?* in which he argued that the power elite operating behind the scenes made decisions in much the same way the traditionalistic view of political culture says they work.

Think about your own beliefs and those of your family and friends about the proper role of government and citizen involvement in the political process. Which view of political culture matches that of your family and friends? Do you think the labels traditionalistic and individualistic correctly identify the way Texas works and how Texans think? If you disagree and think that Texas is moralistic, list examples of politics and programs that support your point of view. If you agree with the labels for Texas, list examples of policies and programs that support your point of view. Examples might be Texas's ranking on things such as spending priorities, education, and the death penalty.

traditionalistic subculture

Political culture that sees the role of government as maintaining the existing political order for the benefit of a small elite.

reasons, to handle those functions demanded by the people it is created to serve."[9] Government is not concerned with the creation of a "good society," and government intervention in the private sector should be kept to a minimum. Politics is viewed not as high calling but as something that should be left to those willing to dirty their hands. Participation in politics is a necessary evil, not an obligation of each citizen.

The **traditionalistic subculture** holds as government's primary function the maintenance of the existing political order, and participation in politics is confined to a small, self-perpetuating elite. The public has only limited power and influence. Policies that benefit the public are enacted only when the elite allows them to be. Most policies enacted by government benefit the ruling elite and not the general public. Political participation by the public is discouraged, and a class-based social structure helps maintain the existing order.

Most of the old southern states have traditionalistic or individualistic political cultures. The southern Anglo settlers of East Texas brought with them a strong traditionalistic culture. Settlers in West Texas in the late nineteenth and early twentieth centuries, on the other hand, were from Midwestern states where the individualistic political culture predominates. These two political cultures (traditionalistic and individualistic) coexist and blend together in the state. They share some views regarding the role of government. Both see a limited role for government and discourage broad-based citizen participation in political processes. Both have a conservative view of government, believing that individuals should do for themselves whenever possible and that government should do only those things individuals cannot do for themselves—such as paving the roads, keeping the peace, and putting out fires—and leave the rest to the private sector. Both hold that government should keep taxes low, limit social services, and limit the advancement of civil rights. However, most state government institutions and political processes are more consistent with the traditionalistic political culture than with the individualistic political culture. Immigrants to East Texas from the lower South (Louisiana, Arkansas, Alabama, Georgia, South Carolina, and Florida) supported the traditionalistic idea of rule by an elite as a natural extension of slavery. This culture was maintained after the Civil War, even in the absence of slavery.

Immigrants from the upper South (Missouri, Tennessee, Kentucky, southern Illinois, southern Ohio, and parts of Pennsylvania) tended to support the individualistic political culture. Most were of German, Scotch-Irish, and English ethnic origins. Few were slave owners, but almost all were hard-core individualists. The many settlers from the upper South far outnumbered the slave owners from the lower South.[10] Similar immigrant patterns persisted among the late-nineteenth-century settlers in West Texas, contributing an individualistic political culture to that area of the state. Thus, the first Anglo settlers to Texas brought with them both individualistic and traditionalistic views on the role of government, beliefs that remain dominant in modern-day Texas politics. German immigrants also came to Texas in search of individual opportunities and viewed government as having a limited role.[11]

Mexican American immigrants contributed a traditionalistic view to the Texas political culture. Spanish culture in the eighteenth century was dominated by a landed aristocracy, a small elite that controlled government for its own benefit. Elements of this traditionalistic Mexican culture have remained vital into the twenty-first century—both in Mexico itself and in the United States among Mexican Americans. A great respect for the extended family is one of those elements. Another is a rigid role structure for family members, such as husbands and wives. Adherence to the Catholic faith is a third. Indeed, some scholars have argued that Mexican culture still places considerably more emphasis on family and religious values than on individual achievement.[12]

Mexicans in Texas have also been subjected to domination by Anglo culture for a large part of their history in the state, reinforcing their preordained view of the role of government. Their segregation from Anglo society and their limited access to the political process due to restrictive voter registration procedures also have reinforced their traditional Mexican cultural predispositions. Some have argued that their adherence to Mexican culture is a defensive reaction to Anglo domination.[13]

African Americans were forced participants in a traditionalistic political culture during pre–Civil War days. After the Civil War, especially at the end of Reconstruction in 1876, they were subjected to similar restraints. Their involvement in Texas political processes was effectively restricted until the late 1960s and early 1970s with passage of the 1965 Federal Voting Rights Act and its application to Texas in the 1970s. Before that time, the poll tax, the Democratic party white primary (in which only Anglos were allowed to vote), and fear and intimidation severely limited African Americans' participation in Texas politics. Segregated public schools and restrictive housing laws reinforced the traditionalistic political culture.

Patterns of political culture are slow to change and persist for long periods of time. For example, these were the primary planks of the platforms of the Democratic governors in the 1940s and 1950s:

- Opposition to expanding civil rights
- Limits on the role of the federal government in state affairs
- Opposition to federal control over natural resources (oil and gas)
- Opposition to organized labor unions
- No new taxes[14]

Except for minor differences, most of these planks would fit well into the platforms of former Republican governor George W. Bush in 1994 and 1998 and Governor Rick Perry in 2002, 2004, and 2006. A review of the platform of the Republican party in Texas in 2002 shows support for all these points.[15] The party in control of the governor's mansion and most statewide offices has a different name, but the political culture has not changed. It is safe to say that in the past

How Texas Compares

Per Capita Income in 2002 for the Fifteen Most Populous States

Per capita income is a measure of the wealth of the state. If you compare Texas with the fourteen other most populous states, it does not compare well. Only two states in this group have lower personal per capita incomes, and Texas ranks well below the national average.

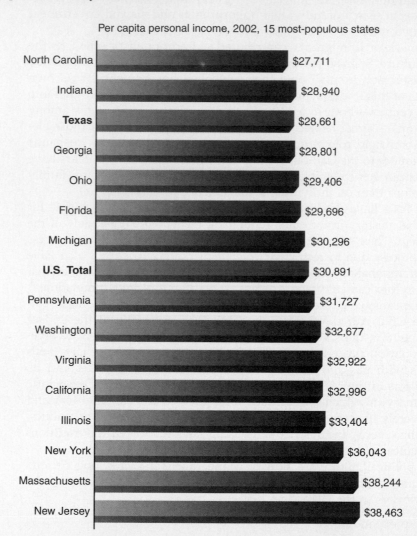

Per capita personal income, 2002, 15 most-populous states

North Carolina	$27,711
Indiana	$28,940
Texas	$28,661
Georgia	$28,801
Ohio	$29,406
Florida	$29,696
Michigan	$30,296
U.S. Total	$30,891
Pennsylvania	$31,727
Washington	$32,677
Virginia	$32,922
California	$32,996
Illinois	$33,404
New York	$36,043
Massachusetts	$38,244
New Jersey	$38,463

Source: Legislative Budget Board, *Texas Fact Book* (2004), 33.

twenty-five years Texas has gone from a state dominated by the Democratic party to a state dominated by the Republican party with little change in philosophy, ideology, or public policy. The concept of political culture helps explain how and why state governments differ on important determinants. Political culture influences the basic structure of state government, defines government policy, and influences the degree of citizen involvement in government.

The basic structure of state government in Texas fits the traditionalistic/individualistic model quite well. Government is limited, with power divided among many elected officials. Executive authority is weak, and most power rests with the state legislature. Few state regulations are imposed on business, and many that do exist benefit specific businesses. Regulation of the environment is modest. Despite the repeal of the poll tax, intervention by the federal government, and the passage of the Voting Rights Acts, voter participation in Texas remains quite low, ranking near the bottom of the fifty states in terms of percentage of population voting. Political corruption often is tolerated as the necessary cost of doing the business of government. Except on rare occasions, the state legislature protects the status quo and places few restrictions on lobbying and other activities of interest groups. The office of governor is formally very weak. The state bar and business interest groups heavily control the selection of the state judiciary in partisan elections. State finances reflect the philosophy of limited government—Texas often ranks near the bottom of the fifty states on government expenditures. Limited state expenditures are financed with a regressive tax system that relies on property taxes and sales taxes.

In summary, the political culture of Texas supports a conservative, limited government. Later chapters expand on these ideas to demonstrate the differences and similarities between Texas and other states.

THE ECONOMY OF TEXAS

The economy of a state also plays a role in its politics. The economy of Texas has changed greatly in the past twenty to thirty years. Texas is no longer a rural state with an economy dominated by cattle, cotton, and oil, although these are still important elements in the state's economy.

Land has always been an important factor in Texas economy and politics. Many settlers originally were lured to Texas by offers of free land. The Spanish and later the Mexican government provided generous land grants to any family that settled in the state. Each family could receive one *sitio* or *legua* (Spanish for "league"), about 4,428 acres of land. A single person could receive 1,500 acres. In the 1820s, it took a generous incentive to get people to live in Texas, given

Wheat harvest on the High Plains near Amarillo in the 1920s.

the hardships of travel and simple survival. General P. H. Sheridan, best known for his remark "The only good Indian I ever saw was dead," wrote in a letter from Fort Clark, Texas, dated 1855: "If I owned Hell and Texas, I'd rent out Texas and live in Hell."[16] Other people supposedly came to Texas from more comfortable environments in order to escape the law. "GTT" ("Gone to Texas") was supposedly a common sign left by those escaping the sheriff.

Land issues drove the Texas revolution in 1836 and the annexation of Texas by the United States in 1845. When Texas entered the Union, it retained both its public debt and its public lands. The U.S. government had to purchase from Texans all land that was to be federal land. The U.S. government also purchased lands that formerly were the west and northwest parts of Texas and that make up much of present-day New Mexico and parts of Colorado, Utah, and Wyoming.[17]

land-based economy

An economic system in which most wealth is derived from the use of the land.

For most of its history, the Lone Star State has had a **land-based economy.** Cotton farming dominated from the 1820s to the 1860s. After the Civil War, cattle became the economic mainstay. In the early twentieth century, abundant oil was discovered in East Texas. Only in the past thirty to forty years has the economy begun to diversify and become less dependent on the land and its cotton, cattle, and oil. Some regions of the state remain more dependent on land economies than others, and vast differences can be found from one region to another.

The State of Texas Comptroller's Office has divided Texas into a number of economic regions as a convenient way to collect data. For purposes of discussion, these have been combined into six regions (see Figure 18–2).

The East Texas or Piney Woods region was traditionally dominated by agriculture, timber, and oil. Today, agriculture is less important and oil's importance is declining. While timber is still important, some diversification has occurred, with manufacturing becoming a more significant element in the economy.

The Plains region, with Lubbock and Amarillo the major cities, was traditionally dominated by agriculture (especially cotton, wheat, and maize) and by

Figure 18–2
Economic Regions of Texas

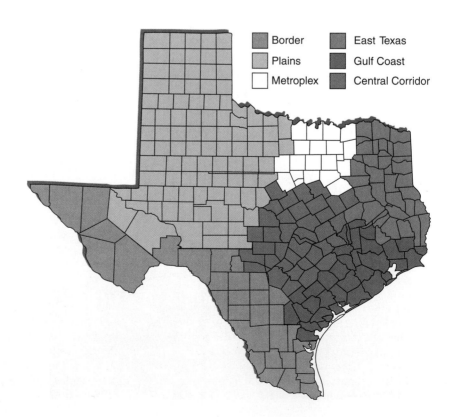

Border	East Texas
Plains	Gulf Coast
Metroplex	Central Corridor

ranching and cattle feedlots. In recent years, the economy of this region has become more diversified and less dominated by agriculture.

The Gulf Coast region, extending from Corpus Christi to Beaumont/Port Arthur/Orange and including Houston, is dominated by petrochemical industries, manufacturing, shipping, and fishing. In recent years, the economy of this area has diversified into manufacturing and high-tech industries. It is also the area with the highest concentration of organized labor unions.

The border area of South Texas and the Rio Grande Valley, stretching from Brownsville to El Paso, is noted primarily for its agricultural production of citrus fruits and vegetables. In recent years, trade with Mexican border cities has led to diversification in this region, and this process has increased with the passage of the North American Free Trade Agreement (NAFTA). Some would distinguish the El Paso area and the border area as separate economic units because the two regions are several hundred miles apart and have limited economic contact. Many citizens of El Paso often feel more closely associated with New Mexico than with Texas. In fact, the six counties in Southeast New Mexico are referred to by New Mexicans as "Little Texas."

The Metroplex or Dallas/Fort Worth area is considered the financial center of the state. This economic region is the most diversified in the state, with a combination of banking, manufacturing, high-tech, and aerospace industries.

The Central Corridor or mid-state region is the area stretching roughly from College Station in the east to Waco in the north and Austin and San Antonio in the southwest. This economic area is dominated by two large state universities (Texas A&M University and the University of Texas at Austin), by high-tech industries in Austin and San Antonio, and by major military bases in the Waco/Temple/Killeen and San Antonio areas.

The economic recession of the early 1980s showed a need for a more diversified economy for the state. It was felt that the old land-based economy could not carry the state into the twenty-first century. Since 1988, there has been significant restructuring of the state economy. NAFTA promised some significant economic growth due to increased trade with Mexico, and new high-tech industries, especially in Austin, Dallas, and Houston, have significantly influenced the Texas economy.

Summary

Self-Test www.mhhe.com/pattersontexas8

As Texas enters the twenty-first century, the economy of the state is far more diverse than it was even twenty years ago. While energy and agriculture are still important elements in the state's economy, they are balanced by many new elements. This trend is expected to continue.

Texas is very much a land of contrasts. The culture of the state is made up of many diverse parts. The Hispanic, Anglo and German immigrants contributed greatly to the culture of the state. More recent arrivals from other states have contributed to the culture of the state. People from other states are often bored with Texans who brag about their state. Some Texans think they have the right to brag, because the history and diversity of the state are unique, and the state is truly a land of contrasts. Others might say that Texas is also a land of contradictions and that Texans have no right to brag. Texas is still one of the lowest ranking states on many factors such as school expenditures, levels of voter participation, and fair treatment of all citizens. These contrasts and the contradictions have contributed to and can be partially explained by its cultural legacy. As we will see in later chapters, these cultural patterns and clashes help explain much of what occurs in the legislative, executive, and judicial branches of the state government.

While these various migrations of people have contributed to the diversity of the state, they have also contributed to a political culture that does not see government as the solver of problems. As discussed the traditionalistic/ individualistic culture does not encourage citizens to participate in politics or to view government intervention in private affairs to be appropriate. This political culture in large part explains why Texas ranks low in public expenditures, especially on education.

Texas is no longer a rural backwater state dependent upon a land-based economy. It is now a large urban industrial state and a major player in national politics. The expanding population of the state and the increase in minority groups in the state will continue to contribute to the challenges facing state government. The challenges facing Texas today are many and varied. Only time will tell how well the government of Texas deals with these challenges.

STUDY CORNER

Key Terms

comparative approach (*p. 529*)

individualistic subculture (*p. 537*)

land-based economy (*p. 542*)

majority-minority (*p. 533*)

moralistic subculture (*p. 537*)

political culture (*p. 537*)

traditionalistic subculture (*p. 537*)

Self-Test

1. All of the following views are shared by Texans characterized by the state's two dominant political subcultures **except** a belief that:
   a. government involvement should take place only to do the things that individuals cannot do for themselves.
   b. political participation is reserved for only a few citizens who are willing to become involved in order to maintain the existing social order.
   c. government should keep taxes low, limit social services, and limit the advancement of civil rights.
   d. involvement in politics is the responsibility of all citizens, who have an obligation to participate in government.

2. The Texas Democratic party platforms of the 1940s and 1950s included all of the following primary planks **except:**
   a. opposition to organized labor.
   b. opposition to expanding civil rights.
   c. limitation of the role of government in state affairs.
   d. acceptance of federal oil and gas regulation and control.

3. The set of attitudes, values, and beliefs that most people in a state have about the proper role of government is called:
   a. political socialization.
   b. political culture.
   c. political behavior.
   d. politics.

4. All of the following play a critical role in Texas politics **except:**
   a. state taxing policies.
   b. population growth and ethnic composition.
   c. political culture.
   d. urban versus rural demographics.

5. Of the three political subcultures described by Daniel Elazar, Texas is best described as:
   a. moralistic and traditionalistic.
   b. individualistic and traditionalistic.
   c. moralistic and traditionalistic.
   d. idealistic and traditionalistic.

6. By the year 2020, the three largest ethnic groups in Texas, in descending order, will be:
   a. Anglos, Hispanics, and African Americans.
   b. Hispanics, African Americans, and Anglos.
   c. Hispanics, Anglos, and Asian Americans.
   d. Hispanics, Anglos, and African Americans.

7. Since the late 1980s, the focus of the Texas economy has shifted from farming, cattle ranching, and oil production to all of the following **except:**
   a. shipping.
   b. banking.
   c. gambling and entertainment.
   d. high-tech industries.

8. In Texas, government is limited, power is divided among many elected officials, executive authority is weak, and most power resides with the state legislature. (T/F)

9. Since the 1970s, Texas has experienced staggering population growth attributed to legal migration of people from other states and legal and illegal immigration from Mexico. (T/F)

10. The population of African Americans in Texas is concentrated in selected areas of the state and is expected to increase to nearly 20 percent. (T/F)

Critical Thinking

The political culture of Texas is described as traditionalistic/individualistic. How well does this characterization fit your idea of Texans and their political beliefs? How do you personally benefit from this political subculture?

Suggested Readings

Calvert, Robert A., and Arnold DeLeon. *The History of Texas.* Arlington Heights, Ill.: Harland Davidson, 1990. Good general history of Texas.

Davidson, Chandler. *Race and Class in Texas Politics.* Princeton, N.J.: Princeton University Press, 1976. Good review of critical issues in Texas politics.

Elazar, Daniel J. *American Federalism: A View from the States.* New York: HarperCollins, 1984. More detailed explanation of concept of political culture.

Fehrendbach, T. R. *Lone Star: A History of Texas and Texans.* New York: Collier, 1980. Excellent history of Texas.

Jordon, Terry G. *German Seed in Texas Soil: Immigrant Farmers in Nineteenth Century Texas.* Austin: University of Texas Press, 1966. Excellent review of impact of German immigration.

Soukup, James R., Clifton McCleskey, and Harry Holloway. *Party and Factional Division in Texas.* Austin: University of Texas Press, 1964. Very comprehensive review of transition of Texas from a one-party state to a two-party state.

List of Websites

http://www.lbb.state.tx.us/
The Texas Facts Book site; gives information on Texas past and present and is a good source of data on the state budget.

http://www.tsha.utexas.edu/handbook/online/
The Texas Handbook, published online by the Texas Historical Society; it has a lot of information on the history of the state and its people.

http://www.state.tx.us/#government
State of Texas home page; general guide to state agencies.

http://www.window.state.tx.us/
Comptroller of Public Accounts website; a good source on state expenditures and economic regions.

http://www.usnpl.com/txnews.html
State newspaper links with information on Texas newspapers.

Participate!

What kinds of activities could you become involved in that would change an individual's or a group of individuals' basic view of the proper role in government? You might consider forming a student political forum group at your campus and invite a political speaker to appear.

Extra Credit

Find an article in your local newspaper that supports the idea of Texas as a conservative state. Editorials may be your best source of such information. Follow the newspaper's stories and editorials for a few days to see if an obvious political bias emerges.

(Self-Test Answers: 1. d   2. d   3. b   4. a   5. b   6. a   7. c   8. T   9. T   10. F)

The State Constitution

Chapter Outline

Texas Constitutions
Constitutions Under the Republic
of Mexico
The Republic of Texas Constitution of 1836
The Statehood Constitution of 1845
The Civil War and Reconstruction
Constitutions of 1861, 1866, and 1869
The Constitution of 1876
State Constitutions as Reflections of Texas
Culture

Political Culture and Institutions

**Principles of Constitutional
Government**

**Characteristics Common to State
Constitutions**
Separation of Powers
Bill of Rights
Supreme Law of the State

**Comparing the Structure of State
Constitutions**

**Amending and Revising State
Constitutions**
Patterns of Constitutional Change
Amending the Texas Constitution

CHAPTER 19

A constitution in the American sense of the word is a written instrument by which the fundamental powers of government are established, limited and defined, and by which those powers are distributed among several departments for their more safe and useful exercise for the benefit of the body politic.

—*Justice Samuel Miller, U.S. Supreme Court*[1]

On November 8, 2005, the voters of Texas voted for nine new amendments to the Texas constitution. Voter turnout was almost 20 percent of registered voters, almost double the normal turnout in such biennial constitutional amendment elections. This increase in turnout was driven by the second amendment on the ballot, a proposal to ban same-sex marriage. There is evidence that churches used the Sunday before the election to encourage voter participation. The ban will not be part of the Bill of Rights in the Texas constitution.

All states and the national government have written constitutions that provide the broad outlines of government. These constitutions are contracts between the government and the people, and they stand as a measure against which government actions must be judged. Constitutions also reveal something about a state. The previous chapter discussed the traditionalistic/individualistic political culture of Texas. The Texas constitution is very much an embodiment of this culture. It reflects the conservative nature of the state, the distrust of government, the desire to limit the government's ability to act, and the desire to protect certain special interests. This chapter looks at the constitutions that have governed Texas over its history.

In addition, this chapter will examine how Texas and other states operate within a federal system of government—American federalism. This system both limits and enhances what state and local governments can do and is one of the great compromises in American history.

TEXAS CONSTITUTIONS

An examination of the several constitutions that have governed Texas helps explain the importance of political culture and its impact on the formal structure of government. Texas has been governed by seven constitutions, five since its annexation by the United States in 1845.

The Alamo, in San Antonio, has long been a symbol of the struggle for Texas independence.

Constitutions Under the Republic of Mexico

The first constitution to govern Anglos in Texas was the Republic of Mexico's constitution of 1824. This constitution was federalist in concept and marked a clear break with the Spanish centralist tradition.[2] Under the 1824 national constitution, Texas was governed by a provincial constitution of the state of Coahuila y Tejas that was approved in 1827. The 1827 constitution provided for a unicameral (single-chamber) legislature, and Texas elected two representatives to the provincial legislature. This constitution, which lacked a bill of rights, provided a government structure with which the Anglos were comfortable. Texans ignored certain sections of the constitution of 1827, most notably those that imposed Catholicism as the state religion and those that did not recognize slavery.

The suspension by Mexican president Santa Anna of the Mexican national constitution of 1824—and with it the provincial constitution of 1827—was one factor that led to the Texas revolution. One of the early Texas flags, supposedly flown at the Alamo, had the numbers *1824* superimposed on a red, green, and white emblem of the Mexican flag. This symbolized a demand to restore the constitution of 1824.[3]

The Republic of Texas Constitution of 1836

In 1836, when Texas declared itself a republic independent of Mexico, a new constitution was adopted. This document was a composite of the U.S. Constitution and the constitutions of several southern states. It provided for a unitary, rather than a federal, form of government. Signs of the distrust of government held by the traditionalistic southerners who wrote the document are evident. They limited the term of the president of the Republic to one three-year term, with prohibitions against consecutive terms. The president also was prohibited from raising an army without the consent of the legislature. Features such as freedom of religion and protection of property rights, which had been absent in the 1824 and 1827 constitutions, were included. Slavery, which had been ignored by the Mexican government, was legalized.[4]

The Texas Declaration of Independence was signed in February and March 1836 in a building like this replica at Washington-on-the-Brazos State Park.

The Statehood Constitution of 1845

When Texas joined the Union in 1845, a state constitution was adopted. This document also reflected the traditionalistic southern culture of Texas, with a few notable exceptions that were adaptations of Spanish law. Women were granted property rights equal to those of men, with married women given half the value of all property acquired during the marriage (community property). In addition, a person's homestead was protected against forced sale to pay debts. These ideas were later adopted by many other states. The 1845 constitution also provided for limited executive authority, biennial sessions of the legislature, and two-year terms for most officials. Most of these features were included in later constitutions.

The Civil War and Reconstruction Constitutions of 1861, 1866, and 1869

In 1861, when Texas joined the Confederacy, another state constitution was adopted. It was essentially the same as the 1845 document, with the exception of a prohibition against the emancipation of slaves, a provision to secede from the Union, and a provision to join the Confederacy.

In 1866, a third state constitution was approved as a condition of rejoining the Union following the Civil War. This document abolished slavery, nullified the ordinances of secession, renounced the right of future secession, and repudiated the wartime debts of the state. The constitution of 1866 was short-lived. It was overturned by Reconstruction acts of the U.S. Congress.

Military rule was again imposed on Texas, and a new constitution was adopted in 1869. This fourth state constitution, which was approved under the supervision of the federal government's military rule, is called the Reconstruction constitution or the "carpetbaggers' constitution." It represented a radical departure from past documents and reflected the centralization aspirations of the national Republicans. A four-year term was provided for the governor, who was also given strong appointive authority—the governor could appoint most state and many local officials. County courts were abolished, and much local authority and control were removed from the class that had governed Texas before the Civil War. Public schools were centralized under state control and funded by a poll tax and the sale of public lands. African Americans were given the right to vote, and whites who had participated in the "rebellion" (the Civil War) were disenfranchised.[5]

From 1836 until 1845, Texas was an independent nation known as the Republic of Texas. In the treaty forced on Mexico by Texas, Mexico ceded land stretching to the headwaters of the Rio Grande. While this land was never fully occupied by the government of the Republic, Texas claimed land in what is now part of the states of New Mexico, Oklahoma, Kansas, Colorado, and Utah.

The Constitution of 1876

The current state constitution was written in 1875, at the end of Reconstruction, and approved by the voters in 1876. The constitutional convention was assembled in 1875. "Not one man who had written the constitution of 1869 sat in this delegation. The convention was composed almost entirely of old Texans."[6] These men were landowners who had objected strongly to the centralist government imposed under Reconstruction. The new document reflected the antigovernment sentiments of the traditionalistic/individualistic political culture of the state. It reimposed shorter terms of office, reestablished many statewide and local elected offices, and severely restricted the ability of government to act. The powers of both the legislature and the governor were restricted.[7]

None of these changes were especially controversial. The controversial issues were the poll tax for the right to vote, women's suffrage, and public schools. The centralized state school system was abolished and replaced by local control of schools, with some state funding provided. In addition, provisions were made for a state-funded university system.[8]

HISTORICAL BACKGROUND

HISTORICAL BACKGROUND

State Constitutions as Reflections of Texas Culture

Texas has been governed by a number of state constitutions. The Spanish constitutions under Mexico contributed several key elements, including community property rights for women, that were a clear departure from English laws. The 1845 constitution provided for limited government with little centralized power. The constitutions of 1861 and 1866 continued these principles of limited government, and the present constitution, approved in 1876, not only reinstated but expanded them. Only the Reconstruction constitution of 1869, which provided for a strong, centralized government, was a departure from these principles. Its swift repeal at the end of Reconstruction indicates how completely the southern whites rejected centralization. As recently as 1999, voters rejected two amendments that would have expanded the power of the governor to appoint and remove minor state officials.

POLITICAL CULTURE AND INSTITUTIONS

To a large degree, culture drives institutions. The Reconstruction constitution of 1869 was a fundamental departure from earlier constitutions and conflicted with the political culture of the state. As described, this document centralized power in state government and reduced the authority of local governments, provided for four-year terms for many officeholders, and gave the governor the power to appoint most state and many local officials, including the state judiciary. In addition, it provided for annual sessions of the legislature, gave African Americans the right to vote, and provided for state-controlled schools and a state police system. Most of these provisions are not supported by a traditionalistic/individualistic political culture that supports decentralized, weak government while discouraging political participation and involvement in government by non-elites.

Except for the four-year terms for governor and other statewide officials, most of the ideas in the 1869 constitution (gubernatorial appointment of state and local officials, annual sessions of the legislature, and state control of local affairs) enjoy little support in Texas today. Voters have rejected annual sessions of the legislature on several occasions, and despite decentralization of local schools, demand has grown for even greater decentralization of decision making down to the local level. Culture drives institutions by influencing the basic structure and organization of government. Thus, the current constitution is quite compatible with the political culture of the state.

PRINCIPLES OF CONSTITUTIONAL GOVERNMENT

popular sovereignty
Idea that the power granted in state constitutions rests with the people.

contract theory of state constitutions
Principle that state constitutions are contracts between the citizens and the government and place limitations on the power of government.

History, culture, and traditions have a general impact on constitutions, but several important principles specifically underpin the idea of constitutional government. The first of these principles is **popular sovereignty,** the idea that all power rests with the people.[9] Constitutions are written by a popularly elected convention of citizens and not by state legislatures. Thus, the citizens must also approve any changes to state constitutions (except in Delaware, where the state legislature can amend the state constitution). The current Texas constitution strongly supports this idea in its preamble and bill of rights.

Second, by the **contract theory of state constitutions,** constitutions are a contract or compact between the citizens and the government and cannot be violated. The laws passed by legislatures must fit within the framework of the constitution.

Third, constitutions impose a limit on the power of government. The assumption here is that government can do anything not prohibited by the constitution and thus it is necessary to expressly limit its power. As has been pointed out, the current (1876) Texas constitution is an example of placing limitations on the power of state government. When the current constitution was drafted in 1874–75, Governor Richard Coke addressed the assembled constitutional convention:

Texas Capitol: Often called the grandest state house in the nation.
Source: House & Senate Office

> The accepted theory of American constitutional government is that State Constitutions are limitations upon, rather than grants of power: and as a rule, not without its exceptions, that power not prohibited exists in State government. Therefore, express prohibitions are necessary upon the power of state government. . . . These restrictions . . . have multiplied in the more recently created instruments of fundamental law.[10]

Some would say that Governor Coke was "preaching to the choir" with his opening statement. The men (women could not vote until 1920 in Texas) who assembled in a constitutional convention in 1875 had as their primary aim limiting the power of state government. The actions of the Radical Republicans during Reconstruction might have intensified the desires of these men to weaken and limit government, but they were predisposed to this philosophy even before the Civil War. While the Texas constitution embraces all three principles, the idea of limiting government is wholeheartedly embraced.

CHARACTERISTICS COMMON TO STATE CONSTITUTIONS

Besides the principles of popular sovereignty, compact or contract theory, and limited government, state constitutions share some other characteristics.

Separation of Powers

All state constitutions embrace the idea of separation of powers provided in the U.S. Constitution: power is divided among an elected executive, an elected legislature, and a judiciary. This separation of powers provides a check on the actions of government. Fear of a concentration of power in a single person led the Framers of the U.S. Constitution to separate powers. Fragmented power was deemed safer. This fear of strong executive authority, experienced in Texas under Governor Edmund J. Davis and the Radical Republicans, led the framers of the 1876 document to break up executive control. The voters were to elect a governor, a lieutenant governor, a comptroller, an attorney general, a commissioner of the land office, and a state treasurer. The elected positions of agricultural commissioner, railroad commissioners, and a state board of education were added later. The office of treasurer was abolished in 1995.

Bill of Rights

Like the U.S. Constitution, most state constitutions include very strong statements on civil liberties that grant basic freedoms. Most civil liberties protections in state constitutions duplicate those found in the federal document, but many state constitutions are more generous in the granting of liberties than is the U.S. Constitution. The Texas constitution is no exception. The average citizen, upon reading the bill of rights section of the Texas constitution, might well conclude that it is a very liberal document. Besides those rights provided by the federal document, the Texas constitution also grants equality under the law to all citizens regardless of "sex, race, color, creed or national origin."[11] This is almost the exact wording of the failed Equal Rights Amendment to the U.S. Constitution. Citizens often are granted more freedoms under their state constitutions than under the national Constitution, but most are unaware of this situation. Attention is often focused on the national Bill of Rights and not on the state bill of rights.

Supreme Law of the State

Article 6 of the U.S. Constitution contains the supremacy clause, which makes the U.S. Constitution the supreme law of the land. Most state constitutions have a similar statement that makes the state constitution superior to state law and to actions by local governments. Any state or local law that conflicts with the state constitution is invalid.

A recent example of local laws potentially conflicting with state law involves the state's issuing of permits to allow citizens to carry concealed handguns. Many local governments (cities, counties, and metropolitan transit authorities) passed regulations prohibiting the carrying of concealed handguns in some public places. Supporters of the "concealed carry law" charged that these local regulations violate state law. The state court system, however, determined that the local regulations do not violate the concept of "supreme law of the state."

COMPARING THE STRUCTURE OF STATE CONSTITUTIONS

Although they share some common characteristics, state constitutions also have vast differences. According to legal experts and political theorists, there are some ideal characteristics that constitutions should possess and that form a basis for comparison. Ideally, a constitution should be brief and explicit, embody only the general principles of government, and provide the broad outlines of government subject to interpretation, especially through the courts' power of judicial review. Constitutions should not be detailed and specific but rather should be broad and flexible. Furthermore, constitutions should provide broad grants of power to specific agencies and hold government officials accountable for their actions. Finally, formal amendments to the constitution should be infrequent, deliberate, and significant.

The U.S. Constitution embodies these ideals. The original document has only 4,300 words. It broadly outlines the basic principles of government and has been amended only twenty-seven times. All but eight of these amendments involved questions of civil liberty, voting, and electoral procedures; very few of them have altered the basic structure of the federal government. The document is flexible enough to allow for change without altering the basic document.

Get Involved!

Concepts from the Bill of Rights in the Texas Constitution

Food for Thought:

Listed below are the rights granted in the Texas Constitution. Compare these rights with those granted in the U.S. Constitution. What rights grated in the Texas Constitution are absent form the U.S. document?

Article 1 of the Texas Constitution grants basic rights to citizens, as the following examples illustrate.

Texas is a free and independent State, subject only to the Constitution of the United States, and the maintenance of our free institutions and the perpetuity of the Union depends upon the preservation of the right of local self-government, unimpaired to all the States. (Section 1)

All political power is inherent in the people, and all free governments are founded on their authority, and instituted for their benefit. The faith of the people of Texas stands pledged to the preservation of a republican [representative] form of government, and, subject to this limitation only, they have at all times the inalienable right to alter, reform or abolish their government in such manner as they may think expedient. (Section 2)

Equality under the law shall not be denied or abridged because of sex, race, color, creed or national origin. (Section 3a)

All men have a natural and indefeasible right to worship Almighty God according to the dictates of their own conscience. No man shall be compelled to attend, erect or support any place of worship, or to maintain any ministry against his consent. . . . and no preference shall ever be given by law to any religious society or mode of worship. (Section 6)

No money shall be appropriated or drawn from the Treasury for the benefit of any sect, or religious society, theological or religious seminary; nor shall property belonging to the State be appropriated for any such purposes. (Section 7)

Every person shall be at liberty to speak, write or publish his opinions on any subject, being responsible for the abuse of that privilege; and no law shall ever be passed curtailing the liberty of speech or of the press. . . . in all indictment for libels, the jury shall have the right to determine the law and the facts, under the direction of the court, as in other cases. (Section 8)

The people shall be secure in their persons, houses, papers and possessions, from unreasonable seizures or searches. (Section 9)

In all criminal prosecutions the accused shall have a speedy trial by an impartial jury. (Section 10)

All prisoners shall be bailable by sufficient sureties, unless for capital offenses. (Section 11)

The writ of habeas corpus is a writ of right, and shall never be suspended. (Section 12)

Excessive bail shall not be required, nor excessive fines imposed, nor cruel or unusual punishment inflicted. (Section 13)

No person, for the same offense, shall be twice put in jeopardy of life or liberty . . . after a verdict of not guilty in a court of [law]. (Section 14)

The right to trial by jury shall remain inviolate. (Section 15)

No bill of attainder, ex post facto law, retroactive law, or any law impairing the obligations of contracts, shall be made. (Section 16)

No person shall ever be imprisoned for debt. (Section 18)

No citizen of this state shall be deprived of life, liberty, property, privileges or immunities, or in any manner disfranchised, except by the due course of the law of the land. (Section 19)

No citizen shall be outlawed. No person shall be transported out of the State for any offense committed within the same. (Section 20)

No conviction shall work corruption of blood, or forfeiture of estate, and the estates of those who destroy their own lives shall descend or vest as in case of natural death. (Section 21)

Treason against the State shall consist only in levying war against it. (Section 22)

Every citizen shall have the right to keep and bear arms in the lawful defense of himself or the State; but the legislature shall have power, by law, to regulate the wearing of arms, with a view to prevent crime. (Section 23)

The military shall at all times be subordinate to the civil authority. (Section 24)

No soldier shall in time of peace be quartered in the house of any citizen without consent of the owner, nor in time of war but in a manner prescribed by law. (Section 25)

Perpetuities and monopolies are contrary to the genius of free government, and shall never be allowed, nor shall the law of primogeniture or entailments ever be in force in this state. (Section 26)

The citizens shall have the right, in a peaceable manner, to assemble together for their common good; and apply to those invested with the powers of government for redress of grievances or other purposes, by petition, address or remonstrance. (Section 27)

No power of suspending laws in this State shall be exercised except by the Legislature. (Section 28)

Debating the Issues

Should Gay Marriage Be Banned?

During the 2005 session of the Texas legislature, an amendment to the constitution to ban gay marriage was approved by the legislature. On November 8, 2005, the voters of the state overwhelmingly approved the amendment by a vote of 76 percent to 24 percent statewide. About 20 percent of registered voters voted, up from 12 percent in November 2003 and 7 percent in 2001. Opponents of the measure say they will fight it in court and hope to have it overturned. Social conservatives obviously turned out their voters.

Yes This amendment is about protecting marriage and defining it as a union between one man and one woman. Laws should not protect homosexuals, because there is no right in the constitution protecting sodomy. It is a sexual deviation that is intrinsically evil and a perversion of natural law. It destroys the meaning of marriage, which is for purposes of procreation of children.

The ban of gay marriages has wide support among all Christian denominations. It is not a liberal or conservative issue but an attempt to save the institution of marriage. The Southern Baptist Convention states: "The Bible condemns it as sin. Homosexuality is not a 'valid alternative lifestyle.' It is not, however, unforgivable sin. The same redemption available to all sinners is available to homosexuals. They, too, may become new creations in Christ."

In Catholic belief, "marriage is a faithful, exclusive and lifelong union between one man and one woman, joined as husband and wife in an intimate partnership of life and love," the forty-seven-bishop committee said . . . "What are called 'homosexual unions,' because they do not express full human complementarity and because they are inherently nonprocreative, cannot be given the status of marriage." The Lutheran position is this: "The Lord teaches us through His Word that homosexuality is a sinful distortion of His desire that one man and one woman live together in marriage as husband and wife. God categorically prohibits homosexuality. Our church, The Lutheran Church—Missouri Synod, has declared that homosexual behavior is 'intrinsically sinful.' While gay marriage would be a catastrophic revision of the most fundamental institution in human culture, civil unions have the potential of undermining heterosexual marriage."

In addition, this constitutional amendment would prevent liberal activist judges from overruling the current state law, which bans homosexual marriage.

—*Marriage Alliance website (http://www.txmarriage.com/getinfo.php)*

No This amendment was cooked up by the political leadership as a hot-button, distraction issue. It is little more than gay bashing. "Defending marriage against a mostly imaginary assault is a lot easier than, say, lowering local property taxes and figuring out a fair and adequate way to pay for public schools, feats that [Governor] Perry and other state Republican leaders have repeatedly promised and repeatedly failed to deliver. A strong public educational system and a spouse's ability to hold and retain a well-paying job would be much more critical to the next generation of families than whether the Texas Constitution has provisions officially defining marriage as a union between one man and one woman. So would improved health care. While Perry and other state leaders piously extol the virtues of a 'traditional marriage,' one-fifth of Texas' children still don't have health insurance, a rate almost double the national average. Texas already has a law restricting marriage to heterosexual unions. Proponents of the constitutional ban . . . claim the extra step is necessary to head off legal challenges to the law." Governor Perry in an address before the Marriage Alliance, which supported the amendment, said, "This is your chance to protect marriage from fringe groups and liberal judges that would undermine marriage to fit their radical agendas. Nonsense! There are very few liberal judges in Texas and almost all of the appellate court judges and all nine members of the Texas Supreme Court are conservative Republicans, many of whom were initially appointed by Perry."

The same-sex marriage amendment promotes prejudice and divisiveness and liberal/gay bashing. It is of questionable constitutionality. It prohibits persons of different sexes to enter into contracts but allows citizens of same sexes to do just that. It will also work hardships on same-sex couples who have adopted children and on employee benefits such as health insurance.

—*Clay Robinson, "Rev. Gov. Perry hitching re-election to conservatives" Houston Chronicle, June 18, 2005.*

Few state constitutions meet the standards of brevity and a limited number of amendments. This is especially true of the Texas constitution. Table 19–1 compares all fifty state constitutions. Several conclusions are obvious from examining this table. For one thing, most states have had several constitutions. Only nineteen states are still operating under their first constitution, and most of these are newer states in the western part of the United States. Massachusetts is the only one of the "original thirteen" states still operating under its first constitution. The Civil War and its aftermath resulted in multiple constitutions for the former Confederate states.

Most state constitutions are very lengthy documents. Alabama's is the longest, with 310,328 words including amendments. The mean word count of state constitutions is 19,300, compared with only 4,300 for the U.S. Constitution.[12] Some writers have pointed out that state constitutions have to be longer than the U.S. document because of the nature of state responsibility. While this is true to some extent, it can also be argued that most state documents are of excessive length for other reasons that will be discussed later.

Also, most state constitutions have been amended more often than the U.S. Constitution, with the mean being about 117 times. Alabama is again the leader, with 743 amendments. Finally, state constitutions have a limited life span compared to the U.S. Constitution, with an average life span of ninety-five years.[13]

Compared to the "average" state constitution, the Texas constitution is longer than most, at 93,000 words, and has more amendments, currently 432.[14] Only five states have drafted more constitutions. It is obvious that most state constitutions, including that of Texas, do not meet the criteria outlined previously for an ideal constitution. Most are lengthy, detailed documents that require frequent alteration. Most state constitutions might more accurately be described as statutory or legislative acts than as constitutional law. This is especially true of the document that governs Texas.

Several other generalizations can be made about state constitutions. First, most create weak executives and strong legislatures. Second, all state constitutions contain articles on taxation and finance that limit how funds can be spent. Often, taxes are earmarked for specific purposes (for example, the gasoline tax for state highways). Third, all but a few constitutions prohibit deficit spending unless approved by voters in the form of a bond election. Finally, most state constitutions contain large amounts of trivia. For example, the original Texas constitution contained a detailed list of items protected by the homestead protection provisions from forced sale for payment of debts. The list specified the number of chickens, ducks, cows, pigs, dogs, and horses exempt from forced sale.

AMENDING AND REVISING STATE CONSTITUTIONS

All state constitutions provide procedures for amending and revising the document. Except in the state of Delaware, two steps are involved in changing constitutions: proposal of an amendment and citizen approval. Some states provide a variety of methods for proposing or recommending changes to the constitution. All state constitutions allow the legislature to propose changes. Eleven states require only a majority vote of both houses of the legislature, but most states require a two-thirds majority vote.[15]

A second method of proposing amendments to state constitutions is the voter initiative, which requires the collection of a prescribed number of signatures on a

| TABLE 19–1 | Comparison of State Constitutions, January 2005 |

STATE	NUMBER OF CONSTITUTIONS	DATE OF CURRENT CONSTITUTION	APPROXIMATE WORD LENGTH	NUMBER OF AMENDMENTS SUBMITTED	NUMBER OF AMENDMENTS APPROVED
Alabama	6	1901	310,328	1,063	776
Alaska	1	1959	15,988	41	29
Arizona	1	1912	28,876	246	136
Arkansas	5	1874	59,500	186	91
California	2	1879	54,645	860	513
Colorado	1	1876	45,679	304	145
Connecticut	4	1965	16,608	30	29
Delaware	4	1879	19,000	*	138
Florida	6	1969	38,000	135	104
Georgia	10	1983	25,000	83	63
Hawaii	1	1959	20,774	123	104
Idaho	1	1890	23,239	204	117
Illinois	4	1971	13,200	17	11
Indiana	2	1851	10,230	78	46
Iowa	2	1857	12,500	57	52
Kansas	1	1861	12,246	122	92
Kentucky	4	1891	23,911	75	41
Louisiana	11	1975	54,112	189	129
Maine	1	1820	13,500	201	169
Maryland	4	1867	46,600	254	218
Massachusetts	1	1780	36,700	148	120
Michigan	4	1964	27,000	63	25
Minnesota	1	1858	11,547	213	118
Mississippi	4	1890	24,323	158	123
Missouri	4	1945	42,600	165	105
Montana	2	1973	13,218	53	30
Nebraska	2	1875	20,048	336	222
Nevada	1	1864	31,377	220	132
New Hampshire	2	1784	9,200	285	144
New Jersey	3	1948	22,956	69	36
New Mexico	1	1912	27,200	280	151
New York	4	1895	51,700	290	216
North Carolina	3	1971	11,000	42	34
North Dakota	1	1889	20,564	258	145
Ohio	2	1851	36,900	266	161
Oklahoma	1	1907	79,133	335	171
Oregon	1	1859	63,372	473	238
Pennsylvania	5	1968	27,503	34	28
Rhode Island	2	1986	10,908	8	8
South Carolina	7	1896	22,300	672	485
South Dakota	1	1889	27,703	219	212
Tennessee	3	1870	13,300	59	36
Texas	5	1876	93,000	605	432
Utah	1	1896	11,000	157	106
Vermont	3	1793	8,295	211	53
Virginia	6	1971	21,319	48	40
Washington	1	1889	50,237	168	95
West Virginia	2	1872	26,000	119	68
Wisconsin	1	1848	14,392	181	133
Wyoming	1	1890	31,800	120	94

*In Delaware, the legislature amends the state constitution without voter approval.

Source: *Book of the States 2005* (Lexington, KY: Council of State Governments, 2005), vol. 37, Table 1.1, p. 10.

How Texas Compares

Constitutional Amendments Among the States

The map below shows the number of amendments to state constitutions. Note that Texas, with more than three hundred amendments, is at the high end. Some western states have lots of amendments due to initiative provisions in their constitutions.

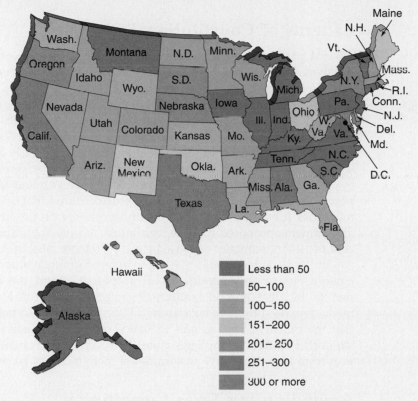

Less than 50
50–100
100–150
151–200
201–250
251–300
300 or more

Source: *Book of the States 2005* (Lexington, KY: Council of State Governments, 2005), vol. 37, Table 1.1, p. 10.

petition within a set time. Seventeen states allow the initiative, most of them western states that entered the Union in the late-nineteenth or early-twentieth century when the initiative was a popular idea. Only four states with the initiative option are east of the Mississippi River. The Texas Republican party pushed the idea of the initiative for many years, but in 1996 it was dropped from the party platform.

Most states, including Texas, allow the legislature to submit to the voters the question of calling a **constitutional convention** to propose amendments. This method normally is used for general revision, not for single amendments. Fourteen states have some provision for automatically submitting the question of a general convention to the voters periodically. If the voters approve, a convention is elected, assembles, and proposes amendments for voter approval.

Constitutional commissions are most often created by acts of the legislature, although other methods are provided. These commissions usually submit a report to the legislature recommending changes. If the legislature approves, the

constitutional convention

An assembly of citizens who may propose to voters changes to state constitutions.

proposed amendments are submitted to the voters. In Florida, the commission can bypass the legislature and go directly to the voters. Texas last used a commission in 1973, when the legislature created a thirty-seven-member commission.[16] This commission then submitted recommendations to the Texas legislature, which acted as a constitutional convention.

Except for Delaware, where the state legislature can unilaterally amend the constitution, all the states require that amendments be approved by voters in an election. Most states, including Texas, require a majority of those voting on the amendment to approve. Some states require a majority of the voters voting for some office (usually the governor) to approve. New Hampshire requires a two-thirds voter approval for all amendments.

Patterns of Constitutional Change

Several patterns of state constitutional change can be observed. One pattern involves the frequency of change. State constitutions are amended more frequently than is the U.S. Constitution. A key reason is that state constitutions deal with a wider range of functions. About 63 percent of state amendments deal with issues not covered by the U.S. Constitution, for example, education. However, even if issues not covered in the U.S. Constitution are excluded, the rate of amendment is still 3.5 times the national rate. Change is also related to length: longer state constitutions are more likely than shorter ones to be amended.[17]

Another pattern involves the method used to amend. Most amendments (90 percent) are proposed by state legislatures. States that require large legislative majorities for initiation have fewer amendments proposed and approved. Most amendments proposed by state legislatures receive voter ap-proval. About 63 percent of all amendments proposed since 1970 have been approved by the voters.[18]

In the seventeen states that allow voters to initiate amendments, two patterns emerge. First, more amendments are proposed; second, the voter approval success rate for initiative- and referendum-generated amendments is about that for amendments proposed by state legislatures (32 percent versus 64 percent).[19] This indicates that the initiative process fails to screen out amendments that lack broad public support. Proposal by the legislature, however, does. Amendments that gain support from large legislative majorities are more likely to be politically acceptable.

Amending the Texas Constitution

As indicated above all amendments to the Texas constitution must be proposed by a two-thirds vote of each house of the legislature. Between 1975 and 2003, the legislature proposed 241 amendments for voter approval. Of these, the voters approved 199 and rejected 42 (an 82 percent approval rate). Most amendments appear on the ballot in November of odd-numbered years, when no statewide offices are up for election. Since 1960, the Texas legislature has proposed 346 amendments to the constitution. Of these, 249 were voted on in odd-numbered years and 97 were voted on in even-numbered years. Voter turnout for odd-year elections generally is lower than for even-year elections (see Table 19–2). In odd-year elections, only about 10 percent of the voting-age population participates on average.[20] This means that as few as 5 percent (plus one voter) of the voting-age population could approve an amendment to the constitution. Voter turnout rates are further complicated by the fact that many city and school board elections are held in Harris County (Houston) on the same date. The Harris County vote could significantly affect the overall vote if turnout statewide is very low. A strongly contested race for mayor of Houston could inflate the turnout rate in that city and affect statewide election results.

TABLE 19-2	Voter Turnout in Odd-Year Constitutional Amendment Elections
YEAR	**PERCENTAGE OF VOTING-AGE POPULATION VOTING**
2005	19.0% (Gay marriage amendment on ballot)
2003	9.03
2001	5.60
1999	6.69
1997	5.32
1997 (Special election)	8.45
1995	5.55
1993	8.25
1991	16.6 (School finance on ballot)
1989	9.33
1987	18.6 (School finance on ballot)
1985	8.24
1983	6.19
1981	8.07

Source: Texas Secretary of State, www.sos.state.tx.us/elections/historic/70-03.shtml.

Ballot wording can contribute to voter confusion and also to voter support for amendments. The state legislature dictates the ballot wording of all amendments. Sometimes this wording can be misleading or noninstructive if the voter has not studied the issue before the election. This example from the 1978 election is illustrative:

> For or against the constitutional amendment providing for tax relief for residential homesteads, elderly persons, disabled persons, and agricultural land; for personal property exceptions; truth in taxation procedures, including citizen involvement; for a redefinition of the tax base; for limitations on state spending; and for fair property tax administration.[21]

Most voters probably found this wording irresistible. Could any voter not favor tax exemptions for the elderly, the handicapped, homeowners, and farmers? Does any citizen oppose fair tax administration or citizen involvement? The amendment passed by an overwhelming majority. Another example of ballot wording bias involves an amendment exempting personal property from taxation in Texas ports. The "freeport" amendment, which failed in 1987, read on the ballot: "rendering to the exemption from ad valorem taxation, certain tangible personal property temporarily located within the states." In 1989, an amendment on the ballot that read. "The constitutional amendment promoting economic growth, job creation and fair tax treatment for Texans who export goods" passed by a large majority. Ballot wording apparently is an important factor in the passage or rejection of amendments.

The number of amendments and the subject matter of most amendments are not of interest to most voters. For example, in 1993 Texas voters were asked to approve sixteen amendments to the state constitution. The subjects of most of these amendments were financial issues: to authorize the issuance of bonds for economic development, pollution control, veterans' land, higher education, prisons, pensions, and agricultural development. In addition, one amendment prohibited the establishment of an income tax without voter approval and another concerned delinquent taxes. Two separate amendments (Propositions 6 and 8) abolished the office of land surveyor in Jefferson and McLennan Counties, and another amendment (Proposition 15) allowed voters in any county to abolish the office of land surveyor. Other amendments cleared up Spanish land-grant titles in two counties, allowed

LEADERS

BILL RATLIFF

(1937–)

State Senator Bill Ratliff, Republican from Mount Pleasant in the Texarkana area, has been a true leader in the battle to reform the Texas constitution. Along with Representative Robert Junell, he proposed sweeping changes in the Texas constitution—a bold step given the lack of support for doing this. This act by Senator Ratliff was one of many such acts of leadership during his tenure in the Texas legislature. At the time of his retirement in 2004, he was the most respected member in either house. When Lieutenant Governor Perry become governor following the election of George W. Bush to the White House, the members of the Senate unanimously selected Ratliff to be the acting lieutenant governor. He had the reputation of being a nonpartisan who worked both sides of the aisle to reach compromises beneficial to Texas as a whole. While serving on the Redistricting Commission, he resisted the partisan efforts of the attorney general, now U.S. Senator Cronyn. He did not seek election for lieutenant governor, saying that he did not want to be involved in the fierce partisan battle that accompanies statewide races in Texas.

Ratliff was very effective as a legislator, achieving passage of most of the bills he authored and sponsored. He was so well liked and respected that he had no opponents the last three times he ran for re-election.

the legislature to set qualifications for county sheriffs, and allowed corporations additional means of raising capital. Except for the income tax prohibition, little in the amendments was of interest to the average voter. This election is typical of most constitutional amendment elections. The generally trivial subject matter contributes to low voter interest and voter turnout. People most affected by an amendment are likely to understand it and to vote on it. Most voters, however, stay home because there is little of interest to bring them to the polls on election day.

Voter ignorance of the issues is yet another factor in voter turnout. Even though the issues are widely discussed in newspapers and in brochures provided by the League of Women Voters, many people do not take advantage of these sources of information.

Thus, odd-year elections, confusing or noninstructive ballot wording, issues of interest to few voters, and voter ignorance all contribute to low voter turnout in elections to amend the state constitution. A very small number of voters, stimulated by personal interests and supported by an active interest group, can amend the constitution without involving a majority of the voters. Many voters often are not even aware that an election is being held.

Other observations can be made regarding the amendment process in Texas. First, most amendments pass and face little opposition. Since 1876, Texans have approved 439 amendments and rejected 173.[22] Most amendments are supported

Political Culture

Constitutional Change in Texas

The Texas constitution was written in 1876 by a group of men who had just experienced what they felt was an oppressive government imposed by a "Yankee carpetbagger government." Many restrictions were placed on state government, most power was vested in the legislature, and the executive branch was placed under the control of many elected officials. As of November 2005, the constitution had been amended 439 times. Only three other states have more amendments: Alabama, California and South Carolina.

Every November of odd-numbered years the voters of Texas are asked to vote and approve many more amendments. The subject matter of these amendments often is trivial.

Often, fewer than 10 percent of the voters bother to vote, meaning that as few as 5 percent of the voters can change the constitution. This process will continue into the future unless efforts are made to revise the Texas constitution to redistribute power among the branches. The present process allows small minorities to get constitutional protection for changes that advantage them. Most of these amendments are passed.

What do you think? Should the Texas constitution undergo a general revision by a constitutional convention called for this purpose? What are the difficulties of undertaking this task? Who are the potential groups that would support such an effort? Who are the groups who might oppose change?

by an organized interest group willing to spend money, gain support, and get the amendment passed. Second, interest groups attempt to protect their interests through the constitution. A vested interest with constitutional protection is more difficult to alter than one protected by state law alone. Rights that are protected only by state law can be changed easily in the next session of the legislature. An old Texas saying is "Neither man nor property is safe as long as the legislature is in session." The process of constitutional change, on the other hand, requires a two-thirds vote of the legislature plus electoral approval.

A good example of constitutional protection is the **Permanent University Fund (PUF).** The University of Texas and Texas A&M University are the only state schools that benefit from this fund, which has a value of approximately $5 billion. Other state universities long felt that they deserved a share of this money. To protect their funds, Texas A&M and the University of Texas formed a coalition with non-PUF schools to support an amendment creating the Higher Education Assistance Fund (HEAF). This fund provides money to non-PUF universities. In the end, higher-education funding for all state universities became protected in the state constitution.

Permanent University Fund (PUF)

An example of how special interests are protected within the state constitution.

Summary

Self-Test www.mhhe.com/pattersontexas8

The state of Texas has been governed by five state constitutions since entering the Union in 1845. Except for the constitution of 1869, which granted broad powers to the Reconstruction government, all others have provided for a government with very limited powers. Texans want a government that is limited in its power and authority. They do not want government that is broad and expansive in its power and authority.

This limitation on government is very much in keeping with the traditionalistic/individualistic political culture of the state. The dominant political forces of the state also want a government that is both limited in its power and authority and one which protects their interest.

While the current constitution, written in 1876, has been amended over 400 times there is little agreement or support in the state for a general revision of the state constitution. Each session of the Legislature sees many amendments proposed to the voters. These amendments are voted on in off-year (odd-numbered years) November elections. Unless there is a very controversial amendment on the ballot, such as the anti–gay marriage amendment in 2005, only 10 percent or less of the qualified voters will bother to vote. A very small number of voters can effectively amend the constitution. Often these amendments are designed to protect special interests or to provide advantages to some group.

The piecemeal process of amending the constitution every two years will likely continue. Several reasons are generally cited. First, there is a lack of support for reform on the part of significant political forces in the state. Strong political leadership from someone like the governor would be necessary. Former governor George W. Bush did not indicate an interest in supporting the effort. Given his status and support in the state and the nation, Bush could have led an effort at general revision that would have been the hallmark of his tenure as governor. The ambition to become president of the United States was far more attractive, and supporting controversial issues such as revision of the constitution held little appeal. No other statewide leader currently enjoys the necessary status. Governor Perry may face challenges within

his own party for reelection. He is not likely to support revision given the prospects of controversy and the small likelihood of political payoff.

Second, the political culture of the state and the basic conservative nature of state politics do not support broad-scale change. The current constitution supports the traditionalistic/individualistic political culture of the state by serving select groups of people and protecting their interests and privileges. These groups have the resources to maintain those protections. Senator Ratliff's and Representative Junell's proposal in the 1999 legislature avoided many of the major controversies by leaving intact important interests that are well protected by the constitution; however, not all interests were protected.

Third, strong opposition from powerful lobbying groups whose interests currently are protected by the state constitution would make change difficult, if not impossible. In his opening address to the constitutional convention assembled in 1974, the vice-chair of the convention, Lieutenant Governor William Hobby, made this observation: "The special interests of today will be replaced by new and different special interests tomorrow, and any attempt to draft a constitution to serve such interests would be futile and also dishonorable."[23]

Fourth, there is a general lack of interest in and support for change among the citizens of the state. Constitutional revision simply is not a subject that excites the average citizen. The average Texan probably does not see the need for revision, and some proud Texans likely would take offense at the suggestion that the state document is flawed. The document drafted at the end of Reconstruction probably will continue to serve Texans for many years. The prospects for general revisions seem slim. Evidence of this can be found in the 1999 election, when the voters rejected three amendments that might be considered mildly progressive. Two of these amendments would have provided that the adjutant general of the National Guard and the commissioner of health and human services would serve at the pleasure of the governor. Another would have created a judicial compensation commission. These proposed amendments are standard in most state constitutions today.

STUDY CORNER

Key Terms

constitutional convention (*p. 560*)
contract theory of state
  constitutions (*p. 553*)

Permanent University Fund (PUF)
  (*p. 564*)

popular sovereignty (*p. 553*)

Self-Test

1. Which of the following is **not** a general principle of the Texas constitution?
   a popular sovereignty.
   b. limited government.
   c. compact or contract theory.
   d. universal suffrage for women and minorities.

2. Passage of a proposed constitutional amendment in Texas requires:
   a. approval by two-thirds of the house and senate and adoption by the citizens with a majority vote.
   b. approval by three-fifths of the house and senate and adoption by the citizens with a majority vote.
   c. approval by two-thirds of the house and senate and adoption by the citizens with a two-thirds vote.
   d. approval by a majority vote of the house and senate and adoption by the citizens with a majority vote.

3. Generally, most state constitutions do all of the following **except:**
   a. contain provisions pertaining to taxation and finance.
   b. prohibit deficit spending without voter approval.
   c. require only infrequent alteration.
   d. create weak executives and strong legislatures.

4. Which of the following is **not** a contributing factor to voter apathy toward proposed constitutional amendments in Texas?
   a. the number and subject matter of amendments.
   b. city and school board elections.
   c. ballot wording.
   d. elections in odd-numbered years.
   e. none of the above.

5. Which of the following has **not** been a hindrance to constitutional reform in Texas?
   a. the level of voter excitement about revision.
   b. attitudes of influential politicians.
   c. attitudes of powerful lobby groups and special interests.
   d. the conservative nature of state citizens.
   e. none of the above.

6. All of the following describe fundamental systems or structures of government **except:**
   a. bureaucratic.
   b. federal.
   c. unitary.
   d. confederal.

7. Because Texans consistently have displayed characteristics of an individualistic subculture, all of the constitutions governing the state have included a bill of rights. (T/F)

8. The constitution of 1876 reimposed lengthier terms of office for government officials, eliminated many statewide and local elected offices, and empowered the government to act with few restrictions. (T/F)

9. Most state constitutions, including the Texas constitution, more generously grant liberties to citizens than does the U.S. Constitution. (T/F)

10. A federal system of government is a system in which powers and resources are shared by the federal and state governments. (T/F)

Critical Thinking

Go to the Internet and get a copy of the state constitution of Delaware. Compare that state constitution with the Texas constitution. What major differences do you see?

Suggested Readings

Chandler, Davidson. *Race and Class in Texas Politics* (Princeton, N.J.: Princeton University Press, 1976). Good discussion of how race and class have played a role in state constitutional politics in Texas.

Lutz, Donald S. "Toward a Theory of Constitutional Amendments," *American Political Science Review* 88 (June 1994): 355–70. Good review of changes in state constitution.

May, Janice C. "State Constitutional Development in 2004," in *Book of the States 2005*, vol. 37, pp. 3–9. Provides a summary of trends in revision of state constitution.

List of Websites

http://www.sos.state.tx.us/
The secretary of state's website; a copy of the Texas constitution can be found here, as well as votes in all elections and recent votes on constitutional amendments.

http://www-camlaw.rutgers.edu/statecon/
Website of the Center for State Constitutional Studies; contains general information on state constitutional revisions among the states.

www.texasbar.com/
The website of one of the many state organizations that favor constitutional revision in Texas.

Participate!

Go to the Texas League of Women Voters website (www.lwvtexas.org) and get copies of their discussions of the amendments on the ballot in the last election. Study these and decide which you support and which you oppose. Then go to the Texas secretary of state website (www.sos.state.tx.us) and see if your opinion matched the outcome of the election.

Extra Credit

Obtain a copy of your local newspaper and read the editorials on the last proposed amendments to the Texas constitution. Does your opinion agree with that of the local newspaper?

(Self-Test Answers: 1. d   2. a   3. c   4. c   5. e   6. a   7. F   8. F   9. T   10. T)

Participation Politics and Interest Groups in Texas Politics

Chapter Outline

Voter Turnout in Texas
    Poll Tax and Annual Registrations
    White Primary
    Gender Discrimination
    Impact of These Restrictions
    Social and Economic Factors
    Party Competition
    Regional Variations
    Other Factors Affecting Voter Turnout

Interest Groups in State Politics

State Regulation of Interest Groups

Techniques Used by Interest Groups
    Lobbying
    Electioneering

Factors Determining the Strength of Interest Groups
    Leadership and Organization
    Geographic Distribution
    Money

The Varying Strength of Interest Groups
    Economic Diversity
    Political Party Competition
    Professionalism of the State Legislature
        and Government Fragmentation

CHAPTER 20

The Greek philosopher Aristotle said that we are political animals. By this Aristotle meant that we are, by our very nature, predisposed to participate in politics. Some would say that Aristotle was an optimist.

In November 2004, the voters of Texas went to the polls to elect many statewide officials, local officials, and electors for the office of president. Despite the importance of this election, most Texans stayed home. One citizen, asked by a TV reporter why he did not vote, said, "It does not make any difference to me who is president. I will still be working in a low-paying job regardless of who's in office."

Most U.S. citizens share this individual's view and choose not to participate in state politics. Before discussing the reasons for this, let us review what opportunities are available for participation. **Political participation** refers to taking part in activities related to governance. Table 20–1 lists some of these activities along with the percentages of people who participate in them. As can be seen from the table, most people do not take an active part in politics, even in national elections. Voter participation at the national level is lower than in most other industrialized nations (see Chapter 7). Participation is lower in state politics than at the national level and still lower at the local level. Texas ranks below all but a few states in voter participation in both national and state elections (see "How Texas Compares" and Table 20–2). Note that the states with the highest voter turnout tend to be states with a moralistic political culture (see Chapter 18).

political participation
All forms of involvement citizens can have that are related to governance.

TABLE 20–1	Political Participation by American Citizens The data in this table are average levels of participation over several years. For example, on the activity "Vote," the percentage is a composite for voting in several elections.

Run for public office	<1%
Become active in political parties and campaigns	4–5%
Contribute money to campaigns	10%
Wear a button or display a bumper sticker	15%
Write or call a public official	17–20%
Belong to a political organization	30–33%
Talk to others about politics	30–35%
Do not participate	30–45%
Vote	30–55%

Source: Survey Research Center, Inter-University Consortium for Political Research, *Federal Election Studies (1952–2000)* (Ann Arbor: University of Michigan).

TABLE 20–2	Texas Rank as a Percentage of Voting-Age Population Voting in National Elections, 1976–2004

YEAR	TEXAS RANK[*]	NATIONAL TURNOUT[†]	TEXAS TURNOUT[‡]
Presidential Election Years			
1976	44	53%	47%
1980	44	52	44
1984	45	53	47
1988	46	50	45
1992	46	55	49
1996	47	52	41
2000	47	50	43
2004	44	60	44
Congressional/Statewide Office Elections			
1978	46	35%	24%
1982	46	38	26
1986	45	33	25
1990	42	33	27
1994	45	36	31
1998	47	38	24
2002	46	38	26

[*]Texas ranking compared to the forty-nine other states.
[†]Average turnout for all fifty states as a percentage of voting-age population voting in the election.
[‡]Percentage of voting-age population voting in Texas elections.

Source: *Statistical Abstracts of the United States,* 1976, 1998 (Washington, D.C.: U.S. Government Printing Office). Data for 2002 and 2004 calculated by the author using Texas secretary of state data. Data for national turnout in 2002 and 2004: *Statistical Abstract of the United States,* 2004, Table 408.

How Texas Compares
Voter Turnout Among the Fifteen Most Populous States

Texas ranks near the bottom of voter turnout among the fifteen largest states by population. Some of this is due to its large minority population. Note that California, also with a large minority population, ranks lower than Texas. Minnesota, which has same-day voter registration, ranks at the top.

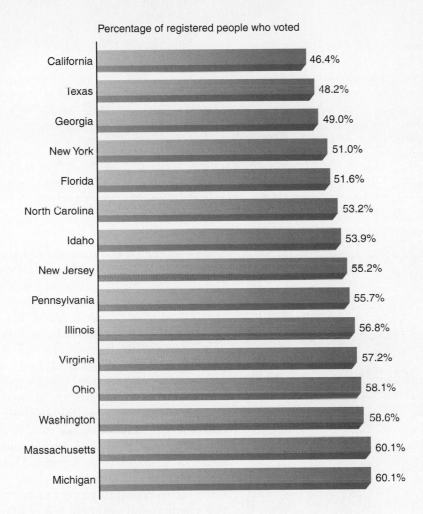

Percentage of registered people who voted

State	Percentage
California	46.4%
Texas	48.2%
Georgia	49.0%
New York	51.0%
Florida	51.6%
North Carolina	53.2%
Idaho	53.9%
New Jersey	55.2%
Pennsylvania	55.7%
Illinois	56.8%
Virginia	57.2%
Ohio	58.1%
Washington	58.6%
Massachusetts	60.1%
Michigan	60.1%

Source: *Statistical Abstract of the United States,* 2004, Table 408.

VOTER TURNOUT IN TEXAS

There are two ways to measure **voter turnout.** One measure is the percentage of **registered voters** voting. A second measure, and the one used most often by political scientists, is the percentage of the voting-age population voting (see Figure 20–1). The **voting-age population** is those persons eligible to

voter turnout
The percent of the voting-age population that votes.

registered voters
Citizens who have formally registered to vote.

Figure 20–1

Percentage of Eligible
Voters Voting in 2000
Presidential Election

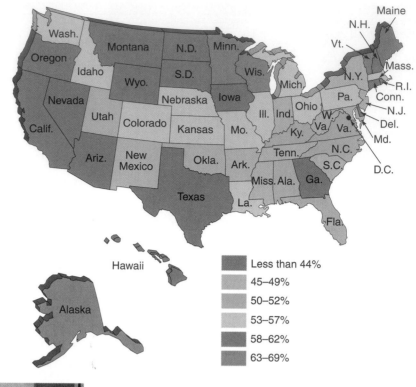

■	Less than 44%
■	45–49%
■	50–52%
■	53–57%
■	58–62%
■	63–69%

voting-age population
Citizens who meet the
formal requirements to
register to vote.

same-day registration
The practice by which voters
are allowed to register on
election day, with no
preregistration before the
election required.

Election Day in Texas

vote—persons who are at least eighteen years of age and
citizens of the United States. Voting-age population is
the preferred measure because it discounts variations in
state voting requirements and elections among the states
that might affect voter turnout. Most, but not all, states
make it easy to register to vote. Five states even allow
same-day registration on election day.

The secretary of state of Texas often releases figures
expressed as a percentage of registered voters voting, always
a much higher figure than the percentage of the voting-age
population voting (see Table 20–3). Even though Texas
makes it very easy to register to vote, Texans are not big voters. As seen in Table 20–2, Texas ranks quite low among all
states in terms of voter turnout. During elections held in
November of odd-numbered years, voting levels are even
lower, often below 10 percent of the voting-age population.
Participation also might fall below 10 percent in March party
primary elections. In local elections for city council and
school board, which usually are held in May, voting can
decline to below 5 percent of the voting-age population.

What explains the low level of voting among Texans?
Many factors are involved: a political culture that discourages participation, a legacy of restricted access to the ballot
for many groups, and social, economic, and political factors.

Like other southern states, Texas has a history of
restrictive voter registration laws. In the past, these laws
made it difficult to qualify to vote and limited potential
avenues of political participation. Due largely to actions by
the federal government, most legal restrictions to voter

Get Involved!

New Efforts to Limit Voting Rights—Voter ID Cards

Finding ways to keep citizens from voting is a time-honored tradition in this country. Poll taxes, grandfather clauses, annual registration, and many other tactics have been used in the past. The latest effort being launched in many states, primarily by the Republican party, is to require a voter ID on election day. The claim is that the primary reason for requiring a voter ID is to prevent fraud. Arizona, which has passed such a requirement, claims it is aimed at keeping illegal immigrants—primarily noncitizens from Mexico—from voting. Getting the ID requires proof of U.S. citizenship. New Mexico is considering requiring a picture ID to vote but not a separate card. Georgia has a law requiring citizens to pay a fee to get a voter picture ID card, prompting some to call this a new poll tax.

The Democratic party in these states has opposed this effort, fearing that it will have an impact on their supporters who might not have ID cards or access to proof of citizenship or residency. Also, many working-class citizens might lack the time or initiative to go to the courthouse to get an ID card.

Many others feel that there is little evidence of voter fraud. Five states—Maine, Minnesota, New Hampshire, Wisconsin, and Wyoming—have same-day voter registration, allowing voters to register on election day. There is no evidence in these states of any increase in voter fraud. In fact, these are all states with high voter turnout. Citizens should be concerned with proposals to restrict the right to vote. While some citizens would take advantage of easy voting rules, most citizens would not. Most citizens have a sense of trust in the election process and would not think of violating the rules.

TABLE 20–3	Comparison of Percentage of Registered and Eligible Voters Voting in Texas Elections, 1970–2004	
YEAR	**PERCENTAGE REGISTERED WHO VOTED**	**PERCENTAGE VOTING-AGE POPULATION WHO VOTED**
Congressional Election Years		
1970	53.9%	31.1%
1974	30.9	20.0
1978	41.7	25.2
1982	49.7	30.0
1986	47.2	29.0
1990	50.5	31.0
1994	50.8	33.6
1998	32.4	26.5
2002	34.2	36.7
2004	36.2	29.3
Presidential Election Years		
1972	89.6%	44.8%
1976	64.8	46.0
1980	68.4	45.5
1984	68.3	47.5
1988	66.2	44.3
1992	72.9	47.6
1996	53.2	40.9
2000	51.8	43.3
2004	56.6	46.1

Source: Texas Secretary of State, election data from website (www.sos.tx.us.gov).

State capitol rotunda, with picture of Texas governors in order of service.
Source: House and Senate.

poll tax

A tax citizens were required to pay each year between November and January to be eligible to vote the following November. Used from 1902 until 1972 in Texas.

HISTORICAL BACKGROUND

registration have been removed. It is easy to register and vote in Texas today, but this has not always been the case. The state's history of restricting access to voting is very much in keeping with its traditionalistic political culture. Although past restrictions have been removed from Texas law, they still have an effect today. Political behavior does not change quickly. A few of the many restrictions once common in southern political cultures are discussed next.

Poll Tax and Annual Registrations

In 1902, the Texas legislature adopted, with voter approval, the payment of a **poll tax** as a requirement for voting. The poll tax restricted the ballot access of African Americans as well as Hispanics, who were disproportionately poor; other barriers to their voting are discussed later.

Certificate of Exemption from Poll Tax.

ORIGINAL   CERTIFICATE OF EXEMPTION FROM POLL TAX

STATE OF TEXAS, COUNTY OF WICHITA

PRECINCT NO 24   Date   4 - 19   1962   N⁰   6732

MR   John Smith   Address   2609 Lawrence

	YEARS
Age	20
Resided in State	20
Resided in County	10
Resided in City	10

Will be or was   21   years old on the 4   day of June 1962. Male   Female   White   Colored

Occupation ....   Native born ... Naturalized

Was born in Texas   Reason for Exemption Minor

I, the undersigned authority, do hereby certify that the within named party personally appeared before me, and being duly sworn, says that the above is correct and that .... he .... is a qualified voter under the constitution and laws of Texas.

Party Affiliation Democratically

By .... , Deputy

BILL CARNES
Assessor and Collector of Taxes, Wichita Co., Tex.

This 1961 exemption certificate to be used in **1962** and through January 1963

The poll tax had to be paid each year between October 1 and January 31 before a person could vote in the primary election, which was not held until September, nine months later. The poll tax was in effect in Texas for about sixty years. It had the intended effect of reducing the number of qualified voters. In 1964–65, 2.4 million Texans paid the tax. In 1968, the first election cycle after the poll tax was abolished, voter registration rose to over 4 million, an increase of about 41 percent.[1]

A 1971 court decision prohibited annual registration systems.[2] Following this decision, the Texas legislature passed a progressive voter registration law that eliminated annual registrations. In 1972, the first year Texas used a permanent registration system, voter registration increased by almost 1.4 million.[3] All states now use some form of permanent registration.[4]

White Primary

Another practice previously used by many southern states, including Texas, to eliminate participation in elections by African Americans was the **white primary.** Beginning in 1923 and continuing until 1945, the Texas legislature passed bills prohibiting African Americans from participating in the Democratic party primary election. The U.S. Supreme Court declared these legislative acts unconstitutional.[5] In 1932, the state Democratic party passed rules that prohibited African Americans from participating in any activity of the party, including voting in the Democratic party primary. This led to another U.S. Supreme Court ruling.[6] The issue before the court was whether a political party was an agent of government or a private organization. The Supreme Court ruled in 1935 that political parties were private organizations and were free to decide who could participate in primary elections. This ruling effectively prevented African Americans from participating in the Democratic party primary. Because there was no Republican opposition at this time in the general election, the primary became the "general election." Thus, from 1932 until 1945, African Americans in Texas were denied the right to vote not by state law but by the rules of the Democratic party.

In 1944, the U.S. Supreme Court in *Smith v. Allwright* outlawed all white primaries in southern states.[7] This ruling overturned earlier rulings that political parties were private organizations. The Supreme Court ruled that political parties were agents of the state and could not exclude people from participating in primary elections because of their race.

white primary
Party primary that excluded African Americans from participating in the Democratic party primary in Texas from 1923 to 1945.

HISTORICAL BACKGROUND

Gender Discrimination

Women's access to voting was restricted in Texas until 1920, when the Nineteenth Amendment to the U.S. Constitution was approved. By 1914, eleven states had granted women the right to vote.[8] In 1915, the Texas legislature considered granting women the right to vote, but the measure failed. However, in 1918 women were given the right to participate in Texas primary elections, and in 1919 Texas became the first southern state to approve the Nineteenth Amendment.[9]

HISTORICAL BACKGROUND

Impact of These Registrations

All these restrictions combined to produce the state's tradition of discouraging participation. The elimination of these restrictions and the present day's easy access to voter registration have increased the number of registered voters in Texas; however, this has not translated into significant increases in the level of

In Texas, private-sector labor unions are not powerful and represent only a small fraction of workers. Strong labor unions do not fit the traditionalistic/individualistic political culture of Texas. In many industrialized states, organized labor unions are important and powerful interest groups, although their influence has declined in recent years. Except in a few counties on the Texas Gulf Coast, where organized labor represents petrochemical workers and longshoremen, organized labor in Texas is very weak. Texas is one of twenty states with "right-to-work" laws. These laws prohibit union shops where all workers, based on a majority vote of the workers, are forced to join the union within ninety days of employment in order to retain their jobs.

African Americans and Hispanics are the two most active ethnic groups in the state. Hispanics are represented by a variety of groups that sometimes are at odds with one another. The League of United Latin American Citizens (LULAC) is the largest such group in the state. Other organizations include the Mexican American Democrats (MAD), the Mexican American Legal Defense and Education Fund (MALDEF), and the Political Association of Spanish-Speaking Organizations (PASSO). The National Association for the Advancement of Colored People (NAACP) and the Congress of Racial Equality (CORE) represent African Americans in Texas. These groups are concerned primarily with advancing civil rights, ending discrimination, improving government services, and gaining political power. While they do not always share common interests, they do share a desire to gain economic and political equality.

Texas has a history of active religious groups. As in the rest of the Old South, Protestant churches fought to eliminate the sale of alcoholic beverages in the state. Even today, large sections of the state are "dry," meaning that alcohol is not sold there. In areas where alcohol can be sold, only beer and wine can be sold on Sunday, and only after 12:00 noon.

Recent years have seen increased activity by fundamentalist religious groups on the national level. This has happened in Texas as well. Organizations such as the Christian Coalition attempt to promote antiabortion campaigns, abstinence-based sex education, home schooling, a school voucher system, prayer in school, and, of course, "family values." These groups have had some success at electing local school boards and now control the Texas State Board of Education, which governs some aspects of school policy statewide. They have also had success in gaining control of the Republican party State Executive Committee in Texas. In 1994, they gained control of the Republican party and have remained in control until the present.

Local government officials also organize in groups to protect and advance their interests. Examples include the Texas Municipal League, the Texas Association of Police Chiefs, the Combined Law Enforcement Association of Texas, the Texas Association of Fire Fighters, the City Attorneys Association, the Texas Association of County Officials, and the Texas School Board Association.

STATE REGULATION OF INTEREST GROUPS

Texas Ethics Commission
State agency responsible for enforcing the requirement for interest groups and candidates for public office to report information on money collected and activities.

Most states have laws regulating two kinds of activities engaged in by interest groups: lobbying and making financial contributions to political campaigns. Lobbying regulations generally consist of requiring organizations that have regular contact with legislators to register and to provide reports on their activities. The **Texas Ethics Commission** is responsible for enforcing these laws. Often this requirement exerts little force, and the reports might not reflect the true activities of the organizations. Some states limit the amount of money PACs can donate to candidates. Texas does not. (See "States in the Nation" in Chapter 9.)

Political Culture

Lobbying Texas Style

Sometime after Franklin Roosevelt died and before Swatch watches, Lubbock elected a state senator who proceeded to Austin, where he holed up in the Driskill Ho-tell with another senator-elect; they's drinkin wiskey and "interviewin" secretaries. Comes a knock-knock-knock on the door and there's the lobbyist for the chiropractors; he offers 'em each $200 to vote for the chiropractor bill. Guy from Lubbock takes the money. Damn ol' bill comes up first week of the session. Guy from Lubbock votes against it. Hacks off the chiropractor lobbyist something serious.

"You take my money and you vote against me!" he says.

Guy from Lubbock says, "Yeah, but the doctors offered me $400 to vote against you."*

Such activity would not be common in Texas today. New rules make it illegal to accept campaign contributions thirty days before the legislative session begins.

*Source: Molly Ivins, *Molly Ivins Can't Say That, Can She?* (New York: Random House, 1991), 91.

The ethics of interest-group activity will vary from state to state as dictated by the political culture of the state. Molly Ivins, a well-known Texas newspaper writer and observer of Texas politics, once said that, in the Texas legislature, "what passes for ethics is if you're bought, by God, you stay bought."[16]

TECHNIQUES USED BY INTEREST GROUPS

Interest groups use a variety of techniques to influence public policy. The type of technique depends on the type of group and the resources available to that group.

Lobbying

Perhaps the best-known and most common technique is **lobbying** the state legislature. Interest groups are often called "lobby groups." The term *lobbying* refers to the practice of waiting in the lobby of the legislative chamber. Commonly, in the past, legislators did not have offices; their office was a desk on the floor of the chamber. Only members of the legislature were allowed on the floor, and they met with other people "in the lobby." Today the term *lobbying* covers many more activities.

Lobbying efforts aimed specifically at influencing the members of the state legislature during legislative sessions include the following:

- Contacting members of the legislature before the session begins
- Getting members of the legislature to file a bill favorable to the group
- Testifying before a committee to inform legislators of the effect a bill will have on their district
- Keeping group members informed about legislative activities
- Asking members of the group to contact legislators (letter-writing campaigns)

lobbying
The practice of attempting to influence the legislature, originally by catching members in the lobby of the capitol.

Citizens exercising right to actively campaign.

- Issuing press releases and buying newspaper and television ads
- Presenting written material to members of the legislature[17]

Additionally, interest groups often provide research information to members of the legislature. The information provided can be self-serving, but it is often accurate and can be an important resource for state legislators. An interest group that provides good, high-quality research and information can have an impact on public policy. An example is the Texas Taxpayers and Research Association, headquartered in Austin.

Besides making an effort to present a favorable face to the public, interest groups also try to curry favor with public officials. Inviting public officials to address organizational meetings is a technique used to advance the group's standing in the eyes of public officials. Presenting awards to public officials at such gatherings, thanking them for their service to the public, is another common technique.

Lobbying doesn't stop when the legislature adjourns. Most legislation requires the governor's signature, and persuading the governor to either sign or veto a bill is an important part of lobbying activity.

When the governor signs a bill, it requires an administrative agency to enforce it. Administrative discretion in enforcement of a law can also be the object of lobbying. Interest groups devote great effort to influencing how agencies interpret and enforce laws. Enforcement can be made compatible with group interests by the appointment of people who favor the interest group to governing boards and commissions. Lobbying goes far beyond simply waiting in the lobby of the legislative chamber for a chance to talk with legislators.

Electioneering

electioneering
Various activities engaged in by interest groups to try to influence the outcome of elections.

Interest groups devote considerable time and effort to **electioneering,** that is, trying to influence the outcome of elections. Their most important resource is money, usually funneled to candidates through political action committees (PACs). Most states require some formal registration of PACs. In Texas, a PAC created by a corporation or a labor union must be formed exclusively to support or oppose a ballot issue and may not be created to support or oppose a candidate for office. PACs must register with the Texas Ethics Commission, designate a treasurer, and file periodic reports.[18]

Interest groups might also become directly involved in campaigns, from running television and newspaper ads explaining the record of officials or the virtues of a nonincumbent to working in voter registration drives and get-out-the-vote campaigns. Interest groups might also aid candidates by helping them write speeches and organize rallies and by staging political fund-raisers. Some groups keep track of legislators' voting records and circulate "good guy/bad guy" score cards to members of the organization, instructing members to vote for or against candidates.

Political Culture

Money Spent by Lobby Groups

Listed below is the total amount of money spent on lobbying the Texas legislature in 2005. Almost everyone would agree that $275.5 million is a lot of money to spend in attempts to influence the legislative process. Note that most of the money is from business interests and only $4.7 million from labor unions. Does this kind of money buy legislation that is slanted toward business and against consumers?

INTEREST CATEGORY	MAXIMUM VALUE OF CONTRACTS	NUMBER OF CONTRACTS	PERCENTAGE (OF MAXIMUM VALUE)
Agriculture	$6,815,001	174	2%
Communications	$18,095,500	367	7
Construction	$12,180,002	249	4
Electronics	$10,055,000	217	4
Energy and natural resources	$42,800,004	908	16
Finance	$13,595,001	342	5
Health	$32,720,001	822	12
Ideological and single issue	$35,850,047	917	13
Insurance	$16,485,000	548	6
Labor	$4,775,000	117	2
Lawyers and lobbyists	$16,590,018	286	6
Miscellaneous business	$29,045,002	694	11
Other	$6,305,000	156	2
Real estate	$10,825,002	219	4
Transportation	$12,585,000	289	5
Unknown	$6,865,000	288	2
Total	$275,585,578	6,593	100%

Source. Texans for Public Justice, *Austin's Oldest Profession;* http://www.tpj.org/docs/2004b/08/lobby04/clients.html#clientsbyinterest.

FACTORS DETERMINING THE STRENGTH OF INTEREST GROUPS

While some interest groups spend large amounts of money, others have very little. Available resources depend on the kind of group, the number of members in the group, and who the members are. For example, the Texas State Teachers Association (TSTA) is strong because it has so many members (hence voters). The Texas Municipal League (TML), which represents Texas city officials, has very little money and fewer members than TSTA, but it has influential members including mayors and council members.

The status and number of the members of an interest group are important determinants of power. Obviously, the presidents of large banks and corporations in Dallas can command the ear of most senators and representatives from the Dallas area. Groups with many members can initiate a barrage of telephone

The Texas Association of School Administrators is an example of an interest group that represents state and local interests. This group, which is dominated by rural school districts, has worked to prevent school vouchers. Its headquarters (pictured here) is a few blocks from the state capitol.

calls and messages to legislators to influence legislative actions.

Leadership and Organization

Leadership quality and organizational ability can also be important factors in the power exerted by interest groups. Many interest groups hire former legislators. Some groups are decentralized, with a loose-knit membership, making mobilization difficult. Other groups, like the Texas Municipal League, are highly organized, monitor legislation under consideration, and can easily contact selected members to influence bills still in committee.

Geographic Distribution

Groups that have representatives in all geographic areas of the state and thus can command the attention of many legislators have more influence than others. The Texas Municipal League, for example, has city officials in every senator's and representative's district. Legislators will listen to citizens from their district but might not listen to citizens from other districts. Legislators, while they might not always agree with local elected officials, will listen to them. Obviously, some groups cannot have geographic distribution. Commercial shrimp fishers are limited to the Gulf Coast region of Texas while Texas bankers and lawyers are everywhere in the state.

Money

Money is always an important resource for any organization. Interest groups that can afford to hire a full-time staff and to travel to meet with legislators obviously have more influence than those that must depend on volunteers and part-time staffs. Money also helps groups develop their public image.

With enough money, small groups can have an impact on government policy, often by mobilizing nonmember citizens to their cause. For example, through the use of television ads, newspaper ads, and "talk radio," groups with money but limited membership can influence legislation. One writer has referred to such nonmembership groups, which lack a grassroots organization, as "astroturf organizations."[19]

THE VARYING STRENGTH OF INTEREST GROUPS

The strength and influence of interest groups vary among the states. Most writers base this variation on four factors: economic diversity, party strength, the professionalism of the legislature, and government fragmentation.[20] Political culture is also a factor.

Political Culture

Grassroots or Astroturf?

Astroturf is a political term for phony grassroots organizations supported with corporate money. In one of the more bizarre developments in the history of modern politics, astroturf has become such a profitable (estimated $1 billion a year) and sophisticated business that public relations firms now war with one another about who provides astroturf and who provides "real" grassroots organizations. "Real" in the context of the PR industry does not mean real; it means PR campaigns that are harder to spot as astroturf. In other words, "real" means a better grade of phony.

Source: Molly Ivins, "Getting to the Grass Roots of the Problem," *Bryan-College Station Eagle*, July 13, 1995, A4. Reprinted by permission of Pom, Inc.

Economic Diversity

States differ in their economic diversity. States that are highly industrialized and have a great variety of industries will have a multitude of interest groups. The diversity and complexity of the state's economy ensure that no single industry or group can dominate.

In the past, the Texas economy was dominated by only a few industries: cotton, cattle, banking, and oil. Today, the Texas economy is more diversified, and the number of interest groups has grown accordingly. States that today are dominated by a single industry include Alaska, where oil is dominant, and Wyoming, where coal mining drives the economy and provides most of the state's revenues.

Political Party Competition

The strength of the political parties in the state can influence the strength of interest groups. Two strongly competitive parties that recruit and support candidates for office can offset the influence of interest groups. Members of the legislature in competitive-party states might owe their election to the political party and be less influenced by interest groups. Texas's history of weak party structure has contributed to the power of interest groups.

Professionalism of the State Legislature and Government Fragmentation

A professional legislature is one that has a full-time staff, is well paid, serves full-time, and has good research and advisory services available. Full-time, well-paid legislators served by a professional staff are less dependent on information supplied by interest groups. As indicated previously, interest groups spend much of their effort in trying to influence the administration of state laws. The degree to which interest groups succeed depends on the structure of the state government. If the government is centralized under a governor who appoints and removes most heads of departments, interest groups will need to lobby the governor directly and the agencies indirectly. Texas has a **fragmented governmental structure.** The governor of Texas makes few significant appointments of agency heads.[21]

fragmented governmental structure

A governmental structure whereby power is dispersed to many state agencies with no central control.

Get Involved!

The Texas Public Utility Commission

In 1975, the Texas legislature passed the Public Utilities Regulatory Act and created the Public Utility Commission (PUC). This act created three classes of electrical public utilities: investor-owned or private electrical companies, rural electrical cooperatives (RECs), and municipally owned systems. Each class of utility was subject to varying degrees of regulation by the PUC. Municipal groups were under the least amount of regulation, and some municipal officials felt that the act did not apply to city electrical systems. The PUC gradually began to extend regulatory control over the municipal systems and by 1978–79 issued orders requiring municipal certification of areas served by these systems.

The electrical cooperatives had an active interest group going back to the late 1930s, when Congress created the Rural Electrification Administration. The investor-owned

systems were represented by a long-standing organization that originally had fought the creation of the PUC. With the energy crisis of the 1970s, the investor-owned group sought statewide regulation of rates.

Until 1980, the municipally owned electrical systems in Texas had no statewide organization. When the PUC gradually began to exert control over the municipal systems, the Texas Public Power Association was created to represent this group. Three interest groups, representing each type of electrical distributor, now attempt to exert influence over the PUC, but no one group is dominant. Citizen "watchdog" groups have also formed to monitor the PUC.

Pick a state regulatory commission; there are about 40 such agencies. Follow its ruling on their web page and see if there are any patterns to their rulings.

HISTORICAL BACKGROUND

capture

Term used to describe the situation in which a state agency or board falls under the heavy influence of its constituency interest groups.

Close relationships exist between many state agencies and interest groups. Until the Texas Sunset Commission was created in 1977 to review most state agencies every twelve years, the members of most state licensing boards (such as the Texas State Bar, the State Board of Medical Examiners, and the State Board of Morticians) were professionals in that field. Members of the profession still dominate these boards, which were created to "protect the public interest" but more often spend their time protecting the profession by limiting the number of persons who can be licensed and by enacting rules favorable to the group. Many people have suggested that the review procedure is unnecessary and only serves to demonstrate the degree to which interest groups control rule making and influence the amount of money earned by the group.

When the relationship between the state agency and the interest group becomes very close, it is referred to as **capture**. The interest group is said to have "captured" the agency. However, capture of the agency by the interest group probably is more the exception than the rule. Often, competing interest groups vie for influence with the agency, reducing the likelihood of its capture by a single interest group. The creation of the Texas Public Utility Commission is a good example of this (see "Get Involved!" above). Political scientists often refer to the "iron triangle" to describe the policymaking process (see Figure 9–9). In this model, the interest group, the state agency, and the legislative committee with oversight of the agency all share in the process of making policy.

Shared policymaking does not mean that interest groups do not exert influence, however. In Texas, the fragmented nature of the state government, the many independent boards and commissions, and the separately elected state agency heads all increase the strength of interest groups and their influence on state government.

Summary

Political participation is affected by many factors. Some states—mostly the southern states, including Texas—have a legacy of restricting access to the ballot and discouraging voter participation. Even with the removal of these restrictions, it can take generations to change political behavior. Social and economic factors also play a role in participation in the political process. Race and ethnicity, along with the lack of party competition, help explain lower voter turnout rates in Texas. All these factors, combined with the individualistic/traditionalistic political culture of Texas, help explain the low levels of participation in the political processes of the Lone Star State.

Even though they are often criticized, interest groups play an important role in state politics. The First Amendment to the U.S. Constitution protects free speech and association, and interest groups are a necessary part of the political process in a democratic society. Efforts by government to control interest groups are—and should be—limited. Knowing the tactics used to influence government is crucial to understanding how politics works in state government.

There is little doubt that the influence of interest groups will continue to grow in the years ahead. In some campaigns, political action committees have replaced the political party as a nominating and electing agent. PAC money unquestionably influences legislation. In a mass media age, little can be done to curb the influence of these groups.

Given the low levels of voter turnout in Texas, it is likely that interest groups will continue to dominate Texas state politics. The traditionalistic/individualistic political culture also supports such domination. A reorganization of state agencies into a centrally controlled administration seems unlikely. The present decentralized state administrative structure, which assists interest groups in their control of state agencies, will likely persist for many years to come.

Political Parties and Elections in Texas

Chapter Outline

Fifty State Party Systems

Party Ideology

Democratic and Republican Party
Strength in Texas

The One-Party Era in Texas

Party Realignment in Texas
   The Beginning of Change
   The Election of John Tower
   The Election of Bill Clements
   The "Conversion" and Election of Phil
      Gramm
   The Move Toward Republican Parity with
      the Democrats, 1988–94
   Governor Bush and the Republican
      Dominance, 1995–2001
   Republican Dominance in 2002–4

The Strength of the Republican
Party

The Death of the Yellow Dog
Democrat?

Party Dealignment

Elections and Party Organization
   Election Cycles
   Ballot Form
   Ballot Access to the November General
      Election
   Political Differences Between Open and
      Closed Primary Systems
   Runoff Primary Elections
   The Administration and Finance of
      Primary Elections
   Absentee and Early Voting

Campaigns
   Political Consultants
   Money in Campaigns

Conclusions

CHAPTER 21

The institutions developed to perform functions in each state differ markedly from the national parties. It is an error to assume that the political parties of each state are but miniatures of the national party system.

V. O. Key[1]

In June 2006 the Republican and Democratic parties met in statewide conventions. While generally much press attention is focused on these meetings, to a large degree they are little more than a formality. Most decisions already will have been made, either in primary elections or in county and precinct meetings. The state convention is more an attempt by both parties to showcase their candidates and those issues that attract attention in the state press. Often, the people who attend are political junkies who get great pleasure from involvement in politics. The Democrats attract a large portion of the state population who are not afraid to admit to being liberal, and the Republicans attract those from the Christian right who are proud to call themselves social conservatives.

FIFTY STATE PARTY SYSTEMS

The origin and purposes of political parties are discussed in Chapter 8. As was intimated there, the United States does not have strong national parties but instead has fifty state party systems. The lack of elected national officials contributes to this situation. President and vice president are the only elected national offices. All others are state offices. The only time anything resembling a national party organization is apparent is every four years when the Democrats and Republicans hold conventions to nominate their candidates for president.

Most laws that govern the election of candidates and the activities of political parties are state, not national, laws. Voters elect members to the U.S. Congress at the state level. Technically, even voting for president is a state function, because members of the Electoral College are elected by state. This lack of national offices is one factor that weakens the role of national parties and shifts the emphasis to the state parties. Another is that each of the fifty state party organizations can act independently of the others and of the national party organization.

There is often a clear distinction between officials elected to state offices and those elected to congressional offices. For example, Texans elect two U.S. senators and thirty-two U.S. representatives. These members of Congress spend most of their time in Washington, focusing on national—not state—policy. Texans also elect thirty-one state senators and 150 representatives to the state legislature. The members of the state legislature have a state focus. Occasionally, the two groups of legislators (in the U.S. Congress and in the state legislature) might come together on common ground, as they did in 2004 for midterm redistricting of the U.S. House seats. Most often, however, they have different interests, agendas, and priorities. Thus, although state-elected officials might carry common party labels—Democratic or Republican—there is little interaction between state and national party officials.

Years ago, V. O. Key Jr. observed this about state party systems:

> The institutions developed to perform functions in each state differ markedly from the national parties. It is an error to assume that the political parties of each state are but miniatures of the national party system. In a few states that condition is approached, but . . . each state has its own pattern of action and often it deviates markedly from the forms of organization commonly thought of as constituting party systems.[2]

Professor Key's observation is as valid today as it was in the 1950s. State party systems vary widely, and often the only common link is the name *Democrat* or *Republican*.

States can be classified according to the strength of party organization within each state. In Texas and other southern states, the Democratic party dominated state politics from Reconstruction in the 1870s until the 1960s. Few Republicans even placed their names on the ballot.

Most studies of competition between the parties rely on several measures: the percentage of votes won by each party in races for governor and the state legislature, the length of time each party controls the legislature and the office of governor, and the frequency with which parties divide control of the governorship and the legislature. (See "How Texas Compares.") These studies do not rely on voting for the office of president of the United States. For reasons discussed later, the vote for presidential candidates is not a good measure of party strength within a state.

The Republican party in Texas has been gaining strength for the past twenty years. It now controls both houses of the Texas legislature, and it has captured the governor's office six times in the last eight elections (1978, 1986, 1994, 1998, 2002, and 2004). Republicans presently hold all statewide elected offices. These victories have changed the classification of Texas from a modified one-party Democratic state to a **two-party competitive state.** Table 21–1 shows party identification changes in Texas over the past fifty years.

two-party competitive state

A state in which the two major parties switch control of statewide elected offices and of the state legislature.

HISTORICAL
BACKGROUND

	Party Realignment in Texas, 1952 to 2002 Figures give the percentage of the population identifying as Democrat, Republican, and Independent.		
TABLE 21–1			
YEAR	**DEMOCRATIC**	**REPUBLICAN**	**INDEPENDENT**
1952	66%	6%	28%
1972	57	14	29
1983	39	23	38
1985	34	33	33
1994	30	29	41
1996	31	31	38
1998	33	33	34
2002	33	33	34
2005	25	39	33

Sources: Data for 1952–85 from James A. Dyer, Arnold Vedlitz, and David B. Hill, "New Voters, Switchers, and Political Party Realignment in Texas" in *The Western Political Quarterly* 41 (March 1988): 156. Data for 1994 from *The Texas Poll*, 1994, Harte-Hanks Communications. Figures for 1996 and 1998 from Texas Poll data. Scripps Howard Inc., University of Texas at Austin. Figures for 2002 from Texas Poll data. Scripps Howard Inc., Texas Tech University. Data for 2005 from Scripps Howard News Service, Texas Poll, 2005. See Table 21.5. In all cases, data on independents include those identified as other party and as don't know.

How Texas Compares

Party Competition in the States

The map below shows party competition in the fifty states. Note that some of the strong Democratic states are part of the Old South, where one-party systems prevailed for years. The strong Republican states are concentrated in the West, with the exception of Ohio and Florida.

Modified one-party Republican

Two-party Competitive

Modified one-party Democratic

Source: John F. Bibby and Thomas M. Holbrook, "Parties and Elections," *Politics in the American States: A Comparative Analysis*, 8th ed., ed. Virginia Gray and Russell L. Hanson (Washington, D.C.: Congressional Quarterly Press, 2004), 88, Table 3.4.

Table 21–2 shows party competition in the fifty states from 1998 to 2005. These data have been updated since 1946 in seven separate studies and reflect changes in state party competitive patterns (see Table 21–3). Three patterns are obvious. First, one-party Democratic states have disappeared and now are classified as either modified Democratic or two-party competitive states. Second, modified Republican states have increased slightly in the past ten years. Third, the number of two-party competitive states has increased from twenty-five to thirty-one between 1946 and 2003. Most of these changes in party competitive patterns are explained by changes in the southern states, where one-party Democratic states have become two-party competitive states. In most other parts of the country, changes in party competitiveness have been less dramatic.

TABLE 21–2	**Index of Party Competitiveness in the Fifty States, 1998–2003** The number shows the degree of inter-party competitiveness. The index ranges from 0 (total Republican success) to 1 (total Democratic success). There are no one-party Republican or one-party Democratic states.

MODIFIED ONE-PARTY DEMOCRATIC

Hawaii	0.735	West Virginia	0.689
Mississippi	0.716	Alabama	0.684
Maryland	0.702	California	0.683
Rhode Island	0.700	Arkansas	0.657
Massachusetts	0.694		

TWO-PARTY COMPETITIVE

Kentucky	0.629	Oregon	0.461
North Carolina	0.619	Minnesota	0.452
New Mexico	0.617	Iowa	0.435
Georgia	0.599	New York	0.435
Vermont	0.585	South Carolina	0.435
Louisiana	0.577	Wisconsin	0.424
Tennessee	0.576	Colorado	0.417
Oklahoma	0.570	Nevada	0.415
Connecticut	0.567	Michigan	0.389
Washington	0.557	Virginia	0.385
Delaware	0.551	Texas	0.378
Maine	0.537	Nebraska	0.365
Missouri	0.532	New Hampshire	0.358
Illinois	0.519	Pennsylvania	0.356
Indiana	0.514	North Dakota	0.354
New Jersey	0.479		

MODIFIED ONE-PARTY REPUBLICAN

Arizona	0.348	Wyoming	0.284
Alaska	0.340	Kansas	0.284
Montana	0.314	Utah	0.249
Florida	0.302	South Dakota	0.247
Ohio	0.289	Idaho	0.167
Fifty-state average	0.483		

Source: John F. Bibby and Thomas M. Holbrook, "Parties and Elections" in *Politics in the American States: A Comparative Analysis.* 8th ed., ed. Virginia Gray and Russell L. Hanson, 88, Table 3.4. Copyright © 2004 Congressional Quarterly Press, Washington, D.C. Reprinted by permission.

Compare the map in Chapter 12 showing electoral votes for president in the 2004 election (page 351) with the map of state party systems. Note that they are very different. Voting for president and for the offices of governor and state legislator follows different patterns. Voters split their votes between the parties.

TABLE 21–3	Patterns of Party Competition in the Fifty States, 1946–2003 Data on Alaska and Hawaii are not included for the years 1946–53. Nebraska has nonpartisan legislative elections, so data are for governor only. There are some problems with the accuracy of this party index when used to measure competitiveness over long periods of time. The accuracy decreases with time.				
YEARS	ONE-PARTY DEMOCRATIC	MODIFIED DEMOCRATIC	TWO-PARTY	MODIFIED REPUBLICAN	ONE-PARTY REPUBLICAN
1946–63	8	9	25	8	0
1956–70	7	13	23	7	0
1974–80	8	19	22	1	0
1981–88	1	21	22	6	0
1989–94	0	13	31	6	0
1995–98	0	9	29	12	0
1999–2003	0	9	31	10	0

Sources: Data for 1946–63: Austin Ranney, "Parties in State Politics," Politics in the American States, ed. Herbert Jacob and Kenneth Vines (Boston: Little, Brown, 1965), 65. Data for 1956–70: Jacob and Vines, 2d ed. Data for 1974–80: John F. Bibby, Cornelius P. Cotter, James L. Gibson, and Robert J. Huchshorn, "Parties in State Politics," Politics in the American States, 3d ed., ed. Virginia Gray, Herbert Jacob, and Kenneth Vines (Boston: Little, Brown, 1983), 99. Data for 1981–88: Politics in the American States, 5th ed., ed. Virginia Gray, Herbert Jacob, and Robert B. Albritton (Boston: Little, Brown, 1990), 85–122. Data for 1989–94: John F. Bibby and Thomas M. Holbrook, "Parties and Elections," Politics in the American States, 6th ed., ed. Virginia Gray and Herbert Jacob (Washington, D.C.: Congressional Quarterly Press, 1996), 105. John F. Bibby and Thomas Holbrook, "Parties and Elections," Politics in the American States: A Comparative Analysis, 7th ed., ed. Virginia Gray & Russell Hanson (Washington, D.C.: Congressional Quarterly Press, 1998), 81. Data for 1999–2003; John F. Bibby and Thomas M. Holbrook, "Parties and Elections," Politics in the American States: A Comparative Analysis, 8th ed., ed. Virginia Gray and Russell L. Hanson (Washington, D.C.: Congressional Quarterly Press, 2004), 88.

PARTY IDEOLOGY

The party labels Democratic and Republican do not necessarily indicate ideology. **Party ideology** is the basic belief system that guides the party. The Democratic party in one state can be quite different ideologically from the Democratic party in another state. For many years in Texas, the Democratic party has had strong conservative leanings. The Democratic party in Massachusetts, the home of Senator Edward Kennedy, has a liberal orientation. The conservatism of Texas Democrats is apparent in voter support for presidential candidates. Since the end of World War II, Texans have most often supported Republican presidential candidates. Texas supported Dwight Eisenhower in 1952 and 1956, Richard Nixon in 1972, Ronald Reagan in 1980 and 1984, George Bush in 1988 and 1992, Bob Dole in 1998, and George W. Bush in 2000 and 2004. In the past thirteen presidential elections, Texas has voted Democratic only four times. In two of these cases, a native-son Democrat was on the ballot: Lyndon Johnson, in 1960 and 1964. Texans also voted for Hubert Humphrey, vice president under Johnson, in 1968, and for Jimmy Carter in 1978, in part because he was a southerner and in part because of the Watergate scandal. This strong support for Republican presidential candidates results from ideological differences between the more conservative Texas Democratic party and the more liberal national Democratic party organization.

Texas is a noncompetitive, non-policy-relevant state. In recent years, a change in the person holding the office of governor has not resulted in policy changes. The policies under Democrat Dolph Briscoe did not change when Republican Bill Clements was elected governor in 1976, nor did policies change much when Democrat Mark White replaced Bill Clements in 1982 or when Clements in turn replaced White in 1986. When Ann Richards was elected governor as a Democrat in 1990, replacing Bill Clements, only a few

party ideology
Basic belief system that guides the party.

policy changes occurred. George W. Bush, a Republican, defeated Ann Richards in 1994 and was reelected in 1998. In 2001, new governor Rick Perry continued the conservative policies of the past. A close examination of the 1995, 1997, 1999, 2001, 2003, and 2005 sessions of the Texas legislature shows little change from past conservative policies. The traditionalistic/individualistic political culture of the state preserves the status quo and protects elite interests, regardless of the party of the governor or the majority party in the legislature. Bipartisan cooperation, so evident during the three Bush sessions of the legislature, is made easier because of philosophical agreements between the governor and the house and senate leadership. Texas has gone from a one-party Democratic-controlled state to one dominated by the Republicans with no change in philosophy or policy. In the 2003 session of the legislature, however, this bipartisan cooperation disappeared.

DEMOCRATIC AND REPUBLICAN PARTY STRENGTH IN TEXAS

Texas has moved from being a one-party Democratic state to being a two-party competitive state, and this movement is reflected in public opinion polls. In 1952, only about 6 percent of Texans identified themselves as Republican. By the mid-1970s this number had increased to about 14 percent, and by 1994 to 29 percent. More important, in the same period, Democratic party support decreased from 66 percent in 1952 to about 30 percent in 1994 and 39 percent in 2005. In 2005 Democrats had declined to 25 percent and Independents also stood at about 30 percent. This is similar to the national party identification data, which show Democrats, Republicans, and Independents evenly divided at one-third each (see Figure 8–2). Claims by either party at the state or national level that they have majority support are simply not supported by citizens' party identifications. Table 21–1 shows this data for Texas.

THE ONE-PARTY ERA IN TEXAS

From the end of Reconstruction in 1874 until the 1960s, Texas was a one-party Democratic state. When Reconstruction ended, the switch from Republican control to Democratic control was almost immediate and absolute. From 1874 until 1961, no Republican was elected to statewide office in Texas, and only a few Republicans were elected to other offices. In 1928, the state did vote Republican, casting its Electoral College votes for Herbert Hoover. President Hoover's opponent was Al Smith, a Roman Catholic, and the vote was more anti-Catholic and anti–New Yorker than pro-Republican. This anti-Republicanism can be traced to the Civil War and Reconstruction. Following the Civil War and the experiences of Reconstruction, southerners felt a strong resentment toward the rest of the nation that bound the South as a unit, and southerners voted against all Republicans.[3]

Until at least the 1950s, Republicans were held in disrespect and were the subject of joke and insult. Some called the Republican party the "party of Yankee aggression." While living in Austin in the 1890s, the famous writer O. Henry supposedly said, "We have only two or three laws [in Texas], such as against murder before witnesses and being caught stealing horses and voting Republican."

PARTY REALIGNMENT IN TEXAS

From 1940 to 1960, political conflicts and competition were confined to the Democratic party. As noted in 1964:

> Until recently, only Democratic Party nominees had an opportunity to capture state offices, and, therefore, ambitious men representing all shades of opinion tried to squeeze in under the same Democratic roof. The old guard Republicans failed not only to win elections, but even to provide mild criticism. Consequently, public officials saw little need for openly declaring themselves; in fact, they often felt that taking a stand would alienate rather than impress prospective voters. The resulting confusion of the general public reinforced the frequently observed American tendency to vote according to personalities rather than principles—thus making it difficult for political organizers to mobilize votes on the basis of well-defined politics.[4]

HISTORICAL BACKGROUND

Writing about Texas political parties in 1949, V. O. Key Jr. observed: "In Texas the vague outlines of a politics are emerging in which irrelevancies are pushed into the background and the people divided broadly along liberal and conservative lines." This division, according to Professor Key, is due to "personal insecurity of men suddenly made rich who are fearful lest they lose their wealth. . . . The Lone Star State is concerned about money and how to make it, about oil and sulphur and gas, about cattle and dust storms and irrigation, about cotton and banking and Mexicans."[5]

In Texas until the late 1960s, politics revolved almost exclusively around personality and economic issues. Race issues, which dominated the politics of many southern states, were less important in Texas.[6] The liberal element in Texas was also based on economic considerations. Liberalism in Texas encouraged welfare spending, by means of deficit spending if necessary; promoted equal treatment for African Americans, Latin Americans, and other minorities; and increased government regulation of business with the aim of expanding national government powers, trade union organization, and taxes on business—especially on large, interstate corporations—rather than on sales or individuals. Furthermore, liberals in Texas at this time made loyalty to the national Democratic party a part of their creed.[7]

People voted Democratic partially out of habit and because of a lack of competition from the Republicans. Party primary elections replaced November general elections in the absence of opposition from Republicans. On those few occasions when Republicans mounted a challenge to Democrats in the November general election, most Texans still voted a straight Democratic ticket. They were called **Yellow Dog Democrats.** The saying "I would vote for a yellow dog before I'd vote for a Republican" summarizes the attitude of these voters.

Yellow Dog Democrats
Texans who voted a straight Democratic ticket.

The Beginning of Change

In the 1952 and 1956 presidential elections, many Yellow Dog Democrats broke with tradition and voted for Dwight Eisenhower. The leader of this movement was the Democratic governor, Allan Shivers, the leader of the conservative faction of the party. This faction chose to dissociate themselves from the New Deal/Fair Deal element of the national Democratic party and from any candidate it might put forward. This group became known as the **Shivercrats.** The liberal faction of the Democratic party became known as the Loyalists and associated with the national Democratic party.[8]

Shivercrats
Democrats who followed Governor Allen Shiver's example and voted for Eisenhower in 1952 and 1956.

Democratic governor Allan
Shivers led a group of
Democrats, the "Shivercrats,"
who endorsed Republican
candidate Dwight D.
Eisenhower.

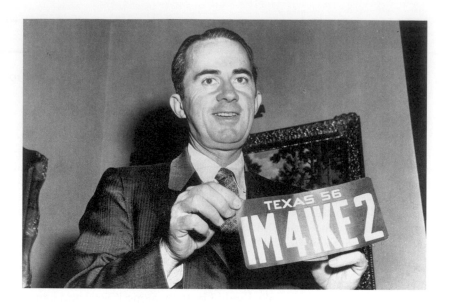

This action began the Texas tradition of supporting Republican presidential candidates while retaining Democratic party dominance over state offices. Presidential politics in 1952 broke the Texas tradition of voting a straight ticket, at least with regard to the top of the ticket.

The Election of John Tower

HISTORICAL BACKGROUND

In 1960, Lyndon Johnson, the senior senator from Texas, ran as the Democratic candidate for the U.S. Senate and also as the vice presidential candidate with John F. Kennedy. Johnson's presence on the Democratic ticket temporarily stayed the movement toward the Republican party. In a special election in 1961, John Tower was elected U.S. senator to fill the seat formerly held by Lyndon Johnson. Tower's win was helped by a special election that attracted seventy-one candidates. He received 41 percent of the vote in the first election and managed to win a slight majority in the runoff election. The election of Senator John Tower as the first Republican statewide officeholder since the end of Reconstruction originally was heralded as the beginning of a new era of two-party politics in the state. In the 1962 elections, Republicans managed to field candidates for many statewide, congressional, and local races. For a variety of reasons, however, they had few successes. Some of the candidates were weak, and some proved an embarrassment for the Republicans. Tower won reelection in 1966, 1972, and 1978, but it would be seventeen years before another Republican (Bill Clements in 1978) won statewide office.

The Election of Bill Clements

HISTORICAL BACKGROUND

After 1961, Republicans had some success in electing legislators and local officeholders, but it was the election of Bill Clements as governor in 1978 that marked the real beginning of two-party politics in Texas. Governor Clements used his power to make appointments to boards, commissions, and judgeships (see Chapter 23) and to recruit people who would publicly declare themselves Republicans. Some referred to these new converts as "closet Republicans" who had finally gone public. These appointments helped build the Republican party in Texas. In 1986, Republican fortunes improved when Bill Clements was returned to the governor's office, defeating Mark White in what many termed a "revenge match."

The "Conversion" and Election of Phil Gramm

In 1983, John Tower announced that he would not seek reelection to the U.S. Senate in 1984. Phil Gramm, the Democratic representative from the Sixth Congressional District, used Tower's retirement to advance from the U.S. House to the Senate. Gramm had first been elected as a Democrat in 1976. By early 1981, he had gained some national prominence by helping President Reagan "cut the federal budget." (The budget actually increased during this time period.)

In a savvy political move, Gramm used the loss of his budget committee seat as an excuse to switch to the Republican party. When Gramm resigned his seat in the U.S. House in 1983, outgoing Republican governor Clements called a special election, which was held thirty days after Gramm's resignation. Because no other candidate could possibly put together a successful campaign in so short a time, Gramm easily won reelection to Congress as a Republican. In 1984, "fully baptized" a Republican, Gramm won election to the U.S. Senate, pulled along on the coattails of President Ronald Reagan.

The Move Toward Republican Parity with the Democrats, 1988–94

In 1988, the Republicans made significant gains, aided by Bill Clements's return in 1987 to the governor's mansion and George H. W. Bush's election to the presidency. The party won four statewide offices, and three Republicans won election to the Texas supreme court.

In 1990, Republicans captured the offices of state treasurer and agricultural commissioner and another seat on the state supreme court. The setback for the Republicans in 1990 was the loss of the governor's office. When Bill Clements did not seek reelection, Clayton Williams, a political newcomer, used his considerable wealth to win the Republican nomination. His campaign for governor was something of a disaster, and he lost to Democrat Ann Richards. This loss by Williams enabled George W. Bush to be elected governor in 1994. Clayton Williams probably would have served two terms, denying George W. Bush the opportunity to be elected governor until 1998. Bush then would not have had enough experience to make a race for president in 2000.

In 1992, Democrat Lloyd Bentsen, after serving as U.S. senator from Texas for twenty years, resigned to become secretary of the treasury under President Bill Clinton. His resignation allowed Republicans to capture their second seat in the U.S. Senate with the election of Kay Bailey Hutchison.

In 1994, the Republicans captured all three seats on the Railroad Commission and a majority of the seats on the state supreme court. They also retained control of the agriculture commissioner's office. In addition, Republicans captured three additional seats on the state board of education, for a total of eight seats. More important, George W. Bush was elected governor. When the dust settled, Republicans controlled a total of twenty-three statewide offices. These wins, coupled with additional seats in the Texas legislature, substantially changed Texas party structure. Texas moved into the two-party era.

Governor Bush and the Republican Dominance, 1995–2001

The son of former President George Bush ran for governor of Texas in 1994, beating the Democratic incumbent Ann Richards. Governor George W. Bush, to a large degree, won because of family name recognition rather than political experience. Governor Bush had no statewide electoral experience before

TABLE 21-4	Voting by Demographic Neighborhoods in Harris County in 2002 Voting precincts in Harris County were broken down by income, race, and ethnic background to determine voting patterns. Upper-income black and Asian Americans were not included in the survey because registered voters in those categories do not live in concentrated areas in large enough numbers to constitute a voting block. More than 75 percent of the Hispanic registered voters in Harris County are Mexican Americans and are predominantly lower to middle income.

TYPE OF NEIGHBORHOOD	% VOTED	% PERRY	% SANCHEZ	% OTHERS
Mexican American	27.6	10.4	88.5	1.1
Low-income Anglo/Hispanic	23.8	30.1	68.5	1.4
Low-income black	29.5	5.0	94.3	0.7
Middle-income black	43.1	8.8	90.5	0.7
Middle-income Anglo	39.2	73.5	24.6	1.9
Upper-income Anglo	55.0	72.3	25.9	1.8

TYPE OF NEIGHBORHOOD	% VOTED	% KIRK	% CORNYN	% OTHERS
Mexican American	25.6	85.3	12.8	1.9
Low-income Anglo/Hispanic	22.3	66.7	31.8	1.5
Low-income black	29.3	97.5	1.9	0.5
Middle-income black	42.8	95.5	4.1	0.4
Middle-income Anglo	38.9	27.6	71.2	1.2
Upper-income Anglo	54.8	30.1	69.1	0.8

Source: *Houston Chronicle*, November 14, 2002, 32A. Data collected by Richard Murray, University of Houston.

running for governor. In 1976, he had run for Congress in his hometown of Midland.

In 1998, Governor Bush won reelection with 67 percent of the popular vote in a low-voter-turnout election, which almost always favors Republicans. While Bush touted this as a huge victory, only 18 percent of qualified voters actually voted for him. Even so, it was a landslide victory of sorts. Bush's popularity also helped down-ballot candidates win election for all statewide executive offices and many judicial offices. For the first time in over one hundred twenty years, Texans elected Republicans to all but one statewide elected office.

Republican Dominance in 2002–4

straight-ticket party voting

Casting all your votes for candidates of one party.

In the 2002 election, the Republican party captured all statewide elected offices, controlled the Texas senate, and for the first time in 125 years controlled the Texas house. The 2002 election is evidence of **straight-ticket party voting** across the board. The exceptions were legislative races in which Democrats were able to hold onto some county-level offices and to retain sixty-two state house seats, twelve state senate seats, and seventeen of thirty-two congressional districts. In 2004, with no statewide offices up for election, the Republicans lost one house seat and gained five congressional seats due to the DeLay-engineered redistricting discussed in Chapter 22.

Republicans likely will continue to be the dominant party in Texas for the near future. As Texas becomes a majority-minority state, it remains to be seen whether these new participants in the political process (Hispanics and African

Americans) will continue to show strong support for Democratic candidates. If they do, the dominance of the Republican party will be reduced over the next thirty years. While Republicans claim to have made strong inroads into the Hispanic community, most Hispanics still show strong support for Democratic candidates. Table 21–4 shows that in the 2002 election in Harris County Hispanics gave strong support to Democratic candidates in statewide races. The same is true of black voters. As can be seen in Table 21–4, Hispanics and blacks do not vote in large numbers; until they do, the likelihood of Democratic candidates being elected is slim. Low voter turnout among minority groups was evident in the 1998 and 2002 elections. Until Hispanic and black voting increases, Texas is likely to remain a dominant Republican party state.

THE STRENGTH OF THE REPUBLICAN PARTY

In the 1950s and 1960s, Republicans began to gain strength in the suburban areas of Dallas and Houston, in oil-producing counties in East Texas, and in the Midland-Odessa area of West Texas. Voters in oil-producing areas supported Republican candidates largely because of national Republican party policies that favored the oil industry. The suburban areas of Houston and Dallas contained many people who relocated from states with Republican loyalties.

Republican support is found today in the traditional areas and also among young professionals and new immigrants to the state who have settled in the suburbs of Dallas/Fort Worth, Houston, and San Antonio. These new residents have not been socialized into voting a straight Democratic ticket, as were older native Texans. Republicans also draw disproportionally from among young voters. Of voters 18–29 years old, 41 percent identify with the Republican party; of voters over 60 years old, 36 percent support the Republican party (see Table 21–5).

A profile of the average Republican supporter in Texas would include the following: young, high income, well-educated, Anglo, professional, living in the suburbs of a large metropolitan area. In addition, Republican voters are likely to be newcomers to the state. One study concluded that about one-fourth of Texas Republicans are new arrivals in the state.[9]

By contrast, the Democratic party draws support from older residents, native Texans, lower-income groups, the less educated, and minority groups, especially Mexican Americans in South Texas and African Americans in urban areas and East Texas. There is also some variation among religious groups, with Catholics—especially Catholic Mexican Americans—showing strong support for the Democratic party and Protestant fundamentalists showing more support for the Republican party. Table 21–5 illustrates these differences between Texas Republicans and Democrats.

Party realignment in Texas is in part the result of regional and national trends. Increased support nationally for Republicans has an impact on Texas. Texas voters, like voters elsewhere in the Old South, have switched from the Democratic to the Republican party. As stated previously, immigration to Texas from other states has also helped the growth of the Republican party.

In 2000 and 2002, Republicans dominated most races in East Texas, with the exception of some house, senate, and congressional races. The era of the Yellow Dog Democrat may be at an end. In part, it has been replaced by straight-ticket-voting Republicans, referred to by one sage as **Yellow Pup Republicans.**

Yellow Pup Republicans
Young Republicans who vote a straight Republican ticket.

TABLE 21–5	Party Identification Among Texans by Socioeconomic Factors, 2005			
TOTAL	REPUBLICAN 39%	DEMOCRAT 25%	INDEPENDENT 23%	OTHER 10%
Age				
18–29	41	25	22	7
30–39	43	23	19	13
40–49	43	21	18	15
50–59	39	24	26	9
60 and older	36	30	26	7
Race/Ethnicity				
Hispanic	26	34	29	8
Anglo	47	21	22	9
Black	8	58	17	12
Gender				
Male	40	20	27	10
Female	29	30	18	10
Region				
East	39	23	26	9
West	43	25	27	5
South	34	31	22	11
North	42	24	22	9
Gulf	47	28	18	7
Central	33	27	30	8
Income				
Less than $10,000	27	42	22	7
$10,001–$20,000	27	38	19	12
$20,001–$30,000	33	34	26	7
$30,001–$40,000	33	27	25	14
$40,001–$50,000	40	22	23	11
$50,001–$60,000	41	32	16	9
$60,001 and above	52	16	21	9
Education				
Some High School	29	40	20	8
High School Grad	34	30	22	9
Some College	43	25	16	14
College Grad	45	18	29	7
Graduate Work	40	22	26	11

Source: Scripps Howard News Service, *Texas Poll*, 2005.

THE DEATH OF THE YELLOW DOG DEMOCRAT?

In 1995, then state agricultural commissioner Rick Perry (the current Republican governor) pronounced, "Yellow Dog Democrats are dead."[10] Some Democrats disagree. Ed Martin, executive director of the Texas Democratic party at that time, said, "Anybody who thinks Yellow Dogs are dead may be looking for tooth

marks." Martin attributes much of the success of the Republicans in East Texas to hot-button issues: "They focus on hot-button issues, get Texans to look the other way while picking their pockets. The old saw is that Republicans have successfully used guns, gays and God as polarizing wedges to define themselves. We have nothing equally emotional to define ourselves."[11]

While there is emphasis on straight-ticket voting by the Republican party, the clean sweep by the Republicans may well spell the end of the Yellow Dog Democrat. In the 2002 election, Republicans managed to win many additional seats in the Yellow Dog stronghold of East Texas. According to Dick Murray, a political scientist at the University of Houston, in past elections Democrats managed to get about 35 percent of the white vote. In 2002, however, Ron Kirk, the Democratic candidate for senator (who was black), managed to get only 31 percent of the white vote, and gubernatorial candidate Tony Sanchez got only 27 percent of the white vote. Murray estimates that for every Hispanic voter the Democrats gain, they lose one white voter.[12]

If Republican efforts to encourage straight-ticket voting are successful, especially among younger Texans, perhaps the Yellow Dogs are not so much dead as changed from Yellow Dog Democrats to Yellow Pup Republicans. In the final analysis, this might not mean much in terms of a change in state policy. The traditionalistic/individualistic political culture has not changed and will not change anytime soon. Texas is experiencing party realignment while maintaining continuity of political ideology.[13] The change can be described as a change in party label rather than as a change in ideology or policy.

PARTY DEALIGNMENT

An alternate view of party realignment is party dealignment. This view holds that the growing number of voters who do not identify with either party but instead call themselves independent is an indication of the low esteem in which American voters hold political parties and politics in general.[14] Many citizens do not see any difference in the two major parties and do not identify with either major party. In addition, candidates can operate independently of any party and capture a nomination without party support. With enough money, candidates can gain the party nomination. In recent years, Clayton Williams, Kay Bailey Hutchison, and Richard Fisher have all gained nomination using media-driven campaigns with limited support from party officials. More recently, Victor Morales gained the Democratic party nomination for the U.S. Senate without support from party officials. In 1996, Steve Forbes made inroads in the Republican primaries using mass-media campaign techniques. Similarly, in 2002, Democrat Tony Sanchez used the mass media to gain recognition in the governor's race, although he had the support of the state party organization. The media also play a large role in screening candidates. The net effect of party dealignment is that parties play a less important role today in state politics. Parties no longer perform traditional functions because other institutions—such as interest groups, professional campaign managers, and the media—have assumed these functions. For parties to regain their prominence, they must begin to again perform these functions. The changing nature of parties in Texas is not unique to the state but is part of a much larger national change in the role played by political parties.

ELECTIONS AND PARTY ORGANIZATION

Elections are at the heart of any democratic system and perform a number of important functions that make government work. Elections bestow legitimacy upon government. Without elections, all actions by governments are questionable. Elections also provide for an orderly transition of power from one group to another. One of the great stabilizing forces in the American system of government has been this orderly transfer of power. Further, elections allow citizens to express their opinions about public policy choices. By voting in elections, citizens tell government officials what they want the government to do. As indicated earlier in this chapter, many citizens do not participate in elections. Nonetheless, elections are still the most essential element of any democracy. In the rest of this chapter, we will examine a number of institutional factors—such as election cycles, ballot access, and party primaries—that influence the conduct of elections.

Election Cycles

Elections occur at regular election cycles as determined by state and federal laws. All states conduct elections on two-year cycles. The date established by federal law for electing members of the U.S. Congress and the president is the first Tuesday after the first Monday in November of even-numbered years. States must elect members of Congress and vote for the president on this date. Most states also use this November date to elect governors, state officials, state legislators, and some local officials.

general elections
Regular elections held every two years to elect state officeholders.

Texas holds **general elections** every two years. During nonpresidential election years, voters elect candidates to statewide offices: governor, lieutenant governor, attorney general, land commissioner, agricultural commissioner, comptroller, some members of the Texas Railroad Commission and the Texas State Board of Education, and some members of the two supreme courts in the state. Before 1976, all nonjudicial officeholders served two-year terms. In 1977, the state constitution was amended to allow for four-year terms beginning in 1978. Every two years, voters also elect all 150 members of the Texas house of representatives (for two-year terms), half the members of the Texas senate (for four-year terms), many judges to various courts, and county officials.

Ballot Form

Each county in Texas decides the **ballot form** and method of casting ballots. The method used to cast votes (e.g., paper ballots or electronic voting) must be approved by the secretary of state's office. Some systems are cleared in advance by the secretary of state's office, with counties able to choose among any of these systems. In the 2004 election, 145 counties used optical scanner systems, 9 counties used the punch-card system made famous in Florida, 89 rural counties used paper ballots, and 11 counties used touch-screen voting, The new touch-screen voting machines do not have a paper backup and thus leave no audit trail. Many computer experts have raised questions about the accuracy of many of these machines. No doubt these new machines will be closely watched during future elections.

Counties in Texas that use paper ballots usually use a **party column format,** with candidates listed by party and by office. The party that holds the governor's office occupies the first party column on the ballot. Being listed first on the ballot is an advantage—voters often choose the first name listed when all the candidates are unfamiliar to them. The party column ballot also encourages straight-ticket voting and was advocated strongly by the Democratic party for many years. In recent years, straight-ticket voting has worked to the advantage of the Republicans in some elections, especially those for judicial offices.

Most computer and optical scanner ballots use the **office block.** This ballot form lists the office (e.g., president), followed by the candidates by party (e.g., Republican: George W. Bush; Democrat: John F. Kerry; Libertarian: Michael Badnarik). The ballot for each county in Texas is available before each election on the secretary of state's web page, www.sos.state.tx.us. The office-block format is often advocated as a way of discouraging straight-ticket voting.

Texas law allows computer-readable ballots to enable voters to vote a straight ticket. By marking a single place on the ballot, the voter can vote for all candidates from that party. The voter can override this mark by voting in individual races. For example, a voter could vote a straight Republican ticket but override this and vote for the Democratic candidate for a selected office.

ballot form
The kind of ballot used during general elections. Each county decides its ballot form in Texas.

party column format
A paper ballot form that lists candidates by party and by office.

office block
A ballot form that lists candidates by office, with party affiliation given by their name. Most often used with computer ballots.

Ballot Access to the November General Election

To appear on the November general election ballot, candidates must meet criteria established by state law. These criteria prevent the lists of candidates on a ballot from being unreasonably long. The Texas Election Code specifies three ways for names to be placed on the ballot: as an independent or third-party candidate, by nomination at a party caucus, or by nomination in a primary election.

Independent and Third-Party Candidates

To run as an Independent, a candidate must file a petition with a specified number of signatures. For statewide office, a number of signatures equal to 1 percent of the votes cast for governor in the last general election is required. For example, in the 2002 governor's race, a total of 4.5 million votes were cast. An independent candidate for statewide office in 2004 needed to collect 45,000 signatures. For multicounty offices, such as state representative, a number of signatures equal to 5 percent of the votes cast for that office in the last election is needed. On average, 30,000 to 40,000 votes are cast in house races.[15] For county offices such as county commissioner, the number of signatures must be at least 5 percent of the votes cast for those offices. This might seem like a large number of signatures, but the process is intended to weed out people who do not

General Election Ballot

No. 0000

GENERAL ELECTION *(ELECCION GENERAL)*
***(Condado de)* SAMPLE COUNTY, TEXAS**
NOVEMBER 2, 2004 *(2 de noviembre de 2004)*
SAMPLE BALLOT *(BOLETA DE MUESTRA)*

INSTRUCTION NOTE: Vote for the candidate of your choice in each race by placing an "X" in the square beside the candidate's name. You may cast a straight-party vote (that is, cast a vote for all the nominees of one party) by placing an "X" in the square beside the name of the party of your choice. If you cast a straight-party vote for all the nominees of one party and also cast a vote for an opponent of one of that party's nominees, your vote for the opponent will be counted as well as your vote for all the other nominees of the party for which the straight-party vote was cast.

(NOTA DE INSTRUCCION: Vote por el candidato de su preferencia para cada candidatura marcando una "X" en el espacio cuadrado a la izquierda del nombre del candidato. Usted podrá votar por todos los candidatos de un solo partido político ("straight ticket") marcando una "X" en el espacio cuadrado a la izquierda del nombre de ese partido político. Si usted vota por uno de los partidos políticos y también vota por el contrincante de uno de los candidatos de dicho partido político, se contará su voto por el contrincante tanto como su voto por todos los demás candidatos del partido político de su preferencia.)

Candidates for: *(Candidatos para:)*	☐ REPUBLICAN PARTY *(Partido Republicano)*	☐ DEMOCRATIC PARTY *(Partido Democrático)*	☐ LIBERTARIAN PARTY *(Partido Libertariano)*	INDEPENDENT *(Independiente)*	WRITE-IN *(Voto Escrito)*
President and Vice President *(Presidente y Vice Presidente)*	☐ George W. Bush/ Dick Cheney	☐ John F. Kerry/ John Edwards	☐ Michael Badnarik/ Richard V. Campagna		☐
United States Representative, District *(Representante de los Estados Unidos, Distrito Núm _____)*					☐
Railroad Commissioner *(Comisionado de Ferrocarriles)*	☐ Victor G. Carrillo	☐ Bob Scarborough	☐ Anthony Garcia		
Justice, Supreme Court, Place 3 *(Juez, Corte Suprema, Núm 3)*	☐ Harriet O'Neill				
Justice, Supreme Court, Place 5 *(Juez, Corte Suprema, Núm 5)*	☐ Paul Green				
Justice, Supreme Court, Place 9 *(Juez, Corte Suprema, Núm 9)*	☐ Scott Brister	☐ David Van Os			
Judge, Court of Criminal Appeals, Place 2 *(Juez, Corte de Apelaciones Criminales, Lugar Núm 2)*	☐ Lawrence "Larry" Meyers		☐ Quanah Parker		
Judge, Court of Criminal Appeals, Place 5 *(Juez, Corte de Apelaciones Criminales, Lugar Núm 5)*	☐ Cheryl Johnson		☐ Tom Oxford		
Judge, Court of Criminal Appeals, Place 6 *(Juez, Corte de Apelaciones Criminales, Lugar Núm 6)*	☐ Michael E. Keasler	☐ J.R. Molina			
Member, State Board of Education, District *(Miembro de la Junta Estatal de Instrucción Pública, Distrito Núm _____)*					
State Senator, District _____ *(Senador Estatal, Distrito Núm _____)*					
State Representative, District _____ *(Representante Estatal, Distrito Núm _____)*					
Chief Justice, _____ Court of Appeals District *(Juez Presidente, Corte de Apelaciones, Distrito Núm _____)*					
Chief Justice, _____ Court of Appeals District, Unexpired Term *(Juez Presidente, Corte de Apelaciones, Distrito Núm _____, Duración Restante del Cargo)*					
Justice, _____ Court of Appeals District *(Juez, Corte de Apelaciones, Distrito Núm _____)*					
Justice, _____ Court of Appeals District, Place _____ *(Juez, Corte de Apelaciones, Distrito Núm _____, Lugar Núm _____)*					
Justice, _____ Court of Appeals District, Place _____, Unexpired Term *(Juez, Corte de Apelaciones, Distrito Núm _____, Lugar Núm _____, Duración Restante del Cargo)*					
District Judge, _____ Judicial District *(Juez del Distrito, Distrito Judicial Núm _____)*					
District Judge, _____ Judicial District, Unexpired Term *(Juez del Distrito, Distrito Judicial Núm _____, Duración Restante del Cargo)*					
Criminal District Judge, Court No. _____ *(Juez Criminal Del Distrito, Corte Núm _____)*					
Family District Judge, _____ Judicial District *(Juez Familiar del Distrito, Distrito Judicial Núm _____)*					

Political Culture

Judge Upholds "Sore Loser" Law

A federal judge . . . upheld Texas' sore loser law that bans commentator Pat Buchanan from appearing on the general election ballot as a presidential candidate because he already ran unsuccessfully in the Republican Primary.

U.S. District Judge James Nowlin rejected arguments from the U.S. Taxpayers Party that the law violates the U.S. Constitution. He said the law merely guarantees that internal party fights will not be carried over to the general election.

"Once you select a team in (an election cycle) that season you've got to stay on that team," Nowlin said. "Professional sports would be a lot better off if they followed a similar rule."

U.S. Taxpayers Party lawyers said they will appeal the ruling to the 5th U.S. Circuit . . . and continue a petition drive to get the party listed on the Texas ballot in the November general election. . . . The party has until May 28 [1996] to gather the signatures of 43,962 registered voters to get on the ballot this fall.

The Taxpayers Party lawyers Herb Titus and Bill Malone had argued that the Texas sore loser law is invalid because only the U.S. Constitution determines who is eligible to be a presidential candidate. "Texas has exceeded its authority under the Constitution," Titus said. Titus said that the current case [Buchanan] is different from the 1974 Supreme Court case that ruled sore loser laws were valid in U.S. Senate and House races. He said the difference in a presidential race is that no single state primary determines who will be a national party's nominee. "A person who loses a party's presidential primary in Texas could be a party's presidential nominee," Titus said.

Source: R.G. Racliff, Judge Upholds "Sore Loser" Law: Law, Blocks Buchanan from Ballot, In Houston Chronicle, 25 April 1996, pages 1A and 29A

have a serious chance of being elected. Few candidates file for statewide office as independents although the 2006 governors' race in Texas is an exception to this. Two candidates qualified to run for governor. The then current Comptroller, Carolyn M. Strayhorn, and Kinky Friedman, a country and western singer and mystery writer, both qualified for a position on the ballot as an Independent. By November the picture had changes. Kinky Freeman's had just 12.6 percent and Strayhorn 18 percent. Governor Perry managed to win with a plurality of 38.1 percent. Chris Bell, the Democratic candidate did better than expected with 30.0 percent. The primary role of the write in candidates were to help reelect an unpopular governor, who after six years in office managed to get less than 40 percent. Candidates who are defeated in the primary election may not file as independents in the general election held that year. This is known as the **sore loser law.**

Gathering signatures on a petition is not easy. Each signer must be a registered voter and must not have participated in the primary elections of other parties in that electoral cycle. For example, persons who voted in either the Democratic or Republican party primary in 1996 were not eligible to sign a petition to have Ross Perot's Reform party placed on the 1996 ballot. The same is true for all election years. If you vote in the primary of either the Democratic or Republican party, you cannot sign the nominating petition of an Independent or minor-party candidate. Signing such a petition is considered the same as voting. This provision of state law makes it all the more difficult for Independents and third-party candidates to acquire the necessary signatures to get on the ballot.

Write-in candidates sometimes are confused with people who file and are listed on the ballot as Independents. The process of filing as a write-in candidate is a separate procedure. To be an "official" write-in candidate, a person must file his or her intention before the election. This applies to all elections, including local, city, and school board elections. If a person does not file before the election, votes for that person are not counted. For some state offices, a filing fee may be

sore loser law
Law in Texas that prevents a person who lost the party primary from running as an Independent or minor-party candidate.

required to have your name listed on the ballot as a write–in. The amount varies from $3,000 for statewide office to as little as $300 for local justices of the peace. People sometimes write in things like "Mickey Mouse" or "None of the above." These votes are recorded but not counted. In 1990, nineteen write-in candidates filed for governor. Bubbles Cash, a retired Dallas stripper, led the pack with 3,287 out of a total of 11,700 write-in votes.[16]

Party Caucus

party caucus
A meeting of members of a political party used by minor political parties in Texas to nominate candidates for office.

The state election code defines a minor party (sometimes called a third party) as any political organization that receives between 5 percent and 19 percent of the total votes cast for any statewide office in the last general election. In the last thirty years, there have been three minor parties in Texas: the Raza Unida party in South Texas in the 1970s, the Socialist Workers party in 1988, and the Libertarian party in the 1990s. Parties that achieve minor-party status must nominate their candidates in a **party caucus** or convention and are exempt from the petition requirement discussed previously.

primary elections
Elections used by major political parties in Texas to nominate candidates for the November general election.

In 1998 and 2000, only the Libertarian party held the status of a minor political party. In 1998, the party fielded twenty-two candidates in the thirty U.S. House races, all statewide offices, and a few state house races. None were elected. Nearly the same pattern prevailed with the Libertarian party in the 2000 election. They fielded candidates for most statewide and congressional offices but elected no one. In the 2002 election, they received less than 1 percent of the statewide vote and lost their status as a minor party. However, the Libertarians still had candidates on the ballot in some races in the 2004 election by petition.

closed primaries
Nominating elections that are closed to all voters except those who have registered as a member of the particular political party.

Primary Election

The Texas Election Code defines a major party as any organization receiving 20 percent or more of the total votes cast for governor in the last election. Only the Democratic and Republican parties hold this status today. By law, these party organizations must nominate their candidates in **primary elections.**

Texas has an open primary system. Some states have closed primary elections. There are several important variations on open and closed primaries that deserve discussion (see Table 21–6).

Closed primaries are currently used in fourteen states. This system requires voters to declare their party affiliation when they register to vote. They then can vote only in the primary of the party in which they are registered. Most of these states have a set time before the election after which a voter may not change party affiliation.

semi-closed primaries
Nominating elections that are open to all registered voters but that require voters to declare party affiliation when they vote in the primary election.

Semi-closed primaries allow voters to register or change their party registration on election day. Registration as a member of a party is required in order to vote on election day. In a **semi-open primary,** the voter can choose to vote in the primary of either party on election day. Voters are considered "declared" for the party in whose primary they vote. This is the system used in Texas. If you vote in the Republican party primary, you are in effect declaring that you are a member of the Republican party. You cannot participate in any activity of any other party for the remainder of that election year. For example, if you vote in the Republican primary, you may not attend the precinct convention of the Democratic party.

semi-open primary
Voters must publicly declare their choice of a party ballot on election day at the polling place.

open primaries
Nominating elections that are open to all registered voters regardless of party affiliation.

Open primaries allow the voter to vote in any primary without declaring a party. The voter can vote as a Democrat and attend the Republican precinct convention or participate in any activity of the opposite party.

TABLE 21–6	Primary Systems Used in State Elections

Closed Primary: Party Registration Required Before Election Day

Connecticut	Nebraska	Oklahoma
Delaware	Nevada	Pennsylvania
Florida	New Jersey	South Dakota
Kentucky	New Mexico	Wyoming
Maine	New York	

Semi-Closed Primary: Voters May Register or Change Registration on Election Day

Alaska	Kansas	Oregon
Arizona	Maryland	Rhode Island
California	Massachusetts	Utah
Colorado	New Hampshire	West Virginia
Iowa	North Carolina	

Semi-Open Primary: Voters Are Required to Request Party Ballot

Alabama	Mississippi	Virginia
Arkansas	Ohio	
Georgia	South Carolina	
Illinois	Tennessee	
Indiana	Texas	

Open Primary: Voters May Vote in Any Party Primary

Hawaii	Montana
Idaho	North Dakota
Michigan	Vermont
Minnesota	Wisconsin
Missouri	

Nonpartisan: Voters May Switch Parties Between Races

Louisiana	Washington

Blanket

Formerly used in Alaska, California, and Washington. Declared unconstitutional by the U.S. Supreme Court in 2000.

Source: John F. Bibby and Thomas M. Holbrook, "Parties and Elections," in *Politics in the American States: A Comparative Analysis*, 8th ed., ed. Virginia Gray and Russell L. Hanson. Copyright © 2004, Congressional Quarterly Press, Washington, D.C. Reprinted by permission.

In the past, three states—Alaska, California, and Washington—used a **blanket primary.** This system allowed voters to switch parties between offices. A voter might vote in the Republican primary for the races for governor and U.S. House and in the Democratic primary for the U.S. Senate race. Blanket primaries have been ruled unconstitutional by the U.S. Supreme Court. Alaska and California currently use a closed primary with voter registration by party. Washington has

blanket primary
Voters may vote in more than one party's primary, but one candidate per office. No longer used. Declared unconstitutional.

How Texas Compares
Primary Systems Among the States

The map below shows the different types of primary elections used among the states. Southern states tend to have open or semi-open primaries due to their history of one-party systems in which winning the primary election was the same as winning the general election.

Source: John F. Bibby and Thomas M. Holbrook, "Parties and Elections," in *Politics in the American States: A Comparative Analysis*, 8th ed., ed. Virginia Gray and Russell L. Hanson. Copyright © 2004, Congressional Quarterly Press, Washington, D.C. Reprinted by permission.

nonpartisan primary

Top two vote getters, regardless of party, are nominated for the general election ballot.

adopted Louisiana's system of a **nonpartisan primary** for all statewide and U.S. House and Senate races. Under this system, all candidates are listed on the ballot by office. The voter can choose one candidate per office. If no person receives a majority, the top two candidates face each other in a runoff election.

Political Differences Between Open and Closed Primary Systems

The primary system a state uses may affect the party system in the state. Advocates of the closed primary system say that it encourages party identification and loyalty and thereby helps build stronger party systems. Open primary systems, they say, allow participation by independents with no loyalty to the party, weakening party organization. There is no strong evidence that such is the case.

Open primaries do allow crossover voting, which occurs when voters abandon their party to vote in the other party's primary. Occasionally, voters in one party might vote in the other party's primary in hopes of nominating a candidate from the other party whose philosophy is similar to their own. For example, Republicans have been accused of voting in the Democratic primary in Texas to ensure the nomination of a conservative. This occurred in the 1970 U.S. Senate race, when Republicans voted for the more conservative Lloyd Bentsen over the liberal Ralph Yarborough. Many voting precincts carried by Bentsen in the Democratic primary voted for the Republican candidate for the U.S. Senate, George H. W. Bush, in the general election.

From 1996 to 2000, more Texans voted in the Republican primaries than in the Democratic primaries. Republicans claimed that this was evidence that their party had become the majority party. Democrats, on the other hand, suggested that these differences in turnout could be explained by the low levels of opposition in the Democratic primaries. For instance, President Clinton faced no opposition in his primary election, while both Bob Dole and Pat Buchanan were still actively seeking the Republican nomination. Some Democratic party leaders claim that many traditional Democratic party voters crossed over and voted in the Republican primary in an attempt to affect who the Republican nominee would be. In the 2000 primary season, there were few reasons to vote in the Democratic primary except in those few cases where local House or Senate races were being contested.

As it turned out, the Democrats' explanation might be the more accurate. In the 2002 primary election, 400,000 more people voted in the Democratic party primary than in the Republican party primary. The difference is due almost entirely to the lack of contested races in the Republican primary and the highly contested races for U.S. Senate and governor in the Democratic primary. Among Republican candidates, Governor Rick Perry had no opponents, and John Cornyn had little opposition for his U.S. Senate seat.

Party raiding and crossover voting are difficult to orchestrate. Once such an effort becomes public, it can be countered by the other party and can work to stimulate voter participation in the opposite direction. Such practices can have an effect on individual races, as in the 1970 U.S. Senate race and again in 1976 when conservative Democrats voted for Ronald Reagan in the special Republican presidential primary. Reagan won the Republican primary over President Gerald Ford, who lost the general election to Democrat Jimmy Carter in November 1976. Except for one case in a runoff primary, the 1980s and 1990s provided few examples of orchestrated crossover voting. The candidates and issues have simply been absent.

Runoff Primary Elections

Runoff primaries are held in eleven southern and border states, as well as South Dakota. A runoff primary is required if no candidate receives a majority vote in the first primary. Until recently in the South, winning the Democratic party primary was the same as winning the general election. The runoff primary became a fixture, supposedly as a way of ensuring that the winner had "majority" support. In reality, voter turnout in the runoff primary is always lower than in the first primary—sometimes substantially lower. The "majority" winner often is selected by the small percentage of the electorate who bother to vote in the runoff primary.

Racial and ethnic minority candidates have challenged the runoff primary system in Southern and border states. They charge that because voter turnout decreases in the runoff and minorities are less likely to vote in runoff elections,

runoff primaries
Elections that are required if no person receives a majority vote in the primary election. Primarily used in southern and border states.

the system is racially biased. The only evidence available suggests that this might not be the case. A study in Georgia examined 215 runoff elections between 1965 and 1982 and found no support for the presence of racial bias in runoff primary elections.[17]

Crossover voting and party raiding might occur in the runoff primary. The Texas Election Code specifies that voters who voted in the primary election of one party may not participate in the runoff primary of the other party. Occasionally in the past decade, it has been charged that this has in fact happened. In a 1992 Democratic primary congressional race in Houston, the Houston congressional district had been drawn to "ensure" that a Mexican American could be elected, but the primary was won by an Anglo, Gene Green. His opponent, Ben T. Reyes, charged that Republicans had "raided" and voted for Green. There was some evidence of this, but it did not appear to have changed the results of the election. The current system of record keeping and the difficulty of checking voter lists make it almost impossible to prevent party raiding or crossover voting in runoff primaries.

Occasionally, runoff primary elections get voter attention. In 2002, former mayor of Dallas Ron Kirk and Victor Morales were locked in a bitter runoff primary. This contest generated 620,517 votes, more than the total vote in the Republican primary election (614,716) that same year. Turnout is obviously related to a number of factors, among them the degree of competition in the election.

The Administration and Finance of Primary Elections

In the past, primary elections were considered functions of private organizations and the state did not regulate them. However, courts have ruled that political parties are not private organizations and that their functions are subject to control by state law. The Texas Election Code governs primary elections. It specifies the time and method of conducting primary elections. The cost of conducting primary elections previously was borne entirely by political parties. Persons wanting to file for an office in the primary election had to pay a **filing fee.** In 1970, court cases forced Texas to alter its filing fee system.

Before 1970 the cost of filing for county offices had increased substantially; for example, the cost of filing for a countywide race in Dallas County was $9,000 in 1970. In 1972, the state of Texas assumed most of the cost of financing primary elections. Filing fees remain, but they are lower than in the past. Currently the cost of filing for a statewide office is $4,000, and for countywide races the fee is $500.

Absentee and Early Voting

All states allow some form of **absentee voting.** This practice began as a way to allow members of the U.S. armed services who were stationed in other states or overseas to vote. In all but a few states, the practice has been extended to other voters. In most states, persons who will be out of the county on election day may file for absentee voting. In Texas before 1979, in order to vote absentee, voters had to sign an affidavit saying they would be out of the county and unable to vote on election day. They also could file for an absentee ballot to be sent to them if they were living out-of-state or confined to a hospital or nursing home. In 1979, the state legislature changed the rules to allow anyone to vote absentee without restrictions. In Texas this is called "early voting." Early voting now begins twenty-two days before an election and closes six days before the election. During that period, polls are open from 7 A.M. to 7 P.M. Voters simply go to an early voting polling place and present their voter registration cards; they are then allowed to vote.

filing fee
A fee or payment required to put a candidate's name on the primary or general election ballot.

absentee voting
A process that allows a person to vote early, before the regular election. Applies to all elections in Texas. (Also called early voting.)

Guns Don't Kill Killdeers
PEOPLE DO

For additional bumper stickers call 512-477-7500
Pd. Pol. Ad. Travis County Democratic Party • P.O. Box 13262 • Austin • Texas • 78711 • Beverly Reeves • Treasurer

Democrats tried to turn George W. Bush's opening-day mistake to their political advantage.

CAMPAIGNS

Campaign activity in Texas has changed considerably in the past two or three decades. These changes are not unique to Texas but are part of a national trend. Norman Brown, in his book on Texas politics, describes the form of political campaigning in the state as "local affairs."[18] In the past, candidates would travel from county seat to county seat and give speeches at political rallies arranged by local supporters. Brown devotes special attention to the campaigns of Governors Jim and Miriam Ferguson ("Ma" and "Pa" Ferguson). Jim Ferguson, when campaigning for himself and later for his wife, would travel from county to county, telling each group what it wanted to hear—often saying different things in different counties. Brown contends that Ferguson and other candidates could do this because of the lack of a statewide press to report on the inconsistencies in political speeches.

In modern-day Texas, the media play a significant role in political campaigns. Reporters often follow candidates for statewide office as they travel the vast expanses of Texas. Political rallies are still held, but most often they are used to gain media attention and to convey the candidate's message to a larger audience. Candidates hope these events will present a favorable image of them to the public.

Heavy media coverage can have its disadvantages for the candidates. For instance, in 1990, Clayton Williams, the Republican candidate for governor, held a media event on one of his West Texas ranches. He and "the boys" were to round up cattle for branding in a display designed to portray Williams as a hardworking rancher. Unfortunately for Williams, rain spoiled the event and caused it to be postponed. Resigned to the rain delay, Williams told the reporters, "It's like rape. When it's inevitable, relax and enjoy it." The state press had a field day with this remark, and it probably hurt Williams's chances with many women voters. The fact that his opponent was a woman (Ann Richards) helped magnify the significance of his statement.

In 1994, Republican candidate George W. Bush made a similar gaffe in his race for governor against incumbent Ann Richards. In Texas the opening day of dove season is in September, and the event marks the beginning of the fall hunting season. Both Bush and Richards participated in opening-day hunts in an attempt to appeal to the strong hunting and gun element in the state. Unfortunately for Bush, by mistake he shot a killdeer rather than a dove. Pictures of

Media & Politics

Texas Blogs: The New Vocal Minority?

One of the newest factors in politics at both the national and state levels is Internet sites, called blogs, where citizens hold forth on all manner of politics. Here are a few examples at the state level.

Juanita's Beauty Shop (http://www.brazosriver.com/)

This web page is devoted to removing Congressman Tom DeLay from office. The writer (who says this ain't a blog) is a witty woman with a homespun "good ol' Texas gal" sense of humor. The official title is *News and Views from Congress Varmit Tom DeLay's Home County.* Any action, regardless of how small, that involves DeLay gets lampooned on the nonblog web page. It is well worth the view and provides links to other satirical pages and news articles.

The Pink Dome (http://pinkdome.com/)

Another blog is called the Pink Dome after the color of the pink stone used to build the state capitol. Actually, the dome is painted to match the stone. While this blog is somewhat more serious than Juanita's, it does have its satirical moments. It is a "take no prisoners" site and covers many issues across the state. When the "Leg" is in session, it often provides information not found in the mainstream media (MSM). It also provides links to many other blogs and web pages dealing with Texas politics. It does have a liberal slant, but even if you are a humor-impaired Republican you might enjoy the site.

The Burnt Orange Report
(http://www.burntorangereport.com/mt/)

For the Aggies in the state, the name might turn you off. If you are a Republican, the content might turn you off. This blog covers both state and national politics. It has a very definite liberal bias and is much more serious and less satirical than the two previously described. It can serve as a good source of information during the legislative sessions. This blog has been known to circulate vicious rumors about the governor in the past.

Clean Up Texas Politics
(http://www.cleanuptexaspolitics.com/scandalblog)

This blog is the most serious of the group. It is less a blog and more a useful source of information on news articles from across the state.

Texas Bloggers (http://www.texasblogs.net/)

This blog lists links for most of the other blogs in Texas. Many are regional and provide local political information. Some are written by people who need serious help.

Bush holding the dead bird appeared in most state papers and on television. He was fined for shooting a migratory bird. A Texas Democratic group in Austin produced bumper stickers reading "Guns don't kill killdeers. People do." In 1998, Governor Bush did not stage a media event for the opening day of dove season. He was so far ahead in the polls that even opening the issue would only result in a painful reminder.

Most campaign events are not as disastrous as the cattle-branding and dove-hunting incidents. Some gain attention and free media coverage for the candidate; however, free media attention is never enough. Candidates must purchase time on television and radio and space in newspapers. In a state as large as Texas, this can be quite costly. Candidates try to make the most of the expensive time they purchase by conveying simple messages. The result is the **"sound bite" commercial**, a thirty-second message that, it is hoped, will be remembered by the voters. This is not unique to Texas but is a nationwide phenomenon.

Sound bites can be classified into at least five types. The **"feel good" spot** lacks substance or issues and is designed to make the public feel good about the candidate or the party. In 1984, Ronald Reagan told us it was "morning in America." His commercial featured scenes of a "middle America" town filled

"sound bite" commercial
A short, usually thirty-second TV political advertisement that conveys a simple message about the candidate or the opponent.

Campaigns often give voters something they can keep to help them remember the candidates' names on election day.

with happy people. In 1988, President Bush told us he saw "a thousand points of light." Others promise "fresh, bold leadership" or claim to have "common sense and uncommon courage." Still others, including Clayton Williams, bid us "Share my vision." In 1998, Governor George W. Bush ran a number of TV spots that asked voters to support his effort to have every child read and become a productive member of society. **"Sainthood" spots** try to depict the candidate as having saintly qualities:[20] "Senator Smith is a Christian family man, Eagle Scout, Little League coach, Sunday school teacher, involved, concerned, committed, community leader who fights the people's fights. Let's keep him working for us."

"Good ol' boy" (or **"good ol' girl"**) **spots** are testimonials from other citizens on the candidate's qualifications. In a staged "person on the street" interview, the citizen says something like "Senator Smith is the most effective leader this state has seen since Sam Houston. He's so effective it's frightening. He is committed to his job, and we need him to fight the coming battles with the liberals." In Texas, cattle and horses in the background provide a down-to-earth backdrop for ranchers' good ol' boy testimonials.

"NOOTS" ("No One's Opposed to This") commercials are also common. In these ads, candidates take courageous stands on issues everyone supports: sound fiscal management, planned orderly growth, good schools, open government, getting tough on crime, no new taxes, and so on.

In **"basher" spots**, the last type of sound bite, candidates play on voters' emotions by painting their opponent in an unfavorable light. If your opponent is a lawyer, you can point out that he or she defends criminals. You can also play the "gay card" by pointing out that your opponent has received money from gay rights organizations. Governor Rick Perry, running for secretary of agriculture in 1990, defeated Democratic incumbent Jim Hightower. In one of his commercials, Perry claimed that Hightower had once visited the home of Jane Fonda, who is often used as a symbol of the radical war protesters of the 1960s because of her visit to Hanoi during the Vietnam War. When pressed for details on the visit, Perry said that Hightower had visited Los Angeles, and that Los Angeles was the home of Jane Fonda.

Basher spots have developed into a fine art. Newt Gingrich, former speaker of the U.S. House of Representatives, extended the art when he used his GOPAC political action committee to help "train local Republican candidates." In 1990, GOPAC mailed a glossary of 131 words to over four thousand state Republican candidates. This glossary included a list of "optimistic positive governing words" that Republican candidates should use to describe themselves and a list of "contrasting negative words" they should use to describe their opponents. For

"feel good" spot
A short political message, often devoid of meaning, aimed at conveying a message that makes the voters have good feelings about the candidate.

"sainthood" spots
Political advertisements that portray the candidate as a virtuous person.

good ol' boy or girls spots
Political advertisement where people/friends declare you to be a regular guy or gal.

"NOOTS"
Political advertisements that contain messages few citizens oppose.

"basher" spots
Political advertisements that portray the opponent in a very negative way.

example, Republicans are described as having common sense and Democrats as being big-spending liberals.

These types of advertisements are used because most often they work to the advantage of the candidate. Occasionally, basher spots can backfire on the candidate. These ads plant in the voters' minds a simple message that they carry into the voting booth. Most citizens do not spend much time studying issues or candidates' backgrounds and they are often entirely dependent on advertisements for information. While the news media (which receive most of the money spent in campaigns) often denounce such ads, they do not refuse to run them.

Political Consultants

The use of professional campaign consultants is becoming more common. Most candidates find it necessary to have these professionals help run their campaigns. If their opponents use professionals, candidates might be disadvantaged by not using them. Professional campaign consultants use many techniques. They take public opinion polls to measure voter reaction to issues so the candidate knows what stands to take. They run focus groups in which a panel of "average citizens" is asked to react to issues or words. Consultants also help the candidate design written and visual advertisements and generally "package" the candidate to the voters. In 2002, David Dewhurst filmed a TV spot for his consulting firm praising its effectiveness in making him look professional.

Money in Campaigns

Using media advertisements, professional consultants, and a full-time paid campaign staff increases the cost of running for state office. The cost can run into the millions. In 1992, U.S. Senator Phil Gramm spent $9.8 million to win reelection.[20] Kay Bailey Hutchison managed to get elected U.S. Senator in 1993 by spending a mere $3.6 million.[21] Clayton Williams spent $21.3 million in 1990 in his losing race for governor, while Ann Richards spent $13.9 million in winning that race.[22] The average Texas congressional race in 1990 cost over $750,000. The range was from $43,147 for Henry B. Gonzalez, who faced little opposition, to $1.6 million for Martin Frost.[23] Campaigns for Texas state senate races can cost as much as a race for the U.S. Congress. In large urban counties, races for the Texas legislature can cost several hundred thousand dollars. Even county-level races can cost candidates more than $50,000.

In 2000, one open seat for the Texas senate broke records for spending for that office. This race would decide which party controlled the Texas senate and the election of a replacement lieutenant governor if (when) Governor Bush became president and Lieutenant Governor Perry became governor. Republican Todd Stapes, who won the race, raised $2.4 million, and his Democratic opponent, David Fisher, raised $1.7 million. Both political parties donated heavily to these campaigns. The Republican party gave Stapes $341,744, while the Democratic party gave Fisher $323,623. Trial lawyers contributed to the Democratic candidate, and big business contributed to the Republican candidate. Also, money from outside the state flowed to both candidates. Candidates often make a big point about their opponents receiving money from outside the state even though they themselves might also have received money from out-of-state supporters.

Money for political campaigns is supplied primarily by political action committees (PACs) (see Chapter 9). In a few cases, such as the races of Clayton Williams and Kay Bailey Hutchison, personal wealth supplies large sums of money. The 1994 race between Republican Kay Bailey Hutchison and Democrat

How Texas Compares

Limitations on Campaign Contributions in Statewide Races

While Texas places no limit on the amount of money candidates can spend for statewide races, many states do. The map below shows these spending limitations. Texas is one of twelve states with no limitations.

- $500 or less
- $500–999
- $1,000–2,000
- $2,001–5,000
- $5,000 or greater
- No limit

Source: National Conference of State Legislatures. http://NCSL.org/programs/legman/about/contriblimits_htm

Richard Fisher was between two wealthy Dallas residents. Fisher refused to take PAC money and used his family wealth to finance his campaign.

In 1996, Senator Phil Gramm spent in excess of $5.3 million defeating Victor Morales, who spent about $417,000. Morales, a newcomer to politics and a political novice, refused to take money from PACs and was outspent by Gramm by a ratio of 12.5 to 1. In the 2002 Democratic primary, Morales ran for Senate and again made a big point of not taking PAC money. He lost again.

In 1998, the governor's race was very lopsided. With polls showing Governor Bush far in front of his opponent, Garry Mauro wasn't able to raise enough money to become competitive. The PACs simply did not think Mauro had a chance to win. The lieutenant governor's race in 1998 was much different. In the contest between the incumbent state comptroller, John Sharp, and the state agriculture commissioner, Rick Perry, both candidates were able to raise money because the race was so close. After the election, the winning candidate, Rick Perry, injected a new term into state politics—"late train contributors." The

Debating the Issues

Do Campaign Contributions Buy Influence with the Governor?

All governors are forced to collect large sums of money to use in their campaigns. While a few candidates, such as Tony Sanchez in 2002, can afford to finance their campaigns from personal wealth, most cannot and must rely on contributions from citizens. Texas is a large state with many media markets, and money is needed to campaign on such a vast scale. While no one doubts the need for money in campaigns, the question is what impact these contributions have on decisions made by the governor.

Yes While all candidates for office will deny that campaign contributions have any influence on their decisions, there is little doubt that such money does buy access and influence. Politicians accused of being bought can and often do act with great indignation and accuse the accusers of being sinister and jaded in their view of government. One must ask why some individuals give vast sums of money to many candidates if they do not expect something in return. Why does Bob Perry of Perry Homes in Houston, Texas, give hundreds of thousands of dollars to Republicans? Are he and others like him trying to influence state policy? Recently it was reported that the governor was using campaign contributions to supplement the salaries of some of his top staff members, a potential conflict of interest.

No Not everyone who gives money to a candidate for governor expects special treatment or appointment to some prestigious board or commission. Some people are interested in government programs that they think are in the best interest of Texas. While giving money may buy a person access, it does not ensure that actions favorable to his or her interests will result. In the 2002 election cycle, gaming and Indian reservations interests donated over $500,000 to Governor Perry's campaign in an attempt to get slot machines at race tracks and on reservations. This measure did not pass the legislature. While some people may donate money expecting appointment to some board or commission, many are disappointed. Governors often appoint those individuals who they think best represent their interests and will do so as a member of that board or commission.

lieutenant governor–elect let it be known that PACs that had not contributed enough could make a late train donation to his campaign before the start of the legislative session.

The 2002 race for governor was the most expensive in Texas history, with both candidates spending close to $90 million. Tony Sanchez supplied much of the money for his candidacy from his private fortune. Republicans gave Governor Rick Perry large sums of money from both state and national sources. President Bush and his father and mother all helped Perry raise money and campaign.

Money supplied by PACs obviously has an impact on elected officials. At the least, PAC money buys the group access to the official. At worst, PAC money buys the vote of the elected official. Distinguishing between the two is almost impossible. Most states, including Texas, have passed laws designed to regulate campaign finances. Many other states have passed laws limiting the amount of money spent on campaigns, but these laws have been invalidated by the U.S. Supreme Court. (See Chapter 20 on interest groups in Texas politics.)

Candidates sometimes loan themselves money that they later repay with "late train" contributions. Special interest groups seldom retire the debt of losers. State law limits the amount of money a candidate can collect to retire personal campaign debts for each election (primary, runoff, general) to $500,000 in personal loans. In 2002, several candidates far exceeded this amount in personal loans, chief among them gubernatorial candidate Tony Sanchez, with $22,262,662 in personal loans, and lieutenant governor–elect David Dewhurst, with $7,413,887 in outstanding debt.[24]

Today, the regulation of campaign finances in Texas is limited to requiring all candidates and PACs to file reports with the Texas State Ethics Commission. All contributions over $50 must be reported along with the name of the contributor. An expenditure report must also be filed. These reports must be filed before and after the election. The idea behind the reporting scheme is to make public the sources of the funds received by candidates and the ways the candidates spend their funds. Sometimes these reports are examined closely by the news media and are given significant media coverage, but such scrutiny is not common. Citizens mostly are left to get such information on their own, a difficult undertaking for the average citizen.

Summary

Self-Test www.mhhe.com/pattersontad8

In the past, the state executive committees of both parties were likely to be part-time organizations with limited staff. Today, both parties have a permanent headquarters, a full-time paid professional staff, and financial resources to help party development. They are actively engaged in organizing and building their party through voter identification and registration, candidate recruitment, candidate education, get-out-the-vote drives, and support for candidates during the general election.

The average citizen has little awareness of party organization at the state and local levels, where political control is left to the active elite of the party; however, it is not difficult to become part of this group. Any citizen with a little time can become active in precinct, county, and state party activities. Most of these positions are not paid. Individuals must be willing to contribute their time and money to serving the party.

Texas is emerging as a two-party state. Party organization at the local level is still not well developed. In an era of candidate-centered politics, the role of the political party has changed. Both the Democratic party and the Republican party in Texas are redefining the role of the state party organization in state politics. State party organizations must continue to expand their services to help candidates and develop local party organizations if they are to remain major forces in state politics.

Elections and campaigns are essential to any democracy. The rules governing the conduct of elections have an impact on who gets elected and on the policies enacted by government. For reasons discussed in Chapter 20, active involvement in Texas politics is limited to a small number of citizens. The electoral process is dominated by the Anglo population, which controls a disproportionate share of state offices. Most citizens choose not to participate in elections or in the activities of political parties. As in other states, campaigns in Texas have become media affairs dominated by political consultants, sound bite ads, and money.

The big unknown in Texas politics is the role of the Hispanic voter. Thus far, voting among Hispanics has remained quite low. In 2002, many thought that the presence of a Hispanic (Tony Sanchez) at the top of the ticket would bring out the Hispanic vote. This did not happen. Hispanic voters stayed away in droves, and an effort to register more minority votes was not successful. The votes Sanchez received from Anglo voters were much fewer than the number normally received by Democratic candidates. If Hispanic voters begin to vote in greater numbers, it is not certain that they will remain strong Democratic party voters.

STUDY CORNER

Key Terms

absentee voting (*p. 612*)
ballot form (*p. 605*)
"basher" spots (*p. 615*)
blanket primary (*p. 610*)
closed primaries (*p. 608*)
"feel good" spot (*p. 615*)
filing fee (*p. 612*)
general elections (*p. 604*)
"good ol' boy"/"good ol' girl"
   spots (*p. 615*)

nonpartisan primary (*p. 611*)
"NOOTS" (*p. 615*)
office block (*p. 605*)
open primaries (*p. 610*)
party caucus (*p. 608*)
party column format (*p. 605*)
party ideology (*p. 595*)
primary elections (*p. 608*)
runoff primaries (*p. 611*)
"sainthood" spots (*p. 615*)

semi-closed primaries (*p. 608*)
semi-open primary (*p. 609*)
Shivercrats (*p. 597*)
sore loser law (*p. 607*)
"sound bite" commercial (*p. 614*)
straight-ticket party voting (*p. 600*)
two-party competitive state (*p. 592*)
Yellow Dog Democrats (*p. 597*)
Yellow Pup Republicans (*p. 601*)

Self-Test

1. Which of the following does **not** describe changes in state party competitive patterns since the mid-1940s?
   a. The number of two-party competitive states has increased.
   b. Most changes in party competitive patterns are explained by changes in the southern states.
   c. One-party Democratic states have evolved into either modified one-party Democratic states or two-party competitive states.
   d. Modified one-party Republican states have increased slightly.
   e. None of the above.

2. Texas's permanent party organization includes all of the following **except:**
   a. the county executive committee.
   b. the precinct chair.
   c. the country or district convention.
   d. the county chair.
   e. the state party chair and vice chair.

3. General elections for statewide offices in Texas are held:
   a. the first Tuesday after the first Monday of presidential election years.
   b. the first Tuesday after the first Monday in odd-numbered years after even-numbered presidential election years.
   c. the first Tuesday after the first Monday in even-numbered years when there is no presidential election.
   d. the first Tuesday after the first Monday in odd-numbered years before even-numbered presidential election years.

4. The Voting Rights Act of 1965, which was extended to Texas in 1975, does all of the following **except:**
   a. require the U.S. Justice Department to approve any changes in the form of Texas ballots, the time and place of elections, and the method of electing legislators.

   b. nullify the Texas runoff primary system that has been challenged by racial and ethnic minorities.
   c. permit the federal government to oversee elections at the state level.
   d. require Texas to use bilingual ballots for all elections in counties with at least 20 percent minority population.

5. Texas has what type of primary system?
   a. semi-closed.
   b. blanket.
   c. closed.
   d. nonpartisan.
   e. semi-open.

6. Traditional election functions on behalf of candidates are now performed not by political parties but by:
   a. political consultants.
   b. political action committees.
   c. special interest groups.
   d. lobbyists.

7. Because the Republican party in Texas now controls both houses of the Texas legislature, the governor's mansion, and all statewide elected offices, Texas has officially been redesignated a two-party competitive state. (T/F)

8. Because of the extremely strong alliance between landowners and low-income Anglos, Texas was a one-party Democratic state from the end of Reconstruction until the 1960s, no Republican was elected to statewide office during that period, and very few Republican candidates were elected in other elections. (T/F)

9. The election of 1998 was critical in Texas because it marked the first time in 120 years that all elected statewide executive offices were held by Republicans. (T/F)

10. Texas Democrats generally favor early voting, which begins twenty-two days before an election and closes six days before an election, because it favors lower- and working-class voters. (T/F)

Critical Thinking

Go the websites for both the Democratic and the Republican parties in Texas and look at the party platforms. What are the major differences between the two parties in Texas? Which party platform do you most agree with?

Suggested Readings

Anderson, James E., Richard W. Murray, and Edward L. Farley. *Texas Politics: An Introduction*. New York: Harper & Row, 1989.

Key, V. O., Jr. *Southern Politics in State and Nation*. New York: Knopf, 1949.

Key, V. O., Jr. *Politics and Pressure Groups*, 4th ed. New York: Thomas Y. Crowell, 1958.

Soukup, James R., Clifton McCleskey, and Harry Holloway. *Party and Factional Division in Texas*. Austin: University of Texas Press, 1962.

Weeks, Douglas O. *Texas Presidential Politics in 1952*. Austin: University of Texas, Institute of Public Affairs, 1953.

List of Websites

http://www.txdemocrats.org/
The Texas Democratic party website.

http://www.texasgop.org/
The Texas Republican party website.

http://www.ethics.state.tx.us/
Website of the Texas Ethics Commission. Has information on campaign contributions reported by candidates for office as well as interest groups.

http://www.sos.state.tx.us/
Texas secretary of state website. Provides information on election laws and voter turnout.

www.tpj.org/
Website of Texans for Public Justice. Provides information on campaign spending and lobbying.

http://www.fairvote.org/
Website of the Center for Voting and Democracy, an organization promoting other election systems. This organization has a slight Republican lean.

Participate!

Both political parties are always looking for volunteers to help work at their headquarters. In larger cities, these party offices will be open much of the year. Volunteer to help work at the headquarters of the party of your choice. As elections approach, there is much work you can do, from very exciting—helping to organize events—to very boring—stuffing envelopes. As you "do your time in the trenches," you will be given more responsible and interesting jobs.

Extra Credit

After working in a campaign as a volunteer, write a paper describing your experiences. What experiences were positive and which were negative? Did your work leave you with a positive view of the political process?

(Self-Test Answers: 1. e   2. c   3. c   4. b   5. e   6. a   7. T   8. F   9. T   10. F)

The Texas Legislature

Chapter Outline

The Size of the Texas Legislature

Methods of Election

Reapportionment and
Redistricting Issues
    Equity of Representation
    Minority Representation
    Political and Racial Gerrymandering

Impact of Redistricting

Re-redistricting in 2003

Qualifications for State Legislators

Getting Elected

Turnover in State Legislatures

Characteristics of State Legislatures
    Term Limits
    Sessions
    Salaries

Formal Procedures of the
Legislature
    Leadership Positions in the Texas
        Legislature
    Committees in the House and Senate
    Formal Rules: How a Bill Becomes Law
    Major and Minor Calendars and Bills
    Legislative Workload and Logjams

Informal Rules

Role-Playing
    Representational Roles
    Partisan Roles

Rating the Texas Legislature

CHAPTER 22

The representatives of the people are sometimes inclined to fancy that they are the people and to assert an imperious control over the other departments. As they commonly have the people on their side, they always act with such momentum as to make it very difficult for the other members of government to maintain the balance of the constitution.

Alexander Hamilton, Federalist No. 20

In the summer of 2005, the Texas legislature adjourned. For two regular sessions and three special sessions, the governor and the Texas legislature had again failed to come up with a solution to how to fund the state's education system—despite being under a court order to change the system. This leads many people to conclude that there is a lack of political will on the part of the leadership to support public education. Many are wondering whether members of the legislature think education is a public good.

While Hamilton's statement is more polished, Texans have a more succinct way of saying the same thing: "Neither man nor property is safe while the Texas legislature is in session." This statement suggests the importance of the Texas legislature in state politics and the fear people have of government. While the office of governor is important, as are the courts and state agencies, the legislature is the most important agency. There are many things that cannot happen without legislative action. Money cannot be spent, taxes cannot be levied, state laws cannot be enacted or changed, and, finally, in most states the constitution cannot be amended without the approval of the legislature. Simply put, without action by the legislature, most state governments would come to a halt. In recent years, the federal government has shifted more responsibility to state governments, with the result that state legislatures have become more important as policymaking bodies.

The Texas constitution makes the legislature the most important decision-making body in the state. The framers of the 1876 constitution distrusted government generally, but they were especially leery of executive authority and gave more power to the legislature than to the executive. This does not mean that the office of governor is insignificant in state politics. Governors play an important role. However, whatever power the governor of Texas possesses is derived primarily from informal, not formal, sources (see Chapter 23).

THE SIZE OF THE TEXAS LEGISLATURE

The Texas legislature consists of two houses. The Texas senate has 31 members elected for four-year overlapping terms; half the membership is elected every two years. The Texas house of representatives now consists of 150 members elected for two-year terms. The first house, elected following the adoption of the 1876 constitution, consisted of 93 members. After 1880, a new house seat was added for every 50,000 inhabitants until the membership reached 150 members.[1]

State legislatures vary in size. Nevada has the smallest senate, with 21 members, and Minnesota has the largest, with 67. Lower-house membership ranges from 41 in Delaware to 400 in New Hampshire. The New Hampshire house is unusually large—the next largest house is Pennsylvania's, at 203 members.[2] The median size of state senates is 40 members; for the lower houses, the median size is 100.

The size of state legislatures raises several issues. Large bodies might promote the representation of diverse interests within the state; however, statewide interests might go unrepresented. Large legislatures also can become inefficient at decision making or, in part because of inefficiency, be dominated by a few members. There is no doubt that decision-making dynamics depend on the size of the legislative body. The Texas senate, with 31 members, generally is regarded as sedate and genteel in its proceedings. Historically, few people have dominated it, and senators act relatively independently. While the Texas lieutenant governor is powerful, his power comes from the senate rules. The house, on the other hand, generally is more "disputatious" in its proceedings and historically is dominated by the speaker of the house.

METHODS OF ELECTION

single-member districts
System in which voters elect one member of the legislature from a district.

Members of legislative bodies most often are elected from **single-member districts.** Under this system, each legislative district has one member in the legislative body. Texas has 31 senatorial districts and 150 house districts. The voters living in these districts elect one house member and one senate member to represent their district. This system allows for geographical representation—all areas of the state choose representatives to the state legislature. In 2002, each house member in Texas represented about 139,000 citizens, and each state senator represented about 673,000 citizens. Figures 22–1 and 22–2 show the details of the single-member election districts in the major metropolitan areas of the state. Figures 22–3 and 22–4 show the senate and house districts for the entire state.

multimember districts
System in which voters elect more than one member of the legislature from a district.

Some states use **multimember districts** for some legislative elections. Twelve percent of all lower-house districts are multimember districts, but only 3 percent of senate seats are filled from multimember districts.[3] While multimember election methods vary widely, the most common method is to elect two or three members per district. Voters get one vote for each seat in the multimember district, and more than one state representative represents each voter. Table 22–1 shows the various multimember district systems used in other states.

The Texas house chamber.

The Texas senate chamber.

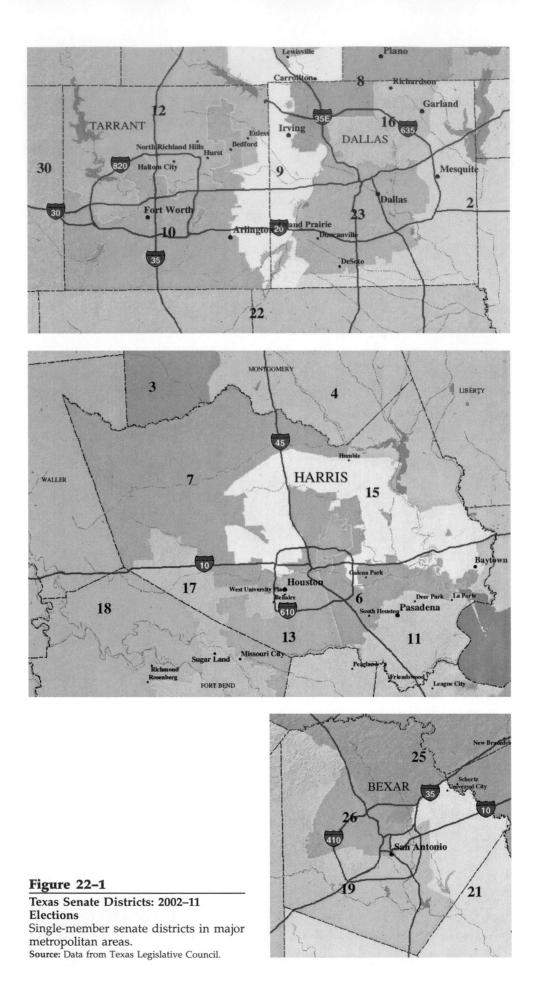

Figure 22–1

Texas Senate Districts: 2002–11 Elections

Single-member senate districts in major metropolitan areas.

Source: Data from Texas Legislative Council.

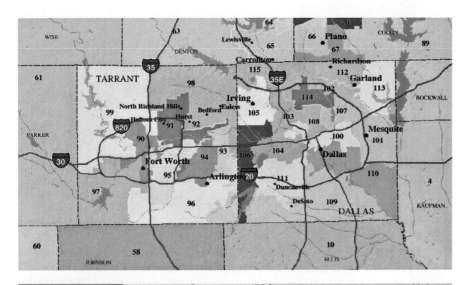

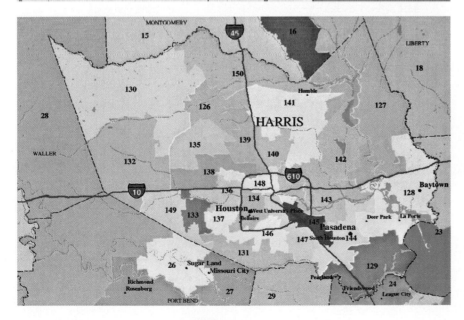

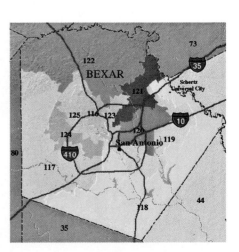

Figure 22–2

Texas House of Representative Districts: 2002–11 Elections
Single-member house districts in major metropolitan areas.
Source: Data from Texas Legislative Council.

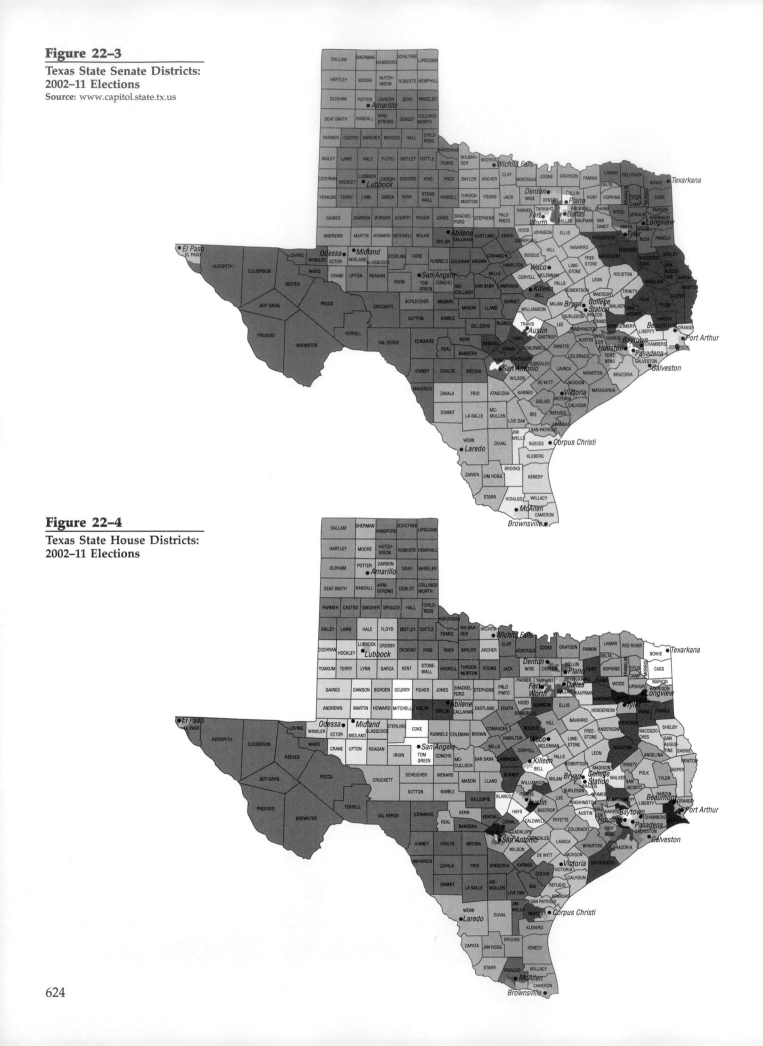

Figure 22–3

Texas State Senate Districts:
2002–11 Elections

Source: www.capitol.state.tx.us

Figure 22–4

Texas State House Districts:
2002–11 Elections

TABLE 22–1	Multimember State Legislative Districts		
STATE	LEGISLATIVE BODY	NUMBER OF MULTIMEMBER DISTRICTS	LARGEST NUMBER OF SEATS IN A DISTRICT
Arizona	House	30 of 30	2
Arkansas	House	3 of 96	2
Idaho	House	35 of 35	2
Maryland	House	44 of 63	3
Nevada	Senate	5 of 16	2
New Hampshire	House	99 of 193	11
New Jersey	House	40 of 40	2
North Carolina	Senate	8 of 42	2
North Dakota	House	49 of 49	2
South Dakota	House	35 of 35	2
Vermont	Senate	10 of 13	6
	House	41 of 109	2
Washington	House	40 of 40	2
West Virginia	House	23 of 56	7
	Senate	17 of 17	2

Source: National Council of State Legislatures, www.ncsl.org.

REAPPORTIONMENT AND REDISTRICTING ISSUES

The U.S. Constitution requires that Congress reapportion the seats in the U.S. House of Representatives among the states following each federal census (every ten years). The Texas constitution likewise requires the state legislature to reapportion the seats following each federal census.[4] Two terms usually used to describe this process are *reapportionment* and *redistricting*. The term *reapportionment* refers to the process of allocating representatives to districts; *redistricting* refers to the drawing of district lines. The terms generally are interchangeable and will be used interchangeably in this text.

Apportioning seats in any legislative body is a highly political process. Each interest within the state tries to gain as much as possible from the process. Existing powers, such as the majority party in the legislature, try to protect their advantages. Incumbent legislators try to ensure their reelection. The primary issues raised by reapportionment are equity of representation, minority representation, and gerrymandering (drawing district boundaries for political advantage).

Equity of Representation

The issue of **equity of representation** is not new; it is perhaps as old as legislative bodies. Thomas Jefferson noted the problem in the Virginia legislature in the eighteenth century.[5] During most of the nineteenth century, legislative apportionment most often resulted in equity. Each representative represented an equal number of citizens. Some states had provisions that limited the number of seats a single county could have. In the early twentieth century, population shifted from rural to urban areas, and gradually the rural areas became overrepresented

equity of representation
Situation where each member of a legislative district represents about the same number of people.

in many state legislatures. In the 1960s, only two states (Wisconsin and Massachusetts) had rural/urban representation in the legislature that equaled population distributions in the state.[6]

From 1876 until the 1920s, the Texas legislature made an effort to reapportion the seats after each census. This process was made easier by the addition of one seat for each increase of 50,000 in the population. From 1880 until 1920, a total of 57 seats were added to the legislature, bringing the total to 150 members. However, in 1930 and 1940, the legislature failed to reapportion legislative seats, and no new seats were added. Thus, in 1951 Texas legislative seats had not changed for thirty years.[7] Major population shifts from rural to urban areas, however, had occurred, especially during and immediately after World War II. These shifts in population created a serious disparity in representation between rural and urban areas of the state. Most urban counties were vastly underrepresented.

In an attempt to resolve the inequality of representation in the state, the Texas constitution was amended in 1948 to create the **Legislative Redistricting Board (LRB).** This board was given the authority to reapportion the seats in the state house and senate if the legislature failed to act. The LRB is made up of the lieutenant governor, the speaker of the house, the attorney general, the comptroller of public accounts, and the commissioner of the general land office.[8]

The creation of the LRB and the threat of action forced the legislature to act in 1951. Representation shifted from rural to urban areas, but large urban counties were still underrepresented in 1952. This underrepresentation was due in part to a 1936 amendment to the Texas constitution that limited the number of representatives any county could have to seven until the population reached 700,000, at which point the county could have one additional representative for each 100,000 increase in population.[9] For example, in 1952, if apportionment had been based on population alone, each state representative would have represented about 50,000 people. This means that Dallas County would have increased from seven to twelve representatives, Harris County from eight to sixteen, and Bexar County (San Antonio) from seven to ten. The constitution also prohibited any county from having more than one senator, no matter how large the county's population.

In 1962, in *Baker v. Carr,* the U.S. Supreme Court decided that these inequalities in the apportionment of legislative districts denied voters "equal protection of the law" and ruled that "as nearly as practicable, one man's vote would be equal to another's."[10] Two years later, in *Reynolds v. Sims,* the court ruled that both houses of state legislatures had to be apportioned based on population. The court rejected the analogy to the U.S. Senate, which is based on geographic units, saying "Legislators represent people, not trees or acres. Legislators are elected by voters, not farms or cities or economic interests."[11] These two cases forced all states to redistrict based on population and led to the "one person, one vote" rule. Over time, the general rule on reapportionment became that legislative districts could vary no more than 5 percent, plus or minus, from the mean population for districts. In Texas in 2002, the deviation from the mean for house districts was 2.65 percent and for senate districts 2.60 percent.

In 1965, a federal district court ruled that the provisions in the Texas constitution that limited a county to seven house seats and one senate seat were unconstitutional.[12] This court action forced the apportionment of both houses of the Texas legislature to be based on population. The political consequences of these court decisions shifted power from rural to urban areas. The impact of these decisions on the makeup of today's Texas legislature is discussed later in this chapter.

By the 1970s, the issue of equity of representation had been settled and is no longer of concern. With advancements in computers, drawing districts with

Legislative Redistricting Board (LRB)
State board composed of elected officials that can draw new legislative districts for the house and senate if the legislature fails to act.

approximately the same number of people is quite easy. Other issues—just as contentious—have replaced the equity issue.

Minority Representation

Another issue raised by redistricting is **minority representation.** Not only should legislative districts be approximately equal in population, they should also allow for minority representation. This issue was first raised in Texas in the 1970s when Texas used multimember districts in some large urban counties. Multimember districts in Texas were invalidated by court actions.[13]

The 1981 session of the legislature produced a redistricting plan that advanced minority representation in both houses. However, Republican Governor Bill Clements vetoed the senate plan, and the Texas supreme court invalidated the house plan. This forced the Legislative Redistricting Board to draw new districts. The new plan was challenged in federal courts and by the U.S. Justice Department, which ruled that the plan violated the federal Voting Rights Act because it did not achieve maximum minority representation. African Americans and Mexican Americans felt that the plan diluted their voting strength. A new plan, drawn up by federal courts, maximized minority representation by creating districts that contained a majority of ethnic minorities—"majority-minority" districts.

> **minority representation**
> Requirement that in drawing legislative districts racial and ethnic minorities should be given seats to which they can elect representatives.

Political and Racial Gerrymandering

Political party gerrymandering is the drawing of legislative districts to achieve the political advantage of one political party over another. Racial gerrymandering refers to the drawing of legislative districts to achieve an advantage for racial minorities. The practice dates to the early days of the Republic. In 1812, Governor Elbridge Gerry of Massachusetts drew a legislative district shaped somewhat like a salamander. A political cartoonist for the *Boston Globe* dressed up the outlines of the district with eyes, wings, and claws and dubbed it a "Gerrymander" (see Figure 11–5).

With the rise of the Republican party, political gerrymandering in Texas has intensified. Until 2003, Republicans repeatedly charged that the Democrats had reduced the number of potential Republican districts, especially in suburban areas. In the 1980s, the Republicans forged alliances with minority groups. Republicans supported the creation of **racially gerrymandered majority-minority districts,** and minority groups supported Republican efforts. It turned out that the creation of majority-minority districts aided the Republicans as well as minorities.

A legal challenge to overturn the practice of creating majority-minority districts has been reviewed by the U.S. Supreme Court.[14] This challenge was aimed at U.S. congressional districts rather than state house and senate districts, but it eventually will affect these as well. In ruling against three Texas U.S. congressional districts, the Court gave several reasons. Writing for the majority, Justice Sandra Day O'Connor stated that these districts were "formed in utter disregard for traditional redistricting criteria" (compactness) and that the shapes of the districts "are ultimately unexplainable on grounds other than the racial quotas established for these districts," resulting in "unconstitutional racial gerrymandering." Justice O'Connor also stated in her opinion that "districts can be oddly shaped but not bizarrely so."[15] While such a vague legal "standard" does not provide clear guidance, the Court is establishing a limit to the use of race as a criterion for drawing legislative district lines.

> **political party gerrymandering**
> Drawing legislative districts to advantage a political party.

> **racially gerrymandered majority-minority districts**
> Legislative districts drawn to advantage a minority group.

In April 2001, the U.S. Supreme Court, in *Hunt v. Cromartie*[16], placed further limitations on the use of racial gerrymandering in drawing legislative districts. The Court said that while race can be a factor, it can't be the primary factor in determining the makeup of legislative districts. Partisan makeup can be a primary factor; race cannot. This is an obvious departure from the past practice of packing minorities into safe districts. This new court ruling clearly reduced the practice of racial gerrymandering. However, political party and race often coincide. It is now possible to pack minority Democrats into districts as long as your intent is politics and not race.

The fine art of gerrymandering has been with us since the development of political parties and will remain a part of the political landscape for years to come. Only the limits of political gerrymandering remain in question.

IMPACT OF REDISTRICTING

What impact has state redistricting had on the Texas legislature and, more generally, on Texas politics? Equity of representation has been achieved. Each member of the house and senate represents about the same number of people. Representation has shifted from rural to urban areas, especially to suburban areas around the major metropolitan centers. Initially, redistricting increased turnover in the state legislature. Turnover increased from around 30 percent in the 1960s to 40 percent in the 1970s; however, it declined to about 20 percent in the 1990s. The 2002 and 2004 election cycle resulted in less than 20 percent turnover in the Texas legislature, despite the drawing of new districts.

Redistricting has had an impact on minority representation in the Texas legislature. Redistricting efforts in the 1990s increased the number of majority-minority districts. This concentration of minority populations in districts has also had the effect of increasing the number of legislative districts that have an Anglo majority and that vote Republican.

RE-REDISTRICTING IN 2003

Redistricting normally takes place every decade following the new federal census. In the 2003 session, Republicans controlled both houses of the Texas legislature for the first time in 130 years and used their new control to redistrict the state's thirty-two U.S. congressional districts. This mid-decade redistricting, or re-redistricting, is unprecedented.

In the 2001 session of the legislature, Republicans in the senate had refused to approve any redistricting plans. The house and senate districts were drawn by the Republican-controlled Legislative Redistricting Board, which drew districts greatly favoring Republicans in both Texas house and senate elections. This board cannot redistrict congressional districts, and Governor Perry refused to call a special session in 2001 to consider the issue. Instead he stated that the matter was best left to the courts.

The congressional district map used in the 2002 election cycle was drawn by a special three-judge federal court. While the map might have favored Republicans in a majority of the districts, Democrats managed to win election in seventeen of the thirty-two districts, leaving the Republicans with fifteen districts. Five districts that heavily favored the Republicans were won by Democrats. With these unexpected results, U.S. House Majority Leader Tom DeLay, a Republican

Get Involved!

Know Your State Representative and Senator

You can view maps of the Texas Legislative Council's web page at www.tlc.state.tx.us/searchridistrin/redist.htm. Using the marker Red Viewer, you can retrieve all legislative maps as well as all proposed plans. Using the zoom feature, you can zoom in on your district. If you don't know the name of your representative or senator, you can find it by going to the main page for the state legislature and entering your zip code. This same website allows you to find out what bills your representatives have introduced, sponsored, or cosponsored. Read these bills and see if you agree that they should be passed. You can e-mail your representatives and let them know how you feel about this legislation. You can also watch your state representatives and senators during committee hearings by using streaming video.

Information about congressional districts is also provided on this website. You can examine the congressional districts before and after they were changed by the DeLay redistricting and see how your district changed.

from Sugarland, Texas, forwarded a plan to the Texas legislature in the 2003 session to redraw the 2001 court-ordered congressional district map.

The Texas house, under the direction of newly elected Speaker Tom Craddick, took up the cause, and a new congressional district map was reported out of committee. The Texas senate, under the direction of newly elected Lieutenant Governor David Dewhurst, did not debate the issue during the regular session due to the senate's two-thirds rule, which required that twenty-one members of the senate agree to allow a bill to be considered by the whole senate. Senate Democrats, with twelve members, refused to consider any such bills.

Texas house rules state that a quorum is two-thirds of the whole membership, or 100 members. A quorum must be present before the house can act. During the last week of the regular session in 2003, fifty-two Democrats left the state and took up residence in the Holiday Inn in Ardmore, Oklahoma. This boycott by the Democrats effectively prevented the house from acting, and the re-redistricting bill failed to pass. The boycott infuriated most of the state and national Republican leadership. Texas Rangers were sent to bring the renegades back to Austin, but all efforts failed. Despite much statewide opposition to continuing the re-redistricting battle, on June 19, 2003, Governor Rick Perry called a special session of the legislature, to begin June 30, to reconsider the re-redistricting proposal.

Despite many misgivings, on July 8, 2003, the Texas house quickly approved a new congressional map by a highly partisan vote of 83 to 62. In this first special session, Lieutenant Governor Dewhurst left in place the two-thirds rule for consideration of a bill on the senate floor.

As long as the Democrats held twelve seats, they could block the house-passed bill from being considered by the senate. However, several Democrats at first withheld their support for blocking the legislation. Some minority Democratic senators were offered passage of legislation favorable to their districts, and others were offered "safe" congressional seats in exchange for favoring re-redistricting. On July 15, 2003, Senator Bill Ratliff, a Republican from Mount Pleasant, joined ten Democrats in blocking the re-redistricting bill.

Great pressure was applied to Lieutenant Governor Dewhurst to drop the two-thirds rule, but many senators, both Democrats and Republicans, opposed the change. Newspapers across the state urged Dewhurst to hold the line and retain the rule. Statewide polls showed Governor Perry losing support over the re-redistricting issue.

On July 28, 2003, eleven Texas senators fled to Albuquerque, New Mexico. Two things prompted their action. First, they anticipated that the governor was going to adjourn the first special legislative session early and call a second special session immediately thereafter (which he did). The rumor was that the senate sergeant-at-arms had been ordered to lock the senators in the senate chamber as soon as the session was called to prevent them from busting a quorum. Second, Lieutenant Governor Dewhurst had stated that he would suspend the two-thirds rule for future sessions. A few hours after the second special session began and a quorum was present, the house passed the same redistricting bill it had passed in the first special session. The quick passage of the bill led some Democrats to question the fairness of the process, because no debate or discussion had been allowed.

Eventually, the Democratic senate boycott was broken, and the governor called a third special session that finally resulted in a new congressional map (see Figure 22–5). Although many predicted that the DeLay redistricting map would be found in violation of the federal Voting Rights Act because it split minority voters rather than concentrating them in majority-minority districts, they were wrong. U.S. Attorney General John Ashcroft issued a one-sentence letter saying that he did not object to the new map. Democratic Texas house members claim that the professional staff of the U.S. Justice Department did object to the map and have asked that the report be made public, but it has not been released. The report was later made public and became part of the court case. The U.S. supreme court directed that 4 districts in Texas be redrawn. See the Texas legislative web page for new districts.

Figure 22–5

U.S. Congressional Districts: 2004 Elections

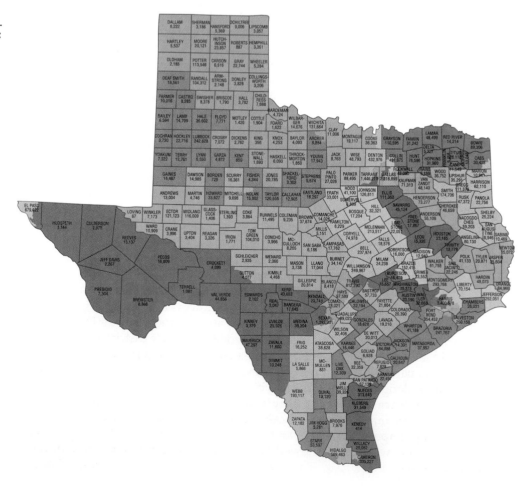

Get Involved!

Competition in State Legislative Races

There is almost no competition for state legislative seats, not only in Texas but in most states. The political party of your local senator and representative is selected by those drawing the district lines. U.S. Representative Tom DeLay used his influence to create safe seats for Republicans and gain control of the Texas house. This allowed DeLay to redraw Congressional District in the 2003 special session and to unseat five Texas congressmen and replace them with people he chose. As a voter, you have very little say in the primary election unless there is competition and almost no say in the general election. In the past, parties would gain or lose seats depending on their standing with the public. If the party that controlled the legislature lost favor with the public, it could be held accountable during elections by losing seats.

Several years ago, many citizens wanted to impose term limits on legislators, and a few states have done so. Some citizens feel term limits are a way of forcing incumbents out of office; however, most legislators voluntarily retire rather than suffer electoral defeat. Even with term limits or voluntary retirement, most legislative seats remain with the same political party. As a citizen, you should be concerned that elections have been made less meaningful. Citizens who support democracy should care very much about this recent turn of events.

A three-judge special court consisting of two Republicans and one Democrat approved the map, voting along party lines. The logic that prevailed in essence sets aside the Voting Rights Act by allowing minority voters to be divided into many congressional districts as long as the intention is to divide Democrats and not to divide minority voters. Partisan gerrymandering is considered legal. Because most minority-group members vote for Democrats, they can be split into many districts as long as the gerrymandering is partisan in intent. This decision established a new standard for redistricting on which the U.S. Supreme Court eventually will have to rule.

Governor Perry, Congressman Tom DeLay, and the Republicans were successful in their redistricting efforts. In the 2004 election, the Republicans gained five U.S. congressional seats and now control the Texas delegation to Congress, with twenty-one of the thirty-two seats. Democrats entered the decade with a seventeen to fifteen majority. All targeted Democrats either were defeated or chose not to run. Only Congressmen Chet Edwards and Lloyd Dogget won reelection in new districts. A new dimension has been added to the redistricting game: legislatures can redistrict any time to gain an advantage. It may very well be that rather than voters picking congressmen, congressmen will pick the voters they need to get elected.

QUALIFICATIONS FOR STATE LEGISLATORS

Setting aside for a moment the politics of state legislatures, let us examine the formal and informal qualifications for membership. Formal qualifications include age, citizenship, state residency, district residency, and qualified voter status. Among the states, the lowest minimum age for house membership is eighteen years, and the upper minimum age is twenty-five. Most states require U.S. citizenship, residency in the state for from one to five years, and district residency for a year or less.

A Texas house member must be a U.S. citizen, a registered voter, at least twenty-one years of age, and a resident of the state for two years and of the district for one year. To be a Texas state senator, a person must be twenty-six years of age and reside in the district for one year preceding the election and must have resided in the state for five years before the election.

The formal requirements are minimal and keep few citizens from serving in the state legislature. More important are informal qualifications that limit many people's ability to serve. These include income, education, and occupation. On these dimensions, state legislators tend not to represent the general population. Nationwide, state legislators tend to be well-educated male professionals (often lawyers).

Other dimensions, sometimes called "birthright" characteristics, include race, ethnicity, religion, and national background. On these dimensions, representatives tend to represent their district.[17] If the legislative district is predominantly Mexican American, the representative will likely be Mexican American. If the district is predominantly Anglo, the legislator is likely to be Anglo. The same is true for African American districts. Even though legislators generally represent their constituents based on these characteristics, legislators usually are better educated and come from selected occupational groups. Thus, legislators are *of the people* in terms of ethnicity but *above the people* in terms of income, education, and occupation. An African American legislator generally is better educated than his or her constituents and is drawn from a selected occupational group. For example, in the 2001 session of the Texas house, nine of the fourteen African Americans were attorneys, and sixteen of the thirty-one Mexican Americans were attorneys. All had a higher level of education than their constituents.[18] The same is also true of Anglo legislators.

Gender is another birthright characteristic. Nationally, the number of women serving in state legislatures has increased in recent years. In 2005, a total of 1,669 legislators, or 22.6 percent of all state legislators nationwide, were women, an increase of 2 percent since 1993 (see Table 22–2). In 1969, only 301 women (4 percent of all legislators nationwide) served in state legislatures.[19] In Texas, the number of women legislators has increased from one woman in each chamber in 1971 to thirty-six in both chambers in 2005 (See Table 22–3). Four are senators, and thirty-two are state representatives. There has been little change on the national level since 1997, when thirty women served in the House and three in the Senate.[20] (See "States in the Nation" in Chapter 11, page 000.)

The number of Hispanics and African Americans has also increased in legislatures across the nation, in part due to reapportionment. Both ethnic groups are underrepresented in the Texas legislature compared with their numbers in the population. In 2000, Hispanics made up 25 percent of the population of Texas and held 19.3 percent of the house seats and 22.5 percent of the senate seats. African Americans made up 13.4 percent of the Texas population and held 9.3 percent of the seats in the state legislature. (See "States in the Nation" in Chapter 5, page 000.)

Even with the changes in apportionment, minorities and women are still underrepresented in state legislatures. Most legislators are upwardly mobile white males. Most are from old, established, often very wealthy families. The state legislature is a good place to begin a political career, and having family and money helps launch that career. In addition, some professions, especially law, allow a person time to devote to legislative duties. Most states do not pay their legislators well, and having other sources of income is essential. Also, unlike the U.S. Congress, most state legislatures are part-time bodies, meeting for a set number of days annually or biennially. A survey by the National Conference of State Legislatures shows that most legislators do not consider themselves full-time legislators, although the number who do has been increasing nationwide. In Texas, only about 13 members identify themselves as full-time legislators (see Table 22–4).

TABLE 22–2	Women in State Legislatures, 1971 to 2005	
YEAR	NUMBER OF WOMEN	PERCENTAGE
1971	344	4.5%
1973	424	5.6
1975	604	8.0
1977	688	9.1
1979	770	10.3
1981	908	12.1
1983	991	13.1
1985	1,103	14.8
1987	1,170	15.7
1991	1.368	18.3
1993	1,524	20.6
1995	1,532	20.6
1997	1,605	21.6
1998	1,617	21.8
1999	1,664	22.4
2000	1,670	22.5
2001	1,666	22.4
2002	1,682	22.7
2003	1,654	22.4
2004	1,659	22.5
2005	1,669	22.6

Source: National Conference of State Legislatures and Center for American Women and Politics, www.cawp.org.

TABLE 22–3	Background of Members of the Texas Legislature, 2005	
	HOUSE	SENATE
Sex		
Male	118	27
Female	31	4
Race		
Anglo	104	22
Hispanic	30	7
African American	14	2
Asian	2	
Longevity		
Incumbent	132	31
Freshman	16	0
Party		
Democratic	63	12
Republican	86	19

Source: Texas legislature web page, www.lrl.state.tx.us

OCCUPATION	1999	2001	2003
TABLE 22–4 Background/Occupation of Texas State Legislators (Percentages), 1999–2003			
Full-time legislator	4.4%	2.6%	7.3%
Retired	1.6	0.6	2.6
Attorney	35.3	32.6	34.0
Business owner	17.6	11.3	12.6
Business executive/manager	9.3	10.0	5.3
Business, nonmanagement	1.6	6.6	8.6
Consultant/professional	4.9	6.0	11.3
Real estate	3.3	7.3	5.3
Insurance	7.7	7.3	3.3
Farmer/rancher	3.3	4.6	3.3
Educator, K–12	1.1	1.3	0.0
Educator, college	1.6	1.3	2.6
Medical*	2.2	4.0	1.3
Government, employee, local	0.5	0.6	0.0
Government, employee, state	0.0	0.0	0.0
Homemaker	0.5	0.0	0.0
Engineer/architect	2.7	2.6	2.6
Accountant	0.5	0.6	0.0
Clergy	0.0	0.0	0.0
Labor union	0.0	0.0	0.0
Student	0.0	0.0	0.0
Not available	0.0	0.0	0.0
Insufficient information	1.6	0.6	0.0

Source: Texas legislature website, www.capitol.state.tx.us.

The percentage of attorneys in the Texas legislature (34.0 percent in 2003) is much higher than in the average state legislature (16.5 percent). In addition, Texas has fewer full-time legislators. Texas legislators are not well paid ($7,200 per year), which might contribute to their feeling that their legislative jobs are only a part-time pursuit. A higher-than-average percentage of businesspersons serve in the Texas legislature, and a lower-than-average percentage of school-teachers. In some states, state employees can serve in the state legislature and keep their jobs as teachers, but this is prohibited in Texas. A Texas state employee may not hold an elective and an appointive office and receive pay for both.

GETTING ELECTED

We now turn our attention to what it takes to get elected. In Chapter 21, we saw that running for office can be costly. Although most candidates for the state legislature face little or no opposition in either the primary or the general election, there are exceptions. Even candidates who do not face opposition are likely to collect large amounts of money from various groups, especially from PACs.

In the 2002 races for the Texas state legislature, house winners raised an average of $123,000 and senate winners raised an average of $450,000. The range for the house was from $11,500 to $1,973,830 for Speaker Tom Craddick. In the senate the range was from $31,989 to $2,102,633.[21]

Most money comes from contributors who live outside the senator's or representative's district. In the house, only seven members received 50 percent or more of their money from within the district. On average, only 19 percent of the money received by house members comes from within their districts. Speaker Craddick received only 1 percent from within his district. In the senate, three members received 50 percent or more from residents living in their district, and on average 22 percent of senators' money came from residents living in their districts. Races in both the house and the senate are financed by PACs and large contributors living outside the candidates' congressional districts.

Most candidates in house and senate races face little opposition in either the primary or the general election. In the house, ninety-six members (64 percent) received 100 percent of the vote in primary elections, and sixty-two members (41 percent) received 100 percent of the vote in the general election. Similar percentages are found in the senate, where twenty-one members (68 percent) received 100 percent of the vote in the primary. The general election, however, is more competitive for the senate. Only eight members (26 percent) received 100 percent of the vote.[22]

Members of the legislature receive money from PACs because of their incumbent status. They face little opposition in the primary and general elections. Incumbents' war chest of money serves to keep competition at a low level. In 2004, for example, few members of the Texas legislature faced opposition in the primaries or in the general election (see Table 22–5). Only a few members faced opposition in both the primary and the general election in either house. In the 2002 November elections, sixty-five house seats (43 percent) and twelve senate seats had major-party opponents in the general election. The 2002 elections had more contested races than usual because of redistricting and the number of open seats.

The lack of competition in Texas legislative races is the result of several factors. The major factor is the degree to which districts are politically and racially gerrymandered, creating safe election districts for both parties. This can be seen by comparing two characteristics of Texas legislative districts in 2002: the strength of party voting in the district and the percentage of the minority

| TABLE 22–5 | Primary and General Election Opponents by Party Affiliation in Texas House and Senate Races, 2004 |

	OPPONENTS IN PRIMARY		
	DEMOCRATS	REPUBLICANS	TOTAL
House	22	23	45 (30%)
Senate	3	1	4 (13%)

	OPPONENTS IN GENERAL ELECTION		
House	25		25 (17%)
Senate	3		3 (10%)

Source: Calculated from election returns, secretary of state web page.

Figure 22–6

Texas House of
Representatives Party
Competition in 2002

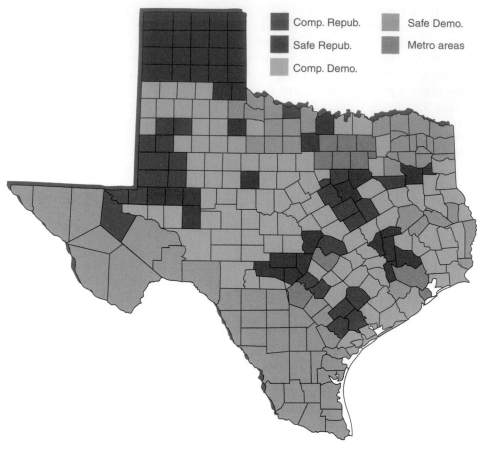

Figure 22–7

Texas Senate Party
Competition in 2002

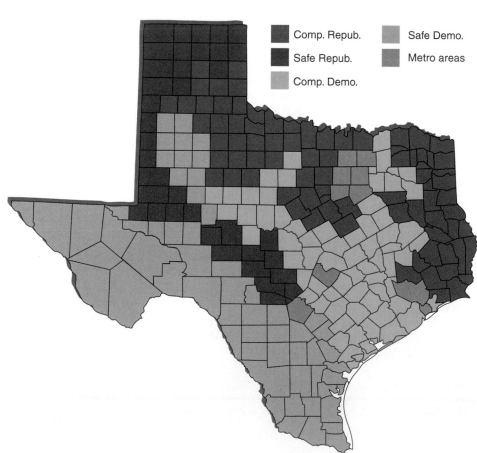

TABLE 22–6	Competitive and Noncompetitive Seats in the Texas House and Senate, 2002 Safe seats are those in which the combined party vote for all offices in the district was 55 percent or greater.		
	SAFE DEMOCRATIC	**SAFE REPUBLICAN**	**COMPETITIVE**
House	58 (39%)	55 (37%)	37 (24%)
Senate	11 (35%)	11 (35%)	9 (30%)

Source: Calculated from data on the home page of the Texas secretary of state, http://www.sos.state.tx.us.

population in the district. As Figures 22–6 and 22–7 clearly show, house and senate seats are clustered in **safe Democratic and safe Republican districts,** with only a few competitive seats.

Party voting is a measure of the strength of a political party in the legislative district based on voter support for the party's candidates in previous elections. It is also a measure of party competition. Studies of party competition in the U.S. House and Senate seats define as noncompetitive any district in which either party receives 55 percent or more of the votes. Thus, a district in which the party vote is between 44 and 54 percent is considered competitive.[23] The measure used here to gauge party competitiveness is the composite party vote, the combined vote received by either party for all offices/candidates in the district. Thus, a house or senate district in which the Republican party candidates for statewide office collectively received 55 percent or more of the votes is considered a safe Republican district. Table 22–6 shows the number of competitive and noncompetitive seats in the Texas house and senate in the 2002 election.

The second variable in the lack of competition in legislative races in Texas is the racial composition of the district. This is simply the percentages of the minority and nonminority populations in the district. Comparing party competition and minority population in the district using some simple statistics shows that most Texas house and senate seats fall into two categories—noncompetitive Republican Anglo districts and noncompetitive Democratic minority districts (see Figure 22–8). The creation of minority-majority districts results in the creation of safe Republican districts. Because minority support for Democratic candidates is always very high, concentrating minorities in districts also concentrates Democratic party support in these districts. Many remaining

safe Democratic and safe Republican districts
Noncompetitive districts that can only be won by the party with 55 percent or more of the votes in the district.

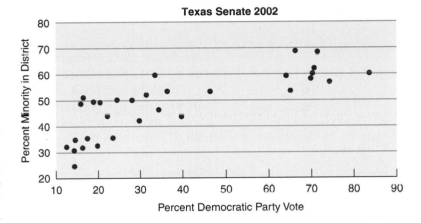

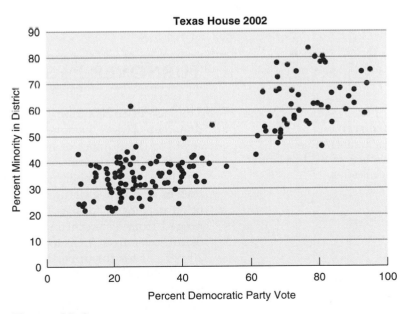

Figure 22–8

The Relationship Between Minorities and Party Votes
Each dot on the graph represents a legislative district. In the lower left are the high-Anglo, high-Republican voting districts, and in the upper right are the high-minority, high-Democratic voting districts. As the percentage of minority voters increases, the percentage of support for the Democratic party increases.

Media & Politics

Texas Legislature Blogs

The advent of the Internet has greatly increased the number and amount of information that is available on the Texas legislature while it is in session. A web search of Texas legislative blogs will yield several hundred. Some are from individuals who have an ax to grind about a special issue (e.g., http://www.thecarpetbaggerreport.com/archives/503.html). Others have more broad-based interest. For example, most of the major newspapers in the state have their own in-house blog that covers many issues (e.g., http://www.dallasnews.com/texassouthwest/legislature//). Still others are aimed at ethnic groups (e.g., http://latinosfortexas.com/blog/). A sample of these sites will provide you with a sample of opinions from all shades of the political spectrum.

districts are noncompetitive Republican districts. The same has been found to be true for U.S. congressional districts.[24]

Thus, the low level of competition in Texas legislative races is due in large part to racial and political gerrymandering. Competition in gerrymandered districts is most likely to occur at the primary level and in races with no incumbent. Competition in the general election is less likely. Safe Democratic districts exist primarily in two places: in South Texas, where there are concentrations of Mexican Americans, and in inner-city districts. Republicans are strong in the Panhandle and in the German Hill Country. Metropolitan areas of the state also contain both safe Democratic and safe Republican districts—Democratic in the inner city and Republican in the suburbs. Unless legislators are in a competitive district, they generally can serve as long as they like. Most voluntarily retire after a few years of service.

TURNOVER IN STATE LEGISLATURES

turnover

The number of new members of the legislature each session.

The lack of competition for Texas legislative seats could lead you to conclude that there is low turnover of the membership. This is not the case. **Turnover** refers to the number of new members of the legislature each session. Turnover is high in all state legislatures and normally is higher for the lower house than for the upper chamber.[25] In elections from 1992 to 1998, turnover in the lower houses of state legislatures ranged from a low of 2 percent in Alabama to a high of 58 percent in Alaska. The average is about 30 percent. State senate turnover ranged from 4 percent in Maryland to 70 percent in Arizona. The median rate of turnover from 1992 to 2002 was 25 percent for the lower house and about 20 percent for the upper house.[26]

Table 22–7 lists the number of years of service for members of the Texas legislature. In 2003, almost 48.5 percent of the house and 57 percent of the senate had served less than five years. Over time, turnover rates in Texas are very high. The turnover rate in 2003 was one of the smallest, with only four new house members and one new senator. Turnover is not due mainly to electoral defeat; rather, most members voluntarily retire from service. Retirement is prompted by poor pay, the lack of professional staff assistance, redistricting, the requirements of the job, the demands on one's family, fund-raising demands,

TABLE 22–7	Years of Service of Members of the Texas Legislature, 2003			
	HOUSE		**SENATE**	
1ST YEAR OF SERVICE	**NUMBER**	**PERCENTAGE**	**NUMBER**	**PERCENTAGE**
1979 or before	7	4.7	1	3.2
1981–85	10	6.7	2	6.5
1987–89	12	8.0	5	16.1
1991	18	12.0	2	6.5
1993	13	8.7	5	16.1
1995	20	13.3	3	9.7
1997	18	12.0	4	12.9
1999	9	6.0	3	9.7
2001	36	24.0	4	12.9
2003	36	24.0	4	12.9

Sources: Texas house of representatives, http://www.house.state.tx.us/members; Texas senate, http://www.senate.state.tx.us

and the rigors of seeking reelection.[27] Some use the office as a stepping-stone to higher office and leave to become members of Congress or to take statewide office (see Table 22–8).

Why is turnover significant in state legislatures? It can be argued that high turnover contributes to the amateurish nature of state legislatures and reduces their effectiveness. In recent years, this has been especially significant in those states where term limits have kicked in. If 20 percent to 25 percent of the members of the legislature are new each session, these new members are learning the rules and finding their way, allowing a few "old-timers" to control the legislative process.

TABLE 22–8	Continuity and Turnover in the Texas Legislature, 2001 and 2003			
	SENATE	**HOUSE**	**SENATE**	**HOUSE**
	2001		**2003**	
Continuity				
Seat not up for reelection	15	0	0	0
Incumbent won election	14	145	26	141
Turnover				
Died	0	0	0	0
Retired	1	4	4	9
Sought other office	0	1	1	0
Lost primary election	0	1	0	0
Lost general election	0	0	0	0

Source: Data from secretary of state web page, http://www.sos.state.tx.us.

CHARACTERISTICS OF STATE LEGISLATURES

Term Limits

term limits

Laws in twenty-one states that limit the number of times a person can be elected to an office in the state legislature.

Although turnover in state legislatures is quite high nationwide, in recent years voters have supported formal term limits for state legislators. From 1990 to 1996, twenty-one states approved **term limits** for both house and senate seats. Fourteen of these states have imposed term limits through constitutional amendments and seven by statute.[28] These limits were approved despite the fact that self-limiting of terms had been working for many years. For example, "nationally, 72 percent of the house members and 75 percent of the senators who served in 1979 had left their respective chamber by 1989."[29] Most legislatures in fact have self-imposed term limits.

Sessions

biennial sessions

Meetings of the legislature every two years in regular session.

The Texas legislature meets in **biennial sessions** (every two years) lasting 140 days in odd-numbered years, beginning in January. Texas is one of only six states that still meet in biennial sessions. Arkansas, Montana, North Dakota, Nevada, and Oregon are the others. In recent years, the trend has been toward annual sessions. At the end of World War II, only four states held annual sessions. There were twenty state legislatures meeting annually by 1966 and forty-two by 1974.[30]

Voters in Texas rejected a move to annual legislative sessions in 1969 and again in 1972. In keeping with the traditionalistic/individualistic political culture of the state, there is some concern that the more often the legislature meets, the more damage it can do. One political wag once remarked that there was a typographical error in the original Texas constitution and that the founders had intended the legislature to meet for two days every 140 years.

sine die

Requirement that the legislature must adjourn at the end of the regular session and cannot continue to meet.

At the end of the 140-day session, the Texas legislature must adjourn (**sine die**) and cannot call longer sessions. In recent years, many state governments have placed limits on the number of days the legislature can stay in session. Thirteen states place no limit on the length of legislative sessions.[31] Another important factor is the ability of the legislature to call itself into special session. In Texas and twelve other states, the legislature cannot call itself into special session. The lack of ability to call special sessions makes the limit on the regular session even more meaningful—the legislature must finish its work in the prescribed time and then leave.

special sessions

Sessions called by the governor to consider legislation proposed by the governor.

In Texas, only the governor can call **special sessions,** of not more than thirty days each. There is no limit on the number of special sessions the governor can call. The governor also decides the subject matter of the session, thereby limiting the range of topics the legislature can consider. This gives the governor of Texas tremendous power to set the agenda of the legislature during special sessions as well as a bargaining chip to get the legislature to do what the governor wants. The inability of the Texas legislature to call itself into special session (called **extraordinary sessions**) also gives the governor stronger veto powers. If a bill is vetoed by the governor and the legislature has adjourned, the veto stands. This in part explains why so few vetoes by the governor are overridden.

extraordinary sessions

Legislative sessions called by the legislature rather than by the governor. Not used in Texas.

States like Texas that limit the number of days of regular legislative sessions often are forced to resort to special sessions. Budgetary problems, reapportionment issues, school finance, and prison funding have forced the Texas legislature to hold many special sessions in the past decades. Many critics of the Texas

Debating the Issues

Should the Legislature Meet in Annual Sessions?

Texas and five other states have biennial sessions of the legislature. Most of these meet in odd-numbered years following the November general election. Before World War II, most states met in biennial sessions; only four met annually. Voters in Texas have twice (1966 and 1974) rejected approval of a constitutional amendment that would provide for annual sessions. Some people feel that the more often the legislature meets, the more damage it can do. At the end of the 140-day session, the legislature must adjourn and cannot call itself back into special session. Only the governor can call special sessions, and he or she sets the agenda. Should Texas follow the lead of other states and move to annual sessions?

Yes The current session is one of the longest sessions among the states. The first 60 days of the session are not very productive. Most of the time is spent on agenda setting and few bills are passed. Having annual sessions would enable the legislature to divide up the work between the two sessions, with some subject matters included in one session, and other types of bills in the other.

Also, budgeting for a two-year period can prove difficult, especially considering the nature of the state revenue system. Most revenue comes from taxes placed on consumer goods, and economic conditions can change quickly. During the 1980s, bad economic times forced the legislature to meet in five special sessions to deal with financial matters. Annual sessions would make the process more continuous as the same group of legislators would be involved in both sessions in a two-year period.

No Annual sessions would be more costly. The legislature would become a continuous body, and staff and other personnel would have to be added. Lobbying activity would become a continuous process and would give the lobby yet more power in Austin. Some people think the legislature does enough damage meeting every two years and would simply do more damage to the interests of the average Texan. Legislators would demand more pay, because they would have to work almost full time. This would further erode the concept of the citizen legislature.

biennial sessions point to the frequency of special sessions as evidence that the state needs to go to annual sessions. State revenues are closely tied to economic conditions in the state and predicting state revenues for a two-year period is extremely difficult.

Salaries

Some citizens feel that because the legislature meets for only 140 days every two years, it is a part-time body and its members should be paid accordingly. Legislative pay reflects this attitude. Texas pays the 181 members of the legislature $7,200 a year plus an additional $124 per day for the first 120 days the legislature is in session. In years when the legislature meets, the total compensation is the $7,200 in salary plus the $14,880 in per diem pay, for a total of $22,080. The Texas Ethics Commission recommends the per diem rate. In recent years, it has used the per diem rate set by the federal government for travel. Most legislators must have a second home in Austin during the legislative session, so the per diem pay is not high. Housing costs in Austin are among the highest in the state.

TABLE 22–9	Legislative Salaries in the Ten Most Populous States
STATE	**ANNUAL SALARY, 2002**
California	$99,000
Texas	7,200
New York	79,500
Florida	27,900
Pennsylvania	61,889
Illinois	55,788
Ohio	53,706
Michigan	77,400
North Carolina	14,951
Georgia	16,200

Source: Council of State Governments, *The Book of the States 2003* (Lexington, Ky.: Council of State Governments, 2003), vol. 35, 127–8, Table 3.9.

In years when the legislature is not in session, legislators receive their $7,200 in salary and may receive some additional per diem pay for off-session committee work and special sessions.

The salary of the Texas legislature has not been increased in the past thirty years. Several attempts to change the state constitutional limit have been rejected by the voters. Low pay contributes to the small number of legislators who consider themselves full-time (see Table 22–4). The current pay in Texas qualifies legislators who have no other income for food stamps and other federal assistance. Obviously, most legislators have other sources of income. Many are attorneys or successful business leaders. Lack of compensation is very much in keeping with the traditionalistic political culture of the state, according to which only the elite should serve in the legislature. As shown in Table 22–9, other southern states (Florida, Georgia, and North Carolina) also have low legislative salaries.

Most citizens are excluded from being legislators because they would not be able to devote the large amount of time to legislative work and still earn a living. Service in the Texas legislature is possible only for the independently wealthy, "political consultants," and those who can find a person or group to support them while they are in the legislature. In Texas, attorney-legislators who have cases in court while the legislature is in session can have their cases delayed until the legislature adjourns. Some attorney-legislators receive cases from people who want to delay court action. Unlike many other states, Texas does not have a financial disclosure law that forces members to disclose their sources of income, which leaves the sources of members' income an open question. Some might receive income as "consultants" to businesses with interests involved in current legislation. Speaker Craddick received pay as a consultant for oil companies while he carried a bill to reduce the franchise tax. The objectivity of members under these circumstances is in question.

Legislative pay in other states varies greatly. The states with the lowest salaries are New Hampshire ($100 per year), Alabama ($10 per day for the 105 days of the session), and Rhode Island ($5 per day for the 60 days of the session). At the high end are California, at $99,000 per year, and eleven other states that pay salaries of more than $30,000 per year (see Table 22–9).[32] Per diem expenses also vary greatly among the states. Texas, at $124 per diem, is at the high end. Four states pay no expenses, and some provide a fixed amount for the year. Most states also provide additional expenses and salary

Texas currently pays members of the state legislature only $600 per month. Among the fifteen large states, Texas has the lowest pay. Eleven states pay more than $30,000 per year. Many states pay less than Texas, some as little as $5 per day. Some, like New Mexico, pay only a per diem and no salary. Texas legislators currently receive $124 per day when in session or while doing interim committee work.

On two occasions in the last half of the twentieth century, voters in Texas rejected an amendment that would have let the legislature set its own salary by statute. This attitude is very much in keeping with the political culture of the state.

No

Citizens should be willing to serve their state without being drawn to the job by pay. Serving as a citizen legislator is in keeping with our founders' view of public service. One serves in the legislature and makes policy that is in the best interest of all citizens. A living wage would encourage members to become full-time legislators. They might broaden their view of their role from one of citizen legislators to one of professional legislators seeking to serve themselves rather than the public interest. Members currently receive a salary and per-day compensation that equal over $15,000 per year. This is not bad pay for a part-time job.

Yes

Low pay greatly limits the number of citizens who can serve in the legislature to a few wealthy citizens or those members who can afford to be away from their jobs for long periods of time. Lawyers who serve in the legislature can have any cases delayed as long as the legislature is in session. Some lawyer members are hired by people wanting to delay cases. Other members may be hired as consultants by companies seeking favors in the legislature. The average citizen, especially the working poor, is not represented in the legislature. If you examine the financial disclosure statements filed by members of the house and senate you will discover a plethora of millionaires. If the Texas legislature is to become a representative body as envisioned by the founders, the pay should be that of a living wage.

to people in leadership positions, such as committee chairs and presiding officers. Most states, including Texas, provide money to legislators for office and staff expenses, although there is great variation among the states.

At least forty-one states offer members of the legislature retirement benefits. In Texas, legislators' retirement pay is tied to the retirement pay of state district judges, which is tied to the judges' salaries. The Texas legislature sets the salary of district judges, and most sessions result in pay raises for district judges. This in turn produces an increase in retirement pay for legislators.

Texas appears to have the most generous retirement benefits among the states. Legislators can retire at sixty years of age with eight years of service, and at fifty-five years of age with twelve years of service. Compensation ranges from $5,000 to $7,000 per month depending on years of service and age at retirement. This high retirement pay might prompt some members to retire after putting in the minimum time. They can count on cost-of-living pay raises as the legislature increases the salaries of district judges. Additional increases can come from cost-of-living adjustments given to all state retirees. In short, an active member of the legislature is worth only $600 per month, but retirement can bring a pay increase of $5,000 to $7,000 per month.

Tom Craddick is the current speaker of the house. The speaker is elected every two years by a majority of the house members. Craddick is serving in his second term as speaker. He is the first Republican speaker of the house since 1875.

Get Involved!

From Lawmaker to Lobbyist in One Short Step: Harvest Time

"Three state lawmakers who lost or surrendered their House seats last year have resurfaced as lobbyists, collectively reporting 17 clients that are paying them up to $1.5 million this year."

"Medical interests coughed up most of the money reported by the two new lobbyists who made the biggest killing: Jaime Capelo and Arlene Wohlgemuth. This same industry may have been the leading beneficiary of these lobbyists' parting legislative session. In 2003 Rep. Capelo co-authored a Wohlgemuth-backed bill that now caps the damages paid by medical interests that commit malpractice."

"Two years later, the medical interests behind this legislation are the top clients of former lawmakers Capelo and Wohlgemuth. One of the main medical groups pushing medical malpractice caps, the Texas Alliance for Patient Access, is a leading client of Capelo, who has reported up to $925,000 in 2005 lobby contracts. Dominating Capelo's client list are medical businesses and associations, including PatientsFirst. This doctors' group fights turf wars to curtail competition from non-physicians, including psychologists, podiatrists and optometrists (the latter of which hired Wohlgemuth)."

"Wohlgemuth's other top clients include trade groups for hospitals, nurse anesthetists and the home care industry. Wohlgemuth gave up her statehouse seat in 2004 to challenge Democratic Congressman Chet Edwards. Edwards confounded Republican redistricting schemes by winning 51 percent of the vote—driving Wohlgemuth into the lobby."

Capelo reported contracts worth between $560,000 and $925,000, while Wohlgemuth reported contracts worth between $220,000 and $460,000. Former Rep. Telford, working for retired teachers, received much less, reporting between $100,000 and $150,000. In the last session, all three received only $7,200 per year in salary as members of the legislature.

Many more former legislators work as lobbyists. This revolving-door practice is common.

Source: Texans for Public Justice, www.tpj.org/page_view.jsp?pageid=927&pf=1.

FORMAL PROCEDURES OF THE LEGISLATURE

All legislatures have formal rules of procedure that govern their operations. These rules prescribe how bills are passed into law and make the process of passing laws more orderly and fair. The rules also make it difficult to pass laws. A bill must clear many hurdles before it becomes law. Rules that make it difficult to pass bills have two results: they prevent bills from becoming law without first undergoing careful review, and they preserve the status quo. In the traditionalistic/ individualistic political culture of Texas, formal procedural rules protect the ruling elite and enable them to control the legislative process. Thus, it is more important to understand the impact of rules on legislation than to have a detailed understanding of the actual rules. This is the basic approach used here to explain how laws are made in Texas.

Leadership Positions in the Texas Legislature

In any legislative body, those holding formal leadership positions possess considerable power to decide the outcome of legislation. In the Texas legislature, power is very much concentrated in the hands of two individuals: the speaker of the house and the lieutenant governor. These two individuals essentially control the output of legislation.

The speaker of the house and the lieutenant governor also have other, extra-legislative powers. They appoint members of other state boards or serve as members of those boards. For example, they appoint the members of the Legislative Budget Board, which writes the state budget, and they serve as the chair and vice-chair of this board. These are important powers, because these boards make policy. The state budget is a policy statement in monetary terms, deciding what agencies and programs will be funded and in what amounts.

Speaker of the House

The members of the house elect the speaker of the Texas house of representatives by majority vote. The election of the **speaker of the house** is the first formal act of the session. The secretary of state presides over the election. Only occasionally is the outcome of this election in doubt. Who the speaker will be generally is known far in advance of the beginning of the session, and this individual spends considerable time lining up supporters before the session begins. In almost all cases, the person elected is a longtime member of the house and enjoys the support of current members. When one-third of the members are new, the person elected speaker might also have to gain support from some of these new members. It is illegal for candidates for speaker to formally promise members something in exchange for their vote, but key players in the election of the speaker often receive choice committee assignments.

It should be noted that for many years the Texas house of representatives operated on a bipartisan basis. In the 2003 session, much of this bipartisanship disappeared when the Republicans gained a majority of the seats in the house and Representative Tom Craddick became speaker. In the 2001 session of the legislature, when Democrats controlled the house and Democrat Pete Laney was speaker, bipartisanship was much more apparent in committee assignments and in the overall tone of the session. In the 2003 session, partisanship was the order of the day, with the tone set by Speaker Craddick. Representative Dawnna Dukes (Democrat from Houston) stated that the Republicans did not feel the need to compromise on issues because they controlled a majority of the seats. This was especially evident on the issue of redistricting of the U.S. House seats.

Retiring Speaker Laney had served in the Texas house since 1973 and chaired several important committees. Incumbent speakers are almost always reelected. Usually, a new speaker is chosen only after the death, retirement, or resignation of a sitting speaker. Traditionally, speakers served for two terms and retired or moved to higher office. From 1951 to 1975, no speaker served more than two terms. In 1975, Billy Clayton broke with this tradition and served for four terms. Gib Lewis, who succeeded Clayton, served five terms.[33]

Many feel that speaker of the house is the most powerful position in Texas government. There is no doubt that the speaker is extremely powerful. Generally, the speakers has the power to direct what legislation passes the house. The speaker gains power from the formal rules adopted by the house at the beginning of each session. These rules allow the speaker to do the following:

- *Appoint the chairs of all house committees.*
- *Appoint most of the members of each standing committee.* About half of these committee seats are assigned based on a limited seniority system. In reality, the backers of the speaker often use their seniority to choose a committee assignment, thereby freeing up an appointment for the speaker.
- *Appoint members of the calendar and procedural committees, conference committees, and other special and interim committees.*
- *Serve as presiding officer over all sessions.* This power allows the speaker to recognize members on the floor who wish to speak, generally interpret house rules, decide when a vote will be taken, and decide the outcome of voice votes.
- *Refer all bills to committees.* As a rule, bills go to subject matter committees. However, the speaker has discretion in deciding what committee will receive

speaker of the house
Member of the Texas house elected by the house members to serve as presiding officer. Generally controls the passage of legislation.

a bill. Billy Clayton used the State Affairs Committee as his "dead bill committee." Bills assigned to this committee usually had little chance of passing. Likewise, the speaker can assign a bill to a favorable committee to enhance its chances of passing.

These rules give the speaker control over the house agenda. The speaker decides the chairs of standing committees, selects a majority of the members of all committees, and refers bills to committees. The selected chairs are members of the "speaker's team." Few bills pass the house without the speaker's approval. In the 2006 election, the Democrats won five new seats in the house giving them 71 seats to the Republican 80 seats. There is speculation that this is enough of a shift in seats to allow for a challenge of the current Speaker Craddick. Several members have indicated that they will challenge the speaker for the leadership of the House. However, with this small change, it is unlikely that the speaker will suffer defeat.

Lieutenant Governor

lieutenant governor
Presiding officer of the Texas senate. Elected by the voters of the state.

Unlike the speaker of the house, the **lieutenant governor** is elected by the voters for a four-year term in the general election. The lieutenant governor does not owe his or her election to the legislative body, is not formally a senator, and cannot vote in the senate except in the case of a tie. It might be assumed that the office is not a powerful legislative office. In most states this is true; however, the lieutenant governor in Texas possesses powers very similar to those of the speaker of the house. Lieutenant governors have power to do the following:

- *Appoint the chairs of all senate committees.*
- *Select all members of all senate committees.* No formal seniority rule applies in the senate.
- *Appoint members of the conference committees.*
- *Serve as presiding officer and interpret rules.*
- *Refer all bills to committees.*

David Dewhurst is serving in his second term as lieutenant governor. Lieutenant governors are elected by the voters for a four-year term in a statewide race.

On the surface, the lieutenant governor appears to be more powerful than the speaker. He does not owe his election to the senate, and he has all powers possessed by the speaker. The reality is different. The powers of the lieutenant governor are assigned by the formal rules of the senate, which are adopted at the beginning of each session. What the senate gives, it can take away. Lieutenant governors must play the delicate balancing act of working with powerful members of the senate and often compromising in the assignment of committee chairs and committee membership. The same is true for all the other powers. Thus, the lieutenant governor must forge an alliance with key senators to effectively utilize his or her powers.[34]

From 1876 to 1999, the Democrats controlled the lieutenant governor's office. They controlled the senate from 1876 to 1997. Until recently, party control was not a factor. It is often suggested that if the lieutenant governor and the senate are ever of opposite parties, the powers of the lieutenant governor could be diminished. Such concerns have been voiced in the past few years, and, given the pattern in other states, this possibility seems quite likely. A powerful lieutenant governor is unusual among the states. In only five other states—Alabama, Georgia, Mississippi, South Carolina, and Vermont—can the lieutenant governor appoint committee members and assign bills to committees. In Arkansas, the lieutenant governor can assign bills to committees but does not appoint committees.[35]

In most states the lieutenant governor is not a powerful leader. Eight states (Arizona, Maine, New Hampshire, New Jersey, Oregon, Tennessee, West Virginia, and Wyoming) do not have a lieutenant governor.[36] In the twenty-six states where the only legislative duty of the lieutenant governor is to serve as the presiding officer, most lieutenant governors attend a senate session only when their vote is needed to break a tie.[37] Most lieutenant governors are figureheads who stand in for the governor when she or he is out of state. In states where the lieutenant governor is a figurehead or where there is no lieutenant governor, the senate elects one of its members to be the presiding officer, called the pro tempore president of the senate or speaker of the senate. (In Tennessee, the speaker of the senate also holds the title of lieutenant governor.)

Thus, the office of lieutenant governor in Texas is quite different from the office in most other states. This has not always been true. J. William Davis, in his book *There Shall Also Be a Lieutenant Governor,* traces the concentration of power in this office to the actions of Allen Shivers and Ben Ramsey during the 1940s and 1950s. Apparently, over a period of several years the office gained power in the senate.[38]

The 1999 session was the first since Reconstruction in which Republicans held both the majority of the senate seats and the lieutenant governor's office. Lieutenant Governor Rick Perry retained the powers usually given to lieutenant governors. Retaining those powers depends on a lieutenant governor's ability to compromise and to get along with the thirty-one members of the senate. Republican senators ensured that Dewhurst kept these powers. It was not in the interests of the Republicans, with nineteen seats, to break with the lieutenant governor, because it takes twenty-one votes to bring a bill up for debate on the floor of the senate.

Committees in the House and Senate

Most of the work of the legislature is done in **standing committees** established by house and senate rules. Besides the standing committees, there are also

standing committees
Committees of the house and senate that consider legislation during sessions.

Many citizens mistakenly believe that state legislators spend a lot of time "goofing off."
SARGENT © 1994 Austin American-Statesmen. Reprinted with permission of Universal Press Syndicate.

conference committees
Joint committees of the
house and senate that work
out differences in bills
passed in each chamber.

interim committees
Temporary committees of the
legislature that study issues
between regular sessions and
make recommendations on
legislation.

subcommittees of the standing committees, **conference committees** to work out differences in bills passed by the two houses, temporary committees to study special problems, and **interim committees** to study issues between sessions of the state legislature. Of these, the standing committees are the most important. There are fourteen standing committees in the senate and forty-one in the house (see Table 22–10).

TABLE 22–10	Standing Committees of the Texas House and Senate, 2003 and 2005 Sessions
SENATE COMMITTEES	**HOUSE COMMITTEES**
Administration	Agriculture and Livestock
Business & Commerce	Appropriations
Subcommittee on Border Affairs	Border and International Affairs
Committee of the Whole Senate	Business and Industry
Criminal Justice	Calendars
Education	Child Welfare and Foster Care
Finance	Civil Practices
Health & Human Services	Corrections
Intergovernmental Relations	County Affairs
Jurisprudence	Criminal Jurisprudence
Natural Resources	Defense Affairs and State-Federal Relations
Subcommittee on Agriculture	Economic Development
Nominations	Elections
Redistricting	Energy Resources
State Affairs	Environmental Regulations
Veteran Affairs & Military Institutions	Financial Institutions
	General Investigating
	Government Reform
	Higher Education
	House Administration
	Human Services
	Insurance
	Judicial Affairs
	Juvenile Justice and Family Issues
	Land and Resource Management
	Licensing and Administrative Procedures
	Local and Consent Calendars
	Natural Resources
	Pensions and Investments
	Public Education
	Public Health
	Public Safety
	Redistricting
	Rules and Resolutions
	Select Committee
	State Affairs
	State Cultural and Recreational Resources
	State, Federal and International Relations
	Transportation
	Urban Affairs
	Ways and Means

Source: Texas Legislature Online, www.capitol.state.tx.us.

The chairs of the standing committees have powers similar to those of the speaker and lieutenant governor at the committee level. They decide the times and agendas for meetings of the committee. In doing so, they decide how much time is devoted to bills and which bills get the attention of the committee. A chair who strongly dislikes a bill often can prevent the bill from passing. Even if the bill is given a hearing, the chair can decide to give that bill to a subcommittee that might kill the bill.

Thus, as in most legislative bodies, in Texas the power is concentrated in a few powerful individuals who control the agendas and actions of the legislature. Few bills can pass the legislature without the support of these individuals.

Formal Rules: How a Bill Becomes Law

Figure 22–9 lists the formal procedures in the Texas house and senate for passing a bill. Each bill, to become law, must clear each step. The vast majority of bills that are introduced fail to pass. Few bills of major importance are passed in any given legislative session. Most bills make only minor changes to existing law.

At each stage in the process, a bill can receive favorable or unfavorable actions. At each step, a bill can die by either action or inaction. There are many ways to kill a bill but only one way to pass a bill. To pass, a bill must clear all hurdles.

Before the sixtieth day of the legislative session, a bill can clear the senate with a simple majority vote. Few bills pass before the sixtieth day. After the sixtieth day, before a bill can be considered on the floor of the senate a two-thirds vote is required. Technically, after the sixtieth day, senate rules state that bills must be considered in the order they are reported out of committee. If bills are not considered in the order reported out of committee, a two-thirds vote is required to change the order. By design, bills are never considered in the order reported out of committee. If two-thirds of the senators agree to consider the bill, it can pass by a simple majority. Because of this rule, few bills clear the senate that are not supported by more than a simple majority of the senators, making the senate a conserving force in the legislative process.

In some cases, the formal rules can be used to hide actions of the legislature. It is not uncommon in legislative bodies to attach **riders** to appropriations bills. A rider can be a subject matter item (creation of a new state regulatory board) or a budget item (money for a park in a legislator's district). In the Texas legislature, the practice has a new twist. Riders called **closed riders** can be attached to appropriations bills and not be made known to the public or media. They are closed to public inspection and appear only after the appropriation bills have passed the house and senate and go to conference committee. In the conference committee, the cloak is removed and the riders appear for public inspection for the first time. At this stage, which is always near the end of the session, the likelihood of change is remote. Unless the governor vetoes the bill, these closed riders become law without public comment.

A recent example of this is a rider that dealt with the Bush School at Texas A&M University. In the 1999 session of the legislature, the Bush School was separated from the College of Liberal Arts and made a separate school within the university, and its budget was increased by several million dollars. This was done at the request of Governor George W. Bush.

Major and Minor Calendars and Bills

To fully understand the legislative process, it is necessary to distinguish between major and minor bills, because state legislators treat them very differently. The Texas house has two different **calendars** for minor bills—the local calendar and the consent calendar. To be assigned to these calendars, a bill must meet tests

riders
Provisions attached to bills that might not be of the same subject matter as the main bill.

closed riders
Provisions attached to appropriations bills that are not made public until the conference committee meets.

calendars
Procedures in the house used to consider different kinds of bills. Major bills and minor bills are considered under different procedures.

Figure 22–9

Basic Steps in the Texas Legislative Process
This diagram displays the sequential flow of a bill from the time it is introduced in the house of representatives to its final passage and transmittal to the governor. A bill introduced in the senate follows the same procedure in reverse.

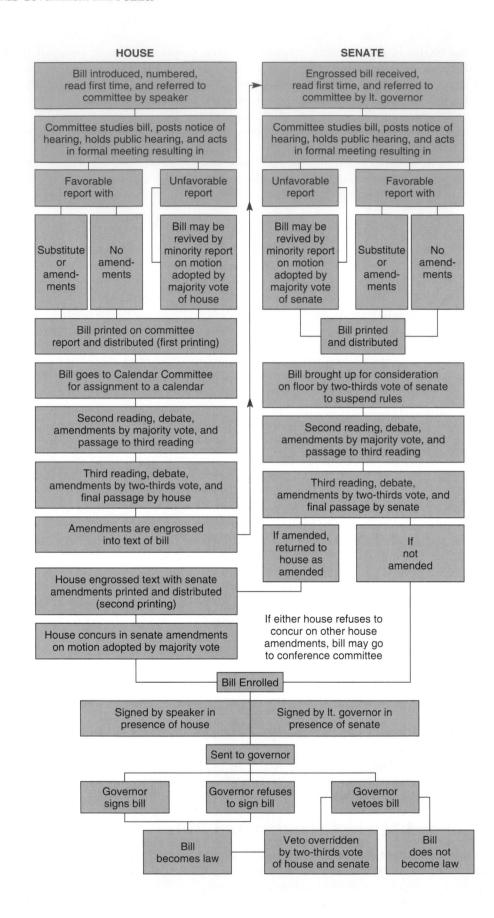

TABLE 22-11	Bill Survival in the 79th Session of Texas Legislature, 2005					
	SENATE BILLS	PERCENT	HOUSE BILLS	PERCENT	TOTAL BILLS	PERCENT
Total bills introduced	1,892	100%	3,592	100%	5,484	100
Committee action in origination chamber	1,139	60*	2,427	68	3,629	65
Passed by committee originating chamber	986	52	1,685	47	2,671	49
Floor consideration originating chamber	875	46	1,247	35	2,122	39
Pass originating chamber	861	46	1,186	33	2,047	37
Committee action in second chamber	747	39	986	27	1,733	32
Passed committee in second chamber	716	38	963	26	1,679	31
Floor consideration second chamber	538	28	903	25	1,441	36
Pass second chamber	522	28	900	25	1,422	26
Passed both	513	27	876	24	1,389	25
Passed into law	502	27	868	24	1,370	25
Vetoed	11		8		19	

Source: Adapted from Harvey J. Tucker, "Legislation Deliberation in the Texas House and Senate." Paper presented at Annual Meeting of Midwest Political Science Association, Chicago, Illinois, April 15-18, 2004. Data in this table updated for 2005 session by Harvey Tucker.

established by house rules. Local bills must not have an effect on more than one of the 254 counties in the state. Bills for the consent calendar must be minor, non-controversial bills. To be placed on either the local or the consent calendar, bills must meet two further criteria. First, they must receive unanimous support in the substantive house committee handling the bill. Second, the Local and Consent Calendars Committee must approve them. If this committee does not approve the bill, it is sent to the Calendars Committee (regular calendars) for assignment to another calendar. A bill can be removed from the local or consent calendar if there is objection by five members during floor debate or if debate exceeds ten minutes; in either case, the bill is withdrawn and effectively killed.[39] These procedures safeguard against important bills being approved without adequate review by the whole house.

There are three calendars for major bills: the emergency calendar, the major state calendar, and the general state calendar. The **Calendars Committee** alone has the authority to assign bills to these calendars, and this power is rarely challenged. The distinction among the major calendars is not important until the final days of the legislative session, when time is limited.

Table 22–11 demonstrates the fate of bills in the seventy-ninth session of the Texas legislature. As can be seen, only about 25 percent of all bills introduced in the house and senate make it into law. Most bills (66 percent) are introduced in the house. While the senate introduces only a third as many as the house, more make it into law (27 percent in the senate and 25 percent in the house). Along the way bills are not advanced. While most make it to a committee for deliberation (60 percent in the senate and 68 percent in the house), about a third are given approval at the committee level and are considered on the floor of either chamber (46 percent in the senate and 35 percent in the house). Most bills die at the committee level, and some are dead on arrival and never see the light of day.

Calendars Committee
Standing committee of the house that decides which bills will be considered for floor debate and to which committee bills will be assigned.

Some bills are introduced to satisfy a constituency, and the member has no intention of working to pass the bill.

Legislative Workload and Logjams

According to much of the literature on state legislatures, most bills pass the legislature in the final days of the session. This scenario suggests that the legislature "goofs off" for most of the session and then frantically passes bills just before adjournment, producing laws that are given only "hasty consideration, [are] of poor quality and are confused and inferior."[40]

In Texas, it is true that most legislation is passed in the final two weeks of the session. In 1985, almost 80 percent of all bills passed were passed in this time period. The question remains, does this result in poor quality and inferior legislation? The answer is probably not. It is necessary to understand the process of setting the agenda in the Texas legislature.

First, bills may be introduced at any time prior to the session and up until the sixtieth day of the 140-day session. After the sixtieth day only local bills, emergency appropriations, emergency matters submitted by the governor, and bills with a four-fifths vote of the house may be introduced. Thus, for the first sixty days the agendas for both houses are being set. After the sixtieth day, the legislature begins to clear these agendas. As indicated, most bills (68 percent) die in committee and are never assigned to a calendar. Killing a bill in committee is an action by the legislature, and it occurs at a regular rate during the session.[41] This leaves only 32 percent of all bills for further consideration later in the session. As Harvey Tucker observes:

> Once the agenda has been set it is cleared at a fairly even rate. Final action on most bills passed occurs at the end of the session by design. Conflicting and complementary bills are reconciled. Bills tied directly or indirectly to the state budget are delayed until the final days of necessity. The legislature is not able to appropriate funds until the Comptroller of Public Accounts certifies the amount of revenues that will be available. The "certification estimate" is not made until the very end of the legislative session, because, among other reasons, the estimate must be informed by any actions the legislature takes that would affect state revenues.[42]

Thus, the image of the legislature as goofing off for most of the session is not accurate. The nature of the legislative process requires the passage of major legislation near the end of the session. Also, about half the bills that pass toward the end of the session are minor bills, and they are cleared late for different reasons than the reasons for major bills.

INFORMAL RULES

informal rules
Set of norms or rules that govern legislative behavior.

In addition to the formal procedures, there are also **informal rules,** or legislative norms, that all state legislators must learn if they are to be successful. Examples include the following:

Do not:

- conceal the real purpose of a bill
- deal in personalities in floor debate
- be a thorn in the side of the majority by refusing unanimous consent
- speak on issues you know nothing about
- seek publicity from the press to look good to the people back home
- talk to the press about decisions reached in private[43]

Political Culture

You Better Be Good—the Lobby Is Watching

In the upper-right-hand gallery of the Texas house chamber, looking toward the speaker's podium, is a section "reserved" for the most powerful members of the lobby.

Some lobbyists are almost always there when business is being conducted on the floor. They watch members of the house, and the house members know they are being watched. Members sometimes are contacted by these lobbyists and "encouraged" to vote right.

Members of the house call this space the "Owners' Box."

Each legislature will have a different set of norms and will place a different value on them. Dealing in personalities during floor debate was viewed as acceptable behavior by a large number of Texas legislators, whereas in the other states only a few members viewed this behavior as acceptable.[44] Legislators must learn the norms of their legislature and adhere to them. Otherwise, they might find themselves isolated and ineffective. The informal rules are as important as the formal rules governing the conduct of the legislature.

ROLE-PLAYING

Members of the legislature are expected to play many roles during the legislative session. We have already discussed formal leadership roles. Each speaker will approach the job differently. Historically, most speakers have exerted very tight control over the house. This was true of Billy Clayton, speaker from 1975 to 1983. However, Gib Lewis, who followed Clayton, exerted much less control. He allowed the members of his team—namely, committee chairs—to control the process while he himself took a much more "laid back" approach. Pete Laney was more like Billy Clayton in that he controlled the house. Speaker Tom Craddick, of Midland, plays a role similar to that of Speakers Laney and Clayton, only with a stronger partisan use of power.

There can also be great differences in the leadership styles of lieutenant governors. For instance, Bill Hobby, the son of a former governor, served as lieutenant governor for eighteen years (1972–90). Hobby, a very quiet-spoken, low-key person, seldom forced his will on the members of the senate, preferring to work behind the scenes and forge compromises. Hobby chose not to run for reelection in 1990, and Bob Bullock succeeded him. Bullock had served for sixteen years as the state comptroller and had developed a reputation for strong, effective leadership, but he often went out of his way to make enemies. Bullock's leadership style as lieutenant governor was almost the opposite of Hobby's. Stories have circulated of shouting matches and angry behavior, sometimes even in open sessions of the senate. The senate seemed to adjust to Bullock's style of leadership, however, and he managed to get much of his agenda passed. Hobby and Bullock illustrate very different ways to be effective leaders of the state senate.

Rick Perry, while serving as Texas agricultural commissioner, did not have the reputation of a compromiser, but he performed quite effectively in the 1999 session. Lieutenant Governor Dewhurst was something of a political unknown, having served only four years as land commissioner prior to his election in 2002.

Dewhurst's performance received mixed reviews. He was an effective leader in the regular session and exhibited partisanship in the three special sessions and the regular session in 2005. Despite weak performances, Republican leaders have ensured that Dewhurst will keep the broad powers normally given to lieutenant governors.

Leadership in legislative bodies can take many forms. In addition to formal leadership roles, some members develop reputations as experts in certain areas of legislation and are looked to by other members as leaders in those areas. Being recognized by other members as the expert in some area of legislation obviously increases a legislator's influence. For instance, a member who is a recognized expert on taxation issues can use this reputation to forge coalitions and pass tax legislation.

Representational Roles

delegates

Representational role of members that states that they represent the wishes of the voters.

trustees

Representational role of members that states that they will make decisions based on their own judgment about what is best for voters.

Constituencies have expectations about their legislators' role. For centuries, members of legislatures have argued about the representational role of a legislator. Whom do legislators represent? Are they **delegates,** sent by the voters to represent the voters' interests, or are they **trustees,** entrusted by the voters to make decisions based on their best judgment? The delegate role is perceived as being more democratic—as doing what the people want. The trustee role can be characterized as elitist—as doing what the politician thinks is best.

In reality, members may play either the delegate role or the trustee role depending on the issue before them. For example, in 1981 the Texas legislature passed a bill prohibiting the catching of redfish by commercial fishermen in some waters in the Gulf of Mexico. The bill was written and advanced by sport fishermen. Representatives from coastal communities in Texas voted as delegates—voting with the commercial fishermen and against the bill. Representatives from the Panhandle, however, were free to vote as trustees. In matters affecting the livelihood of Panhandle ranchers but not coastal fisheries, the voting roles of these representatives would be reversed. Which role representatives play is largely dependent on how the issues affect their district. The problem is that local interests can take the forefront, leading legislators to neglect long-term statewide or larger public interests.

Partisan Roles

As seen earlier, party is becoming a major factor in the Texas legislature today. While members of both parties are given committee assignments, fewer are going to the Democrats. Even today, partisan roles are confined to the speaker and a few leadership positions. Texas contrasts with states with a long tradition of strong partisanship, where party leadership roles are important, formal leadership positions are assigned on the basis of party, and party leaders try to ensure that party members support party positions on issues.

In the past, coalitions in the Texas legislature organized more around ideology than around party. The 1970s saw the formation of the "Dirty Thirty" coalition of liberal Democratic and conservative Republican house members to oppose the conservative Democrats. This uneasy alliance of members excluded from leadership positions was short-lived.

In more recent years, conservative Republicans and Democrats organized the Texas Conservative Coalition to fight what they view as liberal ideas. Other caucuses represent Hispanics and African Americans. In 1993, the Republicans formed a caucus to promote the election of Pete Laney as speaker. As a reward, they were assigned several committee chairs.

Partisan factors will play a much larger role in the Texas legislature in the next decade. In the 2001 and 2003 sessions, bipartisanship was evident in the redistricting battles. Some of this bipartisanship may be the result of incumbents being interested in protecting their seats, perhaps making stronger feelings of partisan gains. Republican control of both the house and the senate in the 2003 and 2005 sessions gave promise of bipartisan cooperation. The new speaker, Tom Craddick of Midland, promised to continue bipartisanship. Speaker Craddick did appoint fourteen (29.2 percent) Democrats as committee chairs; however, there was little evidence of bipartisanship elsewhere during the sessions. What few Democrats were given important assignments by Speaker Craddick were intended to increase his hold on the office. If the Republicans add to their majority in the house, the need to continue appointing Democrats to important committee assignments to retain control might disappear.

RATING THE TEXAS LEGISLATURE

How does the Texas legislature compare to the legislatures of other states? Making comparisons is always difficult. Thirty years ago, the Citizens Conference on State Legislatures developed the "FAIIR" index, based on five criteria: function factors, accountability, informed factors, independence, and representativeness.[45] Unfortunately, this index has not been updated; however, some other ratings have reached the same general conclusions. Several political scientists have developed indexes to measure the "professionalism" of state legislatures.

Most indexes of professionalism rely on several measures. Two important measures are the annual salary and the number of days the legislature is in session. A third measure often employed is the amount of money available for staff assistance. Based on these criteria, three types of state legislatures emerge:

- *Professional legislatures* are those who receive annual salaries in excess of $35,000, meet annually for nine to twelve months, and have annual allowances for office staff.
- *Hybrid legislatures* are those who get $32,000 or less in annual salaries, meet for fewer days each year, and have adequate staff assistance.
- *Citizen, nonprofessional legislatures* are those that meet for fewer days, are paid little or no salary, and have very limited staff assistance.[46]

Other writers have also used the criterion of "percent metropolitan" as a factor in explaining the level of professional development of state legislatures. Their argument is that large, metropolitan states will have an increased number of bills introduced because of the increased number of problems that come with urban growth. This requires more time on the part of the legislature, which results in longer sessions. When sessions become longer, lasting most of the year, pay and staff assistance tend to increase.[47]

Given these criteria, how does the Texas legislature stack up compared to other states on the professionalism ranking? Texas is a mixed bag.

On the criterion of staff assistance, the state provides more money than any other state. Most members keep open offices on a full-time basis in their district, and many do so in the state capital as well. Texas senators each receive $25,000 per month for staff salary support plus office expenses. House members each receive $8,500 per month for staff salary plus office expenses. In addition, standing committees receive staff salary support during and between legislative sessions. In comparison, California provides $20,000 to both house and senate members. New York provides staff support similar to that of Texas for its legislature. The Texas Legislative Council has a large, professional staff to assist the legislature. It has produced one of the best websites of any of the states and provides easy access to citizens during and between legislative sessions. The House Research Organization also provides professional assistance to the legislature.

With regard to building facilities, recent renovations to the state capitol building have provided each senator and house member with excellent office space. The Texas legislature has excellent facilities for its staff, for committee hearings, and for legislative work.

As indicated, among the large urban states, Texas pays the lowest salary at $7,200 per year. The voters have failed to approve amendments to the state constitution that would raise salaries. In most studies ranking legislators, salary is an important indicator of professionalism. Perhaps it is a factor. However, factors such as staff assistance and building facilities are also important, and on these Texas ranks above average.

Texas is only one of only five states that do not meet in annual sessions. Also, the sessions are limited to 140 days, and the legislature cannot call itself into special session.

Texas is a large urban state with many problems, and many bills are introduced each session. Annual sessions have been considered by past legislatures and rejected by the voters. This situation is not likely to change anytime soon. Texas will continue to be a low-pay, part-time legislature with a very professional staff. It is interesting to note that when voter approval is required for a constitutional amendment to raise pay and have annual sessions, the voters reject these changes. When voter approval is not required in areas such as staff and facilities, the legislature has provided increases. In 1994, the National Conference of State Legislatures produced a professionalism ranking based on four factors: full-time or part-time, pay, staff size, and turnover. In this ranking, Texas was classified as a moderate professional/citizen legislature.[48]

Summary

Self-Test www.mhhe.com/pattersontad8

Thomas R. Dye comes to three conclusions about state legislatures, all of which apply well to the Texas legislature. First, Dye observes:

> State legislatures reflect socioeconomic conditions of their states. These conditions help to explain many of the differences one encounters in state legislative politics: the level of legislative activity, the degree of inter-party competition, the extent of party cohesion, the professionalism of the legislature . . . the level of interest group activity.[49]

This means that the legislature is greatly influenced by the social and economic conditions in the state and that policies passed by the legislature reflect those conditions. This observation certainly applies to Texas.

Second, legislatures function as "arbiters of public policy rather than initiators" of policy change.[50] This means that state legislatures wait for others—state agencies, local governments, interest groups, and citizens—to bring issues to them for resolution. Someone other than members of the legislature writes most bills introduced. The rules make it much easier to delay legislation than to pass it. Leadership most often comes from people outside the legislature, often the governor. With a few exceptions, this applies to Texas.

Third, legislatures "function to inject into public decision making a parochial influence."[51] By this Dye means that state legislatures tend to represent local legislative interests and not statewide interests. Legislators are recruited, elected, and reelected locally. Local interests will always be dominant in determining how legislators vote on proposed legislation. Frequently, no one represents statewide interests. This conclusion certainly applies to Texas, where statewide interests are often lost in the effect to protect and promote local interests.

STUDY CORNER

Key Terms

biennial sessions (*p. 640*)
calendars (*p. 649*)
Calendars Committee (*p. 651*)
closed riders (*p. 649*)
conference committees (*p. 648*)
delegates (*p. 654*)
equity of representation (*p. 625*)
extraordinary sessions (*p. 640*)
informal rules (*p. 652*)
interim committees (*p. 648*)

Legislative Redistricting Board (LRB) (*p. 626*)
lieutenant governor (*p. 646*)
minority representation (*p. 627*)
multimember districts (*p. 620*)
political party gerrymandering (*p. 627*)
racially gerrymandered majority-minority districts (*p. 627*)
riders (*p. 649*)

safe Democratic and safe Republican districts (*p. 637*)
sine die (*p. 640*)
single-member districts (*p. 620*)
speaker of the house (*p. 645*)
special sessions (*p. 640*)
standing committees (*p. 647*)
term limits (*p. 640*)
trustees (*p. 654*)
turnover (*p. 638*)

Self-Test

1. Which of the following accurately describes turnover in the Texas legislature?
   a. Turnover is due mainly to the defeat of an incumbent either in the primary or in the general election.
   b. Retirement of legislators is prompted by increased and demanding staffs, pressures from political contributors, and a desire for increased salaries in higher public office or in the private sector.
   c. Turnover is higher in the senate because senatorial districts are larger and more populous and, as a result, senators become detached or distanced from their constituents.
   d. High turnover contributes to an amateur legislature, reduces its effectiveness, and permits a few individuals to control the legislative process.
   e. None of the above.

2. Which of the following is **not** true about sessions of the Texas legislature?
   a. The governor may call special sessions of not more than thirty days and decides the subject matter of the session.
   b. Critics of Texas's biennial sessions contend that the legislature should meet annually to address budgetary matters.
   c. Texas voters with traditionalistic and individualistic tendencies have opposed the concept of biennial sessions.
   d. If the governor calls a special session before the conclusion of Texas's 140-day regular session, the legislature will not adjourn and will continue its regular session for the additional thirty-day special session.
   e. None of the above.

3. Which of the following is **not** a power shared by the Texas speaker of the house and the lieutenant governor?

   a. appointing chairs of committees
   b. voting on all bills after the third reading
   c. serving as presiding officer
   d. referring all bills to committees
   e. none of the above

4. Which of the following is **not** a current factor in rating the Texas legislature?
   a. annual salary
   b. staff assistance
   c. accountability
   d. length of session
   e. building facilities

5. Which of the following is true regarding legislative workload during each regular legislative session?
   a. The agendas of both houses are set during the first thirty days.
   b. During the last thirty days of the session, conflicting bills are killed and complementary bills are reconciled.
   c. Only about one-third of all bills initially introduced for passage remain for consideration late in the legislative session.
   d. Bills may be introduced at any time prior to the session and through the one-hundredth day of the 140-day session.
   e. None of the above.

6. Both the U.S. Constitution and the Texas constitution require the Texas legislature to reapportion U.S. House of Representatives seats after the completion of the federal census. (T/F)

7. *Baker v. Carr* and *Reynolds v. Sims* were U.S. Supreme Court cases that essentially outlawed racial and political gerrymandering, a practice that prevailed throughout Texas until the 1960s. (T/F)

8. The three most common occupations among Texas legislators are attorney, business owner, and real estate broker. (T/F)

9. Although legislators' party affiliations are not currently a strong factor in the Texas legislature, it is anticipated that legislators will become more partisan in their decision making during the next ten years. (T/F)

10. Due to the lack of competition for Texas legislative seats, there is a low turnover of membership. (T/F)

Critical Thinking

Write an essay pointing out the importance of the offices of lieutenant governor and speaker of the house in deciding what gets passed in both houses of the Texas legislature. How would you change this system to make it more democratic?

Suggested Readings

Hamm, Keith E., and Gary F. Moncrief. "Legislative Politics in the Sates," in *Politics in the American States: A Comparative Analysis*, 8th ed., ed. Virginia Gray and Russell L. Hanson. Washington, D.C.: CQ Press, 2004.

Jewell, Malcolm E., and Samuel C. Patterson. *The Legislative Process in the United States* New York: Random House, 1985.

List of Websites

http://www.capitol.state.tx.us/
Website of the Texas legislature. This is an excellent site. You can find your state representative or senator if you know your postal zip code. You can also look up bills by subject matter or by bill number, author, and session.

http://www.lrl.state.tx.us/
Website of the Texas Legislative Reference Library. Has an excellent collection of information about the current and past legislatures.

http://www.ncsl.org/
Website of the National Conference of State Legislatures. Has information on state legislatures.

http://www.tlc.state.tx.us/research/redist/redist.htm
At this site you can examine the various redistricting plans introduced in the past session of the Texas legislature, as well as redistricting worldwide.

Participate!

Go to the Texas legislature website (www.capitol.state.tx.us) and find your state representative and senator. Look at the information provided in their biographies and decide if they represent you. Are you typical of other residents living in your house and senate legislative districts?

Extra Credit

Go to the Texas legislature web page and find your state representative and senator. Do a bill search and find out how many bills he or she has introduced. What subject matters do these bills cover? Does the bill have any direct reference to problems in your area of the state? Write an essay explaining these bills and their implications.

The Office of Governor and State Agencies in Texas

Chapter Outline

Roles of the Governor

Qualifications for Governor

Salary

Postgubernatorial Offices

Succession to Office
and Acting Governor

Removal from Office

Formal Powers of the Governor
  Tenure
  Appointive and Executive Powers
  Budgetary Powers
  Legislative Powers
  Judicial Powers
  Military Powers

Powers of the Texas Governor
Compared

Informal Powers
  Party Leadership
  The Governor's Staff

Administrative Agencies of
State Government
  Agencies with Elected Officials
  Single-Head Agencies
  Boards and Commissions
  Legislative Agencies
  Other State Agencies and Boards
  Sunset Review
  State Employees

CHAPTER 23

The Texas governor has only two happy days: The day he takes office and the
day he retires.

J. D. Sayers, governor of Texas 1898–1903

The *Fort Worth Star Telegram*, on November 27, 2005, reported: "In a very
real sense there is no reason for the Texas Tax Reform Commission to exist.
The commission, created by Republican Rich Perry and headed by his one
time political rival, Democrat John Sharp, includes 24 high-powered business
leaders hand-picked by the Governor from across the state. The commission's
task—finding ways to modernize the state's tax structure is of critical importance." However, the commission's existence indicated the weak nature of the
formal powers of the governor and the need for leadership from the governor
at a critical time.

The governor is the most salient political actor in state government. Whether
the true power center of the state is embodied in the occupant of the office or
elsewhere, the office is the focal point of state government and politics. The
governor is expected to perform many tasks and is blamed for not doing others,
even if the office is formally very weak. The expectation is that governors will
be leaders in their state.

The power and respect accorded to governors have varied greatly over time.
During the colonial period, little power or respect was afforded the office—some
have argued that the American Revolution was a war against colonial governors.
The experiences of southern states following Reconstruction led to a return of
weak governors in the South. There is an old Texas saying: "The governor should
have only enough power to sign for his paycheck." In recent times, the power
and prestige of the office have increased, as evidenced by recent presidential
politics. In both the Democratic and the Republican parties, many presidential
candidates have been former governors. In the past twenty-seven years, only
President George H. Bush had not served as governor prior to becoming president. The office of governor has assumed new significance because of a change
in attitude toward the role of the federal government. The Republican Congress
of the 1990s promised to return power and responsibility to state governments
and to allow states more flexibility in administering programs funded by the
federal government. Even without the renewed significance of the office—and
even though many governors have little formal power—governors are important
players in state politics.

ROLES OF THE GOVERNOR

chief legislator
The role of governors play when they recommend an active legislative agenda to the legislature and work to pass it.

ceremonial duties
The role of governors in attending functions and representing the state. Some governors become so active at this role that they get caught in a "ceremonial trap" and neglect other duties.

intergovernmental coordinator
The role governors play when they coordinate activities with other state governments and with Mexico.

Citizens expect governors to play many roles. They should be the chief policy-makers, formulating long-term goals and objectives. This requires selling their programs to state legislators and coordinating with state agencies that administer those programs.

The governor also is expected to act as **chief legislator.** Governors do not formally introduce bills, but they must have the support of some significant members of the legislature who will carry their program. This requires considerable time and energy to be spent developing these relationships. If the governor is of one party and the other party dominates the legislature, it might be more difficult to get legislation passed, and the governor might have to spend considerable resources to accomplish his or her goals.

The governor must also act as party chief. As the most important partisan official in the state, the governor should lead the party and aid its development and growth. This role involves helping legislators and other elected officials in their reelection efforts, raising money for the party, and creating a favorable image of the party in the state.

The governor also serves as the ceremonial leader of the state. The demands of **ceremonial duties** are extreme. "Where two or more are gathered together," there also is the governor expected to be. The governor receives many invitations to speak, make presentations, and cut ribbons. Some governors become trapped in the safe, friendly environment of ceremonial duties and neglect or avoid the other duties of their office. For governors with an agenda for action, ceremony is a diversion from more important and more difficult objectives. Governors can, however, use ceremonial duties as communication opportunities to promote their programs. They must wisely choose which invitations to accept and which to delegate to others or decline. Ceremonial appearances, such as speaking at a graduation, provide an opportunity to generate favorable press coverage and support for favored programs. Former governor George W. Bush used these opportunities both to promote his state programs and to promote his race for the presidency.

The governor is also the chief **intergovernmental coordinator,** working with federal officials and officials in other states. The governor works with the state congressional delegation of U.S. senators and representatives, the president, and cabinet officials to promote the interests of the state.

Thus governors are assigned many roles. In Texas the formal powers of the governor are very weak, and this complicates things. The governor cannot rely on formal authority but must develop and use the power and prestige of the office to persuade others to accept his or her program. This informal leadership trait—the power to persuade others—is perhaps the most important and necessary "power" the governor must develop.

QUALIFICATIONS FOR GOVERNOR

In most states the formal qualifications for governor are minimal. All but six states set a minimum age requirement, and most require a candidate to be a resident of the state for five to ten years preceding election. Also, most states require governors to be U.S. citizens and qualified voters.

In Texas the formal qualifications are simple: a person must be at least thirty years of age, a citizen of the United States, and a resident of the state for five

Governor and Mrs. Thomas M. Campbell pose with their family on the steps of the governor's mansion, circa 1909.

years preceding election. There is no requirement to be a registered voter. In the 1930s, W. Lee O'Daniel ran for governor stressing that he was not a "professional politician." To prove this, he made a point of not being a registered voter.

Informal qualifications are more important. Nationwide, most governors have held elected office before becoming governor. An examination of the 979 people serving as governor between 1900 and 2003 reveals that the most common career path to the office is to begin in the legislature, move to statewide office, and then move to the governor's office.[1] Others who are elected governor have served as U.S. senator or representative, and a few have served in local elected offices (such as mayor). Thus, having held elected office is an important informal qualification for becoming governor. Some governors gain experience as appointed administrators or as party officials. Between 1970 and 2002, only 10 percent of all people elected governor had no prior political office experience.[2]

These observations generally apply to Texas governors. Table 23–1 lists the men and women who have served as governor in Texas since 1949 and their prior office experience. Most had served in an elected office, five in statewide offices. Only two had not held elected office. The current governor, Rick Perry, followed a rather typical pattern. He served in the state legislature, as agricultural commissioner, and as lieutenant governor prior to becoming governor when George W. Bush resigned to assume the office of president of the United States. He was elected governor in his own right in 2002.

There are many other informal qualifications besides electoral experience. Nationwide, most people who have served as governors have been white, male, Protestant, well-educated, wealthy individuals. Only one African American, Douglas Wilder of Virginia, has been elected governor. Several Hispanics have served as governor: Tony Anaya, Jerry Abodaca, and Bill Richardson in New Mexico; Bob Martinez in Florida; and Raul Castro in Arizona.

More women have served as governor in recent years than in the past. In 1924, Wyoming elected the first woman governor, Nellie T. Ross, who served one term.

informal qualifications
Additional qualifications beyond the formal qualifications that men and women need to have to be elected governor. Holding statewide elected office is an example.

The governor's mansion located on Colorado Street between 10th and 11th streets is at least the second governor's mansion in Austin, Texas. The house is used for receptions and formal affairs. Unfortunately, an ugly parking lot is located across the street. One recent governor's wife found the "small house" not to her standards and rented space elsewhere. She also disliked the public tours of the home.

She succeeded her husband, who died in office. Later in 1924 Texas elected Miriam A. Ferguson governor. She was reelected in 1932. Mrs. Ferguson was a "stand-in" for her husband, Jim Ferguson, who had been impeached, removed from office, and barred from seeking reelection. Similarly, in 1968 Lurleen Wallace was elected governor of Alabama as a stand-in governor for her husband, George Wallace, who

TABLE 23–1	Previous Office Experience of Texas Governors, 1949–2006	
GOVERNOR	**TERM OF OFFICE**	**PREVIOUS OFFICES**
Allan Shivers	1949–57	State Senate, Lieutenant Governor
Price Daniel	1957–63	U.S. Senate
John Connally	1963–69	U.S. Secretary of the Navy*
Preston Smith	1969–73	Texas House and Senate, Lieutenant Governor
Dolph Briscoe	1973–79	Texas House
Bill Clements	1979–83	Assistant Secretary of Defense*
	1987–91	
Mark White	1983–87	Attorney General
Ann Richards	1991–94	County office, State Treasurer
George W. Bush	1995–2001	None
Rick Perry	2001–present	State legislature, Agricultural Commissioner, and Lieutenant Governor

*Appointive offices. No electoral experience before becoming governor.

Source: James Anderson, Richard W. Murray, and Edward L. Farley, *Texas Politics: An Introduction*, 6th ed. (New York: HarperCollins, 1992), 166–88. Governors Bush and Perry from other sources.

could not be reelected because of term limits. While Ferguson and Wallace were stand-in governors for husbands ineligible for reelection, several women besides Wyoming's Ross have been elected in their own right. Since 1974, twenty-five women have served as governor, as shown in Table 23–2.[3] The number of women serving as governor undoubtedly will increase. There are currently seventy-three women serving in statewide offices, fifteen as lieutenant governors and fifty-eight in other statewide elected offices. As indicated previously, service in statewide office often is a stepping-stone to the governor's office.

Historically, the men who have served as governor of Texas have generally had one thing in common—wealth. A few, including Dolph Briscoe and Bill Clements, were very wealthy. Most have been successful in law, business, or politics before becoming governor. Ann Richards was an exception to these informal qualifications. She was not wealthy or from a wealthy family, and she had no business or law experience. Former governor Bush of resembles past governors in terms of background, with a famous family name and family wealth. Governor Perry, while claiming the status of a sharecropper's son, came from a moderate, middle-class background.

TABLE 23–2	Women Governors	
GOVERNOR	**STATE**	**SERVED AS GOVERNOR**
Nellie Tayloe Ross (D)	Wyoming	Jan. 1925–1927
Miriam Amanda Ferguson (D)	Texas	Jan. 1925–1927; Jan. 1933–1935
Lurleen Burns Wallace (D)	Alabama	Jan. 1967–1968
Ella Grasso (D)	Connecticut	Jan. 1975–1980
Dixy Lee Ray (D)	Washington	Jan. 1977–1981
Vesta M. Roy (R)	New Hampshire	Dec. 1982–Jan. 1983
Martha Layne Collins (D)	Kentucky	Dec. 1983–1987
Madeleine M. Kunin (D)	Vermont	Jan. 1985–1991
Kay A. Orr (R)	Nebraska	Jan. 1987–Jan. 1991
Rose Mofford (D)	Arizona	April 1988–Jan. 1991
Joan Finney (D)	Kansas	Jan. 1991–Jan. 1995
Barbara Roberts (D)	Oregon	Jan. 1991 Jan. 1995
Ann W. Richards (D)	Texas	Jan. 1991–Jan. 1995
Christine T. Whitman (R)	New Jersey	Jan. 1994–Jan. 2001
Jane Dee Hull (R)	Arizona	Sep. 1997–Jan. 2003
Nancy P. Hollister (R)	Ohio	Dec. 31, 1998–Jan. 11, 1999
Jeanne Shaheen (D)	New Hampshire	Jan. 1997–Jan. 2003
Jane Swift (R)	Massachusetts	April 2001–Jan. 2003
Ruth Ann Minner (D)	Delaware	Jan. 2001–present
Judy Martz (R)	Montana	Jan. 2001–present
Sila M. Calderón (D)	Puerto Rico	Jan. 2001–present
Linda Lingle (R)	Hawaii	Dec. 2002–present
Janet Napolitano (D)	Arizona	Jan. 2003–present
Kathleen Sebelius (D)	Kansas	Jan. 2003–present
Jennifer Granholm (D)	Michigan	Jan. 2003–present
Olene S. Walker (R)	Utah	Nov. 2003–present
Kathleen Blanco (D)	Louisiana	Jan. 2004–present
M. Jodi Rell (R)	Connecticut	Jan. 2004–present

Sources: National Governors Association Web page, *www.nga.org/governors;* Center for American Women and Politics, www.cawp.rutgers.edu.

SALARY

Governors receive much higher pay than state legislators. As of 2002, salaries ranged from a low of $65,000 in Nebraska to a high of $179,000 in New York. The Texas salary of $116,000 per year is slightly above the mean salary of $90,000 in 2002.[4] In addition, Texas provides the governor with a home in Austin, an automobile with a driver, an airplane, and reimbursement for actual travel expenses. Texas governors also receive a budget for entertaining and maintaining the Governor's Mansion. Compared with members of the state legislature, the governor in Texas is extremely well paid. Given the demands and responsibilities of the job, the governor is not overpaid compared to executives of large corporations who receive many times the governor's salary.

POSTGUBERNATORIAL OFFICES

Some governors use the office is a stepping-stone to other offices. Some go on to serve in the U.S. Senate, and several have been elected president of the United States. For example, former governor W. Lee O'Daniel served as U.S. senator from 1941 to 1949, and George W. Bush became president in 2001. Post-gubernatorial administrative service in the federal government is also common. Presidents often call on former governors to head departments of government. President George H. Bush chose former governor John Sununu of New Hampshire as his chief of staff. Bruce Babbitt, former governor of Arizona, was chosen to be secretary of interior by President Clinton, who also appointed former governor Richard Riley of South Carolina as secretary of education. Former Texas governor John Connally served as secretary of the treasury under President Richard Nixon. President George W. Bush selected several governors to be in his cabinet. However, for most governors (64 percent nationwide) the office is the peak of their political career, and they retire to private life.[5] This is true of most Texas governors. George W. Bush was the first Texas governor since 1941 to move on to higher elected office.

The governor's original private office is furnished with a Victorian desk that was first used by Sul Ross. The capitol was completed during his initial term in office. (Photo courtesy of State Preservation Board.)

SUCCESSION TO OFFICE AND ACTING GOVERNOR

Most states provide for a successor if the governor dies or leaves office early. Forty-three states have lieutenant governors who advance to the office if it is vacant for any reason. In the seven states without lieutenant governors, another officeholder, usually the leader of the state senate, succeeds to the governor's office. In nineteen states, the lieutenant governor and the governor are elected separately. In twenty-four states, the governor and lieutenant governor are jointly elected, they run as a "team" much as candidates for president and vice president do. In these cases, the candidate for governor picks the lieutenant governor. Former governor Paul Cellucci, who resigned to become ambassador to Canada, selected Jane Swift as his lieutenant governor. She became governor of Massachusetts in February 2001 when he resigned office.

When the governor leaves the state, the lieutenant governor becomes **acting governor.** This is unlike the situation for the vice president of the United States, who does not become acting president if the president leaves the country. Some governors have experienced problems with their lieutenant governor when they have left the state. For instance, in 1995, Jim Guy Tucker of Arkansas had problems with senate president pro tem Jerry Jewell, who was acting as governor in the absence of the lieutenant governor. Jewell "granted two pardons and executive clemency to two prison inmates."[6] Also, the Arkansas lieutenant governor, Republican Mike Huckabee, "signed a proclamation designating a Christian Heritage Week after Tucker had declined to do so earlier."[7]

In Texas, present governor Rick Perry may hold the record for serving the most time as acting governor, holding the position when Governor George W. Bush was campaigning for president outside the state. While serving as acting governor, the lieutenant governor in Texas receives the same salary as the governor.

acting governor
The role of the lieutenant governor when he or she becomes acting governor and performs the functions of the office when the governor leaves the state.

REMOVAL FROM OFFICE

All states except Oregon have a procedure for removing governors by a process generally called impeachment. Technically, the lower house of the legislature adopts articles of impeachment and then the senate conducts a trial on these articles of impeachment. If the senate finds the governor guilty, he or she is removed from office. Together, the two steps—the adoption of articles of **impeachment and conviction** by the senate—are commonly called impeachment. Sixteen governors have been the subject of impeachment trials, and eight have been removed from office.[8]

Technically, impeachment is a judicial process, but it is also a very political process. Impeached governors generally have been guilty of some wrongdoing, but they often are removed for political reasons. For example, one of the eight impeached governors was Jim Ferguson of Texas (1915–17). Ferguson was indicted by the Texas house, technically for misuse of state funds, and was convicted and removed from office by the senate. In reality, he was impeached because of his fight with the University of Texas board of regents. When the governor could not force the board of regents to terminate several professors who had been critical of the governor or force the resignation of board members, he vetoed the entire appropriations bill for the University of Texas.[9] This veto led to his removal from office. Ferguson tried to prevent his impeachment by calling the legislature into special session. Because only the governor can decide the agenda of a special session, Governor Ferguson told the legislature they could consider any item they wanted, except impeachment. His ploy did not work, and he was removed from office. Courts later upheld Ferguson's impeachment.

A few years after the Ferguson affair in Texas, Oklahoma impeached two consecutively elected governors. These two impeachments were as political as Ferguson's in Texas. In 1921, several "race riots" broke out in which many African Americans were killed. The most noted of these was in the Greenwood area of Tulsa, Oklahoma. Thirty-five square blocks of this segregated African

impeachment and conviction
Some elected officials, including governors, may be impeached (accused of an impeachable offense) by the state senate and convicted and removed from office by the lower house of the state legislature.

American community were burned and destroyed, and over forty people were killed. In 1922, John C. Walton was elected governor as a member of the Farmer-Laborite party. Walton tried to break up the Ku Klux Klan (KKK) in the state, and this effort led to his impeachment. The lieutenant governor, Martin Trapp, served out the remainder of Walton's term but was unable to run for reelection because Oklahoma at that time had a limit of one term. Henry S. Johnson was elected governor in 1926 as a pro-KKK candidate and refused to use his office to quell Klan activity in the state. Johnson used the National Guard to try to prevent the legislature from meeting to consider his impeachment. The legislature was kept out of the state capitol building and had to meet in a hotel in Oklahoma City. Johnson was convicted and removed from office. He had been indicted on eighteen counts and found not guilty on all but one—"general incompetence," for which he was impeached.[10]

The impeachment of Evan Mecham in Arizona in 1988 was equally political. Mecham had made a number of racist remarks and had become a source of embarrassment in the state. Technically, he was impeached for misuse of state funds during his inaugural celebration.

These four impeachments illustrate the highly political nature of the process. All the impeached governors technically had committed some malfeasance of office yet were impeached for political reasons.

Fifteen states also allow **recall** of the governor. Texas does not provide for recall of state officials. Many Texas home-rule cities do allow recall of city councils and mayors. Recall involves getting petitions signed by some number of voters, followed by an election by which, if a majority approves, the governor can be recalled or removed from office. Two governors have been recalled. Lynn J. Frazier of North Dakota was recalled in 1921, the same time governors were being impeached in Texas and Oklahoma. In 1988, Governor Mecham of Arizona was spared a recall election when he was impeached by the legislature.[11] In 2003, Gray Davis of California was recalled. With so few examples, it is impossible to make any generalizations about the politics of recall.

FORMAL POWERS OF THE GOVERNOR

As indicated previously, most governors do not have great formal powers. The formal powers of the office of governor can be measured on five factors: tenure of office, appointive/administrative powers, budgetary powers, legislative authority, and judicial powers. By examining each of these factors, we can compare the formal powers of governors and, more specifically, the powers of the Texas governor.

Tenure

Tenure of office refers to the legal ability of governors to succeed themselves in office and the length of the governor's term. Historically, the tenure of governors has been less than that of most other statewide-elected state officials, in part because of term limits.[12] Term limits for governors have been a fixture since the beginning of the Republic. Ten of the governors in the original thirteen states had one-year terms. States moved first to two-year terms, then to four-year terms. In the 1960s, several states borrowed from the federal constitution the idea of limiting governors to two four-year terms.[13] Southern states were the last to move to longer terms. Many southern states once prohibited the governor from

recall
The removal of an elected official by a petition signed by the required number of registered voters and an election in which a majority votes to remove the official from office.

tenure of office
The ability of governors or other elected officials to be reelected to office.

How Texas Compares

Term Limits for Governors

While term limits for legislators are a recent phenomenon, historically governors have always been limited in the number of terms they could serve. Most states limit the governor to two terms, just like the president of the United States. Texas is one of twelve states that do not limit the number of terms a governor can serve.

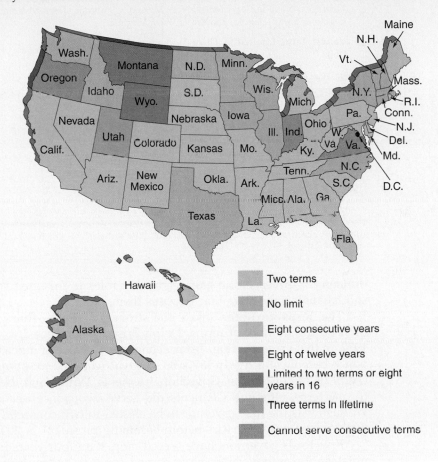

Legend:
- Two terms
- No limit
- Eight consecutive years
- Eight of twelve years
- Limited to two terms or eight years in 16
- Three terms in lifetime
- Cannot serve consecutive terms

serving consecutive terms in office. Today, only Virginia retains this provision. (See "How Texas Compares" and Table 23–3.)

Tenure is an important determinant of power. Governors who can be continually reelected retain the potential to influence government until they decide to leave office. Only fourteen states do not limit how long a person can serve as governor. Governors who are prevented from being reelected by term limits suffer as "lame ducks" toward the end of their terms. Long tenure also enables governors to carry out their programs, while short terms (two years) force governors to continually seek reelection and to make political compromises. Only two states—Vermont and New Hampshire—retain the two-year term.

Longer tenure is also an important factor in the governor's role as intergovernmental coordinator. The important task of building up associations with officials in other states and in Washington takes time. Short tenure makes it

TABLE 23–3 Gubernatorial Term Limits

Two-Year Term, No Limit of Terms
Vermont and New Hampshire

Four-Year Term, No Consecutive Reelection
Virginia

Four-Year Term, Limited to Two Terms in Lifetime
Alabama, Alaska, Arizona, Arkansas, California, Colorado, Delaware, Florida, Georgia, Hawaii, Kansas, Kentucky, Louisiana, Maine, Maryland, Michigan, Mississippi, Missouri, Nebraska, Nevada, New Jersey, New Mexico, Oklahoma, Pennsylvania, Rhode Island, South Carolina, South Dakota, Tennessee, West Virginia

Four-Year Term, Limited to Three Terms in Lifetime
Utah

Four-Year Term, No Limit
Connecticut, Idaho, Illinois, Iowa, Massachusetts, Minnesota, New York, North Carolina, North Dakota, Texas, Washington, Wisconsin

Four-Year Term, No More Than Two Terms in Sixteen Years
Montana and Wyoming

Eight Out of Twelve Years
Indiana and Oregon

Eight Consecutive Years
Ohio

Source: Council of State Governments, *The Book of the States 2003* (Lexington, Ky.: Council of State Governments, 2002). vol. 34, 199–200, Table 4.9.

difficult for governors to gain leadership roles in this area and has the effect of shortchanging the state that imposes them.[14]

The Texas governor enjoys the strongest tenure—four-year terms with no limit on the number of terms. Dolph Briscoe was elected to a two-year term in 1972. In that same election, Texas changed the tenure of office to a four-year term, which became effective in 1975. Briscoe was reelected to serve one four-year term (1975–79). After Briscoe, Governors Clements, White, and Richards were limited to one term, although Clements did serve two nonconsecutive terms. George W. Bush was the first governor to be elected to two consecutive four-year terms. Bush served only six years before becoming president in 2001.

Few Texas governors have served more than four years in office. Since 1874, nineteen Texas governors have served for four years; most of these (fifteen) served consecutive two-year terms. Seven served for two years, four served for six years, and only one (Allan Shivers, 1949–57) served for eight consecutive years—four two-year terms. Bill Clements served for eight nonconsecutive years. Thus, the history of Texas governors is not one of long tenure. Serving two two-year terms was the norm for most of the state's history. From 1874 until 1953, no person served more than four years as governor in Texas.[15] Had Governor Bush not been elected president in 2000, he would have been the first Texas governor to serve two consecutive four-year terms.

Appointive and Executive Powers

More important than tenure of office is the power of the governor to make appointments and control the agencies of state government. Obviously, if the governor can appoint and remove the heads of most state agencies, he or she can better control the administration of programs.

Historically, governors have not had strong **appointive powers.** For most of the nineteenth century, the traditional method of selecting the heads of state agencies was by election—a tradition known as "Jacksonian statehouse democracy." President Andrew Jackson expressed ultimate faith in the ballot box for selecting administrators. Toward the end of the nineteenth century, there was a proliferation of agencies headed by appointed or elected boards and commissions. The governor was just one of many elected state officials and had little formal control over state administration.[16] Thus, governors often share power with many other elected individuals, an arrangement called a plural executive structure.

Equally important to appointive power is the power to remove administrators, which is discussed later in this chapter. Without the power of removal, the appointive powers of the governor are greatly diminished. Beginning in the early twentieth century, the powers of the governor to appoint and remove officials were increased in some states. This expansion of executive authority has grown in the last three decades in many states.[17] This has not been the pattern for

One of the most elegant spaces in the capitol is the governor's public reception room, which reflects the sumptuous Victorian style popular during the late 1800s. Known as "the Living Room of Texas," the reception room is used by the governor for hosting visiting dignitaries, holding press conferences, signing bills, and performing other ceremonial and official functions. It is open to the public weekdays from 8 A.M. to 5 P.M., except for the noon hour and when it is in use by the governor or the governor's staff. (Photo courtesy of State Preservation Board.)

much of the South or for the office of governor in Texas. In 2001, the voters in Texas rejected an amendment that would have made the adjutant general of the Texas National Guard subject to removal by the governor. The traditionalistic culture does not support the idea of strong executive authority even for relatively minor offices.

The ability of the Texas governor to control administrative functions through formal appointive and removal powers is exceptionally weak. The voters elect many important state administrators, making Texas a good example of the plural executive structure. Voters elect a lieutenant governor, an attorney general, a comptroller of public accounts, a state land commissioner, an agricultural commissioner, the Railroad Commission, and the Texas State Board of Education.

The governor does appoint a few agency heads, the most significant being the secretary of state, who serves as the chief record keeper and election official for the state. The governor also appoints the executive directors of the Departments of Commerce, Health and Human Services, Housing and Community Affairs, and Insurance; the Office of State-Federal Relations; and the Fire Fighters Pension Commission. The governor appoints the head of the Texas National Guard and appoints the executive director of the Texas Education Agency based on recommendations made by the elected Texas State Board of Education. The governor also appoints the chief counsels for the Public Utility Commission, the Insurance Commission, and the State Office of Administrative Hearings.

Significant portions of state government are beyond the control of the governor because several agency heads are elected. Most agencies are controlled by independent boards and commissions over which the governor has little control. These independent state agencies usually are governed by three-, six-, or

appointive powers
The ability of a governor to appoint (and sometimes remove) important state administrators.

TABLE 23–4	Texas Governor Appointments to Policymaking and Governing Boards, Commissions, and Agencies	
TYPE OF AGENCY	**NUMBER OF AGENCIES**	**NUMBER OF APPOINTEES**
General government	31	244
Health and human services	31	366
Higher education boards of regents	12	117
Other education	16	149
Business regulation	9	37
Business and economic development	24	176
Regional economic development	32	276
Licensing and professional examining boards	38	461
Public safety and criminal justice	22	158
Natural resources	16	156
Employee retirement boards	8	53
Interstate compact commissions	8	24
Water and river authorities	18	210
Judicial	18	151
Others	18	251
Totals	301	2,829

Source: Data supplied by the Texas State Governor's Appointment Secretary, Freedom of Information Request, August 2000. Categories for state agencies are by the author. List can be obtained from Governor's Appointment Secretary, State Capitol, Austin, Texas

nine-member boards or commissions appointed by the governor for six-year, overlapping, staggered terms. Usually, one-third of the membership is appointed every two years. In total, the number of governing and policymaking positions filled by gubernatorial appointment is about 2,800.[18] (See Table 23–4.) If the governor stays in office for two terms (eight years), she or he will have appointed all members of these agencies and boards and might have indirect influence over them. The governing board chooses the heads of these agencies. For example, the president of a state university is selected by the board of regents, whose members are appointed by the governor. The governor often exercises influence with his or her appointees on the board of regents. In 2002, it was rumored that Governor Perry strongly supported the selection of retiring Senator Phil Gramm for president of Texas A&M University. All of Governor Perry's appointees supported Gramm for the position.

The governor also appoints a number of persons to nonpolicymaking and governing boards that recommend policy and programs to the governor or other state officials. These agencies are not included in this discussion. Many of these nonpolicymaking boards recommend changes in policy and programs. Others are simply window dressing and allow the governor to reward supporters. Most often, appointments to these boards do not require senate approval.

Some gubernatorial appointments are subject to approval by a two-thirds vote of the senate. In these cases, the governor must clear his or her appointments with the state senator from the appointee's home district. This process, known as "senatorial courtesy," limits the discretion of the governor. If the senator from an appointee's home district disapproves of the appointment, the senate might not confirm the appointees. Senatorial courtesy does not apply to all gubernatorial appointments, most notably the nonpolicymaking boards.

The discretion of the governor also is limited by other factors. For example, some boards require geographic representation. Members of river authority

boards must live in the area covered by the river authority. Examples of this are the Trinity River Authority and the Lower Colorado River Authority. Other boards require specified professional backgrounds. Membership on the Texas Municipal Retirement Board, for instance, is limited to certain types of city employees, such as firefighters, police, and city managers.[19]

Of course, there are always political limits placed on the governor's ability to appoint people. Interest groups pay close attention to the governor's appointments to these boards and commissions and try to influence the governor's choices. The governor might have to bend to demands from such groups. Chapter 20 discussed this subject in more detail.

In Texas, the appointive power of the governor—even with its formal limitations—allows the governor to indirectly influence policy. It is unlikely that a governor will select men and women to serve on boards and commissions who do not agree with the governor on major policy issues. Ann Richards used her appointive powers to increase the number of women and minorities serving on state boards and commissions. This broad appointive power allows the governor to influence policy even after leaving office, because some of the appointees will continue to serve on the boards and commissions. Richards's successor, George W. Bush, appointed some women and minorities but tended to appoint mainly businessmen to these positions. Governor Perry, for the most part, also appoints business leaders.

Thus, the governor exerts indirect, not direct, control over policy by appointing people who hold similar policy views. This influence continues for some time after the governor leaves office, because his or her appointees will remain in office for four to six years after the governor's term ends.

Debating the Issues

Do Campaign Contributions Buy Influence with the Governor?

All governors are forced to collect large sums of money to use in their campaigns. While a few candidates, such as Tony Sanchez in 2002, can afford to finance their campaigns from personal wealth, most cannot and must rely on contributions from citizens. Texas is a large state with many media markets, and money is needed to campaign on such a vast scale. While no one doubts the need for money in campaigns, the question is what impact these contributions have on decisions make by the governor.

Yes While all candidates for office will deny that campaign contributions have any influence on their decisions, there is little doubt that such money does buy access and influence. Politicians accused of being bought can and often do act with great indignation and accuse the accusers of being sinister and jaded in their view of government. One must ask why some individuals give vast sums of money to many candidates if they do not expect something in return. Why does Bob Perry of Perry Homes in Houston, Texas, give hundreds of thousands of dollars to Republicans? Are he and others like him trying to influence state policy? Recently it was reported that the governor was using campaign contributions to supplement the salary of some of his top staff members, producing a potential conflict of interest.

No Not everyone who gives money to a candidate for governor expects special treatment or appointment to some prestigious board or commission. Some people are interested in government programs that they think are in the best interest of Texas. While giving money may buy a person access, it does not ensure that actions favorable to his or her interests will result. In the 2002 election cycle, gaming and Indian reservations interests donated over $500,000 to Governor Perry's campaign attempting to get slot machines installed at race tracks and on reservations. This measure did not pass the legislature. While some people might donate money expecting appointment to some board or commission, many are disappointed. Governors often appoint those individuals who they think best represent their interests and will do so as a member of the board or commission.

Appointments and Campaign Contributions

Governors also have been known to appoint people to governing boards and commissions who supported them in their campaigns. People who were loyal supporters, especially those giving large campaign contributions, are often rewarded with appointment to prestigious state boards and commissions. University governing boards are especially desired positions. Table 23–5 lists the contributions given by individuals appointed to state boards and commissions by then governor Bush.

Removal Powers

The other side of the power to appoint is the power to remove persons from office. The president of the United States may remove many of his appointees, but state governors often are restricted by either the state constitution, statutes creating the agency, or term limits set for appointees. Some states allow the governor to remove a person only for cause. This requires the governor to make a

TABLE 23–5	Campaign Contributions and Appointment to Boards and Commissions by Governor George Bush	
STATE BODY	**TOTAL CONTRIBUTIONS**	**NUMBER OF APPOINTMENTS**
University of Texas Regents	$432,606	10
Parks and Wildlife Commission	201,877	10
Texas Tech University Regents	106,000	9
Texas A&M University Regents	85,000	9
Texas Transportation Department	65,000	3
Lottery Commission	30,000	3
Medical Examiners Board (Physicians)	17,500	18
University of North Texas	17,500	9
University of Houston	17,000	9
Alcoholic Beverages Commission	15,000	3
Stephen F. Austin University Regents	13,000	9
Optometry Board	9,500	10
Texas Southern University Regents	8,000	11
Pharmacy Board	5,760	10

Source: Texans for Public Justice. *Well Appointed State Boards*, October 2000, www.tpj.org/appointments/boards.

case for wrongdoing by the individual. Of course, the governor can force the resignation of a person without formal hearings, but the political cost of such forced resignations can be quite high and beyond what the governor is willing to pay.

In Texas, the removal power of the governor is very weak. Before 1981, Texas state law was silent on the issue of removal. In 1981, the constitution was amended to allow governors to remove any person they had personally appointed, subject to approval by a two-thirds vote of the senate. Governors may not remove any of their predecessors' appointees. To date no person has been formally removed from office under this procedure, but it does provide the governor with some leverage to force an appointee to resign. It might also be used to force a policy change the governor wants. It does not, however, allow the governor to control the day-to-day administration of state government.

Budgetary Powers

Along with tenure of office and appointive/executive authority, the power to control budgets is an important determinant of executive authority. Control over how money is spent is at the very heart of the policymaking process. Some define a budget as a statement of policy in monetary terms. If the governor can control budget formation and development (the preparation of the budget for submission to the legislature) and budget execution (deciding how money is spent), the governor can have a significant influence on state policy. Four kinds of constraints can undercut the governor's budgetary authority:

- The extent to which the governor must share budget formation with the legislature or with other state agencies
- The extent to which funds are earmarked for specific expenditures and the choice on how to spend money is limited by previous actions
- The extent to which the governor shares budget execution authority with others in state government
- Limits on the governor's use of a line-item veto for the budget

In forty states, the governor is given "full" authority over budget formation and development.[20] In those states, agencies must present their requests for expenditures to the governor's office, which combines them and presents a unified budget to the legislature. In some states, the governor is limited in how much he or she can reduce the budget requests of some state agencies. If the governor can change the budgetary requests of agencies, he or she will have tremendous control over the final form of the budget submitted to the legislature. A common practice of state governments is to earmark revenue for specific purposes. For example, funds received through the gasoline tax commonly are earmarked for state highways. This practice also limits the discretion of the governor.

Budget execution authority is more involved. Governors and others control budget execution in a variety of ways. If the governor controls the appointment of the major department heads of state government, he or she will have some discretion in how money is spent. The governor might decide, for example, not to spend all the money appropriated for a state park. Administrative discretion over how money is spent is a time-honored way to expand executive authority over the budget.

Another area in which governors often can exercise control over budgets is through the veto. All but seven governors have a line-item veto that allows them to exercise a great deal of influence over the budgetary process.[21]

In Texas, the governor's budgetary powers are exceptionally weak. The governor is not constitutionally mandated to submit a budget. Instead, this power is given to the Legislative Budget Board (LBB), an agency governed by the speaker of the house and the lieutenant governor. Agencies of the state must present budget requests to the LBB. The LBB then produces a budget that is submitted to the legislature. Historically, governors have submitted budget messages to the legislature, often in the form of reactions to the LBB-proposed budget. Someone once said that the "governor's budget" has the same effect as a letter to Santa Claus because it has little effect on the final budget form. In 2003, Governor Perry presented a budget with all zeros, claiming it was a "zero-based" budget. It was not, and many saw the move as an attempt to avoid dealing with the $10 billion budget shortfall. Many funds are earmarked by the previous actions of the Texas legislature. One estimate from the LBB is that more than 80 percent of all funds are earmarked for specific expenditures, such as highways, teachers' retirement, parks, and schools.

The governor of Texas has very limited authority over budget execution. Outside the governor's immediate office, control over the budget rests with other state agencies over which the governor has little or no control. Only in cases of fiscal crisis can the governor exercise influence. A constitutional amendment approved in 1985 created the Budget Execution Committee, composed of the governor, the lieutenant governor, the comptroller, the speaker of the house, and the chairs of the Finance and Appropriations Committees in the senate and house. The Budget Execution Committee can impose restraints on the budget in the case of a fiscal crisis, such as a shortfall in projected revenue.

The one area where the Texas governor does have influence over budget decisions is use of the **line-item veto.** The governor can veto part of an appropriations bill without vetoing the entire bill. The legislature determines what a line item is. It can be a department within an agency or the entire agency. For example, Governor Clements once vetoed the line items appropriating money to operate the systems administration offices of the University of Texas and Texas A&M University. He did not veto all money appropriated to these schools, only those funds earmarked for the operation of the systems offices. The governor might veto the appropriation of money for a state park without having to veto the money for all state parks.

line-item veto
The ability of a governor to veto part of an appropriation bill without vetoing the entire bill.

The legislature can override the governor's line-item veto by a two-thirds vote of each house. However, as we saw in chapter 22, appropriations bills generally pass in the last days of the session, so the legislature has adjourned by the time the governor exercises veto power. Because the legislature cannot call itself back into session (call "extraordinary" sessions), overriding a line-item veto is impossible. The governor may call special sessions, but he or she controls the agenda. If the governor thought there was a chance of a veto override, it would not be included in the agenda of the special session.

Thus, the line-item veto is a very important power possessed by the Texas governor. More important than the actual veto is the threat of a veto. Historically in Texas, governors have used this threat to discipline the legislature. It is not uncommon for the governor to threaten to veto a local line item, such as an item creating a new state park in a legislator's district, to gain legislative support for items important to the governor but unrelated to the park. It should be noted that governors typically do not veto many bills. While there are occasional exceptions, as a general rule threats are more important than an actual veto.

Nationally, the U.S. Congress granted the president of the United States a limited line-item veto. The U.S. Supreme Court declared this act unconstitutional. While many have advocated that the president needs the line item veto to control congressional spending, a constitutional amendment will be required to grant this power. If this power is granted, presidents might use the threat of veto to control members of Congress and to get their support for other programs.

Legislative Powers

While the line-item veto can be viewed as a budgetary power, it is also a **legislative power.** There are also other types of vetoes. All governors possess some form of veto authority, but the form varies among the states (see Table 23–6). Forty-three states have formalized **partial vetoes,** where by the legislature can recall a bill from the governor so that objections raised by the governor can be changed and a veto avoided.[22] Texas does not have a formal partial veto process; however, the governor can state objections to a bill before it is passed and seek to effect changes in legislation. Formalizing the process would shift some power to the office of governor and give the governor more say in the legislative process.

Requirements for overriding a governor's veto also vary widely among the states. Most states require a two-thirds vote to override, although a few allow a

legislative power

The formal power, especially the vote authority, of the governor to force the legislature to enact legislation.

partial vetoes

The ability of some governors to veto part of a bill without vetoing the entire bill. The Texas governor does not have this power except on appropriations bills.

TABLE 23–6	Veto Authority of State Governors, with Override Provisions
TYPE OF VETO	**NUMBER OF GOVERNORS**
General veto and item veto: two-thirds needed to override	37
General veto and item veto: majority elected needed to override	6
General veto, no item veto: special legislative majority to override*	6
General veto, no item veto: simple majority to override	1

*Most common is 3/5 vote. Data change slightly.

Source: Thad L. Beyle, "Governors: The Middlemen and Women in Our Political System" in *Politics in the American States,* 8th ed., ed. Virginia Gray and Russell L. Hanson. Copyright ©2004 Congressional Quarterly Press, Washington, D.C. Reprinted by permission.

simple majority.[23] In Texas, the governor has very strong veto authority. The office possesses a general veto and a line-item veto, with a two-thirds vote of each house required for override. Very few vetoes have been overturned in Texas. From 1876 to 1968, only 25 of 936 vetoes were overridden by the legislature, most before 1940. This low number of veto overrides is due primarily to the late passage of bills and adjournment of the legislature. Only one veto has been overturned in recent years, and the bill was not significant. In 1979, during his first term, Bill Clements vetoed fifty-two bills. The legislature, in an attempt to get the governor's attention, overrode the veto on a bill that limited the ability of county governments to prohibit hunters from killing female deer.[24] Since 1979, no votes have been overridden by the legislature in Texas.

In fifteen other states besides Texas, the legislature cannot call "special" sessions, usually called extraordinary sessions to distinguish them from special sessions called by the governor. In states where the legislature cannot call extraordinary sessions, the governor has additional power to veto bills. In the 2003 session of the Texas legislature, Governor Perry set a new record by vetoing eighty-two bills. If the Texas legislature could have called an extraordinary session, there is little doubt that it would have done so and that some vetoes would have been overridden.

Some governors have a pocket veto, meaning that they can veto a bill by not signing it. The governor just "puts the bill in a pocket" and forgets about it. The Texas governor does not have a pocket veto. If the legislature is in session, the governor has ten days to sign a bill or it becomes law without the governor's signature. If the legislature has adjourned, the governor has twenty days to sign a bill or it becomes law without a signature. Sometimes governors do not like a bill but do not want to veto it for some reason. Letting the bill become law without a signature can be a way of expressing displeasure short of an actual veto.

Judicial Powers

judicial powers
The ability of a governor to issue pardons, clemency, and parole for citizens convicted to a crime.

Governors also are given limited **judicial powers** to grant pardons, executive clemency, and parole. Historically, governors have misused this power. This abuse has led to the creation of some checks on the ability of governors to exercise judicial authority. In Texas, James "Pa" Ferguson was accused of misusing this power, especially during the second term of his wife, Miriam Amanda "Ma" Ferguson (1933–35). It was charged that Jim Ferguson sold pardons and paroles to convicted felons.[25] The process was so open that this joke circulated around the capitol: A man steps off the elevator in the state capitol in Austin and accidentally bumps into Governor "Ma" Ferguson. "Oh! Pardon me, Governor," he says. Governor Ferguson says, "I'm sorry, you'll have to see Pa about that." This story is probably not true, but it illustrates the extent to which power to pardon was misused. The charges against Ferguson led to the creation of the state Pardons and Paroles Board. Today this eighteen-member board, appointed by the governor, recommends to the governor the action he or she can take in such matters and serves as a check on the process. Independent of board action, the governor may grant only one thirty-day stay of execution for any condemned prisoner. The board must recommend all other actions taken by the governor.

In the Fergusons' defense, many of the pardons were given to people who were in prison because they had violated the Prohibition laws. Laws prohibiting the use of alcoholic beverages were the war on drugs of several generations ago. Former lieutenant governor Hobby put it this way: "Prohibition's laws filled the prisons and ruined lives then just as marijuana laws do now. The Fergusons may have rightly concluded that the state was better served by these men being home supporting their families."[26]

Military Powers

The **military powers** of the governor are limited and come into play only in times of natural disaster or civil unrest. The governor appoints the adjutant general of the National Guard and can direct the Guard to protect the lives and property of Texas citizens. The most common use of this power is during natural disasters, when the Guard is deployed to help evacuate people, protect property, and supply food and water to victims.

military powers
Powers giving the governor the right to use the National Guard in times of disaster or civil insurrections.

POWERS OF THE TEXAS GOVERNOR COMPARED

If we take the five main indexes of power—tenure of office, appointive powers, budgetary powers, veto powers, and judicial powers—and compare the Texas governor with the other forty-nine governors, the Texas office is comparatively weak in formal powers (see Table 23–7).[27] The office is formally weak because of the limitations placed on its administrative and budgetary powers. On tenure and veto authority, the office is strong. The formal weakness in the office of governor is in keeping with the traditionalistic/individualistic political culture of the state.

TABLE 23–7	Summary of Institutional Powers of Governors by State, 2004 Scores were computed using six variables: election of other statewide executives, tenure of office, governor's appointive powers, governor's budgetary powers, veto powers; and governor's control over party. Five points were given for each variable and the total divided by six to get the score.

STRONGEST . . . . .WEAKEST

5.0		4.5		4.0		3.5		3.0		2.5		2.0
Illinois		4.1	Alaska	4.0	California	3.4		Alabama	2.7			
New York		4.1	Colorado	3.8	Delaware	3.5		Arizona	2.9			
Utah		4.1	Connecticut	3.8	Florida	3.4		Arkansas	3.0			
			Hawaii	3.7	Idaho	3.5		Georgia	2.8			
			Iowa	3.6	Indiana	3.1		North Carolina	2.8			
			Maine	3.8	Kansas	3.4		Rhode Island	2.8			
			Maryland	3.8	Kentucky	3.4		Vermont	2.8			
			Michigan	3.6	Louisiana	3.1						
			Minnesota	4.0	Massachusetts	3.4						
			Montana	3.6	Mississippi	3.4						
			New Jersey	3.9	Missouri	3.2						
			North Dakota	3.9	New Hampshire	3.2						
			Nebraska	3.7	Nevada	3.2						
			New Mexico	3.7	Oklahoma	3.1						
			Ohio	3.9	Oregon	3.3						
			Pennsylvania	3.7	Overall State Average:	3.5						
			South Dakota	3.8	South Carolina	3.1						
			Tennessee	3.9	Texas	3.1						
			West Virginia	4.0	Virginia	3.2						
			Wisconsin	3.6	Washington	3.2						
					Wyoming	3.3						

Overall State Average: 3.5

Source: Thad L. Beyle, "Governors" in *Politics in the American States*, 8th ed., ed. Virginia Gray and Russell L. Hanson. Copyright © 2004 Congressional Quarterly Press, Washington, D.C. Table 7.5, page 212. Reprinted by permission.

Political Culture

The Weak Governor in Texas

As indicated, the powers of the Texas governor are weak. The men who wrote the present constitution in 1876 had experienced what they felt were excesses under the Reconstruction governors and wanted a weak executive. This also fit well into the political culture of Texas. Today, some feel that with the many problems facing Texas the weak governor model does not fit modern Texas. The state administrative structure is a collection of agencies governed by other elected officials or by independent boards and commissions over which the governor has little control.

What's your opinion? Does modern-day Texas need to increase the power of the governor and his or her ability to control the administration of state government by expanding the governor's administrative and budgetary powers? See "States in the Nation" in Chapter 12, page 000 showing how governors share power with other elected officials in the fifty states.

As was discussed earlier, the present constitution was written in a time when limited government was very much on the minds of its framers. Having experienced strong executive authority during Reconstruction, the framers wanted to limit the governor's ability to act, especially in budgetary and administrative matters. They succeeded. In recent years, the powers of the Texas governor have been increased somewhat, but the office is still very weak in the budgetary and administrative dimensions. Given this formal weakness, Texas governors must use all their informal powers of persuasion and their political skills if they are to be successful. In recent years, the voters have rejected constitutional amendments that would expand the governor's ability to appoint and remove agency heads.

INFORMAL POWERS

While the office of Texas governor is formally very weak, it can be strong politically. The governor's primary political resource is the ability to exert influence. The governor is the most visible officeholder in the state and can command the attention of the news media by holding press conferences and announcing new decisions on policy issues. Such news conferences usually are well covered and reported by the press and other media. This enables the governor to impact the direction of state government. The governor also can stage events that are newsworthy to emphasize things she or he is interested in changing.

The popularity of the governor in public opinion polls is another important aspect of informal leadership. Governors who consistently rank high in popularity polls can use this fact to overcome opposition to their policies and reduce the likelihood of opposition, to both policies and electoral challenges. A governor who is weak in public opinion polls becomes an easy target for political opponents.

In very general ways, governors are judged on their leadership abilities. Some governors develop reputations as being indecisive, while others become known as effective, decisive leaders. The characterization attached to the governor affects his or her ability to be effective. The press will begin to repeat the reputational description of the governor, and with frequent repetition the reputation will become "fact." Therefore, developing a good image is very important.

Get Involved!

Campaign Money Used to Pay Members of Governor's Staff

Michael Toomey, chief of staff to Governor Rick Perry, has a state salary of $135,000. From his political campaign fund, Perry adds an additional $113,281, for a total of $248,281. President Bush started the practice when he was governor but the amount paid from campaign funds has increased dramatically. Bush paid his chief of staff an additional amount of only $9,228.

In addition to the supplemental pay given to Toomey, other members of Perry's staff also get additional pay. The State Comptroller, Carole Keeton Strayhorn, pays her deputy comptroller Billy Hamilton an additional $72,000.

"The potential for corruption is huge. The employees frequently know their salary is coming from political con-

tributions and may well know whose contribution was solicited to pay for their salary," said Tom "Smitty" Smith of *Public Citizen*.

The governor and other state officials justify the additional pay to attract quality people. For example, Mike Toomey earned from $600,000 to $1.4 million as a lobbyist in 2002 before joining the governor's staff. The other side of this argument is that when these people leave office they will be able to command even higher salaries as lobbyists and should not expect additional pay that may compromise their judgments or decisions.

Source: *Houston Chronicle*, "Political Stipends Sweeten State Pay," February 1, 2004, 1A and 14A.

Party Leadership

As indicated earlier, governors are expected to be leaders of their political party and in most states are recognized as the leader of the party. In the one-party era in Texas, the Democratic candidate for governor picked the state party chair and controlled the state party organization. Often, such control was based on a personal following rather than on a well-organized party structure. Republican governor Bill Clements made use of his election to build the party in the state, especially during his second term. He managed to gain enough control over the Republican party and its elected house members to thwart Democratic control of the legislature on some issues.

Today, governors might influence the choice of party leadership, but they do not control the party. George W. Bush found himself in the uncomfortable position of having to work with a state party chair chosen by the Social Conservatives. Governor Bush probably would have picked a different person for party chair. He did not attend the 2000 meeting of the Republican party convention, claiming to be busy campaigning for president. This might have been the first time a sitting governor did not attend his or her state party convention and indicated the degree of disagreement between the governor and the party leaders. As the two-party system matures in Texas, party leadership by the governor will need to become more of a fixture in state politics. Governor Perry has not embraced the Social Conservatives' program or party platform and has avoided becoming closely attached to or associated with this wing of the Republican party.

The Governor's Staff

In Texas, the trend in recent years has been to expand the staff of the governor's office. In 1963, when he became governor, John Connally made the first use of a professional staff of advisers. Previous governors often appointed only a handful of individuals, who were loyal to them politically but not necessarily highly professional. Other governors since Connally have added to the governor's staff. Today an organizational chart is necessary to maintain lines of authority and responsibility. Currently the governor has a staff of about two hundred.

Each governor will make different uses of her or his staff. In recent years, most governors have used their staff to keep track of state agencies over which the governor has little or no direct control. The staff also gathers information and makes recommendations on policy changes that impact most areas of state government. A message from a member of the governor's staff to a state agency is taken seriously. A report issued by the governor's office automatically attracts the attention of significant state leaders and the news media. Often the governor uses the information gathered to wage a public relations war with the legislature or state agencies. Increases in the size, professionalism, and complexity of the governor's staff have become necessary to offset the limited formal control the Texas governor has over state government.

ADMINISTRATIVE AGENCIES OF STATE GOVERNMENT

In addition to the office of governor, a number of state agencies make up what might be called the state bureaucracy. The term *bureaucracy* often implies a hierarchy of offices with levels of power leading to a centralized controlling authority. This term does not accurately describe the overall structure of state government in Texas, because there is no overall central governing authority. Government authority in Texas is very much decentralized and resides within many independent state agencies. The structure can best be described as a plural executive. That is, the governor is not the only executive—there are other elected officials with whom the governor must share power. In addition, many independent boards, commissions, and agencies operate independently of the governor. Power is decentralized among many officials. This decentralized power structure is in keeping with the traditionalistic/individualistic political culture of the state.

There are three basic kinds of state agencies in Texas: agencies headed by an elected official, appointed single-head agencies, and, the most numerous, agencies headed by a multimember appointed board or commission (see Table 23–8). The governor obviously has little or no authority over agencies headed by other elected officials, who are responsible to the voters who elected them. As was indicated earlier, while the Texas governor appoints citizens to these 301-plus state boards and commissions, he or she has very limited removal authority. Each state board and commission operates independently of the others, and there is no central controlling authority. The governor obviously has the greatest authority in the single-head agencies whose head he or she appoints. Except for the secretary of state, these agency heads have limited significance. Most of the work of state government is conducted by agencies controlled either by elected officials or by independent boards and commissions operating quite independently of the governor. Only the legislature, through its oversight and budgetary authority, exercises control over all state agencies.

Jacksonian statehouse government
A system in which most of the major department heads in state government are chosen by the voters at the ballot box.

Agencies with Elected Officials

The election of people to head administrative units of government is a concept dating to the 1820s with the election of Andrew Jackson. Known as **Jacksonian statehouse government,** the concept is that the ballot box is the best way to select administrators and make them accountable to the public. In the aftermath of

TABLE 23–8	The Administrative Structure of State Government in Texas

VOTERS IN STATE ELECT

Comptroller of public Accounts
Commissioner of the General Land Office
Attorney general
Commissioner of agriculture
Railroad Commission (3 members)
State Board of Education (15 members)
Lieutenant governor

GOVERNOR APPOINTS

Agency Heads
Secretary of state
Adjutant general of the National Guard
Director of housing and community affairs
Director of Office of State-Federal Relations
Executive director of Texas Education Agency
Commissioner for health and human services
Eight other minor agencies

Boards and Commissions
General government
Health and human services
Higher education boards of regents
Other education
Business regulation
Business and economic Development
Regional economic development
Licensing and professional examining boards
Public safety and criminal justice
Natural resources
Employee retirement boards
Interstate compact commissions
Water and river authorities
Judicial

Sources: *Guide to Texas State Agencies*, 9th ed., LBJ School, The University of Texas at Austin, Austin, Texas. Legislative Budget Board, *Fiscal Size Up, 1999–2000 Biennium, Texas State Services*. Legislative Budget Board, Austin, Texas. Some information was supplied by Governor's Appointments Office. The governor makes about one thousand appointments to task forces or ad hoc adviory committees who make recommendations to the governor or other state officials. They are not governing or policymaking bodies.

Reconstruction in the 1870s, the current Texas constitution reintroduced the idea of electing almost all officeholders and limiting the ability of the governor to appoint them.

Office of the Attorney General

The office of the **attorney general** was created under the 1876 constitution. The officeholder serves as the legal counsel to the governor, the legislature, and most of the other agencies, boards, and commissions in state government. Most of the

attorney general
Chief counsel to the governor and state agencies; has limited criminal jurisdiction.

work of the attorney general involves civil law and not criminal law. The attorney general's office, with some 3,700 state employees, is responsible for representing the state in litigation, enforcing state and federal child support laws, providing legal counsel to state officials, and enforcing state laws. Criminal functions of the office are limited primarily to those cases appealed to federal courts. The most common example of these criminal cases are death penalty appeals. Occasionally the attorney general's office may assist local criminal prosecutors when invited to do so. Although for the most part the functions of the attorney general are civil and not criminal in nature, this does not prevent most candidates who run for the office from emphasizing their commitment to law enforcement and getting tough on criminals.

Most of the resources of this office are devoted to collection of child support payments, collection of delinquent state taxes, administration of the Crime Victims Compensation program, and investigation of Medicare fraud. Despite this rather "mundane" list of functions, the office has important political functions. The most important of these is to issue so-called AG opinions on legal questions. Often, when the legislature is in session, the attorney general (AG) will be asked for an opinion on a pending piece of legislation. These AG opinions can have an impact on the course of legislation. A negative AG opinion often will kill a bill's chances of passing.

The office of attorney general is also an important stepping-stone to the governor's office. In recent years several candidates for governor have been former attorneys general (John Hill, Mark White, and Jim Mattox). Dan Morales was the first Mexican American to be elected to the office. He did not seek reelection in 1998, and in 2002 he lost a bid to become the Democratic party nominee for governor. John Cornyn, the attorney general from 1998 to 2002, was elected to the U.S. Senate in 2002.

Comptroller of Public Accounts

comptroller of public accounts

Chief tax collector and investor of state funds; does not perform financial audits.

A constitutional office created in 1876, the **comptroller of public accounts** has been assigned many additional duties over the years and currently functions as the chief fiscal and revenue forecasting office. In 1966, the office of treasurer was abolished, and the comptroller became responsible for investing state funds.

In many states and in the private sector, the term is "controller" rather than "comptroller" as used in Texas. Generally in government the "controller" has a pre-audit responsibility for assuring that funds can be spent for specific functions. In Texas the comptroller not only has pre-audit responsibility but also serves as the chief tax collector (a function normally associated with the office of treasurer), revenue forecaster, and investor of state funds.

The comptroller is responsible for collecting thirty-one different taxes for the state and collects the sales tax for some 1,169 local governments (1,018 cities, 117 counties, and 34 special districts).[28] The property tax division also conducts annual audits of property appraisal districts in the state to ensure uniformity in appraisals of the value of property across the state. Uniformity is important to improve the equity of state aid to local school districts. (See Chapter 25 on local governments.)

Former governor Bob Bullock served as comptroller for many years. During his tenure the office expanded its information and management functions and developed a fiscal forecasting model essential to projecting revenues in a two-year budget cycle. John Sharp, who followed Bob Bullock as comptroller, continued and expanded the office's information management programs. Also under Sharp the office developed Texas Performance Review teams to evaluate the effectiveness of government operations and ensure the most efficient use of state funds. These reviews were estimated to have saved the state over $1.3 billion in the 1998–99 biennium fiscal years. Similar management information and efficiency audits are available to assist local governments. Most of these programs were kept in place by Carole Keeton Strayhorn, who succeeded John Sharp.

The office also provides assistance to the private sector through the provision of information. The State of Texas Econometric Model is used to forecast state economic growth, keep track of business cycles, and provide information on the general health of the economy of the state. Finally, the office is responsible for investing state funds. This involves investing and securing fund balances that average $8.6 billion during the year.[29]

Commissioner of the General Land Office

Texas is one of only four states to have a **land commissioner**.[30] The office was created under the 1836 constitution to administer state-owned land. When Texas entered the Union in 1845, the agreement between the former republic and the U.S. government was that Texas would keep its public debt and its public land. When Texas became a state, most of the land was state-owned. Today the state of Texas owns and manages 20.3 million acres of land, including open beaches and submerged land extending 10.3 miles into the Gulf of Mexico.[31]

The land commissioner's office is responsible for leasing state lands and generating funds from oil and gas production. The office also is responsible for overseeing the Veterans Land Board and the Veterans Land Fund. This fund loans money to Texas veterans to purchase rural land. Finally, the land office is responsible for maintaining the environmental quality of the state's open beaches along the Gulf Coast.

land commissioner
Elected official responsible for administration and oversight of state-owned lands.

Commissioner of Agriculture

The Texas Department of Agriculture (TDA) was created by statute in 1907. A commissioner of agriculture is elected by the voters in a statewide election to head the department. The TDA has the dual, and sometimes contradictory, roles of promoting agriculture products and production and regulating agricultural practices, while protecting the public health from unsafe agricultural practices. For example, the TDA must both promote cotton production and sales in the state and regulate the use of pesticides.

The TDA has six major functions: marketing of Texas agricultural products, development and promotion of agricultural businesses' product production, pesticide regulation, pest management, product certification and safety inspection, and inspection and certification of measuring devices (including gasoline pumps, electronic scanners, and scales).

While the TDA and the agricultural commissioner are not as publicly visible as the other statewide elected officials, they are important to a large section of the state's economy—those engaged in agriculture. While the economy of Texas has become more diversified in recent years, agriculture is still a significant player in the state's economy. Major agribusinesses and other agricultural interests in the state pay close attention to who serves as the commissioner of agriculture.

The Texas Railroad Commission

The **Texas Railroad Commission (RRC)** was created in 1891 during the administration of Governor James S. Hogg to regulate the railroad monopolies that had developed in the state. The commission was also given regulatory authority over terminals, wharves, and express companies. The commission consists of three

Texas Railroad Commission (TRC)
State agency charged with regulation over some aspects of transportation and the oil and gas industry of the state.

members elected statewide by the voters for six-year staggered terms, with one member elected every two years. The member up for election, by convention, always serves as chair of the commission.

In the 1920s, when oil and natural gas production developed in the state, the task of regulating the exploration, drilling, and production of oil and natural gas was assigned to the RRC in part because it was the only state regulatory agency in the state at the time. When motor truck transport developed in the state, regulation of the trucking industry was also assigned to the RRC. In part because of federal rules and regulations, the original role of regulating railroads and the later role of regulating trucking have become minor roles of the agency, reduced primarily due to concern with safety issues. The regulation of the oil and gas industry is its primary function today.

Many have been critical of the RRC over the years because of close ties between the elected commissioners and the oil and gas industry it regulates (see Chapter 20 on interest groups). Large campaign contributions from oil and gas PACs have raised questions about whether the commission has been co-opted by the industry it regulates. Also, like the Department of Agriculture, the RRC has the dual role of promoting oil and gas production in the state and regulating the safety and environmental aspects of the industry (e.g., promoting the development of pipelines to carry petroleum products as well as ensuring the safety of those pipelines). A similar conflict may exist between the RRC's task of regulating and promoting the mining of minerals (especially lignite coal) in the state.

The role of the RRC that most directly affects citizens in the state is that of setting the rates charged by local natural gas companies. Natural gas companies must have the rates they charge residential and commercial customers approved by the RRC. The RRC also regulates the safety of natural gas systems.

The State Board of Education

Unlike the other offices discussed in this section, the governing body for public elementary and secondary education in the state has varied greatly in form and structure over the years. Originally, in 1884, an elected school superintendent governed Texas schools. In 1929, an appointed state board was created. In 1949, the Gilmer-Aikin Act created the Texas Education Agency (TEA) headed by an appointed superintendent of education. In the 1960s, an elected state board was added. In 1984, the elected board was reduced from twenty-one members, elected from congressional districts in the state, to fifteen members appointed by the governor. In 1986, the board again was changed from appointed members to members elected from districts. The current board, called the State Board of Education, nominates a person to be named commissioner of education by the governor.

In recent years the authority of the State Board has been greatly reduced by actions of the state legislature. The political battle over the power of the State Board revolves around the Social Conservatives' (Christian Right's) success in electing members to the board and the actions taken in setting curriculum standards and selecting textbooks. Public infighting among members of the board has diminished its effectiveness. The legislature has removed several functions, most significantly the selection of textbooks, from the State Board in part because of infighting and control by the conservative faction.

Single-Head Agencies

In some states, a single person, appointed and serving at the pleasure of the governor, heads most agencies. The structure is similar to that of the federal government, where the president appoints his own cabinet members who serve at the president's pleasure. Only a handful of state agencies in Texas follow this model, and few are of great importance.

Secretary of State

The **secretary of state** (SOS) is a constitutional office, appointed by the governor with approval of the state senate. The constitution and state statutes assign many duties to this office, which can be put into three broad categories: elections, record keeping/information management, and international protocol. As the chief election official, the SOS is responsible for overseeing voter registration, preparation of election information, and supervision of elections. The SOS issues rules, directives, and opinions on the conduct of elections and voter registration. These duties allow the secretary some latitude in the interpretation and application of the state Election Code. For example, the SOS has some latitude in how vigorously citizens are encouraged to register and vote.

secretary of state
Chief election official and keeper of state records; appointed by the governor.

A second duty of the secretary of state is to serve as the official keeper of state records. This includes records of business corporations and some other commercial activities. The office also publishes the *Texas Register*, the source of official notices or rules, meetings, executive orders, and opinions of the attorney general that are required to be filed by state agencies. Through the protocol functions of the office, the SOS provides support services to state officials who interact with representatives of foreign countries.

In a few cases, the office of secretary of state has been an important stepping-stone to higher office. It is a highly visible office, and the secretary is often in the public eye, especially in regard to the duties as chief election official. SOS is without doubt the most important single-head agency appointment the governor makes. The most noted example is Mark White, who became attorney general and later governor. Former governor Bush picked his secretary of state, Alberto Gonzales, to become White House counsel in his administration.

Commissioner for Health and Human Services

The office of commissioner for health and human services was created in 1991 to coordinate a number of health-related programs and agencies. The governor appoints the commissioner for a two-year term with the approval of the state senate. The commissioner has oversight responsibility over eleven separate health and welfare programs, which are directed by boards, councils, or commissions. The commissioner is not directly responsible for the administration of these programs but has oversight and review functions. Programs overseen include aging; alcohol and drug abuse; the blind, deaf, and hard-of-hearing; early childhood intervention; juvenile probation; mental health and retardation; rehabilitation; and the Departments of Health, Human Services, and Protective and Regulatory Services. While this office has little direct administrative control, it can and often does impact policy. The commissioner serves as a spokesperson for the governor in health and welfare matters.

Office of State-Federal Relations

The governor appoints the executive director of the Office of State-Federal Relations. As the name suggests, this office coordinates relations between state and federal officials. The office has existed since 1971 and is the primary liaison between the governor's office and federal officials. To some degree this office becomes an advocate (lobbyist) for the state in dealings with the Texas congressional delegation and federal agencies.

Adjutant General of the National Guard

The office of adjutant general, created by the Texas constitution, is responsible for directing the state military force under the direction of the governor. The governor serves as commander in chief of the National Guard. The size of the National Guard (nationwide and in Texas) is determined and funded by Congress as a reserve force to the regular army. The Guard also provides emergency aid and protection of property and persons in times of natural disaster.

In the November 1999 election, the voters of Texas rejected a constitutional amendment that would have allowed the governor to appoint and remove the head of the National Guard. As with other appointees, the governor may appoint the head of the National Guard but may not remove except on approval of the state senate.

Other Single-Head Agencies

The remaining state agencies to which the governor makes a single appointment are not of great significance in terms of policy or politics. This is not to say that they are insignificant, but they are simply of less importance. These agencies often receive little or no attention from the average citizen or the press. They include the following: Department of Housing and Community Affairs, Department of Commerce, State Office of Administrative Hearings, Executive Director of Health Care Information Council, Insurance Commissioner, Public Utility Commission Council, and Fire Fighters (volunteers) Pension Commission Executive Director. In addition, five interstate compact commissions govern the rivers in Texas. The governor appoints the executive director of each of these commissions.

Boards and Commissions

state boards and commissions

State agencies whose members are appointed by the governor for a fixed term.

In addition to the previously described elected and appointed officials, the governor appoints about 2,800 members to 301 **state boards and commissions** (see Table 23–4). These administrative units carry out most of the work of state government. The board or commission usually appoints the head of the agency (e.g., chancellor of a university or executive director of a state agency) and in varying degrees is responsible for the policy and administration of the agency. Most operate quite independently of other agencies of state government, with the exception of the legislature.

Given the lack of central control and the decentralized nature of state government in Texas, it is surprising that things work as well as they do. For example, some eighteen separate agencies provide health and welfare services. In addition to the Department of Agriculture, the General Land Office, and the Railroad Commission—all exercising some control over environmental and natural resources—there are at least seven other agencies with independent boards or commissions with some authority in this area. These include the Texas Commission of Environmental Quality, the Texas Parks and Wildlife Department, the Soil and Water Conservation Board, and the Water Development Board.

In this conservative state with a strong belief in the free market, there are nonetheless no fewer than thirty-eight separate professional licensing and examining boards. Think of a profession, and there is probably a state agency that licenses and regulates that profession, including accountants, architects, barbers, chiropractors, cosmetologists, dentists, exterminators, funeral directors, land surveyors, medical doctors, two kinds of nurses, pharmacists, physical therapists, podiatrists, and veterinarians, to name just a few. Most often the professional group asks for regulation by the state. When such groups advocate government regulation and licensing, they claim to be primarily interested in protecting the public from incompetent or dishonest practitioners. This might be partially true; however, regulation also has the added benefit of limiting entry into the profession and fostering development of rules favorable to the group. Two examples are the water well drillers and landscape architects. (See Chapter 20 on interest groups.) Also, professionals make the argument that the people appointed to the boards by the governor should be knowledgeable of the profession they are governing. While knowledge is an important factor, the danger is that these boards and commissions, dominated by members of the profession, will be more inclined to make rules and regulations favorable to that group than to protect the public. Because of this fear, in recent years the appointment of at least some members of such boards from outside the profession has become the norm, for example, the appointment of nonphysicians to the State Board of Medical Examiners.

Twelve college governing boards oversee the institutions of higher education in the state. These boards are required to coordinate their activities and gain approval for some activities and programs from the State Higher Education Coordinating Board. Within these broad guidelines, each university governing board is relatively free to set policy, approve budgets, and govern their universities. Once again governance is decentralized, with only a minimum of control from the state and almost none from the governor.

Legislative Agencies

In addition to the executive agencies, there are also several legislative agencies. These units are controlled by the leadership in the Texas house and senate. Their purpose is to provide legislative oversight of the "executive" agencies and to assist the legislature in its lawmaking functions.

Legislative Budget Board (LBB)

The **Legislative Budget Board** is primarily responsible for preparing the state budget. It is composed of the lieutenant governor, the speaker of the house, four senators, and four state representatives. All agencies that receive state funds from the state budget must submit their requests for appropriations to the LBB. The LBB reviews these requests and proposes a budget to the state legislature. As indicated earlier, unlike in most other states, in Texas the governor plays a very limited role in the budget process.

Legislative Budget Board
State agency, controlled by the leadership in the state legislature, that writes the state budget.

Texas Legislative Council

The speaker, the lieutenant governor, four senators, and four state representatives control this agency. They appoint the executive director. The Texas Legislative Council was created in 1949 to assist the legislature in drafting bills, conducting research on legislation, producing publications, and providing technical support services. This highly professional agency produces information for the legislature that is made available to the public in various ways.

Legislative Audit Committee and State Auditor's Office

The **Legislative Audit Committee** consists of the lieutenant governor, the speaker of the house, and the chairs of the senate Finance Committee and State Affairs Committee and the house Appropriations Committee and Ways and Means Committee. This committee appoints the state auditor, who is responsible for auditing state agencies and assisting the legislature in its oversight functions.

Legislative Audit Committee
Legislative agency that performs audits of all state agencies.

Get Involved!

Democratic Control and Bureaucratic Responsiveness

The concept of democratic control requires that state agencies be responsible to the people—that is, that state agencies respond to demands placed on them by citizens. With Texas state administrative agencies operating quite independently of each other and overall administrative control being absent from state government, agencies often are able to respond only to clientele groups they serve and not to the public generally. Thus, most state agencies are accountable only to small groups of attentive citizens. See Chapter 20 on interest groups for a more complete discussion of agency capture.

In other states, accountability in a more general sense is ensured by the governor's broader power to appoint agency heads (rather than independent boards and commissions) that serve at the pleasure of the governor. Also,

some states have given the governor broad budgetary control over state agencies. Agencies are required to submit budget requests to the governor, who produces a state budget that is submitted to the state legislature. As indicated previously, in Texas the governor plays almost no role in the budgetary process. The Legislative Budget Board instead performs this function.

Thus, state government in Texas is so fragmented and responsibility so divided that holding anyone responsible for state government is impossible. While citizens might blame the governor when things go wrong and governors might claim credit when things go right, in truth the governor of Texas is responsible for very little and deserves credit for much less than he or she usually claims.

Legislative Reference Library

This organization assists the legislature in doing research and serves as a depository of records for the legislature. The library, located in the state capitol, is open to members of the public who want to do research on the Texas legislature.

Other State Agencies and Boards

Judicial Agencies

There are several agencies that can be called judicial agencies and are under the supervision of the state supreme court (civil matters). Except for budgeting of money by the legislature, these agencies are relatively free of legislative oversight. The State Bar, which licenses attorneys, receives no state appropriations. The remaining agencies are responsible for court administration (Office of Court Administration), operations of the state law library, and certification of legal licenses and specializations.

Ex Officio Boards and Commissions

A number of state agencies are headed by boards whose membership is completely or partially made up of designated state officials who are members because of the position they hold. Examples of these officials are the statewide elected officials—governor, lieutenant governor, speaker of the house, attorney general, and land commissioner. Examples of these agencies are the Bond Review Board, the Legislative Redistricting Board, and the Budget Execution Committee.

Multi-Appointment Boards

Finally, some state agencies have governing boards whose members are appointed by more than one elected official. The reason for this is to prevent any one individual from dominating the selection process and the outcome of decisions. The Texas Ethics commission is a good example of this type of agency. This commission has four members appointed by the governor and two members each appointed by the lieutenant governor and speaker of the house. It oversees campaign finance and lobbying activities.

Sunset Review

Given the lack of overall, central control in state government and the limited and weak authority of the governor, in 1977 the Texas legislature created the ten-member **Sunset Advisory Commission** to review most state agencies every twelve years and recommend changes. This commission consists of four state senators, four members of the house of representatives, and two public members.

The sunset process basically involves the "idea that legislative oversight of government operations can be enhanced by a systematic evaluation of state agencies."[32] The process works by establishing a date on which an agency of state government is abolished if the legislature does not pass a law providing for its continuance. The act does not apply to agencies created in the Texas constitution or to some state agencies that are exempt. For example, state universities are not subject to sunset review. Sunset review asks this basic question: Do the policies carried out by an agency need to be continued?[33]

In the first twenty-five years of sunset review in Texas, very few (thirty-two) state agencies were abolished. Most were minor state agencies with few functions. Most notable among them were the Boll Weevil Commission, the Battle Ship Texas Commission, and the Stonewall Jackson Memorial Board. More important than abolition is the review process. By forcing a review of an agency every twelve years, the legislature is given the opportunity to recommend changes to improve the efficiency and effectiveness of state government. In many cases, functions of state agencies are transferred to other agencies, and agencies are combined or merged. Table 23–9 lists the activities of the Texas Sunset Advisory Commission over the years 1979 through 2003.

Finally, sunset review has forced public evaluation of many agencies that for the most part operate out of the public's attention. This is especially true of those agencies that license professions. Sunset review resulted in the appointment of nonprofessionals to these agencies in an effort to promote the broader interests of the public over the narrow interests of the agency and its clientele.

State Employees

Most of the funds appropriated by the state legislature go to pay for personnel salaries. This is the largest single expenditure item for all state governments. Table 23–10 shows the number of employees of the top fifteen agencies in Texas, excluding institutions of higher education. Schoolteachers, who are employed by local school districts, also are not included in this ranking.

There is no general civil service system or central personnel agency in Texas. Each agency creates its own set of rules and regulations regarding personnel practices and procedures. Most states have a central personnel system and some form of civil service system that formulates personnel policies and procedures. In keeping with the decentralized nature of its state government, the personnel system in Texas is also very decentralized.

Approximately 76 percent of Texas state employees work in the five major functional areas of state government: corrections, highways, public welfare, hospitals, and higher education. The number of state employees has declined

Sunset Advisory Commission
Agency responsible for making recommendations to the legislature for changes in the structure and organization of most state agencies.

TABLE 23–9	Overview of Sunset Actions in Texas, 1979–2003						
YEAR	SESSION	REVIEWS	AGENCIES CONTINUED	AGENCIES ABOLISHED	FUNCTIONS TRANSFERRED	FUNCTIONS MERGED	SEPARATED
1979	66	26	12	8	1	4	1
1981	67	28	22	2	3	1	0
1983	68	32	29	3	0	0	0
1985	69	31	24	6	0	0	1
1987	70	20	18	1	1	0	0
1989	71	30	25	3	2	0	0
1991	72	30	23	3	3	1	0
1993	73	31	27	1	1	2	0
1995	74	18	16	0	2	0	0
1997	75	21	19	0	2	0	0
1999	76	25	22	1	0	2	0
2001	77	25	23	1	0	1	0
2003	78	26	23	3	0	0	0
2005	79	22	19	2	0	1	0
	Total	365	302	34	15	12	2

Source: www.sunset.state.tx.us/79htm

slightly in recent years due in part to the performance review audits conducted by Comptroller John Sharp. Among the fifteen most populous states, Texas ranks tenth in the number of state employees per ten thousand population. Still, the state of Texas is the largest single employer in Texas.

TABLE 23–10	Top Fifteen State Agencies Ranked by the Number of State Government Employees, 1998–99, 2000–01, and 2002–03 Bienniums Higher-education institutions and local schoolteachers are not included.			
		NUMBER OF EMPLOYEES		
RANK	AGENCY	1998–99	2000–01	2002–03
1	Department of Criminal Justice (most employed in state prisons)	39,868	42,765	42,701
2	Department of Mental Health and Retardation	23,575	20,803	19,718
3	Department of Human Services (welfare)	15,524	14,335	14,555
4	Department of Transportation (state highways)	15,021	14,626	14,726
5	Department of Public Safety (Highway Patrol and Texas Rangers)	7,059	7,216	7,315
6	Department of Protective and Regulatory Services (business regulation)	6,214	6,682	6,882
7	Texas Department of Health	5,783	5,695	5,098
8	Texas Workforce Commission	5,513	5,017	3,914
9	Texas Youth Commission (juvenile criminal offenders)	4,283	3,931	5,529
10	Office of the Attorney General	3,660	3,774	3,817
11	Natural Resources Conservation Commission	2,983	3,027	3,044
12	Parks and Wildlife Department	2,954	2,954	3,036
13	Comptroller of Public Accounts	2,938	2,831	2,845
14	Rehabilitation Commission	2,578	2,603	2,603
15	Worker's Compensation Commission	1,128	1,128	1,118

Sources: *Fiscal Size Up, 1998–99.* Legislative Budget Board, *www.lbb.state.tx.us; Texas Fact Book 2002–03 www.state.tx.us.*

Summary

Self-Test www.mhhe.com/pattersontad8

Even though governors in most states do not have much formal power, the office has great importance in state politics. In recent years, the importance of the office has increased. Four of the last five U.S. presidents have been former governors. As the office becomes increasingly visible in both state and national politics, the need for strong leadership in this office continues to increase.

Texas is now the second-largest state in population and one of the leading states in industrial growth. The governor's lack of formal power makes the task of governing this large, diverse, and economically important state both difficult and challenging. Some reform of the powers of the governor is needed, but it is doubtful that changes will occur. The political culture of the state does not support increasing the authority of the governor's office. Leadership will have to come from force of will and personality and not from formal changes in the structure of the office.

Interest groups do not support transferring power from state agencies they can dominate to agencies under the control of a single individual appointed by the governor. While the Sunset Advisory Commission has had a positive impact on some agencies, a general reorganization of Texas state government is not likely anytime soon.

STUDY CORNER

Key Terms

acting governor (p. 667)
appointive powers (p. 671)
attorney general (p. 683)
ceremonial duties (p. 662)
chief legislator (p. 662)
comptroller of public accounts (p. 000)
impeachment and conviction (p. 667)
informal qualifications (p. 663)
intergovernmental coordinator (p. 662)

Jacksonian statehouse government (p. 682)
judicial powers (p. 678)
land commissioner (p. 685)
Legislative Audit Committee (p. 689)
Legislative Budget Board (p. 689)
legislative power (p. 677)
line-item veto (p. 676)
military powers (p. 679)

partial vetoes (p. 677)
recall (p. 668)
secretary of state (p. 687)
state boards and commissions (p. 688)
Sunset Advisory Commission (p. 691)
tenure of office (p. 668)
Texas Railroad Commission (TRC) (p. 685)

Self-Test

1. Which of the following does **not** accurately describe a role played by the Texas governor?
   a. chief governmental coordinator, in an attempt to promote the interests of the state
   b. chief budget officer, which requires the governor to prepare the budget for the legislature's consideration
   c. ceremonial leader, in an attempt to generate favorable press coverage and support for the governor's programs
   d. chief policymaker, which requires the governor to sell his or her programs to state legislators and to coordinate state agencies that administer those programs
   e. chief legislator, which requires the governor to develop close relationships with legislators who introduce bills for legislative consideration

2. Which of the following is **not** a limitation or restriction on the Texas governor's appointive and removal powers?
   a. The governor shares power with other independently elected officials.
   b. Many of the governor's proposed appointees must be confirmed by the senate.
   c. The governor appoints many individuals to nonpolicymaking and governing boards that recommend policy and programs.
   d. The governor must give geographic and political consideration to his or her appointments.
   e. The governor's appointive powers do not allow the governor to influence policy after leaving office.

3. Which of the following does **not** accurately describe the Texas governor's budgetary powers?
   a. The legislature may override a governor's veto by calling itself into a special session, the budgetary agenda of which is controlled by the speaker of the house.

   b. The governor's budgetary authority is hindered by four different types of constraints.
   c. The governor's limited appointment power gives the governor less discretion in how money is spent.
   d. The governor's strongest budgetary power is the line-item veto.
   e. Earmarked funds limit the governor's authority to control a majority of the funds expended pursuant to the state budget.

3. Which of the following is **not** a state executive officer who is elected independently of the Texas governor?
   a. attorney general
   b. secretary of state
   c. comptroller of public accounts
   d. commissioner of agriculture
   e. commissioner of the General Land Office

4. Which of the following accurately describes sunset review in Texas?
   a. It is performed by a ten-member, bipartisan public commission created by the legislature.
   b. It is designed to enhance the evaluation of state agencies that operate out of the public spotlight.
   c. An agency of the state government is abolished if the legislature does not pass a law providing for its continuance.
   d. b and c only.
   e. All of the above.

5. Like the office of the vice-president of the United States, the lieutenant governor becomes the acting governor when the governor leaves the state. (T/F)

6. Removal of the governor requires a two-step process in which formal articles of impeachment are adopted by the house and conviction occurs in the senate. (T/F)

7. The Texas governor has the strongest tenure because he or she may serve four-year terms with no limit on the number of terms. (T/F)

8. Both the governor and the president of the United States share the budgetary power of the line-item veto. (T/F)

9. If the legislature is in session and the governor chooses not to sign a bill forwarded by the legislature, the bill becomes law after twenty days. (T/F)

10. The governor of Texas has full independent pardoning power of condemned prisoners. (T/F)

Critical Thinking

The office of governor in Texas is relatively weak in terms of formal power. What would be the advantages and disadvantages of making this office stronger? What arguments could be used to persuade the legislature to give up power to the executive?

Suggested Readings

Anderson, James, Richard W. Murray, and Edward L. Farley. *Texas Politics: An Introduction*, 6th ed. New York: Harper-Collins, 1992.

Beyle, Thad. "Governors: The Middlemen and Women in Our Political System," in *Politics in the American States*, 8th ed., ed. Virginia Gray and Russell L. Hanson. Washington, D.C.: Congressional Quarterly Press, 2004.

Brown, Norman D. *Hood, Bonnet and Little Brown Jug: Texas Politics 1921–1928*. College Station: Texas A&M Press, 1983.

Gantt, Fred Jr. *The Chief Executive in Texas: A Study in Gubernatorial Leadership*. Austin: University of Texas Press, 1964.

List of Websites

http://www.governor.state.tx.us/
Website of the Texas Governor's Office.

http://www.lbb.state.tx.us/
Information on the governor's budget proposals from the Legislative Budget Board.

http://www.nga.org/governors/
Useful information on governors in other states, including background and biographical information.

http://www.csg.org/
Website of the Council of State Governments. Provides up-to-date information on state governments and governors.

http://www.nga.org/
Website of the national association of American state governors.

http://www.texasonline.state.tx.us/
Contains Web pages for each Texas state agency, with links to other organizations

Participate!

Send a letter to the governor of Texas and express your opinion on some current issue, for example, school finance. The legislature and governor are at odds on this issue. Ask the governor what tax increases he is willing to support to adequately fund education in Texas. Ask specifically about an income tax.

Extra Credit
Go to the web page for the Texans for Public Justics—www.TPJ.org.

Here you will find a report on Governor Perry's Patronage. Read this article and write an essay giving your opinion on this article. Do you think the governor is influenced by campaign contributions in his appointment of members of state boards and commissions? What are the implications of this practice on state policy produced by these boards and commissions?

(Self-Test Answers: 1. b   2. e   3. a   3. b   4. e   5. F   6. T   7. T   8. F   9. F   10. T)

The Court System in Texas

Chapter Outline

Court Decision Making

Judicial Federalism

Trial and Appellate Courts

The Structure of State Courts
Magistrate or Minor Courts
County Courts
District Courts
Appellate Courts
Supreme Courts

Judicial Selection

Issues in Judicial Selection in Texas
Familiar Names
Straight-Ticket Voting
Campaign Contributions
Minority Representation
Conclusions on Elected Judges

The "Appointive-Elective" System in Texas

Is There a Best System?

Removal and Discipline of Judges

The Legal System
Grand Jury
Petit Jury

Crime and Punishment in Texas
The Crime Rate
Factors Contributing to Crime
The Effect of Punishment on Crime Rates
The Death Penalty
The Harris County Factor

CHAPTER 24

Whoever attentively considers the different departments of power must perceive, that, in a government in which they are separated from each other, the judiciary, from the nature of its functions, will always be the least dangerous to the political rights of the Constitution; because it will be least in a capacity to annoy or injure them.

—*Alexander Hamilton, Federalist No. 78*

On November 22, 2005, the Texas supreme court partially overturned the system used to finance Texas schools. The court ordered the state legislature to fix this problem by June 2006. Some citizens do not like the idea that the court system can be used to fix what they consider to be political problems.

Most citizens hold two conflicting views of the appropriate role of courts in a democratic society. First, citizens think the court system should be above politics. Courts are expected to act in nonpolitical ways. Justice is often portrayed as a "blindfolded woman holding the scales of justice in her hand. Most Americans firmly believe that courts should be blind to political bias: fairness, it would seem, requires neutrality."[1] Second, Americans also want state courts to be responsive to the electorate, "especially if they play prominent roles in molding and implementing public policy."[2] Obviously, courts cannot be both above politics and responsive to the electorate.

Most citizens do not see a conflict between these two ideas. They think that courts should both dispense pure justice and do so according to the wishes of the electorate. Courts are placed in this position because they make decisions on matters ranging from domestic and family law to criminal law and serve as the final arbitrator of highly political decisions. In playing the dual roles of decision-maker and policymaker, courts function very differently from other governmental institutions.

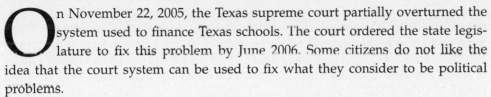

COURT DECISION MAKING

The courts' approach to decision making is quite different from the way the executive and legislative branches make decisions.[3] Courts must maintain a **passive appearance.** Unlike the legislature or the governor, who can initiate policy changes, courts must wait for a case to come to them. Most cases do not involve policy questions but instead deal with controversies between individuals. Courts enforce existing rules and laws; they are arbitrators of conflict, not initiators of laws.

passive appearance
Condition that courts do not initiate cases but must wait for cases to be brought to the court.

697

strict rules of access

Lesser accessibility of courts because of special rules that determine whether the court will or can hear a case.

strict procedural rules

Very tight rules regarding how cases must proceed and what evidence can be presented in court.

specifics of the case

Condition that court decisions apply only to the case heard in court and not to other cases or issues.

stare decisis

Principle that courts base their decisions on previous rulings of other courts.

appearance of objectivity

Condition that courts must appear to make objective decisions and not political ones.

Also, courts have **strict rules of access.**[4] While any citizen may approach the legislature or the governor, courts have rules that limit access to them. Individuals must have "standing." This means that a court case must involve real controversies between two or more parties and that someone must have suffered real damage. Courts do not deal in hypothetical or imaginary controversies. In short, they do not play "what if" ("What if I hit this person? What will the court do?").

Courts are governed by **strict procedural rules** that determine when and how facts and arguments can be presented.[5] These rules prevent the introduction of some evidence in a criminal case. For example, evidence gathered by the police in an illegal search might not be allowed.

Generally, a court's decisions affect only the cases being considered by the court and not other cases before other courts.[6] Courts rule on the **specifics of the case** and do not make general policy decisions. This means that court decisions do not have an effect beyond the specific case being considered. Rarely do trial court decisions have the effect of making general policy. Actions by the legislature do have the effect of making general policy. For example, if a trial court rules that a city ordinance in one city is invalid, this ruling does not invalidate all similar ordinances in other cities. Ordinances in other cities, with slightly different details, might be legal. The court must decide each case separately. There is an exception to this general rule. The rulings of appellate and supreme courts establish rules of law, called precedent, which lower courts must follow. Under English law this is called **stare decisis** ("to stand by that which was decided before"). Courts follow principles announced in former cases and diverge from these only when they can show good cause for doing so. In this way, appellate courts affect how trial courts make decisions; however, each case in a lower court might be affected slightly differently.

Courts also differ from other branches of government in that they must maintain the **appearance of objectivity.**[7] Unlike governors and legislators, courts may not appear to be political in their decision making, even though judges might be affected in their decisions by political considerations. Judges must base their decisions on points of law. The result might be quite political, but the process must not appear to be.

Thus, courts differ from governors and legislators in the way they make decisions. They must maintain a passive role, enforce rules that restrict access to the courts, uphold strict rules of procedure, confine their decisions to the specifics of the cases before them, and maintain the appearance of objectivity. By doing this, courts reinforce the legitimacy of their decisions and their place as the final arbitrators of conflict. This in turn reinforces the concept that the rule of law, and not the rule of arbitrary actions by individuals, governs.

JUDICIAL FEDERALISM

supreme law of the land

Constitutional principle that federal law is superior to state law.

The U.S. Constitution established the U.S. Supreme Court and gave Congress the authority to create other lower federal courts. Article 6 of the U.S. Constitution makes national law the **"supreme law of the land."** The states also create state-level courts. This results in a dual court system of both federal and state courts. Federal courts hear cases involving federal laws, and state courts hear cases involving state laws. While some cases might be filed in either state or federal court, most cases go to state courts and not to federal courts. An example of a case that could have gone to either court system is the case of the bombing of the federal office building in Oklahoma City. While murder is a crime in Oklahoma, a bombing of a federal facility that results in the death of a federal government employee is a federal crime. Another example is the case

Political Culture

The Application of Court Rulings

Court rulings in one case do not automatically apply to all similar cases. Two Texas cities (Missouri City and College Station) both had park land dedication ordinances. The Missouri City ordinance was ruled unconstitutional and the College Station ordinance was upheld. Both dealt with park land dedication, but the ordinances were different.

Most cities require land developers to donate land for streets and public rights-of-way when they subdivide land. Missouri City required land developers to donate park land or money for neighborhood park development, but the city could spend the money collected from developers on parks many miles from that development. The development did not directly benefit from the dedication of money by the developer. This ordinance was tried in the Texas courts. The court of appeals ruled the Missouri City ordinance unconstitutional because it took property from developers for which they received no benefit.

College Station also had a park land and money dedication ordinance, but it differed from the Missouri City ordinance in one significant way. Money collected from developers for parks had to be spent in the immediate neighborhood. If the money was not spent within three years, it would be returned to the developer. The Turtle Rock Corporation, a land development company in College Station, refused to pay the park fee, citing the Missouri City case as their reason.

College Station sued, and the Texas supreme court upheld the city ordinance. Money spent for parks in College Station benefited the development by providing parks in the neighborhood of the development. This was not true with the Missouri City ordinance. (*Turtle Rock Development Corporation v. City of College Station*)

of the so-called Unabomber, in which persons were murdered by bombs, most of which were sent through the U.S. mail. Both of these cases were tried in federal court. State prosecutors initially indicated that they might also file state murder charges against the Unabomber suspect, but this did not happen.

Few other countries have dual court systems. The dual system in the United States developed because of our federal system of government. State courts existed during the colonial period and continued after the adoption of the U.S. Constitution in 1789. State courts act primarily in areas in which the federal government lacks authority to act.

TRIAL AND APPELLATE COURTS

There are two kinds of state courts: trial courts and appellate courts. They differ in several important ways. First, **trial courts** are localized. Jurisdiction is limited to a geographic area such as a county.[8] Second, only one judge presides over a trial court, and each court is considered a separate court. Third, citizens participate in trial court activity, serving as members of juries and as witnesses during trials. Fourth, trial courts are concerned primarily with establishing the facts of a case (such as a determination that a person is guilty). Fifth, trial courts announce decisions immediately after the trial is finished.[9]

Appellate courts, on the other hand, are centralized, often at the state level. More than one judge presides, citizen participation is virtually absent, and, most important, appellate courts decide points of law, not points of fact. An appeal of a murder conviction from a trial court to a higher court is based not on points of fact (Is the person guilty?) but on points of law (Were legal procedures followed?). Trial courts establish guilt, and appellate courts decide whether proper procedures have been followed in the trial courts.

trial courts
Local courts that hear cases for which juries determine the outcome.

appellate courts
Higher-level courts that decide cases on points of law and not on questions of guilt or innocence.

In Texas, all death penalty cases are automatically appealed to the Texas Court of Criminal Appeals. The issue is not the guilt or innocence of the person but whether all procedures were properly followed in the trial court.

THE STRUCTURE OF STATE COURTS

Most states provide for three levels of courts: trial courts, appellate courts, and a supreme court. The structure of courts in Texas is more complicated, as can be seen in Figure 24–1. Texas has several levels of trial courts and appellate courts. Trial courts include the justices of the peace, municipal courts, county courts, district courts, and special purpose courts such as probate, juvenile, and domestic relations courts. Texas has fourteen intermediate appellate courts and two "supreme" appellate courts, one for civil (the state supreme court) and one for criminal cases (the Court of Criminal Appeals).

Magistrate or Minor Courts

All states provide for some type of minor or magistrate court, usually called the justice of the peace. These courts hear cases involving misdemeanors, most often traffic violations and minor civil cases. In Texas, there are two courts at this level: justices of the peace (JPs) and municipal courts. Municipal courts hear cases involving violations of city ordinances, most often traffic tickets. In 2003, 85 percent of all cases in Texas municipal courts involved traffic violations.[10]

magistrate functions
Preliminary hearings held for persons charged with a serious criminal offense.

Municipal courts also have **magistrate functions,** which involve preliminary hearings for persons charged with a serious offense. These persons are informed of the charges against them and told of their rights, and bail is set. As magistrates, municipal judges and JPs can also issue search-and-arrest warrants. JP courts also perform magistrate functions and hear minor criminal cases. JP courts also serve as small claims courts in Texas; municipal courts do not.[11] Jurisdiction in small claims is limited to a maximum of $15,000. Ninety percent of the cases in the JP courts are criminal misdemeanor cases, most (66 percent) traffic cases. Only 10 percent are civil cases.

County Courts

In Texas there are two kinds of county courts: constitutional county courts and county courts at law. The state constitution creates a county court in each of the 254 counties in the state, and the state legislature has created 209 statutory county courts at law and 17 probate courts. County courts at law are created in large urban counties. In those counties, the constitutional county court ceases to function as a court, and the "county judge" becomes the administrative officer or county executive but retains the title *judge* and some limited judicial functions.

The state constitution determines the jurisdiction of constitutional county courts. The jurisdiction of county courts at law is set by the act passed by the legislature creating the court and varies from court to court. The general levels of jurisdiction are shown in Figure 24–1.

County courts hear primarily intermediate criminal and civil cases. Most criminal cases are misdemeanors. Driving while intoxicated (DWI) cases make up a large portion of the docket, as do probate of wills and family law cases such as divorce and child custody. In 2003, there were 1,169,000 cases filed in county

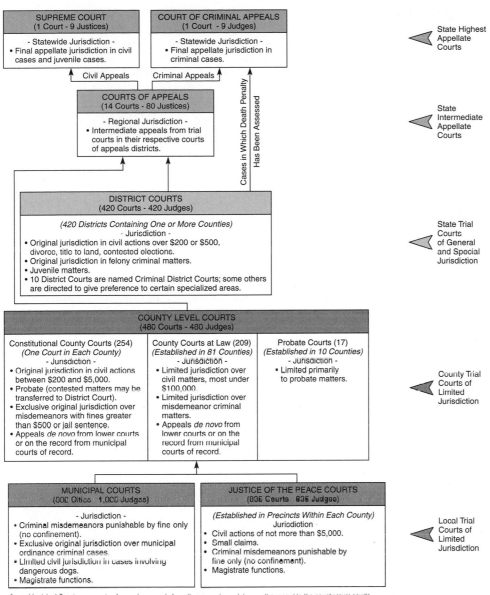

Figure 24–1

The Texas Court Structure, September 1, 2003
Source: Office of Court Administration. Austin, Texas. Reprinted by permission.

courts. Of these, 20 percent were for theft or worthless checks, 18 percent were for DWI, 10 percent were for assault, 9 percent were for violation of drug laws, 14 percent were traffic ticket appeals from JP and municipal courts, and 29 percent were for other criminal offenses.

County courts also serve as appellate courts for cases heard by JP and municipal courts. All JP and most municipal courts in Texas are trial de novo courts and not courts of record. In trial de novo courts, no record of the proceeding is kept and cases may be appealed for any reason. It is a common practice in Texas to appeal traffic tickets to the county court, where, due to heavy caseloads, they get buried. If a person has the resources to hire a lawyer, there is a good chance the ticket will be "forgotten" in case overload.

District Courts

In most states, major trial courts are called district or superior courts. These courts hear major criminal and civil cases. Examples of major criminal cases (felonies) are murder, armed robbery, and car theft. Whether a civil case is major is generally established by the dollar amount of damages claimed in the case. In Texas in 2003, there were 420 district courts. These courts are created by the state legislature. Large urban counties generally have several district courts. In rural areas, district courts might serve several counties. The jurisdiction of these courts often overlaps with county courts, and cases may be filed in either court. Other cases must begin in district courts (see Figure 24–1).

Appellate Courts

Ten states do not have courts of appeal, and twenty-three states have only one court of appeals. The other states, primarily large urban states, have several courts of appeal.[12] Texas has fourteen courts of appeal with eighty judges elected by district in the state. Only California has more judges and courts at the appellate level. These courts hear all civil appeals cases and all criminal appeals except those involving the death penalty, which go directly to the Court of Criminal Appeals (see Figure 24–1).

Supreme Courts

All states have a supreme court or court of last resort. Texas, like Oklahoma, has two supreme courts.[13] Oklahoma copied the idea from Texas when it entered the Union in 1907. The highest court in Texas for civil matters is the Texas supreme

The Texas supreme court's original walnut bench is the capitol's largest and most elaborate furniture piece. It recently was restored to its original length and location (officials had extended it and moved it to the room's south side in the 1930s). The bench bears this Latin inscription in gold leaf: "Sicut Patribus, Sit Deus Nobis" (As God Was To Our Father, May He Also Be To Us).

TABLE 24–1	Methods of Selecting Judges	
		NUMBER OF STATES USING METHOD
Appellate Court Judges		
Legislative election		2
Appointment by governor		3
Partisan election		7
Nonpartisan election		14
Merit plan		24
Trial Court Judges		
Legislative election		2
Appointment by governor		2
Partisan election		11
Nonpartisan election		16
Merit plan		19

Source: Council of State Governments. *The Book of the States 2006* (Lexington, Ky.: Council of State Governments. 2006), 256–258, Table 5.6

court, and the highest court in Texas for criminal cases is the Court of Criminal Appeals. Each court consists of nine judges elected statewide for six-year staggered terms.

JUDICIAL SELECTION

Under the U.S. Constitution, all federal judges are appointed by the president and serve for life. A lifetime appointment means that a judge continues to serve subject to good behavior and can be removed only for cause. Among the states, a variety of methods is used to select judges. Seven of the original thirteen states allow some judges to be appointed by the governor and to serve for life. Two states, also among the original thirteen, allow the legislature to elect judges.[14] Some states use partisan elections to select some judges. Candidates must run in a primary and a general election. Still other states elect some state judges in nonpartisan general elections. Finally, some states use the **merit system** or **Missouri system** to select some judges. Under this plan, the governor appoints judges from a list submitted by a screening committee of legal officials. After appointment, a judge serves for a set term and is then subjected to a retention election in which the voters decide whether the judge retains her or his office.

The method of selection also varies among courts within some states. For example, in some states, appellate court judges are chosen by a merit system while the voters elect trial court judges. Table 24–1 shows the number of states using each selection method for appellate and trial courts. Most states have moved away from partisan election of judges and use either a nonpartisan election or a merit system.

merit system or Missouri system
A system of electing judges that involves appointment by the governor and a periodic retention election.

ISSUES IN JUDICIAL SELECTION IN TEXAS

Trial court judges in Texas are elected in **partisan elections** for four-year terms, and all appellate court judges are elected in partisan elections for six-year terms. The only exceptions to this are municipal court judges. Most municipal judges are

partisan elections
Method used to select all judges in Texas except municipal court judges.

appointed by the mayor or the city council (812 are appointed and only 18 are elected). The question of judicial selection has been an issue in Texas for many years. In 1995, the Texas supreme court established the Commission on Judicial Efficiency to make recommendations on the method of judicial selection, as well as other issues, to the 1997 session of the Texas legislature. The legislature took no action on the recommendations. In the 1999 session of the legislature, several bills were introduced to change judicial selections, but none passed. In 2001, seven bills were introduced calling for the appointment or nonpartisan election of some judges in Texas. None passed. In 2003, six such bills were introduced, and again none passed. In the 2005 regular session four bills were filed and none passed.

Several electoral problems have brought the issue of judicial selection to the forefront in Texas, including name familiarity, straight-ticket voting, campaign contributions, and minority representation.

Familiar Names

Although elections are at the very heart of any democracy, they are imperfect instruments for deciding the qualifications of persons seeking office. This is especially true of judicial offices, for which qualifications are extremely important. The average voter in Texas will be asked to vote for judges for the Texas supreme court and the Court of Criminal Appeals and, in large urban counties, for several district judges, county judges, and JPs. Most voters go to the election booth with scant knowledge about the qualifications of judicial candidates and often end up voting by **name familiarity.** There are two good examples of this in Texas.

name familiarity
Practice of voting for candidates with familiar or popular names.

In 1976, voters elected Don Yarbrough to the Texas supreme court. Yarbrough was an unknown attorney from Houston who won nomination as the Democratic candidate and claimed after the election that God had told him to run. Many voters had confused him with Don Yarborough, who had run unsuccessfully for governor. Still others thought he was Ralph Yarborough, who had served in the U.S. Senate for two terms. Judge Yarbrough was forced to resign after about six months when criminal charges were filed against him. He later was convicted of perjury and sentenced to five years in jail, but he jumped bond. He then attended medical school in Grenada, which refused extradition to the United States. He was arrested in St. Thomas, Virgin Islands, while attending medical school classes, and was returned to Texas, where he was eventually sentenced to five years in prison.[15]

In 1990, there was a similar case of voting based on name familiarity. In that year, Gene Kelly won the Democratic party primary for a seat on the Texas supreme court. Some citizens thought he was the famous dancer and film star from the 1950s and 1960s. However, this Gene Kelly was a retired Air Force judge with little nonmilitary experience. Kelly lost to Republican John Cornyn after extensive television commercials questioned his competency. Some have suggested that Justice Sam Houston Clinton might also have benefited from name recognition in his election to the Texas Court of Criminal Appeals.

Straight-Ticket Voting

straight-ticket voting
System that allows voters to vote for all candidates of a single political party that has resulted in an increase in the number of Republican judges.

Another electoral problem that has surfaced in recent years is straight-ticket voting. Texas is one of fourteen states that allow straight-ticket voting. **Straight-ticket voting** allows a voter to vote for all candidates in a party by making a single mark. In 1984, many incumbent Democratic judges lost their seats in large urban counties to unknown Republican challengers because of Republican straight-ticket voting. Other instances have occurred since 1984. In Harris County in 1994, only one incumbent Democrat was reelected and sixteen Democrats were defeated because of straight-ticket voting. Many of their Republican replacements lacked judicial experience, and one had no courtroom experience. Also in 1994, Steve Mansfield, an individual with very limited legal experience and no experience in criminal law, was elected to the Texas Court of Criminal Appeals, the highest court for criminal matters in Texas. After the election, questions were raised about Mansfield's qualifications. In his state bar application, he had failed to acknowledge that he was behind in his child-support payments. This raised the possibility that he could be disbarred and therefore become ineligible to serve. Some statewide officials called for his resignation. This would have been no loss to the Republicans; if he resigned, then Governor Bush would make an appointment to fill the vacancy, and he likely would choose a Republican.

A similar situation occurred in the 2002 election. Steven W. Smith, the chief litigant behind the Hopwood case that limited the use of racial quotas in selecting law school students at the University of Texas, won election to the Texas supreme court. Despite being a Republican, he had little support from statewide party officials and few endorsements from state bar associations. He still managed to win election due to straight-ticket voting. He received about the same percentage of votes as other Republican candidates for statewide judicial office. A study by Richard Murray at the University of Houston demonstrated that about 54 percent of the votes cast in Harris County in both 1998 and 2002 were straight-ticket votes. A Republican running for countywide office had a 14,000 vote head start.[16]

BUT I THOUGHT IT WAS THE OTHER DON YARBOROUGH!

Ignorance about candidates often leads voters to vote on the basis of name familiarity.

These recent cases of straight-ticket voting have caused some to call for **nonpartisan election** of state judges. In 1995, 1997, 2001, 2003, and 2005, bills were introduced that called for the nonpartisan election of district judges and a merit system for appellate judges. Yet another suggestion is to prohibit straight-ticket voting in judicial races, an idea that has been considered in past sessions. This would force voters to mark the ballot for each judicial race. Given the recent success of Republicans in gaining control of the legislature and the judiciary, this idea might lack strong support in the legislature.

nonpartisan election
Selection of judges using a ballot on which party identification does not appear.

Campaign Contributions

Another electoral issue is campaign contributions. Under the Texas partisan election system, judges must win in both the party primary and the general election. Two elections stretching over ten months (January to November) can be a costly process. In 1984, John L. Hill spent over $1 million to win the race for chief justice. The cost of this race and other experiences caused Hill and two other Democratic justices to resign from the supreme court in 1988. They called for a merit system to replace partisan elections. Their resignations, along with other openings on the court, resulted in six of the nine seats on the supreme court being up for election. The total cost of these six races exceeded $10 million. One candidate alone spent over $2 million.[17]

Races for district judgeships can also be very costly. Money often comes from law firms that have cases before the judges who receive the money. Other money comes from interest groups such as the Texas Medical Association, which has an interest in limiting malpractice tort claims in cases before the courts. The Public Broadcasting System's *Frontline* television series recently ran a program titled "Justice for Sale" on the Texas courts and money (see the Internet site listed at the end of this chapter). This report details how eight justices on the supreme court in 1994 received over $9 million, primarily from corporations and law firms. In the 2002 election cycle, five of nine seats on the court were up for election, including that of the chief justice. Close to $5 million had been raised by November 2002. Many of the contributions came from large law firms that had cases before the court.

The basic question raised by campaign contributions is their impact on judicial impartiality. Do these contributions influence the decisions made by judges? According to a poll by the Texans for Public Justice, the average Texan thinks this money influences judges (73 percent). Even court personnel (69 percent) felt that the money influences judges. Lawyers were even more certain (77 percent); because they contribute about 40 percent of the money, they should be in a position to know. About half of the judges (47 percent) thought the money raised influences their decisions. When people lose confidence in courts, the respect for law declines. It is this result that should be of concern to all citizens.

Minority Representation

minority representation
Election of judges from single-member districts in major urban counties to allow for the election of minority judges.

A fourth electoral issue is **minority representation** in the judiciary. District and county court judges all run for election on a countywide basis. Countywide races for judgeships create the same problem for minorities as do multimember legislative districts (see Chapter 22). Minority judges have not been successful in races for at-large, countywide offices. The problem is especially difficult in nine urban counties (Harris, Dallas, Bexar, Tarrant, Jefferson, Lubbock, Ector, Midland, and Travis). In 1989, the League of United Latin American Citizens (LULAC) sued, claiming that at-large election of judges in these counties was a violation of the Voting Rights Act. In 1989, the federal district court in Midland, Texas, ruled that the Texas system was in violation of the Voting Rights Act. On appeal, the Fifth Federal Circuit Court, in 1994, reversed this decision, and the U.S. Supreme Court refused to hear the case, thus upholding the ruling of the federal circuit court.[18]

Opponents of single-member district elections in urban counties claim that partisan voting was more significant than ethnicity in these judicial elections. The two obviously are related. The same argument could be made if all twenty-four delegates from Harris County to the Texas house of representatives were elected at large. Few minorities would be elected because of straight-ticket voting. The issue of minority representation in the state judiciary remains politically active but is judicially dead. Any change would have to come from the legislature.

Conclusions on Elected Judges

Over the last two decades, several highly political issues have driven demands for change in the way Texas selects its judges. Voting based on name recognition and party label has resulted in the election of persons of questionable qualifications. Campaign contributions from groups with vested interests in cases before the courts have raised the specter of judicial bias or justice for sale. For various reasons, the legislature has not acted to correct any of these problems. Finally, in large urban counties, minority representation on state district and county courts is biased due to at-large elections at the county level.

Get Involved!

Justice for Sale?

The current system of electing judges in partisan elections causes much money to be given by law firms with cases before the state courts. This report by the Texans for Public Justice summarizes some of the problems with the current system that could be overcome by the adoption of a merit system. A merit system would free judges from dependency on campaign contributions and give them more independence.

Austin, TX: Lawyers and law firms—the very donors who have the greatest recurring interest in state court rulings—supply 72 percent of the campaign funds that Texas' intermediate court judges raise to win office, a ground-breaking Texans for Public Justice (TPJ) study finds. In *Lowering the Bar: Lawyers Keep Texas Appeals Judges on Retainer*, TPJ analyzes campaign contributions to 73 judges who sat on intermediate state appeals courts in January 2003. These judges raised $6.8 million for 87 winning campaigns to sit on Texas' 14 intermediate appeals courts between 1997 and 2002. Led by leading defense and plaintiff firms that have numerous cases in state courts, lawyers and law firms supplied 72 percent ($4.9 million) of all the money in the justices' war chests.

The justices' financial dependency on attorneys leapt from 61 percent of their total in 1996 to 76 percent in the 2002 election cycle. By comparison, Texas Supreme Court justices take 48 percent of their campaign funds from lawyers and law firms. The fact that Texas judges depend heavily on campaign donors with vested interest in state court rulings fosters widespread perceptions that justice is for sale in Texas.

Members of the Texas Bar could jump-start badly needed judicial reforms if they would just say "No" to

pleas for campaign funds," said TPJ Director Craig McDonald. "We suspect that Texas attorneys give money because they share the public's perception that few politicians—judicial or otherwise—are blind to big campaign contributions.

Other major findings of *Lowering the Bar* include:

- Republicans, who held 55 percent of Texas' intermediate appeals judge seats in 1997, controlled 76 percent in January 2003;
- The average winning Democratic justice in the age of George W. Bush had to raise $114,739—or 78 percent more than the $64,614 average for winning Republicans;
- Attorneys contributed 82 percent of the money that Democratic justices raised, much more than the 65 percent share that lawyers supplied to Republican justices;
- Led by San Antonio's Fourth District Chief Justice Alma Lopez, Democrats raised eight of the ten largest war chests;
- On average, justices in Dallas' Fifth District and El Paso's Eighth District raised the largest share of their war chests from attorneys (89 percent);
- The top sources of non-lawyer contributions were: the oil-rich Bass family; the Texas Medical Association; Perry Homes and Texans for Lawsuit Reform.

Source: Texans for Public Justice Report, "Texas Lawyers Fund 72 Percent of Appeals Judges' Campaigns: An Endangered Species, Democratic Judges Pay Huge Premiums to Win," http://www.tpj.org/press_releases/appealscourt_pr.html.

THE "APPOINTIVE-ELECTIVE" SYSTEM IN TEXAS

Reformers who include some of the best legal minds in the state are calling for change from the current partisan election system. Both nonpartisan and merit systems are being suggested. Some have pointed out that the state already has an "appointive-elective" system. The Texas governor can fill any seat for district or appellate court that becomes vacant due to death or resignation as well as any new district court position created by the legislature. Vacancies in the county

TABLE 24–2	Texas Judges Serving in 2003 Who Were Appointed to Their Initial Seat on the Court				
	APPOINTED			ELECTED	
COURT	N	%		N	%
Supreme Court	4	44		5	56
Court of Criminal Appeals	1	11		8	89
Courts of Appeals	37	47		42	53
District Courts	168	41		241	59
County Courts at Law	59	31		132	69
Probate Courts	8	53		7	47
Constitutional County Courts	40	17		200	83
Justice of the Peace Courts	115	16		591	84
Municipal Courts	837	98		18	2

Source: Office of Court Administration, Profile of Justices in 2003. See website at end of the chapter. Note that appellate and district court judges are appointed by the governor. County court judges and JPs are appointed by the County Commissioner Court.

courts and justice-of-the-peace courts are filled by the county governing body, the County Commissioners Court. Persons appointed to fill vacancies serve until the next regular election for that office, when they must stand for regular election.

Historically, many judges in Texas have initially received their seats on the courts by appointment. The data are not complete for all time periods, but enough data are available to show that this practice is common. Between 1940 and 1962, about 66 percent of district and appellate judges were appointed by the governor to their first term on the court. In 1976, 150 sitting district court judges were appointed.[19] Table 24–2 shows data on the appointment of sitting judges in 2003. It is evident that many judges in all state courts are appointed to serve.

IS THERE A BEST SYSTEM?

The debate in Texas over judicial selection will continue in future sessions of the legislature. This debate revolves around three basic issues. Citizens expect judges to be competent, independent and not subject to political pressures, and responsive and subject to democratic control. Each method used by the states to select judges has strengths and weaknesses regarding each of these issues (see Table 24–3; also see "States in the Nation" in Chapter 14, page 000). The merit system is used primarily in the Midwest and appointive methods primarily in New England and on the West Coast. Partisan elections are widely used in the South.

Judicial appointment by the governor has great potential for selection of judges who are competent; however, it does not ensure competence. Governors can use judicial appointments to reward friends and repay political debts. All U.S. presidents, some more than others, have used their judicial appointive powers to select federal judges with political philosophies similar to their own. Governors do the same thing. In such cases, questions of judicial competence sometimes are raised.

TABLE 24–3	Strengths and Weaknesses of Judicial Selection Methods		
	ISSUE		
METHOD OF SELECTION	**COMPETENCE**	**INDEPENDENCE**	**RESPONSIVENESS**
Appointment by governor	Strong	Strong	Weak
Election by legislature	Mixed	Strong	Weak
Merit/Missouri method	Moderate	Moderate	Weak
Partisan election	Weak	Weak	Strong
Nonpartisan election	Mixed/weak	Mixed/weak	Strong

Source: Ann O. Bowman and Richard C. Kearney, *State and Local Government* (Boston: Houghton Mifflin, 1990), 286–97.

While governors are not likely to select unqualified people for judicial appointments, governors might not be able to convince the best candidates to agree to serve. The appointive system probably rules out complete incompetents, but it does not necessarily result in the appointment of the most competent people to serve as judges. Once appointed, judges are not responsive to voters and exercise independence in their decisions.

Election by the legislature is a system left over from colonial America, when much power rested with the state legislature. Used only in South Carolina and Virginia, this system tends to select former legislators as judges. In South Carolina, the number of judges who are former legislators is very close to 100 percent. Judicial appointment is viewed as a capstone to a successful legislative career.[20]

Nonpartisan elections are one system being given serious consideration in Texas. Such a system would reduce the cost of campaigns and eliminate the problem of straight-ticket voting. Voters would have to base their decisions on something other than party label. It would not necessarily result in the selection of more competent judges, but it would prevent the kind of large-scale changes in judgeships that happened in Harris County in 1994. As indicated earlier, it has also been suggested that Texas prohibit straight-ticket voting for judicial candidates, requiring voters to mark the ballot for each judicial race.

The merit or Missouri plan is also being given consideration as a method of selecting judges in Texas. Under this system, the governor appoints judges from a list of acceptable (and, it is to be hoped, competent) candidates supplied by a judicial panel and perhaps ranked by the state bar association. Once appointed, a judge serves for a set term and stands for retention in an election. In this retention election, voters vote to either retain or remove the judge from office. The system is used by many states—twenty-one states use it for appellate judges, and fifteen for trial judges.

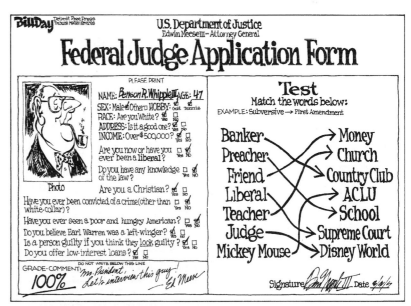

Some methods of selecting judges do not always result in the selection of qualified individuals.

BILL DAY Reprinted by permission of United Features Syndicate, Inc.

The merit plan would seem to be strong on the issues of competency and responsiveness; however, there is little evidence that it results in the selection of more competent judges.[21] There is also evidence that it is weak on responsiveness. In retention elections, the judge does not have an opponent.[22] Voters vote only to retain or remove. Several writers have pointed out that it is difficult to defeat someone with no one.[23] In the states that use this system, most judges are retained; fewer than 1 percent are ever removed.[24] One study showed that between 1964, when the system was first used, and 1984 only 22 of 1,864 trial judges were defeated in retention elections.[25] When judges are removed, it is usually because of either an organized political effort to remove them from office or gross incompetence.

There are also some variations on these plans. In Illinois, judges are elected using a partisan ballot, but they must win 60 percent of the vote in a retention election to remain in office. In Arizona, judges in rural counties are elected in nonpartisan elections, but judges in the most populous counties are appointed. These variations might also be considered in Texas.

In short, there is no perfect system for selecting judges. All methods have problems. Also, there is no evidence that, compared with the other methods, any one of these judicial selection methods results in the selection of judges with "substantially different credentials."[26] The only exception is the fact that in states where the legislature elects judges, more former legislators serve as judges.

REMOVAL AND DISCIPLINE OF JUDGES

Most states provide some system for removing judges for misconduct. Impeachment, a little used and very political system, is provided for in forty-three states, including Texas. Five states allow for recall of judges by the voters.[27] One state, New Hampshire, allows the governor to remove a judge after a hearing. In five states, the legislature can remove judges by a supermajority vote (a two-thirds vote is most common). In recent years, the trend in the states has been to create a commission on judicial conduct to review cases of misconduct by judges and remove them from office. To date, forty-nine states have established judicial conduct commissions. Also, the method of removal of judges can depend on the level of the judgeship—for instance, trial judges versus appellate judges.

In Texas, the state supreme court may remove any judge from office. District judges may remove county judges and justices of the peace. The State Commission on Judicial Conduct may recommend the removal of judges at all levels. This twelve-member commission conducts hearings and decides whether "the judge in question is guilty of willful or persistent conduct that is inconsistent with the proper performance of a judge's duties."[28] The commission can privately reprimand, publicly censure, or recommend the judge for removal by the state supreme court. The use of review commissions to reprimand, discipline, and remove judges is a good check on the actions of judges. If Texas adopts the merit or Missouri plan, this commission would probably increase in importance as a check on judges.

THE LEGAL SYSTEM

The American legal system can be broadly divided into civil and criminal branches. Civil cases are those between individual citizens and involve the idea of responsibilities and not guilt. Criminal cases are those cases brought against individuals for violations of law—crimes against society. Most (65.9 percent) of the cases heard by the district courts in Texas are civil cases, whereas most (75.6 percent) of the cases heard in county court are criminal.[29]

Under civil law, all individuals who feel they have cause or have been injured by others may file a civil lawsuit. Courts decide whether the case has validity and should be heard in court.

Grand Jury

While any citizen may file a civil suit in court, a screening body must review criminal cases. The U.S. Constitution requires the use of grand juries to serve as a screening mechanism to prevent arbitrary actions by federal prosecutors. Some states use the grand jury system for some criminal cases, although in recent years the use of a formal hearing before a judge, called an information hearing or an administrative hearing, has become more common. The judge reviews the facts and decides whether there is enough evidence to try the case.

Texas uses both grand juries and administrative hearings. A citizen may waive his or her right to review by a grand jury and ask that a judge review the charges. In Texas, grand juries consist of twelve citizens chosen by district judges in one of two ways. The district judge may appoint a grand jury commission that consists of three to five people.[30] Each grand jury commissioner then supplies the judge with three to five names of citizens qualified to serve on a grand jury. From these names, the judge selects twelve citizens to serve as a grand jury. In the second method, the district judge can have twenty to seventy-five prospective grand jurors summoned in the same manner used for petit juries. From this group, the district judge selects twelve citizens who are called grand jurors.[31]

Most grand juries serve for six months. They often screen major criminal cases to decide whether enough evidence exists to go to trial. Grand juries are supposed to serve as filters to prevent arbitrary actions by prosecuting attorneys, but they do not always serve this function. Often, the district attorney dominates grand juries. Most grand jury members are lay people who have never served

before, and they frequently follow the advice of the prosecuting attorney. Although grand juries may conduct investigations on their own, few do. Those that do conduct investigations are sometimes termed "runaway grand juries" by the media.

A recent study by the *Houston Chronicle* presented evidence that some judges in Harris County had been given names of citizens for the grand jury by prosecutors from the district attorney's office. The study also demonstrated that many of the same citizens serve on grand juries year after year. Judges justified the repeated use of the same people for grand juries based on the difficulty of getting people to serve. Older, retired citizens often volunteer to serve.[32]

Thus, a grand jury might not always serve the function of protecting the citizen from arbitrary action by prosecutors. For this reason, a person might ask for an administrative hearing before a judge. During grand jury proceedings, the accused may not have his or her attorney present during the hearing; during an administrative hearing, however, the attorney is present and can protect the accused.

Texas does not use grand juries for minor cases. In Texas, the county or district attorney files minor criminal cases in county courts. The county court judge, who determines whether the case should proceed to trial, holds an "administration" hearing. Criminal cases in the county court generally are less serious than those filed in district courts. They consist of DWI/DUI, minor theft, drug, assault, and traffic cases.

Petit Jury

Both criminal and civil cases can be decided by a petit (pronounced *petty*) jury. Petit juries are randomly selected from voter registration lists or, more recently in Texas, from lists of licensed drivers. In criminal and civil cases, the defendant has the right to a trial by jury but may waive this right and let a judge decide the case.

Very few cases involve jury trials. In 2003, Texas county courts heard 698,844 cases, only 5,288 of which were jury trials. In district courts, 791,294 cases were disposed of, and only 6,150 were jury trials. The lack of jury trials in criminal cases is often the subject of concern to some citizens. Most people charged with a crime plead guilty, often in exchange for a lighter sentence in a process known as plea bargaining. The person charged agrees to plead guilty in exchange for a lesser sentence agreed to by the accused and the prosecuting attorney. The judge hearing the case can accept or reject the agreement.

If all criminal cases were subject to jury trials, the court system would have to be greatly expanded. Many additional judges, prosecuting attorneys, and public defenders would be needed. In addition, many more citizens would have to serve on juries. The cost of this expanded process would be excessive. Even though citizens support "getting tough on criminals," they would balk at paying the bill.

CRIME AND PUNISHMENT IN TEXAS

Today we hear a lot about crime and the rising crime rate. Political candidates often use crime as a campaign issue to prove to voters they will be "tough on criminals." It is a safe issue that offends few voters. This section examines several questions regarding crime and punishment: How much crime is there nationally and in Texas? What factors seem to contribute to higher crime rates?

TABLE 24–4	Texas and U.S. Crime Rates, 1989–2001			
YEAR	**TEXAS CRIME RATE**	**% CHANGE YEARLY**	**U.S. CRIME RATE**	**% CHANGE YEARLY**
1989	7,926.9		5,741.0	
1990	7,826.8	−1.3	5,820.3	1.4
1991	7,819.1	−0.1	5,897.8	1.3
1992	7,057.9	−9.7	5,660.2	−4.0
1993	6,439.1	−8.8	5,484.4	−3.1
1994	5,872.4	−8.8	5,373.5	−2.0
1995	5,684.3	−3.2	5,275.9	−1.8
1996	5,708.9	0.4	5,086.6	−3.6
1997	5,480.5	−4.0	4,930.0	−3.1
1998	5,111.6	−6.7	4,619.3	−6.3
1999	5,031.7	−1.6	4,266.5	−7.6
2000	4,955.5	−1.5	4,124.0	−3.3
2001	5,152.7	4.0	4,160.5	0.9

Source: Texas Criminal Justice Policy Council, www.cjpc.state.tx.us.

What impact does punishment have on crime rates? What is the cost of crime and punishment?

The Crime Rate

Table 24–4 shows total violent crime in the United States and Texas from 1989 through 2001. As can be seen, crime has increased, but the increase is not as great as suggested by the news media or by campaign rhetoric. Violent crime has increased in Texas more than in the nation as a whole. In 2001, Texas ranked third among the fifteen most populous states in total crimes committed per hundred thousand population.[33] Crime in Texas generally increased between 1984 and 1989 and has decreased since that time. The same has been true for the United States as a whole—crime has decreased.

Factors Contributing to Crime

Many factors contribute to the crime rate. Most crimes are committed in larger cities. A comparison of the fifty states shows that there is a strong correlation between the percentage of the population living in urban (metropolitan) areas and the crime rate. This in part explains the crime rate in Texas, because about 80 percent of the population of Texas lives in metropolitan areas.

There is also a strong relationship between age, sex, and crime rate (see Table 24–5). People below age twenty-five commit almost 46 percent of all crimes, and males commit almost 82 percent of all crimes. It has been suggested that if society could lock up all men between eighteen and twenty-five years of age, crime would decline tremendously. Race is also a factor in crime. African Americans constitute about 12 percent of the U.S. population, yet, as shown in Table 24–5, they constitute almost 30 percent of persons arrested for crime.

TABLE 24–5	Persons Arrested for Crime by Sex, Race, and Age
	PERCENTAGE OF ARRESTS, 1990
Sex	
Male	81.6%
Female	18.4
Race	
White	69.2
Black	28.9
Others	1.9
Age	
Under 18	15.6
18–24	30.1
25–34	32.1
35–44	14.9
45–54	4.9
55 and over	2.5

Source: Data from Thomas R. Dye, *Politics in States and Communities*, 8th ed. (Englewood Cliffs, N.J.: Prentice Hall, 1994), 262, Table 9.4.

In Texas, the number of young men ages eighteen to twenty-four has decreased in recent years. This has contributed to the reduced crime rate since 1989 in Texas.[34]

The Effect of Punishment on Crime Rates

The attitude among most Texans is "If you do the crime, you do the time." Juries in Texas give out longer sentences than the average nationwide (see Table 24–6).

TABLE 24–6	Average Time Served by Texas Prisoners and Prisoners Nationwide				
	LENGTH OF AVERAGE SENTENCE (YEARS)		AVERAGE TIME SERVED (YEARS)		PERCENTAGE OF SENTENCE SERVED
TYPE OF OFFENSE	NATION	TEXAS	NATION	TEXAS	NATION	TEXAS
All violent offenses	7.4	12.0	3.6	3.6	48%	30%
Homicide	12.4	15.6	5.9	5.0	48	32
Rape	9.8	12.9	5.4	4.4	56	34
Kidnapping	8.7	12.1	4.3	4.4	50	37
Robbery	7.9	13.0	3.7	3.4	46	26
Assault	5.1	7.1	2.4	2.0	48	28

Source: Data from Texas Criminal Justice Policy Council, *Testing the Case for More Incarceration in Texas: The Record So Far* (Austin: State of Texas, 1995), 13.

Political Culture

Incarceration Rates: How Much Justice Can We Afford?

Texas has one of the highest incarceration rates of any state or Western industrialized nation. Rate of incarceration is the number of persons put in prison per hundred thousand population. In 2001, Texas incarcerated 711 prisoners per 100,000. Texas ranked third, with Louisiana (800 per 100,000) ranking first and Mississippi (715 per 100,000) ranking second. The rates of incarceration for other states are shown in the table below.

The argument advanced for more incarceration is that it will lead to a reduction in the crime rate. Studies of Texas crime show that between 1989 and 1993, when the incarceration rate increased by 4 percent, there was a 1 percent decrease in the crime rate. Even if no other factors affecting crime rate were involved, this is a high cost for such a small reduction in crime.

Dr. Tony Fabelo, former executive director of the Texas Criminal Justice Policy Council, made this observation:

Texans should carefully consider what the cost of continuing to increase incarceration rates means in terms of cost: funding increasingly more adult prison and jail space results in proportionately fewer dollars available for juvenile justice initiatives. Under present policies, most offenders are incarcerated after their criminal career has peaked, limiting the impact of more incarceration on the crime rate. Despite dramatic increases in the incarceration rate in 1993, Texas had the fifth highest crime rate in the country. Perhaps funding meaningful early interventions in the juvenile justice system, ranging from accountable community based programs to residential institutional interventions, will achieve better returns on lowering crime for each new dollar spent. However, if "you do the crime, you do the time" is the driving correctional philosophy in Texas, then we need to expect that more new dollars will continue to be spent expanding capacity in the adult correctional system to support more incarceration. The paradox of this policy is that more punishment for adults may do very little to continue lowering the state's crime rate, and may actually divert funds that could more effectively impact a decline in crime, if spent on juvenile justice policies or related areas.

| | RATE OF INCARCERATION (PER 100,000 POPULATION) | | |
STATE/NATION	1995	1999	2001
Louisiana	587	776	800
Mississippi	464	626	715
Texas	636	762	711
Michigan	428	472	488
Florida	406	456	437
California	384	481	453
Ohio	377	389	355
New York	367	400	310
Pennsylvania	235	305	422
United States average	387	476	521
Canada	116		
Mexico	97		
England	93		
Spain	90		
France	84		
Italy	80		
Germany	80		

Sources: Data from Texas Criminal Justice Policy Council, *Testing the Case for More Incarceration in Texas: The Record So Far* (Austin: State of Texas, 1995), 29. Data for 1999, Texas Criminal Justice Policy Council web page. Data for 2001, *Fiscal Size Up.* Table 56. Quote from Texas Criminal Justice Policy Council, *Testing the Case for More Incarceration in Texas,* 2.

However, the average time served in Texas is less than the national average, and the percentage of the sentence served by violent offenders in Texas is also lower than the national average, due to the longer sentences imposed by juries. The length of time served has increased in recent years because of an increase in available prison space. It probably will continue to increase, and the cost of keeping people in jail for longer periods of time will have to be weighed against the cost of programs that might reduce crime.

The Death Penalty

It has often been suggested that the death penalty can reduce crime. The death penalty was outlawed in the United States in 1972 (*Furman v. Georgia*) because it was unfairly applied to many crimes and because it lacked safeguards in many states. In 1976, the U.S. Supreme Court established guidelines under which a state could reinstate the death penalty. To date, only twelve states have *not* reinstated the death penalty: Alaska, Hawaii, Iowa, Maine, Massachusetts, Michigan, Minnesota, North Dakota, Rhode Island, Vermont, West Virginia, and Wisconsin (see Chapter 4, page 000, for a map of the United States showing the application of the death penalty among the states). Note that the southern, traditionalistic states have a higher number of executions. States with the lowest rates or no death penalty are northern, moralistic states.

There is little evidence that the death penalty is a deterrent to crime. Endless delays and appeals and the long time span between the sentence and the execution reduce the effectiveness of the death penalty. In Texas, the average time from sentence to execution is 9.1 years. One person, Jerry Joe Bird, spent 16.8 years on death row. No public officials are advocating a return to public executions, but it has been suggested that they might increase the power of the death sentence as a deterrent to crime. However, most crimes are not capital crimes. The death penalty would do little, even under "ideal circumstances," to reduce the crime rate. Also, the cost to taxpayers of executing felons is quite high.

Additionally, inmates on death row are invariably poor and disproportionately African American or Hispanic. Few middle- or upper-class Anglos are sentenced to death in capital cases. This disparity in sentencing raises questions about equality under the law. Of the 448 inmates on death row in Texas in 2001, 182 were African Americans, 164 were Anglos, 99 were Hispanics, and 3 were of other races. Additionally, most death-row inmates are male—439 males and 7 females in 2001.[35]

Texas is the leading state in both sentencing people to death and number of prisoners executed. Since the death penalty was reinstated in the state in 1976 and executions began in 1982, Texas has executed 317 of the 892 people executed nationwide (see Table 24–7). Texas, with about 7 percent of the total population of the United States, has carried out 35 percent of the executions. Also, there is no shortage of people in Texas waiting to be executed. In May 2003, 451 people were on death row awaiting execution in Texas. At the rate of one execution per week, it would take 8.6 years to execute those persons. In 1995 alone, Texas executed nineteen of the fifty-one people executed nationwide. In 2000, Texas executed forty of the eighty-four people executed nationwide.

Most executions (82 percent, 850 of 1039) have been in the southern states. The death penalty fits well within the dominant traditionalistic culture of the South. In Texas and many other southern states, juries can set the sentence for all crimes, and juries might be more inclined than judges to impose the death penalty. As table 24–7 shows, some states sentence many prisoners to death but carry out few executions. For example, California had 652 prisoners on death row in August 2006 but has executed only 13 since 1976. From 1995 to 2003, California executed only two people.

TABLE 24–7	Executions by State from 1976 to August 2006. Note that 36 percent of all executions since 1976 are from Texas. Twelve states do not have the death penalty.		
STATE	**NUMBER OF EXECUTIONS**	**NUMBER WAITING TO BE EXECUTED 2005**	

STATE	NUMBER OF EXECUTIONS	NUMBER WAITING TO BE EXECUTED 2005	Executions by Region
Texas	373	404	South 850
Virginia	97	22	West 66
Florida	60	392	Midwest 121
Missouri	66	52	Northeast 4
Oklahoma	81	93	Texas alone 373
South Carolina	36	71	
Louisiana	27	88	
Georgia	39	107	
Alabama	34	191	
Arkansas	27	38	
Arizona	22	126	
North Carolina	31	188	
Delaware	14	17	
Illinois	12	9	
California	13	652	
Indiana	17	24	
Nevada	12	81	
Utah	6	9	
Mississippi	7	67	
Ohio	23	195	
Nebraska	3	10	
Washington	4	9	
Maryland	3	8	
Pennsylvania	3	232	
Montana	3	4	
Kentucky	2	37	
Wyoming	1	2	
Idaho	1	20	
Colorado	1	2	
Tennessee	2	108	
South Dakota	0	4	
New Mexico	0	2	
Oregon	2	33	
New Jersey	0	13	
New York	0	1	
New Hampshire	0		
Connecticut	1		
Wisconsin	0		
Totals	1039		

*The governor of Illinois commuted the sentences of most people on death row.
Source: Death Penalty Information Center, Washington, D.C.

TABLE 24–8	**Death-Row Inmates from Selected Counties in Texas.** There have been 864 total death penalty convictions in Texas since 1977.

TOP FIVE COUNTIES	NUMBER OF DEATH ROW INMATES
Harris (Houston)	246
Dallas	78
Bexar (San Antonio)	57
Tarrant (Ft. Worth)	48
Jefferson	24

Source: *Houston Chronicle*, February 5, 2000. 11A.

The Harris County Factor

While Texas leads the nation both in the number of persons sentenced to death and the number of executions, Harris County (Houston) contributes a disproportionate share. In fact, Harris County has contributed more death-row inmates than the other large urban counties in Texas combined (see Table 24–8). Only five states have condemned more people to death (Texas, California, Florida, Pennsylvania, and North Carolina). Most counties in Texas contribute very few death-row inmates. Of the 245 counties in Texas, 138 have no death-row convictions, 15 have two, and 53 have one. Twenty percent of the counties contribute most of the death-row convictions. Convictions also come primarily from East Texas, where the traditionalistic political culture is strongest.

What factors contribute to the large number of death sentences in Texas, and in Harris County in particular? First, the statutes in Texas for assigning a death sentence are among the least complicated among the states. A jury must first answer two questions: Did the defendant act intentionally? and Is the defendant a future threat to society? A person who commits murder while committing another crime (rape, robbery) or who kills two or more people, a police officer, a firefighter, or a child or who is a murderer for hire and did it intentionally and is a threat, can receive the death sentence. These standards make it easy for juries to approve a death sentence.

Second, the Texas Court of Criminal Appeals almost never reverses a death sentence. Only 11 of 300 capital cases have been reversed or sent back to lower courts. Recently this court failed to reverse a death sentence when the defense attorney slept during part of the trial. The chief justice of the court, Judge Sharon Keller, in her campaign for election, stated that failure to execute condemned murderers was a violation of human rights.[36] Likewise, the U.S. Fifth Circuit is reluctant to overturn appeals. This court upheld the conviction in the case of the sleeping defense attorney. Thus, the likelihood of winning a case on appeal in Texas is not great. The purpose of appellate courts is to check the procedures and processes in lower courts and make sure no mistakes are made. Judging by the number of reversals, few mistakes are made in Texas district criminal courts. Those that are found are ruled not important in most cases. Finally, the Texas Board of Pardons and Paroles, often the final recourse for those with failed appeals, is even less apt to change a sentence. Since 1990, the Board of Pardons and Paroles has recommended clemency in only 10 of 140 capital cases.[37]

Debating the Issues

Does the Death Penalty Reduce Crime?

Texas is one of the leading states in executing people convicted of murder. Most Texans strongly support the death penalty and the execution of those convicted of murder. Other Texans oppose the death penalty for moral reasons and do not feel it is a deterrent of crime. Still others point out that most democracies around the world have abolished the death penalty. What do you think?

Yes There is a strong sense of justice among many Americans that demand retribution for heinous crimes—a life for a life. The death penalty dramatically signifies that society does not excuse or condone the taking of innocent lives. It symbolizes the value that society places on innocent lives. A mere jail sentence for murder devalues the life of the innocent victim. In most cases, a life sentence means less than ten years in prison under the current parole and probation policies of most states. Convicted murders have been set free, and some have killed again. Moreover, prison guards and other inmates are exposed to convicted murderers who have a "license to kill," because they are already serving life sentences and have nothing to loose by killing again.—Thomas R. Dye and Susan A. MacManus, authors

No While Texas is the leading state in the execution of prisoners, there is little evidence that these executions have been a deterrent to crime. One big problem is the length of time between a person's sentencing and execution. On average, ten years pass between the time a person is sentenced and the person's execution. In a few cases, it has been over twenty years. Most people have no memory of the crime, and news accounts have to outline the details. Respect for the court system has declined because of the long time that passes between trial and execution. People feel that the appeal process and delays are due to "liberal" judges and do not understand that safeguards must be in place to protect individual rights.

The death penalty in some people's mind is cruel and unusual punishment prohibited by the Eighth Amendment to the U.S. Constitution. In recent years, several states have had death sentences overturned due to problems such as prosecutors withholding information. In Texas, inadequate defense is a major problem in some Texas counties (such as Harris County). Texas should consider giving life sentences without possibility of parole.

Money is also a factor in determining whether the prosecuting attorney will ask for a death sentence. Smaller, rural counties often lack the money to prosecute a death sentence case. Even large urban counties often find that death sentence cases strain their budgets. Harris County is an exception, and this partly explains why the county has so many death sentence convictions. The budget for the Harris County district attorney's office is $30 million, and the county has a staff of 230 assistant district attorneys. Dallas County, by contrast, has a budget of about $20 million. Some of the difference is due to a lower caseload in Dallas. Harris County has a total of twenty-two felony courts (compared to eight in Dallas County). In these twenty-two Harris County courts, all but two judges are former prosecutors in the Harris County district attorney's office.[38]

The high rate of death sentences in Texas and the procedures for appeal might be questioned, but despite its shortcomings the public heavily favors the

TABLE 24–9	Public Opinion on the Death Penalty	
	TEXAS	**NATION**
Do you support the death penalty?		
Yes	69.1%	58.1%
Has an innocent person been executed?		
Very likely	38.9	39.4
Somewhat likely	24.4	24.7
Very unlikely	18.2	17.0
Somewhat unlikely	15.3	15.4
Not sure	3.3	3.6
Is Texas a safer place because of executions?		
Safer	51.5	30.0
Less safe	14.1	27.3
Not sure	34.4	42.7
Is the death penalty a deterrent to crime?		
Yes	58.4	47.7
No	36.6	46.6
Not sure	4.4	5.7

Source: *Houston Chronicle*, February 4, 2001. 24A–25A.

death penalty. Table 24–9 provides public-opinion data on several aspects of the death penalty. Texas favors the death penalty more strongly than the nation as a whole and considers the death penalty a deterrent to crime. Also, Texans say they feel safer because of the death penalty.

Summary

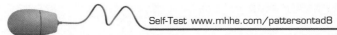

In the twenty-first century, the court system in Texas faces many challenges. Methods of selecting judges will continue to be controversial, and some change in these methods will likely occur. Texans might want to think about their approach to dealing with the high crime rate in the state. While voters seem anxious to approve bonds for the construction of more prisons, they are reluctant to consider other approaches to crime control. The long-term costs of having the highest prison population and the highest execution rate in the world should be weighed against the cost of alternative programs that might more effectively reduce crime.

STUDY CORNER

Key Terms

appearance of objectivity *(p. 698)*

appellate courts *(p. 699)*

magistrate functions *(p. 700)*

merit system or Missouri system *(p. 703)*

minority representation *(p. 706)*

name familiarity *(p. 704)*

nonpartisan election *(p. 705)*

partisan elections *(p. 703)*

passive appearance *(p. 697)*

specifics of the case *(p. 698)*

stare decisis *(p. 698)*

straight-ticket voting *(p. 704)*

strict procedural rules *(p. 698)*

strict rules of access *(p. 698)*

supreme law of the land *(p. 698)*

trial courts *(p. 699)*

Self-Test

1. Which of the following does **not** describe a difference between the approach to decision making by the courts and that by the other branches of Texas government?
   a. Courts demand that the cases brought before them must involve real controversies between at least two parties, one of which has sustained real, rather than hypothetical, damages.
   b. Court decisions generally affect only the cases being considered by those courts and not cases before other courts.
   c. Courts must maintain a passive appearance and generally cannot initiate policy changes.
   d. Courts must maintain an appearance of objectivity by basing their decisions on points of law rather than on political considerations.
   e. none of the above.

2. Which of the following are issues pertaining to judicial selection in Texas?
   a. straight-ticket voting
   b. campaign contributions
   c. minority representation
   d. a and b only
   e. all of the above

3. With regard to the options for judicial selection, which of the following often prompts judges to demonstrate strong competence and independence but weak responsiveness to voters?
   a. judges elected in nonpartisan elections
   b. judges appointed by the governor
   c. judges selected by the merit or Missouri method
   d. judges elected by the legislature
   e. judges elected in partisan elections

4. Which of the following accurately describe(s) Texas's punishment of crime and resulting crime rates?
   a. The average time served by inmates in Texas is less than the national average.

   b. Most Texans believe that the cost of keeping people in jail for longer periods of time should be weighed against the cost of programs that might reduce crime.
   c. Texas leads the nation in both sentencing people to death and the number of prisoners executed.
   d. a and c only.
   e. a, b, and c.

5. Which of the following is **not** a factor contributing to the large number of death sentences in Texas and in Harris County in particular?
   a. the reluctance of state and federal courts to overturn verdicts
   b. a traditionalistic subculture
   c. state statutes pertaining to assessment of the death penalty
   d. the availability of funds to prosecute cases
   e. none of the above

6. The court structure of Texas courts is comparatively more complicated because it includes several levels of trial and appellate courts. (T/F)

7. Texas judicial elections are costly because a candidate must win in the party primary and in the general election, but these costs often are satisfied by business and other interest groups. (T/F)

8. Texas has an "appointive-elective" system of selecting judges because the governor, county governing bodies, and city councils fill seats that become vacant due to death or resignation. (T/F)

9. A plea bargain occurs when a judge accepts an agreement between a criminal defendant and a prosecuting attorney that permits the defendant to serve a lesser sentence upon a plea of guilty. (T/F)

10. Texas is the leading state in both sentencing people to death and the number of prisoners executed. (T/F)

Critical Thinking

How are Americans' attitude toward the courts shaped by mass communications? Many citizens think that courts should not legislate but should make decisions based on the law. If courts reverse decisions made by previous courts, are they legislating or basing their decisions on the law? If the new Bush appointments swing the balance of the Supreme Court to the conservative side and reverse *Roe v. Wade*, would that be legislating or interpreting the law?

Suggested Readings

Abramson, Jeffrey. *We, The Jury.* New York: Basic Books, 1994.

Cheek, Kyle, and Anthony Champagne. "Money in Texas Supreme Court Elections," *Judicature* 84 (2000): 20–25.

Eisenstein, James, and Herbert Jacob. *Felony Justice.* Boston: Little Brown, 1977.

Herbert, Jacob, "Courts: The Least Visible Branch," in *Politics in the American States*, 8th ed., ed. Virginia Gray and Russell L. Hanson. Washington, D.C.: Congressional Quarterly Press, 2004.

Lawrence, Susan. *The Poor in Court.* Princeton, N.J.: Princeton University Press, 1990.

List of Websites

http://www.pbs.org/wgbh/pages/frontline/shows/justice/howshould

The *Frontline* website, with information on campaign finances in Texas judicial races.

http://www.cjpc.state.tx.us/

Website of the Texans Criminal Justice Policy Council. Good source of information on crime and imprisonment.

http://www.deathpenaltyinfo.org/

Website of the Death Penalty Information Center. Keeps track of the death penalty in all states.

http://www.oca.courts.state.tx.us/

Good source of information on state courts in Texas from the Office of Court Administration. Keeps track of court data and serves as a watchdog agency for all state courts.

http://www.tpj.org/

Website of the Texas for Public Justice, an advocacy group keeps track of many aspects of state government, including information on state courts and campaign contributions.

http://www. courts.state.tx.us

Website that contains the organizational structure of state courts and a profile of Texas judges.

Participate!

Attend a session of a local County or District court in your county. It might be helpful to call before you attend and ask for time and information that might be covered in court on the days you can attend. Write as essay describing what happened in court that day. What kind of cases were heard and what was the disposition of these cases?

Extra Credit

Attend a session of a local County or District court in your county. It might be helpful to call before you attend and ask for time and information that might be covered in court on the days you can attend. Write as essay describing what happened in court that day. What kind of cases were heard and what was the disposition of these cases?

(Self-Test Answers: 1. e   2. e   3. b   4. e   5. e   6. T   7. T   8. T   9. T   10. T)

Local Governments in Texas

Chapter Outline

"Creatures of the State"

General Law and Home
Rule Cities

Incorporation: The Process of
Creating a City

Forms of City Government
  Mayor-Council Government
  Council-Manager Government

Role of the Mayor

Role of the City Manager

The Commission Form of
Government

Methods of Electing City Councils
and Mayors
  Election of City Councils
  Election of Mayors
  Nonpartisan Elections

Voter Turnout in City Elections

County Governments
  Urban and Rural Counties
  The Structure of County Government
  Weaknesses of County Government
    in Texas
  Possible Reform of County Government

Special District Governments
  School Districts
  Issues in School Politics

CHAPTER 25

What shall we do with our great cities? What will our great cities do with us? These are the two problems which confront every thoughtful American. For the question involved in these two questions does not concern the city alone. The whole country is affected, if indeed its character and history are not determined.

—Lyman Abbot, 1891[1]

On November 27, 2005, New Orleans mayor Ray Nagin spoke with a gathering of evacuees in a church in the Fifth Ward in Houston, Texas. The gathering of about 500 of the estimated 150,000 evacuees in the Houston area had met to hear the mayor's plans for rebuilding the city. He did not receive a kind reception and heard many angry residents' complaints. The almost total destruction of New Orleans is a good example of both the importance of modern cities and their fragility. American cities are the linchpin of the economy and at the same time are subject to outside forces of nature that can wreak havoc.

Although the attention of the news media most often focuses on state and national government, in many respects local governments have a greater impact on the daily lives of citizens. Many services that local governments provide are taken for granted or expected by citizens, who notice local government only when it fails to properly perform its functions—when the water mains fail, the garbage is not collected, the pothole is not filled, or stray animals are not impounded. When things work, local government goes unnoticed.

Citizens depend on local governments for many life-support services, such as water, sewers, and police and fire protection. Local governments also help maintain the environment and the lifestyles of citizens by protecting neighborhoods through zoning and the regulation of land development. Finally, local governments assume the important, perhaps critical, function of educating children.

While some citizens live in rural areas without services, most people do not find this lifestyle very appealing. Eighty percent of Texans live in urban areas and are dependent on local governments. Even the 20 percent who live in rural areas expect services from county governments and special districts. Thus, local governments are critical linchpins in modern society. Without the services provided by local governments, modern urban society would not be possible. Understanding how local governments work and affect our lives is very important.

Citizens expect local governments not only to provide services but also to be decentralized. In this respect, the United States is the most decentralized nation in the world. Nationwide there are about 87,534 local government units, almost 5,000 of which are in Texas (see Table 25–1). Decentralization allows for local control. In 2002, there were 507,179 local elected officials nationwide and

TABLE 25–1	Number of Local Governments and Elected Officials in the United States and Texas in 2002			
	UNITED STATES		TEXAS	
	LOCAL GOVERNMENTS	ELECTED OFFICIALS	LOCAL GOVERNMENTS	ELECTED OFFICIALS
Counties	3,043	58,818	254	4,491
Cities	19,429	136,632	1,196	7,520
Townships*	16,504	125,209	—	—
School districts	13,506	78,022	1,089	7,423
Special districts	35,052	108,498	2,254	7,187
Totals	87,534	507,179	4,793	26,621

*Texas does not have townships. New England towns in the five New England states are included in township forms of government.

Source: U.S. Department of Commerce, Bureau of the Census, *Statistical Abstract of the United States, 1998* (Washington, D.C.: U.S. Government Printing Office, 2002); http://www.census.gov/prod/2003pubs/g021xI.pdf.

26,621 in Texas. Many citizens become involved in their local governments, which has the effect of reducing conflict and increasing support for government at all levels. Average citizens feel they can have an impact on their local governments and influence outcomes. It is quite easy to attend a meeting of the school board, city council, or county government and participate in the deliberations, and many citizens do so. Participation at the national and state levels, in contrast, is difficult, and few citizens have an opportunity to become involved.

Thus, local governments, decentralized and locally controlled, are central to the American system of government. Few citizens in other countries have the opportunity to become involved in their local government to the extent Americans do.

"CREATURES OF THE STATE"

creatures of the state
Describes the fact that all local governments are created by state government and all powers are derived from the state government.

The city of Houston is the state's largest city.

When citizens become involved in local governments, they do so under the power and authority given them by state governments. All local governments are **creatures of the state,** and whatever power or authority they possess is

Political Culture

Advantages of Decentralized Governments

The United States is perhaps the most decentralized nation in the world. There are over 80,000 units of local government in the United States and over 4,000 in Texas. Some will argue that there are too many governments and that this can lead to problems in uniformity of programs and standards of operation. While this is certainly true, there are also many advantages to decentralization. While the lack of uniformity of policy can be a problem, it can also be a strength in terms of new programs. For example, several years ago many thought that governments could save money by contracting with the private sector to perform services. There were some successes but also many failures. Cities learned which services could best be contracted out and how to do it in areas that proved a success.

Having many local elected officials in many governments might seem to be a source of confusion, but it allows more people to become involved in local government and participate in governing. Nationally, over 500,000 people serve in elected office. This has the effect of increasing citizen support for government and fosters a healthy attitude toward government generally.

Also, government that is decentralized allows for quicker action on problems. If all decisions had to go from local to state to federal governments, the time involved and bureaucratic complexity would be unacceptable to most. Citizens develop a positive attitude that they can, as the saying goes, "fight city hall and win."

derived from state constitutions and statutes. Local governments are not mentioned in the U.S. Constitution. They are created under state constitutions to serve the interests of the state.

The amount of local authority granted and the degree to which local governments can act independently of state government vary greatly from state to state and within states by type of government. One way to sort out this variety is to distinguish between general-purpose and limited-purpose governments. General-purpose governments are those units given broad discretionary authority by the state government. They have the authority to perform many functions and can control their own finances, personnel, and government structure. Limited-purpose governments have very limited authority or control over their finances and are governed by a set structure, with personnel decisions controlled by state law.[1]

A good example of a limited-purpose government in Texas is a school district. It performs only one function (education), has limited revenue sources (property taxes and state funds), is governed by a seven-member school board, and is controlled in regard to many personnel decisions (such as teacher certification) by a state agency. Texas counties are also good examples of limited-purpose governments. State laws limit their authority and revenue, they all operate under the same form of government (see subsequent discussion), and state law often dictates personnel decisions.

Texas cities, on the other hand, are excellent examples of general-purpose governments. Under home rule (discussed next), Texas cities have the authority to pass any ordinance not prohibited by state law and have many sources of revenue. The structure of government varies greatly from city to city, and the state exerts limited control over personnel decisions.[2]

Thus, although all units of local government are "creatures of the state," some units are granted discretionary authority and are relatively free of state control and supervision. Texas cities have very broad authority, but other units of local government in Texas are limited-purpose governments. This chapter examines cities, counties, and special districts (including school districts) in Texas and the differences among these units of local government.

GENERAL LAW AND HOME RULE CITIES

home rule cities:
Cities that are chartered under the home rule provisions of state law. Local citizens write and approve a charter that is unique for that city and that complies with broad guidelines of state law.

general law cities:
Cities that are chartered under the general laws of the state. Their charter is spelled out in the state statutes and is the same for each city using that form in the state.

In Texas, city governments are the principal providers of urban services, and they have been granted great authority to act independently of state government. A study in 1982 by the Federal Advisory Commission on Intergovernmental Relations ranked Texas cities first in terms of local discretionary authority.[3] By comparison, this same study ranked Texas counties forty-third among the forty-eight states with county governments. Since 1982, there have been only a few minor changes in state law that affect the power and resources of Texas cities.

Technically, city governments are municipal corporations. The term *municipality* is derived from the Roman *municipium,* which means "a free city capable of governing its local affairs, even though subordinate to the sovereignty of Rome."[4] Texas cities are granted charters by the state government. A city charter is a document much like a state constitution in that it provides the basic structure and organization of government and the broad outlines of powers and authorities. In Texas, cities are chartered as either general law cities or home rule cities. General law charters are specified in state statutes, and cities can choose from seven charters provided in the statutes.[5] These options allow considerable choice as to form of city government. There are 938 general law cities in Texas.[6]

Since the passage of a constitutional amendment in 1912, any city in Texas with a population of at least 5,000 can be chartered as a home rule city.[7] Most of these cities adopt home rule charters. Of the 309 cities with a population of more than 5,000, only nineteen operate under general law charters.[8] Home rule means that the local citizens may adopt any form of government they want and pass any ordinance not prohibited by state law, a surrender of state power called devolution of authority. There can be implicit or explicit prohibitions on city ordinance power. For example, state law is silent on the number of members on city councils, but the state constitution limits the term of office to four years. There is no specific grant of power to cities in the state constitution. Cities can pass any ordinance (local law) unless there is a prohibition against local governments acting on the matter at issue, and the prohibition might be only implied. For example, there is no explicit prohibition against cities passing an ordinance prohibiting open alcohol containers in vehicles. Several Texas cities passed such ordinances in the 1980s before there was a state law prohibiting open containers. However, state courts ruled that the regulation of alcohol was a state function and by implication (implicitly) Texas cities could not pass no-open-container ordinances.

The home rule provisions of the Texas constitution allow great latitude in governing local affairs. Once approved, home rule charters may be amended only with the approval of the city voters. Usually, the city council or a charter commission proposes changes. While voters are not granted initiative to change the state constitution, 243 home rule charters in Texas allow voters to initiate charter changes.[9]

City hall in Bryan, Texas.

Political Culture

The Creation of Impact, Texas

Texas and some other states make it easy to create city governments. In 1960, Impact, Texas, was created for the sole purpose of allowing for the sale of liquor, a questionable use of the power to create local governments.

Impact, Texas, is a small city now surrounded by the city of Abilene. It was incorporated in February 1960. The primary purpose of its incorporation was to allow for the sale of liquor. Under Texas law, the citizens of a city may vote to allow the sale of alcohol in so-called wet-dry elections. The city of Abilene is noted for being a center of Christian fundamentalism and is the home of three religious colleges, Abilene Christian, Hardin-Simmons and McMurrey University (Methodist). Some citizens of Abilene were scandalized at the prospect of liquor sales in this

dry corner of the state and attempted to block the incorporation. After several trips to the courthouse, (*Perkins v. Ingalsbe*, 1961), the incorporation was allowed and liquor sales took place for many years. Impact was the only place for miles around where liquor could be purchased.

The city of Abilene, using its annexation powers, surrounded the city of Impact, eliminating any chance for it to grow. In 1963, the Texas legislature passed the law creating the extraterritorial jurisdiction for all Texas cities and limiting the incorporation of cities within the ETJ of an existing city. The incorporation of Impact was a factor in the passage of this act.

In the 1980s, Abilene allowed the sale of liquor within the city limits. The liquor store in Impact is now closed.

INCORPORATION: THE PROCESS OF CREATING A CITY

The process of creating a city is known as **incorporation**, because technically cities are municipal corporations. Creating a city normally involves the following steps: first, local citizens must petition the state and ask to be incorporated as a city; second, an election is held and voters must approve the creation of the city; finally, the state issues a charter.

In Texas the requirements of incorporation are as follows:

- There must be a population of at least 201 citizens living within a two-square-mile area (this is a measure of density).

- Petitions requesting that an election be called must be signed by 10 percent of the registered voters and 50 percent of the landowners in the area to be incorporated.

- If the petition is valid, the county judge calls an election.

- If voters approve, the city is created and a general law charter is adopted. A second election is held to elect city officials.[10]

While these procedures are not difficult, there are limitations as to where cities can be created. Under Texas law, all cities have what is called **extraterritorial jurisdiction (ETJ)**.[11] The ETJ extends beyond the city limits of an existing city. General law cities have one-half mile of ETJ. The distance increases as population increases, to as much as five miles for cities above 250,000 in population.[12] A city may not be incorporated within the ETJ of an existing city unless that city approves. This provision is intended to prevent the growth of smaller cities on the fringes of larger cities and to allow existing cities room to grow.

Also, cities may annex land within their ETJ. Annexation is the taking into the city of adjoining land that is unincorporated (not a part of another city). Texas

incorporation
The process of creating a city government.

extraterritorial jurisdiction (ETJ)
City powers that extend beyond the city limits to an area adjacent to the city limits.

cities have broad annexation powers. The city council, by majority vote, can unilaterally annex land, and the residents living in the area being annexed have no voice or vote in the process. This provision in state law, coupled with the ETJ provisions, provides Texas cities with room to expand. In the 1999, 2001, and 2003 sessions of the Texas legislature, over twenty bills were introduced to restrict the ability of Texas cities to annex land. Some restrictions were placed on home rule cities; however, they still have broad annexation authority compared to cities in many other states.

FORMS OF CITY GOVERNMENT

Two basic forms of city government are used by cities in the United States, including Texas: mayor-council and council-manager. A third form, commission, is not used by any Texas city and is used by only a few cities nationwide. The commission form is discussed later in this chapter because it once played an important role in the development of Texas local government.

Mayor-Council Government

Mayor-council government, the more traditional form of city government, developed in the nineteenth century. There are two variations of mayor-council government: weak executive and strong executive. Under the weak executive or **weak mayor form of government** (Figure 25–1), the formal powers of the mayor are limited in much the same way the Texas governor's formal powers are limited. First, the mayor shares power with other elected officials and with the city council, limiting the weak mayor's executive/administrative authority. Second, the mayor has only limited control over budget formation and execution. Third, the number of terms the mayor can serve is limited. Fourth, the mayor has little or no veto authority.[13]

Under a strong executive or **strong mayor form of government** (Figure 25–2), the mayor can appoint and remove the major heads of departments, has control over budget formation and execution, is not limited by short terms or term limits, and can veto actions of the city council.

Only 39 of the 290 home rule cities in Texas use the mayor-council form of government. Houston, El Paso, and Pasadena are the three largest cities using this form.[14] Of these three, only Houston has a strong mayor form. The Houston mayor can appoint and remove department heads and is responsible for budget formation and execution; however, the office has no veto authority, has a short term (two years), and is limited to three terms. In El Paso, the mayor's control over administration is limited by the requirement of city council approval for appointment of department heads and the chief administrative officer and by the lack of veto power. Most Texas cities do not have a strong mayor form of government.

There are many more mayor-council forms in the general law cities in Texas than in

weak mayor form of government

Form of local government in which the mayor shares power with the city council and other elected officials.

strong mayor form of government

Form of local government in which most power rests with the mayor.

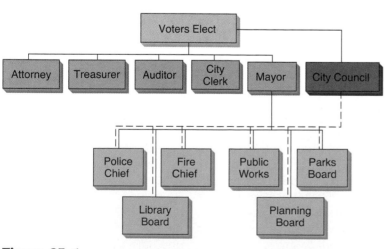

Figure 25–1

Mayor-Council Form of City Government, with a Weak Mayor

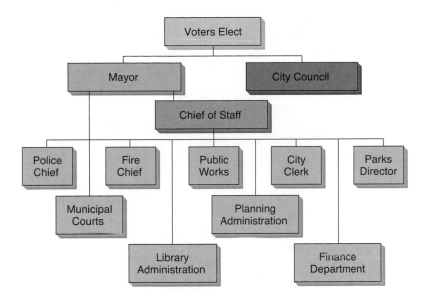

Figure 25–2
Mayor-Council Form of City
Government, with a Strong
Mayor

the home rule cities; however, all have formally very weak mayors. Their powers are provided by state statutes, and no form provided in state law can be classified as a strong executive.

Council-Manager Government

The most popular form of government among Texas cities is the **council-manager form of government** (see Figure 25–3). Except for Houston and El Paso, all major cities in Texas use this form. Under this system, the voters elect a mayor and a small city council (usually seven members). The council hires a city manager, who has administrative control over city government. The city manager appoints and removes the major heads of departments of government and is responsible for budget preparation and execution. The city manager is the chief administrative officer of the city government.

Administrative authority rests with the city manager, and the council is the policymaking body of city government. The mayor and city council are responsible for establishing the mission, policy, and direction of city government and

council-manager form of government

Form of government in which voters elect a mayor and a city council and the mayor and city council appoint a professional administrator to manage the city.

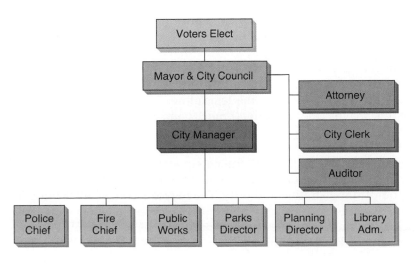

Figure 25–3
Council-Manager Form
of City Government

Figure 25–4

Roles in the Council-Manager Form of Government

The curved line suggests the division between the council's and the manager's spheres of activity (the council's tasks are to the left of the line, and the manager's are to the right). This division roughly approximates a "proper" degree of separation and sharing; shifts to the left or right would indicate improper incursions.

Source: James Svara, "Dichotomy and Duality: Reconceptualizing the Relationship Between Policy and Administration in Council-Manager Cities," *Public Administration Review* 450 (1): 228, 1985. Reprinted with permission from Blackwell Publishing, Ltd.

Mission-Management Separation with Shared Responsibility for Policy and Administration

Dimensions of Governmental Process

Illustrative Tasks for Council	Council's Sphere	Illustrative Tasks for Administrators
Determine "purpose," scope of services, tax level, constitutional issues.	**Mission**	Advise (what city "can" do may influence what it "should" do), analyze conditions and trends.
Pass ordinances, approve new projects and programs, ratify budget.	**Policy**	Make recommendations on all decisions, formulate budget, determine service distribution formulas.
Make implementing decisions, e.g., site selection, handle complaints, oversee administration.	**Administration**	Establish practices and procedures and make decisions for implementing policy.
Suggest management changes to manager, review organizational performance in manager's appraisal.	**Management**	Control the human, material, and informational resources of organization to support policy and administrative functions.

Manager's Sphere

have greatly reduced roles in administration and management. Figure 25–4 shows the roles of the council and the city manager on the four dimensions of city government: mission, policy, administration, and management. The council and city manager share power in each of these areas, with the council dominating in mission and policy and the city manager dominating in administration and management.

ROLE OF THE MAYOR

The role of the mayor in city governments is often misunderstood due to the variations in the role of the office in strong mayor, weak mayor, and council-manager governments. These differences often escape the average citizen.

In the strong mayor–council form, the mayor is the chief executive officer of the city, in charge of the city government. If the mayor possesses veto authority, she or he can use the threat of a veto to extract some things from the council, just as the governor does with the legislature. There is a separation of powers between the mayor (the executive branch) and the city council (the legislative branch).

In the weak mayor–council form, the mayor is not the chief executive officer. The mayor might be the first among equals and the most visible member of city government, but he or she does not control administrative matters, despite having some administrative authority. The mayor's control over budgetary matters is limited and generally requires approval of the council even for minor matters such as paying bills. The mayor usually serves as a member of the council and generally lacks veto authority.

In council-manager government, the mayor is not the chief executive officer and does not control the city administration or budget. These powers rest with the city manager. The mayor is a member of the city council, and there is no separation of powers. The mayor serves as a leader of the council, presides over council meetings, usually helps set the council agenda, and serves as the official representative of the city. Some mayors in council-manager cities have been very successful leaders. They rule not from the formal powers granted in the charter but from their personal abilities or informal leadership traits. Henry Cisneros of San Antonio was one of the best examples of a successful mayoral leader in a council-manager city. Cisneros led "by sheer personal magnetism and intellect, facilitating local successes through joint action of the total city council and professional staff."[15] Thus, mayors in council-manager cities are leaders, although

College Station, Texas, police station.

the leadership style is quite different. They are not a driving force, as they can be in mayor-council governments, but they can serve as a guiding force.[16]

No matter the form of city government, the successful mayor must have political support within the community, the support and confidence of community leaders, popular support among the citizens, charisma, and the energy and stamina to lead, mold a coalition, and gain acceptance of his or her programs.

ROLE OF THE CITY MANAGER

Because so many cities in Texas use the council-manager form of government, some understanding of the role of the city manager is essential. Texas has always been a leader in the use of this form of government. In 1913, Amarillo became the first city in the state to adopt the form. O. M. Carr, the first city manager in Amarillo, strongly influenced the formation of the International City Managers (Management) Association.[17]

Under the council-manager form of government, the voters elect a city council and mayor. Generally these are the only elected officials in city government. The council in turn appoints the city manager and may remove the manager for any reason at any time; managers serve at the pleasure of the city council. In smaller general law cities in Texas, the position might be called a city administrator rather than manager, but the duties are essentially the same.

Most managers are trained professionals. Today many managers have a Masters of Public Administration degree and have served as an assistant city manager for several years before becoming a city manager. All but a few city managers are members of the International City Management Association (ICMA) and, in Texas, of the Texas City Management Association (TCMA). These organizations have a code of ethics and help promote professionalism in the management of local governments. This expertise and professionalism set city governments apart from county governments in Texas. In county governments, the voters elect almost all officeholders, and professionalism often is absent.

Because city managers appoint and can remove all major department heads and are in charge of the day-to-day management of city government, they can instill a high level of professionalism in the city staff. Although the manager's primary role is to administer city government, managers can and do have an impact on the policies of the city as set by the city council. Managers provide information and advice to the council on the impact of policy changes in city government. Professional managers attempt to provide information that is impartial so that the council can make the final decision. Councils sometimes delegate this policymaking role to city managers, either openly or indirectly by failure to act. When this happens, councils are neglecting their duty of office and are failing to serve the citizens who elected them.

Over the last ninety years, the council-manager form of government has functioned well in Texas. Texas cities have a national reputation of being well managed and of maintaining a high degree of professionalism in their operations.

THE COMMISSION FORM OF GOVERNMENT

commission form of government

Form of local government in which voters elect department heads who also serve as members of the city council.

The **commission form of government** is not used by any home rule city in Texas or by any significant-size city in the United States, but it deserves mention because of its impact on Texas local governments. The city of Galveston popularized this form of government in the early part of the twentieth century. In 1901, a major hurricane destroyed most of Galveston and killed an estimated five thousand people. Galveston was the only major port on the Texas Gulf Coast and a linchpin in the cotton economy of the state. It was in the interests of all Texans to have the city and port rebuilt. A delegation of Galveston citizens approached the Texas legislature for funds to help in the rebuilding. Joseph D. Sayers, the governor at the time, was opposed to state funding without some state control. The governor proposed that he be allowed to appoint five commissioners to oversee the rebuilding of the city and threatened a line-item veto of any appropriations lacking this control. The legislature balked at the idea of locally appointed officials because of the experiences during Reconstruction under the administration of Edmund J. Davis. John Nance Garner, who was speaker of the Texas house, said that without the threat of a line-item veto you could not have found five men in Galveston who supported the commission form of government. The governor and legislature compromised, and initially the governor appointed three commissioners and the voters elected two. Later all were elected.[18]

The new commission in Galveston worked expeditiously to rebuild the port city. This efficiency attracted nationwide attention. Many other cities adopted this new form of government, assuming that the commission form was the reason for the efficiency. It was a very simple form (see Figure 25–5) compared to the older weak mayor system and its attendant lengthy ballot of elected officials. In most commission forms, the voters elected five commissioners. Each commissioner was elected citywide by the voters as the head of a department of city government and was also a member of the city commission—the legislative body. Thus, the system combined both the executive and the legislative functions into a single body of government.

This combination of functions seemed to allow for quick action, but it also created many problems. Between 1901 and 1920, many cities adopted the commission form of government. After 1920, there were very few adoptions, and many cities began to abandon the form. By the end of World War II, few commission governments remained. Even Galveston abandoned the form in the

1950s.[19] These abandonments were the result of several fundamental weaknesses in the commission form.

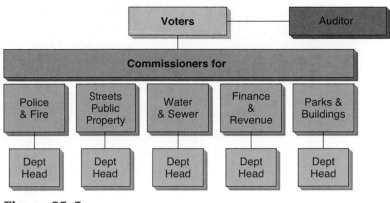

Figure 25–5

The Commission Form of City Government

The first weakness was that voters did not always elect competent administrators. Citizens voted for people based on their apparent qualifications. For example, a failed banker might run for finance commissioner and stress his banking experience.[20] Voters might have no way of knowing that his banking experience had led to failure and would vote on his apparent qualifications. The bank where the person worked might want to see the person depart and not challenge his qualifications.

Second, the combination of legislative and executive functions, while efficient, eliminated the separation of powers and its checks and balances. Commissioners were reluctant to scrutinize the budget and the actions of other commissioners for fear of retaliation. Logrolling set in: you look the other way on my budget and programs, and I will on yours.

Third, the commission initially had no leader. The commissioners rotated the position of mayor among themselves. This "mayor" presided over meetings and served as the official representative of the city but did not hold a leadership position. This lack of a single, strong leader was a major shortcoming in the commission government. One writer described it as a ship with five captains.[21] Later variations called for a separately elected mayor with budget and veto authority. Tulsa, Oklahoma, one of the last larger cities to use the form, gave the mayor these powers.[22]

The major contribution of the commission form of government was that it served as a transition between the old weak mayor form, with many elected officials and a large city council, and the council-manager form, with no elected executives and a small city council. Many cities altered their charters, stripping administrative power from the commissioners and assigning it to a city manager. Many Texas cities retained the term *commission* as a name for the city council. Lubbock retained the five-member commission until the 1980s, when it was forced to increase the size of the council and hold single-member-district elections.

METHODS OF ELECTING CITY COUNCILS AND MAYORS

Election of City Councils

The traditional method to elect city council members, used for most of the nineteenth century, was the single-member-district system (see Chapter 22 on the Texas legislature) or ward system. In this method, the city is divided into election districts of approximately equal populations, and the voters in these districts elect a council member. There are a few cases of multimember districts, all outside Texas.

In the beginning of the twentieth century, many cities, led by early commission adoptions, moved away from the single-member-district system and began to elect council members at large by all voters in the city. There are several variations on the **at-large election system.**

At-large election system

System in which all voters in the city elect the mayor and city council members.

At-large by place is the most common such system used in Texas. In this system, candidates file for at-large ballot positions, which usually are given a number designation—Place 1, Place 2, and so on. Voters cast one vote for each at-large ballot position, and the candidate who wins a majority is elected to that place on the city council

At-large by place with residence wards required is another system. Under this system, candidates file for a specific place as in at-large by place elections; however, the candidates must live in a section, area, or ward of the city to file for a specific place. Abilene, Texas, uses this form. The city is divided into two wards with three council seats in each ward. The mayor can live anywhere in the city. All voters in the city elect the city council members and the mayor at large.

At-large no place is the least common system used in Texas. Under this system, all candidates seeking election to the council have their names placed on the ballot. If there are ten candidates seeking election and five open seats, each voter is instructed to cast one vote each for five candidates. The top five vote-getters are elected. With this method it is not uncommon for a candidate to win election with only a plurality (less than a majority).[23]

Finally, some cities use a combination of at-large and single-member district systems. Houston is a prime example (see Figure 25–6). Voters elect nine council members from single-member districts and elect five council members and the mayor at large.[24]

Two other systems are used to elect council members. One system is called **cumulative voting.** Under this system, each voter has votes equal to the number of city council seats open in the election. If there are five seats open, each voter has five votes and may cast all five votes for one candidate (accumulating their votes), one vote each for five candidates, or any combination or variation of five votes. Several cities have adopted this system as an alternative to going to single-member districts. Since 1991, forty school districts and fourteen cities in Texas have adopted cumulative voting. The Amarillo Independent School District is the largest government body using the system in Texas (160,000 people).[25]

Preferential voting is another system. It allows voters to rank-order the candidates for city council. All candidates' names are listed on the ballot, and the voter indicates the order of his or her preferences (first, second, third, and so on). Using a complicated ballot-counting system, the most preferred candidates are elected. This system was used in Gorman and Sweetwater, Texas, in the past. Neither city uses the system today. The only other city in the United States currently using this system is Cambridge, Massachusetts, which has used the system for almost sixty years.[26]

Cumulative voting and preferential voting supposedly allow a minority of voters to elect members to city councils without the baggage of single-member districts. There is no evidence that either system results in more minority candidates being elected.

Whatever the system used to elect city council members, some cities require a plurality vote and others require a majority vote. Where a majority vote is required, runoff elections might be necessary.

Since the Voting Rights Act was amended in 1975 and applied to Texas, many cities have changed from an at-large system to single-member districts. Prior to 1975, almost no Texas cities used the single-member-district system (SMD). Most major cities have since been forced to change to SMD for at least some of their city council seats. In cities that have changed from at-large to SMD systems, the number of minority candidates elected to the city council has increased substantially. There is some evidence that SMD council members approach their role differently than do at-large council members. A study of council members in

cumulative voting
System that allows voters to concentrate (accumulate) all their votes on one candidate rather than casting one vote for each office up for election.

preferential voting
System that allow voters to rank-order candidates for the city council.

CITY OF HOUSTON

MAYOR
100% precincts counted

Bell	45,591	16%
Brown (i) (r)	125,187	43%
DeVoy	487	0%
Dutrow	235	0%
Sanchez (r)	115,965	40%
Ullrich	572	0%

COUNCIL, DISTRICT A
100% precincts counted

Lawrence	12,165	43%
Tatro (i)	15,811	57%

COUNCIL, DISTRICT B
100% precincts counted

Cole	1,462	6%
Galloway (i)	16,185	65%
Glenn-Johnson	7,436	29%

COUNCIL, DISTRICT C
100% precincts counted

Goldberg (i)	22,140	68%
Hardy	6,417	20%
Kuhleman	4,096	13%

COUNCIL, DISTRICT D
100% precincts counted

Carter	6,893	17%
Clark	975	2%
Edwards (r)	15,814	39%
McKinney	665	2%
Oliver	3,343	9%
Womack (r)	13,096	32%

COUNCIL, DISTRICT E
100% precincts counted

Jones	4,036	16%
Kish	2,483	10%
Maristany (r)	4,161	16%
Orellana	1,690	7%
Rogers	2,291	9%
Wiseman (r)	10,735	42%

COUNCIL, DISTRICT F
100% precincts counted

Ellis (i)	11,161	76%
Nguyen	3,534	24%
Amadi	117	0%

COUNCIL, DISTRICT G
100% precincts counted

Keller (i)	21,979	58%
Osso	12,212	32%
Varkadoz	3,883	10%

COUNCIL, DISTRICT H
100% precincts counted

Vasquez (i)	11,248	100%

COUNCIL, DISTRICT I
100% precincts counted

Alvarado	9,136	56%
Flores	4,819	29%
Morris	2,397	15%

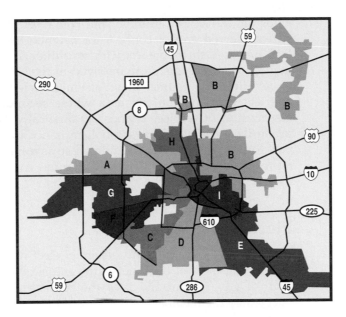

COUNCIL, AT-LARGE POSITION 1
100% precincts counted

Ayres	48,903	22%
Neal	62,762	28%
Parker (i)	114,657	51%

COUNCIL, AT-LARGE POSITION 2
100% precincts counted

Quan (i)	130,371	61%
Terence	84,776	39%

COUNCIL, AT-LARGE POSITION 3
100% precincts counted

Anawaty	9,095	4%
Biggs	15,803	7%
Burks (r)	30,558	14%
Hicks	24,269	11%
O'Brien	20,373	10%
Rodriguez (r)	85,742	40%
Whitehead	26,398	12%

COUNCIL, AT-LARGE POSITION 4
100% precincts counted

Ashley	34,427	17%
Berry (r)	82,088	40%
Griffin	27,961	14%
Lark	9,825	5%
Williamson (r)	49,282	24%

COUNCIL, AT-LARGE POSITION 5
100% precincts counted

Galvan	72,417	36%
Robinson (i)	126,573	64%

CONTROLLER
100% precincts counted

Garcia (i)	202,722	100%

Figure 25–6

Voting Results for the City of Houston Election, November 6, 2001

Source: From *Houston Chronicle*, November 8, 2001. Copyright © 2001 Houston Chronicle Publishing Company. Reprinted with permission. All rights reserved.

Houston, Dallas, San Antonio, and Fort Worth found that council members from SMDs showed greater concern for neighborhood issues, engaged in vote trading, increased their contacts with constituents in their districts regarding service requests, and became more involved in the administrative affairs of the city.[27]

While SMD council members might view their job as representing their districts first and the city as a whole second, there is no evidence that the distribution of services changes dramatically. District representation might be primarily symbolic. Such symbolism is not insignificant, though, because support for local governments can increase as minority groups come to feel they are represented on city councils and become comfortable contacting their council member with problems.

Election of Mayors

The voters of the entire city generally elect mayors at large, the prevailing system during most of the nineteenth century. With the coming of the commission form of government and later the council-manager form, mayors often were selected by the members of the council from among its members. In recent years, the trend both nationwide and in Texas has been toward at-large election of mayors in council-manager cities.

There are thirty-nine home rule, mayor-council cities in Texas. In all of these, the voters elect the mayor at large. Among the 251 council-manager cities, the voters elect 228 mayors at large; the mayors in 23 smaller council-manager cities (9 percent of the total) are elected by the city council. Nationwide, about 35 percent of all council-manager mayors are elected by the city council.[28] The direct election of mayors by the voters of the city gives the mayor some independence from the council and the opportunity to function as the city council's leader.

Nonpartisan Elections

nonpartisan elections
Ballot form in which voters are unable to determine the party of candidates for local office by looking at the election ballot.

Nationwide, about 70 percent of city council members are elected in **nonpartisan elections**.[29] In Texas, all city elections are technically nonpartisan. Officially, a nonpartisan election is one in which no party labels appear on the ballot. Unlike with the November general election ballot, it is not possible for the voter to determine party affiliation by looking at the ballot.

Nonpartisan elections were a feature of the reform movement in the early part of the twentieth century and were aimed at undercutting the power of partisan big-city political machines. Reformers said that there is no Democratic or Republican way to collect garbage, pave streets, or provide police and fire protection, so partisanship should not be a factor in city decisions.

Texas cities adopted the nonpartisan system largely because the state was a one-party Democratic state for over a hundred years and partisanship, even in state elections, was not a factor as long as you ran as a Democrat. It was only natural that city elections used nonpartisan ballots. The Texas Election Code allows for partisan city elections in home rule cities. To date, no Texas city has officially used partisan elections.[30]

It should be noted, however, that the use of a nonpartisan ballot does not eliminate partisanship in local politics. Partisanship simply takes new forms, and new labels are applied. For decades in several Texas cities, "nonpartisan organizations" successfully ran slates of candidates and dominated city politics. Most noted among these organizations were the Citizens Charter Association in Dallas, the Good Government League in San Antonio, and the Business and Professional Association in Wichita Falls and Abilene.[31] The influence of these groups has declined, but slate making is not unknown today in Texas city politics. While the ballot form might continue to be nonpartisan, partisanship can be a big factor in Texas city politics. There is some indication that it is a factor even in smaller cities.

In the 1996 mayoral race in College Station, Texas (population 56,000), there was an undercurrent of partisanship. Supporters of the winner, Lynn McIlhaney, in door-to-door campaigns, reminded voters that McIlhaney was a Republican and her opponent, Nancy Crouch, was a Democrat. On election day, the chair of the local Republican party was campaigning for McIlhaney at the polling places. Republican voters were telephoned before the election and reminded that Lynn was the Republican candidate. In a city where Republicans dominate national and state elections, often winning up to 80 percent of the vote in such elections, this partisan electioneering may have been a critical factor in McIlhaney's decisive victory.

In 2001, the mayor's race in Houston was openly partisan. The current mayor of Houston, Lee Brown, was openly supported and aided by the local, state, and national Democratic party organizations. Mayor Brown's opponent in that race was Orlando Sanchez, who was openly supported by the Republican party. Brown faced Sanchez in a runoff election. Both national parties supplied resources in the runoff election to increase turnout. The turnout in the runoff primary actually exceeded the first primary. In the end, incumbent Mayor Brown managed to win, but not by a large margin. This race highlights the increased role partisanship will likely play in city elections in Texas.

VOTER TURNOUT IN CITY ELECTIONS

Nationwide, voter turnout in city elections is quite low—often lower than in state elections. Turnout rates as low as 4 percent are not uncommon in Texas cities, and seldom do they exceed 25 percent. A number of factors contribute to low turnout.

The first factor is off-year elections. State law provides four dates during the year when Texas cities may hold city council elections: the third Saturday in January, the first Saturday in May, the second Saturday in August, and the first Tuesday after the first Monday in November of odd-numbered years.[32] Most city elections in Texas are held on the May date. In the Houston area, many cities follow Houston's lead and use the November date.

The second factor is the lack of contested races. This situation is so common in Texas that in 1996 a new state law went into effect that allows cities and school boards to dispense with elections if all seats are uncontested. The city or school board simply declares the uncontested candidates elected. An often told local joke is that a person was sitting on a bench by city hall with a sign reading "Will run for mayor for food."

The third factor in low turnout is a lack of publicity and interest in city elections. The news media might cover races in the major cities, especially in years when the mayor's office is up for election, but news coverage of suburban elections in a major metropolitan area is scant. Also, the average citizen does not think local elections are important. The races for president, governor, and other state offices are viewed as more important and are given more attention by the news media.

Off-year elections, a lack of contested races, and low levels of voter interest all contribute to low voter turnout in city elections. Participation is largely class-based—higher socioeconomic groups vote at higher rates (see Table 25–2). The 1991 Houston city charter election to increase the size of the city council was

TABLE 25–2	Voter Turnout in the 1991 Houston Charter Election to Increase the Number of Single-Member Seats on the City Council from Nine to Sixteen		
GROUP	PERCENTAGE WHO VOTED	PERCENTAGE FOR	PERCENTAGE AGAINST
Low-income African American	4.1%	64.5%	35.5%
Middle-income African American	9.1	60.5	39.5
Hispanic	6.9	74.4	25.6
Low-income white	12.2	20.4	79.6
Middle-income white	14.6	11.1	88.9
Affluent	24.4	7.0	93.0

Source: *Houston Chronicle* August 12, 1991, 8A. Copyright © 1991, Houston Chronicle Publishing Company. Reprinted with permission. All rights reserved.

aimed at increasing minority representation on the city council. Despite the obvious benefits to minorities, or perhaps because of them, voter turnout was higher in high-income white precincts and lower in low-income precincts.

Thus, lower overall voter turnout tends to benefit the high-income, non-minority areas of a city, whose residents often dominate city elections and city politics. Single-member-district (SMD) systems might overcome the class bias in voting and increase the number of minority members on the city council, but there is little evidence that great changes in policy result. Also, SMD elections often lead to council members being elected with very few votes. For example, in a city with a population of 25,000 and six council seats elected from districts, it is quite common for someone to be elected with only a few hundred votes.

Low voter turnout can also have a heavy impact on towns where a large percentage of the population is made up of students. Students generally do not participate in local city elections, even though city governments have a big impact on the student population. For example, in Denton, the home of the University of North Texas, most students live off-campus, and the city provides electrical, water, sewer, and other services, for which it charges fees. These services affect off-campus students just as they do nonstudents. One consequence of students' not voting or participating in city government is that others make decisions that can have profound effects on the cost and availability of student housing.

Finally, while city governments are important providers of local services that are essential to urban living, most citizens pay scant attention to elections. It could be argued that this means most citizens are satisfied with the levels and kinds of service they are receiving. The major Texas cities have a reputation of being well run by professionals, in stark contrast with county government in the state. Professionalism often is lacking in county government, where patronage and politics more accurately describe what happens.

COUNTY GOVERNMENTS

The oldest type of local government in the United States is county government, an adaptation of the British county unit of government that was transported to this country. County governments exist in all states except Connecticut (which abolished them in 1963) and Rhode Island (which never needed them). Louisiana calls them "parishes," due to the French influence, and Alaska calls

The courthouse in Anderson, Texas. County government for the most part is still oriented toward providing services to rural areas as opposed to providing services to urban residents.

them "boroughs." The number of counties varies greatly among the states. Alaska, Delaware, and Hawaii each have three county governments, while Texas has 254.[33]

County governments originally were intended to be a subdivision, or an "arm," of state government charged with performing state functions at the local level. For example, counties in Texas still serve as voter registrar, a state function; voters register to vote with the local county government. In issuing marriage licenses, birth certificates, and automobile registrations and in operating state courts, county governments are acting as an arm of state government.

Besides performing state functions, county governments also provide some local services—in some states, they provide many local services. In Texas, counties provide only very limited local services. All Texas counties provide road construction and repair and police protection through the sheriff's department. Some urban county governments in Texas operate hospitals or health units, libraries, and parks.

county governments
Local units of government that are primarily administrative arms of state government. Do not provide urban-type services in most states.

Urban and Rural Counties

The distinguishing feature of county government is population. Of the 3,043 counties in the United States, most are rural counties with small populations. About 700 counties have populations of less than 10,000, and fewer than 200 have populations of over 250,000. In Texas, 56 percent of the population lives in the ten largest urban counties (see Table 25–3). Texas also has the distinction of having the smallest county in the United States. Loving County had a population of seventy in 2000, an increase from eighteen in 1980 due to the oil boom.[34]

In some states, urban counties are major providers of urban services. In Texas, city governments usually provide these services. Urban services include water supply, sewage disposal, planning and zoning, airports, building codes and enforcement, mass transit systems, and fire protection. With a few exceptions, Texas counties cannot perform these functions. Texas counties most closely

TABLE 25–3	The Ten Largest Counties in Texas in 1990 and 2000 by Population		
		POPULATION	
COUNTY AND MAJOR CITY		1990	2000
Harris (Houston)		2,925,965	3,400,578
Dallas (Dallas)		2,049,666	2,218,899
Bexar (San Antonio)		1,232,098	1,446,219
Tarrant (Fort Worth)		1,208,986	1,392,931
El Paso (El Paso)		614,927	679,622
Travis (Austin)		599,357	812,280
Hidalgo (McAllen)		398,648	569,463
Fort Bend (Richmond)		255,412	313,645
Denton (Denton)		212,792	432,976
Collin (Plano)		234,172	491,675
Total		9,732,023	11,758,288
Total state population		17,655,650	20,851,820
Percentage of population in the ten largest counties		55%	56%

Source: Texas State Data Center, Texas A&M University, *www.txsde.tamu.edu.*

resemble the traditional rural county governments that perform functions for the state—recording vital statistics, operating state courts and jails, administering elections, and maintaining roads and bridges. Texas counties also can assist in the creation of rural fire protection districts. In Harris County, the government can assist in the creation of master water and sewer districts that combine many smaller such districts.

Urban Texans tend to identify with city government rather than with county government. People think of themselves as residents of Houston, not of Harris County. Some city residents might not even be able to name the county where they reside. This stems in part from their identification with a particular service being provided, such as police protection. Residents of rural areas are more likely to identify with the county rather than with the city, for much the same reason. The county sheriff responds to calls for assistance in rural areas.

The Structure of County Government

All county governments in Texas have the same basic structure, regardless of the county's size. This structure mirrors the fragmented structure of state government. It can most accurately be described as weak or plural executive (see Figure 25–7). Voters elect the heads of major departments of county government. The provisions for county government appeared in the constitution of 1876. The writers of this document distrusted appointive authority and trusted the electorate to choose reliable administrators.[35]

county commissioners court

Legislative body that governs Texas counties.

In Texas, the governing body of county government is the **county commissioner's court,** which is composed of the constitutional county judge and four county commissioners. The county judge is elected at large, and each commissioner is elected from a single-member district called a "commissioner precinct." Like most other state officeholders, these officials are elected for four-year terms in partisan elections. Even though this body is termed the "commissioners court," it is not a court but a legislative body. Its duties include passing local ordinances, approving budgets and new programs, and overseeing county government.

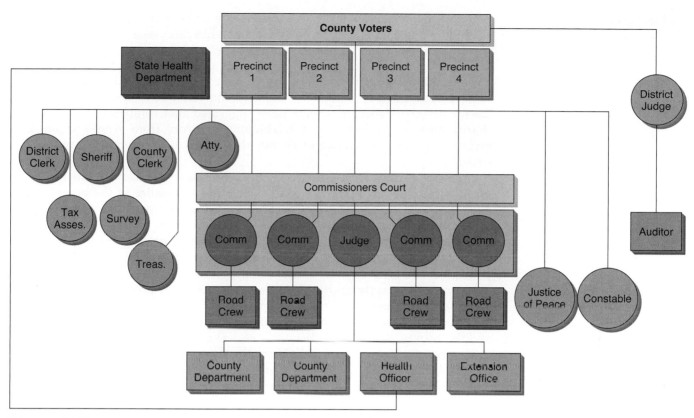

Figure 25–7

The Structure of County Government in Texas

Source: John A. Gilmartin and Joe M. Rothe. *County Government in Texas,* issue 2. (V.G. Young Institute of County Government, Texas Agricultural Extension Service, Texas A&M University).

The county judge presides as the chair of the commissioners court, participates as a full member in deliberations, and has a vote on all matters. The constitution assigns judicial duties to this office, but the occupant does not have to be a licensed attorney; the constitution states only that the **constitutional county judge** must be "well informed in the law." In seventy-two urban counties where the state legislature has created county courts of law, the constitutional county judge performs only very limited judicial functions. The judicial functions of constitutional county courts (described in Chapter 24) are transferred to the county courts of law, and the constitutional county judge acts as the primary administrative officer of the county.

Like other legislative districts, commissioner precincts eventually became mal-apportioned. In 1968, the U.S. Supreme Court ruled that the one-person-one-vote rule applied to these election districts. The commissioners court in Midland County claimed it was a court and not a legislative body and therefore that the one-person-one-vote rule did not apply. The U.S. Supreme Court disagreed, ruling that it was a legislative body and not a court and that election districts must be equally apportioned.[35]

There are seven constitutionally prescribed county officers elected by the voters: sheriff, district attorney, county attorney, tax assessor-collector, district clerk, county clerk, and county treasurer. These officials act as heads of departments of government. Some counties also have other, minor elected officials, such as county surveyor and inspector of hides and wools.

constitutional county judge

Chief administrative officer of county government in Texas. May also have judicial duties in rural counties.

county sheriff
Elected head of law enforcement in a Texas county.

The **county sheriff** is elected countywide for a four–year term and serves as the law enforcement officer for the county. Sheriffs can appoint deputy sheriffs. In rural counties, the sheriff might be the primary law-enforcement officer. In urban counties, city police departments carry out most law-enforcement duties, and the sheriff's primary duty might be to operate the county jail. In smaller counties (below 1,800 residents), state law allows the sheriff to act as the tax assessor-collector.[37] Some have suggested that combining the offices of sheriff and tax collector is a frightening leftover from Anglo-Saxon law, inspiring visions of Sherwood Forest, the Sheriff of Nottingham, and Robin Hood.

The voters also elect constables, who serve as law-enforcement officers. Their primary function is to serve as court officers for the justice of the peace courts, delivering subpoenas and other court orders. Constables may also provide police protection in the precinct they serve.

The county and district attorneys are the chief prosecuting attorneys for criminal cases in the county. Not all counties have county attorneys. In counties with a county attorney, this office usually prosecutes the less serious criminal offenses before county courts while the district attorney prosecutes major crimes before district courts.

The tax assessor-collector is responsible for collecting revenues for the state and the county. Before 1978, this office also assessed the value of all property in the county for property tax collection purposes. In 1978, these functions were transferred to a countywide assessment district. There are 180 of these tax assessment districts in the state, and they are governed by a board elected by the governing bodies of all governments in the jurisdiction—counties, cities, school districts, and special districts. While this office still has the title assessor, few occupants serve in this capacity today. Most collect county property taxes, sell state vehicle licenses and permits, and serve as voter registrars. The voter registration function is a carryover from the days of the poll tax.[38]

The county clerk is the chief record keeper for the county. The county clerk keeps track of all property records and issues marriage licenses, birth certificates, and other county records. Although normally the function of voter registration rests with the tax assessor-collector, in some counties this function has been transferred to the county clerk, who in all counties is responsible for conducting elections.

The district clerk is primarily a court official whose main task is to maintain court records for county and district courts. The clerk also schedules cases in these courts.

The county treasurer is responsible for receiving, maintaining, and disbursing county funds. In many counties, this office has been eliminated by constitutional amendment because the county auditor duplicates the functions. There is probably no reason to retain the office of treasurer in any Texas county.

The district judge or judges in the county appoint the county auditor, whose responsibility is to oversee the collection and disbursement of county funds. The auditor reports to the district judge or judges. Not all counties have auditors. Counties with populations of less than 10,000 are not required to have auditors. In larger counties (population over 250,000), the auditor acts as a budget officer unless the commissioner's court appoints its own budget officer.[39]

Weaknesses Of County Government In Texas

The weaknesses of county government in Texas can be broadly divided into two kinds: inherent weaknesses in the plural executive form of government and the powerlessness of county governments to confront many of the problems of urban areas.

As we have seen, the plural executive structure of county government in Texas is a product of the nineteenth century and the general distrust of centralized executive authority. The plural executive structure lacks centralized authority, and elected officials can, and often do, act quite independently of one another. While the county commissioner's court does exercise some control over department heads, it is primarily limited to budgetary matters. After a budget is approved, elected county officials can make many independent decisions.

Elected officials also hire their own staffs. After each election, the personnel at the county courthouse can change dramatically. For example, new sheriffs hire their own deputy sheriffs. The patronage ("spoils") system in some courthouses results in a less professional staff.

As indicated in the discussion of the judiciary in Chapter 24 and in the discussion of the commission form of city government in this chapter, elections are imperfect instruments for determining the qualifications of candidates and do not always select the most competent person to administer departments. The appointment of department heads is more likely to result in the selection of qualified persons. A lack of professionalism and competence is a frequently noted problem associated with county officials in some counties.

In most (201 of 254) Texas counties, each county commissioner is responsible for road repair within the boundaries of the precinct in which the commissioner is elected.[40] Basically, this means that there are four road crews, each under the direction of a commissioner. While there is some sharing of equipment, duplications and inefficiencies occur with four separate crews. Commissioners also have been known to use their road crews to reward supporters with more favorable attention to road repairs that directly affect them.

County government was designed to meet the needs of and provide services to a rural population. In rural areas of the state, it still functions adequately; in large urban counties, however, this form of government has many weaknesses. One of these weaknesses is the inability of county government to provide urban-type services. Dense urban populations demand and need services that are unnecessary in rural areas. Usually, county governments are powerless under state law to provide even the most basic services common to city governments, such as water and sewer services. In the 1999 session of the legislature, Harris County was given limited authority to assist in the formation of "master" water and sewer districts by consolidating many small suburban districts.

Citizens living on the fringes of cities are forced to provide essential services themselves or to form other governments, such as a water district, to provide these services. In recent years, garbage (solid waste) collection and disposal have become a problem in urban fringe areas. Many citizens must contract with private collectors for this service. Some counties help residents by providing collection centers, often operated by private contractors. In the area of fire protection, counties often help rural residents establish volunteer fire departments; however, counties are not permitted to operate fire departments. Each rural fire department goes its own way, and there is often a lack of coordination between departments. Training and equipment generally are below the standards of full-time city fire departments. Counties sometimes contract with city governments in the county to provide fire protection for the county, although this practice has declined in recent years.

Another weakness is that county governments lack general ordinance authority. City governments in Texas can pass any ordinance not prohibited by state law, but county governments must seek legislative approval to pass specific ordinances. For example, county governments may not pass ordinances on land use (zoning) or building codes that regulate construction standards. A citizen buying a home in a rural area is largely dependent on the integrity of the builder.

Even where counties have been given the authority to regulate activities, they often fall short. For example, counties were given the authority to pass ordinances regulating the construction of septic systems. Some counties failed to pass such ordinances, and many failed to adequately inspect the installation of septic systems. This function was transferred to the state health department in 1992.

A final problem related to county governments is the inequity of financial resources and expenditures. A few counties have a sales tax, but most rely almost exclusively on the property tax. Most property tax is paid by citizens living inside cities and not in the unincorporated, rural areas of the county. For example, in the tax year 2004 in Brazos County, the total taxable property was $9.6 billion. Most of this value ($8.2 billion) was located within the cities of Bryan and College Station, leaving only $1.4 million in rural Brazos County.[41] Most (85 percent) of the cost of county government is paid for by city residents paying county taxes. While county residents pay little of the cost to operate county governments, they receive many services from those governments (such as road construction and repair and police protection) that are not provided to city residents by the county. City residents receive these services from their city and pay city taxes. Thus, city residents pay twice for services they receive only once. This financial inequity goes unnoticed by most citizens.

Possible Reform of County Government

Since the 1930s, suggestions have been made to reform county government in Texas. The rhetoric has often called for county government to be "brought into the twentieth century." In Texas, apparently all such reforms skipped the twentieth century and have to wait for the twenty-first century. While other states have modernized county governments, Texas has steadfastly refused all efforts for change. A frequent agenda item over the past seventy years has been to allow county home rule, which would allow the voters in each county to adopt a local option charter.[42] Voters then could approve any form of government not prohibited by state law, and no county would be forced to change its form of government. This might result in the adoption of a strong executive form of county government similar to the strong mayor and council-manager forms popular with Texas cities. Even though this suggestion seems reasonable, it has been strongly opposed by the many elected county officials in Texas who see it as a threat to their jobs.

The Texas Association of Counties (TAC) is an umbrella organization that represents elected county officials—sheriffs, tax assessor-collectors, treasurers, judges, commissioners, and so on. TAC has opposed granting county governments home rule. This group is politically powerful and has many supporters throughout the state. One group within TAC, the Conference of Urban Counties (CUC), has shown mild support for home rule. CUC represents thirty metropolitan county governments in Texas where home rule would have the greatest impact. CUC is not pushing home rule issues, however, and is more concerned with representing the unique interests of urban counties.

County officials often have provincial attitudes about the role of county government. The idea of expanding county services is foreign to many county officials, who seem content with the status quo. Prospects are dim for any great change in Texas county government in the short term. Urban counties will continue to face many problems that have only a mild impact on rural counties. Also, proposed changes in Medicare funding could have a great impact on the seven most populous counties, which operate hospitals. In the short term, urban counties will have to seek solutions to their problems that do not involve the major structural changes that home rule would bring.

Get Involved!

More Books Than Anyone Can Read, Just Do It Right, and Sick Horses

Why should you care if county government is firmly entrenched in the nineteenth century? County officials traditionally have resisted any change in their power to deal with urban problems. They have a provincial attitude toward providing service, and their view of county government does not extend much beyond that of a nineteenth-century official. This means that urban problems faced by citizens living outside of cities—even simple things like the safety of home construction and septic systems—often are neglected. This neglect can have an effect on life and health.

County officials often will not even consider providing things that might enhance a community. For example, the city council in College Station once proposed that the city libraries be combined and made into a County Library operated by Brazos County. A county commissioner was quoted as saying, "The last thing in the world we need is a bigger library. I was down at the Bryan Library once and they already got more books than anyone can read and every

year they ask the county for more money to buy more books." The city council cooled on the idea of a county-run library given this provincial attitude among county officials.

County government was given the responsibility of inspecting septic systems in rural areas. One county never passed an ordinance or put in place an inspection system. When asked why the county did not have an ordinance or inspections, a citizen was told "We just expect you to do it right." The state has since given this authority to the state health department, and septic installers must be licensed.

County government often is more concerned with problems of rural residents than with those of urban residents. When the Brazos Animal Shelter confiscated a number of horses it felt were being mistreated and had become malnourished, the county commissioners court, at the request of rural residents, prevented the animal shelter from doing this in the future by turning the function over to the sheriff, who is oriented toward policing in rural areas.

Improving the professionalism of county staff might prove difficult, because elected county officials can hire their own people. Some county officials in some counties place great emphasis on professionalism. Other officials reward faithful campaign workers with appointments. In rural counties, these jobs often are well paid and are much sought after by supporters.

SPECIAL DISTRICT GOVERNMENTS

Special district governments are another form of local government that provides services to local residents. Special districts have been referred to as "shadow governments" because they operate out of the view of most citizens. These governments are created for many reasons and perform many functions. Some districts are single-function (e.g., fire), and others are multipurpose (e.g., water, sewer, and street repair). Some special districts (such as metropolitan transit districts) cover several counties, and others (such as municipal utility districts) cover only a few acres.

The primary reason special districts are created is to provide services when no other unit of government exists to provide that service. Sometimes the need extends beyond the geographical boundaries of existing units of government. A good example of this is mass transportation. Dallas/Fort Worth, Houston, San Antonio, Austin, El Paso, and other metropolitan areas have created transit districts that serve several counties. Sometimes the service involves natural boundaries that extend over county lines. Soil and water conservation and flood control are examples of this. In still other cases, the need for a service might be

special district governments
Form of local government that provides specific services to citizens, such as water, sewage, fire protection and public transportation.

confined to a single county but no government unit exists to provide the service. An excellent example of this is municipal utility districts (MUDs), multifunction districts generally created outside cities to provide water, sewage treatment, and other services. In Texas, MUDs are created because county governments cannot provide these services. Finally, some districts are created for political reasons—because no existing unit of government wants to solve the service problem due to potential political conflicts. In this case, the creation of another unit of government to deal with a hot political issue is preferable. The Gulf Coast Waste Disposal Authority, created to clean up water pollution in the Houston area, is a good example of this.

Special districts often are an efficient and expedient way to solve a problem, but they also can generate problems. One problem citizens face is keeping track of the many special districts that provide services to them. For example, a MUD, a soil and water conservation district, a flood control district, a fire protection district, a metropolitan transit authority, a hospital district, and a waste disposal district all can govern a citizen living in the Houston suburbs. Most citizens have trouble distinguishing among a school district, a county, and a city. Dealing with seven or more units of government is even more complicated.

The governing boards of special districts in Texas are selected in two ways. Multicounty special districts (such as DART in Dallas and METRO in Houston) are governed by boards appointed by the governmental units (cities, counties) covered by the district. Single-county special districts (such as MUDs and flood control districts) usually have a board of directors elected by the voters.

Many special districts have taxation authority and can raise local property taxes. The remoteness of these districts from the electorate, their number, and their potential impact on the lives of citizens raise questions of democratic control.[43] The average citizen cannot be expected to know about, understand, and keep track of the decisions made by these remote governments. The alternatives are to consolidate governments, expand cities through the annexation of land, or expand the power of county governments. None of these alternatives is generally acceptable. Citizens demand and expect local governments to be decentralized, even if they have only limited ability to watch and control the actions of local government and the government is ineffective. Big government is something most Texans want to avoid.

School Districts

A type of special district government that generally is watched and controlled very closely by citizens is the school district. Because school districts play an important role in the lives of all citizens, we will focus on them for discussion.

Since 1942, the number of school districts in the United States has decreased dramatically—from 108,579 in 1942 to 14,851 by 1982, to 14,422 by 1992, to 13,726 in 1997, and to 13,506 in 2002. Texas experienced a similar decline in the number of school districts—from 1,100 in 1992 to 1,087 in 1997 and 1,089 in 2002.[44] District consolidation has been driven by several factors. First, there have been demands for improved curriculum, especially in science and math. Many small rural school districts were not able to provide the desired range and diversity of curriculum. Second, there has been increased state financial aid to school districts that consolidate. Third, road conditions improved. Texas developed the farm-to-market road system in the 1950s. This system, coupled with improved all-weather county roads, made possible the busing of students to urban schools.

The rural areas of Texas still have many school districts with a small student body that could consolidate with neighboring districts. Sometimes resistance to consolidation is driven by considerations for the school football program and the realization that closing the school will lead to the death of the town. Often, the school is the only glue that holds a community together. Football and community pride are powerful forces, even if the local football team has only six players.

The future will likely see few additional consolidations. The demand today is not for consolidation but for decentralization with the "open-enrollment charter school." In 1995, the legislature authorized the creation of "up to 20 charters for open-enrollment charter schools. These schools can be operated in school districts or non–school district facilities, by public or private higher education institutions, non-profit organizations or governmental entities."[45] Additional charter schools were authorized in the 1997 and 1999 sessions of the legislature. In 1998–99, 89 charter schools were operating in the state; by 2000–2001, the number had increased to 140. The exact implications of these charter schools are not quite clear. Some preliminary reports and data are available from the Texas Education Agency. It is unclear whether these schools will produce substantial improvements in student achievement.[46] Thirty-two other states have some version of charter schools. What is clear from the passage of these laws is that many citizens want to decentralize control over local schools, so further consolidation seems unlikely.

All but one of the 1,089 school districts in Texas are **independent school districts**. This means that they are independent of any other unit of government. In seventeen states, 1,412 school systems are attached, or dependent on another unit of government, most commonly a city or a county.[47] Most attached school systems are located in the East and the Midwest, with few in the West and South. In Texas, the Stafford school district in the Houston suburbs is the only school district attached to a city government. Reformers advocated making the school district independent of city government early in this century. Independence was said to isolate the schools from the evil political influences of city government.

A seven-member elected school board governs most independent school districts in Texas. School board elections often are held in April or May with city elections. Some school boards are elected from single-member districts, but most are elected at large, and all are chosen in nonpartisan ballot elections.

independent school districts
School districts that are not attached to any other unit of government and operate schools in Texas.

Issues in School Politics

While the creation of independent school districts might reduce the influence of city politics, school district elections still are quite political. Over the past several decades, many contentious issues have dominated school politics.

One issue, and perhaps the most difficult to resolve, is school finance. The state of Texas pays for part of the cost of education. Over the past twenty years, the state's share of the cost of education has declined, and local school districts have been forced to pick up a larger part of the cost. Today, the state of Texas pays about 35 percent of the cost of education, and local districts provide the remainder.[48] Because the only source of local financial support is the property tax, some school districts have been better able than others to absorb the higher local share. Some school districts have a high per-pupil property tax base (so-called rich districts), and others have a low per-pupil property tax base (so-called poor districts). While the state does show preference to poor districts with increased funding, this support is still inadequate, and great disparities exist in the amount of money available to school districts on a per-pupil basis.

These inequities became a statewide issue in 1968 when parents in the Edgewood School District in San Antonio filed a lawsuit challenging the financing of schools in Texas (*Rodriguez v. San Antonio Independent School District*). The U.S. Supreme Court found the system of school financing to be unfair but said that it was a state problem and that its resolution rested with the state. Because of this case, the state increased aid to poor school districts, but severe inequities continued. In 1984, another lawsuit (*Edgewood v. Kirby*) brought education finance to the forefront in Texas. This case was filed in state district court and, due to efforts of the Mexican American Legal Defense and Education Fund and the Equity Center in Austin, the Texas supreme court in 1989 ruled the system of school finance in the state unconstitutional.

Data used in this court case indicate the disparities among school districts (see Table 25–4). The critical variable in the table is the par value, an index of the per-pupil/student value of property in a district compared with the statewide average, with an index of 100 being average. A district with a par value index above 100, it has more wealth per pupil; districts below 100 have less wealth per pupil. Changes in state law have narrowed these disparities, but inequities still exist. While state aid makes up for some of these differences, most aid is aimed at providing the basic foundations of education. Rich districts can provide additional funds for so-called "enrichments."

In an attempt to correct these inequities, the state legislature in 1991 consolidated property taxes within 188 units called county education districts. These districts collected property taxes to be used for school operations and distributed it to the school districts in their jurisdiction on a per-student basis. This system, which became known as the **"Robin Hood Plan,"** was challenged in court by some rich districts. The courts ruled that the plan violated the Texas constitution. The state legislature then proposed a constitutional amendment to make

"Robin Hood Plan"

Name for the provision in the education statutes that requires "rich" school districts with a property tax base per pupil in excess of $305,000 to share their wealth with other school districts.

| TABLE 25–4 | Per-Student Property Tax Value Among Selected School Districts in Texas in 1997 and 2002 Par value is an index of average property values per pupil in the state. An index of 100 is the statewide average, which in 1997 was $202,587 per pupil. If the district is below the statewide average, it has an index of less than 100. Above 100 means the district has an above-average property tax value per pupil. |

SCHOOL DISTRICT	TOTAL STUDENTS 1997	TOTAL STUDENTS 2002	MARKET VALUE PER STUDENT 1997	MARKET VALUE PER STUDENT 2002	PAR VALUE INDEX 1997	PAR VALUE INDEX 2002
Kingsville	5,136	4,644	$ 79,623	$ 113,995	39	49
Santa Gertudis	263	275	561,398	516,853	277	220
Houston	209,375	210,670	218,539	313,871	108	138
Spring	21,044	24,429	151,327	198,109	75	84
Alamo Heights	4,160	4,493	455,614	611,442	225	261
Edgewood	14,180	13,435	29,893	38,150	14	16
San Antonio	61,361	57,421	94,342	127,469	47	54
Dallas	154,847	163,562	245,753	343,973	121	147
Highland Park	5,483	5,869	740,857	1,116,216	366	476
Plano	40,864	48,944	362,159	523,561	178	223
Harlingen	16,156	16,049	81,171	117,559	40	50
Port Isabel	2,228	2,349	403,515	539,691	199	230
College Station	6,939	7,424	260,347	362,352	128	155
Navasota	3,074	3,049	167,953	201,866	82	86

Sources: Data for 1997 from Texas Education Agency data set. Data provided by Ken Meier and John Bohte, faculty members at Texas A&M University.

the system legal. In May 1993, the voters rejected this amendment by a large margin (63 percent against).[49]

The rejection of this issue had political implications in the 1995 governor's race. According to the *Dallas Morning News*, the Republican National Committee spent $400,000 to help defeat the amendment and to promote negative views about the governor, Ann Richards. The campaign ads tied Richards to the amendment.[50] Richards was defeated by George W. Bush in 1994, although Richards might have lost even without the ads.

Following the defeat of this amendment, the legislature passed a new law that gave several options to so-called rich districts. This plan was acceptable to the courts. Under this plan, a school district's property tax wealth is capped at $305,000 per pupil. At that point a district has several choices. It may send its excess wealth to the state, which will send the money to poor district, or it can combine its wealth with a specific district. Most districts send the excess money to the state. After a district reaches the $305,000 per-pupil cap, it receives very little state money. It still receives some federal funds, however. Ninety percent of the school districts in Texas are poor districts, and only 10 percent must give money to the state.

The 2003 and 2005 sessions of the legislature again faced the problem of school finances. An issue that has grown out of the present system is that school district taxes are capped by state law at no more than $1.50 per $100 of valuation for operations. School bonds can be repaid with additional taxes. Many districts have reached the $1.50 limit and still do not have enough money to operate. A few districts are suggesting that they may have to close due to lack of funds. The legislature will have to find a solution to this problem. The state faced a $10 billion shortfall, and equity in school finance was ignored. The legislature in both 2003 and 2005 and in three special sessions has been unable to agree on a change in school finance, making one wonder if the leadership of the house and the senate truly believes in public education.

The current system is, at best, only a partial solution to the problem of differences in resources among the school districts in the state. The legislature has had over thirty-five years to address the issues initially raised in *Rodriguez v. San Antonio Independent School District* and has failed to do so. Equity in education funding is not a value supported by the political culture of Texas.[51]

Governor Bush made education improvement a "cornerstone" of his programs. In the 1995 session of the legislature, he made some progress in getting minor changes that might improve education in Texas. Prior to the 1997 session, an interim study group appointed by Governor Bush failed to develop meaningful ideas for improving the financing of state schools. The legislature eventually developed a program to provide for an additional homeowners exemption. While it was billed as the "largest tax decrease" in Texas history, it was not a tax decrease. It was an increase in the amount of state money appropriated to schools with the requirement that homeowners be given an additional $5,000 in exemptions in the value on which they had to pay property taxes. In some school districts, most property is owner-occupied, single-family property. If the value of each property is reduced by $5,000, the total taxable property declines; some districts actually had to raise their tax rate. The 1999 session of the legislature gave additional money to schools with the hope that local districts would decrease property taxes. This also was billed as a tax decrease, when in fact it was an increase in appropriations to schools with the hope of tax reductions by school districts. Once again the impact varied from district to district. This required exemption for owner-occupied dwellings has contributed to the problem some districts face of being at the $1.50 tax limit discussed earlier.

Under pressure from a decision by the Texas supreme court to close the schools in the Fall of 2006, the legislature met to consider the changes in school finance. The legislature eventually produced a plan that will provide some modest reduction of property tax for homeowners, additional property tax for businesses, an increase by $1.00 per pact on cigarettes and an increase in the franchise tax paid by businesses. This act has probably solved the school finance issue for the next year or two. Some estimates are that the state will face funding shortfalls over the next five years of several million dollars.

Another issue in school politics is the quality of education students receive. In the early 1980s, Governor Mark White raised the profile of this issue. Working with Lieutenant Governor Hobby and House Speaker Gib Lewis, he appointed a select committee on public education. Texas billionaire Ross Perot was appointed chair of the committee. The recommendations of the committee led to the passage of House Bill 72, which contained two very controversial provisions. While it provided funding for a teacher pay raise, it also required the state's teachers to pass a test to prove their competency. There was great resistance to this test by teachers, although it apparently was a rather simple test designed to weed out the completely unqualified. Some referred to the test as a literacy test. Many teachers resented having to take the test and saw it as a personal affront. Many blame this test and the teachers' reactions to it for Mark White's loss to Bill Clements in the 1986 governor's race. The second controversial provision in House Bill 72 was the no-pass, no-play provision. This new rule prohibited students from participating in extracurricular activities if they were not passing all their courses. Of course, the most important no-play was football. In a state where Friday night football is an institution—and in many small towns the premier social event—preventing students from participating simply because they failed a course was viewed not only as un-Texan but also as perhaps a little "communistic." Students were also prohibited from participating in band, tennis, soccer, swimming, and cheerleading, but no one really much cared beyond football (although some communities cared about baseball). The no-pass, no-play rule also contributed to Mark White's defeat in 1986. In the long run, the effects of no-pass, no-play and teacher literacy tests probably were more symbolic than real.

In school board elections in Texas and much of the nation, three curriculum issues in particular have caused controversy: sex education; "creation science," or its newest form, **intelligent design;** and bilingual education. Sex education and creation science/intelligent design are issues that are driven by the Christian Right or Social Conservatives, who have a comfortable majority on the state board of education and have elected members to local school boards. These candidates often run as "stealth" candidates, not openly revealing their agenda during the campaign. Their aim is to limit sex education to abstinence-based programs and to require the teaching of creation science/intelligent design as an alternative to evolution or along with evolution. The extent to which these groups have managed to control school boards is unknown. It is unlikely that the issues will be resolved anytime soon. The Christian Right or Social Conservatives have had an impact in choosing the state school board, which is elected by districts in the state. Some of the authority of this board has been reduced by actions of the legislature in the past ten years. More restrictions are likely in the next session of the legislature, especially in the area of textbook selection.

Bilingual education is a controversy dating to the early twentieth century, when Germans and Czechs in Texas wanted to teach their native languages in the schools. Following World War I, anti-German sentiment in the state killed these efforts, and in the 1920s the legislature prohibited the teaching of languages other than English. There is an old story in the lore of Texas politics

intelligent design
Faith-based pseudoscience used to counter the teaching of evolution in public schools.

Debating the Issues

Should an Alternative to Evolution Be Taught in Public Schools?

In 2005, President George W. Bush made public his belief that Intelligent Design (ID) should be taught as another point of view along with evolution in biology classes. The state school board in Kansas has tried to include some alternative to evolution in the state school curriculum. In Pennsylvania, the Dover school district school board required the reading of a statement on ID in biology classes before evolution could be taught. That case is currently under consideration in federal court. The battle over this issue will continue. Many citizens have strong feelings about the teaching of the scientific theory of evolution. They feel that some alternative Creation Science or Intelligent Design should be presented as "another point of view" in science classes.

Yes

The theory of intelligent design (ID) holds that certain features of the universe and of living things are best explained by an intelligent cause rather than an undirected process such as natural selection. ID is thus a scientific disagreement with the core claim of evolutionary theory that the apparent design of living systems is an illusion.

In a broader sense, Intelligent Design is simply the science of design detection—how to recognize patterns arranged by an intelligent cause for a purpose. Design detection is used in a number of scientific fields, including anthropology, forensic sciences that seek to explain the cause of events such as a death or fire, cryptanalysis and the search for extraterrestrial intelligence (SETI). An inference that certain biological information may be the product of an intelligent cause can be tested or evaluated in the same manner as scientists daily test for design in other sciences.

ID is controversial because of the *implications* of its evidence, rather than the significant *weight* of its evidence. ID proponents believe science should be conducted objectively, without regard to the implications of its findings. This is particularly necessary in origins science because of its historical (and thus very subjective) nature, and because it is a science that unavoidably impacts religion.

Positive evidence of design in living systems consists of the semantic, meaningful or functional nature of biological information, the lack of any known law that can explain the sequence of symbols that carry the "messages," and statistical and experimental evidence that tends to rule out chance as a plausible explanation. Other evidence challenges the adequacy of natural or material causes to explain both the origin and diversity of life.

Intelligent Design is an intellectual movement that includes a scientific research program for investigating intelligent causes and that challenges naturalistic explanations of origins which currently drive science education and research.

— *Intelligence Design Network. (http://www.intelligentdesignnetwork.org/)*

No

Science is the attempt to study things in a systematic way. Observations are made, and based on these observations hypotheses are formulated and tested. This is followed by publication of the result and the formulation of theories about the relationship between observations and testing. Such theories are retested many times in an attempt to find fault. All scientific findings are just theories. To say that evolution is just a theory is but a truism. Einstein's theory of relativity is just that—a theory. As time passed, other scientists found problems with Einstein's theory and a whole new area of physics opened—quantum mechanics.

We are told that evolution has many missing links and that this disproves evolution. The absence of evidence is not evidence of absence. All scientific theories have missing links. ID opposes the basis methodology of science by assuming that some type of supernatural force intervenes in the process and directs evolution. This cannot be subjected to experiment, and no new hypothesis will be formulated. ID is not science despite the new packaging. ID is nothing more than Creationism in a "cheap new suit of clothing." Religion is a belief system. People believe things based on faith. These belief systems are not subject to testing and cannot be proved or disproved. That is why they are called faith.

Today no modern person would believe that a comet in the sky was the work of supernatural forces, design, or a sign from God. Modern persons accept the scientific findings of the solar system and the origins of comets. However, some still are unable to accept evolution and cling to religious explanations of the origins of man. Galileo was punished by religious leaders for his beliefs about comets, and science was set back for years. Teaching ID will have the effect of causing distrust of the scientific method itself.

claiming that when Governor Ma Ferguson signed the bill prohibiting the teaching of children in any language other than English, she reportedly said: "If English was good enough for Jesus Christ, it's good enough for the school children of Texas." Currently the bilingual issue revolves around teaching in both Spanish and English to Hispanic children in the elementary schools. Many Anglo Texans object to the use of tax money for bilingual education. Some take the inconsistent position that everyone should speak English but no tax money should be spent to ensure that they can. Governors Bush and Perry both helped soften the resistance to these education programs and reached out to Hispanic voters in the state.

Summary  Self-Test www.mhhe.com/pattersontad8

While local governments do not generate the same degree of interest that national and state governments do, they have extremely important effects on the daily lives of citizens. Without the services provided by local governments, modern urban life would not be possible.

In Texas, city governments are the principal providers of local services. Council-manager governments govern most major cities. This system has brought a degree of professionalism to city government that often is lacking in county and some other units of local government. In many respects, the contrast between county and city government is remarkable. County governments have resisted change and seem content to operate under a form of government designed by and for an agrarian society. It is a paradox that council-manager city government and plural executive county government could exist in the same state, given the political culture. Economy, efficiency, and professionalism are not values supported by the traditionalistic political culture of the state, yet they are widely practiced in council-manager government.

While many problems of public education remain unresolved, the most pressing is school finance. The current solution does not address the problems of high property taxes in many school districts or the degree to which the state finances local government. Finding new sources of state revenue to reduce local property taxes seems unlikely.

STUDY CORNER

Key Terms

at-large election system *(p. 735)*

commission form of government
  (p. 734)

constitutional county judge *(p. 743)*

council-manager form of government
  (p. 731)

county commissioners court *(p. 742)*

county governments *(p. 741)*

county sheriff *(p. 744)*

creatures of the state *(p. 726)*

cumulative voting *(p. 736)*

extraterritorial jurisdiction (ETJ)
  (p. 729)

incorporation *(p. 729)*

independent school districts *(p. 749)*

intelligent design *(p. 752)*

nonpartisan elections *(p. 738)*

preferential voting *(p. 736)*

"Robin Hood Plan" *(p. 750)*

special district governments *(p. 747)*

strong mayor form of government
  (p. 730)

weak mayor form of government
  (p. 730)

Self-Test

1. Which of the following is **not** a requirement to be met by a city seeking to incorporate in Texas?
   a. There must be a population of at least 201 citizens living within a two-square-mile area.
   b. Petitions requesting that an election be called must be signed by 10 percent of registered voters and 50 percent of the landowners in the area to be incorporated.
   c. If the petition is valid, the governor calls an election.
   d. If voters approve, the city is created and a general law charter is adopted.
   e. A second election is held to elect the newly created city's officials.

2. Which of the following does **not** describe the characteristics of a weak executive or weak mayor in Texas?
   a. The number of terms the mayor may serve is limited.
   b. The mayor has little or no veto authority.
   c. The mayor has limited control over budget formation.
   d. The mayor shares power with other elected officials and with the city council.
   e. None of the above.

3. Which of the following is **not** an effect of single-member-district voting systems in city council elections in Texas?
   a. Distribution of services changes dramatically.
   b. Elected officials approach their roles differently than do at-large council members.
   c. Council members show greater concern for neighborhood issues.
   d. The number of minority candidates elected to the city council has increased substantially.
   e. Council members increase their contacts with their constituents in their districts.

4. Which of the following is **not** a true statement regarding public school financing in Texas?
   a. The "Robin Hood Plan" does not address the basic problem of the differences in resources among the school districts in the state.
   b. Wealthy school districts may send their excess wealth either to the state for redistribution or directly to poorer school districts.
   c. Because the state's share of the cost of education has declined over the past twenty years, local school districts have been forced to assume a larger part of education costs.
   d. In *Rodriguez v. San Antonio Independent School District*, the U.S. Supreme Court held that Texas's system of school finance was unconstitutional.
   e. In 1991, the Texas legislature consolidated property taxes within county education districts, which collected property taxes to be used for school operations and distributed the tax monies to the schools in their jurisdiction on a per-student basis.

5. Which of the following is **not** true with regard to nonpartisan elections?
   a. Texas adopted the nonpartisan system largely because the state became a two-party state after almost a century of Democratic dominance.
   b. In Texas, all municipal elections are technically nonpartisan.
   c. Use of the nonpartisan ballot has not completely eliminated partisanship from local politics because of the influence of organizations that run slates of candidates.
   d. Nationwide, nearly 70 percent of city council members are elected in nonpartisan elections.
   e. It is not possible to determine the party affiliation of candidates by looking at the ballot.

6. The most common form of city council elections in Texas is:
   a. at-large by place.
   b. at-large by place with residence wards required.
   c. at-large no place.
   d. single-member districts.

7. In Texas, county governments often are providers of urban-oriented services such as water supply, sewage disposal, planning and zoning, airports, building codes and enforcement, mass transit systems, and fire protection. (T/F)

8. Home rule cities are inhabited by citizens who may adopt any form of government they want and pass any ordinance not prohibited by state law as long as the city has a population of at least 10,000. (T/F)

9. For cities with a population exceeding 250,000, the extraterritorial jurisdiction extends five miles beyond the limits of those cities. (T/F)

10. The City of Galveston popularized the commission form of government in the early 1900s. (T/F)

Critical Thinking

How does the decentralized nature of local government in the United States and in Texas contribute to democracy?

Suggested Readings

Blodgett, Terrell. *Texas Home Rule Charters*. Austin: Texas Municipal League, 1994.

Frank, Nancy. *Charter Schools: Experiments in Reform, an Update*. Austin: Texas Legislative Budget Board, Public Education Team, 1995.

Halter, Gary M., and Gerald L. Dauthery. "The County Commissioners Court in Texas," in *Governing Texas: Documents and Readings*, 3d ed., ed. Fred Gantt Jr. et al. New York: Thomas Y. Crowell, 1974.

Johnson, David R., John A. Booth, and Richard J. Harris. *The Politics of San Antonio: Community Progress and Power*. Lincoln: University of Nebraska Press, 1983.

Lyndon B. Johnson School of Public Affairs. *Local Government Election Systems*, Policy Research Report No. 62. Austin: University of Texas Press, 1984.

Martin, David L. *Running City Hall: Municipal Administration in the United States*. Tuscaloosa: University of Alabama Press, 1990.

Pernod, Virginia. *Special District, Special Purposes: Fringe Governments and Urban Problems in the Houston Area*. College Station: Texas A&M University Press, 1984.

Rice, Bradley Robert. *Progressive Cities: The Commission Government Movement in America, 1901–1920*. Austin: University of Texas Press, 1977.

Smith, Richard A. "How Business Failed Dallas," in *Governing Texas: Documents and Readings*, 2d ed., ed. Fred Gantt Jr. et al. New York: Thomas Y. Crowell, 1970.

Stillman, Richard. *The Rise of the City Manager: A Public Professional in Local Government*. Albuquerque: University of New Mexico Press, 1974.

Svara, James A. *Official Leadership in the City: Patterns of Conflict and Cooperation*. New York: Oxford University Press, 1990.

List of Websites

http://fairvote.org/
Website of the Center for Voting and Democracy.

http://usacitylink.com/
Website with information on cities across the nation. You might be able to locate your hometown page and get information on your city government.

http://teep.tamu.edu/
Information on state education funding.

http://icma.org/
Website of the International City/County Management Association.

http://www.nlc.org/
Website of the National League of Cities, a national organization representing city governments in the United States.

http://www.county.org/
Information from the Texas Association of Counties.

http://www.courts.state.tx.us/
Texas Judiciary Online.

http://www.tml.org/
Website of the Texas Municipal League.

www.txregionalcouncil.org/
Website of the Texas Association of Regional Council.

http://dir.yahoo.com/Regional/U_S_States/Texas/Government
Yahoo site on Texas government.

www.texasalmanac.com/
Texas Almanac Online.

Participate!

Attend a meeting of your local city government, school board, or county commission. All meetings are open to the public, and most allow public comment. Observe what role the presiding officer (mayor, president of school board, county judge) plays in the meeting. What role does the city manager play? What role do legislators and citizens play in these meetings?

Extra Credit

Obtain a copy of the home rule charter for your home town. If you do not live in a home rule city you may pick another charter. Also, the charter for the City of Houston is difficult to use because it is complicated, legalistic and out of date.

Do a written report on your city charter and indicate the following things.

1. Form of government.
2. Number of city council member and method of election.
3. Terms of office and term limits.
4. Method of electing the mayor.
5. Qualifications for holding office.
6. How are vacancies on the council filled.
7. Compensation for council members and mayor-how determined or how much.
8. Describe the procedures for initiative, referendum and recall if provided in the charter.
9. Powers of the mayor.

(Self-Test Answers: 1. c   2. e   3. a   4. d   5. a   6. a   7. F   8. F   9. T   10. T)

APPENDIXES

The Declaration of Independence

The Constitution of the United States of America

Federalist No. 10

Federalist No. 51

758

THE DECLARATION OF INDEPENDENCE

IN CONGRESS, JULY 4, 1776

The Unanimous Declaration of the Thirteen United States of America

When, in the course of human events, it becomes necessary for one people to dissolve the political bands which have connected them with another, and to assume, among the powers of the earth, the separate and equal station to which the laws of nature and of nature's God entitle them, a decent respect to the opinions of mankind requires that they should declare the causes which impel them to the separation.

We hold these truths to be self-evident, that all men are created equal; that they are endowed by their Creator with certain unalienable rights; that among these, are life, liberty, and the pursuit of happiness. That, to secure these rights, governments are instituted among men, deriving their just powers from the consent of the governed; that, whenever any form of government becomes destructive of these ends, it is the right of the people to alter or to abolish it, and to institute a new government, laying its foundation on such principles, and organizing its powers in such form, as to them shall seem most likely to effect their safety and happiness. Prudence, indeed, will dictate that governments long established, should not be changed for light and transient causes; and, accordingly, all experience hath shown, that mankind are more disposed to suffer, while evils are sufferable, than to right themselves by abolishing the forms to which they are accustomed. But, when a long train of abuses and usurpations, pursuing invariably the same object, evinces a design to reduce them under absolute despotism, it is their right, it is their duty, to throw off such government and to provide new guards for their future security. Such has been the patient sufferance of these colonies, and such is now the necessity which constrains them to alter their former systems of government. The history of the present King of Great Britain is a history of repeated injuries and usurpations, all having, in direct object, the establishment of an absolute tyranny over these States. To prove this, let facts be submitted to a candid world:

He has refused his assent to laws the most wholesome and necessary for the public good.

He has forbidden his governors to pass laws of immediate and pressing importance, unless suspended in their operation till his assent should be obtained; and, when so suspended, he has utterly neglected to attend to them.

He has refused to pass other laws for the accommodation of large districts of people, unless those people would relinquish the right of representation in the legislature; a right inestimable to them, and formidable to tyrants only.

He has called together legislative bodies at places unusual, uncomfortable, and distant from the depository of their public records, for the sole purpose of fatiguing them into compliance with his measures.

He has dissolved representative houses repeatedly for opposing, with manly firmness, his invasions on the rights of the people.

He has refused, for a long time after such dissolutions, to cause others to be elected; whereby the legislative powers, incapable of annihilation, have returned to the people at large for their exercise; the state remaining, in the meantime, exposed to all the danger of invasion from without, and convulsions within.

He has endeavored to prevent the population of these States; for that purpose, obstructing the laws for naturalization of foreigners, refusing to pass others to encourage their migration hither, and raising the conditions of new appropriations of lands.

He has obstructed the administration of justice, by refusing his assent to laws for establishing judiciary powers.

He has made judges dependent on his will alone, for the tenure of their offices, and the amount and payment of their salaries.

He has erected a multitude of new offices, and sent hither swarms of officers to harass our people, and eat out their substance.

He has kept among us, in time of peace, standing armies, without the consent of our legislatures.

He has affected to render the military independent of, and superior to, the civil power.

He has combined, with others, to subject us to a jurisdiction foreign to our Constitution, and unacknowledged by our laws; giving his assent to their acts of pretended legislation:

For quartering large bodies of armed troops among us:

For protecting them by a mock trial, from punishment, for any murders which they should commit on the inhabitants of these States:

For cutting off our trade with all parts of the world:

For imposing taxes on us without our consent:

For depriving us, in many cases, of the benefit of trial by jury:

For transporting us beyond seas to be tried for pretended offences:

For abolishing the free system of English laws in a neighboring province, establishing therein an arbitrary government, and enlarging its boundaries, so as to render it at once an example and fit instrument for introducing the same absolute rule into these colonies:

For taking away our charters, abolishing our most valuable laws, and altering, fundamentally, the powers of our governments:

For suspending our own legislatures, and declaring themselves invested with power to legislate for us in all cases whatsoever.

He has abdicated government here, by declaring us out of his protection, and waging war against us.

He has plundered our seas, ravaged our coasts, burnt our towns, and destroyed the lives of our people.

He is, at this time, transporting large armies of foreign mercenaries to complete the works of death, desolation, and tyranny, already begun, with circumstances of cruelty and perfidy scarcely paralleled in the most barbarous ages, and totally unworthy of the head of a civilized nation.

He has constrained our fellow citizens, taken captive on the high seas, to bear arms against their country, to become the executioners of their friends, and brethren, or to fall themselves by their hands.

He has excited domestic insurrections amongst us, and has endeavored to bring on the inhabitants of our frontiers, the merciless Indian savages, whose known rule of warfare is an undistinguished destruction of all ages, sexes, and conditions.

In every stage of these oppressions, we have petitioned for redress, in the most humble terms; our repeated petitions have been answered only by repeated injury. A prince, whose character is thus marked by every act which may define a tyrant, is unfit to be the ruler of a free people.

Nor have we been wanting in attention to our British brethren. We have warned them, from time to time, of attempts made by their legislature to extend an unwarrantable jurisdiction over us. We have reminded them of the circumstances of our emigration and settlement here. We have appealed to their native justice and magnanimity, and we have conjured them, by the ties of our common kindred, to disavow these usurpations, which would inevitably interrupt our connections and correspondence. They, too, have been deaf to the voice of justice and of consanguinity. We must, therefore, acquiesce in the necessity which denounces our separation, and hold them as we hold the rest of mankind, enemies in war, in peace, friends.

We, therefore, the representatives of the United States of America, in general Congress assembled, appealing to the Supreme Judge of the world for the rectitude of our intentions, do, in the name, and by the authority of the good people of these colonies, solemnly publish and declare, that these united colonies are, and of right ought to be, free and independent states: that they are absolved from all allegiance to the British Crown, and that all political connection between them and the state of Great Britain is, and ought to be, totally dissolved; and that, as free and independent states, they have full power to levy war, conclude peace, contract alliances, establish commerce, and to do all other acts and things which independent states may of right do. And, for the support of this declaration, with a firm reliance on the protection of Divine Providence, we mutually pledge to each other our lives, our fortunes, and our sacred honor.

The foregoing Declaration was, by order of Congress, engrossed, and signed by the following members:

John Hancock

New Hampshire
Josiah Bartlett
William Whipple
Matthew Thornton

Massachusetts Bay
Samuel Adams
John Adams
Robert Treat Paine
Elbridge Gerry

Rhode Island
Stephen Hopkins
William Ellery

Connecticut
Roger Sherman
Samuel Huntington
William Williams
Oliver Wolcott

New York
William Floyd
Philip Livingston
Francis Lewis
Lewis Morris

New Jersey
Richard Stockton
John Witherspoon
Francis Hopkinson
John Hart
Abraham Clark

Pennsylvania
Robert Morris
Benjamin Rush
Benjamin Franklin
John Morton
George Clymer
James Smith
George Taylor
James Wilson
George Ross

Delaware
Caesar Rodney
George Reed
Thomas M'Kean

Maryland
Samuel Chase
William Paca
Thomas Stone
Charles Carroll, of Carrollton

Virginia
George Wythe
Richard Henry Lee
Thomas Jefferson
Benjamin Harrison
Thomas Nelson, Jr.
Francis Lightfoot Lee
Carter Braxton

North Carolina
William Hooper
Joseph Hewes
John Penn

South Carolina
Edward Rutledge
Thomas Heyward, Jr.
Thomas Lynch, Jr.
Arthur Middleton

Georgia
Button Gwinnett
Lyman Hall
George Walton

Resolved, That copies of the Declaration be sent to the several assemblies, conventions, and committees, or councils of safety, and to the several commanding officers of the continental troops; that it be proclaimed in each of the United States, at the head of the army.

THE CONSTITUTION OF THE UNITED STATES OF AMERICA[1]

We the People of the United States, in Order to form a more perfect Union, establish Justice, insure domestic Tranquility, provide for the common defence, promote the general Welfare, and secure the Blessings of Liberty to ourselves and our Posterity, do ordain and establish this CONSTITUTION for the United States of America.

ARTICLE I

SECTION 1

All legislative Powers herein granted shall be vested in a Congress of the United States, which shall consist of a Senate and House of Representatives.

SECTION 2

The House of Representatives shall be composed of Members chosen every second Year by the People of the several States, and the Electors in each State shall have the Qualifications requisite for Electors of the most numerous Branch of the State Legislature.

No Person shall be a Representative who shall not have attained to the Age of twenty-five Years, and been seven Years a Citizen of the United States, and who shall not, when elected, be an Inhabitant of that State in which he shall be chosen.

[Representatives and direct Taxes[2] shall be apportioned among the several States which may be included within this Union, according to their respective Numbers, which shall be determined by adding to the whole Number of free Persons, including those bound to Service for a Term of Years, and excluding Indians not taxed, three fifths of all other Persons.][3] The actual Enumeration shall be made within three Years after the first Meeting of the Congress of the United States, and within every subsequent Term of ten Years, in such Manner as they shall by Law direct. The Number of Representatives shall not exceed one for every thirty Thousand, but each State shall have at Least one Representative; and until such enumeration shall be made, the State of New Hampshire shall be entitled to chuse three, Massachusetts eight, Rhode-Island and Providence Plantations one, Connecticut five, New York six, New Jersey four, Pennsylvania eight, Delaware one, Maryland six, Virginia ten, North Carolina five, South Carolina five, and Georgia three.

When vacancies happen in the Representation from any State, the Executive Authority thereof shall issue Writs of Election to fill such Vacancies.

The House of Representatives shall chuse their Speaker and other Officers; and shall have the sole Power of Impeachment.

SECTION 3

The Senate of the United States shall be composed of two Senators from each State, chosen by the Legislature thereof, for six Years; and each Senator shall have one Vote.

Immediately after they shall be assembled in Consequence of the first Election, they shall be divided as equally as may be into three Classes. The Seats of the Senators of the first Class shall be vacated at the Expiration of the second Year, of the second Class at the Expiration of the fourth Year, and of the third Class at the Expiration of the sixth Year, so that one-third may be chosen every second Year; and if Vacancies happen by Resignation, or otherwise, during the Recess of the Legislature of any State, the Executive thereof may make temporary Appointments until the next Meeting of the Legislature, which shall then fill such Vacancies.

No Person shall be a Senator who shall not have attained to the Age of thirty Years, and been nine Years a Citizen of the United States, and who shall not, when elected, be an Inhabitant of that State for which he shall be chosen.

The Vice President of the United States shall be President of the Senate, but shall have no vote, unless they be equally divided.

The Senate shall chuse their other Officers, and also a President pro tempore, in the absence of the Vice President, or when he shall exercise the Office of President of the United States.

The Senate shall have the sole Power to try all Impeachments. When sitting for that purpose they shall be on Oath or Affirmation. When the President of the United States is tried, the Chief Justice shall preside: And no person shall be convicted without the Concurrence of two thirds of the Members present.

Judgment in Cases of Impeachment shall not extend further than to removal from Office, and disqualification to hold and enjoy any Office of honor, Trust, or Profit under the United States: but the Party convicted shall nevertheless be liable and subject to Indictment, Trial, Judgment and Punishment, according to Law.

[1] This version, which follows the original Constitution in capitalization and spelling, was published by the United States Department of the Interior, Office of Education, in 1935.
[2] Altered by the Sixteenth Amendment.

[3] Negated by the Fourteenth Amendment.

SECTION 4

The Times, Place and Manner of holding Elections for Senators and Representatives, shall be prescribed in each State by the Legislature thereof; but the Congress may at any time by Law make or alter such Regulations, except as to the Places of Chusing Senators.

The Congress shall assemble at least once in every Year, and such Meeting shall be on the first Monday in December, unless they shall by Law appoint a different Day.

SECTION 5

Each House shall be the Judge of the Elections, Returns and Qualifications of its own Members, and a Majority of each shall constitute a Quorum to do Business; but a smaller number may adjourn from day to day, and may be authorized to compel the Attendance of absent Members, in such Manner, and under such Penalties, as each House may provide.

Each House may determine the Rules of its Proceedings, punish its Members for disorderly Behaviour, and, with the Concurrence of two thirds, expel a Member.

Each House shall keep a Journal of its Proceedings, and from time to time publish the same, excepting such Parts as may in their Judgment require Secrecy; and the Yeas and Nays of the Members of either House on any question shall, at the Desire of one fifth of those Present, be entered on the Journal.

Neither House, during the Session of Congress, shall, without the Consent of the other, adjourn for more than three days, nor to any other Place than that in which the two Houses shall be sitting.

SECTION 6

The Senators and Representatives shall receive a Compensation for their Services, to be ascertained by Law, and paid out of the Treasury of the United States. They shall in all Cases, except Treason, Felony, and Breach of the Peace, be privileged from Arrest during their Attendance at the Session of their respective Houses, and in going to and returning from the same; and for any Speech or Debate in either House, they shall not be questioned in any other Place.

No Senator or Representative shall, during the Time for which he was elected, be appointed to any civil Office under the Authority of the United States, which shall have been created, or the Emoluments whereof shall have been increased, during such time; and no Person holding any Office under the United States shall be a Member of either House during his continuance in Office.

SECTION 7

All Bills for raising Revenue shall originate in the House of Representatives; but the Senate may propose or concur with Amendments as on other bills.

Every Bill which shall have passed the House of Representatives and the Senate, shall, before it becomes a Law, be presented to the President of the United States; if he approve he shall sign it, but if not he shall return it, with his Objections, to that House in which it shall have originated, who shall enter the Objections at large on their Journal, and proceed to reconsider it. If after such Reconsideration two thirds of that House shall agree to pass the bill, it shall be sent, together with the objections, to the other House, by which it shall likewise be reconsidered, and if approved by two thirds of that House, it shall become a Law. But in all such Cases the Votes of both Houses shall be determined by Yeas and Nays, and the Names of the Persons voting for and against the Bill shall be entered on the Journal of each House respectively. If any Bill shall not be returned by the President within ten Days (Sundays excepted) after it shall have been presented to him, the Same shall be a Law, in like Manner as if he had signed it, unless the Congress by their Adjournment prevent its Return, in which Case it shall not be a Law.

Every Order, Resolution, or Vote to which the Concurrence of the Senate and House of Representatives may be necessary (except on a question of Adjournment) shall be presented to the President of the United States; and before the Same shall take Effect, shall be approved by him, or being disapproved by him, shall be repassed by two thirds of the Senate and House of Representatives, according to the Rules and Limitations prescribed in the Case of a Bill.

SECTION 8

The Congress shall have Power To lay and collect Taxes, Duties, Imposts and Excises, to pay the Debts and provide for the common Defence and general Welfare of the United States; but all Duties, Imposts and Excises shall be uniform throughout the United States;

To borrow money on the credit of the United States;

To regulate Commerce with foreign Nations, and among the several States, and with the Indian Tribes;

To establish a uniform rule of Naturalization, and uniform Laws on the subject of Bankruptcies throughout the United States;

To coin Money, regulate the Value thereof, and of foreign Coin, and fix the Standard of Weights and Measures;

To provide for the Punishment of counterfeiting the Securities and current Coin of the United States;

To establish Post Offices and post Roads;

To promote the Progress of Science and useful Arts, by securing for limited Times to Authors and Inventors the exclusive Right to their respective Writings and Discoveries;

To constitute Tribunals inferior to the Supreme Court;

To define and punish Piracies and Felonies committed on the high Seas, and Offenses against the Law of Nations;

To declare War, grant Letters of Marque and Reprisal, and make Rules concerning Captures on Land and Water;

To raise and support Armies, but no Appropriation of Money to that Use shall be for a longer Term than two Years;

To provide and maintain a Navy;

To make Rules for the Government and Regulation of the land and naval forces;

To provide for calling forth the Militia to execute the Laws of the Union, suppress Insurrections and repel Invasions;

To provide for organizing, arming, and disciplining the Militia, and for governing such Part of them as may be employed in the Service of the United States, reserving to the States respectively, the Appointment of the Officers, and the Authority of training the Militia according to the discipline prescribed by Congress;

To exercise exclusive Legislation in all Cases whatsoever, over such District (not exceeding ten Miles square) as may, by Cession of particular States, and the acceptance of Congress, become the Seat of the Government of the United States, and to exercise like Authority over all Places purchased by the Consent of the Legislature of the State in which the Same shall be, for the Erection of Forts, Magazines, Arsenals, Dock-yards, and other needful Buildings;—And

To make all Laws which shall be necessary and proper for carrying into Execution the foregoing Powers, and all other Powers vested by this Constitution in the Government of the United States, or in any Department or Officer thereof.

SECTION 9

The Migration or Importation of such Persons as any of the States now existing shall think proper to admit, shall not be prohibited by the Congress prior The Constitution of the United States of America to the Year one thousand eight hundred and eight, but a tax or duty may be imposed on such Importation, not exceeding ten dollars for each Person.

The privilege of the Writ of Habeas Corpus shall not be suspended, unless when in Cases of Rebellion or Invasion the public Safety may require it.

No bill of Attainder or ex post facto Law shall be passed.

No capitation, or other direct, Tax shall be laid unless in Proportion to the Census or Enumeration herein before directed to be taken.

No Tax or Duty shall be laid on Articles exported from any State.

No Preference shall be given by any Regulation of Commerce or Revenue to the Ports of one State over those of another: nor shall Vessels bound to, or from, one State, be obliged to enter, clear, or pay Duties in another.

No Money shall be drawn from the Treasury, but in Consequence of Appropriations made by Law; and a regular Statement and Account of the Receipts and Expenditures of all public Money shall be published from time to time.

No Title of Nobility shall be granted by the United States: And no Person holding any Office of Profit or Trust under them, shall, without the Consent of the Congress, accept of any present, Emolument, Office, or Title, of any kind whatever, from any King, Prince, or foreign State.

SECTION 10

No State shall enter into any Treaty, Alliance, or Confederation; grant Letters of Marque and Reprisal; coin Money; emit Bills of Credit; make any Thing but gold and silver Coin a Tender in Payment of Debts; pass any Bill of Attainder, ex post facto Law, or Law impairing the Obligation of Contracts, or grant any Title of Nobility.

No State shall, without the Consent of the Congress, lay any Imposts or Duties on Imports or Exports, except what may be absolutely necessary for executing its inspection Laws; and the net Produce of all Duties and Imposts, laid by any State on Imports or Exports, shall be for the use of the Treasury of the United States; and all such Laws shall be subject to the Revision and Control of the Congress.

No state shall, without the Consent of Congress, lay any duty of Tonnage, keep Troops, or Ships of War in time of Peace, enter into any Agreement or Compact with another State, or with a foreign Power, or engage in War, unless actually invaded, or in such imminent Danger as will not admit of delay.

ARTICLE II

SECTION 1

The executive Power shall be vested in a President of the United States of America. He shall hold his Office during the Term of four years, and, together with the Vice President, chosen for the same Term, be elected, as follows:

Each State shall appoint, in such Manner as the Legislature thereof may direct, a Number of Electors, equal to the whole Number of Senators and Representatives to which the State may be entitled in the Congress: but no Senator or Representative, or Person holding an Office of Trust or Profit under the United States, shall be appointed an Elector.

[The Electors shall meet in their respective States, and vote by Ballot for two persons, of whom one at least shall not be an Inhabitant of the same State with themselves. And they shall make a List of all the Persons voted for, and of the Number of Votes for each; which List they shall sign and certify, and transmit sealed to the Seat of the Government of the United States, directed to the President of the Senate. The President of the Senate shall, in the Presence of the Senate and House of Representatives, open all the Certificates, and the Votes shall then be counted. The Person having the greatest Number of Votes shall be the President, if such Number be a Majority of the whole Number of Electors appointed; and if there be more than one who have such Majority, and have an equal Number of Votes, then the House of Representatives shall immediately chuse by Ballot one of them for President; and if no Person have a Majority, then from the five highest on the List the said House shall in like Manner chuse the President. But in chusing the President, the Votes shall be taken by States, the Representation from each State having one Vote; a quorum for this Purpose shall consist of a Member or Members from two-thirds of the States, and a Majority of all the States shall be necessary to a Choice. In every Case, after the Choice of the President, the Person having the greatest Number of Votes of the Electors shall be the Vice President. But if there should remain two or more who have equal votes, the Senate shall chuse from them by Ballot the Vice President.][4]

The Congress may determine the Time of chusing the Electors, and the Day on which they shall give their Votes; which Day shall be the same throughout the United States.

No person except a natural-born Citizen, or a Citizen of the United States, at the time of the Adoption of this

[4.] Revised by the Twelfth Amendment.

Constitution, shall be eligible to the Office of President; neither shall any Person be eligible to that Office who shall not have attained to the Age of thirty-five years, and been fourteen Years a Resident within the United States.

In Case of the Removal of the President from Office, or of his Death, Resignation, or Inability to discharge the Powers and Duties of the said Office, the same shall devolve on the Vice President, and the Congress may by Law provide for the Case of Removal, Death, Resignation, or Inability, both of the President and Vice President, declaring what Officer shall then act as President, and such Officer shall act accordingly, until the disability be removed, or a President shall be elected.

The President shall, at stated Times, receive for his Services a Compensation, which shall neither be increased nor diminished during the Period for which he shall have been elected, and he shall not receive within that Period any other Emolument from the United States, or any of them.

Before he enter on the execution of his Office, he shall take the following Oath or Affirmation:—"I do solemnly swear (or affirm) that I will faithfully execute the Office of President of the United States, and will, to the best of my Ability, preserve, protect, and defend the Constitution of the United States."

SECTION 2

The President shall be Commander in Chief of the Army and Navy of the United States, and of the Militia of the several States, when called into the actual Service of the United States; he may require the Opinion, in writing, of the principal Officer in each of the executive Departments, upon any subject relating to the Duties of their respective Offices, and he shall have Power to Grant Reprieves and Pardons for Offenses against the United States, except in Cases of Impeachment.

He shall have Power, by and with the Advice and Consent of the Senate, to make Treaties, provided two-thirds of the Senators present concur; and he shall nominate, and by and with the Advice and Consent of the Senate, shall appoint Ambassadors, other public Ministers and Consuls, Judges of the supreme Court, and all other Officers of the United States, whose Appointments are not herein otherwise provided for, and which shall be established by Law: but the Congress may by Law vest the Appointment of such inferior Officers, as they think proper, in the President alone, in the Courts of Law, or in the Heads of Departments.

The President shall have Power to fill up all Vacancies that may happen during the Recess of the Senate, by granting Commissions which shall expire at the End of their next Session.

SECTION 3

He shall from time to time give to the Congress Information of the State of the Union, and recommend to their Consideration such Measures as he shall judge necessary and expedient; he may, on extraordinary occasions, convene both Houses, or either of them, and in Case of Disagreement between them, with respect to the Time of Adjournment, he may adjourn them to such Time as he shall think proper; he shall receive Ambassadors and other public Ministers; he shall take care that the Laws be faithfully executed, and shall Commission all the Officers of the United States.

SECTION 4

The President, Vice President and all civil Officers of the United States, shall be removed from Office on Impeachment for, and Conviction of, Treason, Bribery, or other high Crimes and Misdemeanors.

ARTICLE III

SECTION 1

The judicial Power of the United States, shall be vested in one supreme Court, and in such inferior Courts as the Congress may from time to time ordain and establish. The Judges, both of the supreme and inferior Courts, shall hold their Offices during good Behaviour, and shall, at stated Times, receive for their Services, a Compensation, which shall not be diminished during their Continuance in Office.

SECTION 2

The judicial Power shall extend to all Cases, in Law and Equity, arising under this Constitution, the Laws of the United States, and Treaties made, or which shall be made, under their Authority;—to all Cases affecting ambassadors, other public ministers and consuls;—to all cases of admiralty and maritime Jurisdiction;—to Controversies to which the United States shall be a Party;—to Controversies between two or more states;—between a State and Citizens of another State;[5]—between Citizens of different States—between Citizens of the same State claiming Lands under Grants of different States, and between a State, or the Citizens thereof, and foreign States, Citizens, or Subjects.

In all Cases affecting Ambassadors, other public Ministers and Consuls, and those in which a State shall be Party, the supreme Court shall have original Jurisdiction. In all the other Cases before mentioned, the supreme Court shall have appellate Jurisdiction, both as to Law and Fact, with such Exceptions, and under such Regulations as the Congress shall make.

The trial of all Crimes, except in Cases of Impeachment, shall be by Jury; and such Trial shall be held in the State where the said Crimes shall have been committed; but when not committed within any State, the Trial shall be at such Place or Places as the Congress may by Law have directed.

SECTION 3

Treason against the United States, shall consist only in levying War against them, or in adhering to their Enemies, giving them Aid and Comfort. No Person shall be convicted of Treason unless on the Testimony of two Witnesses to the same overt Act, or on Confession in open Court.

[5.] Qualified by the Eleventh Amendment.

The Congress shall have power to declare the Punishment of Treason, but no Attainder of Treason shall work Corruption of Blood, or Forfeiture except during the Life of the Person attainted.

ARTICLE IV

SECTION 1

Full Faith and Credit shall be given in each State to the public Acts, Records, and judicial Proceedings of every other State. And the Congress may by general Laws prescribe the Manner in which such Acts, Records and Proceedings shall be proved, and the Effect thereof.

SECTION 2

The Citizens of each State shall be entitled to all Privileges and Immunities of Citizens in the several States.

A Person charged in any State with Treason, Felony, or other Crime, who shall flee from Justice, and be found in another State, shall on demand of the executive Authority of the State from which he fled, be delivered up, to be removed to the State having Jurisdiction of the crime.

No Person held to Service or Labour in one State, under the Laws thereof, escaping into another, shall, in Consequence of any Law or Regulation therein, be discharged from such Service or Labour, but shall be delivered up on Claim of the Party to whom such Service or Labour may be due.

SECTION 3

New States may be admitted by the Congress into this Union; but no new State shall be formed or erected within the Jurisdiction of any other State; nor any State be formed by the Junction of two or more States, or parts of States, without the Consent of the Legislatures of the States concerned as well as of the Congress.

The Congress shall have Power to dispose of and make all needful Rules and Regulations respecting the Territory or other Property belonging to the United States; and nothing in this Constitution shall be so construed as to Prejudice any Claims of the United States, or of any particular State.

SECTION 4

The United States shall guarantee to every State in this Union a Republican Form of Government, and shall protect each of them against Invasion; and on Application of the Legislature, or of the Executive (when the Legislature cannot be convened) against domestic Violence.

ARTICLE V

The Congress, whenever two-thirds of both Houses shall deem it necessary, shall propose Amendments to this Constitution, or, on the Application of the Legislatures of two-thirds of the several States, shall call a Convention for proposing Amendments, which, in either Case, shall be valid to all Intents and Purposes, as part of this Constitution, when ratified by the Legislatures of three-fourths of the several States, or by Conventions in three-fourths thereof, as the one or the other Mode of Ratification may be proposed by the Congress; Provided that no Amendment which may be made prior to the Year One thousand eight hundred and eight shall in any Manner affect the first and fourth Clauses in the Ninth Section of the first Article; and that no State, without its Consent, shall be deprived of its equal Suffrage in the Senate.

ARTICLE VI

All Debts contracted and Engagements entered into, before the Adoption of this Constitution, shall be as valid against the United States under this Constitution, as under the Confederation.

This Constitution, and the Laws of the United States which shall be made in Pursuance thereof; and all Treaties made, or which shall be made, under the Authority of the United States, shall be the supreme Law of the Land; and the Judges in every State shall be bound thereby, any Thing in the Constitution or Laws of any State to the Contrary notwithstanding.

The Senators and Representatives before mentioned, and the Members of the several State Legislatures, and all executive and judicial Officers, both of the United States and of the several States, shall be bound by Oath or Affirmation to support this Constitution; but no religious Tests shall ever be required as a qualification to any Office or public Trust under the United States.

ARTICLE VII

The Ratification of the Conventions of nine States shall be sufficient for the Establishment of this Constitution between the States so ratifying the same.

Done in Convention by the Unanimous Consent of the States present the Seventeenth Day of September in the Year of our Lord one thousand seven hundred and Eighty seven, and of the Independence of the United States of America the Twelfth. In Witness whereof We have hereunto subscribed our Names.[6]

[6.] These are the full names of the signers, which in some cases are not the signatures on the document.

George Washington
President and deputy from Virginia

New Hampshire
John Langdon
Nicholas Gilman

Massachusetts
Nathaniel Gorham
Rufus King

Connecticut
William Samuel Johnson
Roger Sherman

New York
Alexander Hamilton

New Jersey
William Livingston
David Brearley
William Paterson
Jonathan Dayton

Pennsylvania
Benjamin Franklin
Thomas Mifflin
Robert Morris
George Clymer
Thomas FitzSimmons
Jared Ingersoll
James Wilson
Gouverneur
   Morris

Delaware
George Read
Gunning Bedford, Jr.
John Dickinson
Richard Bassett
Jacob Broom

Maryland
James McHenry
Daniel of St. Thomas
   Jenifer
Daniel Carroll

Virginia
John Blair
James Madison, Jr.

North Carolina
William Blount
Richard Dobbs Spaight
Hugh Williamson

South Carolina
John Rutledge
Charles Cotesworth
   Pinckney
Charles Pinckney
Pierce Butler

Georgia
William Few
Abraham Baldwin

Articles in Addition to, and Amendment of, the Constitution of the United States of America, Proposed by Congress, and Ratified by the Legislatures of the Several States, Pursuant to the Fifth Article of the Original Constitution[7]

AMENDMENT I

Congress shall make no law respecting an establishment of religion, or prohibiting the free exercise thereof; or abridging the freedom of speech, or of the press; or the right of the people peaceably to assemble, and to petition the Government for a redress of grievances.

AMENDMENT II

A well regulated Militia, being necessary to the security of a free State, the right of the people to keep and bear Arms shall not be infringed.

[7.] This heading appears only in the joint resolution submitting the first ten amendments, which are collectively known as the Bill of Rights. They were ratified on December 15, 1791.

AMENDMENT III

No Soldier shall, in time of peace, be quartered in any house, without the consent of the Owner, nor in time of war, but in a manner to be prescribed by law.

AMENDMENT IV

The right of the people to be secure in their persons, houses, papers, and effects, against unreasonable searches and seizures, shall not be violated, and no Warrants shall issue, but upon probable cause, supported by Oath or affirmation, and particularly describing the place to be searched, and the persons or things to be seized.

AMENDMENT V

No person shall be held to answer for a capital or otherwise infamous crime, unless on a presentment or indictment of a Grand Jury, except in cases arising in the land or naval forces, or in the Militia, when in actual service in time of War or public danger; nor shall any person be subject for the same offence to be twice put in jeopardy of life or limb; nor shall be compelled in any criminal case to be a witness against himself, nor be deprived of life, liberty, or property, without due process of law; nor shall private property be taken for public use, without just compensation.

AMENDMENT VI

In all criminal prosecutions, the accused shall enjoy the right to a speedy and public trial, by an impartial jury of the State and district wherein the crime shall have been committed, which district shall have been previously ascertained by law, and to be informed of the nature and cause of the accusation; to be confronted with the witnesses against him; to have compulsory process for obtaining witnesses in his favour, and to have the Assistance of Counsel for his defence.

AMENDMENT VII

In suits at common law, where the value in controversy shall exceed twenty dollars, the right of trial by jury shall be preserved, and no fact tried by a jury, shall be otherwise reexamined in any Court of the United States, than according to the rules of the common law.

AMENDMENT VIII

Excessive bail shall not be required, nor excessive fines imposed, nor cruel and unusual punishments inflicted.

AMENDMENT IX

The enumeration of the Constitution, of certain rights, shall not be construed to deny or disparage others retained by the people.

AMENDMENT X

The powers not delegated to the United States by the Constitution, nor prohibited by it to the States, are reserved to the States respectively, or to the people.

AMENDMENT XI [1795]

The Judicial power of the United States shall not be construed to extend to any suit in law or equity, commenced or prosecuted against one of the United States by Citizens of another State, or by Citizens or Subjects of any Foreign State.

AMENDMENT XII [1804]

The Electors shall meet in their respective States and vote by ballot for President and Vice-President, one of whom, at least, shall not be an inhabitant of the same State with themselves; they shall name in their ballots the person voted for as President, and in distinct ballots the person voted for as Vice-President, and they shall make distinct lists of all persons voted for as President, and of all persons voted for as Vice-President, and of the number of votes for each, which lists they shall sign and certify, and transmit sealed to the seat of the government of the United States, directed to the President of the Senate;—The President of the Senate shall, in the presence of the Senate and House of Representatives, open all the certificates and the votes shall then be counted;—The person having the greatest number of votes for President, shall be the President, if such number be a majority of the whole number of Electors appointed; and if no person have such majority, then from the persons having the highest numbers not exceeding three on the list of those voted for as President, the House of Representatives shall choose immediately, by ballot, the President. But in choosing the President, the votes shall be taken by states, the representation from each state having one vote; a quorum for this purpose shall consist of a member or members from two-thirds of the states, and a majority of all the states shall be necessary to a choice. And if the House of Representatives shall not choose a President whenever the right of choice shall devolve upon them, before the fourth day of March next following, then the Vice-President shall act as President, as in the case of the death or other constitutional disability of the President.—The person having the greatest number of votes as Vice-President, shall be the Vice-President, if such number be a majority of the whole number of Electors appointed, and if no person have a majority, then from the two highest numbers on the list, the Senate shall choose the Vice-President; a quorum for the purpose shall consist of two-thirds of the whole number of Senators, and majority of the whole number shall be necessary to a choice. But no person constitutionally ineligible to the office of President shall be eligible to that of Vice-President of the United States.

AMENDMENT XIII [1865]

SECTION 1

Neither slavery nor involuntary servitude, except as a punishment for crime whereof the party shall have been duly convicted, shall exist within the United States, or any place subject to their jurisdiction.

SECTION 2

Congress shall have power to enforce this article by appropriate legislation.

AMENDMENT XIV [1868]

SECTION 1

All persons born or naturalized in the United States, and subject to the jurisdiction thereof, are citizens of the United States and of the State wherein they reside. No State shall abridge the privileges or immunities of citizens of the United States; nor shall any State deprive any person of life, liberty, or property, without due process of law; nor deny to any person within its jurisdiction the equal protection of the laws.

SECTION 2

Representatives shall be apportioned among the several States according to their respective numbers, counting the whole number of persons in each State, excluding Indians not taxed. But when the right to vote at any election for the choice of electors for President and Vice-President of the United States, Representatives in Congress, the Executive and Judicial officers of a State, or the members of the Legislature thereof, is denied to any of the male inhabitants of such State, being twenty-one years of age, and citizens of the United States, or in any way abridged, except for participation in rebellion, or other crime, the basis of representation therein shall be reduced in the proportion which the number of such male citizens shall bear to the whole number of male citizens twenty-one years of age in such State.

SECTION 3

No person shall be a Senator or Representative in Congress, or elector of President and Vice-President, or hold any office, civil or military, under the United States, or under any State, who, having previously taken an oath, as a member of Congress, or as an officer of the United States, or as a member of any State legislature, or as an executive or judicial officer of any State, to support the Constitution of the United States, shall have engaged in insurrection or rebellion against the same, or given aid or comfort to the enemies thereof. But Congress may by a vote of two-thirds of each House, remove such disability.

SECTION 4

The validity of the public debt of the United States, authorized by law, including debts incurred for payment of pensions and bounties for services in suppressing insurrection or rebellion, shall not be questioned. But neither the United States nor any State shall assume or pay any debts or obligation incurred in aid of insurrection or rebellion against the United States, or any claim for the loss or emancipation of any slave; but all such debts, obligations, and claims shall be held illegal and void.

SECTION 5

The Congress shall have the power to enforce, by appropriate legislation, the provisions of this article.

AMENDMENT XV [1870]

SECTION 1

The right of citizens of the United States to vote shall not be denied or abridged by the United States or by any State on account of race, color, or previous condition of servitude.

SECTION 2

The Congress shall have power to enforce this article by appropriate legislation.

AMENDMENT XVI [1913]

The Congress shall have power to lay and collect taxes on incomes, from whatever source derived, without apportionment among the several States, and without regard to any census or enumeration.

AMENDMENT XVII [1913]

The Senate of the United States shall be composed of two Senators from each State, elected by the people thereof, for six years; and each Senator shall have one vote. The electors in each State shall have the qualifications requisite for electors of the most numerous branch of the State legislatures.

When vacancies happen in the representation of any State in the Senate, the executive authority of such State shall issue writs of election to fill such vacancies: Provided, That the legislature of any State may empower the executive thereof to make temporary appointments until the people fill the vacancies by election as the legislature may direct.

This amendment shall not be so construed as to affect the election or term of any Senator chosen before it becomes valid as part of the Constitution.

AMENDMENT XVIII [1919]

SECTION 1

After one year from the ratification of this article the manufacture, sale, or transportation of intoxicating liquors within, the importation thereof into, or the exportation thereof from the United States and all territory subject to the jurisdiction thereof for beverage purposes is hereby prohibited.

SECTION 2

The Congress and the several States shall have concurrent power to enforce this article by appropriate legislation.

SECTION 3

This article shall be inoperative unless it shall have been ratified as an amendment to the Constitution by the legislatures of the several States, as provided in the Constitution, within seven years from the date of the submission hereof to the States by the Congress.

AMENDMENT XIX [1920]

The right of citizens of the United States to vote shall not be denied or abridged by the United States or by any State on account of sex.

Congress shall have power to enforce this article by appropriate legislation.

AMENDMENT XX [1933]

SECTION 1

The terms of the President and Vice-President shall end at noon on the 20th day of January, and the terms of Senators and Representatives at noon on the 3d day of January, of the years in which such terms would have ended if this article had not been ratified; and the terms of their successors shall then begin.

SECTION 2

The Congress shall assemble at least once in every year, and such meeting shall begin at noon on the 3d day of January, unless they shall by law appoint a different day.

SECTION 3

If, at the time fixed for the beginning of the term of the President, the President elect shall have died, the Vice-President elect shall become President. If a President shall not have been chosen before the time fixed for the beginning of his term or if the President elect shall have failed to qualify, then the Vice-President elect shall act as President until a President shall have qualified; and the Congress may by law provide for the case wherein neither a President elect nor a Vice-President elect shall have qualified, declaring who shall then act as President, or the manner in which one who is to act shall be selected, and such person shall act accordingly until a President or Vice-President shall have qualified.

SECTION 4

The Congress may by law provide for the case of the death of any of the persons from whom the House of Representatives may choose a President whenever the right of choice shall have devolved upon them, and for the case of the death of any of the persons from whom the Senate may choose a Vice- President whenever the right of choice shall have devolved upon them.

SECTION 5

Sections 1 and 2 shall take effect on the 15th day of October following the ratification of this article.

SECTION 6

This article shall be inoperative unless it shall have been ratified as an amendment to the Constitution by the legislatures of three-fourths of the several States within seven years from the date of its submission.

AMENDMENT XXI [1933]

SECTION 1

The eighteenth article of amendment to the Constitution of the United States is hereby repealed.

SECTION 2

The transportation or importation into any State, Territory, or possession of the United States for delivery or use therein of intoxicating liquors, in violation of the laws thereof, is hereby prohibited.

SECTION 3

This article shall be inoperative unless it shall have been ratified as an amendment to the Constitution by conventions in the several States, as provided in the Constitution, within seven years from the date of the submission hereof to the States by the Congress.

AMENDMENT XXII [1951]

No person shall be elected to the office of the President more than twice, and no person who has held the office of President, or acted as President, for more than two years of a term to which some other person was elected President shall be elected to the office of the President more than once.

But this Article shall not apply to any person holding the office of President when this Article was proposed by the Congress, and shall not prevent any person who may be holding the office of President, or acting as President, during the term within which this Article becomes operative from holding the office of President or acting as President during the remainder of such term.

This article shall be inoperative unless it shall have been ratified as an amendment to the Constitution by the legislatures of three-fourths of the several states within seven years from the date of its submission to the states by the Congress.

AMENDMENT XXIII [1961]

SECTION 1

The District constituting the seat of Government of the United States shall appoint in such manner as the Congress may direct:

A number of electors of President and Vice- President equal to the whole number of Senators and Representatives in Congress to which the District would be entitled if it were a State, but in no event more than the least populous State; they shall be in addition to those appointed by the States, but they shall be considered, for the purposes of the election of President and Vice-President, to be electors appointed by a State; and they shall meet in the District and perform such duties as provided by the twelfth article of amendment.

SECTION 2

The Congress shall have power to enforce this article by appropriate legislation.

AMENDMENT XXIV [1964]

SECTION 1

The right of citizens of the United States to vote in any primary or other election for President or Vice President, for electors for President or Vice President, or for Senator or Representative in Congress, shall not be denied or abridged by the United States or any state by reason of failure to pay any poll tax or other tax.

SECTION 2

The Congress shall have the power to enforce this article by appropriate legislation.

AMENDMENT XXV [1967]

SECTION 1

In case of the removal of the President from office or of his death or resignation, the Vice President shall become President.

SECTION 2

Whenever there is a vacancy in the office of the Vice President, the President shall nominate a Vice President who shall take office upon confirmation by a majority vote of both Houses of Congress.

SECTION 3

Whenever the President transmits to the President Pro Tempore of the Senate and the Speaker of the House of Representatives his written declaration that he is unable to discharge the powers and duties of his office, and until he transmits to them a written declaration to the contrary, such powers and duties shall be discharged by the Vice President as Acting President.

SECTION 4

Whenever the Vice President and a majority of either the principal officers of the executive departments or of such other body as Congress may by law provide, transmit to the President Pro Tempore of the Senate and the Speaker of the House of Representatives their written declaration that the President is unable to discharge the powers and duties of his office, the Vice President shall immediately assume the powers and duties of the office as Acting President.

Thereafter, when the President transmits to the President Pro Tempore of the Senate and the Speaker of the House of Representatives his written declaration that no inability exists, he shall resume the powers and duties of his office unless the Vice President and a majority of either the principal officers of the executive departments or of such other body as Congress may by law provide, transmit within four days to the President Pro Tempore of the Senate and the Speaker of the House of Representatives their written declaration that the President is unable to discharge the powers and duties of his office. Thereupon Congress shall decide the issue, assembling within forty-eight hours for that purpose if not in session. If the Congress, within twenty-one days after receipt of the latter written declaration, or, if Congress is not in session, within twenty-one days after Congress is required to assemble, determines by two-thirds vote of both Houses that the President is unable to discharge the powers and duties of his office, the Vice President shall continue to discharge the same as Acting President; otherwise, the President shall resume the powers and duties of his office.

AMENDMENT XXVI [1971]

SECTION 1

The right of citizens of the United States, who are eighteen years of age or older, to vote shall not be denied or abridged by the United States or by any State on account of age.

SECTION 2

The Congress shall have the power to enforce this article by appropriate legislation.

AMENDMENT XXVII [1992]

No law varying the compensation for the service of Senators and Representatives shall take effect until an election of Representatives shall have intervened.

FEDERALIST NO. 10
(JAMES MADISON)

Among the numerous advantages promised by a well-constructed union, none deserves to be more accurately developed than its tendency to break and control the violence of faction. The friend of popular governments never finds himself so much alarmed for their character and fate as when he contemplates their propensity to this dangerous vice. He will not fail, therefore, to set a due value on any plan which, without violating the principles to which he is attached, provides a proper cure for it. The instability, injustice, and confusion introduced into the public councils have, in truth, been the mortal diseases under which popular governments have everywhere perished, as they continue to be the favorite and fruitful topics from which the adversaries to liberty derive their most specious declamations. The valuable improvements made by the American constitutions on the popular models, both ancient and modern, cannot certainly be too much admired; but it would be an unwarrantable partiality to contend that they have as effectually obviated the danger on this side, as was wished and expected. Complaints are everywhere heard from our most considerate and virtuous citizens, equally the friends of public and private faith and of public and personal liberty, that our governments are too unstable, that the public good is disregarded in the conflicts of rival parties, and that measures are too often decided, not according to the rules of justice and the rights of the minor party, but by the superior force of an interested and overbearing majority. However anxiously we may wish that these complaints had no foundation, the evidence of known facts will not permit us to deny that they are in some degree true. It will be found, indeed, on a candid review of our situation, that some of the distresses under which we labor have been erroneously charged on the operation of our governments; but it will be found, at the same time, that other causes will not alone account for many of our heaviest misfortunes; and, particularly, for that prevailing and increasing distrust of public engagements and alarm for private rights which are echoed from one end of the continent to the other. These must be chiefly, if not wholly, effects of the unsteadiness and injustice with which a factious spirit has tainted our public administration.

By a faction I understand a number of citizens, whether amounting to a majority or minority of the whole, who are united and actuated by some common impulse of passion, or of interest, adverse to the rights of other citizens, or to the permanent and aggregate interests of the community.

There are two methods of curing the mischiefs of faction: the one, by removing its causes; the other, by controlling its effects.

There are again two methods of removing the causes of faction: the one, by destroying the liberty which is essential to its existence; the other, by giving to every citizen the same opinions, the same passions, and the same interests.

It could never be more truly said than of the first remedy that it was worse than the disease. Liberty is to faction what air is to fire, an aliment without which it instantly expires. But it could not be a less folly to abolish liberty, which is essential to political life, because it nourishes faction than it would be to wish the annihilation of air, which is essential to animal life, because it imparts to fire its destructive agency.

The second expedient is as impracticable as the first would be unwise. As long as the reason of man continues fallible, and he is at liberty to exercise it, different opinions will be formed. As long as the connection subsists between his reason and his self-love, his opinions and his passions will have a reciprocal influence on each other; and the former will be objects to which the latter will attach themselves. The diversity in the faculties of men, from which the rights of property originate, is not less an insuperable obstacle to a uniformity of interest. The protection of these faculties is the first object of government. From the protection of different and unequal faculties of acquiring property, the possession of different degrees and kinds of property immediately results; and from the influence of these on the sentiments and views of the respective proprietors ensues a division of the society into different interests and parties.

The latent causes of faction are thus sown in the nature of man; and we see them everywhere brought into different degrees of activity, according to the different circumstances of civil society. A zeal for different opinions concerning religion, concerning government, and many other points, as well of speculation as of practice; an attachment to different leaders ambitiously contending for pre-eminence and power; or to persons of other descriptions whose fortunes have been interesting to the human passions, have, in turn, divided mankind into parties, inflamed them with mutual animosity, and rendered them much more disposed to vex and oppress each other than to co-operate for their common good. So strong is this propensity of mankind to fall into mutual animosities that where no substantial occasion presents itself the most frivolous and fanciful distinctions have been sufficient to kindle their unfriendly passions and excite their most violent conflicts. But the most common and durable source of factions has been the various and unequal distribution of property. Those who hold and those who are without property have ever formed distinct interests in society. Those who are creditors, and those who are debtors, fall under a like discrimination. A landed interest, a manufacturing interest, a mercantile interest, a moneyed interest, with many lesser interests, grow up of necessity in civilized nations, and divide them into different classes, actuated by different sentiments and views. The regulation of these various and interfering interests forms the principal task of modern legislation and involves the spirit of party and faction in the necessary and ordinary operations of government.

No man is allowed to be a judge in his own cause, because his interest would certainly bias his judgment, and, not improbably, corrupt his integrity. With equal, nay with greater reason, a body of men are unfit to be both judges and parties at the same time; yet what are many of the most important acts of legislation but so many judicial determinations, not indeed concerning the rights of single persons, but concerning the rights of large bodies of citizens? And what are the different classes of legislators but advocates and parties to the causes which they determine? Is a law proposed concerning private debts? It is a question to which the creditors are parties on one side and the debtors on the other. Justice ought to hold the balance between them. Yet the parties are, and must be, themselves the judges; and the most numerous party, or in other words, the most powerful faction must be expected to prevail. Shall domestic manufacturers be encouraged, and in what degree, by restrictions on foreign manufacturers? [These] are questions which would be differently decided by the landed and the manufacturing classes, and probably by neither with a sole regard to justice and the public good. The apportionment of taxes on the various descriptions of property is an act which seems to require the most exact impartiality; yet there is, perhaps, no legislative act in which greater opportunity and temptation are given to a predominant party to trample on the rules of justice. Every shilling with which they overburden the inferior number is a shilling saved to their own pockets.

It is in vain to say that enlightened statesmen will be able to adjust these clashing interests and render them all subservient to the public good. Enlightened statesmen will not always be at the helm. Nor, in many cases, can such an adjustment be made at all without taking into view indirect and remote considerations, which will rarely prevail over the immediate interest which one party may find in disregarding the rights of another or the good of the whole.

The inference to which we are brought is that the *causes* of faction cannot be removed and that relief is only to be sought in the means of controlling its *effects*.

If a faction consists of less than a majority, relief is supplied by the republican principle, which enables the majority to defeat its sinister views by regular vote. It may clog the administration, it may convulse the society; but it will be unable to execute and mask its violence under the forms of the Constitution. When a majority is included in a faction, the form of popular government, on the other hand, enables it to sacrifice to its ruling passion or interest both the public good and the rights of other citizens. To secure the public good and private rights against the danger of such a faction, and at the same time to preserve the spirit and the form of popular government, is then the great object to which our inquiries are directed. Let me add that it is the great desideratum by which alone this form of government can be rescued from the opprobrium under which it has so long labored and be recommended to the esteem and adoption of mankind.

By what means is this object attainable? Evidently by one of two only. Either the existence of the same passion or interest in a majority at the same time must be prevented, or the majority, having such coexistent passion or interest, must be rendered, by their number and local situation, unable to concert and carry into effect schemes of oppression. If the impulse and the opportunity be suffered to coincide, we well know that neither moral nor religious motives can be relied on as an adequate control. They are not found to be such on the injustice and violence of individuals, and lose their efficacy in proportion to the number combined together, that is, in proportion as their efficacy becomes needful.

From this view of the subject it may be concluded that a pure democracy, by which I mean a society consisting of a small number of citizens, who assemble and administer the government in person, can admit of no cure for the mischiefs of faction. A common passion or interest will, in almost every case, be felt by a majority of the whole, a communication and concert result from the form of government itself; and there is nothing to check the inducements to sacrifice the weaker party or an obnoxious individual. Hence it is that such democracies have ever been spectacles of turbulence and contention; have ever been found incompatible with personal security or the rights of property; and have in general been as short in their lives as they have been violent in their deaths. Theoretic politicians, who have patronized this species of government, have erroneously supposed that by reducing mankind to a perfect equality in their political rights, they would at the same time be perfectly equalized and assimilated in their possessions, their opinions, and their passions.

A republic, by which I mean a government in which the scheme of representation takes place, opens a different prospect and promises the cure for which we are seeking. Let us examine the points in which it varies from pure democracy, and we shall comprehend both the nature of the cure and the efficacy which it must derive from the Union.

The two great points of difference between a democracy and a republic are: first, the delegation of the government, in the latter, to a small number of citizens elected by the rest; secondly, the greater number of citizens and greater sphere of country over which the latter may be extended.

The effect of the first difference is, on the one hand, to refine and enlarge the public views by passing them through the medium of a chosen body of citizens, whose wisdom may best discern the true interest of their country and whose patriotism and love of justice will be least likely to sacrifice it to temporary or partial considerations. Under such a regulation it may well happen that the public voice, pronounced by the representatives of the people, will be more consonant to the public good than if pronounced by the people themselves, convened for the purpose. On the other hand, the effect may be inverted. Men of factious tempers, of local prejudices, or of sinister designs, may, by intrigue, by corruption, or by other means, first obtain the suffrages, and then betray the interests of the people. The question resulting is, whether small or extensive republics are most favorable to the election of proper guardians of the public weal; and it is clearly decided in favor of the latter by two obvious considerations.

In the first place it is to be remarked that however small the republic may be the representatives must be raised to a certain number in order to guard against the cabals of a few; and that however large it may be they must be limited to a certain number in order to guard against the confusion of a multitude. Hence, the number of representatives in the two cases not being in proportion to that of the constituents, and being proportionally greatest in the small republic, it follows that if the proportion of fit characters be not less in the large than in the small republic, the former will present a greater option, and consequently a greater probability of a fit choice.

In the next place, as each representative will be chosen by a greater number of citizens in the large than in the small republic, it will be more difficult for unworthy candidates to practice with success the vicious arts by which elections are too often carried; and the suffrages of the people being more free, will be more likely to center on men who possess the most attractive merit and the most diffusive and established characters.

It must be confessed that in this, as in most other cases, there is a mean, on both sides of which inconveniencies will be found to lie. By enlarging too much the number of electors, you render the representative too little acquainted with all their local circumstances and lesser interests; as by reducing it too much, you render him unduly attached to these, and too little fit to comprehend and pursue great and national objects. The federal Constitution forms a happy combination in this respect; the great and aggregate interests being referred to the national, the local and particular to the State legislatures.

The other point of difference is the greater number of citizens and extent of territory which may be brought within the compass of republican than of democratic government; and it is this circumstance principally which renders factious combinations less to be dreaded in the former than in the latter. The smaller the society, the fewer probably will be the distinct parties and interests composing it; the fewer the distinct parties and interests, the more frequently will a majority be found of the same party; and the smaller the number of individuals composing a majority, and the smaller the compass within which they are placed, the more easily will they concert and execute their plans of oppression. Extend the sphere and you take in a greater variety of parties and interests; you make it less probable that a majority of the whole will have a common motive to invade the rights of other citizens; or if such a common motive exists, it will be more difficult for all who feel it to discover their own strength and to act in unison with each other. Besides other impediments, it may be remarked that, where there is a consciousness of unjust or dishonorable purposes, communication is always checked by distrust in proportion to the number whose concurrence is necessary.

Hence, it clearly appears that the same advantage which a republic has over a democracy in controlling the effects of faction is enjoyed by a large over a small republic—is enjoyed by the Union over the States composing it. Does this advantage consist in the substitution of representatives whose enlightened views and virtuous sentiments render them superior to local prejudices and to schemes of injustice? It will not be denied that the representation of the Union will be most likely to possess these requisite endowments. Does it consist in the greater security afforded by a greater variety of parties, against the event of any one party being able to outnumber and oppress the rest? In an equal degree does the increased variety of parties comprised within the Union increase this security. Does it, in fine, consist in the greater obstacles opposed to the concert and accomplishment of the secret wishes of an unjust and interested majority? Here again the extent of the Union gives it the most palpable advantage.

The influence of factious leaders may kindle a flame within their particular States but will be unable to spread a general conflagration through the other States. A religious sect may degenerate into a political faction in a part of the Confederacy; but the variety of sects dispersed over the entire face of it must secure the national councils against any danger from that source. A rage for paper money, for an abolition of debts, for an equal division of property, or for any other improper or wicked project, will be less apt to pervade the whole body of the Union than a particular member of it, in the same proportion as such a malady is more likely to taint a particular county or district than an entire State.

In the extent and proper structure of the Union, therefore, we behold a republican remedy for the diseases most incident to republican government. And according to the degree of pleasure and pride we feel in being republicans ought to be our zeal in cherishing the spirit and supporting the character of Federalists.

FEDERALIST NO. 51
(JAMES MADISON)

To what expedient, then, shall we finally resort, for maintaining in practice the necessary partition of power among the several departments as laid down in the Constitution? The only answer that can be given is that as all these exterior provisions are found to be inadequate, the defect must be supplied, by so contriving the interior structure of the government as that its several constituent parts may, by their mutual relations, be the means of keeping each other in their proper places. Without presuming to undertake a full development of this important idea I will hazard a few general observations which may perhaps place it in a clearer light, and enable us to form a more correct judgment of the principles and structure of the government planned by the convention.

In order to lay a due foundation for that separate and distinct exercise of the different powers of government, which to a certain extent is admitted on all hands to be essential to the preservation of liberty, it is evident that each department should have a will of its own; and consequently should be so constituted that the members of each should have as little agency as possible in the appointment of the members of the others. Were this principle rigorously adhered to, it would require that all the appointments for the supreme executive, legislative, and judiciary magistracies should be drawn from the same fountain of authority, the people, through channels having no communication whatever with one another. Perhaps such a plan of constructing the several departments would be less difficult in practice than it may be in contemplation appear. Some difficulties, however, and some additional expense would attend the execution of it. Some deviations, therefore, from the principle must be admitted. In the constitution of the judiciary department in particular, it might be inexpedient to insist rigorously on the principle; first, because peculiar qualifications being essential in the members, the primary consideration ought to be to select that mode of choice which best secures these qualifications; second, because the permanent tenure by which the appointments are held in that department must soon destroy all sense of dependence on the authority conferring them.

It is equally evident that the members of each department should be as little dependent as possible on those of the others for the emoluments annexed to their offices. Were the executive magistrate, or the judges, not independent of the legislature in this particular, their independence in every other would be merely nominal.

But the great security against a gradual concentration of the several powers in the same department consists in giving to those who administer each department the necessary constitutional means and personal motives to resist encroachments of the others. The provision for defense must in this, as in all other cases, be made commensurate to the danger of attack. Ambition must be made to counteract ambition. The interest of the man must be connected with the constitutional rights of the place. It may be a reflection on human nature that such devices should be necessary to control the abuses of government. But what is government itself but the greatest of all reflections on human nature? If men were angels no government would be necessary. If angels were to govern men, neither external nor internal controls on government would be necessary. In framing a government which is to be administered by men over men, the great difficulty lies in this: you must first enable the government to control the governed; and in the next place oblige it to control itself. A dependence on the people is, no doubt, the primary control on the government; but experience has taught mankind the necessity of auxiliary precautions.

This policy of supplying, by opposite and rival interests, the defect of better motives, might be traced through the whole system of human affairs, private as well as public. We see it particularly displayed in all the subordinate distributions of power, where the constant aim is to divide and arrange the several offices in such a manner as that each may be a check on the other—that the private interest of every individual may be a sentinel over the public rights. These inventions of prudence cannot be less requisite in the distribution of the supreme powers of the State.

But it is not possible to give to each department an equal power of self-defense. In republican government, the legislative authority necessarily predominates. The remedy for this inconveniency is to divide the legislature into different branches; and to render them, by different modes of election and different principles of action, as little connected with each other as the nature of their common functions and their common dependence on the society will admit. It may even be necessary to guard against dangerous encroachments by still further precautions. As the weight of the legislative authority requires that it should be thus divided, the weakness of the executive may require, on the other hand, that it should be fortified. An absolute negative on the legislature appears, at first view, to be the natural defense with which the executive magistrate should be armed. But perhaps it would be neither altogether safe nor alone sufficient. On ordinary occasions it might not be exerted with the requisite firmness, and on extraordinary occasions it might be perfidiously abused. May not this defect of an absolute negative be supplied by some qualified connection between this weaker department and the weaker branch of the stronger department, by which the latter may be led to support the constitutional rights of the former, without being too much detached from the rights of its own department?

If the principles on which these observations are founded be just, as I persuade myself they are, and they be applied as a criterion to the several State constitutions, and to the federal Constitution, it will be found that if the latter does not perfectly correspond with them, the former are infinitely less able to bear such a test.

There are, moreover, two considerations particularly applicable to the federal system of America, which place that system in a very interesting point of view.

First. In a single republic, all the power surrendered by the people is submitted to the administration of a single government; and the usurpations are guarded against by a division of the government into distinct and separate departments. In the compound republic of America, the power surrendered by the people is first divided between two distinct governments, and then the portion allotted to each subdivided among distinct and separate departments. Hence a double security arises to the rights of the people. The different governments will control each other, at the same time that each will be controlled by itself.

Second. It is of great importance in a republic not only to guard the society against the oppression of its rulers, but to guard one part of the society against the injustice of the other part. Different interests necessarily exist in different classes of citizens. If a majority be united by a common interest, the rights of the minority will be insecure. There are but two methods of providing against this evil: the one by creating a will in the community independent of the majority—that is, of the society itself; the other, by comprehending in the society so many separate descriptions of citizens as will render an unjust combination of a majority of the whole very improbable, if not impracticable. The first method prevails in all governments possessing an hereditary or self-appointed authority. This, at best, is but a precarious security; because a power independent of the society may as well espouse the unjust views of the major as the rightful interests of the minor party, and may possibly be turned against both parties. The second method will be exemplified in the federal republic of the United States. Whilst all authority in it will be derived from and dependent on the society, the society itself will be broken into so many parts, interests and classes of citizens, that the rights of individuals, or of the minority, will be in little danger from interested combinations of the majority. In a free government the security for civil rights must be the same as that for religious rights. It consists in the one case in the multiplicity of interests, and in the other in the multiplicity of sects. The degree of security in both cases will depend on the number of interests and sects; and this may be presumed to depend on the extent of country and number of people comprehended under the same government. This view of the subject must particularly recommend a proper federal system to all the sincere and considerate friends of republican government, since it shows that in exact proportion as the territory of the Union may be formed into more circumscribed Confederacies, or States, oppressive combinations of a majority will be facilitated; the best security, under the republican forms, for the rights of every class of citizen, will be diminished; and consequently the stability and independence of some member of the government, the only other security, must be proportionately increased. Justice is the end of government. It is the end of civil society. It ever has been and ever will be pursued until it be obtained, or until liberty be lost in the pursuit. In a society under the forms of which the stronger faction can readily unite and oppress the weaker, anarchy may as truly be said to reign as in a state of nature, where the weaker individual is not secured against the violence of the stronger; and as, in the latter state, even the stronger individuals are prompted, by the uncertainty of their condition, to submit to a government which may protect the weak as well as themselves; so, in the former state, will the more powerful factions or parties be gradually induced, by a like motive, to wish for a government which will protect all parties, the weaker as well as the more powerful. It can be little doubted that if the State of Rhode Island was separated from the Confederacy and left to itself, the insecurity of rights under the popular form of government within such narrow limits would be displayed by such reiterated oppressions of factious majorities that some power altogether independent of the people would soon be called for by the voice of the very factions whose misrule had proved the necessity of it. In the extended republic of the United States, and among the great variety of interests, parties, and sects which it embraces, a coalition of a majority of the whole society could seldom take place on any other principles than those of justice and the general good; whilst there being thus less danger to a minor from the will of a major party, there must be less pretext, also, to provide for the security of the former, by introducing into the government a will not dependent on the latter, or, in other words, a will independent of the society itself. It is no less certain than it is important, notwithstanding the contrary opinions which have been entertained, that the larger the society, provided it lie within a practicable sphere, the more duly capable it will be of self-government. And happily for the republican cause, the practicable sphere may be carried to a very great extent by a judicious modification and mixture of the federal principle.

GLOSSARY

affirmative action A term that refers to programs designed to ensure that women, minorities, and other traditionally disadvantaged groups have full and equal opportunities in employment, education, and other areas of life.

age-cohort tendency The tendency for a significant break in the pattern of political socialization to occur among younger citizens, usually as the result of a major event or development that disrupts preexisting beliefs.

agency point of view The tendency of bureaucrats to place the interests of their agency ahead of other interests and ahead of the priorities sought by the president or Congress.

agenda setting The power of the media through news coverage to focus the public's attention and concern on particular events, problems, issues, personalities, and so on.

agents of socialization Those agents, such as the family and the media, that have significant impact on citizens' political socialization.

air wars A term that refers to the fact that modern campaigns are often a battle of opposing televised advertising campaigns.

alienation A feeling of personal powerlessness that includes the notion that government does not care about the opinions of people like oneself.

Anti-Federalists A term used to describe opponents of the Constitution during the debate over ratification.

apathy A feeling of personal noninterest or unconcern with politics.

appellate jurisdiction The authority of a given court to review cases that have already been tried in lower courts and are appealed to it by the losing party; such a court is called an appeals court or appellate court. (See also **original jurisdiction**.)

authoritarian government A form of government in which leaders, though they admit to no limits on their powers, are effectively limited by other centers of power in the society.

authority The recognized right of an individual or institution to exercise power. (See also **power**.)

autocracy A form of government in which absolute control rests with a single person.

balanced budget When the government's tax revenues for the year are roughly equal to its expenditures.

bicameral legislatures Legislatures having two chambers.

bill A proposed law (legislative act) within Congress or another legislature. (See also **law**.)

Bill of Rights The first ten amendments to the Constitution. They include such rights as freedom of speech and trial by jury.

bipolar (power structure) A power structure dominated by two powers only, as in the case of the United States and the Soviet Union during the cold war.

block grants Federal grants-in-aid that permit state and local officials to decide how the money will be spent within a general area, such as education or health. (See also **categorical grants**.)

brief A written statement by a party in a court case that details its argument.

budget deficit When the government's expenditures exceed its tax revenues.

budget surplus When the government's tax and other revenues exceed its expenditures.

bureaucracy A system of organization and control based on the principles of hierarchical authority, job specialization, and formalized rules. (See also **formalized rules; hierarchical authority; job specialization**.)

bureaucratic accountability The degree to which bureaucrats are held accountable for the power they exercise.

bureaucratic rule The tendency of large-scale organizations to develop into the bureaucratic form, with the effect that administrators make key policy decisions.

cabinet A group consisting of the heads of the (cabinet) executive departments, who are appointed by the president, subject to confirmation by the Senate. The cabinet was once the main advisory body to the president but no longer plays this role. (See also **cabinet departments**.)

cabinet (executive) departments The major administrative organizations within the federal executive bureaucracy, each of which is headed by a secretary (cabinet officer) and has responsibility for a major function of the federal government, such as defense, agriculture, or justice. (See also **cabinet; independent agencies**.)

candidate-centered politics Election campaigns and other political processes in which candidates, not political parties, have most of the initiative and influence. (See also **party-centered politics**.)

capital-gains tax Tax that individuals pay on money gained from the sale of a capital asset, such as property or stocks.

capitalism An economic system based on the idea that government should interfere with economic transactions as little as possible. Free enterprise and self-reliance are the collective and individual principles that underpin capitalism.

categorical grants Federal grants-in-aid to states and localities that can be used only for designated projects. (See also **block grants**.)

charter The chief instrument by which a state governs its local units; it spells out in detail what a local government can and cannot do.

checks and balances The elaborate system of divided spheres of authority provided by the U.S. Constitution as a means of controlling the power of government. The separation of powers among the branches of the national government, federalism, and the different methods of selecting national officers are all part of this system.

citizens' (noneconomic) groups Organized interests formed by individuals drawn together by opportunities to promote a cause in which they believe but that does not provide them significant individual economic benefits. (See also **economic groups; interest group.**)

city manager system Form of municipal government that entrusts the executive role to a professionally trained manager, who is chosen, and can be fired, by the city council.

civic duty The belief of an individual that civic and political participation is a responsibility of citizenship.

civil law Laws governing relations between private parties where no criminal act is alleged and where the parties are making conflicting claims or are seeking to establish a legal relationship.

civil liberties The fundamental individual rights of a free society, such as freedom of speech and the right to a jury trial, which in the United States are protected by the Bill of Rights.

civil rights (equal rights) The right of every person to equal protection under the laws and equal access to society's opportunities and public facilities.

civil service system See **merit system.**

clear-and-present-danger test A test devised by the Supreme Court in 1919 to define the limits of free speech in the context of national security. According to the test, government cannot abridge political expression unless it presents a clear and present danger to the nation's security.

clientele groups Special-interest groups that benefit directly from the activities of a particular bureaucratic agency and are therefore strong advocates of the agency.

cloture A parliamentary maneuver that, if a three-fifths majority votes for it, limits Senate debate to thirty hours and has the effect of defeating a filibuster. (See also **filibuster.**)

cold war The lengthy period after World War II when the United States and the USSR were not engaged in actual combat (a "hot war") but were nonetheless locked in a state of deep-seated hostility.

collective (public) goods Benefits that are offered by groups (usually citizens' groups) as an incentive for membership but that are nondivisible (e.g., a clean environment) and therefore are available to nonmembers as well as members of the particular group. (See also **free-rider problem; private goods.**)

commerce clause The clause of the Constitution (Article I, Section 8) that empowers the federal government to regulate commerce among the states and with other nations.

commission system Form of municipal government that invests executive and legislative authority in a commission, with each commissioner serving as a member of the local council but also having a specified executive role, such as police commissioner or public works commissioner.

common-carrier role The media's function as an open channel through which political leaders can communicate with the public. (See also **public-representative role; signaler role; watchdog role.**)

communism An economic system in which government owns most or all major industries and also takes responsibility for overall management of the economy.

compliance The issue of whether a court's decisions will be respected and obeyed.

concurring opinion A separate opinion written by a Supreme Court justice who votes with the majority in the decision on a case but who disagrees with their reasoning. (See also **dissenting opinion; majority opinion; plurality opinion.**)

confederacy A governmental system in which sovereignty is vested entirely in subnational (state) governments. (See also **federalism; unitary system.**)

conference committees Temporary committees that are formed to bargain over the differences in the House and Senate versions of a bill. The committee's members are usually appointed from the House and Senate standing committees that originally worked on the bill.

conservatives Those who believe government does too many things that should be left to firms and individuals but look to government to uphold traditional social values. (See also **liberals; libertarians; populists.**)

constituency The individuals who live within the geographical area represented by an elected official. More narrowly, the body of citizens eligible to vote for a particular representative.

constitution The fundamental law that defines how a government will legitimately operate.

constitutional democracy A government that is democratic in its provisions for majority influence through elections and constitutional in its provisions for minority rights and rule by law.

constitutional initiative The process by which a citizen or group can petition to place a proposed amendment on the ballot at the next election by obtaining the signatures of a certain number of registered voters, and if the amendment gets majority support, it becomes part of the constitution.

constitutionalism The idea that there are definable limits on the rightful power of a government over its citizens.

containment A doctrine, developed after World War II, based on the assumptions that the Soviet Union was an aggressor nation and that only a determined United States could block Soviet territorial ambitions.

Cooley's rule The term used to describe the idea that cities should be self-governing, articulated in an 1871 ruling by Michigan judge Thomas Cooley.

cooperative federalism The situation in which the national, state, and local levels work together to solve problems.

criminal law Laws governing acts deemed illegal and punishable by government, such as robbery. Government is always a party to a criminal law case; the other party is the individual accused of breaking the law.

de facto discrimination Discrimination on the basis of race, sex, religion, ethnicity, and the like that results from social, economic, and cultural biases and conditions. (See also **de jure discrimination.**)

de jure discrimination Discrimination on the basis of race, sex, religion, ethnicity, and the like that results from a law. (See also **de facto discrimination.**)

decision A vote of the Supreme Court in a particular case that indicates which party the justices side with and by how large a margin.

deficit spending When the government spends more than it collects in taxes and other revenues.

delegates Elected representatives whose obligation is to act in accordance with the expressed wishes of the people whom they represent. (See also **trustees**.)

demand-side economics A form of fiscal policy that emphasizes "demand" (consumer spending). Government can use increased spending or tax cuts to place more money in consumers' hands and thereby increase demand. (See also **fiscal policy; supply-side economics**.)

democracy A form of government in which the people govern, either directly or through elected representatives.

demographic representativeness The idea that the bureaucracy will be more responsive to the public if its employees at all levels are demographically representative of the population as a whole.

denials of power A constitutional means of limiting governmental action by listing those powers that government is expressly prohibited from using.

deregulation The rescinding of excessive government regulations for the purpose of improving economic efficiency.

détente A French word meaning "a relaxing" and used to refer to an era of improved relations between the United States and the Soviet Union that began in the early 1970s.

deterrence policy The idea that nuclear war can be discouraged if each side in a conflict has the capacity to destroy the other with nuclear weapons.

devolution The passing down of authority from the national government to states and localities.

Dillon's rule The term used to describe relations between state and local government; it holds that local governments are creatures of the state, which in theory even has the power to abolish them.

direct primary See **primary election**.

dissenting opinion The opinion of a justice in a Supreme Court case that explains his or her reasons for disagreeing with the majority's decision. (See also **concurring opinion; majority opinion; plurality opinion**.)

diversity The principle that individual and group differences should be respected and are a source of national strength.

dual federalism A doctrine based on the idea that a precise separation of national power and state power is both possible and desirable.

due process clause (of the Fourteenth Amendment) The clause of the Constitution that has been used by the judiciary to apply the Bill of Rights to the actions of state governments.

economic depression A very severe and sustained economic downturn. Depressions are rare in the United States; the last one was in the 1930s.

economic globalization The increased interdependence of nations' economies. The change is a result of technological, transportation, and communication advances that have enabled firms to deploy their resources across the globe.

economic groups Interest groups that are organized primarily for economic reasons but that engage in political activity in order to seek favorable policies from government. (See also **citizens' groups; interest group**.)

economic recession A moderate but sustained downturn in the economy. Recessions are part of the economy's normal cycle of ups and downs.

economy A system of production and consumption of goods and services that are allocated through exchange among producers and consumers.

effective tax rate The actual percentage of a person's income that is spent to pay taxes.

efficiency An economic principle that holds that firms should fulfill as many of society's needs as possible while using as few of its resources as possible. The greater the output (production) for a given input (for example, an hour of labor), the more efficient the process.

elastic clause See **"necessary and proper" clause**.

Electoral College An unofficial term that refers to the electors who cast the states' electoral votes.

electoral votes The method of voting that is used to choose the U.S. president. Each state has the same number of electoral votes as it has members in Congress (House and Senate combined). By tradition, electoral voting is tied to a state's popular voting; thus, the presidential candidate with the most popular votes overall has usually also had the most electoral votes.

elitism The view that the United States is essentially run by a tiny elite (composed of wealthy or well-connected individuals) who control public policy through both direct and indirect means.

entitlement program Any of a number of individual benefit programs, such as social security, that require government to provide a designated benefit to any person who meets the legally defined criteria for eligibility.

enumerated (expressed) powers The seventeen powers granted to the national government under Article I, Section 8 of the Constitution. These powers include taxation and the regulation of commerce as well as the authority to provide for the national defense.

equal-protection clause A clause of the Fourteenth Amendment that forbids any state to deny equal protection of the laws to any individual within its jurisdiction.

equal rights See **civil rights**.

equality The notion that all individuals are equal in their moral worth, in their treatment under the law, and in their political voice.

equality of opportunity The idea that all individuals should be given an equal chance to succeed on their own.

equality of result The objective of policies intended to reduce or eliminate the effects of discrimination so that members of traditionally disadvantaged groups will have the same benefits of society as do members of advantaged groups.

equity (in relation to economic policy) The situation in which the outcome of an economic transaction is fair to each party. An outcome can usually be considered fair if each party enters into a transaction freely and is not knowingly at a disadvantage.

establishment clause The First Amendment provision that government may not favor one religion over another or favor religion over no religion, and that prohibits Congress from passing laws respecting the establishment of religion.

exclusionary rule The legal principle that government is prohibited from using in trials evidence that was obtained by unconstitutional means (for example, illegal search and seizure).

executive departments See **cabinet departments.**

executive leadership system An approach to managing the bureaucracy that is based on presidential leadership and presidential management tools, such as the president's annual budget proposal. (See also **merit system; patronage system.**)

expressed powers See **enumerated powers.**

externalities Burdens that society incurs when firms fail to pay the full cost of resources used in production. An example of an externality is the pollution that results when corporations dump industrial wastes into lakes and rivers.

facts (of a court case) The relevant circumstances of a legal dispute or offense as determined by a trial court. The facts of a case are crucial because they help determine which law or laws are applicable in the case.

federalism A governmental system in which authority is divided between two sovereign levels of government: national and regional. (See also **confederacy; unitary system.**)

Federalists A term used to describe supporters of the Constitution during the debate over ratification.

filibuster A procedural tactic in the U.S. Senate whereby a minority of legislators prevents a bill from coming to a vote by holding the floor and talking until the majority gives in and the bill is withdrawn from consideration. (See also **cloture.**)

fiscal federalism A term that refers to the expenditure of federal funds on programs run in part through states and localities.

fiscal policy A tool of economic management by which government attempts to maintain a stable economy through its taxing and spending decisions. (See also **demand-side economics; monetary policy; supply-side economics.**)

formalized rules A basic principle of bureaucracy that refers to the standardized procedures and established regulations by which a bureaucracy conducts its operations. (See also **bureaucracy.**)

free-exercise clause A First Amendment provision that prohibits the government from interfering with the practice of religion or prohibiting the free exercise of religion.

free-rider problem The situation in which the benefits offered by a group to its members are also available to nonmembers. The incentive to join the group and to promote its cause is reduced because nonmembers (free riders) receive the benefits (e.g., a cleaner environment) without having to pay any of the group's costs. (See also **collective goods.**)

free-trade position The view that the long-term economic interests of all countries are advanced when tariffs and other trade barriers are kept to a minimum. (See also **protectionism.**)

freedom of expression Americans' freedom to communicate their views, the foundation of which is the First Amendment rights of freedom of conscience, speech, press, assembly, and petition.

gender gap The tendency of women and men to differ in their political attitudes and voting preferences.

gerrymandering The process by which the party in power draws election district boundaries in a way that advantages its candidates.

government corporations Bodies, such as the U.S. Postal Service and Amtrak, that are similar to private corporations in that they charge for their services, but different in that they receive federal funding to help defray expenses. Their directors are appointed by the president with Senate approval.

graduated personal income tax A tax on personal income in which the tax rate increases as income increases; in other words, the tax rate is higher for higher income levels.

grants-in-aid Federal cash payments to states and localities for programs they administer.

grants of power The method of limiting the U.S. government by confining its scope of authority to those powers expressly granted in the Constitution.

grassroots lobbying A form of lobbying designed to persuade officials that a group's policy position has strong constituent support.

grassroots party A political party organized at the level of the voters and dependent on their support for its strength.

Great Compromise The agreement of the constitutional convention to create a two-chamber Congress with the House apportioned by population and the Senate apportioned equally by state.

hard money Campaign funds given directly to candidates to spend as they choose.

hierarchical authority A basic principle of bureaucracy that refers to the chain of command within an organization whereby officials and units have control over those below them. (See also **bureaucracy.**)

hired guns The professional consultants who run campaigns for high office.

home rule A device designed to give local governments more leeway in their policies; it allows a local government to design and amend its own charter, subject to the laws and constitution of the state and also subject to veto by the state.

honeymoon period The president's first months in office, a time when Congress, the press, and the public are more inclined than usual to support presidential initiatives.

ideology A consistent pattern of opinion on particular issues that stems from a core belief or set of beliefs.

imminent lawless action test A legal test that says government cannot lawfully suppress advocacy that promotes lawless action unless such advocacy is aimed at producing, and is likely to produce, imminent lawless action.

implied powers The federal government's constitutional authority (through the "necessary and proper" clause) to take action that is not expressly authorized by the Constitution but that supports actions that are so authorized. (See also **"necessary and proper" clause.**)

in-kind benefit A government benefit that is a cash equivalent, such as food stamps or rent vouchers. This form of benefit ensures that recipients will use public assistance in a specified way.

inalienable (natural) rights Those rights that persons theoretically possessed in the state of nature, prior to the formation of governments. These rights, including those of life, liberty, and property, are considered inherent and as such are inalienable. Since government is established by people, government has the responsibility to preserve these rights.

independent agencies Bureaucratic agencies that are similar to cabinet departments but usually have a narrower area of responsibility. Each such agency is headed by a presidential appointee who is not a cabinet member. An example is the National Aeronautics and Space Administration. (See also **cabinet departments.**)

individual goods See **private goods.**

individualism The idea that people should take the initiative, be self-sufficient, and accumulate the material advantages necessary for their well-being.

inflation A general increase in the average level of prices of goods and services.

initiative The process by which citizens can place legislative measures on the ballot through signature petitions, and if the measure receives a majority vote, it becomes law.

inside lobbying Direct communication between organized interests and policymakers, which is based on the assumed value of close ("inside") contacts with policymakers.

interest group A set of individuals who are organized to promote a shared political interest. (See also **citizens' groups; economic groups.**)

interest-group liberalism The tendency of public officials to support the policy demands of self-interested groups (as opposed to judging policy demands according to whether they serve a larger conception of "the public interest").

intermediate-scrutiny test A test applied by courts to laws that attempt a gender classification. In effect, the test eliminates gender as a legal classification unless it serves an important objective and is substantially related to the objective's achievement.

internationalist A person who holds the view that the country should involve itself deeply in world affairs. (See also **isolationist.**)

iron triangle A small and informal but relatively stable group of well-positioned legislators, executives, and lobbyists who seek to promote policies beneficial to a particular interest. (See also **issue network.**)

isolationist A person who holds the view that the country should deliberately avoid a large role in world affairs and, instead, concentrate on domestic concerns. (See **also internationalist.**)

issue network An informal network of public officials and lobbyists who have a common interest and expertise in a given area and who are brought together temporarily by a proposed policy in that area. (See also **iron triangle.**)

job specialization A basic principle of bureaucracy that holds that the responsibilities of each job position should be explicitly defined and that a precise division of labor within the organization should be maintained. (See also **bureaucracy.**)

judicial activism The doctrine that the courts should develop new legal principles when judges see a compelling need, even if this action places them in conflict with the policy decisions of elected officials. (See also **judicial restraint.**)

judicial conference A closed meeting of the justices of the U.S. Supreme Court to discuss and vote on the cases before them; the justices are not supposed to discuss conference proceedings with outsiders.

judicial restraint The doctrine that the judiciary should be highly respectful of precedent and should defer to the judgment of legislatures. The doctrine claims that the job of judges is to work within the confines of laws set down by tradition and lawmaking majorities. (See also **judicial activism.**)

judicial review The power of courts to decide whether a governmental institution has acted within its constitutional powers and, if not, to declare its action null and void.

jurisdiction (of a congressional committee) The policy area in which a particular congressional committee is authorized to act.

jurisdiction (of a court) A given court's authority to hear cases of a particular kind. Jurisdiction may be original or appellate.

laissez-faire doctrine A classic economic philosophy that holds that owners of businesses should be allowed to make their own production and distribution decisions without government regulation or control.

large-state plan See **Virginia Plan.**

law (as enacted by Congress) A legislative proposal, or bill, that is passed by both the House and Senate and is either signed or not vetoed by the president. (See also **bill.**)

lawmaking function The authority (of a legislature) to make the laws necessary to carry out the government's powers. (See also **oversight function; representation function.**)

laws (of a court case) The constitutional provisions, legislative statutes, or judicial precedents that apply to a court case.

legitimacy (of judicial power) The issue of the proper limits of judicial authority in a political system based in part on the principle of majority rule.

libel Publication of material that falsely damages a person's reputation.

liberals Those who believe government should do more to solve the nation's problems but reject the notion that government should favor a particular set of social values. (See also **conservatives; libertarians; populists.**)

libertarians Those who believe government tries to do too many things that should be left to firms and individuals and who oppose government as an instrument of traditional values. (See also **conservatives; liberals; populists.**)

liberty The principle that individuals should be free to act and think as they choose, provided they do not infringe unreasonably on the rights and freedoms of others.

limited government A government that is subject to strict limits on its lawful uses of powers and hence on its ability to deprive people of their liberty.

lobbying The process by which interest-group members or lobbyists attempt to influence public policy through contacts with public officials.

logrolling The trading of votes between legislators so that each gets what he or she most wants.

majoritarianism The idea that the majority prevails not only in elections but also in determining policy.

majority opinion A Supreme Court opinion that results when a majority of the justices is in agreement on the legal basis of the decision. (See also **concurring opinion; dissenting opinion; plurality opinion**.)

material incentive An economic or other tangible benefit that is used to attract group members.

means test The requirement that applicants for public assistance must demonstrate they are poor in order to be eligible for the assistance. (See also **public assistance.**)

merit (civil service) system An approach to managing the bureaucracy whereby people are appointed to government positions on the basis of either competitive examinations or special qualifications, such as professional training. (See also **executive leadership system; patronage system.**)

metropolitan government Form of local government created when local governments join together and assign it responsibility for a range of activities, such as police and sanitation, so as to reduce the waste and duplication that results when every locality in a densely populated area provides its own services.

military-industrial complex The three components (the military establishment, the industries that manufacture weapons, and the members of Congress from states and districts that depend heavily on the arms industry) that mutually benefit from a high level of defense spending.

momentum (in campaigns) A strong showing by a candidate in early presidential nominating contests, which leads to a buildup of public support for the candidate.

monetary policy A tool of economic management, available to government, based on manipulation of the amount of money in circulation. (See also **fiscal policy.**)

money chase A term used to describe the fact that U.S. campaigns are very expensive and that candidates must spend a great amount of time raising funds in order to compete successfully.

multilateralism The situation in which nations act together in response to problems and crises.

multinational corporations Business firms with major operations in more than one country.

multiparty system A system in which three or more political parties have the capacity to gain control of government separately or in coalition.

national debt The total cumulative amount that the U.S. government owes to creditors.

natural rights See **inalienable rights.**

"necessary and proper" clause (elastic clause) The authority granted Congress in Article I, Section 8 of the Constitution "to make all laws which shall be necessary and proper" for the implementation of its enumerated powers. (See also **implied powers.**)

negative government The philosophical belief that government governs best by staying out of people's lives, thus giving individuals as much freedom as possible to determine their own pursuits. (See also **positive government.**)

neutral competence The administrative objective of a merit-based bureaucracy. Such a bureaucracy should be "competent" in the sense that its employees are hired and retained on the basis of their expertise and "neutral" in the sense that it operates by objective standards rather than partisan ones.

New Jersey (small-state) Plan A constitutional proposal for a strengthened Congress but one in which each state would have a single vote, thus granting a small state the same legislative power as a larger state.

news The news media's version of reality, usually with an emphasis on timely, dramatic, and compelling events and developments.

news media See **press.**

nomination The designation of a particular individual to run as a political party's candidate (its "nominee") in the general election.

noneconomic groups See **citizens' groups.**

North-South Compromise The agreement over economic and slavery issues that enabled northern and southern states to settle differences that threatened to defeat the effort to draft a new constitution.

objective journalism A model of news reporting that is based on the communication of "facts" rather than opinions and that is "fair" in that it presents all sides of partisan debate. (See also **partisan press.**)

oligarchy Government in which control rests with a few persons.

open party caucuses Meetings at which a party's candidates for nomination are voted on and that are open to all the party's rank-and-file voters who want to attend.

open-seat election An election in which there is no incumbent in the race.

opinion (of a court) A court's written explanation of its decision, which serves to inform others of the legal basis for the decision. Supreme Court opinions are expected to guide the decisions of other courts. (See also **concurring opinion; dissenting opinion; majority opinion; plurality opinion.**)

ordinances Laws issued by a local government under authority granted by the state government.

original jurisdiction The authority of a given court to be the first court to hear a case. (See also **appellate jurisdiction.**)

outside lobbying A form of lobbying in which an interest group seeks to use public pressure as a means of influencing officials.

oversight function A supervisory activity of Congress that centers on its constitutional responsibility to see that the executive carries out the laws faithfully and spends appropriations properly. (See also **lawmaking function; representation function.**)

packaging (of a candidate) A term of modern campaigning that refers to the process of recasting a candidate's record into an appealing image.

partisan press Newspapers and other communication media that openly support a political party and whose news in significant part follows the party line. (See also **objective journalism.**)

party caucus A group that consists of a party's members in the House or Senate and that serves to elect the party's leadership, set policy goals, and determine party strategy.

party-centered politics Election campaigns and other political processes in which political parties, not individual candidates, hold most of the initiative and influence. (See also **candidate-centered politics.**)

party coalition The groups and interests that support a political party.

party competition A process in which conflict over society's goals is transformed by political parties into electoral competition in which the winner gains the power to govern.

party discipline The willingness of a party's House or Senate members to act together as a cohesive group and thus exert collective control over legislative action.

party identification The personal sense of loyalty that an individual may feel toward a particular political party. (See also **party realignment.**)

party leaders Members of the House and Senate who are chosen by the Democratic or Republican caucus in each chamber to represent the party's interests in that chamber and who give some central direction to the chamber's deliberations.

party organizations The party organizational units at national, state, and local levels; their influence has decreased over time because of many factors. (See also **candidate-centered politics; party-centered politics; primary election.**)

party realignment An election or set of elections in which the electorate responds strongly to an extraordinarily powerful issue that has disrupted the established political order. A realignment has a lasting impact on public policy, popular support for the parties, and the composition of the party coalitions. (See also **party identification.**)

patronage system An approach to managing the bureaucracy whereby people are appointed to important government positions as a reward for political services they have rendered and because of their partisan loyalty. (See also **executive leadership system; merit system; spoils system.**)

pluralism A theory of American politics that holds that society's interests are substantially represented through the activities of groups.

plurality opinion A court opinion that results when a majority of justices agree on a decision in a case but do not agree on the legal basis for the decision. In this instance, the legal position held by most of the justices on the winning side is called a plurality opinion. (See also **concurring opinion; dissenting opinion; majority opinion.**)

police power A term that refers to the broad power of government to regulate the health, safety, and morals of the citizenry.

policy Generally, any broad course of governmental action; more narrowly, a specific government program or initiative.

policy implementation The primary function of the bureaucracy; it refers to the process of carrying out the authoritative decisions of Congress, the president, and the courts.

political action committee (PAC) The organization through which an interest group raises and distributes funds for election purposes. By law, the funds must be raised through voluntary contributions.

political culture The characteristic and deep-seated beliefs of a particular people.

political movements See **social movements.**

political participation Involvement in activities intended to influence public policy and leadership, such as voting, joining political parties and interest groups, writing to elected officials, demonstrating for political causes, and giving money to political candidates.

political party An ongoing coalition of interests joined together to try to get their candidates for public office elected under a common label.

political socialization The learning process by which people acquire their political opinions, beliefs, and values.

political system The various components of American government. The parts are separate, but they connect with each other, affecting how each performs.

politics The process through which society makes its governing decisions.

population In a public opinion poll, the people (for example, the citizens of a nation) whose opinions are being estimated through interviews with a sample of these people.

populists Those who believe government should do more to solve the nation's problems and who look to it to uphold traditional values. (See also **conservatives; liberals; libertarians.**)

pork-barrel projects Legislative acts whose tangible benefits are targeted at a particular legislator's constituency.

positive government The philosophical belief that government intervention is necessary in order to enhance personal liberty when individuals are buffeted by economic and social forces beyond their control. (See also **negative government.**)

poverty line As defined by the federal government, the annual cost of a thrifty food budget for an urban family of four, multiplied by three to allow also for the cost of housing, clothes, and other expenses. Families below the poverty line are considered poor and are eligible for certain forms of public assistance.

power The ability of persons or institutions to control policy. (See also **authority.**)

precedent A judicial decision in a given case that serves as a rule of thumb for settling subsequent cases of a similar nature; courts are generally expected to follow precedent.

preemptive war doctrine The idea, espoused by president George W. Bush, that the United States could attack a potentially threatening nation even if the threat had not yet reached a serious and immediate level.

presidential approval ratings A measure of the degree to which the public approves or disapproves of the president's performance in office.

presidential commissions Organizations within the bureaucracy that are headed by commissioners appointed by the president. An example is the Commission on Civil Rights.

press (news media) Those print and broadcast organizations that are in the news-reporting business.

primary election (direct primary) A form of election in which voters choose a party's nominees for public office. In most states, eligibility to vote in a primary election is limited to voters who designated themselves as party members when they registered to vote. A primary is direct when it results directly in the choice of a nominee; it is indirect (as in the case of presidential primaries) when it results in the selection of delegates who then choose the nominee.

prior restraint Government prohibition of speech or publication before the fact, which is presumed by the courts to be unconstitutional unless the justification for it is overwhelming.

private (individual) goods Benefits that a group (most often an economic group) can grant directly and exclusively to the individual members of the group. (See also **collective goods.**)

probability sample A sample for a poll in which each individual in the population has a known probability of being selected randomly for inclusion in the sample. (See also **public opinion poll.**)

procedural due process The constitutional requirement that government must follow proper legal procedures before a person can be legitimately punished for an alleged offense.

procedural law Laws governing the legal process that define proper courses of action by government or private parties.

proportional representation A form of representation in which seats in the legislature are allocated proportionally according to each political party's share of the popular vote. This system enables smaller parties to compete successfully for seats. (See also **single-member districts.**)

prospective voting A form of electoral judgment in which voters choose the candidate whose policy promises most closely match their own preferences. (See also **retrospective voting.**)

protectionism The view that the immediate interests of domestic producers should have a higher priority (through, for example, protective tariffs) than should free trade between nations. (See also **free-trade position.**)

public assistance A term that refers to social welfare programs funded through general tax revenues and available only to the financially needy. Eligibility for such a program is established by a means test. (See also **means test; social insurance.**)

public goods See **collective goods.**

public opinion The politically relevant opinions held by ordinary citizens that they express openly.

public opinion poll A device for measuring public opinion whereby a relatively small number of individuals (the sample) is interviewed for the purpose of estimating the opinions of a whole community (the population). (See also **probability sample.**)

public policy A decision of government to pursue a course of action designed to produce an intended outcome.

public policy process The political interactions that lead to the emergence and resolution of public policy issues.

public-representative role A role whereby the media attempt to act as the public's representatives. (See also **common-carrier role; signaler role; watchdog role.**)

purposive incentive An incentive to group participation based on the cause (purpose) that the group seeks to promote.

realignment See **party realignment.**

reapportionment The reallocation of House seats among states after each census as a result of population changes.

reasonable-basis test A test applied by courts to laws that treat individuals unequally. Such a law may be deemed constitutional if its purpose is held to be "reasonably" related to a legitimate government interest.

recall The process by which citizens can petition for the removal from office of an elected official before the scheduled completion of his or her term.

redistricting The process of altering election districts in order to make them as nearly equal in population as possible. Redistricting takes place every ten years, after each population census.

referendum The process through which the legislature may submit proposals to the voters for approval or rejection.

registration The practice of placing citizens' names on an official list of voters before they are eligible to exercise their right to vote.

regulation Government restrictions on the economic practices of private firms.

regulatory agencies Administrative units, such as the Federal Communications Commission and the Environmental Protection Agency, that have responsibility for the monitoring and regulation of ongoing economic activities.

representation function The responsibility of a legislature to represent various interests in society. (See also **lawmaking function; oversight function.**)

representative democracy A system in which the people participate in the decision-making process of government not directly but indirectly, through the election of officials to represent their interests.

republic Historically, the form of government in which representative officials met to decide on policy issues. These representatives were expected to serve the public interest but were not subject to the people's immediate control. Today, the term *republic* is used interchangeably with *democracy.*

reserved powers The powers granted to the states under the Tenth Amendment to the Constitution.

retrospective voting A form of electoral judgment in which voters support the incumbent candidate or party when their policies are judged to have succeeded and oppose the candidate or party when their policies are judged to have failed. (See also **prospective voting.**)

rider An amendment to a bill that deals with an issue unrelated to the content of the bill. Riders are permitted in the Senate but not in the House.

sample In a public opinion poll, the relatively small number of individuals interviewed for the purpose of estimating the opinions of an entire population. (See also **public opinion poll.**)

sampling error A measure of the accuracy of a public opinion poll. It is mainly a function of sample size and is usually expressed in percentage terms. (See also **probability sample.**)

selective incorporation The absorption of certain provisions of the Bill of Rights (for example, freedom of speech) into the Fourteenth Amendment so that these rights are protected from infringement by the states.

self-government The principle that the people are the ultimate source and proper beneficiary of governing authority; in practice, a government based on majority rule.

senatorial courtesy The tradition that a U.S. senator from the state in which a federal judicial vacancy has arisen should have a say in the president's nomination of the new judge if the senator is of the same party as the president.

seniority A member of Congress's consecutive years of service on a particular committee.

separated institutions sharing power The principle that, as a way to limit government, its powers should be divided among separate branches, each of which also shares in the power of the others as a means of checking and balancing them. The result is that no one branch can exercise power decisively without the support or acquiescence of the others.

separation of powers The division of the powers of government among separate institutions or branches.

service relationship The situation where party organizations assist candidates for office but have no power to require them to accept or campaign on the party's main policy positions.

service strategy Use of personal staff by members of Congress to perform services for constituents in order to gain their support in future elections.

signaling (signaler) role The accepted responsibility of the media to alert the public to important developments as soon as possible after they happen or are discovered. (See also common-carrier role; public representative role; watchdog role.)

single-issue politics The situation in which separate groups are organized around nearly every conceivable policy issue and press their demands and influence to the utmost.

single-member districts The form of representation in which only the candidate who gets the most votes in a district wins office. (See also proportional representation.)

slander Spoken words that falsely damage a person's reputation.

small-state plan See New Jersey Plan.

social capital The sum of face-to-face interactions among citizens in a society.

social contract A voluntary agreement by individuals to form a government, which is then obligated to work within the confines of that agreement.

social insurance Social welfare programs based on the "insurance" concept, so that individuals must pay into the program in order to be eligible to receive funds from it. An

example is social security for retired people. (See also public assistance.)

social (political) movements Active and sustained efforts to achieve social and political change by groups of people who feel that government has not been properly responsive to their concerns.

socialism An economic system in which government owns and controls many of the major industries.

soft money Campaign contributions that are not subject to legal limits and are given to parties rather than directly to candidates.

solicitor general The high-ranking Justice Department official who serves as the government's lawyer in Supreme Court cases.

sovereignty The ultimate authority to govern within a certain geographical area.

split ticket The pattern of voting in which the individual voter in a given election casts a ballot for one or more candidates of each major party.

spoils system The practice of granting public office to individuals in return for political favors they have rendered. (See also patronage system.)

standing committees Permanent congressional committees with responsibility for a particular area of public policy. An example is the Senate Foreign Relations Committee.

state constitutional convention A state convention convened to amend the state constitution or draft a new one.

stewardship theory A theory that argues for a strong, assertive presidential role, with presidential authority limited only at points specifically prohibited by law. (See also Whig theory.)

strict-scrutiny test A test applied by courts to laws that attempt a racial or ethnic classification. In effect, the strict scrutiny test eliminates race or ethnicity as legal classification when it places minority group members at a disadvantage. (See also suspect classifications.)

strong mayor–council system Most common form of municipal government, consisting of the mayor as chief executive and the local council as the legislative body, in which the mayor has veto power and a prescribed responsibility for budgetary and other policy actions.

suffrage The right to vote.

sunset law A law containing a provision that fixes a date on which a program will end unless the program's life is extended by Congress.

supply-side economics A form of fiscal policy that emphasizes "supply" (production). An example of supply-side economics would be a tax cut for business. (See also demand-side economics; fiscal policy.)

supremacy clause Article VI of the Constitution, which makes national law supreme over state law when the national government is acting within its constitutional limits.

suspect classifications Legal classifications, such as race and national origin, that have invidious discrimination as their purpose and are therefore unconstitutional. (See also strict-scrutiny test.)

symbolic speech Action (for example, the waving or burning of a flag) for the purpose of expressing a political opinion.

totalitarian government A form of government in which the leaders claim complete dominance of all individuals and institutions.

transfer payment A government benefit that is given directly to an individual, as in the case of social security payments to a retiree.

trustees Elected representatives whose obligation is to act in accordance with their own consciences as to what policies are in the best interests of the public. (See also delegates.)

two-party system A system in which only two political parties have a real chance of acquiring control of the government.

tyranny of the majority The potential of a majority to monopolize power for its own gain and to the detriment of minority rights and interests.

unilateralism The situation in which one nation takes action against another state or states.

unipolar (power structure) A power structure dominated by a single powerful actor, as in the case of the United States after the collapse of the Soviet Union.

unitary system A governmental system in which the national government alone has sovereign (ultimate) authority. (See also confederacy; federalism.)

unit rule   The rule that grants all of a state's electoral votes to the candidate who receives most of the popular votes in the state.

unity   The principle that Americans are one people and form an indivisible union.

veto   The president's rejection of a bill, thereby keeping it from becoming law unless Congress overrides the veto.

Virginia (large-state) Plan   A constitutional proposal for a strong Congress with two chambers, both of which would be based on numerical representation, thus granting more power to the larger states.

voter turnout   The proportion of persons of voting age who actually vote in a given election.

watchdog role   The accepted responsibility of the media to protect the public from deceitful, careless, incompetent, and corrupt officials by standing ready to expose any official who violates accepted legal, ethical, or performance standards. (See also **common-carrier role; public-representative role; signaler role.**)

weak mayor–council system   Form of municipal government in which the mayor's policymaking powers are less substantial than the council's; the mayor has no power to veto the council's actions and often has no formal role in such activities as budget making.

Whig theory   A theory that prevailed in the nineteenth century and held that the presidency was a limited or restrained office whose occupant was confined to expressly granted constitutional authority. (See also **stewardship theory.**)

whistle-blowing   An internal check on the bureaucracy whereby individual bureaucrats report instances of mismanagement that they observe.

writ of certiorari   Permission granted by a higher court to allow a losing party in a legal case to bring the case before it for a ruling; when such a writ is requested of the U.S. Supreme Court, four of the Court's nine justices must agree to accept the case before it is granted certiorari.

NOTES

CHAPTER 1

[1]Alexis de Tocqueville, *Democracy in America (1835–1840)*, ed. J. P. Mayer and A. P. Kerr (Garden City, N.Y.: Doubleday/Anchor, 1969), 640.

[2]See John Harmon McElroy, *American Beliefs: What Keeps a Big Country and a Diverse People United* (Chicago: I. R. Dee, 1999); but see Michael B. Katz and Mark J. Stern, *One Nation Divisible: What America Was and What It's Becoming* (New York: Russell Sage Foundation, 2006).

[3]Clinton Rossiter, *Conservativism in America* (New York: Vintage, 1962), 67; see also Robert A. Ferguson, *Reading the Early Republic* (Cambridge, Mass.: Harvard University Press, 2004).

[4]Tocqueville, *Democracy in America*, 310.

[5]James Bryce, *The American Commonwealth*, vol. 2 (New York: Macmillan, 1960), 247–54. First published in 1900.

[6]See Gabriel Almond and Sidney Verba, *The Civic Culture* (Boston: Little, Brown, 1965); Richard Merelman, *Making Something of Ourselves: On Culture and Politics in the United States* (Berkeley: University of California Press, 1984); but see also John Kenneth White, *The Values Divide* (Washington, D.C.: CQ Press, 2002).

[7]Paul Gagnon, "Why Study History?" *Atlantic Monthly*, November 1988, 47.

[8]Ralph Barton Perry, *Puritanism and Democracy* (New York: Vanguard, 1944), 124–25; see also Peter D. Salins, *Assimilation, American Style* (New York: Basic Books, 1996).

[9]Louis Hartz, *The Liberal Tradition in America* (New York: Harcourt, Brace, 1953), 12; see also Jeffrey Stout, *Democracy and Tradition* (Princeton, N.J.: Princeton University Press, 2004).

[10]James Bryce, *The American Commonwealth*, vol. 2 (Indianapolis, Ind.: Liberty Fund, 1995), 1419.

[11]The Pew Research Center for the People and the Press's Global Attitudes Survey, 2002.

[12]See Douglas Muzzio and Richard Behn, "Thinking About Welfare," *The Public Perspective*, February/March 1995, 35–38.

[13]See Seymour Martin Lipset, *American Exceptionalism: A Double-Edged Sword* (New York: Norton, 1996); Claude Levi-Strauss, *Structural Anthropology* (Chicago: University of Chicago Press, 1983); Clifford Geertz, *Myth, Symbol, and Culture* (New York: Norton, 1974).

[14]U.S. Census Bureau, 2006.

[15]Quoted in Ralph Volney Harlow, *The Growth of the United States*, vol. 2 (New York: Henry Holt, 1943), 497.

[16]Survey of American Political Culture, James Davison Hunter and Carol Bowman, directors, University of Virginia, 1996; Debra L. DeLaet, *U.S. Immigration Policy in an Age of Rights* (Westport, Conn.: Praeger Publishers, 2000).

[17]Harold D. Lasswell, *Politics: Who Gets What, When, How* (New York: McGraw-Hill, 1938).

[18]See Charles H. McIlwain, *Constitutionalism: Ancient and Modern* (Ithaca, N.Y.: Cornell University Press, 1983).

[19]Alan S. Rosenbaum, ed., *Constitutionalism: The Philosophical Dimension* (Westport, Conn.: Greenwood, 1988), 4; see also Russell Hardin, *Liberalism, Constitutionalism, and Democracy* (New York: Oxford University Press, 1999).

[20]Tocqueville, *Democracy in America*, ch. 6.

[21]Harold D. Lasswell and Abraham Kaplan, *Power and Society* (New Haven, Conn.: Yale University Press, 1950), 75–77.

[22]Benjamin I. Page and Robert Shapiro, "Effects of Public Opinion on Policy," *American Political Science Review* 77 (March 1983): 178; see also Lawrence R. Jacobs and Robert Shapiro, *Politicians Don't Pander* (Chicago: University of Chicago Press, 2000).

[23]See Robert Dahl, *On Democracy* (New Haven, Conn.: Yale University Press, 2000).

[24]C. Wright Mills, *The Power Elite* (New York: Oxford University Press, 1965).

[25]G. William Domhoff, *Who Rules America? Power and Politics*, 4th ed. (New York, McGraw-Hill, 2002).

[26]See, for example, Dahl, *On Democracy*.

[27]See H. H. Gerth and C. Wright Mills, eds., *From Max Weber: Essays in Sociology* (New York: Oxford University Press, 1958).

[28]Roberto Michels, *Political Parties* (New York: Collier Books, 1962). First published in 1911.

[29]David Easton, *The Political System* (New York: Knopf, 1965), 97.

[30]E. E. Schattschneider, *Two Hundred Million Americans in Search of a Government* (New York: Holt, Rinehart & Winston, 1969), 42.

CHAPTER 2

[1]Quoted in Charles S. Hyneman, "Republican Government in America," in George J. Graham Jr. and Scarlett G. Graham, eds., *Founding Principles of American Government*, rev. ed. (Chatham, N. J.: Chatham House, 1984), 19.

[2]See Russell Hardin, *Liberalism, Constitutionalism, and Democracy* (New York: Oxford University Press, 1999); A. John Simmons, *The Lockean Theory of Rights* (Princeton, N. J.: Princeton University Press, 1994).

[3]George Bancroft, *History of the Formation of the Constitution of the United States of America*, 3d ed., vol. 1 (New York: D. Appleton, 1883), 166.

[4]Quoted in "The Constitution and Slavery," Digital History Website, December 1, 2003.

[5]Gaillard Hunt, ed., *The Writings of James Madison* (New York: Putnam,

1904), 274; see also Garret Ward Sheldon, *The Political Philosophy of James Madison* (Baltimore: Johns Hopkins University Press, 2000).

[6]*Federalist* No. 47.

[7]See *Federalist* Nos. 47 and 48.

[8]Richard Neustadt, *Presidential Power* (New York: Macmillan, 1986), 33.

[9]Henry J. Abraham, *The Judicial Process,* 6th ed. (New York: Oxford University Press, 1993), 320–22.

[10]*Marbury v. Madison,* 1 Cranch 137 (1803).

[11]Martin Diamond, *The Founding of the Democratic Republic* (Itasca, Ill.: Peacock, 1981), 62–71.

[12]*Federalist* No. 10.

[13]Leslie F. Goldstein, "Judicial Review and Democratic Theory: Guardian Democracy vs. Representative Democracy," *Western Political Quarterly* 40 (1987): 391–412.

[14]Benjamin Ginsberg, *The Consequences of Consent* (New York: Random House, 1982), 22.

[15]Robert Dahl, *Pluralist Democracy in the United States* (Chicago: Rand McNally, 1967), 92.

[16]This interpretation is taken from Walter Lippmann, *Public Opinion* (New York: Free Press, 1965), 178–79; for a general discussion of the uncertain meaning of the Constitution, see Lawrence H. Tribe and Michael C. Dorf, *On Reading the Constitution* (Cambridge, Mass.: Harvard University Press, 1991).

[17]Michael McGeer, *A Fierce Discontent: The Rise and Fall of the Progressive Movement in America, 1870–1920.* (New York: Free Press, 2005).

[18]Charles S. Beard, *An Economic Interpretation of the Constitution* (New York, Macmillan, 1941). First published in 1913.

[19]See Randall G. Holcombe, *From Liberty to Democracy* (Ann Arbor: University of Michigan Press, 2002).

CHAPTER 3

[1]Woodrow Wilson, *Constitutional Government in the United States* (New York: Columbia University Press, 1908), 173.

[2]*Gonzales, Attorney General, et al. v. Oregon, et al.,* No. 04-623 (2006).

[3]See Samuel Beer, *To Make a Nation: The Rediscovery of American Federalism* (Cambridge, Mass.: The Belknap Press of Harvard University, 1993).

[4]*Federalist* No. 2; for the Anti-Federalist view, see Saul Cornell, *The Other Founders* (Chapel Hill: University of North Carolina Press, 1999).

[5]*McCulloch v. Maryland,* 4 Wheaton 316 (1819).

[6]*Gibbons v. Ogden,* 22 Wheaton 1 (1824).

[7]Oliver Wendell Holmes Jr., *Collected Legal Papers* (New York: Harcourt, Brace, 1920), 295–96.

[8]See John C. Calhoun, *The Works of John C. Calhoun* (New York: Russell & Russell, 1968).

[9]*Dred Scott v. Sanford,* 19 Howard 393 (1857).

[10]*U.S. v. Cruikshank,* 92 U.S. 452 (1876).

[11]*Slaughter-House Cases,* 16 Wallace 36 (1873); *Civil Rights Cases,* 109 U.S. 3 (1883).

[12]*Plessy v. Ferguson,* 163 U.S. 537 (1896).

[13]*Santa Clara County v. Southern Pacific Railroad Co.,* 118 U.S. 394 (1886).

[14]*U.S. v. E. C. Knight Co.,* 156 U.S. 1 (1895).

[15]*Hammer v. Dagenhart,* 247 U.S. 251 (1918).

[16]*Lochner v. New York,* 198 U.S. 25 (1905).

[17]Alfred H. Kelly, Winifred A. Harbison, and Herman Belz, *The American Constitution,* 7th ed. (New York: Norton, 1991), 529.

[18]James E. Anderson, *The Emergence of the Modern Regulatory State* (Washington, D.C.: Public Affairs Press, 1962), 2–3.

[19]*Schechter Poultry Co. v. United States,* 295 U.S. 495 (1935).

[20]*NLRB v. Jones and Laughlin Steel,* 301 U.S. 1 (1937).

[21]*American Power and Light v. Securities and Exchange Commission,* 329 U.S. 90 (1946); see also Richard A. Maidment, *The Judicial Response to the New Deal: The U.S. Supreme Court and Economic Regulation* (New York: Manchester University Press, 1992).

[22]Louis Fisher, *American Constitutional Law,* 6th ed. (Durham, N.C.: Carolina Academic Press, 2005), 390.

[23]See Maidment, *Judicial Response to the New Deal.*

[24]*Brown v. Board of Education,* 347 U.S. 483 (1954).

[25]*Miranda v. Arizona,* 384 U.S. 436 (1966).

[26]See Thomas Anton, *American Federalism and Public Policy* (Philadelphia: Temple University Press, 1989).

[27]Morton Grodzins, *The American System: A New View of Government in the United States* (Chicago: Rand McNally, 1966).

[28]Rosella Levaggi, *Fiscal Federalism and Grants-in-Aid* (Brookfield, Vt.: Avebury, 1991).

[29]Timothy J. Conlan, *From New Federalism to Devolution* (Washington, D.C.: Brookings Institution, 1998).

[30]*Garcia v. San Antonio Authority,* 469 U.S. 528 (1985).

[31]See Tinsley E. Yarbrough, *The Rehnquist Court and the Constitution* (New York: Oxford University Press, 2000).

[32]*United States v: Lopez,* 514 U.S. 549 (1995).

[33]*Printz v. United States,* 521 U.S. 98 (1997).

[34]*Kimel v. Florida Board of Regents,* 528 U.S. 62 (2000).

[35]*Board of Trustees of the University of Alabama v. Garrett,* 531 U.S. 356 (2002).

[36]*Nevada Department of Human Resources v. Hibbs,* No. 01-1368 (2003).

[37]See Pran Chopra, *Supreme Court Versus the Constitution: A Challenge to Federalism* (Thousand Oaks, Calif.: Sage Publications, 2006).

[38]See Robert F. Nagel, *The Implosion of American Federalism* (New York: Oxford University Press, 2001).

[39]*Gonzales v. Raich,* No. 03-1454 (2005).

[40]Andrew W. Dobelstein, *Politics, Economics, and Public Welfare* (Englewood Cliffs, N.J.: Prentice-Hall, 1980), 5.

[41]Lloyd A. Free and Hadley Cantril, *The Political Beliefs of Americans* (New York: Simon & Schuster, 1968), 21; see also William Lunch, *The Nationalization of American Politics* (Berkeley: University of California Press, 1987).

[42]Survey for the Times Mirror Center for the People and the Press by Princeton Survey Research Associates, July 12–27, 1994; see also Tommy Thompson, *Power to the People* (New York: HarperCollins, 1996).

[43]Daniel J. Boorstin, *The Americans: The Democratic Experience* (New York: Vintage Books, 1974).

CHAPTER 4

[1]Julian P. Boyd, ed., *The Papers of Thomas Jefferson,* vol. 12 (Princeton, N.J.: Princeton University Press, 1955), 440.

[2]*Anderson v. Creighton,* 483 U.S. 635 (1987).

[3]*Bose Corp. v. Consumers Union of the United States,* 466 U.S. 485 (1984).

[4]*Schenck v. United States*, 249 U.S. 47 (1919).

[5]*Dennis v. United States*, 341 U.S. 494 (1951).

[6]See, for example, *Yates v. United States*, 354 U.S. 298 (1957); *Noto v. United States*, 367 U.S. 290 (1961); *Scales v. United States*, 367 U.S. 203 (1961).

[7]*United States v. Carolene Products Co.*, 304 U.S. 144 (1938).

[8]*United States v. O'Brien*, 391 U.S. 367 (1968).

[9]*Texas v. Johnson*, 109 S. Ct. 2544 (1989).

[10]*United States v. Eichman*, 496 U.S. 310 (1990).

[11]*New York Times Co. v. United States*, 403 U.S. 713 (1971).

[12]*Nebraska Press Assn. v. Stuart*, 427 U.S. 539 (1976).

[13]*Barron v. Baltimore*, 7 Peters 243 (1833).

[14]*Gitlow v. New York*, 268 U.S. 652 (1925).

[15]*Fiske v. Kansas*, 274 U.S. 30 (1927); *Near v. Minnesota*, 283 U.S. 697 (1931); *Hamilton v. Regents, U. of California*, 293 U.S. 245 (1934); *DeJonge v. Oregon*, 299 U.S. 253 (1937).

[16]*Near v. Minnesota*, 283 U.S. 697 (1931).

[17]*Brandenburg v. Ohio*, 395 U.S. 444 (1969).

[18]*R.A.V. v. St. Paul*, No. 90-7675 (1992).

[19]*Wisconsin v. Mitchell*, No. 92-515 (1993).

[20]*National Socialist Party v. Skokie*, 432 U.S. 43 (1977).

[21]*Forsyth County v. Nationalist Movement*, No. 91-538 (1992).

[22]*Milkovich v. Lorain Journal*, 497 U.S. 1 (1990); see also *Masson v. The New Yorker*, No. 89-1799 (1991).

[23]*New York Times Co. v. Sullivan*, 376 U.S. 254 (1964).

[24]*Roth v. United States*, 354 U.S. 476 (1957).

[25]*Miller v. California*, 413 U.S. 15 (1973).

[26]*Barnes v. Glen Theatre*, No. 90-26 (1991).

[27]*Stanley v. Georgia*, 394 U.S. 557 (1969).

[28]*Osborne v. Ohio*, 495 U.S. 103 (1990).

[29]*Ashcroft v. Free Speech Coalition*, No. 00-795 (2002).

[30]*Denver Area Consortium v. Federal Communications Commission*, No. 95-124 (1996); *Reno v. American Civil Liberties Union*, No. 96-511 (1997); *Ashcroft v. ACLU*, No. 03-0218 (2004).

[31]*Engel v. Vitale*, 370 U.S. 421 (1962).

[32]*Abington School District v. Schempp*, 374 U.S. 203 (1963).

[33]*Wallace v. Jaffree*, 472 U.S. 38 (1985).

[34]*Santa Fe Independent School District v. Does*, No. 99-62 (2000).

[35]*Van Orden v. Perry*, No. 03-1500 (2005).

[36]*McCreary County v. American Civil Liberties Union*, No. 03-1693 (2005).

[37]*Board of Regents v. Allen*, 392 U.S. 236 (1968).

[38]*Lemon v. Kurtzman*, 403 U.S. 602 (1971).

[39]Ibid.

[40]*Mitchell v. Helms*, No. 98-1648 (2000).

[41]*Zelman v. Simmons-Harris*, No. 00-1751 (2002); see also *Locke v. Davey*, No. 02-1315 (2004).

[42]*Locke v. Davey*, No. 02-1315 (2004).

[43]*Wisconsin v. Yoder*, 406 U.S. 295 (1972); see also *Church of the Lukumi Babalu Aye v. City of Hialeah*, No. 91-948 (1993).

[44]*Edwards v. Aguillard*, 487 U.S. 578 (1987).

[45]*Griswold v. Connecticut*, 381 U.S. 479 (1965).

[46]*Roe v. Wade*, 401 U.S. 113 (1973).

[47]*Webster v. Reproductive Health Services*, 492 U.S. 490 (1989); see also *Rust v. Sullivan*, No. 89-1391 (1991).

[48]*Planned Parenthood v. Casey*, No. 91-744 (1992).

[49]*Ayotte v. Planned Parenthood of Northern New England*, No. 04-1144 (2006).

[50]*Stenberg v. Carhart*, No. 99-830 (2000).

[51]*Bowers v. Hardwick*, 478 U.S. 186 (1986).

[52]*Lawrence v. Texas*, 539 U.S. 558 (2003).

[53]*Vacco v. Quill*, 117 S.C. 36 (1996); *Washington v. Glucksberg*, No. 96-110 (1997).

[54]*Gregg v. United States*, No. 00-939 (2001).

[55]*Powell v. Alabama*, 287 U.S. 45 (1932).

[56]*Palko v. Connecticut*, 302 U.S. 319 (1937).

[57]*Mapp v. Ohio*, 367 U.S. 643 (1961).

[58]*Gideon v. Wainwright*, 372 U.S. 335 (1963).

[59]*Malloy v. Hogan*, 378 U.S. 1 (1964).

[60]*Miranda v. Arizona*, 384 U.S. 436 (1966); see also *Escobedo v. Illinois*, 378 U.S. 478 (1964).

[61]*Pointer v. Texas*, 380 U.S. 400 (1965).

[62]*Klopfer v. North Carolina*, 386 U.S. 213 (1967).

[63]*Duncan v. Louisiana*, 391 U.S. 145 (1968).

[64]*Benton v. Maryland*, 395 U.S. 784 (1969).

[65]*Dickerson v. United States*, No. 99-5525 (2000).

[66]*Missouri v. Siebert*, 542 U.S. 600 (2004).

[67]*Michigan v. Sitz*, No. 88-1897 (1990).

[68]*Indianapolis v. Edmund*, No. 99-1030 (2001).

[69]*Kyllo v. United States*, No. 99-8508 (2001).

[70]*Ferguson v. Charleston*, No. 99-936 (2001).

[71]*Board of Education of Independent School District No. 92 of Pottawatomie County v. Earls*, No. 01-332 (2002).

[72]*Weeks v. United States*, 232 U.S. 383 (1914).

[73]*Nix v. Williams*, 467 U.S. 431 (1984); see also *United States v. Leon*, 468 U.S. 897 (1984).

[74]*Whren v. United States*, 517 U.S. 806 (1996).

[75]*Hudson v. Michigan*, No. 04-1360 (2006).

[76]*Townsend v. Sain*, 372 U.S. 293 (1963).

[77]*Keeney v. Tamaya-Reyes*, No. 90-1859 (1992); see also *Coleman v. Thompson*, No. 89-7662 (1991).

[78]*Brecht v. Abrahamson*, No. 91-7358 (1993); see also *McCleskey v. Zant*, No. 89-7024 (1991).

[79]*Felker v. Turpin*, No. 95-8836 (1996); but see *Stewart v. Martinez-Villareal*, No. 97-300 (1998).

[80]*Williams v. Taylor*, No. 99-6615 (2000).

[81]*Miller-El v. Cockrell*, No. 01-7662 (2003); *Wiggins v. Smith*, No. 02-311 (2003).

[82]Kurt Heine, "Philadelphia Cops Beat One of Their Own," *Syracuse Herald-American*, January 15, 1995, A13.

[83]*Wilson v. Seiter*, No. 89-7376 (1991).

[84]*Harmelin v. Michigan*, No. 89-7272 (1991).

[85]*Lockyer v. Andrade*, No. 01-1127 (2003); see also *Ewing v. California*, No. 01-6978 (2003).

[86]*Atkins v. Virginia*, No. 01-8452 (2002); see also Roger Hood, *The Death Penalty: A Worldwide Perspective* (New York: Oxford University Press, 2003).

[87]*Roper v. Simmons*, No. 03-633 (2005).

[88]*Hill v. McDonough*, No. 05-8794 (2006).

[89]*Ring v. Arizona*, No. 01-488 (2002).

[90]*Blakely v. Washington*, No. 02-1632 (2004).

[91]*Korematsu v. United States*, 323 U.S. 214 (1944).

[92]Case cited in Charles Lane, "In Terror War, 2nd Track for Suspects," *Washington Post*, December 1, 2001, A1.

[93]Bill Mears, "Supreme Court Rejects Appeal over Secret 9/11 Detentions," *Washington Post*, January 12, 2004. Internet copy.

[94]*Rasul v. Bush*, No. 03-334 (2004); *al-Odah v. United States*, No. 03-343 (2004).

[95]*Hamdi v. Rumsfeld,* No. 03-6696 (2004); see also, *Rumsfeld v. Padilla,* No. 03-1027 (2004).

[96]*Hamdan v. Rumsfeld,* No. 05-184 (2006).

[97]Quoted in "Feds Get Wide Wiretap Authority," CBSNEWS.com, November 18, 2002.

[98]Lane, "In Terror War, 2nd Track for Suspects," A1.

[99]See Alpheus T. Mason, *The Supreme Court: Palladium of Freedom* (Ann Arbor: University of Michigan Press, 1962); see also Henry J. Abraham, *Freedom and the Court* (New York: Oxford University Press, 1998).

CHAPTER 5

[1]Speech of Martin Luther King Jr. in Washington, D.C., August 2, 1963.

[2]*Washington Post* wire story, May 14, 1991.

[3]"African-American Health," amednews.com (online newspaper of the American Medical Association), May 1, 2000.

[4]Robert Nisbet, "Public Opinion Versus Popular Opinion," *Public Interest* 41 (1975): 171.

[5]See, for example, John R. Howard, *The Shifting Wind* (Albany: State University of New York Press, 1999).

[6]The classic analysis of this system of legalized segregation is C. Vann Woodward, *The Strange Career of Jim Crow,* 3d rev. ed. (New York: Oxford University Press, 1974).

[7]*Plessy v. Ferguson,* 163 U.S. 537 (1896).

[8]Ada Lois Sipuel Fisher, Danney Gable, and Robert Henry, *A Matter of Black and White: The Autobiography of Ada Lois Sipuel Fisher* (Norman: University of Oklahoma Press, 1996).

[9]*Brown v. Board of Education of Topeka,* 347 U.S. 483 (1954).

[10]See Sar Levitan, William Johnson, and Robert Taggert, *Still a Dream* (Cambridge, Mass.: Harvard University Press, 1975).

[11]Data from National Office of Drug Control Policy, 1997.

[12]See Keith Reeves, *Voting Hopes or Fears?* (New York: Oxford University Press, 1997); Tali Mendelberg, *The Race Card* (Princeton, N.J.: Princeton University Press, 2001).

[13]See Glenna Matthews, *The Rise of Public Women* (New York: Oxford University Press, 1994).

[14]*Tinker v. Colwell,* 193 U.S. 473 (1904).

[15]See Jane Mansbridge, *Why We Lost the ERA* (Chicago: University of Chicago Press, 1986).

[16]*Pennsylvania State Police v. Suder,* No. 03-95 (2004).

[17]*Burlington Northern and Santa Fe Railroad Company v. White,* No. 05-259 (2006).

[18]Linda Witt, Karen M. Paget, and Glenna Matthews, *Running as a Woman* (New York: Free Press, 1994).

[19]Timothy Bledsoe and Mary Herring, "Victims of Circumstance: Women in Pursuit of Political Office," *American Political Science Review* 84 (1990): 213–24.

[20]U.S. Department of Education, 2006.

[21]See, Sara M. Evans and Barbara Nelson, *Wage Justice* (Chicago: University of Chicago Press, 1989).

[22]See Joane Nagel, *American Indian Ethnic Renewal* (New York: Oxford University Press, 1996).

[23]James G. Gimpel, "Latinos and the 2002 Election: Republicans Do Well When Latinos Stay Home," Center for Immigration Studies, University of Maryland, January 2003, web download; see also Louis DeSipio, *Counting on the Latino Vote* (Charlottesville: University of Virginia Press, 1996).

[24]James Truslow Adams, *The March of Democracy,* vol. 4 (New York: Scribner's, 1933), 284–85.

[25]*Lau v. Nichols,* 414 U.S. 563 (1974).

[26]See Gordon Chang, ed., *Asian Americans and Politics* (Stanford, Calif.: Stanford University Press, 2001).

[27]*Kimel v. Florida Board of Regents,* No. 98-791 (2000).

[28]*Board of Trustees of the University of Alabama v. Garrett,* No. 99-1240 (2002); *Tennessee v. Lane,* No. 02-1667 (2004).

[29]*Romer v. Evans,* 517 U.S. 620 (1996).

[30]*Lawrence v. Texas,* 539 U.S. 558 (2003).

[31]*Boy Scouts of America v. Dale,* No. 99-699 (2000).

[32]*Rumsfeld v. Forum for Academic and Institutional Rights,* No. 04-1152 (2006).

[33]Kaiser Family Foundation poll, 2001.

[34]*Craig v. Boren,* 429 U.S. 190 (1976).

[35]*Rostker v. Goldberg,* 453 U.S. 57 (1980).

[36]*United States v. Virginia,* No. 94-1941 (1996).

[37]U.S. Conference of Mayors Report, 1998; see also Survey by Federal Financial Institutions Examination Council, 1998.

[38]V. O. Key Jr., *Southern Politics* (New York: Knopf, 1949), 495.

[39]*Smith v. Allwright,* 321 U.S. 649 (1944).

[40]*Muller v. Johnson,* No. 94-631 (1995); *Bush v. Verg,* No. 94-805 (1996); *Shaw v. Hunt,* No. 94-923 (1996).

[41]*Easley v. Cromartie,* No. 99-1864 (2001).

[42]*League of United Latin American Voters v. Perry,* No. 05-204 (2006).

[43]Terry H. Anderson, *The Pursuit of Happiness: A History of Affirmative Action* (New York: Oxford University Press, 2005).

[44]*University of California Regents v. Bakke,* 438 U.S. 265 (1978).

[45]*Steelworkers v. Weber,* 443 U.S. 193 (1979); *Fullilove v. Klutnick,* 448 U.S. 448 (1980).

[46]*Local No. 28, Sheet Metal Workers v. Equal Employment Opportunity Commission,* 478 U.S. 421 (1986); see also *Local No. 93, International Association of Firefighters v. Cleveland,* 478 U.S. 501 (1986); *Firefighters v. Stotts,* 459 U.S. 969 (1984); *Wygant v. Jackson,* 476 U.S. 238 (1986).

[47]*Adarand v. Pena,* No. 94-310 (1995).

[48]*Gratz v. Bollinger,* No. 02-516 (2003).

[49]*Grutter v. Bollinger,* No. 02-241 (2003).

[50]See J. Edward Kellough, *Understanding Affirmative Action: Politics, Discrimination, and the Search for Justice* (Washington, D.C.: Georgetown University Press, 2006).

[51]*Swann v. Charlotte-Mecklenburg County Board of Education,* 402 U.S. 1 (1971).

[52]Christopher Jencks and Meredith Phillips, eds., *The Black-White Test Score Gap* (Washington, D.C.: Brookings Institution Press, 1998).

[53]*Milliken v. Bradley,* 418 U.S. 717 (1974).

[54]*Board of Education of Oklahoma City v. Dowell,* 498 U.S. 237 (1991).

[55]Sam Dillon, "Schools 'Efforts Hinge on Justices' Ruling in Cases on Race and School Assignments," *New York Times,* June 24, 2660, A11.

[56]Gunnar Myrdal, *An American Dilemma: The Negro Problem and Modern Democracy* (New York: Harper, 1944).

CHAPTER 6

[1]V. O. Key Jr., *Public Opinion and American Democracy* (New York: Knopf, 1961), 8.

[2]See Brandice Canes-Wrone, *Who Leads Whom? Presidents, Policy, and the Public* (Chicago: University of Chicago Press, 2005).

[3]See Jeremy Bentham, *An Introduction to the Principles of Morals and Legislation* (Oxford, England: Clarendon Press, 1996; originally published in 1789).

[4]Jerry L. Yeric and John R. Todd, *Public Opinion*, 3d ed. (Itasca, Ill.: Peacock, 1996), 3.

[5]Elisabeth Noelle-Neumann, *The Spiral of Silence*, 2d ed. (Chicago: University of Chicago Press, 1993), ch. 1.

[6]"Study Finds Widespread Misperceptions on Iraq Highly Related to Support for War," web release of the Program on International Policy Attitudes, School of Public Affairs, University of Maryland, October 2, 2003.

[7]Times-Mirror Center for the People and the Press survey, 1994.

[8]Survey of students of the eight Ivy League schools by Luntz & Weber Research and Strategic Services, for the University of Pennsylvania's Ivy League Study, November 13–December 1, 1992.

[9]See R. Michael Alvarez and John Brehm, *Hard Choices, Easy Answers* (Princeton, N.J.: Princeton University Press, 2002); see also Samuel L. Popkin, *The Reasoning Voter* (Chicago: University of Chicago Press, 1991).

[10]See Herbert Asher, *Polling and the Public*, 6th ed. (Washington, D.C.: Congressional Quarterly Press, 2004).

[11]Example from Adam Clymer, "Wrong Number: The Unbearable Lightness of Public Opinion Polls," *New York Times*, July 22, 2001. Internet copy.

[12]M. Kent Jennings and Richard G. Niemi, *Generations and Politics* (Princeton, N.J.: Princeton University Press, 1981).

[13]See Orit Ichilov, *Political Socialization, Citizenship Education, and Democracy* (New York: Teachers College Press, 1990).

[14]Thomas E. Patterson, *Out of Order* (New York: Vintage, 1994), ch. 2.

[15]Noelle-Neumann, *Spiral of Silence*.

[16]Jon Western, *Selling Intervention and War: The Presidency, the Media, and the American Public* (Baltimore, Md.: Johns Hopkins University Press, 2005).

[17]See, however, Dietram A. Scheufele, Matthew C. Nisbet, and Dominique Brossard, "Pathways to Political Participation: Religion, Communication Contexts, and Mass Media," *International Journal of Public Opinion Research* 15 (Autumn 2003): 300–324.

[18]John L. Sullivan, James E. Pierson, and George E. Marcus, "Ideological Constraint in the Mass Public," *American Journal of Political Science* 22 (May 1978): 233–49.

[19]CNN/USA Today poll conducted by the Gallup Organization, 1997.

[20]Philip Converse, "The Nature of Belief Systems in Mass Publics," in David Apter, ed., *Ideology and Discontent* (New York: Free Press, 1965), 206.

[21]Susan A. MacManus, *Young v. Old: Generational Combat in the Twenty-first Century* (Boulder, Colo.: Westview Press, 1996).

[22]See Angus Campbell, Philip Converse, Warren Miller, and Donald Stokes, *The American Voter* (New York: Wiley, 1960), chs. 3 and 4.

[23]Martin P. Wattenberg, *The Decline of American Political Parties, 1952–1996* (Cambridge, Mass.: Harvard University Press, 1998).

[24]Donald Green, Bradley Palmquist, and Eric Schickler, *Partisan Hearts and Minds* (New Haven, Conn.: Yale University Press, 2002).

[25]See William Domhoff, *Who Rules America?* 4th ed. (New York: McGraw-Hill, 2001).

[26]Benjamin I. Page and Robert Y. Shapiro, "Effects of Public Opinion on Policy," *American Political Science Review* 77 (March 1983): 178; see also Richard Sobel, *The Impact of Public Opinion on U.S. Foreign Policy* (New York: Oxford University Press, 2001); James Stimson, *Tides of Consent: How Public Opinion Shapes American Politics* (New York: Cambridge University Press, 2004).

[27]Lawrence R. Jacobs and Robert Y. Shapiro, *Politicians Don't Pander* (Chicago: University of Chicago Press, 2000).

CHAPTER 7

[1]Walter Lippmann, *Public Opinion* (New York: Free Press, 1965), 36.

[2]Quoted in Ralph Volney Harlow, *The Growth of the United States* (New York: Henry Holt, 1943), 312.

[3]Example from Gus Tyler, "One Cheer for the Democrats," *New Leader*, November 3, 1986, 6.

[4]Turnout figures provided by Washington, D.C., embassies of the respective countries, 2000.

[5]Thomas E. Patterson, *The Vanishing Voter* (New York: Knopf, 2002), 134.

[6]Russell Dalton, "The Myth of the Disengaged American," web publication of the Comparative Study of Electoral Systems, October 2005, 2.

[7]Ivor Crewe, "Electoral Participation," in David Butler, Howard R. Penniman, and Austin Ranney, eds., *Democracy at the Polls* (Washington, D.C.: American Enterprise Institute, 1981), 251–53.

[8]Malcom Jewell and David Olson, *American State Politics and Elections* (Homewood, Ill.: Irwin Press, 1978), 50.

[9]A. Karnig and B. Walter, "Municipal Elections," in *Municipal Yearbook, 1977* (Washington, D.C.: International City Management Assn., 1977).

[10]Richard Boyd, "Decline of U.S. Voter Turnout," *American Politics Quarterly* 9 (April 1981): 142.

[11]G. Bingham Powell, "Voting Turnout in Thirty Democracies," in Richard Rose, ed., *Electoral Participation: A Comparative Analysis* (Beverly Hills, Calif.: Sage, 1980), 6.

[12]See Joseph Nye, David King, and Philip Zelikow, *Why People Don't Trust Government* (Cambridge, Mass.: Harvard University Press, 1997).

[13]John M. Strate, Charles J. Parrish, Charles D. Elder, and Coit Ford III, "Life Span Civic Development and Voting Participation," *American Political Science Review* 83 (June 1989): 443–65.

[14]M. Margaret Conway, *Political Participation in the United States*, 3d ed. (Washington, D.C.: Congressional Quarterly Press, 2000), 23–25; Sidney Verba, Kay Schlozman, and Henry Brady, *Voice and Equality* (Cambridge, Mass.: Harvard University Press, 1995); Jan Leighley, *Strength in Numbers* (Princeton, N.J.: Princeton University Press, 2001).

[15]Vanishing Voter Survey, 2000; but see Jeffrey Stonecash, *Class and Party in American Politics* (Boulder, Colo.: Westview Press, 2000).

[16]W. Russell Neuman, *The Paradox of Mass Politics* (Cambridge, Mass.: Harvard University Press, 1986), 176.

[17]Samuel H. Barnes et al., eds., *Political Action* (Beverly Hills, Calif.: Sage, 1979), 541–42.

[18]Theda Skocpol, *Diminished Democracy: From Membership to Management in American Civic Life* (Norman: University of Oklahoma Press, 2003).

[19]Russell J. Dalton, *Citizen Politics,* 4th ed. (Washington, D.C.: CQ Press, 2005).

[20]Robert Putnam, *Bowling Alone* (New York: Simon & Schuster, 2000); but see Cliff Zukin et al., *A New Engagement: Political Participation, Civic Life, and the Changing American Citizen* (New York: Oxford University Press, 2006).

[21]Pew Research Center for the People and the Press, "Cable and Internet Loom Large in Fragmented Political News Universe," January 11, 2004, 1; web release.

[22]See Bruce Bimber and Richard Davis, *Campaigning Online* (New York: Oxford University Press, 2003); Bruce Bimber, *Information and American Democracy* (New York: Cambridge University Press, 2003); Joe Trippi, *The Revolution Will Not Be Televised* (New York: HarperCollins, 2004).

[23]See Benjamin Ginsberg, *The Consequences of Consent* (New York: Random House, 1982), ch. 2.

[24]See Laura R. Woliver, *From Outrage to Action* (Urbana: University of Illinois Press, 1993).

[25]ABC News/Washington Post poll, March 23, 2003.

[26]Dalton, *Citizen Politics,* 38.

[27]Gallup poll, January 2003.

[28]William Watts and Lloyd A. Free, eds., *The State of the Nation* (New York: University Books, Potomac Associates, 1967), 97.

[29]Robert E. Lane, "Market Justice, Political Justice," *American Political Science Review* 80 (1986): 383; see also Jennifer Nedelsky, *Private Property and the Limits of American Constitutionalism* (New York: Oxford University Press, 1990).

[30]Sidney Verba and Norman Nie, *Participation in America* (New York: Harper & Row, 1972), 131.

[31]See Verba and Nie, *Participation in America,* 332; V. O. Key Jr., *Southern Politics* (New York: Vintage Books, 1949), 527; Lawrence Jacobs and Robert Shapiro, *Politicians Don't Pander* (Chicago: University of Chicago Press, 2000).

CHAPTER 8

[1]E. E. Schattschneider, *Party Government* (New York: Rinehart, 1942), 1.

[2]See John Aldrich, *Why Parties? The Origin and Transformation of Political Parties in America* (Chicago: University of Chicago Press, 1995); L. Sandy Maisel, *Parties and Elections in America,* 4th ed. (Latham, Md.: Rowman and Littlefield, 2004), 27.

[3]E. E. Schattschneider, *The Semisovereign People: A Realist's View of Democracy in America* (New York: Holt, Rinehart & Winston, 1961), 140.

[4]Thomas E. Patterson, *The Vanishing Voter* (New York: Knopf, 2002), ch. 2.

[5]See Richard P. McCormick, *The Second American Party System: Party Formation in the Jacksonian Era* (Chapel Hill: University of North Carolina Press, 1966).

[6]Alexis de Tocqueville, *Democracy in America (1835–1840),* ed. J. P. Mayer and A. P. Kerr (Garden City, N.Y.: Doubleday/Anchor, 1969), 60.

[7]Aldrich, *Why Parties?* 151.

[8]See Kristi Andersen, *The Creation of a Democratic Majority, 1928–1936* (Chicago: University of Chicago Press, 1979).

[9]See Kevin Phillips, *The Emerging Republican Majority* (New Rochelle, N.Y.: Arlington House, 1969).

[10]See Harold W. Stanley, "Southern Partisan Changes: Dealignment, Realignment or Both?" *Journal of Politics* 50 (1988): 64–88; Earl Black and Merle Black, *Politics and Society in the South* (Cambridge, Mass.: Harvard University Press, 1987); Robert H. Swansbrough and David M. Brodsky, eds., *The South's New Politics: Realignment and Dealignment* (Columbia: University of South Carolina Press, 1988); Dewey L. Grantham, *The Life and Death of the Solid South* (Lexington: University of Kentucky Press, 1988).

[11]Gallup Organization, January 2006.

[12]William H. Flanigan and Nancy Zingale, *Political Behavior of the American Electorate,* 9th ed. (Washington, D.C.: Congressional Quarterly Press, 1998), 58–63.

[13]See Lewis L. Gould, *Grand Old Party* (New York: Random House, 2003); but see also Jacob S. Hacker and Paul Pierson, *Off-Center: The Republican Revolution and the Erosion of American Democracy* (New Haven, Conn.: Yale University Press, 2006).

[14]See John B. Judis and Ruy Teixeira, *The Emerging Democratic Majority* (New York: Scribner, 2002).

[15]CNN exit polls, November 2004.

[16]Clinton Rossiter, *Parties and Politics in America* (Ithaca, N.Y.: Cornell University Press, 1960), 11.

[17]Nancy Gibbs and Michael Duffy, "Fall of the House of Newt," *Time,* November 16, 1998, 47.

[18]John F. Bibby, *Politics, Parties, and Elections in America,* 5th ed. (Belmont, Calif.: Wadsworth, 2002), 275–83.

[19]John Green, Mark Rozell, and William Clyde Wilcox, eds., *The Christian Right in American Politics* (Washington, D.C.: Georgetown University Press, 2003).

[20]Micah L. Sifrey, *Spoiling for a Fight: Third-Party Politics in America* (New York: Routledge, 2003).

[21]Daniel A. Mazmanian, *Third Parties in Presidential Elections* (Washington, D.C.: Brookings Institution, 1984), 143–44.

[22]See Lawrence Goodwyn, *The Populist Movement* (New York: Oxford University Press, 1978).

[23]Anthony King, *Running Scared* (New York: Free Press, 1997).

[24]See Alan Ehrenhalt, *The United States of Ambition* (New York: Times Books, 1991).

[25]See Paul S. Herrnson and John C. Green, eds., *Responsible Partisanship* (Lawrence: University Press of Kansas, 2003).

[26]See Sarah McCally Morehouse, "Money Versus Party Effort," *American Journal of Political Science* 34 (1990): 706–24.

[27]David Adamany, "Political Parties in the 1980s," in Michael J. Malbin, ed., *Money and Politics in the United States* (Chatham, N.J.: Chatham House, 1984), 114.

[28]*Senator Mitch McConnell et al. v. Federal Election Commission et al.,* No. 02-1674 (2003).

[29]Joseph Napolitan, *The Election Game and How to Win It* (New York: Doubleday, 1972).

[30]Federal Elections Commission data, 2006.

[31]David B. Magleby and Candice J. Nelson, *The Money Chase: Congressional Campaign Finance Reform* (Washington, D.C.: Brookings Institution, 1990); see also David B. Magelby, J. Quin Monson, and Kelly D. Patterson, eds., *Dancing Without Partners: How Candidates, Parties and Interest Groups Interact in the New Campaign Finance Environment* (Provo, Utah: Brigham Young University Press, 2005).

[32]David Chagall, *The New King-Makers* (New York: Harcourt Brace Jovanovich, 1981).

[33]Lawrence R. Jacobs and Robert Y. Shapiro, *Politicians Don't Pander: Political Manipulation and the Loss of Democratic Responsiveness* (Chicago: University of Chicago Press, 2000).

[34]Darrell M. West, *Air Wars: Television Advertising in Election Campaigns, 1952–2000* (Washington, D.C.: Congressional Quarterly Press, 2001), 140–46.

[35]Stephen Ansolabehere and Shanto Iyengar, *Going Negative* (New York: Free Press, 1995), ch. 5.

[36]West, *Air Wars,* 12.

[37]Peter J. Peterson, *Running on Empty: How the Democratic and Republican Parties Are Bankrupting Our Future and What Americans Can Do About It* (New York: Farrar, Straus, and Giroux, 2005).

CHAPTER 9

[1]E. E. Schattschneider, *The Semisovereign People: A Realist's View of Democracy in America* (New York: Holt, Rinehart & Winston, 1960), 35.

[2]Alexis de Tocqueville, *Democracy in America (1835–1840),* ed. J. P. Mayer and A. P. Kerr (Garden City, N.Y.: Doubleday/Anchor, 1969), bk. 2, ch. 4.

[3]Mancur Olson, *The Logic of Collective Action,* rev. ed. (Cambridge, Mass.: Harvard University Press, 1971), 147; see also Theda Skocpol, *Diminished Democracy* (Norman: University of Oklahoma Press, 2003).

[4]See Jack L. Walker, *Mobilizing Interest Groups in America* (Ann Arbor: University of Michigan Press, 1991).

[5]See Jeffrey M. Berry, *The New Liberalism: The Rising Power of Citizen Groups* (Washington, D.C.: Brookings Institution Press, 1999).

[6]Olson, *Logic of Collective Action,* 64.

[7]Christopher J. Bosso, "The Color of Money: Environmental Groups and the Pathologies of Fund Raising," in Allan J. Cigler and Burdett Loomis, *Interest Group Politics,* 4th ed. (Washington, D.C.: Congressional Quarterly Press, 1995), 101–3.

[8]Kay Lehman Schlozman and John T. Tierney, *Organized Interests and American Democracy* (New York: Harper & Row, 1986), 54.

[9]Norman J. Ornstein and Shirley Elder, *Interest Groups, Lobbying, and Policymaking* (Washington, D.C.: Congressional Quarterly Press, 1978), 82–86.

[10]See John Mark Hansen, *Gaining Access* (Chicago: Chicago University Press, 1991); Bruce Wolpe and Bertram Levine, *Lobbying Congress* (Washington, D.C.: Congressional Quarterly Press, 1996).

[11]Robert H. Salisbury and Paul Johnson, "Who You Know Versus What You Know," *American Journal of Political Science* 33 (February 1989): 175–95; see also William P. Browne, *Cultivating Congress* (Lawrence: University Press of Kansas, 1995).

[12]Quoted in Ornstein and Elder, *Interest Groups, Lobbying, and Policymaking,* 77.

[13]Paul J. Quirk, *Industry Influence in Federal Regulatory Agencies* (Princeton, N.J.: Princeton University Press, 1981); John E. Chubb, *Interest Groups and the Bureaucracy: The Politics of Energy* (Stanford, Calif.: Stanford University Press, 1983), 200–201; Charles T. Goodsell, *The Case for Bureaucracy,* 3d ed. (Chatham, N.J.: Chatham House, 1994), 55–60.

[14]Lee Epstein and C. K. Rowland, "Interest Groups in the Courts," *American Political Science Review* 85 (1991): 205–17.

[15]Hugh Heclo, "Issue Networks and the Executive Establishment," in Anthony King, ed., *The New American Political System* (Washington, D.C.: American Enterprise Institute, 1978), 87–124.

[16]Ornstein and Elder, *Interest Groups, Lobbying, and Policymaking,* 88–93.

[17]Quoted in Mark Green, "Political PAC-Man," *The New Republic,* December 13, 1982, 20; see also Frank J. Sorauf, *Inside Campaign Finance* (New Haven, Conn.: Yale University Press, 1992).

[18]Quoted in Larry Sabato, *PAC Power: Inside the World of Political Action Committees* (New York: Norton, 1984), 72.

[19]Federal Elections Commission data, 2006.

[20]See Thomas L. Gatz, *Improper Influence* (Ann Arbor: University of Michigan Press, 1996); Gene M. Grossman and Elhanan Helpman, *Interest Groups and Trade Policy* (Princeton, N.J.: Princeton University Press, 2002).

[21]Walker, *Mobilizing Interest Groups in America,* 112.

[22]Theodore J. Lowi, *The End of Liberalism: The Second Republic of the United States* (New York: Norton, 1979).

CHAPTER 10

[1]Theodore H. White, *The Making of the President, 1972* (New York: Bantam Books, 1973), 327.

[2]See Richard Davis, *The Press and American Politics,* 3d ed. (Upper Saddle River, N.J.: Prentice-Hall, 2000), 24–27.

[3]See Geneva Overholser and Kathleen Hall Jamieson, eds., *The Press* (New York: Oxford University Press, 2005).

[4]Frank Luther Mott, *American Journalism, a History: 1690–1960* (New York: Macmillan, 1962), 114–15.

[5]Culver H. Smith, *The Press, Politics, and Patronage* (Athens: University of Georgia Press, 1977), 163–68.

[6]Doris A. Graber, *Mass Media and American Politics,* 6th ed. (Washington, D.C.: Congressional Quarterly Press, 2001), 36; Mark Wahlgren Summers, *The Press Gang* (Chapel Hill: University of North Carolina Press, 1994).

[7]Mott, *American Journalism,* 122–23, 220–27.

[8]Ibid., 220–27, 241, 243.

[9]Edwin Emery, *The Press and America: An Interpretive History of the Mass Media* (Englewood Cliffs, N.J.: Prentice-Hall, 1977), 350.

[10]Quoted in Mott, *American Journalism,* 529.

[11]See Bill Kovach and Tom Rosenstiel, *The Elements of Journalism* (New York: Three Rivers Press, 2001).

[12]Quoted in David Halberstam, *The Powers That Be* (New York: Knopf, 1979), 208–9.

[13]See Ben Bagdikian, *The New Media Monopoly* (Boston: Beacon Press, 2004).

[14]See Timothy E. Cook, *Governing with the News* (Chicago: University of Chicago Press, 1997); Bartholomew Sparrow, *Uncertain Guardians* (Baltimore: Johns Hopkins University Press, 1999).

[15]Bernard Goldberg, *Bias: A CBS Insider Exposes How the Media Distort News* (New York: Harper Paperbacks, 2003).

[16]David H. Weaver, Randal A. Beam, Bonnie J. Brownlee, Paul S. Voakes, G. Cleveland Wilhoit, *The American Journalist in the 21st Century* (Mahwah, N.J.: LEA, 2006).

[17]Center for Media and Public Affairs, *Media Monitor,* various dates.

[18]Michael Robinson, "Public Affairs Television and the Growth of Political Malaise," *American Political Science Review* 70 (1976): 409–32.

[19]Center for Media and Public Affairs, *Media Monitor,* various dates.

[20]*Ibid.*

[21]Thomas Patterson, *Out of Order* (New York: Knopf, 1993), ch. 4.

[22]Project for Excellence in Journalism, "The Debate Effect," web release, October 27, 2004.

[23]William Cole, ed. *The Most of A.J. Leibling* (New York: Simon, 1963), 7.

[24]Walter Lippmann, *Public Opinion* (New York: Free Press, 1965), 214. First published in 1922.

[25]Donald Shaw and Maxwell McCombs, *The Emergence of American Political Issues: The Agenda-Setting Function of the Press* (St. Paul, Minn.: West Publishing, 1977).

[26]Bernard C. Cohen, *The Press and Foreign Policy* (Princeton, N.J.: Princeton University Press, 1963), 13.

[27]Figures from Center for Media and Public Affairs, various dates.

[28]Kiku Adatto, "Sound Bite Democracy," Joan Shorenstein Center on the Press, Politics, and Public Policy, Research Paper R-2, Harvard University, Cambridge, Mass., June 1990.

[29]Quoted in Doreen Carvajal, "For News Media, Some Introspection," *New York Times,* April 5, 1998, 28.

[30]Quoted in Max Kampelman, "The Power of the Press, *Policy Review* 6 (1978): 19.

[31]James Reston, "End of the Tunnel," *New York Times,* April 30, 1975, 41.

[32]Quoted in Edward J. Epstein, *News from Nowhere* (New York: Random House, 1973), ix.

[33]See Matthew Baum, *Soft News Goes to War* (Princeton, N.J.: Princeton University Press, 2003); James T. Hamilton, *All the News That's Fit to Sell* (Princeton, N.J.:Princeton University Press, 2004).

[34]Study Finds Widespread Misperceptions on Iraq," Program on International Policy Attitudes, University of Maryland, October 2, 2003.

[35]Lippmann, *Public Opinion,* 221.

CHAPTER 11

[1]Roger H. Davidson and Walter J. Oleszek, *Congress and Its Members,* 9th ed. (Washington, D.C.: Congressional Quarterly Press, 2004), 4.

[2]See Paul S. Herrnson, *Congressional Elections: Campaigning at Home and in Washington,* 4th ed. (Washington, D.C.: Congressional Quarterly Press, 2003).

[3]See Gary C. Jacobson, *The Politics of Congressional Elections,* 5th ed. (New York: Longman, 2001).

[4]Bruce Cain, John Ferejohn, and Morris P. Fiorina, *The Personal Vote* (Cambridge, Mass.: Harvard University Press, 1987).

[5]Information provided by Clerk of the House.

[6]U.S. Code Online, 2006.

[7]Edward Sidlow, *Challenging the Incumbent: An Underdog's Undertaking* (Washington, D.C.: Congressional Quarterly Press, 2003).

[8]Jennifer Babson and Kelly St. John, "Momentum Helps GOP Collect Record Amounts from PACs," *Congressional Quarterly Weekly Report,* December 3, 1994, 3456.

[9]Quoted in "A Tale of Myths and Measures: Who Is Truly Vulnerable?" *Congressional Quarterly Weekly Report,* December 4, 1993, 7; see also Dennis F. Thompson, *Ethics in Congress* (Washington, D.C.: Brookings Institution Press, 1995).

[10]James E. Campbell, *The Presidential Pulse of Congressional Elections* (Lexington: University Press of Kentucky, 1993).

[11]Robert Erikson, "The Puzzle of Midterm Losses, *Journal of Politics* 50 (November 1988): 1011–29.

[12]Linda L. Fowler and Robert D. McClure, *Political Ambition* (New Haven, Conn.: Yale University Press, 1989).

[13]Keith R. Poole and Howard Rosenthal, "Patterns of Congressional Voting," *American Journal of Political Science* 35 (February 1991): 228.

[14]*Congressional Quarterly Weekly Report,* various dates.

[15]Linda Witt, Karen M. Paget, and Glenna Matthews, *Running as a Woman: Gender and Power in American Politics* (New York: Free Press, 1993); Sue Thomas, *How Women Legislate* (New York: Oxford University Press, 1994); Tali Mendelberg, *The Race Card* (Princeton, N.J.: Princeton University Press, 2001).

[16]See Barbara Sinclair, *Legislators, Leaders, and Lawmaking* (Baltimore, Md.: Johns Hopkins University Press, 1998).

[17]Barbara Sinclair, *Majority Leadership in the U.S. House* (Baltimore, Md.: Johns Hopkins University Press, 1983); Barbara Sinclair, *Unorthodox Lawmaking: New Legislative Processes in the U.S. Congress,* 2nd ed. Washington, D.C.: CQ Press, 2000).

[18]See Stephen E. Frantzich and Steven E. Schier, *Congress: Games and Strategies* (Dubuque, Iowa: Brown & Benchmark, 1995), 127.

[19]David King, *Turf Wars* (Chicago: University of Chicago Press, 1997).

[20]See Gerald S. Strom, *The Logic of Lawmaking* (Baltimore, Md.: Johns Hopkins University Press, 1990).

[21]See Sinclair, *Unorthodox Lawmaking.*

[22]See Jon R. Bond and Richard Fleisher, eds., *Polarized Politics: Congress and the President in a Partisan Era* (Washington, D.C.: Congressional Quarterly Press, 2000).

[23]See Gary Orfield, *Congressional Power: Congress and Social Change* (New York: Harcourt Brace Jovanovich, 1975).

[24]James L. Sundquist, "Congress and the President: Enemies or Partners?" in Lawrence C. Dodd and Bruce I. Oppenheimer, eds., *Congress Reconsidered* (New York: Praeger, 1977), 240.

[25]Keith Krehbiel, "Are Congressional Committees Composed of Preference Outliers?" *American Political Science Review* 84 (1990): 149–64; Richard L. Hall and Bernard Grofman, "The Committee Assignment Process and the Conditional Nature of Committee Bias," *American Political Science Review* 84 (1990): 1149–66.

[26]Joel A. Aberbach and Mark A. Peterson, eds., *The Executive Branch* (New York: Oxford University Press, 2005), 534–35.

[27]Davidson and Oleszek, *Congress and Its Members,* 7.

CHAPTER 12

[1]Woodrow Wilson, *Constitutional Government in the United States* (New York: Columbia University Press, 1908), 67.

[2]Sidney Milkis and Michael Nelson, *The American Presidency: Origins and Development, 1790–2002,* 4th ed. (Washington, D.C.: Congressional Quarterly Press, 2003).

[3]James W. Davis, *The American Presidency* (New York: Harper & Row,

1987), 13; see also Bruce Ackerman, *The Failure of the Founding Fathers* (Cambridge, Mass.: Belknap Press of Harvard University Press, 2005).

[4]See Barry M. Blechman and Stephen S. Kaplan, *Force Without War* (Washington, D.C.: Brookings Institution, 1978); Arthur M. Schlesinger, Jr., *War and the American Presidency* (New York: W. W. Norton, 2004).

[5]*United States v. Belmont*, 57 U.S. 758 (1937).

[6]Robert DiClerico, *The American President*, 5th ed. (Englewood Cliffs, N.J.: Prentice-Hall, 1999), 47.

[7]Quoted in Wilfred E. Binkley, *President and Congress*, 3d ed. (New York: Vintage, 1962), 142.

[8]Theodore Roosevelt, *An Autobiography* (New York: Scribner's, 1931), 383.

[9]See Richard M. Pious, *The American Presidency* (New York: Basic Books, 1979), 83.

[10]Harry S Truman, *Years of Trial and Hope* (New York: Signet, 1956), 535.

[11]See Joseph A. Pika and John Anthony Maltese, *The Politics of the Presidency*, 6th ed. (Washington, D.C.: Congressional Quarterly Press, 2004).

[12]James Bryce, *The American Commonwealth* (New York: Commonwealth Edition, 1908), 230.

[13]Hugh Heclo, "Introduction: The Presidential Illusion," in Hugh Heclo and Lester M. Salamon, eds., *The Illusion of Presidential Government* (Boulder, Colo.: Westview Press, 1981), 6.

[14]James W. Ceaser, *Presidential Selection: Theory and Development* (Princeton, N.J.: Princeton University Press, 1979).

[15]Thomas E. Patterson, *The Vanishing Voter* (New York: Vintage, 2003); John S. Jackson and William J. Crotty, *The Politics of Presidential Selection* (New York: Longman, 2001).

[16]Sidney Kraus, ed., *The Great Debates* (Bloomington: Indiana University Press, 1962), 190.

[17]John P. Burke, *The Institutionalized Presidency* (Baltimore: Johns Hopkins University Press, 1992); Charles E. Walcott and Karen M. Hult, *Governing the White House* (Lawrence: University Press of Kansas, 1995).

[18]Quoted in Stephen J. Wayne, *Road to the White House, 1992* (New York: St. Martin's Press, 1992), 143.

[19]See Shirley Anne Warshaw, *Powersharing: White House–Cabinet Relations in the Modern Presidency* (Albany: State University of New York Press, 1995).

[20]See Jeffrey E. Cohen, *The Politics of the United States Cabinet* (Pittsburgh: University of Pittsburgh Press, 1988).

[21]James Pfiffner, *The Modern Presidency* (New York: St. Martin's Press, 1994), 123.

[22]Quoted in James MacGregor Burns, "Our Super-Government—Can We Control It?" *New York Times*, April 24, 1949, 32.

[23]See Paul C. Light, *Thickening Government: Federal Hierarchy and the Diffusion of Accountability* (Washington, D.C.: Brookings Institution, 1995).

[24]Erwin Hargrove, *The Power of the Modern Presidency* (New York: Knopf, 1974); see also John H. Kessel, *Presidents, the Presidency, and the Political Environment* (Washington, D.C.: Congressional Quarterly Press, 2001).

[25]James P. Pfiffner, *The Strategic Presidency: Hitting the Ground Running*, 2d ed. (Chicago: Dorsey Press, 1996).

[26]Aaron Wildavsky, "The Two Presidencies," *Trans-Action*, December 1966, 7.

[27]Pfiffner, *The Modern Presidency*, ch. 6.

[28]Thomas P. (Tip) O'Neill, with William Novak, *Man of the House: The Life and Political Memoirs of Speaker Tip O'Neill* (New York: Random House, 1987), 297.

[29]Fred I. Greenstein, ed., *Leadership in the Modern Presidency* (Cambridge, Mass.: Harvard University Press, 1988), ch. 10.

[30]Richard E. Neustadt, *Presidential Power and the Modern Presidents* (New York: Free Press, 1990), 71–72.

[31]Ibid., 33.

[32]Charlie Savage, "Senator Considers Suit Over Bush Law Challenge," *Boston Globe*, June 28, 2006, Internet copy.

[33]John E. Mueller, "Presidential Popularity from Truman to Johnson," *American Political Science Review* 64 (March 1970): 18–34; Kathleen Frankovic, "Public Opinion in the 1992 Campaign," in Gerald M. Pomper, ed., *The Election of 1992* (Chatham, N.J.: Chatham House, 1993).

[34]Samuel Kernell, *Going Public: New Strategies of Presidential Leadership*, 3d ed. (Washington, D.C.: Congressional Quarterly Press, 1997), 1; see also Robert M. Eisinger, *The Evolution of Presidential Polling* (New York: Cambridge University Press, 2003).

[35]Heclo, "Introduction: The Presidential Illusion," 2.

[36]Theodore J. Lowi, *The "Personal" Presidency: Power Invested, Promise Unfulfilled* (Ithaca, N.Y.: Cornell University Press, 1985).

CHAPTER 13

[1]Norman Thomas, *Rule 9: Politics, Administration, and Civil Rights* (New York: Random House, 1966), 6.

[2]James P. Pfiffner, "The National Performance Review in Perspective," working paper 94-4, Institute of Public Policy, George Mason University, 1994, 2.

[3]Ibid., 12.

[4]Max Weber, *Economy and Society*, trans. Guenther Roth and Claus Wittich (New York: Bedminster Press, 1968), 23; see also Paul Du Gay, *The Values of Bureaucracy* (New York: Oxford University Press, 2005).

[5]See Cornelius M. Kerwin, *Rulemaking*, 3d ed. (Washington, D.C.: Congressional Quarterly Press, 2003).

[6]Michael Lipsky, *Street-Level Bureaucracy* (New York: Russell Sage Foundation, 1980); see also George Serra, "Citizen-Initiated Contact and Satisfaction with Bureaucracy," *Journal of Public Administration* 5 (April 1995): 175–88.

[7]Paul Van Riper, *History of the United States Civil Service* (Evanston, Ill.: Peterson, 1958), 36.

[8]David H. Rosenbloom, *Federal Service and the Constitution* (Ithaca, N.Y.: Cornell University Press, 1971), 83.

[9]Herbert Kaufman, "Emerging Conflicts in the Doctrine of Public Administration," *American Political Science Review* 50 (December 1956): 1060.

[10]Ibid., 1062.

[11]Quoted in Hugh Heclo, *A Government of Strangers* (Washington, D.C.: Brookings Institution, 1977), 225.

[12]Norton E. Long, "Power and Administration," *Public Administration Review* 10 (Autumn 1949): 269; Joel D. Aberbach and Bert A. Rockman, *In the Web of Politics* (Washington, D.C.: Brookings Institution Press, 2000).

[13]See Heclo, *A Government of Strangers*, 117–18.

[14]Quoted in Aaron Wildavsky, *The Politics of the Budgetary Process*, 4th ed.

(Boston: Little, Brown, 1984), 19; see also Dennis D. Riley, *Bureaucracy and the Policy Process: Keeping the Promises* (Latham, Md.: Rowman & Littlefield, 2005).

[15]Joel D. Aberbach and Bert A. Rockman, "Clashing Beliefs Within the Executive Branch," *American Political Science Review* 70 (June 1976): 461.

[16]See B. Dan Wood and Richard W. Waterman, *Bureaucratic Dynamics* (Boulder, Colo.: Westview Press, 1994); Edward C. Page and Bill Jenkins, *Policy Bureaucracy: Government with a Cast of Thousands* (New York: Oxford University Press, 2005).

[17]See John Brehm and Scott Gates, *Working, Shirking, and Sabotage* (Ann Arbor: University of Michigan Press, 1996).

[18]Long, "Power and Administration," 269; see also John Mark Hansen, *Gaining Access* (Chicago: University of Chicago Press, 1991).

[19]Charles T. Goodsell, *The Case for Bureaucracy*, 2d ed. (Chatham, N.J.: Chatham House, 1985), 55–60, see also B. Guy Peters, *The Politics of Bureaucracy*, 5th ed. (New York: Routledge, 2001).

[20]William T. Gormley Jr. and Steven J. Balla, *Bureaucracy and Democracy* (Washington, D.C.: Congressional Quarterly Press, 2003).

[21]See Paul Light, *Thickening Government* (Washington, D.C.: Brookings Institution, 1995).

[22]James G. March and Johan P. Olson, "Organizing Political Life: What Administrative Reorganization Tells Us About Government," *American Political Science Review* 77 (June 1983): 281–96.

[23]Kenneth J. Meier, *Regulation* (New York: St. Martin's Press, 1985), 110–11.

[24]See Heclo, *A Government of Strangers*.

[25]See Donald Kettl, *Deficit Politics* (New York: Macmillan, 1992).

[26]See Joel D. Aberbach, *Keeping a Watchful Eye* (Washington, D.C.: Brookings Institution, 1990).

[27]David Rosenbloom, "The Evolution of the Administrative State, and Transformations of Administrative Law," in David Rosenbloom and Richard Schwartz, eds., *Handbook of Regulation and Administrative Law* (New York: Marcel Dekker, 1994), 3–36.

[28]See *Vermont Yankee Nuclear Power Corp. v. National Resources Defense Council, Inc.*, 435 U.S. 519 (1978); *Chevron v. National Resources Defense Council*, 467 U.S. 837 (1984); *Heckler v. Chaney*, 470 U.S. 821 (1985); but see *FDA v. Brown & Williamson Tobacco Co.* (2000).

[29]*Pigeford v. Veneman*, U.S. District Court for the District of Columbia, Civil Action No. 97-1978 (1999).

[30]"Clark: Bush Didn't See Terrorism as 'Urgent,'" *CNN.com*, March 25, 2004.

[31]See Brian J. Cook, *Bureaucracy and Self-Government* (Baltimore, Md.: Johns Hopkins University Press, 1996).

[32]Ibid.

[33]David Osborne and Ted Gaebler, *Reinventing Government: How the Entrepreneurial Spirit Is Transforming the Public Sector* (New York: Addison-Wesley, 1992); see also Michael Barzelay and Babak J. Armajani, *Breaking Through Bureaucracy* (Berkeley: University of California Press, 1992); Robert D. Behn, *Leadership Counts* (Cambridge, Mass.: Harvard University Press, 1991).

[34]Pfiffner, "The National Performance Review in Perspective," 7.

[35]Ronald C. Moe, "The 'Reinventing Government' Exercise: Misinterpreting the Problem, Misjudging the Results," *Public Administration Review*, March/April 1994, 125–36.

CHAPTER 14

[1]*Marbury v. Madison*, 5 U.S. 137 (1803).

[2]*Bush v. Gore*, No. 00-949 (2000).

[3]Rebecca Mae Salokar, *The Solicitor General: The Politics of Law* (Philadelphia: Temple University Press, 1992); see also Cornell W. Clayton, *The Politics of Justice: The Attorney General and the Making of Legal Policy* (Armonk, N.Y.: Sharpe, 1992).

[4]See Bernard Schwartz, *Decision: How the Supreme Court Decides Cases* (New York: Oxford University Press, 1996).

[5]Henry Glick, *Courts, Politics, and Justice*, 3d ed. (New York: McGraw-Hill, 1993), 214.

[6]Lawrence Baum, *The Supreme Court*, 8th ed. (Washington, D.C.: Congressional Quarterly Press, 2003), 120.

[7]*Gideon v. Wainwright*, 372 U.S. 335 (1963).

[8]From a letter to the author by Frank Schwartz of Beaver College; this section reflects substantially Professor Schwartz's recommendations to the author, as does the later section that addresses the federal court myth. See also Robert A. Carp and Ronald Stidham, *The Federal Courts*, 4th ed. (Washington, D.C.: Congressional Quarterly Press, 2001).

[9]*Hutto v. Davis*, 370 U.S. 256 (1982).

[10]*Lawrence v. Texas*, No. 02-102 (2003).

[11]*Bowers v. Hardwick*, 478 U.S. 186 (1986).

[12]See Richard Davis, *Electing Justices* (New York: Oxford University Press, 2005).

[13]See Lee Epstein and Jeffrey Segal, *Advice and Consent: The Politics of Judicial Appointments* (New York: Oxford University Press, 2005).

[14]Robert Scigliano, *The Supreme Court and the Presidency* (New York: Free Press, 1971), 146; see also Lee Epstein and Jack Knight, *The Choices Justices Make* (Washington, D.C.: Congressional Quarterly Press, 1998).

[15]Quoted in Baum, *The Supreme Court*, 37.

[16]See Virginia A. Hettinger et al., *Judging on a Collegial Court: Influences on Federal Appellate Decision Making* (Charlottesville, Va.: University of Virginia Press, 2006).

[17]John Gottschall, "Reagan's Appointments to the U.S. Courts of Appeals," 70 *Judicature* 48 (1986): 54.

[18]Carp, *The Federal Courts*.

[19]Joseph B. Harris, *The Advice and Consent of the Senate* (Berkeley: University of California Press, 1953), 313.

[20]Quoted in Louis Fisher, *American Constitutional Law* (New York: McGraw-Hill, 1990), 5.

[21]Quoted in Charles P. Curtis, *Law and Large as Life* (New York: Simon & Schuster, 1959), 156–57.

[22]See Lee Epstein and Jack Knight, *The Choices Justices Make* (New York: Longman, 1995); Thomas G. Hansford and James F. Spriggs II, *The Politics of Precedent on the Supreme Court* (Princeton, N.J.: Princeton University Press, 2006).

[23]*Faragher v. City of Boca Raton*, No. 97-282 (1998).

[24]Stephen L. Wasby, *The Supreme Court in the Federal Judicial System*, 4th ed. (Chicago: Nelson-Hall, 1993), 53.

[25]Linda Greenhouse, "Sure Justices Legislate. They Have To," *New York Times*, July 5, 1998, sect. 4, p. 1.

[26]John Schmidhauser, *The Supreme Court* (New York: Holt, Rinehart & Winston, 1964), 6.

[27]Linda Greenhouse, "In a Momentous Term, Justices Remake the Law, and

the Court," *New York Times*, July 1, 2003, A1.

[28]*Bush v. Gore*, No. 00-949 (2000).

[29]See, however, James L. Gibson, Gregory A. Caldeira, and Lester Kenyatta Spence, "The Supreme Court and the U.S. Presidential Election of 2000," *British Journal of Political Science* 33 (2003): 535–56.

[30]David M. O'Brien, *Storm Center: The Supreme Court in American Politics,* 7th ed. (New York: Norton, 2005), 14–15.

[31]Ross Sandler and David Schoenbrod, *Democracy by Decree* (New Haven, Conn.: Yale University Press, 2003).

[32]Some of the references cited in the following sections are taken from Henry J. Abraham, "The Judicial Function Under the Constitution," *News for Teachers of Political Science* 41 (Spring 1984): 12–14; see also Louis Michael Seidman, *Our Unsettled Constitution* (New Haven, Conn.: Yale University Press, 2002).

[33]Abraham, "The Judicial Function," 14.

[34]Alexander M. Bickel, *The Supreme Court and the Idea of Progress* (New Haven, Conn.: Yale University Press, 1978), 173–81; see also Antonin Scalia, *A Matter of Interpretation* (Princeton, N.J.: Princeton University Press, 1997).

[35]Abraham, "The Judicial Function," 13.

[36]*Colegrove v. Green*, 328 U.S. 549 (1946).

[37]*Baker v. Carr*, 369 U.S. 186 (1962).

[38]Frank H. Easterbrook, "Do Liberals and Conservatives Differ in Judicial Activism?" *University of Colorado Law Review* 73 (2002): 1401.

[39]Randy E. Barnett, "Is the Rehnquist Court an 'Activist' Court? The Commerce Clause Cases," *University of Colorado Law Review* 73 (2002): 1275.

[40]Quoted in Linda Greenhouse, "The Justices Decide Who's in Charge," *New York Times*, June 27, 1999, sect. 4, p. 1.

[41]Epstein and Knight, *The Choices Justices Make*; see also Mark Tushnet, *A Court Divided* (New York: W. W. Norton, 2005).

[42]*Vieth v. Jubelirer*, 504 U.S. 267 (2004).

[43]Quoted in Curtis, *Law and Large as Life*, 157.

CHAPTER 15

[1]E. E. Schattschneider, *The Semisovereign People* (New York: Holt, Rinehart and Winston, 1960).

[2]Aaron Wildausky, *The Politics of the Budgetary Process*, 4th ed. (Glenview, Ill.: Scott Foresman & Co., 1984).

[3]John W. Kingdon, *Agendas, Alternatives, and Public Policies*, 2nd ed. (New York: Longman, 2002).

[4]James Kuhnhenn, "Lawmakers Fear Another Senior Citizens' Revolt Against Medicare Bill," Knight Ridder newspapers, November 23, 2003; Internet copy.

[5]The section titled "Efficiency Through Government Intervention" relies substantially on Alan Stone, *Regulation and Its Alternatives* (Washington, D.C.: Congressional Quarterly Press, 1982).

[6]See Marc Allen Eisner, *Regulatory Politics in Transition*, 2d ed. (Baltimore: Johns Hopkins University Press, 1999).

[7]Paul Portney, "Beware of the Killer Clauses Inside the GOP's 'Contract,'" *The Washington Post National Weekly Edition*, January 23–29, 1995, 21.

[8]See Richard A. Harris and Sidney M. Milkis, *The Politics of Regulatory Change* (New York: Oxford University Press, 1996).

[9]Lawrence E. Mitchell, *Corporate Irresponsibility* (New Haven, Conn.: Yale University Press, 2003).

[10]H. Peyton Young, *Equity: In Theory and Practice* (Princeton, N.J.: Princeton University Press, 1995).

[11]"Hill Foes of New Clean Air Rules Unite Behind Moratorium Bill," *Congressional Quarterly Weekly Report*, Spring 1998 (Washington, D.C.: Congressional Quarterly Press, 1998), 61.

[12]See Thomas Streeter, *Selling the Air* (Chicago: University of Chicago Press, 1996); Robert McChesney, *The Problem of the Media* (New York: Monthly Review Press, 2004).

[13]See Christopher J. Bosso, *Environment, Inc.: From Grassroots to Beltway* (Lawrence: University Press of Kansas, 2005).

[14]Rachel Carson, *The Silent Spring* (Boston: Houghton Mifflin, 1962); see also Lester R. Brown, *Plan B2.0: Rescuing a Planet Under Stress and a Civilization in Trouble* (New York: W. W. Norton, 2006).

[15]Robert B. Keiter, *Keeping Faith with Nature* (New Haven, Conn.: Yale University Press, 2003).

[16]*U.S. News & World Report*, June 30, 1975, 25.

[17]*Whitman v. American Trucking Association*, No. 99-1257 (2001).

[18]See Walter A. Rosenbaum, *Environmental Politics and Policy*, 6th ed. (Washington, D.C.: Congressional Quarterly Press, 2004); Norman J. Vig and Michael E. Kraft, eds., *Environmental Policy: New Directions for the Twenty-First Century* (Washington, D.C.: Congressional Quarterly Press, 2003).

[19]See Robert Lekachman, *The Age of Keynes* (New York: Random House, 1966); see also Richard Kopke, Geoffrey M. B. Tootell, and Robert K. Trist, eds., *The Macroeconomics of Fiscal Policy* (Cambridge, Mass.: MIT Press, 2006).

[20]See Bruce Bartlett, *Reaganomics: Supply-Side Economics* (Westport, Conn.: Arlington House, 1981).

[21]See Richard Duncan, *The Dollar Crisis: Causes, Consequences, Cures*, rev. ed. (New York: John Wiley & Sons, 2005).

[22]See Allen Schick, *The Federal Budget*, rev. ed. (Washington, D.C.: Brookings Institution Press, 2000).

[23]U.S. Senate clerk, 2002.

[24]Martin Mayer, *FED: The Inside Story of How the World's Most Powerful Financial Institution Drives the Markets* (New York: Free Press, 2001).

CHAPTER 16

[1]Quoted in E. J. Dionne Jr., "Reflecting on 'Reform,'" *Washington Post*, web download, February 15, 2004.

[2]Press releases of House Committee on Ways and Means and National Conference of State Legislatures, September 19 and June 26, 2002, respectively.

[3]Michael Harrington, *The Other America: Poverty in the United States* (New York: Macmillan, 1962); see also James T. Patterson, *America's Struggle Against Poverty in the Twentieth Century* (Cambridge, Mass.: Harvard University Press, 2000).

[4]Charles Murray, *Losing Ground: American Social Policy, 1950–1980* (New York: Basic Books, 1984).

[5]Signe-Mary McKernan and Caroline Ratcliffe, "Events That Trigger Poverty Entries and Exits," *Social Science Quarterly* 86 (2005): 1146–69.

[6]See Katherine S. Newman, *No Shame in My Game* (New York: Alfred A. Knopf and Russell Sage Foundation, 1999), 41.

[7] V. O. Key Jr., *The Responsible Electorate* (Cambridge, Mass.: Belknap Press of Harvard University, 1966), 43.

[8] Everett Carll Ladd, *American Political Parties* (New York: Norton, 1970), 205.

[9] Institute on Taxation and Economic Policy poll, 2002.

[10] For a general overview of 1950s and 1960s policy disputes, see James Sundquist, *Politics and Policy* (Washington, D.C.: Brookings Institution, 1968).

[11] See Jason DeParle, *American Dream: Three Women, Ten Kids, and a Nation's Drive to End Welfare* (New York: Penguin, 2005).

[12] Quoted in Malcolm Gladwell, "The Medicaid Muddle," *The Washington Post National Weekly Edition*, January 16–22, 1995, 31.

[13] Jill Quadagno, *One Nation, Uninsured: Why the United States Has No National Health Insurance* (New York: Oxford University Press, 2005).

[14] Alberto Alesina and Edward Glaeser, *Fighting Poverty in the U.S. and Europe* (New York: Oxford University Press, 2006).

[15] Robert D. Ebel, Tuan Minh Le, and Zicheng Li Swift, "National Tax Levels and the Rich vs. the Poor," publication of the Tax Policy Center, Washington, D.C., June 6, 2005.

[16] Paul Krugman, "Hey, Lucky Duckies," *New York Times*, December 3, 2002, A31.

[17] Said of George H.W. Bush at the 1988 Democratic Convention. The quote is variously attributed to Ann Richards or Jim Hightower.

[18] Based on Organization for Economic Cooperation and Development (OECD) data, 2006; see Douglas S. Reed, *On Equal Terms: The Constitutional Politics of Educational Opportunity* (Princeton, N.J.: Princeton University Press, 2003).

[19] Kaiser Family Foundation/Washington Post/Kennedy School of Government poll, September 1999.

[20] See John E. Chubb and Terry M. Moe, *Politics, Markets, and America's Schools* (Washington, D.C.: Brookings Institution, 1990); Tony Wagner and Thomas Vander Ark, *Making the Grade* (New York: Routledge, 2001).

[21] See Jeffrey R. Henig, *Rethinking School Choice* (Princeton, N.J.: Princeton University Press, 1995).

[22] Phi Delta Kappa/Gallup poll, 2002.

[23] Press release, Congressman John Boehner, January 4, 2003.

[24] Phi Delta Kappa/Gallup poll, 2005.

[25] Stanley Feldman and John Zaller, "The Political Culture of Ambivalence: Ideological Responses to the Welfare State," *American Journal of Political Science* 36, no. 1 (1992): 268–307.

[26] Robert E. Lane, "Market Justice, Political Justice," *American Political Science Review* 80 (1986): 383.

CHAPTER 17

[1] American Assembly Report (co-sponsored by the Council on Foreign Relations), *Rethinking America's Security* (New York: Harriman, 1991), 8.

[2] See Mr. X. (George Kennan), "The Sources of Soviet Conduct," *Foreign Affairs* 25 (July 1947): 566–82.

[3] David M. Barrett, *Uncertain Warriors: Lyndon Johnson and His Vietnam Advisors* (Lawrence: University Press of Kansas, 1993); see also Stanley Karnow, *Vietnam: A History* (New York: Penguin, 1983).

[4] See Mark Sauter and James Carafano, *Homeland Security* (New York: McGraw-Hill, 2005).

[5] West Point speech, June 1, 2002; for an opposing view, see Gary Hart, *The Shield and the Cloak: The Security of the Commons* (New York: Oxford University Press, 2006).

[6] PIPA-Knowledge Network survey, October 29–November 10, 2003.

[7] See Ole Holsti, *Public Opinion and American Foreign Policy* (Ann Arbor: University of Michigan Press, 1996); Richard Sobel, *The Impact of Public Opinion on U.S. Foreign Policy Since Vietnam* (New York: Oxford University Press, 2001).

[8] George C. Wilson, *This War Really Matters: Inside the Fight for Defense Dollars* (Washington, D.C.: Congressional Quarterly Press, 2000).

[9] U.S. government data, various agencies, 2006.

[10] *The World Competitiveness Yearbook* (Lausanne, Switzerland: International Institute for Management Development, 2006).

[11] American Assembly Report, *Rethinking America's Security*, 9.

[12] Manfred B. Steger, *Globalism: The New Market Philosophy* (New York: Rowman & Littlefield, 2002).

[13] Ted C. Fishman, *China, Inc.: How the Rise of the Next Superpower Challenges America and the World* (New York: Scribner, 2005).

[14] See Joseph S. Nye, *Soft Power: The Means to Success in World Politics* (New York: PublicAffairs, 2003); Michael Lind, *The American Way of Strategy* (New York: Oxford University Press, 2006).

[15] U.S. Department of State data, 2006.

[16] Hobart Rowen, "The Budget: Fact and Fiction," *The Washington Post National Weekly Edition*, January 16–22, 1995, 5.

[17] Tom Masland, "Going Down the Aid 'Rathole'?" *Newsweek*, December 5, 1994, 39.

[18] Philip Gordon, "September 11 and American Foreign Policy," website of the Brookings Institution, downloaded on June 21, 2002. The chapter's last section is based substantially on Gordon's observations.

CHAPTER 18

[1] John Steinbeck, *Travels with Charley: In Search of America* (1962). Taken from *The Columbia World of Quotations* (1996), no. 55679.

[2] *Houston Chronicle*, November 15, 2005.

[3] Terry G. Jordan, *German Seed in Texas Soil: Immigrant Farmers in Nineteenth Century Texas* (Austin: University of Texas Press, 1966).

[4] Robert A. Calvert and Arnold DeLeon, *The History of Texas* (Arlington Heights, Ill.: Harland Davidson, 1990), 99–100.

[5] David Easton, *The Political System* (New York: Knopf, 1953), 129.

[6] Daniel J. Elazar, *American Federalism: A View from the States* (New York: HarperCollins, 1984).

[7] Ibid., 90.

[8] Ibid.

[9] Ibid., 86.

[10] See Elazar, *American Federalism*; Terry Jordan, "The Imprint of the Upper and Lower South on Mid-Nineteenth-Century Texas," *Annals of the Association of American Geographers* 57 (December 1967): 667–90.

[11] Jordan, "Imprint of the Upper and Lower South," 668.

[12] Kenneth R. Mladenka and Kim Q. Hill, *Texas Government: Politics and Economics*, 2d ed. (Pacific Grove, Calif.: Brooks/Cole, 1989), 56.

[13] Joan W. Moore and Harry Pachon, *Mexican Americans*, 2d ed. (Englewood Cliffs, N.J.: Prentice Hall, 1976), 135–36.

[14]Platforms of Beauford Jester, 1946 and 1948; Allan Shivers, 1950, 1952, and 1954; Price Daniel, 1956, 1958, and 1960; see James R. Soukup, Clifton McCleskey, and Harry Holloway, *Party and Factional Division in Texas* (Austin: University of Texas Press, 1964).

[15]www.texasgop.org.

[16]Roy Morris, *Sheridan: The Life and Wars of General Phil Sheridan* (New York: Crown, 1992).

[17]T. R. Fehrendbach, *Lone Star: A History of Texas and the Texans* (New York: Collier, 1980), 276–78.

CHAPTER 19

[1]Wilbourn E. Benton, *Texas: Its Government and Politics*, 2d ed. (Englewood Cliffs, N.J.: Prentice Hall, 1966), 33.

[2]I. R. Fehrendbach, *Lone Star: A History of Texas and the Texans*, (New York: Collier, 1980), 146–47.

[3]Ibid., 206.

[4]Ibid., 222 23.

[5]Ibid., 411–14.

[6]Ibid., 434.

[7]Ibid., 436.

[8]Ibid.

[9]Donald S. Lutz, "Toward a Theory of Constitutional Amendment," *American Political Science Review* 88 (June 1994): 355–70.

[10]Texas Constitution, article 1, section 3a.

[11]Lutz, "Toward a Theory," 359.

[12]Ibid.

[13]*Book of the States 2005* (Lexington, Ky.: Council of State Governments, 2005), vol. 37, table 1.1, p. 12.

[14]Lutz, "Toward a Theory."

[15]Texas Constitution, article 117, section 2.

[16]Lutz, "Toward a Theory," 359.

[17]Ibid., 360.

[18]Ibid.

[19]Number of amendments and dates of elections: Secretary of State, *Vote on Proposed Amendments to Texas Constitution, 1875–November 1993* (Austin: State of Texas, 1993), 12–29. Data for 1995–2003: Secretary of State website, www.sos.state.tx.us.

[20]Constitutional amendments ballot, general election November 7, 1978, tax relief amendment, H.J.R. 1.

[21]*Book of the States 2003* (Lexington, Ky.: Council of State Governments, 2003), vol. 35, table 1.1, p. 10.

[22]*Houston Chronicle*, January 8, 1974.

CHAPTER 20

[1]*Texas Almanac and State Industrial Guide, 1970–1971* (Dallas: A. H. Belo, 1969), 529.

[2]*Beare v. Smith*, 321 F. Supp. 1100.

[3]*Texas Almanac and State Industrial Guide, 1974–1975* (Dallas: A. H. Belo, 1973), 529.

[4]*Book of the States* (Lexington, Ky.: Council of State Governments, 1994), 30:23, Table 5.6.

[5]*Nixon v. Herndon et al.*, 273 U.S. 536 (1927); *Nixon v. Condon et al.*, 286 U.S. 73 (1932).

[6]*Grovey v. Townsend*, 295 U.S. 45 (1935).

[7]*Smith v. Allwright*, 321 U.S. 649 (1944). See also *United States v. Classic*, 313 U.S. 299 (1941).

[8]George McKenna, *The Drama of Democracy: American Government and Politics*, 2d ed. (Guilford, Conn.: Dushkin, 1994), 129.

[9]Wilbourn E. Benton, *Texas Politics: Constraints and Opportunities*, 5th ed. (Chicago: Nelson-Hall, 1984), 65.

[10]Population Estimates and Projections Program, Texas State Data Center, Department of Rural Sociology, Texas A&M University System, *Projections of the Population of Texas and Counties in Texas by Age, Sex, Race/Ethnicity for 1990 to 2030*, February 1994.

[11]Robert R. Brischetto, unpublished report, Southwest Voter Research Institute, San Antonio, 1993; estimate for 1996, Southwest Voter Research Institute, *Southwest Voter Research Notes* X, (no. 1), 3.

[12]C. Richard Hoffstedder, "Inter-Party Competition and Electoral Turnout: The Case of Indiana," *American Journal of Political Science* 17 (May 1973): 351–66.

[13]Norman R. Luttbeg, "Differential Voting Turnout Decline in the American States," *Social Science Quarterly* 65 (March 1984): 60–73.

[14]Ibid.

[15]Alexis de Tocqueville, *Democracy in America*, trans. George Lawrence, ed. J. P. Mayer (Garden City, N.J.: Anchor Books, 1969), 190–91.

[16]Molly Ivins, *Molly Ivins Can't Say That, Can She?* (New York: Random House, 1991), 58.

[17]Adapted from Ronald Hrebenar, Melanee Cherry, and Kathanne Green, "Utah: Church and Corporate Power in the Nation's Most Conservative State," in *Interest Group Politics in the American West*, ed. Ronald Hrebenar and Clive Thomas (Salt Lake City: University of Utah Press, 1987), 117.

[18]Clive S. Thomas and Ronald J. Hrebenar, "Interest Groups in State Politics," in *Politics in the American State*, 5th ed., ed. Virginia Gray, Herbert Jacob, and Robert Albritton (Glenview, Ill.: Scott Foresman/Little Brown, 1990), 154.

[19]Molly Ivins, "Getting to the Grass Roots of the Problem," *Bryan-College Station Eagle*, July 13, 1995, A4. Reprinted by permission of Pan, Inc.

[20]Thomas R. Dye, *Politics in States and Communities*, 7th ed. (Englewood Cliffs, N.J.: Prentice Hall, 1991), 112–13.

[21]David F. Prindel, *Petroleum Politics and the Texas Railroad Commission* (Austin: University of Texas Press, 1981).

CHAPTER 21

[1]V. O. Key Jr., *Politics and Pressure Groups*, 4th ed. (New York: Thomas Y. Crowell, 1958), 331.

[2]Ibid.

[3]V. O. Key Jr., *Southern Politics in State and Nation* (New York: Knopf, 1949), 7.

[4]Soukup, McCleskey, and Holloway, *Party and Factional Division*, 6. (Austin: University of Texas Press, 1962), 6.

[5]V. O. Key Jr., *Southern Politics*, 225.

[6]Soukup, McCleskey, and Holloway, *Party and Factional Division*, 8.

[7]Ibid., 11.

[8]Douglas O. Weeks, *Texas Presidential Politics in 1952* (Austin: University of Texas, Institute of Public Affairs, 1953), 3–4.

[9]James A. Dyer, Arnold Vedlitz, and David B. Hill, "New Voters, Switchers, and Political Party Realignment in Texas," *Western Political Quarterly* 41 (March 1988): 164.

[10]Allan Turner, "Snapping Back: GOP Nipping on Heels of Yellow Dog Democrats," *Houston Chronicle*, March 5, 1995, 1D.

[11]Ibid.

[12]John Williams, "Yellow Dogs Lose Bite in East Texas," *Houston Chronicle*, November 18, 2002, 17A and 24A.

[13]James A. Dyer, Jan E. Leighley, and Arnold Vedlitz, "Party Identification and Public Opinion: Establishing a

Competitive Two Party System," in *Texas Reader,* ed. Tony Champagne and Ted Harpham (New York: Norton, 1997), 113–28.

[14]Walter D. Burnham, *The Current Crisis in American Politics* (Oxford: Oxford University Press, 1982).

[15]Texas secretary of state home page, http://www.sos. state.tx.us.

[16]James A. Anderson, Richard W. Murray, and Edward L. Farley, *Texas Politics: An Introduction,* 6th ed. (New York: HarperCollins, 1992), 34.

[17]Ann O. Bowman and Richard C. Kearney, *State and Local Government* (Boston: Houghton Mifflin, 1990), 158–59. See also Charles S. Bullock III and Loch K. Johnson, *Runoff Elections in the United States* (Chapel Hill: University of North Carolina Press, 1992).

[18]Norman D. Brown, *Hood, Bonnet and Little Brown Jug: Texas Politics, 1921–1928* (College Station: Texas A&M University Press, 1984).

[19]Ann O. Bowman and Richard C. Kearney, *State and Local Government,* 158–59. See also Charles S. Bullock III and Loch K. Johnson, *Runoff Elections in the United States,* 166.

[20]Michael Barone and Grant Ujifusa, *The Almanac of American Politics, 1994* (Washington, D.C.: National Journal, 1993), 1212.

[21]Ibid.

[22]Anderson, Murray, and Farley, *Texas Politics,* 44.

[23]Michael Barone and Grant Ujifusa, *Almanac of American Politics, 1994,* 1222 and 1257.

[24]Lobby Watch, "Texas Loan Stars Incurred $48 Million in Political Debts," www.tpj.org/lobby_Watch/latetrain.html.

CHAPTER 22

[1]Texas Constitution, 1876, art. 3, sec. 2.

[2]Council of State Governments, *Book of the States, 1997–98* (Lexington, Ky.: Council of State Governments, 1998), 68, Table 3.3.

[3]Malcolm E. Jewell and Samuel C. Patterson, *The Legislative Process in the United States* (New York: Random House, 1985), 21.

[4]Texas Constitution, art. 3, sec. 26.

[5]Leroy Hardy, Alan Heslop, and Stuart Anderson, *Reapportionment Politics* (Beverly Hills, Calif.: Sage, 1981), 18.

[6]Gordon E. Baker, *The Reapportionment Revolution: Representation, Political*

Power and the Supreme Court (New York: Random House, 1966).

[7]Wilbourn E. Benton, *Texas: Its Government and Politics,* 2d ed. (Englewood Cliffs, N.J.: Prentice Hall, 1966), 141.

[8]Texas Constitution, art. 3, sec. 28.

[9]Ibid., sec. 26a.

[10]*Baker v. Carr,* 369 U.S. 186 (1962).

[11]*Reynolds v. Sims,* 377 U.S. 533 (1964).

[12]*Kilgarlin v. Martin,* 1965.

[13]*Graves v. Barnes,* 343 F. Supp. 704 (W.D. Tex. 1972); *White v. Register,* 412 U.S. 755 (1973).

[14]*Bush, Governor of Texas et al. v. Vera et al.,* no. 94-805. Case decided on June 13, 1996.

[15]Ibid.

[16]*Hunt v. Cromartie,* no. 99-1864 (2001).

[17]Dye, *Politics in States and Communities,* 157.

[18]Harvey Tucker and Gary Halter, *Texas Legislative Almanac 2001* (Texas A&M University Press, 2001).

[19]Rich Jones, "State Legislatures," in *Book of the States, 1994–95,* 101.

[20]Harvey Tucker and Gary Halter, *Texas Legislative Almanac 1999.*

[21]Texans for Public Justice, http://www.tpj.org.

[22]Texas Secretary of State, Electoral Data, www.sos.states.tx.us.

[23]Gary C. Jacobson, *The Politics of Congressional Elections,* 3d ed. (New York: HarperCollins, 1992).

[24]Kevin A. Hill, "Does the Creation of Majority Black Districts Aid Republicans? An Analysis of the 1992 Congressional Election in Eight Southern States," *Journal of Politics* 57 (May 1995): 348–401.

[25]Samuel C. Patterson, "Legislative Politics in the States," in *Politics in the American States,* 6th ed., ed. Virginia Gray and Herbert Jacob (Washington, D.C.: Congressional Quarterly Press, 1996), 179–86.

[26]*Book of the States, 2004.*

[27]Lawrence W. Miller, *Legislative Turnover and Political Careers: A Study of Texas Legislators, 1969–75,* Ph.D. dissertation, Texas Tech University, 1977, 43–45.

[28]*Book of the States, 1994–95,* 29, Table A; see also the website of the National Conference of State Legislatures, http://www.ncsl.org.

[29]*Book of the States, 1994–95,* 27.

[30]Rich Jones, "State Legislatures," *Book of the States, 1994–95,* 99.

[31]*Book of the States, 1998–99,* 64–67, Table 7.2.

[32]Ibid., 123, Table 3.9.

[33]*Presiding Officers of the Texas Legislature, 1846–2002* (Austin: Texas Legislative Council, 2002).

[34]Interview with William P. Hobby, 1993, Texas A&M University, College Station.

[35]*Book of the States, 1998–99,* 48, Table 2.13.

[36]Ibid., 33, Table 2.9.

[37]Ibid., 48, Table 2.13.

[38]J. William Davis, *There Shall Also Be a Lieutenant Governor* (Austin: University of Texas, Institute of Public Affairs, 1967).

[39]Harvey Tucker, "Legislative Calendars and Workload Management in Texas," *Journal of Politics* 51 (August 1989): 633.

[40]Harvey J. Tucker, "Legislative Workload Congestion in Texas," *Journal of Politics* 49 (1987): 557.

[41]Ibid., 569.

[42]Ibid., 575.

[43]E. Lee Bernick and Charles W. Wiggins, "Legislative Norms in Eleven States," *Legislative Studies Quarterly* 7 (May 1983): 194–95.

[44]Ibid., 194.

[45]Citizens Conference on State Legislatures, *The Sometime Governments: A Critical Study of the Fifty American State Legislatures,* 2d ed. (Kansas City: Citizens Conference on State Legislatures, 1973).

[46]National Conference of State Legislatures, *State Legislature* 20 (November 1994), 5.

[47]Keith E. Hamm and Gary F. Moncrief, "Legislative Politics in the States," in *Politics in the American States: A Comparative Analysis,* 7th ed., ed. Virginia Gray, Russell L. Hanson, and Herbert Jacob (Washington, D.C.: Congressional Quarterly Press, 1999), 145, Table 5.1.

[48]See Norman R. Luttbeg, *Comparing the States* and *Communities: Politics, Government, and Policy in the United States* (Dubuque, Iowa: Eddie Bower Publishing, 1999), 242–43.

[49]Dye, *Politics in States and Communities,* 192.

[50]Ibid., 193.

[51]Ibid.

CHAPTER 23

[1]Thad L. Beyle, "Governors: The Middlemen and Women in Our Political System," in *Politics in the American*

States, 8th ed., ed. Virginia Gray and Russell l. Hanson (Washington, D.C.: Congressional Quarterly Press, 2004), 196.

[2]Ibid., 196.

[3]National Governors Association, www.nga.org/governors/.

[4]*Book of the States, 1998–99*, 20, Table 2.3.

[5]Thad Beyle, "Governors," 217.

[6]*Book of the States, 1994–95*, 66.

[7]Ibid.

[8]Bowman and Kearney, *State and Local Government*, 206.

[9]Benton, *Texas*, 222–24.

[10]Victor E. Harlow, *Harlow's History of Oklahoma*, 5th ed. (Norman, Okla.: Harlow, 1967), 294–315.

[11]Daniel R. Grant and Lloyd B. Omdahl, *State and Local Government in America* (Madison, Wis.: Brown & Benchmark, 1987), 260.

[12]S. M. Morehouse, *State Politics, Parties and Policy* (New York: Holt, Rinehart & Winston, 1981), 206.

[13]Thad Beyle, "Governors," 230.

[14]Ibid., 231.

[15]*Texas Almanac 1994–95*, 519.

[16]Thad Beyle, "Governors," 221.

[17]Ibid., 231.

[18]*Guide to Texas State Agencies* (Austin: University of Texas, Lyndon B. Johnson School of Public Affairs, 1994).

[19]Ibid.

[20]*Book of the States, 1998–99*, 22, Table 2.4

[21]Ibid.

[22]Thad Beyle, "Governors," 234–35.

[23]*Book of the States, 1998–99*, 20, Table 2.3.

[24]James Anderson, Richard W. Murray, and Edward L. Farley, *Texas Politics: An Introduction*, 6th ed. (New York: Harper Collin, 1992), 122.

[25]Deborah K. Wheeler, *Two Men, Two Governors, Two Pardons: A Study of Pardon Policy of Governor Miriam Ferguson*. Unpublished copyrighted paper, presented at State Historical Society Meeting, March 1998, Austin, Texas.

[26]Bill Hobby, "Speaking of Pardons, Texas Has Had Its Share." *Houston Chronicle*, February 18, 2001, 4c.

[27]Thad Beyle, "Governors," 237.

[28]Legislative Budget Board, *Fiscal Size Up 1998–99 Biennium: Texas State Services* (Austin, Texas: Publisher), 4–6.

[29]Ibid., 4–7.

[30]*Book of the States, 1996–97*, 33–34.

[31]*Fiscal Size Up 2002–03*, 242.

[32]Texas Sunset Advisory Commission, *Guide to the Texas Sunset Process, 1997* (Austin, Texas: Publisher), 1997: 1.

[33]Ibid.

CHAPTER 24

[1]Herbert Jacob, "Courts: The Least Visible Branch," in *Politics in the American States*, 8th ed., ed. Virginia Gray and Russell L. Hanson (Washington, D.C.: Congressional Quarterly Press, 2004), 332.

[2]Ibid.

[3]Dye, *Politics in States and Communities*, 8th ed., 227.

[4]Ibid.

[5]Ibid.

[6]Ibid.

[7]Ibid., 228.

[8]Herbert Jacob, "Courts," 253.

[9]Ibid., 256–58.

[10]Office of Court Administration, Texas Judicial Council, *Texas Judicial System Annual Report* (Austin: Office of Court Administration, 2003).

[11]Office of Court Administration, Texas Judicial Council, *Texas Judicial System Annual Report* (Austin: Office of Court Administration, 1994), 31–33.

[12]*Book of the States, 1998–99*, 131–32, Table 4.2.

[13]Ibid., 186–89.

[14]See *Book of the States, 2004–2005*, 318, Table 5.6

[15]Anderson, Murray, and Farley, *Texas Politics*, 246–47.

[16]"A Closer Look at Harris County's Vote," *Houston Chronicle*, November 14, 2002, 32A.

[17]Anthony Champagne, "Campaign Contributions in Texas Supreme Court Races," *Crime, Law and Social Change* 17 (1992): 91–106.

[18]Gibson and Robison, *Government and Politics in the Lone Star State*, 281.

[19]Kraemer and Newell, *Texas Politics*, 3d ed. (New York: West, 1987), 281.

[20]Herbert Jacob, "The Effect of Institutional Differences in the Recruitment Process: The Case of State Judges," *Journal of Public Law* 33, no. 113 (1964): 104–19.

[21]Bradley Canon, "The Impact of Formal Selection Processes on Characteristics of Judges—Reconsidered," *Law and Society Review* 13 (May 1972): 570–93.

[22]Richard Watson and Rondal G. Downing, *The Politics of the Bench and Bar: Judicial Selection Under the Missouri Nonpartisan Court Plan* (New York: John Wiley, 1969).

[23]Dye, *Politics in States and Communities*, 8th ed., 236.

[24]William Jenkins, "Retention Elections: Who Wins When No One Loses," *Judicature* 61 (1977): 78–86.

[25]William K. Hall and Larry T. Aspin, "What Twenty Years of Judicial Retention and Elections Have Told Us," *Judicature* 70 (1987): 340–47.

[26]Craig F. Emmert and Henry R. Glick, "The Selection of Supreme Court Judges," *American Politics Quarterly* 19 (October 1988): 444–65.

[27]*Book of the States, 1998–99*, 138–48, Table 4.5.

[28]Commission on Judicial Conduct, *Annual Report, 1994* (Austin: Commission on Judicial Conduct, State of Texas, 1994).

[29]Office of Court Administration, Texas Judicial Council, *Texas Judicial System Annual Report* (1994), 173, 179.

[30]Interview with District Court Judge John Delaney, Brazos County Courthouse, November 1995.

[31]*Texas Code of Criminal Procedure*, arts. 19.01–20.22.

[32]"Murder Case Testing Grand Jury Selection," *Houston Chronicle*, March 2, 2002, 1A, 16A.

[33]Texas Criminal Justice Policy Council, *Biennial Report to the Governor and the 78th Texas Legislature*, January 2001.

[34]Texas Criminal Justice Policy Council, *Testing the Case for More Incarceration in Texas: The Record So Far* (Austin: State of Texas, 1995), 43.

[35]*Houston Chronicle*, February 9, 2001, 6.

[36]*Houston Chronicle*, February 6, 2001, 6.

[37]*Houston Chronicle*, February 4, 2001, 1A, 24A–27A.

[38]Death Penalty Information Center, www.deathpenaltyinfo.org.

CHAPTER 25

[1]Federal Advisory Commission on Intergovernmental Relations, *State and Local Roles in the Federal System: A–88* (Washington, D.C.: U.S. Government Printing Office, 1982), 59.

[2]Ibid.

[3]Ibid., 59, Table 20.

[4]Terrell Blodgett, *Texas Home Rule Charters* (Austin: Texas Municipal League, 1994), 1.

[5]See *Vernon's Texas Statutes and Codes Annotated*, vol. 1, 5.001–5.003.

[6]Texas Municipal League, *Handbook for Mayors and Councilmembers in General Law Cities* (Austin: Texas Municipal League, 1994).

[7]"Local Government," *Vernon's Texas Statutes and Codes Annotated*, vol. 1, 9.001–9.008.

[8]Blodgett, *Texas Home Rule Charters*, 4.

[9]Ibid., 113–14.

[10]"Local Government," *Vernon's Texas Statutes and Codes Annotated*, vol. 1, 7.005.

[11]David L. Martin, *Running City Hall: Municipal Administration in the United States* (Tuscaloosa: University of Alabama Press, 1990), 21–22.

[12]"Local Government," *Vernon's Texas Statutes and Codes Annotated*, vol. 1, 42.021.

[13]James A. Svara, *Official Leadership in the City: Patterns of Conflict and Cooperation* (New York: Oxford University Press, 1990), ch. 2 and 3.

[14]Blodgett, *Texas Home Rule Charters*, 30–31.

[15]Ibid., 39.

[16]Svara, *Official Leadership in the City.*

[17]Richard Stillman, *The Rise of the City Manager: A Public Professional in Local Government* (Albuquerque: University of New Mexico Press, 1974), 15.

[18]Bradley Robert Rice, *Progressive Cities: The Commission Government Movement in America, 1901–1920* (Austin: University of Texas Press, 1977), 12.

[19]Ibid., 109.

[20]Ibid., 85.

[21]Ibid., 52.

[22]Tulsa City Charter, June 1954, 6.

[23]For a good discussion of electoral systems in American cities, see Joseph Zimmerman, *The Federal City: Community Control in Large Cities* (New York: St. Martin's Press, 1972), ch. 4.

[24]Blodgett, *Texas Home Rule Charters*, 46–47.

[25]See http://fairvote.org/cumultive/texas.html for more information.

[26]Martin, *Running City Hall*, 78, see also *Computerizing a Cambridge Tradition: An Analysis of Cambridge's 1991 City Council Election Count Using a Computer Program* (1992), Center for Voting and Democracy, 6905 Fifth St., NW, Suite 200, Washington, D.C.

[27]Svara, *Official Leadership in the City*, 136; see also Lyndon B. Johnson School of Public Affairs, *Local Government Election Systems*, Policy Research Report No. 62 (Austin: University of Texas Press, 1984), 46–55, 145–46.

[28]Blodgett, *Texas Home Rule Charters*, 48.

[29]International City Management Association, *Municipal Year Book* (Washington, D.C.: International City Management Association, 1988), 17.

[30]"Elections," *Vernon's Texas Statutes and Codes Annotated*, 41.003.

[31]See David R. Johnson, John A. Booth, and Richard J. Harris, *The Politics of San Antonio: Community Progress and Power* (Lincoln: University of Nebraska Press, 1983); Richard A. Smith, "How Business Failed Dallas," in *Governing Texas: Documents and Readings*, 2d ed., ed. Fred Gantt Jr. et al. (New York: Thomas Y. Crowell, 1970), 122–29.

[32]"Elections," *Vernon's Texas Statutes and Codes Annotated*, 41.003.

[33]U.S. Department of Commerce, Bureau of the Census, *1997 Census of Governments: Government Organization*, vol. 1, no. 1 (Washington, D.C.: U.S. Government Printing Office, 1997), 18, Table 13.

[34]U.S. Census of Population 2000, www.census.gov.

[35]Gary M. Halter and Gerald L. Dauthery, "The County Commissioners Court in Texas," in *Governing Texas: Documents and Readings*, 3d ed., ed. Fred Gantt Jr. et al. (New York: Thomas Y. Crowell, 1974), 340–50.

[36]*Avery v. Midland County*, 88 S. Ct. 1114 (1968).

[37]Robert E. Norwood and Sabrina Strawn, *Texas County Government: Let the People Choose*, 2d ed. (Austin: Texas Research League, 1984).

[38]Ibid., 24; see also John A. Gilmartin and Joe M. Rothe, *County Government in Texas: A Summary of the Major Offices and Officials*, Issue No. 2 (College Station: Texas Agricultural Extension Service).

[39]Norwood and Strawn, *Texas County Government*, 27.

[40]Information supplied by the Texas Association of Counties, Austin.

[41]Property tax records of the Brazos County Central Appraisal District, 1673 Briarcrest Dr., Bryan, TX.

[42]See Wilborn E. Benton, *Texas: Its Government and Politics*, 2d ed. (Englewood Cliffs, N.J.: Prentice Hall, 1966), 317–81.

[43]See Virginia Pernod, *Special District, Special Purposes: Fringe Governments and Urban Problems in the Houston Area* (College Station: Texas A&M University Press, 1984).

[44]*2002 Census of Governments* 2:17, Table 3.

[45]Texas Legislative Budget Board, http://www.lbb.state.tx.us.

[46]Nancy Frank, *Charter Schools: Experiments in Reform, an Update* (Austin: Texas Legislative Budget Board, Public Education Team, 1995).

[47]*2002 Census of Governments* 2:17, Table 15.

[48]Texas Legislative Budget Board.

[49]Secretary of State, State of Texas, *Votes on Proposed Amendments to the Texas Constitution, 1875–November 1993* (Austin: Secretary of State, 1994), 73.

[50]*Dallas Morning News*, January 12, 1994, 1A.

[51]Secretary of State, State of Texas, *Votes on Proposed Amendments*, 28.

CREDITS

PART OPENERS:

p. 2: © Hulton Archive/Getty Images and The National Archives (composite); p. 162, 298, 434: © AP/Wide World Photos

Chapter 1

6: © Spencer Platt/Getty Images; 7: © Damian Dovarganes/Pool/Reuters/Corbis Images; 11: Library of Congress, Prints & Photographs Division, [LC-USZC4-2474]; 13: © Spencer Platt/; 15: © Ernest C. Withers, Courtesy, Panopticon Gallery, Waltham, MA; 18: © AP/Wide World Photos; 21: © Bob Daemmrich/Image Works; 22: Collection, The Supreme Court Historical Society. Photo by Richard Strauss, Smithsonian Institution. 23: © Bob Daemmrich/Image Works; 25: USHMM, courtesy of The National Archives; 29: © John Neubauer/PhotoEdit

Chapter 2

p. 36: © Jim Wells; p. 37: © The Granger Collection; p. 38: © Bettmann/Corbis Images; p. 40: Library of Congress, Prints & Photographs Division; p. 41, 43: © Bettmann/Corbis Images; p. 45: © Burstein Collection/Corbis Images; p. 49: © The Granger Collection; p. 56: Library of Congress, Prints & Photographs Division, [LC-USZ62-54940]; p. 57: © The Granger Collection; p. 59: Architect of the Capitol

Chapter 3

p. 68: © Don Ryan/AP/Wide World Photos; p. 69: The Granger Collection; p. 72: © Archivo Iconografico, S.A./Corbis Images; p. 76: © The Granger Collection; p. 78: © The Granger Collection; p. 79: "Home, Sweet Home," by Winslow Homer/Christie's Images; p. 81: © Bettmann/Corbis Images; p. 82: Library of Congress, Prints & Photographs Division; p. 83: Houghton Library of the Harvard College Library; p. 85: © Rick Wilking/Reuters/Corbis Images; p. 89: © AP/Wide World Photos

Chapter 4

p. 99: © AP/Wide World Photos; p. 100: Library of Congress, Prints & Photographs Division, [LC-USZ62-47817]; p. 103: © AP/Wide World Photos; p. 105: © Paul Conklin/PhotoEdit; pp. 108, 111: © AP/Wide World Photos; p. 113: © Greg Gibson/Wide World Photos; p. 124: © Paul Conklin/PhotoEdit; p. 125: © AP/Wide World Photos

Chapter 5

p. 133: Charles Moore/Black Star; p. 134: © Library of Congress; p. 136: © Peter Bryon/PhotoEdit; p. 141(both): © AP/Wide World Photos; p. 143: © Rob Lewine//Corbis Images; p. 148: © AP/Wide World Photos; p. 153: © Jay Mallin/Impact Visuals; p. 155: © Danny Moloshok/AP/Wide World Photos

Chapter 6

p. 167: © AP/Wide World Photos; p. 168: © Joel Stettenheim/Corbis Images; pp. 171, 172: © Bettmann/Corbis Images; p. 175: © Charles Gupton/Corbis Images; p. 176: © Ann Johansson/Corbis Images; p. 180: © Charles E. Rotkin/Corbis Images; p. 183: © Mario Tama/Getty Images; p. 184: © AP/Wide World Photos

Chapter 7

p. 190: Culver Pictures; p. 192: © The Granger Collection; p. 194: © AP/The Charlotte Observer/AP/Wide World Photos; p. 196: © Jonathon Nourok/Stone/Getty Images; p. 202: © Frederic Larson/Corbis Images; p. 205: © Corbis Images; p. 207(top): © The Granger Collection; p. 207 (bottom): © AP/Wide World Photos

Chapter 8

p. 214: © Jeff Roberson/AP/Wide World Photos; pp. 216, 217: Library of Congress; p. 218: © Bettmann/Corbis Images; p. 222: © I.P.O.L., NYC; p. 223: Courtesy of the Ronald Reagan Presidential Library; pp. 227, 229: © AP/Wide World Photos; p. 230: © Alex Wong/Getty Images; p. 235: © Allan Tannenbaum; p. 239: © AP/Wide World Photos

Chapter 9

p. 246: www.aarp.org reprinted with permission.; p. 249: © Getty Images; p. 251: Library of Congress, Prints & Photographs Division; p. 253: © Noah Berger/AP/Wide World Photos; pp. 254-256: AP/Wide World Photos; p. 260: © Jonathan Blair/Corbis Images; p. 262: © AP/Wide World Photos; p. 266: © Chip Somodevilla/Getty Images

Chapter 10

p. 274: © Thorne Anderson/Corbis Images; p. 275: © Stock Montage; p. 280: © Brown Brothers; p. 281: © AP/Wide World Photos; p. 284(top): © Patrick Olear/PhotoEdit; p. 284 (bottom): © AP/Wide World Photos; p. 289: © AFP/Getty Images; p. 291: © AP/Wide World Photos; p. 294: © Jeff Greenberg/PhotoEdit

Chapter 11

p. 302: © Vanessa Vick/Photo Researchers; p. 306: © Bettmann/Corbis Images; p. 309: © James Leynse/Corbis Images; p. 312: © Dennis Cook/AP/Wide World Photos; p. 315: © AP/Wide World Photos; p. 316: © Douglas Graham/Corbis Images; p. 319: © Johathan Nourok/PhotoEdit; p. 325: © Bob Daemmrich/Corbis Images; p. 327: © Bettmann/Corbis Images; p. 329: © John Van Hasselt/Corbis Images

Chapter 12

p. 338: © AP/Wide World Photos; p. 341: © Christie's Images/Corbis Images; p. 342: © UPI/Bettmann/Corbis

Images; p. 343: © James P. Blair; p. 347: © AP/Wide World Photos; p. 354: © UPI/Bettmann/Corbis Images; p. 356: © AP/Wide World Photos; p. 360: © Rene Burri/Magnum Photos; pp. 363, 367: © AP/Wide World Photos

Chapter 13
p. 374: © AP/Wide World Photos; p. 380: © Bob Daemmrich/Stock Boston; p. 381: © Royalty-free/Corbis; p. 383: © Bettmann/Corbis Images; p. 388: © Don Perdue/Getty Images; p. 392: © Wally McNamee/Woodfin Camp & Assoc.; p. 394: White House Historical Association (White House Collection) (22); p. 395: © Mark Wilson/Getty Images

Chapter 14
p. 404: © AP/Wide World Photos; p. 408: © Collection of the Supreme Court of the United States; p. 413: © AP/Wide World Photos; p. 414: Collection, The Supreme Court Historical Society. Photo by Steve Petteway, Supreme Court; p. 415: © AP/Wide World Photos; p. 421: © Michael C. York/AP/Wide World Photos; p. 426: © Landon Nordeman/Getty Images; p. 429(right): © AP/Wide World Photos; p. 430: Library of Congress

Chapter 15
p. 440: © Damian Dovarganes/Wide World Photos; p. 442: By courtesy of the National Portrait Gallery, London.; p. 445: © Najlah Feanny/Corbis Images; p. 447: © AP/Wide World Photos; p. 448: © Reed Saxon/AP/Wide World Photos; p. 450: © Alfred Eisenstaedt//Time Life Pictures//Getty Images; p. 451: © John M. Roberts; p. 453: © Win McNamee/Getty Images; p. 466: © Mandel Ngan/AFP/Getty Images

Chapter 16
p. 474: © Michael Newman/PhotoEdit; p. 476: Library of Congress, Prints & Photographs Division, [LC-USZ62-117121]; p. 477: © William Johnson/Stock Boston; p. 480: © Dana Fineman-Appel/Corbis; p. 481: © Stephen Jaffe/Getty Images; p. 482: © Evan Agostini/Getty Images; p. 486: © Glenn Kulbako/Index Stock Imagery; p. 486: © Sally Weigand/Index Stock Imagery; p. 488: © Bob Daemmrich/Stock Boston; p. 490: Bob Daemmrich/The Image Works

Chapter 17
p. 500: © AP/Wide World Photos; p. 501: Michael Barson Collection/Past Perfect; p. 503: Bettmann/Corbis; p. 506: © Robert Nickelsberg/Getty Images; p. 512: © Mathew B. Brady/Corbis Images; p. 514: © Ed Clark/Life Magazine/Time & Life Pictures/Getty Images; p. 515: © Wolfgang Kaehler/Corbis Images; p. 517: Photo Courtesy of U.S. Army; p. 520: © AP/Wide World Photos

Chapter 18
p. 526: © Andy Jackson/Alamy; p. 532: TxDOT Photo for Mission Espiritu Santo; p. 533: © Kevin Stillman/TxDOT; pp. 535, 524: Courtesy of Gary Halter

Chapter 19
p. 550 (top): Photo by J. Griffis Smith/TxDOT; p. 550 (bottom): Courtesy of Gary Halter; p. 553: Courtesy, Texas House of Representatives

Chapter 20
p. 572: © Bob Daemmrich/PhotoEdit; p. 574: Courtesy, Texas House of Representatives; p. 576: © AP/Wide World Photos; p. 579: Courtesy of Gary Halter; p. 582: © Bob Daemmrich/Image Works; p. 584: Courtesy of Gary Halter

Chapter 21
p. 597: Courtesy of Gary Halter; p. 598: © Bettmann/Corbis Images; p. 615: Courtesy of Gary Halter

Chapter 22
p. 625(both): Courtesy of Gary Halter; p. 647: Courtesy, Texas House of Representatives; p. 650: Courtesy, Lt. Governor David Dewhurst/photo by Senate Media Services

Chapter 23
p. 667: Austin History Center, Austin Public Library; p. 668: Courtesy of Gary Halter; p. 670: Courtesy of the State Preservation Board, Austin, Texas. P7-C4.f1 1/27/97, frame 3.; p. 675: Courtesy of the State Preservation Board, Austin, Texas. P7-C4.f2 6/95, frame 1

Chapter 24
p. 706: © Aker/Zvonkovic Photography; p. 715: © Bob Daemmrich/Image Works

Chapter 25
p. 730: Photo by J. Griffis Smith/TxDOT; pp. 732, 737, 745: Courtesy of Gary Halter.

INDEX

AARP. *See* American Association of Retired Persons (AARP)

AAUP. *See* American Association of University Professors (AAUP)

ABA. *See* American Bar Association (ABA)

Abbot, Lyman, 729

ABC, 203, 277, 280, 283

ABC News/Los Angeles Times poll, 207

Abodaca, Jerry, 667

Abolitionists, 43

Abortion
    Clinton and, 340
    court system and, 258
    group thinking and, 180
    partial-birth abortion, 113
    public opinion and, 114, 168
    Reagan and, 340
    right to privacy and, 110, 112–113
    single-issue groups and, 254
    value differences and, 17–18

Abramoff, Jack, 256, 261–262

Abu Ghraib, 124

Accountability, 240, 291, 326, 388–396, 441

Acting governors, 670–671

Acton Institute, 170

Adamany, David, 230

Adams, John, 53, 56, 58, 72, 100, 215, 423

Adams, John Quincy, 350, 381

Adarand Constructors, 154

Adarand v. Pena, 154, 155

Addams, Jane, 484

Adelsverein Society, 532

AFDC. *See* Aid for Families with Dependent Children (AFDC)

Affirmative action, 16, 152–156

Affirmative action, 422

Afghanistan, 124, 165, 176, 337, 343, 391, 503, 506

AFL–CIO, 250

African Americans, *See also* Slavery
    civil rights movement of, 134–135
    discrimination and, 13–14, 131, 150, 157
    domination of, 80
    education and, 83, 133–134
    gerrymandering and, 631–632
    judiciary and, 134
    party affiliations and, 601
    percentage of population by state 1790, 44
    political associations and, 580
    in public office, 135, 636, 667
    racial profiling and, 120
    segregation and, 13–14, 79, 132–134, 156–157, 439
    in Texas, 532, 536, 539, 551, 597
    voting and, 62, 136, 150, 190, 208, 223, 539, 574, 576, 631
    white primary and, 575

African Americans and, equality and, 132–133

Age
    age discrimination, 92, 144
    group thinking and, 181–182
    voting and, 199–200

Age Discrimination Act of 1975, 144

Age Discrimination in Employment Act of 1967, 144

Age-cohort tendency, definition of, **173**

Agency point of view, 386

Agenda setting, 286–287

Agents of socialization, 173–176

Agricultural interest groups, 250, 251

AHA. *See* American Hospital Association (AHA)

Aid for Families with Dependent Children (AFDC), 482–483

AIDS, 439

Ailes, Roger, 234, 238, 282

Air wars, 236–237

Airlines Deregulation Act, 446

Al Qaeda, 165, 167, 176, 506

Alienation, definition of, **199**

Alito, Samuel Jr., 113, 415, 416

AMA. *See* American Medical Association (AMA)

American Association of Retired Persons (AARP), 245–246, 261, 480

American Association of University Professors (AAUP), 251

American Bar Association (ABA), 251

American Civil Liberties Union, 120, 125, 258, 421

American Creed, 11, *See also* Core values

American Dilemma (Myrdal), 157

American Federalism: A View from the States (Elazar), 537

American Federation of State, County, Municipal Employees, 250

American Hospital Association (AHA), 257

American Independent party, 226

American Medical Association (AMA), 251, 481

American Petroleum Institute, 249, 257

American Political Science Association, 323

American Relief Organization, 394

American Revolution, 8, 11, 21, 38–39

American Soybean Association, 251

Americans with Disabilities Act, 144

AmeriCorps, 520

Ames, Fisher, 35

An Economic Interpretation of the Constitution (Beard), 61

Anaya, Tony, 667

Anderson, Desiree, 305

Anderson, Russell, 97, 98

Anglicanism, 20, 109

Anthony, Susan B., 5, 190, 192

Anti-Federalists, 45, 71, 74, 80

AP. *See* Associated Press (AP)

Apathy, definition of, **197**

Appellate jurisdiction, 406

Appointive powers, 674–679, **675**

Arab Americans, 157–158

Arctic National Wildlife Refuge, 451

Aristotle, 61, 569

Articles of Confederation, 39–40, 69, 72, 191

Ashcroft, John, 67, 68, 125, 634

Ashcroft v. Free Speech Coalition, 109

Asian Americans, 123, 143–144, 536

Assisted suicide, 67, 114–115

Associated Press (AP), 276–277

Association Milk Producers, 251

Association of Wheat Growers, 216, 251

AT&T, 380

At-large election system, 739–740

Atkins v. Virginia, 121

Atlantic Monthly, 191

Attorney general, 587–588, 687–688

Austin, Stephen F., 533

Austria, 193, 201, 359, 503

Austria-Hungary, 8

Authoritarian governments, definition of, **24**

Authority, definition of, **25**

Autocracy, definition of, **21**

"Axis of evil," 506

Babbitt, Bruce, 670

Baker v. Carr, 477, 430, 630

Bakke, Alan, 154

Balanced budget, 458

Balcones Escarpment, 532

Ballor, Jordon J., 170

Ballot form, 562, **605–609**

Banking
    depressions and, 217
    economic panics and, 217
    federal banking system, 72, 76
    Federal Deposit Insurance Corporation (FDIC), 83
    Federal Reserve Board, 29, 466–467
    national currency and, 73
    redlining and, 150
    regulation of, 442, 447

Banking Act of 1934, 447

Barton, Clara, 484

"Basher" spots, 615

Baumgartner, Jody, 26

Bay of Pigs, 360

Bazelon, David, 417

BCRA. *See* Bipartisan Campaign Reform Act (BCRA)

Beard, Charles S., 61

Beeson, Ann, 125

Belarus, 503

Belgium, 8, 192, 193, 221, 359, 387, 394

Bell companies, 380

Bentham, Jeremy, 166

Benton v. Maryland, 117

Bentsen, Lloyd, 599, 611

Berkshire Hathaway, 488

Berlin Wall, 503

Biennial sessions, 644, 645

Bilingual education, 141, 143, 756, 758

Bill, Chris, 607

Bill of Rights, *See also* U.S. Constitution
    definition of, **52,** 98
    historical background, 51–53
    Jefferson and, 11
    limited government and, 47
    state constitutions and, 554–555

Bills, 320–324

Bin Laden, Osama, 26, 158, 165, 235

Bipartisan Campaign Reform Act (BCRA), 231

Bipolar (power structure), definition of, **502**

Birth control, 112

"Birthright" characteristics, 636

Black, Hugo, 409

Blades, Joan, 253

Blair, Tony, 239

Blakely v. Washington, 123

Blanco, Kathleen, 669

Blanket primary, 609, **610**

Block grants, 87

Blogs, 39, 614

Board of Education of Independent School District No. 92 of Pottawatomie County v. Earls, 118

Board of Trustees of the University of Alabama v. Garrett, 92

Boing Boing, 285

Boorstin, Daniel, 93

Boroughs, 745

Boston Globe, 631

Boston Tea Party, 38, 206

Bowers v. Hardwick, 114

Bowling Alone, (Putnam), 191, 202, 248, 252

Boxer, Barbara, 137

Boxer Rebellion, 394

Boy Scouts of America (BSA), 145

Boyd, Wes, 253

Brady Bill. *See* Handgun Violence Prevention Act

Brandeis, Louis D., 416

Brandenburg v. Ohio, 105

Breckinridge, John C., 216

Brennan, William, 415, 427

Breyer, Stephen, 119, 416, 423

Briefs, 407

Briscoe, Dolph, 595, 668, 669, 674

Broadcast news, 277–282

Broder, David S., 263

Brooks, Garth, 388

Brown, Lee, 743
Brown, Linda Carol, 133
Brown, Norman, 613
Brown v. Board of Education of Topeka, 83,
    133–134, 148, 407, 421, 424
Brownback, Sam, 107
Brownlow Commission, 373
Bryan, William Jennings, 286
Bryant, Kobe, 293
Bryce, James, 7, 10, 46, 343
BSA. *See* Boy Scouts of America (BSA)
Buchanan, Pat, 227, 607, 611
Budget
    balanced budget, **458**
    budget deficit, **459**, 460–461
    budget surplus, **458**
    budgetary process, 393, 462–464
    Congressional Budget Office (CBO),
        326, 463
    governors and, 679–681
    Office of Management and Budget
        (OMB), 383, 462
    presidency and, 376
Budget deficit, 459, 460–461
Budget Impoundment and Control Act of
    1974, 326, 364
Budget surplus, 458
Buffett, Warren, 488
Bull Moose Party, 226
Bullock, Bob, 657, 688
Bureau of Indian Affairs, 139–140
Bureaucracy, *See also* Local governments;
        State governments
    accountability and, 388–396
    agency point of view, **386**
    cabinet (executive departments),
        376–377
    clientele groups and, **387**–388
    definition of, **374**
    demographic representativeness and,
        395–**396**
    executive leadership system, **383**, 385
    federal employment, 374–381, 382
    formalized rules and, **374**
    government corporations, **378**
    hierarchical authority and, 374
    independent agencies, **377**–378
    job specialization and, 374
    merit system and, **382**–383, 385
    neutral competence, **383**
    overview of, 373–375
    patronage system and, 381–**382**, 385
    policy implementation and, **380**–381
    power of, 365–388
    presidential commissions, **378**
    regulatory agencies, **377**
    reinvention of government and,
        396–398
    spoils system and, **382**
    state bureaucracies, 375
    sunset laws and, **394**
    whistle blowing, 3
Bureaucratic accountability, 388–396, **390**
Bureaucratic rule, definition of, **29**
Burke, Edmund, 56
Burr, Aaron, 56, 72
Bush, George H. W., 255, 338, 416, 422, 599,
        611, 615, 665, 670
Bush, George W.
    accountability and, 397
    approval ratings and, 337, 366, 367
    Arctic National Wildlife Refuge and, 451

Bush, George W.—*cont.*
    banking and, 290
    campaign financing, 348–349
    Cheney and, 354–355
    debates and, 352
    election to presidency, 59, 208, 213,
        220, 226, 237, 345, 349–352,
        403, 405, 423
    enemy combatant detention,
        123–125
    fiscal policies of, 460–461
    as forceful, 341
    as governor of Texas, 539, 562, 576,
        596, 599–600, 614, 616–618,
        668, 674, 755
    guest–worker program of, 19, 142
    humor about, 26
    intelligent design theory and, 757
    Iraq War and, 165, 219, 273, 276, 285,
        289, 337, 361–362, 368, 383,
        384, 508
    Kyoto Agreement and, 454, 455, 505
    McCain and, 183
    new world order, 503
    Perry and, 667
    press coverage of, 281–282, 282, 293
    protestors and, 99
    Richards and, 755
    September 11, 2001 terrorist attacks
        and, 5, 223, 337, 342–343, 390
    signing statements and, 364–365
    social security reform and, 184,
        245–246, 480
    sound bites and, 615
    speeches of, 6, 245
    stem-cell research and, 266, 362
    Supreme Court nominations, 416, 423
    surveillance of suspected terrorists,
        125–126
    tax policy of, 441, 460–461, 487
    Texas support for, 595
    torture policy, 309
    vetoes, 362
    war on terrorism, 504–506
    wealth of, 669
    wiretapping and, 54, 289, 292, 421
Bush School at Texas A&M University, 653
Bush v. Gore, 403, 405, 423, 424
Business, 7, 73, 80–81
Business groups, 249–250
Business and Professional Association, 742
Busing, 156–157

C-SPAN, 277
Cabinet (executive departments), 356–357,
        376–377
Cable News Network (CNN), 238, 277,
        283, 290
Cable television, 238, 277, 279, 282–283,
        283, 290
Calderón, Sila M., 669
Calendars, 655
Calendars Committee, 655
Calhoun, John C., 59, 77
Calvinists, 20
Campaign consultants, 616
Campaign finance
    campaign reform and, 231
    congressional elections and, 304–305
    federal funding, 348–349
    governors and, 616–618

Campaign finance—*cont.*
    interest groups and, 248–251,
        261–265, 582
    "late train contributors," 617–619
    media and, 352
    overview of, 347–348
    political action committees (PACs)
        and, 261–265
    political parties and, 230–234
    in Texas, 616–619, 638–639
    U.S. Congress and, 304–305, 618
Canada
    accountability and, 389
    child poverty rates, 477
    as colony, 72
    core values and, 12
    defense spending, 510
    environmental protection and, 455
    form of government, 71
    homosexuality and, 147
    immigration and, 8
    legislature of, 314
    marriage in, 139
    NAFTA and, 518
    national pride, 174
    policy leadership in, 359
    political parties in, 221
    television campaigning and, 236
    voter turnout in, 193
    women in elective office and, 137
Cancer, 450, 453
Candidate-centered campaigns, 233–237
Candidate-centered politics, definition
        of, **213**
Cantwell, Maria, 309
Capelo, Jaime, 648
Capitalism, definition of, **23**, 24, 80, 442
Capture, 586
CARE packages, 394
Carr, O. M., 737
Carson, Rachel, 450
Carter, Jimmy, 332, 337, 341, 362, 366, 595,
        611
Carveill, James, 234
Casey, Bob, 233, 308
Castro, Fidel, 360
Castro, Raul, 667
Categorical grants, 87
CBO. *See* Congressional Budget Office
        (CBO)
CBS, 203, 277, 280, 283
CBS News/New York Times polls, 172
Center on Budget and Policy Priorities, 473
Center for Media and Public Affairs, 281
Center for Voting and Democracy, 307
Central Intelligence Agency (CIA), 500
Ceremonial duties, 666
Chagall, David, 233
Chavez, Hugo, 255
Checks and balances
    definition of, **49**
    interest groups and, 267
    judiciary and, 51–53
    limited government and, 49–51
    U.S. Constitution and, 21, 35–36, 49–51,
        267, 302
Cheney, Dick, 213, 290, 291, 354–355, 395
Chesterton, G. K., 20
Chicago Tribune, 277
Chief legislator, 666
Child labor, 81
Child Online Protection Act, 109

Children's Defense Fund, 484
China, 8, 122, 143, 394, 455, 501, 515, 519
Christian Broadcasting Network, 110, 255
Christian Coalition of America, 254, 255, 580
Christian Heritage Week, 671
Christian Moral Government Fund,
        264–265
Chrysler Corporation, 250
Church. *See* Religion; specific religions
Churchill, Winston, 342
CIA. *See* Central Intelligence Agency (CIA)
Cisneros, Henry, 737
Citizen, nonprofessional legislatures, 659
Citizens Charter Association, 742
Citizens Conference on State Legislatures,
        659
Citizen's (noneconomic) groups, 251–254
Citizens party, 226
City Attorneys Association, 580
Civic community, 252
Civic duty, definition of, **197**
Civil law, 418
Civil liberties, 97–99, **98**, *See also* **Bill
        of Rights**
Civil rights, *See also* African Americans;
        Discrimination; **Equality;**
        Segregation
    affirmative action and, 16, 152–156
    black civil rights movement, 134–135
    definition of, **132**
    education and, 83, 133–134, 141, 143
    employment and, 149–150
    equal protection and, 147–149
    gays and lesbians and, 145–147
    Hispanic Americans and, 140–143
    housing and, 150
    Native Americans and, 139–140
    older people and, 144
    persons with disabilities and, 144–145
    voting and, 134, 150, 150–152, 191, 205,
        361, 631, 634–635, 740
    women and, 135–139
Civil Rights Act of 1964, 134, 136, 140, 144,
        149–150, 205, 361, 420
Civil Rights Act of 1968, 150
Civil War, 13, 216, 217, 512, 532, 551, 596
Clarke, Richard, 395
Clay, Henry, 59, 354
Clayton, Billy, 649, 650, 657
Clean Air Act of 1963, 445, 450
Clear Channel, 84
Clear-and-present-danger test, **101**
Cleland, Max, 235
Clements, Bill, 595, 598, 631, 668–669, 674,
        680, 682, 685, 756
Cleveland, Grover, 217
Clientele groups, 387–388
Clinton, Bill
    abortion and, 340
    approval ratings, 336
    Arctic National Wildlife Refuge
        and, 451
    Bentsen and, 599
    Bosnia and, 504
    fiscal policies of, 459, 464
    as governor of Arkansas, 670
    health care reform and, 208–209
    impeachment of, 338, 364
    Lewinsky and, 285, 289, 332, 338
    NAFTA and, 518
    National Performance Review and,
        373, 397

Clinton, Bill—cont.
  press coverage of, 26, 276, 279,
    281–282, 285, 289
  primaries and, 611
  reelection of, 220
  Supreme Court nominations, 416, 422
  welfare reform and, 483
Clinton, Chelsea, 279
Clinton, Hilary, 235, 279, 319, 347
Closed primaries, definition of, **608**–609
Closed riders, 653
Cloture, definition of, **322**
CNN, 505
CNN. *See* Cable News Network (CNN)
Cobb, David, 226
Cohen, Bernard, 287
Coke, Richard, 553–554
Cold War, 101, **502**
Colegrove v. Green., 405, 427
Collective bargaining, 579
Collective (public) goods, definition of,
  251
Collins, Martha Layne, 669
Colombia, 8, 25
Columbia University, 478
Combined Law Enforcement Association of
  Texas, 580
Commerce and business, 7, 73, 80–81
Commerce clause, 80, 91, 92
Commission form of government, 738
Committee system in Congress, 316–320
Common Cause, 246, 254
Common Sense (Paine), 39, 190
Common-carrier role, 288
Communications Act, 277, 278
Communications Workers of America, 250
Communism, 23, 442–443, 502
Communist party, 101
Comparable worth, 138
Comparative approach, 529
Compassionate Use Act of California, 91
Compliance, 426
Comptroller of public accounts, 688–689
Concurring opinions, 408
Confederacy, definition of, **70**
Conference on Catholic Bishops, 172
Conference committees, 318, 652
Conflict. *See* Political conflict
Congress of Racial Equality (CORE), 580
Congress. *See* U.S. Congress
Congressional Budget Office (CBO), 326,
  393–394, 463
Connally, John, 668, 670, 685–686
Connor, Eugene "Bull," 134
Conservatives, 177, **178**
Constables, 748
Constituency, definition of, **304**
Constitutional conventions, 560
Constitutional county judge, 747
Constitutional democracy, 62
Constitutionalism, definition of, **22**
Constitutions, *See also* Bill of Rights; specif-
  ic amendments; State constitu-
  tions; U.S. Constitution
  amendment process, 48, 560–564
  ballot wording bias and, 562
  definition of, **46**, 549
  life span of, 559
  of State of Texas, 549–552, 554–564
Consumer Product Safety Commission, 448
Containment, definition of, **502**
Contract with America, 326

Contract theory of state constitutions, 553
Controlled Substances Act (CSA), 91
Coolidge, Calvin, 15
Cooperative federalism, 85–86
Core ideals
  allegiance and, 7
  conflict resolution and, 17–24
  as habits of heart, 6
  limits of, 13–17
  other countries and, 12
  power of, 11–13
  presidential speeches and, 5
CORE. *See* Congress of Racial Equality
  (CORE)
Cornyn, John, 536, 611, 688
Corporation for Public Broadcasting (CPB),
  387, 397
Council of State Governments, 255
Council-manager government, 735–737
County commissioners court, 746–748
County governments, 744–751, **745**
County sheriff, 748
Courts. *See* Judiciary; U.S. Supreme Court
CPB. *See* Corporation for Public
  Broadcasting (CPB)
Craddick, Tom, 633, 639, 649, 657, 659
Craig v. Boren, 148
Creationism, 112
Creatures of state, 730–731
Creighton, Robert, 97
Creighton, Sarisse, 97
Criminal law, 418
Criminal procedure. *See* **Procedural due
  process**
Crosscutting cleavages, 182
Crouch, Nancy, 743
CSA. *See* Controlled Substances Act (CSA)
Cuba, 8, 124, 140, 275–276
Cultural thinking, 176–177
Cumulative voting, 740
Cuomo, Mario, 379
Cureton, Adrienne, 120
Currency, 73
Czechoslovakia, 8

Dahl, Robert, 28
Daily Kos, 202, 285
Daily Show, 26
Daily Telegram, 278, 286
Daniel, Price, 668
Das Kapital (Marx), 443
Daschle, Tom, 474
Davidson, Roger, 301, 332
Davis, Edmund J., 554, 738
Davis, Gray, 672
Davis, J. William, 651
DCCC. *See* Democratic Congressional
  Campaign Committee (DCCC)
De facto discrimination, 152
De jure discrimination, 152
Dean, Howard, 202, 204–205, 230, 237, 283,
  348
Death with Dignity Act, 67
Death penalty, 83, 119–123, 529
Decisions, 407
Declaration of Independence (U.S.), *See also*
  Texas Declaration of
  Independence
  American Revolution and, 8, 11, 21,
    38–39
  as founding U.S. document, 8

Declaration of Independence (U.S.)—*cont.*
  inalienable rights and, 9
  Jefferson and, 11
  self-government and, 10
  slavery and, 5, 10
Defense policy. *See* Foreign policy
Deficit spending, 458
DeJonge v. Oregon, 104
Delahunt, William D., 346
DeLay, Tom, 261–262, 308, 312, 600, 614,
  632, 634–635
Delegates, 59, **658**
Dellinger, Walter, 429
Demand-side economics, 458–461
Democracy
  constitutional democracy, **62**
  definition of, **21, 56**
  Jacksonian Democracy, 59
  Jeffersonian Democracy, 58
  overview of, 21
  pluralist democracy, 166
  representative democracy, **57**
  republic versus, 55–56
Democratic Congressional Campaign
  Committee (DCCC), 231
Democratic National Committee (DNC),
  230–233, 289
Democratic party
  Dred Scott decision and, 78
  founding of, 46, 58, 215
  loyalty to, 173
  partisan thinking and, 182–184
  party realignments and, 216–218,
    597–603
  voter turnout and, 197
  voting statistics and, 224
  yellow dog democrats, **597**
Democratic Senatorial Campaign
  Committee (DSCC), 231
Demographic representativeness, 395–396
Denials of power, 47, 48
Denmark, 8, 192, 193, 221
Denver Post, 276
Department of Homeland Security (DHS),
  390, 505–506
Deregulation, 446–447
Deterrence policy, definition of, **509**–510
Devolution
  block grants and, 87
  causes of, 88–90
  definition of, 84–85, **88**
  judiciary and, 90–92
  Republican party and, 89–90, 93
Dewey, John, 252
Dewey, Thomas, 171
Dewhurst, David, 616, 619, 633, 634, 651, 657
DHS. *See* Department of Homeland
  Security (DHS)
Dickerson v. United States, 117
Disabilities. *See* Persons with disabilities
Discrimination
  African Americans and, 13–14, 131,
    150, 157
  age discrimination, 92, 144
  Asian Americans and, 143
  de facto discrimination, 152
  de jure discrimination, 152
  housing and, 150
  immigration and, 15–16, 19
  persons with disabilities and, 86, 92
  religious discrimination, 15–16, 19, 20,
    48, 180

Discrimination—*cont.*
  "separate but equal" ruling, 79, 133
  voting and, 575
Dissenting opinions, definition of, 408, **409**
Diversity, definition of, **11**
Dix, Dorothea, 484
DNC. *See* Democratic National Committee
  (DNC)
"Doctrine of nullification," 77
Dogget, Lloyd, 635
Dole, Robert, 255, 595, 611
Domhoff, G. William, 28
Dominican Republic, 8
Double jeopardy, 115
Douglas, Stephen A., 216
Douglass, Frederick, 78
Draft card burning, 206
Drake University, 172
Dred Scott v. Sanford, 77–78, 414
Drudge, Matt, 285
Drudge Report, 285
Drug searches, 118
Drug testing, 118
DSCC. *See* Democratic Senatorial
  Campaign Committee (DSCC)
Dual federalism, 78–80
Due process, *See also* Procedural due
  process
**Due process clause (of Fourteenth
  Amendment),** 103–104, 114
Dukes, Dawnna, 649
Duncan v. Louisiana, 117

E pluribus unum, 11
Earned Income Tax Credit (EITC), 487–489
Earth Day, 452
Easley v. Cromartie, 151
Easton, David, 30
Economic depression, 458
Economic globalization, definition of, **518**
Economic groups, 247, 248–249, 253
Economic Growth and Tax Relief
  Reconciliation Act of 2001,
  460, 465
Economic policy, *See also* Budget; **Fiscal
  policy; Regulation**
  agriculture promotion, 457
  business promotion, 456
  environmental protection and, 150–455
  Federal Reserve Board and, 466–467
  foreign policy and, 514–521
  global trade and, 514–520
  labor promotion, 456
  laissez-faire doctrine, **442**
  overview of, 437–438
  policy formation, 440
  public policy process, 438–442
  trade deficit, 515–516, 519–520
Economic recession, 458
Economy, definition of, **442**
Edelman, Marian Wright, 484
Edgewood v. Kirby, 754
Education
  affirmative action in, 154
  bilingual education, 141, 143, 756, 758
  busing and, 156–157
  children with disabilities and, 144–145
  civil rights and, 83, 133–134, 141, 143
  college graduate statistics by state, 14
  creationism and, 112, 756
  Education Amendment of 1972, 136

Hamilton, Alexander—*cont.*
  on presidential authority, 340
  on representation, 623
  on war, 339
Hamilton, Billy, 685
Hamilton v. Regents, U. of California, 104
Hammer v. Dagenhart, 81
Handgun Violence Prevention Act, 90
Hannity, Sean, 238
Hanseatic League, 70
Hanson, Mark, 191
Hard money, definition of, **231**
Harding, Warren, 394
Hargrove, Erwin, 359–360
Harlan, John Marshall, 79, 427
Harrington, Michael, 476
Harrison, Benjamin, 59, 345, 351
Hartz, Louis, 9
Harvard University, 174, 191, 202, 203, 252, 379, 478
Hastert, Dennis, 222
Hatch, Orin, 266, 316, 422, 427
Hate crimes, 105, 158
Hate speech, 105
Hayes, Rutherford B., 59, 345
Head Start, 484
Health care. *See* Medical care
Hearst, William Randolph, 275
Heclo, Hugh, 368
Heflin, Talmadge, 536
Henry, O., 596
Henry, Patrick, 68–69
Heritage Foundation, 488
Hibbing, John, 308
Hierarchical authority, definition of, **374**
Hightower, Jim, 615
Hill, John, 688
Hired guns, 233–237
Hispanic Americans
  civil rights movement and, 140–143
  demographics, 140
  elective office and, 135
  party affiliations and, 601
  political associations and, 580
  political office and, 636, 667, 688
  Texas and, 530
  voting and, 142–143, 539, 574, 576, 631
Hitler, Adolf, 24, 25, 158, 502
Hobart, Garret Augustus, 286
Hobbes, Thomas, 18, 20
Hobby, Bill, 657, 682, 756
Hogg, James S., 689–690
Hollister, Nancy P., 669
Holmes, Oliver Wendell Jr., 77, 100, 417, 430
Home rule cities, 732
Homestead Act of 1862, 457
Honeymoon period, 360
Hong Kong, 8
Hoover Commission, 373, 394
Hoover, Herbert, 217–218, 341, 356, 394, 596
House Rules Committee, 312, 322
Housing, 150, 539
Houston, Sam, 533
Huckabee, Mike, 671
Hudson, Booker, 119
Hudson v. Michigan, 119
Hull, Jane Dee, 669
Humphrey, Hubert, 345, 595
Hungary, 502
Hussein, Saddam, 165, 235, 361–362, 383, 504, 506, 508, 517

Hutchison, Kay Bailey, 325, 599, 616
Hybrid legislatures, 659

ICBL. *See* International Campaign to Ban Landmines (ICBL)
ICC. *See* International Criminal Court (ICC); Interstate Commerce Commission (ICC)
ICMA. *See* International City Managers Association (ICMA)
Ideals. *See* Core ideals
Ideological, definition of, **177**–179
Ideological groups, 254, 262
Ideological parties, 226–227
IMF. *See* International Monetary Fund (IMF)
Immigration
  attitudes about, 16
  discrimination and, 15–16, 19
  guest worker program, 19, 142, 238
  immigration reform, 142, 325–326
  period 1820–2000 in various countries, 8
  to U.S. by region of origin 1950–2000, 15
Imminent lawless action, 105
Impeachment and conviction, 35, 338, 364, **671**
Implied powers, 74, 76
In-kind benefits, 484
Inalienable rights, 9, 20, **38**
Incorporation of cities, **733**
Incumbents, 304–305, 307–309
Independent agencies, 377–378
Independent candidates, 607–608
Independent school districts, 753
India, 8, 143, 455
Indianapolis v. Edmund, 118
Individualism
  definition of, **11**
  family and, 174
  social programs and, 12, 176, 207–209
  tax policies and, 486–488
Individualist subculture, 537
Industrial Revolution, dual federalism and, 78
Inefficiency, 485–486
Inflation, 461
Influence
  federalism and, 92–93
  on judicial decision, 420–423
  political participation and, 207–209, 238–240
  press influence on public opinion, 275, 294–295
  public influence on political parties, 238–240
  of public opinion on policy making, 184–185
Informal qualification for governors, **667**
Initiative & Referendum Institute, 263
Initiatives, 560
Inside lobbying, 256–260
Instapundit, 285
Intelligence Design Network, 757
Intelligence Surveillance Act (FISA), 54
Intelligent design, 112, **756,** 757
Interest groups
  campaign financing and, 248–251, 261–265, 582
  capture and, 586
  citizen's groups, 251–254
  definition of, **246**
  economic groups, 247–254

Interest groups—*cont.*
  electioneering and, 582
  government interest groups, 254–255
  interest-group liberalism, 267
  iron triangles and, 258–259, 267
  judicial decisions and, 421
  lobbying and, 255–265, 540, 581–582
  overview of, 245–246
  pluralism and, 265–267
  political action committees (PACs) and, 261–265
  political parties and, 245–247
  power of, 583–586
  state politics and, 578–586
Interest-group liberalism, definition of, **267**
Intergovernmental coordinators, 666
Interim committees, 652
Intermediate-scrutiny test, 148–149
International Association of Machinists, 250
International Brotherhood of Electrical Workers, 250
International Brotherhood of Teamsters, 250
International Campaign to Ban Landmines (ICBL), 284
International City Managers Association (ICMA), 737
International Criminal Court (ICC), 505
International Monetary Fund (IMF), 520
Internationalist, definition of, **501**
Internet
  campaigning and, 237, 352
  as news source, 203, 283–285
  political participation and, 198, 204–205
  polling and, 170
  pornography and, 109
  voting and, 198
Internships, 323
Interstate Commerce Commission (ICC), 444
Iran, 517
Iran-Contra scandal, 289, 332
Iraq War
  blogs about, 285
  George W. Bush and, 165, 219, 273, 276, 285, 289, 337, 361–362, 368, 383, 384
  enemy combatant detention and, 124
  international attitudes, 506–507
  press coverage of, 293
  prisoner abuse, 289, 391
  public opinion and, 165, 167, 183, 219, 276
  rebuilding Iraq, 507, 509
  war protests and, 22
  war on terrorism and, 337
Ireland, 8, 201, 206, 290
Iron triangles, 258–259, 267
Iroquois Confederacy, 37
Isolationist, definition of, **501**
Israel, 314, 359, 514
Issue networks, 259–260
Italy
  bureaucratic accountability and, 389
  civil servants and, 387
  core values and, 12
  defense spending, 510
  environmental protection and, 455
  form of government of, 71
  homosexuality and, 147

Italy—*cont.*
  immigration and, 8
  marriage in, 139
  national pride, 174
  partisan journalism and, 278
  policy leadership in, 359
  political parties in, 221
  poverty and, 477, 482
  television campaigning and, 236
  voter turnout in, 193
Izaak, Walton League, 254

Jackson, Andrew
  ballot box and, 675, 686–687
  on doctrine of nullification, 77
  electoral college and, 345
  grassroots parties and, 215–216
  Jacksonian Democracy, 59, 216
  Jacksonian statehouse government, **686**–687
  patronage system and, 381
  presidency of, 59, 235, 340
  War of 1812 and, 45
Jackson, Janet, 108
Jackson, Michael, 293
Jackson State University, 206
Jacksonian Democracy, 59, 216
Jacksonian statehouse government, 686–687
Jacobs, Lawrence, 184
Jamaica, 8
James, Marquis, 533
Japan
  automobile industry and, 444
  bureaucratic accountability and, 389
  core values and, 12
  defense spending, 510
  as economic center, 515
  environmental protection and, 455
  form of government of, 71
  immigration to U.S. and, 8, 143
  incarceration rates, 122
  legislature of, 314
  national pride, 174
  policy leadership in, 359
  voter turnout in, 193
  women in elective office and, 137
Japanese detention camps, 123
Jay, John, 45
Jefferson, Thomas
  Bill of Rights and, 52, 97
  communities and, 252
  correspondence of, 40, 47
  Declaration of Independence (U.S.) and, 11
  Democratic party and, 45, 58
  equality and, 10
  federal banking system and, 76
  Hamilton and, 72
  Iroquois Confederacy and, 37
  on Locke, 38
  Madison and, 45
  Marshall and, 56, 430
  negative campaigning and, 235
  newspapers and, 275
  presidency of, 53, 58
  Republican party and, 72, 214
  Sedition Act and, 100
  veto and, 362
Jeffersonian Democracy, 58
Jeffords, James, 337
Jewell, Jerry, 671

Jim Crow, 13
Job specialization, definition of, **374**
Johns Hopkins University, 450
Johnson, Andrew, 512
Johnson, Gregory Lee, 102
Johnson, Henry S., 672
Johnson, Lyndon
    civil rights and, 359
    foreign policy of, 360
    Great Society program, 84–86, 93, 478
    Medicare and, 440, 478
    political spectrum and, 222
    Texas party realignment and, 598
    Texas support for, 595
    Vietnam War and, 337, 365, 502
    VISTA and, 520
Joint committees, 318
Ju Jintao, 520
Judaism, discrimination against, 16, 19, 180
Judicial activism, 426–431
Judicial conferences, 407
Judicial powers of state governors, **682–683**
Judicial restraint, 424–431
Judicial review, 47, 53, 428
Judiciary, *See also* specific cases; U.S.
        Supreme Court
    abortion and, 258
    accountability and, 394
    African Americans and, 134
    appellate jurisdiction, **406**
    checks and balances and, 51–53
    compliance and, **426**
    county commissioners court, **746–748**
    decisions, 78, 407, 417–423, 753–756
    equal protection and, 147–149
    "federal court myth," 411
    federal judicial system, 409
    impeachment of judges, 405
    interest groups and, 421
    judicial activism, **426–431**
    judicial restraint, **424–431**
    jurisdiction (of courts), 406
    legitimacy and, **424–425**
    original jurisdiction and, **406**
    overview of, 403–405
    power of, 423–431
    presidency and, 414–416, 422
    procedural due process and, 115–123
    protection of individual and, 126
    requirements for federal judicial
        officers, 404
    selection of judiciary, 57, 411, 413–417
    special U.S. courts, 410
    state courts, 411–413
    U.S. Courts of Appeals, 410
    U.S. District Courts, 409–410
Junell, Robert, 562
Jurisdiction (of congressional committee), **320**
Jurisdiction (of courts), **406**
Justice, presidential speeches and, 5
Juveniles, 121

Kaplan, Robert, 191
Katrina hurricane, 301, 391
Kay, David, 507
Kennedy, Anthony, 403, 416, 439
Kennedy, Edward, 595
Kennedy, John F., 337, 352, 354, 359, 360,
    379, 481, 520, 598
Kent State University, 206

Kernell, Samuel, 367
Kerry, John
    campaign finance and, 233
    Edwards and, 239, 349
    McCain and, 309
    presidential campaign, 26, 213, 220,
        233, 351–352, 352
    press coverage of, 282, 293
Key, V. O. Jr., 165, 591, 592, 597
Keynes, John Maynard, 458
Kimel v. Florida Board of Regents, 92
King, Martin Luther Jr., 131, 134, 205
King, Peter, 290
Kingdon, John, 441
Kirk, Ron, 536, 603, 612
KKK;. *See* Ku Klux Klan (KKK)
Klopfer v. North Carolina, 117
Knock-and-announce rule, 119
Korea, 8, 143
Kosovo, 183, 504
Ku Klux Klan (KKK), 105, 672
Kunin, Madeleine M., 669
Kuwait, 165, 504, 517
Kyoto Agreement, 454, 455, 505

Labor unions
    get-out-the-vote efforts and, 237
    government employees and, 250, 380
    National Labor Relations Act, 82
    as special interest groups, 248–250
Laissez-faire capitalism, 80
Laissez-faire doctrine, **442**
Land commissioner, **689**
Land grants, 542
Land-based economy, **542**
Lane, Robert, 207
Laney, Pete, 649, 657, 658
Larry King Live, 277, 352
"Late train contributions," 617–619
Lau v. Nichols, 143
Law (as enacted by Congress), definition
    of, **324**
Lawmaking function, definition of, **324**
Lawrence v. Texas, 114, 145, 413
Laws (of court case), **418**
Lay, Kenneth, 447
League of Nations, 501
League of United Latin American Citizens
    (LULAC), 580
League of United Latin American Voters v.
    Perry, 151
League of Women Voters, 254, 563
Leahy, Patrick, 54, 316
Legislative Audit Committee, **693**
Legislative Budget Board (LBB), **693**
Legislative powers of state governors,
    681–682
Legislative process, 320–324, 653–656
Legislative Redistricting Board (LRB),
    630, 631
Legislative Reorganization Act of 1946, 319
Legitimacy (of judicial power), **424–425**
Letter of the Sheriffs of Bristol (Burke), 56
Leviathan (Hobbes), 18
Levin, Carl, 384
Lewinsky, Monica, 285, 289, 338, 364
Lewis, Gib, 649, 657, 756
Libel, **106**, 274, 290
Liberals, 177, **178**
Libertarian party, 226
Libertarians, definition of, **178**

Liberty, *See also* Freedom
    affirmative action and, 17
    Anti-Federalists and, 71
    Declaration of Independence (U.S.)
        and, 8
    definition of, 9–10, **9**
    Great Depression and, 9
    as inalienable right, 20
    presidential speeches and, 5
    social welfare spending and, 12
Liebling, A. J., 285
Lieutenant governor, **650**
Limbaugh, Rush, 26, 277, 279
Limited government
    Bill of Rights and, 47
    checks and balances and, 49–51
    definition of, **36**
    denials of power, 47, 48
    elections, 47
    federalism, 47
    grants of power, 47, 48
    historical background for, 37
    judicial review, 47, 53
    overview of, 47
    separated institutions sharing power,
        47, 49
Limited popular rule, 56–57
Lincoln, Abraham
    biography of, 217
    Civil War and, 216, 217
    core ideals and, 5
    Dred Scott decision and, 78
    election of, 216
    negative campaigning and, 235
    on self-government, 10
    speeches, 159, 168, 217
Line-item veto, **680**, 681
Lingle, Linda, 669
Lippmann, Walter, 163, 189, 293, 294
Lipsky, Michael, 381
Literacy, 275
Literary Digest poll, 172
Lobbying
    definition of, **255**
    grassroots lobbying, 261
    inside lobbying, 256–260
    iron triangles and, 258–259, 267
    issue networks and, 259–260
    outside lobbying, 260–265
    overview of, 255–256
    political participation and, 201–202
    state governments and, 540, 581–582
Lobbying Disclosure Act of 1995, 256
Local governments
    city council elections, 739–742
    city managers, 737–738
    commission form of government, **738**
    council-manager government,
        735–736
    county commissioners court, **746–748**
    county governments, 744–**751**
    creatures of state and, **730–731**
    general law cities, **732**
    home rule cities, **732**
    incorporation process, 733–734
    mayoral-council governments,
        734–735
    mayors and, 736–737, 742
    minority representation and, 744
    nonpartisan elections, **742–743**
    overview of, 729–730
    school districts, 752–753

Local governments—*cont.*
    special district governments, **751–758**
    voter turnout and, 743–744
Local party organization, 228–229
Lochner v. New York, 81
Locke, John, 20, 38, 71
Locke v. Davey, 111
Logrolling, definition of, **328**
Loose constructionism, 422
Los Angeles Police Department, 158
Los Angeles Times, 277
Losing Ground (Murray), 476
Lott, Trent, 314
Louisiana Territory, 11
Lowi, Theodore, 266
LRB. *See* **Legislative Redistricting Board
    (LRB)**
LULAC. *See* League of United Latin
    American Citizens (LULAC)
Luther, Martin, 5

McCain, John, 183, 309, 347, 454
*McCreary County v. American Civil Liberties
    Union*, 110
McCulloch, Edwin, 76
McCulloch v. Maryland, 76–77, 409, 424
McGavick, Mike, 309
McGovern, George, 222, 349
McIlhaney, Lynn, 743
McInturff, Bill, 170
McKernan, Signe-Mary, 477
McKinley, William, 286
MacManus, Susan, 181
McNabb v. United States, 116
MAD. *See* Mexican American Democrats
    (MAD)
Madison, James
    authority and, 25
    Bill of Rights and, 52
    biography of, 45
    as federalist, 80, 93
    interest groups and, 267–268, 578–579
    Jefferson and, 45
    judicial review and, 53
    on liberty, 47
    political parties and, 214
    as supporter of U.S. Constitution,
        45–46
    writings of, 25, 35, 45, 48, 72, 249,
        578–579
Majoritarianism, definition of, **27**
Majority leaders, 312, 313
Majority opinions, 167, **408**
Majority rule, checks and balances and, 21
Majority whips, 312
Majority-minority populations, **533–536**,
    631–632
Making Democracy Work (Putnam), 252
MALDEF. *See* Mexican American Legal
    Defense and Education Fund
    (MALDEF)
Malloy v. Hogan, 117
Malone, Bill, 607
Mandates., 89–90
Mao Zedong, 502
Mapp, Dollree, 116, 117
Mapp v. Ohio, 116, 118
Marbury v. Madison, 53, 56, 409, 424,
    428, 430
March on Washington for Jobs and
    Freedom, 134

Professional interest groups, 251
Professional legislatures, 659
Progressive era, 59–62, 383, 439, 448
Progressive Republicans, 226, 263, 345
Project for Excellence in Journalism, 282
Proportional representation, 221–222
Prospective voting, definition of, **220**
Protectionism, 518, 519
Public assistance, 481–482
Public assistance. See Social programs
Public opinion
  on abortion, 114, 180
  bureaucratic accountability and,
    388–390
  cultural thinking and, 176–177
  definition of, **167**
  environmental protection and, 450
  frames of reference and, 176–184
  of free trade, 519
  group thinking and, 179–182
  ideological thinking and, 177–179
  influence on policy making, 184–185
  judicial decisions and, 421
  majority opinion, 167
  measurement of, 168–172
  nonopinions, 172
  overview of, 165–167
  partisan thinking and, 182–184
  press influence on, 275, 294–295
  social security and, 480
Public opinion polls
  ABC News/Los Angeles Times poll,
    207
  campaigning and, 235
  CBS News/New York Times polls, 172
  definition of, **169**
  Gallup polls, 92, 134, 172, 178, 181, 218
  Internet polls, 170
  Literary Digest poll, 172
  NBC News/Wall Street Journals polls,
    172
  Washington Post/ABC News poll, 181
Public policy, definition of, **24**
public policy process, 438–442
Public-interest groups, 253–254
Public-representative role, 291, 293
Puerto Rico, 140
Pulitzer, Joseph, 275
Purposive incentive, definition of, **251**
Putnam, Robert, 191, 202, 248, 252

Quakers, 48

Race and ethnicity, 120, 133, 181, *See also*
    specific ethnic groups
**Racially gerrymandered majority-minority
    districts, 631**–632
Radio, 84, 277–279
Ramsey, Ben, 651
Rapid response, 236
Ratliff, Bill, 562, 633
Raven (James), 533
Ray, Dixy Lee, 669
Raza Unidad party, 608
Reagan, Ronald
  abortion and, 340
  accountability and, 392
  affirmative action and, 422
  approval ratings of, 337–338, 367
  effectiveness of, 359

Reagan, Ronald—cont.
  fiscal policies of, 460
  Gramm and, 599
  honeymoon period of, 360
  Iran-Contra scandal and, 289, 332
  new federalism and, 89
  political spectrum and, 222
  sound bites and, 615
  Supreme Court nominations, 22, 137,
    416
  tax cuts and, 487
  Texas support for, 595
RealNetworks, 309
Reapportionment, 306, 427
Reasonable-basis test, 147
Recall, 672
Reconstruction, 596, 665
Red Cross, 124
Redistricting
  Fourteenth Amendment, 151, 427, 430
  gerrymandering and, **306,** 307, 430,
    631–632, 635
  impact of, 632–635
  Legislative Redistricting Board (LRB),
    630, 631
  Texas legislature and, 629–635
  U.S. Congress and, 151, **306,** 427, 430
Redlining, 150
Reform party, 226, 607
Registration, definition of, **194**
Regulation
  definition of, **443**
  deregulation and, **446**–447
  efficiency and, **443**–447
  equity and, **447**–448
  externalities and, **445**
  indirect costs and, 444–445
  overview of, 442–443
  politics and, 448–449
  restraint of trade and, 444
Regulatory agencies, 377
Rehnquist, William, 403, 428–429
Reid, Harry, 245
Reinventing Government (Osborne and
    Gaebler), 396
Religion
  crosscutting cleavages and, 182
  discrimination and, 15–16, 19, 20, 48,
    180
  free-exercise clause, 111–112
  freedom of religion, 9, 20, 37, 104,
    109–112
  group thinking and, 180
  ideological groups and, 254
  political socialization and, 176
  prayer in public schools, 109–110, 254
  same-sex marriage and, 556
  Texas political culture and, 539
Rell, M. Jodi, 669
Remington, Frederic, 275–276
Removal from office, 35, 338, 364, 671,
    671–672, 678–679
Representation function, 327–329
Representative democracy, 57
Representative function, 327–329
Representative government, 56
Republic, 55–56
Republican National Committee (RNC),
    230–233
Republican party
  devolution and, 89–90, 93
  founding of, 72, 214, 216

Republican party—cont.
  loyalty to, 173
  partisan thinking and, 182–184
  party realignments and, 216–218,
    597–603
  presidency and, 218
  socioeconomic status and, 576–577
  voter turnout and, 197
Reservations, 139–140
Reserved powers, 74
Reston, James, 291
Retrospective voting, definition of, **220**
Revolutionary War, 341
Reyes, Ben T., 612
Reynolds v. Sims, 630
Rhetoric, 61
Rice, Condoleeza, 26, 363, 395
Richards, Ann, 595–596, 599, 613, 616, 668,
    669, 674, 755
Richardson, Bill, 667
Riders, 322, 653
Right, *See also* **Bill of rights;** headings
    beginning Freedom;
    Inalienable rights; specific
    rights
Right of privacy, abortion and, 110, 112–115
Riker, William, 80
Riley, Richard, 670
Ring v. Arizona, 123
RNC. See Republican National Committee
    (RNC)
Roberts, Barbara, 669
Roberts, John Jr., 416
Roberts, Owen, 82
Robertson, Pat, 110, 255
"Robin Hood Plan," 754–755
Robinson, Clay, 556
Robinson, Michael, 281
Robinson v. California, 117
Rocky Mountain News, 276
*Rodriguez v. San Antonio Independent School
    District,* 753, 755
Roe v. Wade, 112–113, 315, 424
Rogers, Will, 26
Roman Catholics
  discrimination against, 16, 19, 180
  Mexican culture and, 539
  as preferential, 20
  same-sex marriage and, 556
Romania, 8
Romer v. Evans, 145
Roosevelt, Franklin D.
  approval ratings and, 337
  election of, 222
  fiscal policy and, 457
  Gallup polls and, 172
  honeymoon period of, 360
  Japanese detention camps and, 123
  New Deal, 81–83, 92, 173, 222, 341, 344,
    359, 382, 478
  party realignment and, 217–218
  press and, 280
  social security and, 480
  speeches and, 5, 9
Roosevelt, Theodore, 100, 226, 342, 363, 367
Roper v. Simmons, 121
Rosenberg, Chuck, 293
Rosenstone, Steve, 191
Ross, Nellie Taylor, 667, 669
Rossiter, Clinton, 6, 222
Rostenkowsky, Dan, 441

Rostker v. Goldberg, 148
Rousseau, J.-J., 20, 252
Roy, Vesta M., 669
RRC. See Texas Railroad Commission
    (RRC)
Rudman, Warren, 232
Rumsfeld, Donald, 289, 367–368
Runoff primaries, 611–612
*Rush Limbaugh Is a Big Fat Idiot and Other
    Observations* (Franklin), 279
Russia, 122, 123, 174, 445, 506, 509–510, 516,
    See also USSR

Safe Drinking Water Act, 445
Safire, William, 276
"Sainthood" spots, 615
SALT. See Strategic Arms Limitation Talks
    (SALT)
Same-day registration, 572
Same-sex marriage, 145–147, 549, 556
Samples, definition of, **169**
Sampling errors, definition of, **171**
San Francisco Call, 286
Sanchez, Orlando, 743
Sanchez, Tony, 603, 619, 678
Santa Anna, 533, 550
Santorum, Rick, 233, 308
Saudi Arabia, 124
Sawer, Marian, 174
Sayers, Joseph D., 738
Scalia, Anthony, 232, 403, 416, 423
Scarcity, 17
Schattschneider, E. E., 213, 245, 268, 439
Schectre v. United States, 82
Schenck v. United States, 100–101
Schools. See Education; specific universities
Schultz, Ed, 279
Schwarzenegger, Arnold, 61
Scigliano, Robert, 415
Scott, Dred, 77
Sea Around Us (Carson), 450
Search and seizure
  knock-and-announce rule, 119
  limitations on, 117–118
  overview of application, 97–98
  procedural due process and, 115
  wire tapping and, 54
Sebelius, Kathleen, 669
Second Bank of the United States, 76
Second Treatise on Civil Government
    (Locke), 20
Secretary of state (SOS), 691
Securities and Exchange Act of 1934, 447
Sedition Act of 1798, 100
See, I Told You So (Limbaugh), 279
Segregation
  education and, 83, 133–134, 148,
    156–157, 407, 421, 424, 539
  housing laws and, 539
  Jim Crow era and, 13–14
  "separate but equal" ruling, 79, 133
  World War II and, 439
Select committees, 318
Selective incorporation, 104
Self-government
  American Revolution and, 21
  Anti-Federalists and, 71
  definition of, **10,** 36
  delegates and, 59
  democracy versus republic, 55–56
  Jacksonian Democracy, 59

Self-government—*cont.*
    Jeffersonian Democracy, 58
    limited popular rule and, 56–57
    overview of, 10–11, 55
    Progressive era, 59–62
    tyranny of majority and, 55
Self-incrimination, 115
Semi-closed primaries, 608–609
Semi-open primaries, 609
Senatorial courtesy, 415
Seniority, 316–317
Separated institutions sharing power, 47, **49**
Separation of power, 48–49, 554
September 11, 2001 terrorist attacks
    George W. Bush and, 5, 223, 337,
        342–343, 390
    foreign aid and, 521
    military readiness and, 499
    Muslim prejudice and, 157–158
    political socialization and, 175–176
    problem recognition and, 439
    public opinion and, 165–166
    rights and, 123
    surveillance of suspected terrorists
        and, 125–126
Serbs, 504
Service Employees International, 250
Service relationship, definition of, **231**
Service strategy, definition of, **304**
700 Club, 110, 255
Seventeenth Amendment, 61
Sewell, 286
Sex education, 756
Sexual harassment, 136–137, 420
Sexual relations, 112, 114, 145, 413
Shaheen, Jeanne, 669
Shapiro, Robert, 27, 184
Sharp, John, 617, 665, 688–689
Shays, Daniel, 41
Shays's Rebellion, 40–42
Sheet Metal Workers, 250
Sheridan, P. H., 542
Sheriffs, 748
Sherman Antitrust Act, 80
Sherman, William Tecumseh, 512
Shivercrats, 597
Shivers, Allan, 597–598, 651, 668
Sierra Club, 254, 258, 449
Signaling (signaler) role, 286–287
Signing statements, 364–365
Sikhs, 158
Silent Spring (Carson), 450
Sine die, 644
Singapore, 122
Single-issue groups, 254, 262
Single-issue parties, 225
Single-issue politics, definition of, **246**
Single-member districts, 221–222, 624, 626,
        740, 742, 744, 746
Sipuel, Ada, 133
Sixth Amendment
    procedural due process and, 115
    right to confront witnesses, 115, 117
    right to counsel and, 98, 115, 117
    right to speedy trial, 98, 115, 117
    trial by jury and, 115, 117, 122
Slander, 106
Slavery, *See also* African Americans
    abolitionists, 43
    core ideals and, 13–14
    Declaration of Independence (U.S.)
        and, 5, 10

Slavery—*cont.*
    Dred Scott decision and, 77–78
    North-South Compromise and, 42–44
    percentage of population by state
        1790, 44
    taxation and, 43
    Texas and, 532, 539, 551
    Three-Fifths Compromise, 43
    Union and, 77
Smith, Adam, 442
Smith, Al, 596
Smith, Preston, 668
Smith, Tom "Smitty," 685
Smith v. Allwright, 575
Social capital, 202–204
Social Conservative party, 685, 756
Social Contract (Rousseau), 20
Social contracts, 18, 20–21
social (political) movements, 134–135,
        140–143, 192, **205**–207, *See also*
        Civil rights
Social programs
    entitlement programs, **479,** 479–480
    historical perspective, 477–478
    in-kind benefits, **484**
    individualism value and, 12, 176,
        207–209
    inefficiency and, 485–486
    inequity and, 485–486
    partisan thinking and, 183
    poverty and, 473–477
    public assistance, 481–485
    religious doctrine and, 180
    social insurance programs, 480–481
    spending on, 12
    transfer payments and, **479**
    welfare policies, 27, 90, 473–474, 597
Social security, 184, 245–246, 478, 480
Social Security Act of 1935, 478, 480
Socialism, definition of, **22**
Socialist Workers party, 226, 608
Socioeconomic status, 180, 200, 576–577
Sodomy laws, 114, 556
Soft money, 231–233
Solicitor general, 406
Sore loser law, 607–608
SOS. *See* **Secretary of state (SOS)**
Sossen, Ed, 110
"Sound-bite" commercials, 614–615
Souter, David, 416
South Africa, 122
Southeast Missouri State University, 279
Southern Baptist Church, 255, 556
Sovereignty, definition of, **69**
Soviet Union. *See* USSR
Spain, 8, 12, 72
Spanish-American War, 275
Speaker of the House, 312, **649**
Special district governments, 751–758
Special sessions, 644
Specter, Arlen, 315, 365
Spiral of Silence (Noelle-Neumann), 175
Split tickets, definition of, **219**
Spoils system, 382
Springer, Jerry, 279
SSI. *See* **Supplemental Security**
        Income (SSI)
Stalin, Josef, 24
Stamp Act, 38
Standing committees, 316–320, **651**
Stanford University, 22
Stanton, Elizabeth Cady, 136, 192

Starr, Kenneth, 364
State boards and commissions, 692–693
State constitutions
    amendment process, 560–564
    characteristics common to, 554,
        557–560
    constitutional conventions, **560**
    structure of, 557–560
    Texas constitutions, 549–552, 555, 556
State courts, 411–413
State governments, *See also* Governors;
        headings beginning Texas;
        Local governments
    bureaucracies of, 375, 686–696
    constitutions of, 549–552, 554–564
    devolution and, 84–85, 88–90, 93
    "doctrine of nullification," 77
    Dred Scott decision and, 77–78
    federal government and state sover-
        eignty, 67–69
    federal grants and, 86–87
    Fourteenth Amendment and, 79–80,
        103–104
    freedom of expression and, 103–106
    initiatives and, 560
    interest groups and, 578–586
    legislatures, 644–656
    powers of, 74
    reserved powers and, 74
    salaries and, 645–647
    separation of powers and, 554
    single-head agencies, 690–692
    women in, 637
State of the Nation (Watts), 12
State party organization, 229–230
Statutory law, 419
Steinbeck, John, 529
Stem-cell research, 266, 362
Stenberg v. Carhart, 113
Stevens, John Paul, 91, 97, 107, 111, 403,
        405, 416, 423
Stewardship theory, 341
Stewart, Jon, 26
Stewart, Martha, 293
Stone, Harlan Fiske, 102
Straight-ticket party voting, 600–601
Strategic Arms Limitation Talks (SALT),
        503
Strategic presidency, 360
Strayhorn, Carole Keeton, 685
Strayhorn, Carolyn M., 607
Street, John, 229
Strict constructionism, 422
Strict-scrutiny test, 148
Strong mayor form of government, 734, 736
Subcultures, 537, 538
Subsidized housing, 484–485
Suez Canal, 514
Suffrage, *See also* Voting
    definition of, **190**
Suicide, 67, 114–115, 273, 507
Sundquist, James, 326
Sunset Advisory Commission, 695–696
Sunset laws, 394
Sununu, John, 670
Superfund program, 453
Supplemental Security Income (SSI), 482
Supply-side economics, 460–461
Supremacy clause, 74, 76–77, 557
Suspect classifications, 148
*Swann v. Charlotte-Mecklenburg County
        Board of Education,* 156

Sweden
    campaign activity in, 201
    child poverty rates, 477
    core values and, 12
    form of government, 71
    immigration and, 8
    legislature of, 314
    partisan journalism and, 278
    policy leadership in, 359
    political parties in, 221
    protest activity in, 206
    women in elective office and, 137
Swift, Jane, 669
Swing voters, 237
Switzerland, 8, 12, 515
Symbolic speech, 102

Taft, William Howard, 226
Taliban, 176, 343, 506
Taney, Roger, 77
TANF. *See* Temporary Assistance for
        Needy Families (TANF)
Tax assessor-collector, 748
Taxation
    American Revolution and, 38
    Articles of Confederation and, 69, 72
    George W. Bush tax policies, 411,
        460–461, 487
    Earned Income Tax Credit (EITC),
        487–489
    Economic Growth and Tax Relief
        Reconciliation Act of 2001,
        460, 465
    effective tax rate, **487**
    on federal banks, 76
    graduated personal income tax, **465**
    individualism and, 486–488
    poll taxes, 62, 150, 190, 539, 540, 551,
        552, 572
    public opinion statistics on, 167
    slavery and, 43
    tax cuts, 441, 485, 487
    U.S. Constitution, and, 42–43, 45
    U.S. Supreme Court and, 83
TCMA. *See* Texas City Management
        Association (TCMA)
TDA. *See* Texas Department of Agriculture
        (TDA)
TEA. *See* Texas Education Agency (TEA)
Tejanos, 531, *See also* Hispanic Americans
Telecommunications Act of 1996, 380
Telegraph, 275
Television, 277–282, 288
Temperance movement, 192
Temporary Assistance for Needy Families
        (TANF), 90, 482–484
Temporary Mexican worker program, 19,
        142, 236
Tenet, George J., 384
Tennessee Valley Authority, 443
Tenth Amendment, 90, 411, 477–478
Tenure of office, 672–674
Term limits, 644
Term limits, 672–674
Texas, *See also* Governors; Local govern-
        ments; State governments
    attorney general, **587**–588
    ballot form, 562, **605**
    ballot wording bias and, 562
    Bill of Rights of, 555
    bureaucracy, 686–696

Texas—*cont.*

campaign finance in, 616–619
campaigns in, 613–619
candidate access to ballot in, 607–608
Civil War and, 532, 551, 596
commissioner for health and human services, 691
comparative approach and, 529
comparisons with other legislatures, 659–660
comptroller of public accounts, **688**–689
congressional offices and, 521–522
constitutions of, 549–552, 554–564, 623
county governments, 744–751
death penalty and, 529
economy of, 541–544
education and, 529, 551, 623, 680, 752–756
election process in, 604–613
fragmented governmental structure and, **585**
general elections, **604**
governors of, 539, 540, 556, 562, 576, 595–596, 598–600, 614, 616–618
historical background, 531–532
individualist subculture, **537**
interest groups in, 578–586
judiciary, 694
land commissioner, 682, **689**
land-based economy, **542**
legislative agencies, 693–694
majority-minority populations in, 533–536
multi-appointment boards, 694–695
Office of State-Federal Relations, 691
one-party era in, 596
party dealignment and, 603–604
party ideology in, **595**–596
party realignment in, 597–603
party system and, 591–595
per capita income in, 541
Permanent University Fund (PUF), **564**
political corruption and, 540
political culture of, 537–540, 552, 755
political participation in, **569**
political parties and, 539–540, 577, 591–613
poll tax and, 539, 541, 551, 552, 573
population growth and, 533–536
race issues in, 597
Reconstruction and, 596, 665
redistricting in, 629–635
registered voters, **571**–576
Republican party strength in, 601
"Robin Hood Plan" and, 754–755
same-sex marriage and, 549, 556
school districts, 752–753
secretary of state (SOS), **691**
settlement patterns in, 530–532
slavery and, 532, 539, 551
social programs in, 597
sore loser law, 607–608
special district governments, **751**–758
state boards and commissions, **692**–693
Sunset Advisory Commission, **695**–696
traditionalistic subculture, **537**
as two-party state, **592**
unions and, 579–580
urban/rural contrasts ink, 532–533
voter participation and, 540, 561, 563, 570–578

Texas—*cont.*

white primary and, **575**
yellow dog democrats and, **597**, 602–603
yellow pup Republicans and, 601
Texas A&M University, 653, 676, 680
Texas Alliance for Patient Access, 648
Texas Association of County Officials, 580
Texas Association of Fire Fighters, 580
Texas Association of Police Chiefs, 580
Texas City Management Association (TCMA), 737
Texas Conservative Coalition, 658
Texas Declaration of Independence, 533, *See also* Declaration of Independence (U.S.)
Texas Department of Agriculture (TDA), 689, 692
Texas Education Agency (TEA), 534, 690
Texas Election Code, 612, 742
Texas Ethics Commission, 580–582, 619, 645
Texas governors, *See also* Governors
acting governors, 670–**671**
background of governors 1949–2006, 668
budgetary powers of, 679–681
campaign finance and, 616–618
legislative powers of, **681**–682
party leadership and, 685
postgubernatorial offices of, 670
power of, 623, 665
qualifications for, 666–669
removal from office, 671–672
salaries of, 670
succession to office of governor, 670–671
veto power, 680–682
Texas Legislative Council, 660
Texas legislature
campaign finance and, 616–619
committees in, 651–653
as delegates, **658**
demographics of, 637
districts, 624, 626, 627, 628
election to, 604–613, 624–629, 638–642
formal procedures of, 648–656
informal rules, 656
leadership positions in, 648–651
leadership styles in, 657–659
legislative process, 653–656
Legislative Redistricting Board, **630**, 631
minority representation and, **631**
multimember districts, **624**
occupations of members of, 638
partisan roles in, 658–659
photographs of chambers, 625
qualifications for membership, 635–638
reapportionment and, 629–635
redistricting and, 629–635
salaries of, 645–647
sessions of, 644–645
single-member districts, **624**, 626
size of, 624
term limits and, **644**
as trustees, **658**
turnover in, 642–643
Texas Municipal League (TML), 580, 583, 584
Texas Pardons and Parole Board, 682
Texas Performance Review, 688

Texas Public Utility Commission, 586
Texas Railroad Commission (RRC), 604, 689–690, 692
Texas Revolutionary War, 532
Texas School Board Association, 580
Texas State Board of Education, 580, 604
Texas State Teachers Association (TSTA), 579, 583
Texas Sunset Commission, 586
Texas Tax Reform Commission, 665
Texas Taxpayers and Research Association, 582
Texas v. Johnson, 107
Theory of Moral Sentiments (Smith), 442
Third-party candidates, 607–608
Thomas, Bill, 473
Thomas, Clarence, 416, 423
Thomas, Norman, 373, 403
Timberlake, Justin, 108
Tinsdale, Elkanah, 306
Titus, Herb, 607
TML. *See* Texas Municipal League (TML)
Tocqueville, Alexis de
on American democracy, 5
on American freedom, 10, 101
American political groups and, 248, 252
core values and, 6
interest groups and, 579
judicial issues and, 22
on people's power, 216
Toomey, Michael, 685
Torture, 309, 337
Totalitarian governments, definition of, **24**
Tower, John, 598, 599
Townshend Act, 38
Trade deficit, 515–516, 519–520
Trade restraint, 444
Traditionalistic subculture, 537
Trancredo, Tom, 19
Transfer payments, 479
Trapp, Martin, 672
Trinity College, 315
Truman, Harry, 171, 337, 341, 342, 358, 360, 481, 502
Trustees, 56, 57, 658
TSTA. *See* Texas State Teachers Association (TSTA)
Tucker, Jim Guy, 671
Turkey, 8
Turner, Ted, 282
Turnover, 642–643
Twain, Mark, 26
Twelfth Amendment, 350
Twenty-Fourth Amendment, 150, 190
Twenty-Second Amendment, 341
Two-party state, 592, 594–595
Two-party system
definition of, **220**
minor parties, 224–227
overview of, 220–221
party coalitions and, 222–224
single-member districts, 221–222
Tyranny of the majority, definition of, **55**

UAW. *See* United Auto Workers (UAW)
Ukraine, 503
UN. *See* United Nations (UN)
Underregulation, 446
Unemployment, 82

Unemployment insurance, 480–481
Unfunded mandates, 89–90
Unfunded Mandates Reform Act of 1995, 90
Union, *See also* Labor unions; specific associations
federalism and, 72–73
historical perspective, 75–78
slavery and, 77
Unipolar (power structure), 503
Unit rule, definition of, **350**
Unitary system, definition of, **70**
United Airlines flight 93, 5
United Auto Workers (UAW), 248–249
United Brotherhood of Carpenters & Joiners, 250
United Food and Commercial Workers International, 250
United Mine Workers, 250
United Nations (UN), 501–502, 505
United States v. Lopez, 90
United States v. Virginia, 149
United Steel Workers, 250
Unity, definition of, **11**
University of California Regents v. Bakke, 154, 155
University of Houston, 603
University of Iowa, 172
University of Maryland, 238
University of Michigan, 155
University of Oklahoma, 133
University of Texas, 680
University of Virginia, 11
"Upper court myth," 409
Urban Institute, 131
Urban and rural governments, 745–746
U.S. Bureau of Labor, 481
U.S. Bureau of Statistics, 477
U.S. Chamber of Commerce, 249
U.S. Conference of Mayors, 150, 255
U.S. Congress
bills and, **320**–324
campaign finance and, 304–305, 618
checks and balances and, 49–50, 302
committee system, 316–320
constituency and, 304
election to Congress, 303–310
functions of, 324
gerrymandering and, **306**, 307
gun control policy, 25
incumbents and, 304–305, 307–309
internships, 323
judiciary and, 415, 422–423
lawmaking process, **324**–327
leadership of, 311–317
lobby and, 257
logrolling and, **328**
misconduct and, 308
open-seat elections, 305
oversight function of, 329–332, **330**
overview of, 301–302
pluralism and, 332
pork-barrel projects, 301, **304**
press coverage, 281–282
reapportionment and, **306**, 626
redistricting and, 151, 306, **306**, 430
religious discrimination and, 16
representation function of, **327**–329
roll-call votes and, 315–316
seniority principle and, **316**–317
service strategy and, **304**
welfare reform bill, 27

U.S. Constitution, *See also* Bill of Rights; specific Amendments; U.S. Supreme Court
amendment process, 48
checks and balances and, 21, 35–36, 49–51, 267, 302
commerce clause, 80, 91, 92
core ideals and, 5
elastic clause, 74
enumerated (expressed) powers and, 73–74
Framer's goals, 46, 52, 56, 301–302, 339–340, 361, 449
historical background, 42–44, 52
implied powers and, 74, 76
limited government and, 47
"necessary and proper" clause, 74, 76
as new model of government, 46
opponents to, 45
overview of, 3
political systems and, 30
preamble, 9
procedural due process and, 115
ratification of, 44–46
reapportionment and, 629
reserved powers, 74
self-government and, 11
separation of power and, 48–49
slavery and, 5
social contract theory and, 21
supremacy clause, 74, 76–77, 557
taxation and, 42–43, 45
U.S. Courts of Appeals, 97, 410
U.S. Department of Education, 138
U.S. Department of Justice, 67, 292, 293, 631
U.S. Department of Labor, 477, 634
U.S. Department of State, 499
U.S. District Courts, 409–410
U.S. Fish and Wildlife Services, 450
U.S. Forest Service, 259–260, 450
U.S. House of Representatives
campaign finance and, 304–305
creation of, **42**
gerrymandering and, **306**, 307
House Rules Committee, 312, 322
leadership of, 312–313
overview of, 301–302
reapportionment and, **306**, 427, 626
redistricting and, 151, **306**, 430
requirements for holding office, 310
selection of members of, 57
slaves and, 43
U.S. Senate
campaign finance and, 304–305
creation of, 42
election and, 303–305, 309–310
leadership of, 313
overview of, 301–302
requirements for holding office, 310
selection of members of, 57
Supreme Court justice selection and, 414
U.S. Supreme Court, *See also* Judiciary
abortion and, 112–113, 258
affirmative action and, 154–156
appellate jurisdiction of, 406
appointment to, 413–415
apportionment of legislative districts and, 630
briefs and, **407**
characteristics of judicial appointees, 416

U.S. Supreme Court—*cont.*
clear-and-present-danger test, 101
concurring opinions, **408**
death penalty and, 121–123
decisions of, **407**, 417–423
devolution and, 90–92
dissenting opinions, 408, **409**
dual federalism and, 78
enemy combatant detention and, 124
environmental issues and, 453
equal protection and, 147–149
establishment clause and, 109–111
exclusionary rule and, 118–119
flag-burning and, 107
free expression protection and, 101–107, 109
free-exercise clause and, 111–112
habeas corpus appeals and, 119–120
imminent lawless action and, 105
judicial conferences and, **407**
jurisdiction of, 406
libel and, 106, 274
majority opinions, **408**
majority-minority districts and, 631–632
obscenity and, 108–109
opinions, **407**
original jurisdiction and, 406
overview of, 405–406
per curiam opinions, 408
plurality opinions, **408**
political influence on decisions of, 420–423
power of, 53, 56, 409, 423–424
precedent and, 406
privacy rights and, 112–115
school funding decisions, 753–756
school integration and, 83, 133–134, 148, 156–157, 407, 421, 424
sentences for crimes and, 120–121
"separate but equal" ruling, 79, 133
slander and, 106
solicitor general and, **406**
state sovereignty and, 67, 77
taxation and, 83
"upper court myth," 409
Watergate and, 35
white primary and, 575
writ of certiorari and, 406
U.S. Taxpayers Party, 607
U.S. Uniform Code of Military Justice, 124
USA Patriot Act, 322
USSR, 8, 24, 101, 443, 501, 502–503, *See also* Russia

Van Buren, Martin, 216
Van Orden v. Perry, 110
Venezuela, 255, 359
Veterans Land Board, 689
Veterans Land Fund, 689
Veto, 324, 340, 362, **680–682**
Vice presidency, 313, 349, 354–355
Vieth v. Jubelirer, 429–430
Vietnam, 8, 143
Vietnam War, 206, 222, 288–289, 291, 337, 365, 502
Virginia (large-state) Plan, 42
Virginia Military Institute (VMI), 149
VISTA. *See* Volunteers in Service to America (VISTA)
VMI. *See* Virginia Military Institute (VMI)

Vo, Hubert, 536
Volcker Commission, 373
Volunteers in Service to America (VISTA), 520
Voter turnout, 191, 197, 308–309, 561, 563, 570–578, 743–744
Voting, *See also* **Elections; Political participation**
absentee voting, **612**–613
African Americans and, 62, 136, 150, 190, 208, 223, 539, 574, 576, 631
age and, 199–200
alienation and, 199
apathy and, 197
civic attitudes and, 197–199
cumulative voting, **740**
Fifteenth Amendment and, 136, 150
gender and, 136, 137, 138
get-out-the-vote efforts, 237
Hispanic Americans and, 142–143, 539, 574, 576, 631
initiatives and, 60
literacy tests and, 190
Nineteenth Amendment and, 136, 190, 575
Political parties and, 220
poll taxes, 62, 150, 190, 539, 540, 551, 552, 573
preferential voting, **740**
prospective voting, 220
redistricting and, 151, **306**, 430
referendums and, 60
registration laws, 62
registration requirements, 194–195
retrospective voting, 220
socioeconomic factors, 200, 576–577
split tickets and, 219
swing voters, 237
turnout, 62, 150, 151
Twenty-Fourth Amendment and, 150, 190
voting rights, 134, 150, 190–191, 205, 361, 631, 634–635, 740
Voting Integrity Project, 198
Voting Rights Act of 1965, 134, 150, 191, 205, 361, 631, 634–635, 740
Voting-age population, 572

Walker, Jack, 266
Walker, Mary Edwards, 512
Walker, Olene S., 669
Wall Street Journal, 277
Wallace, George, 226, 668–669
Wallace, Lurleen, 668–669
Walton, John C., 672
War, *See also* Iraq War
Civil War, 13, 216, 217, 512, 532, 551, 596
Cold War, 101, 502
French and Indian War, 37–38, 341
Great Depression and, 514
guerilla war, 510, 512–513
justification of, 339
Persian Gulf War, 282, 504
preemptive war doctrine, 506
press coverage of, 505
Revolutionary War, 341
Spanish-American War, 275
undeclared war, 339–340

War—*cont.*
Vietnam War, 206, 222, 288–289, 291, 337, 365, 502
war on terrorism, 123–126, 337, 504–506
War Powers Act, 365
Warren, Earl, 415
Washington, George
biography of, 341
constitutional convention and, 49
core ideals and, 5
correspondence of, 40
Hamilton and, 72, 76
influence of, 46
newspapers and, 275
patronage system and, 381
political parties and, 214
Washington Post, 263, 277, 289
Washington Post/ABC News poll, 181
Watchdog role, 288–290
Water Quality Act of 1965, 445, 450
Watergate scandal, 35, 231, 288, 289, 291, 595
Waters, M. Dane, 263
Watts, William, 12, 207
Weak may form of government, 734, 736
Weapons of mass destruction (WMDs), 383, 384, 506–507
Weaver, James B., 226
Weber, Max, 29
Webster, Daniel, 59, 354
Webster v. Reproductive Health Services, 113
WEF. *See* World Economic Forum (WEF)
Weigel, Lori, 170
Welfare policies, 27, 90, 473–474, 597
Welfare Reform Act, 27, 90, 473, 478, 483, 484
West, Darrell, 236
West Indies, 8
West Point, 514
Whig party, 216
Whig theory, 340–341
Whistle blowing, 395
White House Office (WHO), 355–356
White, Mark, 535, 595, 598, 668, 674, 688, 756
White primary, 575
White, Theodore H., 28, 273
Whitman, Christine T., 669
WHO. *See* White House Office (WHO)
Whren v. United States, 118–119
Wickard v. Filburn, 91
Wildavsky, Aaron, 360, 440–441
Wilderness Society, 254
Williams, Clayton, 599, 613, 615, 616
Williams, Jody, 283–284
Williams, Roger, 20
Williams, Stanley, 103
Wilson, Woodrow, 217, 226, 337, 341, 342
Wire services, 276–277
Wiretapping, 289, 332, 421
Wittington, Harry, 291
WMDs. *See* Weapons of mass destruction (WMDs)
Wohlgemuth, Arlene, 648
Women, *See also* Gender
affirmative action, 17
civil rights and, 135–139
education and, 138, 149
elective office and, 137
employment and, 138
FMLA and, 92

group thinking and, 181
marriage and, 135
military service and, 148
in political office, 310, 353,
    667–668, 669
political parties and, 223
sexual harassment, 136–137, 420
voting and, 136, 137, 138, 190–192,
    512, 575

Wong, Martha, 536
World Economic Forum, 515
World Economic Forum (WEF), 446
World Trade Center disaster. *See*
    September 11, 2001 terrorist
    attacks
World Trade Organization (WTO), 519
World Wildlife Fund, 246
WorldCom, 358

Writ of certiorari, 406
Writ of mandamus, 53
WTO. *See* World Trade Organization
    (WTO)

Yale University, 255, 484
Yarborough, Ralph, 611
Yellow dog democrats, 597, 602–603

Yellow journalism, 275
Yellow pup Republicans, 601
Young & Rubicam, 172
Young, Don, 301
Young v. Old (MacManus), 181
Yugoslavia, 8

Zelman v. Simmons–Harris, 111